Sample Student Drafts and Revisions

Annotated Student Research Papers

Arguing about Literature

A GUIDE AND READER

John Schilb
Indiana University

John Clifford
University of North Carolina at Wilmington

BEDFORD / ST. MARTIN'S   Boston ▪ New York

For Bedford/St. Martin's

Publisher for Composition: Leasa Burton
Senior Executive Editor: Stephen A. Scipione
Senior Production Editor: Lori Chong Roncka
Senior Production Supervisor: Lisa McDowell
Marketing Manager: Stacey Propps
Editorial Assistant: Rachel Greenhaus
Production Assistant: Erica Zhang
Copy Editor: Lisa Wehrle
Indexer: Mary White
Photo Researcher: Sarah D'Stair
Senior Art Director: Anna Palchik
Text Design: Jean Hammond
Cover Design: Marine Miller
Cover Art: Robert Adrian Hillman/Alamy
Composition: Jouve
Printing and Binding: Quad/Graphics

President, Bedford/St. Martin's: Denise B. Wydra
Editorial Director, English and Music: Karen S. Henry
Director of Marketing: Karen R. Soeltz
Production Director: Susan W. Brown
Director of Rights and Permissions: Hilary Newman

For information, write: Bedford/St. Martin's, 75 Arlington Street, Boston, MA 02116 (617-399-4000)

ISBN 978-1-4576-6209-6

Acknowledgments

Sherman Alexie. "Capital Punishment." Reprinted from *The Summer of Black Widows* © 1996 by Sherman Alexie, by permission of Hanging Loose Press.

Acknowledgments and copyrights are continued at the back of the book on pages 1115–1121, which constitute an extension of the copyright page. It is a violation of the law to reproduce these selections by any means whatsoever without the written permission of the copyright holder.

Preface for Instructors

In a sense, *Arguing about Literature: A Guide and Reader* combines two books. One is a guide to writing skills, especially means of argument. The other is a collection of literature, organized by themes. Similarly, we have designed this book for two common kinds of courses. The first is a composition course where students learn techniques of argument by practicing them through essays they write about literature. The second is a literature course that helps students craft good arguments about their readings. Often, each of these courses also stresses research, an activity we therefore explain in detail.

If you are familiar with our book *Making Literature Matter*, you may see *Arguing about Literature* as a compact version. In major respects, you'd be right. Several fans of our larger volume have asked for a condensation, and this new book — about a third shorter than its parent — meets their request. Our abridgment preserves what teachers report as its predecessor's key strengths. The literary selections, though fewer, still stir thought and represent several genres. The book also resembles *Making Literature Matter* in giving instructors the opportunity to connect the teaching of literature with the teaching of composition. We continue to include numerous exercises, questions, and assignments that help students write responses to the readings. We provide substantial advice about writing and provide numerous sample papers. In particular, we give students much aid in writing *arguments* on various topics. As before, we emphasize that an argument is ideally not a form of war but instead a civilized effort that people make to show their ideas are reasonable.

We don't mean to suggest, however, that *Arguing about Literature* merely shortens our original text. In crucial ways, it's an expansion. In particular, we significantly enlarge our coverage of argument, helping students grasp even better what such writing entails. At all levels of their education, students are increasingly expected to be or become resourceful critical thinkers with strong argumentative skills. We give these subjects extended attention in both "books" of the book: the guide (Part One) and the reader (Part Two).

A Closer Look at the Guide

As in *Making Literature Matter*, Part One, A Brief Guide to Arguing about Literature, focuses on effective ways of writing and reading. But it begins with a brand-new chapter introducing basic elements of argument. With a provocative essay on cell phones serving as our chief example, we carefully elaborate terms such as *rhetoric, issues, claims, audience, evidence,* and *ethos*. Then, Chapter 2 reinforces the principles we have outlined, by explaining how students can use these to write analyses of literary works. Chapter 3 describes and demonstrates methods of close reading, a concept we turn into concrete strategies that students can actually wield. The subsequent chapter returns to the writing process, familiarizing students with other moves that foster good argument essays. Chapter 5 shows how to write arguments about the main literary genres: poems, short stories, plays, and essays. This first part of the book then concludes with a chapter on how to write researched arguments. Although *Making Literature Matter* treats this subject at length, we have significantly updated our discussion, in part by adding advice about online searches and about properly crediting sources. The chapter includes not one but four annotated papers — concrete examples that show students how they can address various common types of research-based assignments such as using a literary work as a springboard to examine social issues, or placing a work in historical and cultural context.

A Closer Look at the Reader

Arguing about Literature echoes its predecessor by featuring the bulk of our literary selections in the theme-based chapters that make up Part Two, Literature and Arguments. We have also carried over the main subjects of these chapters, for they continue to loom in students' lives. Specifically, in order of appearance the topics are families, love, freedom and confinement, doing justice, and journeys. Each chapter, too, continues to draw from multiple genres. For example, Chapter 7 deals with families not only through short fiction (e.g., stories about mothers and daughters by Tillie Olsen, Amy Tan, and Alice Walker) but also verse (e.g., poems about grandparents by Nikki Giovanni and Gary Soto). Then, various chapters turn to drama. Chapter 8's treatment of love includes William Shakespeare's tragedy *Othello*; Chapter 9's concern with freedom and confinement includes plays by Henrik Ibsen, Susan Glaspell, and Lynn Nottage; and Chapter 10 investigates justice partly through Sophocles' *Antigone* and a radio theater piece by Holocaust survivor Ida Fink. Part Two also features essays: for instance, Richard Rodriguez and Jose Antonio Vargas express different perspectives on issues of justice that immigrants face. As perhaps you can tell from this preview, the book reflects a variety of cultural backgrounds, and its authors range from long-esteemed names to talented new voices.

In each of Part Two's chapters, we again arrange works in small clusters so that students can gain insights by comparing texts. In keeping with our enhanced emphasis on argument, however, each chapter of the reader now concludes with a group of opinion pieces (Arguments about an Issue) on a current controversy. These provocative issues include overparenting, contemporary marriage, freedom of speech, neuroscience's role in criminal trials, and the impact of social media. For example, Chapter 11's consideration of journeys includes arguments by Sherry Turkle and Nathan Jurgensen about the digital

world's effect on people's sense of place. Some clusters include excerpts from published scholarship on a work (such as Sylvia Plath's "Daddy" in Chapter 7), while others feature documents (Contexts for Research) from the author's era. Such materials can serve as models of academic writing and can facilitate students' own research projects. Like *Making Literature Matter*, the book ends with an appendix that identifies and demonstrates contemporary critical approaches to literature, ranging from reader-response and feminist criticism to postcolonial criticism. The appendix uses these approaches to analyze a particular short story, in part by presenting a sample student paper on it.

The Guide Is Available Separately, in Print, and as an e-Book

In the event that some instructors want to assign the guide chapters but would rather choose their own literary or argumentative texts for the course, we offer Part One as its own book (or e-book if that's the preferred option): *Arguing about Literature: A Brief Guide*. A print-only evaluation copy of *Arguing about Literature: A Brief Guide* comes with some teaching advice bound into it; use ISBN 978-1-4576-6513-4 to order an evaluation copy or visit the Bedford/St. Martin's catalog (**bedfordstmartins.com**) for further information. You can also find further information about the PDF-style e-book via the online catalog page; visit **bedfordstmartins.com/arguingaboutlit/catalog**.

An Instructor's Manual for the Guide and Reader Is Available for Download

Particularly if you have never taught argument and literature together, you may want to access the instructor's manual, *Resources for Teaching Arguing about Literature: A Guide and Reader*, through the online catalog page; visit **bedfordstmartins.com/arguingaboutlit/catalog**. Prepared by John Schilb, John Clifford, Joyce Hollingsworth, and Laura Sparks, these instructor resources include sample syllabi; advice on teaching argumentation, composition, and literature (including an annotated bibliography for further research); and, especially, substantial commentaries on the individual arguments and literary works in the book to aid class preparation and discussion.

Acknowledgments

The terrific staff at Bedford/St. Martin's continue to be wise and generous collaborators in our efforts. Once again, we have relied especially on three people who are wonderful guides and true friends: senior executive editor Steve Scipione; editorial director, English, Karen Henry; and co-president of Macmillan Higher Education Joan Feinberg. Moreover, we want to express thanks to the highly supportive president of Bedford/St. Martin's, Denise Wydra, and former editorial assistant Laura Horton. In production, we are grateful to director Susan W. Brown and associate director Elise Kaiser; to managing editor Michael Granger and

assistant managing editor John Amburg; and especially to our gracious, wise, and attentive production editor Lori Roncka and her assistant Erica Zhang, who kept us on track and on schedule. In the permissions department, manager Kalina Ingham, editor Caryn Burtt, photo researcher Sarah D'Stair, and photo research manager Martha Friedman expertly and efficiently negotiated and obtained reprint rights. In marketing, we are most grateful to director Karen Soeltz, associate director Jane Helms, and marketing manager Stacey Propps.

We thank Janet E. Gardner, formerly of the University of Massachusetts–Dartmouth, for her contributions to the chapter on research, as well as Joyce Hollingsworth of the University of North Carolina at Wilmington and Laura Sparks of Indiana University for their ample and timely work on the instructor's manual.

As always, John Schilb is indebted to his former University of Maryland colleague Jeanne Fahnestock and his current colleagues at Indiana University, especially Christine Farris, Kathy Smith, and Lisa Ottum. He also thanks Gary Weissman from the University of Cincinnati for calling his attention to Ira Sher's story "The Man in the Well." John Clifford thanks poet Daniel Terry for his help.

Of course, we remain grateful as well to the instructors whose comments on various editions of *Making Literature Matter* honed our thinking on literature and argument, and many of whom urged us to consider a shorter, more argument-intensive version of the book: Julie Aipperspach Anderson, Texas A&M University; Jonathan Alexander, University of Southern Colorado; Donna Allen, Erie Community College; Virginia Anderson, University of Texas at Austin; Liana Andreasen, South Texas College; Sonja L. Andrus, Collin County Community College; Andrew Armond, Belmont Abbey College; Carolyn Baker, San Antonio College; Rance G. Baker, San Antonio College; Barbara Barnard, Hunter College; Charles Bateman, Essex County College; Linda Bensel-Meyers, University of Tennessee, Knoxville; Elaine Boothby, South River High School; Colleen Brooks-Edgar, South Texas College; Elizabeth L. Cobb, Chapman University; Chauna Craig, Indiana University of Pennsylvania; Timothy R. Cramer, Santa Monica College; Michael A. Cronin, Northern Oklahoma College; Rosemary B. Day, Central New Mexico Community College–Montoya Campus; Thomas Deans, Kansas State University; Kevin J. H. Dettmar, Pomona College; Jennifer Dorfield, Westfield State College; Michael Doyle, Blue Ridge Community College; Penelope Dugan, Richard Stockton College of New Jersey; Thomas Dukes, University of Akron; Mary Dutterer, Howard Community College; Kelly Edmisten, University of North Carolina at Wilmington; Irene R. Fairley, Northeastern University; Joli Furnari, Montclair State University; Selma Goldstein, Rider University; Martha K. Goodman, Central Virginia Community College; Christopher Gould, University of North Carolina at Wilmington; Maureen Groome, Brevard Community College; Chad Hammett, Texas State University; Martin Harris, Belmont Abbey College; William Harrison, Northern Virginia Community College; Iris Rose Hart, Santa Fe Community College; Carol Peterson Haviland, California State University, San Bernardino; Ana Hernandez, Miami-Dade College–Wolfson; John Heyda, Miami University–Middletown; Jeff Hoogeveen, Lincoln University;

Richard Dean Hovey, Pima Community College; Karen Howard, Volunteer State Community College; Clark Hutton, Volunteer State Community College; Joan Kellerman, University of Massachusetts–Dartmouth; Sabine A. Klein, Purdue University; Sonya Lancaster, University of Kansas; Kasee Clifton Laster, Ashland University; Marianne Layer, Armstrong Atlantic State University; Margaret Lindgren, University of Cincinnati; Betty Mandeville, Volunteer State Community College; Kelly Martin, Collin County Community College; Phillip Mayfield, Fullerton College; Miles S. McCrimmon, J. Sargeant Reynolds Community College; Christopher McDermott, University of Georgia; Mandy McDougal, Volunteer State Community College; Steven Newman, University of Nebraska–Omaha; Dana Nichols, Gainesville State College; Jim O'Loughlin, University of Northern Iowa; Gordon O'Neal, Collin County Community College; Christine Peter, University of Massachusetts–Dartmouth; Brenton Phillips, Cloud County Community College; Nancy Lawson Remler, Armstrong Atlantic State University; David Rollison, College of Marin; Jane Rosecrans, J. Sargeant Reynolds Community College; Teri Rosen, Hunter College; Lisa Roy-Davis, Collin County Community College; Donna Samet, Broward Community College; Jamie Sanchez, Volunteer State Community College; Daniel Schierenbeck, University of Central Missouri; Meryl F. Schwartz, Lakeland Community College; Pauline Scott, Alabama State University; Julie Segedy, Chabot College; Lucia Seranyan, Northern Virginia Community College, Woodbridge Campus; Kimberly Alford Singh, Northern Virginia Community College; Jason Skipper, Miami University at Oxford; Jennifer Smith, Miami University at Oxford; Debra L. Snyder, Livingstone College; Jamieson Spencer, St. Louis Community College; Pam Stinson, Northern Oklahoma College; Jonathan Taylor, Ferris State University; Julie Tilton, San Bernardino Valley College; Larry A. Van Meter, Texas A&M University; William Verrone, University of North Carolina at Wilmington; Phillippe (Phil) West, Concordia University; Sharon Winn, Northeastern State University; Bertha Wise, Oklahoma City Community College; Pauline G. Woodward, Endicott College.

As with *Making Literature Matter*, we dedicate this book to our wives, Wendy Elliot and Janet Ellerby. May our relationships with them never be compact, always expanding.

John Schilb, *Indiana University*
John Clifford, *University of North Carolina at Wilmington*

*   *   *

You get more resources for *Arguing about Literature*

Arguing about Literature doesn't stop with a book. Online, you'll find both free and affordable premium resources to help students get even more out of the book and your course. You'll also find convenient instructor resources and even a nationwide community of teachers. To learn more about or order any of the products below, contact your Bedford/St. Martin's sales representative, e-mail sales support (**sales_support@bfwpub.com**), or visit the online catalog at **bedfordstmartins.com/catalog**.

Visit *Re:Writing 2* and *Re:Writing for Literature*
bedfordstmartins.com/rewriting
bedfordstmartins.com/rewritinglit

Supplement your print text with our open resources for literature and flexible premium content.

Get free online help for your students. *Re:Writing 2* and *Re:Writing for Literature* provide help in composition and literature:

- Videos of real writers
- Tutorial on visual analysis
- Sample documents in design
- Help on building a bibliography
- Checklists for better writing
- Exercises for grammar and writing
- *VirtuaLit* tutorials for close reading (fiction, poetry, and drama)
- *AuthorLinks* and biographies for 800 authors
- *Quizzes* on poetic elements and hundreds of literary works
- Glossary of literary terms
- MLA-style student papers
- A sampler of author videos and additional literature
- Help for finding and citing sources

Access video interviews with today's writers. *VideoCentral: Literature*, our growing library of more than 50 video interviews with today's writers, includes Ha Jin on how he uses humor, Chitra Banerjee Divakaruni on how she writes from experience, and T. C. Boyle on how he works with language and style. Biographical notes and questions make each video an assignable module. See **bedfordstmartins.com/videolit/catalog**.

This resource can be packaged for free with new student editions of this book. An activation code is required. To order *VideoCentral: Literature* with this print text, use ISBN 978-1-4576-8801-0.

Access Your Instructor Resources
bedfordstmartins.com/arguingaboutlit/catalog

You have a lot to do in your course. Bedford/St. Martin's wants to make it easy for you to find the support you need—and to get it quickly.

Download your instructor's manual. *Resources for Teaching Arguing about Literature* includes sample syllabi; advice on teaching argumentation, composition, and literature (including an annotated bibliography for further research); and, especially, substantial commentaries on the individual arguments and literary works in the book to aid class preparation and discussion. For the PDF, go to **bedfordstmartins.com/arguingaboutlit/catalog**.

Get teaching ideas you can use today. Are you looking for professional resources for teaching literature and writing? How about some help with planning classroom activities?

- ***TeachingCentral.*** We've gathered all of our print and online professional resources in one place. You'll find landmark reference works, sourcebooks on pedagogical issues, winning collections, and practical advice for the classroom—all free for instructors and available at **bedfordstmartins.com/teachingcentral**.
- ***LitBits* Blog: Ideas for Teaching Literature and Creative Writing.** Our *LitBits* blog—hosted by a growing team of instructors, poets, novelists, and scholars—offers a fresh, regularly updated collection of ideas and assignments. You'll find simple ways to teach with new media, excite your students with activities, and join an ongoing conversation about teaching. Go to **bedfordstmartins.com/litbits/catalog** and **bedfordstmartins.com/litbits**.

Order content for your course management system. Content cartridges for the most common course management systems—Blackboard, Canvas, Angel, and Desire2Learn—allow you to easily download Bedford/St. Martin's digital materials for your course. For more information, visit **bedfordstmartins.com/coursepacks**.

Package one of our best-selling brief handbooks at a discount. Do you need a pocket-sized handbook for your course? Package *EasyWriter*, by Andrea Lunsford, or *A Pocket Style Manual*, by Diana Hacker and Nancy Sommers, with this text at a 20% discount. For more information, go to **bedfordstmartins.com/easywriter/catalog** or **bedfordstmartins.com/pocket/catalog**.

Teach longer works at a nice price. Our literary reprints series—the Case Studies in Contemporary Criticism series, the Bedford Cultural Edition series, and the Bedford Shakespeare series—can be shrink-wrapped with *Arguing about Literature*. For a complete list of available titles, visit **bedfordstmartins.com/literaryreprints/catalog**.

Package works from our video and DVD library. Qualified adopters can choose from selected videos and DVDs of plays and stories included in *Arguing about Literature*. To learn more, contact your Bedford/St. Martin's sales representative, e-mail sales support (**sales_support@bfwpub.com**), or visit the online catalog at **bedfordstmartins.com/catalog**.

Trade up and save 50%. Add more value and choice to your students' learning experiences by packaging their Bedford/St. Martin's textbook with one of a thousand titles from our sister publishers such as Farrar, Straus and Giroux and St. Martin's Press — at a discount of 50% off the regular price. Visit **bedfordstmartins.com/tradeup**.

Contents

■ PART TWO   Literature and Arguments

Contents by Genre

Poems

Plays

Contexts for Research

PART ONE

A Brief Guide to Arguing about Literature

CHAPTER 1

What Is Argument?

The first word in our book's title may puzzle you. Why would we want you to *argue*? Are we really inviting you to yell or sneer? The word *arguing* may remind you of spats you regret. Most everyone has suffered arguments like these. They arise in the media all the time. Talk radio hosts and their callers mix strong opinion with insult. Television's political panels routinely lapse into squabbles; guests feel required to clash. Quarrels explode on daytime talkfests; couples fight over who's cheated on whom. Online forums are plagued by "trolls," writers who crudely mock others' posts. No wonder many people define *arguing* as combat. It often seems like war.

But our book is about *arguing* in a positive sense. We define it as a calm, courteous process in which you

identify a subject of current or possible debate;

analyze why you view the subject the way you do;

address others who may not share your view; and

try to persuade them that your view is worth accepting or at least makes sense.

This better kind of arguing occurs at various times and places. You may try to coax friends who dread horror films into joining you at *Saw 12*. In class, you may need to explain the logic of your stand on climate change. Beyond campus, you may advocate for social causes. For instance, you might petition your city to launch recycling sites.

Let's face it: to argue *is* to disagree, or to air views that not all may hold. Still, at its best, argument is an *alternative* to war. It's *not* a contest you try to "win" by insisting you're right. Ideally, argument is a form of **inquiry**, a process in which you test your beliefs, consider other views, and stay open to changing your mind. Rather than immediately attack your critics, you note principles you share with them. When their thinking differs from yours, you treat their positions fairly. If any of their ideas strike you as wise, you adjust your thinking. In the meantime, you recognize the limits of your knowledge and understanding. You admit, too, your inner conflicts: how your thoughts are divided, your values in conflict, your feelings mixed. Indeed, essayist Phillip Lopate observes that "the real argument should be with yourself." Columnist David

Brooks goes even further: "If you write in a way that suggests combative certitude," he warns, "you may gradually smother the inner chaos that will be the source of lifelong freshness and creativity." In their own fashion, these writers point to something important about argument: at its best, it teaches you about yourself and your world, while alerting you to what you still must learn.

Students regularly encounter this kind of arguing in college. Academic subjects aren't just pools of information. They go beyond proven facts. Disciplines grapple with uncertainties: problems, questions, and conflicts they haven't yet solved. Physicists disagree about the origins of the universe. Historians write conflicting accounts of Hitler's Germany; they debate how much his extreme anti-Semitism was traditional there. Two sociologists may scan the same figures on poverty and make different inferences from them. Typically, scholars draw conclusions that are open to challenge. They must explain why their judgments are sound. They expect to engage in reasoned debate with their colleagues. They see this as their field's best chance for truth.

In your classes, expect disagreements. They're crucial to learning in college. Often, classmates will voice ideas you don't immediately accept. Just as often, they'll hesitate to adopt some opinion of yours. Authors you read will deal with controversies, from their own points of view. As a writer yourself, you will enter debates and have to defend your stands.

No one naturally excels at this type of arguing. It takes practice. Our book is a series of opportunities to become skilled in this art. Our book's chief springboard for argument is works of literature. Those we include don't deliver simple straightforward messages. They offer puzzles, complications, metaphors, symbols, and mysteries. In short, they stress life's complexity. They especially encourage you to ponder multiple dimensions of language: how, for example, shifts of context can change a word's meaning. Each of our literary works calls for you to interpret. As you read the text, you must figure out various features of it. Then, other readers may not see the text as you do. So, next you'll *argue* for your view. Often you'll do this by composing essays and perhaps online posts. From Chapter 2 on, we offer strategies for you to argue about literature as a writer.

The Elements of Argument

This chapter is a general introduction to arguing. Let's start with an example: an article entitled "Disconnected Urbanism" by noted architecture critic Paul Goldberger (b. 1950). He wrote it for the February 22, 2003, issue of *Metropolis* magazine. Goldberger worries about cell phones. He believes they lead cities to lose a sense of community and place. At the time he wrote, these phones weren't yet packed with apps. Nor could they connect to the Internet. Still, they were a big development, which pained Goldberger. As you read, note his key points and his efforts to sway his readers to them. Afterward, we raise questions to help you study his text. Then, we refer to it as we explain the basic elements of argument.

PAUL GOLDBERGER

Disconnected Urbanism

There is a connection between the idea of place and the reality of cellular telephones. It is not encouraging. Places are unique — or at least we like to believe they are — and we strive to experience them as a kind of engagement with particulars. Cell phones are precisely the opposite. When a piece of geography is doing what it is supposed to do, it encourages you to feel a connection to it that, as in marriage, forsakes all others. When you are in Paris you expect to wallow in its Parisness, to feel that everyone walking up the Boulevard Montparnasse is as totally and completely there as the lampposts, the kiosks, the facade of the Brasserie Lipp — and that they could be no place else. So we want it to be in every city, in every kind of place. When you are in a forest, you want to experience its woodsiness; when you are on the beach, you want to feel connected to sand and surf.

This is getting harder to do, not because these special places don't exist or because urban places have come to look increasingly alike. They have, but this is not another rant about the monoculture and sameness of cities and the suburban landscape. Even when you are in a place that retains its intensity, its specialness, and its ability to confer a defining context on your life, it doesn't have the all-consuming effect these places used to. You no longer feel that being in one place cuts you off from other places. Technology has been doing this for a long time, of course — remember when people communicated with Europe by letter and it took a couple of weeks to get a reply? Now we're upset if we have to send a fax because it takes so much longer than e-mail.

But the cell phone has changed our sense of place more than faxes and computers and e-mail because of its ability to intrude into every moment in every possible place. When you walk along the street and talk on a cell phone, you are not on the street sharing the communal experience of urban life. You are in some other place — someplace at the other end of your phone conversation. You are there, but you are not there. It reminds me of the title of Lillian Ross's memoir of her life with William Shawn, *Here But Not Here*. Now that is increasingly true of almost every person on almost every street in almost every city. You are either on the phone or carrying one, and the moment it rings you will be transported out of real space into a virtual realm.

This matters because the street is the ultimate public space and walking along it is the defining urban experience. It is all of us — different people who lead different lives — coming together in the urban mixing chamber. But what if half of them are elsewhere, there in body but not in any other way? You are not on Madison Avenue if you are holding a little object to your ear that pulls you toward a person in Omaha.

The great offense of the cell phone in public is not the intrusion of its ring, although that can be infuriating when it interrupts a tranquil moment. It is the fact that even when the phone does not ring at all, and is being used quietly and discreetly, it renders a public place less public. It turns the boulevardier

5

into a sequestered individual, the flaneur into a figure of privacy. And suddenly the meaning of the street as a public place has been hugely diminished.

I don't know which is worse—the loss of the sense that walking along a great urban street is a glorious shared experience or the blurring of distinctions between different kinds of places. But these cultural losses are related, and the cell phone has played a major role in both. The other day I returned a phone call from a friend who lives in Hartford. He had left a voice-mail message saying he was visiting his son in New Orleans, and when I called him back on his cell phone—area code 860, Hartford—he picked up the call in Tallahassee. Once the area code actually meant something in terms of geography: it outlined a clearly defined piece of the earth; it became a form of identity. Your telephone number was a badge of place. Now the area code is really not much more than three digits; and if it has any connection to a place, it's just the telephone's home base. An area code today is more like a car's license plate. The downward spiral that began with the end of the old telephone exchanges that truly did connect to a place—RHinelander 4 and BUtterfield 8 for the Upper East Side, or CHelsea 3 downtown, or UNiversity 4 in Morningside Heights—surely culminates in the placeless area codes such as 917 and 347 that could be anywhere in New York—or anywhere at all.

It's increasingly common for cell-phone conversations to begin with the question, "Where are you?" and for the answer to be anything from "out by the pool" to "Madagascar." I don't miss the age when phone charges were based on distance, but that did have the beneficial effect of reinforcing a sense that places were distinguishable from one another. Now calling across the street and calling from New York to California or even Europe are precisely the same thing. They cost the same because to the phone they are the same. Every place is exactly the same as every other place. They are all just nodes on a network—and so, increasingly, are we.   [2003]

≡ THINKING ABOUT THE TEXT

1. Imagine that Goldberger could observe how people now use cell phones in places you ordinarily go, such as a college campus. To what extent would he see the kind of behavior that he worried about in his 2003 piece? How much evidence could he find for his argument that cell phones are diminishing people's sense of place and *disconnecting* them from one another?

2. Goldberger does not say much about the advantages of a cell phone. Which, if any, do you think he should have mentioned, and why? How, if at all, could he have said more about the advantages while still getting his readers to worry about these phones?

3. Goldberger wrote before smartphones came along, enabling use of apps and the Internet. In what ways, if any, does this newer technology affect your view of his argument?

4. As he indicates by including the word *urbanism* in his title, Goldberger is chiefly concerned with how cell phones affect their users' experiences of cities. If he had written about cell-phone use in suburbs or in rural areas,

do you think he would have changed his argument in some way? If so, in what respect?

5. It seems quite possible that Goldberger himself uses a cell phone. If this is the case, does it make his concern less valid? Why, or why not? Moreover, he does not end his piece by proposing that humanity abandon the technology. Why, conceivably, does he avoid making this recommendation? What might he want his readers to do instead?

Goldberger's article is an example of **rhetoric**. This is a term from ancient Greek. It means writing, speech, and visual images used for a certain purpose: to affect how people think and act. Rhetorical texts don't just convey a message. They aim to *shape* beliefs and conduct. Often they're efforts to *alter* these things. Probably several of Goldberger's readers are joyously addicted to cell phones; he nudges them to reconsider their overattachment.

A related term is the **rhetorical situation**. It's the specific context you have in mind when you engage in rhetoric. Major circumstances include the following:

- **The particular *topic* you choose.** It may already interest the public. The December 2012 massacre of children in Newtown, Connecticut, immediately provoked disputes over gun control, school safety, mental illness, and screen violence. But the topic needn't be a calamity. When Goldberger wrote, cell phones were booming as a trend, so their effects were debated a lot. He didn't have to alert his readers to this subject or remind them of it. Other writers must do one or the other. This was the situation for legal scholars Woodrow Hartzog and Evan Zelinger in 2013, when they posted an online argument about Facebook. At the time, people worried that Facebook's privacy protocols wouldn't securely protect users' personal data. Hartzog and Zelinger deliberately shift to another subject. They recommend thinking less about *privacy* and more about *obscurity*, which they note is a word "rarely used" in debates about Facebook's risks. To them, *privacy* is so vague a concept that brooding about how the site guards it is futile. They call for pushing Facebook to keep personal facts *obscure*: "hard to obtain or understand" when cyberstalkers hunt them.

- **The main readers, listeners, or viewers you decide to address; your *audience*.** Goldberger wrote for readers of the city-oriented magazine *Metropolis*. Its mission statement declares that it "examines contemporary life through design," publishing articles that "range from the sprawling urban environment to intimate living spaces to small objects of everyday lives." This magazine also seeks to put design in "economic, environmental, social, cultural, political, and technological contexts." Readers of *Metropolis* would expect it to probe cell phones' impact on cities. Perhaps Goldberger hoped his piece would someday circulate more widely, as it now does on the Web. But surely his target group loomed in his mind as he decided on content, form, and words.

■ **Possible "channels" for the text.** These include available institutions, media, and genres. Goldberger composed his article for a particular magazine. He used the medium of print. He resorted to a specific genre: the type of writing often called an opinion piece. Such choices do constrain an author. Writing for *Metropolis* forced upon Goldberger certain space limits; otherwise, he might have lengthened his argument. Today a critic like him might film a video for YouTube, perhaps showing callers so absorbed in their cell-phone conversations that they forget friends alongside them.

Current politicians fling the word *rhetoric* as an insult. They accuse their rivals of indulging in it. They treat the word with contempt because they think it means windy exaggeration. But before the modern age, it meant something nobler. Rhetoric was the valuable attempt to *influence* readers, listeners, or viewers. In this sense, almost all of us resort to rhetoric daily. We need to learn rhetorical strategies if we're to have impact on others. For centuries, then, schools have seen rhetoric as a vital art. They've deemed it important to study, practice, and teach. In ancient Greece and Rome as well as Renaissance Europe, it was a core academic subject. American colleges of the nineteenth century also made it central. This focus survives in many courses today, especially ones about writing or speech. Our book reflects their commitment to rhetoric, especially through our advice about writing.

Within the field of rhetoric, arguments are a more specific category. They involve eight basic elements. When you argue, you attempt to **persuade** an **audience** to accept your **claims** regarding an **issue**. To achieve this aim, you present **evidence**, explain your **reasoning**, rely on **assumptions**, and make other kinds of **appeals**. The boldfaced words play key roles in this book; we mention them often. Here we briefly explain them, using them to make suggestions for writing an argument. Taking Goldberger's piece as a sample, we begin with *issue* and then move to *claims, persuasion, audience, evidence, reasoning, assumptions,* and *appeals*. We'll return to these elements in Chapter 2, where we explain their role in arguments about literature.

ISSUES

An **issue** is a question not yet settled. People have disagreed—or might disagree—over how to answer it. Goldberger's question seems to be this: How are cell phones transforming culture? But he doesn't state his question flat out. He presumes his readers will guess it. Other writers of arguments put their questions plainly. They want to ensure their readers know them. This seems Jeremy Rozansky's goal in an argument he wrote for the January 19, 2013, issue of *The New Atlantis*. His article's topic is steroid-using athletes. To him, debates about men like Barry Bonds and Roger Clemens focus too much on whether they played "fair" or are naturally talented. Rozansky calls for thinking about something else: "What are athletes doing when they play sports, and what are we watching when we watch?" His own answer is "a certain kind of human excellence." Then he explains how the men proved incapable of such virtue.

But notice that he bluntly announces his question to begin with. By doing this, he stresses it. He signals that it's the most important issue raised by the steroid scandals.

When you write an argument, readers should find your main issue *significant*. It must be a question they believe is worth caring about. Sometimes they'll immediately see its value. But often you'll need to explain what's at stake. Scholars of rhetoric describe the task as establishing the issue's **exigence**, the urgency or importance of the situation. Goldberger brings up exigence at the start of his fourth paragraph. There he states that on city streets, the use of cell phones "matters," for "the street is the ultimate public space and walking along it is the defining urban experience."

For another statement of exigence, let's turn to a 2013 piece from the online magazine *Slate*. It's about a strange topic: animals put on trial. Author James McWilliams points out that in 1457, a French village brought a sow and six piglets to court, charging them with killing a boy. The piglets were declared innocent; the sow was found guilty and hanged. McWilliams notes that this was just one of many animal trials in past ages. Then, he states his chief issue: "What are we to make of this evidence that our ancestors imputed to animals a sense of moral agency?" McWilliams realizes that his readers may find his question trivial. They may not see its relevance to the present. So he states the question's stakes: "These seemingly odd trials have much to teach us about how fundamentally our relationship with animals has changed and how, more poignantly, we've lost the ability to empathize with them as sentient beings." McWilliams goes on to praise how courts of the past treated animals. Even guilty verdicts respected these creatures, he says. Putting them on trial credited them with powers of thought and the potential to act well. McWilliams wants modern humans to adopt the same attitude. At present, he believes, they treat animals as objects. Whether or not you agree with McWilliams, he resembles Goldberger in stating why his issue matters.

CLAIMS

Perhaps you associate the word *claims* with insurance companies. It's familiar as a term for the forms you fill out when someone bashes your car. You may not be used to calling other things you say or write *claims*. But even when you utter a simple observation about the weather—for instance, "It's beginning to rain"—you make a claim. A **claim** is a statement that is spoken or written so that people will think it true. With this definition in mind, you may spot claims everywhere. Most of us make them every day. Most claims *are* accepted as true by the people to whom we make them. Imagine how difficult life would be if the opposite were so. Human beings would constantly fret if they distrusted everything told them.

But claims may conflict with other claims. We've defined an *issue* as a question with various debatable answers. *Claims*, as we use the term, are the debatable answers. In this sense, most of Goldberger's statements are claims, for readers might resist them. Take his main claim, which he identifies at the start of paragraph 6. There he argues that cell phones are prime forces in a pair of "cultural losses." These are "the loss of the sense that walking along a great urban street is a glorious shared experience" and "the blurring of distinctions between different kinds of places." Readers might object to Goldberger's view in various ways. Some might argue that neither of these losses has occurred. Others might say that these losses have happened but that cell phones didn't cause them. So, Goldberger has more work to do. Like all debatable statements, his requires support.

When you write a college paper, typically you'll raise an issue. Then, you'll make one main claim about it. This can also be called your **thesis**, a term you may know from high school. It won't be your *only* point. You'll make smaller claims as your essay continues. But stating your main claim, and remaining focused on it, will be important.

PERSUASION

It's commonly assumed that if two people argue, they are dogmatic. Each insists on being proclaimed correct. But at its best, argument involves efforts to **persuade**. You argue in the first place because you want others to accept your claims. Yet you can't expect them to applaud at once. To attempt **persuasion** is to concede that your claims need defense. Goldberger knew that much of his readership adored the phones that disturb him. He'd have to justify his stance.

Most likely he figured that he couldn't turn all the fans into critics. Such conversions can be hard to pull off. But he could pursue a more modest goal: showing that his claims merit study. Whether or not they gained approval from everyone, he could make them seem reasonable. Probably he'd be happy if a reader said, "I'm fonder of cell phones than Goldberger is, but I can't dismiss his criticisms. I'm willing to keep reflecting on them." A response like this can be your aim, too. Realistically, *persuasion* doesn't mean everyone eventually agrees with you. An argument you write may leave some readers maintaining another view. But you've done much if they conclude that your ideas are credible—worth their bearing in mind.

AUDIENCE

The word **audience** may first make you think of people at plays, concerts, movies, or lectures. Yet it also describes readers. Not everything you write is for other human eyes; in college courses, you may produce notes, journal entries, blog posts, and essays for yourself alone. But in most any course, you'll also do public writing. You'll try to persuade audiences to accept claims you make.

This task requires you to consider more than your subject. You must take your readers into account. McWilliams realized that his audience wouldn't know about animal trials. He'd have to begin with anecdotes explaining what these hearings were like. By contrast, Goldberger's average readers would be aware of cell phones. Also, he supposed that they had a certain vocabulary—that they knew "boulevardier" and "flaneur" meant someone who likes to explore city streets. Evidently he saw his audience, too, as holding two beliefs about cell phones. One is that they help people connect. The other is that they make private life more public, for chatter on them is often overheard. Deliberately, Goldberger challenges both ideas. He argues that because cell phones distract people from their surroundings, they lead to "*dis*connected urbanism" and turn "a public place less public." Unfortunately, sometimes your audience will have a vaguer profile than his. You may have to guess what your target group knows, assumes, and values.

EVIDENCE

Evidence is support you give your claims so others will accept them. What sort of evidence must it be? That depends on what your audience expects. Disciplines differ in this respect. In literary studies, claims about a text seem more plausible if they're backed by quotations from it. (We discuss this standard more in Chapter 2.) Scientists must not only conduct experiments, but also describe them so that others can repeat them and see if the results are the same. Anthropologists feel pressured to base their conclusions on field research. Not that your audience will always be academic scholars. It can easily be more diverse. Goldberger's audience included experts in design, but also nonprofessionals with interests like theirs. In short, his readership was mixed.

To persuade this group, Goldberger offered two kinds of evidence. His climax is a personal tale, about a Hartford-based friend of his who called him from New Orleans and then from Tallahassee. Clearly Goldberger wanted his audience to find this story typical of modern life. He hoped it would serve as what rhetorical theorist Kenneth Burke calls a *representative anecdote*. Its effect would be to reinforce his claim that cell phones ruin callers' sense of place. In addition, Goldberger presses his readers to consult their *own* experiences. He bids them recall how *they've* used cell phones on city strolls. At such moments, he seeks to remind them, they "are not on the street sharing the communal experience of urban life." Similarly, he prods them to remember how "increasingly common" it is "for cell-phone conversations to begin with the question, 'Where are you?' and for the answer to be anything from 'out by the pool' to 'Madagascar.'"

As a writer, you might have to guess your audience's standards of proof. You'll be influenced by experiences you've had with such readers. Perhaps you'll also have opportunities to review drafts with them.

REASONING

Philosopher Gary Gutting observes that "facts alone are necessary but not sufficient for a good argument. As important as getting the facts right is putting the facts into a comprehensible logical structure that supports your conclusion." This advice can help you as you strive to persuade others through writing. Besides evidence, your readers will expect you to show careful **reasoning**. Ideally, they'll come away feeling that your ideas truly connect. They should sense that your main claim derives from your other ones. Goldberger's logic seems this:

> People should sense the distinctiveness of a place and feel a bond with other people there.
>
> These things should especially happen on a city street, which is "the ultimate public space."
>
> For the last several years, these things have been threatened by faxes, computers, and e-mail, which speedily link people to some other place than the one where they actually are.
>
> The cell phone is a more dramatic development in technology, however, for it can "intrude into every moment in every possible place."
>
> Cell phones let people make contact with other places quickly and easily, so that one result is "the blurring of distinctions between different kinds of places." Indeed, these devices even render area codes meaningless. Furthermore, they prevent a city street from being "a glorious shared experience."
>
> Therefore, cell phones are a "major" factor in two big "cultural losses."

Goldberger doesn't arrange these ideas as a list. He might bore readers if he did! Still, ideally readers will see his claims as a methodical sequence. When you write an argument, guide your audience step by step through your reasoning. Help them follow your logic. Make your essay seem an orderly train of thought.

ASSUMPTIONS

Already we've mentioned certain **assumptions** of Goldberger's. But other beliefs appear to have steered him. They include some that readers may reject. Assumptions behind an argument may be numerous and debatable. That's why we single them out as an element here.

One category is beliefs about the audience's *experiences*. As Goldberger asks his readers to imagine "When you are in Paris," he supposes that all of them have visited Paris or might go there some day. Another type of assumption concerns the writer's *values*. When Goldberger laments cities' loss of uniqueness, he assumes that uniqueness is good. A third type is what rhetorical theory calls *warrants*. This term refers to the writer's beliefs about what can serve as evidence. Recall that Goldberger climaxes his argument with a personal story. He relies on a warrant when he offers this tale. It's the assumption that the story is evidence for his argument's main claim.

We can imagine readers skeptical about these premises. If low-wage workers saw Goldberger's reference to Paris, they might grumble or scoff. How could *they* ever afford to go there? Others may believe that uniqueness isn't always a benefit. Similarly, for some of Goldberger's audience, his personal story may lack weight. As author, Goldberger must decide which of his assumptions are safe or trivial—and which, if any, he has to state and defend.

When you write an argument, try to identify its assumptions. Detecting them isn't always easy. You may need to have friends and classmates read each of your drafts. But the effort pays. Growing alert to a premise helps you anticipate challenges to it. You can then revise to head off these criticisms.

APPEALS

To make their arguments persuasive, writers employ three basic kinds of appeals. Rhetorical theory calls them **logos**, **ethos**, and **pathos**, terms drawn from ancient Greek. In practice, they don't always play equal roles. An argument may depend on one or two of these strategies, not the entire trio. But all three are potential resources.

In a way, we've already introduced **logos**. The term refers to the logical substance of an arguer's case. When you rely on logos, you focus on showing your claims are sound. You do this by emphasizing your evidence and your reasons. Most audiences will demand anyway that these features be strong. No surprise, then, that logos is the most common type of appeal.

Ethos often operates, too. When applied to writing, this term refers to the image you project as an author. Actually, there are two types of ethos. One is your audience's image of you before you present your analysis. It's your prior reputation. Many readers of *Metropolis* know that Paul Goldberger is a leading, Pulitzer Prize–winning critic of architecture. Their awareness inclines them to respect his arguments, whether or not they agree with him. Advertisers have reputational ethos in mind when they hire celebrities for endorsements. The hope is that you'll join Weight Watchers because Jennifer Hudson did. This ethos also comes into play with self-help manuals. Often their covers boast that the writer is an academic. You're supposed to buy *How to Find Lovers by Loving Yourself* because its author has a Ph.D.

Most of us, however, aren't famous or highly credentialed. There remains a second kind of ethos: the picture of you that people form as they read your text. To gain their trust, you should patiently lay out your claims, reasons, and evidence. This is what Goldberger does. True, cell phones bother him enough that he uses the word *offense* and points out that their ring "can be infuriating." But he doesn't lash out against them. He avoids blatant, righteous anger. He signals that his argument won't become a "rant." He declares the phones' impact "not encouraging"—a fairly mild criticism. He doesn't demand they be smashed to bits. He simply mourns "losses" they cause.

When arguers are scornful, some of their audience may object. John Burt points out a problem that Stephen Douglas's ethos created in his famous debates with Abraham Lincoln. When the two men competed for a U.S. Senate seat in 1858, the main issue was slavery. On this topic, Douglas planned to come across as a seeker of compromise. But on stage he fiercely insulted Lincoln, showing nastiness and not tact. As Burt observes, "Douglas's own management of his case was so intemperate, so inflammatory, and so personal that whatever case one could make for his position, he himself was the last person who could plausibly carry the day for that case." Sometimes anger *is* right, especially when injustice must be noticed and stopped. But for much of your writing, especially in college, Goldberger's tone will serve better.

Writers enhance their ethos through **concessions** and **qualifications**. Concessions are civil (or even kind or admiring) acknowledgments of views or experiences other than yours. One appears in Goldberger's piece. Largely he claims that cell phones wreck people's sense of place. But he does admit that unique geography survives to some extent. In paragraph 2, he notes that here and there you can find "a place that retains its intensity, its specialness, and its ability to confer a defining context on your life." He's quick to add that these settings fall short of an "all-consuming effect." Nevertheless, he grants that they've somehow remained distinct. Most readers will like his recognizing this fact.

In rhetorical theory, qualifications aren't credentials for a job. They are two kinds of words. One kind helps writers strengthen their claims. A common example is the word *very*, as in a sentence like "Cell phones are very bad for cities' sense of community." Yet many readers think terms of this sort are unnecessary. "Bad" is already emphatic; why stick "very" before it? The second kind of qualification has the opposite effect. Words in this category weaken a claim. They help writers sound cautious, often an attractive trait. Goldberger uses words of this type:

- In paragraph 1, where a more reckless writer might have simply declared "Places are unique," he adds "or at least we like to believe they are."
- In paragraph 3, he doesn't just proclaim that *all* city dwellers have lost a sense of place. He makes use of the word *almost*, saying this is becoming the experience of "almost every person on almost every street in almost every city."
- In paragraph 4, he resists generalizing about *every* inhabitant of a city. Instead, he asks "what if half of them are elsewhere, there in body but not in any other way?"
- In the next paragraph, he doesn't claim that a cell phone's ring *is* infuriating. Rather, he more softly notes that it "can be."
- In paragraph 6, he doesn't simply announce that an area code has become *just* a set of numbers. Rather, he laments that it "is really not much more than" them.

Such language makes Goldberger look careful. Similar terms include *probably*, *maybe*, *perhaps*, and *possibly*. These words suggest that the writer isn't self-righteously certain. Take this claim from Hartzog and Zelinger's article about Facebook: "Many contemporary privacy disputes are probably better classified as concern over losing obscurity." With "probably," the authors identify their claim as a hypothesis. They grant that it isn't sure fact. Like Goldberger, they project restraint.

Pathos is an appeal to the heart. You find it in charities' ads. Many show photos of suffering children — kids hungry, injured, or poor. These pictures are meant to rouse pity. If they succeed, viewers sob and donate. At other times, pathos stirs fear. Activists warn that if society ignores them, apocalypse will come. Pathos-filled arguments aren't dry in tone. Their language expresses *moods*. Pathos targets its audience's *emotions*. When you write such arguments, you push readers to *feel* the stakes of your issue. You hope they'll *passionately* favor your claims. Sure, you risk sounding excessive: too sad, too mad, too scared, or too hurt. But pathos can be a respectable tool, as well as a powerful one. Plenty of subjects even demand an emotional tone. Readers expect essays on genocide to anguish over its victims. Further, pathos can join logos and ethos. Arguments that move readers may also awe them with logic; the author's image may impress them, too.

Goldberger's piece oozes despair and sorrow. He deeply regrets cell phones' impact on cities and prods his audience to share his grief. He saves his most notable pathos for the end. There he claims that cell technology is turning all of us into "nodes on a network." It's a chilling final image. He wants to leave readers worried that cell phones will destroy their souls.

Developing an Effective Style of Argument

When you write an argument, you need to consider the elements we have discussed. Also good to study are features of an effective **style**. The words authors choose and the order they put them in are tools of style. Goldberger uses various tools to make his prose compelling. Try practicing these methods yourself:

Mark transitions.   Readers want to know how each sentence relates to the ones immediately before and after it. Usually a word or two can show this. Goldberger's second sentence starts with "It," a pronoun that looks back to the previous sentence's "connection." Especially crucial is the language of shifts from one paragraph to the next. When Goldberger begins his third paragraph with "This is getting harder to do," he builds on his second paragraph's final point. Similarly helpful is the word that starts his third paragraph: "But." It signals that this new paragraph turns from older technology to a new, more disturbing kind.

Create coherence by repeating words and by using similar words. Readers appreciate signs that you have carefully focused and structured your argument. Through repeating its key words, you can show that it follows a coherent line of thought. Goldberger notably repeats "cell phones" and "places," making clear that these are central concerns of his piece. More than once he uses "increasingly" when referring to cell phones' impact. It pops up in paragraphs 2 and 3; then it appears twice in paragraph 7, his conclusion. By echoing this word, he stresses that he's discussing an ongoing trend. Your audience will also sense organization if you use words related in meaning. Notice what Goldberger does in paragraph 1. Near its end, he uses "want" three times. But he previews this repetition with earlier language: what "we strive to experience" and what "you expect to wallow in." Together, these words stress that he's consistently concerned with desire.

Balance the parts of a sentence.   Look again at these two sentences from Goldberger:

> When you are in a forest, you want to experience its woodsiness; when you are on a beach, you want to feel connected to sand and surf. (para. 1)

> It turns the boulevardier into a sequestered individual, the flaneur into a figure of privacy. (para. 5)

In each sentence, the parts balance. It's an engaging feat. Readers like rhythmic symmetry. They won't demand it of every sentence you write, but they'll appreciate it when they see it.

Vary the lengths of sentences.   A series of long sentences may confuse your readers, while also losing their attention. On the other hand, a series of short sentences may come across as choppy, obscuring how ideas connect. Usually, your audience will prefer variety. Try to mix sentence lengths, as Goldberger does here:

> Once the area code actually meant something in terms of geography: it outlined a clearly defined piece of the earth; it became a form of identity. Your telephone number was a badge of place. Now the area code is really not much more than three digits; and if it has any connection to a place, it's just the telephone's home base. An area code today is more like a car's license plate. (para. 6)

Even in long sentences, however, be as concise as possible. Don't use more words than necessary; make each one count.

Use active verbs, not just passive ones.   *Active* and *passive* are terms of grammar. When a verb is in active voice, the subject of that verb *performs an action*. When a verb is in passive voice, its subject is *acted upon*. The active tends to make a sentence more dramatic and concise. Also, it better identifies who or what is doing something. Interestingly, Goldberger uses active voice even when the verb's subject is phone technology:

> "the cell phone has changed our sense of place" (para. 3)

> a cell phone "pulls you toward a person in Omaha" (para. 4)

> "the cell phone has played a major role in both" (para. 6)

> an area code "outlined a clearly defined piece of the earth" (para. 6)

> "the old telephone exchanges that truly did connect to a place" (para. 6)

Notice, too, that at key points—the ends of paragraphs 3 and 5—he uses passive voice:

> "the moment it rings you will be transported out of real space into a virtual realm" (para. 3)

"And suddenly the meaning of the street as a public place has been hugely diminished." (para. 5)

In looking at these last two sentences, consider the alternatives: In active voice, "you" would *transport* something, rather than *be transported*. And something would *diminish* "the meaning of the street," rather than that meaning's *being* diminished. Goldberger's use of the passive implies that we humans have lost control of our lives. Rather than *act*, we are *acted upon*. Specifically, we no longer take charge of "real space" or uphold "the meaning of the street." When, by contrast, cell phones become subjects of his active verbs, Goldberger implies they rule us. Overall, his practice suggests that both kinds of voice are resources. Neither is *automatically* preferable. But of the two, active voice is of course more dynamic. And again, it identifies the action's performer more clearly.

Use figurative language.   Arguments may register more strongly with their audience if they explain ideas through figurative language. Such phrases can make concepts more vivid. Three main types are analogies, metaphors, and similes.

An **analogy** calls attention to a similarity between two things while still regarding them as largely distinct. Goldberger creates this analogy in paragraph 6: "An area code today is more like a car's license plate." He recognizes that an area code and a license plate are different in many ways. But he emphasizes what they have in common: both are numbers that fail to convey people's current location. He also uses analogy in paragraph 1, when he explains how people can feel bonded to places. For him, this tie resembles marriage.

A **metaphor**, on the other hand, implies that two things are the same. An example appears in paragraph 6. Ordinarily, people assume that phone numbers and badges are quite different, but Goldberger blends them: "Your telephone number was a badge of place." He resorts to metaphor, too, when he concludes by labeling all of us "nodes on a network."

A **simile** also equates two things, but uses the word *like* or *as* to connect them. No similes appear in Goldberger's text, but they might have:

Today, a cell phone is like a toothbrush. People think you're uncivilized if you don't own one, if you don't use it daily, if you don't think it fundamental to your health, and if you don't replace it the moment it wears out.

Today, people walk along city streets gazing worshipfully down at their cell phone. This posture makes them look as if they are praying over rosary beads or a Bible.

Identify a word's multiple meanings.   Arguers perform a striking move when they seize upon a common word and show that it has more than one possible meaning. Goldberger does this in the middle of paragraph 3, with his sentence "You are there, but you are not there." He has in mind two definitions of the ordinary word *there*. One deals with physical location. If a woman is walking through downtown Manhattan, she is literally "there." The other meaning is psychological connection. If the woman ignores her surroundings in favor of talking on her cell phone, to Goldberger she isn't "there" in Manhattan at all. He reinforces this distinction by noting that Lillian Ross's title implies there are also multiple meanings of the word *here*.

Create "perspectives by incongruity." This term, probably unfamiliar to you, was coined by Kenneth Burke. It refers to a certain means of provoking thought. To create a "perspective by incongruity" is to tamper with traditional oppositions. An example from Goldberger's text appears in paragraph 4. People assume that a typical city street is outdoors, but he describes it as a room. Specifically, he calls it a "chamber." With this metaphor, he presses his readers to associate the street with cozy domestic intimacy—an atmosphere he thinks is lost when walkers chat on their phones. He creates another "perspective by incongruity" at the end of the same paragraph. This one overthrows the usual contrast between what's small and what's powerful. Specifically, he imagines a scene on New York City's Madison Avenue. Even though you're walking there, "a little object"—a cell phone—"pulls you toward a person in Omaha." Ordinarily, people don't think little objects can exert such massive force. Goldberger stresses, however, that cell phones can spirit minds away. Actually, his whole article is a "perspective by incongruity," for it argues that phones *dis*connect people while supposedly linking them.

Sample Argument for Analysis

We've specified elements of argument and style. Now, try to spot their presence in the following opinion piece. "A New Moral Compact" was originally published in November 2012, right around Veterans' Day. The author, David W. Barno (b. 1954), is a retired lieutenant general. He served the U.S. Army in key leadership roles, his experiences including combat campaigns in Afghanistan, Grenada, and Panama. Barno is now Senior Advisor and Senior Fellow at the Center for a New American Security, a group whose mission is "to develop strong, pragmatic, and principled national security and defense policies." His article appeared simultaneously on the Center's Web site and in the digital edition of *Foreign Policy* magazine. Anyone might come upon his piece through a search engine. But probably he took his main audience to be elected officials, their staffs, other policy experts, military professionals, and academic scholars who study national defense.

As you read, consider the following questions:

- What is Barno's main *issue*, and what is his main *claim* about it?
- What smaller claims does he make as he develops his main one?
- Where in his article are you especially conscious of Barno's attempting *persuasion?*
- Where are you especially conscious of how Barno views his *audience?*
- What *evidence* does Barno offer?
- What are the steps in his *reasoning?*
- What are his major *assumptions?*

- To what extent does his argument rely on *logos?*
- To what extent might his *reputational ethos* matter to his readers?
- What sort of *ethos* does he create through his words?
- How much, and where, does his argument use *pathos?*
- What are some words he uses for *transitions?*
- What are some uses he makes of *repetition* and *words similar in meaning?*
- Which, if any, of his sentences strike you as *balanced* in their structure?
- To what extent does he *vary the lengths* of his sentences?
- What are some uses he makes of *active* and *passive* voice?
- Where, if anywhere, does he use *figurative language*, such as *analogies, metaphors*, and *similes?*
- Where, if anywhere, does he draw out a word's *multiple meanings?*
- Where, if anywhere, does he create a *perspective by incongruity?*

DAVID W. BARNO

A New Moral Compact

As our nation enters its second decade of armed conflict overseas, it is appropriate to reflect on the moral compact between our government, our people, and our soldiers. Eleven years of conflict in Afghanistan and Iraq, combined with the prospect for open-ended global warfare against terrorists, has blurred the lines between peace and war, perhaps forever. It has also effectively lowered our national threshold for decisions to conduct military operations or go to war. The reasons have as much to do with our declining personal stake in these conflicts as with the dangerous state of the world.

I recently attended an event honoring former Pennsylvania governor Tom Ridge for his public service. Ridge came from a working class family, won a scholarship to Harvard, and went on to law school. Upon completing his first year, he unexpectedly received his draft notice from Uncle Sam.

Tom Ridge did not seek to dodge his unwelcome summons. In his family, when you were called, you dropped whatever you were doing in your life and you went, as his father did in World War II. But as a Harvard grad and law student, he clearly had other options.

The Army decided to make Tom Ridge an infantryman. He soon became a sergeant and shipped out to Vietnam, where he joined the 101st Airborne for a year in combat from 1969 to 1970. None of the handful of young men he led in his small infantry rifle squad was graduate of Harvard or any other college, but they were draftees from all social strata across the United States. Ridge observed: "The military is a great leveler. Nobody cares who you are, where you went to school, who your parents were. None of that mattered."

The only reason Ridge was in the Army and ultimately fought for a year in Vietnam was the draft lottery system. The Selective Service system randomly   5 assigned numbers to each draft age male by birth date in an annual "lottery"; depending on the needs of the war that year, if your number came up, you were called. Theoretically, your chances of being drafted as a college grad under the lottery system were equal to those of a high school drop-out born on the same date. In the real world, however, both college deferments (see: Dick Cheney, Bill Clinton) and clever manipulation of the system allowed many of the well-off and well-educated to avoid service altogether. And for each of those who side-stepped the call, some other, less fortunate young man was called up to take his place. Some of whom, of course, never came back—a sharp point little noted in discussions about the complex national legacy of the Vietnam War.

In the Vietnam era, draftees were called up for a maximum of two years of service, with one of those almost inevitably spent in Vietnam. And unlike in today's "all-volunteer" military, no draftee was ever sent back to Vietnam for another tour unless he volunteered—probably with a voluntary re-enlistment for longer service. With draftees serving only two years in uniform, it would have been nearly impossible to send a soldier for a second 12-month combat tour within the scope of his two-year service obligation. It simply wasn't done. If you were unfortunate enough to be drafted, you at least knew that the nation drew the line at one year of combat.

Contrast Tom Ridge's world of 1969 with that of America's combat soldiers today. In 2012, there is no draft, and our all-volunteer force has spent the last eleven years in prolonged, bloody ground wars in Iraq and Afghanistan. The Army of this era fields about 560,000 troops on active duty, in comparison to 1.2 million at the height of the Vietnam war. Nearly 3 million Americans are veterans of the post-9/11 wars, with large numbers having served multiple combat tours. It seems obvious that some of the stress on the force—manifested by unprecedented rates of suicide and creeping indiscipline—has come from these widespread repeat deployments, the likes of which no soldier of the Vietnam era ever involuntarily faced. In fact, even career officers and sergeants in the Vietnam-era force—distinct from the two-year draftees—rarely served more than two one-year tours in Vietnam over the entire course of that ten-year war.

In today's military, it is not uncommon to see Army lieutenant colonels and senior sergeants deployed three or four times for 12- to 15-month combat tours over the past decade—a back-breaking, family-stressing commitment the likes of which we have never before asked of our men and women in uniform. Even in World War II, only a small fraction of our nearly 16 million uniformed men and women served more than three years in a combat zone, and the entire war was finished for the United States in 45 months. Our war in Afghanistan has lasted 134 months. It now has eclipsed the American Revolution and Vietnam as the longest war in U.S. history. Stunningly, sizable numbers of the very same sergeants and officers fighting the war today are the men and women that led the way into the earliest campaigns in Afghanistan and Iraq. If you are a career officer or NCO in today's Army and Marines, by and large you either continue to deploy—or you leave the service. There are few other options. Across our volunteer force, over 6,500 have been killed and more than 50,000 wounded since 2001. Consider the burden of that stark reality upon career military families.

Both of my sons have served one-year combat tours in Afghanistan. When our youngest son, an Army pilot, was called to go back after completing his first tour, I was suddenly angry. Not an anger that derived from misunderstanding our rotation system, nor from seeing the war as somehow unjust. My anger was visceral, unbidden, reflexive. And as I examined my unexpected reaction, it came down to this: my son was going back, yet 99 percent of his military age contemporaries were not—and never would, no matter how long the war lasted. Neither his civilian peers, their parents, nor their spouses or siblings would ever be exposed in any way to the gut-wrenching dangers of being in the middle of a lethal national enterprise. It simply wasn't important enough for our nation to insist that all of us shared the sacrifice of unlimited liability that war demands from those who fight it. Having a cadre of admirably willing volunteers simply has made it too easy for us to go to war.

For we Americans as a people, that's just wrong. There must be some limit   10
to what we will ask of our men and women in uniform before the rest of us feel some moral obligation to step in. Tom Ridge—representing all of the people of the United States in 1969—got the telegram, put his life on hold, stepped forward and served in combat alongside a broad cross-section of America's youth. Today, we call on no one to make this kind of sacrifice. We have even made that a matter of some pride, a nation that has moved beyond the dark days of "conscription."

Yet at what point are we morally compelled to in some way expose every American family to our fights abroad, to invest some moral equity as a nation and a society into fighting our wars? Absent any prospect whatsoever for our current or future wars to touch any of us personally, where is the moral hazard—the personal "equity stake"—that shapes our collective judgment, giving us pause when we decide to send our remarkable volunteer military off to war? They are fully prepared to go—but they trust the rest of us to place sufficient weight and seriousness into that decision to ensure that their inevitable sacrifices of life and limb will be for a worthy and essential cause.

Throughout our history, American decisions on going to war have been closely connected to our people because they remain matters of life and death. And they were always seen as matters of deep import to the nation as a whole, since all could be called upon to fight. Today such profound decisions are all but free of consequences for the American people. When the lives and the deaths of our soldiers no longer personally impact the population at large, have we compromised our moral authority on war? How can our elites and our broader populace make wartime decisions in good conscience when those paying the price are someone else's kids—but assuredly never their own?

The past ten years suggest that relying on a professional military comprised only of willing volunteers has eroded the core societal seriousness that we have always accorded to national decisions of war and peace. One wonders if we would have entered our recent conflicts as quickly—or let them drag on so long—if our Army was filled with draftees, drawn from a random swath of families across all segments of America.

One policy to better connect our wars to our people might be to determine that every use of military force over 60 days would automatically trigger an annual draft lottery to call up 10,000 men and women. They would serve in every branch of service for the duration of the conflict, replaced by future draft tranches in limited, like-sized numbers. Ten thousand draftees would comprise only about 5 percent of the number of new recruits the military takes in each year, but they would signify a symbolic commitment of the entire nation. Every family in the country would now be exposed to the potential consequences of our wars and come to recognize in a personal way that they had a stake in the outcome. The national calculus on go-to-war decisions subtly changes when all families can be called upon to answer the call to arms.

In the last decade, war has become something done by "the 1 percent"— our rightly acclaimed force of volunteers—with 99 percent of America uninvolved, and sometimes seemingly uninterested. But with war becoming this easy, our historic caution in committing our troops abroad has frayed dramatically. Partly as a result, "America at war" is slowly becoming a permanent condition. We have gradually, almost imperceptibly, eroded the bonds of responsibility linking our soldiers, our people, and our government. It's time to reestablish that moral compact between our people and our wars.   *[2012]*

Writing a Response to an Argument

Often a college course will require you to read arguments. Just as often, you will respond to them by writing an argument yourself. As you compose your reactions to these texts, you will make, develop, and support claims. Here are some tips to help you:

- Before you write about the text, be sure you understand it in its entirety. Identify its main claim, its other claims, and how they all relate. In your essay, don't treat these claims one by one in isolated fragments, stating your opinion of each. Instead, put in context any claim you discuss. Explain its role in the author's overall reasoning process. You can begin to establish this larger framework in your introduction, by summarizing what the author basically argues.
- Perhaps you'll disagree with the argument. Even then, show respect for its author. Avoid snarky remarks like "What planet is this guy on?" Audiences tend to prefer a more civil ethos. Calling the author stupid, evil, or crazy may drive your readers away. Let your tone suggest that you're reflective, not mean.
- When you first read the argument, you may strongly approve or object. But don't settle for extreme verdicts. Let your written response include concessions and qualifications, not just big evaluative claims. Your readers will appreciate learning what's complex about the argument and how reactions to it can be mixed. Whatever your

attitude toward it, show the reasoning and evidence behind your view.

- When writing about the argument, refer to its author. Make this person the subject of several active verbs: for example, "Barno claims," "Barno argues," "Barno proposes," "Barno calls for." After all, the argument isn't an orphan. Nor is it a random series of free-floating ideas. You're studying an entire case put forth by a particular human being. Take opportunities to remind your readers— and yourself—of this fact. Start doing so with your introduction.
- For each sentence you write, make clear whose view it expresses. Are you conveying an idea brought up in the argument you're analyzing, or is this your own idea? Help your readers distinguish between the two. If you write about Barno's argument, for example, let them know when you're reporting *his* claims and when you're stating *yours*.
- Give your response a title that previews what you'll say.

A Student Response to an Argument

The following essay demonstrates several of the strategies we've discussed in this chapter. The author, Justin Korzack, composed it for a course on debating social issues. Basically, he wrote an argument that reacts to Barno's. To support his response, he investigated presidential history. Still, his essay isn't a full-blown research paper, a genre we discuss in Chapter 6. Nor, probably, is it the finest response ever written. But it does perform moves worth adding to your rhetorical repertoire.

Justin Korzack
Professor Hartfield
English 111
10 April - - - -
How to Slow Down the Rush to War
In "A New Moral Compact," David W. Barno worries about
the United States' current reliance on an all-volunteer military. He claims that this policy allows civilians to feel too
complacent about the country's committing itself to major
hostilities. Barno is a retired lieutenant general with a substantial combat record. Therefore, you might assume that he
himself is comfortable with war. But this is not so, at least
with respect to our recent long-term conflicts. He feels that
these engagements have had serious consequences for the
professional soldiers required to carry them out. In his view,
the public at large needs to become more aware of war's human costs. To make all citizens more alert to these, he proposes "that every use of military force over 60 days would
automatically trigger an annual draft lottery to call up 10,000

men and women" (20). Obviously this measure would disrupt the lives of many people. Whether or not they ever planned to become soldiers, they might now be forced to serve. Nevertheless, Barno believes, this threat would be worthwhile, for it would function as a brake. He expects that it would make Americans more reluctant to send troops into extensive and deadly combat campaigns.

Is Barno's solution useful enough to justify the widespread anxiety it might cause? Not really, because Barno misdiagnoses the problem in the first place. What needs more attention and criticism is not public apathy. Rather, it's the institution of the Presidency. For the last several decades, the nation's Chief Executive has sought to initiate military action without interference from public opinion and even the U.S. Congress. The President should consult more widely and thoroughly before dispatching Americans to the battlefield.

Barno makes a valuable contribution when he reminds his readers of how terrible war can be. Moreover, he raises a legitimate concern when he points out that our nation's current military commitments have imposed awful burdens on recruits. Using the appeal of pathos, he stresses the suffering undergone by soldiers who have had to serve several tours of duty in deadly, traumatic places like Iraq and Afghanistan. He contrasts their experience with that of people like former governor Tom Ridge. Even though Ridge was, after being drafted into the army, sent to fight in Vietnam, at least his time there lasted only one year. Barno emphasizes that many members of today's military are repeatedly assigned to combat. These soldiers include one of Barno's own sons, a fact that he reports while admitting that he's angry about it. Some readers may feel that because of his personal connection, Barno's complaint about repeated rounds of service is nothing but self-interest. But his use of his son's situation as a representative anecdote seems appropriate, for numerous other people in the military have been required lately to return to war. In light of this unfortunate trend, it would be understandable if Barno called for reviving the draft as a gesture of fairness. He could argue that exempting civilians from military service is morally wrong, given that the professional defenders of our nation have had to fight so much. Not everyone would agree with him, but his position would be credible.

A somewhat different motive, however, leads Barno to suggest that a draft lottery be held every year if a military action extends beyond two months. He makes this proposal because he feels that Americans outside the military have

Summarizes Barno's argument so that readers understand his overall reasoning. Also points out which claims are his. Makes him the subject of several active verbs.

Identifies main issue by phrasing it as a question.

The paragraph varies the lengths of sentences and ends with the student's own main claim.

The first of several concessions in this paragraph.

Clear transition from previou[s] paragraph.

grown indifferent to the challenges it faces. In his view, the lottery would make civilians more conscious of combat deployments. At the same time, they would question more the necessity of going to war, for they might be drawn into combat themselves. This skepticism is something that Barno would welcome. To him, the government has grown too inclined to hurl troops into conflicts. He wants our leaders to make such decisions more slowly and carefully. He expects the lottery would achieve this goal, by raising public awareness and concern.

Probably Barno is right to sense that exposing significant numbers of Americans to a draft lottery would make the country uneasier about entering into war. Some greater unrest would most likely occur. Yet he provides no evidence for his claim that dependence on an all-volunteer force "has eroded the core societal seriousness that we have always accorded to national decisions of war and peace" (19). Why must his readers assume that the public is, at present, absolutely indifferent to the ordeals faced by our soldiers in Iraq and Afghanistan? Contrary to what he suggests, many civilians do seem to show "sufficient weight and seriousness" about the U.S.'s current military ventures (19). For instance, numerous cars display "Support our Troops" signs, and supportive crowds regularly turn out for ceremonies welcoming reservists as well as National Guard members home from combat. Barno might respond that these are rituals of cheerful robots, propaganda that hardly shows deep thinking about the government's choices. But civilians are perhaps able to appreciate soldiers' service while being thoughtful about the policies that demanded it. Barno appears to forget that when the invasion of Iraq was beginning, thousands of people marched in several cities to protest it. Moreover, critical attitudes toward current American wars have certainly mounted in the last few years. President Obama's decision to pull our military out of Afghanistan soon, along with his earlier decision to withdraw us from Iraq, stems in part from his awareness that much of our country has already grown tired of these commitments. He knows that we have woken up to how fatigued we are.

Yet even if our nation adopted Barno's proposal and became considerably more skeptical about war, chances seem slight that these developments would inhibit our leaders. Beginning with Harry S. Truman's "police action" in Korea during the early 1950s, no U.S. President has asked Congress for an official declaration of war. Instead, each President has essentially used the military as he has seen fit, seeking Congres-

Another concession, just before criticisms begin.

Provides supporting examples.

Figurative language.

Perspective by incongruity.

Begins another set of examples.

sional permission only at times and only in thin ways. The
procedure has been to "consult" Congress in a superficial
manner but not in a profound one. Lyndon Johnson took   *Identifies two possible
Congress's Gulf of Tonkin Resolution as a pretext for dramati-   meanings of the same word.*
cally escalating the U.S. troop presence in Vietnam. Richard
Nixon ignored massive antiwar protests and continued to
bomb the same region. Ronald Reagan felt free to send sol-   *Balances the two halves of*
diers to Grenada; Bill Clinton felt able to put them in Kosovo.   *the sentence.*
George W. Bush had fairly minimal Congressional authoriza-
tion to attack Iraq, on the basis of what turned out to be
false information about Saddam Hussein's weapons stockpile.
Similarly, after 9/11, Congress authorized Bush to pursue terrorists in Afghanistan. But that campaign was never officially
declared as a war, even though it has managed to become the
longest war in American history. Moreover, the current president is similarly determined to act independently. For all the
sensitivity that Barack Obama has shown to the country's war
fatigue, he has tried as much as possible to keep his policies
on drone attacks secret from Congress and from Americans at
large.

Therefore, devoting energy to Barno's proposed policy
may be counterproductive. His recommendation is thought-   *Concession; use of*
provoking and based on vast military experience, but probably   *qualifications ("may be,"*
his readers would do better to focus on Presidential power. In   *"probably," "has tended").*
military matters, the head of the country has tended to act
on his instincts rather than seek meaningful advice from others. Figuring out ways to change or curb this habit seems an
agenda more worthwhile than implementing the threat of a
draft.

Two Closing Arguments for Analysis

We end this chapter by offering two additional arguments. In their own ways,
they deal with topics we've covered at length. The first selection is an argument
about the process of argument itself. The second returns to the subject of cell
phones, though its angle differs from Goldberger's. You might write responses
to one or both of these texts. In any case, consider their main ideas and study
their techniques of persuasion. To help, we pose questions after each piece.

The first originally appeared as a contribution to the *New York Times*'s
Opinionator blog on September 2, 2012. The blog is a digital supplement to the
newspaper's print op-ed section. Author Carlos Fraenkel (b. 1971) grew up in
Germany and Brazil. He holds joint appointments in the Departments of Philosophy and Jewish Studies at McGill University in Montreal, Canada. Fraenkel
has also taught at universities in Jerusalem and Indonesia. Usually he writes
for other academic scholars, but on occasion he addresses a more general audience. He does so with the following argument about argument.

CARLOS FRAENKEL

In Praise of the Clash of Cultures

About twelve years ago, while studying Arabic in Cairo, I became friends with some Egyptian students. As we got to know each other better we also became concerned about each other's way of life. They wanted to save my soul from eternally burning in hell by converting me to Islam. I wanted to save them from wasting their real life for an illusory afterlife by converting them to the secular worldview I grew up with. In one of our discussions they asked me if I was sure that there is no proof for God's existence. The question took me by surprise. Where I had been intellectually socialized it was taken for granted that there was none. I tried to remember Kant's critique of the ontological proof for God. "Fine," Muhammad said, "but what about this table, does its existence depend on a cause?" "Of course," I answered. "And its cause depends on a further cause?" Muhammad was referring to the metaphysical proof for God's existence, first formulated by the Muslim philosopher Avicenna in the eleventh century: since an infinite regress of causes is impossible, Avicenna argues, things that depend on a cause for their existence must have something that exists through itself as their first cause. And this necessary existent is God. I had a counter-argument to that to which they in turn had a rejoinder. The discussion ended inconclusively.

I did not convert to Islam, nor did my Egyptian friends become atheists. But I learned an important lesson from our discussions: that I hadn't properly thought through some of the most basic convictions underlying my way of life and worldview—from God's existence to the human good. The challenge of my Egyptian friends forced me to think hard about these issues and defend views that had never been questioned in the European student milieu where I came from.

The other thing I realized was how contested my views were. I completed high school in a West German town in 1990 in the middle of Germany's turbulent reunification (I ended my final exam in history describing the newest political developments I had heard on the radio that same morning). For a few years after the breakdown of the Soviet bloc many thought that everyone would be secular and live in a liberal democracy before long. The discussions with my Egyptian friends brought home that I better not hold my breath.

Since that time I have organized philosophy workshops at a Palestinian university in East Jerusalem, at an Islamic university in Indonesia, with members of a Hasidic community in New York, with high school students in Salvador da Bahia (the center of Afro-Brazilian culture), and in a First Nations community in Canada. These workshops gave me first-hand insight into how deeply divided we are on fundamental moral, religious, and philosophical questions. While many find these disagreements disheartening, I will argue that they can be a good thing—if we manage to make them fruitful for a culture debate.

Can we be sure that our beliefs about the world match how the world actually is and that our subjective preferences match what is objectively in our best interest? If the truth is important to us these are pressing questions.   5

We might value the truth for different reasons: because we want to live a life that is good and doesn't just appear so; because we take knowing the truth to be an important component of the good life; because we consider living by the truth a moral obligation independent of any consequences; or because, like my Egyptian friends, we want to come closer to God who is the Truth (al-Haqq in Arabic, one of God's names in Islam). Of course we wouldn't hold our beliefs and values if we weren't *convinced* that they are true. But that's no evidence that they are. Weren't my Egyptian friends just as convinced of their views as I was of mine? More generally: don't we find a bewildering diversity of beliefs and values, all held with great conviction, across different times and cultures? If considerations such as these lead you to concede that your present convictions could be false, then you are a *fallibilist*. And if you are a fallibilist you can see why valuing the truth and valuing a culture of debate are related: because you will want to critically examine your beliefs and values, for which a culture of debate offers an excellent setting.

Of course we don't need to travel all the way to Cairo to subject our beliefs and values to critical scrutiny; in theory we can also do so on our own. In practice, however, we seem to need some sort of unsettling experience that confronts us with our fallibility, or, as the great Muslim thinker al-Ghazâlî (d. 1111) puts it in his intellectual autobiography *The Deliverance from Error*, that breaks the "bonds of taqlîd"—the beliefs and values stemming from the contingent circumstances of our socialization rather than from rational deliberation.

In his own case, al-Ghazâlî writes, the bonds of taqlîd broke when he realized that he would have been just as fervent a Jew or Christian as he was a Muslim, had he been brought up in a Jewish or Christian community. He explains taqlîd as the authority of "parents and teachers," which we can restate more generally as all things other than rational argument that influence what we think and do: from media, fashion, and marketing to political rhetoric and religious ideology.

The problem of taqlîd (or what social psychologists today call "conformism") has a long history. Socrates explained the need for his gadfly mission by comparing Athenian citizens to a "sluggish" horse that "needed to be stirred up." Note that philosophers, too, fall prey to taqlîd. Galen, the second century Alexandrian doctor and philosopher, complained that in his time Platonists, Aristotelians, Stoics, and Epicureans simply "name themselves after the sect in which they were brought up" because they "form admirations" for the school founders, not because they choose the views supported by the best arguments.

If we take taqlîd to be a fact about human psychology and agree that it is an undesirable state to be in—at least when it comes to the core convictions that underlie our way of life and worldview—then we should particularly welcome debates across cultural boundaries. For if we engage someone who does not share the cultural narratives we were brought up in (historical, political, religious, etc.), we cannot rely on their authority, but are compelled to argue for our views—as I had to in my discussions with Egyptian students in Cairo.

Consider a theological debate in the multicultural world of medieval Islam, described by the historian al-Humaydi (d. 1095):

> At the [. . .] meeting there were present not only people of various [Islamic] sects but also unbelievers, Magians, materialists, atheists, Jews, and Christians, in short unbelievers of all kinds. Each group had its own leader, whose task it was to defend its views [. . . .] One of the unbelievers rose and said to the assembly: we are meeting here for a debate; its conditions are known to all. You, Muslims, are not allowed to argue from your books and prophetic traditions since we deny both. Everybody, therefore, has to limit himself to rational arguments [hujaj al-'aql]. The whole assembly applauded these words.

We can consider ourselves lucky to live at a time in which societies are becoming increasingly heterogeneous and multicultural and globalization forces us to interact across national, cultural, religious, and other boundaries; for all this is conducive to breaking the bonds of taqlîd.

Of course diversity and disagreement on their own are not sufficient to bring about a culture of debate (otherwise the Middle East, the Balkans, and many other places would be philosophical debating clubs!). Instead they often generate frustration and resentment or, worse, erupt in violence. That's why we need a *culture* of debate. In my view, the last years of high school are the best place to lay the groundwork for such a culture.

The high school curriculum already includes subjects such as evolution, which are much more controversial than the skills required for engaging difference and disagreement in a constructive way. To provide the foundation for a culture of debate, the classes I have in mind would focus on two things: conveying techniques of debate—logical and semantic tools that allow students to clarify their views and to make and respond to arguments (a contemporary version of what Aristotelians called the Organon, the "toolkit" of the philosopher). And cultivating virtues of debate—loving the truth more than winning an argument, and trying one's best to understand the viewpoint of the opponent.

When we can transform the disagreements arising from diversity into a culture of debate, they cease to be a threat to social peace. I now live in Montréal, one of the world's most multicultural cities. When a couple of years ago I had to see a doctor, the receptionist was from China, in the waiting room I sat between a Hasidic Jew and a secular Québécois couple, the doctor who attended me was from Iran, and the nurse from Haiti. This was an impressive example of how Canadians, despite their deep moral, religious, and philosophical differences, can work together to provide the basic goods and services that we all need irrespective of our way of life and worldview.

But while I certainly didn't want to get into a shouting match about God's existence in the doctor's office, or wait for treatment until everyone had agreed on how to live, I see no reason why we should ignore our differences altogether. Some advocates of multiculturalism ask us to celebrate, rather than just tolerate, diversity, as if our differences weren't a reason for disagreement in the first   15 place, but something good and beautiful—a multicultural "mosaic"! Others argue that our moral, religious, and philosophical convictions shouldn't leave the private sphere. A good example is French laïcité: you are a *citoyen* in public and a Jew, Christian, or Muslim at home. Both models try to remove our reasons for objecting to beliefs and values we don't share—one tries to remove them altogether, the other tries at least to keep them out of sight. A culture of debate, on the other hand, allows us to engage our differences in a way that is serious, yet respectful and mutually beneficial.

Some object that a culture of debate is of no value to religious citizens. Don't they take God's wisdom to be infallible, claim to have access to it through revelation, and accept its contents on faith rather than arguments? Yet a brief look at the history of religions shows that plenty of arguing was going on about how to understand God's wisdom—within a religious tradition, with members of other religious traditions, and, more recently, with secular opponents. Al-Ghazâlî for one writes how, after the bonds of taqlîd were broken, he "scrutinized the creed of every sect" and "tried to lay bare the inmost doctrines of every community" in order to "distinguish between true and false."

The rich philosophical literatures we find in Judaism, Christianity, and Islam, as well as in the Eastern religious traditions offer plenty of resources for a culture of debate. The privatization of moral, religious, and philosophical views in liberal democracies and the cultural relativism that often underlies Western multicultural agendas are a much greater obstacle to a culture of debate than religion. My friends in Cairo at any rate, and the participants in the workshops I subsequently organized, all enjoyed arguing for their views and criticizing mine.   *[2012]*

≡ THINKING ABOUT THE TEXT

1. Fraenkel is a scholar of Jewish studies, and probably Muslims are only a small part of his readership. Yet he draws several examples and principles from Islam. Why, do you think?

2. Fraenkel makes significant use of "I" and of anecdotes about himself. How much do these personal references help his argument for a "culture of debate"?

3. How does he define this "culture"? What does it consist of? Evidently he thinks it can be distinguished from violent, counterproductive clashing. How much do you share his optimism?

4. In paragraphs 12–13, he envisions this "culture" being taught in high school. How similar was your own high school experience to what he has in mind? If many schools adopted his model, would students benefit from it? Why, or why not?

5. Fraenkel stresses the value of arguing across cultural and religious differences. But he does address challenges to this idea. What are the real or possible objections he identifies? What's his response to them?

6. In his first paragraph, Fraenkel recalls a debate he participated in. Evidently he is glad that he went through this experience. But many people would probably be nervous about getting involved in something like this. How might they feel after reading Fraenkel's entire piece? What parts of it, if any, might reassure them, and what else would they perhaps want him to say?

7. In paragraph 6, what's Fraenkel's definition of a *fallibilist*? If you're *not* a fallibilist, should anyone bother to argue with you? Why, or why not?

8. In paragraph 10, Fraenkel includes a medieval Islamic account of a religious debate. How fair is the rule imposed on the debate's Muslims? Explain your reasoning.

9. When discussing the Islamic principle of taqlīd, in paragraph 7, Fraenkel seems to agree with it. He would like us to see how our beliefs might be culturally influenced rather than truly rational. But he admits that "we seem to need some sort of unsettling experience" if we're to realize this distinction. Have you had any such experience? If so, what? What might Fraenkel say to someone who values such experiences but claims that people can have them without entering debates?

The second selection originally appeared in March 2013 as a post to the blog of the *New York Review of Books*, a magazine that not only evaluates new books but also examines culture and politics. The author, Francine Prose (b. 1947), is chiefly known as a novelist. But besides her several works of fiction, she has published books about Anne Frank, about women who were "muses" for famous writers, and about the craft of writing itself. The audience for the magazine's print and digital editions extends beyond New York City but is less general than that of the *New York Times*. It tends to consist of highly educated and well-off people who wouldn't be familiar with the lower-income schools that Prose describes. As you'll see, she draws her readers' attention to these schools' policies on cell phones.

FRANCINE PROSE
Why Are Poor Kids Paying for School Security?

When I asked the students at the Collegiate Institute for Math and Science, a public high school in the Bronx, what they thought of the metal detectors they have to pass through on their way into school, they replied that they hardly thought about them at all. The scan machines had been installed in the entry hall years before they arrived. Lining up outside, often in the cold, removing their belts, surrendering their backpacks and purses to the conveyor belt, and producing their ID cards was a part of their morning routine. But what really bothered them, what seemed unfair, and what they wanted to talk about, was a more recent development: the cell phone trucks. Cell phones are officially banned from public schools in New York City, and each morning, the students, many of whom are poor enough to qualify for the free lunch program, pay a dollar apiece to leave their phones in the privately owned trucks parked outside. Why, they asked, are the students in more prosperous neighborhoods unofficially allowed to ignore the ban, as long as they aren't caught? And why are the poor kids in the eighty-eight New York schools that have been equipped with metal detectors forced to spend five dollars a week—an expense that, for some, means going without food?

For almost a decade, I have been visiting classrooms in Harlem, the Bronx, and Far Rockaway under the auspices of a nonprofit organization, Behind the Book. The students (usually but not exclusively in honors or advanced placement classes) are assigned to read one of my novels, to come up with questions, and to write brief essays that I then discuss with them. I always find these visits interesting, highly enjoyable—and immensely educational. Each time, I'm given a glimpse of a city very different from the New York in which I live.

I usually spend the first part of each class talking about whatever book of mine the students have read and about books in general; the kids want to know how I became a writer, what my typical day is like, how I make a living. After that, I ask them what *they* have been thinking, about what concerns them, about their lives—which, I know, are often extremely difficult. The fact that they are excelling in their studies seems all the more remarkable given how often their teachers have told me about the challenge of educating kids who may not have enough to eat, a safe place to do their homework, or, for that matter, a home. One hears that teenagers are secretive and shy, but in my experience they are often so astonished that an adult is interested in what they have to say, they'll start talking before they realize that's what they're doing. In one class, in Far Rockaway, the students, many of whom lived in the projects, wanted to complain about the omnipresence of surveillance cameras in their lobbies, hallways, and elevators. They laughed when I asked if the cameras made them feel safer.

A girl said, "They're watching *us*."

Last week, I visited the Collegiate Institute, one of the seven schools included within the Christopher Columbus Educational Campus, an enormous institution (most of whose 3,000 students are black or Latino) that has been broken up into smaller units, partly in response to the city's repeated efforts to close it for poor performance; Collegiate is considered the most academically challenging of the schools within the larger complex.

The students had read my novel *After*, which is set in a school that becomes an Orwellian police state, a transformation effected by following, then exceeding, a series of guidelines I found on the internet simply by typing in "Preventing School Violence." The students hadn't failed to notice that, in my novel, one of the first steps on the road to dystopia is the installation of metal detectors. And they said what kids in the so-called "scan schools" always say. The students who want to smuggle in weapons find ways to smuggle in weapons. And the scans just make everyone else late for class.

On the other hand, the cell phone trucks were, they felt, an outrage. Their phones are not merely a way of getting in touch with friends, but a necessity for their safety. Many have long and late commutes through dangerous neighborhoods and need to be able to reach their parents and to get help in case of emergencies.

The kids told me that they had asked the administration about the possibility of having a storage area in the school where they could check their phones, but were told that this would be "too chaotic." Yet a Philadelphia school principal, quoted in the *Huffington Post* in October, said that her city does indeed have an on-site student-run storage area. In the same article, the PTA president of the Frank McCourt High School on Manhattan's Upper West Side, which is also equipped with metal detectors, said that the parents' organization had offered to run a cell phone storage room in the school, and that their offer had been rejected.

Meanwhile the cell phone trucks are generating large amounts of cash for the companies that operate them. With seven trucks, Pure Loyalty is the largest of the firms; others include Safe Mobile Storage, Cell Secure Electronic Storage, Smart Dock, Archangel, and Holding Cell. According to the *New York Post*, the cell phone storage business takes in $22,800 a day, or $4.2 million a year—most of this from poor kids, and in a city that is slashing its school budget. When the City Council suggested lifting the ban on cell phones to ameliorate the problem, its recommendation was countermanded by DOE Chancellor Walcott and Mayor Bloomberg.

During the two hours I spent at the school, a request came over the loud-speakers (the lessons are routinely interrupted by messages that erupt at random and last for minutes, announcing the start of the Toys for Tots Program, and so forth) for back-up to help deal with a "situation"—indicating some kind of violent incident involving one or more students. It would be naïve to deny that these kids inhabit a frequently violent culture from which we want to protect them—just as it would be naïve to deny that the majority of New York's middle-class white parents have found a way for their children to attend school that does not involve metal detectors.

Everyone who has ever driven north along Park Avenue has noticed how dramatically the scenery changes around 100th Street. Not only do the luxury apartment buildings give way to tenements and bodegas, but the smooth, well-maintained streets of the Upper East Side become the rutted, pocked roads and sidewalks of Spanish Harlem. On the northern side of that divide, minority kids are being forbidden something that their more fortunate white counterparts are freely allowed, and poor students are being heavily taxed for the privilege of being harassed and inconvenienced. Were it not for my own brief trips across that border, I would never have known about the cell phone trucks. I might never have noticed them, as I do now, in my own neighborhood, outside Washington Irving High School, another "scan school."

I hope that my visit to their class energized or inspired some of the students. I know that I'm grateful to have learned about something I might otherwise

10

not have been aware of, about yet another example of what is allowed to happen when no one is paying attention, or when no one cares sufficiently about
the inequities that exist, when no one sees a problem when companies, with
the full endorsement of the mayor and the schools chancellor, are able to ex-
ploit the security requirements of schools in poorer neighborhoods to make
millions of dollars from the students who can least afford to pay.   *[2013]*

≡ THINKING ABOUT THE TEXT

1. What is Prose's main issue? Try to put it in the form of a question. What is her main claim (her apparent answer)?

2. Prose refers to herself a lot. How would you describe her ethos? List a few specific adjectives. To what extent do her personal references help make her essay persuasive?

3. Evidently Prose bases her essay on a two-hour visit she made to the Collegiate Institute. Should she have conducted more research before writing? If so, what sorts of research?

4. What might be the arguments of those who support New York City's ban on cell phones in public schools? Should Prose have mentioned and addressed these arguments? Why, or why not?

5. According to the students that Prose met, administrators at the Collegiate Institute refused to offer storage space for cell phones because it would become "too chaotic." What other arguments, if any, might these administrators make? Should Prose have mentioned and addressed such possible arguments more? Why, or why not?

6. What concessions, if any, does Prose make?

7. In paragraph 9, Prose seems critical of the cell phone trucks that students must turn to. How critical do you feel toward the companies in this business? Do you consider them evil? Why, or why not? What arguments might these companies make to defend themselves?

8. How does Prose feel about metal detectors in schools? Identify specific passages where you sense her attitude toward them. Did you attend a school that used these detectors? If so, how necessary did you think they were? In general, how "secure" were the schools you attended? What factors seemed to determine their level of "security"? How would you define these terms with respect to schools?

9. Read Paul Goldberger's essay on cell phones, which opens this chapter. What might he say about Prose's criticisms?

10. In paragraph 7, Prose seems to share the students' feeling that cell phones are necessary for them. But these phones didn't always exist in the first place. Many people can recall a time before them. Imagine someone — perhaps Goldberger? — who argues that cell phones can't possibly be "a necessity" (para. 7) because humanity managed to get along without them for ages. How might Prose respond to this argument?

11. At the end of her first paragraph, Prose says the Collegiate Institute students informed her that "the students in more prosperous neighborhoods" are "unofficially allowed to ignore the ban, as long as they aren't caught." In paragraph 10, she herself claims "it would be naïve to deny that the majority of New York's middle-class white parents have found a way for their children to attend school that does not involve metal detectors." How much *should* a city's school board consider the relative prosperity of neighborhoods in setting policies on cell phones and metal detectors? Explain your reasoning.

CHAPTER 2

How to Argue about Literature

What Is Literature?

Most people would say that *literature* consists of fiction (novels as well as short stories), poetry, and drama. It's a reasonable definition. But limiting the term to these genres can be misleading. After all, they connect to everyday life. Often they employ ordinary forms of talk and blend them with less common ones. Also, things that function as symbols in stories, poems, and plays may do so in daily conversation. As we speak with one another, we may associate fire with passion, water with life, evening with death. Throughout the day, actually, people put literary genres into practice. Perhaps you have commented on situations by quoting a song lyric or citing a line of verse. No doubt you are often theatrical, following scripts and performing roles. Certainly you tell stories. Imagine this scenario: a traffic jam has made you late for a class; now, you must explain your delay. You may relate a tale of suspense, with you the hero struggling to escape the bumper-to-bumper horde. Almost all of us spin narratives day after day, because doing so helps us meaningfully frame our existence. As writer Joan Didion observes, "We tell ourselves stories in order to live."

You may admit that literature is grounded in real life and yet still tend to apply the term only to written texts of fiction, poetry, and drama. But this tendency is distinctly modern, for the term *literature* has not always been applied so restrictively. *Literature* was at first a characteristic of *readers*. From the term's emergence in the fourteenth century to the middle of the eighteenth, *literature* was more or less a synonym for *literacy*. People of literature were assumed to be well read.

In the late eighteenth century, however, the term's meaning changed. Increasingly it referred to books and other printed texts rather than to people who read them. At the beginning of this shift, the scope of literature was broad, encompassing nearly all public writing. But as the nineteenth century proceeded, the term's range shrank. More and more people considered literature to be imaginative or creative writing, which they distinguished from nonfiction. This trend did take years to build; in the early 1900s, literature anthologies still featured *nonfiction* such as essays and excerpts from histories and biographies. By the mid-1900s, though, the narrower definition of literature prevailed.

This limited definition has become vulnerable. From the early 1970s, a number of literature faculty have called for widening it. In 1979, for instance, a National Endowment for the Humanities–Modern Language Association institute entitled "Women's Nontraditional Literature" applied the term *literature* to genres that had not been thought of as such. Participants studied essays, letters, diaries, autobiographies, and oral testimonies. To each of these genres, women have contributed much; in fact, the institute's participants concluded that a literature curriculum slights many works by women if it focuses on fiction, poetry, and drama alone.

Of course, even within these three categories, the term *literature* has been selectively applied. Take the case of novelist and short-story writer Stephen King, whose books have sold millions of copies. Despite his commercial success, a lot of readers—including some of his fans—refuse to call King's writing literature. They assume that to call something literature is to say that it has artistic merit, and for them King's tales of horror fall short.

Yet people who use the term *literature* as a compliment may still disagree about whether a certain text deserves it. Plenty of readers do praise King's writing as literature, even as others deem it simply entertainment. In short, artistic standards differ. To be sure, some works have been constantly admired through the years; regarded as classics, they are frequently taught in literature classes. *Hamlet* and other plays by William Shakespeare are obvious examples. But in the last twenty years, much controversy has arisen over the *literary canon*, those works taught again and again. Are there good reasons why the canon has consisted mostly of works by white men? Or have the principles of selection been skewed by sexism and racism? Should the canon be changed to accommodate a greater range of authors? Or should literary studies resist having any canon at all? These questions have provoked various answers and continued debate.

Also in question are attempts to separate literature from nonfiction. Much nonfiction shows imagination and relies on devices found in novels, short stories, poems, and plays. The last few years have seen emerge the term *creative nonfiction* as a synonym for essays, histories, and journalistic accounts that use evocative language and strong narratives. Conversely, works of fiction, poetry, and drama may stem from real-life events. Charlotte Perkins Gilman based her 1892 short story "The Yellow Wallpaper" (see p. 778) on trauma she went through when her doctor, treating her for depression, made her stop work and vegetate. Gilman's heroine suffers torment similar to hers. A note of caution is in order, though. A literary text may seem autobiographical but not directly reflect the author's life. The situation of Gilman's heroine doesn't completely resemble her own. It differs in certain ways. Indeed, the character is too distressed to write a story as Gilman herself did. In short, Gilman didn't merely transmit her experience. Rather, she *transformed* it. So, her artistic strategies merit study, especially since she could have tapped her experience in other ways. Keep in mind, too, that the author of a work isn't always the best guide to it. It may raise for its readers issues and ideas that the author didn't foresee. Besides, the author's comments about the text may leave aspects of it unexplained.

Some people argue that literature about real events is still "literary" because it inspires contemplation rather than action. This view of literature has traditionally been summed up as "art for art's sake." This notion brushes aside, however, all the novels, short stories, poems, and plays that encourage audiences to undertake certain acts. Famous examples are Harriet Beecher Stowe's antislavery novel *Uncle Tom's Cabin* (1852) and Upton Sinclair's *The Jungle* (1906) about the horrors of immigrant exploitation in the Chicago meatpacking industry. True, not every work of literature is so conspicuously action-oriented. But even when a text seems more geared toward reflection, it may move readers to change their behavior.

In our book, we resist endorsing a single definition of *literature*. Rather, we encourage you to review and perhaps rethink what the term means to you. At the same time, to expand the realm of literature, we include several essays in addition to short stories, poems, and plays. We also present numerous critical commentaries as well as various historical documents. Throughout the book, we invite you to make connections among these different kinds of texts. You need not treat them as altogether separate species.

Why Study Literature in a College Writing Course?

We assume you are reading this book in a course aimed at helping you write. Quite likely the course is meant to prepare you for writing assignments throughout college, including papers in fields beyond English. It's natural to wonder how reading literature serves this purpose.

Much academic writing is, in fact, based on reading. You'll find the two interconnected in course after course. Many classes will ask you to produce essays that analyze published texts. To *analyze* means going beyond your first impressions, carefully noting a text's ideas, techniques, and effects. You'll also find yourself needing to *synthesize*: that is, to trace how the text is patterned, as well as how it relates to other works. Together, these acts of analysis and synthesis have been called reading *closely*, a process we explain and model in Chapter 3. We encourage you to practice this method with the selections in our book.

Often, college courses will ask you to write about some text that isn't easily understood. The purpose of your paper will be to help other readers of the text grasp its meanings and, perhaps, judge its worth. Literature is a good training ground for these skills of interpretation and evaluation. The poems, stories, plays, and essays in this book repeatedly invite inquiry. They don't settle for delivering simple straightforward messages. Rather, they offer puzzles, complications, metaphors, symbols, and mysteries, thereby recognizing that life is complex. In particular, literary works encourage you to ponder the multiple dimensions of language: how, for example, a word's meaning can vary depending on context. Furthermore, much literature can help you understand your own life and conduct it better. In this capacity, literature serves as "equipment for living," scholar-critic Kenneth Burke's description of its function.

Some people *dislike* literature because they find it too vague and indirect. They resent that it often forces them to figure out symbols and implications when they would rather have ideas presented outright. Perhaps you'll wish that the narrator in Gilman's story had made clear why her observations prompted her to destroy her room's wallpaper. But in life, truth can be complicated and elusive. In many ways, literature is most realistic when it suggests the same. Besides, many readers — perhaps including you — appreciate literature most when it resists simple decoding, forcing them to adopt new assumptions and learn new methods of analysis. Indeed, throughout this book we suggest that the most interesting and profitable conversations about literature are those in which the issues are not easily resolved. One of the best things your course can provide you and your classmates is the chance to exchange insights about texts such as Gilman's.

We have been suggesting that one value of studying literature in a writing class is that it often engages not just thought but feeling. The two interweave so that readers find themselves engaging in interpretation and evaluation because they *care* about lives depicted in the text. Most of the works in this book appeal to your emotions, encouraging you to identify with certain characters, to be disturbed by others, and to wonder what happens next in the plot. Indeed, many readers of literature prize the moments when it makes them laugh or cry or gasp as well as think. To be sure, it can be argued that the most worthwhile literature gets us to comprehend, and perhaps even appreciate, certain kinds of people who would normally confuse or disturb us. "When it's the real thing," critic Frank Lentricchia suggests, "literature enlarges us, strips the film of familiarity from the world; creates bonds of sympathy with all kinds, even with evil characters, who we learn are all in the family." This "enlargement" is both intellectual *and* emotional.

Finally, writing about literature is good training for other fields because literary analysis often involves taking an interdisciplinary perspective. A typical interpretation of "The Yellow Wallpaper" will bring in principles of psychology to explain the speaker's distressed state of mind. To evaluate the character's condition, readers also grapple with philosophical questions about what constitutes a "productive" or "good" or "free" life. Moreover, the heroine's entrapment in nineteenth-century gender roles has political, historical, and sociological significance.

Two Stories for Analysis

As we discuss the process of arguing about literature, we mention arguments that might be made about the following pair of stories. Each features a speaker who is introducing someone else to certain kinds of work. It is useful to compare these texts. Indeed, we emphasize comparison throughout this book. As you read each story, take a few moments to reflect on the questions we ask after each one, perhaps jotting down your responses to keep them in your mind as you read the rest of the chapter.

The first story, "Orientation," originally appeared in a 1994 issue of *Seattle Review* and was subsequently selected for *The Best American Short Stories 1995*.

DANIEL OROZCO
Orientation

The son of Nicaraguan immigrants, California-born Daniel Orozco (b. 1957) currently teaches at the University of Idaho. His award-winning short fiction has appeared in a variety of magazines, including Harper's *and* Zoetrope, *and has been collected in* Orientation and Other Stories *(2011). He received a B.A. from Stanford University, an M.A. from San Francisco State University, and an M.F.A. from the University of Washington. He has also held a writing fellowship at Stanford.*

Those are the offices and these are the cubicles. That's my cubicle there, and this is your cubicle. This is your phone. Never answer your phone. Let the Voicemail System answer it. This is your Voicemail System Manual. There are no personal phone calls allowed. We do, however, allow for emergencies. If you must make an emergency phone call, ask your supervisor first. If you can't find your supervisor, ask Phillip Spiers, who sits over there. He'll check with Clarissa Nicks, who sits over there. If you make an emergency phone call without asking, you may be let go.

These are your IN and OUT boxes. All the forms in your IN box must be logged in by the date shown in the upper left-hand corner, initialed by you in the upper right-hand corner, and distributed to the Processing Analyst whose name is numerically coded in the lower left-hand corner. The lower right-hand corner is left blank. Here's your Processing Analyst Numerical Code Index. And here's your Forms Processing Procedures Manual.

You must pace your work. What do I mean? I'm glad you asked that. We pace our work according to the eight-hour workday. If you have twelve hours of work in your IN box, for example, you must compress that work into the eight-hour day. If you have one hour of work in your IN box, you must expand that work to fill the eight-hour day. That was a good question. Feel free to ask questions. Ask too many questions, however, and you may be let go.

That is our receptionist. She is a temp. We go through receptionists here. They quit with alarming frequency. Be polite and civil to the temps. Learn their names, and invite them to lunch occasionally. But don't get close to them, as it only makes it more difficult when they leave. And they always leave. You can be sure of that.

The men's room is over there. The women's room is over there. John LaFountaine, who sits over there, uses the women's room occasionally. He says it is accidental. We know better, but we let it pass. John LaFountaine is harmless, his forays into the forbidden territory of the women's room simply a benign thrill, a faint blip on the dull flat line of his life.

Russell Nash, who sits in the cubicle to your left, is in love with Amanda Pierce, who sits in the cubicle to your right. They ride the same bus together after work. For Amanda Pierce, it is just a tedious bus ride made less tedious by the idle nattering of Russell Nash. But for Russell Nash, it is the highlight of his day. It is the highlight of his life. Russell Nash has put on forty pounds, and grows fatter with each passing month, nibbling on chips and cookies while peeking glumly over the partitions at Amanda Pierce, and gorging himself at home on cold pizza and ice cream while watching adult videos on TV.

Amanda Pierce, in the cubicle to your right, has a six-year-old son named Jamie, who is autistic. Her cubicle is plastered from top to bottom with the boy's crayon artwork—sheet after sheet of precisely drawn concentric circles and ellipses, in black and yellow. She rotates them every other Friday. Be sure to comment on them. Amanda Pierce also has a husband, who is a lawyer. He subjects her to an escalating array of painful and humiliating sex games, to which Amanda Pierce reluctantly submits. She comes to work exhausted and freshly wounded each morning, wincing from the abrasions on her breasts, or the bruises on her abdomen, or the second-degree burns on the backs of her thighs.

But we're not supposed to know any of this. Do not let on. If you let on, you may be let go.

Amanda Pierce, who tolerates Russell Nash, is in love with Albert Bosch, whose office is over there. Albert Bosch, who only dimly registers Amanda Pierce's existence, has eyes only for Ellie Tapper, who sits over there. Ellie Tapper, who hates Albert Bosch, would walk through fire for Curtis Lance. But Curtis Lance hates Ellie Tapper. Isn't the world a funny place? Not in the ha-ha sense, of course.

Anika Bloom sits in that cubicle. Last year, while reviewing quarterly reports in a meeting with Barry Hacker, Anika Bloom's left palm began to bleed. She fell into a trance, stared into her hand, and told Barry Hacker when and how his wife would die. We laughed it off. She was, after all, a new employee. But Barry Hacker's wife is dead. So unless you want to know exactly when and how you'll die, never talk to Anika Bloom.

Colin Heavey sits in that cubicle over there. He was new once, just like you. We warned him about Anika Bloom. But at last year's Christmas Potluck, he felt sorry for her when he saw that no one was talking to her. Colin Heavey brought her a drink. He hasn't been himself since. Colin Heavey is doomed. There's nothing he can do about it, and we are powerless to help him. Stay away from Colin Heavey. Never give any of your work to him. If he asks to do something, tell him you have to check with me. If he asks again, tell him I haven't gotten back to you.

This is the Fire Exit. There are several on this floor, and they are marked accordingly. We have a Floor Evacuation Review every three months, and an Escape Route Quiz once a month. We have our Biannual Fire Drill twice a year, and our Annual Earthquake Drill once a year. These are precautions only. These things never happen.

For your information, we have a comprehensive health plan. Any catastrophic illness, any unforeseen tragedy is completely covered. All dependents are completely covered. Larry Bagdikian, who sits over there, has six daughters. If anything were to happen to any of his girls, or to all of them, if all six were to simultaneously fall victim to illness or injury—stricken with a hideous degenerative muscle disease or some rare toxic blood disorder, sprayed with semiautomatic gunfire while on a class field trip, or attacked in their bunk

10

beds by some prowling nocturnal lunatic—if any of this were to pass, Larry's girls would all be taken care of. Larry Bagdikian would not have to pay one dime. He would have nothing to worry about.

We also have a generous vacation and sick leave policy. We have an excellent disability insurance plan. We have a stable and profitable pension fund. We get group discounts for the symphony, and block seating at the ballpark. We get commuter ticket books for the bridge. We have Direct Deposit. We are all members of Costco.

This is our kitchenette. And this, this is our Mr. Coffee. We have a coffee pool, into which we each pay two dollars a week for coffee, filters, sugar, and CoffeeMate. If you prefer Cremora or half-and-half to CoffeeMate, there is a special pool for three dollars a week. If you prefer Sweet 'n Low to sugar, there is a special pool for two-fifty a week. We do not do decaf. You are allowed to join the coffee pool of your choice, but you are not allowed to touch the Mr. Coffee.

This is the microwave oven. You are allowed to *heat* food in the microwave oven. You are not, however, allowed to *cook* food in the microwave oven.

We get one hour for lunch. We also get one fifteen-minute break in the morning, and one fifteen-minute break in the afternoon. Always take your breaks. If you skip a break, it is gone forever. For your information, your break is a privilege, not a right. If you abuse the break policy, we are authorized to rescind your breaks. Lunch, however, is a right, not a privilege. If you abuse the lunch policy, our hands will be tied, and we will be forced to look the other way. We will not enjoy that.

This is the refrigerator. You may put your lunch in it. Barry Hacker, who sits over there, steals food from this refrigerator. His petty theft is an outlet for his grief. Last New Year's Eve, while kissing his wife, a blood vessel burst in her brain. Barry Hacker's wife was two months pregnant at the time, and lingered in a coma for half a year before dying. It was a tragic loss for Barry Hacker. He hasn't been himself since. Barry Hacker's wife was a beautiful woman. She was also completely covered. Barry Hacker did not have to pay one dime. But his dead wife haunts him. She haunts all of us. We have seen her, reflected in the monitors of our computers, moving past our cubicles. We have seen the dim shadow of her face in our photocopies. She pencils herself in in the receptionist's appointment book, with the notation: To see Barry Hacker. She has left messages in the receptionist's Voicemail box, messages garbled by the electronic chirrups and buzzes in the phone line, her voice echoing from an immense distance within the ambient hum. But the voice is hers. And beneath her voice, beneath the tidal *whoosh* of static and hiss, the gurgling and crying of a baby can be heard.

In any case, if you bring a lunch, put a little something extra in the bag for Barry Hacker. We have four Barrys in this office. Isn't that a coincidence?

This is Matthew Payne's office. He is our Unit Manager, and his door is always closed. We have never seen him, and you will never see him. But he is here. You can be sure of that. He is all around us.

This is the Custodian's Closet. You have no business in the Custodian's Closet.

And this, this is our Supplies Cabinet. If you need supplies, see Curtis Lance. He will log you in on the Supplies Cabinet Authorization Log, then give you a Supplies Authorization Slip. Present your pink copy of the Supplies Authorization Slip to Ellie Tapper. She will log you in on the Supplies Cabinet Key Log, then give you the key. Because the Supplies Cabinet is located outside the Unit Manager's office, you must be very quiet. Gather your supplies quietly. The Supplies Cabinet is divided into four sections. Section One contains letterhead stationery, blank paper and envelopes, memo and note pads, and so on. Section Two contains pens and pencils and typewriter and printer ribbons, and the like. In Section Three we have erasers, correction fluids, transparent tapes, glue sticks, et cetera. And in Section Four we have paper clips and push pins and scissors and razor blades. And here are the spare blades for the shredder. Do not touch the shredder, which is located over there. The shredder is of no concern to you.

Gwendolyn Stich sits in that office there. She is crazy about penguins, and collects penguin knickknacks: penguin posters and coffee mugs and stationery, penguin stuffed animals, penguin jewelry, penguin sweaters and T-shirts and socks. She has a pair of penguin fuzzy slippers she wears when working late at the office. She has a tape cassette of penguin sounds which she listens to for relaxation. Her favorite colors are black and white. She has personalized license plates that read PEN GWEN. Every morning, she passes through all the cubicles to wish each of us a *good* morning. She brings Danish on Wednesdays for Hump Day morning break, and doughnuts on Fridays for TGIF afternoon break. She organizes the Annual Christmas Potluck, and is in charge of the Birthday List. Gwendolyn Stich's door is always open to all of us. She will always lend an ear, and put in a good word for you; she will always give you a hand, or the shirt off her back, or a shoulder to cry on. Because her door is always open, she hides and cries in a stall in the women's room. And John LaFountaine—who, enthralled when a woman enters, sits quietly in his stall with his knees to his chest—John LaFountaine has heard her vomiting in there. We have come upon Gwendolyn Stich huddled in the stairwell, shivering in the updraft, sipping a Diet Mr. Pibb and hugging her knees. She does not let any of this interfere with her work. If it interfered with her work, she might have to be let go.

Kevin Howard sits in that cubicle over there. He is a serial killer, the one they call the Carpet Cutter, responsible for the mutilations across town. We're not supposed to know that, so do not let on. Don't worry. His compulsion inflicts itself on strangers only, and the routine established is elaborate and unwavering. The victim must be a white male, a young adult no older than thirty, heavyset, with dark hair and eyes, and the like. The victim must be chosen at random, before sunset, from a public place; the victim is followed home, and must put up a struggle; et cetera. The carnage inflicted is precise: the angle and direction of the incisions; the layering of skin and muscle tissue; the rearrangement of the visceral organs; and so on. Kevin Howard does not let any of this interfere with his work. He is, in fact, our fastest typist. He types as if he were on fire. He has a secret crush on Gwendolyn Stich, and leaves a red-foil-wrapped

Hershey's Kiss on her desk every afternoon. But he hates Anika Bloom, and keeps well away from her. In his presence, she has uncontrollable fits of shaking and trembling. Her left palm does not stop bleeding.

In any case, when Kevin Howard gets caught, act surprised. Say that he   25
seemed like a nice person, a bit of a loner, perhaps, but always quiet and polite.

This is the photocopier room. And this, this is our view. It faces southwest. West is down there, toward the water. North is back there. Because we are on the seventeenth floor, we are afforded a magnificent view. Isn't it beautiful? It overlooks the park, where the tops of those trees are. You can see a segment of the bay between those two buildings there. You can see the sun set in the gap between those two buildings over there. You can see this building reflected in the glass panels of that building across the way. There. See? That's you, waving. And look there. There's Anika Bloom in the kitchenette, waving back.

Enjoy this view while photocopying. If you have problems with the photocopier, see Russell Nash. If you have any questions, ask your supervisor. If you can't find your supervisor, ask Phillip Spiers. He sits over there. He'll check with Clarissa Nicks. She sits over there. If you can't find them, feel free to ask me. That's my cubicle. I sit in there.   *[1994]*

≡ THINKING ABOUT THE TEXT

1. Orozco reports that since his story was published, "it has even been included in an employee orientation manual, which is either very funny or very disturbing." What is *your* reaction to this news? Does this orientation resemble other orientations with which you are familiar? In what ways? Consider the kinds of advice given and language used.

2. Does the office described here resemble other offices with which you are familiar? In what ways? At what points in the story does this office seem unusual?

3. List at least three adjectives that describe Orozco's narrator. What influences your evaluation of this narrator? What would you say to someone who claims that the story is more about the narrator than about the office?

4. What assumptions do you make about the narrator's audience, that is, the listener being oriented? Write a page or two from this person's point of view, stating his or her response to the orientation.

5. Does the order of the narrator's statements matter? Explain.

The next story, Jamaica Kincaid's "Girl," first appeared in *The New Yorker* in 1978 and was later reprinted in her first book, a 1984 collection of short stories entitled *At the Bottom of the River*.

JAMAICA KINCAID
Girl

Originally named Elaine Potter Richardson, Jamaica Kincaid (b. 1949) was born on the island of Antigua in the West Indies. At the time, Antigua was a British colony. Kincaid lived there until she was seventeen, when she emigrated to the United States. Soon she became a nanny for the family of Michael Arlen, television critic for The New Yorker. *Eventually, the magazine published her own short stories and during the early 1990s her gardening columns. Although she continues to live in the United States, almost all of her writing deals with her native land. In particular, she has written about Antiguan women growing up under British domination. She has published the novels* Annie John *(1985),* Lucy *(1990),* Autobiography of My Mother *(1996), and* Mr. Potter *(2002). Her books of nonfiction include* A Small Place, *an analysis of Antigua (1988); a memoir,* My Brother *(1997);* My Garden (Book) *(1999); and* Talk Stories *(2001), a collection of brief observations that she originally wrote for* The New Yorker. *In 2009, she was inducted into the American Academy of Arts and Sciences and is currently a professor of literature at Claremont McKenna College in California. Her latest novel is* See Now Then *(2013).*

Wash the white clothes on Monday and put them on the stone heap; wash the color clothes on Tuesday and put them on the clothesline to dry; don't walk barehead in the hot sun; cook pumpkin fritters in very hot sweet oil; soak your little cloths right after you take them off; when buying cotton to make yourself a nice blouse, be sure that it doesn't have gum on it, because that way it won't   5
hold up well after a wash; soak salt fish overnight before you cook it; is it true that you sing benna° in Sunday school?; always eat your food in such a way that it won't turn someone else's stomach; on Sundays try to walk like a lady and not like the slut you are so bent on becoming; don't sing benna in Sunday school; you mustn't speak to wharf-rat boys, not even to give directions; don't   10
eat fruits on the street—flies will follow you; *but I don't sing benna on Sundays at all and never in Sunday school*; this is how to sew on a button; this is how to make a button-hole for the button you have just sewed on; this is how to hem a dress when you see the hem coming down and so to prevent yourself from looking like the slut I know you are so bent on becoming; this is how you iron your   15
father's khaki shirt so that it doesn't have a crease; this is how you iron your father's khaki pants so that they don't have a crease; this is how you grow okra—far from the house, because okra tree harbors red ants; when you are growing dasheen, make sure it gets plenty of water or else it makes your throat itch when you are eating it; this is how you sweep a corner; this is   20
how you sweep a whole house; this is how you sweep a yard; this is how you smile to someone you don't like too much; this is how you smile to someone you don't like at all; this is how you smile to someone you like completely; this is how you set a table for tea; this is how you set a table for dinner; this is how

benna: Calypso music.

you set a table for dinner with an important guest; this is how you set a table for   25
lunch; this is how you set a table for breakfast; this is how to behave in the presence of men who don't know you very well, and this way they won't recognize
immediately the slut I have warned you against becoming; be sure to wash every day, even if it is with your own spit; don't squat down to play marbles — you
are not a boy, you know; don't pick people's flowers — you might catch some-   30
thing; don't throw stones at blackbirds, because it might not be a blackbird at
all; this is how to make a bread pudding; this is how to make doukona;° this is
how to make pepper pot; this is how to make a good medicine for a cold; this is
how to make a good medicine to throw away a child before it even becomes a
child; this is how to catch a fish; this is how to throw back a fish you don't like,   35
and that way something bad won't fall on you; this is how to bully a man; this
is how a man bullies you; this is how to love a man, and if this doesn't work
there are other ways, and if they don't work don't feel too bad about giving up;
this is how to spit up in the air if you feel like it, and this is how to move quick
so that it doesn't fall on you; this is how to make ends meet; always squeeze   40
bread to make sure it's fresh; *but what if the baker won't let me feel the bread?*; you
mean to say that after all you are really going to be the kind of woman who the
baker won't let near the bread?   *[1978]*

doukona: A spicy plantain pudding.

≡ THINKING ABOUT THE TEXT

1. Is "Girl" really a story? What characteristics of a story come to mind as you consider this issue?

2. Describe the culture depicted in "Girl" as well as the role of females in that culture. Is either the culture or the role of females in it different from what you are familiar with? Explain.

3. Do you think that the instructions to this girl are all given on the same occasion? Why, or why not? Who do you suppose is giving the instructions? Would you say that the instructor is oppressive or domineering? Identify some of the assumptions behind your position.

4. What effect does Kincaid achieve by making this text a single long sentence? By having the girl speak at only two brief moments?

5. At one point, the girl is shown "how to make a good medicine to throw away a child before it even becomes a child" (lines 33–34). What do you think of the instructor's willingness to give such advice? What do you conclude from its position in the text between "how to make a good medicine for a cold" (line 33) and "how to catch a fish" (line 35)? Does the order of the various pieces of advice matter? Could Kincaid have presented them in a different order without changing their effects?

≡ A WRITING EXERCISE

Once you have read both stories, write brief responses to each. You might jot down things you especially notice about them, feelings they evoke in you, and questions you have about them. You might also note your own work experiences that they lead you to recall. With each story, freewrite for ten minutes without stopping.

Strategies for Arguing about Literature

We return now to the specific elements of argument we discussed in Chapter 1. Remember that when you argue, you try to **persuade** an **audience** to accept your **claims** about an **issue**, working toward this aim by offering **evidence**, showing your **reasoning**, making **assumptions**, and employing other kinds of **appeals**. Here, with Orozco's and Kincaid's stories as our sample texts, we show how you can turn these elements into strategies for writing arguments about literature.

IDENTIFY ISSUES

Recall that an **issue** is something about which people have disagreed or might disagree. Even as you read a text, you can try to guess what features of it will lead to disagreements in class. You may sense that your own reaction to certain aspects of the text is heavily influenced by your background and values, which other students may not share. Some parts of the text may leave you with conflicting ideas or mixed feelings, as if half of you disagrees with the other half. At moments like these, you come to realize what topics are issues for you, and next you can urge the rest of your class to see these topics as issues, too.

An issue is best defined as a question with no obvious, immediate answer. Thus, you can start identifying issues by noting questions that occur to you as you read. Perhaps this question-posing approach to texts is new for you. Often readers demand that a text be clear, and they get annoyed if it leaves them puzzled. Certain writing ought to be immediately clear in meaning; think of operating instructions on a plane's emergency doors. But the value of a literary work often lies in the work's complexities, which can lead readers to reexamine their own ways of perceiving the world. Also, your discussions and papers about literature are likely to be most useful when they go beyond the obvious to deal with more challenging matters. When your class begins talking about a work, you may feel obliged to stay quiet if you have no firm statements to make. But you can contribute a lot by bringing up questions that occurred to you as you read. Especially worth raising are questions that continue to haunt you.

In the case of Daniel Orozco's "Orientation," one possible issue concerns the reliability of the narrator. Should we accept as true everything the narrator says, or should we be suspicious of the orientation this person gives? A possible issue with Jamaica Kincaid's "Girl" concerns how much affection the main speaker has for the girl she addresses. A logical hypothesis is that these two are mother and daughter, but to what degree is the speaker showing motherly love? In fact, people may disagree over how to define this term. What does it mean to *you*?

You may feel unable to answer questions like these. But again, you achieve much when you simply formulate questions and bring them up in class. As other students help you ponder them, you will grow better able to explore issues through writing as well as through conversation.

You are more likely to come up with questions about a text if you assume that for every decision the writer made, alternatives existed. In "Orientation," Orozco might have had the many characters speak, but instead he chose to write the story as a mostly uninterrupted monologue. Similarly, Kincaid might have given the girl of her title more of a speaking voice. When you begin to explore why authors made the choices they did, you also begin to examine the effects of those choices.

You will recognize writers' options more easily if you compare their texts with others. For instance, with "Orientation" you cannot be sure how old the narrator and new employee are, but Kincaid's story is pointedly entitled "Girl," and its speaker is clearly a female adult. Although both stories are about education, Kincaid's is concerned with the transition from youth to adulthood. She shows how a girl's transition to womanhood involves learning certain gender "rules" of her sex. Thinking of Kincaid's focus can strengthen your awareness that Orozco has chosen not to reveal whether his story's two characters are male or female.

Next we identify ten kinds of issues that arise in literature courses. Our list will help you detect the issues that come up in your class and discover others to bring up in discussions or in your writing. The list does not include every kind of issue; you may think of others. Moreover, you may find that an issue can fit into more than one of the categories we name. But when you do have an issue that seems hard to classify, try to assign it to a single category, if only for the time being. You will then have some initial guidance for your reading, class discussions, and writing. If you later feel that the issue belongs to another category, you can shift your focus.

1. Issues of fact.   Rarely does a work of literature provide complete information about its characters and events. Rather, literature is usually marked by what literary theorist Wolfgang Iser calls "gaps," moments when certain facts are omitted or obscured. At such times, readers may give various answers to the question, What is happening in this text? Readers tackle questions of fact only if they suspect that the answers will affect their overall view of a text. It may not matter, for example, that we fail to learn the exact product or service of the company described in Orozco's "Orientation." More consequential seems the question of whether Barry Hacker's dead wife is really sending messages to the office. Imagine a reader who believes that Orozco's narrator is merely fantasizing a ghost. Imagine a second reader who thinks the wife is truly haunting the office. How might these two readers see the whole story differently because of their different assumptions?

2. Issues of theme.   You may be familiar with the term **theme** from other literature courses. By *theme* critics usually mean the main claim that an author seems to be making with his or her text. Sometimes a theme is defined in terms of a single word—for example, *work* or *love*. But such words are really mere topics. Identifying the topics addressed by a text can be a useful way of starting to analyze that text (see pp. 81–88). A text's theme, however, is best seen as an assertion that you need at least one whole sentence to express.

With many texts, an issue of theme arises because readers can easily disagree about the text's main idea. In literature classes, such disagreements often occur, in part because literary works tend to express their themes indirectly. This is especially the case with stories like "Orientation" and "Girl," in which the main speaker's views are not necessarily the same as the author's. Readers of these two stories may give various answers to the question, What is the author ultimately saying? Perhaps some readers will take Kincaid to imply that mothers always know best. Other readers may conclude that Kincaid thinks that excessively controlling mothers are damaging to children.

If you try to express a text's theme, avoid making a statement that is so general that it could apply to many other works. Arguing that Kincaid's theme is "Girls are pressured to fit stereotyped roles" does not get at her story's details. On the other hand, do not let a text's details restrict you so much that you make the theme seem relevant only to a small group. If you argue that Kincaid's theme is "Antiguan women are domineering," then the many readers who are *not* from Antigua will wonder why they should care. In short, try to express themes as *midlevel generalizations*. With Kincaid's story, one possible theme is "In some cultures, women prepare girls for adulthood by teaching them to follow conventions *and* to assert themselves." A statement like this seems both attentive to Kincaid's specific text and applicable to a large portion of humanity. You are free to challenge this version of Kincaid's theme by proposing an alternative. Moreover, even if you do accept this statement as her theme, you are then free to decide whether it is a sound observation. Identifying a theme is one thing; evaluating it is another.

Keep in mind that a theme ties together various parts of a text. Focusing on a single passage, even if it seems thematic, may lead you to ignore other passages that a statement of theme should encompass. For instance, the last words of "Girl" may tempt you to believe that its theme is "be the kind of woman who feels the bread." Yet in other parts of the story, the main speaker seems to be calling for a compliant attitude. You need to take these moments into account as well.

Often you will sense a work's theme but still have to decide whether to state it as an **observation** or as a **recommendation**. You would be doing the first, for example, if you expressed Kincaid's theme as we did above: "In some cultures, women prepare girls for adulthood by teaching them to follow conventions *and* to assert themselves." You would be doing the second if you said Kincaid's theme is "Women should teach girls to follow conventions *and* to assert themselves." Indeed, people who depict a theme as a recommendation often use a word like *should*. Neither way of expressing a theme is necessarily better than the other. But notice that each way conjures up a particular image of the author. Reporting Kincaid's theme as an observation suggests that she is writing as a psychologist, a philosopher, or some other analyst of human nature. Reporting her theme as a recommendation suggests that she is writing as a teacher, preacher, manager, or coach: someone who is telling her readers what to do. Your decision about how to phrase a theme will depend in part on which image of the author you think is appropriate.

You risk obscuring the intellectual, emotional, and stylistic richness of a text if you insist on reducing it to a single message. Try stating the text's theme as a problem for which there is no easy solution, which suggests that the text is complex. For instance, if you say that Kincaid's theme is "In some cultures, women who prepare girls for adulthood are caught in a contradiction between wanting to empower them and wanting to keep them safe," you position yourself to address various elements of the story.

Also weigh the possibility that a text is conveying more than one theme. If you plan to associate the text with any theme at all, you might refer to *a* theme of the text rather than *the* theme of the text. Your use of the term *theme* would still have implications. Above all, you would still be suggesting that you have identified one of the text's major points. Subsequently, you might have to defend this claim, showing how the point you have identified is indeed central to the text.

Issues of theme have loomed large in literary studies. We hope that you will find them useful to pursue. But because references to theme are so common in literary studies, students sometimes forget that there are other kinds of issues. As you move through this list, you may find some that interest you more.

3. Issues of definition.   In arguments about literature, issues of **definition** arise most often when readers try to decide what an author means by a particular word. The titles of Orozco's and Kincaid's stories are puzzling. In the first case, what does "orientation" mean, given that the narrator's description of life in this office might easily *dis*orient someone? In the second case, what does it mean to be a "girl" in this kind of culture? Notice that an issue of definition can arise even with ordinary language. Look at how the narrator of "Orientation" uses the word *free* in the story's third paragraph: "Feel free to ask questions. Ask too many questions, however, and you may be let go." To what extent, and in what sense, do the characters in the story seem "free"? Answering this question involves, we think, considering how much the office workers are able to assert themselves through their eccentric behavior.

4. Issues of symbolism.   In literary studies, an issue of **symbolism** usually centers on a particular image. In question are the image's meaning and purpose, including whether the image is more than just a detail. In "Orientation," the artwork of Amanda Pierce's autistic son is "sheet after sheet of precisely drawn concentric circles and ellipses, in black and yellow" (para. 7). Some readers may argue that the boy's art is one of many indications that life in this office is bizarre. Other readers may contend that the drawings have greater significance but may differ about what their significance is—that the narrator's thinking is circular, in the sense that the narrator is obsessed with describing the employees' eccentricities, or that the employees' actions are circular, in the sense that they are stuck repeating their strange conduct.

5. Issues of pattern. With issues of **pattern**, you observe how a text is organized and try to determine how certain parts of the text relate to other parts. But think, too, about the meaning and purpose of any pattern you find, especially since readers may disagree about the pattern's significance. Also ponder the implications of any moment when a text *breaks* with a pattern it has been following. Disruptions of a pattern may be as important as the pattern itself.

A conspicuous pattern in "Girl" is the main speaker's series of commands, which includes repeated use of the words *this is how.* Indeed, **repetition** is a common pattern in literature. Yet at two points in Kincaid's story, the speaker is interrupted by italicized protests from the girl: "*but I don't sing benna on Sundays at all and never in Sunday school*" (lines 11–12) and "*but what if the baker won't let me feel the bread?*" (line 41). What should we conclude about the main speaker from her string of orders? What should we conclude about the girl from her two disruptions? Readers may have various answers to these questions.

A text's apparent oppositions are also patterns that may be debated. An example in "Orientation" is the distinction that the narrator makes between the majority of the office workers and those who should be avoided (Anika Bloom and Colin Heavey). Does this distinction make sense, or do the two groups seem more similar than the narrator admits? Again, different answers are possible.

6. Issues of evaluation. Consciously or unconsciously, **evaluation** always plays a central role in reading. When you read a work of literature, you evaluate its ideas and the actions of its characters. You judge, too, the views you assume the author is promoting. Moreover, you gauge the artistic quality of the text.

Specifically, you engage in three kinds of evaluation as you read. One kind is *philosophical*: you decide whether a particular idea or action is wise. Another kind is *ethical*: you decide whether an idea or action is morally good. The third kind is *aesthetic*: you decide whether the work as a whole or parts of the text succeed as art. Another reader may disagree with your criteria for wisdom, morality, and art; people's standards often differ. It is not surprising, then, that in the study of literature issues of evaluation come up frequently.

Sometimes you may have trouble distinguishing the three types of judgment from each other. Philosophical evaluation, ethical evaluation, and aesthetic evaluation can overlap. Probably the first two operate in the mind of a reader who is judging the advice given by the main speaker in "Girl." This reader may, for instance, find the speaker insensitive: that is, neither smart nor humane. Moreover, if this reader thinks Kincaid sympathizes with the speaker, then he or she may consider "Girl" flawed as a work of art. Keep in mind, however, that you can admire many aspects of a literary work even if you disagree with the ideas you see the author promoting. Someone may relish Kincaid's colorful language regardless of the views presented in the story.

But whose works should be taught? Many scholars argue that literary studies have focused too much on white male authors, and some refuse to assume that the works of these authors are great and universally relevant. They criticize the long neglect of female and minority writers like Kincaid, a black woman born and raised in the West Indies. In part because of these scholars' arguments, "Girl" now appears in many literature anthologies. Yet other people continue to prize "classics" by William Shakespeare, John Milton, and William Blake. This ongoing debate about the literature curriculum includes disagreements about the worth of recent texts. After all, contemporary literature has yet to pass a "test of time." Does Orozco's 1994 story deserve to be anthologized and taught? We think so and have included "Orientation" in our own book. What, though, is *your* evaluation of it? Also, what particular standards have you used to judge it?

7. Issues of historical and cultural context. Plenty of literary works have engaged readers who are quite unlike their authors. These readers may include much-later generations and inhabitants of distant lands. Nevertheless, an author's own **historical and cultural context** may significantly shape his or her text. Although "Orientation" has elements that probably strike you as strange, many details of this story no doubt remind you of life in offices throughout the present-day United States. Still, readers may disagree over exactly which features of the story are typical of the contemporary American workplace. Consider as well Jamaica Kincaid's use of her past in "Girl." Though she has lived in the United States since she was seventeen, she evidently tapped memories of her childhood on Antigua to write this story and to represent the island's culture. Since many of the story's readers would be unfamiliar with Antigua, she had to decide what aspects of it to acquaint them with. What features of it does she emphasize, and what features does she downplay or omit? When Kincaid was born, Antiguans were under British control, and many labored hard for little money. Do these historical facts matter in "Girl"? If so, in what conceivable ways? Notice that answering such political and economic questions usually requires research. Even then, answers may be complicated. Indeed, rarely does a literary text straightforwardly reflect its author's background. Debate arises over how text and context relate.

We provide some background for each literary work we present to help you begin to situate it historically and culturally. In Chapter 6, we explain how to put literature in context, especially by doing research in the library and on the Internet. For now, we want to emphasize that contextualizing a work involves more than just piling up facts about its origin. In the study of literature, issues of historical and cultural context are often issues of *relevance*: which facts about a work's creation are important for readers to know, and *how* would awareness of these facts help readers better understand the work? Readers can inform themselves about a particular author's life, for instance, but they may disagree about the extent to which a given text is autobiographical.

Perhaps you like to connect a literary work with its author's own life. The authors of the two stories we have been discussing apparently drew to some extent on their personal experiences. Orozco has worked in an office, and Kincaid was a girl on Antigua. Of course, it is unlikely that Orozco's coworkers included a serial killer and a woman whose palms bled. You may be tempted, though, to think that "Girl" consists of advice Kincaid herself received. Yet when you assert that a work is thoroughly autobiographical, you risk over-looking aspects of the text that depart from the author's own experiences, im-pressions, and beliefs. We are not urging you to refrain from ever connecting the author's text to the author's life. Rather, we are pointing out that whatever links you forge may be the subject of debate.

Even the term *history* can be defined in various ways. When you refer to a work's historical context, you need to clarify whether you are examining (1) the life of the work's author; (2) the time period in which it was written; (3) any time period mentioned within the text; (4) its subsequent reception, including responses to it by later generations; or (5) the forms in which the work has been published, which may involve changes in its spelling, punctuation, wording, and overall appearance.

8. Issues of genre.   So far we have been identifying categories of issues. Is-sues of **genre** are *about* categorization, for they involve determining what *kind* of text a particular work is. You might categorize the works by Orozco and Kincaid as belonging to the short-story genre, but someone might disagree be-cause they do not seem to have a conventional plot. This debate would involve deciding what the essential characteristics of a "short story" are. Even if you argue that Orozco's and Kincaid's texts belong to this genre, you could attempt to classify them more precisely by aiming for terms that better sum up their specific content and form. Issues of genre often arise with such further classifi-cation.

A literary text may relate in some way to a characteristic of ordinary, real-life interactions. Orozco's title—"Orientation"—signals that he is having fun with the guided tour that many offices give their new workers. Similarly, Kincaid's story "Girl" belongs to the parental-advice genre. Try, though, to dis-tinguish between text genre and real-life genre. Orozco's story can be labeled a *parody* (a comic imitation) or *satire* (an ironic critique) of an orientation, and Kincaid's story can be categorized as *an exploration of how gender roles are rein-forced.* In any case, you may find that two or more labels are appropriate for a particular text. For instance, perhaps you see Orozco's "Orientation" as both a *parody* and a *horror story.* If so, you must decide whether these labels are equally helpful. Much of the time, issues of genre are issues of priority. Readers debate not whether a certain label for a work is appropriate but whether that label is the best.

9. Issues of social policy.   In many works of literature, writers have at-tempted to instigate social reform by exposing defects in their cultures and en-couraging specific cures. We earlier mentioned Upton Sinclair's 1906 novel, *The Jungle,* which vividly depicts horrible conditions in Chicago's stockyards and thereby led the meat-processing plant owners to adopt more humane and hygienic practices. Even a work of literature that is not blatantly political or that seems rooted in the distant past may make you conscious of your own so-ciety's problems and possible solutions to them. Yet you and your classmates may propose different definitions of and solutions for cultural problems. The result is what we call issues of **social policy**.

Sometimes your position on a current issue of social policy will affect how you read a certain literary work. If you have worked in a highly regimented office, you may empathize with some of the employees described in Orozco's story. Similarly, your view on how girls and boys should be educated may affect your response to Kincaid's text. Even if current issues of social policy do not influence your original reading of a work, you can still use the work to raise such issues in your writing or in class discussion. Imagine discussing Orozco's story at a labor union's convention. What social policies might the story be used to promote there?

10. Issues of cause and effect.   Issues of **causality** are common in literary studies. Often they arise as readers present different explanations for a character's behavior. What causes Orozco's character Gwendolyn Stich to cry in the women's room? Why does the girl in Kincaid's story protest at two particular moments? Remember that even a work's narrator or main speaker is a character with motives worth analyzing. What personal reasons, for example, might lead Orozco's narrator to present the orientation in this way?

Such questions can be rephrased to center on the author. For instance, you can ask why Kincaid ends her story by having the characters speak about feeling the bread. If you look back at our discussion of these ten types of issues, you may see that most issues can be phrased as questions about the author's purposes. But remember your options. Focusing on authorial intent in a given case may not be as useful as sticking with another type of issue. Or you may turn a question about authorial intent into a question about authorial **effect**. How should readers react when Kincaid ends her story the way she does? You can address questions like this without sounding as if you know exactly what the author intended.

MAKE A CLAIM

A **claim** about a literary work is a position on it that not everyone would immediately accept as obvious truth. You have to argue for it. For examples of claims in literary studies, look at our explanations of ten kinds of issues. In that discussion, we mentioned a host of claims: that Orozco's narrator is merely fantasizing a ghost, that Kincaid's theme is "Women should teach girls to follow conventions *and* to assert themselves," that the autistic boy's circles symbolize the circular thinking of Orozco's narrator, that the main speaker in "Girl" is insensitive, and that "Orientation" is a horror story. These claims are debatable because in each case at least one other position is possible.

In literature classes, two types of claims are especially common. To criticize Kincaid's main speaker is to engage in **evaluation**. To identify themes of "Girl" is to engage in **interpretation**. Conventionally, interpretation is the kind of analysis that depends on hypotheses rather than simple observation of plain fact. Throughout this book, we refer to the practice of interpreting a work or certain aspects of it. Admittedly, sometimes you may have trouble distinguishing interpretation from evaluation. When you evaluate some feature of a work or make an overall judgment of that work, probably you are operating with a certain interpretation as well, even if you do not make that interpretation explicit. Similarly, when you interpret part of a work or the text as a whole, probably you have already decided whether the text is worth figuring out. Nevertheless, the two types of claims differ in their emphases. When you attempt to interpret a work, you are mostly analyzing it; when you attempt to evaluate the work, you are mostly judging it.

In class discussions, other students may resist a claim you make about a literary work. Naturally, you may choose to defend your view at length. But remain open to the possibility of changing your mind, either by modifying your claim somehow or by shifting completely to another one. Also, entertain the possibility that a view different from yours is just as reasonable, even if you do not share it.

In much of your writing for your course, you will be identifying an issue and making one main claim about it, which can be called your **thesis**. As you attempt to support your main claim, you will make a number of smaller claims. In drafts of your paper, welcome opportunities to test the claims you make in it. Review your claims with classmates to help you determine how persuasive your thinking is. You will be left with a stronger sense of what you must do to make your paper credible.

AIM TO PERSUADE

As we noted in Chapter 1, persuasion involves defending your claims. But as we also observed, even the best argument essays may fail to convince all their readers. What you *can* do is motivate your audience to keep thinking about your ideas. This is a modest sense of persuasion, but an achievement all the same. Suppose, in an essay on Kincaid's story, you claim that the speaker is loving despite her seeming stern. You may not induce all your readers to regard her as warm. Yet arguing for your idea can still be good, especially if you move people to mull it. Help them find your view worth pondering, whether or not everyone adopts it.

CONSIDER YOUR AUDIENCE

To argue effectively about a work of literature, you need to remember that not everyone will see it as you do. You have to explain and support your understanding of the work, so that skeptics will come to find your view of it sound. Gear every step of your argument toward readers you have to persuade. Focus on what *they* will want you to clarify, elaborate, and defend. Forget about parts of the work irrelevant to your argument. If your main claim is about a certain character in "Orientation" — say, the serial killer — limit your remarks about others, no matter how colorful these figures seem.

Above all, you may wonder how familiar your readers already are with the text you are analyzing. Perhaps your teacher will resolve your uncertainty, telling you exactly how much your audience knows about the text. Then again, you may be left to guess. Should you presume that your audience is totally unfamiliar with the text? This approach is risky, for it may lead you to spend a lot of your paper merely summarizing the text rather than analyzing it. A better move is to write as if your audience is at least a bit more knowledgeable. Here is a good rule of thumb: *Assume that your audience has, in fact, read the text but that you need to recall for this group any features of the text that are crucial to your argument.* Although probably your paper will still include summary, the amount you provide will be limited, and your own ideas will be more prominent.

You can introduce your essay's main claim by referring to the audience of the literary text you're studying:

- **Readers you disagree with:** While some readers may feel that the speaker in "Orientation" gives a thoroughly objective tour of his office, what he chooses to emphasize suggests that his perspective on this workplace is not always trustworthy.
- **Hasty, superficial readers:** Because the physical abuse that Amanda Pierce's husband inflicts on her is so horrifying, readers may overlook the description of her son's artwork in the same paragraph. But his "concentric circles and ellipses" (para. 7) symbolize how life at this office is organized.
- **Puzzled readers:** Many readers may wonder whether Barry Hacker's dead wife has actually returned to haunt the office. Yet, while she may indeed be a ghost, supernatural elements do not seem a major part of the story. Orozco evidently wants us to think more about real features of current office life.
- **Your own divided self:** While at first I thought Gwendolyn Stich is excessive in her devotion to penguin imagery, I have concluded that she deserves credit for striving to maintain a distinct identity in this bureaucratic setting.

GATHER AND PRESENT EVIDENCE

Evidence is the support that you give your claims so that others will accept them. What sort of evidence you must provide depends on what your audience requires to be persuaded. When you make claims during class discussions, your classmates and instructor might ask you follow-up questions, thereby suggesting what you must do to convince them. As a writer, you might often find yourself having to guess your readers' standards of evidence. Naturally, your guesses will be influenced by any prior experiences you have had with your audience. Moreover, you may have opportunities to review drafts with some of its members.

When you make an argument about literature, the evidence most valued by your audience is likely to be details from the work itself. Direct quotations from the text are powerful indications that your claims are well grounded. But when you quote, you need to avoid willful selectivity. If, when writing about Kincaid's story, you quote the girl's question "*but what if the baker won't let me feel the bread?*" without acknowledging the main speaker's response, you may come across as misrepresenting the text. In general, quoting from various parts of a text will help you give your readers the impression that you are being accurate.

If you make claims about the historical or cultural context of a work, your evidence may include facts about its original circumstances. You may be drawn to the author's own experiences and statements, believing these shed light on the text. But again, use such materials cautiously, for they are not always strong evidence for your claims. People are not obliged to accept the author's declaration of his or her intent as a guide to the finished work. Some people may feel that the author's statement of intention was deliberately misleading, while others may claim that the author failed to understand his or her own achievement.

EXPLAIN YOUR REASONING

As we pointed out in Chapter 1, your readers will expect more than evidence. They'll wish to see the process of reasoning behind your main claim. The steps in your logic should be clear in your essay's structure. This may need to differ from the structure of the literary text you analyze. Otherwise, you may confuse your readers—especially if you crawl through the literary work chronologically, commenting on each of its lines. Perhaps your main claim is that although "Orientation" has supernatural touches, the story belongs more to the genre of satire. An essay that simply plods through the story won't help you develop this idea. Probably you should first identify for your audience the story's supernatural elements, whether or not the story itself starts with them. (In fact, Anika Bloom's bleeding palm doesn't show up until paragraph 10, and the ghost of Barry Hacker's wife isn't mentioned until paragraph 19.) You should then identify the story's satirical aspects. In addition, you'll have to define "the supernatural" and "satire" as genres, stating the typical features of each. In general, alert your audience to your stages of thought.

IDENTIFY YOUR ASSUMPTIONS

Writing arguments about literature involves making assumptions, some of which you may need to spell out. One common kind is *warrants*. These are assumptions that lead you to call certain things evidence. Consider in "Orientation" the narrator's remark that "you can see this building reflected in the glass panels of that building across the way" (para. 26). You might argue that through this statement, Orozco suggests that the office has closed in on itself and is not open enough to other kinds of living. As evidence for your claim, you might point out the following things: (1) at this moment in the story a window acts as a mirror, (2) mirrors are sometimes associated with a fixation on the self, and (3) the narrator has already provided many examples of the employees' being stuck in their own routines. But then you may be asked for your warrants—your reasons for presenting this evidence as support for your claim. Some of your assumptions might be about literature: for instance, the transformation of an image (for example, a window into a mirror) is often symbolically significant, and images are often related to how characters in the text behave. Some of your assumptions might be about human nature: for example, if people are trapped in routines, they have trouble seeing how others live in the world at large. Some of your assumptions might be about historical periods and cultures: for instance, many contemporary American offices seem self-enclosed. Often literature classes are most enlightening when students discuss their assumptions about literature, about human nature, and about particular times and places. Your classmates may differ in their assumptions because they differ in the ways they grew up, the experiences they have had, the reading they have done, and the authorities that have influenced them.

Once you state your warrants for a claim you are making, your audience may go further, asking you to identify assumptions supporting the warrants themselves. But more frequently you will have to decide how much you should mention your warrants in the first place. In class discussion, usually your classmates' and instructor's responses to your claims will indicate how much you have to spell out your assumptions. When you write, you have to rely more on your own judgment of what your audience requires. If you suspect that your readers will find your evidence unusual, you should identify your warrants at length. If, however, your readers are bound to accept your evidence, then a presentation of warrants may simply distract them. Again, reviewing drafts of your paper with potential readers will help you determine what to do.

Another potentially significant set of assumptions has to do with your values, which often reflect your own life. You may want to condemn the speaker in "Girl" as a "bad" mother because your own is nicer. But this label requires more support than your personal experience. You'll need to explain why *various* people should apply it to the speaker—whatever particular mothers they've had. In general, be cautious with the terms you apply to literary figures. If you fling at them strong judgments—*bad, crazy, weird, normal, good*—some readers will suspect your mind is controlled by biases you grew up with. They'll prefer more precise, less extreme language, believing it better conveys a character's complexity.

MAKE USE OF APPEALS

As with other arguments, those about literature employ the appeals of **logos**, **ethos**, and **pathos**. You rely on logos when, to support your claims about texts, you stress your evidence and explain your process of thought. Ethos, the image you convey of yourself, often figures when you acknowledge interpretations other than yours. Your readers will appreciate your noting in the first place that these views can exist. You will look even better if you treat such alternatives with respect. Try making *concessions* to them, admitting they're not entirely wrong. For instance, you may want to argue that Kincaid's speaker holds men in contempt. Even so, consider granting that other readers of the story may see her differently. You might admit, for instance, that at moments she suggests her daughter should accept male power. Of course, you would still proceed to argue your own claim about her. But you'll have dealt admirably with a rival idea. In the same spirit, you might *qualify* your generalizations instead of stating them as absolute facts. Rather than declare that "the mother *is* scornful toward men," you might say that this is *probably* her attitude or that it *seems* to be her stance.

With the appeal known as pathos, you try to engage your readers' emotions. This move occurs to some degree in many arguments about literature, for literary works themselves often dramatize and arouse feelings. You can make your analysis compelling if you occasionally use emotional language yourself. You might refer to the "chilling" presence of the serial killer in Orozco's story or to the "intimidating" voice of the mother in Kincaid's. But keep such language limited. If you constantly vent your own passions, you may weaken your case. Take a look at this paragraph:

> Most of the employees in "Orientation" are creepy. They really bother me a lot, because they don't act in ways that strike me as normal. I definitely would not want to work in an office like that. I would fear being killed or interfered with somehow. Even the narrator disturbs me, because he acts like such a know-it-all and often points out what can get a staff member fired. I wouldn't care to have him be the person orienting me.

If you wrote a passage like this, it might annoy your readers. They might think it conveys far more about *you* than about Orozco's text. Probably they'd want more details of the story, fewer bursts of your feelings. Again, emotional words *can* play a role in your argument. They may well add to its force. But they're effective only when you supply them in small doses.

A Sample Student Argument about Literature

The following essay demonstrates several of the strategies we have discussed. Its student author had read Kincaid's "Girl" in a course on composition and literature. Her assignment was to write an argument paper about a specific element of the story. She chose to raise an issue and develop a claim about its ending.

Ann Schumwalt
English 102
Professor Peretti
3 February - - - -

The Mother's Mixed Messages in "Girl"

In Jamaica Kincaid's story "Girl," the speaker is evidently a mother trying to teach her daughter how to behave. The story is basically a single-paragraph speech in which the mother gives various commands, instructions, and lessons, apparently in an effort at training her child to become what their culture considers a proper young woman. Only twice does the daughter herself interrupt the mother's monologue. It's interesting that the second break occurs near the end of the story. Right after the mother orders her to "always squeeze bread to make sure it's fresh," the daughter asks, *"but what if the baker won't let me feel the bread?"* (lines 40–41). There is only one more sentence before the story concludes: the mother responds by asking, "you mean to say that after all you are really going to be the kind of woman who the baker won't let near the bread?" (41–42). Faced with this final exchange, many readers may wonder why author Kincaid chooses to make it the story's conclusion. It could have appeared earlier in the text, and Kincaid might have ended with any of the mother's statements that now come before it. This ending also feels *in*conclusive, for the very last words are a question that does not receive an answer. What, therefore, is Kincaid trying to emphasize with this puzzling finish? A closer look at its language, as well as at other words of the text, suggest that Kincaid is deliberately making us uncertain about whether the mother's stern training will indeed help her daughter become strong enough to survive in their society. The mother may *believe* that she is providing sufficient survival skills, but Kincaid encourages readers to suspect that she is actually *dis*empowering her daughter, not letting her develop the willpower she needs to endure.

When the mother commands her daughter to squeeze the bread, probably she sees herself as pushing her to take charge of her life rather than meekly accept other people's treatment of her. To squeeze something is to perform a vigorous, self-assertive action, and in this case it would involve testing the baker's product instead of just accepting it. Earlier in the text, the mother offers a few other hints that she wishes the daughter to be aggressive, not passive. For example, she advises her on "how to make a good medicine to throw away a child before it even becomes a child" (33–34); on "how to bully a man" (36); and on "how to spit up in the air if you feel like it" (39). A number of readers may infer, too, that even when she is telling the daughter how to perform house-hold chores like washing, ironing, setting meals, and sweeping, she is fostering her independence by enabling her to handle basic demands of daily existence.

But in crucial ways, the mother presses her daughter to play a subservient role in society. More specifically, she attempts to imprison her in a model of femininity that allows

Refers to puzzled readers, as a way of bringing up the main issue. The essay will help these readers with the "closer look" it proceeds to offer.

Introduces the essay's main issue (a cause and effect one) as a question.

The essay's main claim.

Because Ann is mainly concerned with the story's ending, she starts her paper with it, rather than move chronologically through Kincaid's text.

Qualifies this statement rather than expressing it as an absolute fact.

Draws evidence from the text's actual words.

Acknowledges existence of another possible interpretation.

Pathos used with the negatively emotional words presses, subservient, imprison, and dominate. Evidence then offered to support such language.

for men to dominate. Emphasizing that "you are not a boy, you know" (29–30), she demands that she "try to walk like a lady" (8) and take care of her father's clothes. The various chores that she expects her daughter to perform would make life easier for the male head of the household. Moreover, they seem duties that a boy would not be required to fulfill. Similarly, the mother hopes to restrict the daughter's sexual behavior. Repeatedly she warns her "to prevent yourself from looking like the slut I know you are so bent on becoming" (14–15). Again, it is doubtful that a boy would receive warnings like this. Like the United States, perhaps the culture reflected in this story even lacks a masculine equivalent of the derogatory term "slut."

A reasonable assumption.

An assumption, though qualified with the word perhaps.

At the end, I admit, the mother seems to associate her daughter with an image of power. She implies that the girl should become "the kind of woman" whom the baker *does* "let near the bread" so that she can test it by squeezing it (41–42). But even here, actually, the mother does not envision her daughter as actively taking charge. In the scenario she sketches, the baker *allows* the girl to feel the bread. In order to touch it, she must get his permission, rather than straightforwardly exert her own authority. Moreover, she first has to be a certain sort of woman; otherwise, she has not earned the right to examine his product. What type of woman is this? While some readers may argue that the mother wants her daughter to be an *assertive* female, many of the directions she has already given her would greatly limit her sphere of action, leaving her to be a relatively unadventurous housekeeping "lady." Evidently the mother feels that the baker will give her daughter access to the bread only if she is a basically tame and polite version of womanhood.

Concession.

The mother may not realize that she is conveying mixed messages to her child. If we, as readers, take her to be hoping that her daughter becomes empowered *and* subservient, we may be spotting a contradiction that the mother herself is not conscious of. But the daughter may be aware of it. Perhaps the daughter is, in fact, now a grown-up woman who is trying to make sense of the paradoxical pieces of advice her mother gave her during her adolescence. The mother may have offered these supposed bits of wisdom at various different times, but the daughter is now remembering them all as one speech and struggling to figure out their implications. Kincaid's decision to conclude the story with a question mark may be her way of indicating that even in adulthood, the daughter still has not determined whether her mother wanted to *liberate* her or *confine* her. We can regard the daughter as someone who is

"May not" is a qualification, indicating that Ann is less than sure what the mother thinks.

Even the text's punctuation may be significant.

still attempting to "read" her mother's intentions. As actual readers of this story, we would then be in the same position as she is, having to come up with our own interpretation of what her mother wanted her to do and be.

Looking at Literature as Argument

Much of this book concerns arguing *about* literature. But many works of literature can be said to present arguments themselves. Admittedly, not all of literature can be seen as containing or making arguments, but occasionally you will find that associating a literary text with argument opens up productive lines of inquiry. Moreover, as you argue about literature, arguments *within* literature can help you see how you might persuade others.

Some works lay out an argument that the author obviously approves of. For an example, let us turn to the following poem. It was written around 1652, by John Milton (1608–1674), a poet who played a leading role in England's Puritan revolution. Seeking to make dominant their own version of Christianity, the Puritans executed King Charles I and installed their leader, Oliver Cromwell, as head of state. Milton wrote "When I consider how my light is spent" while working as an official in Cromwell's government. This is an autobiographical poem and refers to Milton's growing blindness, which threatened to prevent him from serving both his political leader and his religious one, God.

JOHN MILTON
When I consider how my light is spent

When I consider how my light is spent,
    Ere half my days in this dark world and wide,
    And that one talent which is death to hide
Lodged with me useless, though my soul more bent
To serve therewith my Maker, and present   5
    My true account, lest He returning chide;
    "Doth God exact day-labor, light denied?"
I fondly ask. But Patience, to prevent
That murmur, soon replies, "God doth not need
    Either man's work or His own gifts. Who best   10
    Bear His mild yoke, they serve Him best. His state
Is kingly: thousands at His bidding speed,
    And post o'er land and ocean without rest;
    They also serve who only stand and wait."   *[c. 1652]*

The speaker does not actually spell out his warrants. Consider, however, his reference to Christ's parable of the talents (Luke 19:12–27). In the ancient Middle East, a *talent* was a unit of money. In the parable, a servant is scolded by his master for hoarding the one talent that his master had given him. By telling this story, Christ implies that people should make use of the gifts afforded them by God. For the speaker in Milton's poem, the parable has a lot of authority.

Evidently he feels that he should carry out its lesson. In effect, then, the parable has indeed become a warrant for him: that is, a basis for finding his blindness cause for lament.

Who, exactly, is the speaker's audience? Perhaps he is not addressing anyone in particular. Or perhaps the speaker's mind is divided and one side of it is addressing the other. Or perhaps the speaker is addressing God, even though he refers to God in the third person. Given that the speaker is answered by Patience, perhaps he means to address *that* figure, although Patience may actually be just a part of him rather than an altogether separate being.

At any rate, Patience takes the speaker for an audience in responding. And while Patience does not provide evidence, let alone warrants, Patience does make claims about God and his followers. Furthermore, Milton as author seems to endorse Patience's claims; apparently he is using the poem to advance them. Besides pointing out *how* God is served, Milton suggests that God *ought* to be served, even if God lets bad things happen to good people like Milton.

Every author can be considered an audience for his or her own writing, but some authors write expressly to engage in a dialogue with themselves. Perhaps Milton wrote his poem partly to convince himself that his religion was still valid and his life still worth living. Significantly, he did not publish the poem until about twenty years later. Yet because he did publish it eventually, at some point he must have contemplated a larger audience for it. The first readers of the poem would have been a relatively small segment of the English population: those literate and prosperous enough to have access to books of poetry. In addition, a number of the poem's first readers would have shared Milton's religious beliefs. Perhaps, however, Milton felt that even the faith of this band had to be bolstered. For one thing, not every Protestant of the time would have shared Milton's enthusiasm for the Puritan government. Recall that this regime executed the king, supposedly replacing him with the rule of God. Milton's words "His state / Is kingly" can be seen as an effort to persuade readers that the Puritans did put God on England's throne.

Certain arguments made in literary texts may or may not have the author's endorsement. Faced with a conflict of ideas, readers must engage in interpretation, forced to decide which position is apt to be the author's own view. A classic example is "Mending Wall," a famous poem by Robert Frost (1874–1963), from his 1914 book, *North of Boston*. Troubled by his neighbor's desire to repair the wall between their farms, the poem's speaker argues against its necessity, but literary critics have long debated whether Frost agrees with the speaker's claims and reasons. How persuasive do you find them?

ROBERT FROST

Mending Wall

Something there is that doesn't love a wall,
That sends the frozen-ground-swell under it,
And spills the upper boulders in the sun;
And makes gaps even two can pass abreast.

The work of hunters is another thing: 5
I have come after them and made repair
Where they have left not one stone on a stone,
But they would have the rabbit out of hiding,
To please the yelping dogs. The gaps I mean,
No one has seen them made or heard them made,   10
But at spring mending-time we find them there.
I let my neighbor know beyond the hill;
And on a day we meet to walk the line
And set the wall between us once again.
We keep the wall between us as we go.   15
To each the boulders that have fallen to each.
And some are loaves and some so nearly balls
We have to use a spell to make them balance:
"Stay where you are until our backs are turned!"
We wear our fingers rough with handling them.   20
Oh, just another kind of outdoor game,
One on a side. It comes to little more:
There where it is we do not need the wall:
He is all pine and I am apple orchard.
My apple trees will never get across   25
And eat the cones under his pines, I tell him.
He only says, "Good fences make good neighbors."
Spring is the mischief in me, and I wonder
If I could put a notion in his head:
"*Why* do they make good neighbors? Isn't it   30
Where there are cows? But here there are no cows.
Before I built a wall I'd ask to know
What I was walling in or walling out,
And to whom I was like to give offense.
Something there is that doesn't love a wall,   35
That wants it down." I could say "Elves" to him,
But it's not elves exactly, and I'd rather
He said it for himself. I see him there
Bringing a stone grasped firmly by the top
In each hand, like an old-stone savage armed.   40
He moves in darkness as it seems to me,
Not of woods only and the shade of trees.
He will not go behind his father's saying,
And he likes having thought of it so well
He says again, "Good fences make good neighbors."   *[1914]*   45

Other literary works, though, present an argument that the author is unlikely to endorse. In such cases, we might describe the work as *ironic* because
we sense a distance between the position being expressed and the author's own
view. Probably one of the most famous examples in literature of an ironic

argument is the 1729 essay "A Modest Proposal." Its author, Jonathan Swift (1667–1745), is today chiefly known for his satirical fantasy *Gulliver's Travels* (1726). He also wrote political journalism and served as dean of St. Patrick's Cathedral in Dublin. Swift was moved to write his "Proposal" by the widespread poverty and hunger in his native Ireland, which was then completely under English control. To him, this suffering had human causes, including neglect by the country's absent English landlords, indifference from its government officials, and economic restrictions established in its laws. The solution that Swift puts forth in his essay is not one he actually favored. Indeed, he thought it would shock most people. By making such an outlandish argument, he aimed to disturb his readers so that they would work to solve Ireland's crisis in more realistic and humane ways.

JONATHAN SWIFT

A Modest Proposal

For preventing the children of poor people in Ireland,
from being a burden on their parents or country,
and for making them beneficial to the public.

It is a melancholy object to those, who walk through this great town, or travel in the country, when they see the streets, the roads, and cabin-doors crowded with beggars of the female sex, followed by three, four, or six children, all in rags, and importuning every passenger for an alms. These mothers, instead of being able to work for their honest livelihood, are forced to employ all their time in strolling to beg sustenance for their helpless infants who, as they grow up, either turn thieves for want of work, or leave their dear native country, to fight for the Pretender° in Spain, or sell themselves to the Barbadoes.

I think it is agreed by all parties that this prodigious number of children in the arms, or on the backs, or at the heels of their mothers, and frequently of their fathers, is in the present deplorable state of the kingdom, a very great additional grievance; and therefore whoever could find out a fair, cheap, and easy method of making these children sound and useful members of the commonwealth, would deserve so well of the public, as to have his statue set up for a preserver of the nation.

But my intention is very far from being confined to provide only for the children of professed beggars: it is of a much greater extent, and shall take in the whole number of infants at a certain age, who are born of parents in effect as little able to support them, as those who demand our charity in the streets.

As to my own part, having turned my thoughts for many years, upon this important subject, and maturely weighed the several schemes of our projectors, I have always found them grossly mistaken in their computation. It is true, a child just dropped from its dam, may be supported by her milk, for a

---

Pretender: Son of England's King James II; exiled in Spain but sought his country's throne.

solar year, with little other nourishment: at most not above the value of two shillings, which the mother may certainly get, or the value in scraps, by her lawful occupation of begging; and it is exactly at one year old that I propose to provide for them in such a manner, as, instead of being a charge upon their parents, or the parish, or wanting food and raiment for the rest of their lives, they shall, on the contrary, contribute to the feeding, and partly to the clothing of many thousands.

There is likewise another great advantage in my scheme, that it will pre-   5 vent those voluntary abortions, and that horrid practice of women murdering their bastard children, alas! too frequent among us, sacrificing the poor inno- cent babes, I doubt, more to avoid the expense than the shame, which would move tears and pity in the most savage and inhuman breast.

The number of souls in this kingdom being usually reckoned one million and a half, of these I calculate there may be about two hundred thousand couple whose wives are breeders; from which number I subtract thirty thou- sand couple, who are able to maintain their own children, (although I appre- hend there cannot be so many, under the present distresses of the kingdom) but this being granted, there will remain a hundred and seventy thousand breeders. I again subtract fifty thousand, for those women who miscarry, or whose children die by accident or disease within the year. There only remain a hundred and twenty thousand children of poor parents annually born. The question therefore is, How this number shall be reared, and provided for? which, as I have already said, under the present situation of affairs, is utterly impossible by all the methods hitherto proposed. For we can neither employ them in handicraft or agriculture; we neither build houses (I mean in the coun- try), nor cultivate land: they can very seldom pick up a livelihood by stealing till they arrive at six years old; except where they are of towardly parts, although I confess they learn the rudiments much earlier; during which time they can however be properly looked upon only as probationers: As I have been informed by a principal gentleman in the county of Cavan, who protested to me, that he never knew above one or two instances under the age of six, even in a part of the kingdom so renowned for the quickest proficiency in that art.

I am assured by our merchants, that a boy or a girl before twelve years old, is no saleable commodity, and even when they come to this age, they will not yield above three pounds, or three pounds and half a crown at most, on the exchange; which cannot turn to account either to the parents or kingdom, the charge of nutriments and rags having been at least four times that value.

I shall now therefore humbly propose my own thoughts, which I hope will not be liable to the least objection.

I have been assured by a very knowing American of my acquaintance in London, that a young healthy child well nursed, is, at a year old, a most deli- cious nourishing and wholesome food, whether stewed, roasted, baked, or boiled; and I make no doubt that it will equally serve in a fricassee or a ragout.

I do therefore humbly offer it to public consideration, that of the hundred   10 and twenty thousand children, already computed, twenty thousand may be reserved for breed, whereof only one-fourth part to be males; which is more than we allow to sheep, black cattle, or swine, and my reason is, that these children are seldom the fruits of marriage, a circumstance not much regarded by our savages, therefore, one male will be sufficient to serve four females. That the remaining hundred thousand may, at a year old, be offered in sale to the persons of quality and fortune, through the kingdom, always advising the mother to let them suck plentifully in the last month, so as to render them plump, and fat for a good table. A child will make two dishes at an entertainment for friends, and when the family dines alone, the fore or hind quarter will make a reasonable dish, and seasoned with a little pepper or salt, will be very good boiled on the fourth day, especially in winter.

I have reckoned upon a medium, that a child just born will weigh 12 pounds, and in a solar year, if tolerably nursed, increase to 28 pounds.

I grant this food will be somewhat dear, and therefore very proper for landlords, who, as they have already devoured most of the parents, seem to have the best title to the children.

Infant's flesh will be in season throughout the year, but more plentiful in March, and a little before and after; for we are told by a grave author, an eminent French physician, that fish being a prolific diet, there are more children born in Roman Catholic countries about nine months after Lent, the markets will be more glutted than usual, because the number of Popish infants, is at least three to one in this kingdom, and therefore it will have one other collateral advantage, by lessening the number of Papists among us.

I have already computed the charge of nursing a beggar's child (in which list I reckon all cottagers, laborers, and four-fifths of the farmers) to be about two shillings per annum, rags included; and I believe no gentleman would repine to give ten shillings for the carcass of a good fat child, which, as I have said, will make four dishes of excellent nutritive meat, when he has only some particular friend, or his own family to dine with him. Thus the squire will learn to be a good landlord, and grow popular among his tenants, the mother will have eight shillings neat profit, and be fit for work till she produces another child.

Those who are more thrifty (as I must confess the times require) may flay   15
the carcass; the skin of which, artificially dressed, will make admirable gloves for ladies, and summer boots for fine gentlemen.

As to our City of Dublin, shambles may be appointed for this purpose, in the most convenient parts of it, and butchers we may be assured will not be wanting; although I rather recommend buying the children alive, and dressing them hot from the knife, as we do roasting pigs.

A very worthy person, a true lover of his country, and whose virtues I highly esteem, was lately pleased, in discoursing on this matter, to offer a refinement upon my scheme. He said, that many gentlemen of this kingdom, having of late destroyed their deer, he conceived that the want of venison might be well supplied by the bodies of young lads and maidens, not exceeding fourteen years of age, nor under twelve; so great a number of both sexes in every country being now ready to starve for want of work and service: And these to be disposed of by their parents if alive, or otherwise by their nearest relations. But with due deference to so excellent a friend, and so deserving a patriot, I cannot be altogether in his sentiments; for as to the males, my American acquaintance assured me from frequent experience, that their flesh was generally tough and lean, like that of our schoolboys, by continual exercise, and their taste disagreeable, and to fatten them would not answer the charge. Then as to the females, it would, I think, with humble submission, be a loss to the public, because they soon would become breeders themselves: And besides, it is not improbable that some scrupulous people might be apt to censure such a practice (although indeed very unjustly), as a little bordering upon cruelty, which, I confess, hath always been with me the strongest objection against any project, how well soever intended.

But in order to justify my friend, he confessed, that this expedient was put into his head by the famous Salmanaazor, a native of the island Formosa, who came from thence to London, above twenty years ago, and in conversation told my friend, that in his country, when any young person happened to be put to death, the executioner sold the carcass to persons of quality, as a prime dainty; and that, in his time, the body of a plump girl of fifteen, who was crucified for an attempt to poison the Emperor, was sold to his imperial majesty's prime minister of state, and other great mandarins of the court, in joints from the gibbet, at four hundred crowns. Neither indeed can I deny, that if the same use were made of several plump young girls in this town, who without one single groat to their fortunes, cannot stir abroad without a chair, and appear at a playhouse and assemblies in foreign fineries which they never will pay for; the kingdom would not be the worse.

Some persons of a desponding spirit are in great concern about that vast number of poor people, who are aged, diseased, or maimed; and I have been desired to employ my thoughts what course may be taken, to ease the nation of so grievous an encumbrance. But I am not in the least pain upon that matter, because it is very well known, that they are every day dying, and rotting, by cold and famine, and filth, and vermin, as fast as can be reasonably expected. And as to the young laborers, they are now in almost as hopeful a condition. They cannot get work, and consequently pine away from want of nourishment, to a degree, that if at any time they are accidentally hired to common labor, they have not strength to perform it, and thus the country and themselves are happily delivered from the evils to come.

I have too long digressed, and therefore shall return to my subject. I think   20
the advantages by the proposal which I have made are obvious and many, as well as of the highest importance.

For first, as I have already observed, it would greatly lessen the number of Papists, with whom we are yearly overrun, being the principal breeders of the nation, as well as our most dangerous enemies, and who stay at home on purpose with a design to deliver the kingdom to the Pretender, hoping to take their advantage by the absence of so many good Protestants, who have chosen rather to leave their country, than stay at home and pay tithes against their conscience to an episcopal curate.

Secondly, The poorer tenants will have something valuable of their own, which by law may be made liable to a distress, and help to pay their landlord's rent, their corn and cattle being already seized, and money a thing unknown.

Thirdly, Whereas the maintainance of a hundred thousand children, from two years old, and upward, cannot be computed at less than ten shillings a piece per annum, the nation's stock will be thereby increased fifty thousand pounds per annum, besides the profit of a new dish, introduced to the tables of all gentlemen of fortune in the kingdom, who have any refinement in taste. And the money will circulate among ourselves, the goods being entirely of our own growth and manufacture.

Fourthly, The constant breeders, besides the gain of eight shillings sterling per annum by the sale of their children, will be rid of the charge of maintaining them after the first year.

Fifthly, This food would likewise bring great custom to taverns, where the vintners will certainly be so prudent as to procure the best receipts for dressing it to perfection; and consequently have their houses frequented by all the fine gentlemen, who justly value themselves upon their knowledge in good eating; and a skillful cook, who understands how to oblige his guests, will contrive to make it as expensive as they please. 25

Sixthly, This would be a great inducement to marriage, which all wise nations have either encouraged by rewards, or enforced by laws and penalties. It would increase the care and tenderness of mothers toward their children, when they were sure of a settlement for life to the poor babes, provided in some sort by the public, to their annual profit instead of expense. We should soon see an honest emulation among the married women, which of them could bring the fattest child to the market. Men would become as fond of their wives, during the time of their pregnancy, as they are now of their mares in foal, their cows in calf, or sow when they are ready to farrow; nor offer to beat or kick them (as is too frequent a practice) for fear of a miscarriage.

Many other advantages might be enumerated. For instance, the addition of some thousand carcasses in our exportation of barreled beef: the propagation of swine's flesh, and improvement in the art of making good bacon, so much wanted among us by the great destruction of pigs, too frequent at our tables; which are no way comparable in taste or magnificence to a well grown, fat yearly child, which roasted whole will make a considerable figure at a Lord Mayor's feast, or any other public entertainment. But this, and many others, I omit, being studious of brevity.

Supposing that one thousand families in this city would be constant customers for infants' flesh, besides others who might have it at merry meetings, particularly at weddings and christenings, I compute that Dublin would take off annually about twenty thousand carcasses; and the rest of the kingdom (where probably they will be sold somewhat cheaper) the remaining eighty thousand.

I can think of no one objection that will possibly be raised against this proposal, unless it should be urged that the number of people will be thereby much lessened in the kingdom. This I freely own, and 'twas indeed one principal design in offering it to the world. I desire the reader will observe that I calculate my remedy for this one individual Kingdom of Ireland, and for no other that ever was, is, or, I think, ever can be upon Earth. Therefore let no man talk to me of other expedients: Of taxing our absentees at five shillings a pound: Of using neither clothes, nor household furniture, except what is of our own growth and manufacture: Of utterly rejecting the materials and instruments that promote foreign luxury: Of curing the expensiveness of pride, vanity, idleness, and gaming in our women: Of introducing a vein of parsimony, prudence, and temperance: Of learning to love our country, wherein we differ even from Laplanders, and the inhabitants of Topinamboo: Of quitting our animosities and factions, nor acting any longer like the Jews, who were murdering one another at the very moment their city was taken: Of being a little cautious not to sell our country and consciences for nothing: Of teaching landlords to have at least one degree of mercy toward their tenants. Lastly, of putting a spirit of honesty, industry, and skill into our shopkeepers, who, if a resolution could now be taken to buy only our native goods, would immediately unite to cheat and exact upon us in the price, the measure, and the goodness, nor could ever yet be brought to make one fair proposal of just dealing, though often and earnestly invited to it.

Therefore I repeat, let no man talk to me of these and the like expedients, till he hath at least some glimpse of hope, that there will ever be some hearty and sincere attempt to put them into practice. 30

But, as to myself, having been wearied out for many years with offering vain, idle, visionary thoughts, and at length utterly despairing of success, I fortunately fell upon this proposal, which, as it is wholly new, so it hath something solid and real, of no expense and little trouble, full in our own power, and whereby we can incur no danger in disobliging England. For this kind of commodity will not bear exportation, and flesh being of too tender a consistence, to admit a long continuance in salt, although perhaps I could name a country which would be glad to eat up our whole nation without it.

After all, I am not so violently bent upon my own opinion as to reject any offer, proposed by wise men, which shall be found equally innocent, cheap, easy, and effectual. But before something of that kind shall be advanced in contradiction to my scheme, and offering a better, I desire the author or authors will be pleased maturely to consider two points. First, As things now stand, how they will be able to find food and raiment for a hundred thousand useless mouths and backs. And secondly, There being a round million of creatures in human figure throughout this kingdom, whose whole subsistence put into a common stock, would leave them in debt two million of pounds sterling, adding those who are beggars by profession, to the bulk of farmers, cottagers and laborers, with their wives and children, who are beggars in effect; I desire those politicians who dislike my overture, and may perhaps be so bold to attempt an answer, that they will first ask the parents of these mortals, whether they would not at this day think it a great happiness to have been sold for food at a year old, in the manner I prescribe, and thereby have avoided such a perpetual scene of misfortunes, as they have since gone through, by the oppression of landlords, the impossibility of paying rent without money or trade, the want of common sustenance, with neither house nor clothes to cover them from the inclemencies of the weather, and the most inevitable prospect of entailing the like, or greater miseries, upon their breed forever.

I profess, in the sincerity of my heart, that I have not the least personal interest in endeavoring to promote this necessary work, having no other motive than the public good of my country, by advancing our trade, providing for infants, relieving the poor, and giving some pleasure to the rich. I have no children, by which I can propose to get a single penny; the youngest being nine years old, and my wife past child-bearing.   *[1729]*

CHAPTER 3

The Reading Process

Courses in many disciplines ask for *close reading*. But literature classes strongly emphasize it — one reason they are good preparation for other fields. Nevertheless, the steps involved in close reading are not always clear to students. Perhaps you have been told to engage in this process without knowing what it entails. Because close reading is central to literary studies, plays a big role in other courses, and yet remains murky for many students, this chapter both explains it and models it.

If you are taking a course that asks you to *write* about the literary works you study, close reading of them will help you form ideas about them worth spreading to *your* audiences. Such reading will also help you decide what details of these texts will best support your points about them. So, as we proceed to explain close reading, we treat it mainly as what some would call a method of invention. It's a way for you, as a *writer*, to discover things to say about literature.

Strategies for Close Reading

Actually, close reading consists of not one strategy but several. All of them can help you gain insights into a literary work, which you might then convey through your writing. You need not follow these strategies in the order we list them here, but try each of them.

1. Make predictions as you read. That is, guess what will happen and how the text will turn out. If you wind up being surprised, fine. You may get a richer understanding of the text as you reflect on how it *defies* your expectations.

2. Reread the text. Reread the text several times, focusing each time on a different element of the text and using at least one of these occasions to read aloud. Few readers of a literary work can immediately see everything important and interesting in it. You greatly increase your chances of getting ideas about a text if you read it again and again. At first, you may be preoccupied with following the plot or with figuring out the text's main theme. Only by examining the text repeatedly may you notice several of its other aspects, including features that really stir your thoughts. But don't try to study everything in the text each time you look at it. Use each reading of it to study just one characteristic. In an early stage, for example, you might trace the text's repetitions, and then you might use a later reading to pinpoint its ambiguous words. This division of labor can, in the end, generate many insights that a less focused approach would not.

Reading all of the text or portions of it out loud gives you a better sense of how the text is manipulating language. Reading aloud is especially useful in the case of poems, for you may detect rhymes or soundalike words that you would not notice when reading silently.

3. Test the text against your own experiences.   Keep in mind your experiences, beliefs, assumptions, and values as you read the text, but note ways that it challenges or complicates these things. When you first read a particular literary work, your interpretations and judgments are bound to be influenced by your personal background. This includes your beliefs, assumptions, and values, as well as things that have happened to you. Indeed, many people read a literary work hoping they can personally identify with the characters, situations, and views it presents. Moreover, this is an understandable goal. Pay attention, though, to details of the text that do *not* match your life and current thinking. After all, the author may be deliberately challenging or complicating readers' habitual attitudes. In any case, parts of the text that are hard to identify with will often provide you with great subjects when you write about the work. Bear in mind, though, that you will not interest your readers if you simply criticize characters in the work or sneer at other elements of it. In particular, try not to sum up characters with negative labels such as *immoral, weird,* or *sick.* These terms often strike readers as reflecting mere prejudice — a poor substitute for careful analysis of human complexity.

4. Look for patterns in the text and disruptions of them.   Many a literary work is organized by various patterns, which may not be evident on first reading. In fact, you might not detect a number of these patterns until you read the text several times. You may even see these better if you move back and forth in the text instead of just reading it straight through. Typically, a literary work's patterns include repetitions of words and of actions; oppositions; words similar or related in meaning; and technical methods of organization (such as rhyme schemes or frequent use of flashbacks). Just as important to note are moments in the text that are inconsistent with one or more of its patterns. Locate and think about places where the work makes a significant shift, in meaning, imagery, tone, plot, a character's behavior, narrative point of view, or even physical format (for example, a change in rhyme scheme).

5. Note ambiguities.   These are places where the text's meaning is not crystal clear and therefore calls for interpretation: for example, words that can have more than one definition; symbols that have multiple implications; and actions that suggest various things about a character.

6. Consider the author's alternatives.   That is, think about what the author *could* have done and yet did not do. The author of a literary work faces all sorts of decisions in composing it. And as you study the work, you will have more to say about it if you think about those choices. Try, then, to compare the author's handling of particular passages to other possible treatments of them. By considering, for example, why the author chose a certain word over others, you may better detect implications and effects of the author's actual language. Similarly, by reflecting on how the author *might* have portrayed a certain character more simplistically, you strengthen your ability to analyze the character's variety of traits.

7. Ask questions.   As you read, generate questions that have more than one possible answer. When we first read a literary work, most of us try to get comfortable with it. We search for passages that are clear; we groan when we encounter ones that are mysterious or confusing. Sooner or later, though, we must confront puzzles in the text if we are to analyze it in depth. Furthermore, if we plan to *write* about the text, we are more likely to come up with ideas worth communicating to our readers if we present ourselves as helping them deal with matters *not* immediately clear. After all, our audience will not need our analysis if it centers on what's obvious. Therefore, list multiple questions that the work raises for you, especially ones that have various possible answers. Then, if you focus on addressing one of these questions in your writing — providing and supporting your own particular answer to it — your readers will find value in turning to *your* text. Furthermore, when you come across literary passages that seem easy to understand, consider how they might actually involve more than one possible meaning. Even little words may prove ambiguous and, therefore, worth analyzing in your writing. Of course, you may have to consult a dictionary in order to see the different meanings that a word can have.

The questions you come up with need hardly be restricted to matters of the work's "theme." After all, most any literary text worth studying can't be reduced to a single message. Often, such texts play with multiple ideas, perhaps emphasizing tensions among them. Therefore, it may make more sense for you to refer to a work's *themes*. Actually, as we have been suggesting throughout our catalog of reading strategies, any literary text has several other features. As a writer, you may wind up with much more to say about a literary work if you consider one or more of these other elements: for example, facts obscured or absent in the text; possible definitions of key words; symbols; patterns; evaluations to be made of the characters or the overall work; the text's historical and cultural context; the text's genre; its relevance to current political debates; and cause-effect relationships. In the next chapter, we explain these elements at greater length, identifying them as *issues* you might write about.

8. Jot down possible answers.   Even while reading the text, begin developing and pulling together your thoughts by informally writing about it. See if you can generate not only good questions but also tentative answers to them. Writing need not be the final outcome of your reflections on a literary work. You can jot down ideas about the text even as you first encounter it. Such informal, preliminary writing can actually help you generate insights into the text that you would not have achieved simply by scanning it. The following are some of the specific things you might do:

- *Make notes in the text itself.*   A common method is to mark key passages, either by underlining these passages or by running a highlighter over them. Both ways of marking are popular because they help readers recall main features of the text. But use these techniques moderately if you use them at all, for marking lots of passages will leave you unable to distinguish the really important parts of the text. Also, try "talking back" to the text in its margins. Next to particular passages, you might jot down words of your own, indicating any feelings and questions you have about those parts. On any page of the text, you might circle related words and then draw lines between these words to emphasize their connection. If a word or an idea shows up on numerous pages, you might circle it each time. Furthermore, try cross-referencing, by listing on at least one page the numbers of all those pages where the word or idea appears.

- *As you read the text, occasionally look away from it, and jot down anything in it you recall.*   This memory exercise lets you review your developing impressions of the text. When you turn back to its actual words, you may find that you have distorted or overlooked aspects of it that you should take into account.

- *At various moments in your reading, freewrite about the text for ten minutes or so.*   Spontaneously explore your preliminary thoughts and feelings about it, as well as any personal experiences the text leads you to recall. One logical moment to do freewriting is when you have finished reading the text. But you do not have to wait until then; as you read, you might pause occasionally to freewrite. This way, you give yourself an opportunity to develop and review your thoughts about the text early on.

- *Create a "dialectical notebook."*   So named by composition theorist Ann Berthoff, it involves using pages of your regular notebook in a particular way. On each page, draw a line down the middle to create two columns. In the left column, list various details of the text: specifically, words, images, characters, and events that strike you. In the right column, jot down for each detail one or more sentences indicating *why* you were drawn to it. Take as many pages as you need to record and reflect on your observations. You can also use the two-column format to carry out a dialogue with yourself about the text. This is an especially good way to ponder aspects of the text that you find confusing, mysterious, or complex.

- *Play with the text by revising it.*   Doing so will make you more aware of options that the author rejected and will give you a better sense of the moves that the author chose to make. Specifically, you might rearrange parts of the text, add to it, change some of its words, or shift its narrative point of view. After you revise the text, compare your alternative version with the original, considering especially differences in their effects.

A Poem for Analysis

To demonstrate what it means to read closely, we present observations that various students made about a poem. The poem is by Sharon Olds (b. 1942), who teaches at New York University and has produced many volumes of verse. "Summer Solstice, New York City" appears at the start of her 1987 book *The Gold Cell*. The poem deals with work—in this case, efforts by New York City police to prevent a suicide.

SHARON OLDS

Summer Solstice, New York City

By the end of the longest day of the year he could not stand it,
he went up the iron stairs through the roof of the building
and over the soft, tarry surface
to the edge, put one leg over the complex green tin cornice
and said if they came a step closer that was it. 5
Then the huge machinery of the earth began to work for his life,
the cops came in their suits blue-gray as the sky on a cloudy evening,
and one put on a bullet-proof vest, a
black shell around his own life,
life of his children's father, in case 10
the man was armed, and one, slung with a
rope like the sign of his bounden duty,
came up out of a hole in the top of the neighboring building
like the gold hole they say is in the top of the head,
and began to lurk toward the man who wanted to die. 15
The tallest cop approached him directly,
softly, slowly, talking to him, talking, talking,
while the man's leg hung over the lip of the next world
and the crowd gathered in the street, silent, and the
hairy net with its implacable grid was 20
unfolded near the curb and spread out and
stretched as the sheet is prepared to receive at birth.
Then they all came a little closer
where he squatted next to his death, his shirt
glowing its milky glow like something 25
growing in a dish at night in the dark in a lab and then
everything stopped
as his body jerked and he
stepped down from the parapet and went toward them
and they closed on him, I thought they were going to 30
beat him up, as a mother whose child has been
lost will scream at the child when it's found, they
took him by the arms and held him up and

leaned him against the wall of the chimney and the
tall cop lit a cigarette   35
in his own mouth, and gave it to him, and
then they all lit cigarettes, and the
red, glowing ends burned like the
tiny campfires we lit at night
back at the beginning of the world.   *[1987]*   40

Applying the Strategies

Even before you look at the students' comments, try doing what they did. We asked each of them to read the poem several times (step 2, pp. 70–71). More specifically, they devoted each of their readings to a specific element of the poem:

- First, they focused on how it fulfilled or defied their predictions.
- Then, they considered how the poem matched and diverged from their personal backgrounds.
- Then, they traced the poem's patterns, as well as breaks from these.
- Then, they noted places where the poem is puzzling, ambiguous, or unclear.
- Next, they identified at least one choice that the poem's author faced.
- They then settled on questions that have more than one possible answer and that therefore might be worth addressing in a formal essay about the poem.
- Finally, pulling their thoughts together, they came up with tentative answers to these questions, which they might develop in a formal essay.

Again, the order of these stages is not the only one possible; the important thing is to go through them all. At each stage of their reading, the students also did a few minutes of freewriting, using this strategy to develop thoughts about whatever element was their focus. Below are excerpts from these informal reflections.

MAKE PREDICTIONS

KATHERINE: I was really tense as I read this poem because I thought the man would jump at the end and then we would get a horrible description of him splattering on the sidewalk. I didn't predict the cops would succeed in talking him out of it. When the poet says he "jerked," that could easily have been the start of his jumping, but thank God he is instead stepping back. I'm glad that they persuaded him to remain alive.

MARIA: I was like the poem's speaker expecting that they would physically grab him and treat him roughly, and so I was surprised when they were nice to him and even offered him a cigarette.

TREVOR: I predicted that the poem would end with the man still on the edge of the building deciding whether or not to jump off, because I think that in a way it would be neat to leave us guessing whether he's really going to do it. I wasn't all that surprised when he pulled back and joined the cops, because that was certainly one possible outcome. However, I was surprised when the author had them smoking cigarettes at the end like "at the beginning of the world." I didn't expect that image of prehistoric people to show up here at the end.

REFLECT ON YOUR PERSONAL BACKGROUND

JAMES: It's hard for me to sympathize with someone who commits suicide, especially because someone at my high school killed himself and all of his friends and family were terribly saddened by what he did. I think that no matter how bad things get for you, there's a way out if only you look for it. Suicide is no answer, and it hurts the people you leave behind. So I'm glad that the man in this poem winds up not committing suicide. If he had, I would have thought less of him.

CARLA: I vaguely remember seeing some movies in which a character stands on a ledge and thinks about jumping off it. In real life, I've never seen something like that. What this poem most brings to my mind are reports I heard about people jumping off the World Trade Towers to escape being killed by fire. Of course, they died anyway. As I recall, TV didn't show these people jumping, out of respect for them I guess, and I'm glad that I didn't have to see this happen. Still, I'm aware that it did. Anyway, the man thinking about suicide in this poem isn't facing the same situation. He can easily live if he wants to.

BOB: I guess the police are obligated to try rescuing the man even if they have to risk their own lives. I've never been in this position, so I'm not sure how I'd feel if I'd been assigned to save the man in this poem. Though I disapprove of suicide, maybe I wouldn't have the guts to try confronting him on the edge of the building, and I'm not sure I could talk to him calmly, because if he did jump he might take me down with him. I admire the ability of these cops to stay cool and talk him into joining them. I'm also impressed that they then treat him like a friend instead of like a potentially violent nut case that they have to get under control through force. If it were me, I think I might want to throw him to the ground and pin his arms so that he wouldn't try something like that again.

READ FOR PATTERNS AND FOR BREAKS IN PATTERNS

DOMINICK: This may be too little a thing to think about, but I notice that the word "it" is repeated in the beginning section of the poem. The first line ends with "it," and line 5 does also. I'm not sure what is meant by "it" in "he could not stand it." Obviously on one level "it" here means his life, but he seems to have something specific about his life in mind when he says this, but we don't learn what he's specifically thinking of. The second "it" seems to refer to the fact that he will kill himself if they come closer. But that reference too isn't as clear as it might be. I see that later on "it" comes up again as a word for the cigarette that the cop gives to the man (after lighting it in his own mouth, yuk!). Maybe we're supposed to connect this "it" to the "its" at the start.

BOB: After the middle of the poem we start to get a lot of birth imagery. The word "birth" is even stated, and a little later there's the image of something "growing" in a lab dish.

JARED: "World" is repeated. In the middle of the poem, there's a reference to "the next world," and the very last word of the poem is "world," meaning the world where we currently live.

COURTNEY: I found a number of references to children. There are the words "his children's father," and then toward the end the word "child" is repeated, though this time it's a mother's child. And then the last line refers to "the beginning of the world," as if the world is a child that has just been born.

FRANK: It's funny that the word "end" is one of the first words of the poem, and then the word "beginning" is one of its last words. I can more easily imagine the reverse. Anyway, "end" and "beginning" are opposites that the poet seems to want us to think about. Come to think of it, there is mention of "ends" near the conclusion, but these are the "ends" of the men's cigarettes and not the end of the world.

ALEX: The word "day" appears in the first line (it's "the longest day of the year"), but later there is the word "night" ("growing in a dish at night"), and then "night" is in the next-to-last line. Ironically, things get brighter (the man decides to live) as the poem moves from "day" to "night."

PAUL: As the poem moves along, there's a shift in pronouns. In the first half or so, we get forms of "he" and "they." Then the word "I" suddenly appears, and then the next-to-last line has the word "we."

READ FOR PUZZLES, AMBIGUITIES, AND UNCLEAR MOMENTS

KATHERINE: I just don't learn enough about this man's thinking to know why he's even planning to kill himself. This is something the poem doesn't make clear. But I guess the "I" of the poem doesn't know the man's thinking either, and meanwhile she's in the position of possibly witnessing the man falling to the pavement! Maybe the author doesn't tell us exactly why the man wants to commit suicide because we can then identify more easily with him. We can think about moments when we were incredibly unhappy, whether or not we were depressed by the same things he is.

TIM: We're told that the cop approaching the man is doing a lot of talking, but we don't find out what he specifically says, even though this may have played a big role in getting the man to step back and live.

HILLARY: The gold hole sounds like something from folklore, but I don't know the background.

RACHEL: I'm wondering how much we're supposed to focus on the speaker's reactions to what's going on, or whether we should think more about the man and the policemen.

READ FOR THE AUTHOR'S CHOICES

KATHERINE: Olds could have had the man jump and die. Even if this poem is based on a real incident where the man decided to live, she could have changed what happened. Also, if she still went with the rescue version, she could have had the policemen treat the man roughly after they rescued him.

PAUL: The word "I" could have appeared more often throughout the poem, especially because the poem is written from the point of view of someone observing this suicide attempt.

TIM: We might have been told why the man was thinking of killing himself and what the cops said to him. I realize this information would be hard for the speaker of the poem to give us, since she's just observing the whole business from the street below. Still, maybe Olds could have found a way of telling us at least a little more about what the men on the roof were saying and thinking.

BOB: The author didn't have to use birth images. She could have described this event without them. In fact, death imagery seems more appropriate when a poem is about a possible suicide.

GENERATE QUESTIONS THAT HAVE MORE THAN ONE POSSIBLE ANSWER

JENNIFER: What might the poet be trying to convey when she ends the poem with the image of "the beginning of the world"? The last line really captures my attention.

PAUL: What should we conclude when the pronouns shift from "he" and "they" to "I" and finally "we"?

VICTORIA: How should we interpret the poem's repeated references to children and to parents (both father and mother)?

BOB: How important are the cops as characters in this poem?

STATE TENTATIVE ANSWERS

JENNIFER: Maybe the poet is telling us that each time you overcome depression and decide to go on living, it's like the rebirth of the world, and you're rejoining a "we" in the sense of rejoining the rest of humanity.

PAUL: I believe that the speaker comes to identify with the man and his rescuers and then sees herself and them as all part of a common humanity, as if we all have to decide when to risk our lives and when to preserve them.

VICTORIA: In a paper, I could argue that these child and parent references are used by Olds to suggest that even as adults, we sometimes act like children and sometimes have to act like a parent, but Olds evidently prefers that we not act like a very stern parent.

BOB: The cops are very important in this poem. So much of it is about what they do and how they maybe feel. They're required to save the guy, they're part of "huge machinery," and one of them might end up sacrificing the "life of his children's father" just in order to rescue someone who wants to kill himself anyway, but then the cops turn out to be quite sympathetic toward the guy. There's even this odd religious-type moment with the sharing of a cigarette and then all the men lighting up. I think I would focus my paper on how the cops do their duty to preserve life even when they probably didn't want to, and then something spiritual happens because they didn't give up on the job they were assigned.

DAN: If I'm remembering correctly, the summer solstice is a turning point in the year, and you could say that there's a turning point in this poem when the man steps down from the ledge and chooses not to die. After the summer solstice we're heading toward winter, which is associated with death, but psychologically the poem goes in the opposite direction.

Think about your own developing understanding of Olds's poem. What aspect of it might you focus on in a formal essay? What's a claim that you might make? To us, the students' claims we have quoted seem promising topics for papers. Nevertheless, they could probably stand some polishing and further reflection. After all, they are the outcome of freewriting — an exploratory phase. In any case, what we want to stress is that you are more likely to get ideas about a literary work if you use the reading strategies that this group of students applied.

Reading Closely by Annotating

When you use such strategies, you may come up with several observations about the literary work you are reading. You may even find it helpful to record them directly on the text. Then, by reviewing the points you have annotated and connecting them to one another, you will provide yourself with a solid foundation for a paper. Here we demonstrate this process by showing how student Kara Lundquist annotated a poem by the noted writer and editor X. J. Kennedy (b. 1929) and then composed a possible opening paragraph for an essay about it.

X. J. KENNEDY

Death of a Window Washer

He dropped the way you'd slam an obstinate sash,

His split belt like a shade unrolling, flapping.

Forgotten on his account, the mindless copying

Machine ran scores of memos no one wanted.

Heads stared from every floor, noon traffic halted   5

As though transformed to stone. Cops sealed the block

With sawhorse barricades, laid canvas cover.

Nuns crossed themselves, flies went on being alive,

A broker counted ten shares sold as five,

And by coincidence a digital clock   10

Stopped in front of a second it couldn't leap over.

Struck wordless by his tumble from the sky

To their feet, two lovers held fast to each other

Uttering cries. But he had made no cry.

He'd made the city pause briefly to suffer   15

His taking ample room for once. In rather

A tedious while the rinsed street, left to dry,

Unlatched its gates that passersby might pass.

Why did he live and die? His legacy

Is mute: one final gleaming pane of glass.   20

[2007]

Notes in margin:

Window washer is given no name.

Did his body "split" when he hit the ground? Poem avoids gruesome details to focus mostly on bystanders.

Alliteration: What do "c" words suggest?

Nuns' reaction different from insects'. But are the humans here much more sensitive?

Echoes "account" in line 3. Did the dead man count (matter)?

Do people prefer to "leap over" deaths like this?

At first seems to mean "experience pain," then seems to mean "put up with."

"Tedious" to whom? People soon get impatient for the body to go.

Unusual to ask why he lived in the first place.

Relates to "wordless" in line 12 and "no cry" in line 14.

"Pane of glass " (clear vision) seems opposite of "mute." Connect "pane" to "pain"?

Here is the paragraph that Kara composed, based on her annotations.

> X. J. Kennedy's poem "Death of a Window Washer" emphasizes not the title character's horrible accident, but rather how bystanders react to it. The poem suggests that although people may be *momentarily* affected by the death of an ordinary person whom they do not know, eventually they want to resume their own lives and pay him little attention. The specific situation that the poem dramatizes is the accidental plunge of a window washer from a city building. Certainly this incident shocks, at first, the passersby who witness it. Even though "flies went on being alive" (line 8), various human beings are disturbed by the man's sudden death. But as the poem proceeds, the city's inhabitants want to go back to their personal pursuits. A turning point in the poem is the word "suffer," which the speaker uses to describe the city dwellers at the end of line 15. This word might, at first, lead the reader to believe that they are tormented by the window washer's accident. But in the next line, it becomes clear that they are "suffering" in the sense that they are impatiently waiting for his corpse to be removed. Rather than permanently grieve over his having "passed" (i.e., died), they want to "pass" his body (18) and take up their daily existence once again. Therefore, although his death has been highly visible to them, they don't really bother to learn anything about him. His life is *not* revealed to them like the reality behind a "gleaming pane of glass" (20). The speaker's concluding use of this image is, in fact, ironic.

Using Topics of Literary Studies to Get Ideas

You can also get ideas about the text if, as you read it, you consider how it deals with **topics** that have preoccupied literary studies as a profession. Some of these topics have interested the discipline for many years. One example is work, a common subject of the literature in Chapters 1–6. Traditionally, literary studies has also been concerned with such topics as family relations, love, freedom and confinement, justice, and journeys. Moreover, the discipline has long called attention to topics that are essentially classic conflicts: for example, innocence versus experience, free will versus fate or determinism, the individual versus society, nature versus culture, and eternity versus the passing time.

Over the last few years, however, literary studies has turned to several new concerns. For instance, quite a few literary critics now consider the ways in which literary texts are often *about* reading, writing, interpretation, and evaluation. Critics increasingly refer to some of the following subjects in their analysis of literature:

- Traits that significantly shape human identity, including gender, race, ethnic background, social class, sexual orientation, cultural background, nationality, and historical context
- Representations of groups, including stereotypes held by others
- Acknowledgments — or denials — of differences among human beings
- Divisions, conflicts, and multiple forces *within* the self
- Boundaries, including the processes through which these are created, preserved, and challenged
- Politics and ideology, including the various forms that power and authority can take; acts of domination, oppression, exclusion, and appropriation; and acts of subversion, resistance, and parody
- Ways that carnivals and other festivities challenge or preserve social order
- Distinctions between what's universal and what's historically or culturally specific
- Relations between the public and the private, the social and the personal
- Relations between the apparently central and the apparently marginal
- Relations between what's supposedly normal and what's supposedly abnormal
- Relations between "high" culture and "low" (that is, mass or popular) culture
- Economic and technological developments, as well as their effects
- The role of performance in everyday life
- Values — ethical, aesthetic, religious, professional, and institutional
- Desire and pleasure
- The body
- The unconscious
- Memory, including public commemorations as well as personal memory

If you find that a literary text touches on one of these topics, try next to determine how the work specifically addresses that topic. Perhaps you will consider the topic an element of the text's themes. In any case, remember that, by itself, a topic is not the same as a theme. While a topic can usually be expressed in a word or a short phrase, a theme is a whole claim or assertion that you believe the text makes.

Actually, the topics we have identified may be most worth consulting when you have just begun analyzing a literary text and are far from establishing a theme. By using these topics, you can generate preliminary questions about the text, various issues you can then explore.

To demonstrate how these topics can stimulate inquiry, we apply some of them to the following poem, "Night Waitress." It is from the 1986 book *Ghost Memory*, by the late American poet Lynda Hull (1954–1994). Hull had been developing an impressive career in literature when she died in a car accident. This poem is also about work, the speaker being the night waitress of the title.

LYNDA HULL

Night Waitress

Reflected in the plate glass, the pies
look like clouds drifting off my shoulder.
I'm telling myself my face has character,
not beauty. It's my mother's Slavic face.
She washed the floor on hands and knees   5
below the Black Madonna, praying
to her god of sorrows and visions
who's not here tonight when I lay out the plates,
small planets, the cups and moons of saucers.
At this hour the men all look   10
as if they'd never had mothers.
They do not see me. I bring the cups.
I bring the silver. There's the man
who leans over the jukebox nightly
pressing the combinations   15
of numbers. I would not stop him
if he touched me, but it's only songs
of risky love he leans into. The cook sings
with the jukebox, a moan and sizzle
into the grill. On his forehead   20
a tattooed cross furrows,
diminished when he frowns. He sings words
dragged up from the bottom of his lungs.
I want a song that rolls
through the night like a big Cadillac   25
past factories to the refineries
squatting on the bay, round and shiny
as the coffee urn warming my palm.
Sometimes when coffee cruises my mind
visiting the most remote way stations,   30
I think of my room as a calm arrival
each book and lamp in its place. The calendar
on my wall predicts no disaster
only another white square waiting
to be filled like the desire that fills   35
jail cells, the old arrest
that makes me stare out the window or want
to try every bar down the street.
When I walk out of here in the morning
my mouth is bitter with sleeplessness.   40
Men surge to the factories and I'm too tired
to look. Fingers grip lunch box handles,
belt buckles gleam, wind riffles my uniform

and it's not romantic when the sun unlids
the end of the avenue. I'm fading   4
in the morning's insinuations
collecting in the crevices of buildings,
in wrinkles, in every fault
of this frail machinery.   *[1986]*

≡ A WRITING EXERCISE

After you read "Night Waitress," do a ten-minute freewrite in which you try
to identify how the poem relates to one or more of the topics mentioned
on page 82.

We think that several of the topics now popular in literary studies are relevant to Hull's poem. Here are a few possibilities, along with questions that
these topics can generate.

Gender.   The speaker alludes to conventional roles through which men and
women relate to each other. When the speaker declares that "at this hour the
men all look / as if they'd never had mothers," she indicates that women have
often played a maternal role for men. Furthermore, she implies that often
women have been the primary caretaker of their sons. (Notice that she makes
no reference to fathers.) What is the effect of this attention to women as mothers of men? In most of the poem, the speaker refers to men as potential lovers.
Yet even as she suggests she would like a sexual relationship with a man, she
suggests as well that she has had trouble establishing worthwhile attachments.
Why has she had such difficulty, do you think? Does the problem seem due to
her personality alone, or do you sense larger forces shaping her situation? Notice, too, that the poem refers to the factory workers as male, while the woman
who speaks is a waitress. To what extent does American society perpetuate a
gendered division of labor?

Ethnic background.   Near the start of the poem, the speaker refers to her
"mother's Slavic face" and points out that her mother served "the Black Madonna," a religious icon popular in Central European countries such as the
Czech Republic and Poland. What is the effect of these particular ethnic references? To pursue this line of inquiry, probably you will need to do research into
the Black Madonna, whether in a library or on the Internet.

Social class.   In part, considering social class means thinking about people's
ability to obtain material goods. When the speaker compares her ideal song to
"a big Cadillac," she implies that she doesn't currently possess such a luxurious
car. At the same time, she is expressing her desire for the song, not the car. Why
might the song be more important to her right now? Social class is also a matter of how various workplaces are related to one another. This poem evokes a
restaurant, factories, refineries, and bars. How are these settings connected as

parts of American society? Think, too, about how you would label the social class of the various occupations the poem mentions. What would you say is the social class of a waitress? To what classes would you assign people who work in factories and refineries? Who, for the most part, are the social classes that have to work at night?

Sexual orientation.   The speaker of "Night Waitress" seems heterosexual, an orientation often regarded as the only legitimate one. Because almost all societies have made heterosexuality the norm, a lot of people forget that it is a particular orientation and that not everyone identifies with it. Within literary studies, gay and lesbian critics have pointed out that a literary work may seem to deal with sexuality in general but may actually refer just to heterosexuality. Perhaps "Night Waitress" is examining heterosexuality as a specific social force. If so, how might the speaker's discontent be related to heterosexuality's influence as a particular institution? Keep in mind that you don't have to assume anything about the author's sexuality as you pursue such a question. In fact, heterosexuality may be a more important topic in Hull's poem than she intended.

Divisions, conflicts, and multiple forces within the self.   The poem's beginning indicates that the speaker experiences herself as divided. The first four lines reveal that she feels pride and disappointment in her mirror image: "I'm telling myself my face has character, / not beauty." Later she indicates that within her mind are "remote way stations" that she visits only on occasion. Furthermore, she seems to contradict herself. Although she initially refers to her room as "a calm arrival," she goes on to describe that place negatively, as empty and confined. Early in the evening, she seems sexually attracted to the man playing the jukebox ("I would not stop him / if he touched me"), but by morning her mood is "not romantic" and she is "too tired / to look" at the male factory workers. What may be the significance of these paradoxes?

Boundaries.   In the first line, the speaker is apparently looking at a window, and later she reveals that at times she feels driven to "stare out the window" of her room. What should a reader make of these two references to such a common boundary? When the speaker observes that the men in the restaurant "do not see me," she indicates that a boundary exists between them and her. Do you think she is merely being paranoid, or do you suspect that the men are indeed ignoring her? If they *are* oblivious to her, how do you explain their behavior? Still another boundary explored in the poem is the line between night and day. What happens when the speaker crosses this line? What can night, day, and the boundary between them signify? You might also consider what the author of a literary work does with its technical boundaries. Often a poem creates boundaries in its breaks between stanzas. Yet "Night Waitress" is a continuous, unbroken text; what is the effect of Hull's making it so? At the same time, Hull doesn't always respect sentence boundaries in her lines. At several points in the poem, sentences spill over from one line to another. This poetic technique is called **enjambment**; what is its effect here?

Politics and ideology.   When, in referring to the jukebox man, the speaker declares that "I would not stop him / if he touched me," she can be taken to imply that male customers often flirt with waitresses. How might flirtation be seen as involving power, authority, and even outright domination? Do you see the poem as commenting on such things? Earlier we raised issues of social class; these can be seen as political issues, too. How would you describe a society in which some people have "a big Cadillac" and others do not?

Carnivals and other festivities.   Although the poem does not refer to a "carnival" in any sense of that word, it does mention bars, which today are regarded by many people as places of festive retreat from work. What adjectives would you use to describe the speaker when she says that sometimes she wants "to try every bar down the street"?

Distinctions between what is universal and what is historically or culturally specific.   Try to identify anything that is historically or culturally specific about this poem's setting. Certainly the word *Slavic* and the reference to the Black Madonna indicate that the speaker has a particular background. You might also note her description of the restaurant, her use of the Cadillac as a metaphor, and her mention of the "factories" and the "refineries" that are "squatting on the bay." Although a wide range of places might fit these details, the poem's setting does not seem universal. Indeed, many readers are attracted to literature *because* it deals with specific landscapes, people, and plots. Nevertheless, these same readers usually expect to get some larger, more widely applicable meanings out of literature even as they are engaged by its specific details. Are you inclined to draw general conclusions from "Night Waitress"? If so, what general meanings do you find in it? What sorts of people do you think might learn something about themselves from reading this poem?

Relations between the public and the private, the social and the personal.   The speaker of "Night Waitress" works in a very public place, a restaurant. Yet she seems to feel isolated there, trapped in her own private world. How did she come to experience public life this way, do you think? Later, she initially seems to value her room as a private retreat, calling it "a calm arrival," but then she describes it as a place so lonely that it leads her to "stare out the window or want / to try every bar down the street." How, then, would you ultimately describe the relations between the speaker's public life and her private one? In addressing this issue, probably you need to consider whether the speaker's difficulties are merely personal or reflect a larger social disorder. When, at the end of the poem, she refers to "this frail machinery," is she referring just to herself, or is she suggesting that this phrase applies to her society in general? If she is indeed making a social observation, what do you sense are the "faults" in her society? Who else might be "fading"?

Relations between "high" culture and "low" culture.   Although the speaker does not identify the "songs / of risky love" playing on the jukebox, surely they are examples of what is called low, mass, or popular culture. Just as a lot of us are moved by such music when we hear it, so the jukebox player and the cook are engaged by it. In contrast, the poem itself can be considered an example of high culture. Often poetry is regarded as a serious art even by people who don't read it. In what ways, if any, does this poem conceivably resemble the songs it mentions? Given that author Lynda Hull is in essence playing with combinations of words, can we compare her with "the man / who leans over the jukebox nightly / pressing the combinations / of numbers"? (Actually, *numbers* has been a poetic term; centuries ago, it was commonly used as a synonym for the rhythms of poems.)

The role of performance in everyday life.   The most conspicuous performer in this poem is the cook, who "sings words / dragged up from the bottom of his lungs." But in everyday life, people often perform in the sense of taking on certain roles, even disguising their real personalities. Do you see such instances of performing in this poem? If so, where? Notice that the speaker wears a uniform; can that be considered a costume she wears while performing as a waitress?

Religious values.   The speaker clearly refers to religion when she recalls her mother's devotion to the Black Madonna, behavior that involved "praying / to her god of sorrows and visions." And although that god is "not here tonight," the speaker's description of waitressing has ritualistic overtones reminiscent of religious ceremonies. When she says, "I bring the cups. / I bring the silver," she could almost be describing preparations for Communion. In fact, she depicts the cook as wearing a religious emblem: "On his forehead / a tattooed cross furrows, / diminished when he frowns." What do you make of all this religious imagery? Might the speaker be trying to pursue certain religious values? Can she be reasonably described as looking for salvation?

Desire and pleasure.   The speaker explicitly mentions the word *desire* when she describes the emptiness she feels in her room, a feeling of desolation "that makes me stare out the window or want / to try every bar down the street." These lines may lead you to believe that her desire is basically sexual. Yet when the speaker uses the words *I want* earlier in the poem, she expresses her wish for "a song that rolls / through the night like a big Cadillac." Here, her longing does not appear sexual in nature. Is the speaker referring to at least two kinds of desire, then? Or do you see her as afflicted with basically one kind?

The body.   A notable feature of this poem is its attention to body parts. The speaker mentions her "shoulder," her "face," her mother's "face," her mother's "hands and knees," the cook's "forehead," his "lungs," her "palm," the "way stations" of her "mind," her "mouth," the factory workers' "fingers," and their "belt buckles." At the same time, the speaker never describes any particular body as a whole. What is the effect of this emphasis on mere parts? Does it connect in any way to the speaker's ultimate "fading"?

Memory.   Already we have noted the speaker's reference to her mother at the start of the poem. In what way, if any, is it significant that she engages in recollection? What circumstances in her life might have prompted the speaker to look back at the past?

☰ A WRITING EXERCISE

We have applied several topics from our list to Lynda Hull's poem "Night Waitress." Now see how you can apply topics from the list to another poem in Part One. Try to come up with several questions about the poem you choose, referring to topics on our list. Then select one of the questions you have formulated, and freewrite for ten minutes in response to it.

CHAPTER 4

The Writing Process

In Chapter 5, we discuss how to write about each of the four literary genres featured in this book. Here, however, we suggest how to write about a literary work of any genre. To make our advice concrete, we mostly trace what one student did as she worked on a writing assignment for a course much like yours. Each student chose a single poem from the syllabus and wrote a 600-word argument paper on it for a general audience. We focus on the writing process of a student named Abby Hazelton.

Ultimately, Abby chose to write about William Wordsworth's "The Solitary Reaper." In his own day, Wordsworth (1770–1850) was poet laureate of England, and he continues to be regarded as a major British Romantic poet. He and fellow poet Samuel Taylor Coleridge collaborated on *Lyrical Ballads* (1798), a collection of verse that became a landmark of Romantic poetry. In his preface to the second edition two years later, Wordsworth famously defined *poetry* as "emotion recollected in tranquillity," contended that it should draw on "common life," and called for it to incorporate "language really used by men." Like many other Romantics, Wordsworth celebrated scenes of nature and country life, while deploring the increasing spread of cities. "The Solitary Reaper" appeared in his 1807 *Poems in Two Volumes.*

Before examining Abby's writing process, read Wordsworth's poem.

WILLIAM WORDSWORTH
The Solitary Reaper

Behold her, single in the field,
    Yon solitary Highland Lass!
Reaping and singing by herself;
    Stop here, or gently pass!
Alone she cuts and binds the grain,   5
And sings a melancholy strain;
O listen! for the Vale profound
Is overflowing with the sound.

No Nightingale did ever chaunt
    More welcome notes to weary bands   10
Of travellers in some shady haunt,
    Among Arabian sands:

A voice so thrilling ne'er was heard
In spring-time from the Cuckoo-bird,
Breaking the silence of the seas   15
Among the farthest Hebrides.

Will no one tell me what she sings? —
    Perhaps the plaintive numbers flow
For old, unhappy, far-off things,
    And battles long ago: 20
Or is it some more humble lay,
Familiar matter of to-day?
Some natural sorrow, loss, or pain,
That has been, and may be again?

Whate'er the theme, the Maiden sang   25
    As if her song could have no ending;
I saw her singing at her work,
    And o'er the sickle bending; —
I listen'd, motionless and still;
And, as I mounted up the hill,   30
The music in my heart I bore,
Long after it was heard no more.   *[1807]*

Once she chose to write about Wordsworth's poem for her paper, Abby engaged in four sorts of activities: (1) exploring, (2) planning, (3) composing, and (4) revising. As we describe each, keep in mind that these activities need not be consecutive. Abby moved back and forth among them as she worked on her assignment.

Strategies for Exploring

As you read a literary work, you are bound to interpret and judge it. Yet not all reading is close reading, which can also be called **critical reading**. This process involves carefully and self-consciously analyzing various aspects of a text, including its meanings, its effects, and its treatment of typical elements of its genre. When you read a work closely and critically, you also note questions it raises for you — issues you might explore further in class discussion and writing. Indeed, close reading is a process of self-reflection. During this process, you monitor your own response to the text and try to identify why you see the text the way you do.

Exploring, the first stage of writing an essay about literature, is this particular process of reading. As we explain in Chapter 3, it specifically involves the following:

- Making predictions as you read
- Rereading the text with a different focus each time, including at least one stage in which you read aloud
- Comparing the text with your personal experience
- Tracing patterns and breaks from these patterns

- Noting ambiguities
- Considering the author's alternatives
- Generating questions
- Considering how the text deals with topics that have preoccupied literary studies
- Formulating a tentative claim
- Using informal writing to move through all these steps, including commenting in the text's margins; note-taking; freewriting; creating a "dialectical notebook"; and playfully revising the text

≣ A WRITING EXERCISE

Do at least ten minutes of freewriting about Wordsworth's poem, keeping it nearby so that you can consult it if you need to. In particular, try to raise questions about the poem, and consider which of these may be worth addressing in a more formal paper.

Here is an excerpt from Abby's freewriting.

I see that this poem consists of four stanzas, each of which is eight lines long. But these stanzas have different emphases. The first stanza is a series of commands. The speaker tells people to "Behold," "Stop here, or gently pass," and "listen." The second stanza mainly describes the reaper. The third stanza is basically a bunch of questions. The fourth is the speaker's recollection of his experience in general. So I could write a paper about how this poem changes as it moves along and why the stanzas shift in emphasis. But one problem with a paper like that is that it might get me bogged down in mechanically moving from stanza to stanza. I don't want that to happen. Another thing I could do is answer one of the speaker's own questions, which are about what kind of song the reaper is singing. Evidently this "Highland Lass" is using a Scottish dialect that he doesn't understand. But I'm just as ignorant as he is about the song. I guess I'm more likely to contribute some analysis of my own if I come up with a question myself. I'm struck by the fact that he doesn't give us much sense of the reaper's song. There's no way that a printed poem could convey the reaper's tune, but still. And the words are foreign to the speaker. But I'm surprised that he doesn't make a little effort to convey at least some of the song's lyrics even if they're foreign words that he might hear wrong or misspell. How can I as a reader join him in experiencing the beauty of her song if I don't learn any of its words? I wonder if we're supposed to see the poem as being more about the speaker than about the reaper. More specifically, maybe we're supposed to be a little disturbed that he's a British intellectual who is making a spectacle out of a foreign woman from the working class. At any rate, he seems bent on controlling this experience even as he invites us to share it. Another question for me is, Why does he shift from present tense to past tense in the last stanza? This change is really curious to me. I don't see anything earlier on that prepares me for it. First, we're led to believe that the speaker is observing the reaper right then and there, but at the end he speaks as if this occurred in the past, though maybe the recent past. This inconsistency in the time frame makes me think that in some important way the overall poem is about time. At any rate, I'm drawn to the inconsistency because it's so blatant. If I wrote about it, I might still devote a paragraph to each stanza, but I'd be starting with the last one and referring back to the others in order to explain that stanza. What I still have to figure out, though, is what exactly the poem is saying about time when it makes the shift of tense.

Freewriting enabled Abby to raise several questions. At the same time, she realized that her paper could not deal with everything that puzzled her. When you first get an assignment like hers, you may fear that you will have nothing to say. But you will come up with a lot of material if, like Abby, you take time for exploration. As we have suggested, it's a process of examining potential subjects through writing, discussion, and just plain thinking. One of your challenges will be to choose among the various issues you have formulated. At the end of this excerpt from her freewriting, Abby is on the verge of choosing to analyze the poem's shift of tense in its final stanza. For her, this shift is an interesting change from a pattern, the poem's previous uses of present tense. Abby has not yet decided how to explain this shift; at the moment, it remains for her a mystery. But her paper would achieve little if it focused just on aspects of the poem that are easy to interpret. Though Abby has more thinking to do about the poem's shift of tense, it seems a promising subject for her precisely because it puzzles her.

Strategies for Planning

Planning for an assignment like Abby's involves five main activities:

1. Choosing the text you will analyze
2. Identifying your audience
3. Identifying the main issue, claim, and evidence you will present
4. Identifying your assumptions
5. Determining how you will organize your argument, including how you will demonstrate your process of reasoning

CHOOSE A TEXT

Abby considered several poems before choosing one for her paper. She settled on Wordsworth's for five reasons. First, it was a text that left her with plenty of questions. Second, she believed that these questions could be issues for other readers. Third, she felt increasingly able to *argue* about the poem — that is, to make and support claims about it. Fourth, she believed that she could adequately analyze the poem within the assignment's word limit. Finally, Wordsworth's poem drew her because she had heard about the Romantic movement in English literature and was curious to study an example of it.

Faced with the same assignment, you might choose a different poem than Abby did. Still, the principles that she followed are useful. Think about them whenever you are free to decide which texts you will write about. With some assignments, of course, you may need a while to decide which text is best for you. And later, after you have made your decision, you may want to make a switch. For example, you may find yourself changing your mind once you have done a complete draft. Frustrated by the text you have chosen, you may realize that another inspires you more. If so, consider making a substitution. Naturally, you will feel more able to switch if you have ample time left to write the paper, so avoid waiting to start your paper just before it is due.

IDENTIFY YOUR AUDIENCE

To determine what your readers will see as an issue and to make your claims about it persuasive to them, you need to develop an audience profile. Perhaps your instructor will specify your audience. You may be asked, for example, to imagine yourself writing for a particular group in a particular situation. If you were Abby, how would you analyze "The Solitary Reaper" for an orchestra wanting to know what this poem implies about music? Even when not required of you, such an exercise can be fun and thought-provoking for you as you plan a paper.

Most often, though, instructors ask students to write for a "general" audience, the readership that Abby was asked to address. Assume that a general audience is one that will want evidence for your claims. While this audience will include your instructor, let it also include your classmates, since in class discussions they will be an audience for you whenever you speak. Besides, your class may engage in peer review, with students giving one another feedback on their drafts.

IDENTIFY YOUR ISSUE, CLAIM, AND EVIDENCE

When you have written papers for previous classes, you may have been most concerned with coming up with a thesis. Maybe you did not encounter the term *issue* at all. But good planning for a paper does entail identifying the main issue you will address. Once you have sensed what that issue is, try phrasing it as a question. If the answer would be obvious to your readers, be cautious, for you really do not have an issue if the problem you are raising can be easily resolved.

Also, try to identify what *kind* of issue you will focus on. For help, look at our list of various types (pp. 45–52). Within "The Solitary Reaper," the speaker raises an issue of fact: he wants to know what sort of song the reaper is singing. But as someone writing about Wordsworth's poem, Abby wanted to focus on another kind of issue, which she decided is best regarded as an issue of pattern. More precisely, she thought her main question might be, What should we conclude from the inconsistency in pattern that occurs when the final stanza shifts to past tense? To be sure, Abby recognized that addressing this issue would lead to issues of theme and of cause and effect, for she would have to consider why Wordsworth shifts tenses and how the shift relates to his overall subject.

Now that she had identified her main issue, Abby had to determine her main claim. Perhaps you have grown comfortable with the term *thesis* and want to keep using it. Fine. Bear in mind, though, that your thesis is the main *claim* you will make and proceed to support. And when, as Abby did, you put your main issue as a question, then your main claim is your answer to that question. Sometimes you will come up with question and answer simultaneously. Once in a while, you may even settle on your answer first, not being certain yet how to word the question. Whatever the case, planning for your paper involves articulating both the question (the issue) and the answer (your main claim). Try actually writing both down, making sure to phrase your main issue as a question and your main claim as the answer. Again, Abby's main issue was, What should we conclude from the inconsistency in pattern that occurs when the final stanza shifts to past tense? After much thought, she expressed her main claim this way:

> One possible justification for the shift to past tense is that it reminds us of the speaker's inability to halt the passage of time. He would like to freeze his encounter with the reaper, keeping it always in the present. But as the shift in tense indicates, time goes on, making the encounter part of the speaker's past. Perhaps, therefore, the poem's real subject is the idea that time is always in flux.

Audiences usually want evidence, and as we noted earlier, most arguments you write about literature will need to cite details of the work itself. Because direct quotation is usually an effective move, Abby planned to elaborate her claim by citing several of Wordsworth's references to time. Remember, though, that you need to avoid seeming willfully selective when you quote. While Abby expected to quote from Wordsworth's last stanza, she also knew she had to relate it to earlier lines so that her readers would see her as illuminating the basic subject of the whole poem. In particular, she looked for language in the first three stanzas that might hint at the speaker's lack of control over time, thereby previewing the last stanza's emphasis.

IDENTIFY YOUR ASSUMPTIONS

Often, to think about particular challenges of your paper is to think about your assumptions. Remember that a big category of assumptions is warrants; these are what lead you to call certain things evidence for your claims. Abby knew that one of her warrants was an assumption about Wordsworth himself — that he was not being sloppy when he shifted tenses in his last stanza. Rarely will your paper need to admit all the warrants on which it relies. Most of the time, your task will be to guess which warrants your readers do want stated. Abby felt there was at least one warrant she would have to spell out — her belief that the poem's verb tenses reveal something about the speaker's state of mind.

DETERMINE YOUR ORGANIZATION

To make sure their texts seem organized and demonstrate the process of reasoning, most writers first do an **outline**, a list of their key points in the order they will appear. Outlines are indeed a good idea, but bear in mind that there are various kinds. One popular type, which you may already know, is the **sentence outline**. As the name implies, it lists the writer's key points in sentence form. Its advantages are obvious: this kind of outline forces you to develop a detailed picture of your argument's major steps, and it leaves you with sentences you can then incorporate into your paper. Unfortunately, sentence outlines tend to discourage flexibility. Because they demand much thought and energy, you may hesitate to revise them, even if you come to feel your paper would work better with a new structure.

A second, equally familiar outline is the **topic outline**, a list in which the writer uses a few words to signify the main subjects that he or she will discuss. Because it is sketchy, this kind of outline allows writers to go back and change plans if necessary. Nevertheless, a topic outline may fail to provide all the guidance a writer needs.

We find a third type useful: a **rhetorical purpose outline**. As with the first two, you list the major sections of your paper. Next, you briefly indicate two things for each section: the effect you want it to have on your audience, and how you will achieve that effect. Here is the rhetorical purpose outline that Abby devised for her paper.

INTRODUCTION

The audience needs to know the text I'll discuss.	I'll identify Wordsworth's poem.
The audience must know my main issue.	I'll point out that the poem is puzzling in its shift of tenses at the end.
The audience must know my main claim.	I'll argue that the shift to past tense suggests that the poem's real subject is the inability of human beings to halt the passage of time.

ANALYSIS OF THE POEM'S FINAL STANZA

The audience needs to see in detail how the final stanza's shift to past tense signals the speaker's inability to control the passage of time.	I will point out not only the shift of tense but also other words in the last stanza that imply time moves on. I will note as well that music is an especially fleeting medium, so the reaper's song was bound to fade.

ANALYSIS OF THE PRECEDING STANZAS

To accept that the passage of time is the poem's real concern, the audience must see that the preceding stanzas hint at this subject.	I will analyze the first three stanzas in turn, showing how each implies the speaker is frustrated over his inability to control time.

CONCLUSION

The audience may need to be clearer about what I consider the ultimate *tone* of the poem.	I will say that although the poem can be thought of as a warm tribute to the singing reaper, the final emphasis on the passage of time is pessimistic in tone, and the speaker winds up as "solitary" as the reaper.

For your own rhetorical purpose outlines, you may want to use phrases rather than sentences. If you do use sentences, as Abby did, you do not have to write all that many. Note that Abby wrote relatively few as she stated the effects she would aim for and her strategies for achieving those effects. Thus, she was not tremendously invested in preserving her original outline. She felt free to change it if it failed to prove helpful.

Strategies for Composing

Composing is not always distinguishable from exploring, planning, and revising. As you prepare for your paper, you may jot down words or whole sentences. Once you begin a draft, you may alter that draft in several ways before you complete it. You may be especially prone to making changes in drafts if you use a computer, for word processing enables you to jump around in your text, revisiting and revising what you have written.

Still, most writers feel that doing a draft is an activity in its own right, and a major one at that. The next chapter presents various tips for writing about specific genres, and Chapter 6 discusses writing research-based papers. Meanwhile, here are some tips to help you with composing in general.

DECIDE ON A TITLE

You may be inclined to let your **title** be the same as that of the text you discuss. Were you to write about Wordsworth's poem, then, you would be calling your own paper "The Solitary Reaper." But often such mimicry backfires. For one thing, it may lead your readers to think that you are unoriginal and perhaps even lazy. Also, you risk confusing your audience, since your paper would actually be about Wordsworth's poem rather than being the poem itself. So take the time to come up with a title of your own. Certainly it may announce the text you will focus on, but let it do more. In particular, use your title to indicate the main claim you will be making. With just a few words, you can preview the argument to come.

MAKE CHOICES ABOUT YOUR STYLE

Perhaps you have been told to "sound like yourself" when you write. Yet that can be a difficult demand (especially if you are not sure what your "self" is really like). Above all, the **style** you choose depends on your audience and purpose. In writing an argument for a general audience, probably you would do best to avoid the extremes of pomposity and breezy informality. Try to stick with words you know well, and if you do want to use some that are only hazily familiar to you, check their dictionary definitions first.

At some point in our lives, probably all of us have been warned not to use *I* in our writing. In the course you are taking, however, you may be asked to write about your experiences. If so, you will find *I* hard to avoid. Whether to use it does become a real question when you get assignments like Abby's, which require you chiefly to make an argument about a text. Since you are supposed to focus on that text, your readers may be disconcerted if you keep referring to yourself. Even so, you need not assume that your personal life is irrelevant to the task. Your opening paragraph might refer to your personal encounters with the text, as a way of establishing the issue you will discuss. A personal anecdote might serve as a forceful conclusion to your paper. Moreover, before you reach the conclusion, you might orient your readers to the structure of your paper by using certain expressions that feature the word *I*: for example, *As I suggested earlier, As I have noted, As I argue later.* In general, you may be justified in saying *I* at certain moments. When tempted to use this pronoun, though, consider whether it really is your best move.

Arguments about literature are most compelling when supported by quotations, but be careful not to quote excessively. If you constantly repeat other people's words, providing few of your own, your readers will hardly get a sense of you as an author. Moreover, a paper full of quotation marks is hard to read. Make sure to quote selectively, remembering that sometimes you can simply paraphrase. When you do quote, try to cite only the words you need. You do not have to reproduce a whole line or sentence if one word is enough to support your point.

When summarizing what happens in a literary work, be careful not to shift tenses as you go along. Your reader may be confused if you shift back and forth between past and present. We suggest that you stick primarily to the present tense, which is the tense that literary critics customarily employ. For example, instead of saying that the speaker *praised* the lass, say that he *praises* her.

DRAFT AN INTRODUCTION

As a general principle, use your introduction to identify as quickly and efficiently as possible

- the main text that you will analyze;
- the main issue about it that you will address; and
- the main claim that you will develop in response to that issue.

Don't waste time with grand philosophical statements such as "Society doesn't always appreciate the work that everyone does," or "Over the centuries, much literature has been about work," or "William Wordsworth was a great British Romantic poet."

Remember that your main issue should be a significant question with no obvious answer. Try using one or more of the following strategies to establish that issue at the start of your essay:

- **State the issue as, indeed, a question.** For example: "Why, conceivably, does Wordsworth shift to the past tense in his poem's final stanza?"
- **Apply a word like** *puzzling, confusing, mysterious,* **or** *curious* **to whatever feature your issue will be about.** For example: "Because Wordsworth uses present tense for much of the poem, it is puzzling that he turns to past tense at the very end."
- **Through personal reference, state that you were first puzzled by a particular feature of the work but are now able to interpret it.** For example: "At first, I was confused when Wordsworth shifted to the past tense, but now I have arrived at a possible explanation for this move."
- **Indicate that you aim to help other readers of the work, who may have trouble understanding the feature of it you will focus on.** For example: "Quite a few readers of Wordsworth's poem may have difficulty seeing why he shifts to the past tense at the end. There is, however, a possible explanation for this move."
- **Indicate that you will express disagreement with existing or possible interpretations.** For example: "While some readers of Wordsworth's poem may feel that his shift to the past tense shows a wonderful ability to preserve his experience with the reaper, a more plausible interpretation is that it shows his isolation after meeting her."

LIMIT PLOT SUMMARY

Short stories and plays spin tales. So do many poems and essays. But if you are writing about a literary text that is narrative in form, don't spend much of your paper just summarizing the narrative. Developing a genuine argument about the work involves more than recounting its plot. Here are strategies you can use to limit this:

- Assume that your reader knows the basic plot and needs only a few brief reminders of its key elements.

- Keep in mind that your main purpose is to put forth, explain, and support a *claim* about the text — your answer to some question you raise about it.

- After your introduction, try to begin each new paragraph with a subclaim that helps you develop your main claim. Use the rest of the paragraph to elaborate and provide evidence for this subclaim. *Don't* begin a paragraph simply by recording a plot incident, for doing so is liable to bog you down in sheer summary.

- Instead of reciting plot details, write about how the work you are analyzing is *constructed*. Make observations about specific methods that the author uses to present the story, including techniques of organization and characterization. For example, rather than say "The speaker in Wordsworth's poem wonders what the woman is singing," state and develop a point like "Wordsworth chooses not to translate the woman's song for us; instead, he depicts the speaker as not knowing her words, so that the poem becomes mostly about the effect of her song as sheer musical notes."

- Instead of turning frequently to plot details, try to linger on some of the author's specific language, exploring possible definitions of particular words. For example, rather than say "The speaker in Wordsworth's poem remembers the woman's music," examine possible meanings of the word *bore* in the poem's next-to-last line, "The music in my heart I bore." *Bore* can simply mean "carried," and probably that is one meaning that Wordsworth has in mind here. But it can also mean "engraved, deeply inscribed," and perhaps Wordsworth wants us to think of this definition, too.

DECIDE HOW TO REFER TO THE AUTHOR'S LIFE AND INTENTIONS

Be cautious about relating the work to the author's life. Sometimes a certain character within the work may indeed express the author's own views, but don't simply assume that a character speaks for the author. Even the *I* of a first-person poem may differ significantly from its creator. True, many literary works are at least somewhat autobiographical, based on one or more aspects of the author's life. Nevertheless, even works that are largely autobiographical may not be entirely so. Besides, knowledge of the author's life won't always help you figure out his or her text. Wordsworth may have derived "The Solitary Reaper" from a personal encounter, but we must still interpret the particular poem he proceeded to write. So,

- Be careful in linking a work to the author's own circumstances. Such connections can be legitimate, but the more you push them, the more you may risk distorting the work's exact design. You also risk neglecting the author's artistic achievement. Not everyone who hears a reaper sing could turn this event into a poem!

Much of what you write about a literary work will reflect your understanding of its author's intentions. Needless to say, you can't peer into the author's mind. Rather, you'll make hypotheses about the author's aims. So,

- **Sometimes, at least, admit that you are guessing at what the author thought.** Often, your reader will assume that you are speculating about the author's aims, but your argument about them can be more persuasive if, at times, you acknowledge that you're trying to come up with the best hypothesis rather than stating an absolute fact. Take care, however, to explain why your guesses are logical.
- **If you suspect that the author might object to your view of the text, feel free to acknowledge such possible disagreements.** In fact, many theorists argue that a literary work may differ from how its author sees it. They refuse, therefore, to treat the author as an absolute authority on the work. D. H. Lawrence's advice was "Trust the tale, not the teller." Even if Lawrence is right, of course, you must show how *your* interpretation of a text manages to make sense of it.
- **Feel free to concede that your analysis of the work isn't the only reasonable one.** You can develop your main claim about a literary work partly by noting and addressing ways in which other readers may disagree with you about it. Bear in mind, though, that you will annoy your own audience if you come across as dogmatic. Be as fair as you can to views different from yours. Actually, your readers will appreciate it if at times you concede that yours is not the only reasonable interpretation. You can even specify one or more alternatives. Of course, you would still try to make a case for *your* explanation, perhaps by saying why it is *more plausible* or *more helpful* than its rivals. But speak of these competitors with respect, instead of just dismissing them with scorn.

RECOGNIZE AND AVOID LOGICAL FALLACIES

Although arguments presented in literary texts are often not logical, your arguments about these texts should be. Readers do not expect a poem's speaker, for example, to present cogently reasoned arguments to her lover, nor do they expect a lament for the lost passions of youth to be anything but subjective. But different kinds of writing have different conventions. What works in poetry may not be appropriate in an argument. The kinds of serious arguments you are expected to create cannot be successful using heartfelt emotion alone. When you write about literature, shaky thinking might cause your audience to dismiss your ideas. Your claims and the assumptions behind them should be clear and reasoned. If they are not, you might be committing a **fallacy**, a common term for unsound reasoning.

In the next several paragraphs, we discuss typical logical fallacies. Some of them are especially relevant to literary studies, and for all of them we provide examples related to "The Solitary Reaper." We do not want you to brood over this list, seeing it as a catalog of sins to which you might fall prey. If you constantly fear being accused of fallacies, you might be too paralyzed to make claims at all! In our discussion of fallacies, we also identify circumstances in which your audience might *not* object to a particular fallacy. In addition, we suggest how a writer might revise such claims to be more persuasive. Indeed, the main value in studying fallacies is to identify ways you might develop arguments more effectively.

One of the most common fallacies, ***ad hominem*** (Latin: "toward the man"), is probably the easiest to commit because it is the hardest to resist. Instead of doing the hard work of analyzing the claim and the evidence, we simply ignore them and attack the character of the person making the argument. Instead of trying to figure out what is going on in a complex work of literature, we say, "How can you take seriously a poem about love written by a manic depressive who commits suicide?" It is best to focus on the message, not the messenger.

A related fallacy, **begging the question** (a kind of circular reasoning in which the statement being argued is already assumed to have been decided) is also involved in this example since it is assumed (not proved) that unstable poets cannot have cogent insights about love.

In writing about "The Solitary Reaper," a classmate of Abby's ignored whatever argument the poem is making and focused on Wordsworth's credibility as an observer: "British intellectuals have been either romanticizing or degrading country people for centuries. Whatever Wordsworth thinks about the 'Highland Lass' is almost certainly wrong." First of all, the speaker of the poem should not be automatically equated with the poet. When they write, poets and fictional writers construct personae that may or may not reflect their own views. Second, attacking Wordsworth is a fallacy for several reasons. It first has to be demonstrated that the poet is a British intellectual, that intellectuals have consistently misrepresented rural people, and that the speaker has done so in this particular case. The classmate should revise her claim so that it deals with the words in the text, not her view of the poet's credibility.

Professional historians, mathematicians, and philosophers usually cite other professionals working in their field; that is, they **appeal to authority** to bolster their credibility. Disciplinary knowledge is created by a community of scholars who cite the ideas of its members as evidence for their claims. The warrant is that recognized authorities know what they are talking about. Quoting them is persuasive. But not completely: appeals to authority can also be fallacious. Literary critics, like other thinkers, often disagree. Just citing an expert does not conclusively prove your claim. A classmate of Abby's, for example, quoted a critic, Ian Lancashire, who says that the narrator "transcends the limitations of mortality," but the student did not give his own reasons or his own evidence for thinking this way. This appeal to critical authority without giving reasons or evidence is a fallacy because a sound argument would at least have to consider other critics. An argument is a reasoning process in which claims are supported, not simply asserted, even if they come from an expert.

A related fallacy involves using quotations from unreliable sources. Although the Internet is often a valuable tool, students sometimes use it uncritically. If you went to the search engine Google and entered Wordsworth's "The Solitary Reaper," you would quickly find Ian Lancashire's essay; and since he is a professor at the University of Toronto with many publications on this and other Romantic topics, citing him is appropriate. But some of the commentators noted by the Google search are students, perhaps English majors who have written a paper for a course on the Romantic poets. Using them as authorities would damage your judgment and credibility.

Equally harmful to the soundness of your argument is to rely too heavily on personal experience as evidence for your claim. Personal experience can sometimes be compelling and authoritative. Indeed, many critics have successfully used their own experiences with discrimination to create cogent arguments. But they rarely rely exclusively on personal experience. Instead they blend relevant experience with textual and critical specifics. Telling your readers that "The Solitary Reaper" is factually flawed because you never saw harvesters work alone when you worked on your uncle's farm would be a fallacy.

Actually, the previous example of using personal experience as authority is also unsound because the personal sample is too small to warrant a reasonable conclusion. It is hard to convince your audience if you claim too much based on limited experience. A student arguing that "The Solitary Reaper" demonstrates that field workers are melancholy would be committing a **hasty generalization** fallacy. Simply claiming less would improve the argument. In fact, this student might change the focus of her argument by doing research on other poems by Wordsworth, finding several that deal with young women in nature. Using "She Dwelt among Untrodden Ways" and "She Was a Phantom of Delight," the student might argue that Wordsworth is so enraptured by the natural world that he often blurs the boundaries between people and nature.

Another common fallacy is *post hoc, ergo propter hoc* (Latin: "because of this, then that"). Few of us escape this error in cause and effect. Many superstitions probably began because of this fallacy. A man breaks a mirror and bad luck follows. Did the mirror cause the bad luck? Logic says no, but the next day he breaks a leg, and a week later his car is stolen. The coincidence is often too tempting to resist. Does smoking marijuana lead to hard drugs? Logic says no, since you could argue just as plausibly that almost anything (carrots, beer, coffee) that comes before could be said to cause what comes after. Unless a clear, logical link between the two events is demonstrated, you might be accused of the *post hoc* fallacy.

In writing about "The Solitary Reaper," you might want to argue that the "melancholy strain" the traveler heard caused him to have a deeper appreciation for the beauty and mystery of rural people. But perhaps the narrator held such an opinion for a long time, or perhaps this is just one of dozens of such encounters that the poet remembers fondly. A sounder argument would focus on the cause and effect that do seem to be in the text: the mystery of the song's content adds to the emotional response the poet has.

Most of us commit a version of the **intentional fallacy** when we defend ourselves against someone we offended by saying, "That's not what I meant. It was just a joke." The problem arises because we are not always able to carry out our intentions. Perhaps our language is not precise enough, or perhaps our intention to be sincere or honest or witty gets mixed up with other intentions we have to sound intelligent, confident, or impressive. Students are often surprised when teachers tell them that a writer's stated intentions cannot be taken as the final word on a poem's meaning. "Wordsworth knows the poem better than anyone else" is an understandable retort. But that might not be the case. Wordsworth might not be the most astute reader of his own work. And he may not be fully aware of all that he intended. A student would be committing an intentional fallacy by arguing that "The Solitary Reaper" is written in the language used by the common man because Wordsworth says so in his preface to *Lyrical Ballads.* While this student should be commended for doing extra research, another student might point out that "Vale profound," "plaintive numbers," and "humble lay" seem conventionally poetic. Like others, this fallacy is easily revised by claiming less: "Most of 'The Solitary Reaper' is written in simple diction to approximate the language used by ordinary people."

When you try to destroy someone's argument by ignoring their main point and focusing on something marginal, you are attacking a **straw man**. The student who argues that we should dismiss Wordsworth's credibility as an observer because of "his absurd declaration that 'a voice so thrilling ne'er was heard'" is committing the straw man fallacy. While it is probably true that the song he hears is not the most thrilling in the history of the world, this is hardly Wordsworth's main point. Writers gain more credibility if they deal with a writer's strongest or main claim.

A favorite tactic of traditionalists trying to hold the line against change, the **slippery slope** fallacy is used to claim that if we allow one thing to happen, then slipping into catastrophe is just around the corner. If we do not prevent students from wearing gangsta rap fashions, gangs will eventually roam the hallways; if we allow the morning-after pill, sexual anarchy will follow. A small step is seen as precipitating an avalanche.

The following claim by a student anticipates something that simply is not logically called for: "Although Wordsworth probably means well, his praise for the 'Highland Lass' is a dangerous move since she is probably illiterate and full of rural biases and superstitions. His failure to discriminate will lead to loss of judgment and standards." Again, claiming less improves the argument: Wordsworth is less interested in the content ("Whate'er the theme") than in the "music in my heart," an emotional response that we hope does not carry over into his views on medicine, engineering, and economics.

We are all guilty at times of the fallacy of **oversimplification** — of not seeing the inevitable complexity of things. At the risk of committing a hasty generalization ourselves, it is probably the case that your instructor will be impressed if you look for complexity in literary texts and in your arguments. Seeing complexity is a consequence of hard thinking. There are rarely two sides to a question. More likely, there are a dozen plausible and reasonable per-spectives. The cliché that the truth often appears in shades of gray rather than in black and white gets at the idea that simple solutions are often the result of shallow thinking.

Complexity is not what the following claim reveals: "'The Solitary Reaper' is a poem about a traveler who hears a young girl 'singing by herself,' and like a catchy ad, the tune stays with him." Being exposed to other viewpoints in class discussions and in peer-group revision can help this student avoid over-simplifying the experience Wordsworth has, one that touches on issues of mor-tality, the mysteries of emotional response, the purpose of poetry, and the power of the natural world. When Henry David Thoreau, the author of *Walden* (1854), urged his contemporaries to live simply, he was talking about their life-styles, not their thinking.

Non sequitur is a general catchall fallacy that means "it does not follow." Some principle of logic has been violated when we make a claim that the evi-dence cannot support. In "The Solitary Reaper," it does not follow that because the Highland Lass "sings a melancholy strain," she herself is sad. She could be happy, absentminded, or simply bored. Perhaps the song is a conventional ballad typically sung by workers to pass the time. Revising this fallacy, like many of the others, involves setting aside time in the revision process to look again at your claims and the assumptions behind them, carefully and objec-tively making a clear connection between your claim and the evidence you say supports it.

First Draft of a Student Paper

The following is Abby's first complete draft of her paper. Eventually, she revised this draft after a group of her classmates reviewed it and after she reflected further on it herself. For the moment, though, read this first version, and decide what you would have said to her about it.

Abby Hazelton
Professor Ramsey
English 102
4 March ----
The Passage of Time in
"The Solitary Reaper"
William Wordsworth, one of the most famous writers in the movement known as British Romanticism, liked to write about beautiful features of the countryside. In his poem "The Solitary Reaper," the speaker enthuses over a girl who sings as she works in the fields. Yet although he is enraptured by her "melancholy strain," (line 6), he is unsure what it is *about* because she is using a Scottish dialect that he cannot understand. By contrast, the subject of the poem seems much clearer. The very title of the poem refers to the

singing girl, and the subsequent lines repeatedly praise her song as wonderfully haunting. Nevertheless, the poem has puzzling aspects. Many readers are likely to wonder if they are supposed to find the speaker guilty of cultural and class superiority when he, as a British intellectual, treats a Scottish peasant girl as a spectacle. Another issue, the one I focus on in my paper, arises when the final stanza shifts to past tense. In the first three stanzas, the speaker uses present tense, as if he is currently observing the singer whom he describes. In the concluding stanza, however, the speaker uses verbs such as "sang" (25), "saw" (27), and "listen'd" (29), as if he is *recalling* his encounter with her. How can we explain this inconsistency? One possible justification for the final shift to past tense is that it reminds us of the speaker's inability to halt the passage of time. Even though he would like to freeze the encounter, time goes on. Perhaps, therefore, the poem's real subject is the idea that time is always in flux. Indeed, even before the final stanza, the speaker betrays an awareness that he can't bend time to his will.

Simply by virtue of the shift to past tense, the last stanza indicates that time goes on despite the speaker's wishes. But other elements of this stanza convey the same notion. Recalling his experience of the girl's singing, the speaker reports that he was "motionless and still" (29), yet in the very next line he admits that he eventually moved: "I mounted up the hill" (30). When the speaker says that "the Maiden sang / As if her song could have no ending" (25–26), the words "As if" are significant, implying that the song did end for him in reality. Similarly, the poem itself has to end at some point. In fact, it concludes with the words "no more," which stress that the singer and her song now belong to the speaker's past (32). Only in his "heart" (31), apparently, can he retain them. Furthermore, the medium of print can never convey the sound of music. In fact, prior to recording technology, music was the most fleeting of media, its notes fading with each new moment. By seeking to transmit music, the speaker ensures that he will wind up being frustrated by time.

Even if the final stanza's shift of tense is jarring, the first three stanzas give hints that the speaker will end up defeated by time. Significantly, the poem's very first word is "Behold" (1). In issuing this command, the speaker evidently hopes that other people will abandon all motion and gaze at the singer, basking in her song. The speaker reinforces this call for paralysis with the command that begins line 4: "Stop here." Yet, as if acknowledging limits to his control, he adds "or gently pass!" (4). Besides referring to other human beings, these commands seem directed at time itself. The speaker hopes that time, too, will "Stop" and "Behold." Even at this point in the poem, however, he realizes that time is inclined to "pass," in which case he hopes that it will at least move on "gently" (4).

The second stanza is chiefly concerned with space. Comparing the girl's song to other sounds, the speaker ranges from "Arabian sands" (12) to "the seas / Among the farthest Hebrides" (15–16). In the third stanza, however, he focuses again on time. Trying to determine the subject of the song, he expresses uncertainty about its time frame. He wonders whether the song concerns "old, unhappy, far-off things / And battles long ago" (19-20) or instead deals with "Familiar matter of to-day" (22). Moreover, even if he suspects the song's subject is "Some natural sorrow, loss, or pain" (23), he is unsure whether this experience of despair is confined to the past ("has been") or will reoccur ("may be again") (24). Whichever of the possibilities he raises is true, the speaker is clearly limited in his ability to figure out the song's relation to time. In other words, he cannot force time into a meaningful pattern, let alone prevent its passing.

By the end of the poem, the speaker seems as "solitary" as the reaper. In addition to losing his experience with her as time moves on, he is isolated in other ways.

This situation seems to leave the speaker as "solitary" as the reaper. Throughout the poem, actually, we don't see him in the company of others. His opening "Behold" is directed at no one in particular. Furthermore, we can't be sure he is speaking to actual passersby or, rather, to the poem's hypothetical future readers. Nor, for all his praise of the singer, does he apparently talk to her. Rather, he gives the impression that he keeps at a distance. Even if he did try to converse with the reaper, he himself would still be "solitary" in the sense of failing to understand her language and failing to communicate her song to his readers. He does not even bother trying to reproduce some of the song's words. Therefore, despite the speaker's enchantment over the reaper, this poem is ultimately pessimistic. The speaker is left only with his memories of a wonderful experience. He has lost the experience itself.

Strategies for Revising

Most first drafts are far from perfect. Even experienced professional writers often have to revise their work. Besides making changes on their own, many of them solicit feedback from others. In various workplaces, writing is collaborative, with coauthors exchanging ideas as they try to improve a piece. Remain open to the possibility that your draft needs changes, perhaps several. Of course, you are more apt to revise extensively if you have given yourself enough time. Conversely, you will not feel able to change much of your paper if it is due the next day. You will also limit your ability to revise if you work only with your original manuscript, scribbling possible changes between the lines. This practice amounts to conservatism, for it encourages you to keep passages that really ought to be overhauled.

You may have trouble, however, improving a draft if you are checking many things in it at once. Therefore, read the draft repeatedly, looking at a different aspect of it each time. A good way to begin is to outline the paper you have written and then compare that outline with your original one. If the two outlines differ, your draft may or may not need adjusting; perhaps you were wise to swerve from your original plan. In any case, you should ponder your departures from that plan, considering whether they were for the best.

If, like Abby, you are writing an argument paper, our Checklist for Revising box has some topics and questions you might apply as you review your first draft. Some of these considerations overlap. Nevertheless, take them in turn rather than all at once.

■ **A CHECKLIST FOR REVISING**

Logic

- Will my audience see that the issue I am focusing on is indeed an issue?

- Will the audience be able to follow the logic of my argument?

- Is the logic as persuasive as it might be? Is there more evidence I can provide? Do I need to identify more of my assumptions?

- Have I addressed all of my audience's potential concerns?

Organization

- Does my introduction identify the issue that I will focus on? Does it state my main claim?

- Will my audience be able to detect and follow the stages of my argument?

- Does the order of my paragraphs seem purposeful rather than arbitrary?

- Have I done all I can to signal connections within and between sentences? Within and between paragraphs?

- Have I avoided getting bogged down in mere summary?

- Will my conclusion satisfy readers? Does it leave any key questions dangling?

(continued on next page)

▤ A CHECKLIST FOR REVISING *(continued)*

Clarity

- Does my title offer a good preview of my argument?

- Will each of my sentences be immediately clear?

- Am I sure how to define each word that I have used?

Emphasis

- Have I put key points in prominent places?

- Have I worded each sentence for maximum impact? In particular, is each sentence as concise as possible? Do I use active verbs whenever I can?

Style

- Are my tone and level of vocabulary appropriate?

- Will my audience think me fair-minded? Should I make any more concessions?

- Do I use any mannerisms that may distract my readers?

- Have I used any expressions that may annoy or offend?

- Is there anything else I can do to make my paper readable and interesting?

Grammar

- Is each of my sentences grammatically correct?

- Have I punctuated properly?

Physical Appearance

- Have I followed the proper format for quotations, notes, and bibliography?

- Are there any typographical errors?

We list these considerations from most to least important. When revising a draft, think first about matters of logic, organization, and clarity. There is little point in fixing the grammar of particular sentences if you are going to drop them later because they fail to advance your argument.

As we noted, a group of Abby's classmates discussed her draft. Most of these students seemed to like her overall argument, including her main issue and claim. Having been similarly confused by the poem's shift of tense, they appreciated the light that Abby shed on it. They were impressed by her willingness to examine the poem's specific words. They especially liked her closing analogy between the reaper and the speaker himself. Nevertheless, the group made several comments about Abby's paper that she took as suggestions for improvement. Ultimately, she decided that the following changes were in order.

1. She should make her introduction more concise.   The first draft is so long and dense that it may confuse readers instead of helping them sense the paper's main concerns. This problem is common to first drafts. In this preliminary phase, many writers worry that they will fail to generate *enough* words; they are hardly thinking about how to restrain themselves. Moreover, the writer of a first draft may still be unsure about the paper's whole argument, so the introduction often lacks a sharp focus. After Abby finished and reviewed her first draft, she saw ways of making her introduction tighter.

2. She should rearrange paragraphs.   After her introduction, Abby discussed the poem's last stanza in more detail. Then she moved back to stanza 1. Next, just before her paper's conclusion, she analyzed stanzas 2 and 3. Abby thought that the structure of her paper moved logically from the obvious to the hidden: the poem's last stanza emphasized the passage of time, and the earlier stanzas touched on this subject more subtly. Yet Abby's method of organization frustrated her classmates. They thought her paper would be easier to follow if, after the introduction, it moved chronologically through the poem. For them, her discussion of stanzas 2 and 3 seemed especially mislocated. Though she had positioned this discussion as her paper's climax, her classmates did not sense it to be her most significant and compelling moment of insight. Most important, they believed, were her comments on the *final* stanza, for that seemed to them the most important part of Wordsworth's poem. In other words, they thought the climax of the paper would be stronger if it focused on the climax of the poem. Abby hesitated to adopt her classmates' recommendation, but eventually she did so. When you read her final version, see if you like her rearrangement of paragraphs. Sometimes, though not always, a paper about a literary work seems more coherent if it does follow the work's chronological structure. And papers should indeed build to a climax, even if readers disagree about what its content should be.

3. She should reconsider her claim that "this poem is ultimately pessimistic."   Abby's classmates thought this claim did not fully account for the poem's last two lines: "The music in my heart I bore, / Long after it was heard no more" (31–32). While they agreed with her that the words "no more" emphasize that the singer has faded into the past, they disagreed that her song is lost as well, for it remains in the speaker's "heart." They noted that Abby had acknowledged this fact, but they felt she had done so too briefly and dismissively. In addition, one student encouraged her to think about poetry and music as ways of keeping memories alive. More specifically, he suggested that the speaker of "The Solitary Reaper" is Wordsworth himself, who is using this poem to preserve his memory of an actual encounter. After studying the poem again, Abby decided that her classmates' ideas had merit, and she incorporated them into her revision. Of course, such advice is not always worth heeding. Still, writers should accept the invitation to look more closely at whatever text they are analyzing.

Revised Draft of a Student Paper

Here is the new version of the paper that Abby wrote. Attached to it are marginal comments by us that call your attention to her strategies.

Abby Hazelton
Professor Ramsey
English 102
11 March - - - -

Title clearly indicates the particular work being analyzed and the aspect to be focused on.

The Passage of Time in
"The Solitary Reaper"

In William Wordsworth's poem "The Solitary Reaper," the speaker enthuses over a girl who sings as she works in the fields. Throughout the poem, his rapture is evident. Yet in the last stanza, he makes a puzzling move, shifting to past tense after using present tense in the previous three stanzas. No longer does he seem to be currently observing the singer he describes; rather, now he seems to be *recalling* his encounter with her. One possible justification for this shift in tense is that it reminds us of the speaker's inability to halt the passage of time. Even though he would like to freeze the encounter, time goes on. Perhaps, therefore, the poem's real theme is that time is always in flux. Indeed, even before the final stanza, the speaker betrays an awareness that he can't bend time to his will.

Immediately refers to specific detail of text.

With "puzzling," signals issue to be addressed.

Identifies the main claim.

Connects feature of the poem to be focused on to other parts of it.

Significantly, the poem's very first word is "Behold" (line 1). In issuing this command, the speaker evidently hopes that other people will abandon all motion and gaze at the singer. The speaker reinforces this call for paralysis with the command that begins line 4: "Stop here." Yet, as if acknowledging limits to his control, he adds "or gently pass!" (4). Besides referring to other human beings, these commands seem directed at time itself. The speaker hopes that time, too, will "Stop" and "Behold." Even at this point in the poem, however, he realizes that time is inclined to "pass," in which case he hopes that it will at least move on "gently."

Analyzes an implication of the poem's particular language rather than just beginning with a plot detail.

Develops point that even the poem's early stanzas show concern about the passage of time that final stanza emphasizes.

The second stanza is chiefly concerned with space. Comparing the girl's song to other sounds, the speaker ranges

Moves chronologically through the poem, carefully pointing out how second stanza differs from the first.

from "Arabian sands" (12) to "the seas / Among the farthest Hebrides" (15–16). In the third stanza, however, he focuses again on time. Trying to determine the subject of her song, he expresses uncertainty about its time frame. He wonders whether the song concerns "old, unhappy, far-off things / And battles long ago" (19–20) or instead deals with "Familiar matter of to-day" (22). Moreover, even if he suspects the song's subject is "Some natural sorrow, loss, or pain" (23), he is unsure whether this experience of despair is confined to the past ("has been") or will reoccur ("may be again") (24). Whichever of the possibilities he raises is true, the speaker is clearly limited in his ability to figure out the song's relation to time. In other words, he cannot force time into a meaningful pattern, let alone prevent its passing.

Makes distinctions among stanzas' topics. Returns to main claim of the essay.

Refers to actual words of poem to support points.

Ends paragraph by reminding us what main claim is.

Simply by virtue of the shift to past tense, the last stanza indicates that time goes on despite the speaker's wishes. But other elements of the stanza convey this same notion. Recalling his experience of the girl's singing, the speaker reports that he was "motionless and still" (29), yet in the very next line he admits that he eventually moved: "I mounted up the hill" (30). When the speaker says that "the Maiden sang / As if her song could have no ending" (25–26), the words "As if" are significant, implying that the song did end for him in reality. Similarly, the poem itself has to end at some point. In fact, it concludes with the words "no more" (32), which stress that the singer and her song now belong to the speaker's past. Only in his "heart" (31), apparently, can he retain them.

Directs attention to part of poem with which she is most concerned.

Traces implications of poem's words, especially as these are related to main issue and claim.

This situation seems to leave the speaker as "solitary" as the reaper. Throughout the poem, actually, we don't see him in the company of others. His opening "Behold" is directed at no one in particular. Furthermore, we can't be sure he is speaking to actual passersby or, rather, to the poem's hypothetical future readers. Nor, for all his praise of the singer, does he apparently talk to her. Rather, he gives the impression that he keeps at a distance. Even if he did converse with the reaper, he himself would still be "solitary" in the sense of failing to understand her dialect and failing to communicate her words to his readers. As things stand, he is apparently unable or unwilling to reproduce any of the song's lyrics. Just as important, the medium of print can never convey the sounds of music. In fact, prior to recording technology, music was the most fleeting of media, its notes fading with each new moment. By seeking to transmit music, the speaker ensures that he will wind up being frustrated by time.

Connects last stanza to other parts of poem.

Several observations support idea that the speaker is isolated.

Concludes climactic paragraph with substantial analysis.

Yet perhaps the singer and her song are preserved in more than just the speaker's "heart." It can be argued that they are also preserved by the poem, if only to a limited extent. More generally, we can say that literature is a means by which human beings partially succeed in perpetuating things. This idea seems quite relevant to "The Solitary Reaper" if we suppose that the speaker is the poet himself and that he actually witnessed the scene he describes. If we make such assumptions, we can see Wordsworth as analogous to the speaker. After all, both engage in commemorative verbal art. Because time passes, the "strain[s]" that Wordsworth and the singer produce in their efforts to preserve time are bound to be "melancholy" (6). Still, their art matters, for through it they are imaginatively "[r]eaping" (3) experiences that would otherwise fade.

Signals that she is simply making a suggestion here, rather than asserting a definite new point.

Concluding paragraph reminds us of main issue and claim, but goes beyond mere repetition to bring up some new suggestions.

To us, Abby's revision is more persuasive and compelling than her first draft. In particular, she has nicely complicated her claim about the poem's "pessimism." Nevertheless, we would hesitate to call this revision the definitive version of her paper. Maybe you have thought of things Abby could do to make it even more effective. In presenting her two drafts, we mainly want to emphasize the importance of revision. We hope, too, that you will remember our specific tips as you work on your own writing.

Strategies for Writing a Comparative Paper

Much writing about literature *compares* two or more texts. After all, you can gain many insights into a text by noting how it resembles and differs from others. We refer to the practice of critical comparison in Chapter 2, How to Argue about Literature (pp. 37–45), where we juxtapose stories by Daniel Orozco and Jamaica Kincaid, each of which features a point of comparison: both speakers are introducing someone to a kind of work. But in this section we offer specific advice for writing a comparative paper, a task you may be assigned in your course. We also present a sample paper that models strategies of comparative writing.

To aid our discussion, we ask that you read the following two poems. The first, "Two Trees," appears in the 2009 verse collection *Rain* by Don Paterson (b. 1963), a Scottish writer who is also a jazz musician, a professor at the University of St. Andrews, and the poetry editor for the publisher Picador Macmillan. Next comes "Regarding History," a poem from the 2005 book *Trill & Mordent* by Luisa A. Igloria (b. 1961), a Filipina American writer who is a professor of English and creative writing at Old Dominion University in Norfolk, Virginia.

DON PATERSON
Two Trees

One morning, Don Miguel got out of bed
with one idea rooted in his head:
to graft his orange to his lemon tree.
It took him the whole day to work them free,
lay open their sides, and lash them tight.   5
For twelve months, from the shame or from the fright
they put forth nothing; but one day there appeared
two lights in the dark leaves. Over the years
the limbs would get themselves so tangled up
each bough looked like it gave a double crop,   10
and not one kid in the village didn't know
the magic tree in Miguel's patio.

The man who bought the house had had no dream
so who can say what dark malicious whim
led him to take his axe and split the bole   15
along its fused seam, and then dig two holes.
And no, they did not die from solitude;
nor did their branches bear a sterile fruit;
nor did their unhealed flanks weep every spring
for those four yards that lost them everything   20
as each strained on its shackled root to face
the other's empty, intricate embrace.
They were trees, and trees don't weep or ache or shout.
And trees are all this poem is about.   *[2009]*

LUISA A. IGLORIA
Regarding History

A pair of trees on one side of the walk, leaning
now into the wind in a stance we'd call involuntary —
I can see them from the kitchen window, as I take meat
out of the oven and hold my palms above the crust, darkened
with burnt sugar. Nailed with cloves, small earth of flesh   5
still smoldering from its furnace. In truth I want to take it
into the garden and bury it in soil. There are times
I grow weary of coaxing music from silence, silence
from the circularity of logic, logic from the artifact.
Then, the possibilities of sunlight are less attractive   10
than baying at the moon. I want to take your face
in my hands, grow sweet from what it tells, tend
how it leans and turns, trellis or vine of morning-glory.

I wish for limbs pared to muscle, to climb away from
chance and all its missed appointments, its half-drunk   15
cups of coffee. Tell me what I'll find, in this
early period at the beginning of a century.
Tell me what I'll find, stumbling into a boat
and pushing off into the year's last dark hours.   *[2005]*

LIST SIMILARITIES AND DIFFERENCES

A class like yours sensed value in comparing Paterson's poem with Igloria's. So
the students proceeded to brainstorm lists of specific similarities and differences — something you might do to start analyzing texts you bring together.
For these two poems, the class came up with the following comparisons:

SIMILARITIES

In both poems, a prominent role is played by a real pair of trees, and
  their relation to each other seems important.

Both poems describe labor. In Paterson's, it's the labor of joining and
  then separating the trees; in Igloria's, it's the labor of cooking,
  burying, coaxing, climbing, and "pushing off."

The word *limbs* appears in both poems.

Both poems contain many words that have negative connotations.
  Paterson's poem includes such words as *shame*, *fright*, *dark*
  malicious whim, *die*, *sterile*, *unhealed*, *weep*, *strained*, *shackled*,
  empty, and *ache*, while Igloria's poem includes such words as
  darkened, *burnt*, *Nailed*, *bury*, *weary*, *missed*, and *dark*.

More specifically, both poems contain words associated with death.

Both poems refer to the time frame of a year, with Paterson's
  mentioning "twelve months" and Igloria's concluding with "the
  year's last dark hours."

DIFFERENCES

The speaker in Igloria's poem uses first person, indicated by the
  pronoun *I*, while the speaker in Paterson's poem is no specific,
  identifiable person.

Paterson's poem does, however, name a particular character (Don
  Miguel) and refers to several other people (kids in the village,
  the man who chopped apart the trees), while the only people in
  Igloria's poem seem to be "I" and "you."

Paterson's poem centers on a particular image, the two trees,
  whereas Igloria's poem has other images besides the pair of
  trees.

Paterson's poem seems more like a narrative; it tells a story. Igloria's poem seems to be more the expression of the speaker's mood.

While Igloria's speaker is clearly interested in the pair of trees as metaphors for her relationship with "you," Paterson's poem leaves readers to interpret whether and how the two trees have metaphorical implications.

"Two Trees" rhymes, but "Regarding History" does not.

"Regarding History" seems in many respects a love poem, but "Two Trees" is hard to see in that way.

"Two Trees" comments on the fact that it is a poem, but "Regarding History" does not.

"Regarding History" ends with its speaker wanting to know something ("Tell me what I'll find"), but "Two Trees" may leave its *readers* wanting to know something: whether we're supposed to accept its speaker's claim that "trees are all this poem is about."

As you plan your own comparative paper, lists such as these can help you organize your thoughts. To be sure, this class did not immediately think of all the similarities and differences it ended up noting. Usually, going beyond obvious points of comparison is a gradual process, for which you should give yourself plenty of time. Similarly, once you have made lists such as the one above, take time to decide which similarities and differences truly merit your attention. At most, only a few can be part of your paper's main issue and claim.

CONSIDER "WEIGHTING" YOUR COMPARISON

Unfortunately, many students writing a comparative analysis are content to put forth main claims such as these:

There are many similarities and differences between "Two Trees" and "Regarding History."

While "Two Trees" and "Regarding History" have many similarities, in many ways they are also different.

While "Two Trees" and "Regarding History" are different in many ways, they are similar in others.

Several problems arise with these common methods of introducing a comparative paper. For one thing, they give the reader no preview of the specific ideas to come. Indeed, they could have been written by someone who never bothered to read the two poems, for any two texts are similar in certain ways and different in others. Furthermore, these sorts of claims leave no meaningful and compelling way of organizing the paper. Rather, they encourage the writer to proceed arbitrarily, noting miscellaneous similarities and differences on impulse. More precisely, claims such as these fail to identify the *issue* driving the paper. Why compare Paterson's and Igloria's poems in the first place? Comparison is a means to an end, not an end in itself. What important question is the writer using these two texts to answer? In short, what's at stake?

A more fruitful approach, we think, is to write a *weighted* comparative analysis — that is, an argument chiefly concerned with *one* text more than others. When professional literary critics compare two texts, often they mainly want to answer a question about just one of them. They bring in the second text because they believe that doing so helps them address the issue they are raising about their key text. True, a good paper can result even when you treat equally all texts you discuss. But you might write a paper that seems more purposeful and coherent if you focus basically on one work, using comparisons to resolve some issue concerning it.

A Student Comparative Paper

The following paper by student Jeremy Cooper demonstrates weighted comparative analysis. The author refers to Igloria's "Regarding History" along with Paterson's "Two Trees," but he is mostly concerned with Paterson's poem. He brings up Igloria's poem not to do comparison for its own sake but to address a question he has about Paterson's text.

Jeremy Cooper
Professor Budnoy
English 102
15 October - - - -

Title does not merely repeat title of the poem to be analyzed. Moreover, title specifies what aspect of that poem he will examine.

 Don Paterson's Criticism of Nature's Owners

 Until its last two lines, Don Paterson's poem "Two Trees" tells a fairly straightforward story. The title refers to an orange tree and a lemon tree that stood next to each other on an estate. The speaker in the poem recalls how these trees were treated by two different owners of the property. The first owner, Don Miguel, successfully grafted the trees together. The next owner, a man unnamed by the speaker, separated them with an axe. Given the speaker's clear description of these events, most readers would probably have no trouble understanding what happened to the trees. But the poem's concluding pair of lines is puzzling:

First sentence refers to poem he will focus on, his primary text.

Signals issue that the paper will address.

     They were trees, and trees don't weep or ache or shout.
     And trees are all this poem is about. (23–24)
On the surface, the word "all" seems equivalent to "merely." If this is the case, readers might feel that Paterson is encouraging them to take a limited view of his poem, seeing it as concerned with nothing more than trees. They would then feel

*dis*couraged from looking for additional significance or meaning in his text. But this interpretation of Paterson's focus risks making his poem appear relatively trivial, an impression that he surely does not want to create. A likelier possibility is that the speaker is being ironic in his final declaration, stating the word "all" sarcastically. Such a tone might then move readers to question whether the poem is simply about trees. They might feel compelled to consider how its real subject is something else. Indeed, the poem's actual main topic seems to be the regrettable attitudes that human beings take toward nature when they are able to own it.

Trees play a major role in Paterson's poem, as their presence in the title suggests. In the first of the poem's two stanzas, the speaker describes Don Miguel's effort to fuse the orange tree and the lemon tree together, something that he evidently managed to accomplish so well that the trees became hard to distinguish from each other: "the limbs would get themselves so tangled up / each bough looked like it gave a double crop" (9–10). In the second stanza, the speaker turns to describing how the next owner of the trees did the opposite thing to them, splitting them apart (15–16). The poem presents no other scenic feature to compete with the two trees for the reader's attention. The speaker just briefly mentions a bed (1), a patio (12), a house (13), and an axe (15).

Introductory paragraph ends by stating the claim about the primary text that the paper will support and develop.

That the focus is very much on the trees becomes even more apparent if we compare this poem with another in which two trees figure, Luisa A. Igloria's "Regarding History." Igloria's poem begins with "A pair of trees on one side of the walk, leaning / now into the wind in a stance we'd call involuntary" (1–2). Later, the speaker seems to have these two trees still in mind when she says that she wants to hold her lover's face and feel "how it leans and turns, trellis or vine of morning-glory" (13). The close relation of the word "leans" in this line to "leaning" (1) in the earlier one implies that the trees remain a meaningful symbol for her throughout the poem. But, unlike Paterson's speaker, Igloria's turns her thoughts to a number of images other than trees. For example, besides her beloved's face, she thinks of food she has just prepared ("meat / out of the oven" [3–4], which she has evidently "Nailed with cloves" [5]), her garden (7), sunlight (10), the moon (11), muscle (14), coffee (16), and a boat (18). Basically, the two trees in this poem are just part of its many elements. By contrast, the pair of trees in Paterson's poem is much more prominent.

This is a secondary text, which he uses to reinforce the point he has just made about his primary text.

The question then becomes what we as readers should make of their central role in that poem. Some of us may be inclined to see Paterson's trees as a metaphor, their physical existence being less significant than something else they represent. The pair of trees in "Regarding History" do seem metaphorical, functioning in the speaker's mind as stand-ins for a human relationship. When she observes that the trees are "leaning / now into the wind in a stance we'd call involuntary" (1–2), she appears to be actually thinking of her relationship with her beloved. Specifically, she seems worried about pressures on their relationship that threaten their ability to keep it steady. This concern of hers comes up again later, when she expresses a desire "to take your face" (11) and "tend / how it leans and turns" (12–13). Here, too, she evidently feels that her connection to her loved one is challenged by outside forces. As in her earlier remark about the trees, she fears that she will not be able to protect her relationship from influences that will make her and her lover do "involuntary" (2) things. In comparison, though, the two trees in Paterson's poem do not appear to have a metaphorical function. In the first place, the speaker of "Two Trees" lacks a distinct personality, so that the poem does not encourage readers to interpret the trees he mentions as representing thoughts or feelings of his. Whereas Igloria's speaker dominates "Regarding History" with her clearly marked hopes and concerns, Paterson's speaker writes largely like a reporter narrating news events. Moreover, when he tells what the two property owners did to the trees, he describes these actions so precisely and concretely that he makes it hard for readers to consider the trees as symbolic rather than physical. Also, in such lines as "they did not die from solitude" (17) and "nor did their unhealed flanks weep every spring" (19) the speaker seems to be reminding the reader that they are, in fact, basically vegetation rather than images of something in the human mind. If anything, these lines discourage the reader from interpreting the trees as metaphors.

He has identified a possible interpretation but now offers a different one, which he proceeds to argue for.

He uses comparison with his secondary text to support his argument about his primary text.

But if the two trees in Paterson's poem come across mainly as real elements of nature, the attitudes that their owners show toward them are nevertheless significant. Actually, the poem's main subject is not the trees of the title, but the intense and disturbing emotions that drove Don Miguel and the later owner to handle them roughly. The feelings that led the second owner to separate the trees seem villainous. The speaker suggests that this man "had had no dream" (13) but instead acted on some mysterious "dark

He is working with the claim he put forth in his introduction.

malicious whim" that compelled him to "split" them apart
(14–15), leaving their flanks "unhealed" (19) and their roots
"shackled" (21). This language gives the impression of a
plantation owner in the pre–Civil War American South, the
type of person who cruelly divided slave families and kept
their members separated in bondage. Because the poem ends
with the physical stress inflicted upon the trees by their
second owner, some readers may be more bothered by this
man's behavior than they are by Don Miguel's. They might
even appreciate Don Miguel's interest in uniting the trees,
especially because his labor resulted in the heartening picture
of "two lights in the dark leaves" (8). But the language used
to describe his actions, too, is mostly negative. The words
"lay open" (5), "lash them tight" (5), "shame" (6), "fright"
(6), and "tangled up" (9) imply traumatic destruction, even
rape, rather than blissful harmony. In his willingness to
manipulate the trees, Don Miguel therefore seems no better
than the man who replaced him. Furthermore, Don Miguel's
behavior toward the trees did not have the excuse of being
carefully thought-out and planned. He simply awoke "with
one idea rooted in his head: / to graft his orange to his
lemon tree" (2–3). Just as the word "Don" in the first line is
an indication that he is a man of power in his community, so
the repetition of the word "his" in this line suggests that he
felt able to perform surgery on the trees merely because he
owned them. Both of the men in the poem avoided thinking
of what was best for the trees. Instead, both preferred to
exercise the authority they had as possessors of the trees, no
matter how abusive their handling of the trees might be. The
speaker in Igloria's poem calls attention to what she currently
lacks or is *unable* to do, through statements like "I want to
take your face" (11), "I wish for limbs pared to muscle" (14),
and "Tell me what I'll find" (18). Furthermore, she does not
possess the two trees that figure in "Regarding History."
Rather, she is a mere observer of them: "I can see them from
the kitchen window" (3). In Paterson's poem, on the other
hand, Don Miguel and the second man treat their trees
violently and are able to do so because the trees are legally
theirs.

Paterson does not end his poem by directly indicating
what he thinks is the proper way of treating trees like those
of his title. He does not clearly offer some sort of prescription
for their care. Many readers may, nevertheless, come away
from the poem concluding that human beings should avoid
tampering with trees and, more generally, should leave nature
alone as often as possible. In any case, Paterson's central

Again, he acknowledges the possibility of an interpretation different from his, before advancing his view.

Once more, he uses comparison with his secondary text to reinforce his argument about his primary text.

He suggests that this interpretation is possible but that he is more interested in getting his readers to accept his main claim about the poem: the idea he returns to in his final sentence.

purpose seems to be to make us more aware that when
humans own some of nature, they may treat it arrogantly,
whether in the pursuit of unity (Don Miguel's aim when he
fuses the trees) or separation (the second man's goal when he
breaks them apart).

Jeremy gains much from comparing "Two Trees" with "Regarding History." In paragraph 3, the analysis of the modest role that trees play in Igloria's poem bolsters Jeremy's claim that they are the core of Paterson's poem. In paragraph 4, the discussion of how Igloria uses trees as metaphors strengthens Jeremy's point that Paterson's trees are literal. In paragraph 5, the observation that Igloria's speaker is *not* an owner of trees helps Jeremy stress that Paterson's men possess them. Obviously, though, Jeremy focuses his paper on Paterson's poem, not on both. By concentrating chiefly on "Two Trees," he enables himself to develop a tight and logical argument, whereas focusing on both poems would encourage him to roam through similarities and differences at random.

Perhaps you know the advice usually given about how to organize a comparative paper. Traditionally, writers aiming to compare two texts learn of two options: (1) discuss one text and then move to the other, comparing it with the first; (2) discuss the texts together, noting each of their similarities and differences in turn. Both of these alternatives make sense and provide a ready-made structure for your paper; either can result in a coherent essay. Still, a weighted analysis such as Jeremy's — an analysis that focuses on one text more than another — is more likely than either of the alternatives to seem the logical evolution of a pointed claim.

CHAPTER 5

Writing about Literary Genres

At the beginning of Chapter 2, we discussed how literary works are often understood as examples of particular **genres** (kinds or types of writing). While acknowledging that most readers think of literature as comprising the genres of fiction, poetry, and drama, we invited you to think of nonfiction (such as historical writing), creative nonfiction (such as autobiography and memoir), and essays (sometimes including argumentative prose) as literature as well. In this chapter, we present elements of literary analysis for the genres of fiction, poetry, drama, and the essay, and show how various students have used those elements to generate writing about literary works. You will notice that many of these elements are useful in thinking about most genres, but different genres make different use of elements, emphasizing some more than others. We also devote a section to writing about poems and pictures; over the centuries, many poets have been prompted to create their art in response to visual images created by other kinds of artists.

Writing about Stories

Short stories can be said to resemble novels. Above all, both are works of fiction. Yet the difference in length matters. As William Trevor, a veteran writer of short stories, has observed, short fiction is "the art of the glimpse; it deals in echoes and reverberations; craftily it withholds information. Novels tell all. Short stories tell as little as they dare." Maybe Trevor overstates the situation when he claims that novels reveal everything. All sorts of texts feature what literary theorist Wolfgang Iser calls "gaps." Still, Trevor is right to emphasize that short stories usually tell much less than novels do. They demand that you understand and evaluate characters on the basis of just a few details and events. In this respect, short stories resemble poems. Both tend to rely on compression rather than expansion, seeking to affect their audience with a sharply limited number of words.

Short stories' focused use of language can make the experience of reading them wonderfully intense. Furthermore, you may end up considering important human issues as you try to interpret the "glimpses" they provide. Precisely because short stories "tell as little as they dare," they offer you much to ponder as you proceed to write about them.

In discussing the writing process, we refer often to the story that follows. Published in 1941, "A Visit of Charity" is by a pioneer of American short fiction, Eudora Welty (1909–2001). She spent her life chiefly in her hometown of Jackson, Mississippi, and most of her writing is set in the American South.

EUDORA WELTY
A Visit of Charity

It was mid-morning—a very cold, bright day. Holding a potted plant before her, a girl of fourteen jumped off the bus in front of the Old Ladies' Home, on the outskirts of town. She wore a red coat, and her straight yellow hair was hanging down loose from the pointed white cap all the little girls were wearing that year. She stopped for a moment beside one of the prickly dark shrubs with which the city had beautified the Home, and then proceeded slowly toward the building, which was of whitewashed brick and reflected the winter sunlight like a block of ice. As she walked vaguely up the steps she shifted the small pot from hand to hand; then she had to set it down and remove her mittens before she could open the heavy door.

"I'm a Campfire Girl. . . . I have to pay a visit to some old lady," she told the nurse at the desk. This was a woman in a white uniform who looked as if she were cold; she had close-cut hair which stood up on the very top of her head exactly like a sea wave. Marian, the little girl, did not tell her that this visit would give her a minimum of only three points in her score.

"Acquainted with any of our residents?" asked the nurse. She lifted one eyebrow and spoke like a man.

"With any old ladies? No—but—that is, any of them will do," Marian stammered. With her free hand she pushed her hair behind her ears, as she did when it was time to study Science.

The nurse shrugged and rose. "You have a nice *multiflora cineraria°* there," she remarked as she walked ahead down the hall of closed doors to pick out an old lady.   5

There was loose, bulging linoleum on the floor. Marian felt as if she were walking on the waves, but the nurse paid no attention to it. There was a smell in the hall like the interior of a clock. Everything was silent until, behind one of the doors, an old lady of some kind cleared her throat like a sheep bleating. This decided the nurse. Stopping in her tracks, she first extended her arm, bent her elbow, and leaned forward from the hips—all to examine the watch strapped to her wrist; then she gave a loud double-rap on the door.

"There are two in each room," the nurse remarked over her shoulder.

"Two what?" asked Marian without thinking. The sound like a sheep's bleating almost made her turn around and run back.

---

multiflora cineraria: A houseplant with brightly colored flowers and heart-shaped leaves.

One old woman was pulling the door open in short, gradual jerks, and when she saw the nurse a strange smile forced her old face dangerously awry. Marian, suddenly propelled by the strong, impatient arm of the nurse, saw next the side-face of another old woman, even older, who was lying flat in bed with a cap on and a counterpane° drawn up to her chin.

"Visitor," said the nurse, and after one more shove she was off up the hall.   10

Marian stood tongue-tied; both hands held the potted plant. The old woman, still with that terrible, square smile (which was a smile of welcome) stamped on her bony face, was waiting. . . . Perhaps she said something. The old woman in bed said nothing at all, and she did not look around.

Suddenly Marian saw a hand, quick as a bird claw, reach up in the air and pluck the white cap off her head. At the same time, another claw to match drew her all the way into the room, and the next moment the door closed behind her.

"My, my, my," said the old lady at her side.

Marian stood enclosed by a bed, a washstand, and a chair; the tiny room had altogether too much furniture. Everything smelled wet—even the bare floor. She held on to the back of the chair, which was wicker and felt soft and damp. Her heart beat more and more slowly, her hands got colder and colder, and she could not hear whether the old women were saying anything or not. She could not see them very clearly. How dark it was! The window shade was down, and the only door was shut. Marian looked at the ceiling. . . . It was like being caught in a robbers' cave, just before one was murdered.

"Did you come to be our little girl for a while?" the first robber asked.   15

Then something was snatched from Marian's hand—the little potted plant.

"Flowers!" screamed the old woman. She stood holding the pot in an undecided way. "Pretty flowers," she added.

Then the old woman in bed cleared her throat and spoke. "They are not pretty," she said, still without looking around, but very distinctly.

Marian suddenly pitched against the chair and sat down in it.

"Pretty flowers," the first old woman insisted. "Pretty—pretty . . ."   20

Marian wished she had the little pot back for just a moment—she had forgotten to look at the plant herself before giving it away. What did it look like?

"Stinkweeds," said the other old woman sharply. She had a bunchy white forehead and red eyes like a sheep. Now she turned them toward Marian. The fogginess seemed to rise in her throat again, and she bleated, "Who—are—you?"

To her surprise, Marian could not remember her name. "I'm a Campfire Girl," she said finally.

"Watch out for the germs," said the old woman like a sheep, not addressing anyone.

"One came out last month to see us," said the first old woman.   25

A sheep or a germ? wondered Marian dreamily, holding on to the chair.

"Did not!" cried the other old woman.

counterpane: Bedspread.

"Did so! Read to us out of the Bible, and we enjoyed it!" screamed the first.

"Who enjoyed it!" said the woman in bed. Her mouth was unexpectedly small and sorrowful, like a pet's.

"We enjoyed it," insisted the other. "You enjoyed it—I enjoyed it."   30

"We all enjoyed it," said Marian, without realizing that she had said a word.

The first old woman had just finished putting the potted plant high, high on the top of the wardrobe, where it could hardly be seen from below. Marian wondered how she had ever succeeded in placing it there, how she could ever have reached so high.

"You mustn't pay any attention to old Addie," she now said to the little girl. "She's ailing today."

"Will you shut your mouth?" said the woman in bed. "I am not."

"You're a story."   35

"I can't stay but a minute—really, I can't," said Marian suddenly. She looked down at the wet floor and thought that if she were sick in here they would have to let her go.

With much to-do the first old woman sat down in a rocking chair—still another piece of furniture!—and began to rock. With the fingers of one hand she touched a very dirty cameo pin on her chest. "What do you do at school?" she asked.

"I don't know . . ." said Marian. She tried to think but she could not.

"Oh, but the flowers are beautiful," the old woman whispered. She seemed to rock faster and faster; Marian did not see how anyone could rock so fast.

"Ugly," said the woman in bed.   40

"If we bring flowers—" Marian began, and then fell silent. She had almost said that if Campfire Girls brought flowers to the Old Ladies' Home, the visit would count one extra point, and if they took a Bible with them on the bus and read it to the old ladies, it counted double. But the old woman had not listened, anyway; she was rocking and watching the other one, who watched back from the bed.

"Poor Addie is ailing. She has to take medicine—see?" she said, pointing a horny finger at a row of bottles on the table, and rocking so high that her black comfort shoes lifted off the floor like a little child's.

"I am no more sick than you are," said the woman in bed.

"Oh, yes you are!"

"I just got more sense than you have, that's all," said the other old woman,   45
nodding her head.

"That's only the contrary way she talks when *you all* come," said the first old lady with sudden intimacy. She stopped the rocker with a neat pat of her feet and leaned toward Marian. Her hand reached over—it felt like a petunia leaf, clinging and just a little sticky.

"Will you hush! Will you hush!" cried the other one.

Marian leaned back rigidly in her chair.

"When I was a little girl like you, I went to school and all," said the old woman in the same intimate, menacing voice. "Not here—another town . . ."

"Hush!" said the sick woman. "You never went to school. You never   50
came and you never went. You never were anything—only here. You never

were born! You don't know anything. Your head is empty, your heart and hands and your old black purse are all empty, even that little old box that you brought with you you brought empty—you showed it to me. And yet you talk, talk, talk, talk, talk all the time until I think I'm losing my mind! Who are you? You're a stranger—a perfect stranger! Don't you know you're a stranger? Is it possible that they have actually done a thing like this to anyone—sent them in a stranger to talk, and rock, and tell away her whole long rigmarole? Do they seriously suppose that I'll be able to keep it up, day in, day out, night in, night out, living in the same room with a terrible old woman—forever?"

Marian saw the old woman's eyes grow bright and turn toward her. This old woman was looking at her with despair and calculation in her face. Her small lips suddenly dropped apart, and exposed a half circle of false teeth with tan gums.

"Come here, I want to tell you something," she whispered. "Come here!"

Marian was trembling, and her heart nearly stopped beating altogether for a moment.

"Now, now, Addie," said the first old woman. "That's not polite. Do you know what's really the matter with old Addie today?" She, too, looked at Marian; one of her eyelids dropped low.

"The matter?" the child repeated stupidly. "What's the matter with her?" 55

"Why, she's mad because it's her birthday!" said the first old woman, beginning to rock again and giving a little crow as though she had answered her own riddle.

"It is not, it is not!" screamed the old woman in bed. "It is not my birthday, no one knows when that is but myself, and will you please be quiet and say nothing more, or I'll go straight out of my mind!" She turned her eyes toward Marian again, and presently she said in the soft, foggy voice, "When the worst comes to the worst, I ring this bell, and the nurse comes." One of her hands was drawn out from under the patched counterpane—a thin little hand with enormous black freckles. With a finger which would not hold still she pointed to a little bell on the table among the bottles.

"How old are you?" Marian breathed. Now she could see the old woman in bed very closely and plainly, and very abruptly, from all sides, as in dreams. She wondered about her—she wondered for a moment as though there was nothing else in the world to wonder about. It was the first time such a thing had happened to Marian.

"I won't tell!"

The old face on the pillow, where Marian was bending over it, slowly gathered 60
and collapsed. Soft whimpers came out of the small open mouth. It was a sheep that she sounded like—a little lamb. Marian's face drew very close, the yellow hair hung forward.

"She's crying!" She turned a bright, burning face up to the first old woman.

"That's Addie for you," the old woman said spitefully.

Marian jumped up and moved toward the door. For the second time, the claw almost touched her hair, but it was not quick enough. The little girl put her cap on.

"Well, it was a real visit," said the old woman, following Marian through the doorway and all the way out into the hall. Then from behind she suddenly clutched the child with her sharp little fingers. In an affected, high-pitched whine she cried, "Oh, little girl, have you a penny to spare for a poor old woman that's not got anything of her own? We don't have a thing in the world—not a penny for candy—not a thing! Little girl, just a nickel—a penny—"

Marian pulled violently against the old hands for a moment before she was   65
free. Then she ran down the hall, without looking behind her and without looking at the nurse, who was reading *Field & Stream* at her desk. The nurse, after another triple motion to consult her wrist watch, asked automatically the question put to visitors in all institutions: "Won't you stay and have dinner with *us*?"

Marian never replied. She pushed the heavy door open into the cold air and ran down the steps.

Under the prickly shrub she stooped and quickly, without being seen, retrieved a red apple she had hidden there.

Her yellow hair under the white cap, her scarlet coat, her bare knees all flashed in the sunlight as she ran to meet the big bus rocketing through the street.

"Wait for me!" she shouted. As though at an imperial command, the bus ground to a stop.

She jumped on and took a big bite out of the apple.   *[1941]*   70

A Student's Personal Response to the Story

Here is some freewriting a student did about the story you just read. By simply jotting down some observations and questions, she provided herself with the seeds of a paper.

> I'm not sure which character I should be sympathizing with in Welty's story. Right away I disliked the girl because she wasn't really interested in seeing the old women. I don't know why the story is called "A Visit of Charity," since she just wanted to get more points. And yet I have to admit that when I was younger I was sort of like her. I remember one time when my church youth group had to sing Christmas carols at an old folks' home, and I was uneasy about having to meet all these ancient men and women I didn't know, some of whom could barely walk or talk. It's funny, because I was always comfortable around my grandparents, but I have to confess that being around all those old people at once spooked me a little. I smiled a lot at them and joined in the singing and helped hand out candy canes afterward. But I couldn't wait to leave. Once I did, I felt proud of myself for going there, but I guess I also felt a little guilty because I didn't really want to be there at all. So, maybe I'm being hypocritical when I criticize the girl in Welty's story for insensitivity. Anyway, I expected that Welty would present in a good light any old women that Marian encountered, just to emphasize that Marian was being unkind and that it's really sad for people to have to live in a

retirement home (or senior citizens center or whatever they're calling such places nowadays). And yet the two old women she meets are cranky and unpleasant. Even the receptionist doesn't come off all that good. If I were Marian, I probably would have left even sooner than she did! Maybe Welty didn't want us to sympathize with anyone in the story, and maybe that's OK. I tend to want a story to make at least some of the characters sympathetic, but maybe it's unfair of me to demand that. Still, I'm wondering if I'm not appreciating Welty's characters enough. When the two old women argue, should we side with one of them, or are we supposed to be bothered by them both? Are we supposed to think any better of the girl by the time she leaves? The apple she eats immediately made me think of the Adam and Eve story, but I don't know what I'm supposed to do with that parallel.

The Elements of Short Fiction

Whether discussing them in class or writing about them, you will improve your ability to analyze stories like Welty's if you grow familiar with typical elements of short fiction. These elements include plot and structure, point of view, characters, setting, imagery, language, and theme.

PLOT AND STRUCTURE

For many readers, the most important element in any work of fiction is **plot**. As they turn the pages of a story, their main question is, What will happen next? In reading Welty's story, quite possibly you wanted to know how Marian's visit to the rest home would turn out. Indeed, plots usually center on human beings, who can be seen as engaging in actions, as being acted upon, or both. You might describe Marian as acting, noting among other things that she "jumped off the bus" (para. 1); that "she shifted the small pot from hand to hand" (para. 1); that "she pushed her hair behind her ears" (para. 4); that her "face drew very close" to Addie's (para. 60); that she "jumped up and moved toward the door" (para. 63); that she "pulled violently against the old hands" of the other elderly woman (para. 65); that "she ran to meet the big bus" (para. 68); and that she "jumped on and took a big bite out of the apple" (para. 70). But you might also describe her as being affected by other forces. For example, she is "suddenly propelled by the strong, impatient arm of the nurse" (para. 9); the "claw" of the first old woman "drew her all the way into the room" (para. 11); and she repeats the two women's language "without realizing that she had said a word" (para. 31). In any case, most short stories put characters into high-pressure situations, whether for dark or comic effect. To earn the merit points she desires, Marian has to contend with the feuding roommates.

Besides physical events, a short story may involve psychological developments. Welty's heroine goes through mental changes during her visit. One is that her interest in the two women grows; they are no longer just a dutiful task to her. This change is indicated best by a particular word: "wondered." When the women discuss a previous visitor, Marian "wondered" about the animal imagery suddenly filling her mind (para. 26). When the first old woman perches the plant "high on the top of the wardrobe," the girl "wondered how she had ever succeeded in placing it there" (para. 32). Then, as Marian gazes upon the bedridden Addie, "She wondered about her—she wondered for a moment as though there was nothing else in the world to wonder about" (para. 58). As if to emphasize that the girl is experiencing a psychological transition, the narrator reports: "It was the first time such a thing had happened to Marian" (para. 58). Many stories do show characters undergoing complete or partial conversions. Meanwhile, a number of stories include characters who stick to their beliefs but gain a new perspective on them.

Does Marian's encounter with the two women have something to do with her ultimately biting the apple and leaping onto the bus? If so, what's the specific connection? Questions like these bring up relations of cause and effect, terms that often figure in discussions of plot. The novelist and short-story writer E. M. Forster refers to them in defining the term *plot* itself. To Forster, a plot is not simply one incident after another, such as "the king died and then the queen died." Rather, it is a situation or a whole chain of events in which there are reasons *why* characters behave as they do. Forster's example: "The king died, and then the queen died of grief."

Writers of short stories do not always make cause and effect immediately clear. Another possible plot, Forster suggests, is "The queen died, no one knew why, until it was discovered that it was through grief at the death of the king." In this scenario, all of the characters lack information about the queen's true psychology for a while, and perhaps the reader is in the dark as well. Indeed, many short stories leave the reader ignorant for a spell. For instance, only near the conclusion of her story does Welty reveal that before entering the rest home, Marian had put an apple under the shrub. Why does the author withhold this key fact from you? Perhaps Welty was silent about the apple because, had she reported it right away, its echoes of Eve might have overshadowed your interpretation of the story as you read. Worth considering are issues of effect: what the characters' behavior makes you think of them and what impact the author's strategies have on you.

When you summarize a story's plot, you may be inclined to put events in chronological order. But remember that short stories are not always linear. Alice Adams, author of many short stories, offers a more detailed outline of their typical **structure**. She has proposed the formula ABDCE: these letters stand for **action, background, development, climax**, and **ending**. More precisely, Adams has said that she sometimes begins a story with an action, follows that action with some background information, and then moves the plot forward in time through a major turning point and toward some sort of resolution. Not all writers of short stories follow this scheme. In fact, Adams does not always stick to it. Certainly a lot of short stories combine her background and development stages, moving the plot along while offering details of their characters' pasts. And sometimes a story will have several turning points rather than a single distinct climax. But by keeping Adams's formula in mind, if only as a common way to construct short stories, you will be better prepared to recognize how a story departs from chronological order.

The first paragraph of Welty's story seems to be centered on *action*. Marian arrives at the Old Ladies' Home and prepares to enter it. Even so, Welty provides some basic information in this paragraph, describing Marian and the rest home as if the reader is unfamiliar with both. Yet only in the second paragraph do you learn Marian's name and the purpose of her visit. Therefore, Welty can be said to obey Adams's formula, beginning with *action* and then moving to *background*. Note, however, that the second paragraph features *development* as well. By explaining to the receptionist who she is and why she is there, Marian takes a step closer to the central event, her meeting with the two roommates. The remainder of the story keeps moving forward in time.

What about *climax*, Adams's fourth term? Traditionally, the climax of a story has been defined as a peak moment of drama appearing near the end. Also, it is usually thought of as a point when at least one character commits a significant act, experiences a significant change, makes a significant discovery, learns a significant lesson, or perhaps does all these things. With Welty's story, you could argue that the climax is when Marian asks Addie her age, meets with refusal, sees Addie crying, and tries to bolt. Certainly this is a dramatic moment, involving intense display of emotion resulting in Marian's departure. But Welty indicates, too, that Marian here experiences inner change. When she looks on Addie "as though there was nothing else in the world to wonder about," this is "the first time such a thing had happened to Marian."

Adams's term *ending* may seem unnecessary. Why would anyone have to be reminded that stories end? Yet a story's climax may engage readers so much that they overlook whatever follows. If the climax of Welty's story is Marian's conversation with the tearful Addie, then the ending is basically in four parts: the plea that Addie's roommate makes to Marian as she is leaving; Marian's final encounter with the receptionist; Marian's retrieval of the apple; and her escape on the bus, where she bites into the apple. Keep in mind that the ending of a story may relate somehow to its beginning. The ending of Welty's "A Visit of Charity," for instance, brings the story full circle. Whereas at the start Marian gets off a bus, hides the apple, and meets the receptionist, at the conclusion she rushes by the receptionist, recovers the apple, and boards another bus. However a story ends, ask yourself if any of the characters have changed at some point between start and finish. Does the conclusion of the story indicate that at least one person has developed in some way, or does it leave you with the feeling of lives frozen since the start? As Welty's story ends, readers may have various opinions about Marian. Some may find that she has not been changed all that much by her visit to the home, while others may feel that it has helped her mature.

A common organizational device in short stories is **repetition**. It takes various forms. First, a story may repeat words, as Welty's story does with its multiple uses of the word "wondered." Second, a story may repeatedly refer to a certain image, as you see with Welty's images of the plant and the apple. Third, a story may involve repeated actions. In "A Visit of Charity," the two roommates repeatedly argue; Marian travels by bus at the beginning and at the end; and the nurse consults her wristwatch both when Marian arrives and when she leaves.

POINT OF VIEW

A short story may be told from a particular character's perspective or **point of view**. "When it is written in the **first person**—narrated by someone using the pronoun *I* or, more rarely, *we*—you have to decide how much to accept the narrator's point of view, keeping in mind that the narrator may be psychologically complex. How objective does the narrator seem in depicting other people and events? In what ways, if any, do the narrator's perceptions seem influenced by his or her personal experiences, circumstances, feelings, values, and beliefs? Does the narrator seem to have changed in any way since the events recalled? How reasonable do the narrator's judgments seem? At what moments, if any, do you find yourself disagreeing with the narrator's view of things?

Not every short story is narrated by an identifiable person. Many of them are told by what has been traditionally called an **omniscient narrator**. The word *omniscient* means "all-knowing" and is often used as an adjective for God. An omniscient narrator is usually a seemingly all-knowing, objective voice. This is the kind of voice at work in Welty's story, right from the first paragraph. There, Marian is described in an authoritatively matter-of-fact tone that appears detached from her: "Holding a potted plant before her, a girl of fourteen jumped off the bus in front of the Old Ladies' Home." Keep in mind, though, that a story may rely primarily on an omniscient narrator and yet at some points seem immersed in a character's perspective. This, too, is the case with Welty's story. Consider the following passage about Marian:

> Everything smelled wet—even the bare floor. She held on to the back of the chair, which was wicker and felt soft and damp. Her heart beat more and more slowly, her hands got colder and colder, and she could not hear whether the old women were saying anything or not. She could not see them very clearly. How dark it was! The window shade was down, and the only door was shut. Marian looked at the ceiling. . . . It was like being caught in a robbers' cave, just before one was murdered.

The passage remains in the third person, referring to "she" rather than to "I." Nevertheless, the passage seems intimately in touch with Marian's physical sensations. Indeed, the sentence "How dark it was!" seems something that Marian would say to herself. Similarly, the analogy to the robbers' cave may be Marian's own personal perception, and as such, the analogy may reveal more about her own state of mind than about the room. Many literary critics use the term **free indirect style** for moments like this, when a narrator otherwise omniscient conveys a particular character's viewpoint by resorting to the character's own language.

Throughout this book, we encourage you to analyze an author's strategies by considering the options that he or she faced. You may better understand a short story's point of view if you think about the available alternatives. For example, how would you have reacted to Welty's story if it had focused on Addie's perceptions more than on Marian's?

CHARACTERS

Although we have been discussing plots, we have also referred to the people caught up in them. Any analysis you do of a short story will reflect your understanding and evaluation of its **characters**. Rarely does the author of a story provide you with extended, enormously detailed biographies. Rather, you see the story's characters at select moments of their lives. To quote William Trevor again, the short story is "the art of the glimpse."

You may want to judge characters according to how easily you can identify with them. Yet there is little reason for you to read works that merely reinforce your prejudices. Furthermore, you may overlook the potential richness of a story if you insist that its characters fit your usual standards of behavior. An author can teach you much by introducing you to the complexity of people you might automatically praise or condemn in real life. Many of us would immediately condemn someone reluctant to help old women, but Welty encourages us to analyze carefully the girl in her story rather than just denounce her. You may be tempted to dismiss the roommates in Welty's story as unpleasant, even "sick"; in any case, take the story as an opportunity to explore *why* women in a rest home may express discontent.

One thing to consider about the characters in a story is what each basically desires. At the beginning of Welty's story, for example, Marian is hardly visiting the Old Ladies' Home out of "charity," despite that word's presence in the story's title. Rather, Marian hopes to earn points as a Campfire Girl. Again, characters in a story may change, so consider whether the particular characters you are examining alter their thinking. Perhaps you feel that Marian's visit broadens her vision of life; then again, perhaps you conclude that she remains much the same.

Reading a short story involves relating its characters to one another. In part, you'll need to determine their relative importance. Even a seemingly minor character can perform some noteworthy function; the nurse in "A Visit of Charity" not only ushers Marian in and out but also marks time. Nevertheless, any reader will try to identify a story's *main* figures. When a particular character seems the focus, he or she is referred to as the story's **protagonist**. Many readers would say that Marian is the protagonist of "A Visit of Charity." When the protagonist is in notable conflict with another character, this foe is referred to as the **antagonist**. Because Marian initially finds both roommates unpleasant, you may want to call them her antagonists. But it's not a word that you *must* apply to some character in a story; the work can have a protagonist and yet *not* include an opponent. Moreover, as a story proceeds, characters may alter their relationships with one another. Marian grows more conscious of the tensions *between* the roommates, and then for a moment she sympathizes with Addie. It is possible, too, for one character to be ambivalent toward another, feeling both drawn *and* opposed to that person. Perhaps the roommates have a love-hate relationship, needing each other's company even as they bicker. As perhaps you have found in your own experience, human relationships are often far from simple. Works of literature can prove especially interesting when they suggest as much.

What power and influence people achieve may depend on particular traits of theirs. These include their gender, social class, race, ethnic background, nationality, sexual orientation, age, and the kind of work they do. Because these attributes may greatly affect a person's life, pay attention to them as you analyze characters. For instance, in Welty's story, all the characters are female. How might their gender matter? How might the story's dynamics have differed if it had featured at least one man? Another element of the story is its gap in ages: while the roommates are old, Marian is barely a teenager. What, over their years of living, might the two women have learned that the girl doesn't know yet?

Typically, characters express views of one another, and you have to decide how accurate these are. Some characters will seem wise observers of humanity. Others will strike you as making distorted statements about the world, revealing little more than their own biases and quirks. And some characters will seem to fall in the middle, coming across as partly objective and partly subjective. On occasion, you and your classmates may find yourselves debating which category a particular character fits. One interesting case is Welty's character Addie. Look again at the speech in which she berates her roommate:

> "Hush!" said the sick woman. "You never went to school. You never came and you never went. You never were anything—only here. You never were born! You don't know anything. Your head is empty, your heart and hands and your old black purse are all empty, even that little old box that you brought with you you brought empty—you showed it to me. And yet you talk, talk, talk, talk, talk all the time until I think I'm losing my mind! Who are you? You're a stranger—a perfect stranger! Don't you know you're a stranger? Is it possible that they have actually done a thing like this to anyone—sent them in a stranger to talk, and rock, and tell away her whole long rigmarole? Do they seriously suppose that I'll be able to keep it up, day in, day out, night in, night out, living in the same room with a terrible old woman—forever?"

Some may argue that this speech is merely an unreasonable rant, indicating Addie's dour mood rather than her roommate's true nature. (For one thing, contrary to Addie's declaration, the roommate must have been born!) Yet it can also be argued that Addie shrewdly diagnoses her situation. Perhaps statements like "you never were born," "your head is empty," and "you're a stranger" are true in a metaphorical sense.

SETTING

Usually a short story enables readers to examine how people behave in concrete circumstances. The characters are located in a particular place or **setting**. Moreover, they are shown at particular moments in their personal histories.

Sometimes the story goes further, referring to them as living at a certain point in world history.

As the word *sometimes* implies, short stories vary in the precision with which they identify their settings. They differ as well in the importance of their setting. Sometimes location serves as a mere backdrop for the plot. At other times, the setting can be a looming presence. When Welty's character Marian visits the Old Ladies' Home, we get her vivid impressions of it. Even when a story's setting seems ordinary, it may become filled with drama and meaning as the plot develops. One way of analyzing characters is to consider how they accommodate themselves — or fail to accommodate themselves — to their surroundings. The two roommates in Welty's story are evidently frustrated with living in the Old Ladies' Home, and they take out their frustration on each other.

IMAGERY

Just like poems, short stories often use **imagery** to convey meaning. Sometimes a character in the story may interpret a particular image just the way you do. Some stories, though, include images that you and the characters may analyze quite differently. One example is the apple in Welty's story. Whereas Marian probably views the apple as just something to eat, many readers would make other associations with it, thinking in particular of the apple that Adam and Eve ate from the tree of knowledge in the Garden of Eden. By the end of Welty's story, perhaps Marian has indeed become like Adam and Eve, in that she has lost her innocence and grown more aware that human beings age. At any rate, many readers would call Marian's apple a **symbol**. Traditionally, that is the term for an image seen as representing some concept or concepts. Again, Marian herself probably does not view her apple as symbolic; indeed, characters within stories rarely use the word *symbol* at all.

Images may appear in the form of metaphors or other figures of speech. For example, when Marian enters the Old Ladies' Home, she experiences "a smell in the hall like the interior of a clock." Welty soon builds on the clock image as she describes the receptionist checking her wristwatch, an action that this character repeats near the end. Welty's whole story can be said to deal with time and its effects, both on the old and on the young.

Images in short stories usually appeal to the reader's visual sense. Most often, they are things you can picture in your mind. Yet stories are not limited to rendering visual impressions. They may refer to other senses, too, as when Welty's young heroine notices the odor in the hall.

LANGUAGE

Everything about short stories we have discussed so far concerns **language**. After all, works of literature are constructed entirely out of words. Here, however, we call your attention to three specific uses of language in stories: title, predominant style, and dialogue.

A story's **title** may be just as important as any words in the text. Not always will the relevance of the title be immediately clear to you. Usually you have to read a story all the way through before you can sense fully how its title applies. In any case, play with the title in your mind, considering its various possible meanings and implications. In analyzing the title of Welty's "A Visit of Charity," you may find it helpful to think about this famous passage from the King James translation of the New Testament: "And now abideth faith, hope, charity, these three; but the greatest of these is charity" (1 Corinthians 13:13). You may also want to look up the word *charity* in a dictionary.

Not all short stories have a uniform **style**. Some feature various tones, dialects, vocabularies, and levels of formality. Welty's story incorporates different types of speech almost from its start. When, using rather formal language, the nurse asks Marian, "Acquainted with any of our residents?" (para. 3), the girl puts this question more plainly: "With any old ladies?" (para. 4). Stories that do have a predominant style are often told in the first person, thus giving the impression of a presiding "voice." Charlotte Perkins Gilman's "The Yellow Wallpaper (p. 228) teems with the anguished expressions of its beleaguered narrator.

Dialogue may serve more than one purpose in a short story. By reporting various things, characters may provide you with necessary background for the plot. In Welty's story, it's only from the roommates' fragmentary remarks that Marian — and the reader — can learn anything about their lives up until now. Actually, dialogue can also be thought of as an action in itself, moving the plot along. Try to identify the particular kinds of acts that characters perform when they speak. When the first roommate asks the departing Marian for a coin, she seems to be begging, but perhaps she is also doing whatever she can to hold the girl there; her having "clutched the child" (para. 64) suggests as much. Indeed, dialogue may function to reveal shifts in characters' relations with one another.

THEME

We have already discussed the term **theme** on pages 46–48. There, we identified issues of theme as one kind of issue that comes up in literary studies. At the same time, we suggested that the term *theme* applies to various literary genres, not just short stories. Later in this chapter, we examine theme in connection with poems, plays, and essays. Here, though, we consider theme as an element of short fiction. In doing so, we review some points from our earlier discussion, applying them now to Welty's story.

Recall that we defined the theme of a work as the main claim it seems to make. Furthermore, we identified it as an assertion, a proposition, or a statement rather than as a single word. "Charity" is obviously a *topic* of Welty's story, but because it is just one word, it is not an adequate expression of the story's *theme*. The following exercise invites you to consider just what that theme may be.

1. Try to state a text's theme as a midlevel generalization.   If you were to put it in very broad terms, your audience would see it as fitting a great many works besides the one you have read. If you went to the opposite extreme, tying the theme completely to specific details of the text, your audience might think the theme irrelevant to their own lives.

The phrase "the moral of the story" suggests that a story can usually be reduced to a single message, often a principle of ethics or religion. Plenty of examples can be cited to support this suggestion. In the New Testament, for instance, Jesus tells stories—they are called *parables*—to convey some of his key ideas. In any number of cultures today, stories are used to teach children elements of good conduct. Moreover, people often determine the significance of a real-life event by building a story from it and by drawing a moral from it at the same time. These two processes conspicuously dovetailed when England's Princess Diana was killed in a car crash. Given that she died fleeing photographers, many people saw her entire life story as that of a woman hounded by the media. The moral was simultaneous and clear: thou shalt honor the right to privacy.

It is possible to lose sight of a story's theme by placing too much emphasis on minor details of the text. The more common temptation, however, is to turn a story's theme into an all-too-general cliché. Actually, a story is often most interesting when it *complicates* some widely held idea that it seemed ready to endorse. Therefore, a useful exercise is to start with a general thematic statement about the story and then make it increasingly specific. With "A Visit of Charity," for example, you might begin by supposing that a theme is "everyone must give up their dreams of innocence and paradise, just as Adam and Eve did." Your next step would be to identify the specific spin that Welty's story gives this idea. How does her story differ from others on this theme? Note, for instance, that Marian comes literally face to face with the mortality of women much older than she is, and that the experience fills her momentarily with "wonder." Try to rephrase our version of Welty's theme so that it seems more in touch with these specific details of the text.

2. A theme of a text may be related to its title. It may also be expressed by some statement made within the text. But often various parts of the text merit consideration as you try to determine its theme.

In our discussion of a short story's language, we called attention to the potential significance of its title. The title may serve as a guide to the story's theme. What clues, if any, do you find in the title "A Visit of Charity"? Of course, determining a story's theme entails going beyond the title. You have to read, and usually reread, the entire text. In doing so, you may come across a statement that seems a candidate for the theme because it is a philosophical generalization. Nevertheless, take the time to consider whether the story's essence is indeed captured by this statement alone.

3. You can state a text's theme either as an observation or as a recommendation. Each way of putting it evokes a certain image of the text's author. When you state the theme as an **observation**, you depict the author as a psychologist, a philosopher, or some other kind of analyst. When you state the theme as a **recommendation**—which often involves your using the word *should*—you depict the author as a teacher, preacher, manager, or coach. That is, the author comes across as telling readers what to do.

As we have noted, stories are often used to teach lessons. Moreover, often the lessons are recommendations for action, capable of being phrased as "Do X" or "Do not do X." The alternative is to make a generalization about some state of affairs. When you try to express a particular story's theme, which of these two options should you follow? There are several things to consider in making your decision. First is your personal comfort: do you feel at ease with both ways of stating the theme, or is one of these ways more to your taste? Also worth pondering is the impression you want to give of the author: do you want to portray this person as a maker of recommendations, or do you want to assign the author a more modest role?

4. Consider stating a text's theme as a problem.   That way, you are more apt to convey the complexity and drama of the text.

We have suggested that short stories often pivot around conflicts between people and conflicts within people. Perhaps the most interesting stories are ones that pose conflicts not easily resolved. Probably you will be more faithful to such a text if you phrase its theme as a problem. In the case of Welty's story, for example, you might state the theme as follows: "Young people may sense an older person's infirmity, but, especially if that person is a stranger, they may as yet lack sufficient maturity and confidence to stay and help."

5. Rather than refer to *the* theme of a text, you might refer to *a* theme of the text, implying that the text has more than one.   You would still be suggesting that you have identified a central idea of the text. Subsequently, you might have to defend your claim.

Unlike the average novel, the typical short story pivots around only a few ideas. Yet you need not insist that the story you are analyzing has a single theme. The shortest piece of short fiction may have more than one, and your audience may well appreciate your admitting this. One theme of Welty's story may be that none of us can escape the passage of time. The old roommates aside, teenaged Marian seems on the brink of adulthood, and her concluding bus ride suggests that she is moving further into it. But additional themes are possible. A second idea, dramatized by the roommates' feud, may be that old age can test a person's spirit even as it hurts the person's body. Of course, to call either of these ideas a theme of the story is still to make a claim that requires support.

Perhaps the biggest challenge you will face in writing about short stories is to avoid long stretches of plot summary. Selected details of the plot will often serve as key evidence for you. You will need to describe such moments from the story you are discussing, even if your audience has already read it. But your readers are apt to be frustrated if you just repeat plot at length. They will feel that they may as well turn back to the story itself rather than linger with your rehash. Your paper is worth your readers' time only if you provide insights of your own, *analyzing* the story rather than just *summarizing* it.

To understand what analysis of a short story involves, let's turn to student Tanya Vincent. Assigned to write an argument paper about a short story, Tanya decided to focus on Welty's. She realized that for her paper to be effective, she had to come up with an issue worth addressing, a claim about that issue, and evidence for that claim. Moreover, she had to be prepared to identify her process of reasoning and her assumptions.

For most writing assignments, settling on an issue will be your most important preliminary step. Without a driving question, you will have difficulty producing fresh, organized, and sustained analysis. For her paper on "A Visit of Charity," Tanya chose to address this issue: What does the story suggest charity can mean? In part, she was drawn to this question because the word *charity* appears in the story's title and because it comes up in the famous passage from 1 Corinthians that we quoted earlier. But the question also enticed her because Welty's protagonist doesn't appear truly compassionate. A conventional definition of *charity* is that it is an expression of a sincere desire to help people. Given that Marian appears to lack this desire, is Welty's title ironic? Or does charity in some *other* sense of the word operate in the story? Tanya realized that she would be tackling an issue of definition. She would need to examine various possible meanings of "charity" and determine which are relevant to specific details of Welty's text.

A paper about a short story doesn't have to mention explicitly all the elements of short fiction we've identified. Nevertheless, thinking of these elements can help you plan such a paper, providing you with some preliminary terms for your analysis. Tanya perceived that her paper would be very much about characters and plot; it might also dwell upon imagery and language. She knew, too, that she would be more apt to persuade her readers if she included quotations from the story. Yet, as with plot summary, quoting should be limited, so that the paper seems an original argument — not a recycling of the literary work's own words. Tanya sensed that practically every sentence of Welty's story could be quoted and then interpreted. At the same time, she realized that she should quote only *some* words, not all.

Final Draft of a Student Paper

Here is Tanya's final draft of her paper about "A Visit of Charity." As you read it, keep in mind that it emerged only after she had done several preliminary drafts, in consultation with some of her classmates as well as her instructor. Although Tanya's paper is a good example of how to write about a short story, most drafts can stand to be revised further. What do you think Tanya has done well in her paper? If she planned to do yet another revision, what suggestions would you make?

Tanya Vincent
Professor Stein
English 1A
3 November - - - -

The Real Meaning of "Charity"
in "A Visit of Charity"

Many people would define the word "charity" as an act in which an individual or institution sincerely offers material or

An assumption, but seems a reasonable one.

spiritual comfort to someone less fortunate. In this respect, charity is a form of love. Such is the meaning implied in the King James translation of the most famous statement about charity, 1 Corinthians 13:13: "And now abideth faith, hope, charity, these three; but the greatest of these is charity." In fact, some other translations of this biblical passage use "love" instead of "charity," thereby suggesting that the two terms are more or less equivalent. But Marian, the protagonist of Eudora Welty's short story "A Visit of Charity" does not appear to demonstrate this concept of charity when she visits the Old Ladies' Home. She gives no indication that she sincerely cares about any of its residents. Rather, she approaches the visit as a mechanical task that she must perform to raise her standing as a Campfire Girl. Nor does she seem to become much more empathetic after spending time at the Home. Several readers of the story, therefore, might think its title ironic.

Starts to introduce her issue and claim by referring to readers who are possibly superficial.

This view may, however, be too limited. Welty may be encouraging us to move past our familiar concept of "charity" and give the word a meaning that *can* apply to her text in a nonironic way. It is true that Marian does not act lovingly or even compassionately on her trip to the Home. Yet maybe her brief moments with the two elderly roommates provide charity to Marian herself, making her a beneficiary of it rather than a donor of it. After all, her encounter with the two women helps to make her at least a bit more aware of the stresses that old age can bring. Charity in *this* sense would mean the providing of a necessary lesson about what life can be like as an adult. Even though the two roommates do not intend to be benevolent teachers of the girl, her meeting with them has some value, for it gives her a preview of realities she will have to deal with more extensively as she grows up.

A qualification. Tanya holds back from claiming certainty about Welty's intentions.

Introduction ends with main issue (a definitional kind) and main claim.

When we first meet her in the story, Marian seems anything but passionately devoted to improving life for the Home's inhabitants. Probably "Old Ladies' Home" is not the building's real name to begin with, but instead Marian's own insensitive designation. Clearly she looks upon her visit as a chore. To her, it is just something she must do to earn points. Later, we readers learn that she has even computed the specific amounts available to her: "She had almost said that if Campfire Girls brought flowers to the Old Ladies' Home, the visit would count one extra point, and if they took a Bible with them on the bus and read it to the old ladies, it counted double" (124). When, back at the story's start, she introduces herself to the nurse, she does not even pretend to be a true Angel of Mercy pursuing a higher spiritual purpose: "I'm a

Concession to readers who have trouble finding "charity" in the story.

Campfire Girl. . . . I have to pay a visit to some old lady"
(122). So indifferent is she to the Home's aged occupants
that she candidly announces "any of them will do" (122).
When she does meet with the two roommates, she chooses
not to stay long with them. Nor does she offer charity in a
traditional sense when one of the roommates begs. While the
woman asks, "have you a penny to spare for a poor old woman
that's not got anything of her own?" (126), Marian is anxious
to flee. Nor, when she does leave the pair, is her exit gradual,
patient, and kind: she "jumped up and moved toward the door";
"pulled violently against the old hands"; "ran down the hall,
without looking behind her and without looking at the nurse";
"quickly . . . retrieved a red apple"; "ran to meet the big bus";
"shouted" at the bus; and "jumped on" (126). These frenzied
motions indicate that Marian is ultimately *repelled* by the two
women, not drawn to them as clients for her kindness.

Here and elsewhere in the paper, Tanya quotes from Welty's text.

Nevertheless, perhaps Marian's experience with them con-
fers a sort of charity upon *her* by alerting her to facts she will
eventually have to face. When she first meets the roommate
who is supposedly healthier, she is struck by the "terrible,
square smile (which was a smile of welcome) stamped on her
bony face" (123). This seems more an image of death than of
life, suggesting that Marian is beginning to grow conscious of
mortality. This implication gets even stronger when Marian
comes to the bed of the sicker woman, Addie: "She wondered
about her — she wondered for a moment as though there was
nothing else in the world to wonder about. It was the first
time such a thing had happened to Marian" (125). More precisely, Marian seems to discover that people soon to die may
become a mixture of helplessness and fierce self-assertion. To
the girl, Addie repeatedly comes across as a sheep or lamb, a
species of animal traditionally associated with innocence.
Even before she enters the room, Marian twice experiences
Addie's voice as that of a sheep "bleating" (122), and at Addie's bedside she mentally compares the tearful, suffering
woman to "a little lamb" (125). Yet Addie is also someone capable not only of refusing to tell her age, but also of berating
her roommate: "And yet you talk, talk, talk, talk, talk all the
time until I think I'm losing my mind!" (125). In turn, the
object of this scorn displays to Marian a similar blend of powerlessness and ferocity. "In an affected, high-pitched whine,"
this roommate refers to herself as "a poor old woman," but
at the same time "she suddenly clutched the child with her
sharp little fingers" (125–26). Indeed, if Addie comes across
to Marian as a sheep or lamb, the girl senses right from the
start of the meeting that the other woman is an aggressive

Transition to development of main claim.

As earlier, with "wondered," Tanya shows attention to repetition.

bird: "Suddenly Marian saw a hand, quick as a bird claw, reach up in the air and pluck the white cap off her head" (123). In general, neither of the roommates fits the sentimental stereotype of the sweet old lady. But their difference from this image is precisely what can be educational for Marian. Their nearness to death, and the complex behavior they show in response to their fate, are matters that the girl will have to contend with a lot once she herself becomes a full-fledged adult.

While admitting that the sentence about "the first time" appears significant, some readers may doubt that Marian learns anything from this experience. Their skepticism would be understandable, given that she does not philosophize at length about the visit and ends it rather speedily. Welty does, however, suggest the stirrings of mental change in Marian by drawing our attention to the bodily disorientation she goes through in the old women's room. Immediately upon meeting them, she "stood tongue-tied" (123). Soon, "her heart beat more and more slowly, her hands got colder and colder, and she could not hear whether the old women were saying anything or not" (123). Moreover, "she could not see them very clearly" (123). A moment later, she winds up "pitched against the chair" (123) and forgets her own name. Eventually "her heart nearly stopped beating altogether" (125). These disabilities, though temporary, indicate that at *some* level of consciousness, Marian is having perceptions that she did not have before. Specifically, she seems to have glimmers of how death increasingly enters people's lives as they age.

Concession to readers with a different view.

The story's very last sentence further suggests that Marian either learns this lesson or vaguely intuits it. By taking "a big bite out of the apple" (126), she resembles Adam and Eve, whose own eating of an apple resulted in their becoming mortal. But in writing her story, Welty may also have had in mind a second biblical passage. Occurring just two lines before the famous statement about charity I have quoted, it is a well-known review of life's journey: "When I was a child, I spake as a child, I understood as a child, I thought as a child: but when I became a man, I put away childish things" (1 Corinthians 13:11). Although Marian is female, the line can still apply to her. Before her visit to the Home, she has been "a child," and she acts that way for much of her time there. But the visit may make her more inclined to "put away childish things," in which case she herself would receive a form of charity from it.

Again, acknowledges that she can't be certain about Welty's thinking.

Writing about Poems

Some students are put off by poetry, perhaps because their early experiences with it were discouraging. They imagine that poems have deep hidden meanings they can't uncover. Maybe their high-school English teacher always had the right interpretation, and they rarely did. This need not be the case. Poetry can be accessible to all readers.

The problem is often a confusion about the nature of poetry, since poetry is more compressed than prose. Poetry focuses more on connotative, emotional, or associative meanings and conveys meaning more through suggestion, indirection, and the use of metaphor, symbol, and imagery than prose does. It seldom hands us a specific meaning. Poetic texts suggest certain possibilities, but the reader completes the transaction. Part of the meaning comes from the writer, part from the text itself, and part from the reader. Even students who are the same age, race, religion, and ethnicity are not duplicates of one another. Each has unique experiences, family histories, and emotional lives. If thirty people read a poem about conformity or responsibility, all thirty will have varying views about these concepts, even though they will probably have some commonalities. (Most societies are so saturated with shared cultural experiences that it is nearly impossible to avoid some overlap in responses.)

In a good class discussion, then, we should be aware that even though we might be members of the same culture, each of us reads from a unique perspective, a perspective that might also shift from time to time. If a woman reads a poem about childbirth, her identity as a female will seem more relevant than if she were reading a poem about death, a more universal experience. In other words, how we read a poem and how significant and meaningful the poem is for us depends both on the content of the poem and on our specific circumstances. Suppose you are fourteen when you first read a poem about dating; you would likely have very different responses rereading it at nineteen, twenty-five, and fifty. We read poems through our experiences. As we gain new experiences, our readings change.

One reason to respond in writing to your first reading is to be able to separate your first thoughts from those of your classmates. They too will bring their own experiences, values, and ideas to the discussion. In the give-and-take of open discussion, it may be difficult to remember what you first said. Of course, the point of a classroom discussion is not simply to defend your initial response, for then you would be denying yourself the benefit of other people's ideas. A good discussion should open up the poem, allow you to see it from multiple viewpoints, and enable you to expand your perspective, to see how others make sense of the world.

This rich mixture of the poet's text, the reader's response, and discussion among several readers can create new possibilities of meaning. Even more than fiction or drama, poetry encourages creative readings that can be simultaneously true to the text and to the reader. A lively class discussion can uncover a dozen or more plausible interpretations of a poem, each backed up with valid evidence both from the poem and the reader's experience. You may try to persuade others that your views about the poem are correct; others may do the same to you. This negotiation is at the heart of a liberal, democratic education. In fact, maybe the most respected and repeated notion about being well-educated is the ability to empathize with another's point of view, to see as another sees. Reading, discussing, and writing about poetry can help you become a person who can both create meaning and understand and appreciate how others do. This is one important way literature matters.

The following three poems are about work—about the joys and sorrows, the satisfactions and frustrations of physical labor. Some people might think of poets as intellectuals who are far removed from the experiences of the working class, but this is not the case. Indeed, many poets were themselves brought up in working-class homes and know firsthand the dignity and value of such work. Even among poets who do not toil with their hands, few lack the imaginative empathy that would allow them to write perceptively about firefighters and factory workers, cleaning women and mill workers. These three poems are especially relevant today when physical work is becoming less and less a reality among middle-class Americans. Poems that matter are poems about real life— about love and death, about pain and loss, about beauty and hope. These three poems about work are about all of these and more.

The first poem, Mary Oliver's (b. 1935) "Singapore" appeared in *House of Light* (1992). She has won a Pulitzer Prize for her poetry. "Blackberries" is by Yusef Komunyakaa (b. 1947), who has become known for exploring various aspects of African American experience; the poem is from *Magic City* (1992). Edwin Arlington Robinson's "The Mill" is the oldest poem in the cluster. Robinson (1869–1935) is considered the first major poet of twentieth-century America.

MARY OLIVER
Singapore

In Singapore, in the airport,
a darkness was ripped from my eyes.
In the women's restroom, one compartment stood open.
A woman knelt there, washing something
    in the white bowl.   5

Disgust argued in my stomach
and I felt, in my pocket, for my ticket.

A poem should always have birds in it.
Kingfishers, say, with their bold eyes and gaudy wings.
Rivers are pleasant, and of course trees.   10
A waterfall, or if that's not possible, a fountain
    rising and falling.
A person wants to stand in a happy place, in a poem.

When the woman turned I could not answer her face.
Her beauty and her embarrassment struggled together, and   15
    neither could win.
She smiled and I smiled. What kind of nonsense is this?
Everybody needs a job.
Yes, a person wants to stand in a happy place, in a poem.
But first we must watch her as she stares down at her labor,   20
    which is dull enough.
She is washing the tops of the airport ashtrays, as big as
    hubcaps, with a blue rag.
Her small hands turn the metal, scrubbing and rinsing.
She does not work slowly, nor quickly, but like a river.   25
Her dark hair is like the wing of a bird.

I don't doubt for a moment that she loves her life.
And I want her to rise up from the crust and the slop
    and fly down to the river.
This probably won't happen.   30
But maybe it will.
If the world were only pain and logic, who would want it?

Of course, it isn't.
Neither do I mean anything miraculous, but only
the light that can shine out of a life. I mean   35
the way she unfolded and refolded the blue cloth,
the way her smile was only for my sake; I mean
the way this poem is filled with trees, and birds.   *[1992]*

YUSEF KOMUNYAKAA

Blackberries

They left my hands like a printer's
Or thief's before a police blotter
& pulled me into early morning's
Terrestrial sweetness, so thick
The damp ground was consecrated   5
Where they fell among a garland of thorns.

Although I could smell old lime-covered
History, at ten I'd still hold out my hands
& berries fell into them. Eating from one
& filling a half gallon with the other,   10
I ate the mythology & dreamt
Of pies & cobbler, almost

Needful as forgiveness. My bird dog Spot
Eyed blue jays & thrashers. The mud frogs
In rich blackness, hid from daylight.   15

An hour later, beside City Limits Road
I balanced a gleaming can in each hand,
Limboed between worlds, repeating *one dollar*.
The big blue car made me sweat.
Wintertime crawled out of the windows.   20
When I leaned closer I saw the boy
& girl my age, in the wide back seat
Smirking, & it was then I remembered my fingers
Burning with thorns among berries too ripe to touch.   *[1992]*

EDWIN ARLINGTON ROBINSON
The Mill

The miller's wife had waited long,
    The tea was cold, the fire was dead;
And there might yet be nothing wrong
    In how he went and what he said:
"There are no millers any more,"   5
    Was all that she had heard him say;
And he had lingered at the door
    So long that it seemed yesterday.

Sick with fear that had no form
    She knew that she was there at last;   10
And in the mill there was a warm
    And mealy fragrance of the past.
What else there was would only seem
    To say again what he had meant;
And what was hanging from a beam   15
    Would not have heeded where she went.

And if she thought it followed her,
    She may have reasoned in the dark
That one way of the few there were
    Would hide her and would leave no mark: 20
Black water, smooth above the weir
    Like starry velvet in the night,
Though ruffled once, would soon appear
    The same as ever to the sight.   *[1920]*

A Student's Personal Responses to the Poems

The following are selections from the response journal of student Michaela
Fiorucci, who chose to focus on boundaries — on the various divisions we set
up between ourselves and other people, such as income, race, gender, sexual
preference, and religion. It seemed to her an interesting way to talk about work

since Michaela had observed barriers of all kinds between workers at her job at the university.

Using an explorative strategy, Michaela did some freewriting on the three poems, hoping to discover an argument about boundaries that might fit. The following are selections from her response journal.

> In "Singapore," there is a clear boundary between the middle-class American tourist and the cleaning lady, so much so that at first the narrator says, "Disgust argued in my stomach." The cleaning woman also seems to believe in a barrier and continues to work in a steady way. The narrator finally sees beauty in her dedication to her work. When the narrator does see beauty in her work habits, it helps close the barrier between them. There are also the issues of boundaries between fantasy and reality and between a world of pain and logic and one with birds and rivers. But at the end these boundaries also seem to be closing.
>
> In "Blackberries," the young boy seems to be living in a rural paradise, beyond the city boundaries, outside the usual urban and suburban environment. He lives in a land of bird dogs, jays, thrashers, and mud frogs. He makes comparisons between blackness and light that seem to anticipate the economic boundary that appears in the last stanza, the one between the poor boy and the rich kids in the car. It is this division between the children in air-conditioned comfort and the narrator on the outside looking in that seems to be the main point of this poem. Some boundaries cause us pain.
>
> "The Mill" tells the sad story of a miller who could not see a boundary between himself and his job. When he tells his wife "there are no millers any more," he is really saying that his life is over; he has no reason to live. And so he crosses the boundary between life and death. Tragically, his wife also has difficulty seeing herself outside her role as wife and housekeeper, and so she also crosses that ultimate boundary. She does so, however, in a completely different way: she drowns herself, so no one will know. She passes through life's boundary without leaving a trace.

After reading these brief freewrites to her response group, Michaela still didn't have a focus, but she liked the idea that boundaries, like walls, sometimes serve a purpose and sometimes they don't. She remembered a discussion of Robert Frost's "Mending Wall" from another course that focused on negotiating the walls we build between us. Her professor liked this idea since it helped her considerably narrow the concept of boundaries.

After reviewing her freewriting, Michaela wrote the following first draft and read it to her response group. She then discussed with her instructor her plans for a revision. Her instructor made a number of specific and general comments. After reading her first draft, what feedback would you give Michaela? Her revision appears later in this chapter on pp. 154–56.

First Draft of a Student Paper

Michaela Fiorucci
Mr. Hardy
English 102
15 April - - - -

Boundaries in Robinson, Komunyakaa, and Oliver

Although most sophomores I know at school value their privacy, they also want to create intimate relationships. It is often hard to reconcile these two impulses. Most middle-class students are lucky enough to have their own rooms, private enclaves against annoying sisters and brothers, intrusive mothers and fathers. But a room is also more than a physical boundary; it is also a symbolic assertion of identity. It says, "I'm separate from others, even within the closeness of the family." Such a commitment to physical privacy might be innocent enough, but it does contain dangerous seeds, especially when extended beyond the home to neighborhoods. When different ethnic groups want boundaries between them, it is no longer innocent. When the upper classes need to be separated from workers because they see each other as radically different, a dangerous boundary has been erected.

It would be reductive, however, to say all boundaries need to be erased. Edwin Arlington Robinson's "The Mill" is a good example of the dangerous consequences of a missing boundary. The poem narrates the sad story of a farm couple who commit suicide — the husband because he feels useless, the wife because she can't imagine life without her husband. During my first few readings, I was struck by the lack of communication between the couple. He must have been depressed for a long time, but it seems they never discussed his feelings. Keeping an emotional distance from others was probably a typical part of the way men and women dealt with each other a hundred years ago. It was a boundary not to be crossed. Apparently he could not say, "I feel terrible that I am going to lose my job." And his wife accepts his reticence, even though he might have been having second thoughts as he "lingered at the door" (line 7). Clearly this is a boundary that should have been breached. But after several readings I began to realize that the boundary that should have been established wasn't — the idea that a person's value or worth is synonymous with his or her identity is dehumanizing. And it probably isn't something that just happened in the past. Nor is the equally dehumanizing idea that a wife is nothing without her husband. When the miller's wife decides to "leave no mark" (20) by jumping into the pond, she is admitting she is not a worthwhile person by herself. Both identify totally with a role that in my view should be only one aspect of a complex human life. The final barrier she crosses, from life to death, is symbolically represented in the poem as a feminine domestic gesture: she doesn't want to leave a mess. The boundaries of person and occupation should be made clear; the arbitrary boundaries between genders should not.

When the narrator in Yusef Komunyakaa's "Blackberries" claims that he is "Limboed between worlds" (18), he means the rural paradise of "Terrestrial sweetness" (4) and "rich blackness" (15) he temporarily lives in versus the commercial, urban work that "made me sweat" (19). He has constructed a boundary between the ancient picking of berries and the technology of automobiles, between a natural closeness with nature and the artificial "Wintertime crawled out of the windows" (20). Even though the narrator is only ten, he senses the sensual joys of being one with nature. He seems to reject "old lime-covered / History" (7–8) in favor of "mythology" (11), which seems to suggest a conscious rejection or maybe repression of the contemporary world. But this boundary cannot stand. He needs the outside world to survive, and when the car approaches, it is the modern world and all its pluses and minuses that draw near. When he looks in, he sees "Smirking" (23) children; he sees class prejudice, hierarchy, and economic reality. The smirkers of the world are in charge. This realization dissolves the protective boundary around his Garden of Eden, and he feels physical pain. But really he feels the pain of initiation, the pain of having to cross a boundary he wanted to delay as long as possible. Although we can sympathize with the young narrator, he would probably have fared better by not making his boundary so extreme.

The narrator in Mary Oliver's "Singapore" at first sees a significant boundary between herself as a middle-class traveler and a cleaning woman washing a toilet. It is a separation we might all make, given our socialization to see this kind of physical labor as degrading. College-educated people in America have a tendency to see themselves as distinct from workers. For most, a woman washing something in a compartment is beyond the pale, a clear indication that the woman is other. But Oliver does have some conflicting ideas since she says a "Disgust argued in my stomach" (6). Since we are also socialized to be tolerant and open-minded, she knows she shouldn't think this way. And since she is also a writer with ideas about how a poem should "always have birds in it" (8), she looks harder at the cleaning woman, finally seeing in her face, in her hair, and in the way she works slowly, "like a river" (25), the positive aspects she probably wants to find. Oliver does not simply accept the boundaries that her culture constructs but negotiates with herself, eventually seeing that "light . . . can shine out of a life" (35) even where we do not expect it. In the woman's careful folding and unfolding of her blue work cloth and in her smile, Oliver eclipses the social boundary and ends up with a life-affirming vision "filled with trees, and birds" (38).

Works Cited

Komunyakaa, Yusef. "Blackberries." Schilb and Clifford 143–44.

Oliver, Mary. "Singapore." Schilb and Clifford 142–43.

Robinson, Edwin Arlington. "The Mill." Schilb and Clifford 144.

Schilb, John, and John Clifford, eds. *Arguing about Literature: A Brief Guide*. Boston: Bedford, 2014. Print.

The Elements of Poetry

SPEAKER AND TONE

The voice we hear in a poem could be the poet's, but it is better to think of the speaker as an artistic construction—perhaps a **persona** (mask) for the poet or perhaps a character who does not resemble the poet at all. For example, the speaker in Lynda Hull's "Night Waitress" (p. 83) is not the poet herself but a struggling worker. In large part, to describe any poem's speaker is to pinpoint the person's tone or attitude. Sometimes this is hard to discern. The tone could be ironic or sentimental, joyful or morose, or a combination of emotions. To get a precise sense of it, read the poem aloud, actually performing the speaker's role. Bear in mind that his or her tone may change over the course of the poem. For instance, as the speaker in Yusef Komunyakaa's "Blackberries" recalls a day in his childhood when he picked fruit and then tried to sell it on a highway, he shifts from nostalgia (remembering "Terrestrial sweetness") to bitter recognition of class bias (the "Smirking" of the children who passed him in their car).

The narrator of "The Mill" immediately creates a somber, foreboding tone of anxiety and dread with the tea is "cold" and the fire is "dead," which also foreshadows the death of the miller. Likewise, his brief statement that "there are no millers any more" reinforces and intensifies the sense of impending doom that permeates the plot and theme of the poem. And, of course, such a grim tone is warranted by the dual suicides. Interestingly, the ominous tone of the poem noticeably shifts in the last four lines to one of quiet smooth repose as the once ruffled pond appears "like starry velvet in the night." Perhaps the miller and his wife are finally at peace.

DICTION AND SYNTAX

Although we would all agree that poets rely on the meaning of words to express their feelings and their ideas, what words mean is no simple matter. Perplexed over what a poet might have intended, we often consult a dictionary. And that certainly might help demystify a puzzling passage. But poetry is often more about complicating than clarifying. Most poets are more interested in opening up words than pinning them down. Unlike journalists or science writers, poets often intend to be ambiguous. They like a word's possibilities, its rich emotional overtones. That's one reason readers see in poems different things; one reader may think of the line "Wintertime crawled out of the window" as meaning air conditioning and another as meaning the chilly arrogance and distaste of the privileged for laborers. Only Komunyakaa knows exactly what he meant by "wintertime."

Looking up "wintertime" in the dictionary would give us the denotative meaning, which wouldn't be much help here. But the emotional overtones or associations for individual readers give us the complex multiplicity that poets hope will enrich the poem's meaning. When in "Singapore," for example, the narrator says "a darkness was ripped from my eyes," the objective denotative meaning is probably not what she is after. More likely Oliver is counting on the more subjective, emotional associations of "darkness." Perhaps lack of understanding or ignorance is suggested. Perhaps intolerance or fear of otherness comes to mind. And in the background lie all the negative associations of the unknown, the uncertainty and the danger of things unseen. These are the word's connotations, and they are crucial to the evocative suggestiveness of poems. Oliver wants readers to allow connotation to do its work in expanding and personalizing the meaning of words. In this sense, the word *darkness* contains within it infinite subjective and cultural possibilities.

The same is true for "light" in line 38 of the last stanza. It is the connotative possibilities that infuse "light" with significance, especially when contrasted with the darkness of the first stanza. Seen in the context of the poem, "light" might suggest beauty or integrity or perhaps dedication, commitment, or the ability to find in work something valuable and beautiful. For religious readers, "light" might suggest the beauty and worthiness of each human soul, while for the political thinkers, the dedication and skill of laborers might come to mind. What other connotations can you suggest for these two words?

The last line of the poem offers a clear distinction between denotation and connotation when Oliver says, "this poem is filled with trees, and birds." Literally, of course, trees and birds do not fill the page (except for the actual words), but if we think of trees and birds connoting or suggesting delicate beauty or the majesty of nature or perhaps simply positive and pleasant thoughts, then through her diction, Oliver's meaning is both clarified and expanded.

FIGURES OF SPEECH

When we use figures of speech, we mean something other than the words' literal meaning. In the first sentence of "Singapore," Mary Oliver writes that "a darkness was ripped from my eyes." This direct comparison is a **metaphor**. Had she been more indirect, she might have written "it was like a darkness . . . ," a common literary device called a **simile**. Poets use metaphors and similes to help us see in a fresh perspective. Comparing love to a rose encourages us to think differently about love, helping us see its delicate beauty. Of course, today that comparison is no longer novel and can even be a cliché, suggesting that a writer is not trying to be original and is settling instead for an easy comparison. When Robert Burns wrote "my love is like a red, red rose" more than two hundred years ago, it was a fresh comparison that excited new ways of looking at love. Indeed, some theorists, like the contemporary American philosopher Richard Rorty, think that metaphors can change our ways of looking at the world. Our thinking about time, for example, might be different if we didn't think with linear metaphors about the past being behind us and the future up ahead. What if, as some American Indian languages do, ours used a circular metaphor, having just one day that constantly repeated itself? Would our perceptions of time change?

What if Mary Oliver had begun her poem by saying that "a misunderstanding was corrected," instead of "a darkness was ripped from my eyes"? Her metaphor is not only more dramatic and memorable but also more suggestive. Darkness deepens the idea of lack of knowledge, suggesting not only intellectual blindness but also a host of negative connotations that readers might associate with the dark. Fresh metaphors can be expansive and illuminating. They help us understand the world differently.

Oliver creatively uses metaphors and similes throughout "Singapore." "Disgust argued" is an interesting metaphor or perhaps a personification, in which the speaker's stomach is given the ability to argue. She interrupts her observation of the cleaning woman in the third stanza to make a comment on the function of poetry itself, claiming that poems should have birds, rivers, and trees in them. Is she suggesting metaphorically that poems should be pleasant? Is that the only thing birds, rivers, and trees suggest to you?

She returns to the woman, and they exchange glances. Apparently the speaker is struggling with her own socialization that sees this kind of physical labor as demeaning. She directly describes the woman's "scrubbing and rinsing" but then returns to similes, describing her work as being "like a river" and her hair "like the wing of a bird." These comparisons seem for a moment to clarify the event for the speaker, helping her see this seemingly oppressive job positively. Amazingly, she wants the woman actually to become a bird and "rise up from the crust and the slop and fly."

But in the final stanza, she reminds us that she isn't really expecting that kind of physical miracle; instead, she wants to remind us that how we describe the woman working controls how we feel about her. If we see the folding and unfolding of her washcloth metaphorically, then we might see her differently; we might see her natural dignity, her beauty, and how her "light" was able to illuminate the speaker's "darkness."

Sometimes the poet chooses words like *darkness* and *light* that are so rich in texture that they can be examined as both metaphor and connotation. Such words might also be thought of as examples of synecdoche or metonymy. **Synecdoche** substitutes part of something for the whole, as in "I love my new wheels" referring to a car. **Metonymy** substitutes something associated with a thing, as in "Hollywood is resisting censorship" for the entire film industry. Oliver's "eyes" might be a synecdoche for her mind, and "darkness" and "light" can be metonymies for ignorance and beauty. Locate examples in our three poems of metaphor, connotation, synecdoche, and metonymy, if you can.

Although students often seem perplexed when professors find hidden **symbols** in poems, writers rarely plant such puzzling images deep in the recesses of their texts. The best symbols grow naturally out of the meaning-making process that readers go through. In the context of a particular poem, symbols are usually objects that can stand for general ideas. And like metaphors and similes, they suggest different things to different readers. The whale in *Moby-Dick*, for example, can be read as a symbol for implacable evil or perhaps the mysteries of the universe. In "Singapore," the specific event of the speaker watching a woman washing ashtrays in a toilet could be symbolic of anything we find unpleasant or strange or alien. And the whole event, including her eventual understanding, could easily be an **allegory** or extended symbol for the necessity for all of us to transcend our cultural socialization to understand other cultures and other attitudes toward working.

SOUND

The English poet Alexander Pope hoped that poetry's **sound** could become "an echo to [its] sense," that what the ear hears would reinforce what the mind understands. To many people, **rhyme** is the most recognizable aspect of poetry. The matching of final vowel and consonant sounds can make a poem trite or interesting. The now-familiar rhyming of "moon" and "June" with "swoon" suggests a poet who will settle for a cliché rather than do the hard work of being fresh. Rhyme, of course, is pleasing to the ear and makes the poem easier to remember, but it also gives the poem psychological force. Most contemporary poets choose not to rhyme, preferring the flexibility and freedom of free verse. But sound is still a high priority.

One of the most famous and effective examples of how sound can "echo" its sense is found in Robert Frost's "Stopping by Woods on a Snowy Evening," especially in the last two stanzas:

He gives his harness bells a shake

To ask if there is some mistake.

The only other sound's the sweep

Of easy wind and downy flake.

The woods are lovely, dark and deep,

But I have promises to keep,

And miles to go before I sleep,

And miles to go before I sleep.

Skilled poets like Frost use **alliteration** to connect words near each other by repeating the initial consonant sound. A variation, **assonance**, repeats vowel sounds. Frost obviously and subtly employs these sound techniques to echo both theme and mood. The alliterative -s's in "shake," "some," "sound's," and "sweep" also connect the meaning of these words, which are also reinforced by the -s's in "gives," "his," "harness," "bells," "asks," "is," "mistake," "sound's," and "easy." And when alliteration is combined with the assonance of "sweep" and "easy," as well as "downy" and "sound's," visual, tactile, and aural images are joined to create a soothing, restful, and idyllic scene of beauty and peace. All of these choices prepare the reader for the -e's of "keep" and "deep" and the -s's of the repeated "woods," "promises," "miles," and "sleep." In this way, the serenity and retreat of the woods are verbally and thematically contrasted with the demands of life's duties, culminating in the deadly temptation to escape responsibility by entering the winter woods.

Notice how Mary Oliver uses alliteration in her first stanza to link "women's," "woman," "washing," and "white." Komunyakaa's first stanza too links "printers," "police," and "pulled" as well as "they," "thief's," "Terrestrial," "thick," and "thorns." What effect do these and other elements of sound have on the impact and meaning of the poems?

A WRITING EXERCISE

Note the use of alliteration and assonance in all three poems. How might these devices enhance meaning?

RHYTHM AND METER

Many poets in the early twentieth century chose to have their poems rhyme. Edwin Arlington Robinson's "The Mill" employs a typical **rhyme scheme** in which in each stanza the last words in lines 1 and 3 sound the same and the last words in lines 2 and 4 sound the same. We indicate such a pattern with letters—*abab.* The second half of the first stanza would then be *cdcd* and so forth.

Rhythm in poetry refers to the beat, a series of stresses, pauses, and accents. We are powerfully attuned to rhythm, whether it is our own heartbeat or the throb of the bass guitar in a rock band. When we pronounce a word, we give more **stress** (breath, emphasis) to some syllables than to others. When these stresses occur at a regular interval over, say, a line of poetry, we refer to it as **meter**. When we scan a line of poetry, we try to mark its stresses and pauses. We use ´ to indicate a stressed syllable and ˘ for an unstressed one. The basic measuring unit for these stressed and unstressed syllables in English is the **foot**. There are four usual feet: *iambic, trochaic, anapestic,* and *dactylic.* An **iamb** is an unstressed syllable followed by a stressed one, as in "thĕ wóods." Reversed we have a **trochee**, as in "tígĕr." An **anapest** contains three syllables that are unstressed, then unstressed, then stressed, as in "Whĕn thĕ blúe / wăve rólls níghtlў / ŏn deép Gălĭleé." The reverse, the **dactyl**, can be heard in the Mother Goose rhyme, "Púss̆y cát, / púss̆y cát / whére hăve yŏu / beén?" If you look at the first four lines of "The Mill" again, you can hear a regular beat of iambs:

> Thĕ mill / er's wife / hăd waít / ĕd lóng,
> Thĕ téa / wăs cóld, / thĕ fire / wăs deád;
> Ănd thére / might yét / bĕ nóth / ĭng wróng
> Ĭn hów / hĕ wént / ănd whát / hĕ saíd:

Depending on the number of feet, we give lines various names. If a line contains one foot, it is a **monometer**; two, a **dimeter**; three, a **trimeter**; four, a **tetrameter**; five, a **pentameter**; six, a **hexameter**; seven, a **heptameter**; and eight, an **octometer**. So Robinson's lines are iambic tetrameter. Most lines in Shakespeare's sonnets are iambic pentameter, or five iambs.

Note the punctuation in Robinson's poem. When a line ends with a comma, we are meant to pause very briefly; when a line ends with a period (end stop), we pause a bit longer. But when there is no punctuation (line 7), we are meant to continue on until the end of the next line. This is known as *enjambment*. These poetic techniques improve the sound and flow of the poem and enhance the thoughts and feelings that give poetry its memorable depth and meaningfulness.

THEME

Some readers are fond of extracting ideas from poems, claiming, for example, that the theme of "Blackberries" is the loss of innocence or that the theme of "The Mill" is the loss of identity. In a sense, these thematic observations are plausible enough, but they are limiting and misleading. "Blackberries" certainly seems to have something to do with the interruption of a certain view about physical labor, but the significance for each reader might be much more specific, having to do with the noble savage; the Garden of Eden; hierarchy in society; the arrogance of the rich; or sensitivity, cruelty, and dignity. "The Mill" could also be about gender relations, economic cruelty, or the responsibility of communities. Reducing a complex, ambiguous poem to a bald statement robs the poem of its evocative power, its mystery, and its art.

Some critics stress the response of readers; others care only for what the text itself says; still others are concerned with the social and cultural implications of the poem's meaning. Psychoanalytic readers may see poems as reflections of the psychological health or illness of the poet; source-hunting or intertextual readers want to find references and hints of other literary works hidden deep within the poem. Feminist readers may find sexism, Marxists may find economic injustice, and gay and lesbian readers may find heterosexual bias. Readers can and will find in texts a whole range of issues. Perhaps we find what we are looking for, or we find what matters most to us.

This does not mean that we should think of committed readers as biased or as distorting the text to fulfill their own agenda, although biased or distorted readings are not rare. In a literature course, readers are entitled to read poems according to their own interpretations as long as they follow the general convention of academic discourse. That is, it is possible to make a reasonable case that "Blackberries" is really about rejecting contemporary technology in favor of rural life. The reason that some themes sound more plausible than others is that these critics marshal their evidence from the text and their own experience. Usually the evidence that fits best wins: if you can persuade others that you have significant textual support for your theme and if you present a balanced and judicious persona, you can usually carry the day. Poems almost always have several reasonable themes. The critic's job is to argue for a theme that seems to make the most sense in relation to the support. Often the same evidence can be used to bolster different themes because themes are really just higher-level generalizations than the particulars found in the text. Critics use the concrete elements of a poem to make more general abstract statements. In "Blackberries," for example, the same textual support could be used to uphold a theme about the cruelty of children or the more general notion of an initiation in a class-conscious culture or the even more general idea of the inevitable loss of innocence.

Revised Draft of a Student Paper

Michaela Fiorucci

Mr. Hardy

English 102

25 April - - - -

Negotiating Boundaries

Although most college students value their privacy, they also want to create intimate relationships; it is often hard to reconcile these two impulses. Most middle-class students are lucky enough to have their own bedrooms, private enclaves against annoying sisters and brothers, intrusive mothers and fathers. But such boundaries are more than physical barriers; they are also a symbolic assertion of identity. They say, "I'm separate from you even within the closeness of our family." Such a commitment to physical privacy might be innocent enough, but it does contain dangerous seeds, especially when extended beyond the home to neighborhoods. When different ethnic groups want boundaries between them, it is no longer innocent. When the upper classes want to be separated from workers because they see each other as radically different, a dangerously undemocratic boundary has been erected. Boundaries clearly serve a protective function, but unneeded ones can also prevent us from helping and understanding each other. Writers like Edwin Arlington Robinson, Yusef Komunyakaa, and Mary Oliver understand that we must negotiate boundaries, building them when they increase privacy and self-worth and bridging them when human solidarity can be enhanced.

Creates context about boundaries, moving from the personal to neighborhoods and beyond.

Announces her focus on need to negotiate.

It would be reductive to say that boundaries are either good or bad, since their value depends so much on context. Robinson's "The Mill" is a good example of the dangerous consequences of a failure to cross a boundary that should not exist and then a failure to establish a boundary where one should exist. The poem narrates the sad story of a farm couple who commit suicide — the husband because he feels useless, the wife because she can't imagine life without her husband. A contemporary reader is struck by the lack of communication between the couple. He must have been depressed for a long time, but it seems they never discussed his feelings. Keeping such an emotional boundary between husband and wife was probably typical of the way men and women dealt with each

Begins first concrete supporting example.

other one hundred years ago. Apparently it was a constructed barrier that few could cross. He simply could not bare his heart by saying, "I feel terrible that I am going to lose my job." And his wife accepts his reticence, even though he might have been having second thoughts as he "lingered at the door" (line 7). Clearly this is a boundary that should have been breached. The time for their solidarity was before he kills himself, not after.

Example of harmful tradition boundary.

After several readings it is clear that the boundary that should have been established wasn't. The miller is the victim of the demeaning idea that a person's worth is synonymous with his or her occupation. When his job disappears, so must he. Although Robinson's tone is flat, we sense his frustration with the inevitability of this grim tragedy, one that is compounded by the equally dehumanizing idea that a wife cannot exist without her husband. When the miller's wife decides to "leave no mark" (20) by jumping into the pond, she is admitting that she is useless outside her matrimonial role. Both identify with a role that should be only one aspect of a complex human life. The final barrier she crosses, from life to death, is symbolically represented in the poem as a feminine domestic gesture: she doesn't want to leave a mess. She continues as a housewife even in death. The boundaries between a person and occupation should be clear, but the arbitrary boundaries between husbands and wives should continue to be eradicated.

Concrete reference to poems strengthens argument.

Concludes paragraph with example of a boundary needing negotiating.

When the ten-year-old narrator in "Blackberries" claims that he is "Limboed between worlds" (18), he means the rural paradise of "Terrestrial sweetness" (4) and "rich blackness" (15) he temporarily lives in versus the commercial urban world that seems to make him anxious. He has constructed a boundary between the ancient task of picking berries and the modern technology of automobiles, between a closeness with nature and the artificial air-conditioning of the car. Although the narrator enjoys being one with nature, he seems to be cutting himself off from the realities of the world. He seems to reject "old lime-covered / History" (7–8) in favor of "mythology" (11), which seems to suggest a conscious rejection of the present. But this is a boundary that cannot stand. He needs the outside world to survive financially, and so when the car approaches, it is the modern world and all its complexity that draws near. When he looks into the car, he sees "Smirking" (23) children; he sees class prejudice, hierarchy, and economic reality. The smirkers of the world are in charge. It is this realization that dissolves the protective boundary around his Garden of Eden; consequently, he feels physical pain, but it is really the pain of initiation into reality that he feels. He must now cross a boundary he tried to delay.

Second concrete example of problematic boundary.

Notes consequences of not negotiating.

Although we can sympathize with the young narrator, like the couple in "The Mill," he would have been better off not making his boundary so extreme.

Connection to previous poem increases essay's unity.

The narrator in Mary Oliver's "Singapore" also imagines that she sees a significant boundary, here between herself as a middle-class traveler and a cleaning woman laboring over a toilet. It is a separation we might all make, given our socialization in America to consider this kind of physical labor as degrading. College-educated people have a tendency to see themselves as distinct from the working class. For many, a woman washing an ashtray in a toilet bowl is beyond the pale, a clear indication that the woman is Other. But Oliver does not simply give into her cultural conditioning; she contests the boundary, asserting that a "Disgust argued in my stomach"(6). Since part of our democratic socialization is also to be tolerant and open-minded, Oliver knows that she shouldn't stereotype workers. And since she is also a writer with ideas about how a poem should "always have birds in it" (8), she looks hard at the cleaning woman, finally seeing in her face, in her hair, and in the way she works, slowly "like a river" (25), the positive aspects of the woman that most of us would probably miss.

Third concrete example of boundaries.

Explicit example of negotiating a boundary.

Oliver does not simply accept the boundaries that her culture constructs. Instead, she negotiates internally, eventually seeing that a "light . . . can shine out of a life" (35) even where we would not expect it. In the woman's careful folding and unfolding of her blue work cloth and in her smile, Oliver sees a beauty that helps her eclipse a social boundary, ending with a life-affirming vision "filled with trees, and birds" (38). Such an insight does not come easily to us because we usually accept our given cultural boundaries. The miller and his wife are tragically unequipped to bridge the divide between them. Likewise, the boy in "Blackberries" is unable to sustain his fantasy boundaries. Oliver's traveler, however, struggles to negotiate boundaries and is thereby able to increase human solidarity even across class structures and cultures.

Notes benefits of breaching boundary.

Concludes by uniting all 3 poems in support of claim.

Comparing Poems and Pictures

Although literature and visual art may seem quite different media, they have often been closely connected. For one thing, any page of literature is a visual image, whether or not readers are always conscious of this fact. Also, most publishers of literature carefully design the covers of their books, aiming to lure readers in. Specific genres and authors, however, have forged even stronger relations between literature and art. Beginning in classical times and continuing today, many poems have precisely described existing paintings and sculptures; this tradition of verse is called **ekphrasis**. In the late eighteenth century, William Blake made highly ornamental engravings of his poems, so that they were striking works of art and not just written texts. In the nineteenth century, many novels included illustrations, a tradition evident today in children's picture books. At present, perhaps you are a fan of **graphic novels**: comic books that combine words and images to tell stories aimed at adults.

Aside from this history of connections, comparing a literary text with an image is a good mental exercise. The process can help you acquire more insights into each work. Given this possibility, we present a pairing on pages 158–59 of an Edward Hopper painting and a Rolando Perez poem, both titled *Office at Night*. In this case, the poem was written in response to the image. In other cases you may wish to connect a poem and an image for the first time, to trace their similarities and differences. With any such pairing, comparison can help you generate ideas for writing, a principle we stress throughout this book.

ANALYZING VISUAL ART

You can better understand a work of visual art—and develop ideas for an essay about it—if you raise certain questions about it and try to answer them. These questions apply to various types of pictures. Bear in mind that even photographs are not mere reproductions of reality. People who create them are, consciously or not, choosing their subject and figuring out how best to represent it. Especially in the age of digital technologies such as Photoshop, images caught by the camera can be tweaked in all sorts of ways. Moreover, the scene depicted might be a staged fantasy in the first place.

Here are the questions to ask yourself as you examine a picture with an eye to analyzing it:

1. What details do you see in the picture? Besides recognizable objects and figures (human beings or animals), consider shapes, colors, lighting, and shading. Do not list just the picture's most prominent elements, for those that at first seem trivial may turn out to be important for you.

2. What are aspects of the picture's *style*—the artist's particular way of handling the subject? Among other things, consider what the artist does and does not allow the viewer to see; how realistic or abstract the work seems; and whether anyone in the picture looks directly at the viewer.

3. How has the artist organized the picture? Note especially patterns of resemblance and contrast. Think, too, about whether the picture's design directs the viewer's attention to a particular part of it.

4. What mood does the picture evoke? Consider emotions that you experience as a viewer, as well as those that seem to be felt by any living figures in the scene.

5. What is at least one detail of the picture that strikes you as puzzling (and therefore especially in need of interpretation)?

6. Does the picture seem to tell a story or appear to be part of a story that has already begun and will continue?

7. How does the picture relate to its title and (where applicable) to its caption?

8. What are some options that the artist could have explored but did not pursue?

WRITING AN ESSAY THAT COMPARES LITERATURE AND ART

Before you write an essay comparing a work of literature with a work of art, collect as many details as you can about each. The questions above can help you do this with the artwork. For aid in gathering observations about the literary text, see Chapter 3, The Reading Process, especially the section on Strategies for Close Reading. Then, as you proceed to write, keep the following principles especially in mind:

- You do not have to give equal space to each work. Rather, you may prefer to come up with an issue and a main claim by focusing on interpreting *one* of the works: either the literary text *or* the visual image. Your secondary work will still play some role in the essay, but your primary one will receive greater attention. The result will be what in Chapter 4 we call a *weighted* comparison. (See that chapter for more tips.)
- Assume that your reader is at least somewhat familiar with both the literary work and the image but needs to be reminded of their basic details. In particular, help your audience *visualize* the art you discuss.
- Refer at least sometimes to the author of the literary work and to the artist who created the image. Doing so will help you analyze how their productions involve particular strategies of representation — attempts to affect audiences in particular ways.

ROLANDO PEREZ
Office at Night

It is past nine o'clock, and she has stayed late to help him. How many times did he dream of this very same scenario: her standing there in her tight blue dress, with her black pumps and flesh-colored stockings. And now it has finally happened. Without him having to ask — not that he would have dared — she volunteered all on her own.

He had to "open the window."

"This office at night is a bit stuffy."

A sheet of paper that once lay on top of other papers on his desk, now lies on the green carpet — to his right — gently carried there by the wind. Standing at a black filing cabinet, searching for some old bills, she has noticed the paper lying on the floor. The desk lamp throws a shadow on the desk, and illuminates his hands. And a patch of light, reflected on the wall, touches them both . . . lightly, very lightly . . . as with finger tips.

Will she bend over to pick it up?

If only the phone beside him would ring, then he would do something, he would act, produce the correct combination of words that would elicit the correct series of reactions from her. He might even suggest that they lock up and go for a drink somewhere. But having heard too many truths in the past, now history holds him back. In his suit, with his shirt buttoned to the top, and his tie still on, he hasn't moved, and she hasn't moved; and the wind-swept

Edward Hopper, *Office at Night*. 1940. Oil on canvas. 30-5/16 × 33-15/16 × 2-3/4″ framed. Collection Walker Art Center, Minneapolis. Gift of the T. B. Walker Foundation, Gilbert M. Walker Fund, 1948. Acc.#1948.21.

paper will stay on the floor, halfway between his desk and her cabinet, timidly undisturbed, in this wounded and frozen infinity.   *[2002]*

A Sample Paper Comparing a Poem and a Picture

To give you a better idea of what an essay comparing literature and art looks like, we present a paper by student Karl Magnusson. He connects Edward Hopper's painting *Office at Night* to the prose poem of the same title by Rolando Perez. As you will see, Karl's essay is a weighted comparison; it focuses mostly on Perez's poem.

Karl Magnusson
Professor Kemper
English W350
16 May ----

Lack of Motion and Speech in
Rolando Perez's "Office at Night"

Edward Hopper's painting *Office at Night* depicts a man and a woman working in the kind of setting indicated by the title. The man is apparently the boss of the woman, who seems to be his secretary. He sits at a desk by an

Immediately refers to the painting and then proceeds to summarize its key details.

open window, studying a document that he holds in front of him. She is positioned to the left and slightly to the rear of him. More precisely, she stands at a filing cabinet with her right hand resting on an open drawer. Their respective postures suggest that she is waiting to hear what he will say next. Perhaps she has just asked him a question and he is thinking about how to answer, or perhaps she is simply expecting him, as her superior, to issue her a new order. In any case, viewers of the painting are free to interpret their interaction, and different spectators might come up with different ideas about what these people really mean to each other. Indeed, not everyone would conceive their relationship to be what Rolando Perez imagines it as being in his poem about Hopper's artwork. Also entitled "Office at Night," Perez's poem speculates that the man and woman have a romantic interest in each other that neither he nor she can express. Furthermore, the poem conveys their reticence in terms that have often been used to describe the medium of painting in general.

Now turns to the poem, which will be the primary work in this weighted comparison.

This is the essay's main claim, which is about the poem.

The poem draws attention more to the self-repression of the boss. The secretary, too, evidently does not feel able to speak frankly about their emotions, perhaps because she is after all his employee. But the text tends to focus on *his* reluctance to reveal that he is enamored of her. This mixture of lust and hesitation is evident right near the start of the poem. There, just before describing the secretary's alluring clothes, the poem's speaker wonders, "How many times did he [the boss] dream of this very same scenario" (lines 1–2). The implication is that the boss has entertained sensual visions of his employee in his mind while doing nothing to bring them about. He merely fantasizes a romance with her, not actually helping it come to life. Soon after, the reader learns that *she* had to prompt *him* to "open the window" (5) and let fresh air in. Evidently she wishes to stimulate their senses and admit their real feelings, but this is behavior that he apparently would never "have dared" (4) to engage in on his own. Later, he resists actually inviting her to take their office working relationship in a romantic direction. Although he apparently considers the possibility that "he would do something, he would act, produce the correct combination of words" (14–15) to initiate a courtship, he remains silent and still. The implication is that he is restrained by the memory of his previous disappointments in love — "too many truths in the past" (17). Whatever specific episodes

Proceeds to support the main argument with specific lines from the poem.

in his past he is thinking of, the result is that "now history holds him back" (17). Rather than "suggest[ing] that they lock up and go for a drink somewhere" (16), he stays emotionally locked up, not letting his true attachment to her emerge.

In describing physical details of the office, the poem's speaker sums up the couple's inability to be emotionally open with each other. In part, the speaker does this by sometimes using images of motion that underscore by contrast how the man and woman fail to act on their feelings. The "patch of light" that "touches them both . . . lightly, very lightly . . . as with fingertips" (10–12) is a reminder that these two people do not physically touch each other at all. The phrase "gently carried there by the wind" (8) — used in reference to a piece of paper on the floor — indirectly emphasizes that the couple will not let themselves be carried away by passion. When, however, near the end of the poem, the speaker describes the paper as "timidly undisturbed" (20), the symbolism is more direct: the word "timidly" seems to fit the couple as well, for they have been too scared to confess their emotional bond. Moreover, the speaker's observation that "he hasn't moved, and she hasn't moved" (18–19) directly reinforces their *psychological* paralysis. The poem's final phrase, "wounded and frozen infinity" (20), is not just an overview of this late-night office environment. The speaker is also indicating the basic state of the couple's relationship. They are "wounded" in the sense that they suffer unfulfilled desires for each other. They are "frozen" in the sense that they cannot reveal these desires. The word "infinity" implies that, given their inertia, their situation is unlikely to change.

Not every poem about Hopper's *Office at Night* painting would necessarily focus on its two human figures. Nor would every poem about the painting necessarily depict their relationship in the way that Perez's does. Indeed, a distinctive feature of his poem is that his portrait of the couple attributes to them characteristics often associated with the medium of painting itself. Aware, like most people, that figures in a painting do not move, Perez takes this fact and makes it an element of the couple's behavior. The static nature of painting in general is echoed in their paralytic inhibition. Furthermore, just as people in paintings do not speak aloud, so the couple in Perez's poem resist articulating what they really feel. Also, just as viewers of a painting have to guess the thoughts of anyone shown in it, so Perez's man and woman force themselves to guess what is on each other's mind.

Perez could be seen as tolerating and even encouraging affairs between bosses and their secretaries. In this respect, his text seems more in keeping with the world of 1940, the year Hopper painted *Office at Night*. Back then, expressions of love between a manager and a subordinate might have been smiled upon, perceived as what the poem's speaker calls "the correct combination of words" and "the correct series of reactions" (15–16). The same expressions now, however, might be condemned as politically and even legally *in*correct. Certainly government and company policies on sexual harassment warn executives not to seduce the employees who serve them. Nevertheless, it would be unfair simply to dismiss Perez's poem or Hopper's painting as outdated, especially because the audiences for these works do not have to take them as being just about romance in the office. Both the poem and the painting allow for interpretations that see the couple as universal — as people who might exist anywhere. In this case, their reticence toward each other would be a widespread human problem: the difficulty of communicating the stirrings of one's heart.

> *The concluding paragraph does not simply repeat what has already been said. It touches on a new subject: changes in policies on office affairs.*

Writing about Plays

Most plays incorporate elements also found in short fiction, such as plot, characterization, dialogue, setting, and theme. But, in contrast to short fiction and other literary genres, plays are typically enacted live, in front of an audience. Theater professionals distinguish between the written *script* of a play and its actual *performances*. When you write about a play, you may wind up saying little or nothing about performances of it. When you first read and analyze a play, however, try to imagine ways of staging it. You might even research past productions of the play, noting how scenery, costumes, and lighting — as well as particular actors — were used.

Because a play is usually meant to be staged, its readers are rarely its only interpreters. Audiences at productions of the play also ponder its meanings. So, too, do members of the casts; no doubt you have heard of actors "interpreting" their parts. When a play is put on, even members of the backstage team are involved in interpreting it. The technical designers' choices of sets, costumes, and lighting reflect their ideas about the play, while the director works with cast and crew to implement a particular vision of it. No matter what the author of the script intended, theater is a collaborative art: all of the key figures involved in a play's production are *active* interpreters of the play, in that they influence the audience's understanding and experience of it. Therefore, you can develop good ideas when you read a play if you imagine yourself directing a production of it. More specifically, think what you would say to the actors as you guide them through their parts. As you engage in this thought experiment, you will see that you have options, for even directors keen on staying faithful to the script know it can be staged in any number of ways. Perhaps your course will give you and other students the chance to perform a scene together; if so, you will be deciding what interpretation of the scene to set forth.

To help you understand how to write about plays, we will refer often to the one-act play that follows. *The Stronger* was first performed in 1889. Its Swedish author, August Strindberg (1849–1912), is widely acknowledged as a founder of modern drama. Throughout his career, Strindberg experimented with a variety of theatrical styles. With this particular play, an encounter between two actresses, he dared to have one of the women speak and the other remain silent.

AUGUST STRINDBERG
The Stronger
Translated by Edith and Warner Oland

CHARACTERS

MRS. X, *an actress, married*
MISS Y, *an actress, unmarried*
A WAITRESS

SCENE: *The corner of a ladies' café. Two little iron tables, a red velvet sofa, several chairs. Enter Mrs. X, dressed in winter clothes, carrying a Japanese basket on her arm.*

Miss Y sits with a half empty beer bottle before her, reading an illustrated paper, which she changes later for another.

MRS. X: Good afternoon, Amelie. You're sitting here alone on Christmas eve like a poor bachelor!

Miss Y looks up, nods, and resumes her reading.

MRS. X: Do you know it really hurts me to see you like this, alone, in a café, and on Christmas eve, too. It makes me feel as I did one time when I saw a bridal party in a Paris restaurant, and the bride sat reading a comic paper, while the groom played billiards with the witnesses. Huh, thought I, with such a beginning, what will follow, and what will be the end? He played billiards on his wedding eve! *(Miss Y starts to speak.)* And she read a comic paper, you mean? Well, they are not altogether the same thing.

A waitress enters, places a cup of chocolate before Mrs. X, and goes out.

MRS. X: You know what, Amelie! I believe you would have done better to have kept him! Do you remember, I was the first to say "Forgive him?" Do you remember that? You would be married now and have a home. Remember that Christmas when you went out to visit your fiancé's parents in the country? How you gloried in the happiness of home life and really longed to quit the theater forever? Yes, Amelie dear, home is the best of all, the theater next and children—well, you don't understand that.

Miss Y looks up scornfully.

Mrs. X sips a few spoonfuls out of the cup, then opens her basket and shows Christmas presents.

MRS. X: Now you shall see what I bought for my piggywigs. *(Takes up a doll.)* Look at this! This is for Lisa, ha! Do you see how she can roll her eyes and turn her head, eh? And here is Maja's popgun. *(Loads it and shoots at Miss Y.)*

Miss Y makes a startled gesture.

MRS. X: Did I frighten you? Do you think I would like to shoot you, eh? On my soul, if I don't think you did! If you wanted to shoot *me* it wouldn't be so surprising, because I stood in your way—and I know you can never forget that—although I was absolutely innocent. You still believe I intrigued and got you out of the Stora theater, but I didn't. I didn't do that, although you think so. Well, it doesn't make any difference what I say to you. You still believe I did it. *(Takes up a pair of embroidered slippers.)* And these are for my better half. I embroidered them myself—I can't bear tulips, but he wants tulips on everything.

Miss Y looks up ironically and curiously.

MRS. X *(putting a hand in each slipper):*   What little feet Bob has! What? And you should see what a splendid stride he has! You've never seen him in slippers! *(Miss Y laughs aloud.)* Look! *(She makes the slippers walk on the table. Miss Y laughs loudly.)* And when he is grumpy he stamps like this with his foot. "What! damn those servants who can never learn to make coffee. Oh, now those creatures haven't trimmed the lamp wick properly!" And then there are draughts on the floor and his feet are cold. "Ugh, how cold it is; the stupid idiots can never keep the fire going." *(She rubs the slippers together, one sole over the other.)*

Miss Y shrieks with laughter.

MRS. X: And then he comes home and has to hunt for his slippers which Marie has stuck under the chiffonier—oh, but it's sinful to sit here and make fun of one's husband this way when he is kind and a good little man. You ought to have had such a husband, Amelie. What are you laughing at? What? What? And you see he's true to me. Yes, I'm sure of that, because he told me himself—what are you laughing at?—that when I was touring in Norway that that brazen Frédérique came and wanted to seduce him! Can you fancy anything so infamous? *(Pause.)* I'd have torn her eyes out if she had come to see him when I was at home. *(Pause.)* It was lucky that Bob told me about it himself and that it didn't reach me through gossip. *(Pause.)* But would you believe it, Frédérique wasn't the only one! I don't know why, but the women are crazy about my husband. They must think he has influence about getting them theatrical engagements, because he is connected with the government. Perhaps you were after him yourself. I didn't use to trust you any too much. But now I know he never bothered his head about you, and you always seemed to have a grudge against him someway.

Pause. They look at each other in a puzzled way.

Come and see us this evening, Amelie, and show us that you're not put out with us,—not put out with me at any rate. I don't know, but I think it would be uncomfortable to have you for an enemy. Perhaps it's because I stood in your way or—I really—don't know why—in particular.

Pause. Miss Y stares at Mrs. X curiously.

MRS. X *(thoughtfully)*: Our acquaintance has been so queer. When I saw you for the first time I was afraid of you, so afraid that I didn't dare let you out of my sight; no matter when or where, I always found myself near you—I didn't dare have you for an enemy, so I became your friend. But there was always discord when you came to our house, because I saw that my husband couldn't endure you, and the whole thing seemed as awry to me as an ill-fitting gown—and I did all I could to make him friendly toward you, but with no success until you became engaged. Then came a violent friendship between you, so that it looked all at once as though you both dared show your real feelings only when you were secure—and then—how was it later? I didn't get jealous—strange to say! And I remember at the christening, when you acted as godmother, I made him kiss you—he did so, and you became so confused—as it were; I didn't notice it then—didn't think about it later, either—have never thought about it until—now! *(Rises suddenly.)* Why are you silent? You haven't said a word this whole time, but you have let me go on talking! You have sat there, and your eyes have reeled out of me all these thoughts which lay like raw silk in its cocoon—thoughts—suspicious thoughts, perhaps. Let me see—why did you break your engagement? Why do you never come to our house any more? Why won't you come to see us tonight?

Miss Y appears as if about to speak.

MRS. X: Hush, you needn't speak—I understand it all! It was because—and because—and because! Yes, yes! Now all the accounts balance. That's it. Fie, I won't sit at the same table with you. *(Moves her things to another table.)* That's the reason I had to embroider tulips—which I hate—on his slippers, because you are fond of tulips; that's why *(Throws slippers on the floor.)* we go to Lake Mälarn in the summer, because you don't like salt water; that's why my boy is named Eskil—because it's your father's name; that's why I wear your colors, read your authors, eat your favorite dishes, drink your drinks—chocolate, for instance; that's why—oh—my God—it's terrible, when I think about it; it's terrible. Everything, everything came from you to me, even your passions. Your soul crept into mine, like a worm into an apple, ate and ate, bored and bored, until nothing was left but the rind and a little black dust within. I wanted to get away from you, but I couldn't; you lay like a snake and charmed me with your black eyes; I felt that when I lifted my wings they only dragged me down; I lay in the water with bound feet, and the stronger I strove to keep up the deeper I worked myself down, down, until I sank to the bottom, where you lay like a giant crab to clutch me in your claws—and there I am lying now.

I hate you, hate you, hate you! And you only sit there silent—silent and indifferent; indifferent whether it's new moon or waning moon, Christmas or New Year's, whether others are happy or unhappy; without power to hate or to love; as quiet as a stork by a rat hole—you couldn't scent your prey and capture it, but you could lie in wait for it! You sit here in your corner of the café—did you know it's called "The Rat Trap" for you?— and read the papers to see if misfortune hasn't befallen someone, to see if someone hasn't been given notice at the theater, perhaps; you sit here and calculate about your next victim and reckon on your chances of recompense like a pilot in a shipwreck. Poor Amelie, I pity you, nevertheless, because I know you are unhappy, unhappy like one who has been wounded, and angry because you are wounded. I can't be angry with you, no matter how much I want to be—because you come out the weaker one. Yes, all that with Bob doesn't trouble me. What is that to me, after all? And what difference does it make whether I learned to drink chocolate from you or someone else. *(Sips a spoonful from her cup.)*

Besides, chocolate is very healthful. And if you taught me how to dress— *tant mieux!—[so much the better!]* that has only made me more attractive to my husband; so you lost and I won there. Well, judging by certain signs, I believe you have already lost him; and you certainly intended that I should leave him—do as you did with your fiancé and regret as you now regret; but, you see, I don't do that—we mustn't be too exacting. And why should I take only what no one else wants?

Perhaps, take it all in all, I am at this moment the stronger one. You received nothing from me, but you gave me much. And now I seem like a thief since you have awakened and find I possess what is your loss. How could it be otherwise when everything is worthless and sterile in your hands? You can never keep a man's love with your tulips and your passions—but I can keep it. You can't learn how to live from your authors, as I have learned. You have no little Eskil to cherish, even if your father's name was Eskil. And why are you always silent, silent, silent? I thought that was strength, but perhaps it is because you have nothing to say! Because you never think about anything! *(Rises and picks up slippers.)*

Now I'm going home—and take the tulips with me—*your* tulips! You are unable to learn from another; you can't bend—therefore, you broke like a dry stalk. But I won't break! Thank you, Amelie, for all your good lessons. Thanks for teaching my husband how to love. Now I'm going home to love him. *(Goes.)*   *[1889]*

A Student's Personal Response to the Play

Trish Carlisle was enrolled in a class that read and discussed Strindberg's *The Stronger*. Below is some freewriting that Trish did about the play.

Near the end of Strindberg's play, Mrs. X says that "I am at this moment the stronger one." But is she? I guess that depends on what Strindberg meant by "the stronger" when he gave his play that title. As I was reading, I started to think that the stronger woman is actually the silent one, Miss Y, because she seems to have more self-control than Mrs. X does. I mean, Miss Y doesn't apparently feel that she has to make long, loud speeches in defense of her way of life. I can even believe that with her silence she is manipulating Mrs. X into getting fairly hysterical. Also, I guess we're to think that Amelie has managed to lure away Mrs. X's husband, at least for a while. Furthermore, we don't have to believe Mrs. X when at the end she claims that she has triumphed over Miss Y. Maybe people who have really succeeded in life don't need to proclaim that they have, as Mrs. X does.

Nevertheless, I can see why some students in this class feel that Mrs. X is in fact the stronger. If she has her husband back and wants her husband back, and if Miss Y is really without companionship at the end and has even lost her job at the theater, then probably Mrs. X is entitled to crow. Was Strindberg being deliberately unclear? Did he want his audience to make up their own minds about who is stronger? Maybe neither of these women is strong, because each of them seems dependent on a man, and Mrs. X's husband may not even be such a great person in the first place. If I were Mrs. X, maybe I wouldn't even take him back. I guess someone could say that it's Mrs. X's husband who is the stronger, since he has managed to make the two women fight over him while he enjoys his creature comforts. Anyway, Strindberg makes us guess what he is really like. Because he's offstage, he's just as silent as Miss Y is, although his wife imitates his voice at one point.

In a way, I feel that this play is too short. I want it to go on longer so that I can be sure how to analyze the two women and the man. But I realize that one of the reasons the play is dramatic is that it's brief. I might not be interested in it if it didn't leave me hanging. And it's also theatrical because Miss Y is silent even as Mrs. X lashes out at her. I wonder what the play would be like if we could

> hear Miss Y's thoughts in a sort of voice-over, like we find in some
> movies. It's interesting to me that the play is *about* actresses. I
> wonder if these characters are still "performing" with each other
> even if they're not acting in a theater at the moment.

Trish's freewriting would eventually help her develop ideas for a paper in which she had to analyze Strindberg's play. Compare your responses to the play with hers. Did the same issues come up for you? How do you feel about the women characters? What, if anything, do you wish the playwright had made clearer? What would you advise Trish to think about as she moved from freewriting to drafting a paper?

The Elements of Drama

You strengthen your ability to write about plays if you grow familiar with typical elements of drama. These elements include plot and structure, characterization, stage directions and setting, imagery, language, and theme.

PLOT AND STRUCTURE

Most plays, like most short stories, have a **plot**. When you read them, you find yourself following a narrative, a sequence of interrelated events. Even plays as short as *The Stronger* feature a plot, though the onstage action occurs in just one place and takes just a little while. As with short fiction, the reader of a play is often anxious to know how the events will turn out. The reader may especially feel this way when the play contains a mystery that characters are trying to solve. In Strindberg's play, for example, Mrs. X is apparently bent on discovering what relation her husband has had with her friend.

In summarizing the play, you might choose to depict the plot as a detective story. Then again, you might prefer to emphasize the characters' emotional conflicts as you describe how the play proceeds. In fact, there are various ways you can describe Strindberg's plot; just bear in mind that your account should be grounded in actual details of the text. However you summarize a play will reflect your sense of which characters are central to it. Is the offstage husband Bob in *The Stronger* as important as the two women onstage? More important than they are? Less important? Your summary will also reflect your sense of which characters have power. Do you think the two women in Strindberg's drama equally influence that play's events? In addition, your summary ought to acknowledge the human motives that drive the play's action. Why do you think Mrs. X feels compelled to confront Miss Y?

Summarizing the plot of a play can mean arranging its events chronologically. Yet bear in mind that some of the play's important events may have occurred in the characters' pasts. In many plays, actually, characters learn things about the past that they did not know and must now try to accept. For example, important events mentioned in *The Stronger* take place before the play begins. By the time the curtain rises, Miss Y's close relationship with Bob is well in the past. A typical summary would begin with the events on stage, but you could also summarize Strindberg's play as a chronicle of the relationship that precedes the scene in the café.

In discussing the structure of short stories, we noted that many of them follow Alice Adams's formula *ABDCE* (Action, Background, Development, Climax, and Ending). This scheme, however, does not fit many plays. In a sense, the average play is entirely Action, for its performers are constantly engaged in physical movement of various sorts. Furthermore, as we have been suggesting, information about Background can surface quite often as the play's characters talk. Yet the terms Development, Climax, and Ending do seem appropriate for many plays. Certainly the plot of *The Stronger* develops, as Mrs. X becomes increasingly hostile to Miss Y. Certainly the play can be said to reach a Climax, a moment of great significance and intensity, when Mrs. X moves to another table and declares her hatred for Miss Y. The term *Ending* can also apply to this play, although readers may disagree about exactly when its Climax turns into its Ending. Certainly Mrs. X is in a different state of mind at the play's last moment; at that point, she stops haranguing Miss Y and leaves, declaring that she will save her own marriage.

Like short stories, plays often use repetition as an organizational device. The characters in a play may repeat certain words; Mrs. X's variations on "silence" multiply as Miss Y retreats from interacting with her. Also, a play may show repeated actions, such as Mrs. X's interruptions of Miss Y. In addition, a play may suggest that the onstage situation echoes previous events, as when Mrs. X alludes to confrontations between her husband and Miss Y in the past.

The Stronger is a short, one-act play. But many other plays are longer and divided conspicuously into subsections. The ancient Greek drama *Antigone* alternates choral sections with scenes involving only the title character and her uncle Creon. All of Shakespeare's plays, and most modern ones, are divided into acts, which are often further divided into scenes. Even within a one-act play, however, you can detect various stages in the action. This task is easier when the one-act play is fairly lengthy, but even a very short play like *The Stronger* can be broken down into stages, although you will have to decide exactly what those stages are.

CHARACTERS

Many short stories have a narrator who reveals the characters' inner thoughts. Most plays, however, have no narrator at all. To figure out what the characters think, you must study what they *say* and how they *move*, if the author has indeed provided stage directions. To be sure, some characters say a great deal, leaving you with several clues to their psyche. If you are familiar with Shakespeare's lengthy play *Hamlet*, you may recall that it contains thousands of lines. Moreover, when the title character is alone on stage making long speeches to the audience, he seems to be baring his very soul. Yet despite such moments, Hamlet's mental state remains far from clear; scholars continue to debate his sanity. Thus, as a reader of *Hamlet* and other plays, you have much room for interpretation. Often you will have to decide whether to accept the judgments that characters express about one another. For example, how fair and accurate does Strindberg's Mrs. X seem to you as she berates Miss Y?

As with short stories, a good step toward analyzing a play's characters is to consider what each desires. The drama or comedy of many plays arises when the desires of one character conflict with those of another. Strindberg's Mrs. X feels that Miss Y has been a threat to her marriage, and while we cannot be sure of Miss Y's thoughts, evidently she is determined not to answer Mrs. X's charges. At the end of the play, the women's conflict seems to endure, even though Mrs. X proclaims victory. Many other plays end with characters managing to resolve conflict because one or more of them experiences a change of heart. Whatever the play you are studying, consider whether any of its characters change. Is any character's thinking transformed? If so, whose?

The main character of a play is often referred to as its **protagonist**, and a character who notably opposes this person is often referred to as the **antagonist**. As you might guess without even reading Shakespeare's play, Prince Hamlet is the protagonist of *Hamlet*; his uncle Claudius, who succeeded Hamlet's father to the throne of Denmark, serves as his antagonist. To be sure, applying these terms may be tricky or impossible in some instances. The two women in *The Stronger* oppose each other, but each can be called the protagonist and each can be called the antagonist. Can you think of other plays you have read in which the protagonist and antagonist are not readily identifiable?

In discussing the elements of short fiction, we referred to point of view, the perspective from which a story is told. Since very few plays are narrated, the term *point of view* fits this genre less well. While it is possible to claim that much of Shakespeare's *Hamlet* reflects the title character's point of view, he is offstage for stretches, and the audience may focus on other characters even when he appears. Also, do not overlook the possible significance of characters who are not physically present. A character may be important even when he or she never appears onstage. In *The Stronger*, the two women's conflict is partly about Mrs. X's unseen husband.

In most plays, characters' lives are influenced by their social standing, which in turn is influenced by particular traits of theirs. These may include their gender, their social class, their race, their ethnic background, their nationality, their sexual orientation, and the kind of work they do. Obviously *The Stronger* deals with gender relationships. Mrs. X defines herself in gendered terms: wife, mother, and insecure lover in competition with a rival for her husband's affections. But there are elements of social class too—of the circumstances of upper-middle-class Swedish women in Stockholm in the late nineteenth century—that may require research.

STAGE DIRECTIONS AND SETTING

When analyzing a script, pay attention to the staging directions it gives, and try to imagine additional ways that the actors might move around. Through a slight physical movement, performers can indicate important developments in their characters' thoughts. When Mrs. X fires a popgun at Miss Y, audience members may flinch in surprised sympathy with Miss Y's "startled gesture." But they may be just as startled by Miss Y's mirthful response, culminating in a "shriek of laughter," when Mrs. X uses her husband's slippers to mime and mock him. Is Miss Y's laughter hysterical, or knowing, or something else? How does it set up the "puzzled," curious looks Mrs. X and Miss Y exchange moments later?

You can get a better sense of how a play might be staged if you research its actual production history. Granted, finding out about its previous stagings may be difficult. But at the very least, you can discover some of the theatrical conventions that must have shaped presentations of the play, even one that is centuries old. Consider Sophocles' classical tragedy *Antigone* and Shakespeare's *Hamlet*, canonical plays that you may have read or seen performed in films or theater. While classical scholars would like to learn more about early performances of *Antigone*, they already know that it and other ancient Greek plays were staged in open-air arenas. They know, too, that *Antigone*'s Chorus turned in unison at particular moments, and that the whole cast wore large masks. Although the premiere of *Hamlet* was not videotaped, Shakespeare scholars are sure that, like other productions in Renaissance England, it made spare use of scenery and featured an all-male cast. By contrast, *The Stronger* is anchored in the nineteenth-century realist tradition that values in literary works an accurate and plausible presentation of everyday life and events.

Some plays can be staged in any number of styles and still work well. Shakespeare wrote *Hamlet* back in Renaissance England, but quite a few successful productions of it have been set in later times, such as late-nineteenth-century England. Even modern plays that seem to call for realist productions can be staged in a variety of ways. Note Strindberg's description of the setting for *The Stronger*: "The corner of a ladies' café. Two little iron tables, a red velvet sofa, several chairs." Many productions of this play have remained within the conventions of realism, striving to make the audience believe that it is seeing a late-nineteenth-century Stockholm café. But a production of *The Stronger* may present the audience with only a few pieces of furniture that barely evoke the café. Furthermore, the production might have Mrs. X's husband physically hover in the background, as if he were a ghost haunting both women's minds. You may feel that such a production would horribly distort Strindberg's drama; a boldly experimental staging of a play can indeed become a virtual rewriting of it. Nevertheless, remember that productions of a play may be more diverse in style than the script would indicate.

Remember, too, that a particular theater's architecture may affect a production team's decisions. Realism's illusion of the "fourth wall" works best on a proscenium stage, which is the kind probably most familiar to you. In brief, a proscenium is a boxlike space where the actors perform in front of the entire audience. In a proscenium production of *The Stronger*, the ladies' café can be depicted in great detail. The performing spaces at some theaters, however, are "in the round": that is, the audience completely encircles the stage. What would have to be done with the café then? List some items in the café that an "in the round" staging could accommodate.

In referring to possible ways of staging a play, we have inevitably been referring as well to its setting. A play may not be all that precise in describing its setting; Strindberg provides set designers with few guidelines for creating his Stockholm café. More significant, perhaps, than the place of the action is its *timing*: Mrs. X finds Miss Y sitting alone on Christmas eve. Yet a play may stress to its audience that its characters are located in particular places, at particular moments in their personal histories, and/or at a particular moment in *world* history. For example, *The Stronger* calls attention to the fact that it is set in a ladies' café, a female space. Are there gendered public arenas today where Mrs. X might play out her conflict with Miss Y? Could the play be set in a women's locker room? What would happen if the setting were not for women only?

You can learn much about a play's characters by studying how they accommodate themselves—or fail to accommodate themselves—to their settings. When Strindberg's Mrs. X can no longer bear sitting next to Miss Y, her shift to another table dramatically signifies her feelings. Of course, much of the drama in Strindberg's play occurs because there is a *single* setting, in which at least one character feels confined. Other plays employ a wider variety of settings to dramatize their characters' lives.

IMAGERY

When plays use images to convey meaning, sometimes they do so through dialogue. At the beginning of *The Stronger*, for instance, Mrs. X recalls "a bridal party in a Paris restaurant," where "the bride sat reading a comic paper, while the groom played billiards with the witnesses." The play proceeds to become very much about divisions between husband and wife; moreover, the two women engage in a tense "game" that seems analogous to billiards. But just as often, a play's meaningful images are physically presented in the staging: through gestures, costumes, lighting, and props. For instance, consider the slippers embroidered with tulips that Mrs. X flourishes early in the play. The slippers and the tulips gain meaning as the play progresses. The audience may be ever more inclined to see them as *symbolic*. *Symbol* is the term traditionally used for an image that represents some concept or concepts.

Keep in mind that *you* may interpret an image differently than the characters within the play do. When Strindberg's Mrs. X refers to billiards, she may not think at all that she will be playing an analogous game with Miss Y. You, however, may make this connection, especially as the play proceeds.

LANGUAGE

As we have been suggesting, a play's meaning and impact may be apparent only when the play is physically staged. Nevertheless, you can learn much from studying the language in its script. For example, the play's very title may be important. At the climax of Strindberg's play, Mrs. X even refers to herself as "the stronger." Obviously the playwright is encouraging audiences to think about the title's implications. Yet not always will the meaning of a play's title be immediately clear. In her freewriting, Trish wonders how to define "stronger" and which of Strindberg's characters fit the term. Even if you think the title of a play is easily explainable, pause to see whether that title can actually lead to an issue of definition. In other words, don't take the title for granted.

In most plays, language is a matter of dialogue. The audience tries to figure out the play by focusing on how the characters address one another. But remember that the pauses or silences within a play may be just as important as its dialogue. In fact, a director may *add* moments of silence that the script does not explicitly demand. In many plays, however, the author does specify moments when one or more characters significantly fail to speak. *The Stronger* is a prominent example: Miss Y is notably silent throughout the play, and as a reader you probably find yourself wondering why she is. Ironically, the play's *absence* of true dialogue serves to remind us that plays usually *depend* on dialogue.

Consider this moment in *The Stronger* when Miss Y fails to speak:

MRS. X: . . . Why are you silent? You haven't said a word this whole time, but you have let me go on talking! You have sat there, and your eyes have reeled out of me all these thoughts which lay like raw silk in its cocoon — thoughts — suspicious thoughts, perhaps. Let me see — why did you break your engagement? Why do you never come to our house any more? Why won't you come to see us tonight?

Miss Y appears as if about to speak.

MRS. X: Hush, you needn't speak — I understand it all! . . .

An interesting discussion might result from imagining what Miss Y might have said had she not been cut off. It's also worth reflecting on what Strindberg conceivably gains by *not* having Miss Y speak at that moment.

THEME

We have already discussed *theme* in short fiction (pp. 46–48), and here we will build on some points from our earlier discussion. Again, a *theme* is the main claim — an assertion, a proposition, or a statement — that a work seems to make. As with other literary genres, try to state a play's theme as a midlevel generalization. If expressed in very broad terms, it will seem to fit many other works besides the one you have read; if narrowly tied to the play's characters and their particular situation, it will seem irrelevant to most other people's lives. With *The Stronger*, an example of a very broad theme would be "Women should not fight over a man." At the opposite extreme, a too-narrow theme would be "Women should behave well toward each other on Christmas eve, even if one of them has slept with the other's husband." If you are formulating Strindberg's theme, you might *start* with the broad generalization we have cited and then try to narrow it to a midlevel one. You might even think of ways that Strindberg's play *complicates* that broad generalization. What might, in fact, be a good midlevel generalization in Strindberg's case?

As we have noted, the very title of *The Stronger* seems significant. Indeed, a play's theme may be related to its title or to some other parts of the text. Nevertheless, be wary of couching the theme in terms drawn solely from the title or from some passage within the text. The play's theme may not be reducible to these words alone. Remember that the title of Strindberg's play can give rise to issues of definition in the first place.

You can state a play's theme as an observation or as a recommendation. With Strindberg's play, an observation-type theme would be "Marriage and career may disrupt relations between women." A recommendation-type theme would be either the broad or narrow generalization that we cited above. Neither way of stating the theme is automatically preferable, but remain aware of the different tones and effects they may carry. Consider, too, the possibility of stating the theme as a problem, as in this example: "We may be inclined to defend our marriages when they seem threatened, but in our defense we may cling to illusions that can easily shatter." Furthermore, consider the possibility of referring to *a* theme of the play rather than *the* theme, thereby acknowledging the possibility that the play is making several important claims.

When you write about a play, certainly you will refer to the text of it, its **script**. But probably the play was meant to be staged, and most likely it has been. Thus, you might refer to actual productions of it and to ways it can be performed. Remember, though, that different productions of the play may stress different meanings and create different effects. In your paper, you might discuss how much room for interpretation the script allows those who would stage it. For any paper you write about the play, look beyond the characters' dialogue and study whatever stage directions the script gives.

Undoubtedly your paper will have to offer some plot summary, even if your audience has already read the play. After all, certain details of the plot will be important support for your points. But, as with papers about short fiction, keep the amount of plot summary small, mentioning only events in the play that are crucial to your overall argument. Your reader should feel that you are analyzing the play rather than just recounting it.

To understand more what analysis of a play involves, let's return to Trish Carlisle, the student whose freewriting you read earlier. Trish was assigned to write a 600-word paper about Strindberg's *The Stronger*. She was asked to imagine herself writing to a particular audience: performers rehearsing a production of the play she chose. More specifically, she was to identify and address some question that these performers might have, an issue that might be bothering them as they prepared to put on the play. Trish knew that, besides presenting an issue, her paper would have to make a main claim and support it with evidence. Moreover, the paper might have to spell out some of the warrants or assumptions behind her evidence.

Because finding an issue was such an important part of the assignment, Trish decided to review her freewriting about Strindberg's play, noting questions she had raised there about it. Trish saw that the chief issue posed for her by *The Stronger* was "Which character is the stronger?" Nevertheless, Trish recognized that the issue "Which character is the stronger?" still left her with various decisions to make. For one thing, she had to decide what kind of an is-sue she would call it. Trish saw that it could be considered an issue of fact, an issue of evaluation, or an issue of definition. Although it could fit into all of these categories, Trish knew that the category she chose would influence the direction of her paper. Eventually she decided to treat "Which character is the stronger?" as primarily an issue of definition, because she figured that, no mat-ter what, she would be devoting much of her paper to defining *stronger* as a term.

Of course, there are many different senses in which someone may be "stronger" than someone else. Your best friend may be a stronger tennis player than you, in the sense that he or she always beats you at that game. But you may be a stronger student than your friend, in the sense that you get better grades in school. In the case of Strindberg's play, Trish came to see that a paper focused on which character is *morally* stronger would differ from one focused on who is *emotionally* stronger, and these papers would differ in turn from one focused on which character is *politically* stronger, more able to impose his or her will. These reflections led Trish to revise her issue somewhat. She decided to address the question "Which particular sense of the word 'stronger' is most relevant to Strindberg's play?" In part, Trish came up with this reformulation of her issue because she realized that the two women feuding in the play are actresses, and that they behave as actresses even when they are not profession-ally performing. Trish's answer to her revised question was that the play en-courages the audience to consider which woman is the stronger *actress*—which woman is more able, that is, to convey her preferred version of reality.

When you write about a play, you may have to be selective, for your paper may not be able to accommodate all the ideas and issues that occur to you. Trish was not sure which woman in Strindberg's play is the stronger actress. She felt that a case can be made for Mrs. X or Miss Y; indeed, she suspected that Strindberg was letting his audience decide. But she decided that her paper was not obligated to resolve this matter; she could simply mention the various pos-sible positions in her final paragraph. In the body of her paper, Trish felt she would contribute much if she focused on addressing her main issue with her main claim. Again, her main issue was "Which particular sense of the word 'stronger' is most relevant to Strindberg's play?" Her main claim was that "The play is chiefly concerned with which woman is the stronger actress, 'stronger' here meaning 'more able to convey one's version of reality.'"

Although a paper about a play need not explicitly mention the elements of plays we have identified, thinking about these elements can provide you with a good springboard for analysis. Trish saw that her paper would be very much concerned with the title of Strindberg's play, especially as that title applied to the characters. Also, she would have to refer to stage directions and imagery, because Miss Y's silence leaves the reader having to look at her physical move-ments and the play's props for clues to her thinking. The play does not really include dialogue, a term that implies people talking with each other. Neverthe-less, Trish saw that there are utterances in the script that she could refer to, especially as she made points about the play's lone speaker, Mrs. X. Indeed, a persuasive paper about a play is one that quotes from characters' lines and perhaps from the stage directions, too. Yet the paper needs to quote selectively, for a paper chock full of quotations may obscure instead of enhance the writer's argument.

Final Draft of a Student Paper

Here is Trish's final draft of her paper about *The Stronger*. It emerged out of several drafts, and after Trish had consulted classmates and her instructor. As you read this version of her paper, note its strengths, but also think of any suggestions that might help Trish make the paper even better.

Trish Carlisle

Professor Zelinsky

English 102

28 April - - - -

Which Is the Stronger Actress
in August Strindberg's Play?

You have asked me to help you solve difficulties you may be experiencing with August Strindberg's script for *The Stronger* as you prepare to play the roles of Mrs. X and Miss Y. These female characters seem harder to judge than the three women who are the focus of Susan Glaspell's play *Trifles*, the play you are performing next month. Obviously, Glaspell is pushing us to think well of Mrs. Hale, Mrs. Peters, and Minnie Wright. The two women in Strindberg's play are another matter; in particular, you have probably been wondering which of these two women Strindberg thinks of as "the stronger." If you knew which character he had in mind with that term, you might play the roles accordingly. As things stand, however, Strindberg's use of the term in his title is pretty ambiguous. It is not even clear, at least not immediately, which particular sense of the word *stronger* is most relevant to the play. I suggest that the play is chiefly concerned with which character is the stronger actress. In making this claim, I am defining *stronger* as "more able to convey one's version of reality."

You may feel that Strindberg is clarifying his use of the word *stronger* when he has Mrs. X bring up the word in the long speech that ends the play. In that final speech, she declares to Miss Y that "I am . . . the stronger one" (166) and that Miss Y's silence is not the "strength" that Mrs. X previously thought it was. At this point in the play, Mrs. X is evidently defining *stronger* as "more able to keep things, especially a man." She feels that she is the stronger because she is going home to her husband, while Miss Y is forced to be alone on Christmas Eve. Yet there is little reason to believe that Mrs. X is using the word *stronger* in the sense that the playwright has chiefly in mind. Furthermore, there is little reason to believe that Mrs. X is an accurate judge of the two women's situations. Perhaps she is telling herself that she is stronger because she simply needs to believe that she is. Similarly, perhaps she is telling herself that she now has control over her husband when in actuality he may still be emotionally attached to Miss Y. In addition, because Miss Y does not speak and because Mrs. X sweeps out without giving her any further opportunity to do so, we don't know if Miss Y agrees with Mrs. X's last speech.

Since Mrs. X's final use of the word *stronger* is so questionable, we are justified in thinking of other ways that the term might be applied. In thinking about this play, I have entertained the idea that the stronger character is actually Mrs. X's husband Bob, for he has two women fighting over him and also apparently has the creature comforts that servants provide. But now I tend to think that the term applies to one or both of the two women. Unfortunately, we are not given many facts about them, for it is a brief one-act play and one of the major characters does not even speak. But as we try to figure out how Strindberg is defining the term *stronger,* we should notice one fact that we are indeed given: Each of these women is an actress. Both of them have worked at Stockholm's Grand Theater, although apparently Mrs. X got Miss Y fired from the company. Furthermore, Mrs. X engages in a bit of theatrical illusion when she scares Miss Y by firing the toy pistol at her. Soon after, Mrs. X plays the role of her own husband when she puts her hands in the slippers she has bought for him and imitates not only his walk but also the way he scolds his servants. Miss Y even laughs at this "performance," as if she is being an appreciative audience for it. In addition, if Mrs. X is right about there being an adulterous affair between her husband and Miss Y, then those two people have basically been performing an act for Mrs. X. It is possible, too, that Mrs. X has not been quite so naïve; perhaps she has deliberately come to the café in order to confront Miss Y about the affair and to proclaim ultimate victory over her. In that case, Mrs. X is performing as someone more innocent than she really is. On the other hand, Miss Y might be using her silence as an actress would, manipulating her audience's feelings by behaving in a theatrical way.

Because we do know that these women are professional actresses, and because Strindberg gives us several hints that they are performing right there in the café, we should feel encouraged to think that he is raising the question of which is the stronger *actress.* Of course, we would still have to decide how he is defining the term *stronger.* But if he does have in mind the women's careers and behavior as actresses, then he seems to be defining *stronger* as "more able to convey one's version of reality." Obviously Mrs. X is putting forth her own version of reality in her final speech, although we do not know how close her version comes to the actual truth. Again, we cannot be sure of Miss Y's thoughts because she does not express them in words; nevertheless, she can be said to work at influencing Mrs. X's version of reality by making strategic use of silence.

I realize that the claim I am making does not solve every problem you might have with the play as you prepare to perform it. Frankly, I am not sure who *is* the stronger actress. I suspect that Strindberg is being deliberately ambiguous; he wants the performers to act in a way that will let each member of the audience arrive at his or her own opinion. Still, if you accept my claim, each of you will think of yourself as playing the part of an actress who is trying to shape the other woman's sense of reality.

Writing about Essays

Many readers do not realize that nonfiction is a literary genre. They believe that writing about information and facts, science and technology, history and biography, memories and arguments is far different from writing traditional literary works such as sonnets, short stories, and plays. But what counts as literature is often more a matter of tradition and perspective than a matter of content, language, or merit. Many contemporary critics have noticed that definitions of literature are quite subjective, even arbitrary. We are told that literature must move us emotionally; it must contain imaginative, extraordinary language; it must deal with profound, timeless, and universal themes. If these claims are true of poems, stories, and plays, they might also be true of essays, autobiographies, memoirs, speeches, and historical writing.

Essays demand as much of a reader's attention as fiction, drama, and poetry do. They also demand a reader's active participation. And as with more conventional literature, the intellectual, emotional, and aesthetic rewards of attentively reading essays are significant.

Writing about essays in college is best done as a process that begins with careful reading and a first response and ends with editing and proofreading. Author Henry David Thoreau once noted that books should be read with the same care and deliberation with which they were written. This is as true for essays as it is for complex modern poetry. Few people, even professionals, can read a text and write cogently about it the first time. Writing well about essays — actively participating in a cycle of reading, reflecting, and writing — takes as much energy and discipline as writing about other genres. And the results are always worth it.

The essay presented here deals with women and work — more specifically, with the struggles of gifted African American women in a context of poverty and oppression. "Many Rivers to Cross" by June Jordan (1936–2002) was the keynote address at a 1981 conference on "Women and Work" held at Barnard College in New York City. In the speech, Jordan recalls the suicide of her mother fifteen years earlier. Her essay uses an autobiographical narrative as evidence for her argument about the necessity for women to be strong. In this sense, the essay is inductive as it moves from specifics to a generalization rather than the more typical deductive approach, which begins with a claim that is then supported. What are the advantages and disadvantages of Jordan's structure?

JUNE JORDAN

Many Rivers to Cross

When my mother killed herself I was looking for a job. That was fifteen years ago. I had no money and no food. On the pleasure side I was down to my last pack of Pall Malls plus half a bottle of J and B. I needed to find work because I needed to be able fully to support myself and my eight-year-old son, very fast. My plan was to raise enough big bucks so that I could take an okay apartment inside an acceptable public school district, by September. That deadline left me less than three months to turn my fortunes right side up.

It seemed that I had everything to do at once. Somehow, I must move all of our things, mostly books and toys, out of the housing project before the rent fell due, again. I must do this without letting my neighbors know because destitution and divorce added up to personal shame, and failure. Those same neighbors had looked upon my husband and me as an ideal young couple, in many ways: inseparable, doting, ambitious. They had kept me busy and laughing in the hard weeks following my husband's departure for graduate school in Chicago; they had been the ones to remember him warmly through teasing remarks and questions all that long year that I remained alone, waiting for his return while I became the "temporary," sole breadwinner of our peculiar long-distance family by telephone. They had been the ones who kindly stopped the teasing and the queries when the year ended and my husband, the father of my child, did not come back. They never asked me and I never told them what that meant, altogether. I don't think I really knew.

I could see how my husband would proceed more or less naturally from graduate school to a professional occupation of his choice, just as he had shifted rather easily from me, his wife, to another man's wife—another woman. What I could not see was how I should go forward, now, in any natural, coherent way. As a mother without a husband, as a poet without a publisher, a freelance journalist without assignment, a city planner without a contract, it seemed to me that several incontestable and conflicting necessities had suddenly eliminated the whole realm of choice from my life.

My husband and I agreed that he would have the divorce that he wanted, and I would have the child. This ordinary settlement is, as millions of women will testify, as absurd as saying, "I'll give you a call, you handle everything else." At any rate, as my lawyer explained, the law then was the same as the law today; the courts would surely award me a reasonable amount of the father's income as child support, but the courts would also insist that they could not enforce their own decree. In other words, according to the law, what a father owes to his child is not serious compared to what a man owes to the bank for a car, or a vacation. Hence, as they say, it is extremely regrettable but nonetheless true that the courts cannot garnish a father's salary, nor freeze his account, nor seize his property on behalf of his children, in our society. Apparently this is because a child is not a car or a couch or a boat. (I would suppose this is the very best available definition of the difference between an American child and a car.)

Anyway, I wanted to get out of the projects as quickly as possible. But I was going to need help because I couldn't bend down and I couldn't carry anything heavy and I couldn't let my parents know about these problems because I didn't want to fight with them about the reasons behind the problems—which was the same reason I couldn't walk around or sit up straight to read or write without vomiting and acute abdominal pain. My parents would have evaluated that reason as a terrible secret compounded by a terrible crime; once again an unmarried woman, I had, nevertheless, become pregnant. What's more I had tried to interrupt this pregnancy even though this particular effort required not only one but a total of three abortions—each of them illegal and amazingly expensive, as well as, evidently, somewhat poorly executed.

My mother, against my father's furious rejections of me and what he viewed as my failure, offered what she could; she had no money herself but there was space in the old brownstone of my childhood. I would live with them during the summer while I pursued my crash schedule for cash, and she would spend as much time with Christopher, her only and beloved grandchild, as her worsening but partially undiagnosed illness allowed.

After she suffered a stroke, her serenely imposing figure had shrunk into an unevenly balanced, starved shell of chronic disorder. In the last two years, her physical condition had forced her retirement from nursing, and she spent most of her days on a makeshift cot pushed against the wall of the dining room next to the kitchen. She could do very few things for herself, besides snack on crackers, or pour ready-made juice into a cup and then drink it.

In June, 1966, I moved from the projects into my parents' house with the help of a woman named Mrs. Hazel Griffin. Since my teens, she had been my hairdresser. Every day, all day, she stood on her feet, washing and straightening hair in her crowded shop, the Arch of Beauty. Mrs. Griffin had never been married, had never finished high school, and she ran the Arch of Beauty with an imperturbable and contagious sense of success. She had a daughter as old as I who worked alongside her mother, coddling customer fantasy into confidence. Gradually, Mrs. Griffin and I became close; as my own mother became more and more bedridden and demoralized, Mrs. Griffin extended herself—dropping by my parents' house to make dinner for them, or calling me to wish me good luck on a special freelance venture, and so forth. It was Mrs. Griffin who closed her shop for a whole day and drove all the way from Brooklyn to my housing project apartment in Queens. It was Mrs. Griffin who packed me up, so to speak, and carried me and the boxes back to Brooklyn, back to the house of my parents. It was Mrs. Griffin who ignored my father standing hateful at the top of the stone steps of the house and not saying a word of thanks and not once relieving her of a single load she wrestled up the stairs and past him. My father hated Mrs. Griffin because he was proud and because she was a stranger of mercy. My father hated Mrs. Griffin because he was like that sometimes: hateful and crazy.

My father alternated between weeping bouts of self-pity and storm explosions of wrath against the gods apparently determined to ruin him. These were his alternating reactions to my mother's increasing enfeeblement, her stoic depression. I think he was scared; who would take care of him? Would she get well again and make everything all right again?

This is how we organized the brownstone; I fixed a room for my son on the top floor of the house. I slept on the parlor floor in the front room. My father slept on the same floor, in the back. My mother stayed downstairs.

About a week after moving in, my mother asked me about the progress of my plans. I told her things were not terrific but that there were two different planning jobs I hoped to secure within a few days. One of them involved a study of new towns in Sweden and the other one involved an analysis of the social consequences of a huge hydro-electric dam under construction in Ghana. My mother stared at me uncomprehendingly and then urged me to look for work in the local post office. We bitterly argued about what she dismissed as my "high-falutin" ideas and, I believe, that was the last substantial conversation between us.

From my first memory of him, my father had always worked at the post office. His favorite was the night shift, which brought him home usually between three and four o'clock in the morning.

It was hot. I finally fell asleep that night, a few nights after the argument between my mother and myself. She seemed to be rallying; that afternoon, she and my son had spent a long time in the backyard, oblivious to the heat and the mosquitoes. They were both tired but peaceful when they noisily re-entered the house, holding hands awkwardly.

But someone was knocking at the door to my room. Why should I wake up? It would be impossible to fall asleep again. It was so hot. The knocking continued. I switched on the light by the bed: 3:30 A.M. It must be my father. Furious, I pulled on a pair of shorts and a t-shirt. "What do you want? What's the matter?" I asked him, through the door. Had he gone berserk? What could he have to talk about at that ridiculous hour?

"OK, all right," I said, rubbing my eyes awake as I stepped to the door and opened it. "What?"

To my surprise, my father stood there looking very uncertain.

"It's your mother," he told me, in a burly, formal voice. "I think she's dead, but I'm not sure." He was avoiding my eyes.

"What do you mean," I answered.

"I want you to go downstairs and figure it out."

I could not believe what he was saying to me. "You want me to figure out if my mother is dead or alive?"

"I can't tell! I don't know!!" he shouted angrily.

"Jesus Christ," I muttered, angry and beside myself.

I turned and glanced about my room, wondering if I could find anything to carry with me on this mission; what do you use to determine a life or a death? I couldn't see anything obvious that might be useful.

"I'll wait up here," my father said. "You call up and let me know."

I could not believe it; a man married to a woman more than forty years and he can't tell if she's alive or dead and he wakes up his kid and tells her, "You figure it out."   25

I was at the bottom of the stairs. I halted just outside the dining room where my mother slept. Suppose she really was dead? Suppose my father was not just being crazy and hateful? "Naw," I shook my head and confidently entered the room.

"Momma?!" I called, aloud. At the edge of the cot, my mother was leaning forward, one arm braced to hoist her body up. She was trying to stand up! I rushed over. "Wait. Here, I'll help you!" I said.

And I reached out my hands to give her a lift. The body of my mother was stiff. She was not yet cold, but she was stiff. Maybe I had come downstairs just in time! I tried to loosen her arms, to change her position, to ease her into lying down.

"Momma!" I kept saying. "Momma, listen to me! It's OK! I'm here and everything. Just relax. Relax! Give me a hand, now. I'm trying to help you lie down!"

Her body did not relax. She did not answer me. But she was not cold. Her eyes were not shut.   30

From upstairs my father was yelling, "Is she dead? Is she dead?"

"No!" I screamed at him. "No! She's not dead!"

At this, my father tore down the stairs and into the room. Then he braked. "Milly?" he called out, tentative. Then he shouted at me and banged around the walls. "You damn fool. Don't you see now she's gone. Now she's gone!" We began to argue.

"She's alive! Call the doctor!"   35

"No!"

"Yes!"

At last my father left the room to call the doctor.

I straightened up. I felt completely exhausted from trying to gain a response from my mother. There she was, stiff on the edge of her bed, just about to stand up. Her lips were set, determined. She would manage it, but by herself. I could not help. Her eyes fixed on some point below the floor.

"Momma!" I shook her hard as I could to rouse her into focus. Now she fell   40
back on the cot, but frozen and in the wrong position. It hit me that she might be dead. She might be dead.

My father reappeared at the door. He would not come any closer. "Dr. Davis says he will come. And he call the police."

The police? Would they know if my mother was dead or alive? Who would know?

I went to the phone and called my aunt. "Come quick," I said. "My father thinks Momma has died but she's here but she's stiff."

Soon the house was weird and ugly and crowded and I thought I was losing my mind.

Three white policemen stood around telling me my mother was dead. 45 "How do you know?" I asked, and they shrugged and then they repeated themselves. And the doctor never came. But my aunt came and my uncle and they said she was dead.

After a conference with the cops, my aunt disappeared and when she came back she held a bottle in one of her hands. She and the police whispered together some more. Then one of the cops said, "Don't worry about it. We won't say anything." My aunt signalled me to follow her into the hallway where she let me understand that, in fact, my mother had committed suicide.

I could not assimilate this information: suicide.

I broke away from my aunt and ran to the telephone. I called a friend of mine, a woman who talked back loud to me so that I could realize my growing hysteria, and check it. Then I called my cousin Valerie who lived in Harlem; she woke up instantly and urged me to come right away.

I hurried to the top floor and stood my sleeping son on his feet. I wanted to get him out of this house of death more than I ever wanted anything. He could not stand by himself so I carried him down the two flights to the street and laid him on the backseat and then took off.

At Valerie's, my son continued to sleep, so we put him to bed, closed the 50 door, and talked. My cousin made me eat eggs, drink whiskey, and shower. She would take care of Christopher, she said. I should go back and deal with the situation in Brooklyn.

When I arrived, the house was absolutely full of women from the church dressed as though they were going to Sunday communion. It seemed to me they were, every one of them, wearing hats and gloves and drinking coffee and solemnly addressing invitations to a funeral and I could not find my mother anywhere and I could not find an empty spot in the house where I could sit down and smoke a cigarette.

My mother was dead.

Feeling completely out of place, I headed for the front door, ready to leave. My father grabbed my shoulder from behind and forcibly spun me around.

"You see this?" he smiled, waving a large document in the air. "This am insurance paper for you!" He waved it into my face. "Your mother, she left you insurance, see?"

I watched him. 55

"But I gwine burn it in the furnace before I give it you to t'row away on trash!"

"Is that money?" I demanded. "Did my mother leave me money?"

"Eh-heh!" he laughed. "And you don't get it from me. Not today, not tomorrow. Not until I dead and buried!"

My father grabbed for my arm and I swung away from him. He hit me on my head and I hit back. We were fighting.

Suddenly, the ladies from the church bustled about and pushed, horrified, 60 between us. This was a sin, they said, for a father and a child to fight in the house of the dead and the mother not yet in the ground! Such a good woman she was, they said. She was a good woman, a good woman, they all agreed. Out of respect for the memory of this good woman, in deference to my mother who had committed suicide, the ladies shook their hats and insisted we should not fight; I should not fight with my father.

Utterly disgusted and disoriented, I went back to Harlem. By the time I reached my cousin's place I had begun to bleed, heavily. Valerie said I was hemorrhaging so she called up her boyfriend and the two of them hobbled me into Harlem Hospital.

I don't know how long I remained unconscious, but when I opened my eyes I found myself on the women's ward, with an intravenous setup feeding into my arm. After a while, Valerie showed up. Christopher was fine, she told me; my friends were taking turns with him. Whatever I did, I should not admit I'd had an abortion or I'd get her into trouble, and myself in trouble. Just play dumb and rest. I'd have to stay on the ward for several days. My mother's funeral was tomorrow afternoon. What did I want her to tell people to explain why I wouldn't be there? She meant, what lie?

I thought about it and I decided I had nothing to say; if I couldn't tell the truth then the hell with it.

I lay in that bed at Harlem Hospital, thinking and sleeping. I wanted to get well.

I wanted to be strong. I never wanted to be weak again as long as I lived. I   65
thought about my mother and her suicide and I thought about how my father could not tell whether she was dead or alive.

I wanted to get well and what I wanted to do as soon as I was strong again, actually, what I wanted to do was I wanted to live my life so that people would know unmistakably that I am alive, so that when I finally die people will know the difference for sure between my living and my death.

And I thought about the idea of my mother as a good woman and I rejected that, because I don't see why it's a good thing when you give up, or when you cooperate with those who hate you or when you polish and iron and mend and endlessly mollify for the sake of the people who love the way that you kill yourself day by day silently.

And I think all of this is really about women and work. Certainly this is all about me as a woman and my life work. I mean I am not sure my mother's suicide was something extraordinary. Perhaps most women must deal with a similar inheritance, the legacy of a woman whose death you cannot possibly pinpoint because she died so many, many times and because, even before she became your mother, the life of that woman was taken; I say it was taken away.

And really it was to honor my mother that I did fight with my father, that man who could not tell the living from the dead.

And really it is to honor Mrs. Hazel Griffin and my cousin Valerie and   70
all the women I love, including myself, that I am working for the courage to admit the truth that Bertolt Brecht has written; he says, "It takes courage to say that the good were defeated not because they were good, but because they were weak."

I cherish the mercy and the grace of women's work. But I know there is new work that we must undertake as well: that new work will make defeat detestable to us. That new women's work will mean we will not die trying to stand up: we will live that way: standing up.

I came too late to help my mother to her feet.

By way of everlasting thanks to all of the women who have helped me to stay alive I am working never to be late again. *[1985]*

A Student's Personal Response to the Essay

Isla Bravo wrote in her journal:

> It was shocking to read about Jordan's mother's suicide in the first sentence of "Many Rivers to Cross." I expected the rest of the essay to be about only that one event, but she went on to talk about everything else that was going on in her life around that time first. It is hard to understand how she managed everything in her life. She is out of money and needs to find a way to improve her financial status in just three months. My family may not have everything we've ever wanted, but we've always done pretty well, and I never worried about where we lived.
>
> Even though I have never had to struggle the way Jordan did, I can relate to her descriptions of her friends and neighbors. They all help her out the best they can when her husband leaves her and then when her mother dies. These are the people that she really appreciates in her life. They are the same kind of people that brought food to my parents when my grandmother died. These are the people that she loves, and she creates her own sort of family despite the fact that her father is so mean to her. These are people with whom she creates relationships that aren't defined by specific standards created by society.
>
> When Jordan says that her mother's death may not be extraordinary, that maybe every woman watches someone die over and over, she is really talking about all the little things that can wear a lot of women down and cause their deaths a long time before they actually die. She can't even tell that her mother is dead because she's been wearing down for so long. The image of her mother looking as if she was "just about to stand up" made me think of my grandmother's funeral and how she looked like she was sleeping rather than dead. For Jordan the image of her mother in that sort of paralysis is also an image of her possible future. It is strange to think of someone whose life has been so hard on them that their death doesn't create a jarring difference.
>
> Jordan seems to be trying to keep herself from wearing down just like her mother at the end. Women are given roles by society that prevent them from being able to really enjoy their lives. She

uses her other friends and family as models for how to survive. She has a friend who calms her down on the phone, a cousin that gives her advice in the hospital, and more that take care of her son when she can't. Mrs. Griffin is a good example of the type of person she wants to be. She has to work hard to avoid becoming her mother. It seems as if she is motivated by guilt because she wasn't able to help her mother when she says, "I came too late to help my mother to her feet." Even though it wasn't her fault that her mother put up with so much, it certainly makes her determined to prevent her life from ending up the same way her mother's did.

The Elements of Essays

First impressions are valuable, but writing intelligently about essays should not be completely spontaneous. We can be personal and insightful, but persuading others about the validity of our reading takes a more focused and textually informed presentation. The following discussion of the basic elements of the essay is meant to increase your ability to analyze and write about essays. The elements include voice, style, structure, and ideas.

VOICE

When we read the first few sentences of an essay, we usually hear the narrator's **voice**: we hear a person speaking to us, and we begin to notice if he or she sounds friendly or hostile, stuffy or casual, self-assured or tentative. The voice might be austere and technical or personal and flamboyant. The voice may be intimate or remote. It may be sincere, hectoring, hysterical, meditative, or ironic. The possibilities are endless.

We usually get a sense of the writer's voice from the **tone** the writer projects. In the first paragraph of Jordan's essay, we get a sense of the speaker's voice through the direct and forthright tone that she takes, beginning with the disturbing assertion that her mother killed herself and that she herself was destitute. She is also not afraid to admit that her cigarettes and scotch were running low and informal enough to use "big bucks" and "okay" (para. 1). This is not someone who will be putting on airs or who will skirt the bare-bones truth of her situation, however unflattering or unpleasant.

Given the situation she describes, it is not surprising that Jordan's tone would occasionally be sarcastic and ironic, as when she describes the "difference between an American child and a car" (para. 4) and her abortions as "somewhat poorly executed" (para. 5).

Jordan's concerned and bewildered voice over the death of her mother and the revelation of her suicide turns to anger and outrage over the insensitive and selfish response of her father. And then while recovering in the hospital, Jordan's voice and tone shift drastically with "I wanted to be strong" (para. 65). She is now assertive, confident, and committed. Rejecting any sentimental thoughts of her deceased mother, she is determined not to be as weak as her mother. And so she boldly promises that she is now committed to the "new work that we must undertake" (para. 71). This new work, she asserts in a voice brimming with hope and determination, means that she will live "standing up" (para. 71).

When we speak of a writer's persona, we mean a kind of performance mask or stance the writer assumes. Writers are trying to construct a persona that will serve their purposes. Voice and tone are techniques that help writers create an appropriate persona.

STYLE

We all have stylish friends. They look good. Their shoes and pants and shirts seem to complement each other perfectly. It's not that they are color-coordinated—that would be too obvious for them—it's something more subtle. They seem to make just the right choices. When they go to a party, to the movies, or to school, they have a personal style that is their own.

Writers also have **style**. They make specific choices in words, in syntax and sentence length, in diction, in metaphors, even in sentence beginnings and endings. Writers use parallelism, balance, formal diction, poetic language, even sentence fragments to create their own styles.

Jordan's first three dramatic sentences are a good example of how she adapts her style to the content. Here she uses short, direct sentences to announce her predicament, but then her sentences get longer and more complex. Notice in the second paragraph her cumulative sentence ("Those same neighbors . . ."). In this pattern, writers make a statement and then add modifiers after a colon or a comma that can be words (as in this case) or long phrases. Notice the next long, compound sentence. She then ends the paragraph with a short simple assertion. Skilled writers like Jordan vary their sentence length and type as well as the imaginative ways they begin their sentences. Notice, for example, the different ways Jordan begins her paragraphs. Also notice the way Jordan crafts transitions between paragraphs, sometimes with a simple word ("Anyway" in para. 5), or a pronoun ("This" in para. 10), or a conjunction ("And" in paras. 67–70), or a phrase ("About . . ." in para. 11).

STRUCTURE

The way essayists put their work together is not mysterious. The best writers create a **structure** to fit their needs. Most do not have a prearranged structure in mind or feel the need to obey the composition rules many students think they have to follow: topic sentence first and three examples following. Writers of essays aren't inclined to follow formulas. Essayists begin and end as they see fit; they give explicit topic sentences or create narratives that imply themes; they begin with an assertion and support it, or vice versa. Essayists are inventors of structures that fit the occasion and their own way of seeing the world. The thought of the essay significantly influences its structure. Like the relationship between mind and body, form and thought are inseparable.

Jordan's plan, of course, is to begin her argument with a detailed autobiographical narrative focused on her mother's suicide. After setting the scene with her husband abandoning her and the necessity to move into her childhood home, Jordan focuses on the relationship between her egregious bullying father and her weak mother. And then, after detailing in excruciating detail the night of her mother's death, Jordan begins the generalizations that are at the heart of her argument, which is, essentially: my mother was weak and that cost her her life, and I'm not going to let that happen to me.

IDEAS

All writers have something on their minds when they write. That seems especially true when writers decide to put their **ideas** into a nonfictional form such as the essay. Of course, lots of ideas fill poems and short stories too, but they are usually expressed more indirectly. Although essays seem more idea-driven, this does not mean that as readers we have a responsibility to extract the precise idea or argument the writer had in mind. That may not even be possible since in the creative process of all writing, ideas get modified or changed. Sometimes a writer's original intention is significantly transformed; sometimes writers are not fully conscious of all their hidden intentions. Regardless, readers of essays are not simply miners unearthing hidden meanings; they are more like coproducers. And in creating that meaning, ideas are central.

Of course, Jordan has been developing ideas from the very beginning of her essay. It seems as if she becomes more focused on ideas per se when her narrative concludes at the hospital, but her comments about her husband starting in paragraph 2 clearly develop the idea that choice has been systematically eliminated from her life, and by implication the lives of all working-class women. Paragraph 4 also focuses on the unfairness of the courts and their favorable bias toward men. But the primary emphasis on ideas happens with "I wanted to be strong" in paragraph 65, with Jordan's manifesto-like assertion in the same paragraph that she was never going to "be weak again as long as I lived." Interestingly, she cites the fight with her father, who could not tell the difference between the living and the dead, as a metaphor for the larger fight of all women to assert that a change is coming in the lives of women, that new women will live "standing up" (para. 71). And Jordan's concluding idea in the last sentence announces a new solidarity, a new community of women who will help each other be independent. And now, some thirty years later, Jordan's ideas have proven to be prescient.

Final Draft of a Student Paper

After writing journal entries and a freewrite, Isla planned her essay and then wrote a draft. She used responses from several students in a small-group workshop and from her instructor to help her revise her essay, sharpening her focus and supporting her claims more explicitly. Here is Isla's final version.

Isla Bravo
Ms. Hollingsworth
English 201
21 April - - - -

Resisting Women's Roles

June Jordan takes a strongly feminist stance against the
roles women are forced to contend with in her essay "Many
Rivers to Cross." She begins the essay from her experience as
a woman who has conformed to the social expectations of a
wife, daughter, and mother. Her commitment to these roles
has left her as a single mother who is contending with an unwanted pregnancy, forced to care for a dying mother and a
belligerent father, and without a place of her own to live or
work. This essay supports my argument that women need to *Clear, explicit claim with her*
establish their independence and not allow society to control *plan to support.*
their lives. This argument is substantiated by Jordan's exploration of her own defiance of society's conventions regarding
the roles for women as wife, daughter, and mother in an attempt to preserve herself from the restrictions that destroyed
her mother.

Women are expected by society to place their families *Gives concrete examples of*
before their careers, and part of this sacrifice includes aiding *negative consequences of*
their husband's careers in lieu of their own. Jordan portrays *following convention.*
herself as an example of how this convention is detrimental
to a woman's ability to survive on her own. Jordan sacrifices
her own professional ambition to her husband's pursuit of his
career. The ensuing complications depict the limitations and
perils of the idea that women must always place their own careers behind their husbands. Rather than specifically condemn
this social expectation, she provides an illustration of the destruction it can cause. Her own career is a secondary priority,
subjugated to her roles as a supportive wife and mother, while
her husband pursues graduate school in another city and has
an affair with another man's wife. Jordan squanders a year
of her life waiting for her husband's return and becomes "a
mother without a husband, . . . a poet without a publisher, a
freelance journalist without assignment, a city planner with-
out a contract" (179). She abides by the social conventions *Qualifies her objections.*
that insist she support her husband, and her life remains in
stasis until he steps out of his own commitments. By living
her life under the social guidelines for a wife, she allows herself to be exploited for her husband's convenience. Her needs
are supplanted by her husband's, and his abandonment leaves
her embarrassed and destitute.

Jordan's depiction of her parents' relationship illustrates *Another concrete example*
the generational quality of these social conventions. Her *supporting need for*
independence.

parents' relationship foreshadows the potential outcome of her
marriage if it continues. Her parents' relationship is wholly restricted to the typical gender roles they both inherit from society. Her mother subjugates her own life only to the needs of
her husband, a sacrifice he expects from her. This historical
relationship becomes clear when Jordan describes her father's
response to her mother's fatal illness when she says, "I think
he was scared; who would take care of him? Would she get
well again and make everything all right again?" (181). The
fact that his concern was about his own life — "who would
take care of him?" — makes it clear that their relationship re-
volved around only his own comfort. Jordan is desperate to
prevent her own life from following this path.

Concludes paragraph with reference to claim.

Jordan's relationship with her father explores another aspect of the expectations placed on women by society, that of
a daughter. Jordan's father's reliance on her mother for all of
his comfort turns onto Jordan when her mother is no longer
able to fulfill these duties. Jordan's role as his daughter, her
most important function, is dynamically portrayed when her
father forces her to check her mother's body to see if she is
alive because he is incapable or unwilling to do it himself.
He says to her, "I'll wait up here. . . . You call up and let me
know" (182), only to yell at her inaccurate determination. His
anger appears to stem more from the disruption to his own
life rather than from the loss of his wife; he is angry rather
than sad. He appears almost offended by her death and his
daughter's failure to provide him with the level of comfort he
craves for his life. His own expectations for the superior role
in the household have been created by a male-dominated society and have been enforced by the manner in which his wife
seems to have fulfilled those expectations as well. The role of
a dutiful child is not by itself destructive until it begins to
take precedence in this destructive manner. His expectation is
that Jordan should take on the role of caregiver, waiting on
him despite any reluctance on her part and regardless of the
animosity that exists between them.

Another concrete example of societal expectations.

Qualifies her objections before reinforcing objections to harmful social convention.

Jordan also defies social conventions by her unwillingness
to become a mother again to the new baby she's carrying. She
attempts to abort the child several times until she finally
does lose the baby. Jordan describes the advice she receives
from a friend in the hospital: "Whatever I did, I should not
admit I'd had an abortion or I'd get her into trouble, and myself in trouble" (184). The possibility that Jordan does not
want to be a mother to another child is abhorrent to the social standards that have formed her life and surroundings.
Motherhood is the expected career for a woman, and her

Another concrete example supporting her claim.

choice to not have another baby is a direct rejection of those standards.

As a woman in this particular culture, she has certain designated assignments of work that include being a daughter, wife, and mother. She rejects a caretaker role for her father, her marriage has dissolved, and she has an abortion. These portrayals do not suggest a rejection of these roles in their entirety; rather, they explicitly show how they can become harmful if they force women into situations they might have avoided if not for these societal pressures. From this point, she is able to look toward her own career and her own needs. The role society imposes on her as a woman puts her in a position that deemphasizes her own ambitions and preferences. The end of her mother's life is the catalyst that forces her to fully recognize the restrictions that she has been living with and that her mother succumbed to until her death. Jordan says, "I came too late to help my mother to her feet. . . . I am working never to be late again" (185). She wants to free herself from the limiting standards for women in society and hopefully free other women to be independent and assertive.

Reviews her assigned roles and her objections.

Gives context for her defiance of social expectations.

Concludes by reinforcing and extending her claim to all women.

Works Cited

Jordan, June. "Many Rivers to Cross." Schilb and Clifford
     179–85.

Schilb, John, and John Clifford, eds. *Arguing about Literature:
     A Brief Guide*. Boston: Bedford, 2014. Print.

CHAPTER 6

Writing Researched Arguments

At the conclusion of this chapter, we discuss four specific kinds of research papers, in each case providing a sample student essay on Charlotte Perkins Gilman's short story "The Yellow Wallpaper." (See p. 228.) But first we explain in general the research process and how it can lead to successful writing. You may imagine that writing a research paper for your literature class is a significantly different, and perhaps more difficult, assignment than others you have had. Because more steps are involved in their writing (for example, additional reading and analysis of sources), research papers tend to be long-range projects. They also tend to be more formal than other kinds of papers because they involve integrating and documenting source material.

These differences, however, are essentially of magnitude and appearance, not of substance. Despite the common misconception (cause of much unnecessary anxiety) that writing a research paper requires a special set of knowledge and skills, it draws principally on the same kind of knowledge and skills needed to write other types of papers. You will still need to begin with an arguable **issue** and a **claim**, still need to marshal **evidence** to defend that claim, and still need to display a sound process of **reasoning**, so that your audience will think your claim has merit. The main difference between a researched argument and other types is that the evidence for it comes from a wider variety of sources.

The literary text you focus on is your **primary source**. The other materials you consult for your essay are your **secondary sources**. They may include historical documents along with present-day scholarship. These materials may consist as well of visual artifacts, such as photographs, films, and maps. You may even investigate music recordings or other types of sound. Whatever your sources, your essay will need to **synthesize** them. This means drawing connections between them, explaining how they harmonize or clash. It also means relating your secondary materials clearly to the literature you're analyzing. In a sense, synthesis involves putting the literature and these sources in "conversation" with one another, so your reader can tell how they all bear on your essay's main argument.

Identify an Issue and a Tentative Claim

Your first task in writing most researched arguments is to identify an issue that you genuinely want to think and learn more about. The more interested you are in your issue, the better your essay will be. But here, too, the word *conversation* may apply, for your issue may be a controversy that's come up in class discussions—some topic that you and other students don't agree on. If your essay will focus on literature, any of the types of issues described on pages 46–52 will suit. In any case, read carefully the literary work you choose as your springboard. If it's in this book, review the information we provide about its author; take a look at the questions or commentaries we include along with it. Then, ask questions of your own about it, trying to figure out what really interests you about the text. Don't settle for an issue or a question that you can easily answer with a few factual statements. Strive to come up with a subject that requires serious research.

Before you begin searching for sources, formulate a tentative claim. Consider it a hypothesis to test. Don't worry if it seems a little vague or obvious; you'll have many opportunities to refine it as your research proceeds. Even if you end up changing the claim, having one in mind at the start will help you manage your investigation. It will keep you from feeling overwhelmed by the multitude of sources available.

Search for Sources in the Library and Online

Once you have your topic in mind and have sketched a tentative claim, begin looking for research sources. Many different types of sources for literary research are available, and the types you will need will depend largely on the type of claim you choose to defend. If your issue is primarily one of interpretation—about the theme, patterns, or symbolism of the text, for instance—you will most likely need to consult literary criticism to see what has been said in the past about the literature you are discussing. If your issue concerns historical or cultural context, including issues of social policy, you may need to consult newspapers, magazines, and similar sorts of cultural documents. Some topics might require several different types of sources.

Not many years ago, for most people the word *research* was synonymous with hours spent in the library hunting for books and articles. For many students today, *research* has become synonymous with the Internet, which they turn to in the belief that everything is available online. But this is simply not true. Many of the best and most reliable sources are still available just in print. In particular, lots of potentially useful books haven't been digitized yet. They remain in your school library, so you'll have to go there if you hope to read them. The library may also house relevant documents and scholarly journals that aren't online. The library's computerized **catalog** will alert you to its holdings, helping you locate useful texts. Typically, the catalog entry for a book lists various subject headings for it. By clicking on a heading, you'll find other books on that topic. When you go to the library's shelves for a book, browse through neighboring volumes, for perhaps they also address your subject of study.

Of course, a wealth of information is available on the Internet. As with the library, your goal is to find useful information efficiently, evaluate it carefully, and employ it effectively in your paper. Unfortunately, and unlike a library's sources, information on the Internet is not indexed and organized to make it easily accessible to researchers. Many students go right away to Wikipedia, hoping to find most of their needed data there. Indeed, a Wikipedia entry may contain some useful facts. Nevertheless, you shouldn't accept on faith everything that the entry says. It's the product of anonymous people, many of whom may not really be experts on the subject they claim to know. Wikipedia can be a decent *starting* point for online searches, especially because it provides links to Web sites that may be more authoritative. But many teachers will object if you depend on Wikipedia itself as a source. Consider it a launch pad, not a destination.

You will need to do a certain amount of "surfing" if you are to find appropriate online materials for your project. A number of **search engines** (programs for finding information) are designed to help you track down materials on the Web. If you are an old hand on the Internet, probably you can depend on search engines that have served you well in the past. Bear in mind, however, that relying on just one search engine may not lead you to all the sources that would benefit you. Many students pursuing a research topic go immediately to Google. They type their subject into the box, click a mouse, and expect to see terrific sources pop right up on-screen. Yet often this search method proves exasperating. For one thing, it may suceed all *too* well in generating items. Our four sample researched arguments discuss "The Yellow Wallpaper"; a Google search using this title elicits around 628,000 results. The first paper also deals with postpartum depression; if you Google this term, you'll come up with roughly 3,820,000 results. Even if you combine "The Yellow Wallpaper" with "postpartum depression," you'll get roughly 6,110 results. It can take forever to sift through these avalanches for whatever gems they contain. Faced with such landslides, some writers just pounce on the first few results they obtain. But "first" doesn't necessarily mean "best." An ideal article may surface late in a Google list.

You can narrow your results by adding words to your search, making it more exact. Or, you might turn to Google Scholar, which sticks with academic texts. There, combining "The Yellow Wallpaper" with "postpartum depression" produces about 125 results. This is certainly a more manageable number. Still, Google addiction will limit you as a researcher. See what other Web sites can do for you. If your college or university makes available to you sites such as *JSTOR, Academic Search Premier,* and *Project Muse,* these will give you access to hundreds of scholarly journals and books. The Internet service *LexisNexis* offers current articles from newspapers and magazines, as well as transcripts of radio and TV broadcasts. For literary research, a great service is the *MLA International Bibliography.* Sponsored by the Modern Language Association and carried by many schools, it lists books and articles on a wide range of topics in literary criticism, history, and theory.

When you discover a book or article that fits with your research agenda, examine its bibliography. There, perhaps you'll find listed other texts useful to you. In general, scholars refer to previous works on their subject. They extend, challenge, or refine their predecessors' claims. Notice how they treat these prior views. You'll thereby get a sense of the "conversation" your topic has already stirred. You may also see how to join this "dialogue" with ideas of your own.

Evaluate the Sources

Whatever method you use to locate your research materials, remember that not all sources are created equal. Take care to **evaluate** those you come across. When tempted to use a writer's work, ask yourself the following: What do I want my audience to think about this person? Often, you'll hope your readers will accept him or her as some sort of authority. In a way, you have to think about **ethos**, a term we discussed in our first two chapters. There, you may recall, we defined *ethos* as the image that an author projects. Many writers try to be persuasive by constructing an admirable ethos—a version of themselves that will impress their readers. Similarly, when you incorporate sources into a researched argument, you will often want your audience to respect them. These sources may not agree with one another—heck, *you* may not agree with them all—but they'll need to have recognizable expertise. Otherwise, why should your readers pay attention to them?

Suppose you plan to write a research paper on "The Yellow Wallpaper." An online search leads you to an analysis of the story. You might refer to this study in your essay. But you need to determine whether the author is someone your readers would take seriously. You have to look for credentials. Perhaps the writer is a professor publishing in a scholarly journal. Maybe, like Paul Goldberger in Chapter 1, this person is an award-winning authority in a certain field (in this case, architecture). Another writer in the same chapter, David Barno, is a veteran military officer affiliated with a distinguished think tank. Sometimes you can learn writers' professional status by visiting the Web sites of institutions they work for. At any rate, be skeptical when a Web post's author is shrouded in mystery. The views expressed may be interesting, but if their advocate is a phantom, you can't expect your readers to care about them. Useful to bear in mind is the famous *New Yorker* magazine cartoon about the digital age. One canine, perched at a computer, tells another that "on the Internet, nobody knows you're a dog." In short, the Web can fool you. Although someone posting on it is probably human, hunt for details of the person's background. Your audience will expect you to have this information about a source, even if you don't include every bit of it in your paper.

A teacher may require a number of your sources to be articles from "peer-reviewed" academic journals. Such journals publish a manuscript only after it has been evaluated by experts in its subject. Usually, a journal's Web site will indicate whether it falls into this category. Some search engines have a feature that, when you activate it, confines your results to peer-reviewed works. For example, both *Academic Search Premier* and the *MLA International Bibliography* enable you to restrict your search this way. Most books published by academic and unversity presses have also been peer reviewed. Of course, even when it doesn't come with this label, a book or an article may still be worth consulting. In many popular newspapers (such as the *New York Times* and the *Washington Post*) and magazines (such as *The New Yorker* and the *Atlantic*), you'll find thoughtful, well-grounded reports and opinion pieces.

In general, you should ask the following basic questions of your sources: (1) Is the information recent, and if not, is the validity of the information likely to have changed significantly over time? (2) How credible is the author? Is he or she a recognized expert on the subject? (3) Is the source published by an established, respectable press, or does it appear in a well-respected journal or periodical (the *Los Angeles Times* has more credibility than the *National Enquirer*, for example) or Web site (one supported by a university or library, for instance)? (4) Based on what you've learned about responsible argument, do the arguments in your source seem sound, fair, and thoughtful? Is the evidence convincing? Is the development of the argument logical?

You increase your own credibility with your audience by using the most reliable research materials available to you, so do not just stick with whatever comes to hand if you have the opportunity to find a stronger source.

Strategies for Working with Sources

Once you have identified a number of sources for your paper and tracked down the books, periodicals, or other materials, it is time to begin reading, analyzing, and taking notes. At this point, it is especially important to keep yourself well organized and to write down *everything* that may be of use to you later. No matter how good your memory, do not count on remembering a few days (or even hours) later which notes or quotations come from which sources. Scrupulously write down page numbers and Web addresses, and double-check facts and spellings. Some researchers find it useful to record this information on a stack of note cards, with one entry per card. Many others prefer to do their recording on a computer file. Whatever your method, you will need this information for your paper's bibliography, called **Works Cited**.

Many researchers find it easier to stay organized if they divide the notes they take into three basic categories: summaries, paraphrases, and quotations. (A fourth category is notes of your own ideas, prompted by your research. Write these down as well, keeping them separate and clearly labeled, as you would any other notes.)

Student researchers often rely too heavily on **quotations**, copying verbatim large sections from their research sources. Do not make this mistake. Instead, start your note-taking with a **summary** of the source in question—just one or two sentences indicating in your own words the author's main point. Such summaries guarantee that you understand the gist of an author's argument and (since they are your own words) can readily be incorporated in your paper. You might think of a summary as a restatement of the author's principal claim, perhaps with a brief indication of the types of supporting evidence he or she marshals. You can also write summaries of supporting points—subsections of an author's argument—if they seem applicable to your paper. A summary should not, however, include quotations, exhaustive detail about subpoints, or a list of all the evidence in a given source. A summary is meant to provide a succinct overview—to demonstrate that you have grasped a point and can convey it to your readers.

Chances are you will want to take more specific notes as well, ones that **paraphrase** the most germane passages in a particular source. Unlike a summary, a paraphrase does not condense an argument or leave out supporting evidence; instead it puts the information into new words. A paraphrase is generally no shorter than the material being paraphrased, but it still has two advantages over a quotation. First, as with a summary, an accurate paraphrase proves that you understand the material you've read. Second, again as with a summary, a paraphrase is easier to integrate into your paper than a quotation, since it is already written in your own words and style. When you include a paraphrase in your notes, indicate on the note the page numbers in the original source.

The rule of thumb about summarizing or paraphrasing is that you must always clearly indicate which ideas are yours and which are those of others. It is **plagiarism**—a serious violation of academic standards—to accept credit for another's ideas, even if you put them in your own words. Ideas in your paper that are not attributed to a source will be assumed to be your own, so to avoid plagiarism it is important to leave no doubt in your reader's mind about when you are summarizing or paraphrasing. Always cite the source.

To see better what we mean, look first at the following sentence, which is about the heroine of Charlotte Perkins Gilman's short story "The Yellow Wallpaper." The sentence comes from page 523 of Greg Johnson's article "Gilman's Gothic Allegory: Rage and Redemption in 'The Yellow Wallpaper,'" published in a 1989 issue of the journal *Studies in Short Fiction*. Many readers of Gilman's story believe that its ending is negative. They think the protagonist goes completely mad, to her terrible misfortune. Johnson, however, disagrees:

> Her experience should finally be viewed not as a final catastrophe but as a terrifying, necessary stage in her progress toward self-identity and personal achievement.

Imagine that you are writing a paper on Gilman's story and that you want to express your approval of Johnson's view. You might quote at least part of his statement and give him credit for it:

> A more useful way to interpret the ending is to regard it optimistically, as Greg Johnson does when he says that although the heroine's behavior is "terrifying," it is also a "necessary stage in her progress toward self-identity and personal achievement" (523).

Alternatively, you can paraphrase Johnson's claim, acknowledging that he is the source of it and noting the page where it appears:

> Greg Johnson points out helpfully that at the end of the story, the heroine may seem doomed but actually is not, for she has to engage in such frightening behavior if she is eventually to become a ful-filled, accomplished individual (523).

You would be committing plagiarism, however, if you presented Johnson's claim as your own. This would be the case if you reproduced his exact statement without admitting that it's his. But you would also be plagiarizing if you paraphrased his idea without noting it's his:

> At the end of the story, the heroine may seem doomed but actually is not, for she has to engage in such frightening behavior if she is eventually to become a fulfilled, accomplished individual.

What *does not* need to be referenced is **common knowledge**: factual information that the average reader can be expected to know or that is readily available in many easily accessible sources. For example, it is common knowledge that Charlotte Perkins Gilman was an American writer. It is also common knowledge that she was born in 1860 and died in 1935, even though most people would have to look that information up in an encyclopedia or a biographical dictionary to verify it.

Of course, during your process of research, you will sometimes want to copy quotations directly from a source. Do so sparingly, copying quotations only when the author's own words are especially succinct and pertinent. When you write down a quotation, enclose it in quotation marks, and record the *exact* wording, right down to the punctuation. As with a paraphrase, make note of the original page numbers for the quotation, as you will need to indicate this in your final paper.

Each time you take a note, be it summary, paraphrase, or quotation, take a moment to think about why you wrote it down. Why is this particular note from this source important? Write a brief commentary about the note's importance, maybe just a sentence or a few words, perhaps on the back of a note card (if you are using note cards). When the time comes to draft your paper, such commentaries will help you remember why you bothered to take the note and may restart your train of thought if it gets stuck.

And do not forget: If something you read in a source sparks an original idea, write it down and label it clearly as your own. Keep these notes with your notes from the primary and secondary sources. Without your own ideas, your paper will be little more than a report, a record of what others have said. Your ideas will provide the framework for an argument that is your own.

Strategies for Integrating Sources

With your research completed (at least for the moment), it is time to get down to drafting the paper. At this point, many students find themselves overwhelmed with information and wonder if they are really in any better shape to begin writing than they were before starting their research. But having read and thought about a number of authors' ideas and arguments, you are almost certainly more prepared to construct an argument of your own. You can, of course, use any method that has worked for you in the past to devise a first draft of your paper. If you are having trouble getting started, though, you might look to Chapters 4 and 5 of this book, which discuss general strategies for exploring, planning, and drafting papers as well as more specific ideas for working with individual literary genres.

Start by revisiting your tentative claim. Refine it to take into account what you have learned during your research. With your revised and refined claim at hand, examine your assembled notes, and try to subdivide them into groups of related ideas, each of which can form a single section of your paper or even a single piece of supporting evidence for your claim. You can then arrange the groups of notes according to a logical developmental pattern — for example, from cause to effect or from weakest to strongest evidence — which may provide a structure for the body of your essay. As you write, avoid using your own comments as a kind of glue to hold together other people's ideas. Instead, you are constructing an argument of your own, using secondary sources to support your own structure of claims and evidence.

Anytime you summarize, paraphrase, or quote another author, it should be clear how this author's ideas or words relate to your own argument. Keep in mind that, in your final paper, it is quite unlikely that every note you took deserves a place. Be prepared to discard any notes that do not, in some fashion, support your claim and strengthen your argument. Remember also that direct quotations should be used sparingly for greatest effect; papers that rely too heavily on them make for choppy reading. By contrast, summaries and paraphrases are in your own words and should be a clean and easy fit with your prose style.

When you quote directly from either primary or secondary sources, you will need to follow special conventions of format and style. When quoting up to four lines of prose or three lines of poetry, integrate the quotation directly into your paragraph, enclosing the quoted material in double quotation marks and checking to make sure that the quotation accurately reflects the original. Longer quotations are set off from the text by starting a new line and indenting one inch on the left margin only; these are called **block quotations**. For these, quotation marks are omitted since the indention is enough to indicate that the material is a quotation. Examples of the correct format for both long and short quotations appear in Katie Johnson's paper (pp. 213–17).

When a short quotation is from a poem, line breaks in the poem are indicated by slash marks, with single spaces on either side. The following example demonstrates the format for a short quotation, in this case from Yusef Komunyakaa's poem "Blackberries" (featured in Chapter 5). The numbers in parentheses specify which lines in the poem are being quoted:

> The poem's speaker recalls the scene as sinister, noting: "The big blue car made me sweat. / Wintertime crawled out of the windows" (19–20).

While it is essential to quote accurately, sometimes you may need to alter a quotation slightly, either by deleting text for brevity or by adding or changing text to incorporate it grammatically. If you delete words from a quotation, indicate the deletion by inserting an ellipsis (three periods with spaces between them), as demonstrated by the following quotation from Robert Frost's poem "Mending Wall" (Chapter 2):

> The speaker makes his neighbor sound warlike, describing him as "Bringing a stone . . . / In each hand, like an old-stone savage armed" (39–40).

If you need to change or add words for clarity or grammatical correctness, indicate the changes with square brackets. If, for instance, you wanted to clarify the meaning of "They" in Komunyakaa's opening line "They left my hands like a printer's," you could do so like this:

> The speaker recalls that "[The blackberries] left my hands like a printer's" (1).

In addition to these format considerations, remember a few general rules of thumb as you deploy primary and secondary sources in your paper. First, without stinting on necessary information, keep quotations as short as possible—your argument will flow more smoothly if you do. Quotations long enough to be blocked should be relatively rare. Second, never assume that a quotation is self-sufficient or its meaning self-evident. Every time you put a quotation in your paper, take the time to introduce it clearly and comment on it to demonstrate why you chose to include it in the first place. Finally, quote fairly and accurately, and stick to a consistent format (such as the MLA style explained in the next section) when giving credit to your sources.

Strategies for Documenting Sources (MLA Format)

Documentation is the means by which you give credit to the authors of all primary and secondary sources cited within a research paper. It serves two principal purposes: (1) it allows your readers to find out more about the origin of the ideas you present, and (2) it protects you from charges of plagiarism. Every academic discipline follows slightly different conventions for documentation, but the method most commonly used for writing about literature is the format devised by the Modern Language Association (MLA). This documentation method encompasses **in-text citations**, which briefly identify within the body of your paper the source of a particular quotation, summary, or paraphrase, and a bibliography, called **Works Cited**, which gives more complete publication information.

While mastering the precise requirements of MLA punctuation and format can be time-consuming and even frustrating, getting them right adds immeasurably to the professionalism of a finished paper. More detailed information, including special circumstances and documentation styles for types of sources not covered here, will be found in the *MLA Handbook for Writers of Research Papers*, Seventh Edition (New York: Modern Language Association, 2009). Of course, if your instructor requests that you follow a different documentation method, you should follow his or her instructions instead.

MLA IN-TEXT CITATION

Each time you include information from any outside source—whether in the form of a summary, a paraphrase, or a quotation—you must provide your reader with a brief reference indicating the author and page number of the original. This reference directs the reader to the Works Cited list, where more complete information is available.

There are two basic methods for in-text citation. The first, and usually preferable, method is to include the author's name in the text of your essay and note the page number in parentheses at the end of the citation. The following paraphrase and quotation from "The Yellow Wallpaper" show the format to be followed for this method. Note that the page number (without the abbreviation "pg." or additional punctuation) is enclosed within parentheses and that the final punctuation for the sentence occurs after the parenthetical reference, effectively making the reference part of the preceding sentence. For a direct quotation, the closing quotation marks come before the page reference, but the final period is still saved until after the reference.

Gilman's narrator believes her husband trivializes her disorder (230).

Gilman's narrator sadly reports that her husband considers her disorder to be just "a slight hysterical tendency" (230).

The method is similar for long quotations (those set off from the main text of your essay). The only differences are that the final punctuation mark comes before the parenthetical page reference, and that the quotation is not enclosed within quotation marks.

In those cases where citing the author's name in your text would be awkward or difficult, you may include both the author's last name and the page reference in the parenthetical citation. The following example draws a quotation from Greg Johnson's article about Gilman's story.

According to one interpreter of the story, the heroine's final behavior is a "necessary stage in her progress toward self-identity and personal achievement" (Johnson 523).

Knowing the last name of the author is enough to allow your reader to find out more about the reference in the Works Cited, and having the page number makes it easy to find the original of the quotation, summary, or paraphrase should your reader choose to. The only time more information is needed is if you cite more than one work by the same author. In this case, you will need to specify from which of the author's works a particular citation comes. Electronic sources, such as CD-ROMs and Internet sources, are generally not divided into numbered pages. If you cite from such a source, the parenthetical reference need include only the author's last name (or, if the work is anonymous, an identifying title).

MLA WORKS CITED

The second feature of the MLA format is the Works Cited list, or bibliography. This list should begin on a new page of your paper and should be double-spaced throughout and use hanging indention, which means that all lines except the first are indented one-half inch. The list is alphabetized by author's last name (or by the title in the case of anonymous works) and includes every primary and secondary source referred to in your paper. The format for the most common types of entries is given below. If any of the information called for is unavailable for a particular source, simply skip that element and keep the rest of the entry as close as possible to the given format. An anonymous work, for instance, skips the author's name and is alphabetized under the title.

Books

Entries in your Works Cited for books should contain as much of the following information as is available to you. Follow the order and format exactly as given, with a period after each numbered element below (between author and title, and so on). Not all of these elements will be needed for most books. Copy the information directly from the title and publication pages of the book, not from a library catalog or other reference, because these sources often leave out some information.

1. The name of the author (or editor, if no author is listed, or organization in the case of a corporate author), last name first.
2. The full title, in italics. If the book has a subtitle, put a colon between title and subtitle.
3. The name(s) of the editor(s), if the book has both an author and an editor, following the abbreviation "Ed."
4. The name(s) of the translator or compiler, following the abbreviation "Trans." or "Comp.," as appropriate.
5. The edition, if other than the first.
6. The volume(s) used, if the book is part of a multivolume set.
7. The city of publication (followed by a colon), name of the publisher (comma), and year.
8. The medium of publication (Print, Web, etc.), followed by a period.
9. The name of any series to which the book belongs.

The examples below cover the most common types of books you will encounter.

A book by a single author or editor.   Simply follow the elements and format as listed above. The first example below is for a book by a single author; note also the abbreviation "UP," for "University Press." The second example is a book by a single editor. The third is for a book with both an author (Conrad) and an editor (Murfin); note also that it is a third edition and a book in a series, so these facts are listed as well.

> Cima, Gay Gibson. *Performing Women: Female Characters, Male Playwrights, and the Modern Stage*. Ithaca: Cornell UP, 1993. Print.
>
> Tucker, Robert C., ed. *The Marx-Engels Reader*. New York: Norton, 1972. Print.
>
> Conrad, Joseph. *Heart of Darkness*. Ed. Ross C Murfin. 3rd ed. Boston: Bedford, 2011. Print. Case Studies in Contemporary Criticism.

A book with multiple authors or editors.   If a book has two or three authors or editors, list all names, but note that only the first name is given last name first and the rest are in normal order. In cases where a book has four or more authors or editors, give only the first name listed on the title page, followed by a comma and the phrase "et al." (Latin for "and others").

> Leeming, David, and Jake Page. *God: Myths of the Male Divine*. New York: Oxford UP, 1996. Print.
>
> Arrow, Kenneth Joseph, et al., eds. *Education in a Research University*. Stanford: Stanford UP, 1996. Print.

A book with a corporate author.   When a book has a group, government agency, or other organization listed as its author, treat that organization in your Works Cited just as you would a single author.

> National Conference on Undergraduate Research. *Proceedings of the National Conference on Undergraduate Research*. Asheville: U of North Carolina, 1995. Print.

Short Works from Collections and Anthologies

Many scholarly books are collections of articles on a single topic by several different authors. When you cite an article from such a collection, include the information given below. The format is the same for works of literature that appear in an anthology, such as this one.

1. The name of the author(s) of the article or literary work.
2. The title of the short work, enclosed in quotation marks.
3. The title of the anthology, italicized.
4. The name(s) of the editor(s) of the collection or anthology.
5. All relevant publication information, in the same order and format as it would appear in a book citation.
6. The inclusive page numbers for the shorter work.
7. The medium of publication.

A single work from a collection or an anthology.   If you are citing only one article or literary work from any given collection or anthology, simply follow the format outlined above and demonstrated in the following examples.

Kirk, Russell. "Eliot's Christian Imagination." *The Placing of T. S. Eliot*. Ed. Jewel Spears Brooker. Columbia: U of Missouri P, 1991. 136-44. Print.

Silko, Leslie Marmon. "Yellow Woman." *The Story and Its Writer: An Introduction to Short Fiction*. 8th ed. Ed. Ann Charters. Boston: Bedford, 2011. 1204–10. Print.

Multiple works from the same collection or anthology.   If you are citing more than one short work from a single collection or anthology, it is often more efficient to set up a **cross-reference**. This means first writing a single general entry that provides full publication information for the collection or anthology as a whole. The entries for the shorter works then contain only the author and title of the shorter work, the names of the editors of the book, and the page numbers of the shorter work. The example below shows an entry for a short story cross-referenced with a general entry for this book; note that the entries remain in alphabetical order in your Works Cited, regardless of whether the general or specialized entry comes first.

Charters, Ann, ed. *The Story and Its Writer: An Introduction to Short Fiction*. 8th ed. Boston: Bedford, 2011. Print.

Faulkner, William. "A Rose for Emily." Charters 409–15.

Works in Periodicals

The following information should be included, in the given order and format, when you cite articles and other short works from journals, magazines, or newspapers.

1. The name(s) of the author(s) of the short work.
2. The title of the short work, in quotation marks.
3. The title of the periodical, italicized.
4. All relevant publication information as explained in the examples below.
5. The inclusive page numbers for the shorter work.
6. The medium of publication.

A work in a scholarly journal.   Publication information for works from scholarly and professional journals should include the volume number and the issue number, separated by a period; the year of publication in parentheses, followed by a colon; the page numbers of the shorter work; and the medium of publication.

Charles, Casey. "Gender Trouble in *Twelfth Night*." *Theatre Journal* 49.2 (1997): 121–41. Print.

An article in a magazine.   Publication information for articles in general-circulation magazines includes the month(s) of publication for a monthly (or bimonthly), or the date (day, abbreviated month, then year) for a weekly or bi-weekly, followed by a colon, the page numbers of the article, and the medium of publication.

> Cowley, Malcolm. "It Took a Village." *Utne Reader* Nov.–Dec. 1997:
>   48–49. Print.
> Levy, Steven. "On the Net, Anything Goes." *Newsweek* 7 July 1997:
>   28–30. Print.

An article in a newspaper.   When citing an article from a newspaper, include the date (day, abbreviated month, year) and the edition if one is listed on the masthead, followed by a colon, the page numbers (including the section number or letter, if applicable), and the medium of publication.

> Cobb, Nathan. "How to Dig Up a Family Tree." *Boston Globe* 9 Mar.
>   1998: C7. Print.

CD-ROMs

CD-ROMs come in two basic types: those published in a single edition — including major reference works like dictionaries and encyclopedias — and those published serially on a regular basis. In a Works Cited list, the first type is treated like a book and the second like a periodical. Details of citation appear in the following examples.

Single-edition CD-ROMs.   An entry for a single-edition CD-ROM is formatted like one for a book, but with "CD-ROM" as the medium of publication. Most CD-ROMs are divided into smaller subsections, and these should be treated like short works from anthologies.

> "Realism." *The Oxford English Dictionary*. 2nd ed. Oxford: Oxford UP,
>   1992. CD-ROM.

Serial CD-ROMs.   Treat information published on periodically released CD-ROMs just as you would articles in print periodicals, but also include the title of the CD-ROM, italicized; the word *CD-ROM*; the name of the vendor distributing the CD-ROM; and the date of electronic publication. Many such CD-ROMs contain reprints and abstracts of print works, and in these cases, the publisher and date for the print version should be listed as well, preceding the information for the electronic version.

> Brodie, James Michael, and Barbara K. Curry. *Sweet Words So Brave:*
>   *The Story of African American Literature*. Madison: Knowledge
>   Unlimited, 1996. CD-ROM. *ERIC*. SilverPlatter. 1997.

The Internet

Internet sources fall into several categories — World Wide Web documents and postings to newsgroups, listservs, and so on. Documentation for these sources should include as much of the following information as is available, in the order and format specified.

1. The name of the author(s), last name first (as for a print publication).
2. The title of the section of the work accessed (the subject line for e-mails and postings) in quotation marks.
3. The title of the Web site in italics.
4. The name of the sponsor or publisher of the Web site.
5. The date the material was published or updated.
6. The medium of publication.
7. The date you access a site.

The examples below show entries for a Web site and a newsgroup citation, two of the most common sorts of Internet sources.

> Brandes, Jay. "Maya Angelou: A Bibliography of Literary Criticism."
>   Troy University, 20 Aug. 1997. Web. 10 June 2009.
> Broun, Mike. "Jane Austen Video Package Launched." *Google groups*.
>   Google, 1 Mar. 1998. Web. 10 June 2009.

Personal Communication

In some cases you may get information directly from another person, either by conducting an interview or by receiving correspondence. In this case, include in your Works Cited the name of the person who gave you the information, the type of communication you had with that person, the date of the communication, and the medium if other than a personal interview.

> McCorkle, Patrick. Personal interview. 12 Mar. 2004.
> Aburrow, Clare. Message to the author. 15 Apr. 2004. E-mail.

Multiple Works by the Same Author

If you cite more than one work (in any medium) by a single author, the individual works are alphabetized by title. The author's full name is given only for the first citation in the Works Cited, after which it is replaced by three hyphens. The rest of the citation follows whatever format is appropriate for the medium of the source. The following two entries are for a work in an anthology and a book, both by the same author.

> Faulkner, William. "A Rose for Emily." *The Story and Its Writer: An
>   Introduction to Short Fiction*. 8th ed. Ed. Ann Charters. Boston:
>   Bedford, 2011. 409–15. Print.
> - - - . *The Sound and the Fury*. New York: Modern Library, 1956. Print.

Occasionally, you may have an idea or find a piece of information that seems important to your paper but that you just cannot work in smoothly without interrupting the flow of ideas. Such information can be included in the form of **endnotes**. A small superscript number in your text signals a note, and the notes themselves appear on a separate page at the end of your paper, before the Works Cited.

Four Annotated Student Researched Arguments

A PAPER THAT USES A LITERARY WORK TO EXAMINE SOCIAL ISSUES

Some research papers mention a literary work but then focus on examining a social issue related to that work. An example of such a paper is the following essay by student Sarah Michaels. To prepare for writing her paper, Sarah consulted numerous sources, and she turns to them during the course of her essay. The chief danger in a project like this is that it will become a mere "data dump" — that is, a paper in which the writer uncritically cites one source after another without really making an original argument. In writing an essay like Sarah's, be sure to identify your main issue and claim clearly. Present yourself as someone who is genuinely *testing* your sources, determining the specific ways in which they are relevant to your argument. Keep in mind that even if you are representing a source as useful, you can indicate how its ideas need to be further complicated. With at least some of your sources, analyze specific terms they employ, lingering over their language. Moreover, try to relate your sources to one another, orchestrating them into a well-organized conversation. We think Sarah accomplishes all these objectives. Even if you disagree, aim to practice them yourself.

Sarah Michaels
Professor Swain
English L202
21 May - - - -

"The Yellow Wallpaper" as a Guide
to Social Factors in Postpartum Depression

    In 2005, actor Brooke Shields's memoir *Down Came the Rain: My Journey through Postpartum Depression* drew much public attention to the psychological problem mentioned in its subtitle.[1] But during the last couple of decades, postpartum depression has been the subject of reports by many medical institutions and media outlets. By now, lots of people other than health professionals are aware of this problem and can at least roughly define it. If asked, most of them would probably say that although it can exhibit varying degrees of severity, postpartum depression is basically a state of despair suffered by a significant number of women who have just given birth. This is, in fact, the main image of it presented in a recent document about it, an October 2010 report by Marian Earls and a committee of the American Academy of Pediatrics.

Calls attention to an endnote

Quickly identifies social issue that the paper will focus on.

Besides explaining what postpartum depression is, the report urges pediatricians and other primary care providers to screen new mothers for it. Given that many members of the public already know that the problem is widespread, the report has not sparked much disagreement. Responding to it in the online magazine *Slate*, however, Emily Anthes does challenge its almost total emphasis on mothers. She argues that the Academy's committee makes a questionable assumption in writing as if only females are traumatized by birth. In her article entitled "Dads Get Blue, Too," she criticizes the report's authors for not acknowledging at greater length that new fathers can experience postpartum depression as well.[2] More generally, her article suggests that discussions of this disorder can be skewed by ideological views that need to be recognized. But, more than a century ago, Charlotte Perkins Gilman's story "The Yellow Wallpaper" made pretty much the same point, by showing how a woman diagnosed with a label like postpartum depression is a victim of her domestic circumstances and her society's ideas about gender, not just a person who has become ill on her own. When juxtaposed with the Academy's report, Gilman's 1892 tale is a reminder that today's doctors should look beyond an individual woman's symptoms of post-birth distress, because the social arrangements in which she lives may significantly affect her health.

Introduces the literary work that the paper will relate to the social issue.

    The term *postpartum depression* has for a long time appeared in analyses of "The Yellow Wallpaper" and of the personal experience that Gilman based the story on. Veronica Makowsky points out that this clinical phrase has even "become a critical commonplace" (329) in studies of the relationship between the story and Gilman's life. Gilman does not, however, actually use the term *postpartum depression* in the tale. Instead, the heroine's husband, John, declares that she suffers from "temporary nervous depression — a slight hysterical tendency" (230), and the character herself refers to her "nervous troubles" (232). Nor does Gilman bring up the term in her accounts of the real-life despair she went through when she gave birth to her daughter. In her essay "Why I Wrote 'The Yellow Wallpaper,'" she recalls being tormented much of her life by "a severe and continuous nervous breakdown tending to melancholia" (792). In her book-length autobiography *The Living of Charlotte Perkins Gilman*, she describes herself as suffering from "nervous prostration" (90). Indeed, the *Oxford English Dictionary*'s entry for *postpartum depression* indicates that the term was not recorded until 1929, when it showed up in an issue of the *American Journal of Psychiatry*.

Concedes that the term is used by scholars rather than by the author herself.

Nevertheless, the phrase does seem to fit the condition of Gilman's narrator. According to the American Academy of Pediatrics report, the symptoms of postpartum depression can range from "crying, worrying, sadness, anxiety, and mood swings" to more disturbing signs like "paranoia, mood shifts, hallucinations, [and] delusions" (1033). Gilman's character can be said to display most of these things once her child is born. At the estate that is the story's setting, she has trouble sleeping, she comes to doubt her husband's love, and, most dramatically, she rips off the wallpaper in her bedroom to free a woman whom she imagines wanting to creep away.

Directly connects language o the report to the story.

But simply labeling the heroine's distress as postpartum depression risks ignoring the conditions surrounding her that contribute to her suffering. Commenting on "The Yellow Wallpaper," literary critic Paula A. Treichler points out that a medical diagnosis can block understanding of "social, cultural, and economic practices" (69), even though these may support the doctor's claim to expertise, play a role in the patient's anguish, and become more important to confront than the patient's individual pain. In Gilman's story, John uses his social authority as physician and husband to control his wife. Specifically, he isolates her on the estate and makes her give up real activity, just as Gilman's real-life doctor, S. Weir Mitchell, demanded that she rest. As a result, the heroine feels obligated to surrender to the stereotypical passive female role, even though she would welcome more interaction with others and suspects that "congenial work, with excitement and change, would do me good" (780). When she proceeds to hallucinate the woman in the wallpaper, this is something that she is *driven* to do by John's assertion of masculine power, just as Weir Mitchell's prescription for inertia drove Gilman "near the border line of utter mental ruin" ("Why" 792).

Uses another interpreter of the story to advance this paper's argument.

Key quote from the story.

With "The Yellow Wallpaper" in mind, readers of the American Academy of Pediatrics report might examine how it downplays what Treichler calls "social, cultural, and economic practices" in its focus on diagnosing postpartum depression in women. Although the report does note that "Paternal depression is estimated at 6%" (1032), it does not linger on this fairly significant figure. In addition, the committee mentions only in passing that while "as many as 12% of all pregnant or postpartum women experience depression in a given year," the percentage is twice as much "for low-income women" (1032). Similarly brief is the recognition that "Eighteen percent of fathers of children in Early Head Start had symptoms of depression" (1033), a distinctly high figure that again suggests one's social class can affect one's health.

Uses the story to examine the issue raised by the report.

Paper works with specific examples and language from the report.

Nor does the report develop its brief notice that possible causes of postpartum depression include "domestic violence" (1034), which would be a serious problem in the patient's environment rather than a malfunction within the patient herself. Instead of insisting that "Treatment must address the mother-child dyad relationship" (1036), the committee might also have called for addressing the chance that the mother suffers from a lack of money or the presence of an abusive partner.

Juxtaposing Gilman's story with the Academy's report does not mean that readers of this recent document about postpartum depression have to declare its authors evil. The attitudes and recommendations of the committee are not as morally disturbing as those of Gilman's character John. But her story should encourage the report's readers to notice where, in its call for screening women for postpartum depression, it risks screening *out* social influences on people diagnosed with this clinical problem.

Heads off possible misunderstanding.

Endnotes

[1] Shields also discussed her postpartum depression in a *New York Times* op-ed column, in which she defended herself against actor Tom Cruise's charge that she should have relied on vitamins and exercise rather than on the prescription drug Paxil.

[2] For an article that supports Anthes's attention to fathers even though she does not mention it, see Kim and Swain.

The endnotes provide additional information not easily incorporated into the paper's main text.

Works Cited

Anthes, Emily. "Dads Get Blue, Too." *Slate.com*. Slate, 4 Nov. 2010. Web. 9 Nov. 2010.

Earls, Marian F., and the Committee on Psychosocial Aspects of Child and Family Health. "Clinical Report: Incorporating Recognition and Management of Perinatal and Postpartum Depression into Pediatric Practice." *Pediatrics.org*. Pediatrics, 25 Oct. 2010. Web. 9 Nov. 2010.

Gilman, Charlotte Perkins. *The Living of Charlotte Perkins Gilman: An Autobiography*. 1935. New York: Arno Press, 1972. Print.

- - - . "Why I Wrote 'The Yellow Wallpaper.'" 1913. Schilb and Clifford 792–93.

- - - . "The Yellow Wallpaper." 1892. Schilb and Clifford 778–91.

Kim, Pilyoung, and James E. Swain. "Sad Dads: Paternal Postpartum Depression." *Psychiatry* Feb. 2007: 36–47. Print.

Makowsky, Veronica. "Fear of Feeling and the Turn-of-the-Century Woman of Letters." *American Literary History* 5.2 (1993): 326–34. Print.

Schilb, John, and John Clifford, eds. *Arguing about Literature*. Boston: Bedford, 2014. Print.

Shields, Brooke. *Down Came the Rain: My Journey through Postpartum Depression*. New York: Hyperion, 2005. Print.

- - - . "War of Words." *New York Times* 1 July 2005, late ed.: A17. Print.

Treichler, Paula A. "Escaping the Sentence: Diagnosis and Discourse in 'The Yellow Wallpaper.'" *Tulsa Studies in Women's Literature* 3.1/2 (1984): 61–77. Print.

Citation for an online article.

Citation for a book.

Note style for multiple works by same author. Note, too, that when you cite more than one work from the same book, you give each book its own entry and cite each work from it in the shorthand form you see here.

Citation for a print article.

A PAPER THAT DEALS WITH EXISTING INTERPRETATIONS OF A LITERARY WORK

A research paper assignment may require you to develop a claim about a literary work by relating your analysis to previous interpretations of the text. An example of a paper like this is the following essay, in which student Katie Johnson makes an argument about Charlotte Perkins Gilman's story "The Yellow Wallpaper" by incorporating statements made by people who have already written about it. To prepare for writing her paper, she especially consulted the *MLA International Bibliography*, through which she located several published articles about Gilman's tale. The bibliographies of these articles led her to still more interpretations of the story. The biggest challenge in writing a paper like this is to stay focused on developing an idea of your own, rather than just inserting and echoing opinions held by others. Katie ended up examining an element of Gilman's story that she felt had not been adequately noted, let alone properly interpreted, by literary critics. As her essay proceeds, therefore, she does not simply agree with all the interpreters she cites. She treats with respect, however, those she finds fault with, civilly pointing out how her own thoughts differ. In addition, she clearly takes seriously the specific language of the critics she mentions, pondering their actual words rather than superficially summarizing their views.

Katie Johnson
Professor Van Wyck
English L141
5 May - - - -

The Meaning of the Husband's Fainting
in "The Yellow Wallpaper"

At the end of Charlotte Perkins Gilman's short story "The Yellow Wallpaper," the narrator is in a state that many people observing her would consider madness. She has torn off the wallpaper in her room and now seems proud of being able to "creep smoothly on the floor" (791). Her outwardly bizarre behavior at this point, along with her telling of the whole story beforehand, has led most literary critics to focus on analyzing her final conduct, as if it was the only really noteworthy feature of this concluding scene. Just as striking, however, is the final behavior of the narrator's husband, John. Up until the ending, he has acted as an authority on his wife's medical condition, and he has tried to assert power by always telling her what to do. At the conclusion, though, his mastery plainly vanishes. After finding the key to his wife's room, letting himself in, and beholding her crawling, he faints. Both the narrator and her husband end up on the floor. The narrator herself is highly aware of John's collapse, as she shows when she complains that "I had to creep over him every time!" (791). Because John's fainting is a dramatic reversal of his previous behavior and resembles the narrator's final physical position, it is surprising that only some literary critics have bothered to comment on John's breakdown, and even then the comments are relatively few. This neglect is a shame because, through John's fainting, Gilman seems to imply that he is left without any clear gender role to support him when his wife defies his manly effort to keep her what his society would consider sane.

Concisely summarizes the story's conclusion in first paragraph, which ends by stating main claim the essay will develop.

Until the last scene, John has repeatedly attempted to control his wife in the way that his society would expect of a man. This effort of his is reinforced by the professional standing he has achieved as a doctor. His masculine authority is interconnected with his medical authority. As we readers are made aware, he does not succeed in thoroughly bending his wife's will to his. Much of her narration is about her secret rebellion against him, which takes the form of imagining women trapped in the wallpaper of her room. Despite her hidden thoughts, however, he is often issuing commands to her, and she finds it hard to resist his domination. She admits to us that "I take pains to control myself — before him, at least, and that makes me very tired" (781). His attempts at enforcing his power over her include shutting her up in an odd country house in the first place. When she expresses suspicion of the estate, he simply "laughs" and "scoffs" (780), as he seems to do whenever she reveals independent thinking. She also says that he "hardly lets me stir without special direction" and gives her "a schedule prescription for each hour in the day" (781). Furthermore, he discourages her from writing, does not want to let her have visitors, and refuses to leave the estate when she informs him that she is not getting any better. Actually, he treats her more like his child than his wife, which is revealed when he asks "What is it, little girl?" (786) one night when she wakes up bothered by the wallpaper. All in all, he fits the nineteenth-century image of the ideal man as someone who gives his wife orders and expects her to follow them, though John tries to disguise his bossiness by declaring that he loves her and is looking out for her best interests.

The literary critics who do write about John's fainting at the end of the story tend to see it as a moment of irony, because in their view this masculine authority figure winds up physically collapsing in a way that is stereotypically associated with women. For example, Carol Margaret Davison states that when John faints, he is "assuming the traditional role of frail female" (66). Greg Johnson describes John's fall as "Gilman's witty inversion of a conventional heroine's confrontation with Gothic terror" (529), and similarly, Beverly A. Hume says that what happens is that John is "altering his conventional role as a soothing, masculine figure to that of a stereotypically weak nineteenth-century female" (478). These comments are not unreasonable, because during the nineteenth century, fainting was indeed something that women were believed to do more often than men. But a pair of literary critics has made another observation that, even though it sounds like the ones I have just quoted, points in a different direction that seems worth pursuing. Sandra M. Gilbert and Susan Gubar refer to John's fainting as an "unmasculine swoon of surprise" (91). They sound as if they are saying that he now seems feminine, but actually the word

Synthesizes comments from critics, combining them to indicate the pattern she finds in interpretations of the story.

Does not flatly declare critic "wrong" but will develop an idea they have not mentioned.

"unmasculine" simply indicates that he is no longer acting like a stereotypical male, so that readers of the story have to wonder whether he has any kind of identity left to him now. In fact, John's fainting seems like a total falling apart, as if he has become incapable of performing any further role at all, whether it is stereotypically feminine or masculine. Though his wife is creeping, at least she is still able to move, whereas he lies paralyzed. Overall, he appears to suffer a complete loss of identity rather than take on a female identity. Because his wife has fallen into what he sees as madness despite his efforts to control her, he experiences a shattering of his male ego, the result being not that he is left with a "womanly" self but that he now lacks any sense of self at all. Just as he has only leased the estate instead of owning it, so too has his personhood proven impermanent because his ability to treat his wife as his property has apparently gone. At the very end of the story, the narrator even refers to her husband merely as "that man" (791), suggesting that he is no longer recognizable as an individual human being.

Carefully analyzes a particular word that this pair of critics uses. Rest of paragraph develops main claim.

    More than one literary critic has argued that John has suffered a loss of power only momentarily and that he will soon dominate his wife just as much as he did before. Judith Fetterley contends that "when John recovers from his faint, he will put her in a prison from which there will be no escape" (164), and Paula Treichler claims that

> As the ending of her narrative, her madness will no doubt commit her to more intense medical treatment, perhaps to the dreaded Weir Mitchell of whom her husband has spoken. The surrender of patriarchy is only temporary; her husband has merely fainted, after all, not died, and will no doubt move swiftly and severely to deal with her. Her individual escape is temporary and compromised. (67)

Because quotation from Treichler is somewhat lengthy, Katie puts it in block form.

    Unfortunately, Gilman did not write a sequel called "The Yellow Wallpaper: The Next Day" to let us know exactly what happens to the couple after the husband wakes up. Fetterley and Treichler might have been right if the events of this story had taken place in real life and involved a real married couple. Though it was based on Gilman's actual situation,[1] the story should be treated as a work of fiction, and Gilman has chosen to conclude it by showing John as physically overcome. If she had wanted to suggest that he will quickly regain power, presumably she would have done so. As the text stands, the final scene emphasizes his new weakness, not signs of a strength that will soon be restored to him.

Synthesizes two critics' observations, putting them together as examples of a view that she questions.

Directs readers to endnote.

Disagrees with two critics but carefully explains why and avoids using hostile tone.

Although both the husband and the wife are in a bad physical state at the end, we as readers do not have to sympathize with them equally. Especially by having the wife narrate the story, Gilman has designed it so that we are encouraged to care far more about her than about John. A lot of readers might even feel joy at his collapse, regarding it as the bringing down of a tyrant. In any case, his fainting is worth paying attention to as a sign that he has experienced a loss of masculine power that leaves him unable to function as any kind of self.

Uses final paragraph not only to restate main claim but also to add the point that readers of story do not have to feel as sorry for John as they do for his wife.

Endnote

[1] Gilman recalls the personal experience that motivated her to write her story in her essay "Why I Wrote 'The Yellow Wallpaper.'"

Endnote provides information that could not be easily integrated into main text of essay.

Works Cited

Davison, Carol Margaret. "Haunted House / Haunted Heroine: Female Gothic Closets in 'The Yellow Wallpaper.'" *Women's Studies* 33.1 (2004): 47–75. Print.   *Citation for article in scholarly journal.*

Fetterley, Judith. "Reading about Reading: 'A Jury of Her Peers,' 'The Murders in the Rue Morgue,' and 'The Yellow Wallpaper.'" *Gender and Reading: Essays on Readers, Texts, and Contexts*. Ed. Elizabeth A. Flynn and Patrocinio P. Schweickart. Baltimore: Johns Hopkins UP, 1986. 147–64. Print.   *Citation for work in anthology.*

Gilbert, Sandra M., and Susan Gubar. *The Madwoman in the Attic: The Woman Writer and the Nineteenth-Century Literary Imagination*. New Haven: Yale UP, 1979. Print.   *Citation for book.*

Gilman, Charlotte Perkins. "Why I Wrote 'The Yellow Wall-paper.'" 1913. Schilb and Clifford 792–93.   *Note style for multiple works by the same author. Note, too, that when you cite more than one work from the same book, you give the book its own entry and then cite each work from it in the shorthand form you see here.*

- - -. "The Yellow Wallpaper." 1892. Schilb and Clifford 778–91.

Hume, Beverly A. "Gilman's 'Interminable Grotesque': The Narrator of 'The Yellow Wallpaper.'" *Studies in Short Fiction* 28.4 (1991): 477–84. Print.

Johnson, Greg. "Gilman's Gothic Allegory: Rage and Redemption in 'The Yellow Wallpaper.'" *Studies in Short Fiction* 26.4 (1989): 521–30. Print.

Schilb, John, and John Clifford, eds. *Arguing about Literature*. Boston: Bedford, 2014. Print.   *Citation for anthology.*

Treichler, Paula A. "Escaping the Sentence: Diagnosis and Discourse in 'The Yellow Wallpaper.'" *Tulsa Studies in Women's Literature* 3.1/2 (1984): 61–77. Print.

A PAPER THAT ANALYZES A LITERARY WORK THROUGH THE FRAMEWORK OF A PARTICULAR THEORIST

In the appendix, we explain how to write a research paper that takes one of the critical approaches now popular in literary theory. Some research papers, however, make an argument about a literary work by applying to it the ideas of a single theorist. Often, this is someone whose concepts have already influenced many scholars. Perhaps this person has even pioneered an entire field of thought. Examples include the father of psychoanalysis, Sigmund Freud; the founder of Marxist theory, Karl Marx; leading voices of existentialism such as Friedrich Nietzsche and Martin Heidegger; and the modern feminist writer Virginia Woolf.

If you attempt a paper like this, the theorist you choose might not have read the literary work you discuss. Even so, his or her ideas can illuminate it. Of course, you need to summarize the theorist's thinking in a manner that is both helpful and concise. Instead of just offering scattered, random passages from this person's writing, try to provide an efficient overview of the theorist's basic *framework*: that is, the main ideas that this figure contributes. You will especially want to specify the ideas that are most helpful for interpreting your chosen literary text. In essence, you will be using these concepts as a *lens*. Your paper can, however, admit that the theorist's principles do not cover *everything* important in the text. Probably you will be more credible to your reader if you concede that while the theorist's framework is useful, it provides a less-than-exact explanation. In fact, you will be seen more as developing a claim of your own if you point out the *limits* of the theorist's ideas along with their strengths. This is what student Jacob Grobowicz does in the following paper. His essay applies to "The Yellow Wallpaper" the ideas of the late Michel Foucault, a French theorist whose writings about modern power relations have inspired scholars in the social sciences and humanities. But Jacob does not simply quote from Foucault's writings. Instead, he critically examines the lens he provides, arguing that it clarifies major parts of the story but does not account for them all.

Jacob Grobowicz

Professor Burke

English L202

10 May - - - -

Using Foucault to Understand Disciplinary Power
in Gilman's "The Yellow Wallpaper"

Michel Foucault provides a useful framework for understanding the narrator's experiences in Charlotte Perkins Gilman's 1892 short story "The Yellow Wallpaper." More specifically, the theory of power that Foucault puts forth in his book *Discipline and Punish*[1] sheds light on the narrator's frustration with the "rest cure" that her husband makes her undergo. Of course, any perspective on a literary work may neglect some aspects of it. As a slant on Gilman's story, Foucault's book does have limits. In particular, *Discipline and Punish* does not pay much attention to gender, a significant element of the narrator's life. Still, quite relevant to her situation is Foucault's central argument in the book, which is that "discipline" is the main form of power in the modern age.

When Foucault refers to "discipline" in his book, he has two meanings of the term in mind, though he sees them as closely related to each other. First, human beings have become "disciplined" in the sense that they feel pressured to follow the standards held by all sorts of authorities. According to his historical account, power was previously associated with the figure of the king. Judges were a narrow group of

Directs reader to an endnote

Immediately establishes what literary work the paper will focus on, as well as what theorist and what specific text by that theorist.

The paper's main claim, which identifies which of the theorist's concepts the paper will apply to the story.

Begins a two-paragraph section that summarizes relevant details of theorist's framework and defines a key term of his.

officials who carried out the will of the monarch by punishing blatant violators of the law. Foucault also points out that the punishment usually took the form of physical imprisonment. The emphasis was on confinement of the criminal's body, not on reform of the criminal's soul. Foucault views the modern era, however, as a major shift from this state of affairs. He declares that nowadays, the administrators of power are more widespread: "The judges of normality are everywhere. We are in the society of the teacher-judge, the doctor-judge, the educator-judge, the 'social-worker' judge" (304). Furthermore, these figures look beyond sheer criminals and try to control all humanity. In fact, they aim to mold human beings' basic thinking, a goal they pursue by getting people to adopt conformist ideas and values promoted by various fields of expertise. Increasingly, Foucault claims, human beings are kept in place through forms of training, knowledge, and examination that are developed and advanced by academic and professional specialties — "disciplines" in the second sense of the word. Foucault argues that although these fields pose as benevolent "sciences of man," they actually partici- pate in "the modern play of coercion over bodies, gestures and behavior" (191).

Discipline and Power stresses this idea by spending many pages on the image of the Panopticon. This is a model for a prison, proposed in the nineteenth century by British philoso- pher Jeremy Bentham. He envisioned a penitentiary with a central tower whose guards could observe all of the surround- ing cells. The prisoners would feel constantly threatened by the tower's gaze, even though they could not be sure when the building was actually occupied. Eventually, their insecu- rity would drive them to monitor and restrict their conduct on their own, thereby doing the guards' work. Foucault brings up the Panopticon to argue that while institutions still engage in external surveillance — watching people in various ways — fields of expertise now serve dominant forces by leading people to engage in *self*-surveillance. In this respect, power can be said to *produce* the self rather than simply repress it.

Of all the experts that Foucault mentions in *Discipline and Power*, the one most significant to the narrator of "The Yellow Wallpaper" is "the doctor-judge." Suffering from a depression that seems related to her having recently given birth, she is in the hands of a physician named John who is also her husband. His diagnosis of her is reinforced by her brother, who is a doctor as well. Moreover, when the narrator fails to get physically better as fast as John would like, he threatens to deliver her over to S. Weir Mitchell, the real-life medical

Paper now begins directly connecting theorist's ideas to specific details of the story.

expert whose rest cure proved unendurable to Gilman herself. By linking three physicians to each other — John, the brother, and Weir Mitchell — Gilman suggests that her heroine must cope with principles and values imposed on her by the field of medicine in general, which Foucault calls attention to as a discipline that manipulates people's identities in the name of health. In John's view, his spouse is not experiencing any serious discontentment with her life, even though the reader senses that she is, in fact, distressed at having to accommodate herself to the roles of wife and mother as defined by the field of medicine specifically and by society overall. Proclaiming that she is afflicted by simply "a slight hysterical tendency" (780), John prevents himself from learning "how much I really suffer" (782). Relying on his alleged expertise as a representative of his profession, he values his own clinical precision over her vague reports of unease: "He has no patience with faith, an intense horror of superstition, and he scoffs openly at any talk of things not to be felt and seen and put down in figures" (780). Foucault might say that John wishes for his wife to discipline herself, which involves her obeying the policies that John derives from his scientific background. Indeed, at two different points in the story, she comments that he is basically focused on her achieving "self-control" (785).

It is important for the reader to note that John is not an outright monster in his treatment of the narrator. He does not physically abuse her, at least not in any dramatic way. In fact, even when he is condescending toward her, he seems to believe sincerely that he has her best interests at heart. In an article that interprets the story with Foucault's ideas in mind, John S. Bak overstates the case when he argues that the narrator's husband subjects her to "a dehumanizing imprisonment" (40) and "resembles the penal officers of the eighteenth-century psychiatric wards or penitentiaries" (42). Although he isolates her on a country estate, he does not virtually lock her up and physically torment her, as Bak implies. While much of the plot takes place in a single room, she is free to roam the estate, and it is *she* who denies *him* access to the room for a brief spell at the end. Explaining in his book how power now operates, Foucault points out that it tends to present itself not as a crude, blatant instrument of punishment but as a means of enlightened reform.

Foucault does believe, however, that agents of power like John are presumptuous in assuming that they can produce better human beings through their guidance. So, too, Gilman's narrator does not find that her husband's professional advice

Heads off possible misunderstanding.

Takes a position on an article that has already applied the theorist's ideas to the story.

Resumes connecting the theorist's ideas directly to the story.

is helping her to grow healthier. Inwardly, she disagrees with him when he commands her to avoid physical activity, for she supposes that "congenial work, with excitement and change, would do me good" (780). Though "he hates to have me write a word" (781), she defies him by secretly writing down the story of her lingering unhappiness and tension. Similarly, she tries to conceal from him her inability to comply with his demand that she get plenty of sleep. Eventually, rather than automatically following his prescriptions, she finds herself "getting a little afraid of John" (787). She moves from believing that "he loves me so" (785) to suspecting that in his interrogations of her, he has merely "pretended to be very loving and kind" (789). Of course, the most dramatic form that her alienation from him takes is her preoccupation with the woman she sees lurking behind her room's wallpaper. The narrator's effort to free the woman — including her violent tearing of the paper — vividly demonstrates that Gilman's heroine hopes to escape the forces of domination that her husband symbolizes. She is not as capable as Foucault is of coming up with a full-fledged theory of the modern disciplinary society that her husband represents, but intuitively she associates him with this kind of world, and in essence she protests against it as she strips the paper off.

While Foucault's *Discipline and Punish* provides much context for Gilman's story, it does not offer an adequate account of how lives like the narrator's are affected by their gender. In order to be complete, an analysis of "The Yellow Wallpaper" would have to acknowledge that the narrator's womanhood does matter to the plot. When she originally comes to the estate, clearly she is distressed by her society's expectation that as a mother she will be the prime nurturer of her newborn child. Then, the patriarchal authority that John enjoys in that society as her husband encourages him to tell her what is good for her. His demand that she rest instead of work is no doubt supported by their culture's belief that women of her upper-middle-class standing are not supposed to perform much physical labor in the first place. Most likely Foucault was aware that gender has usually been a key variable in modern society's power structures, and there is no reason to think he would simply ignore how it bears on Gilman's story. But because *Discipline and Punish* does not give gender much attention, its significance for Gilman's narrator is a topic that Foucault leaves other, more explicitly feminist perspectives to discover.

Some feminist theorists have criticized Foucault not only for neglecting gender but also for failing to develop any

Points out limits of this framework, rather than simply matching it to the story.

Concluding paragraph connects the theorist to the story by briefly bringing up new topic, resistance.

model of resistance to domination. For example, Nancy C. M. Hartsock faults him for leaving people with no method of escaping "passivity and immobility," no "hope of transcendence" over "the ways humans have been subjugated" (45). Nor does Gilman offer in her story a clear notion of what resistance to unjust power would look like. One feature of "The Yellow Wallpaper" that has much been debated is whether the narrator's destruction of the wallpaper and her crawling on the floor are a truly effective challenge to disciplinary society. Readers who might otherwise agree on many elements of the story have disagreed on this issue. While Bak, for example, claims that ultimately the narrator "is successful at freeing herself from her male-imposed shackles" (40), Paula A. Treichler argues that "the surrender of patriarchy is only temporary" and that "her madness will no doubt commit her to more intense medical treatment, perhaps to the dreaded Weir Mitchell of whom her husband has spoken" (67). It is possible that Gilman was being deliberately ambiguous with her ending, wishing to provoke discussion about how to define worthwhile resistance instead of attempting to settle the question herself. In any case, Foucault's *Discipline and Punish* sheds light on a lot of her story even if it keeps Gilman's readers wondering exactly what her narrator should have done.

Endnote

[1] *Discipline and Punish* is not the only text by Foucault that can help in analyzing Gilman's story. Another possible work is his book *Madness and Civilization: A History of Insanity in the Age of Reason*, which can be useful for understanding the psychological problems of Gilman's narrator. *Discipline and Punish* is especially good, however, at explaining how power relationships throughout modern societies like the narrator's involve academic and professional disciplines of various sorts.

Endnote provides additional information that is not easily incorporated into main body of the paper.

Works Cited

Bak, John S. "Escaping the Jaundiced Eye: Foucauldian   *Citation for scholarly article.*
   Panopticism in Charlotte Perkins Gilman's 'The Yellow
   Wallpaper.'" *Studies in Short Fiction* 31.1 (1994): 39–46.
   Print.

Foucault, Michel. *Discipline and Punish: The Birth of the*   *Citation for book. Note style*
   Prison. Trans. Alan Sheridan. New York: Vintage, 1979.   *for multiple works by same*
   Print.   *author.*

– – –. *Madness and Civilization: A History of Insanity in the Age*
   of Reason. Trans. Richard Howard. New York: Vintage,
   1988. Print.

Gilman, Charlotte Perkins. "The Yellow Wallpaper." *Arguing*   *Citation for work in an*
   about Literature. Ed. John Schilb and John Clifford.   *anthology.*
   Boston: Bedford, 2014. 778–91. Print.

Hartsock, Nancy C. M. "Postmodernism and Political Change:
   Issues for Feminist Theory." *Feminist Interpretations of*
   Michel Foucault. Ed. Susan J. Hekman. University Park:
   Pennsylvania State UP, 1996. 39–55. Print.

Treichler, Paula A. "Escaping the Sentence: Diagnosis and
   Discourse in 'The Yellow Wallpaper.'" *Tulsa Studies in*
   Women's Literature 3.1/2 (1984): 61–77. Print.

A PAPER THAT PLACES A LITERARY WORK IN HISTORICAL AND CULTURAL CONTEXT

When scholars do research on a literary work, often they are trying to place it in its original situation. They wish to identify how it relates to the historical and cultural context in which it emerged. If you write a research paper aiming to provide such background for a literary text, you will probably incorporate various sources. But your essay needs to focus on developing a claim of your own about the text. This is what the following paper by student Brittany Thomas does. Her essay connects Gilman's "The Yellow Wallpaper" to its original time. To prepare for the paper, Brittany examined autobiographical writings by Gilman as well as a lecture by S. Weir Mitchell, Gilman's own real-life doctor. She also investigated scholarship on nineteenth-century medical treatments of women. Becoming interested in the "rest cure" on which Gilman's story was based, Brittany realized that Gilman's plot leaves out the massages that were normally part of this therapy. In her paper, Brittany states and elaborates the claim that this omission was probably intentional—an effort by Gilman to emphasize the narrator's isolation from human touch.

Brittany Thomas

Professor Schneebaum

English L202

25 April - - - -

The Relative Absence of the Human Touch

in "The Yellow Wallpaper"

In her essay "Why I Wrote 'The Yellow Wallpaper,'" Charlotte Perkins Gilman reveals that her famous story was inspired by a personal depression that got worse when she underwent a "rest cure" prescribed to her by "a noted specialist in nervous diseases, the best known in the country" (792). Though she does not name this doctor in the essay, we are aware today that he was S. Weir Mitchell, a name that she actually brings up briefly in "The Yellow Wallpaper." The rest cure that the story's narrator goes through, however, does not seem to have all the features that Weir Mitchell's did. Interestingly, neither by reading the essay nor by reading Gilman's story would you realize that Weir Mitchell's treatment involved massage. The question for an interpreter of the story thus becomes, Why did Gilman leave massage out of "The Yellow Wallpaper"? Because we can only guess at her intentions, perhaps a better way of putting the question is this: What is the effect of omitting massage from the story? One important consequence is that there is less of a literal human touch in the story than there might have been, and so the heroine's alienation from others and her withdrawal into fantasy seem stronger than they might have been.

Immediately mentions one of her sources, but only to set up main claim about Gilman's story, which she states at end of paragraph.

Using question form helps signal cause/effect issue that the essay will address.

This is the essay's main claim

Weir Mitchell himself seems to have regarded massage as a very big component of his rest cure. He gives it a lot of attention in his 1904 lecture "The Evolution of the Rest Treatment." There he describes at length two cases, one of a man and one of a woman, where he found out that rubbing the body helped the person overcome depression. He recalls arriving at the conclusion "that massage was a tonic of extraordinary value" (796), and he continues his lecture by giving a brief account of the larger world history of what he terms "this invaluable therapeutic measure" (797). Evidently Weir Mitchell did not perform massage himself; in his lecture, he describes having others do it for him. Perhaps he thought that if he personally rubbed a patient's body, he would run the risk of being accused of a sexual advance. Despite his use of stand-ins for him, he clearly considered massage a necessary feature of his rest cure. One reason was that he thought the depressed person's body needed some form of physical stimulation, which the person would not otherwise be getting

Briefly summarizes Weir Mitchell's lecture, focusing o his remarks about massage rather than spending additional time on other topics of his speech.

by lying around so much of the time. He states in his lecture that massage was something that "enabled me to use rest in bed without causing the injurious effects of unassisted rest" (796). Probably this method also reflected a more general be-lief of his, which Jane F. Thrailkill describes as the assump-tion "that the efficacy of his cure lay in its treatment of a patient's material body, not in what we might now term the psychological effects of isolation or of his own charismatic presence" (532). Thrailkill goes on to point out that Weir Mitchell was not alone in this belief: "[T]he medical wisdom of the day . . . conceived of a patient as a conceptually inert bundle of physiological processes" (552).[1] Massage was a means of helpfully manipulating the physique, which for Weir Mitchell and other doctors of his era was the main source of difficulties that today might be seen as chiefly mental.

Analyzes at length one particular source, Weir Mitchell's lecture.

Square brackets indicate alteration of text being quoted. Ellipses indicate words deleted from original text.

Given that massage was so important to Weir Mitchell, it is significant that Gilman's references to it are not consistent. She does recall being massaged when she discusses how Weir Mitchell treated her medically in her autobiography *The Living of Charlotte Perkins Gilman*. In that book, she says that besides being "put to bed and kept there," she was "fed, bathed, [and] rubbed" (96). She does not refer to massage, however, in "Why I Wrote 'The Yellow Wallpaper.'" More important for interpretations of the story, she does not make massage part of "The Yellow Wallpaper" itself. It plays no role at all in the plot. The elements of the rest cure that come up in the story are, instead, physical seclusion and forced abandonment of work.

Synthesis of three texts, comparing what they do with the topic of massage. More specifically, compares Gilman's autobiography, Gilman's essay on writing the story, and the story itself.

If massage were a major element of the rest cure that the narrator goes through in "The Yellow Wallpaper," the story would probably feature a lot more human touching than it presently does. The way the story is written, the heroine experiences relatively little physical contact with other people, or at least she does not tell us that she is having much of this. What is especially interesting is that we do not find many instances of her being physically touched by her husband, John. There are, in fact, a few places in the text where he does touch her. She says that when she informs him that she is disturbed by the wallpaper, "he took me in his arms and called me a blessed little goose" (782). When she weeps because he will not leave the house to visit relatives, "dear John gathered me up in his arms, and just carried me upstairs and laid me on the bed, and sat by me and read to me till it tired my head" (785). When she complains that he is wrong to think she is getting better, he gives her "a big hug"

In effect, admits it would be misleading to claim there are no instances of touching in the story. Proceeds to bring together (to synthesize) vari-ous examples of such contact.

and says "'Bless her little heart! . . . she shall be as sick as she pleases!'" (786). Yet his moments of touching her not only are very few but also reflect his insensitivity toward her. His folding her in his arms seems an effort to control her and trivialize her protests, not an expression of genuine love. Moreover, she takes no real comfort from his touch. If this amounts to rubbing her, then from her point of view, he is rubbing her the wrong way. Again, however, massage is significantly absent from this story, and because what touches there are seem so few and inhumane, readers are led to feel that the narrator is pretty much alone in her concerns. She has only the imaginary woman in the wallpaper to bond with, and she seems drawn to that woman in large part because her human companions have no true understanding of the distress that caused her to need some sort of cure in the first place.

Accounts for details of story that might seem to conflict with main claim.

In calling attention to the role of massage in S. Weir Mitchell's rest cure, I do not mean to minimize the importance of his treatment's other components. The physical rest he demanded of his patients was certainly a big element of the cure, so that we can easily see why Gilman made it central to her story. In his lecture, Weir Mitchell also points out that he applied electrical charges to the patient's body. Historians of women's health Barbara Ehrenreich and Deirdre English argue that Weir Mitchell relied heavily as well on "the technique of healing by *command*" (119, emphasis in original), constantly and firmly giving orders to his patients so that they felt obligated to obey his wishes and to get better on the precise schedule he had in mind. Massage certainly figured, however, in Weir Mitchell's mode of treatment, including his handling of Gilman's own case, so that her omission of it from "The Yellow Wallpaper" seems a deliberate strategy for giving other things emphasis. Above all, the quite limited role of human touching in the story serves to make readers highly aware that the narrator is without the loving, intimate company she really needs to recover from her depression.

Heads off possible misunderstanding of argument; dealing with it enables her to write a concluding paragraph that does more than just repeat main claim.

Endnote

[1] Thrailkill spends much of her article tracing how an emphasis on treating depression through physical means (the approach taken by Weir Mitchell) gave way late in the nineteenth century to a more psychological and verbal form of therapy (such as Sigmund Freud practiced).

Endnote provides informatio that could not be easily integrated into main text of the essay.

Works Cited

Ehrenreich, Barbara, and Deirdre English. *For Her Own Good: 150 Years of the Experts' Advice to Women*. Garden City: Doubleday-Anchor, 1978. Print.

Gilman, Charlotte Perkins. *The Living of Charlotte Perkins Gilman*. 1935. New York: Arno Press, 1972. Print.

- - -. "Why I Wrote 'The Yellow Wallpaper.'" 1913. Schilb and Clifford 792–93.

- - -. "The Yellow Wallpaper." 1892. Schilb and Clifford 778–91.

Schilb, John, and John Clifford, eds. *Arguing about Literature*. Boston: Bedford, 2014. Print.

Thrailkill, Jane F. "Doctoring 'The Yellow Wallpaper.'" *ELH* 69.2 (2005): 525–66. Print.

Weir Mitchell, S. Excerpt from "The Evolution of the Rest Treatment." 1904. Schilb and Clifford 793–97.

Citation for book.

Note style for multiple works by same author.

When you cite more than one work from the same book, you give the book its own entry and cite each work from it in the shorthand form you see here.

Citation for anthology.

Citation for scholarly article.

PART TWO

Literature and Arguments

CHAPTER 7

Families

In the not-too-distant past, family life was the focal point of our emotional existence, the center of all our important psychological successes and failures. It was common for several generations to live together in the same town and even the same home. Grandparents, aunts, and uncles were an intimate part of daily life, not just relatives one saw during the holidays. Besides the usual emotional drama that always takes place between parents and children, there were the additional tensions that inevitably arise when the values of the old clash with those of the young. Of course, there was also the comforting emotional support available from more than just a mother and father as well as the sense of belonging and bonding with the many aunts, uncles, and cousins that usually lived nearby.

As extended families become less common, the emotional stakes of home life seem higher than ever. Since we rely on one another more in today's nuclear family, our sense of disappointment, our sense of rejection, and our sense of unworthiness can be more acute. During childhood, the drama of family life can stamp an indelible mark on our psyches, leaving psychological scars that make safe passage into adulthood difficult. Our status within the family can also offer us a sense of worth and confidence that leads to contentment and success later on. For all of us, however, family life is composed not of psychological and sociological generalities but, rather, of our one-to-one relationships with fathers, sisters, grandmothers. Writers often give us imaginative, honest, and illuminating charts of their successes and failures in negotiating both the calm and the choppy waters of our family journeys. The following clusters do not hope to be complete or representative of your experiences. We do hope, however, that in reading and discussing these poems and stories, you will find them an interesting and provocative catalyst for you to delve into the joys and sorrows of your own life in a family.

The chapter opens with three stories that examine the tensions that arise between mothers and daughters as they work out questions of identity and responsibility. Two stories of brothers in conflict from different economic settings follow. The third cluster traces moments of crisis in parenting in two provocative stories. Poems about fathers are next as four poets paint memorable but not always positive portraits. Then a cluster of poems about grandparents gives us loving, honest, and humorous snapshots. The feelings of gays and lesbians in families is the concern of the next poetry cluster, followed by a cluster that groups Sylvia Plath's "Daddy" with critical commentaries on the poet's brilliant and haunting attempts as a young girl to understand her father's death. The chapter concludes with three essays that argue over the bounds of parental protection.

≣ Mothers and Daughters: Stories

TILLIE OLSEN, "I Stand Here Ironing"

AMY TAN, "Two Kinds"

ALICE WALKER, "Everyday Use"

We all know stories of parents who want to mold their children, stories of mothers and fathers who push their reluctant children to be fashion models or beauty queens or Little League stars. Some studies of adults playing musical instruments in orchestras say the biggest factor in their success was the commitment of their parents. But we also hear about tennis prodigies who burn out at sixteen because of parental pressure. Mothers and daughters have always struggled with each other over life goals and identity. How much guidance is enough? How much is too much? What is a reasonable balance between preparing a child for life's challenges and shaping a child to act out the mother's fantasy or her internal vision of what the good life is? And no matter where parents fall on this continuum, are there childhood events so powerful that we cannot get beyond them? The following three stories chart the difficulties mothers and daughters have with each other and with the social and cultural forces that influence our destiny.

≣ BEFORE YOU READ

Are your parents responsible for your successes? Your failures? Do you wish that your parents had pushed you to succeed more insistently? Are you annoyed that your parents set unreasonable standards for you?

TILLIE OLSEN
I Stand Here Ironing

Born in Omaha, Nebraska, to Russian immigrants of Jewish descent and socialist views, Tillie Olsen (1912–2007) was an activist in social and political causes all of her life, often choosing family, work, union, feminist, or other political causes over writing. Although her publishing record is short, its quality is greatly admired. In addition to critically respected short stories, Olsen wrote a novel, Yonnondio *(1974), which paints a vivid picture of a coal-mining family during the Depression. Her essay collection,* Silences *(1978), stimulated debate about class and gender as factors in the creation of literature and led both directly and indirectly to the revived interest in works by women writers. The mother of four daughters, Olsen often wrote about generational relationships within families. "I Stand Here Ironing" is from her 1961 collection of stories,* Tell Me a Riddle.

I stand here ironing, and what you asked me moves tormented back and forth with the iron.

"I wish you would manage the time to come in and talk with me about your daughter. I'm sure you can help me understand her. She's a youngster who needs help and whom I'm deeply interested in helping."

"Who needs help." . . . Even if I came, what good would it do? You think because I am her mother I have a key, or that in some way you could use me as a key? She has lived for nineteen years. There is all that life that has happened outside of me, beyond me.

And when is there time to remember, to sift, to weigh, to estimate, to total? I will start and there will be an interruption and I will have to gather it all together again. Or I will become engulfed with all I did or did not do, with what should have been and what cannot be helped.

She was a beautiful baby. The first and only one of our five that was beauti- 5 ful at birth. You do not guess how new and uneasy her tenancy in her now-loveliness. You did not know her all those years she was thought homely, or see her poring over her baby pictures, making me tell her over and over how beautiful she had been—and would be, I would tell her—and was now, to the seeing eye. But the seeing eyes were few or nonexistent. Including mine.

I nursed her. They feel that's important nowadays, I nursed all the children, but with her, with all the fierce rigidity of first motherhood, I did like the books then said. Though her cries battered me to trembling and my breasts ached with swollenness, I waited till the clock decreed.

Why do I put that first? I do not even know if it matters, or if it explains anything.

She was a beautiful baby. She blew shining bubbles of sound. She loved motion, loved light, loved color and music and textures. She would lie on the floor in her blue overalls patting the surface so hard in ecstasy her hands and feet would blur. She was a miracle to me, but when she was eight months old I had to leave her daytimes with the woman downstairs to whom she was no miracle at all, for I worked or looked for work and for Emily's father, who "could no longer endure" (he wrote in his good-bye note) "sharing want with us."

I was nineteen. It was the pre-relief, pre-WPA world of the depression. I would start running as soon as I got off the streetcar, running up the stairs, the place smelling sour, and awake or asleep to startle awake, when she saw me she would break into a clogged weeping that could not be comforted, a weeping I can hear yet.

After a while I found a job hashing at night so I could be with her days, 10 and it was better. But it came to where I had to bring her to his family and leave her.

It took a long time to raise the money for her fare back. Then she got chicken pox and I had to wait longer. When she finally came, I hardly knew her, walking quick and nervous like her father, looking like her father, thin, and dressed in a shoddy red that yellowed her skin and glared at the pockmarks. All the baby loveliness gone.

She was two. Old enough for nursery school they said, and I did not know then what I know now—the fatigue of the long day, and the lacerations of group life in the kinds of nurseries that are only parking places for children.

Except that it would have made no difference if I had known. It was the only place there was. It was the only way we could be together, the only way I could hold a job.

And even without knowing, I knew. I knew the teacher that was evil because all these years it has curdled into my memory, the little boy hunched in the corner, her rasp, "why aren't you outside, because Alvin hits you? that's no reason, go out, scaredy." I knew Emily hated it even if she did not clutch and implore "don't go Mommy" like the other children, mornings.

She always had a reason why we should stay home. Momma, you look 15 sick. Momma, I feel sick. Momma, the teachers aren't there today, they're sick. Momma, we can't go, there was a fire there last night. Momma, it's a holiday today, no school, they told me.

But never a direct protest, never rebellion. I think of our others in their three-, four-year-oldness—the explosions, the tempers, the denunciations, the demands—and I feel suddenly ill. I put the iron down. What in me demanded that goodness in her? And what was the cost, the cost to her of such goodness?

The old man living in the back once said in his gentle way: "You should smile at Emily more when you look at her." What *was* in my face when I looked at her? I loved her. There were all the acts of love.

It was only with the others I remembered what he said, and it was the face of joy, and not of care or tightness or worry I turned to them—too late for Emily. She does not smile easily, let alone almost always as her brothers and sisters do. Her face is closed and sombre, but when she wants, how fluid. You must have seen it in her pantomimes, you spoke of her rare gift for comedy on the stage that rouses laughter out of the audience so dear they applaud and applaud and do not want to let her go.

Where does it come from, that comedy? There was none of it in her when she came back to me that second time, after I had to send her away again. She had a new daddy now to learn to love, and I think perhaps it was a better time.

Except when we left her alone nights, telling ourselves she was old enough. 20

"Can't you go some other time, Mommy, like tomorrow?" she would ask. "Will it be just a little while you'll be gone? Do you promise?"

The time we came back, the front door open, the clock on the floor in the hall. She rigid awake. "It wasn't just a little while. I didn't cry. Three times I called you, just three times, and then I ran downstairs to open the door so you could come faster. The clock talked loud. I threw it away, it scared me what it talked."

She said the clock talked loud again that night I went to the hospital to have Susan. She was delirious with the fever that comes before red measles, but she was fully conscious all the week I was gone and the week after we were home when she could not come near the new baby or me.

She did not get well. She stayed skeleton thin, not wanting to eat, and night after night she had nightmares. She would call for me, and I would rouse from exhaustion to sleepily call back: "You're all right, darling, go to sleep, it's just a dream," and if she still called, in a sterner voice, "now go to sleep, Emily, there's nothing to hurt you." Twice, only twice, when I had to get up for Susan anyhow, I went in to sit with her.

Now when it is too late (as if she would let me hold her and comfort her like   25
I do the others) I get up and go to her at once at her moan or restless stirring. "Are you awake, Emily? Can I get you something?" And the answer is always the same: "No, I'm all right, go back to sleep, Mother."

They persuaded me at the clinic to send her away to a convalescent home in the country where "she can have the kind of food and care you can't manage for her, and you'll be free to concentrate on the new baby." They still send children to that place. I see pictures on the society page of sleek young women planning affairs to raise money for it, or dancing at the affairs, or decorating Easter eggs or filling Christmas stockings for the children.

They never have a picture of the children so I do not know if the girls still wear those gigantic red bows and the ravaged looks on the every other Sunday when parents can come to visit "unless otherwise notified" — as we were notified the first six weeks.

Oh it is a handsome place, green lawns and tall trees and fluted flower beds. High up on the balconies of each cottage the children stand, the girls in their red bows and white dresses, the boys in white suits and giant red ties. The parents stand below shrieking up to be heard and the children shriek down to be heard, and between them the invisible wall "Not To Be Contaminated by Parental Germs or Physical Affection."

There was a tiny girl who always stood hand in hand with Emily. Her parents never came. One visit she was gone. "They moved her to Rose Cottage," Emily shouted in explanation. "They don't like you to love anybody here."

She wrote once a week, the labored writing of a seven-year-old. "I am fine.   30
How is the baby. If I write my leter nicly I will have a star. Love." There never was a star. We wrote every other day, letters she could never hold or keep but only hear read — once. "We simply do not have room for children to keep any personal possessions," they patiently explained when we pieced one Sunday's shrieking together to plead how much it would mean to Emily, who loved so to keep things, to be allowed to keep her letters and cards.

Each visit she looked frailer. "She isn't eating," they told us.

(They had runny eggs for breakfast or mush with lumps, Emily said later, I'd hold it in my mouth and not swallow. Nothing ever tasted good, just when they had chicken.)

It took us eight months to get her released home, and only the fact that she gained back so little of her seven lost pounds convinced the social worker.

I used to try to hold and love her after she came back, but her body would stay stiff, and after a while she'd push away. She ate little. Food sickened her, and I think much of life too. Oh she had physical lightness and brightness, twinkling by on skates, bouncing like a ball up and down up and down over the jump rope, skimming over the hill; but these were momentary.

She fretted about her appearance, thin and dark and foreign-looking at a   35
time when every little girl was supposed to look or thought she should look like

a chubby blonde replica of Shirley Temple. The doorbell sometimes rang for her, but no one seemed to come and play in the house or to be a best friend. Maybe because we moved so much.

There was a boy she loved painfully through two school semesters. Months later she told me how she had taken pennies from my purse to buy him candy. "Licorice was his favorite and I brought him some every day, but he still liked Jennifer better'n me. Why, Mommy?" The kind of question for which there is no answer.

School was a worry for her. She was not glib or quick in a world where glibness and quickness were easily confused with ability to learn. To her overworked and exasperated teachers she was an overconscientious "slow learner" who kept trying to catch up and was absent entirely too often.

I let her be absent, though sometimes the illness was imaginary. How different from my now-strictness about attendance with the others. I wasn't working. We had a new baby. I was home anyhow. Sometimes, after Susan grew old enough, I would keep her home from school, too, to have them all together.

Mostly Emily had asthma, and her breathing, harsh and labored, would fill the house with a curiously tranquil sound. I would bring the two old dresser mirrors and her boxes of collections to her bed. She would select beads and single earrings, bottle tops and shells, dried flowers and pebbles, old postcards and scraps, all sorts of oddments; then she and Susan would play Kingdom, setting up landscapes and furniture, peopling them with action.

Those were the only times of peaceful companionship between her and   40
Susan. I have edged away from it, that poisonous feeling between them, that terrible balancing of hurts and needs I had to do between the two, and did so badly, those earlier years.

Oh there were conflicts between the others too, each one human, needing, demanding, hurting, taking—but only between Emily and Susan, no, Emily toward Susan that corroding resentment. It seems so obvious on the surface, yet it is not obvious; Susan, the second child, Susan, golden- and curly-haired and chubby, quick and articulate and assured, everything in appearance and manner Emily was not; Susan, not able to resist Emily's precious things, losing or sometimes clumsily breaking them; Susan telling jokes and riddles to company for applause while Emily sat silent (to say to me later: that was *my* riddle, Mother, I told it to Susan); Susan, who for all the five years' difference in age was just a year behind Emily in developing physically.

I am glad for that slow physical development that widened the difference between her and her contemporaries, though she suffered over it. She was too vulnerable for that terrible world of youthful competition, of preening and parading, of constant measuring of yourself against every other, of envy, "If I had that copper hair," "If I had that skin. . . ." She tormented herself enough about not looking like the others, there was enough of unsureness, the having to be conscious of words before you speak, the constant caring—what are they thinking of me? without having it all magnified by the merciless physical drives.

Ronnie is calling. He is wet and I change him. It is rare there is such a cry now. That time of motherhood is almost behind me when the ear is not one's own but must always be racked and listening for the child cry, the child call. We sit for a while and I hold him, looking out over the city spread in charcoal with its soft aisles of light. *"Shoogily,"* he breathes and curls closer. I carry him back to bed, asleep. *Shoogily.* A funny word, a family word, inherited from Emily, invented by her to say: *comfort.*

In this and other ways she leaves her seal, I say aloud. And startle at my saying it. What do I mean? What did I start to gather together, to try and make coherent? I was at the terrible, growing years. War years. I do not remember them well. I was working, there were four smaller ones now, there was not time for her. She had to help be a mother, and housekeeper, and shopper. She had to get her seal. Mornings of crisis and near hysteria trying to get lunches packed, hair combed, coats and shoes found, everyone to school or Child Care on time, the baby ready for transportation. And always the paper scribbled on by a smaller one, the book looked at by Susan then mislaid, the homework not done. Running out to that huge school where she was one, she was lost, she was a drop; suffering over the unpreparedness, stammering and unsure in her classes.

There was so little time left at night after the kids were bedded down. She would struggle over books, always eating (it was in those years she developed her enormous appetite that is legendary in our family) and I would be ironing, or preparing food for the next day, or writing V-mail to Bill, or tending the baby. Sometimes, to make me laugh, or out of her despair, she would imitate happenings or types at school.

I think I said once: "Why don't you do something like this in the school amateur show?" One morning she phoned me at work, hardly understandable through the weeping: "Mother, I did it. I won, I won; they gave me first prize; they clapped and clapped and wouldn't let me go."

Now suddenly she was Somebody, and as imprisoned in her difference as she had been in anonymity.

She began to be asked to perform at other high schools, even in colleges, then at city and statewide affairs. The first one we went to, I only recognized her that first moment when thin, shy, she almost drowned herself into the curtains. Then: Was this Emily? The control, the command, the convulsing and deadly clowning, the spell, then the roaring, stamping audience, unwilling to let this rare and precious laughter out of their lives.

Afterwards: You ought to do something about her with a gift like that—but without money or knowing how, what does one do? We have left it all to her, and the gift has so often eddied inside, clogged and clotted, as been used and growing.

She is coming. She runs up the stairs two at a time with her light graceful step, and I know she is happy tonight. Whatever it was that occasioned your call did not happen today.

"Aren't you ever going to finish the ironing, Mother? Whistler painted his mother in a rocker. I'd have to paint mine standing over an ironing board." This is one of her communicative nights and she tells me everything and nothing as she fixes herself a plate of food out of the icebox.

She is so lovely. Why did you want me to come in at all? Why were you concerned? She will find her way.

She starts up the stairs to bed. "Don't get me up with the rest in the morning." "But I thought you were having midterms." "Oh, those," she comes back in, kisses me, and says quite lightly, "in a couple of years when we'll all be atom-dead they won't matter a bit."

She has said it before. She *believes* it. But because I have been dredging the past, and all that compounds a human being is so heavy and meaningful in me, I cannot endure it tonight.

I will never total it all. I will never come in to say: She was a child seldom   55
smiled at. Her father left me before she was a year old. I had to work her first six years when there was work, or I sent her home and to his relatives. There were years she had care she hated. She was dark and thin and foreign-looking in a world where the prestige went to blondeness and curly hair and dimples, she was slow where glibness was prized. She was a child of anxious, not proud, love. We were poor and could not afford for her the soil of easy growth. I was a young mother, I was a distracted mother. There were other children pushing up, demanding. Her younger sister seemed all that she was not. There were years she did not want me to touch her. She kept too much in herself, her life was such she had to keep too much in herself. My wisdom came too late. She has much to her and probably little will come of it. She is a child of her age, of depression, of war, of fear.

Let her be. So all that is in her will not bloom—but in how many does it? There is still enough left to live by. Only help her to know—help make it so there is cause for her to know—that she is more than this dress on the ironing board, helpless before the iron.   *[1961]*

≣ THINKING ABOUT THE TEXT

1. Is Olsen's last paragraph optimistic or pessimistic about personal destiny? Is there some support in the story for both perspectives?

2. There is an old expression: "To know all is to forgive all." Does this statement apply to "I Stand Here Ironing"? Some critics want to privilege personal responsibility; others, social conditions. Do you blame Emily's mother? Or is she just a victim?

3. How might this story be different if told from Emily's perspective? From Susan's? From Emily's teacher's? What are the advantages and disadvantages of writing a story from one character's point of view?

4. How would you describe the voice or voices we hear in the story? What qualities, dimensions, or emotions can you infer? Does one dominate? Are you sympathetic to this voice? Is that what Olsen wanted?

5. Do you agree with the mother's decision not to visit the school for a conference? What are her reasons? Are they sound? What do you think the teacher wants to discuss? How involved in a child's life should a teacher be?

AMY TAN

Two Kinds

Born to Chinese immigrants in Oakland, California, Amy Tan (b. 1952) weaves intricate stories about generational and intercultural relationships among women in families, basing much of her writing on her own family history. She earned a double B.A., in English and linguistics, and an M.A. in linguistics at San Jose State University. Her novels dealing with mother-daughter relationships, The Joy Luck Club *(1989) and* The Kitchen God's Wife *(1991), have received awards and critical acclaim.* The Hundred Secret Senses *(1995) explores the relationship between sisters who grew up in different cultures. Her latest novel is* The Bonesetter's Daughter *(2001), and her more recent book is a collection of nonfiction,* The Opposite of Fate *(2003). "Two Kinds" is excerpted from* The Joy Luck Club. *A recent book,* Saving Fish from Drowning *(2005), was called a "witty parable," loosely based on* The Canterbury Tales. *A novel,* The Valley of Amazement, *was published in 2013.*

My mother believed you could be anything you wanted to be in America. You could open a restaurant. You could work for the government and get good retirement. You could buy a house with almost no money down. You could become rich. You could become instantly famous.

"Of course you can be prodigy, too," my mother told me when I was nine. "You can be best anything. What does Auntie Lindo know? Her daughter, she is only best tricky."

America was where all my mother's hopes lay. She had come here in 1949 after losing everything in China: her mother and father, her family home, her first husband, and two daughters, twin baby girls. But she never looked back with regret. There were so many ways for things to get better.

We didn't immediately pick the right kind of prodigy. At first my mother thought I could be a Chinese Shirley Temple. We'd watch Shirley's old movies on TV as though they were training films. My mother would poke my arm and say, *"Ni kan"* —You watch. And I would see Shirley tapping her feet, or singing a sailor song, or pursing her lips into a very round O while saying, "Oh my goodness."

"Ni kan," said my mother as Shirley's eyes flooded with tears. "You already know how. Don't need talent for crying!"

Soon after my mother got this idea about Shirley Temple, she took me to a beauty training school in the Mission district and put me in the hands of a student who could barely hold the scissors without shaking. Instead of getting big fat curls, I emerged with an uneven mass of crinkly black fuzz. My mother dragged me off to the bathroom and tried to wet down my hair.

"You look like Negro Chinese," she lamented, as if I had done this on purpose.

The instructor of the beauty training school had to lop off these soggy clumps to make my hair even again. "Peter Pan is very popular these days," the instructor assured my mother. I now had hair the length of a boy's, with straight-across bangs that hung at a slant two inches above my eyebrows. I liked the haircut and it made me actually look forward to my future fame.

In fact, in the beginning, I was just as excited as my mother, maybe even more so. I pictured this prodigy part of me as many different images, trying each one on for size. I was a dainty ballerina girl standing by the curtains, waiting to hear the right music that would send me floating on my tiptoes. I was like the Christ child lifted out of the straw manger, crying with holy indignity. I was Cinderella stepping from her pumpkin carriage with sparkly cartoon music filling the air.

In all of my imaginings, I was filled with a sense that I would soon become *perfect*. My mother and father would adore me. I would be beyond reproach. I would never feel the need to sulk for anything.   10

But sometimes the prodigy in me became impatient. "If you don't hurry up and get me out of here, I'm disappearing for good," it warned. "And then you'll always be nothing."

Every night after dinner, my mother and I would sit at the Formica kitchen table. She would present new tests, taking her examples from stories of amazing children she had read in *Ripley's Believe It or Not*, or *Good Housekeeping*, *Reader's Digest*, and a dozen other magazines she kept in a pile in our bathroom. My mother got these magazines from people whose houses she cleaned. And since she cleaned many houses each week, we had a great assortment. She would look through them all, searching for stories about remarkable children.

The first night she brought out a story about a three-year-old boy who knew the capitals of all the states and even most of the European countries. A teacher was quoted as saying the little boy could also pronounce the names of the foreign cities correctly.

"What's the capital of Finland?" my mother asked me, looking at the magazine story.

All I knew was the capital of California, because Sacramento was the   15
name of the street we lived on in Chinatown. "Nairobi!" I guessed, saying the most foreign word I could think of. She checked to see if that was possibly one way to pronounce "Helsinki" before showing me the answer.

The tests got harder — multiplying numbers in my head, finding the queen of hearts in a deck of cards, trying to stand on my head without using my hands, predicting the daily temperatures in Los Angeles, New York, and London.

One night I had to look at a page from the Bible for three minutes and then report everything I could remember. "Now Jehoshaphat had riches and honor in abundance and . . . that's all I remember, Ma," I said.

And after seeing my mother's disappointed face once again, something inside of me began to die. I hated the tests, the raised hopes and failed expectations. Before going to bed that night, I looked in the mirror above the bathroom sink and when I saw only my face staring back — and that it would always be this ordinary face — I began to cry. Such a sad, ugly girl! I made high-pitched noises like a crazed animal, trying to scratch out the face in the mirror.

And then I saw what seemed to be the prodigy side of me—because I had never seen that face before. I looked at my reflection, blinking so I could see more clearly. The girl staring back at me was angry, powerful. This girl and I were the same. I had new thoughts, willful thoughts, or rather thoughts filled with lots of won'ts. I won't let her change me, I promised myself. I won't be what I'm not.

So now on nights when my mother presented her tests, I performed list-   20
lessly, my head propped on one arm. I pretended to be bored. And I was. I got so bored I started counting the bellows of the foghorns out on the bay while my mother drilled me in other areas. The sound was comforting and reminded me of the cow jumping over the moon. And the next day, I played a game with myself, seeing if my mother would give up on me before eight bellows. After a while I usually counted only one, maybe two bellows at most. At last she was beginning to give up hope.

Two or three months had gone by without any mention of my being a prodigy again. And then one day my mother was watching *The Ed Sullivan Show* on TV. The TV was old and the sound kept shorting out. Every time my mother got halfway up from the sofa to adjust the set, the sound would go back on and Ed would be talking. As soon as she sat down, Ed would go silent again. She got up, the TV broke into loud piano music. She sat down. Silence. Up and down, back and forth, quiet and loud. It was like a stiff embraceless dance between her and the TV set. Finally she stood by the set with her hand on the sound dial.

She seemed entranced by the music, a little frenzied piano piece with this mesmerizing quality, sort of quick passages and then teasing lilting ones before it returned to the quick playful parts.

"*Ni kan,*" my mother said, calling me over with hurried hand gestures. "Look here."

I could see why my mother was fascinated by the music. It was being pounded out by a little Chinese girl, about nine years old, with a Peter Pan haircut. The girl had the sauciness of a Shirley Temple. She was proudly modest like a proper Chinese child. And she also did this fancy sweep of a curtsy, so that the fluffy skirt of her white dress cascaded slowly to the floor like the petals of a large carnation.

In spite of these warning signs, I wasn't worried. Our family had no piano   25
and we couldn't afford to buy one, let alone reams of sheet music and piano lessons. So I could be generous in my comments when my mother bad-mouthed the little girl on TV.

"Play note right, but doesn't sound good! No singing sound," complained my mother.

"What are you picking on her for?" I said carelessly. "She's pretty good. Maybe she's not the best, but she's trying hard." I knew almost immediately I would be sorry I said that.

"Just like you," she said. "Not the best. Because you not trying." She gave a little huff as she let go of the sound dial and sat down on the sofa.

The little Chinese girl sat down also to play an encore of "Anitra's Dance" by Grieg. I remember the song, because later on I had to learn how to play it.

Three days after watching *The Ed Sullivan Show*, my mother told me what my   30
schedule would be for piano lessons and piano practice. She had talked to Mr. Chong, who lived on the first floor of our apartment building. Mr. Chong was a retired piano teacher and my mother had traded housecleaning services for weekly lessons and a piano for me to practice on every day, two hours a day, from four until six.

When my mother told me this, I felt as though I had been sent to hell. I whined and then kicked my foot a little when I couldn't stand it anymore.

"Why don't you like me the way I am? I'm *not* a genius! I can't play the piano. And even if I could, I wouldn't go on TV if you paid me a million dollars!" I cried.

My mother slapped me. "Who ask you be genius?" she shouted. "Only ask you be your best. For you sake. You think I want you be genius? Hnnh! What for! Who ask you!"

"So ungrateful," I heard her mutter in Chinese. "If she had as much talent as she has temper, she would be famous now."

Mr. Chong, whom I secretly nicknamed Old Chong, was very strange, al-   35
ways tapping his fingers to the silent music of an invisible orchestra. He looked ancient in my eyes. He had lost most of the hair on top of his head and he wore thick glasses and had eyes that always looked tired and sleepy. But he must have been younger than I thought, since he lived with his mother and was not yet married.

I met Old Lady Chong once and that was enough. She had this peculiar smell like a baby that had done something in its pants. And her fingers felt like a dead person's, like an old peach I once found in the back of the refrigerator; the skin just slid off the meat when I picked it up.

I soon found out why Old Chong had retired from teaching piano. He was deaf. "Like Beethoven!" he shouted to me. "We're both listening only in our head!" And he would start to conduct his frantic silent sonatas.

Our lessons went like this. He would open the book and point to different things, explaining their purpose: "Key! Treble! Bass! No sharps or flats! So this is C major! Listen now and play after me!"

And then he would play the C scale a few times, a simple chord, and then, as if inspired by an old, unreachable itch, he gradually added more notes and running trills and a pounding bass until the music was really something quite grand.

I would play after him, the simple scale, the simple chord, and then I just   40
played some nonsense that sounded like a cat running up and down on top of garbage cans. Old Chong smiled and applauded and then said, "Very good! But now you must learn to keep time!"

So that's how I discovered that Old Chong's eyes were too slow to keep up with the wrong notes I was playing. He went through the motions in half-time.

To help me keep rhythm, he stood behind me, pushing down on my right shoulder for every beat. He balanced pennies on top of my wrists so I would keep them still as I slowly played scales and arpeggios. He had me curve my hand around an apple and keep that shape when playing chords. He marched stiffly to show me how to make each finger dance up and down, staccato like an obedient little soldier.

He taught me all these things, and that was how I also learned I could be lazy and get away with mistakes, lots of mistakes. If I hit the wrong notes because I hadn't practiced enough, I never corrected myself. I just kept playing in rhythm. And Old Chong kept conducting his own private reverie.

So maybe I never really gave myself a fair chance. I did pick up the basics pretty quickly, and I might have become a good pianist at that young age. But I was so determined not to try, not to be anybody different that I learned to play only the most ear-splitting preludes, the most discordant hymns.

Over the next year, I practiced like this, dutifully in my own way. And then one day I heard my mother and her friend Lindo Jong both talking in a loud bragging tone of voice so others could hear. It was after church, and I was leaning against the brick wall wearing a dress with stiff white petticoats. Auntie Lindo's daughter, Waverly, who was about my age, was standing farther down the wall about five feet away. We had grown up together and shared all the closeness of two sisters squabbling over crayons and dolls. In other words, for the most part, we hated each other. I thought she was snotty. Waverly Jong had gained a certain amount of fame as "Chinatown's Littlest Chinese Chess Champion."

"She bring home too many trophy," lamented Auntie Lindo that Sunday.   45
"All day she play chess. All day I have no time do nothing but dust off her winnings." She threw a scolding look at Waverly, who pretended not to see her.

"You lucky you don't have this problem," said Auntie Lindo with a sigh to my mother.

And my mother squared her shoulders and bragged: "Our problem worser than yours. If we ask Jing-mei wash dish, she hear nothing but music. It's like you can't stop this natural talent."

And right then, I was determined to put a stop to her foolish pride.

A few weeks later, Old Chong and my mother conspired to have me play in a talent show which would be held in the church hall. By then, my parents had saved up enough to buy me a secondhand piano, a black Wurlitzer spinet with a scarred bench. It was the showpiece of our living room.

For the talent show, I was to play a piece called "Pleading Child" from   50
Schumann's *Scenes from Childhood*. It was a simple, moody piece that sounded more difficult than it was. I was supposed to memorize the whole thing, playing the repeat parts twice to make the piece sound longer. But I dawdled over it, playing a few bars and then cheating, looking up to see what notes followed. I never really listened to what I was playing. I daydreamed about being somewhere else, about being someone else.

The part I liked to practice best was the fancy curtsy: right foot out, touch the rose on the carpet with a pointed foot, sweep to the side, left leg bends, look up and smile.

My parents invited all the couples from the Joy Luck Club to witness my debut. Auntie Lindo and Uncle Tin were there. Waverly and her two older brothers had also come. The first two rows were filled with children both younger and older than I was. The littlest ones got to go first. They recited simple nursery rhymes, squawked out tunes on miniature violins, twirled Hula Hoops, pranced in pink ballet tutus, and when they bowed or curtsied, the audience would sigh in unison, "Awww," and then clap enthusiastically.

When my turn came, I was very confident. I remember my childish excitement. It was as if I knew, without a doubt, that the prodigy side of me really did exist. I had no fear whatsoever, no nervousness. I remember thinking to myself, This is it! This is it! I looked out over the audience, at my mother's blank face, my father's yawn, Auntie Lindo's stiff-lipped smile, Waverly's sulky expression. I had on a white dress layered with sheets of lace, and a pink bow in my Peter Pan haircut. As I sat down I envisioned people jumping to their feet and Ed Sullivan rushing up to introduce me to everyone on TV.

And I started to play. It was so beautiful. I was so caught up in how lovely I looked that at first I didn't worry how I would sound. So it was a surprise to me when I hit the first wrong note and I realized something didn't sound quite right. And then I hit another and another followed that. A chill started at the top of my head and began to trickle down. Yet I couldn't stop playing, as though my hands were bewitched. I kept thinking my fingers would adjust themselves back, like a train switching to the right track. I played this strange jumble through two repeats, the sour notes staying with me all the way to the end.

When I stood up, I discovered my legs were shaking. Maybe I had just been nervous and the audience, like Old Chong, had seen me go through the right motions and had not heard anything wrong at all. I swept my right foot out, went down on my knee, looked up and smiled. The room was quiet, except for Old Chong, who was beaming and shouting, "Bravo! Bravo! Well done!" But then I saw my mother's face, her stricken face. The audience clapped weakly, and as I walked back to my chair, with my whole face quivering as I tried not to cry, I heard a little boy whisper loudly to his mother, "That was awful," and the mother whispered back, "Well, she certainly tried."

55

And now I realized how many people were in the audience, the whole world it seemed. I was aware of eyes burning into my back. I felt the shame of my mother and father as they sat stiffly throughout the rest of the show.

We could have escaped during intermission. Pride and some strange sense of honor must have anchored my parents to their chairs. And so we watched it all: the eighteen-year-old boy with a fake mustache who did a magic show and juggled flaming hoops while riding a unicycle. The breasted girl with white makeup who sang from *Madama Butterfly* and got honorable mention. And the eleven-year-old boy who won first prize playing a tricky violin song that sounded like a busy bee.

After the show, the Hsus, the Jongs, and the St. Clairs from the Joy Luck Club came up to my mother and father.

"Lots of talented kids," Auntie Lindo said vaguely, smiling broadly.

"That was somethin' else," said my father, and I wondered if he was refer- 60
ring to me in a humorous way, or whether he even remembered what I had done.

Waverly looked at me and shrugged her shoulders. "You aren't a genius like me," she said matter-of-factly. And if I hadn't felt so bad, I would have pulled her braids and punched her stomach.

But my mother's expression was what devastated me: a quiet, blank look that said she had lost everything. I felt the same way, and it seemed as if every-body were now coming up, like gawkers at the scene of an accident, to see what parts were actually missing. When we got on the bus to go home, my father was humming the busy-bee tune and my mother was silent. I kept thinking she wanted to wait until we got home before shouting at me. But when my father unlocked the door to our apartment, my mother walked in and then went to the back, into the bedroom. No accusations. No blame. And in a way, I felt dis-appointed. I had been waiting for her to start shouting, so I could shout back and cry and blame her for all my misery.

I assumed my talent-show fiasco meant I never had to play the piano again. But two days later, after school, my mother came out of the kitchen and saw me watching TV.

"Four clock," she reminded me as if it were any other day. I was stunned, as though she were asking me to go through the talent-show torture again. I wedged myself more tightly in front of the TV.

"Turn off TV," she called from the kitchen five minutes later. 65

I didn't budge. And then I decided. I didn't have to do what my mother said anymore. I wasn't her slave. This wasn't China. I had listened to her before and look what happened. She was the stupid one.

She came out from the kitchen and stood in the arched entryway of the living room. "Four clock," she said once again, louder.

"I'm not going to play anymore," I said nonchalantly. "Why should I? I'm not a genius."

She walked over and stood in front of the TV. I saw her chest was heaving up and down in an angry way.

"No!" I said, and I now felt stronger, as if my true self had finally emerged. 70
So this was what had been inside me all along.

"No! I won't!" I screamed.

She yanked me by the arm, pulled me off the floor, snapped off the TV. She was frighteningly strong, half pulling, half carrying me toward the piano as I kicked the throw rugs under my feet. She lifted me up and onto the hard bench. I was sobbing by now, looking at her bitterly. Her chest was heaving even more and her mouth was open, smiling crazily as if she were pleased I was crying.

"You want me to be someone that I'm not!" I sobbed. "I'll never be the kind of daughter you want me to be!"

"Only two kinds of daughters," she shouted in Chinese. "Those who are obedient and those who follow their own mind! Only one kind of daughter can live in this house. Obedient daughter!"

"Then I wish I wasn't your daughter. I wish you weren't my mother," I   75
shouted. As I said these things I got scared. I felt like worms and toads and slimy things were crawling out of my chest, but it also felt good, as if this awful side of me had surfaced, at last.

"Too late change this," said my mother shrilly.

And I could sense her anger rising to its breaking point. I wanted to see it spill over. And that's when I remembered the babies she had lost in China, the ones we never talked about. "Then I wish I'd never been born!" I shouted. "I wish I were dead! Like them."

It was as if I had said the magic words, Alakazam!—and her face went blank, her mouth closed, her arms went slack, and she backed out of the room, stunned, as if she were blowing away like a small brown leaf, thin, brittle, lifeless.

It was not the only disappointment my mother felt in me. In the years that followed, I failed her so many times, each time asserting my own will, my right to fall short of expectations. I didn't get straight As. I didn't become class president. I didn't get into Stanford. I dropped out of college.

For unlike my mother, I did not believe I could be anything I wanted to be.   80
I could only be me.

And for all those years, we never talked about the disaster at the recital or my terrible accusations afterward at the piano bench. All that remained unchecked, like a betrayal that was now unspeakable. So I never found a way to ask her why she had hoped for something so large that failure was inevitable.

And even worse, I never asked her what frightened me the most: Why had she given up hope?

For after our struggle at the piano, she never mentioned my playing again. The lessons stopped, the lid to the piano was closed, shutting out the dust, my misery, and her dreams.

So she surprised me. A few years ago, she offered to give me the piano, for my thirtieth birthday. I had not played in all those years. I saw the offer as a sign of forgiveness, a tremendous burden removed.

"Are you sure?" I asked shyly. "I mean, won't you and Dad miss it?"   85

"No, this your piano," she said firmly. "Always your piano. You only one can play."

"Well, I probably can't play anymore," I said. "It's been years."

"You pick up fast," said my mother, as if she knew this was certain. "You have natural talent. You could been genius if you want to."

"No I couldn't."

"You just not trying," said my mother. And she was neither angry nor sad.   90
She said it as if to announce a fact that could never be disproved. "Take it," she said.

But I didn't at first. It was enough that she had offered it to me. And after that, every time I saw it in my parents' living room, standing in front of the bay windows, it made me feel proud, as if it were a shiny trophy I had won back.

Last week I sent a tuner over to my parents' apartment and had the piano reconditioned, for purely sentimental reasons. My mother had died a few months before and I had been getting things in order for my father, a little bit at a time. I put the jewelry in special silk pouches. The sweaters she had knitted in yellow, pink, bright orange—all the colors I hated—I put those in moth-proof boxes. I found some old Chinese silk dresses, the kind with little slits up the sides. I rubbed the old silk against my skin, then wrapped them in tissue and decided to take them home with me.

After I had the piano tuned, I opened the lid and touched the keys. It sounded even richer than I remembered. Really, it was a very good piano. Inside the bench were the same exercise notes with handwritten scales, the same secondhand music books with their covers held together with yellow tape.

I opened up the Schumann book to the dark little piece I had played at the recital. It was on the left-hand side of the page, "Pleading Child." It looked more difficult than I remembered. I played a few bars, surprised at how easily the notes came back to me.

And for the first time, or so it seemed, I noticed the piece on the right-hand   95 side. It was called "Perfectly Contented." I tried to play this one as well. It had a lighter melody but the same flowing rhythm and turned out to be quite easy. "Pleading Child" was shorter but slower; "Perfectly Contented" was longer but faster. And after I played them both a few times, I realized they were two halves of the same song.

                                                                    [1989]

≡ THINKING ABOUT THE TEXT

1. Most sons and daughters struggle to establish their own identities. Does this seem true in "Two Kinds"? Does the cultural difference between the immigrant mother and Americanized daughter intensify their struggle? Do you think you have different goals in life than your parents do?

2. Do you agree with the mother's belief that "you could be anything you wanted to be in America" (para. 1)? Does race matter? Gender? Ethnicity? Religion? Sexual orientation?

3. What do you believe each character learned from the argument at the piano bench the day after the recital?

4. How does Tan establish the differing personalities of her characters? Through details? Dialogue? Anecdotes? Do the main characters change significantly? Does she tell us or show us?

5. Do you sympathize with the mother or with the daughter? Should parents channel their children toward selected activities? Or should parents let their children choose their own paths? Can parents push their children too much? Why would they do this?

☰ MAKING COMPARISONS

1. Do you think Emily's mother in Olsen's story would want to be like the Chinese mother if given the opportunity? Which mother would you prefer to have? Why?

2. One mother seems to do too little, the other too much. Is this your reading of the two stories? Is the lesson of Olsen's and Tan's stories that mothers can't win no matter what they do? Or do you have a more optimistic interpretation?

3. Which daughter's life seems more difficult? How possible is it to say from the outside looking in?

ALICE WALKER
Everyday Use

A native of Eatonton, Georgia, Alice Walker (b. 1944) attended Spelman College and received her B.A. from Sarah Lawrence College in 1965. During the 1960s, she was active in the civil rights movement, an experience reflected in her 1976 novel Meridian *and in her autobiographical book,* The Way Forward Is with a Broken Heart *(2000). Walker is accomplished in many genres, and her essays, short stories, novels, and poems are widely read. She is perhaps best known for the novel* The Color Purple *(1976), which earned her both a Pulitzer Prize and an American Book Award and was made into a movie. Terming herself a "womanist" rather than a feminist in the essays of* In Search of Our Mothers' Gardens *(1983), Walker has confronted many issues concerning women, including abusive relationships, lesbian love, and the horrors of ritual genital mutilation in some African societies. Her daughter, Rebecca, has written her own memoir,* Black, White and Jewish, *dealing with her childhood and adolescence as the daughter of Alice Walker and activist lawyer Mel Leventhal, to whom Walker was married for nine years, after meeting him during voter registration drives in Mississippi in 1967. The short story "Everyday Use," from the collection* In Love and Trouble: Stories of Black Women *(1973), deals with definitions of history, heritage, and value in a changing world for African Americans in the mid-twentieth century. Her recent work includes a novel,* Now Is the Time to Open Your Heart *(2004);* We Are the Ones We've Been Waiting For *(2006), "a book of spiritual ruminations with a progressive political edge"; and* Hard Times Require Serious Dancing: New Poems *(2010).*

I will wait for her in the yard that Maggie and I made so clean and wavy yesterday afternoon. A yard like this is more comfortable than most people know. It is not just a yard. It is like an extended living room. When the hard clay is swept clean as a floor and the fine sand around the edges lined with tiny, irregular grooves anyone can come and sit and look up into the elm tree and wait for the breezes that never come inside the house.

Maggie will be nervous until after her sister goes: she will stand hopelessly in corners homely and ashamed of the burn scars down her arms and legs, eyeing her sister with a mixture of envy and awe. She thinks her sister has held life always in the palm of one hand, that "no" is a word the world never learned to say to her.

You've no doubt seen those TV shows where the child who has "made it" is confronted, as a surprise, by her own mother and father, tottering in weakly from backstage. (A pleasant surprise, of course: What would they do if parent and child came on the show only to curse out and insult each other?) On TV mother and child embrace and smile into each other's faces. Sometimes the mother and father weep, the child wraps them in her arms and leans across the table to tell how she would not have made it without their help. I have seen these programs.

Sometimes I dream a dream in which Dee and I are suddenly brought together on a TV program of this sort. Out of a dark and soft-seated limousine I am ushered into a bright room filled with many people. There I meet a smiling, gray, sporty man like Johnny Carson who shakes my hand and tells me what a fine girl I have. Then we are on the stage and Dee is embracing me with tears in her eyes. She pins on my dress a large orchid, even though she has told me once that she thinks orchids are tacky flowers.

In real life I am a large, big-boned woman with rough, man-working   5
hands. In the winter I wear flannel nightgowns to bed and overalls during the day. I can kill and clean a hog as mercilessly as a man. My fat keeps me hot in zero weather. I can work outside all day, breaking ice to get water for washing; I can eat pork liver cooked over the open fire minutes after it comes steaming from the hog. One winter I knocked a bull calf straight in the brain between the eyes with a sledge hammer and had the meat hung up to chill before nightfall. But of course all this does not show on television. I am the way my daughter would want me to be: a hundred pounds lighter, my skin like an uncooked barley pancake. My hair glistens in the hot bright lights. Johnny Carson has much to do to keep up with my quick and witty tongue.

But that is a mistake. I know even before I wake up. Who ever knew a Johnson with a quick tongue? Who can even imagine me looking a strange white man in the eye? It seems to me I have talked to them always with one foot raised in flight, with my head turned in whichever way is farthest from them. Dee, though. She would always look anyone in the eye. Hesitation was no part of her nature.

"How do I look, Mama?" Maggie says, showing just enough of her thin body enveloped in pink skirt and red blouse for me to know she's there, almost hidden by the door.

"Come out into the yard," I say.

Have you ever seen a lame animal, perhaps a dog run over by some careless person rich enough to own a car, sidle up to someone who is ignorant enough to be kind to him? That is the way my Maggie walks. She has been like this, chin on chest, eyes on ground, feet in shuffle, ever since the fire that burned the other house to the ground.

Dee is lighter than Maggie, with nicer hair and a fuller figure. She's a woman now, though sometimes I forget. How long ago was it that the other house burned? Ten, twelve years? Sometimes I can still hear the flames and feel Maggie's arms sticking to me, her hair smoking and her dress falling off her in little black papery flakes. Her eyes seemed stretched open, blazed open by the flames reflected in them. And Dee. I see her standing off under the sweet gum tree she used to dig gum out of; a look of concentration on her face as she watched the last dingy gray board of the house fall in toward the red-hot brick chimney. Why don't you do a dance around the ashes? I'd wanted to ask her. She had hated the house that much.

I used to think she hated Maggie, too. But that was before we raised the money, the church and me, to send her to Augusta to school. She used to read to us without pity; forcing words, lies, other folks' habits, whole lives upon us two, sitting trapped and ignorant underneath her voice. She washed us in a river of make-believe, burned us with a lot of knowledge we didn't necessarily need to know. Pressed us to her with the serious way she read, to shove us away at just the moment, like dimwits, we seemed about to understand.

Dee wanted nice things. A yellow organdy dress to wear to her graduation from high school; black pumps to match a green suit she'd made from an old suit somebody gave me. She was determined to stare down any disaster in her efforts. Her eyelids would not flicker for minutes at a time. Often I fought off the temptation to shake her. At sixteen she had a style of her own: and knew what style was.

I never had an education myself. After second grade the school was closed down. Don't ask me why: in 1927 colored asked fewer questions than they do now. Sometimes Maggie reads to me. She stumbles along good-naturedly but can't see well. She knows she is not bright. Like good looks and money, quickness passed her by. She will marry John Thomas (who has mossy teeth in an earnest face) and then I'll be free to sit here and I guess just sing church songs to myself. Although I never was a good singer. Never could carry a tune. I was always better at a man's job. I used to love to milk till I was hooked in the side in '49. Cows are soothing and slow and don't bother you, unless you try to milk them the wrong way.

I have deliberately turned my back on the house. It is three rooms, just like the one that burned, except the roof is tin; they don't make shingle roofs any more. There are no real windows, just some holes cut in the sides, like the portholes in a ship, but not round and not square, with rawhide holding the shutters up on the outside. This house is in a pasture, too, like the other one. No doubt when Dee sees it she will want to tear it down. She wrote me once that no matter where we "choose" to live, she will manage to come see us. But she will never bring her friends. Maggie and I thought about this and Maggie asked me, "Mama, when did Dee ever *have* any friends?"

She had a few. Furtive boys in pink shirts hanging about on washday after school. Nervous girls who never laughed. Impressed with her they worshiped the well-turned phrase, the cute shape, the scalding humor that erupted like bubbles in lye. She read to them.

When she was courting Jimmy T she didn't have much time to pay to us, but turned all her faultfinding power on him. He *flew* to marry a cheap gal from a family of ignorant flashy people. She hardly had time to recompose herself.

When she comes I will meet—but there they are!

Maggie attempts to make a dash for the house, in her shuffling way, but I stay her with my hand. "Come back here," I say. And she stops and tries to dig a well in the sand with her toe.

It is hard to see them clearly through the strong sun. But even the first glimpse of leg out of the car tells me it is Dee. Her feet were always neat-looking, as if God himself had shaped them with a certain style. From the other side of the car comes a short, stocky man. Hair is all over his head a foot long and hanging from his chin like a kinky mule tail. I hear Maggie suck in her breath. "Uhnnnh," is what it sounds like. Like when you see the wriggling end of a snake just in front of your foot on the road. "Uhnnnh."

Dee next. A dress down to the ground, in this hot weather. A dress so loud   20
it hurts my eyes. There are yellows and oranges enough to throw back the light of the sun. I feel my whole face warming from the heat waves it throws out. Earrings gold, too, and hanging down to her shoulders. Bracelets dangling and making noises when she moves her arm up to shake the folds of the dress out of her armpits. The dress is loose and flows, and as she walks closer, I like it. I hear Maggie go "Uhnnnh" again. It is her sister's hair. It stands straight up like the wool on a sheep. It is black as night and around the edges are two long pig-tails that rope about like small lizards disappearing behind her ears.

"Wa-su-zo-Tean-o!" she says, coming on in that gliding way the dress makes her move. The short stocky fellow with the hair to his navel is all grin-ning and he follows up with "Asalamalakim, my mother and sister!" He moves to hug Maggie but she falls back, right up against the back of my chair. I feel her trembling there and when I look up I see the perspiration falling off her chin.

"Don't get up," says Dee. Since I am stout it takes something of a push. You can see me trying to move a second or two before I make it. She turns, showing white heels through her sandals, and goes back to the car. Out she peeks next with a Polaroid. She stoops down quickly and lines up picture after picture of me sitting there in front of the house with Maggie cowering behind me. She never takes a shot without making sure the house is included. When a cow comes nibbling around the edge of the yard she snaps it and me and Maggie *and* the house. Then she puts the Polaroid in the back seat of the car, and comes up and kisses me on the forehead.

Meanwhile Asalamalakim is going through the motions with Maggie's hand. Maggie's hand is as limp as a fish, and probably as cold, despite the sweat, and she keeps trying to pull it back. It looks like Asalamalakim wants to shake hands but wants to do it fancy. Or maybe he don't know how people shake hands. Anyhow, he soon gives up on Maggie.

"Well," I say. "Dee."

"No, Mama," she says. "Not 'Dee,' Wangero Leewanika Kemanjo!"   25

"What happened to 'Dee'?" I wanted to know.

"She's dead," Wangero said. "I couldn't bear it any longer being named after the people who oppress me."

"You know as well as me you was named after your aunt Dicie," I said. Dicie is my sister. She named Dee. We called her "Big Dee" after Dee was born.

"But who was *she* named after?" asked Wangero.

"I guess after Grandma Dee," I said.   30

"And who was she named after?" asked Wangero.

"Her mother," I said, and saw Wangero was getting tired. "That's about as far back as I can trace it," I said. Though, in fact, I probably could have carried it back beyond the Civil War through the branches.

"Well," said Asalamalakim, "there you are."

"Uhnnnh," I heard Maggie say.

"There I was not," I said, "before 'Dicie' cropped up in our family, so why   35
should I try to trace it that far back?"

He just stood there grinning, looking down on me like somebody inspecting a Model A car. Every once in a while he and Wangero sent eye signals over my head.

"How do you pronounce this name?" I asked.

"You don't have to call me by it if you don't want to," said Wangero.

"Why shouldn't I?" I asked. "If that's what you want us to call you, we'll call you."

"I know it might sound awkward at first," said Wangero.   40

"I'll get used to it," I said. "Ream it out again."

Well, soon we got the name out of the way. Asalamalakim had a name twice as long and three times as hard. After I tripped over it two or three times he told me to just call him Hakim-a-barber. I wanted to ask him was he a barber, but I didn't really think he was, so I didn't ask.

"You must belong to those beef-cattle peoples down the road," I said. They said "Asalamalakim" when they met you, too, but they didn't shake hands. Always too busy: feeding the cattle, fixing the fences, putting up salt-lick shelters, throwing down hay. When the white folks poisoned some of the herd the men stayed up all night with rifles in their hands. I walked a mile and a half just to see the sight.

Hakim-a-barber said, "I accept some of their doctrines, but farming and raising cattle is not my style." (They didn't tell me, and I didn't ask, whether Wangero [Dee] had really gone and married him.)

We sat down to eat and right away he said he didn't eat collards and pork   45
was unclean. Wangero, though, went on through the chitlins and corn bread, the greens and everything else. She talked a blue streak over the sweet potatoes. Everything delighted her. Even the fact that we still used the benches her daddy made for the table when we couldn't afford to buy chairs.

"Oh, Mama!" she cried. Then turned to Hakim-a-barber. "I never knew how lovely these benches are. You can feel the rump prints," she said, running her hands underneath her and along the bench. Then she gave a sigh and her hand closed over Grandma Dee's butter dish. "That's it!" she said. "I knew there was something I wanted to ask you if I could have." She jumped up from the table and went over in the corner where the churn stood, the milk in it clabber by now. She looked at the churn and looked at it.

"This churn top is what I need," she said. "Didn't Uncle Buddy whittle it out of a tree you all used to have?"

"Yes," I said.

"Uh huh," she said happily. "And I want the dasher, too."

"Uncle Buddy whittle that, too?" asked the barber.   50

Dee (Wangero) looked up at me.

"Aunt Dee's first husband whittled the dash," said Maggie so low you almost couldn't hear her. "His name was Henry, but they called him Stash."

"Maggie's brain is like an elephant's," Wangero said, laughing. "I can use the churn top as a centerpiece for the alcove table," she said, sliding a plate over the churn, "and I'll think of something artistic to do with the dasher."

When she finished wrapping the dasher the handle stuck out. I took it for a moment in my hands. You didn't even have to look close to see where hands pushing the dasher up and down to make butter had left a kind of sink in the wood. In fact, there were a lot of small sinks; you could see where thumbs and fingers had sunk into the wood. It was beautiful light yellow wood, from a tree that grew in the yard where Big Dee and Stash had lived.

After dinner Dee (Wangero) went to the trunk at the foot of my bed and   55
started rifling through it. Maggie hung back in the kitchen over the dishpan. Out came Wangero with two quilts. They had been pieced by Grandma Dee and then Big Dee and me had hung them on the quilt frames on the front porch and quilted them. One was in the Lone Star pattern. The other was Walk Around the Mountain. In both of them were scraps of dresses Grandma Dee had worn fifty and more years ago. Bits and pieces of Grandpa Jarrell's paisley shirts. And one teeny faded blue piece, about the size of a penny matchbox, that was from Great Grandpa Ezra's uniform that he wore in the Civil War.

"Mama," Wangero said sweet as a bird. "Can I have these old quilts?"

I heard something fall in the kitchen, and a minute later the kitchen door slammed.

"Why don't you take one or two of the others?" I asked. "These old things was just done by me and Big Dee from some tops your grandma pieced before she died."

"No," said Wangero. "I don't want those. They are stitched around the borders by machine."

"That'll make them last better," I said.   60

"That's not the point," said Wangero. "These are all pieces of dresses Grandma used to wear. She did all this stitching by hand. Imagine!" She held the quilts securely in her arms, stroking them.

"Some of the pieces, like those lavender ones, come from old clothes her mother handed down to her," I said, moving up to touch the quilts. Dee

(Wangero) moved back just enough so that I couldn't reach the quilts. They already belonged to her.

"Imagine!" she breathed again, clutching them closely to her bosom.

"The truth is," I said, "I promised to give them quilts to Maggie, for when she marries John Thomas."

She gasped like a bee had stung her.   65

"Maggie can't appreciate these quilts!" she said. "She'd probably be backward enough to put them to everyday use."

"I reckon she would," I said. "God knows I been saving 'em for long enough with nobody using 'em. I hope she will!" I didn't want to bring up how I had offered Dee (Wangero) a quilt when she went away to college. Then she had told me they were old-fashioned, out of style.

"But they're *priceless*!" she was saying now, furiously; for she has a temper. "Maggie would put them on the bed and in five years they'd be in rags. Less than that!"

"She can always make some more," I said. "Maggie knows how to quilt."

Dee (Wangero) looked at me with hatred. "You just will not understand.   70
The point is these quilts, *these* quilts!"

"Well," I said, stumped. "What would *you* do with them?"

"Hang them," she said. As if that was the only thing you *could* do with quilts.

Maggie by now was standing in the door. I could almost hear the sound her feet made as they scraped over each other.

"She can have them, Mama," she said, like somebody used to never winning anything, or having anything reserved for her. "I can 'member Grandma Dee without the quilts."

I looked at her hard. She had filled her bottom lip with checkerberry snuff   75
and it gave her face a kind of dopey, hangdog look. It was Grandma Dee and Big Dee who taught her how to quilt herself. She stood there with her scarred hands hidden in the folds of her skirt. She looked at her sister with something like fear but she wasn't mad at her. This was Maggie's portion. This was the way she knew God to work.

When I looked at her like that something hit me in the top of my head and ran down to the soles of my feet. Just like when I'm in church and the spirit of God touches me and I get happy and shout. I did something I never had done before: hugged Maggie to me, then dragged her on into the room, snatched the quilts out of Miss Wangero's hands and dumped them into Maggie's lap. Maggie just sat there on my bed with her mouth open.

"Take one or two of the others," I said to Dee.

But she turned without a word and went out to Hakim-a-barber.

"You just don't understand," she said, as Maggie and I came out to the car.

"What don't I understand?" I wanted to know.   80

"Your heritage," she said. And then she turned to Maggie, kissed her, and said, "You ought to try to make something of yourself, too, Maggie. It's really a new day for us. But from the way you and Mama still live you'd never know it."

She put on some sunglasses that hid everything above the tip of her nose and her chin.

Maggie smiled; maybe at the sunglasses. But a real smile, not scared. After we watched the car dust settle I asked Maggie to bring me a dip of snuff. And then the two of us sat there just enjoying, until it was time to go in the house and go to bed.   [1973]

≡ THINKING ABOUT THE TEXT

1. Be specific in arguing that Mama is more sympathetic to Maggie than to Dee? Is Mama hostile to Dee? What values are involved in the tension between Mama and Dee and Maggie?

2. Although many students seem to prefer Maggie to Dee, most would probably rather be Dee than Maggie. Is this true for you? Why?

3. Do you think Walker is against "getting back to one's roots"? Does she give a balanced characterization of Maggie? Of Dee? How might she portray Dee if she wanted to be more positive about her? Less positive?

4. Do you think it helps or hinders the social fabric to affirm ethnic differences? Do you think America is a melting pot? Is a quilt a better symbol to capture our diversity? Can you suggest another metaphor?

5. Do you think most mothers would side with daughters with whom they are more politically or culturally sympathetic? What might be the deciding factor? Are most mothers equally supportive of each of their children?

≡ MAKING COMPARISONS

1. How do you think Maggie would fare if she were the first child in "I Stand Here Ironing"? In "Two Kinds"?

2. Which relationship in the stories in this cluster is closest to your own? Explain.

3. Which one of the five daughters seems the kindest? The smartest? The most ambitious? The most troubled? The most likely to succeed? To find love? Do you think the mothers are responsible for how their daughters turn out?

≡ WRITING ABOUT ISSUES

1. After reading Olsen's story, as Emily's teacher, write a letter to Emily's mother persuading her that she should still come in for a conference. Acknowledge her excuses and her side of the issue, but offer objections.

2. Write a brief essay arguing that each of the mothers presented in Olsen's, Tan's, and Walker's stories is either a good or a bad model for parenting.

3. Write a personal-experience narrative about a time when your parents pushed you too hard or too little or wanted you to be someone you

thought you were not. Conclude with your present view of the consequences of their action.

4. Ask six males and six females if they feel their parents tried to shape their personalities, behavior, choice of friends, and so forth. Were the parents' efforts successful? Do the sons and daughters resent it now? Conclude your brief report with some generalizations, including how relevant gender is.

≡ Siblings in Conflict: Stories

TOBIAS WOLFF, "The Rich Brother"

JAMES BALDWIN, "Sonny's Blues"

Although the expression "blood is thicker than water" suggests that brothers and sisters should support each other, the reality is often more complex. Children growing up together share intense emotional ties, but affection and loyalty sometimes conflict with hostility and jealousy. Children often feel they are competing for their parents' attention and love, a rivalry often played out over a lifetime and intensified as siblings choose different lifestyles. Well into adulthood, brothers and sisters often find their relationships with each other conflicted by unresolved issues of mutual responsibility and disparities in values as well as individual issues of financial success, self-esteem, and guilt. The siblings in the following two stories, separated by age and disparate occupations, engage in a psychologically complex dance that ebbs and flows over their lives. They struggle to understand each other and ultimately themselves, for, as with all of us, healthy relationships with siblings start with a healthy relationship with oneself.

≡ BEFORE YOU READ

How would you describe your relationship with your siblings? Did rivalry ever play a part? Does it now? Do you consider your siblings' futures as similar to yours? Is it important for brothers and sisters to look after each other? Or might that create more problems than it solves?

TOBIAS WOLFF

The Rich Brother

Tobias Wolff (b. 1945) is known chiefly for his short stories. The following piece comes from his second collection, Back in the World *(1985). He has produced two other volumes of stories,* In the Garden of the North American Martyrs *(1981) and* The Night in Question *(1996), and a short novel,* The Barracks Thief *(1984). His latest novel is* Old School *(2004). Wolff is also the author of two memoirs. In the first,* This Boy's Life *(1989), he recalls his parents' divorce and subsequent family dramas. These include wanderings with his mother through the West and Northwest; arguments with his abusive stepfather; occasional contact with his real father, who was a habitual liar later imprisoned for fraud; and years of separation from his brother Geoffrey, who eventually became a writer himself.* This Boy's Life *won the* Los Angeles Times *Book Award for biography and later became a movie starring Robert De Niro as the stepfather and Leonardo DiCaprio as the young Toby. Wolff's second memoir,* In Pharaoh's Army: Memories of the Lost War *(1994), deals mostly with his military service in Vietnam. His most recent collection is* Our Story Begins: New and Selected Stories *(2008). Today, Wolff teaches creative writing at Stanford University.*

There were two brothers, Pete and Donald.

Pete, the older brother, was in real estate. He and his wife had a Century 21 franchise in Santa Cruz. Pete worked hard and made a lot of money, but not any more than he thought he deserved. He had two daughters, a sailboat, a house from which he could see a thin slice of the ocean, and friends doing well enough in their own lives not to wish bad luck on him. Donald, the younger brother, was still single. He lived alone, painted houses when he found the work, and got deeper in debt to Pete when he didn't.

No one would have taken them for brothers. Where Pete was stout and hearty and at home in the world, Donald was bony, grave, and obsessed with the fate of his soul. Over the years Donald had worn the images of two different Perfect Masters around his neck. Out of devotion to the second of these he entered an ashram in Berkeley, where he nearly died of undiagnosed hepatitis. By the time Pete finished paying the medical bills Donald had become a Christian. He drifted from church to church, then joined a pentecostal community that met somewhere in the Mission District to sing in tongues and swap prophecies.

Pete couldn't make sense of it. Their parents were both dead, but while they were alive neither of them had found it necessary to believe in anything. They managed to be decent people without making fools of themselves, and Pete had the same ambition. He thought that the whole thing was an excuse for Donald to take himself seriously.

The trouble was that Donald couldn't content himself with worrying   5
about his own soul. He had to worry about everyone else's, and especially Pete's. He handed down his judgments in ways that he seemed to consider subtle: through significant silence, innuendo, looks of mild despair that said, *Brother, what have you come to?* What Pete had come to, as far as he could tell, was prosperity. That was the real issue between them. Pete prospered and Donald did not prosper.

At the age of forty Pete took up sky diving. He made his first jump with two friends who'd started only a few months earlier and were already doing stunts. He never would have used the word *mystical,* but that was how Pete felt about the experience. Later he made the mistake of trying to describe it to Donald, who kept asking how much it cost and then acted appalled when Pete told him.

"At least I'm trying something new," Pete said. "At least I'm breaking the pattern."

Not long after that conversation Donald also broke the pattern, by going to live on a farm outside Paso Robles. The farm was owned by several members of Donald's community, who had bought it and moved there with the idea of forming a family of faith. That was how Donald explained it in the first letter he sent. Every week Pete heard how happy Donald was, how "in the Lord." He told

Pete that he was praying for him, he and the rest of Pete's brothers and sisters on the farm.

"I only have one brother," Pete wanted to answer, "and that's enough." But he kept this thought to himself.

In November the letters stopped. Pete didn't worry about this at first, but   10 when he called Donald at Thanksgiving Donald was grim. He tried to sound upbeat but he didn't try hard enough to make it convincing. "Now listen," Pete said, "you don't have to stay in that place if you don't want to."

"I'll be all right," Donald answered.

"That's not the point. Being all right is not the point. If you don't like what's going on up there, then get out."

"I'm all right," Donald said again, more firmly. "I'm doing fine."

But he called Pete a week later and said that he was quitting the farm. When Pete asked him where he intended to go, Donald admitted that he had no plan. His car had been repossessed just before he left the city, and he was flat broke.

"I guess you'll have to stay with us," Pete said.   15

Donald put up a show of resistance. Then he gave in. "Just until I get my feet on the ground," he said.

"Right," Pete said. "Check out your options." He told Donald he'd send him money for a bus ticket, but as they were about to hang up Pete changed his mind. He knew that Donald would try hitchhiking to save the fare. Pete didn't want him out on the road all alone where some head case would pick him up, where anything could happen to him.

"Better yet," he said, "I'll come and get you."

"You don't have to do that. I didn't expect you to do that," Donald said. He added, "It's a pretty long drive."

"Just tell me how to get there."   20

But Donald wouldn't give him directions. He said that the farm was too depressing, that Pete wouldn't like it. Instead, he insisted on meeting Pete at a service station called Jonathan's Mechanical Emporium.

"You must be kidding," Pete said.

"It's close to the highway," Donald said. "I didn't name it."

"That's one for the collection," Pete said.

The day before he left to bring Donald home, Pete received a letter from a man   25 who described himself as "head of household" at the farm where Donald had been living. From this letter Pete learned that Donald had not quit the farm, but had been asked to leave. The letter was written on the back of a mimeographed survey form asking people to record their response to a ceremony of some kind. The last question said:

> *What did you feel during the liturgy?*
>   *a) Being*
>   *b) Becoming*
>   *c) Being and Becoming*
>   *d) None of the Above*
>   *e) All of the Above*

Pete tried to forget the letter. But of course he couldn't. Each time he thought of it he felt crowded and breathless, a feeling that came over him again when he drove into the service station and saw Donald sitting against a wall with his head on his knees. It was late afternoon. A paper cup tumbled slowly past Donald's feet, pushed by the damp wind.

Pete honked and Donald raised his head. He smiled at Pete, then stood and stretched. His arms were long and thin and white. He wore a red bandanna across his forehead, a T-shirt with a couple of words on the front. Pete couldn't read them because the letters were inverted.

"Grow up," Pete yelled. "Get a Mercedes."

Donald came up to the window. He bent down and said, "Thanks for coming. You must be totally whipped."

"I'll make it." Pete pointed at Donald's T-shirt. "What's that supposed to say?"

"Donald looked down at his shirt front. "Try God. I guess I put it on backwards. Pete, could I borrow a couple of dollars? I owe these people for coffee and sandwiches."

Pete took five twenties from his wallet and held them out the window.

Donald stepped back as if horrified. "I don't need that much."

"I can't keep track of all these nickels and dimes," Pete said. "Just pay me back when your ship comes in." He waved the bills impatiently. "Go on — take it."

"Only for now." Donald took the money and went into the service station office. He came out carrying two orange sodas, one of which he gave to Pete as he got into the car. "My treat," he said.

"No bags?"

"Wow, thanks for reminding me." Donald balanced his drink on the dashboard, but the slight rocking of the car as he got out tipped it onto the passenger's seat, where half its contents foamed over before Pete could snatch it up again. Donald looked on while Pete held the bottle out the window, soda running down his fingers.

"Wipe it up," Pete told him. "Quick!"

"With what?"

Pete stared at Donald. "That shirt. Use the shirt."

Donald pulled a long face but did as he was told, his pale skin puckering against the wind.

"Great, just great," Pete said. "We haven't even left the gas station yet."

Afterwards, on the highway, Donald said, "This is a new car, isn't it?"

"Yes. This is a new car."

"Is that why you're so upset about the seat?"

"Forget it, okay? Let's just forget about it."

"I said I was sorry."

Pete said, "I just wish you'd be more careful. These seats are made of leather. That stain won't come out, not to mention the smell. I don't see why I can't have leather seats that smell like leather instead of orange pop."

"What was wrong with the other car?"

Pete glanced over at Donald. Donald had raised the hood of the blue sweat-   50
shirt he'd put on. The peaked hood above his gaunt, watchful face gave him the
look of an inquisitor.

"There wasn't anything wrong with it," Pete said. "I just happened to like
this one better."

Donald nodded.

There was a long silence between them as Pete drove on and the day darkened toward evening. On either side of the road lay stubble-covered fields. A
line of low hills ran along the horizon, topped here and there with trees black
against the grey sky. In the approaching line of cars a driver turned on his
headlights. Pete did the same.

"So what happened?" he asked. "Farm life not your bag?"

Donald took some time to answer, and at last he said, simply, "It was my   55
fault."

"What was your fault?"

"The whole thing. Don't play dumb, Pete. I know they wrote to you."
Donald looked at Pete, then stared out the windshield again.

"I'm not playing dumb."

Donald shrugged.

"All I really know is they asked you to leave," Pete went on. "I don't know   60
any of the particulars."

"I blew it," Donald said. "Believe me, you don't want to hear the gory details."

"Sure I do," Pete said. He added, "Everybody likes the gory details."

"You mean everybody likes to hear how someone messed up."

"Right," Pete said. "That's the way it is here on Spaceship Earth."

Donald bent one knee onto the front seat and leaned against the door so   65
that he was facing Pete instead of the windshield. Pete was aware of Donald's
scrutiny. He waited. Night was coming on in a rush now, filling the hollows of
the land. Donald's long cheeks and deep-set eyes were dark with shadow. His
brow was white. "Do you ever dream about me?" Donald asked.

"Do I ever dream about you? What kind of a question is that? Of course I
don't dream about you," Pete said, untruthfully.

"What do you dream about?"

"Sex and money. Mostly money. A nightmare is when I dream I don't
have any."

"You're just making that up," Donald said.

Pete smiled.   70

"Sometimes I wake up at night," Donald went on, "and I can tell you're
dreaming about me."

"We were talking about the farm," Pete said. "Let's finish that conversation
and then we can talk about our various out-of-body experiences and the interesting things we did during previous incarnations."

For a moment Donald looked like a grinning skull; then he turned serious
again. "There's not much to tell," he said. "I just didn't do anything right."

"That's a little vague," Pete said.

"Well, like the groceries. Whenever it was my turn to get the groceries I'd   75
blow it somehow. I'd bring the groceries home and half of them would be missing, or I'd have all the wrong things, the wrong kind of flour or the wrong kind
of chocolate or whatever. One time I gave them away. It's not funny, Pete."

Pete said, "Who did you give the groceries to?"

"Just some people I picked up on the way home. Some fieldworkers. They
had about eight kids with them and they didn't even speak English—just nodded their heads. Still, I shouldn't have given away the groceries. Not all of
them, anyway. I really learned my lesson about that. You have to be practical.
You have to be fair to yourself." Donald leaned forward, and Pete could sense
his excitement. "There's nothing actually wrong with being in business," he
said. "As long as you're fair to other people you can still be fair to yourself. I'm
thinking of going into business, Pete."

"We'll talk about it," Pete said. "So, that's the story? There isn't any more
to it than that?"

"What did they tell you?" Donald asked.

"Nothing."   80

"They must have told you something."

Pete shook his head.

"They didn't tell you about the fire?" When Pete shook his head again
Donald regarded him for a time, then folded his arms across his chest and
slumped back into the corner. "Everybody had to take turns cooking dinner. I
usually did tuna casserole or spaghetti with garlic bread. But this one night I
thought I'd do something different, something really interesting." Donald
looked sharply at Pete. "It's all a big laugh to you, isn't it?"

"I'm sorry," Pete said.

"You don't know when to quit. You just keep hitting away."   85

"Tell me about the fire, Donald."

Donald kept watching him. "You have this compulsion to make me look
foolish."

"Come off it, Donald. Don't make a big thing out of this."

"I know why you do it. It's because you don't have any purpose in life.
You're afraid to relate to people who do, so you make fun of them."

"Relate," Pete said.   90

"You're basically a very frightened individual," Donald said. "Very threatened. You've always been like that. Do you remember when you used to try to
kill me?"

"I don't have any compulsion to make you look foolish, Donald—you do it
yourself. You're doing it right now."

"You can't tell me you don't remember," Donald said. "It was after my operation. You remember that?"

"Sort of." Pete shrugged. "Not really."

"Oh yes," Donald said. "Do you want to see the scar?"   95

"I remember you had an operation. I don't remember the specifics, that's
all. And I sure as hell don't remember trying to kill you."

"Oh yes," Donald repeated, maddeningly. "You bet your life you did. All the time. The thing was, I couldn't have anything happen to me where they sewed me up because then my intestines would come apart again and poison me. That was a big issue, Pete. Mom was always in a state about me climbing trees and so on. And you used to hit me there every chance you got."

"Mom was in a state every time you burped," Pete said. "I don't know. Maybe I bumped into you accidentally once or twice. I never did it deliberately."

"Every chance you got," Donald said. "Like when the folks went out at night and left you to baby-sit. I'd hear them say good night, and then I'd hear the car start up, and when they were gone I'd lie there and listen. After a while I would hear you coming down the hall, and I would close my eyes and pretend to be asleep. There were nights when you would stand outside the door, just stand there, and then go away again. But most nights you'd open the door and I would hear you in the room with me, breathing. You'd come over and sit next to me on the bed — you remember, Pete, you have to — you'd sit next to me on the bed and pull the sheets back. If I was on my stomach you'd roll me over. Then you would lift up my pajama shirt and start hitting me on my stitches. You'd hit me as hard as you could, over and over. I was afraid that you'd get mad if you knew I was awake. Is that strange or what? I was afraid that you'd get mad if you found out that I knew you were trying to kill me." Donald laughed. "Come on, you can't tell me you don't remember that."

"It might have happened once or twice. Kids do those things. I can't get all   100
excited about something I maybe did twenty-five years ago."

"No maybe about it. You did it."

Pete said, "You're wearing me out with this stuff. We've got a long drive ahead of us and if you don't back off pretty soon we aren't going to make it. You aren't, anyway."

Donald turned away.

"I'm doing my best," Pete said. The self-pity in his own voice made the words sound like a lie. But they weren't a lie! He was doing his best.

The car topped a rise. In the distance Pete saw a cluster of lights that   105
blinked out when he started downhill. There was no moon. The sky was low and black.

"Come to think of it," Pete said, "I did have a dream about you the other night." Then he added, impatiently, as if Donald were badgering him, "A couple of other nights, too. I'm getting hungry," he said.

"The same dream?"

"Different dreams. I only remember one of them. There was something wrong with me, and you were helping out. Taking care of me. Just the two of us. I don't know where everyone else was supposed to be."

Pete left it at that. He didn't tell Donald that in this dream he was blind.

"I wonder if that was when I woke up," Donald said. He added, "I'm sorry   110
I got into that thing about my scar. I keep trying to forget it but I guess I never will. Not really. It was pretty strange, having someone around all the time who wanted to get rid of me."

"Kid stuff," Pete said. "Ancient history."

They ate dinner at a Denny's on the other side of King City. As Pete was paying the check he heard a man behind him say, "Excuse me, but I wonder if I might ask which way you're going?" and Donald answer, "Santa Cruz."

"Perfect," the man said.

Pete could see him in the fish-eye mirror above the cash register: a red blazer with some kind of crest on the pocket, little black moustache, glossy black hair combed down on his forehead like a Roman emperor's. A rug, Pete thought. Definitely a rug.

Pete got his change and turned. "Why is that perfect?" he asked.   115

The man looked at Pete. He had a soft, ruddy face that was doing its best to express pleasant surprise, as if this new wrinkle were all he could have wished for, but the eyes behind the aviator glasses showed signs of regret. His lips were moist and shiny. "I take it you're together," he said.

"You got it," Pete told him.

"All the better, then," the man went on. "It so happens I'm going to Santa Cruz myself. Had a spot of car trouble down the road. The old Caddy let me down."

"What kind of trouble?" Pete asked.

"Engine trouble," the man said. "I'm afraid it's a bit urgent. My daughter is   120
sick. Urgently sick. I've got a telegram here." He patted the breast pocket of his blazer.

Before Pete could say anything Donald got into the act again. "No problem," Donald said. "We've got tons of room."

"Not that much room," Pete said.

Donald nodded. "I'll put my things in the trunk."

"The trunk's full," Pete told him.

"It so happens I'm traveling light," the man said. "This leg of the trip any-   125
way. In fact, I don't have any luggage at this particular time."

Pete said, "Left it in the old Caddy, did you?"

"Exactly," the man said.

"No problem," Donald repeated. He walked outside and the man went with him. Together they strolled across the parking lot, Pete following at a distance. When they reached Pete's car Donald raised his face to the sky, and the man did the same. They stood there looking up. "Dark night," Donald said.

"Stygian,°" the man said.

Pete still had it in his mind to brush him off, but he didn't do that. Instead   130
he unlocked the door for him. He wanted to see what would happen. It was an adventure, but not a dangerous adventure. The man might steal Pete's ashtrays but he wouldn't kill him. If Pete got killed on the road it would be by some spiritual person in a sweatsuit, someone with his eyes on the far horizon and a wet Try God T-shirt in his duffel bag.

As soon as they left the parking lot the man lit a cigar. He blew a cloud of smoke over Pete's shoulder and sighed with pleasure. "Put it out," Pete told him.

Stygian: Unremittingly dark and frightening.

"Of course," the man said. Pete looked in the rearview mirror and saw the man take another long puff before dropping the cigar out the window. "Forgive me," he said. "I should have asked. Name's Webster, by the way."

Donald turned and looked back at him. "First name or last?"

The man hesitated. "Last," he said finally.

"I know a Webster," Donald said. "Mick Webster."   135

"There are many of us," Webster said.

"Big fellow, wooden leg," Pete said.

Donald gave Pete a look.

Webster shook his head. "Doesn't ring a bell. Still, I wouldn't deny the connection. Might be one of the cousinry."

"What's your daughter got?" Pete asked.   140

"That isn't clear," Webster answered. "It appears to be a female complaint of some nature. Then again it may be tropical." He was quiet for a moment, and added: "If indeed it *is* tropical, I will have to assume some of the blame myself. It was my own vaulting ambition that first led us to the tropics and kept us in the tropics all those many years, exposed to every evil. Truly I have much to answer for. I left my wife there."

Donald said quietly, "You mean she died?"

"I buried her with these hands. The earth will be repaid, gold for gold."

"Which tropics?" Pete asked.

"The tropics of Peru."   145

"What part of Peru are they in?"

"The lowlands," Webster said.

"What's it like down there? In the lowlands."

"Another world," Webster said. His tone was sepulchral. "A world better imagined than described."

"Far out," Pete said.   150

The three men rode in silence for a time. A line of trucks went past in the other direction, trailers festooned with running lights, engines roaring.

"Yes," Webster said at last, "I have much to answer for."

Pete smiled at Donald, but Donald had turned in his seat again and was gazing at Webster. "I'm sorry about your wife," Donald said.

"What did she die of?" Pete asked.

"A wasting illness," Webster said. "The doctors have no name for it, but I   155
do." He leaned forward and said, fiercely, "*Greed.* My greed, not hers. She wanted no part of it."

Pete bit his lip. Webster was a find and Pete didn't want to scare him off by hooting at him. In a voice low and innocent of knowingness, he asked, "What took you there?"

"It's difficult for me to talk about."

"Try," Pete told him.

"A cigar would make it easier."

Donald turned to Pete and said, "It's okay with me."   160

"All right," Pete said. "Go ahead. Just keep the window rolled down."

"Much obliged." A match flared. There were eager sucking sounds.

"Let's hear it," Pete said.

"I am by training an engineer," Webster began. "My work has exposed me to all but one of the continents, to desert and alp and forest, to every terrain and season of the earth. Some years ago I was hired by the Peruvian government to search for tungsten in the tropics. My wife and daughter accompanied me. We were the only white people for a thousand miles in any direction, and we had no choice but to live as the Indians lived — to share their food and drink and even their culture."

Pete said, "You knew the lingo, did you?"   165

"We picked it up." The ember of the cigar bobbed up and down. "We were used to learning as necessity decreed. At any rate, it became evident after a couple of years that there was no tungsten to be found. My wife had fallen ill and was pleading to be taken home. But I was deaf to her pleas, because by then I was on the trail of another metal — a metal far more valuable than tungsten."

"Let me guess," Pete said. "Gold?"

Donald looked at Pete, then back at Webster.

"Gold," Webster said. "A vein of gold greater than the Mother Lode itself. After I found the first traces of it nothing could tear me away from my search — not the sickness of my wife or anything else. I was determined to uncover the vein, and so I did — but not before I laid my wife to rest. As I say, the earth will be repaid."

Webster was quiet. Then he said, "But life must go on. In the years since my   170
wife's death I have been making the arrangements necessary to open the mine. I could have done it immediately, of course, enriching myself beyond measure, but I knew what that would mean — the exploitation of our beloved Indians, the brutal destruction of their environment. I felt I had too much to atone for already." Webster paused, and when he spoke again his voice was dull and rushed, as if he had used up all the interest he had in his own words. "Instead I drew up a program for returning the bulk of the wealth to the Indians themselves. A kind of trust fund. The interest alone will allow them to secure their ancient lands and rights in perpetuity. At the same time, our investors will be rewarded a thousandfold. Two-thousandfold. Everyone will prosper together."

"That's great," said Donald. "That's the way it ought to be."

Pete said, "I'm willing to bet that you just happen to have a few shares left. Am I right?"

Webster made no reply.

"Well?" Pete knew that Webster was on to him now, but he didn't care. The story had bored him. He'd expected something different, something original, and Webster had let him down. He hadn't even tried. Pete felt sour and stale. His eyes burned from cigar smoke and the high beams of road-hogging truckers. "Douse the stogie," he said to Webster. "I told you to keep the window down."

"Got a little nippy back here."   175

Donald said, "Hey, Pete. Lighten up."

"Douse it!"

Webster sighed. He got rid of the cigar.

"I'm a wreck," Pete said to Donald. "You want to drive for a while?"

Donald nodded.   180
Pete pulled over and they changed places.
Webster kept his counsel in the back seat. Donald hummed while he drove, until Pete told him to stop. Then everything was quiet.

Donald was humming again when Pete woke up. Pete stared sullenly at the road, at the white lines sliding past the car. After a few moments of this he turned and said, "How long have I been out?"

Donald glanced at him. "Twenty, twenty-five minutes."

Pete looked behind him and saw that Webster was gone. "Where's our   185
friend?"

"You just missed him. He got out in Soledad. He told me to say thanks and good-bye."

"Soledad? What about his sick daughter? How did he explain her away?"

"He has a brother living there. He's going to borrow a car from him and drive the rest of the way in the morning."

"I'll bet his brother's living there," Pete said. "Doing fifty concurrent life sentences. His brother and his sister and his mom and his dad."

"I kind of liked him," Donald said.   190

"I'm sure you did," Pete said wearily.

"He was interesting. He's been places."

"His cigars had been places, I'll give you that."

"Come on, Pete."

"Come on yourself. What a phony."   195

"You don't know that."

"Sure I do."

"How? How do you know?"

Pete stretched. "Brother, there are some things you're just born knowing. What's the gas situation?"

"We're a little low."   200

"Then why didn't you get some more?"

"I wish you wouldn't snap at me like that," Donald said.

"Then why don't you use your head? What if we run out?"

"We'll make it," Donald said. "I'm pretty sure we've got enough to make it. You didn't have to be so rude to him," Donald added.

Pete took a deep breath. "I don't feel like running out of gas tonight, okay?"   205

Donald pulled in at the next station they came to and filled the tank while Pete went to the men's room. When Pete came back, Donald was sitting in the passenger's seat. The attendant came up to the driver's window as Pete got in behind the wheel. He bent down and said, "Twelve fifty-five."

"You heard the man," Pete said to Donald.

Donald looked straight ahead. He didn't move.

"Cough up," Pete said. "This trip's on you."

"I can't."   210

"Sure you can. Break out that wad."

Donald glanced up at the attendant, then at Pete. "Please," he said, "Pete, I don't have it anymore."

Pete took this in. He nodded, and paid the attendant.

Donald began to speak when they left the station but Pete cut him off. He said, "I don't want to hear from you right now. You just keep quiet or I swear to God I won't be responsible."

They left the fields and entered a tunnel of tall trees. The trees went on and on. "Let me get this straight," Pete said at last. "You don't have the money I gave you."

"You treated him like a bug or something," Donald said.

"You don't have the money," Pete said again.

Donald shook his head.

"Since I bought dinner, and since we didn't stop anywhere in between, I assume you gave it to Webster. Is that right? Is that what you did with it?"

"Yes."

Pete looked at Donald. His face was dark under the hood but he still managed to convey a sense of remove, as if none of this had anything to do with him.

"Why?" Pete asked. "Why did you give it to him?" When Donald didn't answer, Pete said, "A hundred dollars. Gone. Just like that. I *worked* for that money, Donald."

"I know, I know," Donald said.

"You don't know! How could you? You get money by holding out your hand."

"I work too," Donald said.

"You work too. Don't kid yourself, brother."

Donald leaned toward Pete, about to say something, but Pete cut him off again.

"You're not the only one on the payroll, Donald. I don't think you understand that. I have a family."

"Pete, I'll pay you back."

"Like hell you will. A hundred dollars!" Pete hit the steering wheel with the palm of his hand. "Just because you think I hurt some goofball's feelings. Jesus, Donald."

"That's not the reason," Donald said. "And I didn't just *give* him the money."

"What do you call it, then? What do you call what you did?"

"I *invested* it. I wanted a share, Pete." When Pete looked over at him Donald nodded and said again, "I wanted a share."

Pete said, "I take it you're referring to the gold mine in Peru."

"Yes," Donald said.

"You believe that such a gold mine exists?"

Donald looked at Pete, and Pete could see him just beginning to catch on. "You'll believe anything," Pete said. "Won't you? You really will believe anything at all."

"I'm sorry," Donald said, and turned away.

Pete drove on between the trees and considered the truth of what he had just said—that Donald would believe anything at all. And it came to him that it would be just like this unfair life for Donald to come out ahead in the end, by believing in some outrageous promise that would turn out to be true and that he, Pete, would reject out of hand because he was too wised up to listen to any-body's pitch anymore except for laughs. What a joke. What a joke if there really was a blessing to be had, and the blessing didn't come to the one who deserved it, the one who did all the work, but to the other.

And as if this had already happened Pete felt a shadow move upon him, darkening his thoughts. After a time he said, "I can see where all this is going, Donald." 240

"I'll pay you back," Donald said.

"No," Pete said. "You won't pay me back. You can't. You don't know how. All you've ever done is take. All your life."

Donald shook his head.

"I see exactly where this is going," Pete went on. "You can't work, you can't take care of yourself, you believe anything anyone tells you. I'm stuck with you, aren't I?" He looked over at Donald. "I've got you on my hands for good."

Donald pressed his fingers against the dashboard as if to brace himself. "I'll get out," he said. 245

Pete kept driving.

"Let me out," Donald said. "I mean it, Pete."

"Do you?"

Donald hesitated. "Yes," he said.

"Be sure," Pete told him. "This is it. This is for keeps." 250

"I mean it."

"All right. You made the choice." Pete braked the car sharply and swung it to the shoulder of the road. He turned off the engine and got out. Trees loomed on both sides, shutting out the sky. The air was cold and musty. Pete took Donald's duffel bag from the back seat and set it down behind the car. He stood there, facing Donald in the red glow of the taillights. "It's better this way," Pete said.

Donald just looked at him.

"Better for you," Pete said.

Donald hugged himself. He was shaking. "You don't have to say all that," he told Pete. "I don't blame you." 255

"Blame me? What the hell are you talking about? Blame me for what?"

"For anything," Donald said.

"I want to know what you mean by blame me."

"Nothing. Nothing, Pete. You'd better get going. God bless you."

"That's it," Pete said. He dropped to one knee, searching the packed dirt with his hands. He didn't know what he was looking for, his hands would know when they found it. 260

Donald touched Pete's shoulder. "You'd better go," he said.

Somewhere in the trees Pete heard a branch snap. He stood up. He looked at Donald, then went back to the car and drove away. He drove fast, hunched over the wheel, conscious of the way he was hunched and the shallowness of his breathing, refusing to look in the mirror above his head until there was nothing behind him but darkness.

Then he said, "A hundred dollars," as if there were someone to hear.

The trees gave way to fields. Metal fences ran beside the road, plastered with windblown scraps of paper. Tule fog hung above the ditches, spilling into the road, dimming the ghostly halogen lights that burned in the yards of the farms Pete passed. The fog left beads of water rolling up the windshield.

Pete rummaged among his cassettes. He found Pachelbel's Canon and 265 pushed it into the tape deck. When the violins began to play he leaned back and assumed an attentive expression as if he were really listening to them. He smiled to himself like a man at liberty to enjoy music, a man who has finished his work and settled his debts, done all things meet and due.

And in this way, smiling, nodding to the music, he went another mile or so and pretended that he was not already slowing down, that he was not going to turn back, that he would be able to drive on like this, alone, and have the right answer when his wife stood before him in the doorway of his home and asked, Where is he? Where is your brother? *[1985]*

≡ THINKING ABOUT THE TEXT

1. Are you more sympathetic to Donald's side or to Pete's side in this story? Do you agree with the comment that "everybody likes to hear how someone messed up" (para. 63)? Does Donald get conned by Webster? Would you be angry with Donald for giving Webster your money? Does Pete want Donald to look foolish? Is Donald foolish?

2. How do you interpret Donald's story about Pete hitting his stitches? Was Pete trying to get rid of Donald? What could his reason have been?

3. Why doesn't Pete tell Donald he was blind in his dream? How do you interpret this dream? Is the heart of their dispute "prosperity," or is it something else?

4. In his recent book (*Our Story Begins: New and Selected Stories* [2008]), Wolff revises the end of this story. In paragraph 260, he deletes the last two sentences and adds instead, "and took a step toward Donald." Some readers were disappointed that he takes out what they see as an enigmatic action that adds mystery and complexity to the ending. Do you agree? Why do you think Wolff made this change?

5. Why would Pete turn around to get Donald? Why would he keep going? What would you do? Why?

JAMES BALDWIN
Sonny's Blues

James Baldwin (1924–1987) wanted to be a writer from the time he was a boy growing up in Harlem. He continued his writing through high school while also following in his foster father's footsteps by doing some preaching. On his own at age eighteen, Baldwin left Greenwich Village in 1948 and moved to Paris. He lived in France for eight years before returning to New York, where he wrote widely about the civil rights movement.

Indeed, Baldwin's passionate and eloquent essays, like those in Notes of a Native Son *(1955) and* The Fire Next Time *(1963), exploring the place of African Americans in contemporary society are considered among the best nonfiction of his generation.*

Being an artist and an African American were lifelong central issues for Baldwin. His fiction confronts the psychological challenges that were inevitable for black writers searching for identity in America. Themes of responsibility, pain, identity, frustration, and bitterness are woven into his fiction along with understanding, equanimity, love, and tolerance. "Sonny's Blues," from Going to Meet the Man *(1965), is one of his strongest dramatizations of the struggles and achievements of black artists.*

I read about it in the paper, in the subway, on my way to work. I read it, and I couldn't believe it, and I read it again. Then perhaps I just stared at it, at the newsprint spelling out his name, spelling out the story. I stared at it in the swinging lights of the subway car, and in the faces and bodies of the people, and in my own face, trapped in the darkness which roared outside.

It was not to be believed and I kept telling myself that, as I walked from the subway station to the high school. And at the same time I couldn't doubt it. I was scared, scared for Sonny. He became real to me again. A great block of ice got settled in my belly and kept melting there slowly all day long, while I taught my classes algebra. It was a special kind of ice. It kept melting, sending trickles of ice water all up and down my veins, but it never got less. Sometimes it hardened and seemed to expand until I felt my guts were going to come spilling out or that I was going to choke or scream. This would always be at a moment when I was remembering some specific thing Sonny had once said or done.

When he was about as old as the boys in my classes his face had been bright and open, there was a lot of copper in it; and he'd had wonderfully direct brown eyes, and great gentleness and privacy. I wondered what he looked like now. He had been picked up, the evening before, in a raid on an apartment downtown, for peddling and using heroin.

I couldn't believe it: but what I mean by that is that I couldn't find any room for it anywhere inside me. I had kept it outside me for a long time. I hadn't wanted to know. I had had suspicions, but I didn't name them, I kept putting them away. I told myself that Sonny was wild, but he wasn't crazy. And he'd always been a good boy, he hadn't ever turned hard or evil or disrespectful, the way kids can, so quick, so quick, especially in Harlem. I didn't want to believe that I'd ever see my brother going down, coming to nothing, all that light in his face gone out, in the condition I'd already seen so many others. Yet it had happened and here I was, talking about algebra to a lot of boys who might, every one of them for all I knew, be popping off needles every time they went to the head. Maybe it did more for them than algebra could.

I was sure that the first time Sonny had ever had horse,° he couldn't have been much older than these boys were now. These boys, now, were living as we'd been living then, they were growing up with a rush and their heads bumped abruptly against the low ceiling of their actual possibilities. They were

5

horse: Name for heroin in the 1950s.

filled with rage. All they really knew were two darknesses, the darkness of their lives, which was now closing in on them, and the darkness of the movies, which had blinded them to that other darkness, and in which they now, vindictively, dreamed, at once more together than they were at any other time, and more alone.

When the last bell rang, the last class ended, I let out my breath. It seemed I'd been holding it for all that time. My clothes were wet — I may have looked as though I'd been sitting in a steam bath, all dressed up, all afternoon. I sat alone in the classroom a long time. I listened to the boys outside, downstairs, shouting and cursing and laughing. Their laughter struck me for perhaps the first time. It was not the joyous laughter which — God knows why — one associates with children. It was mocking and insular, its intent to denigrate. It was disenchanted, and in this, also, lay the authority of their curses. Perhaps I was listening to them because I was thinking about my brother and in them I heard my brother. And myself.

One boy was whistling a tune, at once very complicated and very simple, it seemed to be pouring out of him as though he were a bird, and it sounded very cool and moving through all that harsh, bright air, only just holding its own through all those other sounds.

I stood up and walked over to the window and looked down into the courtyard. It was the beginning of the spring and the sap was rising in the boys. A teacher passed through them every now and again, quickly, as though he or she couldn't wait to get out of that courtyard, to get those boys out of their sight and off their minds. I started collecting my stuff. I thought I'd better get home and talk to Isabel.

The courtyard was almost deserted by the time I got downstairs. I saw this boy standing in the shadow of a doorway, looking just like Sonny. I almost called his name. Then I saw that it wasn't Sonny, but somebody we used to know, a boy from around our block. He'd been Sonny's friend. He'd never been mine, having been too young for me, and, anyway, I'd never liked him. And now, even though he was a grown-up man, he still hung around that block, still spent hours on the street corners, was always high and raggy. I used to run into him from time to time and he'd often work around to asking me for a quarter or fifty cents. He always had some real good excuse, too, and I always gave it to him, I don't know why.

But now, abruptly, I hated him. I couldn't stand the way he looked at me, partly like a dog, partly like a cunning child. I wanted to ask him what the hell he was doing in the school courtyard. 10

He sort of shuffled over to me, and he said, "I see you got the papers. So you already know about it."

"You mean about Sonny? Yes, I already know about it. How come they didn't get you?"

He grinned. It made him repulsive and it also brought to mind what he'd looked like as a kid. "I wasn't there. I stay away from them people."

"Good for you." I offered him a cigarette and I watched him through the smoke. "You come all the way down here just to tell me about Sonny?"

"That's right." He was sort of shaking his head and his eyes looked strange,   15
as though they were about to cross. The bright sun deadened his damp dark
brown skin and it made his eyes look yellow and showed up the dirt in his
kinked hair. He smelled funky. I moved a little away from him and I said, "Well,
thanks. But I already know about it and I got to get home."

"I'll walk you a little ways," he said. We started walking. There were a
couple of kids still loitering in the courtyard and one of them said goodnight to
me and looked strangely at the boy beside me.

"What're you going to do?" he asked me. "I mean, about Sonny?"

"Look. I haven't seen Sonny for over a year. I'm not sure I'm going to do
anything. Anyway, what the hell *can* I do?"

"That's right," he said quickly, "ain't nothing you can do. Can't much help
old Sonny no more, I guess."

It was what I was thinking and so it seemed to me he had no right to say it.   20

"I'm surprised at Sonny, though," he went on — he had a funny way of
talking, he looked straight ahead as though he were talking to himself — "I
thought Sonny was a smart boy, I thought he was too smart to get hung."

"I guess he thought so too," I said sharply, "and that's how he got hung.
And how about you? You're pretty goddamn smart, I bet."

Then he looked directly at me, just for a minute. "I ain't smart," he said. "If
I was smart, I'd have reached for a pistol a long time ago."

"Look. Don't tell *me* your sad story, if it was up to me, I'd give you one."
Then I felt guilty — guilty, probably, for never having supposed that the poor
bastard *had* a story of his own, much less a sad one, and I asked, quickly,
"What's going to happen to him now?"

He didn't answer this. He was off by himself some place. "Funny thing," he   25
said, and from his tone we might have been discussing the quickest way to get
to Brooklyn, "when I saw the papers this morning, the first thing I asked myself
was if I had anything to do with it. I felt sort of responsible."

I began to listen more carefully. The subway station was on the corner, just
before us, and I stopped. He stopped, too. We were in front of a bar and he
ducked slightly, peering in, but whoever he was looking for didn't seem to be
there. The juke box was blasting away with something black and bouncy and I
half watched the barmaid as she danced her way from the juke box to her place
behind the bar. And I watched her face as she laughingly responded to something someone said to her, still keeping time to the music. When she smiled one
saw the little girl, one sensed the doomed, still-struggling woman beneath the
battered face of the semi-whore.

"I never *give* Sonny nothing," the boy said finally, "but a long time ago I come
to school high and Sonny asked me how it felt." He paused, I couldn't bear to
watch him, I watched the barmaid, and I listened to the music which seemed to
be causing the pavement to shake. "I told him it felt great." The music stopped, the
barmaid paused and watched the juke box until the music began again. "It did."

All this was carrying me some place I didn't want to go. I certainly didn't
want to know how it felt. It filled everything, the people, the houses, the music,
the dark, quicksilver barmaid, with menace; and this menace was their reality.

"What's going to happen to him now?" I asked again.

"They'll send him away some place and they'll try to cure him." He shook   30
his head. "Maybe he'll even think he's kicked the habit. Then they'll let him
loose" — he gestured, throwing his cigarette into the gutter. "That's all."

"What do you mean, that's *all*?"

But I knew what he meant.

"I *mean*, that's *all*." He turned his head and looked at me, pulling down the
corners of his mouth. "Don't you know what I mean?" he asked, softly.

"How the hell *would* I know what you mean?" I almost whispered it, I don't
know why.

"That's right," he said to the air, "how would *he* know what I mean?" He   35
turned toward me again, patient and calm, and yet I somehow felt him shaking, shaking as though he were going to fall apart. I felt that ice in my guts
again, the dread I'd felt all afternoon; and again I watched the barmaid, moving about the bar, washing glasses, and singing. "Listen. They'll let him out and
then it'll just start all over again. That's what I mean."

"You mean — they'll let him out. And then he'll just start working his way
back in again. You mean he'll never kick the habit. Is that what you mean?"

"That's right," he said, cheerfully. "*You* see what I mean."

"Tell me," I said at last, "why does he want to die? He must want to die, he's
killing himself, why does he want to die?"

He looked at me in surprise. He licked his lips. "He don't want to die. He
wants to live. Don't nobody want to die, ever."

Then I wanted to ask him — too many things. He could not have answered,   40
or if he had, I could not have borne the answers. I started walking. "Well, I
guess it's none of my business."

"It's going to be rough on old Sonny," he said. We reached the subway station. "This is your station?" he asked. I nodded. I took one step down. "Damn!"
he said, suddenly. I looked up at him. He grinned again. "Damn it if I didn't
leave all my money home. You ain't got a dollar on you, have you? Just for a
couple of days, is all."

All at once something inside gave and threatened to come pouring out of
me. I didn't hate him any more. I felt that in another moment I'd start crying
like a child.

"Sure," I said. "Don't sweat." I looked in my wallet and didn't have a dollar,
I only had a five. "Here," I said. "That hold you?"

He didn't look at it — he didn't want to look at it. A terrible closed look
came over his face, as though he were keeping the number on the bill a secret
from him and me. "Thanks," he said, and now he was dying to see me go.
"Don't worry about Sonny. Maybe I'll write him or something."

"Sure," I said. "You do that. So long."   45

"Be seeing you," he said. I went on down the steps.

And I didn't write Sonny or send him anything for a long time. When I finally
did, it was just after my little girl died, he wrote me back a letter which made me
feel like a bastard.

Here's what he said:

Dear brother,

You don't know how much I needed to hear from you. I wanted to write you many a time but I dug how much I must have hurt you and so I didn't write. But now I feel like a man who's been trying to climb up out of some deep, real deep and funky hole and just saw the sun up there, outside. I got to get outside.

I can't tell you much about how I got here. I mean I don't know how to tell you. I guess I was afraid of something or I was trying to escape from something and you know I have never been very strong in the head (smile). I'm glad Mama and Daddy are dead and can't see what's happened to their son and I swear if I'd known what I was doing I would never have hurt you so, you and a lot of other fine people who were nice to me and who believed in me.

I don't want you to think it had anything to do with me being a musician. It's more than that. Or maybe less than that. I can't get anything straight in my head down here and I try not to think about what's going to happen to me when I get outside again. Sometime I think I'm going to flip and never get outside and sometime I think I'll come straight back. I tell you one thing, though, I'd rather blow my brains out than go through this again. But that's what they all say, so they tell me. If I tell you when I'm coming to New York and if you could meet me, I sure would appreciate it. Give my love to Isabel and the kids and I was sure sorry to hear about little Gracie. I wish I could be like Mama and say the Lord's will be done, but I don't know it seems to me that trouble is the one thing that never does get stopped and I don't know what good it does to blame it on the Lord. But maybe it does some good if you believe it.

Your brother,

Sonny

Then I kept in constant touch with him and I sent him whatever I could and I went to meet him when he came back to New York. When I saw him many things I thought I had forgotten came flooding back to me. This was because I had begun, finally, to wonder about Sonny, about the life that Sonny lived inside. This life, whatever it was, had made him older and thinner and it had deepened the distant stillness in which he had always moved. He looked very unlike my baby brother. Yet, when he smiled, when we shook hands, the baby brother I'd never known looked out from the depths of his private life, like an animal waiting to be coaxed into the light.

"How you been keeping?" he asked me.

"All right. And you?"

"Just fine." He was smiling all over his face. "It's good to see you again."

"It's good to see you."

The seven years' difference in our ages lay between us like a chasm: I wondered if these years would ever operate between us as a bridge. I was remembering, and it made it hard to catch my breath, that I had been there when he was born; and I had heard the first words he had ever spoken. When he started to walk, he walked from our mother straight to me. I caught him just before he fell when he took the first steps he ever took in this world.

"How's Isabel?"   55
"Just fine. She's dying to see you."
"And the boys?"
"They're fine, too. They're anxious to see their uncle."
"Oh, come on. You know they don't remember me."
"Are you kidding? Of course they remember you."   60

He grinned again. We got into a taxi. We had a lot to say to each other, far too much to know how to begin.

As the taxi began to move, I asked, "You still want to go to India?"

He laughed. "You still remember that. Hell, no. This place is Indian enough for me."

"It used to belong to them," I said.

And he laughed again. "They damn sure knew what they were doing   65
when they got rid of it."

Years ago, when he was around fourteen, he'd been all hipped on the idea of going to India. He read books about people sitting on rocks, naked, in all kinds of weather, but mostly bad, naturally, and walking barefoot through hot coals and arriving at wisdom. I used to say that it sounded to me as though they were getting away from wisdom as fast as they could. I think he sort of looked down on me for that.

"Do you mind," he asked, "if we have the driver drive alongside the park? On the west side—I haven't seen the city in so long."

"Of course not," I said. I was afraid that I might sound as though I were humoring him, but I hoped he wouldn't take it that way.

So we drove along, between the green of the park and the stony, lifeless elegance of hotels and apartment buildings, toward the vivid, killing streets of our childhood. These streets hadn't changed, though housing projects jutted up out of them now like rocks in the middle of a boiling sea. Most of the houses in which we had grown up had vanished, as had the stores from which we had stolen, the basements in which we had first tried sex, the rooftops from which we had hurled tin cans and bricks. But houses exactly like the houses of our past yet dominated the landscape, boys exactly like the boys we once had been found themselves smothering in these houses, came down into the streets for light and air and found themselves encircled by disaster. Some escaped the trap, most didn't. Those who got out always left something of themselves behind, as some animals amputate a leg and leave it in the trap. It might be said, perhaps, that I had escaped, after all, I was a school teacher; or that Sonny had, he hadn't lived in Harlem for years. Yet, as the cab moved uptown through streets which seemed, with a rush, to darken with dark people, and as I covertly studied Sonny's face, it came to me that what we both were seeking through our separate cab windows was that part of ourselves which had been left behind. It's always at the hour of trouble and confrontation that the missing member aches.

We hit 110th Street and started rolling up Lenox Avenue. And I'd known   70
this avenue all my life, but it seemed to me again, as it had seemed on the day I'd first heard about Sonny's trouble, filled with a hidden menace which was its very breath of life.

"We almost there," said Sonny.

"Almost." We were both too nervous to say anything more.

We live in a housing project. It hasn't been up long. A few days after it was up it seemed uninhabitably new, now, of course, it's already rundown. It looks like a parody of the good, clean, faceless life—God knows the people who live in it do their best to make it a parody. The beat-looking grass lying around isn't enough to make their lives green, the hedges will never hold out the streets, and they know it. The big windows fool no one, they aren't big enough to make space out of no space. They don't bother with the windows, they watch the TV screen instead. The playground is most popular with the children who don't play at jacks, or skip rope, or roller skate, or swing, and they can be found in it after dark. We moved in partly because it's not too far from where I teach, and partly for the kids; but it's really just like the houses in which Sonny and I grew up. The same things happen, they'll have the same things to remember. The moment Sonny and I started into the house I had the feeling that I was simply bringing him back into the danger he had almost died trying to escape.

Sonny has never been talkative. So I don't know why I was sure he'd be dying to talk to me when supper was over the first night. Everything went fine, the oldest boy remembered him, and the youngest boy liked him, and Sonny had remembered to bring something for each of them; and Isabel, who is really much nicer than I am, more open and giving, had gone to a lot of trouble about dinner and was genuinely glad to see him. And she's always been able to tease Sonny in a way that I haven't. It was nice to see her face so vivid again and to hear her laugh and watch her make Sonny laugh. She wasn't, or, anyway, she didn't seem to be, at all uneasy or embarrassed. She chatted as though there were no subject which had to be avoided and she got Sonny past his first, faint stiffness. And thank God she was there, for I was filled with that icy dread again. Everything I did seemed awkward to me, and everything I said sounded freighted with hidden meaning. I was trying to remember everything I'd heard about dope addiction and I couldn't help watching Sonny for signs. I wasn't doing it out of malice. I was trying to find out something about my brother. I was dying to hear him tell me he was safe.

"Safe!" my father grunted, whenever Mama suggested trying to move to a   75
neighborhood which might be safer for children. "Safe, hell! Ain't no place safe for kids, nor nobody."

He always went on like this, but he wasn't, ever, really as bad as he sounded, not even on weekends, when he got drunk. As a matter of fact, he was always on the lookout for "something a little better," but he died before he found it. He died suddenly, during a drunken weekend in the middle of the war, when Sonny was fifteen. He and Sonny hadn't ever got on too well. And this was partly because Sonny was the apple of his father's eye. It was because he loved Sonny so much and was frightened for him, that he was always fighting with him. It doesn't do any good to fight with Sonny. Sonny just moves back, inside himself, where he can't be reached. But the principal reason that they never hit it off is that they were so much alike. Daddy was big and rough and loud-talking, just the opposite of Sonny, but they both had—that same privacy.

Mama tried to tell me something about this, just after Daddy died. I was home on leave from the army.

This was the last time I ever saw my mother alive. Just the same, this picture gets all mixed up in my mind with pictures I had of her when she was younger. The way I always see her is the way she used to be on a Sunday afternoon, say, when the old folks were talking after the big Sunday dinner. I always see her wearing pale blue. She'd be sitting on the sofa. And my father would be sitting in the easy chair, not far from her. And the living room would be full of church folks and relatives. There they sit, in chairs all around the living room, and the night is creeping up outside, but nobody knows it yet. You can see the darkness growing against the windowpanes and you hear the street noises every now and again, or maybe the jangling beat of a tambourine from one of the churches close by, but it's real quiet in the room. For a moment nobody's talking, but every face looks darkening, like the sky outside. And my mother rocks a little from the waist, and my father's eyes are closed. Everyone is looking at something a child can't see. For a minute they've forgotten the children. Maybe a kid is lying on the rug, half asleep. Maybe somebody's got a kid in his lap and is absent-mindedly stroking the kid's head. Maybe there's a kid, quiet and big-eyed, curled up in a big chair in the corner. The silence, the darkness coming, and the darkness in the faces frightens the child obscurely. He hopes that the hand which strokes his forehead will never stop—will never die. He hopes that there will never come a time when the old folks won't be sitting around the living room, talking about where they've come from, and what they've seen, and what's happened to them and their kinfolk.

But something deep and watchful in the child knows that this is bound to end, is already ending. In a moment someone will get up and turn on the light. Then the old folks will remember the children and they won't talk any more that day. And when light fills the room, the child is filled with darkness. He knows that every time this happens he's moved just a little closer to that darkness outside. The darkness outside is what the old folks have been talking about. It's what they've come from. It's what they endure. The child knows that they won't talk any more because if he knows too much about what's happened to *them*, he'll know too much too soon, about what's going to happen to *him*.

The last time I talked to my mother, I remember I was restless. I wanted to get out and see Isabel. We weren't married then and we had a lot to straighten out between us.

There Mama sat, in black, by the window. She was humming an old church song, *Lord, you brought me from a long ways off.* Sonny was out somewhere. Mama kept watching the streets.

"I don't know," she said, "if I'll ever see you again, after you go off from here. But I hope you'll remember the things I tried to teach you."

"Don't talk like that," I said, and smiled. "You'll be here a long time yet."

She smiled, too, but she said nothing. She was quiet for a long time. And I said, "Mama, don't you worry about nothing. I'll be writing all the time, and you be getting the checks. . . ."

80

"I want to talk to you about your brother," she said, suddenly. "If anything   85
happens to me he ain't going to have nobody to look out for him."

"Mama," I said, "ain't nothing going to happen to you *or* Sonny. Sonny's
all right. He's a good boy and he's got good sense."

"It ain't a question of his being a good boy," Mama said, "nor of his having
good sense. It ain't only the bad ones, nor yet the dumb ones that gets sucked
under." She stopped, looking at me. "Your Daddy once had a brother," she said,
and she smiled in a way that made me feel she was in pain. "You didn't never
know that, did you?"

"No," I said, "I never knew that," and I watched her face.

"Oh, yes," she said, "your Daddy had a brother." She looked out of the window again. "I know you never saw your Daddy cry. But *I* did — many a time,
through all these years."

I asked her, "What happened to his brother? How come nobody's ever   90
talked about him?"

This was the first time I ever saw my mother look old.

"His brother got killed," she said, "when he was just a little younger than
you are now. I knew him. He was a fine boy. He was maybe a little full of the
devil, but he didn't mean nobody no harm."

Then she stopped and the room was silent, exactly as it had sometimes
been on those Sunday afternoons. Mama kept looking out into the streets.

"He used to have a job in the mill," she said, "and, like all young folks,
he just liked to perform on Saturday nights. Saturday nights, him and your
father would drift around to different places, go to dances and things like that,
or just sit around with people they knew, and your father's brother would
sing, he had a fine voice, and play along with himself on his guitar. Well, this
particular Saturday night, him and your father was coming home from some
place, and they were both a little drunk and there was a moon that night, it
was bright like day. Your father's brother was feeling kind of good, and he was
whistling to himself, and he had his guitar slung over his shoulder. They was
coming down a hill and beneath them was a road that turned off from the
highway. Well, your father's brother, being always kind of frisky, decided to
run down this hill, and he did, with that guitar banging and clanging behind
him, and he ran across the road, and he was making water behind a tree.
And your father was sort of amused at him and he was still coming down
the hill, kind of slow. Then he heard a car motor and that same minute his
brother stepped from behind the tree, into the road, in the moonlight. And
he started to cross the road. And your father started to run down the hill,
he says he don't know why. This car was full of white men. They was all
drunk, and when they seen your father's brother they let out a great whoop
and holler and they aimed the car straight at him. They was having fun, they
just wanted to scare him, the way they do sometimes, you know. But they was
drunk. And I guess the boy, being drunk, too, and scared, kind of lost his head.
By the time he jumped it was too late. Your father says he heard his brother
scream when the car rolled over him, and he heard the wood of that guitar
when it give, and he heard them strings go flying, and he heard them white
men shouting, and the car kept on a-going and it ain't stopped till this day.

And, time your father got down the hill, his brother weren't nothing but blood and pulp."

Tears were gleaming on my mother's face. There wasn't anything I could say.   95

"He never mentioned it," she said, "because I never let him mention it before you children. Your Daddy was like a crazy man that night and for many a night thereafter. He says he never in his life seen anything as dark as that road after the lights of that car had gone away. Weren't nothing, weren't nobody on that road, just your Daddy and his brother and that busted guitar. Oh, yes. Your Daddy never did really get right again. Till the day he died he weren't sure but that every white man he saw was the man that killed his brother."

She stopped and took out her handkerchief and dried her eyes and looked at me.

"I ain't telling you all this," she said, "to make you scared or bitter or to make you hate nobody. I'm telling you this because you got a brother. And the world ain't changed."

I guess I didn't want to believe this. I guess she saw this in my face. She turned away from me, toward the window again, searching those streets.

"But I praise my Redeemer," she said at last, "that He called your Daddy   100
home before me. I ain't saying it to throw no flowers at myself, but, I declare, it keeps me from feeling too cast down to know I helped your father get safely through this world. Your father always acted like he was the roughest, strongest man on earth. And everybody took him to be like that. But if he hadn't had *me* there—to see his tears!"

She was crying again. Still, I couldn't move. I said, "Lord, Lord, Mama, I didn't know it was like that."

"Oh, honey," she said, "there's a lot that you don't know. But you are going to find it out." She stood up from the window and came over to me. "You got to hold on to your brother," she said, "and don't let him fall, no matter what it looks like is happening to him and no matter how evil you gets with him. You going to be evil with him many a time. But don't you forget what I told you, you hear?"

"I won't forget," I said. "Don't you worry, I won't forget. I won't let nothing happen to Sonny."

My mother smiled as though she were amused at something she saw in my face. Then, "You may not be able to stop nothing from happening. But you got to let him know you's *there*."

Two days later I was married, and then I was gone. And I had a lot of things on   105
my mind and I pretty well forgot my promise to Mama until I got shipped home on a special furlough for her funeral.

And, after the funeral, with just Sonny and me alone in the empty kitchen, I tried to find out something about him.

"What do you want to do?" I asked him.

"I'm going to be a musician," he said.

For he had graduated, in the time I had been away, from dancing to the juke box to finding out who was playing what, and what they were doing with it, and he had bought himself a set of drums.

"You mean, you want to be a drummer?" I somehow had the feeling that   110
being a drummer might be all right for other people but not for my brother
Sonny.

"I don't think," he said, looking at me very gravely, "that I'll ever be a good
drummer. But I think I can play a piano."

I frowned. I'd never played the role of the older brother quite so seriously
before, had scarcely ever, in fact, *asked* Sonny a damn thing. I sensed myself in
the presence of something I didn't really know how to handle, didn't understand. So I made my frown a little deeper as I asked: "What kind of musician do
you want to be?"

He grinned. "How many kinds do you think there are?"

"Be *serious*," I said.

He laughed, throwing his head back, and then looked at me. "I *am* serious."   115

"Well, then, for Christ's sake, stop kidding around and answer a serious
question. I mean, do you want to be a concert pianist, you want to play classical music and all that, or—or what?" Long before I finished he was laughing
again. "For Christ's *sake*, Sonny!"

He sobered, but with difficulty. "I'm sorry. But you sound so—*scared*!" and
he was off again.

"Well, you may think it's funny now, baby, but it's not going to be so funny
when you have to make your living at it, let me tell you *that*." I was furious because I knew he was laughing at me and I didn't know why.

"No," he said, very sober now, and afraid, perhaps, that he'd hurt me, "I
don't want to be a classical pianist. That isn't what interests me. I mean"—he
paused, looking hard at me, as though his eyes would help me to understand,
and then gestured helplessly, as though perhaps his hand would help—"I mean,
I'll have a lot of studying to do, and I'll have to study *everything*, but, I mean, I
want to play *with*—jazz musicians." He stopped. "I want to play jazz," he said.

Well, the word had never before sounded as heavy, as real, as it sounded   120
that afternoon in Sonny's mouth. I just looked at him and I was probably
frowning a real frown by this time. I simply couldn't see why on earth he'd
want to spend his time hanging around nightclubs, clowning around on band-
stands, while people pushed each other around a dance floor. It seemed—
beneath him, somehow. I had never thought about it before, had never been
forced to, but I suppose I had always put jazz musicians in a class with what
Daddy called "good-time people."

"Are you *serious*?"

"Hell, *yes*, I'm serious."

He looked more helpless than ever, and annoyed, and deeply hurt.

I suggested, helpfully: "You mean—like Louis Armstrong?"

His face closed as though I'd struck him. "No. I'm not talking about none   125
of that old-time, down home crap."

"Well, look, Sonny, I'm sorry, don't get mad. I just don't altogether get it,
that's all. Name somebody—you know, a jazz musician you admire."

"Bird."

"Who?"

"Bird! Charlie Parker! Don't they teach you nothing in the goddamn army?"

I lit a cigarette. I was surprised and then a little amused to discover that I   130
was trembling. "I've been out of touch," I said. "You'll have to be patient with
me. Now. Who's this Parker character?"

"He's just one of the greatest jazz musicians alive," said Sonny, sullenly, his
hands in his pockets, his back to me. "Maybe *the* greatest," he added, bitterly,
"that's probably why *you* never heard of him."

"All right," I said, "I'm ignorant. I'm sorry. I'll go out and buy all the cat's
records right away, all right?"

"It don't," said Sonny, with dignity, "make any difference to me. I don't
care what you listen to. Don't do me no favors."

I was beginning to realize that I'd never seen him so upset before. With
another part of my mind I was thinking that this would probably turn out to be
one of those things kids go through and that I shouldn't make it seem important by pushing it too hard. Still, I didn't think it would do any harm to ask:
"Doesn't all this take a lot of time? Can you make a living at it?"

He turned back to me and half leaned, half sat, on the kitchen table. "Ev-   135
erything takes time," he said, "and—well, yes, sure, I can make a living at it.
But what I don't seem to be able to make you understand is that it's the only
thing I want to do."

"Well, Sonny," I said, gently, "you know people can't always do exactly
what they *want* to do—"

"*No*, I don't know that," said Sonny, surprising me. "I think people *ought* to
do what they want to do, what else are they alive for?"

"You getting to be a big boy," I said desperately, "it's time you started thinking about your future."

"I'm thinking about my future," said Sonny, grimly. "I think about it all the
time."

I gave up. I decided, if he didn't change his mind, that we could always talk   140
about it later. "In the meantime," I said, "you got to finish school." We had already decided that he'd have to move in with Isabel and her folks. I knew this
wasn't the ideal arrangement because Isabel's folks are inclined to be dicty and
they hadn't especially wanted Isabel to marry me. But I didn't know what else
to do. "And we have to get you fixed up at Isabel's."

There was a long silence. He moved from the kitchen table to the window.
"That's a terrible idea. You know it yourself."

"Do you have a *better* idea?"

He just walked up and down the kitchen for a minute. He was as tall as I
was. He had started to shave. I suddenly had the feeling that I didn't know him
at all.

He stopped at the kitchen table and picked up my cigarettes. Looking at me
with a kind of mocking, amused defiance, he put one between his lips. "You
mind?"

"You smoking already?"   145

He lit the cigarette and nodded, watching me through the smoke. "I just
wanted to see if I'd have the courage to smoke in front of you." He grinned and

blew a great cloud of smoke to the ceiling. "It was easy." He looked at my face. "Come on, now. I bet you was smoking at my age, tell the truth."

I didn't say anything but the truth was on my face, and he laughed. But now there was something very strained in his laugh. "Sure. And I bet that ain't all you was doing."

He was frightening me a little. "Cut the crap," I said. "We already decided that you was going to go and live at Isabel's. Now what's got into you all of a sudden?"

"*You* decided it," he pointed out. "*I* didn't decide nothing." He stopped in front of me, leaning against the stove, arms loosely folded. "Look, brother. I don't want to stay in Harlem no more, I really don't." He was very earnest. He looked at me, then over toward the kitchen window. There was something in his eyes I'd never seen before, some thoughtfulness, some worry all his own. He rubbed the muscle of one arm. "It's time I was getting out of here."

"Where do you want to *go*, Sonny?"   150

"I want to join the army. Or the navy, I don't care. If I say I'm old enough, they'll believe me."

Then I got mad. It was because I was so scared. "You must be crazy. You goddamn fool, what the hell do you want to go and join the *army* for?"

"I just told you. To get out of Harlem."

"Sonny, you haven't even finished *school*. And if you really want to be a musician, how do you expect to study if you're in the *army?*"

He looked at me, trapped, and in anguish. "There's ways. I might be able to   155 work out some kind of deal. Anyway, I'll have the G.I. Bill when I come out."

"*If* you come out." We stared at each other. "Sonny, please. Be reasonable. I know the setup is far from perfect. But we got to do the best we can."

"I ain't learning nothing in school," he said. "Even when I go." He turned away from me and opened the window and threw his cigarette out into the narrow alley. I watched his back. "At least, I ain't learning nothing you'd want me to learn." He slammed the window so hard I thought the glass would fly out, and turned back to me. "And I'm sick of the stink of these garbage cans!"

"Sonny," I said, "I know how you feel. But if you don't finish school now, you're going to be sorry later that you didn't." I grabbed him by the shoulders. "And you only got another year. It ain't so bad. And I'll come back and I swear I'll help you do *whatever* you want to do. Just try to put up with it till I come back. Will you please do that? For me?"

He didn't answer and he wouldn't look at me.

"Sonny. You hear me?"   160

He pulled away. "I hear you. But you never hear anything *I* say."

I didn't know what to say to that. He looked out of the window and then back at me. "OK," he said, and sighed. "I'll try."

Then I said, trying to cheer him up a little, "They got a piano at Isabel's. You can practice on it."

And as a matter of fact, it did cheer him up for a minute. "That's right," he said to himself. "I forgot that." His face relaxed a little. But the worry, the thoughtfulness, played on it still, the way shadows play on a face which is staring into the fire.

But I thought I'd never hear the end of that piano. At first, Isabel would write 165
me, saying how nice it was that Sonny was so serious about his music and how, as soon as he came in from school, or wherever he had been when he was supposed to be at school, he went straight to that piano and stayed there until suppertime. And, after supper, he went back to that piano and stayed there until everybody went to bed. He was at the piano all day Saturday and all day Sunday. Then he bought a record player and started playing records. He'd play one record over and over again, all day long sometimes, and he'd improvise along with it on the piano. Or he'd play one section of the record, one chord, one change, one progression, then he'd do it on the piano. Then back to the record. Then back to the piano.

Well, I really don't know how they stood it. Isabel finally confessed that it wasn't like living with a person at all, it was like living with sound. And the sound didn't make any sense to her, didn't make any sense to any of them— naturally. They began, in a way, to be afflicted by this presence that was living in their home. It was as though Sonny were some sort of god, or monster. He moved in an atmosphere which wasn't like theirs at all. They fed him and he ate, he washed himself, he walked in and out of their door; he certainly wasn't nasty or unpleasant or rude, Sonny isn't any of those things; but it was as though he were all wrapped up in some cloud, some fire, some vision all his own; and there wasn't any way to reach him.

At the same time, he wasn't really a man yet, he was still a child, and they had to watch out for him in all kinds of ways. They certainly couldn't throw him out. Neither did they dare to make a great scene about that piano because even they dimly sensed, as I sensed, from so many thousands of miles away, that Sonny was at that piano playing for his life.

But he hadn't been going to school. One day a letter came from the school board and Isabel's mother got it—there had, apparently, been other letters but Sonny had torn them up. This day, when Sonny came in, Isabel's mother showed him the letter and asked where he'd been spending his time. And she finally got it out of him that he'd been down in Greenwich Village, with musicians and other characters, in a white girl's apartment. And this scared her and she started to scream at him and what came up, once she began—though she denies it to this day—was what sacrifices they were making to give Sonny a decent home and how little he appreciated it.

Sonny didn't play the piano that day. By evening, Isabel's mother had calmed down but then there was the old man to deal with, and Isabel herself. Isabel says she did her best to be calm but she broke down and started crying. She says she just watched Sonny's face. She could tell, by watching him, what was happening with him. And what was happening was that they penetrated his cloud, they had reached him. Even if their fingers had been a thousand times more gentle than human fingers ever are, he could hardly help feeling that they had stripped him naked and were spitting on that nakedness. For he also had to see that his presence, that music, which was life or death to him, had been torture for them and that they had endured it, not at all for his sake, but only for mine. And Sonny couldn't take that. He can take it a little better today than he could then but he's still not very good at it and, frankly, I don't know anybody who is.

The silence of the next few days must have been louder than the sound of   170 all the music ever played since time began. One morning, before she went to work, Isabel was in his room for something and she suddenly realized that all of his records were gone. And she knew for certain that he was gone. And he was. He went as far as the navy would carry him. He finally sent me a postcard from some place in Greece and that was the first I knew that Sonny was still alive. I didn't see him any more until we were both back in New York and the war had long been over.

He was a man by then, of course, but I wasn't willing to see it. He came by the house from time to time, but we fought almost every time we met. I didn't like the way he carried himself, loose and dreamlike all the time, and I didn't like his friends, and his music seemed to be merely an excuse for the life he led. It sounded just that weird and disordered.

Then we had a fight, a pretty awful fight, and I didn't see him for months. By and by I looked him up, where he was living, in a furnished room in the Village, and I tried to make it up. But there were lots of people in the room and Sonny just lay on his bed, and he wouldn't come downstairs with me, and he treated these other people as though they were his family and I weren't. So I got mad and then he got mad, and then I told him that he might just as well be dead as live the way he was living. Then he stood up and he told me not to worry about him any more in life, that he *was* dead as far as I was concerned. Then he pushed me to the door and the other people looked on as though nothing were happening, and he slammed the door behind me. I stood in the hallway, staring at the door. I heard somebody laugh in the room and then the tears came to my eyes. I started down the steps, whistling to keep from crying, I kept whistling to myself, *You going to need me, baby, one of these cold, rainy days.*

I read about Sonny's trouble in the spring. Little Grace died in the fall. She was a beautiful little girl. But she only lived a little over two years. She died of polio and she suffered. She had a slight fever for a couple of days, but it didn't seem like anything and we just kept her in bed. And we would certainly have called the doctor, but the fever dropped, she seemed to be all right. So we thought it had just been a cold. Then, one day, she was up, playing, Isabel was in the kitchen fixing lunch for the two boys when they'd come in from school, and she heard Grace fall down in the living room. When you have a lot of children you don't always start running when one of them falls, unless they start screaming or something. And, this time, Grace was quiet. Yet, Isabel says that when she heard that *thump* and then that silence, something happened in her to make her afraid. And she ran to the living room and there was little Grace on the floor, all twisted up, and the reason she hadn't screamed was that she couldn't get her breath. And when she did scream, it was the worst sound, Isabel says, that she'd ever heard in all her life, and she still hears it sometimes in her dreams. Isabel will sometimes wake me up with a low, moaning, strangled sound and I have to be quick to awaken her and hold her to me and where Isabel is weeping against me seems a mortal wound.

I think I may have written Sonny the very day that little Grace was buried. I was sitting in the living room in the dark, by myself, and I suddenly thought of Sonny. My trouble made his real.

One Saturday afternoon, when Sonny had been living with us, or, anyway, been in our house, for nearly two weeks, I found myself wandering aimlessly about the living room, drinking from a can of beer, and trying to work up the courage to search Sonny's room. He was out, he was usually out whenever I was home, and Isabel had taken the children to see their grandparents. Suddenly I was standing still in front of the living room window, watching Seventh Avenue. The idea of searching Sonny's room made me still. I scarcely dared to admit to myself what I'd be searching for. I didn't know what I'd do if I found it. Or if I didn't. 175

On the sidewalk across from me, near the entrance to a barbecue joint, some people were holding an old-fashioned revival meeting. The barbecue cook, wearing a dirty white apron, his conked hair reddish and metallic in the pale sun, and a cigarette between his lips, stood in the doorway, watching them. Kids and older people paused in their errands and stood there, along with some older men and a couple of very tough-looking women who watched everything that happened on the avenue, as though they owned it, or were maybe owned by it. Well, they were watching this, too. The revival was being carried on by three sisters in black, and a brother. All they had were their voices and their Bibles and a tambourine. The brother was testifying and while he testified two of the sisters stood together, seeming to say, amen, and the third sister walked around with the tambourine outstretched and a couple of people dropped coins into it. Then the brother's testimony ended and the sister who had been taking up the collection dumped the coins into her palm and transferred them to the pocket of her long black robe. Then she raised both hands, striking the tambourine against the air, and then against one hand, and she started to sing. And the two other sisters and the brother joined in.

It was strange, suddenly, to watch, though I had been seeing these street meetings all my life. So, of course, had everybody else down there. Yet, they paused and watched and listened and I stood still at the window. "*Tis the old ship of Zion,*" they sang, and the sister with the tambourine kept a steady, jangling beat, "*it has rescued many a thousand!*" Not a soul under the sound of their voices was hearing this song for the first time, not one of them had been rescued. Nor had they seen much in the way of rescue work being done around them. Neither did they especially believe in the holiness of the three sisters and the brother, they knew too much about them, knew where they lived, and how. The woman with the tambourine, whose voice dominated the air, whose face was bright with joy, was divided by very little from the woman who stood watching her, a cigarette between her heavy, chapped lips, her hair a cuckoo's nest, her face scarred and swollen from many beatings, and her black eyes glittering like coal. Perhaps they both knew this, which was why, when, as rarely, they addressed each other, they addressed each other as Sister. As the singing filled the air the watching, listening faces underwent a change, the eyes focusing on something within; the music seemed to soothe a poison out of them; and time seemed, nearly, to fall away from the sullen, belligerent, battered faces, as though they were fleeing back to their first condition, while dreaming of their last. The barbecue cook half shook his head and smiled, and dropped his cigarette and disappeared into his joint. A man fumbled in his pockets for change and stood holding it in his hand impatiently, as though he had just remembered a pressing appointment further up the avenue. He looked furious. Then I saw Sonny, standing on the edge of the crowd. He was carrying a wide, flat notebook with a green cover, and it made him look, from where I was standing, almost like a schoolboy. The coppery sun brought out the copper in his skin, he was very faintly smiling, standing very still. Then the singing stopped, the tambourine turned into a collection plate again. The furious man dropped in his coins and vanished, so did a couple of the women, and Sonny dropped some change in the plate, looking directly at the woman with a little smile. He started across the avenue, toward the house. He has a slow, loping walk, something like the way Harlem hipsters walk, only he's imposed on this his own half-beat. I had never really noticed it before.

I stayed at the window, both relieved and apprehensive. As Sonny disappeared from my sight, they began singing again. And they were still singing when his key turned in the lock.

"Hey," he said.

"Hey, yourself. You want some beer?"   180

"No. Well, maybe." But he came up to the window and stood beside me, looking out. "What a warm voice," he said.

They were singing *If I could only hear my mother pray again!*

"Yes," I said, "and she can sure beat that tambourine."

"But what a terrible song," he said, and laughed. He dropped his notebook on the sofa and disappeared into the kitchen. "Where's Isabel and the kids?"

"I think they went to see their grandparents. You hungry?"   185

"No." He came back into the living room with his can of beer. "You want to come some place with me tonight?"

I sensed, I don't know how, that I couldn't possibly say no. "Sure. Where?"

He sat down on the sofa and picked up his notebook and started leafing through it. "I'm going to sit in with some fellows in a joint in the Village."

"You mean, you're going to play, tonight?"

"That's right." He took a swallow of his beer and moved back to the window.   190
dow. He gave me a sidelong look. "If you can stand it."

"I'll try," I said.

He smiled to himself and we both watched as the meeting across the way broke up. The three sisters and the brother, heads bowed, were singing *God be with you till we meet again.* The faces around them were very quiet. Then the song ended. The small crowd dispersed. We watched the three women and the lone man walk slowly up the avenue.

"When she was singing before," said Sonny, abruptly, "her voice reminded me for a minute of what heroin feels like sometimes — when it's in your veins. It makes you feel sort of warm and cool at the same time. And distant.

And—and sure." He sipped his beer, very deliberately not looking at me. I watched his face. "It makes you feel—in control. Sometimes you've got to have that feeling."

"Do you?" I sat down slowly in the easy chair.

"Sometimes." He went to the sofa and picked up his notebook again. "Some people do."   195

"In order," I asked, "to play?" And my voice was very ugly, full of contempt and anger.

"Well"—he looked at me with great, troubled eyes, as though, in fact, he hoped his eyes would tell me things he could never otherwise say—"they *think* so. And *if* they think so—!"

"And what do *you* think?" I asked.

He sat on the sofa and put his can of beer on the floor. "I don't know," he said, and I couldn't be sure if he were answering my question or pursuing his thoughts. His face didn't tell me. "It's not so much to *play.* It's to *stand* it, to be able to make it at all. On any level." He frowned and smiled: "In order to keep from shaking to pieces."

"But these friends of yours," I said, "they seem to shake themselves to pieces pretty goddamn fast."   200

"Maybe." He played with the notebook. And something told me that I should curb my tongue, that Sonny was doing his best to talk, that I should listen. "But of course you only know the ones that've gone to pieces. Some don't—or at least they haven't *yet* and that's just about all *any* of us can say." He paused. "And then there are some who just live, really, in hell, and they know it and they see what's happening and they go right on. I don't know." He sighed, dropped the notebook, folded his arms. "Some guys, you can tell from the way they play, they on something *all* the time. And you can see that, well, it makes something real for them. But of course," he picked up his beer from the floor and sipped it and put the can down again, "they *want* to, too, you've got to see that. Even some of them that say they don't—*some*, not all."

"And what about you?" I asked—I couldn't help it. "What about you? Do *you* want to?"

He stood up and walked to the window and remained silent for a long time. Then he sighed. "Me," he said. Then: "While I was downstairs before, on my way here, listening to that woman sing, it struck me all of a sudden how much suffering she must have had to go through—to sing like that. It's *repulsive* to think you have to suffer that much."

I said: "But there's no way not to suffer—is there, Sonny?"

"I believe not," he said and smiled, "but that's never stopped anyone from trying." He looked at me. "Has it?" I realized, with this mocking look, that there stood between us, forever, beyond the power of time or forgiveness, the fact that I had held silence—so long!—when he had needed human speech to help him. He turned back to the window. "No, there's no way not to suffer. But you try all kinds of ways to keep from drowning in it, to keep on top of it, and to make it seem—well, like *you*. Like you did something, all right, and now you're suffering for it. You know?" I said nothing. "Well you know," he said, impatiently, "why *do* people suffer? Maybe it's better to do something to give it a reason, *any* reason."   205

"But we just agreed," I said, "that there's no way not to suffer. Isn't it better, then, just to—take it?"

"But nobody just takes it," Sonny cried, "that's what I'm telling you! *Everybody* tries not to. You're just hung up on the *way* some people try—it's not *your* way!"

The hair on my face began to itch, my face felt wet. "That's not true," I said, "that's not true. I don't give a damn what other people do, I don't even care how they suffer. I just care how *you* suffer." And he looked at me. "Please believe me," I said, "I don't want to see you—die—trying not to suffer."

"I won't," he said, flatly, "die trying not to suffer. At least, not any faster than anybody else."

"But there's no need," I said, trying to laugh, "is there? in killing yourself."   210

I wanted to say more, but I couldn't. I wanted to talk about will power and how life could be—well, beautiful. I wanted to say that it was all within; but was it? or, rather, wasn't that exactly the trouble? And I wanted to promise that I would never fail him again. But it would all have sounded—empty words and lies.

So I made the promise to myself and prayed that I would keep it.

"It's terrible sometimes, inside," he said, "that's what's the trouble. You walk these streets, black and funky and cold, and there's not really a living ass to talk to, and there's nothing shaking, and there's no way of getting it out—that storm inside. You can't talk it and you can't make love with it, and when you finally try to get with it and play it, you realize *nobody's* listening. So *you've* got to listen. You got to find a way to listen."

And then he walked away from the window and sat on the sofa again, as though all the wind had suddenly been knocked out of him. "Sometimes you'll do *anything* to play, even cut your mother's throat." He laughed and looked at me. "Or your brother's." Then he sobered. "Or your own." Then: "Don't worry. I'm all right now and I think I'll *be* all right. But I can't forget—where I've been. I don't mean just the physical place I've been, I mean where I've *been.* And *what* I've been."

"What have you been, Sonny?" I asked.   21⁹

He smiled—but sat sideways on the sofa, his elbow resting on the back, his fingers playing with his mouth and chin, not looking at me. "I've been something I didn't recognize, didn't know I could be. Didn't know anybody could be." He stopped, looking inward, looking helplessly young, looking old. "I'm not talking about it now because I feel *guilty* or anything like that—maybe it would be better if I did, I don't know. Anyway, I can't really talk about it. Not to you, not to anybody," and now he turned and faced me. "Sometimes, you know, and it was actually when I was most *out* of the world, I felt that I was in it, that I was *with* it, really, and I could play or I didn't really have to *play,* it just came out of me, it was there. And I don't know how I played, thinking about it now, but I know I did awful things, those times, sometimes, to people. Or it wasn't that I *did* anything to them—it was that they weren't real." He picked up the beer can; it was empty; he rolled it between his palms: "And other times—well, I needed a fix, I needed to find a place to lean, I needed to clear a space to *listen*—and I couldn't find it, and I—went crazy, I did terrible things to *me*, I was terrible *for* me." He began pressing the beer can between his hands, I watched the metal begin to give. It glittered, as he played with it, like a knife, and I was afraid he would cut himself, but I said nothing. "Oh well. I can never tell you. I was all by myself at the bottom of something, stinking and sweating and crying and shaking, and I smelled it, you know? *my* stink, and I thought I'd die if I couldn't get away from it and yet, all the same, I knew that everything I was doing was just locking me in with it. And I didn't know," he paused, still flattening the beer can, "I didn't know, I still *don't* know, something kept telling me that maybe it was good to smell your own stink, but I didn't think that *that* was what I'd been trying to do—and—who can stand it?" and he abruptly dropped the ruined beer can, looking at me with a small, still smile, and then rose, walking to the window as though it were the lodestone rock. I watched his face, he watched the avenue. "I couldn't tell you when Mama died—but the reason I wanted to leave Harlem so bad was to get away from drugs. And then, when I ran away, that's what I was running from—really. When I came back, nothing had changed, *I* hadn't changed, I was just—older." And he stopped, drumming with his fingers on the windowpane. The sun had vanished, soon darkness would fall. I watched his face. "It can come again," he said, almost as though speaking to himself. Then he turned to me. "It can come again," he repeated. "I just want you to know that."

"All right," I said, at last. "So it can come again. All right."

He smiled, but the smile was sorrowful. "I had to try to tell you," he said.

"Yes," I said. "I understand that."

"You're my brother," he said, looking straight at me, and not smiling at all.   220

"Yes," I repeated, "yes. I understand that."

He turned back to the window, looking out. "All that hatred down there," he said, "all that hatred and misery and love. It's a wonder it doesn't blow the avenue apart."

We went to the only nightclub on a short, dark street, downtown. We squeezed through the narrow, chattering, jam-packed bar to the entrance of the big room, where the bandstand was. And we stood there for a moment, for the lights were very dim in this room and we couldn't see. Then, "Hello, boy," said a voice and an enormous black man, much older than Sonny or myself, erupted out of all that atmospheric lighting and put an arm around Sonny's shoulder. "I been sitting right here," he said, "waiting for you."

He had a big voice, too, and heads in the darkness turned toward us.

Sonny grinned and pulled a little away, and said, "Creole, this is my brother.   225 I told you about him."

Creole shook my hand. "I'm glad to meet you, son," he said, and it was clear that he was glad to meet me *there*, for Sonny's sake. And he smiled, "You got a real musician in *your* family," and he took his arm from Sonny's shoulder and slapped him, lightly, affectionately, with the back of his hand.

"Well. Now I've heard it all," said a voice behind us. This was another musician, and a friend of Sonny's, a coal-black, cheerful-looking man, built close to the ground. He immediately began confiding to me, at the top of his lungs, the most terrible things about Sonny, his teeth gleaming like a lighthouse and his laugh coming up out of him like the beginning of an earthquake. And it turned out that everyone at the bar knew Sonny, or almost everyone; some were musicians, working there, or nearby, or not working, some were simply hangers-on, and some were there to hear Sonny play. I was introduced to all of them and they were all very polite to me. Yet, it was clear that, for them, I was only Sonny's brother. Here, I was in Sonny's world. Or, rather: his kingdom. Here, it was not even a question that his veins bore royal blood.

They were going to play soon and Creole installed me, by myself, at a table in a dark corner. Then I watched them, Creole, and the little black man, and Sonny, and the others, while they horsed around, standing just below the bandstand. The light from the bandstand spilled just a little short of them and, watching them laughing and gesturing and moving about, I had the feeling that they, nevertheless, were being most careful not to step into that circle of light too suddenly: that if they moved into the light too suddenly, without thinking, they would perish in flame. Then, while I watched, one of them, the small, black man, moved into the light and crossed the bandstand and started fooling around with his drums. Then—being funny and being, also, extremely ceremonious—Creole took Sonny by the arm and led him to the piano. A woman's voice called Sonny's name and a few hands started clapping. And Sonny, also being funny and being ceremonious, and so touched, I think, that he could have cried, but neither hiding it nor showing it, riding it like a man, grinned, and put both hands to his heart and bowed from the waist.

Creole then went to the bass fiddle and a lean, very bright-skinned brown man jumped up on the bandstand and picked up his horn. So there they were, and the atmosphere on the bandstand and in the room began to change and tighten. Someone stepped up to the microphone and announced them. Then there were all kinds of murmurs. Some people at the bar shushed others. The waitress ran around, frantically getting in the last orders, guys and chicks got closer to each other, and the lights on the bandstand, on the quartet, turned to a kind of indigo. Then they all looked different there. Creole looked about him for the last time, as though he were making certain that all his chickens were in the coop, and then he—jumped and struck the fiddle. And there they were.

All I know about music is that not many people ever really hear it. And 230 even then, on the rare occasions when something opens within, and the music enters, what we mainly hear, or hear corroborated, are personal, private, vanishing evocations. But the man who creates the music is hearing something else, is dealing with the roar rising from the void and imposing order on it as it hits the air. What is evoked in him, then, is of another order, more terrible because it has no words, and triumphant, too, for that same reason. And his triumph, when he triumphs, is ours. I just watched Sonny's face. His face was troubled, he was working hard, but he wasn't with it. And I had the feeling that, in a way, everyone on the bandstand was waiting for him, both waiting for him and pushing him along. But as I began to watch Creole, I realized that it was Creole who held them all back. He had them on a short rein. Up there, keeping the beat with his whole body, wailing on the fiddle, with his eyes half closed, he was listening to everything, but he was listening to Sonny. He was having a dialogue with Sonny. He wanted Sonny to leave the shoreline and strike out for the deep water. He was Sonny's witness that deep water and drowning were not the same thing — he had been there, and he knew. And he wanted Sonny to know. He was waiting for Sonny to do the things on the keys which would let Creole know that Sonny was in the water.

And, while Creole listened, Sonny moved, deep within, exactly like someone in torment. I had never before thought of how awful the relationship must be between the musician and his instrument. He has to fill it, this instrument, with the breath of life, his own. He has to make it do what he wants it to do. And a piano is just a piano. It's made out of so much wood and wires and little hammers and big ones, and ivory. While there's only so much you can do with it, the only way to find this out is to try; to try and make it do everything.

And Sonny hadn't been near a piano for over a year. And he wasn't on much better terms with his life, not the life that stretched before him now. He and the piano stammered, started one way, got scared, stopped; started another way, panicked, marked time, started again; then seemed to have found a direction, panicked again, got stuck. And the face I saw on Sonny I'd never seen before. Everything had been burned out of it, and, at the same time, things usually hidden were being burned in, by the fire and fury of the battle which was occurring in him up there.

Yet, watching Creole's face as they neared the end of the first set, I had the feeling that something had happened, something I hadn't heard. Then they finished, there was scattered applause, and then, without an instant's warning, Creole started into something else, it was almost sardonic, it was *Am I Blue.* And, as though he commanded, Sonny began to play. Something began to happen. And Creole let out the reins. The dry, low, black man said something awful on the drums, Creole answered, and the drums talked back. Then the horn insisted, sweet and high, slightly detached perhaps, and Creole listened, commenting now and then, dry, and driving, beautiful and calm and old. Then they all came together again, and Sonny was part of the family again. I could tell this from his face. He seemed to have found, right there beneath his fingers, a damn brand-new piano. It seemed that he couldn't get over it. Then, for awhile, just being happy with Sonny, they seemed to be agreeing with him that brand-new pianos certainly were a gas.

Then Creole stepped forward to remind them that what they were playing was the blues. He hit something in all of them, he hit something in me, myself, and the music tightened and deepened, apprehension began to beat the air. Creole began to tell us what the blues were all about. They were not about anything very new. He and his boys up there were keeping it new, at the risk of ruin, destruction, madness, and death, in order to find new ways to make us listen. For, while the tale of how we suffer, and how we are delighted, and how we may triumph is never new, it always must be heard. There isn't any other tale to tell, it's the only light we've got in all this darkness.

And this tale, according to that face, that body, those strong hands on   235
those strings, has another aspect in every country, and a new depth in every
generation. Listen, Creole seemed to be saying, listen. Now these are Sonny's
blues. He made the little black man on the drums know it, and the bright,
brown man on the horn. Creole wasn't trying any longer to get Sonny in the
water. He was wishing him Godspeed. Then he stepped back, very slowly, filling
the air with the immense suggestion that Sonny speak for himself.

Then they all gathered around Sonny and Sonny played. Every now and
again one of them seemed to say, amen. Sonny's fingers filled the air with life,
his life. But that life contained so many others. And Sonny went all the way
back, he really began with the spare, flat statement of the opening phrase of
the song. Then he began to make it his. It was very beautiful because it wasn't
hurried and it was no longer a lament. I seemed to hear with what burning he
had made it his, with what burning we had yet to make it ours, how we could
cease lamenting. Freedom lurked around us and I understood, at last, that he
could help us to be free if we would listen, that he would never be free until we
did. Yet, there was no battle in his face now. I heard what he had gone through,
and would continue to go through until he came to rest in earth. He had made
it his: that long line, of which we knew only Mama and Daddy. And he was giving it back, as everything must be given back, so that, passing through death,
it can live forever. I saw my mother's face again, and felt, for the first time, how
the stones of the road she had walked on must have bruised her feet. I saw the
moonlit road where my father's brother died. And it brought something else
back to me, and carried me past it. I saw my little girl again and felt Isabel's
tears again, and I felt my own tears begin to rise. And I was yet aware that this
was only a moment, that the world waited outside, as hungry as a tiger, and
that trouble stretched above us, longer than the sky.

Then it was over. Creole and Sonny let out their breath, both soaking wet,
and grinning. There was a lot of applause and some of it was real. In the dark,
the girl came by and I asked her to take drinks to the bandstand. There was a
long pause, while they talked up there in the indigo light and after awhile I saw
the girl put a Scotch and milk on top of the piano for Sonny. He didn't seem to
notice it, but just before they started playing again, he sipped from it and looked
toward me, and nodded. Then he put it back on top of the piano. For me, then,
as they began to play again, it glowed and shook above my brother's head like
the very cup of trembling.   *[1957]*

☰ THINKING ABOUT THE TEXT

1. Were you sympathetic to the older brother in the beginning of the story?
   Did this become more so or less so as the story progressed? Is Sonny a
   sympathetic character in the beginning? At the end?

2. In real life, what do you believe is the role of an older brother? Do you
   have a responsibility to the members of your family regardless of their
   behavior? Explain. What is Sonny's mother's view of this?

3. Baldwin refers to the "darkness outside" several times. What do you think this means for Sonny? For Sonny's mother and father? For the older brother?

4. Listening seems to play an important function for Sonny and his brother. Cite specific examples of how they do or do not listen to each other. What might be some definitions of "listening" in this context?

5. One might think that brothers would understand each other better than outsiders do. But is that the case here? In your experience? In other stories or movies? How might you account for this difficulty?

≡ MAKING COMPARISONS

1. The older brothers in "The Rich Brother" and "Sonny's Blues" struggle to understand their younger brothers. Which one seems more successful? Why?

2. Both younger brothers in these two stories seem to march to different drummers. How would you describe their variations from the norm?

3. Some critics claim that these two stories are about responsibility; others claim they are about tolerance; still others see sibling rivalry, blind faith, or ego as the focus. What do you think, and why?

≡ WRITING ABOUT ISSUES

1. Baldwin shows us the letter Sonny writes to his older brother, but we do not see any of the older brother's letters to Sonny. Based on the older brother's insights about Sonny in the closing scene, write a letter to Sonny from the older brother's point of view, explaining the substance of his new understanding of Sonny's life and music.

2. Write an essay that compares the relationship between Pete and Donald to the one between Sonny and his brother. Be sure to comment on similarities and differences.

3. Write a personal essay based on a conflict you had with a sibling, explaining how the relationship evolved. Use at least two specific incidents, and describe how they fit into a larger pattern.

4. Do some library research on birth order as it affects sibling rivalry, especially between brothers. Write a report comparing your findings to the relationships depicted in these two stories.

ERNEST HEMINGWAY, "Hills like White Elephants"

T. CORAGHESSAN BOYLE, "The Love of My Life"

Ambitious politicians are not the only voices extolling the virtues of family life. Millennia of images and narratives have socialized us to accept the naturalness of motherhood and fatherhood and to see parenthood as a concept that is nearly beyond critique, beyond questioning. We look askance at those who fail in their roles as loving, supportive parents—and sometimes even at couples who decide that they do not want children or at least not as a result of a particular pregnancy. Although abortion has been legal since the early 1970s, the decision to abort a fetus is often not easy to make. Some couples agonize during the decision process, especially if they are not married and especially, as in Ernest Hemingway's story, if the procedure is illegal and risky. Under these circumstances, it is not surprising if one partner sees the pressure to abort as signifying something ominous for the relationship's future.

Even though the right to terminate a pregnancy is still an emotionally contested political and ethical issue, there is almost universal condemnation—in America, at least—for parents who harm infants. Our culture does not seem to forgive such behavior, often condemning it regardless of the circumstances. But serious writers are not in the habit of shying away from the dark corners of human experience, and we can profitably turn to a writer like T. Coraghessan Boyle to shine the artist's light on disturbing stories of family life gone awry. In his notes on "The Love of My Life," Boyle writes that at its essence the world "remains a dark and mysterious place. I write fiction to address and measure my response to that darkness and mystery." With Boyle, we can try to sort out the inevitably conflicting feelings we have about the actions of the characters in the following stories.

≡ BEFORE YOU READ

Respond to the following statement: "Neonaticide (the killing of an infant less than a day old) has been going on for centuries. Some societies have allowed the practice if done under extreme stress. Some modern philosophers also agree with this position."

ERNEST HEMINGWAY
Hills like White Elephants

One of the most influential writers of the first half of the twentieth century, Ernest Hemingway (1898–1961) was born in a suburb of Chicago but felt most alive at his parents' summer home in the woods of Michigan, where he could indulge his enthusiastic love of hunting, fishing, and camping. After high school, where he was an active and excellent student, Hemingway decided to become a journalist instead of going to college and worked successfully for the Kansas City Star. *He signed up as an ambulance driver for the Red Cross during World War I and was seriously wounded in Italy. After moving to Paris after the war, he wrote his first important book,* In Our Time *(1925). It was well received, and the next year* The Sun Also Rises, *about the "lost generation," made him a celebrity. He published several popular novels, including* For Whom the Bell Tolls *(1949) and* The Old Man and the Sea *(1952). He received the Nobel Prize for literature in 1954 and committed suicide after difficult mental and physical problems. Always full of contradictions, Hemingway was at once an inveterate sportsman and an omnivorous reader; he loved life while also being obsessed with death, especially his father's suicide. Most people think of him as a famous and intensely masculine writer of adventure tales of big game, hunting, fishing, and war. While this is true, he was also a dedicated and intricate stylist of great delicacy and power. The following story is a good example of Hemingway's technique of developing a story through dialogue. He was a believer in compression, using an analogy to an iceberg to explain his narrative method: "There is seven-eighths of it under water for every part that shows." His laconic style continues to influence today's writers.*

The hills across the valley of the Ebro were long and white. On this side there was no shade and no trees and the station was between two lines of rails in the sun. Close against the side of the station there was the warm shadow of the building and a curtain, made of strings of bamboo beads, hung across the open door into the bar, to keep out flies. The American and the girl with him sat at a table in the shade, outside the building. It was very hot and the express from Barcelona would come in forty minutes. It stopped at this junction for two minutes and went on to Madrid.

"What should we drink?" the girl asked. She had taken off her hat and put it on the table.

"It's pretty hot," the man said.

"Let's drink beer."

"*Dos cervezas*," the man said into the curtain.   5

"Big ones?" a woman asked from the doorway.

"Yes. Two big ones."

The woman brought two glasses of beer and two felt pads. She put the felt pads and the beer glasses on the table and looked at the man and the girl. The girl was looking off at the line of hills. They were white in the sun and the country was brown and dry.

"They look like white elephants," she said.

"I've never seen one," the man drank his beer.   10

"No, you wouldn't have."

"I might have," the man said. "Just because you say I wouldn't have doesn't prove anything."

The girl looked at the bead curtain. "They've painted something on it," she said. "What does it say?"

"Anis del Toro. It's a drink."

"Could we try it?"   15

The man called "Listen" through the curtain. The woman came out from the bar.

"Four reales."

"We want two Anis del Toro."

"With water?"

"Do you want it with water?"   20

"I don't know," the girl said. "Is it good with water?"

"It's all right."

"You want them with water?" asked the woman.

"Yes, with water."

"It tastes like licorice," the girl said and put the glass down.   25

"That's the way with everything."

"Yes," said the girl. "Everything tastes of licorice. Especially all the things you've waited so long for, like absinthe."

"Oh, cut it out."

"You started it," the girl said. "I was being amused. I was having a fine time."

"Well, let's try and have a fine time."   30

"All right. I was trying. I said the mountains looked like white elephants. Wasn't that bright?"

"That was bright."

"I wanted to try this new drink: That's all we do, isn't it—look at things and try new drinks?"

"I guess so."

The girl looked across at the hills.   35

"They're lovely hills," she said. "They don't really look like white elephants. I just meant the coloring of their skin through the trees."

"Should we have another drink?"

"All right."

The warm wind blew the bead curtain against the table.

"The beer's nice and cool," the man said.   40

"It's lovely," the girl said.

"It's really an awfully simple operation, Jig," the man said. "It's not really an operation at all."

The girl looked at the ground the table legs rested on.

"I know you wouldn't mind it, Jig. It's really not anything. It's just to let the air in."

The girl did not say anything.   45

"I'll go with you and I'll stay with you all the time. They just let the air in and then it's all perfectly natural."

"Then what will we do afterward?"

"We'll be fine afterward. Just like we were before."

"What makes you think so?"

"That's the only thing that bothers us. It's the only thing that's made us   50
unhappy."

The girl looked at the bead curtain, put her hand out, and took hold of two of the strings of beads.

"And you think then we'll be all right and be happy."

"I know we will. You don't have to be afraid. I've known lots of people that have done it."

"So have I," said the girl. "And afterward they were all so happy."

"Well," the man said, "if you don't want to you don't have to. I wouldn't   55
have you do it if you didn't want to. But I know it's perfectly simple."

"And you really want to?"

"I think it's the best thing to do. But I don't want you to do it if you don't really want to."

"And if I do it you'll be happy and things will be like they were and you'll love me?"

"I love you now. You know I love you."

"I know. But if I do it, then it will be nice again if I say things are like white   60
elephants, and you'll like it?"

"I'll love it. I love it now but I just can't think about it. You know how I get when I worry."

"If I do it you won't ever worry?"

"I won't worry about that because it's perfectly simple."

"Then I'll do it. Because I don't care about me."

"What do you mean?"   65

"I don't care about me."

"Well, I care about you."

"Oh, yes. But I don't care about me. And I'll do it and then everything will be fine."

"I don't want you to do it if you feel that way."

The girl stood up and walked to the end of the station. Across, on the other   70
side, were fields of grain and trees along the banks of the Ebro. Far away, beyond the river, were mountains. The shadow of a cloud moved across the field
of grain and she saw the river through the trees.

"And we could have all this," she said. "And we could have everything and
every day we make it more impossible."

"What did you say?"

"I said we could have everything."

"We can have everything."

"No, we can't."   75

"We can have the whole world."

"No, we can't."

"We can go everywhere."

"No, we can't. It isn't ours any more."

"It's ours."   80

"No, it isn't. And once they take it away, you never get it back."

"But they haven't taken it away."

"We'll wait and see."

"Come on back in the shade," he said. "You mustn't feel that way."

"I don't feel any way," the girl said. "I just know things."   85

"I don't want you to do anything that you don't want to do ——"

"Nor that isn't good for me," she said. "I know. Could we have another beer?"

"All right. But you've got to realize ——"

"I realize," the girl said. "Can't we maybe stop talking?"

They sat down at the table and the girl looked across at the hills on the dry   90
side of the valley and the man looked at her and at the table.

"You've got to realize," he said, "that I don't want you to do it if you don't want to. I'm perfectly willing to go through with it if it means anything to you."

"Doesn't it mean anything to you? We could get along."

"Of course it does. But I don't want anybody but you. I don't want anyone else. And I know it's perfectly simple."

"Yes, you know it's perfectly simple."

"It's all right for you to say that, but I do know it."   95

"Would you do something for me now?"

"I'd do anything for you."

"Would you please please please please please please please stop talking?"

He did not say anything but looked at the bags against the wall of the station. There were labels on them from all the hotels where they had spent nights.

"But I don't want you to," he said, "I don't care anything about it."   100

"I'll scream," the girl said.

The woman came out through the curtains with two glasses of beer and put them down on the damp felt pads. "The train comes in five minutes," she said.

"What did she say?" asked the girl.

"That the train is coming in five minutes."

The girl smiled brightly at the woman, to thank her.   105

"I'd better take the bags over to the other side of the station," the man said. She smiled at him.

"All right. Then come back and we'll finish the beer."

He picked up the two heavy bags and carried them around the station to the other tracks. He looked up the tracks but could not see the train. Coming back, he walked through the barroom, where people waiting for the train were drinking. He drank an Anis at the bar and looked at the people. They were all waiting reasonably for the train. He went out through the bead curtain. She was sitting at the table and smiled at him.

"Do you feel better?" he asked.

"I feel fine," she said. "There's nothing wrong with me. I feel fine."   110

[1927]

≡ **THINKING ABOUT THE TEXT**

1. At what point in the story do you sense some tension? Is it before the man says, "Oh, cut it out" (para. 28)? At this point, why do you think he says that? Do you think the tension is resolved in the last line, or is the relationship over?

2. Jig says, "That's all we do, isn't it—look at things and try new drinks?" (para. 33). What do you think she really means? How would you phrase this thought if you were trying to be clear and honest about your feelings?

3. Some critics see symbolic significance in the title. What might the phrase "white elephant" mean, and how might this be applied to the situation in the story?

4. When Jig asks, "Then what will we do . . . ?" (para. 47) after the operation (presumably an abortion), what do you think of the man's answer? Does she believe him? Do you? Why, or why not?

5. When Jig says, "And afterward they were all so happy" (para. 54), is she being sarcastic? How about when she says, "I don't care about me" (para. 64)? What does Jig mean by "It isn't ours any more" (para. 79)?

T. CORAGHESSAN BOYLE

The Love of My Life

T. Coraghessan Boyle (b. 1948), who says that his middle name is pronounced with the stress on the second syllable and that his friends call him Tom, has written more than twenty books of fiction, including Drop City *(2003),* The Inner Circle *(2004),* Tooth and Claw *(2005), and* Talk, Talk *(2006). His novel* The Women *(2009) focuses on the women in Frank Lloyd Wright's life.* Wild Child and Other Stories *was published in 2010. His latest novel is* When the Killing's Done *(2011). After graduating from the State University of New York, Potsdam, with a B.A. in English and history, Boyle taught for several years at the high school that he had attended as a teenager, though he continued to follow his interests in creative writing. In the early 1970s, he attended the prestigious University of Iowa Writers' Workshop and went on to receive a Ph.D. in nineteenth-century British literature from the University of Iowa in 1977. His list of awards and publications is long, and he received the O. Henry Award in 2001 for the short story reprinted here, "The Love of My Life." Boyle says that the story is based on a news event of a few years ago that "should break your heart. I know it broke mine."*

They wore each other like a pair of socks. He was at her house, she was at his. Everywhere they went—to the mall, to the game, to movies and shops and the classes that structured their days like a new kind of chronology—their fingers were entwined, their shoulders touching, their hips joined in the slow triumphant sashay of love. He drove her car, slept on the couch in the family room at her parents' house, played tennis and watched football with her father on the big, thirty-six-inch TV in the kitchen. She went shopping with his mother and hers, a triumvirate of tastes, and she would have played tennis with his father, if it came to it, but his father was dead. "I love you," he told her, because he did, because there was no feeling like this, no triumph, no high—it was like being immortal and unconquerable, like floating. And a hundred times a day she said it, too: "I love you. I love you."

They were together at his house one night when the rain froze on the streets and sheathed the trees in glass. It was her idea to take a walk and feel it in their hair and on the glistening shoulders of their parkas, an other-worldly drumming of pellets flung down out of the troposphere, alien and familiar at the same time, and they glided the length of the front walk and watched the way the power lines bellied and swayed. He built a fire when they got back, while she towelled her hair and made hot chocolate laced with Jack Daniel's. They'd rented a pair of slasher movies for the ritualized comfort of them— "Teens have sex," he said, "and then they pay for it in body parts"—and the maniac had just climbed out of the heating vent, with a meat hook dangling from the recesses of his empty sleeve, when the phone rang.

It was his mother, calling from the hotel room in Boston where she was curled up—shacked up?—for the weekend with the man she'd been dating. He tried to picture her, but he couldn't. He even closed his eyes a minute, to concentrate, but there was nothing there. Was everything all right? she wanted to know. With the storm and all? No, it hadn't hit Boston yet, but she saw on the Weather Channel that it was on its way. Two seconds after he hung up—before she could even hit the Start button on the VCR—the phone rang again, and this time it was her mother. Her mother had been drinking. She was calling from the restaurant, and China could hear a clamor of voices in the background. "Just stay put," her mother shouted into the phone. "The streets are like a skating rink. Don't you even think of getting in that car."

Well, she wasn't thinking of it. She was thinking of having Jeremy to herself, all night, in the big bed in his mother's room. They'd been having sex ever since they started going together at the end of their junior year, but it was always sex in the car or sex on a blanket or the lawn, hurried sex, nothing like she wanted it to be. She kept thinking of the way it was in the movies, where the stars ambushed each other on beds the size of small planets and then did it again and again until they lay nestled in a heap of pillows and blankets, her head on his chest, his arm flung over her shoulder, the music fading away to individual notes plucked softly on a guitar and everything in the frame glowing as if it had been sprayed with liquid gold. That was how it was supposed to be. That was how it was going to be. At least for tonight.

She'd been wandering around the kitchen as she talked, dancing with the phone in an idle slow saraband, watching the frost sketch a design on the window over the sink, no sound but the soft hiss of the ice pellets on the roof, and now she pulled open the freezer door and extracted a pint box of ice cream. She was in her socks, socks so thick they were like slippers, and a pair of black leggings under an oversize sweater. Beneath her feet, the polished floorboards were as slick as the sidewalk outside, and she liked the feel of that, skating indoors in her big socks. "Uh-huh," she said into the phone. "Uh-huh. Yeah, we're watching a movie." She dug a finger into the ice cream and stuck it in her mouth.

5

"Come on," Jeremy called from the living room, where the maniac rippled menacingly over the Pause button. "You're going to miss the best part."

"O.K., Mom, O.K.," she said into the phone, parting words, and then she hung up. "You want ice cream?" she called, licking her finger.

Jeremy's voice came back at her, a voice in the middle range, with a congenital scratch in it, the voice of a nice guy, a very nice guy who could be the star of a TV show about nice guys: "What kind?" He had a pair of shoulders and pumped-up biceps, too, a smile that jumped from his lips to his eyes, and close-cropped hair that stood up straight off the crown of his head. And he was always singing—she loved that—his voice so true he could do any song, and there was no lyric he didn't know, even on the oldies station. She scooped ice cream and saw him in a scene from last summer, one hand draped casually over the wheel of his car, the radio throbbing, his voice raised in perfect synch with Billy Corgan's, and the night standing still at the end of a long dark street overhung with maples.

"Chocolate. Swiss-chocolate almond."

"O.K.," he said, and then he was wondering if there was any whipped   10
cream, or maybe hot fudge—he was sure his mother had a jar stashed away somewhere, *Look behind the mayonnaise on the top row*—and when she turned around he was standing in the doorway.

She kissed him—they kissed whenever they met, no matter where or when, even if one of them had just stepped out of the room, because that was love, that was the way love was—and then they took two bowls of ice cream into the living room and, with a flick of the remote, set the maniac back in motion.

It was an early spring that year, the world gone green overnight, the thermometer twice hitting the low eighties in the first week of March. Teachers were holding sessions outside. The whole school, even the halls and the cafeteria, smelled of fresh-mowed grass and the unfolding blossoms of the fruit trees in the development across the street, and students—especially seniors—were cutting class to go out to the quarry or the reservoir or to just drive the backstreets with the sunroof and the windows open wide. But not China. She was hitting the books, studying late, putting everything in its place like pegs in a board, even love, even that. Jeremy didn't get it. "Look, you've already been accepted at your first-choice school, you're going to wind up in the top ten G.P.A.-wise, and you've got four years of tests and term papers ahead of you, and grad school after that. You'll only be a high-school senior once in your life. Relax. Enjoy it. Or at least *experience* it."

He'd been accepted at Brown, his father's alma mater, and his own G.P.A. would put him in the top ten percent of their graduating class, and he was content with that, skating through his final semester, no math, no science, taking art and music, the things he'd always wanted to take but never had time for—and Lit., of course, A.P. History, and Spanish 5. "*Tú eres el amor de mi vida*," he would tell her when they met at her locker or at lunch or when he picked her up for a movie on Saturday nights.

"*Y tú también*," she would say, "or is it '*yo también*'?"—French was her language. "But I keep telling you it really matters to me, because I know I'll never catch Margery Yu or Christian Davenport, I mean they're a lock for val and salut, but it'll kill me if people like Kerry Sharp or Jalapy Seegrand finish ahead of me—you should know that, you of all people—"

It amazed him that she actually brought her books along when they went backpacking over spring break. They'd planned the trip all winter and through the long wind tunnel that was February, packing away freeze-dried entrées, PowerBars, Gore-Tex windbreakers, and matching sweatshirts, weighing each item on a handheld scale with a dangling hook at the bottom of it. They were going up into the Catskills, to a lake he'd found on a map, and they were going to be together, without interruption, without telephones, automobiles, parents, teachers, friends, relatives, and pets, for five full days. They were going to cook over an open fire, they were going to read to each other and burrow into the double sleeping bag with the connubial zipper up the seam he'd found in his mother's closet, a relic of her own time in the lap of nature. It smelled of her, of his mother, a vague scent of her perfume that had lingered there dormant all these years, and maybe there was the faintest whiff of his father, too, though his father had been gone so long he didn't even remember what he looked like, let alone what he might have smelled like. Five days. And it wasn't going to rain, not a drop. He didn't even bring his fishing rod, and that was love.

When the last bell rang down the curtain on Honors Math, Jeremy was waiting at the curb in his mother's Volvo station wagon, grinning up at China through the windshield while the rest of the school swept past with no thought for anything but release. There were shouts and curses, T-shirts in motion, slashing legs, horns bleating from the seniors' lot, the school buses lined up like armored vehicles awaiting the invasion—chaos, sweet chaos—and she stood there a moment to savor it. "Your mother's car?" she said, slipping in beside him and laying both arms over his shoulders to pull him to her for a kiss. He'd brought her jeans and hiking boots along, and she was going to change as they drove, no need to go home, no more circumvention and delay, a stop at McDonald's, maybe, or Burger King, and then it was the sun and the wind and the moon and the stars. Five days. Five whole days.

"Yeah," he said, in answer to her question, "my mother said she didn't want to have to worry about us breaking down in the middle of nowhere—"

"So she's got your car? She's going to sell real estate in your car?"

He just shrugged and smiled. "Free at last," he said, pitching his voice down low till it was exactly like Martin Luther King's. "Thank God Almighty, we are free at last."

It was dark by the time they got to the trailhead, and they wound up camping just off the road in a rocky tumble of brush, no place on earth less likely or less comfortable, but they were together, and they held each other through the damp whispering hours of the night and hardly slept at all. They made the lake by noon the next day, the trees just coming into leaf, the air sweet with the smell of the sun in the pines. She insisted on setting up the tent, just in case—it

15

20

could rain, you never knew — but all he wanted to do was stretch out on a gray neoprene pad and feel the sun on his face. Eventually, they both fell asleep in the sun, and when they woke they made love right there, beneath the trees, and with the wide blue expanse of the lake giving back the blue of the sky. For dinner, it was étouffée and rice, out of the foil pouch, washed down with hot chocolate and a few squirts of red wine from Jeremy's bota bag.

The next day, the whole day through, they didn't bother with clothes at all. They couldn't swim, of course — the lake was too cold for that — but they could bask and explore and feel the breeze out of the south on their bare legs and the places where no breeze had touched before. She would remember that always, the feel of that, the intensity of her motions, the simple unrefined pleasure of living in the moment. Wood smoke. Duelling flashlights in the night. The look on Jeremy's face when he presented her with the bag of finger-size crayfish he'd spent all morning collecting.

What else? The rain, of course. It came midway through the third day, clouds the color of iron filings, the lake hammered to iron, too, and the storm that crashed through the trees and beat at their tent with a thousand angry fists. They huddled in the sleeping bag, sharing the wine and a bag of trail mix, reading to each other from a book of Donne's love poems (she was writing a paper for Mrs. Masterson called "Ocular Imagery in the Poetry of John Donne") and the last third of a vampire novel that weighed eighteen-point-one ounces.

And the sex. They were careful, always careful — *I will never, never be like those breeders that bring their puffed-up squalling little red-faced babies to class*, she told him, and he agreed, got adamant about it, even, until it became a running theme in their relationship, the breeders overpopulating an overpopulated world and ruining their own lives in the process — but she had forgotten to pack her pills and he had only two condoms with him, and it wasn't as if there were a drugstore around the corner.

In the fall — or the end of August, actually — they packed their cars separately and left for college, he to Providence and she to Binghamton. They were separated by three hundred miles, but there was the telephone, there was e-mail, and for the first month or so there were Saturday nights in a motel in Danbury, but that was a haul, it really was, and they both agreed that they should focus on their course work and cut back to every second or maybe third week. On the day they'd left — and no, she didn't want her parents driving her up there, she was an adult and she could take care of herself — Jeremy followed her as far as the Bear Mountain Bridge and they pulled off the road and held each other till the sun fell down into the trees. She had a poem for him, a Donne poem, the saddest thing he'd ever heard. It was something about the moon. *More than moon*, that was it, lovers parting and their tears swelling like an ocean till the girl — the woman, the female — had more power to raise the tides than the moon itself, or some such. More than moon. That's what he called her after that, because she was white and round and getting rounder, and it was no joke, and it was no term of endearment.

She was pregnant. Pregnant, they figured, since the camping trip, and it   25
was their secret, a new constant in their lives, a fact, an inescapable fact that
never varied no matter how many home-pregnancy kits they went through.
Baggy clothes, that was the key, all in black, cargo pants, flowing dresses, a
jacket even in summer. They went to a store in the city where nobody knew
them and she got a girdle, and then she went away to school in Binghamton
and he went to Providence. "You've got to get rid of it," he told her in the motel
room that had become a prison. "Go to a clinic," he told her for the hundredth
time, and outside it was raining—or, no, it was clear and cold that night, a
foretaste of winter. "I'll find the money—you know I will."

She wouldn't respond. Wouldn't even look at him. One of the *Star Wars*
movies was on TV, great flat thundering planes of metal roaring across the
screen, and she was just sitting there on the edge of the bed, her shoulders
hunched and hair hanging limp. Someone slammed a car door—two doors in
rapid succession—and a child's voice shouted, "Me! Me first!"

"China," he said. "Are you listening to me?"

"I can't," she murmured, and she was talking to her lap, to the bed, to the
floor. "I'm scared. I'm so scared." There were footsteps in the room next door,
ponderous and heavy, then the quick tattoo of the child's feet and a sudden
thump against the wall. "I don't want anyone to know," she said.

He could have held her, could have squeezed in beside her and wrapped her
in his arms, but something flared in him. He couldn't understand it. He just
couldn't. "What are you thinking? Nobody'll know. He's a doctor, for Christ's
sake, sworn to secrecy, the doctor-patient compact and all that. What are you
going to do, keep it? Huh? Just show up for English 101 with a baby on your lap
and say, 'Hi, I'm the Virgin Mary'?"

She was crying. He could see it in the way her shoulders suddenly crum-   30
pled and now he could hear it, too, a soft nasal complaint that went right
through him. She lifted her face to him and held out her arms and he was there
beside her, rocking her back and forth in his arms. He could feel the heat of her
face against the hard fibre of his chest, a wetness there, fluids, her fluids. "I
don't want a doctor," she said.

And that colored everything, that simple negative: life in the dorms, roommates, bars, bullshit sessions, the smell of burning leaves and the way the light
fell across campus in great wide smoking bands just before dinner, the unoffi-
cial skateboard club, films, lectures, pep rallies, football—none of it mattered.
He couldn't have a life. Couldn't be a freshman. Couldn't wake up in the morning and tumble into the slow steady current of the world. All he could think of
was her. Or not simply her—her and him, and what had come between them.
Because they argued now, they wrangled and fought and debated, and it was
no pleasure to see her in that motel room with the queen-size bed and the big
color TV and the soaps and shampoos they made off with as if they were treasure. She was pig-headed, stubborn, irrational. She was spoiled, he could see
that now, spoiled by her parents and their standard of living and the socioeconomic expectations of her class—of his class—and the promise of life as
you like it, an unscrolling vista of pleasure and acquisition. He loved her. He

didn't want to turn his back on her. He would be there for her no matter what, but why did she have to be so *stupid?*

Big sweats, huge sweats, sweats that drowned and engulfed her, that was her campus life, sweats and the dining hall. Her dorm mates didn't know her, and so what if she was putting on weight? Everybody did. How could you shovel down all those carbohydrates, all that sugar and grease and the puddings and nachos and all the rest, without putting on ten or fifteen pounds the first semester alone? Half the girls in the dorm were waddling around like the Doughboy, their faces bloated and blotched with acne, with crusting pimples and whiteheads fed on fat. So she was putting on weight. Big deal. "There's more of me to love," she told her roommate, "and Jeremy likes it that way. And, really, he's the only one that matters." She was careful to shower alone, in the early morning, long before the light had begun to bump up against the windows.

On the night her water broke — it was mid-December, almost nine months, as best as she could figure — it was raining. Raining hard. All week she'd been having tense rasping sotto-voce debates with Jeremy on the phone — arguments, fights — and she told him that she would die, creep out into the woods like some animal and bleed to death, before she'd go to a hospital. "And what am I supposed to do?" he demanded in a high childish whine, as if he were the one who'd been knocked up, and she didn't want to hear it, she didn't.

"Do you love me?" she whispered. There was a long hesitation, a pause you could have poured all the affirmation of the world into.

"Yes," he said finally, his voice so soft and reluctant it was like the last gasp   35
of a dying old man.

"Then you're going to have to rent the motel."

"And then what?"

"Then — I don't know." The door was open, her roommate framed there in the hall, a burst of rock and roll coming at her like an assault. "I guess you'll have to get a book or something."

By eight, the rain had turned to ice and every branch of every tree was coated with it, the highway littered with glistening black sticks, no moon, no stars, the tires sliding out from under her, and she felt heavy, big as a sumo wrestler, heavy and loose at the same time. She'd taken a towel from the dorm and put it under her, on the seat, but it was a mess, everything was a mess. She was cramping. Fidgeting with her hair. She tried the radio, but it was no help, nothing but songs she hated, singers that were worse. Twenty-two miles to Danbury and the first of the contractions came like a seizure, like a knife blade thrust into her spine. Her world narrowed to what the headlights would show her.

Jeremy was waiting for her at the door to the room, the light behind him a   40
pale rinse of nothing, no smile on his face, no human expression at all. They didn't kiss — they didn't even touch — and then she was on the bed, on her back, her face clenched like a fist. She heard the rattle of the sleet at the window, the murmur of TV: *I can't let you go like this,* a man protested, and she could picture him, angular and tall, a man in a hat and overcoat in a black-and-white world that might have been another planet, *I just can't.* "Are you —?" Jeremy's

voice drifted into the mix, and then stalled. "Are you ready? I mean, is it time? Is it coming now?"

She said one thing then, one thing only, her voice as pinched and hollow as the sound of the wind in the gutters: "Get it out of me."

It took a moment, and then she could feel his hands fumbling with her sweats.

Later, hours later, when nothing had happened but pain, a parade of pain with drum majors and brass bands and penitents crawling on their hands and knees till the streets were stained with their blood, she cried out and cried out again. "It's like *Alien*," she gasped, "like that thing in *Alien* when it, it—"

"It's O.K.," he kept telling her, "it's O.K.," but his face betrayed him. He looked scared, looked as if he'd been drained of blood in some evil experiment in yet another movie, and a part of her wanted to be sorry for him, but another part, the part that was so commanding and fierce it overrode everything else, couldn't begin to be.

He was useless, and he knew it. He'd never been so purely sick at heart and   45
terrified in all his life, but he tried to be there for her, tried to do his best, and when the baby came out, the baby girl all slick with blood and mucus and the lumped white stuff that was like something spilled at the bottom of a garbage can, he was thinking of the ninth grade and how close he'd come to fainting while the teacher went around the room to prick their fingers one by one so they each could smear a drop of blood across a slide. He didn't faint now. But he was close to it, so close he could feel the room dodging away under his feet. And then her voice, the first intelligible thing she'd said in an hour: "Get rid of it. Just get rid of it."

Of the drive back to Binghamton he remembered nothing. Or practically nothing. They took towels from the motel and spread them across the seat of her car, he could remember that much . . . and the blood, how could he forget the blood? It soaked through her sweats and the towels and even the thick cotton bathmat and into the worn fabric of the seat itself. And it all came from inside her, all of it, tissue and mucus and the shining bright fluid, no end to it, as if she'd been turned inside out. He wanted to ask her about that, if that was normal, but she was asleep the minute she slid out from under his arm and dropped into the seat. If he focused, if he really concentrated, he could remember the way her head lolled against the doorframe while the engine whined and the car rocked and the slush threw a dark blanket over the windshield every time a truck shot past in the opposite direction. That and the exhaustion. He'd never been so tired, his head on a string, shoulders slumped, his arms like two pillars of concrete. And what if he'd nodded off? What if he'd gone into a skid and hurtled over an embankment into the filthy gray accumulation of the worst day of his life? What then?

She made it into the dorm under her own power, nobody even looked at her, and, no, she didn't need his help. "Call me," she whispered, and they kissed, her lips so cold it was like kissing a steak through the plastic wrap, and then he parked her car in the student lot and walked to the bus station. He made Danbury late that night, caught a ride out to the motel, and walked right through the "Do Not Disturb" sign on the door. Fifteen minutes. That was all it took. He bundled up everything, every trace, left the key in the box at the desk, and stood scraping the ice off the windshield of his car while the night opened up above him to a black glitter of sky. He never gave a thought to what lay discarded in the Dumpster out back, itself wrapped in plastic, so much meat, so much cold meat.

He was at the very pinnacle of his dream, the river dressed in its currents, the deep hole under the cutbank, and the fish like silver bullets swarming to his bait, when they woke him—when Rob woke him, Rob Greiner, his roommate, Rob with a face of crumbling stone and two policemen there at the door behind him and the roar of the dorm falling away to a whisper. And that was strange, policemen, a real anomaly in that setting, and at first—for the first thirty seconds, at least—he had no idea what they were doing there. Parking tickets? Could that be it? But then they asked him his name, just to confirm it, joined his hands together behind his back, and fitted two loops of naked metal over his wrists, and he began to understand. He saw McCaffrey and Tuttle from across the hall staring at him as if he were Jeffrey Dahmer° or something, and the rest of them, all the rest, every head poking out of every door up and down the corridor, as the police led him away.

"What's all this about?" he kept saying, the cruiser nosing through the dark streets to the station house, the man at the wheel and the man beside him as incapable of speech as the seats or the wire mesh or the gleaming black dashboard that dragged them forward into the night. And then it was up the steps and into an explosion of light, more men in uniform, stand here, give me your hand, now the other one, and then the cage and the questions. Only then did he think of that thing in the garbage sack and the sound it had made—its body had made—when he flung it into the Dumpster like a sack of flour and the lid slammed down on it. He stared at the walls, and this was a movie, too. He'd never been in trouble before, never been inside a police station, but he knew his role well enough, because he'd seen it played out a thousand times on the tube: deny everything. Even as the two detectives settled in across from him at the bare wooden table in the little box of the overlit room he was telling himself just that: *Deny it, deny it all.*

The first detective leaned forward and set his hands on the table as if he'd come for a manicure. He was in his thirties, or maybe his forties, a tired-looking man with the scars of the turmoil he'd witnessed gouged into the flesh under his eyes. He didn't offer a cigarette ("I don't smoke," Jeremy was prepared to say, giving them that much at least), and he didn't smile or soften his eyes. And when he spoke his voice carried no freight at all, not outrage or threat or cajolery—it was just a voice, flat and tired. "Do you know a China Berkowitz?" he said.

And she. She was in the community hospital, where the ambulance had deposited her after her roommate had called 911 in a voice that was like a bone stuck in the back of her throat, and it was raining again. Her parents were

50

Jeffrey Dahmer: A notorious serial killer and sex offender. He was killed in prison in 1994.

there, her mother red-eyed and sniffling, her father looking like an actor who has forgotten his lines, and there was another woman there, too, a police-woman. The policewoman sat in an orange plastic chair in the corner, dipping her head to the knitting in her lap. At first, China's mother had tried to be pleasant to the woman, but pleasant wasn't what the circumstances called for, and now she ignored her, because the very unpleasant fact was that China was being taken into custody as soon as she was released from the hospital.

For a long while no one said anything — everything had already been said, over and over, one long flood of hurt and recrimination — and the antiseptic silence of the hospital held them in its grip while the rain beat at the windows and the machines at the foot of the bed counted off numbers. From down the hall came a snatch of TV dialogue, and for a minute China opened her eyes and thought she was back in the dorm. "Honey," her mother said, raising a purga-torial face to her, "are you all right? Can I get you anything?"

"I need to — I think I need to pee."

"Why?" her father demanded, and it was the perfect non sequitur. He was up out of the chair, standing over her, his eyes liked cracked porcelain. "Why didn't you tell us, or at least tell your mother — or Dr. Fredman? Dr. Fredman, at least. He's been — he's like a family member, you know that, and he could have, or he would have . . . What were you *thinking*, for Christ's sake?"

Thinking? She wasn't thinking anything, not then and not now. All she 55 wanted — and she didn't care what they did to her, beat her, torture her, drag her weeping through the streets in a dirty white dress with "Baby Killer" stitched over her breast in scarlet letters — was to see Jeremy. Just that. Because what really mattered was what he was thinking.

The food at the Sarah Barnes Cooper Women's Correctional Institute was ex-actly what they served at the dining hall in college, heavy on the sugars, starches, and bad cholesterol, and that would have struck her as ironic if she'd been there under other circumstances — doing community outreach, say, or researching a paper for sociology class. But given the fact that she'd been locked up for more than a month now, the object of the other girls' threats, scorn, and just plain *nastiness*, given the fact that her life was ruined beyond any hope of redemption, and every newspaper in the country had her shrunken white face plastered across its front page under a headline that screamed "MOTEL MOM," she didn't have much use for irony. She was scared twenty-four hours a day. Scared of the present, scared of the future, scared of the reporters waiting for the judge to set bail so that they could swarm all over her the minute she stepped out the door. She couldn't concentrate on the books and magazines her mother brought her, or even on the TV in the rec room. She sat in her room — it was a room, just like a dorm room, except that they locked you in at night — and stared at the walls, eating peanuts, M&M's, sunflower seeds by the handful, chewing for the pure animal gratification of it. She was putting on more weight, and what did it matter?

Jeremy was different. He'd lost everything — his walk, his smile, the muscles of his upper arms and shoulders. Even his hair lay flat now, as if he couldn't bother with a tube of gel and a comb. When she saw him at the arraignment, saw him for the first time since she'd climbed out of the car and limped into the dorm with the blood wet on her legs, he looked like a refugee, like a ghost. The room they were in—the courtroom—seemed to have grown up around them, walls, windows, benches, lights, and radiators already in place, along with the judge, the American flag, and the ready-made spectators. It was hot. People coughed into their fists and shuffled their feet, every sound magnified. The judge presided, his arms like bones twirled in a bag, his eyes searching and opaque as he peered over the top of his reading glasses.

China's lawyer didn't like Jeremy's lawyer, that much was evident, and the state prosecutor didn't like anybody. She watched him—Jeremy, only him—as the reporters held their collective breath and the judge read off the charges and her mother bowed her head and sobbed into the bucket of her hands. And Jeremy was watching her, too, his eyes locked on hers as if he defied them all, as if nothing mattered in the world but her, and when the judge said *First-degree murder* and *Murder by abuse or neglect* he never flinched.

She sent him a note that day—"I love you, will always love you no matter what, More than Moon"—and in the hallway, afterward, while their lawyers fended off the reporters and the bailiffs tugged impatiently at them, they had a minute, just a minute, to themselves. "What did you tell them?" he whispered. His voice was a rasp, almost a growl; she looked at him, inches away, and hardly recognized him.

"I told them it was dead."   60

"My lawyer—Mrs. Teagues?—she says they're saying it was alive when we, when we put it in the bag." His face was composed, but his eyes were darting like insects trapped inside his head.

"It was dead."

"It looked dead," he said, and already he was pulling away from her and some callous shit with a camera kept annihilating them with flash after flash of light, "and we certainly didn't—I mean, we didn't slap it or anything to get it breathing. . . ."

And then the last thing he said to her, just as they were pulled apart, and it was nothing she wanted to hear, nothing that had any love in it, or even the hint of love: "You told me to get rid of it."

There was no elaborate name for the place where they were keeping him. It was   65
known as Drum Hill Prison, period. No reform-minded notions here, no verbal gestures toward rehabilitation or behavior modification, no benefactors, mayors, or role models to lend the place their family names, but then who in his right mind would want a prison named after him anyway? At least they kept him separated from the other prisoners, the gangbangers and dope dealers and sexual predators and the like. He was no longer a freshman at Brown, not officially, but he had his books and his course notes and he tried to keep up as best he could. Still, when the screams echoed through the cell block at night and the walls dripped with the accumulated breath of eight and a half thousand

terminally angry sociopaths, he had to admit it wasn't the sort of college experience he'd bargained for.

And what had he done to deserve it? He still couldn't understand. That thing in the Dumpster—and he refused to call it human, let alone a baby—was nobody's business but his and China's. That's what he'd told his attorney, Mrs. Teagues, and his mother and her boyfriend, Howard, and he'd told them over and over again: *I didn't do anything wrong.* Even if it was alive, and it was, he knew in his heart that it was, even before the state prosecutor presented evidence of blunt-force trauma and death by asphyxiation and exposure, it didn't matter, or shouldn't have mattered. There was no baby. There was nothing but a mistake, a mistake clothed in blood and mucus. When he really thought about it, thought it through on its merits and dissected all his mother's pathetic arguments about where he'd be today if she'd felt as he did when she was pregnant herself, he hardened like a rock, like sand turning to stone under all the pressure the planet can bring to bear. Another unwanted child in an overpopulated world? They should have given him a medal.

It was the end of January before bail was set—three hundred and fifty thousand dollars his mother didn't have—and he was released to house arrest. He wore a plastic anklet that set off an alarm if he went out the door, and so did she, so did China, imprisoned like some fairy-tale princess at her parents' house. At first, she called him every day, but mostly what she did was cry—"I want to see it," she sobbed. "I want to see our daughter's *grave.*" That froze him inside. He tried to picture her—her now, China, the love of his life—and he couldn't. What did she look like? What was her face like, her nose, her hair, her eyes and breasts and the slit between her legs? He drew a blank. There was no way to summon her the way she used to be or even the way she was in court, because all he could remember was the thing that had come out of her, four limbs and the equipment of a female, shoulders rigid and eyes shut tight, as if she were a mummy in a tomb . . . and the breath, the shuddering long gasping rattle of a breath he could feel ringing inside her even as the black plastic bag closed over her face and the lid of the Dumpster opened like a mouth.

He was in the den, watching basketball, a drink in his hand (7UP mixed with Jack Daniel's in a ceramic mug, so no one would know he was getting shitfaced at two o'clock on a Sunday afternoon), when the phone rang. It was Sarah Teagues. "Listen, Jeremy," she said in her crisp, equitable tones, "I thought you ought to know—the Berkowitzes are filing a motion to have the case against China dropped."

His mother's voice on the portable, too loud, a blast of amplified breath and static: "On what grounds?"

"She never saw the baby, that's what they're saying. She thought she had a miscarriage."

"Yeah, right," his mother said.

Sarah Teagues was right there, her voice as clear and present as his mother's. "Jeremy's the one that threw it in the Dumpster, and they're saying he acted alone. She took a polygraph test day before yesterday."

He could feel his heart pounding like it used to when he plodded up that last agonizing ridge behind the school with the cross-country team, his legs sapped, no more breath left in his body. He didn't say a word. Didn't even breathe.

"She's going to testify against him."

Outside was the world, puddles of ice clinging to the lawn under a weak afternoon sun, all the trees stripped bare, the grass dead, the azalea under the window reduced to an armload of dead brown twigs. She wouldn't have wanted to go out today anyway. This was the time of year she hated most, the long interval between the holidays and spring break, when nothing grew and nothing changed—it didn't even seem to snow much anymore. What was out there for her anyway? They wouldn't let her see Jeremy, wouldn't even let her talk to him on the phone or write him anymore, and she wouldn't be able to show her face at the mall or even the movie theater without somebody shouting out her name as if she were a freak, as if she were another Monica Lewinsky or Heidi Fleiss.° She wasn't China Berkowitz, honor student, not anymore—she was the punch line to a joke, a footnote to history.   75

She wouldn't mind going for a drive, though—that was something she missed, just following the curves out to the reservoir to watch the way the ice cupped the shore, or up to the turnout on Route 9 to look out over the river where it oozed through the mountains in a shimmering coil of light. Or to take a walk in the woods, just that. She was in her room, on her bed, posters of bands she'd outgrown staring down from the walls, her high-school books on two shelves in the corner, the closet door flung open on all the clothes she'd once wanted so desperately she could have died for each individual pair of boots or the cashmere sweaters that felt so good against her skin. At the bottom of her left leg, down there at the foot of the bed, was the anklet she wore now, the plastic anklet with the transmitter inside, no different, she supposed, than the collars they put on wolves to track them across all those miles of barren tundra or the bears sleeping in their dens. Except that hers had an alarm on it.

For a long while she just lay there gazing out the window, watching the rinsed-out sun slip down into the sky that had no more color in it than a TV tuned to an unsubscribed channel, and then she found herself picturing things the way they were an eon ago, when everything was green. She saw the azalea bush in bloom, the leaves knifing out of the trees, butterflies—or were they cabbage moths?—hovering over the flowers. Deep green. That was the color of the world. And she was remembering a night, summer before last, just after she and Jeremy started going together, the crickets thrumming, the air thick with humidity, and him singing along with the car radio, his voice so sweet and pure it was as if he'd written the song himself, just for her. And when they got to where they were going, at the end of that dark lane overhung with trees, to a place where it was private and hushed and the night fell in on itself as if it

Monica Lewinsky: A White House intern who was involved in a sex scandal with President Clinton in 1998.
Heidi Fleiss: Known as the "Hollywood Madam"; arrested in 1993 for running a high-priced prostitution ring.

couldn't support the weight of the stars, he was as nervous as she was. She moved into his arms and they kissed, his lips groping for hers in the dark, his fingers trembling over the thin yielding silk of her blouse. He was Jeremy. He was the love of her life. And she closed her eyes and clung to him as if that were all that mattered.   *[2000]*

≡ THINKING ABOUT THE TEXT

1. Both China and Jeremy are condemned by their peers in this story (as they were in real life). Is that your response, too? Did Boyle persuade you to see how such an event is possible? Do you want to understand how such an event is possible? Or is there no explanation for such behavior?

2. After reading the first few pages of the exposition, what do you think Boyle's purpose is in this opening scene? Is the sentence "Teens have sex . . . and then they pay for it in body parts" (para. 2) clever or perhaps even cruel?

3. Look again at the fourth paragraph. What does it tell you about China's frame of mind? Her sense of reality?

4. Is Boyle trying to make an argument about the power of the media? The obliviousness of teens? The power of first love?

5. Have China's and Jeremy's lives been irreparably ruined? Boyle ends the story with China remembering a summer night shortly after she started dating Jeremy. Can this memory save the relationship, or is it proof of her blindness?

≡ MAKING COMPARISONS

1. Through a brief dialogue, Hemingway indirectly sketches the relationship between Jig and the American. Boyle's description is more detailed and expansive. Can you imagine China and Jeremy having the conversation Jig and her boyfriend have? Why? Should they have?

2. If Boyle were given the task of revising "Hills like White Elephants" into his fuller style, what do you think he should include — that is, what would you want to know about Hemingway's characters?

3. Are there indications that Hemingway is sympathetic to Jig's situation? Is Boyle more sympathetic to China or to Jeremy?

≡ WRITING ABOUT ISSUES

1. Some philosophers argue that neonaticide should not be a criminal offense. Write an argument essay that agrees or disagrees.

2. Write an essay that answers the question: What can be done to prevent such events?

3. In the conclusion of Boyle's story, Jeremy thinks: "And what had he done to deserve it? He still couldn't understand" (para. 66). Write a brief analysis of this position.

4. In *Intimate Reading*, her study of the memoir, Janet Ellerby claims that reading memoirs of women who keep secrets "will help those people who rush to damn unfortunate adolescent girls to understand why these desperate girls hide their pregnancies from their families . . . and themselves . . . and help others understand how a panicked and forsaken girl in unimaginable pain might hysterically abandon the newborn she has steadfastly denied, whether she gives birth in a delivery room or a high school bathroom . . . [and] will help our culture understand that we have not yet solved the physical and psychological obstacles that adolescent girls must brave when faced with unwanted pregnancies." Write an essay that agrees or disagrees with this position.

LUCILLE CLIFTON, "forgiving my father"

ROBERT HAYDEN, "Those Winter Sundays"

THEODORE ROETHKE, "My Papa's Waltz"

LI-YOUNG LEE, "My Father, in Heaven, Is Reading Out Loud"

In childhood, our emotions are often intense. Fears about life arise because we feel so powerless. For some of us, our fathers held all the power. Fathers may use their power in various ways—some to control or abuse, others to comfort and protect. We form perceptions about our fathers from these early memories. Often we become judgmental about their failures in the world or their failures as parents. As we grow older, we sometimes come to terms with our fathers and see them simply as human beings with strengths and weaknesses. But it is not always simple; some wounds may be too deep for us to reconcile. The four poets in this cluster approach memories of their fathers with different perspectives and purposes: to forgive their fathers and perhaps themselves, to remember fondly, to come to a closure, to relive a past that still haunts them, to come to terms with loss.

■ **BEFORE YOU READ**

Make a list of four strong memories about your father from your childhood. Are the memories positive or not? Can you remember how you felt then? Is it different from how you feel now? How can you explain the difference?

LUCILLE CLIFTON
forgiving my father

Lucille Clifton (1936–2010) was born in a small town near Buffalo, New York. She attended Howard University and Fredonia State Teacher's College and taught poetry at a number of universities. Her numerous awards for writing include two creative writing fellowships from the National Endowment for the Arts (1970 and 1973), two Pulitzer Prize nominations (for Good Woman: Poems and a Memoir *and for* Next, *both in 1988), several major poetry awards, and an Emmy. The mother of six, Clifton has written fifteen children's books. She was a former poet laureate of Maryland and the Distinguished Professor of Humanities at St. Mary's College. "Forgiving my father" is from her 1980 book,* Two-Headed Woman. Voices, *her most recent book, was published in 2008.*

it is friday. we have come
to the paying of the bills.
all week you have stood in my dreams
like a ghost, asking for more time
but today is payday, payday old man,   5
my mother's hand opens in her early grave
and i hold it out like a good daughter.

there is no more time for you. there will
never be time enough daddy daddy old lecher
old liar. i wish you were rich so i could take it all   10
and give the lady what she was due
but you were the son of a needy father,
the father of a needy son,
you gave her all you had
which was nothing. you have already given her   15
all you had.

you are the pocket that was going to open
and come up empty any friday.
you were each other's bad bargain, not mine.
daddy old pauper old prisoner, old dead man   20
what am i doing here collecting?
you lie side by side in debtor's boxes
and no accounting will open them up.   [1980]

☰ THINKING ABOUT THE TEXT

1. How might you answer the question in line 21? Are the last two lines of
   the poem a kind of answer? Is there some way we can "collect" from the
   dead?

2. Should we bury the dead — that is, should we let the past go and let bygones be bygones? Or is it necessary to settle old scores? What do you
   think Clifton's answer would be?

3. How consistently does Clifton use the payday analogy? Make a list of
   words that reinforce her overall scheme.

4. Would you think differently about the speaker's father if Clifton had
   written "elderly one" instead of "old man" (line 5) or "old playboy / old
   fibber" instead of "old lecher / old liar" (lines 9–10)?

5. Some readers look for tensions or contradictions early in a poem, hoping they will be resolved at the end. Does this poem end in a resolution
   of paying up and forgiving?

ROBERT HAYDEN
Those Winter Sundays

Born in Detroit, Michigan, African American poet Robert Hayden (1913–1980) grew up in a poor neighborhood where his natural parents left him with family friends. He grew up with the Hayden name, not discovering his original name until he was forty. Hayden attended Detroit City College (now Wayne State University) from 1932 to 1936, worked in the Federal Writer's Project, and later earned his M.A. at the University of Michigan in 1944. He taught at Fisk University from 1946 to 1968 and at the University of Michigan from 1968 to 1980 and published several collections of poetry. Although his poems sometimes contain autobiographical elements, Hayden is primarily a formalist poet who preferred that his poems not be limited to personal or ethnic interpretations. "Those Winter Sundays" is from Angle of Ascent *(1966).*

Sundays too my father got up early
and put his clothes on in the blueblack cold,
then with cracked hands that ached
from labor in the weekday weather made
banked fires blaze. No one ever thanked him.   5

I'd wake and hear the cold splintering, breaking.
When the rooms were warm, he'd call,
and slowly I would rise and dress,
fearing the chronic angers of that house,

Speaking indifferently to him,   10
who had driven out the cold
and polished my good shoes as well.
What did I know, what did I know
of love's austere and lonely offices?   *[1962]*

≡ THINKING ABOUT THE TEXT

1. Is the concluding question meant rhetorically—that is, is the answer so obvious that no real reply is expected? Write a response that you think the son might give now.

2. Why did the children never thank their father? Is this common? What specific things might you thank your father (or mother) for? Do parents have basic responsibilities to their children that do not warrant thanks?

3. Is there evidence that the son loves his father now? Did he then? Why did he speak "indifferently" (line 10) to his father? Is it clear what the "chronic angers" (line 9) are? Should it be?

4. How might you fill in the gaps here? For example, how old do you think the boy is? How old is the father? What kind of a job might he have? What else can you infer?

5. What is the speaker's tone? Is he hoping for your understanding? Your sympathy? Are we responsible for the things we do in childhood? Is this speaker repentant or simply explaining?

≡ MAKING COMPARISONS

1. What degrees of forgiveness do you see in Clifton's and Hayden's poems?

2. Writing a poem for one's father seems different from writing a poem about him. Explain this statement in reference to these poems.

3. Compare the purpose of the questions in each poem. How might each poet answer the other poet's questions?

THEODORE ROETHKE
My Papa's Waltz

Born in Saginaw, Michigan, Theodore Roethke (1908–1963) was strongly influenced by childhood experiences with his father, a usually stern man who sold plants and flowers and who kept a large greenhouse, the setting for many of Roethke's poems. Roethke was educated at the University of Michigan, took courses at Harvard, and taught at several universities before becoming poet-in-residence at the University of Washington in 1948. Roethke's books include The Lost Son and Other Poems *(1949), the source for "My Papa's Waltz";* The Waking *(1953), which won a Pulitzer Prize; and* Words for the Wind *(1958), which won the National Book Award. Roethke's intensely personal style ensures his place among the most influential postmodern American poets.*

The whiskey on your breath
Could make a small boy dizzy;
But I hung on like death:
Such waltzing was not easy.

We romped until the pans   5
Slid from the kitchen shelf;
My mother's countenance
Could not unfrown itself.

The hand that held my wrist
Was battered on one knuckle;   10
At every step you missed
My right ear scraped a buckle.

You beat time on my head
With a palm caked hard by dirt,
Then waltzed me off to bed   15
Still clinging to your shirt.
                                        [1948]

≡ THINKING ABOUT THE TEXT

1. Is the narrator looking back at his father with fondness? Bitterness?

2. Would the poem make a different impression if we changed "romped" (line 5) to "fought" and "waltzing" (line 4) to "dancing"?

3. Why did the boy hang on and cling to his father? From fear? From affection?

4. What is the mother's role here? How would you characterize her frown?

5. Readers often have a negative view of the relationship represented here, but many change their minds, seeing some positive aspects to the father and son's waltz. How might you account for this revision?

≡ MAKING COMPARISONS

1. Would you have read this poem differently if the poet had used Clifton's title "forgiving my father"?

2. How would you compare the tone of Roethke's poem with that of Hayden's? Do they miss their fathers?

3. Would you say that Roethke has more complex feelings about his father, whereas Clifton and Hayden seem clearer?

LI-YOUNG LEE
My Father, in Heaven, Is Reading Out Loud

Li-Young Lee (b. 1959) was born in Indonesia to Chinese parents. His father taught medicine and philosophy in Jakarta. During a purge of ethnic Chinese, Lee's father was imprisoned because of his Western interests. He eventually escaped, and the family finally settled in Pittsburgh, where his father became a Presbyterian minister. Lee graduated from the University of Pittsburgh in 1979. He has won many prizes for his poetry, from Rose *(1986) to* Book of My Nights *(2001). He lives in Chicago with his wife and two sons.*

My father, in heaven, is reading out loud
to himself Psalms or news. Now he ponders what
he's read. No. He is listening for the sound
of children in the yard. Was that laughing
or crying? So much depends upon the   5
answer, for either he will go on reading,
or he'll run to save a child's day from grief.
As it is in heaven, so it was on earth.

Because my father walked the earth with a grave,
determined rhythm, my shoulders ached   10

from his gaze. Because my father's shoulders
ached from the pulling of oars, my life now moves
with a powerful back-and-forth rhythm:
nostalgia, speculation. Because he
made me recite a book a month, I forget   15
everything as soon as I read it. And knowledge
never comes but while I'm mid-stride a flight
of stairs, or lost a moment on some avenue.

A remarkable disappointment to him,
I am like anyone who arrives late   20
in the millennium and is unable
to stay to the end of days. The world's
beginnings are obscure to me, its outcomes
inaccessible. I don't understand
the source of starlight, or starlight's destinations.   25
And already another year slides out
of balance. But I don't disparage scholars;
my father was one and I loved him,
who packed his books once, and all of our belongings,
then sat down to await instruction   30
from his god, yes, but also from a radio.
At the doorway, I watched, and I suddenly
knew he was one like me, who got my learning
under a lintel; he was one of the powerless,
to whom knowledge came while he sat among   35
suitcases, boxes, old newspapers, string.

He did not decide peace or war, home or exile,
escape by land or escape by sea.
He waited merely, as always someone
waits, far, near, here, hereafter, to find out: 40
is it praise or lament hidden in the next moment?   *[1990]*

≡ THINKING ABOUT THE TEXT

1. Lee begins his poem by speculating that his father is either reading
   or listening. What does this suggest about the narrator's view of his
   father?

2. What influence does Lee suggest his father had on him in stanza 2? Is it
   positive or negative or both?

3. When Lee says that his father awaited "instruction / from his god, yes,
   but also from a radio" (lines 30–31), what is he suggesting?

4. Does Lee finally identify with his father? In what way?

5. Would you interpret the last stanza as reconciliation? Be specific about
   the resolution that Lee comes to.

☰ MAKING COMPARISONS

1. Unlike Hayden and Roethke, Lee explicitly says he loved his father. What other differences do you note?
2. Is this view of his father more or less balanced than the other three poets?
3. Which of the previous three fathers does Lee's seem most like?

☰ WRITING ABOUT ISSUES

1. Choose one of the four preceding poems to argue that our feelings for our fathers are complex, not simple.
2. In *Words* (1964), Jean-Paul Sartre writes that "there is no good father, that is the rule." Use examples from the four poems to argue that this is, or is not, the case.
3. Do you think all children leave childhood or adolescence with unresolved tensions in their relationships with their fathers? Write a personal narrative that confronts this idea.
4. Locate at least three more poems that deal with memories of fathers. Write a brief report, noting the similarities to the four poems presented here.

ELIZABETH COOK-LYNN, "Grandfather at the Indian Health Clinic"

NIKKI GIOVANNI, "Legacies"

LINDA HOGAN, "Heritage"

GARY SOTO, "Behind Grandma's House"

ALBERTO RÍOS, "Mi Abuelo"

LORNA DEE CERVANTES, "Refugee Ship"

JUDITH ORTIZ COFER, "Claims"

In contemporary middle-class America, the influence, even the presence, of our grandparents has waned. They often live elsewhere, perhaps in retirement communities or nursing homes. But this was not always the case. Grandparents in the past, and in traditional households even today, were active members of the family, exerting influence on the daily decisions of everyday life, from diet to child-rearing. Some of this was beneficial: grandparents gave children a personal understanding of their cultural traditions as well as the benefit of their accumulated wisdom. But they could also create tension in families where change and progress conflicted with the habits and attitudes of the past. The following seven poets present us with different perspectives on their grandparents, some loving and proud, others less positive, and one quite funny.

▤ BEFORE YOU READ

What specific memories do you have of your grandparents? What role do you think they should play in a family's life? What effects might the segregation of the elderly have on a society?

ELIZABETH COOK-LYNN
Grandfather at the Indian Health Clinic

A member of the Crow Creek Sioux tribe, Elizabeth Cook-Lynn (b. 1930) was raised on a reservation in South Dakota by "a family of Sioux politicians and Native scholars." She received a degree in journalism in 1952 and later her doctorate from the University of Nebraska in 1978. She has been a journalist, high-school teacher, university professor, and writer-in-residence. She founded the Native American journal WICAZO Sa Review. In her autobiographical essay "I Tell You Now," she notes that anger over the absence of Native American history compelled her to write. Writing for her is "an act of defiance born of the need to survive. . . . It is the quintessential act of optimism born of frustration." She has written a short-story collection, The Power of Horses and Other Stories *(1990); a novel,* From the River's Edge *(1991); and a poetry collection,* Seek the House of Relatives *(1983), from which the following poem is taken.* Anti-Indianism in Modern America: A Voice from Tatekeya's Earth *was published in 2001. She is currently professor emerita of English and Native American studies at Eastern Washington University and lives in the Black Hills of South Dakota.*

It's cold at last and cautious winds creep
softly into coves along the riverbank. At my insistence
he wears his denim cowboy coat high on his neck; averse to
an unceremonious world, he follows me through
hallways pushing down the easy rage he always has   5
with me, a youngest child, and smiles.
This morning the lodge is closed to the dance
and he reminds me these are not the men who
raise the bag above the painted marks; for the young
intern from New Jersey he bares his chest   10
but keeps a scarf tied on his steel-gray braids
and thinks of days that have no turning: he wore
yellow chaps and went as far as Canada to ride
Mad Dog and then came home to drive the Greenwood Woman's
cattle to his brother's place,   15
two hundred miles
along the timber line
the trees were bright
he turned his hat brim down in summer rain.

Now winter's here, he says, in this white lighted place   20
where lives are sometimes saved by
throwing blankets over spaces where the leaves are brushed away
and giving brilliant gourd-shell rattles
to everyone who comes.   [1983]

≡ THINKING ABOUT THE TEXT

1. What attitude does the narrator seem to have toward her grandfather? Is it affectionate? Wary? Respectful? Caring?

2. How do you explain the phrase "pushing down the easy rage he always has / with me" (lines 5–6)?

3. What can we infer about the grandfather from the line "he turned his hat brim down in summer rain" (line 19)?

4. What significance do you think the grandfather places in giving out "gourd-shell rattles" (line 23)?

5. Indian literature is often concerned with contrasts between cultures. In this sense, how do you explain the grandfather's reaction to the young intern?

NIKKI GIOVANNI
Legacies

Raised near Cincinnati, Ohio, Nikki Giovanni (b. 1943) returned as a teenager to her birthplace and spiritual home in Knoxville, Tennessee, where she experienced the strong influence of her grandmother, Louvenia Watson. She studied at the University of Cincinnati from 1961 to 1963 and earned a B.A. at Fisk University in 1967. She also attended the University of Pennsylvania School of Social Work (1967) and Columbia University School of the Arts (1968). She has taught at a number of universities, since 1987 at Virginia Polytechnic Institute, where she is a professor of English. Her poetry, essays, and works for children reflect her commitment to African American community, family, and womanhood. Her books include Quilting the Black-Eyed Pea: Poems and Not Quite Poems *(2002). Recent books include* On My Journey Now: Looking at African American History through the Spirituals *(2006) and* Acolytes *(2007).* Bicycles: Love Poems *was published in 2009. "Legacies" is from Giovanni's 1972 book,* My House.

her grandmother called her from the playground
    "yes, ma'am"
    "i want chu to learn how to make rolls," said the old
woman proudly
but the little girl didn't want   5
to learn how because she knew
even if she couldn't say it that
that would mean when the old one died she would be less
dependent on her spirit so
she said   10
    "i don't want to know how to make no rolls"
with her lips poked out
and the old woman wiped her hands on
her apron saying "lord
    these children"   15
and neither of them ever
said what they meant
and i guess nobody ever does   *[1972]*

≡ **THINKING ABOUT THE TEXT**

1. Does the dialogue in Giovanni's poem reveal the true feelings of the grandmother and the girl? Be explicit about what is really going on in their minds. Is the girl superstitious?

2. Is it true that "nobody" (line 18) says what she really means? Do you? Is this an indication of honesty or something else — say, tact or convention? Are poets more likely to tell the truth?

3. What makes this piece a poem? Would you prefer more metaphors or similes, allusions, or flowery language? Is *proudly* (line 4) an important word here?

4. Change the grandmother's words to those that reflect more of what is in her heart. Might the girl respond differently if the grandmother were more forthright?

5. The title is only referred to obliquely. Why? What does it refer to? Is contemporary society concerned with legacies? Are you? Are they important or irrelevant?

LINDA HOGAN
Heritage

Born in 1947 in Denver, Colorado, Linda Hogan calls on her Chickasaw heritage to interpret environmental, antinuclear, and other spiritual and societal issues. Her published works include poems, stories, screenplays, essays, and novels. Her novel Power *(1998) has been praised for its beauty of language, mythical structure, and allegorical power. Her works include* The Woman Who Watches Over the World: A Native Memoir *(2001) and* Sightings: The Gray Whales' Mysterious Journey *(2002). Her many honors include an American Book Award for* Seeing through the Sun *(1985), a Colorado Book Award and a Pulitzer nomination for* The Book of Medicines *(1993), fellowships from the Guggenheim Foundation and the National Endowment for the Arts, and a Lannan Award. Hogan received her M.A. from the University of Colorado at Boulder, where she currently teaches creative writing. "Heritage" is from her 1978 book titled* Calling Myself Home.

From my mother, the antique mirror
where I watch my face take on her lines.
She left me the smell of baking bread
to warm fine hairs in my nostrils,
she left the large white breasts that weigh down   5
my body.

From my father I take his brown eyes,
the plague of locusts that leveled our crops,
they flew in formation like buzzards.

From my uncle the whittled wood   10
that rattles like bones
and is white
and smells like all our old houses
that are no longer there. He was the man
who sang old chants to me, the words   15
my father was told not to remember.

From my grandfather who never spoke
I learned to fear silence.
I learned to kill a snake
when you're begging for rain.   20

And Grandmother, blue-eyed woman
whose skin was brown,
she used snuff.
When her coffee can full of black saliva
spilled on me   25
it was like the brown cloud of grasshoppers
that leveled her fields.
It was the brown stain
that covered my white shirt,
my whiteness a shame.   30
That sweet black liquid like the food
she chewed up and spit into my father's mouth
when he was an infant.
It was the brown earth of Oklahoma
stained with oil.   35
She said tobacco would purge your body of poisons.
It has more medicine than stones and knives
against your enemies.
That tobacco is the dark night that covers me.

She said it is wise to eat the flesh of deer   40
so you will be swift and travel over many miles.
She told me how our tribe has always followed a stick
that pointed west
that pointed east.
From my family I have learned the secrets   45
of never having a home.   *[1978]*

☰ THINKING ABOUT THE TEXT

1. The last sentence seems to contain a contradiction. "From my family I
   have learned the secrets" might lead you to expect something positive.
   But maybe the last phrase is not meant to be positive. What is your
   reading of Hogan's conclusion?

2. What does the narrator learn from her mother? Her father? Her uncle? Her grandfather? Her grandmother? What kinds of things did you learn from your family members? Use concrete images.

3. Why does she say "my whiteness a shame" (line 30)? Is this a racial comment?

4. Examine the "black saliva" section in lines 21 to 39. Does it start off negatively? Does it change? Explain.

5. We all learn things from our families, both positive and negative. Is Hogan giving a balanced account? Should she? Would you? Do poets have any responsibility to the larger culture? Or should they just follow their own inner vision?

≡ MAKING COMPARISONS

1. Compare Hogan's grandfather to Cook-Lynn's.

2. Describe the ways the tone of "Heritage" differs from Cook-Lynn's poem.

3. What indications of cultural differences do you find in these two poems?

GARY SOTO

Behind Grandma's House

Born in 1952 in Fresno, California, Gary Soto gives voice to San Joaquin Valley agricultural workers whose deprivations have been part of his experience and social awareness from an early age. After graduating with honors from California State University in 1974, Soto went on to earn an M.F.A. in creative writing from the University of California at Irvine in 1976 and to teach in the university system. He has received numerous writing awards, including the distinction of being the first writer identifying himself as Chicano to be nominated for a Pulitzer Prize. A young adult novel, The Afterlife, *was published in 2003. A book of poems,* One Kind of Faith *(2003), was cited as confirming Soto's "immense talent." His Mexican American heritage continues to be central to his work. The poem reprinted here is from Soto's 1985 book,* Black Hair.

At ten I wanted fame. I had a comb
And two Coke bottles, a tube of Bryl-creem.
I borrowed a dog, one with
Mismatched eyes and a happy tongue,
And wanted to prove I was tough   5
In the alley, kicking over trash cans,
A dull chime of tuna cans falling.
I hurled light bulbs like grenades

And men teachers held their heads,
Fingers of blood lengthening   10
On the ground. I flicked rocks at cats,
Their goofy faces spurred with foxtails.
I kicked fences. I shooed pigeons.
I broke a branch from a flowering peach
And frightened ants with a stream of piss.   15
I said "Shit," "Fuck you," and "No way
Daddy-O" to an imaginary priest
Until grandma came into the alley,
Her apron flapping in a breeze,
Her hair mussed, and said, "Let me help you,"   20
And punched me between the eyes.   *[1985]*

≣ THINKING ABOUT THE TEXT

1. Were you glad or disturbed when the narrator's grandmother hit him? Does he deserve it? Are you angry or sympathetic to his attempts to be tough? Do you understand why he wants to appear older? Is this normal?

2. What did you want at age ten? Did your grandparents know your desires? Did they support you? Did they ever set you straight? Are our grandparents' values too dated to matter?

3. Are the concrete details meaningful to you? Does the profanity help Soto achieve authenticity, or is it unnecessary?

4. Does the speaker learn something here, or is this just a snapshot of an event?

5. How would you describe our culture's ideas of the different roles of parents and grandparents? Do grandparents in today's culture have less influence than in the past? Is this a good thing or not?

≣ MAKING COMPARISONS

1. Is Soto more or less respectful of his grandparent than the writers of the previous two poems?

2. Is this a gendered poem? That is, could a female see herself in a comparable situation? Are the Cook-Lynn and Hogan poems gendered?

ALBERTO RÍOS
Mi Abuelo°

Alberto Ríos (b. 1952) has said that being bilingual is like going through life with a pair of binoculars; having at least two words for everything opens one's eyes to the world. Ríos is a person of the border in several ways: his father was from Chiapas, Mexico, and his mother from Lancashire, England. He grew up in the city of Nogales, Arizona, where he could stand with one foot in the United States and the other in Mexico; as a writer, he crosses the line between poetry and prose, having written seven books of poetry, three collections of short stories, and a memoir. He is an instructor of creative writing, since 1994 the Regents Professor of English at Arizona State University, where he has taught since 1982. He received his B.A. (1974) and his M.F.A. in creative writing (1979) from the University of Arizona. His work appears in 175 anthologies, including the Norton Anthology of Modern Poetry, *and his awards include fellowships from the Guggenheim Foundation and the National Endowment for the Arts and the 1982 Walt Whitman Award for* Whispering to Fool the Wind. *A book of poems,* The Smallest Muscle in the Human Body *(2002), was a finalist for the National Book Award.* The Theater of Night *(2006), was reviewed as "rhapsodic."* The Dangerous Shirt *was published in 2009.*

Where my grandfather is is in the ground
where you can hear the future
like an Indian with his ear at the tracks.
A pipe leads down to him so that sometimes
he whispers what will happen to a man   5
in town or how he will meet the best
dressed woman tomorrow and how the best
man at her wedding will chew the ground
next to her. Mi abuelo is the man
who speaks through all the mouths in my house.   10
An echo of me hitting the pipe sometimes
to stop him from saying *my hair is a*
sieve is the only other sound. It is a phrase
that among all others is the best,
he says, and *my hair is a sieve* is sometimes   15
repeated for hours out of the ground
when I let him, which is not often.
An abuelo should be much more than a man
like you! He stops then, and speaks: *I am a man*
who has served ants with the attitude   20
of a waiter, who has made each smile as only
an ant who is fat can, and they liked me best,

Mi Abuelo: My grandfather (Spanish).

but there is nothing left. Yet I know he ground
green coffee beans as a child, and sometimes
he will talk about his wife, and sometimes   25
about when he was deaf and a man
cured him by mail and he heard groundhogs
talking, or about how he walked with a cane
he chewed on when he got hungry.
At best, mi abuelo is a liar.   30
I see an old picture of him at nani's with an
off-white yellow center mustache and sometimes
that's all I know for sure. He talks best
about these hills, *slowest waves,* and where this man
is going, and I'm convinced his hair is a sieve,   35
that his fever is cooled now underground.
Mi abuelo is an ordinary man.
I look down the pipe, sometimes, and see a
ripple-topped stream in its best suit, in the ground.   *[1990]*

≣ THINKING ABOUT THE TEXT

1. The narrator seems ambivalent about his abuelo. What specific things does he know about him? Can you tell his attitude toward him? How do you read the line "At best, mi abuelo is a liar" (line 30)? What might the worst be?

2. When the grandfather speaks from the grave (*"I am a man . . ."*) (lines 19–23), he seems odd indeed. Is he a bit crazy, or do you see meaning in his ant speech?

3. What does Ríos mean when he writes that his abuelo "speaks through all the mouths in my house" (line 10)? Could this be a positive notion?

4. Ríos seems convinced that his grandfather's "fever is cooled now" (line 36). Should we take this literally?

5. Do you agree that Ríos wants to continue conversing with his dead abuelo? Why? Can we see this as a metaphor?

≣ MAKING COMPARISONS

1. Compare Ríos's attitude toward his grandfather with the attitudes shown in the poems by Cook-Lynn, Hogan, and Soto.

2. Which of the four grandparents featured in these poems would you like to meet? Why?

3. Do all the poems have a sense that grandparents possess some special experience or knowledge?

LORNA DEE CERVANTES
Refugee Ship

Lorna Dee Cervantes (b. 1954), considered one of America's most accomplished Chicana poets, was born in San Francisco. As a child, as a way to avoid widespread racism, she was allowed to speak only English. She has won numerous awards for her poetry collections, including Drive: The First Quartet *(2005), which was nominated for a Pulitzer Prize. She was a professor at the University of Colorado. She currently lives in Boulder, Colorado. The following poem first appeared in* Emplumada *(1981).*

Like wet cornstarch, I slide
past my grandmother's eyes. Bible
at her side, she removes her glasses.
The pudding thickens.

Mama raised me without language.   5
I'm orphaned from my Spanish name.
The words are foreign, stumbling
on my tongue. I see in the mirror
my reflection: bronzed skin, black hair.

I feel I am captive   10
aboard the refugee ship.
The ship that will never dock.
El barco que nunca atraca.°
                                                        [1981]

13 *El barco que nunca atraca*: The ship that never docks.

≡ THINKING ABOUT THE TEXT

1. What does Cervantes mean when she says she is "orphaned from my Spanish name" (line 6)?
2. In what way is the poet "captive / aboard the refugee ship" (lines 10–11)?
3. What is the poet implying with the metaphor of a ship that never docks?
4. How does the poet's looking into the mirror fit into the ideas of the rest of the poem?
5. Why do you think Cervantes repeats the next-to-last line in Spanish?

≡ MAKING COMPARISONS

1. Compare what Cervantes learns about her heritage with what Hogan and Soto learn about theirs.

2. Compare the cooking imagery in this poem with that in "Legacies" and "Heritage."

3. Compare the poet's attitude toward her grandmother with Ríos's attitude toward his grandfather.

JUDITH ORTIZ COFER

Claims

Judith Ortiz Cofer (b. 1952) was born in Puerto Rico but spent most of her childhood traveling between Paterson, New Jersey, and Hormigueros, Puerto Rico. The constant shifting of languages and cultures influenced most of her early work, especially two volumes of poetry: Reaching for the Mainland *and* Terms of Survival, *both published in 1987. Her first novel,* The Line of the Sun *(1989), the first novel ever published by the University of Georgia Press, was widely praised and was nominated for the Pulitzer Prize. Her themes center on the pressures of migratory life and the cultural importance of male–female relationships.* Woman in Front of the Sun *was published in 2000, followed by* A Love Story Beginning in Spanish *(2005). Her recent work includes a number of novels for adolescents, including* If I Could Fly *(2011) and* The Poet Upstairs *(2012). Cofer is a faculty member at the University of Georgia in Athens and is a Regents and Franklin Professor of English and Creative Writing.*

Last time I saw her, Grandmother
had grown seamed as a Bedouin tent.
She had claimed the right
to sleep alone, to own
her nights, to never bear   5
the weight of sex again nor to accept
its gift of comfort, for the luxury
of stretching her bones.
She'd carried eight children,
three had sunk in her belly, *naufragos°*   10
she called them, shipwrecked babies
drowned in her black waters.
Children are made in the night and
steal your days
for the rest of your life, amen. She said this   15
to each of her daughters in turn. Once she had made a pact
with man and nature and kept it. Now like the sea,
she is claiming back her territory.   *[1987]*

10 ***naufragos:*** Victims of shipwrecks (Spanish).

≡ THINKING ABOUT THE TEXT

1. To whom does the title refer?

2. What is the pact the grandmother made with "man and nature" (line 17)?

3. Comment on the simile "like the sea" Cofer uses in the last sentence. Has the reader been prepared for that comparison? Why, or why not?

4. What parts do duty and responsibility play in the grandmother's life? Does her quote (lines 13–15) suggest a negative view of children or sex?

5. Do you think the grandmother's response is typical or unusual?

≡ MAKING COMPARISONS

1. Is Cofer's attitude toward her grandmother more or less respectful than the other poets here?

2. Compare Cofer's grandmother with Cervantes's.

3. Which of the grandparents portrayed here might make the same decision about sex as Cofer's grandmother?

≡ WRITING ABOUT ISSUES

1. Pick one of the seven preceding poems, and argue that it offers an appropriate view of grandparents.

2. Pick two of these poems, and argue that something of value is learned in each.

3. Which poem comes closest to your own experiences? Write a narrative that demonstrates this.

4. Do some research on over-sixty-five communities from a sociological point of view. Write a report about your findings. Include the impact of such places on the family and on the larger culture. Do you think they are a positive development or not?

≡ Gays and Lesbians in Families: Poems

ESSEX HEMPHILL, "Commitments"

AUDRE LORDE, "Who Said It Was Simple"

MINNIE BRUCE PRATT, "Two Small-Sized Girls"

RANE ARROYO, "My Transvestite Uncle Is Missing"

The late Essex Hemphill was gay, as is Rane Arroyo; the late Audre Lorde was a lesbian, as is Minnie Bruce Pratt. All four writers in this cluster remind their audience that families may have gay or lesbian members, but the families depicted in most literature, films, television shows, and songs are heterosexual. Indeed, much of American society prefers this image. Throughout history, plenty of gays and lesbians have concealed their sexual identities from their families, fearing rejection. Families that do have gay or lesbian members may refuse to admit the fact, although most have grown more accepting of their loved ones' differences.

As increasing numbers of gays and lesbians "come out of the closet," many are also publicly claiming the term *family*. They seek acceptance by the families they were raised in and the right to form and raise families of their own. Some are working to get same-sex marriage legalized. In all these efforts, they have quite a few heterosexual allies, but they face heterosexual resistance too. In the 1990s, a lesbian mother, Sharon Bottoms, lost custody of her children for that reason. Also, gays and lesbians are far from winning a universal right to adopt. In 2004, Massachusetts became the first state to legalize same-sex marriage, but as arguments about it raged throughout the United States, the federal government sought to discourage it by passing the Defense of Marriage Act in 1996, and several states passed laws against it. But in June 2013 the Supreme Court passed two landmark decisions, ruling that a law denying same-sex couples federal benefits was unconstitutional and that same-sex marriages in California could continue as legal. Gays and lesbians still face difficulties with adoption and foster parenting, although there are indications that societal attitudes here are changing, albeit slowly. Consider your own position on these matters as you read the following poems. Each refers to American society's widespread assumption that families are heterosexual; each also points out the suffering that can result from this belief.

≡ BEFORE YOU READ

What, at present, is your attitude toward gays and lesbians? Try to identify specific people, experiences, and institutions that have shaped your view. If it has changed over the years, explain how. Finally, describe an occasion that made you quite conscious of the attitude you now hold.

ESSEX HEMPHILL
Commitments

Before his untimely death from AIDS-related complications, Essex Hemphill (1957–
1995) explored through prose, poetry, and film what it meant to live as a black gay
man. The following poem comes from his 1992 book Ceremonies: Prose and Poetry. *His other books include a collection he edited,* Brother to Brother: New Writings by Black Gay Men *(1991). Hemphill also appeared in the documentaries*
Looking for Langston *and* Tongues Untied.

I will always be there.
When the silence is exhumed.
When the photographs are examined
I will be pictured smiling
among siblings, parents,   5
nieces and nephews.

In the background of the photographs
the hazy smoke of barbecue,
a checkered red-and-white tablecloth
laden with blackened chicken,   10
glistening ribs, paper plates,
bottles of beer, and pop.

In the photos
the smallest children
are held by their parents.   15
My arms are empty, or around
the shoulders of unsuspecting aunts
expecting to throw rice at me someday.

Or picture tinsel, candles,
ornamented, imitation trees,   20
or another table, this one
set for Thanksgiving,
a turkey steaming the lens.

My arms are empty
in those photos, too,   25
so empty they would break

around a lover.
I am always there
for critical emergencies,
graduations,   30
the middle of the night.

I am the invisible son.
In the family photos
nothing appears out of character.
I smile as I serve my duty.   *[1992]*   35

≡ **THINKING ABOUT THE TEXT**

1. The speaker begins with the announcement "I will always be there," and yet later he says "I am the invisible son" (line 32). How can these two statements be reconciled? In the second line, he uses the word *exhumed*. Look up this word in a dictionary. What do you infer from the speaker's use of it?

2. Unlike the other stanzas, the second lacks verbs. Should Hemphill have included at least one verb there for the sake of consistency? Why, or why not? Is the scene described in the second stanza characteristic of your own family? Note similarities and differences.

3. What do you think the speaker means when he describes his arms in the photographs as "so empty they would break / around a lover" (lines 26–27)?

4. In line 34, the speaker refers to "character." How does he seem to define the term? He concludes the poem by noting, "I smile as I serve my duty." Should this line be taken as an indication of how he really feels about his family commitments? Why, or why not?

5. List some commitments that you think the speaker's family should be making toward him. What overall attitude of yours toward the family does your list suggest? What is your overall attitude toward the speaker?

AUDRE LORDE
Who Said It Was Simple

Audre Lorde (1934–1992), a prolific writer and speaker, was also active in the civil rights, women's, and gay and lesbian movements. She published several books of poetry, including Cables to Rage *(1970);* From a Land Where Other People Live *(1973), where the following poem appeared;* The New York Head Shop and Museum *(1974);* Coal *(1976);* The Black Unicorn *(1978); and* Our Dead behind Us *(1986). In addition, she wrote several works of nonfiction, including a memoir,* Zami: A New Spelling of My Name *(1982); a collection of essays and speeches,* Sister Outsider *(1984); and an account of her struggle with breast cancer,* The Cancer Journals *(1980). Her last book was* The Marvelous Arithmetic of Distance *(1993). Although Lorde was a lesbian, she had two children and described herself as "black, lesbian, mother, warrior, poet." Lorde was quite controversial, as she saw a clear link among sexism, racism, and homophobia. The key issue for her was mainstream culture's intolerance of difference. This issue alienated her from many white feminists who thought solidarity was crucial. Although Lorde certainly believed in sisterhood, for her the metaphor of family had its limits, as the following poem suggests.*

> There are so many roots to the tree of anger
> that sometimes the branches shatter
> before they bear.
>
> Sitting in Nedicks
> the women rally before they march   5
> discussing the problematic girls
> they hire to make them free.
> An almost white counterman passes
> a waiting brother to serve them first
> and the ladies neither notice nor reject   10
> the slighter pleasures of their slavery.
> But I who am bound by my mirror
> as well as my bed
> see causes in colour
> as well as sex   15
>
> and sit here wondering
> which me will survive
> all these liberations.   *[1973]*

≡ THINKING ABOUT THE TEXT

1. What is the thematic focus that Lorde announces with the tree metaphor of the first three lines?

2. What does the counterman do, and why does that annoy the speaker?

3. Why does Lorde use such a strong word as *slavery* (line 11) to describe the women at the counter who are served before the "brother"?

4. What does Lorde mean by being "bound by my mirror / as well as my bed" (lines 12–13)?

5. Do you see irony in Lorde's final stanza? Do you think Lorde is using "liberations" (line 18) sarcastically?

≡ MAKING COMPARISONS

1. Explain how both Lorde and Hemphill use the idea of invisibility.

2. Lorde mentions anger. Do you think Hemphill is angry, or do you sense other emotions?

3. Lorde was the mother of two children. Do you think that gave her a different perspective when protesting for gay rights?

MINNIE BRUCE PRATT
Two Small-Sized Girls

Minnie Bruce Pratt (b. 1946) has long been active in the women's movement. Her prose writings include Rebellion: Essays, 1980–1991 *(1991) and a 1995 volume of short pieces titled* S/HE. *As a poet, she has published* The Sound of One Fork *(1981);* Crime against Nature *(1990), which won the prestigious Lamont Prize of the American Academy of Poets; and* We Say We Love Each Other *(1992). Her latest books are* Walking Back Up Depot Street *(1999) and* The Dirt She Ate *(2003). In divorce proceedings, Pratt lost custody of her two sons because she is a lesbian. Many of the poems in* Crime against Nature, *including the following, refer to this experience.*

1

Two small-sized girls, hunched in the corn crib,
skin prickly with heat and dust.   We rustle
in the corn husks and grab rough cobs gnawed
empty as bone.   We twist them with papery shreds.
Anyone passing would say we're making our dolls.   5

Almost sisters, like our mothers, we turn and shake
the shriveled beings.   We are not playing at babies.
We are doing, single-minded, what we've been watching
our grandmother do.   We are making someone.   We hunker
on splintered grey planks older than our mothers,   10
and ignore how the sun blazes across us, the straw husks,
the old door swung open for the new corn of the summer.

2

Here's the cherry spool bed from her old room,
the white bedspread crocheted by Grandma,
rough straw baskets hanging on the blank wall,   15
snapshots from her last trip home, ramshackle
houses eaten up by kudzu.   The same past
haunts us.   We have ended up in the same present

where I sit crosslegged with advice on how to keep
her children from being seized by their father   20
ten years after I lost my own.   The charge then:
crime against nature, going too far with women,
and not going back to men.   And hers?   Wanting
to have her small garden the way she wanted it,
and wanting to go her own way.   The memory: 25

      Her father's garden, immense rows of corn,
      cantaloupe and melon squiggling, us squatting,

late afternoon, cool in the four o'clocks;
waiting for them to open, making up stories,
anything might happen, waiting in the garden.   30

3

So much for the power of my ideas about oppression
and her disinterest in them.   In fact we've ended
in the same place.   Made wrong, knowing we've done
nothing wrong:
    Like the afternoon we burned up   35
the backyard, wanting to see some fire.
The match's seed opened into straw, paper,
then bushes, like enormous red and orange
lantana flowers.   We chased the abrupt power
blooming around us down to charred straw,   40
and Grandma bathed us, scorched and ashy,
never saying a word.

    Despite our raw hearts,
guilt from men who used our going to take our children,
we know we've done nothing wrong, to twist and search   45
for the kernels of fire deep in the body's shaken husk.   *[1990]*

≡ THINKING ABOUT THE TEXT

1. Do you think any behavior deserves to be called a "crime against nature" (line 22)? Explain your reasoning.

2. Ironically, one pattern in Pratt's poem is nature imagery. Do you consider some or all of this imagery to be symbolic, or do you accept the images simply as details of a physical scene? Refer to specific examples.

3. Compare the three sections of the poem. What are their common elements? How do they significantly differ from one another? Why does the speaker believe that she and her cousin have "ended / in the same place" (lines 32–33)?

4. How would you describe the two girls' relationship to their grandmother? Support your answer with specific details from the text.

5. Do you think this poem is an affirmation of family ties? A criticism of them? Both? Again, refer to specific details.

≡ MAKING COMPARISONS

1. Compare the tone of the three speakers in Hemphill's, Lorde's, and Pratt's poems.

2. Do you get the impression that all three speakers in this cluster are searching for Pratt's "kernels of fire deep in the body's shaken husk" (line 46)? Show how these words are or are not relevant in each case.

3. Do you sympathize with any of the three speakers more than the others? Why, or why not?

RANE ARROYO
My Transvestite Uncle Is Missing

Rane Arroyo (b. 1954) was born in Chicago to Puerto Rican parents. He received a Ph.D. in American literature from the University of Pittsburgh. Besides being a performance artist, a literary critic, and a playwright, he is currently the director of Creative Writing at the University of Toledo. He is the author of eleven books, including the Ciardi Prize Poetry Winner The Portable Famine *(2005). His latest book is* White as Silver: Poems *(2010). Arroyo's poetic work deals with Caribbean and Latino life and his place as a gay writer in a culture that sees him as an outsider. Many of his poems deal with issues of masculinity and his relationship with his family. The following poem was published in* The Singing Shark *(1996).*

1. Questions

I remember you so Elvis Presley-thin
and ever about to join the army (now I know

the whys of that), and I remember remembering you:
before breasts, before European wigs, when

the etc. of your sexuality was a secret,   5
and you babysat me, and we danced to Aretha,°

and you taught me to scream for the joy of
a song on the radio ("Romeo requests this from

his grave!"), and I can't call you, what's
your new legal name? Is it in the phone book?   10

Are you that official? I've heard you're
dead, call me collect please, I'm on my own,

and Uncle Rachel if you were here tonight I'd . . .
I'd sing to you: "Pretty woman walking down

the street of dreams," and you could tell me   15
that story again where gold is spun out of straw

---

6   Aretha Franklin (b. 1942): Known as the Queen of Soul; has won eighteen Grammy Awards.

2. Answers

News of your old death, first I danced in the shower with
clothes on, cracked my green head against a corner gave you a
bloody birth in my mind, gave myself a satisfying scar,
watched an Annie Lennox° video where she has a red towel on   20
her head, I mirrored her, white towel to stop the bleeding
inside my own nest of a skull, then I screamed and screamed,
but the police never came, snow fell from the constellations,
everything was on fire, fast forward, tumbling and I stupidly
read the *Song of Solomon* for comfort, my eye filled up with   25
blood, I strapped a big bandage around my head, I'm a poor
man's Wilfred Owen,° I'm my own damnation, you're dead,
I won't sing at the funeral that took place without me, the
sun will hear my confessions, my naked body on a rooftop
cruel cock crowing as if another ordinary morning and it is,   30
I did survive, I, someone shows up to make sure I'm not in a
coma, I'm not, not with all these memories, I touch myself as
if I'm still loved, Uncle Rachel, does Death look sexy without
a fig leaf?   *[1996]*

20 Annie Lennox (b. 1954): Lead singer for British band the Eurythmics; called "the greatest white soul singer alive." **27 Wilfred Owen (1893–1914):** British poet of shockingly realistic war verse.

≣ THINKING ABOUT THE TEXT

1. What does the unusual phrase "the etc. of your sexuality" (line 5) suggest about the way Arroyo's family and the culture dealt with Uncle Rachel?

2. Are you surprised that Uncle Rachel teaches Arroyo to scream at the song? Is this an obviously unmasculine response? What seems the response of the adult Arroyo to this?

3. Is the first half of this poem a fond remembrance? How else would you characterize the tone of the speaker?

4. What does the narrator's dramatic response to the news of the uncle's death tell you about their relationship and about the poet's feelings?

5. What significance do memories have for the narrator?

≣ MAKING COMPARISONS

1. Is the speaker here more or less sympathetic than the three speakers in the other poems? Why?

2. Does this poem seem more an affirmation of family ties than do the other poems?

3. Point to any specific lines in the four poems that give you insight into gay life.

☰ WRITING ABOUT ISSUES

1. Choose Hemphill's, Lorde's, or Pratt's poem, and write an essay arguing for or against a position held by someone in the poem. The person can be the speaker. Support your argument with specific details and examples.

2. Choose two of the poems in this cluster, and write an essay comparing how commitments figure in them. Be sure to cite specific words from each poem.

3. In the next week, observe and jot down things on your campus that you think might disturb a gay or lesbian student. (If you are a gay or lesbian student, you may have already thought about such matters.) Then write an essay addressing the issue of whether your campus is inviting to gay and lesbian students. In arguing for your position on this issue, refer to some of the observations you made. If you wish, refer as well to one or more of the poems in this cluster.

4. Increasingly, the United States is grappling with whether same-sex marriage should be legalized. Another debate is whether gays and lesbians should be allowed to become foster parents. Choose one of these issues, and read at least three articles about it. Then write an essay in which you not only put forth and support your own position on the issue but also state whether and how the articles affected your thinking. If you wish, you may refer as well to one or more of the poems in this cluster.

☰ Arguments about a Poem: Sylvia Plath's "Daddy"

SYLVIA PLATH, "Daddy"

CRITICAL COMMENTARIES:

MARY LYNN BROE, From *Protean Poetic: The Poetry of Sylvia Plath*

LYNDA K. BUNDTZEN, From *Plath's Incarnations*

STEVEN GOULD AXELROD, From *Sylvia Plath: The Wound and the Cure of Words*

TIM KENDALL, From *Sylvia Plath: A Critical Study*

As contradictory as it might seem, we sometimes get angry when someone close to us dies. Psychologists tell us that anger is a healthy emotion in the mourning process, following sorrow and preceding acceptance: it is painful to miss loved ones, and we resent it. We might even direct the anger at them, feeling as if they are responsible for depriving us of their love. Sometimes, however, this anger lingers on long after the normal grieving process is over. Perhaps the attachment was abnormally strong, or perhaps the survivor's own life is too unstable to allow him or her to reach the final acceptance stage.

In the following poem, Sylvia Plath writes about her dead father as if he were a terrible person, even though as a young girl she seems to have adored him. Perhaps she is trying to expel his memory so she can find peace; perhaps she is using the poem as an occasion to express a deeper meaning about authority or influence from the past. Regardless, the poem is a powerful, strange, and passionate work of art. Following the poem, we include four critical essays that focus on autobiographial questions while also extending the critical discussion.

Each of the four critics presented here construct arguments about "Daddy," after an obviously careful reading of Plath's poem. Each makes focused assertions that are supported with detailed references to tone, diction, syntax, rhyme, meter, metaphor, alliteration, symbol, and theme—all the elements discussed in Writing about Poems (p. 141). Note how scrupulously all four cite words, lines, and passages to create an informed, judicious, and disciplined persona and hence a convincing argument.

☰ BEFORE YOU READ

Does it make sense to you that we might get angry at those who die because they have somehow deserted us? Do you think we have to "work out" the tensions between us and our parents before we can move into adulthood? Might it be healthy to exaggerate the difficulties of our childhood in poems and stories?

(© Bettmann/Corbis.)

SYLVIA PLATH
Daddy

Born to middle-class parents in suburban New York, Sylvia Plath (1932–1963) became known as an intensely emotional "confessional" poet whose work is primarily autobiographical. Her father, a professor of biology and German, died when she was eight, the year her first poem was published. She graduated with honors from Smith College in 1950, after an internship at Mademoiselle *and a suicide attempt in her junior year, experiences described in her novel* The Bell Jar *(1963). She won a Fulbright Scholarship to study at Cambridge University, in England, where she met and married poet Ted Hughes. The couple had two children; the marriage ended the year before her suicide in 1963. "Daddy" is from* Ariel, *published posthumously in 1965.*

You do not do, you do not do
Any more, black shoe
In which I have lived like a foot

For thirty years, poor and white,
Barely daring to breathe or Achoo.   5

Daddy, I have had to kill you.
You died before I had time —
Marble-heavy, a bag full of God,
Ghastly statue with one gray toe
Big as a Frisco seal   10

And a head in the freakish Atlantic
Where it pours bean green over blue
In the waters off beautiful Nauset.°   *Cape Cod inlet*
I used to pray to recover you.
Ach, du.°   *Oh, you*   15

In the German tongue, in the Polish Town°
Scraped flat by the roller
Of wars, wars, wars.
But the name of the town is common.
My Polack friend   20

Says there are a dozen or two.
So I never could tell where you
Put your foot, your root,
I never could talk to you.
The tongue stuck in my jaw.   25

It stuck in a barb wire snare.
Ich, ich, ich, ich,°   *I, I, I, I*
I could hardly speak.
I thought every German was you.
And the language obscene   30

An engine, an engine
Chuffing me off like a Jew.
A Jew to Dachau, Auschwitz, Belsen.°
I began to talk like a Jew.
I think I may well be a Jew.   35

The snows of the Tyrol, the clear beer of Vienna
Are not very pure or true.
With my gypsy-ancestress and my weird luck
And my Taroc° pack and my Taroc pack
I may be a bit of a Jew.   40

---

16 Polish Town: Plath's father was born in Granbow, Poland.   **33 Dachau . . . Belsen:**
Nazi death camps in World War II.   **39 Taroc:** Tarot cards used to tell fortunes. The prac-
tice may have originated among the early Jewish Cabalists and was then widely adopted by
European Gypsies during the Middle Ages.

I have always been scared of *you*,
With your Luftwaffe,° your gobbledygoo.
And your neat mustache
And your Aryan eye, bright blue.
Panzer-man, panzer-man,° O You —   45

Not God but a swastika
So black no sky could squeak through.
Every woman adores a Fascist,
The boot in the face, the brute
Brute heart of a brute like you.   50

You stand at the blackboard, daddy,
In the picture I have of you,
A cleft in your chin instead of your foot
But no less a devil for that, no not
Any less the black man who   55

Bit my pretty red heart in two.
I was ten when they buried you.
At twenty I tried to die
And get back, back, back to you.
I thought even the bones would do   60

But they pulled me out of the sack,
And they stuck me together with glue.
And then I knew what to do.
I made a model of you,
A man in black with a Meinkampf° look   65

And a love of the rack and the screw.
And I said I do, I do.
So daddy, I'm finally through.
The black telephone's off at the root,
The voices just can't worm through.   70

If I've killed one man, I've killed two —
The vampire who said he was you
And drank my blood for a year,
Seven years, if you want to know.
Daddy, you can lie back now.   75

There's a stake in your fat black heart
And the villagers never liked you.
They are dancing and stamping on you.
They always *knew* it was you.
Daddy, daddy, you bastard, I'm through.   *[1962]* 80

42 Luftwaffe: World War II German air force. **45 panzer-man:** A member of the German armored vehicle division. **65 Meinkampf:** Hitler's autobiography (*My Struggle*).

≡ **THINKING ABOUT THE TEXT**

1. Can this poem be seen as a series of arguments for why Plath has to forget her father? What complaints does the speaker seem to have against her father?

2. Some psychologists claim that we all have a love-hate relationship with our parents. Do you agree? Would Plath's speaker agree?

3. How effective is it for the speaker to compare herself to a Jew in Hitler's Germany? What other similes and metaphors are used to refer to her father? Do they work, or are they too extreme? Perhaps Plath wants them to be outrageous. Why might she?

4. Plath combines childhood rhymes and words with brutal images. What effect does this have on you? Why do you think Plath does this? What odd stylistic features can you point to here?

5. Why do you think it is necessary for the speaker to be finally "through" with her father? Is it normal young adult rebelliousness? What else might it be?

MARY LYNN BROE

From *Protean Poetic: The Poetry of Sylvia Plath*

Mary Lynn Broe (b. 1946) was educated at St. Louis University, where she received her B.A. in 1967, and the University of Connecticut, where she earned an M.A. in 1970 and a Ph.D. in 1976. She currently teaches English at Rochester Institute of Technology in Rochester, New York. She wrote Silence and Power: A Reevaluation of Djuna Barnes *(1991). She publishes and travels extensively and is an international voice in the fields of women's studies and modern literature. Her most recent book is* Black Walking: Selected Letters of Djuna Barnes to Emily Holmes Coleman, 1934–1938 *(2004).*

Among the other poems that display the performing self, "Daddy" and "Lady Lazarus" are two of the most often quoted, but most frequently misunderstood, poems in the Plath canon. The speaker in "Daddy" performs a mock poetic exorcism of an event that has already happened—the death of her father who she feels withdrew his love from her by dying prematurely: "Daddy, I have had to kill you. / You died before I had time—."

The speaker attempts to exorcise not just the memory of her father but her own *Mein Kampf* model of him as well as her inherited behavioral traits that lead her graveward under the Freudian banner of death instinct or Thanatos's libido. But her ritual reenactment simply does not take. The event comically backfires as pure self-parody: the metaphorical murder of the father dwindles into Hollywood spectacle, while the poet is lost in the clutter of the collective unconscious.

Early in the poem, the ritual gets off on the wrong foot both literally and figuratively. A sudden rhythmic break midway through the first stanza interrupts the insistent and mesmeric chant of the poet's own freedom:

> You do not do, you do not do
> Any more, black shoe
> In which I have lived like a foot
> For thirty years, poor and white,
> Barely daring to breathe or Achoo.

The break suggests, on the one hand, that the nursery-rhyme world of contained terror is here abandoned; on the other, that the poet-exorcist's mesmeric control is superficial, founded in a shaky faith and an unsure heart — the worst possible state for the strong, disciplined exorcist.

At first, she kills her father succinctly with her own words, demythologizing him to a ludicrous piece of statuary that is hardly a Poseidon or the Colossus of Rhodes:

> Marble-heavy, a bag full of God,
> Ghastly statue with one grey toe
> Big as a Frisco seal
>
> And a head in the freakish Atlantic
> Where it pours bean green over blue
> In the waters off beautiful Nauset.
> I used to pray to recover you.
> Ach, du.

Then as she tries to patch together the narrative of him, his tribal myth (the "common" town, the "German tongue," the war-scraped culture), she begins to lose her own powers of description to a senseless Germanic prattle ("The tongue stuck in my jaw. / It stuck in a barb wire snare. / Ich, ich, ich, ich"). The individual man is absorbed by his inhuman archetype, the "panzer-man," "an engine / Chuffing me off like a Jew." Losing the exorcist's power that binds the spirit and then casts out the demon, she is the classic helpless victim of the swastika man. As she calls up her own picture of him as a devil, he refuses to adopt this stereotype. Instead he jumbles his trademark:

> A cleft in your chin instead of your foot
> But no less a devil for that, no not
> Any less the black man who
>
> Bit my pretty red heart in two.

The overt Nazi-Jew allegory throughout the poem suggests that, by a simple inversion of power, father and daughter grow more alike. But when she tries to imitate his action of dying, making all the appropriate grand gestures, she

5

once again fails: "But they pulled me out of the sack, / And they stuck me together with glue." She retreats to a safe world of icons and replicas, but even the doll image she constructs turns out to be "the vampire who said he was you." At last, she abandons her father to the collective unconscious where it is *he* who is finally recognized ("They always *knew* it was you"). *She* is lost, impersonally absorbed by his irate persecutors, bereft of both her power and her conjurer's discipline, and possessed by the incensed villagers. The exorcist's ritual, one of purifying, cleansing, commanding silence, and then ordering the evil spirit's departure, has dwindled to a comic picture from the heart of darkness. Mad villagers stamp on the devil-vampire creation.

In the course of performing the imaginative "killing," the speaker moves through a variety of emotions, from viciousness ("a stake in your fat black heart"), to vengefulness ("you bastard, I'm through"), finally to silence ("The black telephone's off at the root"). It would seem that the real victim is the poet-performer who, despite her straining toward identification with the public events of holocaust and destruction of World War II, becomes more murderously persecuting than the "panzer-man" who smothered her, and who abandoned her with a paradoxical love, guilt, and fear. Unlike him, she kills three times: the original subject, the model to whom she said "I do, I do," and herself, the imitating victim. But each of these killings is comically inverted. Each backfires. Instead of successfully binding the spirits, commanding them to remain silent and cease doing harm, and then ordering them to an appointed place, the speaker herself is stricken dumb.

The failure of the exorcism and the emotional ambivalence are echoed in the curious rhythm. The incantatory safety of the nursery-rhyme thump (seemingly one of controlled, familiar terrors) also suggests some sinister brooding by its repetition. The poem opens with a suspiciously emphatic protest, a kind of psychological whistling-in-the-dark. As it proceeds, "Daddy"'s continuous life-rhythms—the assonance, consonance, and especially the sustained *oo* sounds—triumph over either the personal or the cultural-historical imagery. The sheer sense of organic life in the interwoven sounds carries the verse forward in boisterous spirit and communicates an underlying feeling of comedy that is also echoed in the repeated failure of the speaker to perform her exorcism.

Ultimately, "Daddy" is like an emotional, psychological, and historical autopsy, a final report. There is no real progress. The poet is in the same place in the beginning as in the end. She begins the poem as a hesitant but familiar fairy-tale daughter who parodies her attempt to reconstruct the myth of her father. Suffocating in her shoe house, she is unable to do much with that "bag full of God." She ends as a murderous member of a mythical community enacting the ritual or vampire killing, but only for a surrogate vampire, not the real thing ("The vampire who said he was you"). Although it seems that the speaker has moved from identification with the persecuted to identify as persecutor, Jew to vampire-killer, powerless to powerful, she has simply enacted a performance that allows her to live with what is unchangeable. She has used her art to stave off suffocation and performs her self-contempt with a degree of bravado.   *[1980]*

LYNDA K. BUNDTZEN

From *Plath's Incarnations*

Educated at the University of Minnesota, where she earned a B.A. in 1968, and the University of Chicago, where she earned a Ph.D. in 1972, Lynda Bundtzen (b. 1947) teaches at Williams College. A Renaissance scholar with a strong interest in women's issues, she teaches and writes on subjects that range from Shakespeare to Thelma and Louise. Plath's Incarnations *was published in 1983. Her latest book is* The Other Ariel *(2001).*

In "Daddy," Plath is conscious of her complicity in creating and worshiping a father-colossus.

> You stand at the blackboard, daddy,
> In the picture I have of you,
> A cleft in your chin instead of your foot
> But no less a devil for that, no not
> Any less the black man who
>
> Bit my pretty red heart in two.
> I was ten when they buried you.
> At twenty I tried to die
> And get back, back, back to you.
> I thought even the bones would do.

The photograph is of an ordinary man, a teacher, with a cleft chin. She imaginatively transforms him into a devil who broke her heart, and she tells her audience precisely what she is doing. As Plath describes "Daddy," it is "spoken by a girl with an Electra complex. Her father died while she thought he was God. Her case is complicated by the fact that her father was also a Nazi and her mother very possibly part Jewish. In the daughter the two strains marry and paralyze each other—she has to act out the awful little allegory once over before she is free of it." The poem is a figurative drama about mourning—about the human impulse to keep a dead loved one alive emotionally. And it is about mourning gone haywire—a morbid inability to let go of the dead. The child was unready for her father's death, which is why, she says, she must kill him a second time. She resurrected Daddy and sustained his unnatural existence in her psyche as a vampire, sacrificing her own life's blood, her vitality, to a dead man. The worship of this father-god, she now realizes, is self-destructive.

There is nothing unconscious about the poem; instead it seems to force into consciousness the child's dread and love for the father, so that these feelings may be resolved. Plath skillfully evokes the child's world with her own versions of Mother Goose rhymes. Like the "old woman who lived in a shoe and had so many children she didn't know what to do," she has tried to live in the confines of the black shoe that is Daddy. Like Chicken Little, waiting for the sky to fall in, she lives under an omnipresent swastika "So black no sky could squeak through." And Daddy is a fallen giant toppled over and smothering, it seems, the entire United States. He has one grey toe (recalling Otto Plath's gangrened appendage) dangling like a Frisco seal in the Pacific and his head lies in the Atlantic.

The Mother Goose rhythms gradually build to a goose step march as the mourning process turns inward. She feels more than sorrow, now guilt, for Daddy's death and this guilt leads to feelings of inadequacy, acts of self-abasement, and finally self-murder. Nothing she can do will appease the guilt: she tries to learn his language; she tries to kill herself; she marries a man in his image. It will not do.

The self-hatred must be turned outward again into "*You* do not do" by a very self-conscious transformation of a mild-mannered professor into an active oppressor. Her emotional paralysis is acted out as a struggle between Nazi man and Jewess, and, I would argue, the Jewess wins. The poem builds toward the imaginary stake driving, the dancing and stamping and "Daddy, daddy, you bastard, I'm through." Not necessarily through with life, as many critics have read this line, but through with the paralysis, powerlessness, guilt. At last Daddy—the Nazi Daddy she frightened herself with, and not the real one, the professor—is at rest.

Plath's control over ambivalent feelings toward her father is probably the result of their availability for conscious artistic manipulation. She had already written several poems about her dead father when she composed "Daddy," and we also know from a conversation recorded by Steiner that she had "worked through" her emotions in therapy. "She talked freely about her father's death when she was nine and her reactions to it. 'He was an autocrat,' she recalled. 'I adored and despised him, and I probably wished many times that he were dead. When he obliged me and died, I imagined that I had killed him.'" The result in "Daddy" is a powerful and remarkably accessible allegory about her adoration and dread, which ends in emotional catharsis.   *[1983]*

5

STEVEN GOULD AXELROD

From *Sylvia Plath: The Wound and the Cure of Words*

An expert in nineteenth- and twentieth-century American poetry, Steven Gould Axelrod (b. 1944) was educated at the University of California at Los Angeles and served as chair of the English Department at the University of California at Riverside, where he received a Distinguished Teaching Award in 1989. His publications include book-length works on modern and contemporary poets. Sylvia Plath: The Wound and the Cure of Words *was published in 1990.*

The covert protest of "The Colossus" eventually transformed itself into the overt rebellion of "Daddy." Although this poem too has traditionally been read as "personal" or "confessional," Margaret Homans has more recently suggested that it concerns a woman's dislocated relations to speech. Plath herself introduced it on the BBC as the opposite of confession, as a constructed fiction: "Here is a poem spoken by a girl with an Electra complex. Her father died while she thought he was God. Her case is complicated by the fact that her father was also a Nazi and her mother very possibly part Jewish. In the daughter the two strains marry and paralyze each other—she has to act out the awful little allegory once over before she is free of it." We might interpret this preface as an accurate retelling of the poem; or we might regard it as a case of an author's estrangement from her text, on the order of Coleridge's preface to "Kubla Khan" in which he claims to be unable to finish the poem, having forgotten what it was about. However we interpret Plath's preface, we must agree that "Daddy" is dramatic and allegorical, since its details depart freely from the facts of her biography. In this poem she again figures her unresolved conflicts with paternal authority as a textual issue. Significantly, her father was a published writer, and his successor, her husband, was also a writer. Her preface asserts that the poem concerns a young woman's paralyzing self-division, which she can defeat only through allegorical representation. Recalling that paralysis was one of Plath's main tropes for literary incapacity, we begin to see that the poem evokes the female poet's anxiety of authorship and specifically Plath's strategy of delivering herself from that anxiety by making it the topic of her discourse. Viewed from this perspective, "Daddy" enacts the woman poet's struggle with "daddy-poetry." It represents her effort to eject the "buried male muse" from her invention process and the "jealous gods" from her audience.

Plath wrote "Daddy" several months after Hughes left her, on the day she learned that he had agreed to a divorce. George Brown and Tirril Harris have shown that early loss makes one especially vulnerable to subsequent loss, and Plath seems to have defended against depression by almost literally throwing herself into her poetry. She followed "Daddy" with a host of poems that she considered her greatest achievement to date: "Medusa," "The Jailer," "Lady Lazarus," "Ariel," the bee sequence, and others. The letters she wrote to her mother and brother on the day of "Daddy," and then again four days later, brim with a sense of artistic self-discovery: "Writing like mad. . . . Terrific stuff, as if domesticity had choked me." Composing at the "still blue, almost eternal hour before the baby's cry, before the glassy music of the milkman, settling his bottles," she experienced an enormous surge in creative energy. Yet she also expressed feelings of misery: "The half year ahead seems like a lifetime, and the half behind an endless hell." She was again contemplating things German: a trip to the Austrian Alps, a renewed effort to learn the language. If "German" was Randall Jarrell's "favorite country," it was not hers, yet it returned to her discourse like clockwork at times of psychic distress. Clearly Plath was attempting to find and to evoke in her art what she could not find or communicate in her life. She wished to compensate for her fragmenting social existence by investing herself in her texts: "Hope, when free, to write myself out of this hole." Desperately eager to sacrifice her "flesh," which was "wasted," to her "mind and spirit," which were "fine," she wrote "Daddy" to demonstrate the existence of her voice, which had been silent or subservient for so long. She wrote it to prove her "genius."

Plath projected her struggle for textual identity onto the figure of a partly Jewish young woman who learns to express her anger at the patriarch and at his language of male mastery, which is as foreign to her as German, as "obscene" as murder, and as meaningless as "gobbledygoo." The patriarch's death "off beautiful Nauset" recalls Plath's journal entry in which she associated the "green seaweeded water" at "Nauset Light" with "the deadness of a being . . . who no longer creates." Daddy's deadness—suggesting Plath's unwillingness to let her father, her education, her library, or her husband inhibit her any longer—inspires the poem's speaker to her moment of illumination. At a basic level, "Daddy" concerns its own violent, transgressive birth as a text, its origin in a culture that regards it as illegitimate—a judgment the speaker hurls back on the patriarch himself when she labels *him* a bastard. Plath's unaccommodating worldview, which was validated by much in her childhood and adult experience, led her to understand literary tradition not as an expanding universe of beneficial influence . . . but as a closed universe in which every addition required a corresponding subtraction—a Spencerian agon in which only the fittest survived. If Plath's speaker was to be born as a poet, a patriarch must die.

As in "The Colossus," the father here appears as a force or an object rather than as a person. Initially he takes the form of an immense "black shoe," capable of stamping on his victim. Immediately thereafter he becomes a marble "statue," cousin to the monolith of the earlier poem. He then transforms into Nazi Germany, the archetypal totalitarian state. When the protagonist mentions Daddy's "boot in the face," she may be alluding to Orwell's comment in *1984*, "If you want a picture of the future, imagine a boot stomping on a human face—forever." Eventually the father declines in stature from God to a devil to a dying vampire. Perhaps he shrinks under the force of his victim's denunciation, which de-creates him as a power as it creates him as figure. But whatever his size, he never assumes human dimensions, aspirations, and relations—except when posing as a teacher in a photograph. Like the colossus, he remains figurative and symbolic, not individual.

Nevertheless, the male figure of "Daddy" does differ significantly from that of "The Colossus." In the earlier poem, which emphasizes his lips, mouth, throat, tongue, and voice, the colossus allegorically represents the power of speech, however fragmented and resistant to the protagonist's ministrations. In the later poem Daddy remains silent, apart from the gobbledygoo attributed to him once. He uses his mouth primarily for biting and for drinking blood. The poem emphasizes his feet and, implicitly, his phallus. He is a "black shoe," a statue with "one gray toe," a "boot." The speaker, estranged from him by fear, could never tell where he put his "foot," his "root." Furthermore, she is herself silenced by his shoe: "I never could talk to you." Daddy is no "male muse," not even one in ruins, but frankly a male censor. His boot in the face of "every woman" is presumably lodged in her mouth. He stands for all the elements in the literary situation and in the female ephebe's internalization of it, that prevent her from producing any words at all, even copied or subservient ones. Appropriately, Daddy can be killed only by being stamped on: he lives and dies by force, not language. If "The Colossus" tells a tale of the patriarch's speech, his grunts and brays, "Daddy" tells a tale of the daughter's effort to speak.

Thus we are led to another important difference between the two poems. The "I" of "The Colossus" acquires her identity only through serving her "father," whereas the "I" of "Daddy" actuates her gift only through opposition to him. The latter poem precisely inscribes the plot of Plath's dream novel of 1958: "a girl's search for her dead father—for an outside authority which must be developed, instead, from the inside." As the child of a Nazi, the girl could "hardly speak," but as a Jew she begins "to talk" and to acquire an identity. In Plath's allegory, the outsider Jew corresponds to "the rebel, the artist, the odd," and particularly to the woman artist. Otto Rank's *Beyond Psychology*, which had a lasting influence on her, explicitly compares women to Jews, since "woman . . . has suffered from the very beginning a fate similar to that of the Jew, namely, suppression, slavery, confinement, and subsequent persecution." Rank, whose discourse I would consider tainted by anti-Semitism, argues that Jews speak a language of pessimistic "self-hatred" that differs essentially from the language of the majority cultures in which they find themselves. He analogously, though more sympathetically, argues that woman speaks in a language different from man's, and that as a result of man's denial of woman's world, "woman's 'native tongue' has hitherto been unknown or at least unheard." Although Rank's essentializing of woman's "nature" lapses into the sexist clichés of his time ("intuitive," "irrational"), his idea of linguistic difference based on gender and his analogy between Jewish and female speech seem to have embedded themselves in the substructure of "Daddy" (and in many of Plath's other texts as well). For Plath, as later for Adrienne Rich, the Holocaust and the patriarchy's silencing of women were linked outcomes of the masculinist interpretation of the world. Political insurrection and female self-assertion also interlaced symbolically. In "Daddy," Plath's speaker finds her voice and motive by identifying herself as antithetical to her Fascist father. Rather than getting the colossus "glued" and properly jointed, she wishes to stick herself "together with glue," an act that seems to require her father's dismemberment. Previously devoted to the patriarch—both in "The Colossus" and in memories evoked in "Daddy" of trying to "get back" to him—she now seeks only to escape from him and to see him destroyed.

Plath has unleashed the anger, normal in mourning as well as in revolt, that she suppressed in the earlier poem. But she has done so at a cost. Let us consider her childlike speaking voice. The language of "Daddy," beginning with its title, is often regressive. The "I" articulates herself by moving backward in time, using the language of nursery rhymes and fairy tales (the little old woman who lived in a shoe, the black man of the forest). Such language accords with a child's conception of the world, not an adult's. Plath's assault on the language of "daddy-poetry" has turned inward, on the language of her own poem, which teeters precariously on the edge of a preverbal abyss—represented by the eerie, keening "oo" sound with which a majority of the verses end. And then let us consider the play on "through" at the poem's conclusion. Although that last line allows for multiple readings, one interpretation is that the "I" has unconsciously carried out her father's wish: her discourse, by transforming itself into cathartic oversimplifications, has undone itself.

Yet the poem does contain its verbal violence by means more productive than silence. In a letter to her brother, Plath referred to "Daddy" as "gruesome," while on almost the same day she described it to A. Alvarez as a piece of "light verse." She later read it on the BBC in a highly ironic tone of voice. The poem's unique spell derives from its rhetorical complexity: its variegated and perhaps bizarre fusion of the horrendous and the comic. . . . [I]t both shares and remains detached from the fixation of its protagonist. The protagonist herself seems detached from her own fixation. She is "split in the most complex fashion," as Plath wrote of Ivan Karamazov in her Smith College honors thesis. Plath's speaker uses potentially self-mocking melodramatic terms to describe both her opponent ("so black no sky could squeak through") and herself ("poor and white"). While this aboriginal speaker quite literally expresses black-and-white thinking, her civilized double possesses a sensibility sophisticated enough to subject such thinking to irony. Thus the poem expresses feelings that it simultaneously parodies—it may be parodying the very idea of feeling. The tension between erudition and simplicity in the speaker's voice appears in her pairings that juxtapose adult with childlike diction: "breathe or Achoo," "your Luftwaffe, your gobbledygoo." She can expound such adult topics as Taroc packs, Viennese beer, and Tyrolean snowfall; can specify death camps by name; and can employ an adult vocabulary of "recover," "ancestress," "Aryan," "*Meinkampf*," "obscene," and "bastard." Yet she also has recourse to a more primitive lexicon that includes "chuffing," "your fat black heart," and "my pretty red heart." She proves herself capable of careful intellectual discriminations ("so I never could tell"), conventionalized description ("beautiful Nauset"), and moral analogy ("if I've killed one man, I've killed two"), while also exhibiting regressive fantasies (vampires), repetitions ("wars, wars, wars"), and inarticulateness ("panzer-man, panzer-man, O You—"). She oscillates between calm reflection ("You stand at the blackboard, daddy, / In the picture I have of you") and mad incoherence ("Ich, ich, ich, ich"). Her sophisticated language puts her wild language in an ironic perspective, removing the discourse from the control of the archaic self who understands experience only in extreme terms.

The ironies in "Daddy" proliferate in unexpected ways, however. When the speaker proclaims categorically that "every woman adores a Fascist," she is subjecting her victimization to irony by suggesting that sufferers choose, or at least accommodate themselves to, their suffering. But she is also subjecting her authority to irony, since her claim about "every woman" is transparently false. It simply parodies patriarchal commonplaces, such as those advanced . . . concerning "feminine masochism." The adult, sophisticated self seems to be speaking here: Who else would have the confidence to make a sociological generalization? Yet the content of the assertion, if taken straightforwardly, returns us to the regressive self who is dominated by extravagant emotions she cannot begin to understand. Plath's mother wished that Plath would write about "decent, courageous people," and she herself heard an inner voice demanding that she be a perfect "paragon" in her language and feeling. But in the speaker of "Daddy," she inscribed the opposite of such a paragon: a divided self whose veneer of civilization is breached and infected by unhealthy instincts.

Plath's irony cuts both ways. At the same time that the speaker's sophisticated voice undercuts her childish voice, reducing its melodrama to comedy, the childish or maddened voice undercuts the pretensions of the sophisticated voice, revealing the extremity of suffering masked by its ironies. While demonstrating the inadequacy of thinking and feeling in opposites, the poem implies that such a mode can locate truths denied more complex cognitive and affective systems. The very moderation of the normal adult intelligence, its tolerance of ambiguity, its defenses against the primal energies of the id, results in falsification. Reflecting Schiller's idea that the creative artist experiences a "momentary and passing madness" (quoted by Freud in a passage of *The Interpretation of Dreams* that Plath underscored), "Daddy" gives voice to that madness. Yet the poem's sophisticated awareness, its comic vision, probably wins out in the end, since the poem concludes by curtailing the power of its extreme discourse. . . . Furthermore, Plath distanced herself from the poem's aboriginal voice by introducing her text as "a poem spoken by a girl with an Electra complex"—that is, as a study of the *girl's* pathology rather than her father's—and as an allegory that will "free" her from that pathology. She also distanced herself by reading the poem in a tone that emphasized its irony. And finally, she distanced herself by laying the poem's wild voice permanently to rest after October. The aboriginal vision was indeed purged. "Daddy" represents not Dickinson's madness that is divinest sense, but rather an entry into a style of discourse and a mastery of it. The poem realizes the trope of suffering by means of an inherent irony that both questions and validates the trope in the same gestures, and that finally allows the speaker to conclude the discourse and to remove herself from the trope with a sense of completion rather than wrenching, since the irony was present from the very beginning.

Plath's poetic revolt in "Daddy" liberated her pent-up creativity, but the momentary success sustained her little more than self-sacrifice had done. "Daddy" became another stage in her development, an unrepeatable experiment, a vocal opening that closed itself at once. The poem is not only an elegy for the power of "daddy-poetry" but for the powers of speech Plath discovered in composing it.

When we consider "Daddy" generically, a further range of implications presents itself. Although we could profitably consider the poem as the dramatic monologue Plath called it in her BBC broadcast, let us regard it instead as the kind of poem most readers have taken it to be: a domestic poem. I have chosen this term, rather than M. L. Rosenthal's better-known "confessional poem" or the more neutral "autobiographical poem," because "confessional poem" implies a confession rather than a making (though Steven Hoffman and Lawrence Kramer have recently indicated the mode's conventions) and because "autobiographical poem" is too general for our purpose. I shall define the domestic poem as one that represents and comments on a protagonist's relationship to

10

one or more family members, usually a parent, child, or spouse. To focus our discussion even further, I shall emphasize poetry that specifically concerns a father.   [1990]

TIM KENDALL
From *Sylvia Plath: A Critical Study*

Tim Kendall edits Thumbscrew *and is the author of* Paul Muldoon *(1996). He received an Eric Gregory Award for his poetry in 1997 and appears in the* Oxford Poets 2000 *anthology. He was the Thomas Chatterton British Academy Lecturer for 2001 at the University of Bristol and is currently a professor of English literature at the University of Exeter. In 2005, Kendall was awarded the lucrative Philip Leverhulme Prize. This selection is from a book he published in 2001.*

Plath's journals . . . indicate that as late as December 1958, the poet was seriously considering a Ph.D. in psychology: "Awesome to confront a program of study which is so monumental: all human experience."[1] The previous day Plath had discovered in Freud's *Mourning and Melancholia* "an almost exact description of my feelings and reasons for suicide."[2] She felt creatively vindicated when she found parallels between her own life and writings and those of Freud and Jung: "All this relates in a most meaningful way my instinctive images with perfectly valid psychological analysis. However, I am the victim, rather than the analyst."[3] In these examples, experience precedes the psychoanalytical explanation; Freud and Jung confirm what Plath already knows. Despite her emphasis on victimhood, such passages show how she transforms herself into her own case history, becoming simultaneously victim and analyst. The same dual role is apparent in "Daddy," which Plath introduces for BBC radio in terms of Freudian allegory:

> Here is a poem spoken by a girl with an Electra complex. Her father died while she thought he was God. Her case is complicated by the fact that her father was also a Nazi and her mother very possibly part Jewish. In the daughter the two strains marry and paralyze each other—she has to act out the awful little allegory once over before she is free of it.

"Daddy," built on poetic repetition, is therefore a poem about a compulsion to repeat, and its psychology is characterized according to Freudian principles. Repetition necessitates performance—the speaker must "*act out* the awful little allegory once over" in order to escape it. Whether she does succeed in escaping depends on the poem's ambivalent last line: "Daddy, daddy, you bastard, I'm through." "I'm through" can mean (especially to an American ear) "I've had enough of you," but it also means "I've got away from you, I'm free of you," or "I'm done for, I'm beaten," or even "I've finished what I have to say." The speaker's ability to free herself from the urge to repeat remains in the balance.

These dilemmas and uncertainties can be traced back, as Plath suggests, to Freud's accounts of compulsive behavior. "Daddy" adopts a Freudian understanding of infantile sexuality (the Electra complex), a Freudian belief in transference (the vampire-husband "said he was you," and the father also shifts identities), and a Freudian attitude towards repetitive behavior. In a passage from *Beyond the Pleasure Principle* which might conveniently serve to diagnose the speaker of "Daddy," Freud argues that,

> The patient cannot remember the whole of what is repressed in him, and what he cannot remember may be precisely the essential part of it. Thus he acquires no sense of the conviction of the correctness of the construction that has been communicated to him. He is obliged to *repeat* the repressed material as a contemporary experience instead of, as the physician would prefer to see, *remembering* it as something belonging to the past. These reproductions, which emerge with such unwished-for exactitude, always have as their subject some portion of infantile sexual life — of the Oedipus complex, that is, and its derivatives; and they are invariably acted out in the sphere of the transference, of the patient's relation to the physician.[4]

This illuminates Plath's attempts to persuade the dead father to communicate. The refusal of the father-figure, in his various transferred roles of colossus, Nazi, teacher, and vampire, to become "something belonging to the past" is evident in the speaker's need to kill him repeatedly. He must be imaginatively disinterred in order to be killed again, and even as one of the undead, he must be destroyed with a stake in his heart. This repetitive pattern of disappearance and return represents Plath's version of the *fort-da* game as famously described in *Beyond the Pleasure Principle*, where the child's repeated and "long-drawn-out 'o-o-o-o'" is only a slight vowel modulation away from the "oo" repetitions of "Daddy." The father-figure is a "contemporary experience," not a memory; and, as Freud explains, the reason for his continuing presence lies in the speaker's "infantile sexual life." The father's early death ensures that she cannot progress, and her sense of selfhood is stutteringly confined within a compulsion to repeat:

> I never could talk to you.
> The tongue stuck in my jaw.
>
> It stuck in a barb wire snare.
> Ich, ich, ich, ich,
> I could hardly speak.

Repetition occurs when Plath's speaker gets stuck in the barb wire snare of communication with her father. She is unable to move beyond the self. This proposes a more fundamental understanding of repetitive words and phrases than those suggested by Blessing or Shapiro. "Daddy" implies that each local repetition, whatever its microcosmic effects, symptomizes a larger behavioral pattern of repetition compulsion. The poem's title, the "oo" rhymes, and the nursery-rhyme rhythms all reinforce this suggestion of a mind struggling to free itself from the need to repeat infantile trauma. Such infantilism, exhibited by an adult persona, contributes to the poem's transgressive humor: Plath read "Daddy" aloud to a friend, reports Anne Stevenson, "in a mocking, comical voice that made both women fall about with laughter."[5]

Psychoanalyzing the speaker of "Daddy" in the Freudian terms proposed by Plath herself is a valuable exercise which carries important implications for *Ariel's* use of repetition, but it still does not settle the nature of the poet's complex relationship to the "girl with an Electra complex." Plath's introduction for radio seems to reverse the pattern in her journals: now Freud becomes a source as much as an explanation. Her introduction also reverses the reader's experience of the poem. "Daddy" conveys a power and an intimacy which challenge any hygienic separation of poet and poetic voice. With such contradictory evidence, the gulf between poet and persona, cold-blooded technique and blood-hot emotion, analyst and victim, seems unbridgeable. If these divisions can be successfully reconciled, it is through Plath's emphasis on performance and repetition. Freud's account of repetition compulsion shares with Plath's description of "Daddy" a crucial verb: just as Plath's persona must "act out the awful little allegory," so Freud notes that the Oedipus complex and its derivatives are "invariably acted out in the sphere of the transference." Repetition guarantees performance, and performance requires an audience. Freud notes, as if glossing "Daddy," that "the artistic play and artistic imitation carried out by adults, which, unlike children's, are aimed at an audience, do not spare the spectators (for instance, in tragedy) the most painful experiences and can yet be felt by them as highly enjoyable." Plath categorized "Daddy" as "light verse,"[6] a genre which W. H. Auden considered to be "written for performance."[7] "Daddy" may be written for performance, but it pushes the "painful experiences" and the entertainment value to extremes which many readers find intolerable. Freud's Aristotelian concern—why is tragedy pleasurable?—also seems a valid question to ask of Plath's poem: "Daddy" derives its aesthetic pleasures from incest, patricide, suicide, and the Nazi extermination camps.

These taboo-breaking juxtapositions of personal and private realms help explain the poem's notoriety. However, controversy over "Daddy" always returns eventually to Plath's relationship with her persona. Seamus Heaney's principled objection, for example, discerns no difference at all:

> A poem like "Daddy," however brilliant a *tour de force* it can be acknowledged to be, and however its violence and vindictiveness can be understood or excused in light of the poet's parental and marital relations, remains, nevertheless, so entangled in biographical circumstances and rampages so permissively in the history of other people's sorrows that it simply withdraws its rights to our sympathy.[8]

Heaney's pointed phrase "rampages so permissively" might be disputed as an unfair rhetorical flourish, especially in the context of Plath's hard-earned Emersonian desire to assimilate and her wider theological explorations. But Heaney's most revealing word is his last: "sympathy." Heaney refers to one aspect of Aristotelian catharsis—pity for the suffering of others—which he claims that "Daddy" fails to earn. It is not surprising that his critical decorum should come into conflict with a poem which is so consciously and manifestly indecorous. Heaney reads "Daddy" purely as the protest of the poet-victim, who behaves vindictively because of her difficult parental and marital relations. This fails to credit Plath with the self-awareness to be acting deliberately—to be performing. In "Daddy" Plath seeks no one's "sympathy"; she has once more become victim and analyst, the girl with the Electra complex and the physician who diagnoses her condition. Plath wonders in her journal whether "our desire to investigate psychology [is] a desire to get Beuscher's [her psychiatrist's] power and handle it ourselves."[9] "Daddy," as her introduction makes clear, represents a poetic handling of that power. Freud states that the patient must acquire "some degree of aloofness."[10] "Daddy" is the work of a poet so aloof as to render allegorical, act out, and psychoanalyze, her own mental history. [2001]

Notes

1. Sylvia Plath, *The Journals of Sylvia Plath, 1950–1962*, ed. Karen V. Kukil (London: Faber & Faber, 2000), p. 452.
2. Ibid., p. 447.
3. Ibid., p. 514.
4. S. Freud, *Beyond the Pleasure Principle*, tr. and ed. J. Strachey (Hogarth, 1961), p. 12.
5. A. Stevenson, *Bitter Fame: A Life of Sylvia Plath* (Viking, 1989), p. 277.
6. A. Alvarez, "Sylvia Plath," in C. Newman (ed.), *The Art of Sylvia Plath* (Indiana UP, 1970), p. 66.
7. W. H. Auden (ed.), *The Oxford Book of Light Verse* (OUP, 1938), p. ix.
8. S. Heaney, "The Indefatigable Hoof-taps: Sylvia Plath," *The Government of the Tongue* (Faber, 1988), p. 165.
9. *Journals*, p. 449.
10. *Beyond the Pleasure Principle*, p. 13.

≡ MAKING COMPARISONS

1. "Daddy" seems to be a protest, but some critics see it as more than that. Which of the four commentaries makes the best case that it is more than a revolt against the speaker's father?

2. Which critic seems to answer most of the perplexing questions of this poem — for example, the father as Nazi, the father as vampire, the childlike rhythms, the speaker's vengefulness, her viciousness?

3. Do these critics make any similar points? How might you describe them? What is their most striking difference?

≡ WRITING ABOUT ISSUES

1. Choose one of the critical commentaries in this cluster and argue that the textual evidence supporting its assertions is, or is not, adequate.

2. Imagine you are Sylvia Plath. After reading these four essays, write a letter to a literary journal either attacking or praising these critics.

3. Write an essay arguing that your own reading of "Daddy" makes more sense than those of Broe, Bundtzen, Axelrod, or Kendall. Assume that the audience for the criticism is your class.

4. There are dozens of critical commentaries on Plath's "Daddy." Some were written soon after the poem's publication; others are quite recent. Locate an early piece of criticism, and compare it to one published in the past few years. Do these critics make similar or different points? Is one more concerned with the text, with gender issues, with cultural concerns, or with what other critics say? Write a brief comparison of the two, explaining your evidence.

▬ Arguments about an Issue: What Are the Bounds of Parental Protection?

GERARD JONES, "Violent Media Is Good for Kids"

LEE SIEGEL, "The Perils of Parenting in the Digital Age"

HARLAN COBEN, "The Undercover Parent"

Each generation of parents faces challenges and difficulties unknown to the previous generation. But today, with technological advances coming so rapidly, parents' responsibilities in protecting their children have intensified significantly. It is no longer as simple as, "It's 9 p.m., do you know where your child is?" Parents and their children could be at separate computers in the very same room and the dangers to the children could be quite real. The Internet, social media, and violent videogames have complicated parental responsibility as experts debate both the effectiveness of strict rules concerning computer use and easy access to a virtual world children often know more about than their parents. Our three essayists take interesting but different stances toward these problems, opening the door for question and debate. Gerard Jones takes a minority position that violent media are good for children, while Lee Siegel and Harlan Coben are more skeptical about the dangers of the Internet and argue for parental control. All three want what's best for their children in a world where answers are not easy or permanent.

▬ BEFORE YOU READ

How do you think violent video games could do harm? Why do you think they should be or shouldn't be covered under freedom of speech? Why might social media be more dangerous than you first suspected some years ago? What advice would you give parents of twelve-year-olds going on Facebook?

GERARD JONES
Violent Media Is Good for Kids

Gerard Jones (b. 1957) was born in Montana and raised in California. He currently lives in San Francisco, where he writes comic books, short stories, and nonfiction, especially cultural criticism. He has been a contributor to National Lampoon *and written comic book series including* Green Lantern, Justice League, The Shadow, *and* Batman *for Marvel Comics, DC Comics, and other such publishers. His latest book is* The Undressing of America: How a Bodybuilder, a Swimming Queen and a Magician Created Reality Media *(2010). This essay appeared in* Mother Jones *in June 2000.*

At thirteen I was alone and afraid. Taught by my well-meaning, progressive, English-teacher parents that violence was wrong, that rage was something to be overcome and cooperation was always better than conflict, I suffocated my deepest fears and desires under a nice-boy persona. Placed in a small, experimental school that was wrong for me, afraid to join my peers in their bumptious rush into adolescent boyhood, I withdrew into passivity and loneliness. My parents, not trusting the violent world of the late 1960s, built a wall between me and the crudest elements of American pop culture.

Then the Incredible Hulk smashed through it.

One of my mother's students convinced her that Marvel Comics, despite their apparent juvenility and violence, were in fact devoted to lofty messages of pacifism and tolerance. My mother borrowed some, thinking they'd be good for me. And so they were. But not because they preached lofty messages of benevolence. They were good for me because they were juvenile. And violent.

The character who caught me, and freed me, was the Hulk: overgendered and undersocialized, half-naked and half-witted, raging against a frightened world that misunderstood and persecuted him. Suddenly I had a fantasy self to carry my stifled rage and buried desire for power. I had a fantasy self who was a self: unafraid of his desires and the world's disapproval, unhesitating and effective in action. "Puny boy follow Hulk!" roared my fantasy self, and I followed.

I followed him to new friends—other sensitive geeks chasing their own   5
inner brutes—and I followed him to the arrogant, self-exposing, self-assertive, superheroic decision to become a writer. Eventually, I left him behind, followed more sophisticated heroes, and finally my own lead along a twisting path to a career and an identity. In my thirties, I found myself writing action movies and comic books. I wrote some Hulk stories, and met the geek-geniuses who created him. I saw my own creations turned into action figures, cartoons, and computer games. I talked to the kids who read my stories. Across generations, genders, and ethnicities I kept seeing the same story: people pulling themselves out of emotional traps by immersing themselves in violent stories. People integrating the scariest, most fervently denied fragments of their psyches into fuller senses of selfhood through fantasies of superhuman combat and destruction.

I have watched my son living the same story—transforming himself into a bloodthirsty dinosaur to embolden himself for the plunge into preschool, a Power Ranger to muscle through a social competition in kindergarten. In the first grade, his friends started climbing a tree at school. But he was afraid: of falling, of the centipedes crawling on the trunk, of sharp branches, of his friends' derision. I took my cue from his own fantasies and read him old Tarzan comics, rich in combat and bright with flashing knives. For two weeks he lived in them. Then he put them aside. And he climbed the tree.

But all the while, especially in the wake of the recent burst of school shootings, I heard pop psychologists insisting that violent stories are harmful to kids, heard teachers begging parents to keep their kids away from "junk culture," heard a guilt-stricken friend with a son who loved Pokémon lament, "I've turned into the bad mom who lets her kid eat sugary cereal and watch cartoons!"

That's when I started the research.

"Fear, greed, power-hunger, rage: these are aspects of our selves that we try not to experience in our lives but often want, even need, to experience vicariously through stories of others," writes Melanie Moore, Ph.D., a psychologist who works with urban teens. "Children need violent entertainment in order to explore the inescapable feelings that they've been taught to deny, and to reintegrate those feelings into a more whole, more complex, more resilient selfhood."

Moore consults to public schools and local governments, and is also rais-   10
ing a daughter. For the past three years she and I have been studying the ways in which children use violent stories to meet their emotional and developmental needs—and the ways in which adults can help them use those stories healthily. With her help I developed Power Play, a program for helping young people improve their self-knowledge and sense of potency through heroic, combative storytelling.

We've found that every aspect of even the trashiest pop-culture story can have its own developmental function. Pretending to have superhuman powers helps children conquer the feelings of powerlessness that inevitably come with being so young and small. The dual-identity concept at the heart of many superhero stories helps kids negotiate the conflicts between the inner self and the public self as they work through the early stages of socialization. Identification with a rebellious, even destructive, hero helps children learn to push back against a modern culture that cultivates fear and teaches dependency.

At its most fundamental level, what we call "creative violence"— head-bonking cartoons, bloody videogames, playground karate, toy guns— gives children a tool to master their rage. Children will feel rage. Even the sweetest and most civilized of them, even those whose parents read the better class of literary magazines, will feel rage. The world is uncontrollable and incomprehensible; mastering it is a terrifying, enraging task. Rage can be an energizing emotion, a shot of courage to push us to resist greater threats, take more control, than we ever thought we could. But rage is also the emotion our culture distrusts the most. Most of us are taught early on to fear our own. Through immersion in imaginary combat and identification with a violent protagonist, children engage the rage they've stifled, come to fear it less, and become more capable of utilizing it against life's challenges.

I knew one little girl who went around exploding with fantasies so violent that other moms would draw her mother aside to whisper, "I think you should know something about Emily. . . ." Her parents were separating, and she was small, an only child, a tomboy at an age when her classmates were dividing sharply along gender lines. On the playground she acted out "Sailor Moon" fights, and in the classroom she wrote stories about people being stabbed with knives. The more adults tried to control her stories, the more she acted out the roles of her angry heroes: breaking rules, testing limits, roaring threats.

Then her mother and I started helping her tell her stories. She wrote them, performed them, drew them like comics: sometimes bloody, sometimes tender, always blending the images of pop culture with her own most private fantasies. She came out of it just as fiery and strong, but more self-controlled and socially competent: a leader among her peers, the one student in her class who could truly pull boys and girls together.

I worked with an older girl, a middle-class "nice girl," who held herself to-   15
gether through a chaotic family situation and a tumultuous adolescence with gangsta rap. In the mythologized street violence of Ice T, the rage and strutting of his music and lyrics, she found a theater of the mind in which she could be powerful, ruthless, invulnerable. She avoided the heavy drug use that sank many of her peers, and flowered in college as a writer and political activist.

I'm not going to argue that violent entertainment is harmless. I think it has helped inspire some people to real-life violence. I am going to argue that it's helped hundreds of people for every one it's hurt, and that it can help far more if we learn to use it well. I am going to argue that our fear of "youth violence" isn't well-founded on reality, and that the fear can do more harm than the reality. We act as though our highest priority is to prevent our children from growing up into murderous thugs — but modern kids are far more likely to grow up too passive, too distrustful of themselves, too easily manipulated.

We send the message to our children in a hundred ways that their craving for imaginary gun battles and symbolic killings is wrong, or at least dangerous. Even when we don't call for censorship or forbid "Mortal Kombat," we moan to other parents within our kids' earshot about the "awful violence" in the entertainment they love. We tell our kids that it isn't nice to play-fight, or we steer them from some monstrous action figure to a pro-social doll. Even in the most progressive households, where we make such a point of letting children feel what they feel, we rush to substitute an enlightened discussion for the raw material of rageful fantasy. In the process, we risk confusing them about their natural aggression in the same way the Victorians confused their children about their sexuality. When we try to protect our children from their own feelings and fantasies, we shelter them not against violence but against power and selfhood.   [2000]

≡ THINKING ABOUT IDEAS

1. Jones's thinking is certainly counterintuitive since most people do not think of violent videogames as therapeutic. In what specific way does Jones think they are? In what ways might the opposite be true?

2. What specific ideas that Jones raises might be influential in the ongoing debate about possible negative effects of popular culture on children?

3. In citing the example of the young girl influenced by Ice-T, Jones uses the interesting phrase "theater of the mind" (para. 15). What does he mean? In what way does your experience with music, videogames, or movies include this concept?

≡ THINKING ABOUT ARGUMENTATIVE MOVES

1. Jones begins his argument with personal anecdotes about himself and his son. What specific lesson does he learn? How does this jibe with

conventional wisdom? How does an expert, Melanie Moore, "support" Jones?

2. Comment on the significance of the phrase, "Rage can be an energizing emotion" (para. 12). How does this idea fit into Jones's thesis? How do his two examples (Emily and the "nice girl") support his thesis?

3. How does Jones address the opposition? How might his argument about the efficacy of violent games and music be more persuasive if he gave them more attention? What specific objection would you raise to his ideas in the last paragraph about protecting children?

LEE SIEGEL

The Perils of Parenting in the Digital Age

Lee Siegel was born in the Bronx in 1957 and graduated from Columbia, where he also received an M.A. and M.Phil. He is a full-time writer who has worked for the Nation, Slate, Harper's, Raritan, *and the* Daily Beast. *His critique of Web culture,* Against the Machine: Being Human in the Age of the Electronic Mob *(2008), was praised by the* New York Times. *His latest book is* Are You Serious? How to Be True and Get Real in the Age of Silly *(2011). He lives in Montclair, New Jersey, with his wife and children. Siegel's piece was posted on the* Newsweek/Daily Beast *Web site in October 2012.*

When regulators at the Federal Trade Commission take steps within the coming weeks to strengthen the Children's Online Privacy Protection Act of 1998, they could well be acting with Vicki Turner in mind.

Along with raising her three kids, ages 16, 13, and 7, and working a job with handicapped children and adults, the 43-year-old resident of Fullerton, Calif., also spends a big part of her life monitoring her oldest kids' online activities: steering them away from inappropriate content, preventing them from uploading photos of themselves onto commercial sites that invite them to do so, and occasionally making them unfriend a person on Facebook whom Turner considers undesirable. When told about Mark Zuckerberg's declared ambition to open Facebook to children under the age of 13, she sighs. "He just cares about what will profit him," she says.

In fact, Facebook, which hit a billion users last week, has sent a 20-page letter to the FTC imploring the agency to reconsider its planned revision of the 1998 act, which would prohibit the collection of information from children online, a lucrative practice that the social-networking behemoth clearly would not like to give up. Yet the FTC, though sharply criticized by an advertising industry unhappy with the proposed changes, says that current laws meant to shield children on the Internet have fallen way behind advancing technology. Entities, ranging from large corporations to obscure apps to roving data collectors, gather up children's personal information, photographs, and even their physical location. Antiquated laws requiring parental permission for such things are easily circumvented by cookies that document children's online movements the way birds devoured the crumbs of bread that Hansel and Gretel hoped would guide them back home.

For besieged parents, the FTC's proposed revisions cannot arrive a moment too soon. But welcome as those changes will be, they will have little effect on the Internet's social environment, which in many ways has made being a modern American parent more complex than ever before. "It used to be the proverbial question: 'It's 10 o'clock, do you know where your children are?'" says Jamie Wasserman, a child therapist with a practice in Manhattan. "Now your kid can be sitting a few feet away from you in the living room with a laptop, being damaged."

By "damage," Wasserman doesn't mean only the danger of meeting a predator on the Internet. She is also referring to what seems to be an almost infinite spectrum of online harm. A child could be bullied or harshly excluded from an instantly formed clique. At the same time, the pressure to be constantly posting, tweeting, and updating one's status threatens to obstruct the development of what used to be called, in unwired times, a child's "inner resources." With all the frenzied social networking on sites like Facebook, our kids are often forced to be social before they have become socialized.

Even for the most gregarious children, the Web's constant reminder of majority opinion makes them fearful of trying to say or do anything that doesn't please the crowd. Yet appealing to the Web's masses also offers them the temptation to say things they would never ordinarily have uttered in public—things that can come back to haunt them later in life.

I look at my own children, a 6-year-old boy and a 2-year-old girl, and I wonder not just what the world has in store for them, but also how they will be able to find the world. When I was 5, people used a typewriter and talked on a landline. When I was 35, people were still conversing on old-fashioned phones. Between the time my son and my daughter were born, texting overtook both cellphones and emailing, desktop computers became obsolete, Twitter was born, the iPod passed through several generations, and both the Kindle and the iPad were invented.

The process of maturing is a movement from a rich yet defensive inner space to the outer reality of pleasure postponement, setback, and perseverance. But the Internet offers one recessive chamber after another of inwardness; it is a place where distraction and immediate gratification become cognitive tools in themselves. The main barrier between parent and child, which looms gigantic in adolescence, is the stubborn insularity of a child's world. These days that insularity has its own enabling techniques, skills, and idiom. What used to be quaintly called the generation gap is now adorned with the corporate logos of Apple, Google, and Facebook.

This is why few people seem sympathetic to Facebook's desire, publicly announced over the summer, to sign up children under 13, especially parents like Turner, who are fighting against escalating odds to keep up with ever-accelerating technology that they barely understand but which their children have mastered to the point of jadedness. Thomas Hughey, a school counselor at Lancaster High School in Lancaster, Wis., for 20 years, routinely encounters students "so connected to all the digital stimulation that it ruins their day. They're so used to instant stimulation that"—like overburdened business executives—"they don't have downtime."

"For my kids," says Miriam Ancis, an artist in Brooklyn, N.Y., who has   10
three teenage children, "the Internet is the air they breathe, how they function in the world." Professor Howard Gardner, a developmental psychologist at Harvard who believes that intuition, creativity, and interpersonal skills matter as much as the formal intelligence measured in standardized tests and whose theory of "multiple intelligences" has changed the way children are taught, says it's often the case that today's youth "don't know whether they're online or not." That is a sea change in human relations, not to mention in the parent-child dynamic.

Recent studies showing that kids spend at least four hours a day on social and recreational media, distracted and disengaged from the world and each other, have caused yet another ripple of alarm. And increasingly, parents fear that their children's "electronic fingerprints" will hinder their path through life.

"Kids are losing jobs because of things they posted," says Hughey. For Sherry Turkle, a social psychologist who has been studying the effects of computers on personality for nearly 30 years, the Internet's breach of privacy is a public tragedy. "We were absolutely not paying attention," she said. "We taught our children not to care about privacy. A whole generation was let down."

The concern with privacy is precisely what the FTC is now moving to address. Yet throughout the country, parents, educators, and mental-health experts are voicing their concern over not just the commercial invasion of privacy, or Facebook's domination of American life, but also the conventions of digital culture itself. "Our kids are being socialized by each other at warp speed," says Wasserman. "They're never off social duty." For the most hurt, withdrawn children, Wasserman says it's like "Columbine on crack."

Dr. John Huxsahl, co-chairman of the Division of Child Psychiatry and Psychology at the Mayo Clinic in Rochester, Minn., says the Internet "allows you instant access to what other people desire more than to what you desire." Conformity becomes an end in itself—what Hughey calls "a new category of peer pressure." Even Turkle's MIT students are not immune. "They leave their phones on the seminar table" and wait for the little red light to blink, she says, "just to see who wants them."

Of course, it is the transformation of children into desirable objects that   15
alarms parents the most when Zuckerberg speaks of opening Facebook to the very young. "The Internet has created greater access to children," said Cynthia Carreiro, a supervisory special agent in the FBI. Ironically, says Carreiro, it's the very young children whose self-protective mechanisms are sharpest when they see the actual face of a predator. "Young kids are really grossed out," she says. But on the Internet there are no physical danger signs standing between the seductive machinations of a monster and an innocent child.

Recent reports that a new flirting app, called Skout, resulted in three separate cases of children being raped by older men have driven home the dangers confronting minors when they go on the Web. After the rapes, Skout banned minors from the site, but they've since readmitted them, with new safeguards. Carreiro says that "parents have to educate themselves on how to protect their kids online." At the same time, she is concerned about the rapid pace of changing technology. "It's becoming more difficult for parents to block access," she says.

That is, if they want to block access. According to a *Consumer Reports* article published last May, 7.5 million kids twelve and younger are on Facebook. Some of those kids' parents helped their children create a fake birth date to get them access to the site. The fear of being disconnected can be even stronger for parents than for their sons and daughters. Gardner tells the story of parents who get around some summer camps' prohibition against electronic devices by packing in with their children's supplies teddy bears that have a cellphone or iPod sewn, prison-break style, into their tummies.

Then there are the parents who themselves become like children in the hands of the Internet. Several students have come to Hughey seeking help after walking in on a parent watching porn on the Web. They felt "shocked, betrayed, confused," he said. Other students complained to him that their parents were so wrapped up in the Internet they didn't come to ball games or spend time with their kids.

On several occasions, Hughey said, a divorced parent, after connecting with someone online, piled the kids into the car and drove off to start a new life with a person neither the parent nor the children had ever met. In one case, a single mother hauled her family to Texas from Wisconsin, only to get a "bad vibe" once she saw her online lover in the flesh. Returning to the hotel, she took to her laptop to check up on him and discovered that he had a criminal background. Then it was back to Wisconsin with her scared and confused children.

While parents such as these struggle with Internet addiction and disorientation, many children are actually becoming weary of their digital rounds. "Some kids complain about keeping up with the pace of the Internet," says Huxsahl. "It's a time of life when people are so vulnerable, so insecure, so cliquey," he says. The jarring effect of being excluded online, or being "defriended" creates in some children a defensive aversion to the medium that is hurting them.

"Kids will print out postings of harmful things and bring them to me," says Thomas Hughey. A public-school teacher in Metuchen, N.J., says that her high-school students themselves "express concern about what they're exposed to" on the Web, especially porn sites. And, she says, "they get sick of a lot of the gossipy drama" they encounter on social-networking sites like Facebook. Sometimes, she wearily confided, "I just want to tell my students, 'Get off the Internet and go watch TV.'"

C.J. Sprowls, a 22-year-old college student in La Habra, Calif., is not one of the disenchanted. He says that he has been online since he was 8 years old. He now spends between 6 and 11 hours a day on the Internet. His closest friends, he tells me, are people he first encountered online and has never seen, though he has talked to all of them on the phone.

Sprowls says that he has never felt threatened or uncomfortable on the Web. He dismisses the notion that the Internet is a powerful distraction, pointing to the fact that he can carry on "three conversations on three different subjects" simultaneously. I confess to him that I can't imagine this has not badly affected his attention span. "Not at all," he says. "I can read a book and watch TV at the same time."

As for the rising evidence that the Internet is having negative effects on everything from kids' ability to learn to their safety and their privacy to their development as persons, Sprowls concedes the Internet's shortcomings, but he doesn't think all the blame should fall on the Web. "Parents are failing to raise their children," he says. "They should teach them better."

Blaming parents for the Internet's ills hints at a disappointed expectation   25
that parents will fulfill their traditional role as guardians and protectors. In some respects, Sprowls' surprising accusation is a plea for parents to take firmer control. And no doubt the pendulum will swing between a more regulated Internet and a more untrammeled one for some time to come. When, in defiance of advertisers, corporations, and online businesses, the FTC finally overhauls anachronistic laws governing commercial conduct online, that will be one important step toward a new equilibrium between individuals and the economic forces that rule the Web.

In the meantime many parents will continue to approach the Internet in a spirit of poignant improvisation. While Miriam Ancis refuses to employ any of the proliferating new technologies able to monitor her teenage children's online lives, she subtly deploys her own surgeon general–type warning, counseling her kids to put a pillow between themselves and their laptop. "It gives off radiation," she tells them, hoping—as parents have always hoped—that her children will discover for themselves what she really means.   [2012]

≡ THINKING ABOUT IDEAS

1. Siegel claims that a child's inner resources are "damaged" by too much Internet time (para. 4). What does this mean? How might Gerard Jones answer this charge? Why might parents in the past have made the same claim about TV?

2. How might the Internet intensify what Siegel calls the "insularity of a child's world" (para. 8)? Why does Miriam Ancis claim that the Internet causes children not to know "'whether they're online or not'"? How might this be accurate?

3. How might Siegel's last paragraph be optimistic or pessimistic? Why might his use here of "hoping" be ironic? Does he mean that Ancis's strategy is completely ineffective or that it is the best she can do? Something else?

≡ THINKING ABOUT ARGUMENTATIVE MOVES

1. What are some examples of the "infinite spectrum of online harm" Siegel is trying to protect children from (para. 5)? How might Facebook's proposal endanger them even more? How would Jones object to Siegel's examples?

2. How does the expert testimony from Hughey, Gardner, and Turkle support Siegel's claim? What other expert evidence impressed you? Why? What comments by any one of these experts seem dubious? Why?

3. Siegel uses examples of parents misusing the Internet. What point is he trying to make by doing this? What specific opposition to his proposal to oppose Facebook's allowing children does Siegel cite? Does Siegel's conclusion in the last paragraph bolster his argument or weaken it? Why?

HARLAN COBEN
The Undercover Parent

Harlan Coben (b. 1962) was born and grew up in New Jersey, where he lives with his wife, a pediatrician, and their four children. He published his first novel at twenty-six and has since published more than twenty others. He has written mostly mysteries and thrillers, for which he has won numerous awards. His latest novel, Six Years, *was published in 2013. The op-ed essay that follows appeared in the* New York Times *in March 2008.*

Not long ago, friends of mine confessed over dinner that they had put spyware on their fifteen-year-old son's computer so they could monitor all he did online. At first I was repelled at this invasion of privacy. Now, after doing a fair amount of research, I get it.

Make no mistake: If you put spyware on your computer, you have the ability to log every keystroke your child makes and thus a good portion of his or her private world. That's what spyware is—at least the parental monitoring kind. You don't have to be an expert to put it on your computer. You just download the software from a vendor and you will receive reports—weekly, daily, whatever—showing you everything your child is doing on the machine.

Scary. But a good idea. Most parents won't even consider it.

Maybe it's the word: spyware. It brings up associations of Dick Cheney sitting in a dark room, rubbing his hands together, and reading your most private thoughts. But this isn't the government we are talking about—this is your family. It's a mistake to confuse the two. Loving parents are doing the surveillance here, not faceless bureaucrats. And most parents already monitor their children, watching over their home environment, their school.

Today's overprotective parents fight their kids' battles on the playground, berate coaches about playing time, and fill out college applications—yet when   5 it comes to chatting with pedophiles or watching beheadings or gambling away their entire life savings, then . . . then their children deserve independence?

Some will say that you should simply trust your child, that if he is old enough to go on the Internet he is old enough to know the dangers. Trust is one thing, but surrendering parental responsibility to a machine that allows the entire world access to your home borders on negligence.

Some will say that it's better just to use parental blocks that deny access to risky sites. I have found that they don't work. Children know how to get around them. But more than that—and this is where it gets tough—I want to know what's being said in e-mail and instant messages and in chat rooms.

There are two reasons for this. First, we've all read about the young boy unknowingly conversing with a pedophile or the girl who was cyberbullied to the point where she committed suicide. Would a watchful eye have helped? We rely in the real world on teachers and parents to guard against bullies—do we just dismiss bullying on the Internet and all it entails because we are entering difficult ethical ground?

Second, everything your child types can already be seen by the world—teachers, potential employers, friends, neighbors, future dates. Shouldn't he learn now that the Internet is not a haven of privacy?

One of the most popular arguments against spyware is the claim that you are reading your teenager's every thought, that in today's world, a computer is the little key-locked diary of the past. But posting thoughts on the Internet isn't the same thing as hiding them under your mattress. Maybe you should buy your children one of those little key-locked diaries so that they too can understand the difference. 10

Am I suggesting eavesdropping on every conversation? No. With new technology comes new responsibility. That works both ways. There is a fine line between being responsibly protective and irresponsibly nosy. You shouldn't monitor to find out if your daughter's friend has a crush on Kevin next door or that Mrs. Peterson gives too much homework or what schoolmate snubbed your son. You are there to start conversations and to be a safety net. To borrow from the national intelligence lexicon—and yes, that's uncomfortable—you're listening for dangerous chatter.

Will your teenagers find other ways of communicating to their friends when they realize you may be watching? Yes. But text messages and cell phones don't offer the anonymity and danger of the Internet. They are usually one-on-one with someone you know. It is far easier for a predator to troll chat rooms and MySpace and Facebook.

There will be tough calls. If your sixteen-year-old son, for example, is visiting hardcore pornography sites, what do you do? When I was sixteen, we looked at *Playboy* centerfolds and read *Penthouse Forum*. You may argue that's not the same thing, that Internet pornography makes that stuff seem about as harmful as "SpongeBob."

And you're probably right. But in my day, that's all you could get. If something more graphic had been out there, we probably would have gone for it. Interest in those, um, topics is natural. So start a dialogue based on that knowledge. You should have that talk anyway, but now you can have it with some kind of context.

Parenting has never been for the faint of heart. One friend of mine, using spyware to monitor his college-bound, straight-A daughter, found out that not only was she using drugs but she was sleeping with her dealer. He wisely took a deep breath before confronting her. Then he decided to come clean, to let her know how he had found out, to speak with her about the dangers inherent in her behavior. He'd had these conversations before, of course, but this time he had context. She listened. There was no anger. Things seem better now.

Our knee-jerk reaction as freedom-loving Americans is to be suspicious of anything that hints at invasion of privacy. That's a good and noble thing. But it's not an absolute, particularly in the face of the new and evolving challenges presented by the Internet. And particularly when it comes to our children.

Do you tell your children that the spyware is on the computer? I side with yes, but it might be enough to show them this article, have a discussion about your concerns, and let them know the possibility is there.   *[2008]*

≡ THINKING ABOUT IDEAS

1. Why do you think Coben was initially "repelled" by "this invasion of privacy" (para. 1)? What would your response have been when you were a young teenager? What would Gerard Jones's response be?

2. Give examples of the closest you and your friends have ever come to visiting "risky sites." What explanation can you offer for visits to "dangerous" or "risky sites"?

3. What does your experience tell you about the problems involved in negotiating between privacy and protection? In what ways might these problems have changed for you over the past seven or eight years? How might Jones view these problems?

≡ THINKING ABOUT ARGUMENTATIVE MOVES

1. Coben makes the controversial argument that it is a "good idea" (para. 3) to put spyware on a child's computer. To what extent and where does Coben consider possible objections to his claim? What objections does he overlook?

2. Coben's argument turns on the definition of several terms such as *trust*, *independence*, and *eavesdropping*. How does he use these terms to bolster his argument? How would you define "responsibly protective" and "irresponsibly nosy" (para. 11)? How might Jones define them?

3. Coben asks a number of questions. Which ones seem effective in furthering his argument? How might you answer them? How do you think he wants you to answer them?

≣ WRITING ABOUT ISSUES

1. Parental protection and privacy are perhaps two specific examples of a wider tension between freedom and independence, between different versions of what's good for you. Write an essay in which you analyze a time when you experienced such a tension. What claims were involved? What assumptions? What support was there for competing positions?

2. Write an argument in which you demonstrate the complexity of Siegel's assertion that students who spend four hours a day on social and recreational media are "distracted and disengaged from the world and each other." Be sure to include Jones's perspective.

3. As part of a comprehensive attempt to do something about gun violence, some critics propose taxing violent videogames. Write a letter to the editor of your local newspaper opposing or supporting this proposal.

4. Coben argues that privacy is not absolute. Just recently a newspaper published a list of gun owners and their addresses. Many were upset. What about publishing a list of drunken driver arrest records or a list of subscribers to racist magazines? Write an essay that confronts this problem, agreeing or disagreeing with Coben.

CHAPTER 8

Love

Our culture makes many claims about love: stories of the rejected lover who dies of a broken heart abound. Modern kings give up the throne, ancient cities go to war—all for love. Love is thought to be such a powerful emotion that its loss may even make one want to die or to kill. (In some countries, finding one's wife or husband in bed with a lover is a legal excuse for murder.) Men and women seem willing to radically change their lives to be near their beloved. These are a few examples of love's powerful influence on our behavior and our understanding of who we are.

Yet a serious discussion about the nature of love is often frustratingly difficult. We can all make a list of things we love: a cold beer in summer, a great science-fiction film, a new car, a quiet dinner with a good friend, a walk in fresh snow, a football game when our favorite team comes from behind for a dramatic victory. We love our parents, our siblings, our best friends. How can one word cover such diversity?

When we try to generalize about love, we find ourselves relying on specific incidents because giving examples is easier than giving definitions. If clarifying the essence of love seems difficult, perhaps it is because our stories, myths, and songs are filled with contradictions. Love conquers all, we say, but doesn't love fade? We profess our undying love, but divorce statistics soar. Love is complex and frustrating to pin down. Our culture even identifies different types of love: true love, platonic love, maternal love, erotic love. Yet opinions about love are strong; we all have evidence for what it is and isn't that we find persuasive.

But the evidence we find so convincing is influenced by cultural assumptions, probably more than we know. It would be naive to claim otherwise when we are bombarded with so many movies, songs, and stories about love. Indeed, some critics argue that romantic love is only a socially constructed illusion, merely an elaborate rationalization for physical desire. Once the carnal attraction fades, we get restless. At least, this is one argument, and probably not a popular one among college students in search of love. Because we know what we feel about those we love, we often grow impatient with other people's perspectives. We are likely to ignore friends who say, "He wouldn't treat you like that if he really loved you." Perhaps nothing arouses our interest more than a discussion of our hopes and dreams about love.

Our engagement with stories and poems about love is equally complex and ambivalent. Although the stories in this chapter often illuminate the sometimes dark passageways we take in our romantic journeys, there is no consensus about the final destination. Arguing about love stories engages us as much as it may also baffle us. As you read, rely on your own experience, ethical positions, and literary judgment in determining whether specific characters are indeed in love, whether they should continue their relationship, whether they need more commitment or less. The wise and the foolish seem equally perplexed in matters of the heart.

The chapter opens with three stories with young protagonists by James Joyce, John Updike, and Joyce Carol Oates, followed by two stories by twentieth-century masters, William Faulkner and Raymond Carver. The third cluster features three love stories written around 1900 by a surprisingly modern writer, Kate Chopin. Seven classic love poems follow with two famous revisions of Andrew Marvell's "To His Coy Mistress" next. The sixth cluster presents poems by Matthew Arnold and Susan Minot followed by three famous elegies. Shakespeare's great tragedy *Othello* is next, along with three essays that argue about the nature of Othello's journey. We conclude with two contemporary essays arguing over the value of marriage.

≡ Romantic Dreams: Stories

JAMES JOYCE, "Araby"

JOHN UPDIKE, "A & P"

JOYCE CAROL OATES, "Where Are You Going, Where Have You Been?"

Although centuries old, the cliché that the human heart is a mystery still seems valid. We still wonder if falling in love is natural: Is love our inborn impulse to seek romance, or is it simply a physical attraction spurred on by our evolutionary need to procreate? Perhaps Western culture has socialized us to believe in the power of romantic love and the often irrational behavior that follows. Might it serve some deep psychological need to find a substitute for a beloved parent? Is it a giving emotion? A selfish one? Is it a psychological malady or the one thing worth giving up everything for? Do we need to believe in it whether or not it exists? Since we are often driven to irrational behavior, delusions, and heartbreak, might we be better off without romantic love? Or might life without it be intolerably flat?

In the following cluster, three fiction writers explore the ways romantic love can sometimes cloud judgment, encouraging us to act against our best interests.

Joyce shows us a boy in the throes of romantic idealism; Updike gives us a memorable picture of how an indifferent world responds to romantic gestures; and Oates stuns us with the consequences of what could happen when romantic daydreams and evil collide.

≡ BEFORE YOU READ

Can people be truly happy without being in love? Is there one person in the world who is your true love? Or are there only certain types of people you could love? If your love didn't make you "float on a cloud," would you be disappointed? Is true love unconditional? Have you ever been fooled by romantic dreams?

JAMES JOYCE
Araby

James Joyce (1882–1941) is regarded as one of the most innovative and influential writers of the modernist movement of the early twentieth century. His use of interior monologue, wordplay, complex allusions, and other techniques variously delighted, offended, or puzzled readers. Joyce's work demanded attention and was often subject to censorship during his lifetime. A Portrait of the Artist as a Young Man *(1916), set in Joyce's native Dublin, is largely autobiographical. Like his hero at the end of the novel, Joyce left Ireland at the age of twenty to spend the remainder of his life in Paris and other European cities. His long, complex novel* Ulysses *(1922), also set in Dublin, takes the reader through one day in the life of its protagonist and his city. In "Araby," published in Dubliners (1914), as in other stories in the collection, Joyce pictures the limited life of his character and leads him toward a sudden insight, or epiphany.*

North Richmond Street, being blind, was a quiet street except at the hour when the Christian Brothers' School set the boys free. An uninhabited house of two storeys stood at the blind end, detached from its neighbors in a square ground. The other houses of the street, conscious of decent lives within them, gazed at one another with brown imperturbable faces.

The former tenant of our house, a priest, had died in the back drawing-room. Air, musty from having been long enclosed, hung in all the rooms, and the waste room behind the kitchen was littered with old useless papers. Among these I found a few paper-covered books, the pages of which were curled and damp: *The Abbot*, by Walter Scott, *The Devout Communicant*, and *The Memoirs of Vidocq*. I liked the last best because its leaves were yellow. The wild garden behind the house contained a central apple-tree and a few straggling bushes under one of which I found the late tenant's rusty bicycle-pump. He had been a very charitable priest; in his will he had left all his money to institutions and the furniture of his house to his sister.

When the short days of winter came dusk fell before we had well eaten our dinners. When we met in the street the houses had grown sombre. The space of sky above us was the color of ever-changing violet and towards it the lamps of the street lifted their feeble lanterns. The cold air stung us and we played till our bodies glowed. Our shouts echoed in the silent street. The career of our play brought us through the dark muddy lanes behind the houses where we ran the gauntlet of the rough tribes from the cottages, to the back doors of the dark dripping gardens where odors arose from the ashpits, to the dark odorous stables where a coachman smoothed and combed the horse or shook music from the buckled harness. When we returned to the street light from the kitchen windows had filled the areas. If my uncle was seen turning the corner we hid in the shadow until we had seen him safely housed. Or if Mangan's sister came out on the doorstep to call her brother in to his tea we watched her from our shadow peer up and down the street. We waited to see whether she would remain or go in and, if she remained, we left our shadow and walked up to Mangan's steps resignedly. She was waiting for us, her figure defined by the light from the half-opened door. Her brother always teased her before he obeyed and I stood by the railings looking at her. Her dress swung as she moved her body and the soft rope of her hair tossed from side to side.

Every morning I lay on the floor in the front parlor watching her door. The blind was pulled down to within an inch of the sash so that I could not be seen. When she came out on the doorstep my heart leaped. I ran to the hall, seized my books, and followed her. I kept her brown figure always in my eye and, when we came near the point at which our ways diverged, I quickened my pace and passed her. This happened morning after morning. I had never spoken to her, except for a few casual words, and yet her name was like a summons to all my foolish blood.

Her image accompanied me even in places the most hostile to romance. On Saturday evenings when my aunt went marketing I had to go to carry some of the parcels. We walked through the flaring streets, jostled by drunken men and bargaining women, amid the curses of laborers, the shrill litanies of shop-boys who stood on guard by the barrel of pigs' cheeks, the nasal chanting of street-singers, who sang a *come-all-you* about O'Donovan Rossa,° or a ballad about the troubles in our native land. These noises converged in a single sensation of life for me: I imagined that I bore my chalice safely through a throng of foes. Her name sprang to my lips at moments in strange prayers and praises which I myself did not understand. My eyes were often full of tears (I could not tell why) and at times a flood from my heart seemed to pour itself out into my bosom. I thought little of the future. I did not know whether I would ever speak to her or not or, if I spoke to her, how I could tell her of my confused adoration. But my body was like a harp and her words and gestures were like fingers running upon the wires.

One evening I went into the back drawing-room in which the priest had died. It was a dark rainy evening and there was no sound in the house. Through one of the broken panes I heard the rain impinge upon the earth, the fine incessant needles of water playing in the sodden beds. Some distant lamp or lighted window gleamed below me. I was thankful that I could see so little. All my senses seemed to desire to veil themselves and, feeling that I was about to slip from them, I pressed the palms of my hands together until they trembled, murmuring: "*O love! O love!*" many times.

At last she spoke to me. When she addressed the first words to me I was so confused that I did not know what to answer. She asked me was I going to *Araby.* I forgot whether I answered yes or no. It would be a splendid bazaar, she said she would love to go.

"And why can't you?" I asked.

While she spoke she turned a silver bracelet round and round her wrist. She could not go, she said, because there would be a retreat that week in her convent. Her brother and two other boys were fighting for their caps and I was alone at the railings. She held one of the spikes, bowing her head towards me. The light from the lamp opposite our door caught the white curve of her neck, lit up her hair that rested there and, falling, lit up the hand upon the railing. It fell over one side of her dress and caught the white border of a petticoat, just visible as she stood at ease.

"It's well for you," she said.

"If I go," I said, "I will bring you something."

What innumerable follies laid waste my waking and sleeping thoughts after that evening! I wished to annihilate the tedious intervening days. I chafed against the work of school. At night in my bedroom and by day in the classroom

O'Donovan Rossa: Jeremiah O'Donovan (1831–1915) was nicknamed "Dynamite Rossa" for advocating violent means to achieve Irish independence.

her image came between me and the page I strove to read. The syllables of the word *Araby* were called to me through the silence in which my soul luxuriated and cast an Eastern enchantment over me. I asked for leave to go to the bazaar on Saturday night. My aunt was surprised and hoped it was not some Freemason° affair. I answered few questions in class. I watched my master's face pass from amiability to sternness; he hoped I was not beginning to idle. I could not call my wandering thoughts together. I had hardly any patience with the serious work of life which, now that it stood between me and my desire, seemed to me child's play, ugly monotonous child's play.

On Saturday morning I reminded my uncle that I wished to go to the bazaar in the evening. He was fussing at the hallstand, looking for the hat-brush, and answered me curtly:

"Yes, boy, I know."

As he was in the hall I could not go into the front parlor and lie at the window. I left the house in bad humor and walked slowly towards the school. The air was pitilessly raw and already my heart misgave me.   15

When I came home to dinner my uncle had not yet been home. Still it was early. I sat staring at the clock for some time and, when its ticking began to irritate me, I left the room. I mounted the staircase and gained the upper part of the house. The high cold empty gloomy rooms liberated me and I went from room to room singing. From the front window I saw my companions playing below in the street. Their cries reached me weakened and indistinct and, leaning my forehead against the cool glass, I looked over at the dark house where she lived. I may have stood there for an hour, seeing nothing but the brown-clad figure cast by my imagination, touched discreetly by the lamplight at the curved neck, at the hand upon the railings, and at the border below the dress.

When I came downstairs again I found Mrs. Mercer sitting at the fire. She was an old garrulous woman, a pawnbroker's widow, who collected used stamps for some pious purpose. I had to endure the gossip of the tea-table. The meal was prolonged beyond an hour and still my uncle did not come. Mrs. Mercer stood up to go: she was sorry she couldn't wait any longer, but it was after eight o'clock and she did not like to be out late, as the night air was bad for her. When she had gone I began to walk up and down the room, clenching my fists. My aunt said:

"I'm afraid you may put off your bazaar for this night of Our Lord."

At nine o'clock I heard my uncle's latchkey in the halldoor. I heard him talking to himself and heard the hallstand rocking when it had received the weight of his overcoat. I could interpret these signs. When he was midway through his dinner I asked him to give me the money to go to the bazaar. He had forgotten.

"The people are in bed and after their first sleep now," he said.   20

I did not smile. My aunt said to him energetically:

"Can't you give him the money and let him go? You've kept him late enough as it is."

Freemason: A Protestant fraternal society that was in the past viewed by Catholics as hostile.

My uncle said he was very sorry he had forgotten. He said he believed in the old saying: "All work and no play makes Jack a dull boy." He asked me where I was going and, when I had told him a second time he asked me did I know *The Arab's Farewell to His Steed*. When I left the kitchen he was about to recite the opening lines of the piece to my aunt.

I held a florin° tightly in my hand as I strode down Buckingham Street towards the station. The sight of the streets thronged with buyers and glaring with gas recalled to me the purpose of my journey. I took my seat in a third-class carriage of a deserted train. After an intolerable delay the train moved out of the station slowly. It crept onward among ruinous houses and over the twinkling river. At Westland Row Station a crowd of people pressed to the carriage doors; but the porters moved them back, saying that it was a special train for the bazaar. I remained alone in the bare carriage. In a few minutes the train drew up beside an improvised wooden platform. I passed out on to the road and saw by the lighted dial of a clock that it was ten minutes to ten. In front of me was a large building which displayed the magical name.

I could not find any sixpenny entrance and, fearing that the bazaar would   25
be closed, I passed in quickly through a turnstile, handing a shilling to a weary-looking man. I found myself in a big hall girdled at half its height by a gallery. Nearly all the stalls were closed and the greater part of the hall was in darkness. I recognized a silence like that which pervades a church after a service. I walked into the center of the bazaar timidly. A few people were gathered about the stalls which were still open. Before a curtain, over which the words *Café Chantant* were written in colored lamps, two men were counting money on a salver. I listened to the fall of the coins.

Remembering with difficulty why I had come I went over to one of the stalls and examined porcelain vases and flowered tea-sets. At the door of the stall a young lady was talking and laughing with two young gentlemen. I remarked their English accents and listened vaguely to their conversation.

"O, I never said such a thing!"

"O, but you did!"

"O, but I didn't!"

"Didn't she say that?"   30

"Yes. I heard her."

"O, there's a . . . fib!"

Observing me the young lady came over and asked me did I wish to buy anything. The tone of her voice was not encouraging; she seemed to have spoken to me out of a sense of duty. I looked humbly at the great jars that stood like eastern guards at either side of the dark entrance to the stall and murmured:

"No, thank you."

The young lady changed the position of one of the vases and went back to   35
the two young men. They began to talk of the same subject. Once or twice the young lady glanced at me over her shoulder.

---

florin: A silver coin worth two shillings.

I lingered before her stall, though I knew my stay was useless, to make my interest in her wares seem the more real. Then I turned away slowly and walked down the middle of the bazaar. I allowed the two pennies to fall against the sixpence in my pocket. I heard a voice call from one end of the gallery that the light was out. The upper part of the hall was now completely dark.

Gazing up into the darkness I saw myself as a creature driven and derided by vanity; and my eyes burned with anguish and anger.   [1914]

≡ **THINKING ABOUT THE TEXT**

1. Why do the boy's eyes burn with anguish and anger? Has he learned something about romantic love? Was he in love with Mangan's sister? Give evidence.

2. If this story is partly autobiographical, what is Joyce's attitude toward his younger self? Are you sympathetic or critical of your own initiations into the complexities of relationships?

3. Reread the first and last paragraphs. In what ways might they be connected?

4. Find examples of religious imagery. What do you think is its purpose?

5. Do you think the boy's quest has symbolic meaning? Do you think cultures can also search for something?

JOHN UPDIKE
A & P

John Updike (1932–2009) was born in Shillington, Pennsylvania, an only child of a father who taught high-school algebra and a mother who wrote short stories and novels. After graduating from Harvard, Updike studied art in England and later joined the staff of The New Yorker. *In 1959, he published his first novel,* The Poorhouse Fair, *and moved to Massachusetts. His many novels are notable for their lyrical and accurate depiction of the details and concerns of modern America.* Rabbit Run *(1960) and the sequels* Rabbit Redux *(1971),* Rabbit Is Rich *(1981), and* Rabbit at Rest *(1990) are considered important and insightful records of American life. His other works include the novels* Villages *(2004) and* Terrorist *(2006);* Due Considerations: Essays and Criticism *(2007);* The Maples Stories *(2009); and* Hub Fans Bid Kid Adieu: John Updike on Ted Williams *(2010). "A & P" comes from Updike's* Pigeon Feathers and Other Stories *(1962).*

In walks these three girls in nothing but bathing suits. I'm in the third checkout slot, with my back to the door, so I don't see them until they're over by the bread. The one that caught my eye first was the one in the plaid green two-piece. She was a chunky kid, with a good tan and a sweet broad soft-looking can with those two crescents of white just under it, where the sun never seems to hit, at the top of the backs of her legs. I stood there with my hand on a box of HiHo crackers trying to remember if I rang it up or not. I ring it up again and the customer starts giving me hell. She's one of these cash-register-watchers, a witch about fifty with rouge on her cheekbones and no eyebrows, and I know it made her day to trip me up. She'd been watching cash registers for fifty years and probably never seen a mistake before.

By the time I got her feathers smoothed and her goodies into a bag — she gives me a little snort in passing, if she'd been born at the right time they would have burned her over in Salem — by the time I get her on her way the girls had circled around the bread and were coming back, without a pushcart, back my way along the counters, in the aisle between the checkouts and the Special bins. They didn't even have shoes on. There was this chunky one, with the two-piece — it was bright green and the seams on the bra were still sharp and her belly was still pretty pale so I guessed she just got it (the suit) — there was this one, with one of those chubby berry-faces, the lips all bunched together under her nose, this one, and a tall one, with black hair that hadn't quite frizzed right, and one of these sunburns right across under the eyes, and a chin that was too long — you know, the kind of girl other girls think is very "striking" and "attractive" but never quite makes it, as they very well know, which is why they like her so much — and then the third one, that wasn't quite so tall. She was the queen. She kind of led them, the other two peeking around and making their shoulders round. She didn't look around, not this queen, she just walked straight on slowly, on these long white prima-donna legs. She came down a little hard on her heels, as if she didn't walk in her bare feet that much, putting down her heels and then letting the weight move along to her toes as if she was testing the floor with every step, putting a little deliberate extra action into it. You never know for sure how girls' minds work (do you really think it's a mind in there or just a little buzz like a bee in a glass jar?) but you got the idea she had talked the other two into coming in here with her, and now she was showing them how to do it, walk slow and hold yourself straight.

She had on a kind of dirty-pink — beige maybe, I don't know — bathing suit with a little nubble all over it, and what got me, the straps were down. They were off her shoulders looped loose around the cool tops of her arms, and I guess as a result the suit had slipped a little on her, so all around the top of the cloth there was this shining rim. If it hadn't been there you wouldn't have known there could have been anything whiter than those shoulders. With the straps pushed off, there was nothing between the top of the suit and the top of her head except just *her*, this clean bare plane of the top of her chest down from the shoulder bones like a dented sheet of metal tilted in the light. I mean, it was more than pretty.

She had sort of oaky hair that the sun and salt had bleached, done up in a bun that was unravelling, and a kind of prim face. Walking into the A & P with your straps down, I suppose it's the only kind of face you *can* have. She held her head so high her neck, coming up out of those white shoulders, looked kind of stretched, but I didn't mind. The longer her neck was, the more of her there was.

She must have felt in the corner of her eye me and over my shoulder   5
Stokesie in the second slot watching, but she didn't tip. Not this queen. She kept
her eyes moving across the racks, and stopped, and turned so slow it made my
stomach rub the inside of my apron, and buzzed to the other two, who kind of
huddled against her for relief, and then they all three of them went up the cat-
and-dog-food-breakfast-cereal-macaroni-rice-raisins-seasonings-spreads-
spaghetti-soft-drinks-crackers-and-cookies aisle. From the third slot I look
straight up this aisle to the meat counter, and I watched them all the way. The
fat one with the tan sort of fumbled with the cookies, but on second thought
she put the package back. The sheep pushing their carts down the aisle—the
girls were walking against the usual traffic (not that we have one-way signs or
anything)—were pretty hilarious. You could see them, when Queenie's white
shoulders dawned on them, kind of jerk, or hop, or hiccup, but their eyes
snapped back to their own baskets and on they pushed. I bet you could set off
dynamite in an A & P and the people would by and large keep reaching and
checking oatmeal off their lists and muttering "Let me see, there was a third
thing, began with A, asparagus, no, ah, yes, applesauce!" or whatever it is they
do mutter. But there was no doubt, this jiggled them. A few houseslaves in pin
curlers even looked around after pushing their carts past to make sure what
they had seen was correct.

You know, it's one thing to have a girl in a bathing suit down on the beach,
where what with the glare nobody can look at each other much anyway, and
another thing in the cool of the A & P, under the fluorescent lights, against all
those stacked packages, with her feet paddling along naked over our check-
board green-and-cream rubber-tile floor.

"Oh Daddy," Stokesie said beside me. "I feel so faint."

"Darling," I said. "Hold me tight." Stokesie's married, with two babies
chalked up on his fuselage already, but as far as I can tell that's the only difference. He's twenty-two, and I was nineteen this April.

"Is it done?" he asks, the responsible married man finding his voice. I forgot
to say he thinks he's going to be manager some sunny day, maybe in 1990 when
it's called the Great Alexandrov and Petrooshki Tea Company or something.

What he meant was, our town is five miles from a beach, with a big sum-   10
mer colony out on the Point, but we're right in the middle of town, and the
women generally put on a shirt or shorts or something before they get out of
the car into the street. And anyway these are usually women with six children
and varicose veins mapping their legs and nobody, including them, could care
less. As I say, we're right in the middle of town, and if you stand at our front
doors you can see two banks and the Congregational church and the newspaper store and three real-estate offices and about twenty-seven old freeloaders
tearing up Central Street because the sewer broke again. It's not as if we're on
the Cape; we're north of Boston and there's people in this town haven't seen
the ocean for twenty years.

The girls had reached the meat counter and were asking McMahon something. He pointed, they pointed, and they shuffled out of sight behind a pyra-
mid of Diet Delight peaches. All that was left for us to see was old McMahon

patting his mouth and looking after them sizing up their joints. Poor kids, I began to feel sorry for them, they couldn't help it.

Now here comes the sad part of the story, at least my family says it's sad, but I don't think it's so sad myself. The store's pretty empty, it being Thursday afternoon, so there was nothing much to do except lean on the register and wait for the girls to show up again. The whole store was like a pinball machine and I didn't know which tunnel they'd come out of. After a while they come around out of the far aisle, around the light bulbs, records at discount of the Caribbean Six or Tony Martin Sings or some such gunk you wonder they waste the wax on, sixpacks of candy bars, and plastic toys done up in cellophane that fall apart when a kid looks at them anyway. Around they come, Queenie still leading the way, and holding a little gray jar in her hand. Slots Three through Seven are unmanned and I could see her wondering between Stokes and me, but Stokesie with his usual luck draws an old party in baggy gray pants who stumbles up with four giant cans of pineapple juice (what do these bums *do* with all that pineapple juice? I've often asked myself) so the girls come to me. Queenie puts down the jar and I take it into my fingers icy cold. Kingfish Fancy Herring Snacks in Pure Sour Cream: 49¢. Now her hands are empty, not a ring or a bracelet, bare as God made them, and I wonder where the money's coming from. Still with that prim look she lifts a folded dollar bill out of the hollow at the center of her nubbled pink top. The jar went heavy in my hand. Really, I thought that was so cute.

Then everybody's luck begins to run out. Lengel comes in from haggling with a truck full of cabbages on the lot and is about to scuttle into that door marked manager behind which he hides all day when the girls touch his eye. Lengel's pretty dreary, teaches Sunday school and the rest, but he doesn't miss that much. He comes over and says, "Girls, this isn't the beach."

Queenie blushes, though maybe it's just a brush of sunburn I was noticing for the first time, now that she was so close. "My mother asked me to pick up a jar of herring snacks." Her voice kind of startled me, the way voices do when you see the people first, coming out so flat and dumb yet kind of tony, too, the way it ticked over "pick up" and "snacks." All of a sudden I slid right down her voice into her living room. Her father and the other men were standing around in ice-cream coats and bow ties and the women were in sandals picking up herring snacks on toothpicks off a big glass plate and they were all holding drinks the color of water with olives and sprigs of mint in them. When my parents have somebody over they get lemonade and if it's a real racy affair Schlitz in tall glasses with "They'll Do It Every Time" cartoons stencilled on.

"That's all right," Lengel said. "But this isn't the beach." His repeating this   15
struck me as funny, as if it had just occurred to him, and he had been thinking all these years the A & P was a great big sand dune and he was the head lifeguard. He didn't like my smiling — as I say he doesn't miss much — but he concentrates on giving the girls that sad Sunday-school–superintendent stare.

Queenie's blush is no sunburn now, and the plump one in plaid, that I liked better from the back — a really sweet can — pipes up, "We weren't doing any shopping. We just came in for the one thing."

"That makes no difference," Lengel tells her, and I could see from the way his eyes went that he hadn't noticed she was wearing a two-piece before. "We want you decently dressed when you come in here."

"We *are* decent," Queenie says suddenly, her lower lip pushing, getting sore now that she remembers her place, a place from which the crowd that runs the A & P must look pretty crummy. Fancy Herring Snacks flashed in her very blue eyes.

"Girls, I don't want to argue with you. After this come in here with your shoulders covered. It's our policy." He turns his back. That's policy for you. Policy is what the kingpins want. What the others want is juvenile delinquency.

All this while, the customers had been showing up with their carts but, you know, sheep, seeing a scene, they had all bunched up on Stokesie, who shook open a paper bag as gently as peeling a peach, not wanting to miss a word. I could feel in the silence everybody getting nervous, most of all Lengel, who asks me, "Sammy, have you rung up their purchase?"

I thought and said "No" but it wasn't about that I was thinking. I go through the punches, 4, 9, groc, tot—it's more complicated than you think, and after you do it often enough, it begins to make a little song, that you hear words to, in my case "Hello (*bing*) there, you (*gung*) hap-py *pee*-pul (*splat*)!"—the *splat* being the drawer flying out. I uncrease the bill, tenderly as you may imagine, it just having come from between the two smoothest scoops of vanilla I had ever known were there, and pass a half and a penny into her narrow pink palm, and nestle the herrings in a bag and twist its neck and hand it over, all the time thinking.

The girls, and who'd blame them, are in a hurry to get out, so I say "I quit" to Lengel enough for them to hear, hoping they'll stop and watch me, their unsuspected hero. They keep right on going, into the electric eye; the door flies open and they flicker across the lot to their car, Queenie and Plaid and Big Tall Goony-Goony (not that as raw material she was so bad), leaving me with Lengel and a kink in his eyebrow.

"Did you say something, Sammy?"

"I said I quit."

"I thought you did."

"You didn't have to embarrass them."

"It was they who were embarrassing us."

I started to say something that came out "Fiddle-de-doo." It's a saying of my grandmother's, and I know she would have been pleased.

"I don't think you know what you're saying," Lengel said.

"I know you don't," I said. "But I do." I pull the bow at the back of my apron and start shrugging it off my shoulders. A couple customers that had been heading for my slot begin to knock against each other, like scared pigs in a chute.

Lengel sighs and begins to look very patient and old and gray. He's been a friend of my parents for years. "Sammy, you don't want to do this to your Mom and Dad," he tells me. It's true, I don't. But it seems to me that once you begin a gesture it's fatal not to go through with it. I fold the apron, "Sammy" stitched in

20

25

30

red on the pocket, and put it on the counter, and drop the bow tie on top of it. The bow tie is theirs, if you've ever wondered. "You'll feel this for the rest of your life," Lengel says, and I know that's true, too, but remembering how he made that pretty girl blush makes me so scrunchy inside I punch the No Sale tab and the machine whirs "pee-pul" and the drawer splats out. One advantage to this scene taking place in summer, I can follow this up with a clean exit, there's no fumbling around getting your coat and galoshes, I just saunter into the electric eye in my white shirt that my mother ironed the night before, and the door heaves itself open, and outside the sunshine is skating around on the asphalt.

I look around for my girls, but they're gone, of course. There wasn't anybody but some young married screaming with her children about some candy they didn't get by the door of a powder-blue Falcon station wagon. Looking back in the big windows, over the bags of peat moss and aluminum lawn furniture stacked on the pavement, I could see Lengel in my place in the slot, checking the sheep through. His face was dark gray and his back stiff, as if he'd just had an injection of iron, and my stomach kind of fell as I felt how hard the world was going to be to me hereafter.   [1961]

≡ THINKING ABOUT THE TEXT

1. Why do you think Sammy quits? Make a list of several plausible answers.

2. What would you do if you were in Sammy's position? What would your priorities be in this situation?

3. When Sammy hears Queenie's voice, he imagines an elegant cocktail party that he contrasts to his parents' "real racy affair" (para. 14) with lemonade and beer. What does this scene say about Sammy's attitude toward the girls? Toward his own social status?

4. Some critics have objected to Sammy's comment in the last sentence of paragraph 2 about "girls' minds." Is this a sexist observation? Does the time frame of the story figure in your opinion? Should it?

5. Comment on the last paragraph. What is the significance of the young married woman? Why does Sammy mention "sheep"? Why does Sammy think the world will be hard on him? Do you agree? What does "hard" mean?

≡ MAKING COMPARISONS

1. Are the main characters in "Araby" and "A & P" wiser at each story's end? Are they happier?

2. Which character's views about romance are more compatible with your views when you were, say, thirteen? With your views today?

3. Compare the last paragraphs of "Araby" and "A & P." What attitudes toward romantic love do they express?

JOYCE CAROL OATES

Where Are You Going, Where Have You Been?

Joyce Carol Oates (b. 1938) is perhaps the most prolific of major American writers, publishing about two books a year for more than forty years. Always cited as a favorite to win the Nobel Prize for literature, Oates has won numerous awards, including a National Book Award for fiction (1970).

Oates grew up in the countryside of upstate New York. She started writing early and won a scholarship to Syracuse University, where she was valedictorian in 1960. She received her M.A. from the University of Wisconsin a year later. She taught at the University of Detroit and the University of Windsor before joining the faculty at Princeton, where she has taught since 1978. Like Flannery O'Connor and William Faulkner, her work is usually referred to as gothic, probably because of her violent characters, many of whom are filled with enigmatic malice and tormented emotions. Working in the realistic tradition, the "Dark Lady of American Literature" writes compelling narratives about seemingly ordinary people who beneath the surface live in a nightmare world of unconscious forces and sometimes sensational events.

Oates claims the story printed here was written after listening to Bob Dylan's "It's All Over Now, Baby Blue." The story was inspired by the serial killer Charles Schmid, also known as "The Pied Piper of Tucson." Her most recent work includes the novel The Accursed *(2013), which one critic called the first postmodern horror tale, and the short story collection* Black Dahlia and White Rose *(2012).*

For Bob Dylan

Her name was Connie. She was fifteen and she had a quick nervous giggling habit of craning her neck to glance into mirrors, or checking other people's faces to make sure her own was all right. Her mother, who noticed everything and knew everything and who hadn't much reason any longer to look at her own face, always scolded Connie about it. "Stop gawking at yourself, who are you? You think you're so pretty?" she would say. Connie would raise her eyebrows at these familiar complaints and look right through her mother, into a shadowy vision of herself as she was right at that moment: she knew she was pretty and that was everything. Her mother had been pretty once too, if you could believe those old snapshots in the album, but now her looks were gone and that was why she was always after Connie.

"Why don't you keep your room clean like your sister? How've you got your hair fixed—what the hell stinks? Hair spray? You don't see your sister using that junk."

Her sister June was twenty-four and still lived at home. She was a secretary in the high school Connie attended, and if that wasn't bad enough—with her in the same building—she was so plain and chunky and steady that Connie had to hear her praised all the time by her mother and her mother's sisters. June did this, June did that, she saved money and helped clean the house and cooked and Connie couldn't do a thing, her mind was all filled with trashy day-dreams. Their father was away at work most of the time and when he came home he wanted supper and he read the newspaper at supper and after supper he went to bed. He didn't bother talking much to them, but around his bent head Connie's mother kept picking at her until Connie wished her mother was dead and she herself was dead and it was all over. "She makes me want to throw up sometimes," she complained to her friends. She had a high, breath-less, amused voice which made everything she said a little forced, whether it was sincere or not.

There was one good thing: June went places with girl friends of hers, girls who were just as plain and steady as she, and so when Connie wanted to do that her mother had no objections. The father of Connie's best girl friend drove the girls the three miles to town and left them off at a shopping plaza, so that they could walk through the stores or go to a movie, and when he came to pick them up again at eleven he never bothered to ask what they had done.

They must have been familiar sights, walking around that shopping plaza   5
in their shorts and flat ballerina slippers that always scuffed the sidewalk, with charm bracelets jingling on their thin wrists; they would lean together to whis-per and laugh secretly if someone passed by who amused or interested them. Connie had long dark blond hair that drew anyone's eye to it, and she wore part of it pulled up on her head and puffed out and the rest of it she let fall down her back. She wore a pullover jersey blouse that looked one way when she was at home and another way when she was away from home. Everything about her had two sides to it, one for home and one for anywhere that was not home: her walk that could be childlike and bobbing, or languid enough to make anyone think she was hearing music in her head, her mouth which was pale and smirk-ing most of the time, but bright and pink on these evenings out, her laugh which was cynical and drawling at home—"Ha, ha, very funny"—but high-pitched and nervous anywhere else, like the jingling of the charms on her bracelet.

Sometimes they did go shopping or to a movie, but sometimes they went across the highway, ducking fast across the busy road, to a drive-in restaurant where older kids hung out. The restaurant was shaped like a big bottle, though squatter than a real bottle, and on its cap was a revolving figure of a grinning boy who held a hamburger aloft. One night in midsummer they ran across, breathless with daring, and right away someone leaned out a car window and invited them over, but it was just a boy from high school they didn't like. It made them feel good to be able to ignore him. They went up through the maze of parked and cruising cars to the bright-lit, fly-infested restaurant, their faces pleased and expectant as if they were entering a sacred building that loomed out of the night to give them what haven and what blessing they yearned for. They sat at the counter and crossed their legs at the ankles, their thin shoulders rigid with excitement and listened to the music that made everything so good: the music was always in the background like music at a church service, it was something to depend upon.

A boy named Eddie came in to talk with them. He sat backwards on his stool, turning himself jerkily around in semi-circles and then stopping and turning again, and after a while he asked Connie if she would like something to eat. She said she did and so she tapped her friend's arm on her way out—her friend pulled her face up into a brave droll look—and Connie said she would meet her at eleven, across the way. "I just hate to leave her like that," Connie said earnestly, but the boy said that she wouldn't be alone for long. So they went out to his car and on the way Connie couldn't help but let her eyes wander over the windshields and faces all around her, her face gleaming with the joy that had nothing to do with Eddie or even this place; it might have been the music. She drew her shoulders up and sucked in her breath with the pure pleasure of being alive, and just at that moment she happened to glance at a face just a few feet from hers. It was a boy with shaggy black hair, in a convertible jalopy painted gold. He stared at her and then his lips widened into a grin. Connie slit her eyes at him and turned away, but she couldn't help glancing back and there he was still watching her. He wagged a finger and laughed and said. "Gonna get you, baby," and Connie turned away again without Eddie noticing anything.

She spent three hours with him, at the restaurant where they ate hamburgers and drank Cokes in wax cups that were always sweating, and then down an alley a mile or so away, and when he left her off at five to eleven only the movie house was still open at the plaza. Her girl friend was there, talking with a boy. When Connie came up the two girls smiled at each other and Connie said, "How was the movie?" and the girl said, "*You* should know." They rode off with the girl's father, sleepy and pleased, and Connie couldn't help but look at the darkened shopping plaza with its big empty parking lot and its signs that were faded and ghostly now, and over at the drive-in restaurant where cars were still circling tirelessly. She couldn't hear the music at this distance.

Next morning June asked her how the movie was and Connie said, "So-so."

She and that girl and occasionally another girl went out several times a week that way, and the rest of the time Connie spent around the house—it was summer vacation—getting in her mother's way and thinking, dreaming, about the boys she met. But all the boys fell back and dissolved into a single face that was not even a face, but an idea, a feeling, mixed up with the urgent insistent pounding of the music and the humid night air of July. Connie's mother kept dragging her back to the daylight by finding things for her to do or saying suddenly, "What's this about the Pettinger girl?"

And Connie would say nervously, "Oh, her. That dope." She always drew thick clear lines between herself and such girls, and her mother was simple and kindly enough to believe her. Her mother was so simple, Connie thought, that it was maybe cruel to fool her so much. Her mother went scuffling around the house in old bedroom slippers and complained over the telephone to one sister about the other, then the other called up and the two of them complained about the third one. If June's name was mentioned her mother's tone was approving, and if Connie's name was mentioned it was disapproving. This did not really mean she disliked Connie and actually Connie thought that her mother preferred her to June because she was prettier, but the two of them kept up a pretense of exasperation, a sense that they were tugging and struggling over

10

something of little value to either of them. Sometimes, over coffee, they were almost friends, but something would come up—some vexation that was like a fly buzzing suddenly around their heads—and their faces went hard with contempt.

One Sunday Connie got up at eleven—none of them bothered with church—and washed her hair so that it could dry all day long, in the sun. Her parents and sister were going to a barbecue at an aunt's house and Connie said no, she wasn't interested, rolling her eyes, to let mother know just what she thought of it. "Stay home alone then," her mother said sharply. Connie sat out back in a lawn chair and watched them drive away, her father quiet and bald, hunched around so that he could back the car out, her mother with a look that was still angry and not at all softened through the windshield, and in the back seat poor old June all dressed up as if she didn't know what a barbecue was, with all the running yelling kids and the flies. Connie sat with her eyes closed in the sun, dreaming and dazed with the warmth about her as if this were a kind of love, the caresses of love, and her mind slipped over onto thoughts of the boy she had been with the night before and how nice he had been, how sweet it always was, not the way someone like June would suppose but sweet, gentle, the way it was in movies and promised in songs; and when she opened her eyes she hardly knew where she was, the back yard ran off into weeds and a fenceline of trees and behind it the sky was perfectly blue and still. The asbestos "ranch house" that was now three years old startled her—it looked small. She shook her head as if to get awake.

It was too hot. She went inside the house and turned on the radio to drown out the quiet. She sat on the edge of her bed, barefoot, and listened for an hour and a half to a program called XYZ Sunday Jamboree, record after record of hard, fast, shrieking songs she sang along with, interspersed by exclamations from "Bobby King": "An' look here you girls at Napoleon's—Son and Charley want you to pay real close attention to this song coming up!"

And Connie paid close attention herself, bathed in a glow of slow-pulsed joy that seemed to rise mysteriously out of the music itself and lay languidly about the airless little room, breathed in and breathed out with each gentle rise and fall of her chest.

After a while she heard a car coming up the drive. She sat up at once, star- 15 tled, because it couldn't be her father so soon. The gravel kept crunching all the way in from the road—the driveway was long—and Connie ran to the window. It was a car she didn't know. It was an open jalopy, painted a bright gold that caught the sun opaquely. Her heart began to pound and her fingers snatched at her hair, checking it, and she whispered "Christ. Christ," wondering how bad she looked. The car came to a stop at the side door and the horn sounded four short taps as if this were a signal Connie knew.

She went into the kitchen and approached the door slowly, then hung out the screen door, her bare toes curling down off the step. There were two boys in the car and now she recognized the driver: he had shaggy, shabby black hair that looked crazy as a wig and he was grinning at her.

"I ain't late, am I?" he said.

"Who the hell do you think you are?" Connie said.

"Toldja I'd be out, didn't I?"

"I don't even know who you are."   20

She spoke sullenly, careful to show no interest or pleasure, and he spoke in a fast bright monotone. Connie looked past him to the other boy, taking her time. He had fair brown hair, with a lock that fell onto his forehead. His sideburns gave him a fierce, embarrassed look, but so far he hadn't even bothered to glance at her. Both boys wore sunglasses. The driver's glasses were metallic and mirrored everything in miniature.

"You wanta come for a ride?" he said.

Connie smirked and let her hair fall loose over one shoulder.

"Don'tcha like my car? New paint job," he said. "Hey."

"What?"   25

"You're cute."

She pretended to fidget, chasing flies away from the door.

"Don'tcha believe me, or what?" he said.

"Look, I don't even know who you are," Connie said in disgust.

"Hey, Ellie's got a radio, see. Mine's broke down." He lifted his friend's arm   30
and showed her the little transistor the boy was holding, and now Connie began to hear the music. It was the same program that was playing inside the house.

"Bobby King?" she said.

"I listen to him all the time. I think he's great."

"He's kind of great," Connie said reluctantly.

"Listen, that guy's *great*. He knows where the action is."

Connie blushed a little, because the glasses made it impossible for her to see   35
just what this boy was looking at. She couldn't decide if she liked him or if he was just a jerk, and so she dawdled in the doorway and wouldn't come down or go back inside. She said, "What's all that stuff painted on your car?"

"Can'tcha read it?" He opened the door very carefully, as if he was afraid it might fall off. He slid out just as carefully, planting his feet firmly on the ground, the tiny metallic world in his glasses slowing down like gelatine hardening and in the midst of it Connie's bright green blouse. "This here is my name, to begin with," he said. ARNOLD FRIEND was written in tar-like black letters on the side, with a drawing of a round grinning face that reminded Connie of a pumpkin, except it wore sunglasses. "I wanta introduce myself, I'm Arnold Friend and that's my real name and I'm gonna be your friend, honey, and inside the car's Ellie Oscar, he's kinda shy." Ellie brought his transistor up to his shoulder and balanced it there. "Now these numbers are a secret code, honey," Arnold Friend explained. He read off the numbers 33, 19, 17 and raised his eyebrows at her to see what she thought of that, but she didn't think much of it. The left rear fender had been smashed and around it was written, on the gleaming gold background: DONE BY CRAZY WOMAN DRIVER. Connie had to laugh at that. Arnold Friend was pleased at her laughter and looked up at her. "Around the other side's a lot more—you wanta come and see them?"

"No."

"Why not?"

"Why should I?"

"Don'tcha wanta see what's on the car? Don'tcha wanta go for a ride?"   40

"I don't know."

"Why not?"

"I got things to do."

"Like what?"

"Things."   45

He laughed as if she had said something funny. He slapped his thighs. He was standing in a strange way, leaning back against the car as if he were balancing himself. He wasn't tall, only an inch or so taller than she would be if she came down to him. Connie liked the way he was dressed, which was the way all of them dressed: tight faded jeans stuffed into black, scuffed boots, a belt that pulled his waist in and showed how lean he was, and a white pullover shirt that was a little soiled and showed the hard small muscles of his arms and shoulders. He looked as if he probably did hard work, lifting and carrying things. Even his neck looked muscular. And his face was a familiar face, somehow: the jaw and chin and cheeks slightly darkened, because he hadn't shaved for a day or two, and the nose long and hawk-like, sniffing as if she were a treat he was going to gobble up and it was all a joke.

"Connie, you ain't telling the truth. This is your day set aside for a ride with me and you know it," he said, still laughing. The way he straightened and recovered from his fit of laughing showed that it had been all fake.

"How do you know what my name is?" she said suspiciously.

"It's Connie."

"Maybe and maybe not."   50

"I know my Connie," he said, wagging his finger. Now she remembered him even better, back at the restaurant, and her cheeks warmed at the thought of how she sucked in her breath just at the moment she passed him — how she must have looked to him. And he had remembered her. "Ellie and I come out here especially for you." he said. "Ellie can sit in back. How about it?"

"Where?"

"Where what?"

"Where're we going?"

He looked at her. He took off the sunglasses and she saw how pale the skin   55
around his eyes was, like holes that were not in shadow but instead in light. His eyes were like chips of broken glass that catch the light in an amiable way. He smiled. It was as if the idea of going for a ride somewhere, to some place, was a new idea to him.

"Just for a ride, Connie sweetheart."

"I never said my name was Connie," she said.

"But I know what it is. I know your name and all about you, lots of things," Arnold Friend said. He had not moved yet but stood still leaning back against the side of his jalopy. "I took a special interest in you, such a pretty girl, and found out all about you like I know your parents and sister are gone somewheres and I know where and how long they're going to be gone, and I know who you were with last night, and your best friend's name is Betty. Right?"

He spoke in a simple lilting voice, exactly as if he were reciting the words to a song. His smile assured her that everything was fine. In the car Ellie turned up the volume on his radio and did not bother to look around at them.

"Ellie can sit in the back seat," Arnold Friend said. He indicated his friend   60
with a casual jerk of his chin, as if Ellie did not count and she could not bother with him.

"How'd you find out all that stuff?" Connie said.

"Listen: Betty Schultz and Tony Fitch and Jimmy Pettinger and Nancy Pettinger," he said, in a chant. "Raymond Stanley and Bob Hutter—"

"Do you know all those kids?"

"I know everybody."

"Look, you're kidding. You're not from around here."   65

"Sure."

"But—how come we never saw you before?"

"Sure you saw me before," he said. He looked down at his boots, as if he were a little offended. "You just don't remember."

"I guess I'd remember you," Connie said.

"Yeah?" He looked up at this, beaming. He was pleased. He began to mark   70
time with the music from Ellie's radio, tapping his fists lightly together. Connie looked away from his smile to the car, which was painted so bright it almost hurt her eyes to look at it. She looked at that name, ARNOLD FRIEND. And up at the front fender was an expression that was familiar—MAN THE FLYING SAUCERS. It was an expression kids had used the year before, but didn't use this year. She looked at it for a while as if the words meant something to her that she did not yet know.

"What're you thinking about? Huh?" Arnold Friend demanded. "Not worried about your hair blowing around in the car, are you?"

"No."

"Think I maybe can't drive good?"

"How do I know?"

"You're a hard girl to handle. How come?" he said. "Don't you know I'm   75
your friend? Didn't you see me put my sign in the air when you walked by?"

"What sign?"

"My sign." And he drew an X in the air, leaning out toward her. They were maybe ten feet apart. After his hand fell back to his side the X was still in the air, almost visible. Connie let the screen door close and stood perfectly still inside it, listening to the music from her radio and the boy's blend together. She stared at Arnold Friend. He stood there so stiffly relaxed, pretending to be relaxed, with one hand idly on the door handle as if be were keeping himself up that way and had no intention of ever moving again. She recognized most things about him, the tight jeans that showed his thighs and buttocks and the greasy leather boots and the tight shirt, and even that slippery friendly smile of his, that sleepy dreamy smile that all the boys used to get across ideas they didn't want to put into words. She recognized all this and also the singsong way he talked, slightly mocking, kidding, but serious and a little melancholy, and she recognized the way he tapped one fist against the other in homage to the perpetual music behind him. But all these things did not come together.

She said suddenly, "Hey, how old are you?"

His smile faded. She could see then that he wasn't a kid, he was much older—thirty, maybe more. At this knowledge her heart began to pound faster. "That's a crazy thing to ask. Can'tcha see I'm your own age?"   80

"Like hell you are."

"Or maybe a coupla years older, I'm eighteen."

"Eighteen?" she said doubtfully.

He grinned to reassure her and lines appeared at the corners of his mouth. His teeth were big and white. He grinned so broadly his eyes became slits and she saw how thick the lashes were, thick and black as if painted with a black tar-like material. Then he seemed to become embarrassed, abruptly, and looked over his shoulder at Ellie. "*Him,* he's crazy," he said. "Ain't he a riot, he's a nut, a real character." Ellie was still listening to the music. His sunglasses told nothing about what he was thinking. He wore a bright orange shirt unbuttoned halfway to show his chest, which was a pale, bluish chest and not muscular like Arnold Friend's. His shirt collar was turned up all around and the very tips of the collar pointed out past his chin as if they were protecting him. He was pressing the transistor radio up against his ear and sat there in a kind of daze, right in the sun.

"He's kinda strange," Connie said.   85

"Hey, she says you're kinda strange! Kinda strange!" Arnold Friend cried. He pounded on the car to get Ellie's attention. Ellie turned for the first time and Connie saw with shock that he wasn't a kid either—he had a fair, hairless face, cheeks reddened slightly as if the veins grew too close to the surface of his skin, the face of a forty-year-old baby. Connie felt a wave of dizziness rise in her at this sight and she stared at him as if waiting for something to change the shock of the moment, make it all right again. Ellie's lips kept shaping words, mumbling along with the words blasting his ear.

"Maybe you two better go away," Connie said faintly.

"What? How come?" Arnold Friend cried. "We come out here to take you for a ride. It's Sunday." He had the voice of the man on the radio now. It was the same voice, Connie thought. "Don'tcha know it's Sunday all day and honey, no matter who you were with last night today you're with Arnold Friend and don't you forget it!—Maybe you better step out here," he said, and this last was in a different voice. It was a little flatter, as if the heat was finally getting to him.

"No. I got things to do."

"Hey."   90

"You two better leave."

"We ain't leaving until you come with us."

"Like hell I am—"

"Connie, don't fool around with me. I mean—I mean, don't fool *around,*" he said, shaking his head. He laughed incredulously. He placed his sunglasses on top of his head, carefully, as if he were indeed wearing a wig, and brought the stems down behind his ears. Connie stared at him, another wave of dizziness and fear rising in her so that for a moment he wasn't even in focus but was just a blur; standing there against his gold car, and she had the idea that he had driven up the driveway all right but had come from nowhere before that and belonged nowhere and that everything about him and even the music that was so familiar to her was only half real.

"If my father comes and sees you—"   95

"He ain't coming. He's at a barbecue."

"How do you know that?"

"Aunt Tillie's. Right now they're—uh—they're drinking. Sitting around," he said vaguely, squinting as if he were staring all the way to town and over to Aunt Tillie's back yard. Then the vision seemed to clear and he nodded energetically. "Yeah. Sitting around. There's your sister in a blue dress, huh? And high heels, the poor sad bitch—nothing like you, sweetheart! And your mother's helping some fat woman with the corn, they're cleaning the corn—husking the corn—"

"What fat woman?" Connie cried.

"How do I know what fat woman. I don't know every goddamn fat woman   100 in the world!" Arnold Friend laughed.

"Oh, that's Mrs. Hornby. . . . Who invited her?" Connie said. She felt a little light-headed. Her breath was coming quickly.

"She's too fat. I don't like them fat. I like them the way you are, honey," he said, smiling sleepily at her. They stared at each other for a while, through the screen door. He said softly, "Now what you're going to do is this: you're going to come out that door. You're going to sit up front with me and Ellie's going to sit in the back, the hell with Ellie, right? This isn't Ellie's date. You're my date. I'm your lover, honey."

"What? You're crazy—"

"Yes, I'm your lover. You don't know what that is but you will," he said. "I know that too. I know all about you. But look: it's real nice and you couldn't ask for nobody better than me, or more polite. I always keep my word. I'll tell you how it is, I'm always nice at first, the first time. I'll hold you so tight you won't think you have to try to get away or pretend anything because you'll know you can't. And I'll come inside you where it's all secret and you'll give in to me and you'll love me—"

"Shut up! You're crazy!" Connie said. She backed away from the door. She   105 put her hands against her ears as if she'd heard something terrible, something not meant for her. "People don't talk like that, you're crazy," she muttered. Her heart was almost too big now for her chest and its pumping made sweat break out all over her. She looked out to see Arnold Friend pause and then take a step toward the porch lurching. He almost fell. But, like a clever drunken man, he managed to catch his balance. He wobbled in his high boots and grabbed hold of one of the porch posts.

"Honey?" he said. "You still listening?"

"Get the hell out of here!"

"Be nice, honey. Listen."

"I'm going to call the police—"

He wobbled again and out of the side of his mouth came a fast spat curse,   110 an aside not meant for her to hear. But even this "Christ!" sounded forced. Then he began to smile again. She watched this smile come, awkward as if he were smiling from inside a mask. His whole face was a mask, she thought wildly, tanned down onto his throat but then running out as if he had plastered make-up on his face but had forgotten about his throat.

"Honey—? Listen, here's how it is. I always tell the truth and I promise you this: I ain't coming in that house after you."

"You better not! I'm going to call the police if you—if you don't—"

"Honey," he said, talking right through her voice, "honey, I'm not coming in there but you are coming out here. You know why?"

She was panting. The kitchen looked like a place she had never seen before, some room she had run inside but which wasn't good enough, wasn't going to help her. The kitchen window had never had a curtain, after three years, and there were dishes in the sink for her to do—probably—and if you ran your hand across the table you'd probably feel something sticky there.

"You listening, honey? Hey?"   115

"—going to call the police—"

"Soon as you touch the phone I don't need to keep my promise and can come inside. You won't want that."

She rushed forward and tried to lock the door. Her fingers were shaking. "But why lock it," Arnold Friend said gently, talking right into her face. "It's just a screen door. It's just nothing." One of his boots was at a strange angle, as if his foot wasn't in it. It pointed out to the left, bent at the ankle. "I mean, any-body can break through a screen door and glass and wood and iron or any-thing else if he needs to, anybody at all and specially Arnold Friend. If the place got lit up with a fire, honey, you'd come runnin' out into my arms, right into my arms an' safe at home—like you knew I was your lover and'd stopped fooling around, I don't mind a nice shy girl but I don't like no fooling around." Part of those words were spoken with a slight rhythmic lilt, and Connie somehow rec-ognized them—the echo of a song from last year, about a girl rushing into her boy friend's arms and coming home again—

Connie stood barefoot on the linoleum floor, staring at him. "What do you want?" she whispered.

"I want you," he said.   120

"What?"

"Seen you that night and thought, that's the one, yes sir. I never needed to look any more."

"But my father's coming back. He's coming to get me. I had to wash my hair first—" She spoke in a dry, rapid voice, hardly raising it for him to hear.

"No, your daddy is not coming and yes, you had to wash your hair and you washed it for me. It's nice and shining and all for me. I thank you, sweetheart," he said, with a mock bow, but again he almost lost his balance. He had to bend and adjust his boots. Evidently his feet did not go all the way down; the boots must have been stuffed with something so that he would seem taller. Connie stared out at him and behind him at Ellie in the car, who seemed to be looking off toward Connie's right, into nothing. Then Ellie said, pulling the words out of the air one after another as if he were just discovering them, "You want me to pull out the phone?"

"Shut your mouth and keep it shut," Arnold Friend said, his face red from 125 bending over or maybe from embarrassment because Connie had seen his boots. "This ain't none of your business."

"What—what are you doing? What do you want?" Connie said. "If I call the police they'll get you, they'll arrest you—"

"Promise was not to come in unless you touch that phone, and I'll keep that promise," he said. He resumed his erect position and tried to force his shoulders back. He sounded like a hero in a movie, declaring something important. He spoke too loudly and it was as if he were speaking to someone behind Connie. "I ain't made plans for coming in that house where I don't belong but just for you to come out to me, the way you should. Don't you know who I am?"

"You're crazy," she whispered. She backed away from the door but did not want to go into another part of the house, as if this would give him permission to come through the door. "What do you . . . You're crazy, you. . . ."

"Huh? What're you saying, honey?"

Her eyes darted everywhere in the kitchen. She could not remember what 130 it was, this room.

"This is how it is, honey: you come out and we'll drive away, have a nice ride. But if you don't come out we're gonna wait till your people come home and then they're all going to get it."

"You want that telephone pulled out?" Ellie said. He held the radio away from his ear and grimaced, as if without the radio the air was too much for him.

"I toldja shut up, Ellie," Arnold Friend said, "you're deaf, get a hearing aid, right? Fix yourself up. This little girl's no trouble and's gonna be nice to me, so Ellie keep to yourself, this ain't your date—right? Don't hem in on me, don't hog, don't crush, don't bird dog, don't trail me," he said in a rapid, meaningless voice, as if he were running through all the expressions he'd learned but was no longer sure which one of them was in style, then rushing on to new ones, making them up with his eyes closed. "Don't crawl under my fence, don't squeeze in my chipmunk hole, don't sniff my glue, suck my popsicle, keep your own greasy fingers on yourself!" He shaded his eyes and peered in at Connie, who was backed against the kitchen table. "Don't mind him, honey, he's just a creep. He's a dope. Right? I'm the boy for you and like I said, you come out here nice like a lady and give me your hand, and nobody else gets hurt, I mean, your nice old bald-headed daddy and your mummy and your sister in her high heels. Because listen: why bring them in this?"

"Leave me alone," Connie whispered.

"Hey, you know that old woman down the road, the one with the chickens 135 and stuff—you know her?"

"She's dead!"

"Dead? What? You know her?" Arnold Friend said.

"She's dead—"

"Don't you like her?"

"She's dead—she's—she isn't here any more—"   140

"But don't you like her, I mean, you got something against her? Some grudge or something?" Then his voice dipped as if he were conscious of rudeness. He touched the sunglasses on top of his head as if to make sure they were still there. "Now you be a good girl."

"What are you going to do?"

"Just two things, or maybe three," Arnold Friend said. "But I promise it won't last long and you'll like me that way you get to like people you're close to. You will. It's all over for you here, so come on out. You don't want your people in any trouble, do you?"

She turned and bumped against a chair or something, hurting her leg, but she ran into the back room and picked up the telephone. Something roared in her ear, a tiny roaring, and she was so sick with fear that she could do nothing but listen to it—the telephone was clammy and very heavy and her fingers groped down to the dial but were too weak to touch it. She began to scream into the phone, into the roaring. She cried out, she cried for her mother, she felt her breath start jerking back and forth in her lungs as if it were something Arnold Friend was stabbing her with again and again with no tenderness. A noisy sorrowful wailing rose all about her and she was locked inside it the way she was locked inside this house.

After a while she could hear again. She was sitting on the floor, with her   145
wet back against the wall.

Arnold Friend was saying from the door, "That's a good girl. Put the phone back."

She kicked the phone away from her.

"No, honey. Pick it up. Put it back right."

She picked it up and put it back. The dial tone stopped.

"That's a good girl. Now you come outside."   150

She was hollow with what had been fear but what was now just an emptiness. All that screaming had blasted it out of her. She sat, one leg cramped under her, and deep inside her brain was something like a pinpoint of light that kept going and would not let her relax. She thought, I'm not going to see my mother again. She thought, I'm not going to sleep in my bed again. Her bright green blouse was all wet.

Arnold Friend said, in a gentle-loud voice that was like a stage voice, "The place where you came from ain't there any more, and where you had in mind to go is cancelled out. This place you are now—inside your daddy's house—is nothing but a cardboard box I can knock down any time. You know that and always did know it. You hear me?"

She thought, I have got to think. I have got to know what to do.

"We'll go out to a nice field, out in the country here where it smells so nice and it's sunny," Arnold Friend said. "I'll have my arms tight around you so you won't need to try to get away and I'll show you what love is like, what it does. The hell with this house! It looks solid all right," he said. He ran a fingernail down the screen and the noise did not make Connie shiver, as it would have the day before. "Now put your hand on your heart, honey. Feel that? That feels solid too but we know better. Be nice to me, be sweet like you can because what else is there for a girl like you but to be sweet and pretty and give in?—and get away before her people get back?"

She felt her pounding heart. Her hand seemed to enclose it. She thought   155
for the first time in her life that it was nothing that was hers, that belonged to her, but just a pounding, living thing inside this body that wasn't really hers either.

"You don't want them to get hurt," Arnold Friend went on. "Now get up, honey. Get up all by yourself."

She stood.

"Now turn this way. That's right. Come over to me—Ellie, put that away, didn't I tell you? You dope. You miserable creepy dope," Arnold Friend said. His words were not angry but only part of an incantation. The incantation was kindly. "Now come out through the kitchen to me honey and let's see a smile, try it, you're a brave sweet little girl and now they're eating corn and hotdogs cooked to bursting over an outdoor fire, and they don't know one thing about you and never did and honey you're better than them because not a one of them would have done this for you."

Connie felt the linoleum under her feet; it was cool. She brushed her hair back out of her eyes. Arnold Friend let go of the post tentatively and opened his arms for her, his elbows pointing in toward each other and his wrists limp, to show that this was an embarrassed embrace and a little mocking, he didn't want to make her self-conscious.

She put out her hand against the screen. She watched herself push the   160
door slowly open as if she were back safe somewhere in the other doorway, watching this body and this head of long hair moving out into the sunlight where Arnold Friend waited.

"My sweet little blue-eyed girl," he said in a half-sung sigh that had nothing to do with her brown eyes but was taken up just the same by the vast sunlit reaches of the land behind him and on all sides of him—so much land that Connie had never seen before and did not recognize except to know that she was going to it.

[1966]

≡ THINKING ABOUT THE TEXT

1. This story was first published in 1966. What still seems typical of fifteen-year-old Connie's behavior? What seems dated about her?

2. Is Oates making a comment about the effect music has on Connie? Should popular music be accountable for the behavior of its listeners? Can popular culture make us oblivious to the real dangers of the world? Can it make us suspicious and cynical?

3. The suggestions about what will happen to Connie when she leaves the protection of her home are not so subtle. What is your view of her future? What does Connie mean when she says, " 'People don't talk like

that, you're crazy'"? What is your reading of her response? Is Arnold Friend crazy?

4. A common response to this story is frustration with Connie's hesitation and her inability to take appropriate action in the face of serious danger. Was this your response? Why isn't she more assertive?

5. Could Connie have been better prepared for this encounter with evil? What evidence does the author give to show how prepared she is or isn't? What is her relationship with her parents? Is her social awareness primarily her parents' responsibility? If not, whose is it?

≡ MAKING COMPARISONS

1. Compare the influence of romantic dreams on the boy in "Araby," on Sammy, and on Connie. What exactly are their outlooks? How do you think these were shaped?

2. What future do you see for these three characters? Most of us experience the disappointment and pain of romantic illusion but stop short of suffering Connie's fate. What might Oates's point be in such an extreme ending?

3. How might the consequences for the boy and for Sammy be different if they were confronted with an Arnold Friend?

≡ WRITING ABOUT ISSUES

1. Write an essay that argues that the main characters in these stories are or are not adversely affected by romantic dreams.

2. Ever since "A&P" was published, readers have argued about the real reason Sammy quits. Write an essay that considers various plausible reasons on the way to choosing the one you think is the strongest. Be sure to refer to the text as well as your own experience.

3. Look up information about the culture of James Joyce's Ireland, especially about religion and romance. Then research America's culture in the early-mid 1960s, when Updike and Oates wrote their stories. In a brief essay, argue that each story is understood more fully when the cultural context is provided.

4. Look up the lyrics to Bob Dylan's "It's All Over Now, Baby Blue," as well as information on "The Pied Piper of Tucson." Write an essay that argues that these two sources help explain Oates's story.

≡ Is This Love?: Stories

WILLIAM FAULKNER, "A Rose for Emily"

RAYMOND CARVER, "What We Talk About When We Talk About Love"

Although stories about those who die for love are not unknown, those about killing for love are much rarer. Can "killing for love" still be considered love, or is it something quite different, something dark and perverse? Can the world be so stressful, so unjust and cruel that someone batters a beloved in frustration? What if that person is looking to someone else to relieve the disappointments of the world? Is that love or just physical need? What if someone harbors violent fantasies about a person loved years before? Or what if a wife sexually betrays her loving husband so she can get for him the material possessions he desires? And can love be so worn down by cruelty that it turns to hate? These are not simple questions. Trying to understand our emotional contradictions and paradoxes never is. The following two writers grapple with these issues in creative and sometimes painful ways: Faulkner's story focuses on the interaction of tradition, madness, and love; Carver's looks at the complexity of discussing love. See whether you can decide if the characters in these stories are motivated by love or something more dangerous.

≡ BEFORE YOU READ

Have you ever hurt somebody you love? Did you mean to? Has a loved one ever hurt you? Is it possible for an emotionally disturbed person to love?

WILLIAM FAULKNER
A Rose for Emily

William Faulkner (1897–1962) is recognized as a great American novelist and storyteller and a major figure of world literature, having won the Nobel Prize in 1949. This acclaim failed to impress the people of his hometown, however, where his genteel poverty and peculiar ways earned him the title "Count No Count." Born in New Albany, Mississippi, and raised in Oxford, the home of the University of Mississippi, Faulkner briefly attended college there after World War I but was reduced to working odd jobs while continuing his writing. His fiction is most often set in Yoknapatawpha County, a created world whose history, geography, and complex genealogies parallel those of the American South. His many novels and stories blend the grotesquely comic with the appallingly tragic. The Sound and the Fury *(1929) is often considered his finest work. In later years, Faulkner's "odd jobs" included scriptwriting for Hollywood movies, speaking at universities, and writing magazine articles. "A Rose for Emily," first published in* Forum, *presents a story of love as told by citizens of Yoknapatawpha County.*

1

When Miss Emily Grierson died, our whole town went to her funeral: the men through a sort of respectful affection for a fallen monument, the women mostly out of curiosity to see the inside of her house, which no one save an old man-servant—a combined gardener and cook—had seen in at least ten years.

It was a big, squarish frame house that had once been white, decorated with cupolas and spires and scrolled balconies in the heavily lightsome style of the seventies, set on what had once been our most select street. But garages and cotton gins had encroached and obliterated even the august names of that neighborhood; only Miss Emily's house was left, lifting its stubborn and co-quettish decay above the cotton wagons and the gasoline pumps—an eyesore among eyesores. And now Miss Emily had gone to join the representatives of those august names where they lay in the cedar-bemused cemetery among the ranked and anonymous graves of Union and Confederate soldiers who fell at the battle of Jefferson.

Alive, Miss Emily had been a tradition, a duty, and a care; a sort of heredi-tary obligation upon the town, dating from that day in 1894 when Colonel Sartoris, the mayor—he who fathered the edict that no Negro woman should appear on the streets without an apron—remitted her taxes, the dispensation dating from the death of her father on into perpetuity. Not that Miss Emily would have accepted charity. Colonel Sartoris invented an involved tale to the effect that Miss Emily's father had loaned money to the town, which the town, as a matter of business, preferred this way of repaying. Only a man of Colonel Sartoris's generation and thought could have invented it, and only a woman could have believed it.

When the next generation, with its more modern ideas, became mayors and aldermen, this arrangement created some little dissatisfaction. On the first of the year they mailed her a tax notice. February came, and there was no re-ply. They wrote her a formal letter, asking her to call at the sheriff's office at her convenience. A week later the mayor wrote her himself, offering to call or to send his car for her, and received in reply a note on paper of an archaic shape, in a thin, flowing calligraphy in faded ink, to the effect that she no longer went out at all. The tax notice was also enclosed, without comment.

They called a special meeting of the Board of Aldermen. A deputation waited upon her, knocked at the door through which no visitor had passed since she ceased giving china-painting lessons eight or ten years earlier. They were admitted by the old Negro into a dim hall from which a stairway mounted into still more shadow. It smelled of dust and disuse—a close, dank smell. The Negro led them into the parlor. It was furnished in heavy, leather-covered fur-niture. When the Negro opened the blinds of one window, they could see that the leather was cracked; and when they sat down, a faint dust rose sluggishly about their thighs, spinning with slow motes in the single sun-ray. On a tarnished gilt easel before the fireplace stood a crayon portrait of Miss Emily's father.

They rose when she entered—a small, fat woman in black, with a thin gold chain descending to her waist and vanishing into her belt, leaning on an

5

ebony cane with a tarnished gold head. Her skeleton was small and spare; perhaps that was why what would have been merely plumpness in another was obesity in her. She looked bloated, like a body long submerged in motionless water, and of that pallid hue. Her eyes, lost in the fatty ridges of her face, looked like two small pieces of coal pressed into a lump of dough as they moved from one face to another while the visitors stated their errand.

She did not ask them to sit. She just stood in the door and listened quietly until the spokesman came to a stumbling halt. Then they could hear the invisible watch ticking at the end of the gold chain.

Her voice was dry and cold. "I have no taxes in Jefferson. Colonel Sartoris explained it to me. Perhaps one of you can gain access to the city records and satisfy yourselves."

"But we have. We are the city authorities, Miss Emily. Didn't you get a notice from the sheriff, signed by him?"

"I received a paper, yes," Miss Emily said. "Perhaps he considers himself   10
the sheriff. . . . I have no taxes in Jefferson."

"But there is nothing on the books to show that, you see. We must go by the—"

"See Colonel Sartoris. I have no taxes in Jefferson."

"But, Miss Emily—"

"See Colonel Sartoris." (Colonel Sartoris had been dead almost ten years.) "I have no taxes in Jefferson. Tobe!" The Negro appeared. "Show these gentlemen out."

2

So she vanquished them, horse and foot, just as she had vanquished their fa-   15
thers thirty years before about the smell. That was two years after her father's death and a short time after her sweetheart—the one we believed would marry her—had deserted her. After her father's death she went out very little; after her sweetheart went away, people hardly saw her at all. A few of the ladies had the temerity to call, but were not received, and the only sign of life about the place was the Negro man—a young man then—going in and out with a market basket.

"Just as if a man—any man—could keep a kitchen properly," the ladies said; so they were not surprised when the smell developed. It was another link between the gross, teeming world and the high and mighty Griersons.

A neighbor, a woman, complained to the mayor, Judge Stevens, eighty years old.

"But what will you have me do about it, madam?" he said.

"Why, send her word to stop it," the woman said. "Isn't there a law?"

"I'm sure that won't be necessary," Judge Stevens said. "It's probably just a   20
snake or a rat that nigger of hers killed in the yard. I'll speak to him about it."

The next day he received two more complaints, one from a man who came in diffident deprecation. "We really must do something about it, Judge. I'd be the last one in the world to bother Miss Emily, but we've got to do something."

That night the Board of Aldermen met—three graybeards and one younger man, a member of the rising generation.

"It's simple enough," he said. "Send her word to have her place cleaned up. Give her a certain time to do it in, and if she don't. . . ."

"Dammit, sir," Judge Stevens said, "will you accuse a lady to her face of smelling bad?"

So the next night, after midnight, four men crossed Miss Emily's lawn and slunk about the house like burglars, sniffing along the base of the brickwork and at the cellar openings while one of them performed a regular sowing motion with his hand out of a sack slung from his shoulder. They broke open the cellar door and sprinkled lime there, and in all the outbuildings. As they recrossed the lawn, a window that had been dark was lighted and Miss Emily sat in it, the light behind her, and her upright torso motionless as that of an idol. They crept quietly across the lawn and into the shadow of the locusts that lined the street. After a week or two the smell went away.

That was when people had begun to feel really sorry for her. People in our town, remembering how old lady Wyatt, her great-aunt, had gone completely crazy at last, believed that the Griersons held themselves a little too high for what they really were. None of the young men were quite good enough for Miss Emily and such. We had long thought of them as a tableau, Miss Emily a slender figure in white in the background, her father a spraddled silhouette in the foreground, his back to her and clutching a horsewhip, the two of them framed by the backflung front door. So when she got to be thirty and was still single, we were not pleased exactly, but vindicated; even with insanity in the family she wouldn't have turned down all of her chances if they had really materialized. 25

When her father died, it got about that the house was all that was left to her; and in a way, people were glad. At last they could pity Miss Emily. Being left alone, and a pauper, she had become humanized. Now she too would know the old thrill and the old despair of a penny more or less.

The day after his death all the ladies prepared to call at the house and offer condolence and aid, as is our custom. Miss Emily met them at the door, dressed as usual and with no trace of grief on her face. She told them that her father was not dead. She did that for three days, with the ministers calling on her, and the doctors, trying to persuade her to let them dispose of the body. Just as they were about to resort to law and force, she broke down, and they buried her father quickly.

We did not say she was crazy then. We believed she had to do that. We remembered all the young men her father had driven away, and we knew that with nothing left, she would have to cling to that which had robbed her, as people will.

3

She was sick for a long time. When we saw her again, her hair was cut short, making her look like a girl, with a vague resemblance to those angels in colored church windows—sort of tragic and serene.

The town had just let the contracts for paving the sidewalks, and in the 30 summer after her father's death they began the work. The construction company came with niggers and mules and machinery, and a foreman named Homer Barron, a Yankee—a big, dark, ready man, with a big voice and eyes lighter than his face. The little boys would follow in groups to hear him cuss the niggers, and the niggers singing in time to the rise and fall of picks. Pretty soon he knew everybody in town. Whenever you heard a lot of laughing anywhere about the square, Homer Barron would be in the center of the group. Presently, we began to see him and Miss Emily on Sunday afternoons driving in the yellow-wheeled buggy and the matched team of bays from the livery stable.

At first we were glad that Miss Emily would have an interest, because the ladies all said, "Of course a Grierson would not think seriously of a Northerner, a day laborer." But there were still others, older people, who said that even grief could not cause a real lady to forget *noblesse oblige*—without calling it *noblesse oblige*. They just said, "Poor Emily. Her kinsfolk should come to her." She had some kin in Alabama; but years ago her father had fallen out with them over the estate of old lady Wyatt, the crazy woman, and there was no communication between the two families. They had not even been represented at the funeral.

And as soon as the old people said, "Poor Emily," the whispering began. "Do you suppose it's really so?" they said to one another. "Of course it is. What else could. . . ." This behind their hands; rustling of craned silk and satin behind jalousies closed upon the sun of Sunday afternoon as the thin, swift clop-clop-clop of the matched team passed: "Poor Emily."

She carried her head high enough—even when we believed that she was fallen. It was as if she demanded more than ever the recognition of her dignity as the last Grierson; as if it had wanted that touch of earthiness to reaffirm her imperviousness. Like when she bought the rat poison, the arsenic. That was over a year after they had begun to say "Poor Emily," and while the two female cousins were visiting her.

"I want some poison," she said to the druggist. She was over thirty then, still a slight woman, though thinner than usual, with cold, haughty black eyes in a face the flesh of which was strained across the temples and about the eye-sockets as you imagine a lighthouse-keeper's face ought to look. "I want some poison," she said.

"Yes, Miss Emily. What kind? For rats and such? I'd recom——" 35

"I want the best you have. I don't care what kind."

The druggist named several. "They'll kill anything up to an elephant. But what you want is——"

"Arsenic," Miss Emily said. "Is that a good one?"

"Is . . . arsenic? Yes, ma'am. But what you want——"

"I want arsenic." 40

The druggist looked down at her. She looked back at him, erect, her face like a strained flag. "Why, of course," the druggist said. "If that's what you want. But the law requires you to tell what you are going to use it for."

Miss Emily just stared at him, her head tilted back in order to look him eye for eye, until he looked away and went and got the arsenic and wrapped it up.

The Negro delivery boy brought her the package; the druggist didn't come back. When she opened the package at home there was written on the box, under the skull and bones: "For rats."

4

So the next day we all said, "She will kill herself"; and we said it would be the best thing. When she had first begun to be seen with Homer Barron, we had said, "She will marry him." Then we said, "She will persuade him yet," because Homer himself had remarked—he liked men, and it was known that he drank with the younger men in the Elks' Club—that he was not a marrying man. Later we said, "Poor Emily" behind the jalousies as they passed on Sunday afternoon in the glittering buggy, Miss Emily with her head high and Homer Barron with his hat cocked and a cigar in his teeth, reins and whip in a yellow glove.

Then some of the ladies began to say that it was a disgrace to the town and a bad example to the young people. The men did not want to interfere, but at last the ladies forced the Baptist minister—Miss Emily's people were Episcopal—to call upon her. He would never divulge what happened during that interview, but he refused to go back again. The next Sunday they again drove about the streets, and the following day the minister's wife wrote to Miss Emily's relations in Alabama.

So she had blood-kin under her roof again and we sat back to watch developments. At first nothing happened. Then we were sure that they were to be married. We learned that Miss Emily had been to the jeweler's and ordered a man's toilet set in silver, with the letters H.B. on each piece. Two days later we learned that she had bought a complete outfit of men's clothing, including a nightshirt, and we said, "They are married." We were really glad. We were glad because the two female cousins were even more Grierson than Miss Emily had ever been.

So we were not surprised when Homer Barron—the streets had been finished some time since—was gone. We were a little disappointed that there was not a public blowing-off, but we believed that he had gone on to prepare for Miss Emily's coming, or to give her a chance to get rid of the cousins. (By that time it was a cabal, and we were all Miss Emily's allies to help circumvent the cousins.) Sure enough, after another week they departed. And, as we had expected all along, within three days Homer Barron was back in town. A neighbor saw the Negro man admit him at the kitchen door at dusk one evening.

And that was the last we saw of Homer Barron. And of Miss Emily for some time. The Negro man went in and out with the market basket, but the front door remained closed. Now and then we would see her at the window for a moment, as the men did that night when they sprinkled the lime, but for almost six months she did not appear on the streets. Then we knew that this was to be expected too; as if that quality of her father which had thwarted her woman's life so many times had been too virulent and too furious to die.

45

When we next saw Miss Emily, she had grown fat and her hair was turning gray. During the next few years it grew grayer and grayer until it attained an even pepper-and-salt iron-gray, when it ceased turning. Up to the day of her death at seventy-four it was still that vigorous iron-gray, like the hair of an active man.

From that time on her front door remained closed, save during a period of six or seven years, when she was about forty, during which she gave lessons in china-painting. She fitted up a studio in one of the downstairs rooms, where the daughters and granddaughters of Colonel Sartoris's contemporaries were sent to her with the same regularity and in the same spirit that they were sent to church on Sundays with a twenty-five-cent piece for the collection plate. Meanwhile her taxes had been remitted.

Then the newer generation became the backbone and the spirit of the town, and the painting pupils grew up and fell away and did not send their children to her with boxes of color and tedious brushes and pictures cut from the ladies' magazines. The front door closed upon the last one and remained closed for good. When the town got free postal delivery, Miss Emily alone refused to let them fasten the metal numbers above her door and attach a mailbox to it. She would not listen to them. 50

Daily, monthly, yearly we watched the Negro grow grayer and more stooped, going in and out with the market basket. Each December we sent her a tax notice, which would be returned by the post office a week later, unclaimed. Now and then we would see her in one of the downstairs windows—she had evidently shut up the top floor of the house—like the carven torso of an idol in a niche, looking or not looking at us, we could never tell which. Thus she passed from generation to generation—dear, inescapable, impervious, tranquil, and perverse.

And so she died. Fell ill in the house filled with dust and shadows, with only a doddering Negro man to wait on her. We did not even know she was sick; we had long since given up trying to get any information from the Negro. He talked to no one, probably not even to her, for his voice had grown harsh and rusty, as if from disuse.

She died in one of the downstairs rooms, in a heavy walnut bed with a curtain, her gray head propped on a pillow yellow and moldy with age and lack of sunlight.

5

The Negro met the first of the ladies at the front door and let them in, with their hushed, sibilant voices and their quick, curious glances, and then he disappeared. He walked right through the house and out the back and was not seen again.

The two female cousins came at once. They held the funeral on the second day, with the town coming to look at Miss Emily beneath a mass of bought flowers, with the crayon face of her father musing profoundly above the bier and the ladies sibilant and macabre; and the very old men—some in their brushed 55

Confederate uniforms—on the porch and the lawn, talking of Miss Emily as if she had been a contemporary of theirs, believing that they had danced with her and courted her perhaps, confusing time with its mathematical progression, as the old do, to whom all the past is not a diminishing road but, instead, a huge meadow which no winter ever quite touches, divided from them now by the narrow bottleneck of the most recent decade of years.

Already we knew that there was one room in that region above stairs which no one had seen in forty years, and which would have to be forced. They waited until Miss Emily was decently in the ground before they opened it.

The violence of breaking down the door seemed to fill this room with pervading dust. A thin, acrid pall as of the tomb seemed to lie everywhere upon this room decked and furnished as for a bridal: upon the valance curtains of faded rose color, upon the rose-shaded lights, upon the dressing table, upon the delicate array of crystal and the man's toilet things backed with tarnished silver, silver so tarnished that the monogram was obscured. Among them lay a collar and tie, as if they had just been removed, which, lifted, left upon the surface a pale crescent in the dust. Upon a chair hung the suit, carefully folded; beneath it the two mute shoes and the discarded socks.

The man himself lay in the bed.

For a long while we just stood there, looking down at the profound and fleshless grin. The body had apparently once lain in the attitude of an embrace, but now the long sleep that outlasts love, that conquers even the grimace of love, had cuckolded him. What was left of him, rotted beneath what was left of the nightshirt, had become inextricable from the bed in which he lay; and upon him and upon the pillow beside him lay that even coating of the patient and biding dust.

Then we noticed that in the second pillow was the indentation of a head. 60 One of us lifted something from it, and leaning forward, that faint and invisible dust dry and acrid in the nostrils, we saw a long strand of iron-gray hair.

[1931]

☰ THINKING ABOUT THE TEXT

1. Do you think some people can love another so much that they simply cannot bear for that person to leave? Is it possible Emily was like this?

2. Can a disturbed person be in love? Does love have to be healthy? Is sanity culturally defined? Can you imagine a society that would accept Emily's behavior?

3. Who do you think the narrator of "A Rose for Emily" is? Why would Faulkner tell the story from this perspective? Why not from Emily's?

4. Look at the last sentence of paragraph 51. What do you make of the five adjectives used? Are they understandable in terms of the story?

5. Some critics think this story is not a love story but a political allegory about the South. Does this make sense to you? What else does the story suggest to you?

6. Comment on the various kinds of repression—social and psychological—that occur throughout the story. What connections can you draw, and what generalizations might you make about them?

7. Reread "A Rose for Emily." How does your knowledge of the ending of the story affect your second reading? What details of the narrative tend to stand out the second time around?

RAYMOND CARVER
What We Talk About
When We Talk About Love

Raymond Carver (1938–1988) re-creates in what has been called a "stripped-down and muscular prose style" the minutiae of everyday life in mid-twentieth-century America. Brought up in the Pacific Northwest in a working-class family, Carver began writing in high school and married early. While both he and his young wife worked at low-paying jobs, Carver took college courses and struggled to find time to write. In 1958, he studied fiction writing with John Gardner and graduated in 1963 from what is now the California State University at Humboldt. He received national recognition in 1967 when a story was included in the Best American Short Stories *annual anthology. Although Carver was a National Endowment for the Arts fellow in poetry in 1971, fiction remained his primary genre, earning him numerous awards and fellowships, including O. Henry awards in 1974, 1975, and 1980. Despite his success as a writer, alcoholism plagued Carver for most of his life until with the help of Alcoholics Anonymous he stopped drinking in 1982, soon after his divorce. "What We Talk About When We Talk About Love" was the title story in his 1981 collection.*

My friend Mel McGinnis was talking. Mel McGinnis is a cardiologist, and sometimes that gives him the right.

The four of us were sitting around his kitchen table drinking gin. Sunlight filled the kitchen from the big window behind the sink. There were Mel and me and his second wife, Teresa—Terri, we called her—and my wife, Laura. We lived in Albuquerque then. But we were all from somewhere else.

There was an ice bucket on the table. The gin and the tonic water kept going around, and we somehow got on the subject of love. Mel thought real love was nothing less than spiritual love. He said he'd spent five years in a seminary before quitting to go to medical school. He said he still looked back on those years in the seminary as the most important years in his life.

Terri said the man she lived with before she lived with Mel loved her so much he tried to kill her. Then Terri said, "He beat me up one night. He dragged me around the living room by my ankles. He kept saying, 'I love you, I love you, you bitch.' He went on dragging me around the living room. My head kept knocking on things." Terri looked around the table. "What do you do with love like that?"

She was a bone-thin woman with a pretty face, dark eyes, and brown hair   5
that hung down her back. She liked necklaces made of turquoise, and long
pendant earrings.

"My God, don't be silly. That's not love, and you know it," Mel said. "I don't
know what you'd call it, but I sure know you wouldn't call it love."

"Say what you want to, but I know it was," Terri said. "It may sound crazy
to you, but it's true just the same. People are different, Mel. Sure, sometimes he
may have acted crazy. Okay. But he loved me. In his own way maybe, but he
loved me. There was love there, Mel. Don't say there wasn't."

Mel let out his breath. He held his glass and turned to Laura and me. "The
man threatened to kill me," Mel said. He finished his drink and reached for the
gin bottle. "Terri's a romantic. Terri's of the kick-me-so-I'll-know-you-love-me
school. Terri, hon, don't look that way." Mel reached across the table and
touched Terri's cheek with his fingers. He grinned at her.

"Now he wants to make up," Terri said.

"Make up what?" Mel said. "What is there to make up? I know what I know.   10
That's all."

"How'd we get started on this subject, anyway?" Terri said. She raised her
glass and drank from it. "Mel always has love on his mind," she said. "Don't
you, honey?" She smiled, and I thought that was the last of it.

"I just wouldn't call Ed's behavior love. That's all I'm saying, honey," Mel
said. "What about you guys?" Mel said to Laura and me. "Does that sound like
love to you?"

"I'm the wrong person to ask," I said. "I didn't even know the man. I've
only heard his name mentioned in passing. I wouldn't know. You'd have to
know the particulars. But I think what you're saying is that love is an absolute."

Mel said, "The kind of love I'm talking about is. The kind of love I'm talking
about, you don't try to kill people."

Laura said, "I don't know anything about Ed, or anything about the situa-   15
tion. But who can judge anyone else's situation?"

I touched the back of Laura's hand. She gave me a quick smile. I picked up
Laura's hand. It was warm, the nails polished, perfectly manicured. I encircled
the broad wrist with my fingers, and I held her.

"When I left, he drank rat poison," Terri said. She clasped her arms with
her hands. "They took him to the hospital in Santa Fe. That's where we lived
then, about ten miles out. They saved his life. But his gums went crazy from it.
I mean they pulled away from his teeth. After that, his teeth stood out like
fangs. My God," Terri said. She waited a minute, then let go of her arms and
picked up her glass.

"What people won't do!" Laura said.

"He's out of the action now," Mel said. "He's dead."

Mel handed me the saucer of limes. I took a section, squeezed it over my   20
drink, and stirred the ice cubes with my finger.

"It gets worse," Terri said. "He shot himself in the mouth. But he bungled
that too. Poor Ed," she said. Terri shook her head.

"Poor Ed nothing," Mel said. "He was dangerous."

Mel was forty-five years old. He was tall and rangy with curly soft hair. His face and arms were brown from the tennis he played. When he was sober, his gestures, all his movements, were precise, very careful.

"He did love me though, Mel. Grant me that," Terri said. "That's all I'm asking. He didn't love me the way you love me. I'm not saying that. But he loved me. You can grant me that, can't you?"

"What do you mean, he bungled it?" I said.   25

Laura leaned forward with her glass. She put her elbows on the table and held her glass in both hands. She glanced from Mel to Terri and waited with a look of bewilderment on her open face, as if amazed that such things happened to people you were friendly with.

"How'd he bungle it when he killed himself?" I said.

"I'll tell you what happened," Mel said. "He took this twenty-two pistol he'd bought to threaten Terri and me with. Oh, I'm serious, the man was always threatening. You should have seen the way we lived in those days. Like fugitives. I even bought a gun myself. Can you believe it? A guy like me? But I did. I bought one for self-defense and carried it in the glove compartment. Sometimes I'd have to leave the apartment in the middle of the night. To go to the hospital, you know? Terri and I weren't married then, and my first wife had the house and kids, the dog, everything, and Terri and I were living in this apartment here. Sometimes, as I say, I'd get a call in the middle of the night and have to go in to the hospital at two or three in the morning. It'd be dark out there in the parking lot, and I'd break into a sweat before I could even get to my car. I never knew if he was going to come up out of the shrubbery or from behind a car and start shooting. I mean, the man was crazy. He was capable of wiring a bomb, anything. He used to call my service at all hours and say he needed to talk to the doctor, and when I'd return the call, he'd say, 'Son of a bitch, your days are numbered.' Little things like that. It was scary, I'm telling you."

"I still feel sorry for him," Terri said.

"It sounds like a nightmare," Laura said. "But what exactly happened after he shot himself?"   30

Laura is a legal secretary. We'd met in a professional capacity. Before we knew it, it was a courtship. She's thirty-five, three years younger than I am. In addition to being in love, we like each other and enjoy one another's company. She's easy to be with.

"What happened?" Laura said.

Mel said, "He shot himself in the mouth in his room. Someone heard the shot and told the manager. They came in with a passkey, saw what had happened, and called an ambulance. I happened to be there when they brought him in, alive but past recall. The man lived for three days. His head swelled up to twice the size of a normal head. I'd never seen anything like it, and I hope I never do again. Terri wanted to go in and sit with him when she found out about it. We had a fight over it. I didn't think she should see him like that. I didn't think she should see him, and I still don't."

"Who won the fight?" Laura said.

"I was in the room with him when he died," Terri said. "He never came up   35
out of it. But I sat with him. He didn't have anyone else."

"He was dangerous," Mel said. "If you call that love, you can have it."

"It was love," Terri said. "Sure, it's abnormal in most people's eyes. But he
was willing to die for it. He did die for it."

"I sure as hell wouldn't call it love," Mel said. "I mean, no one knows what
he did it for. I've seen a lot of suicides, and I couldn't say anyone ever knew
what they did it for."

Mel put his hands behind his neck and tilted his chair back. "I'm not interested in that kind of love," he said. "If that's love, you can have it."

Terri said, "We were afraid. Mel even made a will out and wrote to his   40
brother in California who used to be a Green Beret. Mel told him who to look for
if something happened to him."

Terri drank from her glass. She said, "But Mel's right—we lived like fugitives. We were afraid. Mel was, weren't you, honey? I even called the police at
one point, but they were no help. They said they couldn't do anything until Ed
actually did something. Isn't that a laugh?" Terri said.

She poured the last of the gin into her glass and waggled the bottle. Mel got
up from the table and went to the cupboard. He took down another bottle.

"Well, Nick and I know what love is," Laura said. "For us, I mean," Laura said.
She bumped my knee with her knee. "You're supposed to say something now,"
Laura said, and turned her smile on me.

For an answer, I took Laura's hand and raised it to my lips. I made a big
production out of kissing her hand. Everyone was amused.

"We're lucky," I said.   45

"You guys," Terri said. "Stop that now. You're making me sick. You're still
on the honeymoon, for God's sake. You're still gaga, for crying out loud. Just
wait. How long have you been together now? How long has it been? A year?
Longer than a year?"

"Going on a year and a half," Laura said, flushed and smiling.

"Oh, now," Terri said. "Wait awhile."

She held her drink and gazed at Laura.

"I'm only kidding," Terri said.   50

Mel opened the gin and went around the table with the bottle.

"Here, you guys," he said. "Let's have a toast. I want to propose a toast. A
toast to love. To true love," Mel said.

We touched glasses.

"To love," we said.

Outside in the backyard, one of the dogs began to bark. The leaves of the aspen   55
that leaned past the window ticked against the glass. The afternoon sun was
like a presence in this room, the spacious light of ease and generosity. We could
have been anywhere, somewhere enchanted. We raised our glasses again and
grinned at each other like children who had agreed on something forbidden.

"I'll tell you what real love is," Mel said. "I mean, I'll give you a good example. And then you can draw your own conclusions." He poured more gin into his glass. He added an ice cube and a sliver of lime. We waited and sipped our drinks. Laura and I touched knees again. I put a hand on her warm thigh and left it there.

"What do any of us really know about love?" Mel said. "It seems to me we're just beginners at love. We say we love each other and we do, I don't doubt it. I love Terri and Terri loves me, and you guys love each other too. You know the kind of love I'm talking about now. Physical love, that impulse that drives you to someone special, as well as love of the other person's being, his or her essence, as it were. Carnal love and, well, call it sentimental love, the day-to-day caring about the other person. But sometimes I have a hard time accounting for the fact that I must have loved my first wife too. But I did, I know I did. So I suppose I am like Terri in that regard. Terri and Ed." He thought about it and then he went on. "There was a time when I thought I loved my first wife more than life itself. But now I hate her guts. I do. How do you explain that? What happened to that love? What happened to it, is what I'd like to know. I wish someone could tell me. Then there's Ed. Okay, we're back to Ed. He loves Terri so much he tries to kill her and he winds up killing himself." Mel stopped talking and swallowed from his glass. "You guys have been together eighteen months and you love each other. It shows all over you. You glow with it. But you both loved other people before you met each other. You've both been married before, just like us. And you probably loved other people before that too, even. Terri and I have been together five years, been married for four. And the terrible thing, the terrible thing is, but the good thing too, the saving grace, you might say, is that if something happened to one of us—excuse me for saying this—but if something happened to one of us tomorrow I think the other one, the other person, would grieve for a while, you know, but then the surviving party would go out and love again, have someone else soon enough. All this, all of this love we're talking about, it would just be a memory. Maybe not even a memory. Am I wrong? Am I way off base? Because I want you to set me straight if you think I'm wrong. I want to know. I mean, I don't know anything, and I'm the first one to admit it."

"Mel, for God's sake," Terri said. She reached out and took hold of his wrist. "Are you getting drunk? Honey? Are you drunk?"

"Honey, I'm just talking," Mel said. "All right? I don't have to be drunk to say what I think. I mean, we're all just talking, right?" Mel said. He fixed his eyes on her.

"Sweetie, I'm not criticizing," Terri said.

She picked up her glass.

"I'm not on call today," Mel said. "Let me remind you of that. I am not on call," he said.

"Mel, we love you," Laura said.

Mel looked at Laura. He looked at her as if he could not place her, as if she was not the woman she was.

60

"Love you too, Laura," Mel said. "And you, Nick, love you too. You know   65
something?" Mel said. "You guys are our pals," Mel said.

He picked up his glass.

Mel said, "I was going to tell you about something. I mean, I was going to prove
a point. You see, this happened a few months ago, but it's still going on right
now, and it ought to make us feel ashamed when we talk like we know what
we're talking about when we talk about love."

"Come on now," Terri said. "Don't talk like you're drunk if you're not
drunk."

"Just shut up for once in your life," Mel said very quietly. "Will you do me a
favor and do that for a minute? So as I was saying, there's this old couple who
had this car wreck out on the interstate. A kid hit them and they were all torn
to shit and nobody was giving them much chance to pull through."

Terri looked at us and then back at Mel. She seemed anxious, or maybe   70
that's too strong a word.

Mel was handing the bottle around the table.

"I was on call that night," Mel said. "It was May or maybe it was June. Terri
and I had just sat down to dinner when the hospital called. There'd been this
thing out on the interstate. Drunk kid, teenager, plowed his dad's pickup into
this camper with this old couple in it. They were up in their midseventies, that
couple. The kid—eighteen, nineteen, something—he was DOA. Taken the
steering wheel through his sternum. The old couple, they were alive, you understand. I mean, just barely. But they had everything. Multiple fractures, internal injuries, hemorrhaging, contusions, lacerations, the works, and they
each of them had themselves concussions. They were in a bad way, believe me.
And, of course, their age was two strikes against them. I'd say she was worse
off than he was. Ruptured spleen along with everything else. Both kneecaps
broken. But they'd been wearing their seatbelts and, God knows, that's what
saved them for the time being."

"Folks, this is an advertisement for the National Safety Council," Terri said.
"This is your spokesman, Dr. Melvin R. McGinnis, talking." Terri laughed.
"Mel," she said, "sometimes you're just too much. But I love you, hon," she said.

"Honey, I love you," Mel said.

He leaned across the table. Terri met him halfway. They kissed.   75

"Terri's right," Mel said as he settled himself again. "Get those seatbelts on.
But seriously, they were in some shape, those oldsters. By the time I got down
there, the kid was dead, as I said. He was off in a corner, laid out on a gurney. I
took one look at the old couple and told the ER nurse to get me a neurologist
and an orthopedic man and a couple of surgeons down there right away."

He drank from his glass. "I'll try to keep this short," he said. "So we took
the two of them up to the OR and worked like fuck on them most of the night.
They had these incredible reserves, those two. You see that once in a while. So
we did everything that could be done, and toward morning we're giving them
a fifty-fifty chance, maybe less than that for her. So here they are, still alive the
next morning. So, okay, we move them into the ICU, which is where they both

kept plugging away at it for two weeks, hitting it better and better on all the scopes. So we transfer them out to their own room."

Mel stopped talking. "Here," he said, "let's drink this cheapo gin the hell up. Then we're going to dinner, right? Terri and I know a new place. That's where we'll go, to this new place we know about. But we're not going until we finish up this cut-rate, lousy gin."

Terri said, "We haven't actually eaten there yet. But it looks good. From the outside, you know."

"I like food," Mel said. "If I had it to do all over again, I'd be a chef, you know? Right, Terri?" Mel said.   80

He laughed. He fingered the ice in his glass.

"Terri knows," he said. "Terri can tell you. But let me say this. If I could come back again in a different life, a different time and all, you know what? I'd like to come back as a knight. You were pretty safe wearing all that armor. It was all right being a knight until gunpowder and muskets and pistols came along."

"Mel would like to ride a horse and carry a lance," Terri said.

"Carry a woman's scarf with you everywhere," Laura said.

"Or just a woman," Mel said.   85

"Shame on you," Laura said.

Terri said, "Suppose you came back as a serf. The serfs didn't have it so good in those days," Terri said.

"The serfs never had it good," Mel said. "But I guess even the knights were vessels to someone. Isn't that the way it worked? But then everyone is always a vessel to someone. Isn't that right? Terri? But what I liked about knights, besides their ladies, was that they had that suit of armor, you know, and they couldn't get hurt very easy. No cars in those days, you know? No drunk teenagers to tear into your ass."

"Vassals," Terri said.

"What?" Mel said.   90

"Vassals," Terri said. "They were called vassals, not vessels."

"Vassals, vessels," Mel said, "what the fuck's the difference? You knew what I meant anyway. All right," Mel said. "So I'm not educated. I learned my stuff. I'm a heart surgeon, sure, but I'm just a mechanic. I go in and I fuck around and I fix things. Shit," Mel said.

"Modesty doesn't become you," Terri said.

"He's just a humble sawbones," I said. "But sometimes they suffocated in all that armor, Mel. They'd even have heart attacks if it got too hot and they were too tired and worn out. I read somewhere that they'd fall off their horses and not be able to get up because they were too tired to stand with all that armor on them. They got trampled by their own horses sometimes."

"That's terrible," Mel said. "That's a terrible thing, Nicky. I guess they'd just lay there and wait until somebody came along and made a shish kebab out of them."   95

"Some other vessel," Terri said.

"That's right," Mel said. "Some vassal would come along and spear the bastard in the name of love. Or whatever the fuck it was they fought over in those days."

"Same things we fight over these days," Terri said.

Laura said, "Nothing's changed."

The color was still high in Laura's cheeks. Her eyes were bright. She   100
brought her glass to her lips.

Mel poured himself another drink. He looked at the label closely as if studying a long row of numbers. Then he slowly put the bottle down on the table and slowly reached for the tonic water.

"What about the old couple?" Laura said. "You didn't finish that story you started."

Laura was having a hard time lighting her cigarette. Her matches kept going out.

The sunshine inside the room was different now, changing, getting thinner. But the leaves outside the window were still shimmering, and I stared at the pattern they made on the panes and on the Formica counter. They weren't the same patterns, of course.

"What about the old couple?" I said.   105

"Older but wiser," Terri said.

Mel stared at her.

Terri said, "Go on with your story, hon. I was only kidding. Then what happened?"

"Terri, sometimes," Mel said.

"Please, Mel," Terri said. "Don't always be so serious, sweetie. Can't you   110
take a joke?"

"Where's the joke?" Mel said.

He held his glass and gazed steadily at his wife.

"What happened?" Laura said.

Mel fastened his eyes on Laura. He said, "Laura, if I didn't have Terri and if I didn't love her so much, and if Nick wasn't my best friend, I'd fall in love with you, I'd carry you off, honey," he said.

"Tell your story," Terri said. "Then we'll go to that new place, okay?"   115

"Okay," Mel said. "Where was I?" he said. He stared at the table and then he began again.

"I dropped in to see each of them every day, sometimes twice a day if I was up doing other calls anyway. Casts and bandages, head to foot, the both of them. You know, you've seen it in the movies. That's just the way they looked, just like in the movies. Little eye-holes and nose-holes and mouth-holes. And she had to have her legs slung up on top of it. Well, the husband was very depressed for the longest while. Even after he found out that his wife was going to pull through, he was still very depressed. Not about the accident, though. I mean, the accident was one thing, but it wasn't everything. I'd get up to his mouth-hole, you know, and he'd say no, it wasn't the accident exactly but it was because he couldn't see her through his eye-holes. He said that was what was making him feel so bad. Can you imagine? I'm telling you, the man's heart was breaking because he couldn't turn his goddamn head and *see* his goddamn wife."

Mel looked around the table and shook his head at what he was going to say.

"I mean, it was killing the old fart just because he couldn't *look* at the fucking woman."

We all looked at Mel.   120

"Do you see what I'm saying?" he said.

Maybe we were a little drunk by then. I know it was hard keeping things in focus. The light was draining out of the room, going back through the window where it had come from. Yet nobody made a move to get up from the table to turn on the overhead light.

"Listen," Mel said. "Let's finish this fucking gin. There's about enough left here for one shooter all around. Then let's go eat. Let's go to the new place."

"He's depressed," Terri said. "Mel, why don't you take a pill?"

Mel shook his head. "I've taken everything there is."   125

"We all need a pill now and then," I said.

"Some people are born needing them," Terri said.

She was using her finger to rub at something on the table. Then she stopped rubbing.

"I think I want to call my kids," Mel said. "Is that all right with everybody? I'll call my kids," he said.

Terri said, "What if Marjorie answers the phone? You guys, you've heard   130
us on the subject of Marjorie? Honey, you know you don't want to talk to Marjorie. It'll make you feel even worse."

"I don't want to talk to Marjorie," Mel said. "But I want to talk to my kids."

"There isn't a day goes by that Mel doesn't say he wishes she'd get married again. Or else die," Terri said. "For one thing," Terri said, "she's bankrupting us. Mel says it's just to spite him that she won't get married again. She has a boyfriend who lives with her and the kids, so Mel is supporting the boyfriend too."

"She's allergic to bees," Mel said. "If I'm not praying she'll get married again, I'm praying she'll get herself stung to death by a swarm of fucking bees."

"Shame on you," Laura said.

"Bzzzzzzz," Mel said, turning his fingers into bees and buzzing them at   135
Terri's throat. Then he let his hands drop all the way to his sides.

"She's vicious," Mel said. "Sometimes I think I'll go up there dressed like a beekeeper. You know, that hat that's like a helmet with the plate that comes down over your face, the big gloves, and the padded coat? I'll knock on the door and let loose a hive of bees in the house. But first I'd make sure the kids were out, of course."

He crossed one leg over the other. It seemed to take him a lot of time to do it. Then he put both feet on the floor and leaned forward, elbows on the table, his chin cupped in his hands.

"Maybe I won't call the kids, after all. Maybe it isn't such a hot idea. Maybe we'll just go eat. How does that sound?"

"Sounds fine to me," I said. "Eat or not eat. Or keep drinking. I could head right on out into the sunset."

"What does that mean, honey?" Laura said.   140

"It just means what I said," I said. "It means I could just keep going. That's all it means."

"I could eat something myself," Laura said. "I don't think I've ever been so hungry in my life. Is there something to nibble on?"

"I'll put out some cheese and crackers," Terri said.

But Terri just sat there. She did not get up to get anything.

Mel turned his glass over. He spilled it out on the table.   145

"Gin's gone," Mel said.

Terri said, "Now what?"

I could hear my heart beating. I could hear everyone's heart. I could hear the human noise we sat there making, not one of us moving, not even when the room went dark.   *[1981]*

☰ THINKING ABOUT THE TEXT

1. The argument between the couples seems to be about the nature of love. Which character's ideas make the most sense to you? What kinds of love are discussed? Are these demonstrated in the story? Do you think true love is an illusion?

2. Do you see similarities between Mel and Ed? Do any of the characters seem aware of any similarities? Is Mel a perceptive person? What are his problems? Is he in love with Terri? How do you interpret his fantasy with the bees and Marjorie?

3. Why does Mel seem so interested in knights? Is this symbolic? Are there other symbols here (light? dark? cardiologist?)? What do you make of the last paragraph? Why does it end with beating hearts and silence?

4. Is this story optimistic or pessimistic about true love? Is the old couple a positive or a negative example of true love? What about Nick and Laura? What about Ed? Could you argue that he was in love?

5. What does the title mean? Be specific, especially about the first word. Do you tell stories about love? Have you heard some recently? What lessons or information do they give about love?

☰ MAKING COMPARISONS

1. Compare Ed to Emily Grierson in Faulkner's story. What similarities do you see in their behavior?

2. Have these stories complicated your idea of love?

3. Do you see Terri and Homer Barron as victims of love? Did they do something wrong?

☰ WRITING ABOUT ISSUES

1. Is love or hate a stronger emotion? Use examples from these stories to support your argument.

2. What difficulties do you encounter when you try to define love? Write an essay in which you use Homer and Emily or Terri and Ed as examples that complicate the definition.

3. Citing evidence from these and other stories, as well as novels, films, and your own experiences, write an essay that explains your view of the necessary ingredients for a loving relationship.

4. Argue that because our culture overemphasizes romantic love, individuals feel pressured to find love, sometimes in all the wrong places.

≡ The Appearance of Love: Stories by Kate Chopin

KATE CHOPIN, "The Storm"

KATE CHOPIN, "The Story of an Hour"

KATE CHOPIN, "Désirée's Baby"

People at weddings often remark how happy and in love the bridal couple looks. But people can *appear* to be in love. Indeed, psychologists tell us that someone can play a loving role for years, at times actually believing the part he or she is playing. To a limited extent, this is true for all of us. We learn what it means to be in love from watching movies, reading books, and absorbing other clues from our culture. A man proposing marriage on one knee is just one cultural notion of how we should act when we are in love.

Suppose a woman acts lovingly toward her husband and then has a passionate sexual encounter with an old boyfriend. Which is her true self? Which is the appearance and which the reality? Sometimes a society's conventions about marriage are so strong that men and women have little choice but to conform. If we were to judge the behavior of a woman toward her husband a hundred years ago, we might not get an accurate reading of how much she loved him. Likewise, people can believe their lives to be quite harmonious until they find out that one of them has a surprising past. William Shakespeare wrote of love that would not change when difficulties arose, but such is not always the case. Does that mean that one's love is not deep enough? Or when a loved one does not live up to expectations, is it natural to readjust one's heart?

The following three stories take on controversial topics. Kate Chopin was not a conformist thinker, and her stories are filled with views of desire, love, and relationships meant to provoke her late-nineteenth-century readers. Indeed, they continue to provoke audiences today.

≡ BEFORE YOU READ

Would you change your mind about loving someone if you found out he or she was having an affair? If that person lied about his or her religion or race? Is it possible to love someone and at the same time want to be free?

KATE CHOPIN
The Storm

Kate Chopin (1851–1904) is known for her evocations of the unique, multiethnic Creole and Cajun societies of late-nineteenth-century Louisiana; however, her characters transcend the limitation of regional genre writing, striking a particularly resonant note among feminist readers. Born Katherine O'Flaherty in St. Louis, Missouri,

(Missouri Historical
Society. St. Louis.
Negative Por C-146.
Kate Chopin carte de
visite photograph by
J. J. Scholten, 1869.)

she married Oscar Chopin in 1870 and went to live with him in New Orleans and on his plantation along the Mississippi River. Her short stories were collected in Bayou Folk *(1894) and* A Night in Acadie *(1897). Chopin's last novel,* The Awakening, *scandalized readers at the time of its publication in 1899 because of its frank portrayal of female sexuality in the context of an extramarital affair. Long ignored by readers and critics, her work was revived in the 1960s and continues to provoke heated discussion of her female characters: are they women who seek freedom in the only ways available to them, or are they willing participants in their own victimhood?*

"The Storm" was written about 1898, but because of its provocative content, Chopin probably did not even try to find a magazine that would risk the publicity.

1

The leaves were so still that even Bibi thought it was going to rain. Bobinôt, who was accustomed to converse on terms of perfect equality with his little son, called the child's attention to certain sombre clouds that were rolling with sinister intention from the west, accompanied by a sullen, threatening roar. They were at Friedheimer's store and decided to remain there till the storm had passed. They sat within the door on two empty kegs. Bibi was four years old and looked very wise.

"Mama'll be 'fraid, yes," he suggested with blinking eyes.

"She'll shut the house. Maybe she got Sylvie helpin' her this evenin'," Bobinôt responded reassuringly.

"No; she ent got Sylvie. Sylvie was helpin' her yistiday," piped Bibi.

Bobinôt arose and going across to the counter purchased a can of shrimps,   5
of which Calixta was very fond. Then he returned to his perch on the keg and sat stolidly holding the can of shrimps while the storm burst. It shook the wooden store and seemed to be ripping great furrows in the distant field. Bibi laid his little hand on his father's knee and was not afraid.

2

Calixta, at home, felt no uneasiness for their safety. She sat at a side window sewing furiously on a sewing machine. She was greatly occupied and did not notice the approaching storm. But she felt very warm and often stopped to mop her face on which the perspiration gathered in beads. She unfastened her white sacque at the throat. It began to grow dark, and suddenly realizing the situation she got up hurriedly and went about closing windows and doors.

Out on the small front gallery she had hung Bobinôt's Sunday clothes to air and she hastened out to gather them before the rain fell. As she stepped outside, Alcée Laballière rode in at the gate. She had not seen him very often since her marriage, and never alone. She stood there with Bobinôt's coat in her hands, and the big rain drops began to fall. Alcée rode his horse under the shelter of a side projection where the chickens had huddled and there were plows and a harrow piled up in the corner.

"May I come and wait on your gallery till the storm is over, Calixta?" he asked.

"Come 'long in, M'sieur Alcée."

His voice and her own startled her as if from a trance, and she seized   10
Bobinôt's vest. Alcée, mounting to the porch, grabbed the trousers and snatched Bibi's braided jacket that was about to be carried away by a sudden gust of wind. He expressed an intention to remain outside, but it was soon apparent that he might as well have been out in the open: the water beat in upon the boards in driving sheets, and he went inside, closing the door after him. It was even necessary to put something beneath the door to keep the water out.

"My! what a rain! It's good two years sence it rain' like that," exclaimed Calixta as she rolled up a piece of bagging and Alcée helped her to thrust it beneath the crack.

She was a little fuller of figure than five years before when she married; but she had lost nothing of her vivacity. Her blue eyes still retained their melting quality; and her yellow hair, dishevelled by the wind and rain, kinked more stubbornly than ever about her ears and temples.

The rain beat upon the low, shingled roof with a force and clatter that threatened to break an entrance and deluge them there. They were in the dining room—the sitting room—the general utility room. Adjoining was her bed room, with Bibi's couch along side her own. The door stood open, and the room with its white, monumental bed, its closed shutters, looked dim and mysterious.

Alcée flung himself into a rocker and Calixta nervously began to gather up from the floor the lengths of a cotton sheet which she had been sewing.

"If this keeps up, *Dieu sait*° if the levees goin' to stan' it!" she exclaimed.   15

"What have you got to do with the levees?"

"I got enough to do! An' there's Bobinôt with Bibi out in that storm—if he only didn' left Friedheimer's!"

"Let us hope, Calixta, that Bobinôt's got sense enough to come in out of a cyclone."

She went and stood at the window with a greatly disturbed look on her face. She wiped the frame that was clouded with moisture. It was stiflingly hot. Alcée got up and joined her at the window, looking over her shoulder. The rain was coming down in sheets obscuring the view of far-off cabins and enveloping the distant wood in a gray mist. The playing of the lightning was incessant. A bolt struck a tall chinaberry tree at the edge of the field. It filled all visible space with a blinding glare and the crash seemed to invade the very boards they stood upon.

Calixta put her hands to her eyes, and with a cry, staggered backward.   20 Alcée's arm encircled her, and for an instant he drew her close and spasmodically to him.

"*Bonté!*"° she cried, releasing herself from his encircling arm and retreating from the window, "the house'll go next! If I only knew w'ere Bibi was!" She would not compose herself; she would not be seated. Alcée clasped her shoulders and looked into her face. The contact of her warm, palpitating body when he had unthinkingly drawn her into his arm, had aroused all the old-time infatuation and desire for her flesh.

"Calixta," he said, "don't be frightened. Nothing can happen. The house is too low to be struck, with so many tall trees standing about. There! aren't you going to be quiet? say, aren't you?" He pushed her hair back from her face that was warm and steaming. Her lips were as red and moist as pomegranate seed. Her white neck and a glimpse of her full, firm bosom disturbed him powerfully. As she glanced up at him the fear in her liquid blue eyes had given place to a drowsy gleam that unconsciously betrayed a sensuous desire. He looked down into her eyes and there was nothing for him to do but to gather her lips in a kiss. It reminded him of Assumption.

"Do you remember—in Assumption, Calixta?" he asked in a low voice broken by passion. Oh! she remembered; for in Assumption he had kissed her and kissed and kissed her; until his senses would well nigh fail, and to save her he would resort to a desperate flight. If she was not an immaculate dove in those days, she was still inviolate; a passionate creature whose very defenselessness had made her defense, against which his honor forbade him to prevail.

Dieu sait: God knows.   *Bonté*: Goodness.

Now—well, now—her lips seemed in a manner free to be tasted, as well as her round, white throat and her whiter breasts.

They did not heed the crashing torrents, and the roar of the elements made her laugh as she lay in his arms. She was a revelation in that dim, mysterious chamber; as white as the couch she lay upon. Her firm, elastic flesh that was knowing for the first time its birthright, was like a creamy lily that the sun invites to contribute its breath and perfume to the undying life of the world.

The generous abundance of her passion, without guile or trickery, was like a white flame which penetrated and found response in depths of his own sensuous nature that had never yet been reached.   25

When he touched her breasts they gave themselves up in quivering ecstasy, inviting his lips. Her mouth was a fountain of delight. And when he possessed her, they seemed to swoon together at the very borderland of life's mystery.

He stayed cushioned upon her, breathless, dazed, enervated, with his heart beating like a hammer upon her. With one hand she clasped his head, her lips lightly touching his forehead. The other hand stroked with a soothing rhythm his muscular shoulders.

The growl of the thunder was distant and passing away. The rain beat softly upon the shingles, inviting them to drowsiness and sleep. But they dared not yield.

The rain was over; and the sun was turning the glistening green world into a palace of gems. Calixta, on the gallery, watched Alcée ride away. He turned and smiled at her with a beaming face; and she lifted her pretty chin in the air and laughed aloud.

3

Bobinôt and Bibi, trudging home, stopped without at the cistern to make themselves presentable.   30

"My! Bibi, w'at will yo' mama say! You ought to be ashame'. You oughtn' put on those good pants. Look at 'em! An' that mud on yo' collar! How you got that mud on yo' collar, Bibi? I never saw such a boy!" Bibi was the picture of pathetic resignation. Bobinôt was the embodiment of serious solicitude as he strove to remove from his own person and his son's the signs of their tramp over heavy roads and through wet fields. He scraped the mud off Bibi's bare legs and feet with a stick and carefully removed all traces from his heavy brogans. Then, prepared for the worst—the meeting with an over-scrupulous housewife, they entered cautiously at the back door.

Calixta was preparing supper. She had set the table and was dripping coffee at the hearth. She sprang up as they came in.

"Oh, Bobinôt! You back! My! but I was uneasy. W'ere you been during the rain? An' Bibi? he ain't wet? he ain't hurt?" She had clasped Bibi and was kissing him effusively. Bobinôt's explanations and apologies which he had been composing all along the way, died on his lips as Calixta felt him to see if he were dry, and seemed to express nothing but satisfaction at their safe return.

"I brought you some shrimps, Calixta," offered Bobinôt, hauling the can from his ample side pocket and laying it on the table.

"Shrimps! Oh, Bobinôt! you too good fo' anything!" and she gave him a 35 smacking kiss on the cheek that resounded. *"J'vous réponds,°* we'll have a feas' to-night! umph-umph!"

Bobinôt and Bibi began to relax and enjoy themselves, and when the three seated themselves at table they laughed much and so loud that anyone might have heard them as far away as Laballière's.

4

Alcée Laballière wrote to his wife, Clarisse, that night. It was a loving letter, full of tender solicitude. He told her not to hurry back, but if she and the babies liked it at Biloxi, to stay a month longer. He was getting on nicely; and though he missed them, he was willing to bear the separation a while longer — realizing that their health and pleasure were the first things to be considered.

5

As for Clarisse, she was charmed upon receiving her husband's letter. She and the babies were doing well. The society was agreeable; many of her old friends and acquaintances were at the bay. And the first free breath since her marriage seemed to restore the pleasant liberty of her maiden days. Devoted as she was to her husband, their intimate conjugal life was something which she was more than willing to forego for a while.

So the storm passed and every one was happy. [1898]

J'vous réponds: I'm telling you.

≡ THINKING ABOUT THE TEXT

1. Does Calixta truly love Bobinôt? What explains the sudden passion of Calixta and Alcée? Are they in love?

2. Are you bothered by the happy ending? Are stories supposed to reinforce the dominant values of a society? What do you think would (or should) have happened in real life?

3. Can you recall other stories, novels, films, or television programs in which someone who is sexually transgressive is not punished?

4. Are the injured parties in this story really injured; that is, if they never find out, will they still suffer somehow?

5. Should extramarital affairs be illegal? Is Chopin suggesting that they are not so terrible, or is she simply saying something about passion?

KATE CHOPIN
The Story of an Hour

"The Story of an Hour" was first published in Bayou Folk *(1894). It is typical of Chopin's controversial works and caused a sensation among the reading public.*

Knowing that Mrs. Mallard was afflicted with a heart trouble, great care was taken to break to her as gently as possible the news of her husband's death.

It was her sister Josephine who told her, in broken sentences; veiled hints that revealed in half concealing. Her husband's friend Richards was there, too, near her. It was he who had been in the newspaper office when intelligence of the railroad disaster was received, with Brently Mallard's name leading the list of "killed." He had only taken the time to assure himself of its truth by a second telegram, and had hastened to forestall any less careful, less tender friend in bearing the sad message.

She did not hear the story as many women have heard the same, with a paralyzed inability to accept its significance. She wept at once, with sudden, wild abandonment, in her sister's arms. When the storm of grief had spent itself she went away to her room alone. She would have no one follow her.

There stood, facing the open window, a comfortable, roomy armchair. Into this she sank, pressed down by a physical exhaustion that haunted her body and seemed to reach into her soul.

She could see in the open square before her house the tops of trees that were all aquiver with the new spring life. The delicious breath of rain was in the air. In the street below a peddler was crying his wares. The notes of a distant song which some one was singing reached her faintly, and countless sparrows were twittering in the eaves. 5

There were patches of blue sky showing here and there through the clouds that had met and piled one above the other in the west facing her window.

She sat with her head thrown back upon the cushion of the chair, quite motionless, except when a sob came up into her throat and shook her, as a child who had cried itself to sleep continues to sob in its dreams.

She was young, with a fair, calm face, whose lines bespoke repression and even a certain strength. But now there was a dull stare in her eyes, whose gaze was fixed away off yonder on one of those patches of blue sky. It was not a glance of reflection, but rather indicated a suspension of intelligent thought.

There was something coming to her and she was waiting for it, fearfully. What was it? She did not know; it was too subtle and elusive to name. But she felt it, creeping out of the sky, reaching toward her through the sounds, the scents, the color that filled the air.

Now her bosom rose and fell tumultuously. She was beginning to recog- 10
nize this thing that was approaching to possess her, and she was striving to beat it back with her will—as powerless as her two white slender hands would have been.

When she abandoned herself a little whispered word escaped her slightly parted lips. She said it over and over under her breath: "free, free, free!" The vacant stare and the look of terror that had followed it went from her eyes. They stayed keen and bright. Her pulses beat fast, and the coursing blood warmed and relaxed every inch of her body.

She did not stop to ask if it were or were not a monstrous joy that held her. A clear and exalted perception enabled her to dismiss the suggestion as trivial.

She knew that she would weep again when she saw the kind, tender hands folded in death; the face that had never looked save with love upon her, fixed and gray and dead. But she saw beyond that bitter moment a long procession of years to come that would belong to her absolutely. And she opened and spread her arms out to them in welcome.

There would be no one to live for her during those coming years: she would live for herself. There would be no powerful will bending hers in that blind persistence with which men and women believe they have a right to impose a private will upon a fellow-creature. A kind intention or a cruel intention made the act seem no less a crime as she looked upon it in that brief moment of illumination.

And yet she had loved him—sometimes. Often she had not. What did it   15
matter! What could love, the unsolved mystery, count for in face of this possession of self-assertion which she suddenly recognized as the strongest impulse of her being!

"Free! Body and soul free!" she kept whispering.

Josephine was kneeling before the closed door with her lips to the keyhole, imploring for admission. "Louise, open the door! I beg; open the door—you will make yourself ill. What are you doing, Louise? For heaven's sake open the door."

"Go away. I am not making myself ill." No; she was drinking in a very elixir of life through that open window.

Her fancy was running riot along those days ahead of her. Spring days, and summer days, and all sorts of days that would be her own. She breathed a quick prayer that life might be long. It was only yesterday she had thought with a shudder that life might be long.

She arose at length and opened the door to her sister's importunities. There   20
was a feverish triumph in her eyes, and she carried herself unwittingly like a goddess of Victory. She clasped her sister's waist, and together they descended the stairs. Richards stood waiting for them at the bottom.

Some one was opening the front door with a latchkey. It was Brently Mallard who entered, a little travel-stained, composedly carrying his gripsack and umbrella. He had been far from the scene of accident, and did not even know there had been one. He stood amazed at Josephine's piercing cry; at Richards's quick motion to screen him from the view of his wife.

But Richards was too late.

When the doctors came they said she had died of heart disease—of joy that kills.

[1894]

≡ THINKING ABOUT THE TEXT

1. Is Louise Mallard really in love with her husband? Regardless of your answer, would she ever leave him? Is it possible to confuse love with duty?

2. Is it possible to assign blame for this tragedy? To Mr. Mallard? Mrs. Mallard? The culture?

3. Why did Chopin keep the story so brief? What would you like to know more about?

4. What specifically do you think Mrs. Mallard was thinking about in the room?

5. Do you think this situation was common during Chopin's time? Is it today?

≡ MAKING COMPARISONS

1. Compare Mrs. Mallard and Calixta. Do you think Mrs. Mallard would have an extramarital affair?

2. Is Chopin sympathetic to Mrs. Mallard and Calixta? Is she judgmental?

3. Calixta and Bobinôt seem to be on more equal terms than Mr. and Mrs. Mallard. Do you think this is the case? Explain why this might be so.

KATE CHOPIN
Désirée's Baby

"Désirée's Baby" was written in 1892 and published in Bayou Folk *(1894). The story reflects her experience among the French Creoles in Louisiana.*

As the day was pleasant, Madame Valmondé drove over to L'Abri to see Désirée and the baby.

It made her laugh to think of Désirée with a baby. Why, it seemed but yesterday that Désirée was little more than a baby herself; when Monsieur in riding through the gateway of Valmondé had found her lying asleep in the shadow of the big stone pillar.

The little one awoke in his arms and began to cry for "Dada." That was as much as she could do or say. Some people thought she might have strayed there of her own accord, for she was of the toddling age. The prevailing belief was that she had been purposely left by a party of Texans, whose canvas-covered wagon, late in the day, had crossed the ferry that Coton Maïs kept, just below the plantation. In time Madame Valmondé abandoned every speculation but the one that Désirée had been sent to her by a beneficent Providence to be the child of her affection, seeing that she was without child of the flesh. For the girl grew to be beautiful and gentle, affectionate and sincere,—the idol of Valmondé.

It was no wonder, when she stood one day against the stone pillar in whose shadow she had lain asleep, eighteen years before, that Armand Aubigny riding by and seeing her there, had fallen in love with her. That was the way all the Aubignys fell in love, as if struck by a pistol shot. The wonder was that he had not loved her before; for he had known her since his father brought him home from Paris, a boy of eight, after his mother died there. The passion that awoke in him that day, when he saw her at the gate, swept along like an avalanche, or like a prairie fire, or like anything that drives headlong over all obstacles.

Monsieur Valmondé grew practical and wanted things well considered: that is, the girl's obscure origin. Armand looked into her eyes and did not care. He was reminded that she was nameless. What did it matter about a name when he could give her one of the oldest and proudest in Louisiana? He ordered the *corbeille*° from Paris, and contained himself with what patience he could until it arrived; then they were married.

Madame Valmondé had not seen Désirée and the baby for four weeks. When she reached L'Abri she shuddered at the first sight of it, as she always did. It was a sad looking place, which for many years had not known the gentle presence of a mistress, old Monsieur Aubigny having married and buried his wife in France, and she having loved her own land too well ever to leave it. The roof came down steep and black like a cowl, reaching out beyond the wide galleries that encircled the yellow stuccoed house. Big, solemn oaks grew close to it, and their thick-leaved, far-reaching branches shadowed it like a pall. Young Aubigny's rule was a strict one, too, and under it his negroes had forgotten how to be gay, as they had been during the old master's easy-going and indulgent lifetime.

The young mother was recovering slowly, and lay full length, in her soft white muslins and laces, upon a couch. The baby was beside her, upon her arm, where he had fallen sleep, at her breast. The yellow nurse woman sat beside a window fanning herself.

Madame Valmondé bent her portly figure over Désirée and kissed her, holding her an instant tenderly in her arms. Then she turned to the child.

"This is not the baby!" she exclaimed, in startled tones. French was the language spoken at Valmondé in those days.

"I knew you would be astonished," laughed Désirée, "at the way he has grown. The little *cochon de lait*!° Look at his legs, mamma, and his hands and fingernails,—real fingernails. Zandrine had to cut them this morning. Isn't it true, Zandrine?"

The woman bowed her turbaned head majestically, "Mais si, Madame."

"And the way he cries," went on Désirée, "is deafening. Armand heard him the other day as far away as La Blanche's cabin."

Madame Valmondé had never removed her eyes from the child. She lifted it and walked with it over to the window that was lightest. She scanned the baby narrowly, then looked as searchingly at Zandrine, whose face was turned to gaze across the fields.

***corbeille*:** Double bed. ***cochon de lait*:** French for "suckling pig"; an endearment.

"Yes, the child has grown, has changed," said Madame Valmondé, slowly, as she replaced it beside its mother. "What does Armand say?"

Désirée's face became suffused with a glow that was happiness itself.   15

"Oh, Armand is the proudest father in the parish, I believe, chiefly because it is a boy, to bear his name; though he says not, — that he would have loved a girl as well. But I know it isn't true. I know he says that to please me. And mamma," she added, drawing Madame Valmondé's head down to her and speaking in a whisper, "he hasn't punished one of them — not one of them — since baby is born. Even Négrillon, who pretended to have burnt his leg that he might rest from work — he only laughed, and said Négrillon was a great scamp. Oh, mamma, I'm so happy; it frightens me."

What Désirée said was true. Marriage, and later the birth of his son had softened Armand Aubigny's imperious and exacting nature greatly. This was what made the gentle Désirée so happy, for she loved him desperately. When he frowned she trembled, but loved him. When he smiled, she asked no greater blessing of God. But Armand's dark, handsome face had not often been disfigured by frowns since the day he fell in love with her.

When the baby was about three months old, Désirée awoke one day to the conviction that there was something in the air menacing her peace. It was at first too subtle to grasp. It had only been a disquieting suggestion; an air of mystery among the blacks; unexpected visits from far-off neighbors who could hardly account for their coming. Then a strange, an awful change in her husband's manner, which she dared not ask him to explain. When he spoke to her, it was with averted eyes, from which the old love-light seemed to have gone out. He absented himself from home; and when there, avoided her presence and that of her child, without excuse. And the very spirit of Satan seemed suddenly to take hold of him in his dealings with the slaves. Désirée was miserable enough to die.

She sat in her room, one hot afternoon, in her *peignoir*, listlessly drawing through her fingers the strands of her long, silky brown hair that hung about her shoulders. The baby, half naked, lay asleep upon her own great mahogany bed, that was like a sumptuous throne, with its satin-lined half-canopy. One of La Blanche's little quadroon boys — half naked too — stood fanning the child slowly with a fan of peacock feathers. Désirée's eyes had been fixed absently and sadly upon the baby, while she was striving to penetrate the threatening mist that she felt closing about her. She looked from her child to the boy who stood beside him, and back again; over and over. "Ah!" It was a cry that she could not help; which she was not conscious of having uttered. The blood turned like ice in her veins, and a clammy moisture gathered upon her face.

She tried to speak to the little quadroon boy; but no sound would come, at   20
first. When he heard his name uttered, he looked up, and his mistress was pointing to the door. He laid aside the great, soft fan, and obediently stole away, over the polished floor, on his bare tiptoes.

She stayed motionless, with gaze riveted upon her child, and her face the picture of fright.

Presently her husband entered the room, and without noticing her, went to a table and began to search among some papers which covered it.

"Armand," she called to him, in a voice which must have stabbed him, if he was human. But he did not notice. "Armand," she said again. Then she rose and tottered towards him. "Armand," she panted once more, clutching his arm, "look at our child. What does it mean? tell me."

He coldly but gently loosened her fingers from about his arm and thrust the hand away from him. "Tell me what it means!" she cried despairingly.

"It means," he answered lightly, "that the child is not white; it means that you are not white." 25

A quick conception of all that this accusation meant for her nerved her with unwonted courage to deny it. "It is a lie; it is not true, I am white! Look at my hair, it is brown; and my eyes are gray, Armand, you know they are gray. And my skin is fair," seizing his wrist. "Look at my hand; whiter than yours, Armand," she laughed hysterically.

"As white as La Blanche's," he returned cruelly; and went away leaving her alone with their child.

When she could hold a pen in her hand, she sent a despairing letter to Madame Valmondé.

"My mother, they tell me I am not white. Armand has told me I am not white. For God's sake tell them it is not true. You must know it is not true. I shall die. I must die. I cannot be so unhappy, and live."

The answer that came was as brief: 30

"My own Désirée: Come home to Valmondé; back to your mother who loves you. Come with your child."

When the letter reached Désirée she went with it to her husband's study, and laid it open upon the desk before which he sat. She was like a stone image: silent, white, motionless after she placed it there.

In silence he ran his cold eyes over the written words. He said nothing. "Shall I go, Armand?" she asked in tones sharp with agonized suspense.

"Yes, go."

"Do you want me to go?" 35

"Yes, I want you to go."

He thought Almighty God had dealt cruelly and unjustly with him; and felt, somehow, that he was paying Him back in kind when he stabbed thus into his wife's soul. Moreover he no longer loved her, because of the unconscious injury she had brought upon his home and his name.

She turned away like one stunned by a blow, and walked slowly towards the door, hoping he would call her back.

"Good-by, Armand," she moaned.

He did not answer her. That was his last blow at fate. 40

Désirée went in search of her child. Zandrine was pacing the sombre gallery with it. She took the little one from the nurse's arms with no word of explanation, and descending the steps, walked away, under the live-oak branches.

It was an October afternoon; the sun was just sinking. Out in the still fields the negroes were picking cotton.

Désirée had not changed the thin white garment nor the slippers which she wore. Her hair was uncovered and the sun's rays brought a golden gleam from its brown meshes. She did not take the broad, beaten road which led to the far-off plantation of Valmondé. She walked across a deserted field, where the stubble bruised her tender feet, so delicately shod, and tore her thin gown to shreds.

She disappeared among the reeds and willows that grew thick along the banks of the deep, sluggish bayou; and she did not come back again.

Some weeks later there was a curious scene enacted at L'Abri. In the center of   45
the smoothly swept back yard was a great bonfire. Armand Aubigny sat in the wide hallway that commanded a view of the spectacle; and it was he who dealt out to a half dozen negroes the material which kept this fire ablaze.

A graceful cradle of willow, with all its dainty furbishings, was laid upon the pyre, which had already been fed with the richness of a priceless *layette*. Then there were silk gowns, and velvet and satin ones added to these; laces, too, and embroideries; bonnets and gloves; for the *corbeille* had been of rare quality.

The last thing to go was a tiny bundle of letters; innocent little scribblings that Désirée had sent to him during the days of their espousal. There was the remnant of one back in the drawer from which he took them. But it was not Désirée's; it was part of an old letter from his mother to his father. He read it. She was thanking God for the blessing of her husband's love: —

"But, above all," she wrote, "night and day, I thank the good God for having so arranged our lives that our dear Armand will never know that his mother, who adores him, belongs to the race that is cursed with the brand of slavery."

                                                                                        [1892]

≡ THINKING ABOUT THE TEXT

1. Does Armand really love Désirée? Explain.

2. Armand seems to have fallen in love "at first sight." Is this possible? Can love conquer all, even racial bias? Is Chopin skeptical?

3. What would you have done if you were Désirée? What will Armand do now that he knows his own racial background?

4. Are we able to break free of our cultural heritage? What are the ways society tries to keep us in line? How do some people break free? Is there a danger in disregarding societal norms? Are there benefits?

5. Could this story happen this way today?

≡ MAKING COMPARISONS

1. Which female character—Calixta, Louise, or Désirée—possesses true love for her husband? Do the husbands love their wives more? In different ways?

2. Which one of these marriages seems the strongest? Why?

3. Compare Chopin's attitude toward marriage in these three stories. Does she support all aspects of marriage? Since she wrote over a century ago, would she be pleased with the present state of marriage (including divorce)?

≡ WRITING ABOUT ISSUES

1. Which ending seems more ethically questionable? Write a brief position paper suggesting that one of Chopin's endings should be changed (or remain the same) for moral reasons before junior high students read it.

2. Compare Alcée and Armand. Write a brief justification for or refutation of the behavior of one of them.

3. Do you think Louise Mallard should have admitted her feelings for her husband and left him? Would you? Why?

4. Chopin's works shocked American audiences. Research the ways sex, love, and relationships were dealt with in the 1890s in America. Write a brief explanation of why Chopin was ahead of her time.

WILLIAM SHAKESPEARE, "Let me not to the marriage of true minds"

JOHN KEATS, "Bright Star"

EMILY DICKINSON, "Wild Nights — Wild Nights!"

EDNA ST. VINCENT MILLAY, "What Lips My Lips Have Kissed, and Where, and Why"

E. E. CUMMINGS, "somewhere i have never travelled"

WISLAWA SZYMBORSKA, "True Love"

MICHAEL S. HARPER, "Discovery"

Think about the term *true love*. Why *true*? Does *love* need this modification? Isn't love supposed to be true? Is there a *false* love? Or is something else implied that *love* doesn't convey by itself? Might it be something like *the one-and-only*? Some writers seem committed to the idea that true love lasts forever, for better or worse, regardless of circumstances. Is this just a fantasy, something we hope will be true? Or is it a reality, delivered to those who are lucky or who work hard to make it true? See if you agree with the seven poets in this cluster, some of whom are direct and clear about the possibilities of true love, while others take a more indirect, even playfully ironic tone.

■ BEFORE YOU READ

Do you believe there is one perfect person in the world for you? Is it possible to love someone forever, even if both of you change over the years from young adulthood to retirement and beyond?

WILLIAM SHAKESPEARE
Let me not to the marriage of true minds

William Shakespeare (1564–1616) is best known to modern readers as a dramatist; however, there is evidence that both he and his contemporaries valued his poetry above the plays. In 1598, for example, a writer praised Shakespeare's "sugared sonnets among his private friends." As with other aspects of his life and work, questions about how much autobiographical significance to attach to Shakespeare's subject matter continue to arise. Regardless of the discussion, there can be no doubt that the sonnets attributed to Shakespeare, at times directed to a man and at others directed to a woman, address the subject of love. Sonnet 116, which was written in 1609 and proposes a "marriage of true minds," is no exception.

Let me not to the marriage of true minds,
Admit impediments. Love is not love
Which alters when it alteration finds,
Or bends with the remover to remove:
Oh, no! it is an ever-fixèd mark,   5
That looks on tempests and is never shaken;
It is the star to every wandering bark,°   *small ship*
Whose worth's unknown, although his height be taken.
Love's not Time's fool, though rosy lips and cheeks
Within his bending sickle's compass come;   10
Love alters not with his brief hours and weeks,
But bears it out even to the edge of doom.
If this be error and upon me proved,
I never writ, nor no man ever loved.   *[1609]*

≡ **THINKING ABOUT THE TEXT**

1. Would you be pleased if your beloved wrote you this sonnet? Is he professing his love or giving a definition of true love as unchanging?

2. What if love didn't last "even to the edge of doom" (line 12)? Would it then be ordinary?

3. Shakespeare uses images to describe true love. Which one strikes you as apt? Can you suggest an image of your own?

4. The concluding couplet seems to be saying something like "I'm absolutely right." Do you think Shakespeare is? Can you think of a situation in which love should bend or alter?

5. The world seems to demonstrate that true love seldom lasts forever. Why then do writers of all kinds profess the opposite? If you really believe that true love does not exist, would you still marry? If your beloved asked you if your love would last forever, would you truthfully answer, "Only time will tell"?

JOHN KEATS
Bright Star

John Keats (1795–1821) was born into a working-class family. He hoped to be a physician but decided that poetry was his calling. His narrative poem Endymion *(1818) received poor reviews, but he was totally committed to his work. He was stricken with tuberculosis shortly after the poem's publication and went to Italy to recover. He died in Rome at age twenty-five.*

In 2009, Jane Campion directed Bright Star, *a film based on the last three years of Keats's life. The film focuses on his intense relationship with Fanny Brawne. Lines from many of his most famous poems are recited, including "La Belle Dame Sans Merci" and "Ode on Melancholy," as well as lines from his poetic letters to Fanny. On his tombstone is his own inscription: "Here lies one whose name was writ in water." Today Keats is considered one of literature's greatest poets.*

Bright star, would I were stedfast as thou art—
Not in lone splendour hung aloft the night
And watching, with eternal lids apart,
Like nature's patient, sleepless Eremite,
The moving waters at their priestlike task　　　　　　　　5
Of pure ablution round earth's human shores,
Or gazing on the new soft-fallen mask
Of snow upon the mountains and the moors—
No—yet still stedfast, still unchangeable,
Pillow'd upon my fair love's ripening breast,　　　　　　10
To feel for ever its soft fall and swell,
Awake for ever in a sweet unrest,
Still, still to hear her tender-taken breath,
And so live ever—or else swoon to death.　　　　　　　　*[1819]*

≡ THINKING ABOUT THE TEXT

1. Discuss how the speaker wants to be like the bright star in some ways, but not in others.

2. Is the speaker trying to stop time (as the pop star Jim Croce sang, "If I could save time in a bottle"), or is he hoping that his love will never change?

3. "Sweet unrest" (line 12) seems to be a contradiction. Is it? What is Keats trying to get at?

4. Is it psychologically healthy to want to have an unchanging love for someone forever? Is it realistic? Is it simply a kind of ritual to say such things?

5. Keats was quite sickly at the end of his short life. Do you think awareness of his serious illness influenced the theme of his poem?

≡ MAKING COMPARISONS

1. Compare the images of change that both Shakespeare and Keats use.

2. Compare Shakespeare's and Keats's use of the star metaphor.

3. Do both poets have similar notions of true love?

EMILY DICKINSON
Wild Nights—Wild Nights!

Emily Dickinson (1830–1886) spent most of her life in her father's house in Amherst, Massachusetts. Except for a year of college and several brief excursions to Philadelphia and Washington, D.C., Dickinson lived a quiet, reclusive life in a house she described as "pretty much all sobriety." Although a few poems were published during her lifetime, Dickinson wrote almost two thousand poems on love, death, immortality, and nature that are universally judged to be some of the most original, lyrical, and artistic works in American literature. Although the specific person to whom Dickinson wrote her love poems is unclear, many critics today believe her interests were both lesbian and heterosexual. As the poem below suggests, Dickinson, although outwardly retiring and isolated, lived a lively, rich, and passionate life in her poetry.

Wild Nights—Wild Nights!
Were I with thee
Wild Nights should be
Our luxury!

Futile—the Winds—   5
To a Heart in port—
Done with the Compass—
Done with the Chart!

Rowing in Eden—
Ah, the Sea!   10
Might I but moor—Tonight—
In Thee   [c. 1861]

≡ THINKING ABOUT THE TEXT

1. Many critics see this poem as an erotic fantasy, perhaps a surprising subject for a reclusive spinster. Are there indications that this is not a poem about a real sexual encounter?

2. Comment on the imagery of the ocean and port. Could the port be Dickinson's isolation? The ocean the actual consummation?

3. How do you read the speaker's claim that she is done with the compass and chart? Is she rejecting convention?

4. Comment on the images in the last stanza. Is the speaker suggesting that sex might bring her paradise on earth?

5. What does the image of "moor[ing] . . . In Thee" (lines 11–12) suggest about her erotic desire?

☰ MAKING COMPARISONS

1. Compare Dickinson's final stanza with the last six lines in Keats's poem.

2. Is Dickinson's poem more erotic than Shakespeare's or Keats's?

3. Compare Dickinson's phrase "a Heart in port" (line 6) to Shakespeare's line "That looks on tempests and is never shaken" (line 6).

EDNA ST. VINCENT MILLAY
What Lips My Lips Have Kissed, and Where, and Why

Edna St. Vincent Millay (1892–1950) was born in Rockland, Maine. Her mother encouraged her to be ambitious and self-sufficient and taught her about literature at an early age. On the strength of her early poems, Millay won a scholarship to Vassar, where she became a romantic legend for breaking the "hearts of half the undergraduate class." She also soon became wildly famous for her love poetry, giving readings in large auditoriums across the country, much like a contemporary rock star. She was openly bisexual, and her fame, talent, beauty, and bohemian aura was said to have driven her many admirers to distraction. A biography by Nancy Milford, Savage Beauty (2001), quotes from dozens of letters to Millay, whining, pleading, and groveling for her favors. Milford writes that "she gave the Jazz Age its lyric voice." In fact, we still use a phrase that Salon.com says Millay "invented to describe a life of impudent abandon":

> My candle burns at both ends;
>   It will not last the night;
> But oh, my foes, and oh, my friends—
>   It gives a lovely light!

Once called "the greatest female poet since Sappho," Millay's reputation in academic circles has fallen off somewhat. Perhaps her work seems a bit obvious compared to the cerebral and allusive free verse of poets like T. S. Eliot. But some critics still think of her as America's "most illustrious love poet." The title poem of Renascence and Other Poems *(1917) ranks as a landmark of modern literature, and the collection itself is ranked fifth on the New York Public Library's Books of the Century. The following poem is from* Collected Poems *(1956).*

What lips my lips have kissed, and where, and why,
I have forgotten, and what arms have lain
Under my head till morning; but the rain
Is full of ghosts tonight, that tap and sigh
Upon the glass and listen for reply,   5
And in my heart there stirs a quiet pain
For unremembered lads that not again

Will turn to me at midnight with a cry.
Thus in winter stands the lonely tree,
Nor knows what birds have vanished one by one,   10
Yet knows its boughs more silent than before:
I cannot say what loves have come and gone,
I only know that summer sang in me
A little while, that in me sings no more.   *[1923]*

≡ THINKING ABOUT THE TEXT

1. What is it the speaker misses if she can't remember who her lovers were?
2. What does Millay mean by "a quiet pain" (line 6)?
3. Is Millay the "lonely tree" in winter (line 9)? Does it surprise you that she was only thirty-one when she wrote this poem?
4. Do you read the last two lines as saying that the speaker is no longer in love?
5. How would you describe the tone of this poem? Is it wistful or nostalgic? Appropriate? Regretful or sentimental? Bittersweet or simply sad?

≡ MAKING COMPARISONS

1. Do you think Shakespeare and Keats would think of Millay's loves as "true"?
2. Compare the rhyme scheme of the sonnets by Shakespeare, Keats, and Millay.
3. Which of the four poems seems the most contemporary in its view of love?

E. E. CUMMINGS
somewhere i have never travelled

Edward Estlin Cummings (1894–1962) often experimented with language on every level, but he did not legally change his name to lowercase and preferred the usual uppercase. Born in Cambridge, Massachusetts, and educated at Harvard, he tried his hand at essays, plays, and other types of prose; in fact, it was a novel based on a World War I concentration camp experience in France, The Enormous Room *(1922), that first brought cummings attention. It is his poetry, however, that most readers immediately recognize for its eccentric use of typography and punctuation, its wordplay and slang usage, its jazz rhythms, and its childlike foregrounding of the concrete above the abstract. Cummings hated pretension and would agree to deliver the prestigious Eliot lectures at Harvard in 1953 only if they were called* nonlectures. *His two large volumes of* The Complete Poems, 1913–1962, *published in 1972, include humor, understated satire, and celebrations of love and sex.*

somewhere i have never travelled,gladly beyond
any experience,your eyes have their silence:
in your most frail gesture are things which enclose me,
or which i cannot touch because they are too near

your slightest look easily will unclose me   5
though i have closed myself as fingers,
you open always petal by petal myself as Spring opens
(touching skilfully,mysteriously)her first rose
or if your wish be to close me,i and
my life will shut very beautifully,suddenly,   10
as when the heart of this flower imagines
the snow carefully everywhere descending;

nothing which we are to perceive in this world equals
the power of your intense fragility:whose texture
compels me with the colour of its countries,   15
rendering death and forever with each breathing

(i do not know what it is about you that closes
and opens;only something in me understands
the voice of your eyes is deeper than all roses)
nobody,not even the rain,has such small hands   *[1931]*   20

≡ THINKING ABOUT THE TEXT

1. In your own words, what is cummings saying about the effect love has
   on him? Is this hyperbolic? Why?

2. Does love open us up? In what ways? Can you give a personal example
   of what a strong feeling did to you?

3. Is this a poem about love or obsession or romantic infatuation? What is
   the difference?

4. What do you think "the power of your intense fragility" (line 14) might
   mean? Is this a contradiction?

5. When cummings says "something in me understands" (line 18), what
   might he mean? Is love located inside us somewhere? In our hearts? Our
   brains?

≡ MAKING COMPARISONS

1. Is cummings's flower imagery more effective than the images that Shakespeare and Keats use?

2. Is this poem closer in theme to Keats's poem or to Millay's?

3. What do you imagine Shakespeare and Keats would think about cummings's sentence structure? His images?

WISLAWA SZYMBORSKA
True Love

Translated by Stanislaw Baránczak and Clare Cavanagh

Wislawa Szymborska (1923–2012) was born in Poland and lived in Krakow from 1931 until her death. She studied literature at Jagiellonian University and worked as a poetry editor for almost twenty years for a well-known literary journal in Krakow. She published sixteen collections of poetry, many of which have been widely translated, and won many prizes, including, most notably, the Nobel Prize for literature in 1996 "for poetry that with ironic precision allows the historical and biological context to come to light in fragments of human reality." Her collection Monologue of a Dog: New Poems *(2005) was called "elegiac, personal, and often profound." The following poem is from* View with a Grain of Sand *(1995).*

True love. Is it normal,
is it serious, is it practical?
What does the world get from two people
who exist in a world of their own?

Placed on the same pedestal for no good reason,   5
drawn randomly from millions, but convinced
it had to happen this way — in reward for what?
    For nothing.
The light descends from nowhere.
Why on these two and not on others?   10
Doesn't this outrage justice? Yes it does.
Doesn't it disrupt our painstakingly erected principles,
and cast the moral from the peak? Yes on both accounts.

Look at the happy couple.
Couldn't they at least try to hide it,   15
fake a little depression for their friends' sake!
Listen to them laughing — it's an insult.
The language they use — deceptively clear.
And their little celebrations, rituals,
the elaborate mutual routines —   20
it's obviously a plot behind the human race's back!

It's hard even to guess how far things might go
if people start to follow their example.
What could religion and poetry count on?
What would be remembered? What renounced?   25
Who'd want to stay within bounds?

True love. Is it really necessary?
Tact and common sense tell us to pass over it in silence,

like a scandal in Life's highest circles.
Perfectly good children are born without its help.   30
It couldn't populate the planet in a million years,
it comes along so rarely.

Let the people who never find true love
keep saying that there's no such thing.

Their faith will make it easier for them to live and die.   *[1972]*   35

≡ THINKING ABOUT THE TEXT

1. The tone of the poem seems to be crucial. Is Szymborska being ironic? Does it really matter to her if true love is practical?

2. Why does the poet ask a series of questions and then answer them? Would you have answered them in the same way she does?

3. Reading between the lines, what kind of behavior do those in "true love" exhibit? Is this true in your experience?

4. Can people just "follow their example" (line 23)? Is falling in love an act of will? Is it an accident? Does she really worry about "how far things might go" (line 22)?

5. How could this poem be seen as an argument against true love? As an argument for true love? Does the last line make you think the poet really does believe in true love? How would you explain the meaning of the last line?

≡ MAKING COMPARISONS

1. How might Shakespeare, Millay, and cummings respond to this poet's tone? Would they find it amusing? Annoying?

2. How might each of the poets respond to the question, Is true love necessary?

3. Which of these four poems is the most realistic? Which is the most idealistic?

MICHAEL S. HARPER
Discovery

Born in Brooklyn, New York, in 1951 to working-class parents, Michael S. Harper and his family soon moved to a predominantly white Los Angeles neighborhood. While attending college in Los Angeles, he worked as a postal worker, where he met educated black men like his father who came of age before the civil rights movement and had not been able to advance economically. Harper received an M.F.A. from the University of Iowa's creative writing program. His first book of poems, Dear John,

Dear Coltrane (1970), from which this selection is taken, was nominated for the National Book Award. He has received many writing awards, including a Guggenheim. Among his ten books of poetry are Songlines in Michaeltree: New and Collected Poems *(2000) and* Use Trouble *(2005). He is a professor of English at Brown University.*

We lay together, darkness all around,
I listen to her constant breath,
and when I thought she slept,
I too fell asleep.
But something stirred me, why I . . .   5
she was staring at me with her eyes,
her breasts still sturdy,
her thigh warming mine.
And I, a little shaken as she stroked
my skin and kissed my brow,   10
reached for the light turned on,
feeling for the heat which would
reveal how long she had looked
and cared.
The bulb was hot. It burned my hand.   *[1970]*   15

≡ THINKING ABOUT THE TEXT

1. The last sentence seems literal. But how might you read it metaphorically?

2. Why do you think Harper used the ellipsis in line 5? Is this an effective device, or should he have tried to say what the "something" was?

3. Why was the speaker "a little shaken" (line 9)? Would you feel that way in a similar situation, or would your response be something else? Surprise? Satisfaction?

4. Why did he want to know "how long she had looked / and cared" (lines 13–14)? Why might it matter to him? Would it to you?

5. Would you interpret the staring as evidence of true love? Would you interpret the speaker's behavior as true love or something else?

≡ MAKING COMPARISONS

1. Does the behavior of the woman in this poem correspond to any of the definitions of true love in the other poems?

2. Compare line 4 of e. e. cummings's poem to the response of the narrator in Harper's poem.

3. Which of the poems come closest to your idea of what true love is? Why?

≡ **WRITING ABOUT ISSUES**

1. Translate the cummings poem into concrete prose. Try not to use images; just explain the individual lines as simply as you can.

2. Write a comparison of the effects these seven poems had on you.

3. Write a position paper arguing for or against the reality of true love. Make reference to three of the poems given here.

4. Find three more love poems by Emily Dickinson or Edna St. Vincent Millay and write a report about the issues of love that this poet raises.

■ A Seductive Argument: Re-Visions of a Poem

ANDREW MARVELL, "To His Coy Mistress"

PETER DE VRIES, "To His Importunate Mistress"

T. S. ELIOT, "The Love Song of J. Alfred Prufrock"

Most poets are influenced by their predecessors, especially by the great canonical poets of the past. Sometimes they try to imitate the language of the great masters; sometimes, according to the critic Harold Bloom in *The Anxiety of Influence,* they misread famous poets on purpose, hoping to carve out a unique niche for themselves. But sometimes poets write parodies of well-known poems, much like Anthony Hecht's "The Dover Bitch," an amusing parody of Matthew Arnold's "Dover Beach." Parodies often make fun of the themes and language (William Carlos Williams's poem "This Is Just to Say" has been a target dozens of times), but Peter De Vries's "To His Importunate Mistress" is a more gentle parody of Andrew Marvell's "To His Coy Mistress," often cited as the greatest of the *carpe diem* poems of the seventeenth century. Marvell's work is frequently seen as a seduction poem, reflective of the attitudes of a privileged male of that time. In this context, his sexual proposal would be filled with danger since unmarried women of the time were expected to be virgins. If they weren't virgins, their marriage prospects would be severely diminished. And there were few other options for young women of that era. Although his seductive argument is not actually logical, readers have enjoyed his language and the emotions involved. De Vries updates the poem by having the male narrator reject the advances of a woman. He seems to be not so much poking fun at Marvell's poem as amusingly continuing a poetic tradition that is centuries old.

We also include here one of the most famous poems of the twentieth century, "The Love Song of J. Alfred Prufrock," not because it directly alludes to Marvell but because Prufrock's journey is often viewed as an attempt to either propose marriage or engage in a seduction. But Prufrock vacillates so much and is so uncertain about love and seems so fearful and so anxious that we wonder if he is up to the task. Prufrock is often seen as a modern antihero who reflects our own doubts and lack of self-esteem about love. Prufrock seems alienated in a meaningless world and as such is surely an ironic modern counterpoint to the confident and heedless narrator of Marvell's poem.

■ BEFORE YOU READ

Are seduction poems (or songs or letters) effective? Is such an offer more effectively made in person? What would the difference be? Could you say some things in a letter, say, that you couldn't (or wouldn't) say in person?

ANDREW MARVELL
To His Coy Mistress

Andrew Marvell (1621–1678) was famous in his own time as an adroit politician and a writer of satire, but modern readers admire him for the style and content of his lyric, metaphysical poetry. Born into a Protestant family, Marvell was tolerant of Catholicism from a young age, and his willingness to somehow circumvent the religious prejudices of seventeenth-century England allowed his continued success. He traveled to Holland, France, Italy, and Spain—possibly to avoid the English civil war as a young man and undoubtedly to spy for England in later years. He tutored Cromwell's ward and later served on his Council of State but was influential enough during the Restoration to get his fellow poet and mentor, John Milton, released from prison. Although admired by the Romantic poets of the early nineteenth century, Marvell's poetry (much of it published after his death) was revived in the twentieth century by T. S. Eliot and has been widely read for its ironic approach to the conventions of love.

Had we but world enough, and time,
This coyness, lady, were no crime.
We would sit down, and think which way
To walk, and pass our long love's day.
Thou by the Indian Ganges'° side   5
Shouldst rubies find; I by the tide
Of Humber° would complain.° I would
Love you ten years before the Flood,
And you should, if you please, refuse
Till the conversion of the Jews.   10
My vegetable love should grow°
Vaster than empires, and more slow;
An hundred years should go to praise
Thine eyes and on thy forehead gaze,
Two hundred to adore each breast,   15
But thirty thousand to the rest:
An age at least to every part,
And the last age should show your heart.
For, lady, you deserve this state,
Nor would I love at lower rate.   20
    But at my back I always hear
Time's wingèd chariot hurrying near;
And yonder all before us lie
Deserts of vast eternity.
Thy beauty shall no more be found,   25

---

5 Ganges: A river in India sacred to the Hindus.   **7 Humber:** An estuary that flows through Marvell's native town, Hull.   **complain:** Sing love songs.   **11 My vegetable love . . . grow:** A slow, insensible growth, like that of a vegetable.

(Photo by Archive
Photos/Getty Images.)

Nor in thy marble vault shall sound
My echoing song; then worms shall try
That long preserved virginity,
And your quaint honor turn to dust,
And into ashes all my lust.   30
The grave's a fine and private place,
But none, I think, do there embrace.
    Now, therefore, while the youthful hue
Sits on thy skin like morning dew,
And while thy willing soul transpires°   35
At every pore with instant fires,
Now let us sport us while we may,

35 transpires: Breathes forth.

And now, like amorous birds of prey,
Rather at once our time devour
Than languish in his slow-chapped° power.   40
Let us roll all our strength and all
Our sweetness up into one ball,
And tear our pleasures with rough strife
Thorough° the iron gates of life.
Thus, though we cannot make our sun   45
Stand still, yet we will make him run.   *[1681]*

40 slow-chapped: Slow-jawed.   **44 Thorough:** Through.

≡ THINKING ABOUT THE TEXT

1. Considered as both an intellectual and an emotional argument, what is the narrator's goal, and what specific claims does he make? Are they convincing? Do you think they were in 1681? Do you think women three hundred years ago worried about virginity? Why?

2. What does this poem say about the needs of Marvell's audience? What assumptions about women does the poem make?

3. How many sections does this poem have? What is the purpose of each? How is the concluding couplet in each related to that section? Is the rhyme scheme related to the meaning of these couplets?

4. Is the speaker passionate? Sincere? How do you make such a decision? Do you look at his language or at his message?

5. Some feminist readers see in the last ten lines a kind of indirect threat, a suggestion of force through the use of violent images. Is this a plausible reading? If this is the case, what do you now think of the narrator's pleading?

PETER DE VRIES
To His Importunate Mistress

Peter De Vries (1910–1993) was born in Chicago and graduated from Calvin College in 1931. Sometimes described as our "national humorist laureate," De Vries is noted for his satiric jabs at our culture's shortcomings. He began a long-lasting career with The New Yorker *magazine in 1944 and over the years contributed numerous short stories and poems. Because of his wit, irony, and inspired wordplay, his novels are often compared to such critically acclaimed humorists as Evelyn Waugh and P. G. Wodehouse. Most of his novels and poems deal with marriage and its problems and delights. A line from* Tents of Wickedness *(1959) from a character who refuses an affair is seen as typical of De Vries's wry style: "Thanks just the same . . . but I don't*

(Photo by Bernard
Gotfryd/Getty Images.

want any pleasures interfering with my happiness." His most famous novel, The
Blood of the Lamb *(1961), was brought back into print in 2005.*

Had we but world enough, and time,
My coyness, lady, were a crime,
But at my back I always hear
Time's winged chariot, striking fear
The hour is nigh when creditors   5
Will prove to be my predators.
As wages of our picaresque,
Bag lunches bolted at my desk
Must stand as fealty to you
For each expensive rendezvous.   10
Obeisance at your marble feet
Deserves the best-appointed suite,

And would have, lacked I not the pelf°   *money*
To pleasure also thus myself;
But amply sumptuous amorous scenes   15
Rule out the rake of modest means.

Since mistress presupposes wife,
It means a doubly costly life;
For fools by second passion fired
A second income is required,   20
The earning which consumes the hours
They'd hoped to spend in rented bowers.
To hostelries the worst of fates
That weekly raise their daily rates!
I gather, lady, from your scoffing   25
A bloke more solvent in the offing.
So revels thus to rivals go
For want of monetary flow.
How vexing that inconsistent cash
The constant suitor must abash,   30
Who with excuses vainly pled
Must rue the undishevelled bed,
And that for paltry reasons given
His conscience may remain unriven.   *[1986]*

☰ THINKING ABOUT THE TEXT

1. Morality doesn't seem to be a major factor in the narrator's apparent rejection of his demanding mistress. What is his main reason?

2. The narrator claims he is being coy, but presumably only because they don't have "world enough, and time" (line 1). What do you think he means?

3. Formulate this poetic argument into simple straightforward prose. What is gained and lost in this translation?

4. Apparently his mistress is "scoffing" (line 25) at his perhaps overly practical reasoning. Would you? Would most people? Do you think this is his real reason or just an excuse?

5. Although he claims to be remorseful for "the undishevelled bed" (line 32), he says that his reasons are paltry. Does he really think so? Since he never mentions ethical concerns, why should his conscience be of any concern to him?

☰ MAKING COMPARISONS

1. Compare the meaning of the opening two lines of each poem.

2. Marvell's argument seems more complicated and serious than De Vries's. Is this your interpretation? Why? Is De Vries's argument really serious?

What about such rhymes as "creditors" and "predators," "pelf" and "myself," "cash" and "abash"? Do they suggest a tongue-in-cheek tone?

3. What would a contemporary woman make of Marvell's seduction argument? Would De Vries's argument have been effective in Marvell's age?

T. S. ELIOT
The Love Song of J. Alfred Prufrock

One of the most respected intellectuals of his time, Thomas Stearns Eliot (1888–1965) was a poet, playwright (Murder in the Cathedral), *and critic* (The Sacred Wood). *His poem "The Waste Land" (1922), considered a modernist masterpiece, is perhaps the last century's most influential poem. The long-running Broadway play* Cats *is based on some of Eliot's lighter poems. Born in America and educated at Harvard, Eliot lived his mature life in England. He was awarded the Nobel Prize for literature in 1948.*

> *S'io credesse che mia risposta fosse*
> *A persona che mai tornasse al mondo,*
> *Questa fiamma staria senza più scosse.*
> *Ma perciocchè giammai di questo fondo*
> *Non tornò vivo alcun, s'i'odo il vero,*
> *Senza tema d'infamia ti rispondo.*°

Let us go then, you and I,
When the evening is spread out against the sky
Like a patient etherized upon a table;
Let us go, through certain half-deserted streets,
The muttering retreats   5
Of restless nights in one-night cheap hotels
And sawdust restaurants with oyster-shells:
Streets that follow like a tedious argument
Of insidious intent

To lead you to an overwhelming question . . .   10
Oh, do not ask, "What is it?"
Let us go and make our visit.

In the room the women come and go
Talking of Michelangelo.

The yellow fog that rubs its back upon the window panes,   15
The yellow smoke that rubs its muzzle on the window panes

EPIGRAPH: **S'io . . . rispondo:** In Dante's *Inferno*, a sufferer in hell says, "If I thought I was talking to someone who might return to earth, this flame would cease; but if what I have heard is true, no one does return; therefore, I can speak to you without fear of infamy."

(Photo by E. O. Hoppe/
Mansell/Time Life
Pictures/Getty Images.)

Licked its tongue into the corners of the evening,
Lingered upon the pools that stand in drains,
Let fall upon its back the soot that falls from chimneys,
Slipped by the terrace, made a sudden leap,   20
And seeing that it was a soft October night,
Curled once about the house, and fell asleep.

        And indeed there will be time°
For the yellow smoke that slides along the street,
Rubbing its back upon the window panes;   25
There will be time, there will be time
To prepare a face to meet the faces that you meet;
There will be time to murder and create,
And time for all the works and days° of hands

23 there will be time: An allusion to Ecclesiastes 3:1–8: "To everything there is a season, and a time to every purpose under heaven." **29 works and days:** Hesiod's eighth-century B.C.E. poem gave practical advice.

That lift and drop a question on your plate: 30
Time for you and time for me,
And time yet for a hundred indecisions,
And for a hundred visions and revisions,
Before the taking of a toast and tea.
In the room the women come and go   35
Talking of Michelangelo.
    And indeed there will be time
To wonder, "Do I dare?" and, "Do I dare?" —
Time to turn back and descend the stair,
With a bald spot in the middle of my hair —   40
(They will say: "How his hair is growing thin!")
My morning coat, my collar mounting firmly to the chin,
My necktie rich and modest, but asserted by a simple pin —
(They will say: "But how his arms and legs are thin!")
Do I dare   45
Disturb the universe?
In a minute there is time
For decisions and revisions which a minute will reverse.

    For I have known them all already, known them all:
Have known the evenings, mornings, afternoons,   50
I have measured out my life with coffee spoons;
I know the voices dying with a dying fall
Beneath the music from a farther room.
    So how should I presume?

    And I have known the eyes already, known them all —   55
The eyes that fix you in a formulated phrase.
And when I am formulated, sprawling on a pin,
When I am pinned and wriggling on the wall,
Then how should I begin
To spit out all the butt-ends of my days and ways?   60
    And how should I presume?

    And I have known the arms already, known them all —
Arms that are braceleted and white and bare
(But in the lamplight, downed with light brown hair!)
    Is it perfume from a dress   65
    That makes me so digress?
Arms that lie along a table, or wrap about a shawl.
    And should I then presume?
    And how should I begin?

    Shall I say, I have gone at dusk through narrow streets,   70
And watched the smoke that rises from the pipes
Of lonely men in shirtsleeves, leaning out of windows? . . .

I should have been a pair of ragged claws
Scuttling across the floors of silent seas.

And the afternoon, the evening, sleeps so peacefully!   75
Smoothed by long fingers,
Asleep . . . tired . . . or it malingers,
Stretched on the floor, here beside you and me.
Should I, after tea and cakes and ices,
Have the strength to force the moment to its crisis?   80
But though I have wept and fasted, wept and prayed,
Though I have seen my head (grown slightly bald) brought in upon a
    platter,°
I am no prophet — and here's no great matter;
I have seen the moment of my greatness flicker,
And I have seen the eternal Footman hold my coat, and snicker,   85
    And in short, I was afraid.

And would it have been worth it, after all,
After the cups, the marmalade, the tea,
Among the porcelain, among some talk of you and me,
Would it have been worth while   90
To have bitten off the matter with a smile,
To have squeezed the universe into a ball°
To roll it toward some overwhelming question,
To say: "I am Lazarus,° come from the dead,
Come back to tell you all, I shall tell you all" —   95
If one, settling a pillow by her head,
    Should say: "That is not what I meant at all;
    That is not it, at all."

And would it have been worth it, after all,
Would it have been worth while,   100
After the sunsets and the dooryards and the sprinkled streets,
After the novels, after the teacups, after the skirts that trail along the
    floor —
And this, and so much more? —
It is impossible to say just what I mean!
But as if a magic lantern° threw the nerves in patterns on a screen: 105
Would it have been worth while
If one, settling a pillow or throwing off a shawl,
And turning toward the window, should say:
    "That is not it at all,
    That is not what I meant, at all."   110

82 head . . . platter: Like John the Baptist (Matt. 14:1–12).   **92 squeezed . . . ball:** See
lines 41–42 of Marvell's "To His Coy Mistress" (p. 450).   **94 "I am Lazarus":** Raised from
the dead by Jesus.   **105 magic lantern:** Precursor of the slide projector.

No! I am not Prince Hamlet, nor was meant to be;
Am an attendant lord,° one that will do
To swell a progress,° start a scene or two
Advise the prince: withal, an easy tool,
Deferential, glad to be of use,   115
Politic, cautious, and meticulous;
Full of high sentence, but a bit obtuse;
At times, indeed, almost ridiculous —
Almost, at times, the Fool.
I grow old . . . I grow old . . .   120
I shall wear the bottoms of my trowsers rolled.

   Shall I part my hair behind?° Do I dare to eat a peach?°
I shall wear white flannel trowsers, and walk upon the beach.
I have heard the mermaids singing, each to each.

I do not think that they will sing to me.   125

I have seen them riding seaward on the waves,
Combing the white hair of the waves blown back
When the wind blows the water white and black.

We have lingered in the chambers of the sea
By seagirls wreathed with seaweed red and brown,   130
Till human voices wake us, and we drown.   *[1917]*

≣ THINKING ABOUT THE TEXT

1. Do you think Prufrock is on a journey to propose marriage, to have a sexual rendezvous, or to do something else?

2. Is Prufrock enchanted with women (lines 62–67) or wary of them (lines 55–61)? What other lines might help to answer this question?

3. How do you interpret the questions "Do I dare" (lines 38, 45), "So how should I presume?" (line 54), "And how should I begin?" (line 69)?

4. How old do you think Prufrock is? Can you cite some evidence in the text? How might his age (young man? middle-aged man?) be a factor in the purpose for his journey toward marriage, casual sex, or something else?

5. Why do you think Prufrock ends his poem with fantasies about mermaids? Do you read this as an admission of failure?

---

112 attendant lord: Like Polonius in Shakespeare's *Hamlet.*   **113 progress:** State procession.   **121–22 trowsers rolled . . . part my hair behind:** The latest fashion; **eat a peach:** Considered a risky fruit.

≡ **MAKING COMPARISONS**

1. In what ways is Eliot's poem closer to De Vries's than to Marvell's?
2. How does the idea of conscience figure into these three poems?
3. What do you think Marvell would make of De Vries's parody and Eliot's reluctant narrator?

≡ **WRITING ABOUT ISSUES**

1. Argue that Prufrock does or does not represent contemporary concerns about romantic relationships.
2. Write a letter to Marvell explaining why contemporary readers of his poem might find his proposal objectionable.
3. Write a letter to Prufrock explaining why you think his attitude toward love is either accurate or ill founded.
4. Argue that contemporary social networks like Facebook and Twitter make verbal seduction easier or more difficult.

MATTHEW ARNOLD, "Dover Beach"

SUSAN MINOT, "My Husband's Back"

Part of our cultural narrative about romance—circulating for centuries in novels, poems, and films—is that love will save us from the disappointments and frustrations of the world. If our society sometimes seems cruel or unfair, if our jobs are tedious, if the economy fails, if war, injustice, and racism persist, we can always find solace in the arms of our beloved. It is here in a loving relationship that one can escape the world's duplicity, finding instead loyalty, acceptance, intimacy, and comfort. It is a popular and widespread scenario. Is romantic love enough to keep the world at bay? Can it help us suffer, with Hamlet, the "slings and arrows of outrageous fortune" or endure "the heart-ache and the thousand natural shocks that flesh is heir to"? Is that perhaps putting too much pressure on romance?

Both poems in this cluster seem to have a fairly dark view of existence, although Minot's woes are more domestic frustrations than Arnold's cosmic angst. Arnold's famous concluding stanza employs the chilling metaphor "Where ignorant armies clash by night" to characterize his pessimistic view of life. Minot begins more locally: "Sunday evening. / Breakdown hour." Both poets are filled with gloomy thoughts, and both hope love will cure what ails them.

≡ BEFORE YOU READ

Do you expect love to be a buffer against the world? To protect you from life's disappointments?

MATTHEW ARNOLD
Dover Beach

Victorian poet Matthew Arnold (1822–1889) was the eldest son of Thomas Arnold, an influential clergyman and historian and headmaster of Rugby, one of England's most prestigious college preparatory schools. He grew up in an educational milieu in which religious, political, and social issues were discussed in depth. He went on to Oxford, where he eventually achieved success despite his irreverence and eccentricity. In 1851, he became an inspector of schools and served in this capacity for thirty-five years. He drew on his experiences with people of diverse social classes to become a keen critic of British education and culture, and he expressed his views of society in critical essays on literary, social, and religious issues as well as in poems. Living during an age in which Charles Darwin published On the Origin of Species *(1859) and religious dogma was being questioned in many ways, Arnold suggests in "Dover Beach" that human love becomes especially important in such a world. The poem may have been written during the months just before or just after Arnold's marriage and honeymoon, which included a ferry ride from Dover, England, to Calais, France.*

The sea is calm tonight.
The tide is full, the moon lies fair
Upon the straits;—on the French coast the light
Gleams and is gone; the cliffs of England stand,
Glimmering and vast, out in the tranquil bay.   5
Come to the window, sweet is the night-air!
Only, from the long line of spray
Where the sea meets the moon-blanched land,
Listen! you hear the grating roar
Of pebbles which the waves draw back, and fling,   10
At their return, up the high strand,
Begin, and cease, and then again begin,
With tremulous cadence slow, and bring
The eternal note of sadness in.

Sophocles long ago   15
Heard it on the Aegean, and it brought
Into his mind the turbid ebb and flow
Of human misery;° we
Find also in the sound a thought,
Hearing it by this distant northern sea.   20

The Sea of Faith
Was once, too, at the full, and round earth's shore
Lay like the folds of a bright girdle furled.
But now I only hear
Its melancholy, long, withdrawing roar,   25
Retreating, to the breath
Of the night-wind, down the vast edges drear
And naked shingles° of the world.

Ah, love, let us be true
To one another! for the world, which seems   30
To lie before us like a land of dreams,
So various, so beautiful, so new,
Hath really neither joy, nor love, nor light,
Nor certitude, nor peace, nor help for pain;
And we are here as on a darkling plain   35
Swept with confused alarms of struggle and flight,
Where ignorant armies clash by night.   *[1867]*

15–18 Sophocles . . . misery: In *Antigone*, Sophocles compares the disasters that beset the house of Oedipus to a mounting tide.   **28 shingles:** Pebble beach.

≣ THINKING ABOUT THE TEXT

1. In trying to re-create this scene — say, for a movie script — what would you have the lovers look like? Where would the couple be positioned? If you were the director, how would you explain the scene to the actors — that is, what is the speaker saying? Put another way, what argument is being made?

2. Arnold uses the sea as a metaphor. What do you think it represents? What other metaphors and similes are used? Are they effective in making his point?

3. Some feminist readers see this poem as yet another example of a man who hopes to escape temporarily from the troubles of the world by finding comfort and support from a woman. Is there some validity to this point? Why, for example, doesn't the woman speak?

4. In the film *The Anniversary Party*, Kevin Kline's character reads the last stanza of this poem to a couple celebrating their sixth wedding anniversary. Some critics saw it as an ironic joke, others as a parody of a "sweet" love poem. What is it about the poem that seems to make it inappropriate for such an occasion? Would you send it to your beloved? Why, or why not?

5. What specific reasons does the speaker give for the lovers to be true to each other, beginning with "for the world" (line 30)? Is this an attitude you share? Do you know others who agree? Is this an extreme position? What would the opposite view be? Is this extreme, as well?

SUSAN MINOT
My Husband's Back

Susan Minot (b. 1956) was born in Boston and grew up in Manchester-by-the-Sea, Massachusetts. She studied writing and painting at Brown University and received an M.F.A. from Columbia University. Minot was an editor of the literary journal Grant Street. *Her first book,* Monkeys *(1986), is a collection of nine stories about a large New England family. Minot's female protagonists are searching for love, usually unsuccessfully. Her best-selling collection* Lust and Other Stories *(1989) focuses on romantic love, although one critic cautions readers not to "look for a happy, mutual, heterosexual relationship in Minot. You will not find it." Her novel* Evening *(1998) was made into a popular film in 2007 starring Vanessa Redgrave, Meryl Streep, and Claire Danes. A volume of her verse,* Poems 4am, *was published in 2002. The women in these poems seem more optimistic about love than do those in her fiction.*

Sunday evening.
Breakdown hour. Weeping into
a pot of burnt rice. Sun dimmed

like a light bulb gone out
behind a gray lawn of snow.   5
The baby flushed with the flu
asleep on a pillow.
The fire won't catch.
The wet wood's caked
with ice. Sitting   10
on the couch my spine
collides with all its bones
and I watch my husband
peer past the glass grate
and blow.   15
His back in a snug plaid shirt
gray and white
leaning into the woodstove
is firm and compact
like a young man's back.   20

And the giant world which swirls
in my head
stopping most thought
suddenly ceases
to spin. It sits   25
right there, the back I love,
animal and gamine,° leaning
on one arm.
I could crawl on it forever
the one point in the world   30
turns out
I have traveled everywhere
to get to.   *[2005]*

gamine: Untamed and mischievous.

≣ THINKING ABOUT THE TEXT

1. Why is the speaker "Weeping" (line 2)? Is she unhappy? Frustrated? Overwhelmed?

2. Why does "the giant world" (line 21) cease to spin?

3. What do you think the speaker means in the last two lines when she says she has "traveled everywhere / to get to" (lines 32–33)?

4. Do you think being in love can help a person deal with global tragedies? Domestic frustration? Cosmic gloom?

5. Do you think Minot's feelings of love are momentary, caused by the "Breakdown hour"?

≣ MAKING COMPARISONS

1. Would you agree with some critics who see the speakers in these two poems as stereotypically male and female? Why?

2. Does Minot seem more in love than Arnold? Is Arnold declaring his love or his loyalty?

3. Is it dangerous to put too many expectations on love? Do these poets?

≣ WRITING ABOUT ISSUES

1. Argue that Arnold's last stanza is or is not an appropriate metaphor for contemporary life.

2. The poet Percy Bysshe Shelley noted that our "sweetest songs are of saddest thought," perhaps commenting on the often melancholy nature of some of our best literature. Argue that this is or is not the case with these two poems. Try to include other favorite texts as examples to support your claim.

3. Argue that people put too much or too little emphasis on love in their lives. Use the works of Arnold and Minot or other poets or songwriters as part of your support.

4. Do you think that one's outlook on life is directly related to age? Do middle-aged writers tend to have a darker vision and younger writers a sunnier perspective? You might examine several early and recent songs by well-established singers or bands that you know and like. Write a report in which you compare the early songs with the later songs and also analyze these songs as either typical or atypical of youth's optimistic view of life.

■ Mourning a Loved One: Poems

W. H. AUDEN, "Funeral Blues"

THEODORE ROETHKE, "Elegy for Jane"

ANNE SEXTON, "Sylvia's Death"

Public and private ways of articulating grief are, of course, historically ancient and diverse. Naturally, tears and cries of lamentation are universal and understandable when expressing grief for the loss of a loved one. But our culture has evolved more stylized and ceremonial ways of mourning. Over the centuries, priests and poets have turned our deepest feelings into words that express personal and communal sorrow. The elegy is perhaps the oldest and most common poetic form used for mourning. From the Middle Ages to the present, poetry written in English has lamented the inevitable loss that is our shared destiny. Some of these poems are among the greatest lyrics ever written. John Milton's "Lycidas," Percy Bysshe Shelley's "Adonaïs," and Walt Whitman's "When Lilacs Last in the Dooryard Bloom'd" are beloved classics that have given private consolation to generations of mourners.

In our own time, technological innovations have allowed millions to participate in the ritual of bereavement. When Diana, Princess of Wales, died in 1997, millions participated by leaving flowers and scrawling messages in cities all over the world. Songs were sung and poems written, but mostly people shared their grief by leaving tributes at impromptu funeral sites. Today those sites would be on the Internet and most probably on Facebook. For several years, people have been leaving comments on Web sites devoted to elegies, but the recent explosion of memorials on Facebook is a significant evolutionary step in the process of public mourning.

On various Web sites for W. H. Auden's "Funeral Blues," people have posted their tributes to friends and relatives, noting that they read the poem at a beloved one's funeral. Ironically, Auden's poem is technically not an elegy because the poem was written not for the deceased but for a lover who left him. But for generations, people have found in the poem a perfect form for their sadness and despair, and so it has become, along with Elton John's song "Candle in the Wind," the most embraced elegy of our time. And ever since it was read in the popular film *Four Weddings and a Funeral*, "Funeral Blues" has taken on iconic status.

We present Auden's poem along with Theodore Roethke's classic lament for one of his students and Anne Sexton's elegy for her friend and fellow poet Sylvia Plath. Today the suicide of such a beloved and famous poet as Plath would elicit thousands of comments online, especially with the phenomenal growth of Facebook memorials. While this new idea is constantly evolving, it seems a contemporary development that will last.

≡ BEFORE YOU READ

How might communicating grief help people cope? Is there a difference between writing a poem, which could be private or public, and joining a community of mourners in a support group or on Facebook? In what other ways do people grieve? How do you prefer to mourn?

W. H. AUDEN
Funeral Blues

Wystan Hugh Auden (1907–1973) was born in England and is widely regarded as the finest English poet of the twentieth century. Yet he moved to the United States in 1939, became an American citizen, and spent his remaining years living alternately in this country and in Austria. Auden's reputation as a poet soared in the 1930s, especially with the publication of his second book, Poems *(1930). In this period of his career, he was much influenced by psychoanalysis and Marxism. During the late 1930s, his leftist sympathies led him to join what was ultimately a losing cause, the fight against Fascist rebels in Spain. The following poem has several titles and versions, including "Stop All the Clocks" and a text with five stanzas. Auden intended this poem to be sung by the soprano Hedli Anderson, but the lyric has taken on a life of its own and has evolved into perhaps the most frequently read elegy at funerals in English-speaking countries. From the innumerable postings online, it is clear that it beautifully and lucidly describes our deep sense of loss at the death of a loved one.*

Stop all the clocks, cut off the telephone.
Prevent the dog from barking with a juicy bone,
Silence the pianos and with muffled drum
Bring out the coffin, let the mourners come.

Let aeroplanes circle moaning overhead   5
Scribbling in the sky the message He is Dead,
Put crêpe bows round the white necks of the public doves,
Let the traffic policemen wear black cotton gloves.

He was my North, my South, my East and West,
My working week and my Sunday rest   10
My noon, my midnight, my talk, my song;
I thought that love would last forever, I was wrong.

The stars are not wanted now; put out every one,
Pack up the moon and dismantle the sun.
Pour away the ocean and sweep up the wood;   15
For nothing now can ever come to any good.   *[1940]*

☰ THINKING ABOUT THE TEXT

1. What is it about this poem that makes it so universally popular?

2. What images in the poem seem most poignant to you?

3. Auden employs hyperbole throughout the poem. Is this an effective device since we are not meant to take his thoughts literally?

4. Are thoughts like those presented here normal for the grieving process?

5. Given the despair of the last line, why do you think so many people read this poem at funerals?

THEODORE ROETHKE
Elegy for Jane

Theodore Roethke (1908–1963) was born in Saginaw, Michigan. The early deaths of Roethke's uncle and father had a profound effect on his career. Not untypically for poets of his generation, he was a heavy drinker and suffered from depression. He suffered a heart attack at age fifty-five in the swimming pool of a friend, who converted it into a public Zen rock garden on Bainbridge Island across from Seattle. The following poem and "My Papa's Waltz" (p. 319) are often thought of as his two best poems.

My Student, Thrown by a Horse

I remember the neckcurls, limp and damp as tendrils;
And her quick look, a sidelong pickerel smile;
And how, once startled into talk, the light syllables leaped for her,
And she balanced in the delight of her thought,
A wren, happy, tail into the wind,   5
Her song trembling the twigs and small branches.
The shade sang with her;
The leaves, their whispers turned to kissing;
And the mold sang in the bleached valleys under the rose.

Oh, when she was sad, she cast herself down into such a pure depth,   10
Even a father could not find her:
Scraping her cheek against straw;
Stirring the clearest water.

My sparrow, you are not here,
Waiting like a fern, making a spiny shadow.   15
The sides of wet stones cannot console me,
Nor the moss, wound with the last light.

If only I could nudge you from this sleep,
My maimed darling, my skittery pigeon.

Over this damp grave I speak the words of my love: 20
I, with no rights in this matter,
Neither father nor lover.

[1950]

≣ THINKING ABOUT THE TEXT

1. What does Roethke remember most about his student? Do these details surprise you?

2. Does the statement "I speak the words of my love" (line 20) surprise you? What do you think he means?

3. Do you think teachers have a complicated emotional connection to their students?

4. Most images in the poem are taken from nature. Is this an effective strategy?

5. Do you think Roethke felt the last line was necessary to prevent readers from misunderstanding his feelings?

≣ MAKING COMPARISONS

1. Compare the images used in Auden's and Roethke's poems.

2. Does the narrator in Auden's poem seem more pained than the speaker in Roethke's poem?

3. Compare the tone in both poems. Which seems more authentic?

ANNE SEXTON
Sylvia's Death

Anne Sexton (1928–1974) had a difficult childhood, growing up in an alcoholic, unstable family. Her biographers now suspect she was sexually abused by her parents. Ironically, that charge has recently been leveled against her by her own daughters. Several breakdowns caused her to be in therapy on and off her whole life, although long bouts of depression, several suicide attempts, and numerous infidelities suggest this therapy was not very successful.

She, along with Robert Lowell and Sylvia Plath, is often referred to as a confessional poet. But that is only partly true since she wrote often of sexist cultural practices and, in her last years, of her religious interests. Plath's suicide upset Sexton so much that she also wanted to take her own life. The following poem is filled with pain and anger. And Sexton, five years later, joined Plath in the death she "wanted so badly and for so long."

For Sylvia Plath

O Sylvia, Sylvia,
with a dead box of stones and spoons,

with two children, two meteors
wandering loose in the tiny playroom,

with your mouth into the sheet,   5
into the roofbeam, into the dumb prayer,

(Sylvia, Sylvia,
where did you go
after you wrote me
from Devonshire   10
about raising potatoes
and keeping bees?)

what did you stand by,
just how did you lie down into?

Thief!—   15
how did you crawl into,

crawl down alone
into the death I wanted so badly and for so long,

the death we said we both outgrew,
the one we wore on our skinny breasts,   20

the one we talked of so often each time
we downed three extra dry martinis in Boston,

the death that talked of analysts and cures,
the death that talked like brides with plots,

the death we drank to,   25
the motives and then the quiet deed?

(In Boston
the dying
ride in cabs,
yes death again,   30
that ride home
with *our* boy.)

O Sylvia, I remember the sleepy drummer
who beat on our eyes with an old story,

how we wanted to let him come   35
like a sadist or a New York fairy

to do his job,
a necessity, a window in a wall or a crib,

and since that time he waited
under our heart, our cupboard,   40

and I see now that we store him up
year after year, old suicides

and I know at the news of your death,
a terrible taste for it, like salt.

(And me,   45
me too.
And now, Sylvia,
you again
with death again,

that ride home   50
with *our* boy.)

And I say only
with my arms stretched out into that stone place,

what is your death
but an old belonging,   55

a mole that fell out
of one of your poems?

(O friend,
while the moon's bad,
and the king's gone,   60
and the queen's at her wit's end
the bar fly ought to sing!)

O tiny mother,
you too!
O funny duchess!   65
O blonde thing!   *[1964]*

≡ **THINKING ABOUT THE TEXT**

1. Why does Sexton call Plath a "thief" (line 15)?

2. What was the apparent topic of the conversations Plath and Sexton had?

3. Who is *"our* boy" (lines 32 and 51)? Why does Sexton use such a term?

4. What does Sexton mean when she says that Plath's death is "an old belonging, / a mole that fell out / of one of your poems" (lines 55–57)?

5. Does the ending seem typical for an elegy about a friend? How do you interpret the last four lines?

≡ MAKING COMPARISONS

1. How does the tone of Sexton's poem differ from the tones of the poems by Auden and Roethke?

2. If you had lost a loved one, which of these poems would you find most comforting? Least comforting? Why?

3. Does Sexton's poem seem more or less personal than Roethke's poem? Explain.

≡ WRITING ABOUT ISSUES

1. Choose one of the elegies in this cluster, and write an essay in which you analyze the extent to which it is about the speaker. Is this poem mostly about the speaker? Mostly about the person being mourned? Equally about both? Refer to specific lines in the poem.

2. Research two or three critical articles on Roethke's "Elegy for Jane" from the 1950s or '60s and compare them to two or three more recent ones. Write an essay on the implications of the similarities and differences.

3. The introduction to this cluster mentions elegies by John Milton, Percy Bysshe Shelley, and Walt Whitman. Read one of these elegies and compare the ideas and feelings found there with one of the three poems in the present cluster. Write a brief essay on your findings.

4. Write an essay analyzing the design of an online memorial that you have discovered through research. Choose a site that you have mixed feelings about, and use your essay to explain what specifically about the memorial leaves you with such divided emotions. If you wish, refer to any of the texts in this cluster.

≡ Arguments about a Play: William Shakespeare's *Othello*

WILLIAM SHAKESPEARE, *Othello*

CRITICAL COMMENTARIES:
A. C. BRADLEY, "The Noble Othello"

MILLICENT BELL, "Othello's Jealousy"

JEFFRIE G. MURPHY, "Jealousy, Shame, and the Rival"

Of all the great tragedies of Shakespeare, *Othello* seems the closest to our own lives. Hamlet is a prince, and Lear and Macbeth are kings with the fate of their nations tied to their destiny. It is sometimes hard for contemporary readers to relate to their struggles or to regicide. But *Othello* is more domesticated, more about a relationship we can understand; few of us would claim that we have never been jealous. We know that relationships thrive on trust and openness, but even if we trust our partner, jealousy can find its way into our consciousness and might especially do so if we are prompted to doubt by a close friend.

Psychologists suggest that insecure people are prone to jealousy, perhaps because their low esteem suggests to them that they are not worthy of love. Is this the case with Othello? Although at first he seems filled with confidence and authority, he is considered a Moorish outsider in Venetian society and as such might be tempted to think that his wife, Desdemona, might find Cassio, one of her "own kind," attractive and desirable. The innocent and devoted Desdemona does not, but the seeds of distrust that are planted early on by Brabantio ("She deceived her father, and may thee") are diabolically nurtured by Iago, "an inhuman dog." The speed with which a great love is destroyed leaves the reader stunned by the potential darkness within us all.

The three essays that follow the play focus on jealousy, but they have different ideas about where that emotion comes from and how it alters our view of Othello's character and the play. A. C. Bradley develops the idea that Othello remains a noble soul and so we admire him to the end. This admiration increases our pity and the force of catharsis, which leaves us "for the moment free from pain, and exulting in the power of 'love and man's unconquerable mind.'" Millicent Bell sees jealousy as connected to philosophical ideas about truth and seeming and connects the play to ideas about skepticism in Elizabethan England and contemporary America. Jeffrie G. Murphy takes a more psychological view of jealousy as personal disintegration strongly linked to shame.

≡ BEFORE YOU READ

Do you think jealousy is a natural emotion? If you loved someone deeply, would you trust him or her? Are only insecure people jealous? Are there any positive elements to jealousy?

(© Bettmann/Corbis.)

WILLIAM SHAKESPEARE
Othello

William Shakespeare's reputation as the greatest dramatist in the English language is built on his five major tragedies: Romeo and Juliet (1594), Hamlet (1600), Othello (1604), Macbeth (1605), and King Lear (1605). But he was also a master in other genres, including comedies (As You Like It in 1599), histories (Henry IV in 1597), and romances (The Tempest in 1611). And his collection of sonnets is considered art of the highest order.

Very little is known about Shakespeare's personal life. He attended the grammar school at Stratford-upon-Avon, where he was born in 1564. He married Anne Hathaway in 1582 and had three children. Around 1590 he moved to London, where he became an actor and began writing plays. He was an astute businessperson, becoming a shareholder in London's famous Globe Theatre. After writing thirty-seven plays, he retired to Stratford in 1611. When he died in 1616, he left behind the most respected body of work in literature. Shakespeare's ability to use artistic language to convey a wide range of humor and emotion is perhaps unsurpassed.

THE NAMES OF THE ACTORS

OTHELLO, *the Moor*
BRABANTIO, *father to Desdemona*
CASSIO, *an honorable lieutenant [to Othello]*
IAGO *[Othello's ancient,] a villain*
RODERIGO, *a gulled gentleman*
DUKE OF VENICE
SENATORS OF VENICE
MONTANO, *governor of Cyprus*
LODOVICO AND GRATIANO, *[kinsmen to Brabantio,] two noble Venetians*
SAILORS
CLOWNS
DESDEMONA, *wife to Othello*
EMILIA, *wife to Iago*
BIANCA, *a courtesan*
[Messenger, Herald, Officers, Venetian Gentlemen, Musicians, Attendants
scene: Venice and Cyprus]

[ACT I, Scene I: A street in Venice.]

Enter Roderigo and Iago.

RODERIGO: Tush, never tell me! I take it much unkindly
    That thou, Iago, who hast had my purse
    As if the strings were thine, shouldst know of this.°
IAGO: 'Sblood,° but you'll not hear me!
    If ever I did dream of such a matter,   5
    Abhor me.
RODERIGO: Thou told'st me thou didst hold him in thy hate.
IAGO: Despise me if I do not. Three great ones of the city,
    In personal suit to make me his lieutenant,
    Off-capped to him;° and, by the faith of man,   10
    I know my price; I am worth no worse a place.
    But he, as loving his own pride and purposes,
    Evades them with a bombast circumstance.°
    Horribly stuffed with epithets of war;
    [And, in conclusion,]   15
    Nonsuits° my mediators; for, "Certes," says he,
    "I have already chose my officer."
    And what was he?
    Forsooth, a great arithmetician,°

ACT I, SCENE I.   **3 this:** I.e., Desdemona's elopement.   **4 'Sblood:** By God's blood.   **10 him:** I.e., Othello.   **13 a bombast circumstance:** Pompous circumlocutions.   **16 Nonsuits:** Rejects.   **19 arithmetician:** Theoretician.

One Michael Cassio, a Florentine   20
(A fellow almost damned in a fair wife°)
That never set a squadron in the field,
Nor the division of a battle knows
More than a spinster; unless the bookish theoric,
Wherein the togèd consuls can propose   25
As masterly as he. Mere prattle without practice
Is all his soldiership. But he, sir, had th' election;
And I (of whom his eyes had seen the proof
At Rhodes, at Cyprus, and on other grounds
Christian and heathen) must be belee'd and calmed°   30
By debitor and creditor; this counter-caster,°
He, in good time, must his lieutenant be,
And I—God bless the mark!—his Moorship's ancient.°
RODERIGO: By heaven, I rather would have been his hangman.
IAGO: Why, there's no remedy; 'tis the curse of service.   35
Preferment goes by letter and affection,°
And not by old gradation, where each second
Stood heir to th' first. Now, sir, be judge yourself,
Whether I in any just term am affined°
To love the Moor.
RODERIGO: I would not follow him then.   40
IAGO: O, sir, content you;
I follow him to serve my turn upon him.
We cannot all be masters, nor all masters
Cannot be truly followed. You shall mark
Many a duteous and knee-crooking knave   45
That, doting on his own obsequious bondage,
Wears out his time, much like his master's ass,
For naught but provender; and when he's old, cashiered.°
Whip me such honest knaves! Others there are
Who, trimmed° in forms and visages of duty,   50
Keep yet their hearts attending on themselves;
And, throwing but shows of service on their lords,
Do well thrive by them, and when they have lined their coats,
Do themselves homage. These fellows have some soul;
And such a one do I profess myself. For, sir,   55
It is as sure as you are Roderigo,
Were I the Moor, I would not be Iago.
In following him, I follow but myself;
Heaven is my judge, not I for love and duty,

---

21 almost . . . wife: (An obscure allusion; Cassio is unmarried, but see IV.i.12).   **30 belee'd and calmed:** Left in the lurch.   **31 counter-caster:** Bookkeeper.   **33 ancient:**
Ensign.   **36 affection:** Favoritism.   **39 affined:** Obliged.   **48 cashiered:** Turned off.
50 trimmed: Dressed up.

But seeming so, for my peculiar end; 60
For when my outward action doth demonstrate
The native act and figure of my heart°
In compliment extern,° 'tis not long after
But I will wear my heart upon my sleeve
For daws to peck at; I am not what I am. 65
RODERIGO: What a full fortune does the thick-lips° owe°
If he can carry't thus!
IAGO: Call up her father,
Rouse him. Make after him, poison his delight,
Proclaim him in the streets. Incense her kinsmen,
And though he in a fertile climate dwell, 70
Plague him with flies; though that his joy be joy,
Yet throw such changes of vexation on't
As it may lose some color.
RODERIGO: Here is her father's house. I'll call aloud.
IAGO: Do, with like timorous° accent and dire yell 75
As when, by night and negligence, the fire
Is spied in populous cities.
RODERIGO: What, ho, Brabantio! Signior Brabantio, ho!
IAGO: Awake! What, ho, Brabantio! Thieves! thieves! thieves!
Look to your house, your daughter, and your bags! 80
Thieves! thieves!

Brabantio at a window.°

BRABANTIO *(above)*:   What is the reason of this terrible summons?
What is the matter there?
RODERIGO: Signior, is all your family within?
IAGO: Are your doors locked?
BRABANTIO: Why, wherefore ask you this? 85
IAGO: Zounds, sir, y' are robbed! For shame, put on your gown!
Your heart is burst; you have lost half your soul.
Even now, now, very now, an old black ram
Is tupping your white ewe. Arise, arise!
Awake the snorting° citizens with the bell. 90
Or else the devil will make a grandsire of you.
Arise, I say!
BRABANTIO: What, have you lost your wits?
RODERIGO: Most reverend signior, do you know my voice?
BRABANTIO: Not I. What are you? 95
RODERIGO: My name is Roderigo.
BRABANTIO: The worser welcome!

---

62 The . . . heart: What I really believe and intend. **63 compliment extern:** Outward appearance. **66 thick-lips:** An Elizabethan epithet for blacks, including Moors; **owe:** Own. **75 timorous:** Terrifying. ***Brabantio at a window:*** (added from quarto). **90 snorting:** Snoring.

I have charged thee not to haunt about my doors.
In honest plainness thou hast heard me say
My daughter is not for thee; and now, in madness,
Being full of supper and distemp'ring draughts,   100
Upon malicious knavery dost thou come
To start my quiet.

RODERIGO: Sir, sir, sir—

BRABANTIO: But thou must needs be sure
My spirit and my place have in them power   105
To make this bitter to thee.

RODERIGO: Patience, good sir.

BRABANTIO: What tell'st thou me of robbing? This is Venice;
My house is not a grange.°

RODERIGO: Most grave Brabantio,
In simple and pure soul I come to you.

IAGO: Zounds, sir, you are one of those that will not serve God if the devil bid   110
you. Because we come to do you service, and you think we are ruffians,
you'll have your daughter covered with a Barbary horse; you'll have your
nephews° neigh to you; you'll have coursers for cousins, and gennets for
germans.°

BRABANTIO: What profane wretch art thou?   115

IAGO: I am one, sir, that comes to tell you your daughter and the Moor are now
making the beast with two backs.

BRABANTIO: Thou are a villain.

IAGO: You are—a senator.

BRABANTIO: This thou shalt answer. I know thee, Roderigo.

RODERIGO: Sir, I will answer anything. But I beseech you,   120
If 't be your pleasure and most wise consent,
As partly I find it is, that your fair daughter,
At this odd-even° and dull watch o' th' night,
Transported, with no worse nor better guard
But with a knave of common hire, a gondolier,   125
To the gross clasps of a lascivious Moor—
If this be known to you, and your allowance,°
We then have done you bold and saucy wrongs;
But if you know not this, my manners tell me
We have your wrong rebuke. Do not believe   130
That, from the sense° of all civility,
I thus would play and trifle with your reverence.
Your daughter, if you have not given her leave,
I say again, hath made a gross revolt,
Tying her duty, beauty, wit, and fortunes   135

---

108 grange: Isolated farmhouse. **113 nephews:** I.e., grandsons. **113–14 gennets for germans:** Spanish horses for near kinsmen. **123 odd-even:** Between night and morning. **127 allowance:** Approval. **131 from the sense:** In violation.

In an extravagant and wheeling° stranger
Of here and everywhere. Straight satisfy yourself.
If she be in her chamber, or your house,
Let loose on me the justice of the state
For thus deluding you.
BRABANTIO: Strike on the tinder, ho!   140
Give me a taper! Call up all my people!
This accident° is not unlike my dream.
Belief of it oppresses me already.
Light, I say! light!   *Exit [above].*
IAGO: Farewell, for I must leave you.
It seems not meet, nor wholesome to my place,   145
To be produced—as, if I stay, I shall—
Against the Moor. For I do know the state,
However this may gall him with some check,°
Cannot with safety cast° him; for he's embarked
With such loud reason to the Cyprus wars,   150
Which even now stand in act,° that for their souls
Another of his fathom° they have none
To lead their business; in which regard,
Though I do hate him as I do hell-pains,
Yet, for necessity of present life,   155
I must show out a flag and sign of love,
Which is indeed but sign. That you shall surely find him,
Lead to the Sagittary° the raisèd search;
And there will I be with him. So farewell.   *Exit.*

Enter [below] Brabantio in his nightgown,° and Servants with torches.

BRABANTIO: It is too true an evil. Gone she is;   160
And what's to come of my despisèd time
Is naught but bitterness. Now, Roderigo,
Where didst thou see her?—O unhappy girl!—
With the Moor, say'st thou?—Who would be a father?—
How didst thou know 'twas she!—O, she deceives me   165
Past thought!—What said she to you?—Get moe° tapers!
Raise all my kindred!—Are they married, think you?
RODERIGO: Truly I think they are.
BRABANTIO: O heaven! How got she out? O treason of the blood!
Fathers, from hence trust not your daughters' minds   170
By what you see them act. Is there not charms
By which the property° of youth and maidhood

---

136 extravagant and wheeling: Expatriate and roving.   **142 accident:** Occurrence.
148 check: Reprimand.   **149 cast:** Discharge.   **151 stand in act:** Are going on.
152 fathom: Capacity.   **158 Sagittary:** An inn.   **nightgown:** Dressing gown.   **166
moe:** More.   **172 property:** Nature.

May be abused? Have you not read, Roderigo,
Of some such thing?

RODERIGO: Yes, sir, I have indeed.

BRABANTIO: Call up my brother.—O, would you had had her!—   175
Some one way, some another.—Do you know
Where we may apprehend her and the Moor?

RODERIGO: I think I can discover him, if you please
To get good guard and go along with me.

BRABANTIO: I pray you lead on. At every house I'll call;   180
I may command at most.—Get weapons, ho!
And raise some special officers of night.—
On, good Roderigo; I'll deserve° your pains.   *Exeunt.*

[Scene II: Before the lodgings of Othello.]

Enter Othello, Iago, and Attendants with torches.

IAGO: Though in the trade of war I have slain men,
Yet do I hold it very stuff o' th' conscience
To do no contrived murther. I lack iniquity
Sometimes to do me service. Nine or ten times
I had thought t' have yerked° him here under the ribs.   5

OTHELLO: 'Tis better as it is.

IAGO: Nay, but he prated,
And spoke such scurvy and provoking terms
Against your honor
That with the little godliness I have
I did full hard forbear him. But I pray you, sir,   10
Are you fast° married? Be assured of this,
That the magnifico° is much beloved,
And hath in his effect a voice potential°
As double° as the Duke's. He will divorce you,
Or put upon you what restraint and grievance   15
The law, with all his might to enforce it on,
Will give him cable.

OTHELLO: Let him do his spite.
My services which I have done the signiory°
Shall out-tongue his complaints. 'Tis yet to know°—
Which, when I know that boasting is an honor,   20
I shall promulgate—I fetch my life and being
From men of royal siege;° and my demerits°

183 deserve: Show gratitude for. **SCENE II. 5 yerked:** Stabbed. **11 fast:** Securely.
12 magnifico: Grandee (Brabantio). **13 potential:** Powerful. **14 double:** Doubly
influential. **18 signiory:** Venetian government. **19 yet to know:** Still not generally known. **22 siege:** Rank; **demerits:** Deserts.

     May speak unbonneted to as proud a fortune
     As this that I have reached.° For know, Iago,
     But that I love the gentle Desdemona,   25
     I would not my unhousèd° free condition
     Put into circumscription and confine
     For the sea's worth. But look what lights come yond?
IAGO: Those are the raisèd father and his friends.
     You were best go in.
OTHELLO: Not I; I must be found.   30
     My parts, my title, and my perfect soul°
     Shall manifest me rightly. Is it they?
IAGO: By Janus, I think no.

Enter Cassio, with torches, Officers.

OTHELLO: The servants of the Duke, and my lieutenant.
     The goodness of the night upon you, friends!   35
     What is the news?
CASSIO: The Duke does greet you, general;
     And he requires your haste-post-haste appearance
     Even on the instant.
OTHELLO: What's the matter, think you?
CASSIO: Something from Cyprus, as I may divine.
     It is a business of some heat. The galleys   40
     Have sent a dozen sequent° messengers
     This very night at one another's heels,
     And many of the consuls, raised and met,
     Are at the Duke's already. You have been hotly called for;
     When, being not at your lodging to be found,   45
     The Senate hath sent about three several quests
     To search you out.
OTHELLO: 'Tis well I am found by you.
     I will but spend a word here in the house,
     And go with you.   *[Exit.]*
CASSIO: Ancient, what makes he here?
IAGO: Faith, he to-night hath boarded a land carack.°   50
     If it prove lawful prize, he's made for ever.
CASSIO: I do not understand.
IAGO: He's married.
CASSIO: To who?

[Enter Othello.]

IAGO: Marry, to—Come, captain, will you go?
OTHELLO: Have with you.

23–24 May speak . . . reached: Are equal, I modestly assert, to those of Desdemona's family. **26 unhousèd:** Unrestrained. **31 perfect soul:** Stainless conscience. **41 sequent:** Consecutive. **50 carack:** Treasure ship.

CASSIO: Here comes another troop to seek for you.

Enter Brabantio, Roderigo, and others with lights and weapons.

IAGO: It is Brabantio. General, be advised.   55
    He comes to bad intent.

OTHELLO: Holla! stand there!

RODERIGO: Signior, it is the Moor.

BRABANTIO: Down with him, thief!

[They draw on both sides.]

IAGO: You, Roderigo! Come, sir, I am for you.

OTHELLO: Keep up° your bright swords, for the dew will rust them.
    Good signior, you shall more command with years   60
    Than with your weapons.

BRABANTIO: O thou foul thief, where hast thou stowed my daughter?
    Damned as thou art, thou hast enchanted her!
    For I'll refer me to all things of sense,
    If she in chains of magic were not bound,   65
    Whether a maid so tender, fair, and happy,
    So opposite to marriage that she shunned
    The wealthy curlèd darlings of our nation,
    Would ever have, t' incur a general mock,
    Run from her guardage to the sooty bosom   70
    Of such a thing as thou—to fear, not to delight.
    Judge me the world if 'tis not gross in sense°
    That thou hast practiced on her with foul charms,
    Abused her delicate youth with drugs or minerals
    That weaken motion.° I'll have't disputed on;   75
    'Tis probable, and palpable to thinking.
    I therefore apprehend and do attach° thee
    For an abuser of the world, a practicer
    Of arts inhibited and out of warrant.
    Lay hold upon him. If he do resist,   80
    Subdue him at his peril.

OTHELLO: Hold your hands,
    Both you of my inclining and the rest.
    Were it my cue to fight, I should have known it
    Without a prompter. Where will you that I go
    To answer this your charge?

BRABANTIO: To prison, till fit time   85
    Of law and course of direct session°
    Call thee to answer.

OTHELLO: What if I do obey?
    How may the Duke be therewith satisfied,

---

59 Keep up: I.e., sheath.   **72 gross in sense:** Obvious.   **75 motion:** Perception.
77 attach: Arrest.   **86 direct session:** Regular trial.

Whose messengers are here about my side
Upon some present business of the state   90
To bring me to him?
OFFICER: 'Tis true, most worthy signior.
The Duke's in council, and your noble self
I am sure is sent for.
BRABANTIO: How? The Duke in council?
In this time of the night? Bring him away.
Mine's not an idle° cause. The Duke himself,   95
Or any of my brothers of the state,
Cannot but feel this wrong as 'twere their own;
For if such actions may have passage free,
Bondslaves and pagans shall our statesmen be.   *Exeunt.*

[Scene III: The Venetian Senate Chamber.]

Enter Duke and Senators, set at a table, with lights and Attendants.

DUKE: There is no composition° in these news
That gives them credit.
1. SENATOR: Indeed they are disproportioned.
My letters say a hundred and seven galleys.
DUKE: And mine a hundred forty.
2. SENATOR: And mine two hundred.
But though they jump° not on a just account—   5
As in these cases where the aim° reports
'Tis oft with difference—yet do they all confirm
A Turkish fleet, and bearing up to Cyprus.
DUKE: Nay, it is possible enough to judgment.
I do not so secure me° in the error   10
But the main article° I do approve°
In fearful sense.
SAILOR *(within):*   What, ho! what, ho! what, ho!
OFFICER: A messenger from the galleys.

Enter Sailor.

DUKE: Now, what's the business?
SAILOR: The Turkish preparation makes for Rhodes.
So was I bid report here to the state   15
By Signior Angelo.
DUKE: How say you by this change?
1. SENATOR: This cannot be
By no assay° of reason. 'Tis a pageant
To keep us in false gaze.° When we consider

95 idle: Trifling.   **SCENE III.   1 composition:** Consistency.   **5 jump:** Agree.
6 aim: Conjecture.   **10 so secure me:** Take such comfort.   **11 article:** Substance;
approve: Accept.   **18 assay:** Test.   **19 in false gaze:** Looking the wrong way.

Th' importancy of Cyprus to the Turk,   20
And let ourselves again but understand
That, as it more concerns the Turk than Rhodes,
So may he with more facile question bear° it,
For that it stands not in such warlike brace,°
But altogether lacks th' abilities   25
That Rhodes is dressed in—if we make thought of this,
We must not think the Turk is so unskillful
To leave that latest which concerns him first,
Neglecting an attempt of ease and gain
To wake and wage° a danger profitless.   30

DUKE: Nay, in all confidence, he's not for Rhodes.

OFFICER: Here is more news.

Enter a Messenger.

MESSENGER: The Ottomites, reverend and gracious,
Steering with due course toward the isle of Rhodes,
Have there injointed them with an after fleet.   35

1. SENATOR: Ay, so I thought. How many, as you guess?

MESSENGER: Of thirty sail; and now they do restem°
Their backward course, bearing with frank appearance
Their purposes toward Cyprus, Signior Montano,
Your trusty and most valiant servitor,   40
With his free duty recommends you thus,
And prays you to believe him.

DUKE: 'Tis certain then for Cyprus.
Marcus Luccicos,° is not he in town?

1. SENATOR: He's now in Florence.   45

DUKE: Write from us to him; post, post-haste dispatch.

1. SENATOR: Here comes Brabantio and the valiant Moor.

Enter Brabantio, Othello, Cassio, Iago, Roderigo, and Officers.

DUKE: Valiant Othello, we must straight employ you
Against the general enemy Ottoman.   *[To Brabantio.]*
I did not see you. Welcome, gentle signior.   50
We lacked your counsel and your help to-night.

BRABANTIO: So did I yours. Good your grace, pardon me.
Neither my place, nor aught I heard of business,
Hath raised me from my bed; nor doth the general care
Take hold on me; for my particular grief   55
Is of so floodgate° and o'erbearing nature
That it engluts° and swallows other sorrows,
And it is still itself.

---

23 with . . . bear: More easily capture.   **24 brace:** Posture of defense.   **30 wake and wage:** Rouse and risk.   **37 restem:** Steer again.   **44 Marcus Luccicos:** (Presumably a Venetian envoy).   **56 floodgate:** Torrential.   **57 engluts:** Devours.

DUKE: Why, what's the matter?
BRABANTIO: My daughter! O, my daughter!
ALL: Dead?
BRABANTIO: Ay, to me.
   She is abused, stol'n from me, and corrupted   60
   By spells and medicines bought of mountebanks;
   For nature so prepost'rously to err,
   Being not deficient,° blind, or lame of sense,
   Sans witchcraft could not.
DUKE: Whoe'er he be that in this foul proceeding   65
   Hath thus beguiled your daughter of herself,
   And you of her, the bloody book of law
   You shall yourself read in the bitter letter
   After your own sense; yea, though our proper° son
   Stood in your action.°
BRABANTIO: Humbly I thank your grace.   70
   Here is the man — this Moor, whom now, it seems,
   Your special mandate for the state affairs
   Hath hither brought.
ALL: We are very sorry for't.
DUKE [to Othello]:   What, in your own part, can you say to this?
BRABANTIO: Nothing, but this is so.   75
OTHELLO: Most potent, grave, and reverend signiors,
   My very noble, and approved° good masters,
   That I have ta'en away this old man's daughter,
   It is most true; true I have married her.
   The very head and front of my offending   80
   Hath this extent, no more. Rude° am I in my speech,
   And little blessed with the soft phrase of peace;
   For since these arms of mine had seven years' pith°
   Till now some nine moons wasted, they have used
   Their dearest action in the tented field;   85
   And little of this great world can I speak
   More than pertains to feats of broil and battle;
   And therefore little shall I grace my cause
   In speaking for myself. Yet, by your gracious patience,
   I will a round° unvarnished tale deliver   90
   Of my whole course of love — what drugs, what charms,
   What conjuration, and what mighty magic
   (For such proceeding am I charged withal)
   I won his daughter.

---

63 deficient: Feeble-minded. **69 our   proper:** My   own. **70 Stood   in   your action:** Were   accused   by   you. **77 approved:** Tested   by   experience. **81 Rude:** Unpolished. **83 pith:** Strength. **90 round:** Plain.

BRABANTIO: A maiden never bold;
    Of spirit so still and quiet that her motion   95
    Blushed° at herself; and she—in spite of nature,
    Of years, of country, credit, everything—
    To fall in love with what she feared to look on!
    It is a judgment maimed and most imperfect
    That will confess perfection so could err   100
    Against all rules of nature, and must be driven
    To find out practices° of cunning hell
    Why this should be. I therefore vouch° again
    That with some mixtures pow'rful o'er the blood,°
    Or with some dram, conjured to this effect,   105
    He wrought upon her.
DUKE: To vouch this is no proof,
    Without more certain and more overt test
    Than these thin habits° and poor likelihoods
    Of modern seeming° do prefer against him.
1. SENATOR: But, Othello, speak.   110
    Did you by indirect and forcèd° courses
    Subdue and poison this young maid's affections?
    Or came it by request, and such fair question°
    As soul to soul affordeth?
OTHELLO: I do beseech you,
    Send for the lady to the Sagittary   115
    And let her speak of me before her father.
    If you do find me foul in her report,
    The trust, the office, I do hold of you
    Not only take away, but let your sentence
    Even fall upon my life.
DUKE: Fetch Desdemona hither.   120
OTHELLO: Ancient, conduct them; you best know the place.

                            Exit [Iago, with] two or three [Attendants].

    And till she come, as truly as to heaven
    I do confess the vices of my blood,
    So justly to your grave ears I'll present
    How I did thrive in this fair lady's love,   125
    And she in mine.
DUKE: Say it, Othello.
OTHELLO: Her father loved me, oft invited me;
    Still° questioned me the story of my life
    From year to year—the battles, sieges, fortunes   130

95–96 her motion Blushed: Her own emotions caused her to blush.   **102 practices:** Plots.   **103 vouch:** Assert.   **104 blood:** Passions.   **108 thin habits:** Slight appearances.   **109 modern seeming:** Everyday supposition.   **111 forcèd:** Violent.   **113 question:** Conversation.   **129 Still:** Continually.

That I have passed.
I ran it through, even from my boyish days
To th' very moment that he bade me tell it.
Wherein I spoke of most disastrous chances,
Of moving accidents by flood and field; 135
Of hairbreadth scapes i' th' imminent deadly breach;
Of being taken by the insolent foe
And sold to slavery; of my redemption thence
And portance° in my travels' history;
Wherein of anters° vast and deserts idle, 140
Rough quarries, rocks, and hills whose heads touch heaven,
It was my hint° to speak—such was the process;
And of the Cannibals that each other eat,
The Anthropophagi,° and men whose heads
Do grow beneath their shoulders. This to hear 145
Would Desdemona seriously incline;
But still the house affairs would draw her thence;
Which ever as she could with haste dispatch,
She'ld come again, and with a greedy ear
Devour up my discourse. Which I observing, 150
Took once a pliant° hour, and found good means
To draw from her a prayer of earnest heart
That I would all my pilgrimage dilate,°
Whereof by parcels° she had something heard,
But not intentively.° I did consent, 155
And often did beguile her of her tears
When I did speak of some distressful stroke
That my youth suffered. My story being done,
She gave me for my pains a world of sighs.
She swore, i' faith, 'twas strange, 'twas passing strange; 160
'Twas pitiful, 'twas wondrous pitiful.
She wished she had not heard it; yet she wished
That heaven had made her such a man. She thanked me;
And bade me, if I had a friend that loved her,
I should but teach him how to tell my story, 165
And that would woo her. Upon this hint° I spake.
She loved me for the dangers I had passed,
And I loved her that she did pity them.
This only is the witchcraft I have used.
Here comes the lady. Let her witness it. 170

Enter Desdemona, Iago, Attendants.

---

139 portance: Behavior. **140 anters:** Caves. **142 hint:** Occasion. **144
Anthropophagi:** Man-eaters. **151 pliant:** Propitious. **153 dilate:** Recount in full.
154 parcels: Portions. **155 intentively:** With full attention. **166 hint:** Opportunity.

DUKE: I think this tale would win my daughter too.
　　　Good Brabantio,
　　　Take up this mangled matter at the best.
　　　Men do their broken weapons rather use
　　　Than their bare hands.
BRABANTIO:　　　　　　　I pray you hear her speak.　　　175
　　　If she confess that she was half the wooer,
　　　Destruction on my head if my bad blame
　　　Light on the man! Come hither, gentle mistress.
　　　Do you perceive in all this noble company
　　　Where most you owe obedience?
DESDEMONA:　　　　　　　My noble father,　　　180
　　　I do perceive here a divided duty.
　　　To you I am bound for life and education;°
　　　My life and education both do learn me
　　　How to respect you: you are the lord of duty;
　　　I am hitherto your daughter. But here's my husband;　　　185
　　　And so much duty as my mother showed
　　　To you, preferring you before her father,
　　　So much I challenge° that I may profess
　　　Due to the Moor my lord.
BRABANTIO:　　　　　　　God be with you! I have done.
　　　Please it your grace, on to the state affairs.　　　190
　　　I had rather to adopt a child than get° it.
　　　Come hither, Moor.
　　　I here do give thee that with all my heart
　　　Which, but thou hast already, with all my heart
　　　I would keep from thee. For your sake,° jewel,　　　195
　　　I am glad at soul I have no other child;
　　　For thy escape° would teach me tyranny,
　　　To hang clogs on them. I have done, my lord.
DUKE: Let me speak like yourself° and lay a sentence°
　　　Which, as a grise° or step, may help these lovers　　　200
　　　[Into your favor.]
　　　When remedies are past, the griefs are ended
　　　By seeing the worst, which late on hopes depended.
　　　To mourn a mischief that is past and gone
　　　Is the next way to draw new mischief on.　　　205
　　　What cannot be preserved when fortune takes,
　　　Patience her injury a mock'ry makes.
　　　The robbed that smiles steals something from the thief;
　　　He robs himself that spends a bootless grief.

---

182 education: Upbringing. **188 challenge:** Claim　the　right.　**191 get:** Beget.
195 For your sake: Because of you. **197 escape:** Escapade. **199 like yourself:**
As you should;　**sentence:** Maxim. **200 grise:** Step.

BRABANTIO: So let the Turk of Cyprus us beguile: 210
   We lose it not so long as we can smile.
   He bears the sentence well that nothing bears
   But the free comfort which from thence he hears;
   But he bears both the sentence and the sorrow
   That to pay grief must of poor patience borrow.   215
   These sentences, to sugar, or to gall,
   Being strong on both sides, are equivocal.
   But words are words. I never yet did hear
   That the bruised heart was piercèd through the ear.
   Beseech you, now to the affairs of state.   220
DUKE: The Turk with a most mighty preparation makes for Cyprus. Othello,
   the fortitude° of the place is best known to you; and though we have there
   a substitute of most allowed° sufficiency, yet opinion,° a more sovereign
   mistress of effects, throws a more safer voice on you. You must therefore be
   content to slubber° the gloss of your new fortunes with this more stubborn   225
   and boist'rous expedition.
OTHELLO: The tyrant custom, most grave senators,
   Hath made the flinty and steel couch of war
   My thrice-driven bed of down. I do agnize
   A natural and prompt alacrity   230
   I find in hardness;° and do undertake
   These present wars against the Ottomites.
   Most humbly, therefore, bending to your state,
   I crave fit disposition for my wife,
   Due reference of place, and exhibition,°   235
   With such accommodation and besort°
   As levels° with her breeding.
DUKE: If you please,
   Be't at her father's.
BRABANTIO: I will not have it so.
OTHELLO: Nor I.
DESDEMONA: Nor I. I would not there reside,   240
   To put my father in impatient thoughts
   By being in his eye. Most gracious Duke,
   To my unfolding lend your prosperous° ear,
   And let me find a charter in your voice,
   T' assist my simpleness.°   245
DUKE: What would you, Desdemona?
DESDEMONA: That I did love the Moor to live with him,

---

222 fortitude: Fortification.   **223 allowed:** Acknowledged;   **opinion:** Public
opinion.   **225 slubber:** Sully.   **229–31 agnize . . . hardness:** Recognize in myself
a natural and easy response to hardship.   **235 exhibition:** Allowance of money.   **236
besort:** Suitable company.   **237 levels:** Corresponds.   **243 prosperous:** Favorable.
245 simpleness: Lack of skill.

My downright violence, and storm of fortunes,
May trumpet to the world. My heart's subdued
Even to the very quality of my lord.   250
I saw Othello's visage in his mind,
And to his honors and his valiant parts
Did I my soul and fortunes consecrate.
So that, dear lords, if I be left behind,
A moth of peace, and he go to the war,   255
The rites for which I love him are bereft me,
And I a heavy interim shall support
By his dear absence. Let me go with him.
OTHELLO: Let her have your voice.
Vouch with me, heaven, I therefore beg it not   260
To please the palate of my appetite,
Not to comply with heat° — the young affects°
In me defunct — and proper satisfaction;
But to be free and bounteous to her mind;
And heaven defend your good souls that you think   265
I will your serious and great business scant
When she is with me. No, when light-winged toys
Of feathered Cupid seel° with wanton dullness
My speculative and officed instruments,°
That° my disports corrupt and taint my business,   270
Let housewives make a skillet of my helm,
And all indign° and base adversities
Make head against my estimation!°
DUKE: Be it as you shall privately determine,
Either for her stay or going. Th' affair cries haste,   275
And speed must answer it.
1. SENATOR: You must away to-night.
OTHELLO: With all my heart.
DUKE: At nine i' th' morning here we'll meet again.
Othello, leave some officer behind,
And he shall our commission bring to you,   280
With such things else of quality and respect
As doth import° you.
OTHELLO: So please your grace, my ancient;
A man he is of honesty and trust
To his conveyance I assign my wife,
With what else needful your good grace shall think   285
To be sent after me.
DUKE: Let it be so.

---

262 heat: Passions;   **young affects:** Tendencies of youth.   **268 seel:** Blind.   **269 My . . . instruments:** My perceptive and responsible faculties.   **270 That:** So that. **272 indign:** Unworthy.   **273 estimation:** Reputation.   **282 import:** Concern.

Good night to every one.
[To Brabantio.]   And, noble signior,
If virtue no delighted° beauty lack,
Your son-in-law is far more fair than black.

1. SENATOR: Adieu, brave Moor. Use Desdemona well.   290
BRABANTIO: Look to her, Moor, if thou hast eyes to see:
She has deceived her father, and may thee.

Exeunt [Duke, Senators, Officers, &c.].

OTHELLO: My life upon her faith!—Honest Iago,
My Desdemona must I leave to thee.
I prithee let thy wife attend on her,   295
And bring them after in the best advantage.°
Come, Desdemona. I have but an hour
Of love, of worldly matters and direction,
To spend with thee. We must obey the time.

Exit Moor and Desdemona.

RODERIGO: Iago,—   300
IAGO: What say'st thou, noble heart?
RODERIGO: What will I do, think'st thou?
IAGO: Why, go to bed and sleep.
RODERIGO: I will incontinently° drown myself.
IAGO: If thou dost, I shall never love thee after. Why, thou silly gentleman!   305
RODERIGO: It is silliness to live when to live is torment; and then have we a pre-
scription to die when death is our physician.
IAGO: O villainous! I have looked upon the world for four times seven years;
and since I could distinguish betwixt a benefit and an injury, I never found
man that knew how to love himself. Ere I would say I would drown myself   310
for the love of a guinea hen, I would change my humanity with a baboon.
RODERIGO: What should I do? I confess it is my shame to be so fond, but it is not
in my virtue to amend it.
IAGO: Virtue? a fig! 'Tis in ourselves that we are thus or thus. Our bodies are
our gardens, to which our wills are gardeners; so that if we will plant   315
nettles or sow lettuce, set hyssop and weed up thyme, supply it with one
gender° of herbs or distract it with many—either to have it sterile with
idleness or manured with industry—why, the power and corrigible
authority° of this lies in our wills. If the balance of our lives had not one
scale of reason to poise° another of sensuality, the blood and baseness° of   320
our natures would conduct us to most preposterous conclusions. But we
have reason to cool our raging motions,° our carnal strings, our unbitted°
lusts; whereof I take this that you call love to be a sect or scion.°

288 delighted: Delightful.   **296 in the best advantage:** At the best opportunity.
304 incontinently: Forthwith.   **317 gender:** Species.   **318–19 corrigible
authority:** Corrective power.   **320 poise:** Counterbalance; **blood and baseness:**
Animal instincts.   **322 motions:** Appetites; **unbitted:** Uncontrolled.   **323 sect or
scion:** Offshoot, cutting.

RODERIGO: It cannot be.

IAGO: It is merely a lust of the blood and a permission of the will. Come, be a   325
man! Drown thyself? Drown cats and blind puppies! I have professed me
thy friend, and I confess me knit to thy deserving with cables of perdurable
toughness. I could never better stead thee than now. Put money in thy
purse. Follow thou the wars; defeat thy favor° with an usurped beard. I say,
put money in thy purse. It cannot be that Desdemona should long con-   330
tinue her love to the Moor—put money in thy purse—nor he his to her.
It was a violent commencement in her, and thou shalt see an answerable
sequestration°—put but money in thy purse. These Moors are change-
able in their wills—fill thy purse with money. The food that to him now is
as luscious as locusts shall be to him shortly as bitter as coloquintida.° She   335
must change for youth: when she is sated with his body, she will find the
error of her choice. [She must have change, she must.] Therefore put
money in thy purse. If thou wilt needs damn thyself, do it a more delicate
way than drowning. Make° all the money thou canst. If sanctimony and a
frail vow betwixt an erring° barbarian and a supersubtle Venetian be not   340
too hard for my wits and all the tribe of hell, thou shalt enjoy her. Therefore make money. A pox of drowning thyself! 'Tis clean out of the way.
Seek thou rather to be hanged in compassing thy joy than to be drowned
and go without her.

RODERIGO: Wilt thou be fast to my hopes, if I depend on the issue?   345

IAGO: Thou art sure of me. Go, make money. I have told thee often, and I retell
thee again and again, I hate the Moor. My cause is hearted;° thine hath no
less reason. Let us be conjunctive in our revenge against him. If thou canst
cuckold him, thou dost thyself a pleasure, me a sport. There are many
events in the womb of time, which will be delivered. Traverse,° go, provide   350
thy money! We will have more of this to-morrow. Adieu.

RODERIGO: Where shall we meet i' th' morning?

IAGO: At my lodging.

RODERIGO: I'll be with thee betimes.

IAGO: Go to, farewell—Do you hear, Roderigo?   355

RODERIGO: What say you?

IAGO: No more of drowning, do you hear?

RODERIGO: I am changed.

IAGO: Go to, farewell. Put money enough in your purse.

RODERIGO: I'll sell all my land.   *Exit.*   360

IAGO: Thus do I ever make my fool my purse;

For I mine own gained knowledge should profane
If I would time expend with such a snipe°
But for my sport and profit. I hate the Moor;

---

329 defeat thy favor: Spoil thy appearance.   **333 sequestration:** Estrangement.
335 coloquintida: A medicine.   **339 Make:** Raise.   **340 erring:** Wandering.
347 My cause is hearted: My heart is in it.   **350 Traverse:** Forward march.   **363
snipe:** Fool.

And it is thought abroad that 'twixt my sheets   365
H'as done my office. I know not if 't be true;
But I, for mere suspicion in that kind,
Will do as if for surety. He holds me well;°
The better shall my purpose work on him.
Cassio's a proper man. Let me see now: 370
To get his place, and to plume up° my will
In double knavery—How, how?—Let's see:—
After some time, to abuse Othello's ears
That he is too familiar with his wife.
He hath a person and a smooth dispose°   375
To be suspected—framed to make women false.
The Moor is of a free° and open nature
That thinks men honest that but seem to be so;
And will as tenderly be led by th' nose
As asses are.   380
I have 't! It is engend'red! Hell and night
Must bring this monstrous birth to the world's light.   *Exit.*

[ACT II, Scene I: An open place in Cyprus, near the harbor.]

Enter Montano and two Gentlemen.
MONTANO: What from the cape can you discern at sea?
1. GENTLEMAN: Nothing at all: it is a high-wrought flood.
   I cannot 'twixt the heaven and the main
   Descry a sail.
MONTANO: Methinks the wind hath spoke aloud at land;   5
   A fuller blast ne'er shook our battlements.
   If it hath ruffianed so upon the sea,
   What ribs of oak, when mountains melt on them,
   Can hold the mortise?° What shall we hear of this?
2. GENTLEMAN: A segregation° of the Turkish fleet.   10
   For do but stand upon the foaming shore,
   The chidden billow seems to pelt the clouds;
   The wind-shaked surge, with high and monstrous mane,
   Seems to cast water on the burning Bear
   And quench the Guards° of th' ever-fixèd pole.°   15
   I never did like molestation° view
   On the enchafèd flood.
MONTANO: If that the Turkish fleet

---

368 well: In high regard.   **371 plume up:** Gratify.   **375 dispose:** Manner.   **377 free:** Frank.   ACT II, SCENE I.   **9 hold the mortise:** Hold their joints together.   **10 segregation:** Scattering.   **15 Guards:** Stars near the North Star;   **pole:** Polestar.   **16 molestation:** Tumult.

Be not ensheltered and embayed, they are drowned;
It is impossible to bear it out.

Enter a third Gentleman.

3. GENTLEMAN: News, lads! Our wars are done.   20
  The desperate tempest hath so banged the Turks
  That their designment halts.° A noble ship of Venice
  Hath seen a grievous wrack and sufferance°
  On most part of their fleet.
MONTANO: How? Is this true?
3. GENTLEMAN: The ship is here put in,   25
  A Veronesa;° Michael Cassio,
  Lieutenant to the warlike Moor Othello,
  Is come on shore; the Moor himself at sea,
  And is in full commission here for Cyprus.
MONTANO: I am glad on't. 'Tis a worthy governor.   30
3. GENTLEMAN: But his same Cassio, though he speak of comfort
  Touching the Turkish loss, yet he looks sadly
  And prays the Moor be safe, for they were parted
  With foul and violent tempest.
MONTANO: Pray heaven he be;
  For I have served him, and the man commands   35
  Like a full soldier. Let's to the seaside, ho!
  As well to see the vessel that's come in
  As to throw out our eyes for brave Othello,
  Even till we make the main and th' aerial blue
  An indistinct regard.°   40
3. GENTLEMAN: Come, let's do so;
  For every minute is expectancy
  Of more arrivance.

Enter Cassio.

CASSIO: Thanks, you the valiant of this warlike isle,
  That so approve the Moor! O, let the heavens
  Give him defense against the elements,   45
  For I have lost him on a dangerous sea!
MONTANO: Is he well shipped?
CASSIO: His bark is stoutly timbered, and his pilot
  Of very expert and approved allowance;
  Therefore my hopes, not surfeited to death,°   50
  Stand in bold cure.°
    (Within.)   A sail, a sail, a sail!   *Enter a messenger.*
CASSIO: What noise?

---

22 designment halts: Plan is crippled.   **23 sufferance:** Disaster.   **26 Veronesa:** Ship furnished by Verona.   **40 An indistinct regard:** Indistinguishable.   **50 surfeited to death:** Overindulged.   **51 in bold cure:** A good chance of fulfillment.

MESSENGER: The town is empty; on the brow o' th' sea
    Stand ranks of people, and they cry "A sail!"
CASSIO: My hopes do shape him for the governor.   55

A shot.

2. GENTLEMAN: They do discharge their shot of courtesy:
    Our friends at least.
CASSIO: I pray you, sir, go forth
    And give us truth who 'tis that is arrived.
2. GENTLEMAN: I shall.   *Exit.*
MONTANO: But, good lieutenant, is your general wived?   60
CASSIO: Most fortunately. He hath achieved a maid
    That paragons° description and wild fame;
    One that excels the quirks° of blazoning° pens,
    And in th' essential vesture of creation
    Does tire the ingener.°

Enter Second Gentleman.

                  How now? Who has put in?   65
2. GENTLEMAN: 'Tis one Iago, ancient to the general.
CASSIO: H'as had most favorable and happy speed:
    Tempests themselves, high seas, and howling winds,
    The guttered° rocks and congregated sands,
    Traitors ensteeped° to clog the guiltless keel,   70
    As having sense of beauty, do omit
    Their mortal° natures, letting go safely by
    The divine Desdemona.
MONTANO: What is she?
CASSIO: She that I spake of, our great captain's captain,
    Left in the conduct of the bold Iago,   75
    Whose footing° here anticipates our thoughts
    A se'nnight's° speed. Great Jove, Othello guard,
    And swell his sail with thine own pow'rful breath,
    That he may bless this bay with his tall ship,
    Make love's quick pants in Desdemona's arms,   80
    Give renewed fire to our extincted spirits,
    [And bring all Cyprus comfort!]

Enter Desdemona, Iago, Roderigo, and Emilia [with Attendants].

                  O, behold!
    The riches of the ship is come on shore!
    You men of Cyprus, let her have your knees.°

---

62 paragons: Surpasses.   **63 quirks:** Ingenuities;   **blazoning:** Describing.
64–65 And . . . ingener: Merely to describe her as God made her exhaust her praiser.
69 guttered: Jagged.   **70 ensteeped:** Submerged.   **72 mortal:** Deadly.   **76
footing:** Landing.   **77 se'nnight's:** Week's.   **84 knees:** I.e., kneeling.

Hail to thee, lady! and the grace of heaven,   85
Before, behind thee, and on every hand,
Enwheel thee round!
DESDEMONA: I thank you, valiant Cassio.
What tidings can you tell me of my lord?
CASSIO: He is not yet arrived; nor know I aught
But that he's well and will be shortly here.   90
DESDEMONA: O but I fear! How lost you company?
CASSIO: The great contention of the sea and skies
Parted our fellowship.
(Within.)   A sail, a sail! *[A shot.]*
But hark. A sail!
2. GENTLEMAN: They give their greeting to the citadel;
This likewise is a friend.
CASSIO: See for the news.   95

[Exit Gentleman.]

Good ancient, you are welcome.
[To Emilia.]   Welcome, mistress. —
Let it not gall your patience, good Iago,
That I extend my manners. 'Tis my breeding
That gives me this bold show of courtesy.

[Kisses Emilia.°]

IAGO: Sir, would she give you so much of her lips   100
As of her tongue she oft bestows on me,
You would have enough.
DESDEMONA: Alas, she has no speech!
IAGO: In faith, too much.
I find it still when I have list to sleep.
Marry, before your ladyship, I grant,   105
She puts her tongue a little in her heart
And chides with thinking.
EMILIA: You have little cause to say so.
IAGO: Come on, come on! You are pictures out of doors,
Bells in your parlors, wildcats in your kitchens,   110
Saints in your injuries, devils being offended,
Players in your housewifery,° and housewives° in your beds.
DESDEMONA: O, fie upon thee, slanderer!
IAGO: Nay, it is true, or else I am a Turk:
You rise to play, and go to bed to work.   115
EMILIA: You shall not write my praise.
IAGO: No, let me not.

Kisses Emilia: (Kissing was a common Elizabethan form of social courtesy).   **112 house-wifery:** Housekeeping;   **housewives:** Hussies.

DESDEMONA: What wouldst thou write of me, if thou shouldst praise me?

IAGO: O gentle lady, do not put me to't,
 For I am nothing if not critical.

DESDEMONA: Come on, assay.°—There's one gone to the harbor?   120

IAGO: Ay, madam.

DESDEMONA: I am not merry; but I do beguile
 The thing I am by seeming otherwise.—
 Come, how wouldst thou praise me?

IAGO: I am about it; but indeed my invention   125
 Comes from my pate as birdlime° does from frieze°—
 It plucks out brains and all. But my Muse labors,
 And thus she is delivered:
 If she be fair and wise, fairness and wit—
 The one's for use, the other useth it.   130

DESDEMONA: Well praised! How if she be black° and witty?

IAGO: If she be black, and thereto have a wit,
 She'll find a white that shall her blackness fit.

DESDEMONA: Worse and worse!

EMILIA: How if fair and foolish?   135

IAGO: She never yet was foolish that was fair,
 For even her folly° helped her to an heir.

DESDEMONA: These are old fond° paradoxes to make fools laugh i' th' alehouse.
 What miserable praise hast thou for her that's foul° and foolish?

IAGO: There's none so foul, and foolish thereunto,   140
 But does foul pranks which fair and wise ones do.

DESDEMONA: O heavy ignorance! Thou praisest the worst best. But what praise
 couldst thou bestow on a deserving woman indeed—one that in the
 authority of her merit did justly put on the vouch° of very malice itself?

IAGO: She that was ever fair, and never proud;   145
 Had tongue at will, and yet was never loud;
 Never lacked gold, and yet went never gay;
 Fled from her wish, and yet said "Now I may";
 She that, being ang'red, her revenge being nigh,
 Bade her wrong stay, and her displeasure fly;   150
 She that in wisdom never was so frail
 To change the cod's head for the salmon's tail;°
 She that could think, and ne'er disclose her mind;
 See suitors following, and not look behind:
 She was a wight (if ever such wight were)—   155

DESDEMONA: To do what?

IAGO: To suckle fools and chronicle small beer.°

---

120 assay: Try.   **126 birdlime:** A sticky paste;   **frieze:** Rough cloth.   **131 black:** Brunette.   **137 folly:** Wantonness.   **138 fond:** Foolish.   **139 foul:** Ugly.   **144 put on the vouch:** Compel the approval.   **152 To . . . tail:** I.e., to exchange the good for the poor but expensive.   **157 chronicle small beer:** Keep petty household accounts.

DESDEMONA: O most lame and impotent conclusion! Do not learn of him, Emilia, though he be thy husband. How say you, Cassio? Is he not a most profane and liberal° counsellor?   160

CASSIO: He speaks home,° madam. You may relish him more in the soldier than in the scholar.

IAGO [aside]:   He takes her by the palm. Ay, well said, whisper! With as little a web as this will I ensnare as great a fly as Cassio. Ay, smile upon her, do! I will gyve thee in thine own courtship.° —You say true; 'tis so, indeed! —If   165 such tricks as these strip you out of your lieutenantry, it had been better you had not kissed your three fingers so oft —which now again you are most apt to play the sir° in. Very good! well kissed! an excellent courtesy! 'Tis so, indeed. Yet again your fingers to your lips? Would they were clyster pipes° for your sake! (Trumpet within.)   170
   The Moor! I know his trumpet.

CASSIO: 'Tis truly so.

DESDEMONA: Let's meet him and receive him.

CASSIO: Lo, where he comes.

Enter Othello and Attendants.

OTHELLO: O my fair warrior!

DESDEMONA: My dear Othello!   175

OTHELLO: It gives me wonder great as my content
   To see you here before me. O my soul's joy!
   If after every tempest come such calms,
   May the winds blow till they have wakened death!
   And let the laboring bark climb hills of seas   180
   Olympus-high, and duck again as low
   As hell's from heaven! If it were now to die,
   'Twere now to be most happy;° for I fear
   My soul hath her content so absolute
   That not another comfort like to this   185
   Succeeds in unknown fate.

DESDEMONA: The heavens forbid
   But that our loves and comforts should increase
   Even as our days do grow.

OTHELLO: Amen to that, sweet powers!
   I cannot speak enough of this content;
   It stops me here; it is too much of joy.   190
   And this, and this, the greatest discords be

They kiss.

   That e'er our hearts shall make!

IAGO [aside]:   O, you are well tuned now!

---

160 profane and liberal: Worldly and licentious. **161 home:** Bluntly. **165 gyve . . . courtship:** Manacle you by means of your courtly manners. **168 sir:** Courtly gentleman. **169–70 clyster pipes:** Syringes. **183 happy:** Fortunate.

But I'll set down° the pegs that make this music,
As honest as I am.

OTHELLO: Come, let us to the castle.
News, friends! Our wars are done; the Turks are drowned.   195
How does my old acquaintance of this isle? —
Honey, you shall be well desired° in Cyprus;
I have found great love amongst them. O my sweet,
I prattle out of fashion, and I dote
In mine own comforts. I prithee, good Iago,   200
Go to the bay and disembark my coffers.
Bring thou the master° to the citadel;
He is a good one, and his worthiness
Does challenge° much respect. — Come, Desdemona,
Once more well met at Cyprus.   205

Exit Othello [with all but Iago and Roderigo].

IAGO *[to an Attendant, who goes out]*:   Do thou meet me presently at the harbor.
[To Roderigo.] Come hither. If thou be'st valiant (as they say base men
being in love have then a nobility in their natures more than is native to
them), list me. The lieutenant to-night watches on the court of guard.°
First, I must tell thee this: Desdemona is directly in love with him.   210

RODERIGO: With him? Why, 'tis not possible.

IAGO: Lay thy finger thus,° and let thy soul be instructed. Mark me with
what violence she first loved the Moor, but for bragging and telling her
fantastical lies; and will she love him still for prating? Let not thy discreet
heart think it. Her eye must be fed; and what delight shall she have to look   215
on the devil? When the blood is made dull with the act of sport, there
should be, again to inflame it and to give satiety a fresh appetite, loveliness
in favor, sympathy in years, manners, and beauties; all which the Moor is
defective in. Now for want of these required conveniences,° her delicate
tenderness will find itself abused, begin to heave the gorge,° disrelish and   220
abhor the Moor. Very nature will instruct her in it and compel her to some
second choice. Now, sir, this granted — as it is a most pregnant° and
unforced position — who stands so eminent in the degree of this fortune as
Cassio does? A knave very voluble; no further conscionable° than in
putting on the mere form of civil and humane° seeming for the better   225
compassing of his salt° and most hidden loose affection? Why, none! why,
none! A slipper° and subtle knave; a finder-out of occasions; that has an
eye can stamp and counterfeit advantages, though true advantage never
present itself; a devilish knave! Besides, the knave is handsome, young, and

---

193 set down: Loosen.   **197 well desired:** Warmly welcomed.   **202 master:** Ship
captain.   **204 challenge:** Deserve.   **209 court of guard:** Headquarters.   **212
thus:** I.e., on your lips.   **219 conveniences:** Compatibilities.   **220 heave the gorge:**
Be nauseated.   **222 pregnant:** Evident.   **224 conscionable:** Conscientious.   **225
humane:** Polite.   **226 salt:** Lecherous.   **227 slipper:** Slippery.

hath all those requisites in him that folly and green minds look after. A   230
pestilent complete knave! and the woman hath found him already.

RODERIGO: I cannot believe that in her; she's full of most blessed condition.°

IAGO: Blessed fig's-end! The wine she drinks is made of grapes. If she had been
blessed, she would never have loved the Moor. Blessed pudding! Didst thou
not see her paddle with the palm of his hand? Didst not mark that?   235

RODERIGO: Yes, that I did; but that was but courtesy.

IAGO: Lechery, by this hand! an index and obscure prologue to the history of
lust and foul thoughts. They met so near with their lips that their breaths
embraced together. Villainous thoughts, Roderigo! When these mutuali-
ties° so marshal the way, hard at hand comes the master and main exer-   240
cise, th' incorporate° conclusion. Pish! But, sir, be you ruled by me: I have
brought you from Venice. Watch you to-night; for the command, I'll lay't
upon you. Cassio knows you not. I'll not be far from you: do you find some
occasion to anger Cassio, either by speaking too loud, or tainting° his discipline, or from what other course you please which the time shall more fa-   245
vorably minister.

RODERIGO: Well.

IAGO: Sir, he's rash and very sudden in choler,° and haply with his truncheon
may strike at you. Provoke him that he may; for even out of that will I
cause these of Cyprus to mutiny; whose qualification° shall come into no   250
true taste° again but by the displanting of Cassio. So shall you have a
shorter journey to your desires by the means I shall then have to prefer°
them; and the impediment most profitably removed with-out the which
there were no expectation of our prosperity.

RODERIGO: I will do this if you can bring it to any opportunity.   255

IAGO: I warrant thee. Meet me by and by at the citadel; I must fetch his necessaries ashore. Farewell.

RODERIGO: Adieu.   *Exit.*

IAGO: That Cassio loves her, I do well believe't;
That she loves him, 'tis apt° and of great credit.   260
The Moor, howbeit that I endure him not,
Is of a constant, loving, noble nature,
And I dare think he'll prove to Desdemona
A most dear husband. Now I do love her too;
Not out of absolute lust, though peradventure   265
I stand accountant° for as great a sin,
But partly led to diet° my revenge,
For that I do suspect the lusty Moor
Hath leaped into my seat; the thought whereof
Doth, like a poisonous mineral, gnaw my inwards;   270

---

232 condition: Character.   **239–40 mutualities:** Exchanges.   **241 incorporate:** Carnal.   **244 tainting:** Discrediting.   **248 sudden in choler:** Violent in anger.
250 qualification: Appeasement.   **251 true taste:** Satisfactory state.   **252 prefer:**
Advance.   **260 apt:** Probable.   **266 accountant:** Accountable.   **267 diet:** Feed.

And nothing can or shall content my soul
Till I am evened with him, wife for wife;
Or failing so, yet that I put the Moor
At least into a jealousy so strong
That judgment cannot cure. Which thing to do,   275
If this poor trash of Venice, whom I trash°
For° his quick hunting, stand the putting on,°
I'll have our Michael Cassio on the hip,°
Abuse him to the Moor in the rank garb°
(For I fear Cassio with my nightcap too),   280
Make the Moor thank me, love me, and reward me
For making him egregiously an ass
And practicing upon° his peace and quiet
Even to madness. 'Tis here, but yet confused:
Knavery's plain face is never seen till used.   *Exit.*   285

[Scene II: A street in Cyprus.]

Enter Othello's Herald, with a proclamation.

HERALD: It is Othello's pleasure, our noble and valiant general, that, upon certain tidings now arrived, importing the mere perdition° of the Turkish fleet,
every man put himself into triumph; some to dance, some to make bonfires,
each man to what sport and revels his addiction leads him. For, besides
these beneficial news, it is the celebration of his nuptial. So much was his   5
pleasure should be proclaimed. All offices° are open, and there is full liberty
of feasting from the present hour of five till the bell have told eleven. Heaven
bless the isle of Cyprus and our noble general Othello!   *Exit.*

[Scene III: The Cyprian Castle.]

Enter Othello, Desdemona, Cassio, and Attendants.

OTHELLO: Good Michael, look you to the guard to-night.
Let's teach ourselves that honorable stop,
Not to outsport discretion.
CASSIO: Iago hath direction what to do;
But not withstanding, with my personal eye   5
Will I look to't.
OTHELLO: Iago is most honest.
Michael, good night. To-morrow with your earliest
Let me have speech with you.

---

276 I trash: I weight down (in order to keep under control).   **277 For:** In order to
develop;   **stand the putting on:** Responds to my inciting.   **278 on the hip:** At my
mercy.   **279 rank garb:** Gross manner.   **283 practicing upon:** Plotting against.
SCENE II. **2 mere perdition:** Complete destruction.   **6 offices:** Kitchens and storerooms.

[To Desdemona.]   Come, my dear love.
The purchase made, the fruits are to ensue;
That profit 's yet to come 'tween me and you.—   10
Good night.

Exit [Othello with Desdemona and Attendants].

Enter Iago.

CASSIO: Welcome, Iago. We must to the watch.

IAGO: Not this hour, lieutenant; 'tis not yet ten o' th' clock. Our general cast°
us thus early for the love of his Desdemona; who let us not therefore
blame. He hath not yet made wanton the night with her, and she is sport   15
for Jove.

CASSIO: She's a most exquisite lady.

IAGO: And, I'll warrant her, full of game.

CASSIO: Indeed, she's a most fresh and delicate creature.

IAGO: What an eye she has! Methinks it sounds a parley to provocation.   20

CASSIO: An inviting eye; and yet methinks right modest.

IAGO: And when she speaks, is it not an alarum to love?

CASSIO: She is indeed perfection.

IAGO: Well, happiness to their sheets! Come, lieutenant, I have a stoup° of
wine, and here without are a brace of Cyprus gallants that would fain have   25
a measure to the health of black Othello.

CASSIO: Not to-night, good Iago. I have very poor and unhappy brains for
drinking; I could well wish courtesy would invent some other custom of
entertainment.

IAGO: O, they are our friends. But one cup! I'll drink for you.   30

CASSIO: I have drunk but one cup to-night, and that was craftily qualified° too;
and behold what innovation° it makes here. I am unfortunate in the infirmity and dare not task my weakness with any more.

IAGO: What, man! 'Tis a night of revels: the gallants desire it.

CASSIO: Where are they?   35

IAGO: Here at the door; I pray you call them in.

CASSIO: I'll do't, but it dislikes me.   *Exit.*

IAGO: If I can fasten but one cup upon him
With that which he hath drunk to-night already,
He'll be as full of quarrel and offense   40
As my young mistress' dog. Now my sick fool Roderigo,
Whom love hath turned almost the wrong side out,
To Desdemona hath to-night caroused
Potations pottle-deep;° and he's to watch.
Three lads of Cyprus—noble swelling spirits,   45
That hold their honors in a wary distance,°
The very elements° of this warlike isle—

SCENE III. 14 cast: Dismissed. 24 stoup: Two-quart tankard. 31 qualified: Diluted.
32 innovation: Disturbance. 44 pottle-deep: Bottoms up. 46 That . . . distance:
Very sensitive about their honor. 47 very elements: True representatives.

Have I to-night flustered with flowing cups,
And they watch too. Now, 'mongst this flock of drunkards
Am I to put our Cassio in some action   50
That may offend the isle.

Enter Cassio, Montano, and Gentlemen [; Servants following with wine].

But here they come.
If consequence do but approve my dream,
My boat sails freely, both with wind and stream.

CASSIO: 'Fore God, they have given me a rouse° already.

MONTANO: Good faith, a little one; not past a pint, as I am a soldier.   55

IAGO: Some wine, ho!

   [Sings.]   And let me the canakin clink, clink;
              And let me the canakin clink
                 A soldier's a man;
                 A life's but a span,   60
               Why then, let a soldier drink.

Some wine, boys!

CASSIO: 'Fore God, an excellent song!

IAGO: I learned it in England, where indeed they are most potent in potting.
Your Dane, your German, and your swag-bellied Hollander—Drink,   65
ho!—are nothing to your English.

CASSIO: Is your Englishman so expert in his drinking?

IAGO: Why, he drinks you with facility your Dane dead drunk; he sweats not
to overthrow your Almain; he gives your Hollander a vomit ere the next
pottle can be filled.   70

CASSIO: To the health of our general!

MONTANO: I am for it, lieutenant, and I'll do you justice.

IAGO: O sweet England!

   [Sings.]   King Stephen was a worthy peer;
               His breeches cost him but a crown;   75
            He held 'em sixpence all too dear,
               With that he called the tailor lown.°
            He was a wight of high renown,
               And thou art but of low degree.
            'Tis pride that pulls the country down;   80
               Then take thine auld cloak about thee.

Some wine, ho!

CASSIO: 'Fore God, this is a more exquisite song than the other.

IAGO: Will you hear't again?

CASSIO: No, for I hold him to be unworthy of his place that does those things.°   85
Well, God's above all; and there be souls must be saved, and there be souls
must not be saved.

IAGO: It's true, good lieutenant.

54 rouse: Bumper.   **77 lown:** Rascal.   **85 does…things:** I.e., behaves in this fashion.

CASSIO: For mine own part—no offense to the general, nor any man of qual
    ity—I hope to be saved.   90
IAGO: And so do I too, lieutenant.
CASSIO: Ay, but, by your leave, not before me. The lieutenant is to be saved
    before the ancient. Let's have no more of this; let's to our affairs.—God for-
    give us our sins!—Gentlemen, let's look to our business. Do not think, gen-
    tlemen, I am drunk. This is my ancient; this is my right hand, and this is my
    left. I am not drunk now. I can stand well enough, and I speak well enough.
ALL: Excellent well!
CASSIO: Why, very well then. You must not think then that I am drunk.

Exit.

MONTANO: To th' platform, masters. Come, let's set the watch.
IAGO: You see this fellow that is gone before.   100
    He's a soldier fit to stand by Caesar
    And give direction; and do but see his vice.
    'Tis to his virtue a just equinox,°
    The one as long as th' other. 'Tis pity of him.
    I fear the trust Othello puts him in,   105
    On some odd time of his infirmity,
    Will shake this island.
MONTANO: But is he often thus?
IAGO: 'Tis evermore his prologue to his sleep:
    He'll watch the horologe a double set°
    If drink rock not his cradle.
MONTANO: It were well   110
    The general were put in mind of it.
    Perhaps he sees it not, or his good nature
    Prizes the virtue that appears in Cassio
    And looks not on his evils. Is not this true?

Enter Roderigo.

IAGO *[aside to him]:*   How now, Roderigo?   115
    I pray you after the lieutenant, go!   *Exit Roderigo.*
MONTANO: And 'tis great pity that the noble Moor
    Should hazard such a place as his own second
    With one of an ingraft° infirmity.
    It were an honest action to say   120
    So to the Moor.
IAGO: Not I, for this fair island!
    I do love Cassio well and would do much
    To cure him of this evil.
        (Within.) Help! help!
              But hark! What noise?

---

103 just equinox: Exact equivalent.   **109 watch . . . set:** Stay awake twice around
the clock.   **119 ingraft:** I.e., ingrained.

Enter Cassio, driving in Roderigo.

CASSIO: Zounds, you rogue! you rascal! 125
MONTANO: What's the matter, lieutenant?
CASSIO: A knave to teach me my duty?
I'll beat the knave into a twiggen° bottle.
RODERIGO: Beat me?
CASSIO: Dost thou prate, rogue? *[Strikes him.]*
MONTANO: Nay, good lieutenant!

[Stays him.]

I pray you, sir, hold your hand.
CASSIO: Let me go, sir,
Or I'll knock you o'er the mazzard.°
MONTANO: Come, come, you're drunk! 130
CASSIO: Drunk?

They fight.

IAGO *[aside to Roderigo]:* Away, I say! Go out and cry a mutiny!

Exit Roderigo.

Nay, good lieutenant. God's will, gentlemen!
Help, ho!—lieutenant—sir—Montano—sir—
Help, masters!—Here's a goodly watch indeed! 135

A bell rung.

Who's that which rings the bell? Diablo, ho!
The town will rise.° God's will, lieutenant, hold!
You'll be shamed for ever.

Enter Othello and Gentlemen with weapons.

OTHELLO: What is the matter here?
MONTANO: Zounds, I bleed still. I am hurt to th' death.
He dies! 140
OTHELLO: Hold for your lives!
IAGO: Hold, hold! Lieutenant—sir—Montano—gentlemen!
Have you forgot all sense of place and duty?
Hold! The general speaks to you. Hold, for shame!
OTHELLO: Why, how now ho? From whence ariseth this? 145
Are we turned Turks, and to ourselves do that
Which heaven hath forbid the Ottomites?
For Christian shame put by this barbarous brawl!
He that stirs next to carve for° his own rage.
Holds his soul light; he dies upon his motion. 150
Silence that dreadful bell! It frights the isle
From her propriety.° What is the matter, masters?
Honest Iago, that looks dead with grieving,

127 twiggen: Wicker-covered. **130 mazzard:** Head. **137 rise:** Grow riotous.
149 carve for: Indulge. **152 propriety:** Proper self.

Speak. Who began this? On thy love, I charge thee.
IAGO: I do not know. Friends all, but now, even now,   155
 In quarter,° and in terms like bride and groom
 Devesting them for bed; and then, but now—
 As if some planet had unwitted men—
 Swords out, and tilting one at other's breast
 In opposition bloody. I cannot speak   160
 Any beginning to this peevish odds,°
 And would in action glorious I had lost
 Those legs that brought me to a part of it!
OTHELLO: How comes it, Michael, you are thus forgot?
CASSIO: I pray you pardon me; I cannot speak.   165
OTHELLO: Worthy Montano, you were wont to be civil;
 The gravity and stillness of your youth
 The world hath noted, and your name is great
 In months of wisest censure.° What's the matter
 That you unlace° your reputation thus   170
 And spend your rich opinion° for the name
 Of a night-brawler? Give me answer to it.
MONTANO: Worthy Othello, I am hurt to danger.
 Your officer, Iago, can inform you,
 While I spare speech, which something now offends° me,   175
 Of all that I do know; nor know I aught
 By me that's said or done amiss this night,
 Unless self-charity be sometimes a vice,
 And to defend ourselves it be a sin
 When violence assails us.
OTHELLO: Now, by heaven,   180
 My blood° begins my safer guides to rule,
 And passion, having my best judgment collied,°
 Assays° to lead the way. If I once stir
 Or do but lift this arm, the best of you
 Shall sink in my rebuke. Give me to know   185
 How this foul rout began, who set it on;
 And he that is approved in° this offense,
 Though he had twinned with me, both at a birth,
 Shall lose me. What! in a town of war,
 Yet wild, the people's hearts brimful of fear,   190
 To manage° private and domestic quarrel?
 In night, and on the court and guard of safety?
 'Tis monstrous. Iago, who began't?

---

156 quarter: Friendliness.   **161 peevish odds:** Childish quarrel.   **169 censure:**
Judgment.   **170 unlace:** Undo.   **171 rich opinion:** High reputation.   **175 offends:**
Pains.   **181 blood:** Passion.   **182 collied:** Darkened.   **183 Assays:** Tries.   **187
approved in:** Proved guilty of.   **191 manage:** Carry on.

MONTANO: If partially affined, or leagued in office,°
    Thou dost deliver more or less than truth,   195
    Thou art no soldier.
IAGO: Touch me not so near.
    I had rather have this tongue cut from my mouth
    Than it should do offense to Michael Cassio;
    Yet I persuade myself, to speak the truth
    Shall nothing wrong him. This it is, general.   200
    Montano and myself being in speech,
    There comes a fellow crying out for help,
    And Cassio following him with determined sword
    To execute° upon him. Sir, this gentleman
    Steps in to Cassio and entreats his pause.   205
    Myself the crying fellow did pursue,
    Lest by his clamor — as it so fell out —
    The town might fall in fright. He, swift of foot,
    Outran my purpose; and I returned then rather
    For that I heard the clink and fall of swords,   210
    And Cassio high in oath;° which till to-night
    I ne'er might say before. When I came back —
    For this was brief — I found them close together
    At blow and thrust, even as again they were
    When you yourself did part them.   215
    More of this matter cannot I report;
    But men are men; the best sometimes forget.
    Though Cassio did some little wrong to him,
    As men in rage strike those that wish them best,
    Yet surely Cassio I believe received   220
    From him that fled some strange indignity,
    Which patience could not pass.°
OTHELLO: I know, Iago,
    Thy honesty and love doth mince this matter,
    Making it light to Cassio. Cassio, I love thee;
    But never more be officer of mine.   225

Enter Desdemona, attended.

    Look if my gentle love be not raised up!
    I'll make thee an example.
DESDEMONA: What's the matter?
OTHELLO: All's well now, sweeting; come away to bed.
    [To Montano.]
    Sir, for your hurts, myself will be your surgeon.
    Lead him off.   230

---

194 partially . . . office: Prejudiced by comradeship or official relations.   **204 execute:** Work his will.   **211 high in oath:** Cursing.   **222 pass:** Pass over, ignore.

[Montano is led off.]

Iago, look with care about the town
And silence those whom this vile brawl distracted.°
Come, Desdemona; 'tis the soldiers' life
To have their balmy slumbers waked with strife.

Exit [with all but Iago and Cassio].

IAGO: What, are you hurt, lieutenant?   235

CASSIO: Ay, past all surgery.

IAGO: Marry, God forbid!

CASSIO: Reputation, reputation, reputation! O, I have lost my reputation! I
have lost the immortal part of myself, and what remains is bestial. My reputation, Iago, my reputation!   240

IAGO: As I am an honest man, I thought you had received some bodily wound.
There is more sense in that than in reputation. Reputation is an idle and
most false imposition; oft got without merit and lost without deserving.
You have lost no reputation at all unless you repute yourself such a loser.
What, man! there are ways to recover° the general again. You are but now   245
cast in his mood° — a punishment more in policy than in malice, even so
as one would beat his offenseless dog to affright an imperious lion. Sue to
him again, and he's yours.

CASSIO: I will rather sue to be despised than to deceive so good a commander
with so slight, so drunken, and so indiscreet an officer. Drunk! and speak   250
parrot!° and squabble! swagger! swear! and discourse fustian° with one's
own shadow! O thou invisible spirit of wine, if thou hast no name to be
known by, let us call thee devil!

IAGO: What was he that you followed with your sword? What had he done
to you?   255

CASSIO: I know not.

IAGO: Is't possible?

CASSIO: I remember a mass of things, but nothing distinctly; a quarrel, but
nothing wherefore. O God, that men should put an enemy in their mouths
to steal away their brains! that we should with joy, pleasance, revel, and   260
applause° transform ourselves into beasts!

IAGO: Why, but you are now well enough. How came you thus recovered?

CASSIO: It hath pleased the devil drunkenness to give place to the devil wrath.
One unperfectness shows me another, to make me frankly despise myself.

IAGO: Come, you are too severe a moraler. As the time, the place, and the con-   265
dition of this country stands, I could heartily wish this had not so befall'n;
but since it is as it is, mend it for your own good.

CASSIO: I will ask him for my place again: he shall tell me I am a drunkard!
Had I as many mouths as Hydra,° such an answer would stop them all. To

---

232 distracted: Excited.   **245 recover:** Regain favor with.   **246 in his mood:**
Dismissed because of his anger.   **251 parrot:** Meaningless phrases;   **fustian:** Bombastic
nonsense.   **261 applause:** Desire to please.   **269 Hydra:** Monster with many heads.

be now a sensible man, by and by a fool, and presently a beast! O strange! 270
Every inordinate cup is unblest, and the ingredient° is a devil.

IAGO: Come, come, good wine is a good familiar creature if it be well used.
Exclaim no more against it. And, good lieutenant, I think you think I
love you.

CASSIO: I have well approved° it, sir. I drunk!   275

IAGO: You or any man living may be drunk at some time, man. I'll tell you
what you shall do. Our general's wife is now the general. I may say so in
this respect, for that he hath devoted and given up himself to the contemplation, mark, and denotement of her parts and graces. Confess yourself
freely to her; importune her help to put you in your place again. She is of so   280
free,° so kind, so apt, so blessed a disposition she holds it a vice in her goodness not to do more than she is requested. This broken joint between you
and her husband entreat her to splinter;° and my fortunes against any lay°
worth naming, this crack of your love shall grow stronger than it was
before.   285

CASSIO: You advise me well.

IAGO: I protest, in the sincerity of love and honest kindness.

CASSIO: I think it freely; and betimes in the morning will I beseech the virtuous Desdemona to undertake for me. I am desperate of my fortunes if they
check me here.   290

IAGO: You are in the right. Good night, lieutenant; I must to the watch.

CASSIO: Good night, honest Iago.   *Exit Cassio.*

IAGO: And what's he then that says I play the villain,
When this advice is free I give and honest,
Probal° to thinking, and indeed the course   295
To win the Moor again? For 'tis most easy
Th' inclining Desdemona to subdue°
In an honest suit; she's framed as fruitful
As the free elements. And then for her
To win the Moor—were't to renounce his baptism,   300
All seals and symbols of redeemèd sin—
His soul is so enfettered to her love
That she may make, unmake, do what she list,
Even as her appetite shall play the god
With his weak function. How am I then villain   305
To counsel Cassio to this parallel° course,
Directly to his good? Divinity° of hell!
When devils will the blackest sins put on,°
They do suggest at first with heavenly shows,
As I do now. For whiles this honest fool   310
Plies Desdemona to repair his fortunes,

---

271 ingredient: Contents.   **275 approved:** Proved.   **281 free:** Bounteous.
283 splinter: Bind up with splints;   **lay:** Wager.   **295 Probal:** Probable.   **297 subdue:** Persuade.   **306 parallel:** Corresponding.   **307 Divinity:** Theology.   **308
put on:** Incite.

And she for him pleads strongly to the Moor,
I'll pour this pestilence into his ear,
That she repeals him° for her body's lust;
And by how much she strives to do him good,   315
She shall undo her credit with the Moor.
So will I turn her virtue into pitch,
And out of her own goodness make the net
That shall enmesh them all.

Enter Roderigo.

                              How, now, Roderigo?

RODERIGO: I do follow here in the chase, not like a hound that hunts, but one   320
   that fills up the cry.° My money is almost spent; I have been to-night
   exceedingly well cudgelled; and I think the issue will be—I shall have so
   much experience for my pains; and so, with no money at all, and a little
   more wit, return again to Venice.

IAGO: How poor are they that have not patience!   325
   What wound did ever heal but by degrees?
   Thou know'st we work by wit, and not by witchcraft;
   And wit depends on dilatory time.
   Does't not go well? Cassio hath beaten thee,
   And thou by that small hurt hast cashiered Cassio.°   330
   Though other things grow fair against the sun,
   Yet fruits that blossom first will first be ripe.
   Content thyself awhile. By the mass, 'tis morning!
   Pleasure and action make the hours seem short.
   Retire thee; go where thou art billeted.   335
   Away, I say! Thou shalt know more hereafter.
   Nay, get thee gone!   *Exit Roderigo.*
                   Two things are to be done:
   My wife must move for Cassio to her mistress;
   I'll set her on;
   Myself the while to draw the Moor apart   340
   And bring him jump° when he may Cassio find
   Soliciting his wife. Ay, that's the way!
   Dull no device by coldness and delay.   *Exit.*

[ACT III, Scene I: Before the chamber of Othello and Desdemona.]

Enter Cassio, with Musicians and the Clown.

CASSIO: Masters, play here, I will content° your pains:
   Something that's brief; and bid "Good morrow, general."

---

314 repeals   him: Seeks   his   recall.   **321 cry:** Pack.   **330 cashiered   Cassio:**
Maneuvered Cassio's discharge.   **341 jump:** At the exact moment.   ACT III, SCENE I. 1
content: Reward.

[They play.]

CLOWN: Why, masters, ha' your instruments been in Naples,° that they speak
    i' th' nose thus?

MUSICIAN: How, sir, how? 5

CLOWN: Are these, I pray you, called wind instruments?

MUSICIAN: Ay, marry, are they, sir.

CLOWN: O, thereby hangs a tail.

MUSICIAN: Whereby hangs a tail, sir?

CLOWN: Marry, sir, by many a wind instrument that I know. But, masters, 10
    here's money for you; and the general so likes your music that he desires
    you, for love's sake, to make no more noise with it.

MUSICIAN: Well, sir, we will not.

CLOWN: If you have any music that may not be heard, to't again: but, as they
    say, to hear music the general does not greatly care. 15

MUSICIAN: We have none such, sir.

CLOWN: Then put up your pipes in your bag, for I'll away. Go, vanish into air,
    away! *Exit Musician [with his fellows].*

CASSIO: Dost thou hear, my honest friend?

CLOWN: No, I hear not your honest friend. I hear you. 20

CASSIO: Prithee keep up thy quillets.° There's a poor piece of gold for thee. If
    the gentlewoman that attends the general's wife be stirring, tell her there's
    one Cassio entreats her a little favor of speech. Wilt thou do this?

CLOWN: She is stirring sir. If she will stir hither, I shall seem to notify unto her.

CASSIO: [Do, good my friend.] *Exit Clown.*

Enter Iago.

                In happy time,° Iago. 25

IAGO: You have not been abed then?

CASSIO: Why, no; the day had broke
    Before we parted. I have made bold, Iago,
    To send in to your wife: my suit to her
    Is that she will to virtuous Desdemona 30
    Procure me some access.

IAGO: I'll send her to you presently;
    And I'll devise a mean to draw the Moor
    Out of the way, that your converse and business
    May be more free.

CASSIO: I humbly thank you for't. *Exit [Iago].*
                I never knew 35
    A Florentine° more kind and honest.

Enter Emilia.

EMILIA: Good morrow, good lieutenant. I am sorry

---

3 Naples: (Notorious for its association with venereal disease). **21 quillets:** Quips.
25 In happy time: Well met. **36 Florentine:** I.e., even a Florentine (like Cassio; Iago
was a Venetian).

For your displeasure: but all will sure be well.
The general and his wife are talking of it,
And she speaks for you stoutly. The Moor replied   40
That he you hurt is of great fame in Cyprus
And great affinity,° and that in wholesome wisdom
He might not but refuse you; but he protests he loves you,
And needs no other suitor but his likings
[To take the safest occasion° by the front°]   45
To bring you in again.

CASSIO: Yet I beseech you,
If you think fit, or that it may be done,
Give me advantage of some brief discourse
With Desdemona alone.

EMILIA: Pray you come in.
I will bestow you where you shall have time   50
To speak your bosom° freely.

CASSIO: I am much bound to you.   *Exeunt.*

[Scene II: The castle.]

Enter Othello, Iago, and Gentlemen.

OTHELLO: These letters give, Iago, to the pilot
      And by him do my duties to the Senate.
      That done, I will be walking on the works;°
      Repair there to me.

IAGO: Well, my good lord, I'll do't.

OTHELLO: This fortification, gentlemen, shall we see't?   5

GENTLEMEN: We'll wait upon your lordship.   *Exeunt.*

[Scene III: The castle grounds.]

Enter Desdemona, Cassio, and Emilia.

DESDEMONA: Be thou assured, good Cassio, I will do
      All my abilities in thy behalf.

EMILIA: Good madam, do. I warrant it grieves my husband
      As if the cause were his.

DESDEMONA: O, that's an honest fellow. Do not doubt, Cassio,   5
      But I will have my lord and you again
      As friendly as you were.

CASSIO: Bounteous madam,
      Whatever shall become of Michael Cassio,
      He's never anything but your true servant.

DESDEMONA: I know't; I thank you. You do love my lord;   10

---

42 affinity: Family   connections.   **45 occasion:** Opportunity;   **front:** Forelock.   **51**
your bosom: Your inmost thoughts.   **SCENE II. 3 works:** Fortifications.

You have known him long; and be you well assured
He shall in strangeness° stand no farther off
Than in a politic distance.°

CASSIO: Ay, but, lady,
That policy may either last so long,
Or feed upon such nice and waterish diet,° 15
Or breed itself so out of circumstance,
That, I being absent, and my place supplied,
My general will forget my love and service.

DESDEMONA: Do not doubt° that; before Emilia here
I give thee warrant of thy place. Assure thee, 20
If I do vow a friendship, I'll perform it
To the last article. My lord shall never rest;
I'll watch him tame° and talk him out of patience;
His bed shall seem a school, his board a shrift;°
I'll intermingle everything he does 25
With Cassio's suit. Therefore be merry, Cassio,
For thy solicitor shall rather die
Than give thy cause away.

Enter Othello and Iago [at a distance].

EMILIA: Madam, here comes my lord.

CASSIO: Madam, I'll take my leave. 30

DESDEMONA: Why, stay, and hear me speak.

CASSIO: Madam, not now: I am very ill at ease,
Unfit for mine own purposes.

DESDEMONA: Well, do your discretion. *Exit Cassio.*

IAGO: Ha! I like not that.

OTHELLO: What dost thou say? 35

IAGO: Nothing, my lord; or if — I know not what.

OTHELLO: Was not that Cassio parted from my wife?

IAGO: Cassio, my lord? No, sure, I cannot think it,
That he would steal away so guilty-like,
Seeing your coming.

OTHELLO: I do believe 'twas he. 40

DESDEMONA: How now, my lord?
I have been talking with a suitor here,
A man that languishes in your displeasure.

OTHELLO: What is't you mean?

DESDEMONA: Why, your lieutenant, Cassio. Good my lord, 45
If I have any grace or power to move you,
His present° reconciliation take;
For if he be not one that truly loves you,

SCENE III. **12 strangeness:** Aloofness. **13 Than . . . distance:** Than wise policy
requires. **15 Or . . . diet:** Or be continued for such slight reasons. **19 doubt:** Fear.
23 watch him tame: Keep him awake until he gives in. **24 shrift:** Confessional. **47
present:** Immediate.

That errs in ignorance, and not in cunning,
I have no judgment in an honest face,   50
I prithee call him back.
OTHELLO: Went he hence now?
DESDEMONA: Yes, faith; so humbled
That he hath left part of his grief with me
To suffer with him. Good love, call him back.
OTHELLO: Not now, sweet Desdemon; some other time.   55
DESDEMONA: But shall't be shortly?
OTHELLO: The sooner, sweet, for you.
DESDEMONA: Shall't be to-night at supper?
OTHELLO: No, not to-night.
DESDEMONA: To-morrow dinner then?
OTHELLO: I shall not dine at home;
I meet the captains at the citadel.
DESDEMONA: Why then, to-morrow night, or Tuesday morn,   60
On Tuesday noon or night, or Wednesday morn.
I prithee name the time, but let it not
Exceed three days. I' faith, he's penitent;
And yet his trespass, in our common reason
(Save that, they say, the wars must make examples   65
Out of their best), is not almost° a fault
T' incur a private check.° When shall he come?
Tell me, Othello. I wonder in my soul
What you could ask me that I should deny
Or stand so mamm'ring on.° What? Michael Cassio,   70
That came a-wooing with you, and so many a time,
When I have spoke of you dispraisingly,
Hath ta'en your part—to have so much to do
To bring him in? By'r Lady, I could do much—
OTHELLO: Prithee no more. Let him come when he will!   75
I will deny thee nothing.
DESDEMONA: Why, this is not a boon;
'Tis as I should entreat you wear your gloves,
Or feed on nourishing dishes, or keep you warm,
Or sue to you to do a peculiar profit
To your own person. Nay, when I have a suit   80
Wherein I mean to touch your love indeed,
It shall be full of poise and difficult weight,
And fearful° to be granted.
OTHELLO: I will deny thee nothing!
Whereon I do beseech thee grant me this,
To leave me but a little to myself.   85

66 not almost: Hardly.   **67 a private check:** Even a private reprimand.   **70 mamm'ring on:** Hesitating about.   **83 fearful:** Dangerous.

DESDEMONA: Shall I deny you? No. Farewell, my lord.

OTHELLO: Farewell, my Desdemon: I'll come to thee straight.

DESDEMONA: Emilia, come. — Be as your fancies teach you;
Whate'er you be, I am obedient.   *Exit [with Emilia].*

OTHELLO: Excellent wretch!° Perdition catch my soul   90
But I do love thee! and when I love thee not,
Chaos is come again.

IAGO: My noble lord—

OTHELLO: What dost thou say, Iago?

IAGO: Did Michael Cassio, when you wooed my lady,
Know of your love?   95

OTHELLO: He did, from first to last. Why dost thou ask?

IAGO: But for a satisfaction of my thought;
No further harm.

OTHELLO: Why of thy thought, Iago?

IAGO: I did not think he had been acquainted with her.

OTHELLO: O, yes, and went between us° very oft.   100

IAGO: Indeed?

OTHELLO: Indeed? Ay, indeed! Discern'st thou aught in that?
Is he not honest?

IAGO: Honest, my lord?

OTHELLO: Honest. Ay, honest.

IAGO: My lord, for aught I know.

OTHELLO: What dost thou think?

IAGO: Think, my lord?

OTHELLO: Think, my lord?   105
By heaven, he echoes me,
As if there were some monster in his thought
Too hideous to be shown. Thou dost mean something:
I heard thee say even now, thou lik'st not that,
When Cassio left my wife. What didst not like?   110
And when I told thee he was of my counsel
In my whole course of wooing, thou cried'st "Indeed?"
And didst contract and purse thy brow together,
As if thou then hadst shut up in thy brain
Some horrible conceit.° If thou dost love me,   115
Show me thy thought.

IAGO: My lord, you know I love you.

OTHELLO: I think thou dost;
And, for I know thou'rt full of love and honesty
And weigh'st thy words before thou giv'st them breath,
Therefore these stops of thine fright me the more;   120
For such things in a false disloyal knave

90 wretch: (A term of endearment). **100 went . . . us:** (I.e., as messenger). **115 conceit:** Fancy.

Are tricks of custom; but in a man that's just
They are close dilations, working from the heart
That passion cannot rule.°

IAGO: For Michael Cassio,
I dare be sworn I think that he is honest.   125

OTHELLO: I think so too.

IAGO: Men should be what they seem;
Or those that be not, would they might seem none!°

OTHELLO: Certain, men should be what they seem.

IAGO: Why then, I think Cassio's an honest man.

OTHELLO: Nay, yet there's more in this.   130
I prithee speak to me as to thy thinkings,
As thou dost ruminate, and give thy worst of thoughts
The worst of words.

IAGO: Good my lord, pardon me:
Though I am bound to every act of duty,
I am not bound to that all slaves are free to.°   135
Utter my thoughts? Why, say they are vile and false,
As where's that palace whereinto foul things
Sometimes intrude not? Who has a breast so pure
But some uncleanly apprehensions
Keep leets and law days,° and in Sessions sit   140
With meditations lawful?

OTHELLO: Thou dost conspire against thy friend, Iago,
If thou but think'st him wronged, and mak'st his ear
A stranger to thy thoughts.

IAGO: I do beseech you—
Though I perchance am vicious in my guess   145
(As I confess it is my nature's plague
To spy into abuses, and oft my jealousy°
Shapes faults that are not), that your wisdom yet
From one that so imperfectly conjects°
Would take no notice, nor build yourself a trouble   150
Out of his scattering and unsure observance.
It were not for your quiet nor your good,
Nor for my manhood, honesty, and wisdom,
To let you know my thoughts.

OTHELLO: What dost thou mean?

IAGO: Good name in man and woman, dear my lord,   155
Is the immediate° jewel of their souls.

123–24 close dilations . . . rule: Secret emotions that well up in spite of restraint.
127 seem none: I.e., not pretend to be men when they are really monsters.   **135
bound . . . free to:** Bound to tell that which even slaves are allowed to keep to themselves.
140 leets and law days: Sittings of the courts.   **147 jealousy:** Suspicion.   **149
conjects:** Conjectures.   **156 immediate:** Nearest the heart.

Who steals my purse steals trash; 'tis something, nothing;
'Twas mine, 'tis his, and has been slave to thousands;
But he that filches from me my good name
Robs me of that which not enriches him   160
And makes me poor indeed.
OTHELLO: By heaven, I'll know thy thoughts!
IAGO: You cannot, if my heart were in your hand;
    Nor shall not whilst 'tis in my custody.
OTHELLO: Ha!
IAGO: O, beware, my lord, of jealousy!   165
    It is the green-eyed monster, which doth mock°
    The meat it feeds on. That cuckold lives in bliss
    Who, certain of his fate, loves not his wronger;
    But O, what damnèd minutes tells he o'er
    Who dotes, yet doubts—suspects, yet strongly loves!   170
OTHELLO: O misery!
IAGO: Poor and content is rich, and rich enough;
    But riches fineless° is as poor as winter
    To him that ever fears he shall be poor.
    Good God, the souls of all my tribe defend
    From jealousy!   175
OTHELLO: Why, why is this?
    Think'st thou I'ld make a life of jealousy,
    To follow still the changes of the moon
    With fresh suspicions? No! To be once in doubt
    Is once to be resolved. Exchange me for a goat   180
    When I shall turn the business of my soul
    To such exsufflicate and blown° surmises,
    Matching this inference. 'Tis not to make me jealous
    To say my wife is fair, feeds well, loves company,
    Is free of speech, sings, plays, and dances;   185
    Where virtue is, these are more virtuous.
    Nor from mine own weak merits will I draw
    The smallest fear or doubt of her revolt,°
    For she had eyes, and chose me. No, Iago;
    I'll see before I doubt; when I doubt, prove;   190
    And on the proof there is no more but this—
    Away at once with love or jealousy!
IAGO: I am glad of this; for now I shall have reason
    To show the love and duty that I bear you
    With franker spirit. Therefore, as I am bound,   195
    Receive it from me. I speak not yet of proof.
    Look at your wife; observe her well with Cassio;

166 mock: Play with, like a cat with a mouse.   **173 fineless:** Unlimited.   **182
exsufflicate and blown:** Spat out and flyblown.   **188 revolt:** Unfaithfulness.

Wear your eyes thus, not jealous nor secure:°
I would not have your free and noble nature,
Out of self-bounty,° be abused. Look to't.   200
I know our country disposition well:
In Venice they do let God see the pranks
They dare not show their husbands; their best conscience
Is not to leave't undone, but keep't unknown.

OTHELLO: Dost thou say so?   205
IAGO: She did deceive her father, marrying you;
And when she seemed to shake and fear your looks,
She loved them most.

OTHELLO: And so she did.
IAGO: Why, go to then!
She that, so young, could give out such a seeming
To seel° her father's eyes up close as oak°—   210
He thought 'twas witchcraft—but I am much to blame.
I humbly do beseech you of your pardon
For too much loving you.

OTHELLO: I am bound to thee for ever.
IAGO: I see this hath a little dashed your spirits.
OTHELLO: Not a jot, not a jot.   215
IAGO: I' faith, I fear it has.
I hope you will consider what is spoke
Comes from my love. But I do see y' are moved.
I am to pray you not to strain my speech
To grosser issues° nor to larger reach
Than to suspicion.   220

OTHELLO: I will not.
IAGO: Should you do so, my lord,
My speech should fall into such vile success°
As my thoughts aim not at. Cassio's my worthy friend—
My lord, I see y' are moved.

OTHELLO: No, not much moved:
I do not think but Desdemona's honest.°   225
IAGO: Long live she so! and long live you to think so!
OTHELLO: And yet, how nature erring from itself—
IAGO: Ay, there's the point! as (to be bold with you)
Not to affect many proposèd matches
Of her own clime, complexion, and degree,   230
Whereto we see in all things nature tends—
Foh! one may smell in such a will most rank,
Foul disproportions, thought unnatural—

---

198 secure: Overconfident.   **200 self-bounty:** Natural goodness.   **210 seel:** Close;
oak: Oak grain.   **219 To grosser issues:** To mean something more monstrous.   **222
vile success:** Evil outcome.   **225 honest:** Chaste.

But pardon me—I do not in position°
Distinctly speak of her; though I may fear   235
Her will, recoiling° to her better judgment,
May fall to match° you with her country forms,
And happily° repent.
OTHELLO: Farewell, farewell!
If more thou dost perceive, let me know more.
Set on thy wife to observe. Leave me, Iago.   240
IAGO: My lord, I take my leave.   *[Going.]*
OTHELLO: Why did I marry? This honest creature doubtless
Sees and knows more, much more, than he unfolds.
IAGO *[returns]:*   My lord, I would I might entreat your honor
To scan this thing no further: leave it to time.   245
Although 'tis fit that Cassio have his place,
For sure he fills it up with great ability,
Yet, if you please to hold off a while,
You shall by that perceive him and his means.
Note if your lady strain his entertainment°   250
With any strong or vehement importunity;
Much will be seen in that. In the mean time
Let me be thought too busy° in my fears
(As worthy cause I have to fear I am)
And hold her free,° I do beseech your honor.   255
OTHELLO: Fear not my government.°
IAGO: I once more take my leave.   *Exit.*
OTHELLO: This fellow's of exceeding honesty,
And knows all qualities,° with a learned spirit
Of° human dealings. If I do prove her haggard,°   260
Though that her jesses° were my dear heartstrings,
I'd whistle her off and let her down the wind
To prey at fortune.° Haply, for I am black
And have not those soft parts of conversation°
That chamberers° have, or for I am declined   265
Into the vale of years—yet that's not much—
She's gone. I am abused, and my relief
Must be to loathe her. O curse of marriage,
That we can call these delicate creatures ours,
And not their appetites! I had rather be a toad   270

---

234 position: Definite assertion. **236 recoiling:** Reverting. **237 fall to match:** Happen to compare. **238 happily:** Haply, perhaps. **250 strain his entertainment:** Urge his recall. **253 busy:** Meddlesome. **255 hold her free:** Consider her guiltless. **256 government:** Self-control. **259 qualities:** Natures. **259–60 learned spirit Of:** Mind informed about. **260 haggard:** A wild hawk. **261 jesses:** Thongs for controlling a hawk. **262–63 whistle . . . fortune:** Turn her out and let her take care of herself. **264 soft . . . conversation:** Ingratiating manners. **265 chamberers:** Courtiers.

And live upon the vapor of a dungeon
Than keep a corner in the thing I love
For others' uses. Yet 'tis the plague of great ones;°
Prerogatived° are they less than the base.
'Tis destiny unshunnable, like death.   275
Even then this forkèd plague° is fated to us
When we do quicken.° Look where she comes.

Enter Desdemona and Emilia.

If she be false, O, then heaven mocks itself!
I'll not believe't.
DESDEMONA: How now, my dear Othello?
Your dinner, and the generous° islanders   280
By you invited, do attend your presence.
OTHELLO: I am to blame.
DESDEMONA: Why do you speak so faintly?
Are you not well?
OTHELLO: I have a pain upon my forehead, here.
DESDEMONA: Faith, that's with watching;° 'twill away again.   285
Let me but bind it hard, within this hour
It will be well.
OTHELLO: Your napkin° is too little;

[He pushes the handkerchief from him, and it falls unnoticed.]

Let it° alone. Come, I'll go in with you.
DESDEMONA: I am very sorry that you are not well.   *Exit [with Othello].*
EMILIA: I am glad I have found this napkin;   290
This was her first remembrance from the Moor,
My wayward husband hath a hundred times
Wooed me to steal it; but she so loves the token
(For he conjured her she should ever keep it)
That she reserves it evermore about her   295
To kiss and talk to. I'll have the work ta'en out°
And give't Iago.
What he will do with it heaven knows, not I;
I nothing but to please his fantasy.°

Enter Iago.

IAGO: How now? What do you here alone?   300
EMILIA: Do not you chide; I have a thing for you.
IAGO: A thing for me? It is a common thing—
EMILIA: Ha?
IAGO: To have a foolish wife.

---

273 great ones: Prominent men. **274 Prerogatived:** Privileged. **276 forkèd plague:** I.e., horns of a cuckold. **277 do quicken:** Are born. **280 generous:** Noble. **285 watching:** Working late. **287 napkin:** Handkerchief. **288 it:** I.e., his forehead. **296 work ta'en out:** Pattern copied. **299 fantasy:** Whim.

EMILIA: O, is that all? What will you give me now   305
    For that same handkerchief?
IAGO: What handkerchief?
EMILIA: What handkerchief!
    Why, that the Moor first gave to Desdemona;
    That which so often you did bid me steal.
IAGO: Hast stol'n it from her?   310
EMILIA: No, faith; she let it drop by negligence,
    And to th' advantage,° I, being here, took't up.
    Look, here it is.
IAGO: A good wench! Give it me.
EMILIA: What will you do with't, that you have been so earnest
    To have me filch it?
IAGO: Why, what is that to you?   315
[Snatches it.]

EMILIA: If it be not for some purpose of import,°
    Give't me again. Poor lady, she'll run mad
    When she shall lack it.
IAGO: Be not acknown on't;° I have use for it.
    Go, leave me.   *Exit Emilia.*   320
    I will in Cassio's lodgings lose this napkin
    And let him find it. Trifles light as air
    Are to the jealous confirmations strong
    As proofs of holy writ. This may do something.
    The Moor already changes with my poison: 325
    Dangerous conceits° are in their nature poisons,
    Which at the first are scarce found to distaste,
    But with a little act upon the blood
    Burn like the mines of sulphur.
Enter Othello.

                      I did say so.
    Look where he comes! Not poppy nor mandragora,°   330
    Nor all the drowsy syrups of the world,
    Shall ever med'cine thee to that sweet sleep
    Which thou owedst yesterday.
OTHELLO: Ha! ha! false to me?
IAGO: Why, how now, general? No more of that!
OTHELLO: Avaunt! be gone! Thou hast set me on the rack.   335
    I swear 'tis better to be much abused
    Than but to know't a little.
IAGO: How now, my lord?
OTHELLO: What sense had I of her stol'n hours of lust?

---

312 to th' advantage: Opportunely.   **316 import:** Importance.   **319 Be . . . on't:** Do not acknowledge it.   **326 conceits:** Ideas.   **330 mandragora:** A narcotic.

I saw't not, thought it not, it harmed not me;
I slept the next night well, fed well, was free° and merry;   340
I found not Cassio's kisses on her lips
He that is robbed, not wanting° what is stol'n,
Let him not know't, and he's not robbed at all.

IAGO: I am sorry to hear this.

OTHELLO: I had been happy if the general camp,   345
Pioneers° and all, had tasted her sweet body,
So I had nothing known. O, now for ever
Farewell the tranquil mind! farewell content!
Farewell the plumèd troop, and the big° wars
That make ambition virtue! O, farewell!   350
Farewell the neighing steed and the shrill trump,
The spirit-stirring drum, th' ear-piercing fife,
The royal banner, and all quality,
Pride, pomp, and circumstance° of glorious war!
And O you mortal engines° whose rude throats   355
Th' immortal Jove's dread clamors counterfeit,°
Farewell! Othello's occupation's gone!

IAGO: Is't possible, my lord?

OTHELLO: Villain, be sure thou prove my love a whore!
Be sure of it; give me the ocular proof;   360
Or, by the worth of mine eternal soul,
Thou hadst been better have been born a dog
Than answer my waked wrath!

IAGO: Is't come to this?

OTHELLO: Make me to see't; or at the least so prove it
That the probation° bear no hinge nor loop   365
To hang a doubt on — or woe upon thy life!

IAGO: My noble lord—

OTHELLO: If thou dost slander her and torture me,
Never pray more; abandon all remorse;
On horror's head horrors accumulate;   370
Do deeds to make heaven weep, all earth amazed;
For nothing canst thou to damnation add
Greater than that.

IAGO: O grace! O heaven forgive me!
Are you a man? Have you a soul or sense? —
God b' wi' you! take mine office. O wretched fool,   375
That liv'st to make thine honesty a vice!
O monstrous world! Take note, take note, O world,
To be direct and honest is not safe.

---

340 free: Carefree.   **342 wanting:** Missing.   **346 Pioneers:** Sappers, laborers.
349 big: Stately.   **354 circumstance:** Pageantry.   **355 mortal   engines:** Deadly
artillery.   **356 counterfeit:** Imitate.   **365 probation:** Proof.

I thank you for this profit;° and from hence
I'll love no friend, sith love breeds such offense.   380
OTHELLO: Nay, stay. Thou shouldst be honest.
IAGO: I should be wise; for honesty's a fool
And loses that it works for.
OTHELLO: By the world,
I think my wife be honest, and think she is not;
I think that thou art just, and think thou art not.   385
I'll have some proof. Her name, that was as fresh
As Dian's visage, is now begrimed and black
As mine own face. If there be cords, or knives,
Poison, or fire, or suffocating streams,
I'll not endure it. Would I were satisfied!°   390
IAGO: I see, sir, you are eaten up with passion:
I do repent me that I put it to you.
You would be satisfied?
OTHELLO: Would? Nay, I will.
IAGO: And may; but how? how satisfied, my lord?
Would you, the supervisor,° grossly gape on?   395
Behold her topped?
OTHELLO: Death and damnation! O!
IAGO: It were a tedious difficulty, I think,
To bring them to that prospect. Damn them then,
If ever mortal eyes do see them bolster°
More than their own! What then? How then?   400
What shall I say? Where's satisfaction?
It is impossible you should see this,
Were they as prime° as goats, as hot as monkeys,
As salt° as wolves in pride,° and fools as gross
As ignorance made drunk. But yet, I say,   405
If imputation and strong circumstances
Which lead directly to the door of truth
Will give you satisfaction, you may have't.
OTHELLO: Give me a living reason she's disloyal.
IAGO: I do not like the office.   410
But sith I am ent'red in this cause so far,
Pricked to't by foolish honesty and love,
I will go on. I lay with Cassio lately,
And being troubled with a raging tooth,
I could not sleep.   415
There are a kind of men so loose of soul
That in their sleeps will mutter their affairs.

---

379 profit: Profitable lesson.   **390 satisfied:** Completely informed.   **395 supervisor:**
Spectator.   **399 bolster:** Lie   together.   **403 prime:** Lustful.   **404 salt:** Lecherous;
pride: Heat.

One of this kind is Cassio.
In sleep I heard him say, "Sweet Desdemona,
Let us be wary, let us hide our loves!"   420
And then, sir, would he gripe and wring my hand,
Cry "O sweet creature!" and then kiss me hard,
As if he plucked up kisses by the roots
That grew upon my lips; then laid his leg
Over my thigh, and sighed, and kissed, and then   425
Cried "Cursèd fate that gave thee to the Moor!"

OTHELLO: O monstrous! monstrous!

IAGO: Nay, this was but his dream.

OTHELLO: But this denoted a foregone conclusion;°
'Tis a shrewd doubt,° though it be but a dream.

IAGO: And this may help to thicken other proofs   430
That do demonstrate thinly.

OTHELLO: I'll tear her all to pieces!

IAGO: Nay, but be wise. Yet we see nothing done;
She may be honest yet. Tell me but this—
Have you not sometimes seen a handkerchief
Spotted with strawberries in your wife's hand?   435

OTHELLO: I gave her such a one; 'twas my first gift.

IAGO: I know not that; but such a handkerchief—
I am sure it was your wife's—did I to-day
See Cassio wipe his beard with.

OTHELLO: If it be that—

IAGO: If it be that, or any that was hers,   440
It speaks against her with the other proofs.

OTHELLO: O, that the slave had forty thousand lives!
One is too poor, too weak for my revenge.
Now do I see 'tis true. Look here, Iago:
All my fond love thus do I blow to heaven.   445
'Tis gone.
Arise, black vengeance, from the hollow hell!
Yield up, O love, thy crown and hearted throne
To tyrannous hate! Swell, bosom, with thy fraught,°
For 'tis of aspics'° tongues!

IAGO: Yet be content.   450

OTHELLO: O, blood, blood, blood!

IAGO: Patience, I say. Your mind perhaps may change.

OTHELLO: Never, Iago. Like to the Pontic sea,°
Whose icy current and compulsive course
Ne'er feels retiring ebb, but keeps due on   455

---

428 foregone conclusion: Previous experience. **429 a shrewd doubt:** Cursedly
suspicious. **449 fraught:** Burden. **450 aspics:** Deadly poisonous snakes. **453
Pontic sea:** Black Sea.

To the Propontic and the Hellespont,
Even so my bloody thoughts, with violent pace,
Shall ne'er look back, ne'er ebb to humble love,
Till that a capable° and wide revenge
Swallow them up.
    (He kneels.)   Now, by yond marble heaven,   460
In the due reverence of a sacred vow
I here engage my words.
IAGO: Do not rise yet.

(Iago kneels.)

Witness, you ever-burning lights above,
You elements that clip° us round about,
Witness that here Iago doth give up   465
The execution° of his wit,° hands, heart
To wronged Othello's service! Let him command,
And to obey shall be in me remorse,°
What bloody business ever.

[They rise.]

OTHELLO: I greet thy love,
Not with vain thanks but with acceptance bounteous,   470
And will upon the instant put thee to't.
Within these three days let me hear thee say
That Cassio's not alive.
IAGO: My friend is dead; 'tis done at your request.
But let her live.   475
OTHELLO: Damn her, lewd minx! O, damn her! damn her!
Come, go with me apart. I will withdraw
To furnish me with some swift means of death
For the fair devil. Now art thou my lieutenant.
    IAGO: I am your own forever.   *Exeunt.*   480

[Scene IV: The environs of the castle.]

Enter Desdemona, Emilia, and Clown.

DESDEMONA: Do you know, sirrah, where Lieutenant Cassio lies?°
CLOWN: I dare not say he lies anywhere.
DESDEMONA: Why, man?
CLOWN: He's a soldier, and for me to say a soldier lies is stabbing.
DESDEMONA: Go to. Where lodges he?   5
CLOWN: To tell you where he lodges is to tell you where I lie.
DESDEMONA: Can anything be made of this?

---

459 capable: All-embracing.   **464 clip:** Encompass.   **466 execution:** Activities;
wit: Mind.   **468 remorse:** Pity.   **Scene IV. 1 lies:** Lives, lodges.

CLOWN: I know not where he lodges; and for me to devise a lodging, and say he
lies here or he lies there, were to lie in mine own throat.

DESDEMONA: Can you enquire him out, and be edified by report?   10

CLOWN: I will catechize the world for him; that is, make questions, and by
them answer.

DESDEMONA: Seek him, bid him come hither. Tell him I have moved° my lord on
his behalf and hope all will be well.

CLOWN: To do this is within the compass of man's wit, and therefore I'll   15
attempt the doing of it.   *Exit.*

DESDEMONA: Where should I lose that handkerchief, Emilia?

EMILIA: I know not, madam.

DESDEMONA: Believe me, I had rather have lost my purse
Full of crusadoes;° and but my noble Moor
Is true of mind, and made of no such baseness   20
As jealous creatures are, it were enough
To put him to ill thinking.

EMILIA: Is he not jealous?

DESDEMONA: Who? he? I think the sun where he was born
Drew all such humors° from him.

Enter Othello.

EMILIA: Look where he comes.   25

DESDEMONA: I will not leave him now till Cassio
Be called to him—How is't with you, my lord?

OTHELLO: Well, my good lady. [Aside.] O, hardness to dissemble!—
How do you, Desdemona?

DESDEMONA: Well, my good lord.

OTHELLO: Give me your hand. This hand is moist, my lady.   30

DESDEMONA: It yet hath felt no age nor known no sorrow.

OTHELLO: This argues fruitfulness and liberal heart.
Hot, hot, and moist. This hand of yours requires
A sequester° from liberty, fasting and prayer,
Much castigation, exercise devout;   35
For here's a young and sweating devil here
That commonly rebels. 'Tis a good hand,
A frank one.

DESDEMONA: You may, indeed, say so;
For 'twas that hand that gave away my heart.   40

OTHELLO: A liberal hand! The hearts of old gave hands;
But our new heraldry° is hands, not hearts.

DESDEMONA: I cannot speak of this. Come now, your promise!

OTHELLO: What promise, chuck?

DESDEMONA: I have sent to bid Cassio come speak with you.   45

13 moved: Made proposals to.   **20 crusadoes:** Portuguese gold coins.   **25 humors:**
Inclinations.   **34 sequester:** Removal.   **42 heraldry:** Heraldic symbolism.

OTHELLO: I have a salt and sorry rheum° offends me.
   Lend me thy handkerchief.
DESDEMONA: Here, my lord.
OTHELLO: That which I gave you.
DESDEMONA: I have it not about me.
OTHELLO: Not?
DESDEMONA: No, faith, my lord.
OTHELLO: That's a fault.
   That handkerchief   50
   Did an Egyptian° to my mother give.
   She was a charmer,° and could almost read
   The thoughts of people. She told her, while she kept it,
   'Twould make her amiable° and subdue my father
   Entirely to her love; but if she lost it   55
   Or made a gift of it, my father's eye
   Should hold her loathèd, and his spirits should hunt
   After new fancies. She, dying, gave it me,
   And bid me, when my fate would have me wive;
   To give it her. I did so; and take heed on't;   60
   Make it a darling like your precious eye.
   To lose't or give't away were such perdition°
   As nothing else could match.
DESDEMONA: Is't possible?
OTHELLO: 'Tis true. There's magic in the web of it.
   A sibyl that had numb'red in the world   65
   The sun to course two hundred compasses,°
   In her prophetic fury sewed the work;
   The worms were hallowed that did breed the silk;
   And it was dyed in mummy° which the skillful
   Conserved of maidens' hearts.
DESDEMONA: I' faith? Is't true?   70
OTHELLO: Most veritable. Therefore look to't well.
DESDEMONA: Then would to God that I had never seen't!
OTHELLO: Ha! Wherefore?
DESDEMONA: Why do you speak so startingly and rash?
OTHELLO: Is't lost? Is't gone? Speak, is it out o' th' way?   75
DESDEMONA: Heaven bless us!
OTHELLO: Say you?
DESDEMONA: It is not lost. But what an if it were?
OTHELLO: How?
DESDEMONA: I say it is not lost.
OTHELLO: Fetch't, let me see't!   80

---

46 salt . . . rheum: Distressing head cold.   **51 Egyptian:** Gypsy.   **52 charmer:**
Sorceress.   **54 amiable:** Lovable.   **62 perdition:** Disaster.   **66 compasses:**
Annual rounds.   **69 mummy:** A drug made from mummies.

DESDEMONA: Why, so I can, sir; but I will not now.
    This is a trick to put° me from my suit:
    Pray you let Cassio be received again.
OTHELLO: Fetch me the handkerchief! My mind misgives.
DESDEMONA: Come, come!   85
    You'll never meet a more sufficient man.
OTHELLO: The handkerchief!
DESDEMONA: I pray talk me of Cassio.
OTHELLO: The handkerchief!
DESDEMONA: A man that all his time°
    Hath founded his good fortunes on your love,
    Shared dangers with you —   90
OTHELLO: The handkerchief!
DESDEMONA: I' faith, you are to blame.
OTHELLO: Zounds!   *Exit Othello.*
EMILIA: Is not this man jealous?
DESDEMONA: I ne'er saw this before.   95
    Sure there's some wonder in this handkerchief;
    I am most unhappy in the loss of it.
EMILIA: 'Tis not a year or two shows us a man.
    They are all but stomachs, and we all but food;
    They eat us hungerly, and when they are full,   100
    They belch us.

Enter Iago and Cassio.

           Look you — Cassio and my husband!
IAGO: There is no other way; 'tis she must do't.
    And lo the happiness!° Go and importune her.
DESDEMONA: How now, good Cassio? What's the news with you?
CASSIO: Madam, my former suit. I do beseech you   105
    That by your virtuous means I may again
    Exist, and be a member of his love
    Whom I with all the office of my heart
    Entirely honor. I would not be delayed.
    If my offense be of such mortal kind   110
    That neither service past, nor present sorrows,
    Nor purposed merit in futurity,
    Can ransom me into his love again,
    But to know so must be my benefit.
    So shall I clothe me in a forced content,   115
    And shut myself up in° some other course,
    To fortune's alms.
DESDEMONA: Alas, thrice-gentle Cassio!

---

82 put: Divert.   **88 all . . . time:** During his whole career.   **103 happiness:** Good
luck.   **116 shut myself up in:** Confine myself to.

My advocation° is not now in tune.
My lord is not my lord; nor should I know him,
Were he in favor° as in humor altered.   120
So help me every spirit sanctified
As I have spoken for you all my best
And stood within the blank° of his displeasure
For my free speech! You must a while be patient.
What I can do I will; and more I will   125
    Than for myself I dare. Let that suffice you.
IAGO: Is my lord angry?
EMILIA: He went hence but now,
    And certainly in strange unquietness.
IAGO: Can he be angry? I have seen the cannon
When it hath blown his ranks into the air   130
And, like the devil, from his very arm
Puffed his own brother — and is he angry?
Something of moment then. I will go meet him.
    There's matter in't indeed if he be angry.
DESDEMONA: I prithee do so.   *Exit [Iago].*
                        Something sure of state,°   135
Either from Venice or some unhatched practice°
Made demonstrable here in Cyprus to him,
Hath puddled° his clear spirit; and in such cases
Men's natures wrangle with inferior things,
Though great ones are their object. 'Tis even so;   140
For let our finger ache, and it endues°
Our other, healthful members even to a sense
Of pain. Nay, we must think men are not gods,
Nor of them look for such observancy
As fits the bridal. Beshrew me much, Emilia,   145
I was, unhandsome warrior° as I am,
Arraigning his unkindness with my soul;°
But now I find I had suborned the witness,
    And he's indicted falsely.
EMILIA: Pray heaven it be state matters, as you think,   150
And no conception nor no jealous toy°
    Concerning you.
DESDEMONA: Alas the day! I never gave him cause.
EMILIA: But jealous souls will not be answered so;
They are not ever jealous for the cause,   155

---

118 advocation: Advocacy.   **120 favor:** Appearance.   **123 blank:** Bull's-eye of the
target.   **135 state:** Public affairs.   **136 unhatched practice:** Budding plot.   **138
puddled:** Muddied.   **141 endues:** Brings.   **146 unhandsome warrior:** Inadequate
soldier.   **147 Arraigning . . . soul:** Indicting his unkindness before the bar of my soul.
151 toy: Fancy.

But jealous for they're jealous. 'Tis a monster
Begot upon itself,° born on itself.
DESDEMONA: Heaven keep that monster from Othello's mind!
EMILIA: Lady, amen.
DESDEMONA: I will go seek him. Cassio, walk here about: 160
    If I do find him fit, I'll move your suit
    And seek to effect it to my uttermost.
CASSIO: I humbly thank your ladyship.

                             Exeunt Desdemona and Emilia.

Enter Bianca.

BIANCA: Save you, friend Cassio!
CASSIO: What make you from home?
    How is't with you, my most fair Bianca?   165
    I' faith, sweet love, I was coming to your house.
BIANCA: And I was going to your lodging, Cassio.
    What, keep a week away? seven days and nights?
    Eightscore eight hours? and lovers' absent hours,
    More tedious than the dial° eightscore times?   170
    O weary reck'ning!
CASSIO: Pardon me, Bianca:
    I have this while with leaden thoughts been pressed;
    But I shall in a more continuate° time
    Strike off this score of absence. Sweet Bianca,

[Gives her Desdemona's handkerchief.]

    Take me this work out.°
BIANCA: O Cassio, whence came this?   175
    This is some token from a newer friend.
    To the felt absence now I feel a cause.
    Is't come to this? Well, well.
CASSIO: Go to, woman!
    Throw your vile guesses in the devil's teeth,
    From whence you have them. You are jealous now   180
    That this is from some mistress, some remembrance.
    No, by my faith, Bianca.
BIANCA: Why, whose is it?
CASSIO: I know not, sweet; I found it in my chamber.
    I like the work° well; ere it be demanded,
    As like enough it will, I'd have it copied.   185
    Take it and do't, and leave me for this time.
BIANCA: Leave you? Wherefore?
CASSIO: I do attend here on the general

---

157 Begot ... itself: Self-engendered.   **170 dial:** Clock.   **173 continuate:** Uninterrupted.   **175 Take ... out:** Copy this embroidery for me.   **184 work:** Needlework.

And think it no addition, nor my wish,
To have him see me womaned.
BIANCA: Why, I pray you?   190
CASSIO: Not that I love you not.
BIANCA: But that you do not love me!
I pray you bring me on the way a little,
And say if I shall see you soon at night.
CASSIO: 'Tis but a little way that I can bring you,
For I attend here; but I'll see you soon.   195
BIANCA: 'Tis very good. I must be circumstanced.°   *Exeunt.*

[ACT IV, Scene I: The environs of the castle.]

Enter Othello and Iago.

IAGO: Will you think so?
OTHELLO: Think so, Iago?
IAGO: What,
To kiss in private?
OTHELLO: An unauthorized kiss.
IAGO: Or to be naked with her friend in bed
An hour or more, not meaning any harm?
OTHELLO: Naked in bed, Iago, and not mean harm?   5
It is hypocrisy against the devil.°
They that mean virtuously, and yet do so,
The devil their virtue tempts, and they tempt heaven.
IAGO: So they do nothing, 'tis a venial slip.
But if I give my wife a handkerchief —   10
OTHELLO: What then?
IAGO: Why, then 'tis hers, my lord; and being hers,
She may, I think, bestow't on any man.
OTHELLO: She is protectress of her honor too;
May she give that?   15
IAGO: Her honor is an essence that's not seen;
They have it very oft that have it not.
But for the handkerchief —
OTHELLO: By heaven, I would most gladly have forgot it!
Thou said'st — O, it comes o'er my memory   20
As doth the raven o'er the infected° house,
Boding to all! — he had my handkerchief.
IAGO: Ay, what of that?
OTHELLO: That's not so good now.
IAGO: What

196 circumstanced: Governed by circumstances. **ACT IV, SCENE I. 6 hypocrisy . . .
devil:** I.e., feigned sin instead of feigned virtue.   **21 infected:** Plague-stricken.

If I had said I had seen him do you wrong?
Or heard him say—as knaves be such abroad   25
Who having, by their own importunate suit,
Or voluntary dotage of some mistress,
Convincèd or supplied° them, cannot choose
But they must blab—

OTHELLO: Hath he said anything?

IAGO: He hath, my lord; but be you well assured,   30
No more than he'll unswear.

OTHELLO: What hath he said?

IAGO: Faith, that he did—I know not what he did.

OTHELLO: What? what?

IAGO: Lie—

OTHELLO: With her?

IAGO: With her, on her; what you will.   35

OTHELLO: Lie with her? lie on her?—We say lie on her when they belie her.—
Lie with her! Zounds, that's fulsome.—Handkerchief—confessions—
handkerchief!—To confess, and be hanged for his labor—first to be
hanged, and then to confess! I tremble at it. Nature would not invest herself
in such shadowing passion without some instruction.° It is not words that   40
shakes me thus.—Pish! Noses, ears, and lips? Is't possible?—Confess?—
Handkerchief?—O devil!

(Falls in a trance.)

IAGO: Work on,
My med'cine, work! Thus credulous fools are caught,
And many worthy and chaste dames even thus,   45
All guiltless, meet reproach.—What, ho! my lord!
My lord, I say! Othello!
Enter Cassio.   How now, Cassio?

CASSIO: What's the matter?

IAGO: My lord is fall'n into an epilepsy.
This is his second fit; he had one yesterday.   50

CASSIO: Rub him about the temples.

IAGO: No, forbear.
The lethargy° must have his quiet course.
If not, he foams at mouth, and by and by
Breaks out to savage madness. Look, he stirs.
Do you withdraw yourself a little while.   55
He will recover straight. When he is gone,
I would on great occasion speak with you.   *[Exit Cassio.]*
How is it, general? Have you not hurt your head?

OTHELLO: Dost thou mock me?

---

28 Convincèd or supplied: Overcome or gratified.   **39–40 Nature . . . instruction:**
My natural faculties would not be so overcome by passion without reason.   **52 lethargy:**
Coma.

IAGO: I mock you? No, by heaven.
   Would you would bear your fortune like a man!   60
OTHELLO: A hornèd man's° a monster and a beast.
IAGO: There's many a beast then in a populous city,
   And many a civil monster.
OTHELLO: Did he confess it?
IAGO: Good sir, be a man.
   Think every bearded fellow that's but yoked   65
   May draw with you. There's millions now alive
   That nightly lie in those unproper° beds
   Which they dare swear peculiar:° your case is better.
   O, 'tis the spite of hell, the fiend's arch-mock,
   To lip a wanton in a secure° couch,   70
   And to suppose her chaste! No, let me know;
   And knowing what I am, I know what she shall be.
OTHELLO: O, thou art wise! 'Tis certain.
IAGO: Stand you awhile apart;
   Confine yourself but in a patient list.°
   Whilst you were here, o'erwhelmèd with your grief —   75
   A passion most unsuiting such a man—
   Cassio came hither. I shifted him away
   And laid good 'scuse upon your ecstasy;°
   Bade him anon return, and here speak with me;
   The which he promised. Do but encave° yourself   80
   And mark the fleers, the gibes, and notable scorns
   That dwell in every region of his face;
   For I will make him tell the tale anew—
   Where, how, how oft, how long ago, and when
   He hath, and is again to cope° your wife.   85
   I say, but mark his gesture. Marry, patience!
   Or I shall say y'are all in all in spleen,°
   And nothing of a man.
OTHELLO: Dost thou hear, Iago?
   I will be found most cunning in my patience;
   But—dost thou hear?—most bloody.
IAGO: That's not amiss: 90
   But yet keep time in all. Will you withdraw?

                                  [Othello retires.]

   Now will I question Cassio of Bianca,
   A huswife° that by selling her desires
   Buys herself bread and clothes. It is a creature

---

61 hornèd man: Cuckold.   **67 unproper:** Not exclusively their own.   **68 peculiar:**
Exclusively their own.   **70 secure:** Free from fear of rivalry.   **74 in a patient list:** With-
in the limits of self-control.   **78 ecstasy:** Trance.   **80 encave:** Conceal.   **85 cope:**
Meet.   **87 all in all in spleen:** Wholly overcome by your passion.   **93 huswife:** Hussy.

That dotes on Cassio, as 'tis the strumpet's plague   95
To beguile many and be beguiled by one.
He, when he hears of her, cannot refrain
From the excess of laughter. Here he comes.

Enter Cassio.

As he shall smile, Othello shall go mad;
And his unbookish° jealousy must conster°   100
Poor Cassio's smiles, gestures, and light behavior
Quite in the wrong. How do you now, lieutenant?

CASSIO: The worser that you give me the addition°
Whose want even kills me.

IAGO: Ply Desdemona well, and you are sure on't.   105
Now, if this suit lay in Bianca's power,
How quickly should you speed!

CASSIO: Alas, poor caitiff!°

OTHELLO: Look how he laughs already!

IAGO: I never knew a woman love man so.

CASSIO: Alas, poor rogue! I think, i' faith, she loves me.   110

OTHELLO: Now he denies it faintly, and laughs it out.

IAGO: Do you hear, Cassio?

OTHELLO: Now he importunes him
To tell it o'er. Go to! Well said, well said!

IAGO: She gives out that you shall marry her.
Do you intend it?   115

CASSIO: Ha, ha, ha!

OTHELLO: Do you triumph, Roman? Do you triumph?

CASSIO: I marry her? What, a customer?° Prithee bear some charity to my wit;
do not think it so unwholesome. Ha, ha, ha!

OTHELLO: So, so, so, so! They laugh that win!   120

IAGO: Faith, the cry goes that you shall marry her.

CASSIO: Prithee say true.

IAGO: I am a very villain else.

OTHELLO: Have you scored me?° Well.

CASSIO: This is the monkey's own giving out. She is persuaded I will marry   125
her out of her own love and flattery, not out of my promise.

OTHELLO: Iago beckons° me; now he begins the story.

CASSIO: She was here even now; she haunts me in every place. I was t' other
day talking on the sea bank with certain Venetians, and thither comes the
bauble,° and, by this hand, she falls me thus about my neck—   130

OTHELLO: Crying "O dear Cassio!" as it were. His gesture imports it.

CASSIO: So hangs, and lolls, and weeps upon me; so shakes and pulls me! Ha,
ha, ha!

---

100 unbookish: Uninstructed; **conster:** Construe, interpret. **103 addition:** Title.
107 caitiff: Wretch. **118 customer:** Prostitute. **124 scored me:** Settled my
account (?). **127 beckons:** Signals. **130 bauble:** Plaything.

OTHELLO: Now he tells how she plucked him to my chamber. O, I see that nose
of yours, but not that dog I shall throw it to.   135

CASSIO: Well, I must leave her company.

Enter Bianca.

IAGO: Before me! Look where she comes.

CASSIO: 'Tis such another fitchew!° marry, a perfumed one. What do you
mean by this haunting of me?

BIANCA: Let the devil and his dam haunt you! What did you mean by that   140
same handkerchief you gave me even now? I was a fine fool to take it. I
must take out the whole work? A likely piece of work that you should find it
in your chamber and know not who left it there! This is some minx's token,
and I must take out the work? There! Give it your hobby-horse.° Whereso-
ever you had it, I'll take out no work on't.   145

CASSIO: How now, my sweet Bianca? How now? how now?

OTHELLO: By heaven, that should be my handkerchief!

BIANCA: An you'll come to supper to-night, you may; an you will not, come
when you are next prepared for.   *Exit.*

IAGO: After her, after her!   150

CASSIO: Faith, I must; she'll rail in the street else.

IAGO: Will you sup there?

CASSIO: Yes, I intend so.

IAGO: Well, I may chance to see you; for I would very fain speak with you.

CASSIO: Prithee come. Will you?   155

IAGO: Go to! say no more.   *Exit Cassio.*

OTHELLO *[comes forward]*:   How shall I murder him, Iago?

IAGO: Did you perceive how he laughed at his vice?°

OTHELLO: O Iago!

IAGO: And did you see the handkerchief?   160

OTHELLO: Was that mine?

IAGO: Your, by this hand! And to see how he prizes° the foolish woman your
wife! She gave it him, and he hath giv'n it his whore.

OTHELLO: I would have him nine years a-killing—A fine woman! a fair
woman! a sweet woman!   165

IAGO: Nay, you must forget that.

OTHELLO: Ay, let her rot, and perish, and be damned to-night; for she shall not
live. No, my heart is turned to stone; I strike it, and it hurts my hand. O, the
world hath not a sweeter creature! She might lie by an emperor's side and
command him tasks.   170

IAGO: Nay, that's not your way.

OTHELLO: Hang her! I do but say what she is. So delicate with her needle! an
admirable musician! O, she will sing the savageness out of a bear! Of so
high and plenteous wit and invention°—

---

138 fitchew: Polecat (slang for whore). **144 hobby-horse:** Harlot. **158 vice:**
I.e., vicious conduct. **162 prizes:** Values. **174 invention:** Imagination.

IAGO: She's the worse for all this.   175

OTHELLO: O, a thousand thousand times! And then, of so gentle a condition!°

IAGO: Ay, too gentle.

OTHELLO: Nay, that's certain. But yet the pity of it, Iago! O Iago, the pity of it, Iago!

IAGO: If you are so fond over her iniquity, give her patent° to offend; for if it   180
touch not you, it comes near nobody.

OTHELLO: I will chop her into messes! Cuckold me!

IAGO: O, 'tis foul in her.

OTHELLO: With mine officer!

IAGO: That's fouler.   185

OTHELLO: Get me some poison, Iago, this night. I'll not expostulate with her,
lest her body and beauty unprovide° my mind again. This night, Iago!

IAGO: Do it not with poison. Strangle her in her bed, even the bed she hath
contaminated.

OTHELLO: Good, good! The justice of it pleases. Very good!   190

IAGO: And for Cassio, let me be his undertaker;° you shall hear more by
midnight.

OTHELLO: Excellent good!

A trumpet.

What trumpet is that same?

IAGO: I warrant something from Venice.

Enter Lodovico, Desdemona, and Attendants.

                                                                'Tis Lodovico.   195
This comes from the Duke; and see, your wife is with him.

LODOVICO: God save you, worthy general!

OTHELLO: With all my heart, sir.

LODOVICO: The Duke and senators of Venice greet you.

[Gives him a letter.]

OTHELLO: I kiss the instrument of their pleasures.

[Opens the letter and reads.]

DESDEMONA: And what's the news, good cousin Lodovico?   200

IAGO: I am very glad to see you, signior.
Welcome to Cyprus.

LODOVICO: I thank you. How does Lieutenant Cassio?

IAGO: Lives, sir.

DESDEMONA: Cousin, there's fall'n between him and my lord
An unkind breach; but you shall make all well.   205

OTHELLO: Are you sure of that?

DESDEMONA: My lord?

OTHELLO *[reads]*:   "This fail you not to do, as you will—"

---

176 condition: Disposition.   **180 patent:** License.   **187 unprovide:** Disarm.
191 be his undertaker: Undertake to deal with him.

LODOVICO: He did not call; he's busy in the paper.
    Is there division 'twixt thy lord and Cassio?   210
DESDEMONA: A most unhappy one. I would do much
    T' atone° them, for the love I bear to Cassio.
OTHELLO: Fire and brimstone!
DESDEMONA: My lord?
OTHELLO: Are you wise?
DESDEMONA: What, is he angry?
LODOVICO: May be the letter moved him;
    For, as I think, they do command him home,   215
    Deputing Cassio in his government.
DESDEMONA: By my troth, I am glad on't.
OTHELLO: Indeed?
DESDEMONA: My lord?
OTHELLO: I am glad to see you mad.°
DESDEMONA: Why, sweet Othello—
OTHELLO: Devil!

[Strikes her.]

DESDEMONA: I have not deserved this.   220
LODOVICO: My lord, this would not be believed in Venice,
    Though I should swear I saw't. 'Tis very much.
    Make her amends; she weeps.
OTHELLO: O devil, devil!
    If that the earth could teem° with woman's tears,
    Each drop she falls would prove a crocodile.°   225
    Out of my sight!
DESDEMONA: I will not stay to offend you.   *[Going.]*
LODOVICO: Truly, an obedient lady.
    I do beseech your lordship call her back.
OTHELLO: Mistress!
DESDEMONA: My lord?
OTHELLO: What would you with her, sir?   230
LODOVICO: Who? I, my lord?
OTHELLO: Ay! You did wish that I would make her turn.
    Sir, she can turn, and turn, and yet go on
    And turn again; and she can weep, sir, weep;
    And she's obedient; as you say, obedient,   235
    Very obedient.—Proceed you in your tears.—
    Concerning this, sir—O well-painted passion!°—
    I am commanded home.—Get you away;
    I'll send for you anon.—Sir, I obey the mandate
    And will return to Venice.—Hence, avaunt!   240

---

212 atone: Reconcile. **218 mad:** I.e.,   waggish. **224 teem:** Breed. **225 crocodile:** Crocodiles were supposed to shed hypocritical tears to lure men to destruction.
237 passion: Grief.

[Exit Desdemona.]

Cassio shall have my place. And, sir, to-night
I do entreat that we may sup together.
You are welcome, sir, to Cyprus—Goats and monkeys!

Exit.

LODOVICO: Is this the noble Moor whom our full Senate
  Call all in all sufficient? Is this the nature   245
  Whom passion could not shake? whose solid virtue
  The shot of accident nor dart of chance
  Could neither graze nor pierce?
IAGO: He is much changed.
LODOVICO: Are his wits safe? Is he not light of brain?
IAGO: He's that he is; I may not breathe my censure.   250
  What he might be—if what he might he is not—
  I would to heaven he were!
LODOVICO: What, strike his wife?
IAGO: Faith, that was not so well; yet would I knew
  That stroke would prove the worst!
LODOVICO: Is it his use?°
  Or did the letters work upon his blood   255
  And new-create this fault?
IAGO: Alas, alas!
  It is not honesty in me to speak
  What I have seen and known. You shall observe him,
  And his own courses will denote him so
  That I may save my speech. Do but go after   260
  And mark how he continues.
LODOVICO: I am sorry that I am deceived in him.   *Exeunt.*

[Scene II: Within the castle.]

Enter Othello and Emilia.

OTHELLO: You have seen nothing then?
EMILIA: Nor ever heard, nor ever did suspect.
OTHELLO: Yes, you have seen Cassio and she together.
EMILIA: But then I saw no harm, and then I heard
  Each syllable that breath made up between them.   5
OTHELLO: What, did they never whisper?
EMILIA: Never, my lord.
OTHELLO: Nor send you out o' th' way?
EMILIA: Never.
OTHELLO: To fetch her fan, her gloves, her mask, nor nothing?

254 use: Custom.

EMILIA: Never, my lord.   10
OTHELLO: That's strange.
EMILIA: I durst, my lord, to wager she is honest,
   Lay down my soul at stake. If you think other,
   Remove your thought; it doth abuse your bosom.°
   If any wretch have put this in your head,   15
   Let heaven requite it with the serpent's curse!°
   For if she be not honest, chaste, and true,
   There's no man happy; the purest of their wives
   Is foul as slander.
OTHELLO: Bid her come hither. Go.   *Exit Emilia.*
   She says enough; yet she's a simple bawd   20
   That cannot say as much. This is a subtle whore,
   A closet lock and key of villainous secrets;
   And yet she'll kneel and pray; I have seen her do't.

Enter Desdemona and Emilia.

DESDEMONA: My lord, what is your will?
OTHELLO: Pray, chuck, come hither.
DESDEMONA: What is your pleasure?
OTHELLO: Let me see your eyes.   25
   Look in my face.
DESDEMONA: What horrible fancy's this?
OTHELLO *[to Emilia]*:   Some of your function, mistress.
   Leave procreants° alone and shut the door;
   Cough or cry hem if anybody come.
   Your mystery, your mystery!° Nay, dispatch!   30

                                                                        Exit Emilia.

DESDEMONA: Upon my knees, what doth your speech import?
   I understand a fury in your words,
   [But not the words.]
OTHELLO: Why, what art thou?
DESDEMONA: Your wife, my lord; your true
   And loyal wife.
OTHELLO: Come, swear it, damn thyself;   35
   Lest, being like one of heaven,° the devils themselves
   Should fear to seize thee. Therefore be double-damned—
   Swear thou art honest.°
DESDEMONA: Heaven doth truly know it.
OTHELLO: Heaven truly knows that thou art false as hell.
DESDEMONA: To whom, my lord? With whom? How am I false?   40
OTHELLO: Ah, Desdemona! away! away! away!

SCENE II. 14 abuse . . . bosom: Deceive your heart. **16 serpent's curse:** (cf. Genesis
3:14). **28 procreants:** Mating   couples. **30 mystery:** Trade,   occupation. **36
being . . . heaven:** Looking like an angel. **38 honest:** Chaste.

DESDEMONA: Alas the heavy day! Why do you weep?
    Am I the motive of these tears, my lord?
    If haply you my father do suspect
    An instrument° of this your calling back,   45
    Lay not your blame on me. If you have lost him,
    Why, I have lost him too.
OTHELLO: Had it pleased heaven
    To try me with affliction, had they rained
    All kinds of sores and shames on my bare head,
    Steeped me in poverty to the very lips,   50
    Given to captivity me and my utmost hopes,
    I should have found in some place of my soul
    A drop of patience. But, alas, to make me
    A fixèd figure for the time of scorn°
    To point his slow unmoving finger at!   55
    Yet could I bear that too; well, very well.
    But there where I have garnered up my heart,
    Where either I must live or bear no life,
    The fountain from the which my current runs
    Or else dries up—to be discarded thence,   60
    Or keep it as a cistern for foul toads
    To knot and gender in—turn thy complexion there,°
    Patience, thou young and rose-lipped cherubin!
    Ay, there look grim as hell!
DESDEMONA: I hope my noble lord esteems me honest.   65
OTHELLO: O, ay; as summer flies are in the shambles,°
    That quicken° even with blowing. O thou weed,
    Who art so lovely fair, and smell'st so sweet,
    That the sense aches at thee, would thou hadst ne'er been born!
DESDEMONA: Alas, what ignorant sin have I committed?   70
OTHELLO: Was this fair paper, this most goodly book,
    Made to write "whore" upon? What committed?
    Committed? O thou public commoner!°
    I should make very forges of my cheeks
    That would to cinders burn up modesty,   75
    Did I but speak thy deeds. What committed?
    Heaven stops the nose at it, and the moon winks;°
    The bawdy wind, that kisses all it meets,
    Is hushed within the hollow mine of earth
    And will not hear it. What committed?   80
    Impudent strumpet!
DESDEMONA: By heaven, you do me wrong!

---

45 An instrument: To be the cause.   **54 time of scorn:** Scornful world.   **62 turn thy complexion there:** Change thy color at that point.   **66 shambles:** Slaughterhouse.   **67 quicken:** Come to life.   **73 commoner:** Harlot.   **77 winks:** Closes her eyes.

OTHELLO: Are not you a strumpet?

DESDEMONA: No, as I am a Christian!
If to preserve this vessel for my lord
From any other foul unlawful touch
Be not to be a strumpet, I am none.   85

OTHELLO: What, not a whore?

DESDEMONA: No, as I shall be saved!

OTHELLO: Is't possible?

DESDEMONA: O, heaven forgive us!

OTHELLO: I cry you mercy° then.
I took you for that cunning whore of Venice
That married with Othello.—[Calling.] You, mistress,   90
That have the office opposite to Saint Peter
And keep the gate of hell!

Enter Emilia.

                        You, you, ay, you!
We have done our course; there's money for your pains:
I pray you turn the key, and keep our counsel.   *Exit.*

EMILIA: Alas, what does this gentleman conceive?   95
How do you, madam? How do you, my good lady?

DESDEMONA: Faith, half asleep.°

EMILIA: Good madam, what's the matter with my lord?

DESDEMONA: With who?

EMILIA: Why, with my lord, madam.   100

DESDEMONA: Who is thy lord?

EMILIA: He that is yours, sweet lady.

DESDEMONA: I have none. Do not talk to me, Emilia.
I cannot weep; nor answer have I none
But what should go by water. Prithee to-night
Lay on my bed my wedding sheets, remember;   105
And call thy husband hither.

EMILIA: Here's a change indeed!   *Exit.*

DESDEMONA: 'Tis meet I should be used so, very meet.
How have I been behaved, that he might stick
The small'st opinion° on my least misuse?°

Enter Iago and Emilia.

IAGO: What is your pleasure, madam? How is't with you?   110

DESDEMONA: I cannot tell. Those that do teach young babes
Do it with gentle means and easy tasks:
He might have chid me so; for, in good faith,
I am a child to chiding.

IAGO: What is the matter, lady?

88 cry you mercy: Beg your pardon.   **97 half asleep:** I.e., stunned.   **109 small'st opinion:** Least suspicion;   **least misuse:** Slightest misconduct.

EMILIA: Alas, Iago, my lord hath so bewhored her,   115
    Thrown such despite and heavy terms upon her
    As true hearts cannot bear.
DESDEMONA: Am I that name, Iago?
IAGO: What name, fair lady?
DESDEMONA: Such as she said my lord did say I was.
EMILIA: He called her whore. A beggar in his drink   120
    Could not have laid such terms upon his callet.°
IAGO: Why did he so?
DESDEMONA: I do not know; I am sure I am none such.
IAGO: Do not weep, do not weep. Alas the day!
EMILIA: Hath she forsook so many noble matches,   125
    Her father and her country, and her friends,
    To be called whore? Would it not make one weep?
DESDEMONA: It is my wretched fortune.
IAGO: Beshrew him for't!
    How comes this trick° upon him?
DESDEMONA: Nay, heaven doth know.
EMILIA: I will be hanged if some eternal villain,   130
    Some busy and insinuating rogue,
    Some cogging, cozening° slave, to get some office,
    Have not devised this slander. I'll be hanged else.
IAGO: Fie, there is no such man! It is impossible.
DESDEMONA: If any such there be, heaven pardon him!   135
EMILIA: A halter pardon him! and hell gnaw his bones!
    Why should he call her whore? Who keeps her company?
    What place? what time? what form? what likelihood?
    The Moor 's abused by some most villainous knave,
    Some base notorious knave, some scurvy fellow.   140
    O heaven, that such companions° thou 'dst unfold,°
    And put in every honest hand a whip
    To lash the rascals naked through the world
    Even from the east to th' west!
IAGO: Speak within door.°
EMILIA: O, fie upon them! Some such squire he was   145
    That turned your wit the seamy side without
    And made you to suspect me with the Moor.
IAGO: You are a fool. Go to.
DESDEMONA: Alas, Iago,
    What shall I do to win my lord again?
    Good friend, go to him; for, by this light of heaven,   150
    I know not how I lost him. Here I kneel:

---

121 callet: Whore.   **129 trick:** Freakish behavior.   **132 cogging, cozening:** Cheating, defrauding.   **141 companions:** Rogues;   **unfold:** Expose.   **144 within door:** With restraint.

If e'er my will did trespass 'gainst his love
Either in discourse° of thought or actual deed,
Or that mine eyes, mine ears, or any sense
Delighted them in any other form,   155
Or that I do not yet, and ever did,
And ever will (though he do shake me off
To beggarly divorcement) love him dearly,
Comfort forswear° me! Unkindness may do much;
And his unkindness may defeat° my life,   160
But never taint my love. I cannot say "whore."
It does abhor me now I speak the word;
To do the act that might the addition earn
Not the world's mass of vanity could make me.

IAGO: I pray you be content. 'Tis but his humor.   165
The business of the state does him offense,
[And he does chide with you.]

DESDEMONA: If 'twere no other—

IAGO: 'Tis but so, I warrant.

[Trumpets within.]

Hark how these instruments summon you to supper.
The messengers of Venice stay the meat: 170
Go in, and weep not. All things shall be well.

                              Exeunt Desdemona and Emilia.

Enter Roderigo.

How now, Roderigo?

RODERIGO: I do not find that thou deal'st justly with me.

IAGO: What in the contrary?

RODERIGO: Every day thou daff'st me with some device,° Iago, and rather, as it   175
seems to me now, keep'st from me all conveniency° than suppliest me with
the least advantage of hope. I will indeed no longer endure it; nor am I yet
persuaded to put up in peace what already I have foolishly suffered.

IAGO: Will you hear me, Roderigo?

RODERIGO: Faith, I have heard too much; for your words and performances are   180
no kin together.

IAGO: You charge me most unjustly.

RODERIGO: With naught but truth. I have wasted myself out of my means. The
jewels you have had from me to deliver to Desdemona would half have
corrupted a votarist.° You have told me she hath received them, and   185
returned me expectations and comforts of sudden respect° and acquaintance; but I find none.

---

153 discourse: Course.   **159 Comfort forswear:** Happiness forsake.   **160 defeat:**
Destroy.   **175 thou . . . device:** You put me off with some trick.   **176 conveniency:**
Favorable   opportunities.   **185 votarist:** Nun.   **186 sudden   respect:** Immediate
notice.

IAGO: Well, go to; very well.

RODERIGO: Very well! go to! I cannot go to, man; nor 'tis not very well. By this hand, I say 'tis very scurvy, and begin to find myself fopped° in it.   190

IAGO: Very well.

RODERIGO: I tell you 'tis not very well. I will make myself known to Desdemona. If she will return me my jewels, I will give over my suit and repent my unlawful solicitation; if not, assure yourself I will seek satisfaction of you.

IAGO: You have said now.   195

RODERIGO: Ay, and said nothing but what I protest intendment of doing.

IAGO: Why, now I see there's mettle in thee; and even from this instant do build on thee a better opinion than ever before. Give me thy hand, Roderigo. Thou has taken against me a most just exception; but yet I protest I have dealt most directly° in thy affair.   200

RODERIGO: It hath not appeared.

IAGO: I grant indeed it hath not appeared, and your suspicion is not without wit and judgment. But, Roderigo, if thou hast that in thee indeed which I have greater reason to believe now than ever, I mean purpose, courage, and valor, this night show it. If thou the next night following enjoy not   205 Desdemona, take me from this world with treachery and devise engines for° my life.

RODERIGO: Well, what is it? Is it within reason and compass?

IAGO: Sir, there is especial commission come from Venice to depute Cassio in Othello's place.   210

RODERIGO: Is that true? Why, then Othello and Desdemona return again to Venice.

IAGO: O, no; he goes into Mauritania and takes away with him the fair Desdemona, unless his abode be lingered here° by some accident; wherein none can be so determinate° as the removing of Cassio.   215

RODERIGO: How do you mean removing of him?

IAGO: Why, by making him uncapable of Othello's place—knocking out his brains.

RODERIGO: And that you would have me to do?

IAGO: Ay, if you dare do yourself a profit and a right. He sups to-night with a   220 harlotry, and thither will I go to him. He knows not yet of his honorable fortune. If you will watch his going thence, which I will fashion to fall out between twelve and one, you may take him at your pleasure. I will be near to second your attempt, and he shall fall between us. Come, stand not amazed at it, but go along with me. I will show you such a necessity in his   225 death that you shall think yourself bound to put it on him. It is now high supper time, and the night grows to waste. About it!

RODERIGO: I will hear further reason for this.

IAGO: And you shall be satisfied.   *Exeunt.*

190 fopped: Duped.   **200 directly:** Straightforwardly.   **207 engines for:** Plots against.
214 abode . . . here: Stay here be extended.   **215 determinate:** Effective.

[Scene III: Within the castle.]

Enter Othello, Lodovico, Desdemona, Emilia, and Attendants.

LODOVICO: I do beseech you, sir, trouble yourself no further.

OTHELLO: O, pardon me; 'twill do me good to walk.

LODOVICO: Madam, good night. I humbly thank your ladyship.

DESDEMONA: Your honor is most welcome.

OTHELLO: Will you walk, sir?

O, Desdemona—   5

DESDEMONA: My lord?

OTHELLO: Get you to bed on th' instant; I will be returned forthwith. Dismiss
your attendant there. Look 't be done.

DESDEMONA: I will, my lord.

Exit [Othello, with Lodovico and Attendants].

EMILIA: How goes it now? He looks gentler than he did.   10

DESDEMONA: He says he will return incontinent.°

He hath commanded me to go to bed,

And bade me to dismiss you.

EMILIA: Dismiss me?

DESDEMONA: It was his bidding; therefore, good Emilia,

Give me my nightly wearing, and adieu.   15

We must not now displease him.

EMILIA: I would you had never seen him!

DESDEMONA: So would not I. My love doth so approve him

That even his stubbornness,° his checks,° his frowns—

Prithee unpin me—have grace and favor in them.   20

EMILIA: I have laid those sheets you bade me on the bed.

DESDEMONA: All's one. Good faith, how foolish are our minds!

If I do die before thee, prithee shroud me

In one of those same sheets.

EMILIA: Come, come! You talk.

DESDEMONA: My mother had a maid called Barbary.   25

She was in love; and he she loved proved mad°

And did forsake her. She had a song of "Willow";

An old thing 'twas; but it expressed her fortune,

And she died singing it. That song to-night

Will not go from my mind; I have much to do   30

But to go hang my head all at one side

And sing it like poor Barbary. Prithee dispatch.

EMILIA: Shall I go fetch your nightgown?°

DESDEMONA: No, unpin me here.

This Lodovico is a proper man.

SCENE III.   **11 incontinent:** At once.   **19 stubbornness:** Roughness;   **checks:** Rebukes.   **26 mad:** Wild, faithless.   **33 nightgown:** Dressing gown.

EMILIA: A very handsome man.   35
DESDEMONA: He speaks well.
EMILIA: I know a lady in Venice would have walked barefoot to Palestine for a
     touch of his nether lip.
DESDEMONA *(sings)*:   "The poor soul sat sighing by a sycamore tree
                    Sing all a green willow;   40
               Her hand on her bosom, her head on her knee,
                    Sing willow, willow, willow.
               The fresh streams ran by her and murmured her moans;
                    Sing willow, willow, willow;
               Her salt tears fell from her, and soft'ned the stones" —   45
     Lay by these.

                    "Sing willow, willow, willow" —
               Prithee hie thee;° he'll come anon.
                    "Sing all a green willow must be my garland.
               Let nobody blame him; his scorn I approve" —   50
     Nay, that's not next. Hark! who is't that knocks?
EMILIA: It's the wind.
DESDEMONA *(sings)*:   "I call my love false love; but what said he then?
                    "Sing willow, willow, willow" —
               If I court moe women, you'll couch with moe men."   55
     So get thee gone; good night. Mine eyes do itch.
     Doth that bode weeping?
EMILIA: 'Tis neither here nor there.
DESDEMONA: I have heard it said so. O, these men, these men!
     Dost thou in conscience think — tell me, Emilia —
     That there be women do abuse their husbands   60
     In such gross kind?
EMILIA: There be some such, no question.
DESDEMONA: Wouldst thou do such a deed for all the world?
EMILIA: Why, would not you?
DESDEMONA: No, by this heavenly light!
EMILIA: Nor I neither by this heavenly light.
     I might do't as well i' th' dark.   65
DESDEMONA: Wouldst thou do such a deed for all the world?
EMILIA: The world's a huge thing; it is a great price for a small vice.
DESDEMONA: In troth, I think thou wouldst not.
EMILIA: In troth, I think I should; and undo't when I had done it. Marry, I
     would not do such a thing for a joint-ring,° nor for measures of lawn, nor   70
     for gowns, petticoats, nor caps, nor any petty exhibition;° but, for all the
     whole world — 'Ud's pity! who would not make her husband a cuckold to
     make him a monarch? I should venture purgatory for't.
DESDEMONA: Beshrew me if I would do such a wrong

48 hie thee: Hurry.   **70 joint-ring:** Ring made in separable halves.   **71 exhibition:** Gift.

For the whole world.   75

EMILIA: Why, the wrong is but a wrong i' th' world; and having the world
for your labor, 'tis a wrong in your own world, and you might quickly make
it right.

DESDEMONA: I do not think there is any such woman.

EMILIA: Yes, a dozen; and as many to th' vantage° as   80
would store° the world they played for.
But I do think it is their husbands' faults
If wives do fall. Say that they slack their duties
And pour our treasures into foreign laps;
Or else break out in peevish° jealousies,   85
Throwing restraint upon us; or say they strike us,
Or scant our former having° in despite—
Why, we have galls;° and though we have some grace,
Yet have we some revenge. Let husbands know
Their wives have sense like them. They see, and smell,   90
And have their palates both for sweet and sour,
As husbands have. What is it that they do
When they change us for others? Is it sport?
I think it is. And doth affection breed it?
I think it doth. Is't frailty that thus errs?   95
It is so too. And have not we affections,
Desires for sport, and frailty, as men have?
Then let them use us well; else let them know,
The ills we do, their ills instruct us so.

DESDEMONA: Good night, good night. God me such usage° send,   100
Not to pick bad from bad, but by bad mend!   *Exeunt.*

[ACT V, Scene I: A street in Cyprus]

Enter Iago and Roderigo.

IAGO: Here, stand behind this bulk;° straight will he come.
Wear thy good rapier bare, and put it home.
Quick, quick! Fear nothing; I'll be at thy elbow.
It makes us, or it mars us—think on that,
And fix most firm thy resolution.   5

RODERIGO: Be near at hand; I may miscarry in't.

IAGO: Here, at thy hand. Be bold, and take thy stand.

[Stands aside.]

RODERIGO: I have no great devotion to the deed,
And yet he hath given me satisfying reasons.

80 to   th'   vantage: Besides.   **81 store:** Populate.   **85 peevish:** Senseless.   **87
having:** Allowance.   **88 galls:** Spirits to resent.   **100 usage:** Habits.   **ACT V, SCENE I.
1 bulk:** Projecting shop-front.

'Tis but a man gone. Forth my sword! He dies!   10

IAGO: I have rubbed this young quat° almost to the sense,°
And he grows angry. Now whether he kill Cassio,
Or Cassio him, or each do kill the other,
Every way makes my gain. Live Roderigo,
He calls me to a restitution large   15
Of gold and jewels that I bobbed° from him
As gifts to Desdemona.
It must not be. If Cassio do remain,
He hath a daily beauty in his life
That makes me ugly; and besides, the Moor   20
May unfold me to him; there stand I in much peril.
No, he must die. Be't so! I hear him coming.

Enter Cassio.

RODERIGO: I know his gait. 'Tis he. Villain, thou diest!

[Makes a pass at Cassio.]

CASSIO: That thrust had been mine enemy indeed
But that my coat° is better than thou know'st.   25
I will make proof of thine.

[Draws, and wounds Roderigo.]

RODERIGO: O, I am slain!

[Iago darts from concealment behind Cassio, wounds him in the leg, and exit.]

CASSIO: I am maimed for ever. Help, ho! Murder! murder!

[Falls.]

Enter Othello.

OTHELLO: The voice of Cassio. Iago keeps his word.
RODERIGO: O, villain that I am!
OTHELLO: It is even so.
CASSIO: O, help, ho! light! a surgeon!   30
OTHELLO: 'Tis he. O brave Iago, honest and just,
That hast such noble sense of thy friend's wrong!
Thou teachest me. Minion,° your dear lies dead,
And your unblest fate hies.° Strumpet, I come.
Forth of my heart those charms, thine eyes, are blotted.   35
Thy bed, lust-stained, shall with lust's blood be spotted.

                                        Exit Othello.

Enter Lodovico and Gratiano.

CASSIO: What, ho? No watch? No passage?° Murder! murder!
GRATIANO: 'Tis some mischance. The cry is very direful.

---

11 quat: Pimple;   **sense:** Quick.   **16 bobbed:** Swindled.   **25 coat:** Undershirt of
mail.   **33 Minion:** Mistress.   **34 hies:** Hurries on.   **37 passage:** Passersby.

CASSIO: O, help!
LODOVICO: Hark!   40
RODERIGO: O wretched villain!
LODOVICO: Two or three groan. It is a heavy° night.
   These may be counterfeits. Let's think't unsafe
   To come in to the cry without more help.
RODERIGO: Nobody come? Then shall I bleed to death.   45
LODOVICO: Hark!

Enter Iago, with a light.

GRATIANO: Here's one comes in his shirt, with light and weapons.
IAGO: Who's there? Whose noise is this that cries on° murder?
LODOVICO: We do not know.
IAGO: Did not you hear a cry?
CASSIO: Here, here! For heaven's sake, help me!
IAGO: What's the matter?   50
GRATIANO: This is Othello's ancient, as I take it.
LODOVICO: The same indeed, a very valiant fellow.
IAGO: What are you here that cry so grievously?
CASSIO: Iago? O, I am spoiled, undone by villains!
   Give me some help.   55
IAGO: O me, lieutenant! What villains have done this?
CASSIO: I think that one of them is hereabout
   And cannot make° away.
IAGO: O treacherous villains!

[To Lodovico and Gratiano.]

   What are you there? Come in, and give some help.
RODERIGO: O, help me here!   60
CASSIO: That's one of them.
IAGO: O murd'rous slave! O villain!

[Stabs Roderigo.]

RODERIGO: O damned Iago! O inhuman dog!
IAGO: Kill men i' th' dark? — Where be these bloody thieves? —
   How silent is this town! — Ho! murder! murder! —
   What may you be? Are you of good or evil?   65
LODOVICO: As you shall prove us, praise us.
IAGO: Signior Lodovico?
LODOVICO: He, sir.
IAGO: I cry you mercy. Here's Cassio hurt by villains.
GRATIANO: Cassio?   70
IAGO: How is't, brother?
CASSIO: My leg is cut in two.
IAGO: Marry,° heaven forbid!
   Light, gentlemen. I'll bind it with my shirt.

42 heavy: Cloudy, dark. **48 cries on:** Raises the cry of. **58 make:** Get. **72 Marry:** (From "By Mary").

Enter Bianca.

BIANCA: What is the matter, ho? Who is't that cried?
IAGO: Who is't that cried?   75
BIANCA: O my dear Cassio! my sweet Cassio!
    O Cassio, Cassio, Cassio!
IAGO: O notable strumpet!—Cassio, may you suspect
    Who they should be that have thus mangled you?
CASSIO: No.   80
GRATIANO: I am sorry to find you thus. I have been to seek you.
IAGO: Lend me a garter. So. O for a chair°
    To bear him easily hence!
BIANCA: Alas, he faints! O Cassio, Cassio, Cassio!
IAGO: Gentlemen all, I do suspect this trash   85
    To be a party in this injury.—
    Patience a while, good Cassio.—Come, come!
    Lend me a light. Know we this face or no?
    Alas, my friend and my dear countryman
    Roderigo? No—Yes, sure.—O heaven, Roderigo!   90
GRATIANO: What, of Venice?
IAGO: Even he, sir. Did you know him?
GRATIANO: Know him? Ay.
IAGO: Signior Gratiano? I cry your gentle pardon.
    These bloody accidents must excuse my manners
    That so neglected you.
GRATIANO: I am glad to see you.   95
IAGO: How do you, Cassio?—O, a chair, a chair!
GRATIANO: Roderigo?
IAGO: He, he, 'tis he!

[A chair brought in.]

    O, that's well said;° the chair.
    Some good man bear him carefully from hence.   100
    I'll fetch the general's surgeon. *[To Bianca.]* For you, mistress,
    Save you your labor.—He that lies slain here, Cassio,
    Was my dear friend. What malice was between you?
CASSIO: None in the world; nor do I know the man.
IAGO *[to Bianca]*:   What, look you pale?—O, bear him out o' th' air.   105

                      [Cassio and Roderigo are borne off.]

    Stay you, good gentlemen.—Look you pale, mistress?—
    Do you perceive the gastness° of her eye?—
    Nay, if you stare, we shall hear more anon.
    Behold her well; I pray you look upon her.
    Do you see, gentlemen? Nay, guiltiness will speak.   110
    Though tongues were out of use.

82 chair: Litter.   **99 well said:** Well done.   **107 gastness:** Terror.

Enter Emilia.

EMILIA: 'Las, what's the matter? What's the matter, husband?
IAGO: Cassio hath here been set on in the dark
    By Roderigo, and fellows that are scaped.
    He's almost slain, and Roderigo dead.   115
EMILIA: Alas, good gentlemen! alas, good Cassio!
IAGO: This is the fruits of whoring. Prithee, Emilia,
    Go know of Cassio where he supped to-night.

[To Bianca.]

What, do you shake at that?
BIANCA: He supped at my house; but I therefore shake not.   120
IAGO: O, did he so? I charge you go with me.
EMILIA: Fie, fie upon thee, strumpet!
BIANCA: I am no strumpet, but of life as honest°
    As you that thus abuse me.
EMILIA: As I? Foh! fie upon thee!
IAGO: Kind gentlemen, let's go see poor Cassio dressed.   125

[To Bianca.]

Come, mistress, you must tell 's another tale.
    Emilia, run you to the citadel
    And tell my lord and lady what hath happed.

[Exit Emilia.]

Will you go on afore?   *Exeunt [all but Iago].*
    This is the night
    That either makes me or fordoes° me quite.   *[Exit.]* 130

[Scene II: A bedchamber in the castle.]

Desdemona [asleep] in her bed. Enter Othello with a light.

OTHELLO: It is the cause, it is the cause,° my soul.
    Let me not name it to you, you chaste stars!
    It is the cause. Yet I'll not shed her blood,
    Nor scar that whiter skin of hers than snow,
    And smooth as monumental alabaster.   5
    Yet she must die, else she'll betray more men.
    Put out the light, and then put out the light.
    If I quench thee, thou flaming minister,°
    I can again thy former light restore,
    Should I repent me; but once put out thy light,   10
    Thou cunning'st pattern of excelling nature,
    I know not where is that Promethean heat°

---

123 honest: Chaste.   **130 fordoes:** Destroys.   **SCENE II. 1 cause:** Cause of justice.
8 minister: Servant.   **12 Promethean heat:** Divine fire.

That can thy light relume.° When I have plucked the rose,
I cannot give it vital growth again;
It needs must wither. I'll smell thee on the tree.   15

(He kisses her.)

O balmy breath, that dost almost persuade
    Justice to break her sword! One more, one more!
    Be thus when thou art dead, and I will kill thee,
    And love thee after. One more, and that's the last!
    So sweet was ne'er so fatal. I must weep,   20
    But they are cruel tears. This sorrow's heavenly;
    It strikes where it doth love. She wakes.

DESDEMONA: Who's there? Othello?
OTHELLO: Ay, Desdemona.
DESDEMONA: Will you come to bed, my lord?
OTHELLO: Have you prayed to-night, Desdemona?
DESDEMONA: Ay, my lord.   25
OTHELLO: If you bethink yourself of any crime°
    Unreconciled as yet to heaven and grace,
    Solicit for it straight.
DESDEMONA: Alack, my lord, what may you mean by that?
OTHELLO: Well, do it, and be brief; I will walk by.   30
    I would not kill thy unprepared spirit.
    No, heaven forfend!° I would not kill thy soul.
DESDEMONA: Talk you of killing?
OTHELLO: Ay, I do.
DESDEMONA: Then heaven
    Have mercy on me!
OTHELLO: Amen, with all my heart!
DESDEMONA: If you say so, I hope you will not kill me.   35
OTHELLO: Hum!
DESDEMONA: And yet I fear you; for you're fatal then
    When your eyes roll so. Why I should fear I know not,
    Since guiltiness I know not; but yet I feel I fear.
OTHELLO: Think on thy sins.
DESDEMONA: They are loves I bear to you.   40
OTHELLO: Ay, and for that thou diest.
DESDEMONA: That death 's unnatural that kills for loving.
    Alas, why gnaw you so your nether lip?
    Some bloody passion shakes your very frame.
    These are portents,° but yet I hope, I hope,   45
    They do not point on me.
OTHELLO: Peace and be still!
DESDEMONA: I will so. What's the matter?

13 relume: Relight. **26 crime:** Sin. **32 forfend:** Forbid. **45 portents:** Signs of
impending violence.

OTHELLO: That handkerchief which I so loved and gave thee
 Thou gav'st to Cassio.
DESDEMONA: No, by my life and soul!
 Send for the man and ask him.
OTHELLO: Sweet soul, take heed,   50
 Take heed of perjury; thou art on thy deathbed.
DESDEMONA: Ay, but not yet to die.
OTHELLO: Yes, presently.°
 Therefore confess thee freely of thy sin;
 For to deny each article with oath
 Cannot remove nor choke the strong conception°   55
 That I do groan withal. Thou art to die.
DESDEMONA: Then Lord have mercy on me!
OTHELLO: I say amen.
DESDEMONA: And have you mercy too! I never did
 Offend° you in my life; never loved Cassio
 But with such general warranty of heaven   60
 As I might love. I never gave him token.
OTHELLO: By heaven, I saw my handkerchief in's hand!
 O perjured woman! thou dost stone my heart,°
 And mak'st me call what I intend to do
 A murder, which I thought a sacrifice.   65
 I saw the handkerchief.
DESDEMONA: He found it then.
 I never gave it him. Send for him hither.
 Let him confess a truth.
OTHELLO: He hath confessed.
DESDEMONA: What, my lord?
OTHELLO: That he hath used thee.
DESDEMONA: How? Unlawfully?
OTHELLO: Ay.   70
DESDEMONA: He will not say so.
OTHELLO: No, his mouth is stopped.
 Honest Iago hath ta'en order° for't.
DESDEMONA: O, my fear interprets. What, is he dead?
OTHELLO: Had all his hairs been lives, my great revenge
 Had stomach for them all.   75
DESDEMONA: Alas, he is betrayed, and I undone!
OTHELLO: Out, strumpet! Weep'st thou for him to my face?
DESDEMONA: O, banish me, my lord, but kill me not!
OTHELLO: Down, strumpet!
DESDEMONA: Kill me to-morrow; let me live to-night!   80
OTHELLO: Nay, if you strive—

---

52 presently: At   once.   **55 conception:** Belief.   **59 Offend:** Wrong.   **63 stone my heart:** Turn my heart to stone.   **72 ta'en order:** Taken measures.

DESDEMONA: But half an hour!

OTHELLO: Being done, there is no pause.

DESDEMONA: But while I say one prayer!

OTHELLO: It is too late.

(Smothers her.)

DESDEMONA: [O Lord, Lord, Lord!]

Emilia at the door.

EMILIA *(calls within)*:   My lord, my lord! What, ho! my lord, my lord!   85

OTHELLO: What noise is this? Not dead? not yet quite dead?
    I that am cruel am yet merciful;
    I would not have thee linger in thy pain.
    So, so.

EMILIA *(within)*:   What, ho! my lord, my lord!

OTHELLO: Who's there?   90

EMILIA *(within)*:   O, good my lord, I would speak a word with you!

OTHELLO: Yes, 'tis Emilia.—By and by.°—She's dead.—
    'Tis like she comes to speak of Cassio's death.
    The noise was here. Ha! no more moving?
    Still as the grave.—Shall she come in? Were't good!—   95
    I think she stirs again. No.—What's best to do?
    If she come in, she'll sure speak to my wife.
    My wife! my wife! what wife? I have no wife.
    O, insupportable! O heavy hour!
    Methinks it should be now a huge eclipse   100
    Of sun and moon, and that th' affrighted globe
    Should yawn° at alteration.

EMILIA *(within)*:   I do beseech you
    That I may speak with you, O good my lord!

OTHELLO: I had forgot thee. O, come in, Emilia.
    Soft, by and by.—Let me the curtains draw.—   105

[Closes the bed-curtains.]

    Where art thou?

[Opens the door.]

Enter Emilia.

                 What's the matter with thee now?

EMILIA: O my good lord, yonder's foul murder done!

OTHELLO: What? Now?

EMILIA: But now, my lord.

OTHELLO: It is the very error° of the moon.   110
    She comes more nearer earth than she was wont
    And makes men mad.

92 By and by: Just a moment (addressed to Emilia).   **102 yawn:** Open, as in an earthquake.   **110 error:** Straying off course.

EMILIA: Cassio, my lord, hath killed a young Venetian
 Called Roderigo.
OTHELLO: Roderigo killed?
 And Cassio killed?
EMILIA: No, Cassio is not killed.   115
OTHELLO: Not Cassio killed? Then murder's out of tune,
 And sweet revenge grows harsh.
DESDEMONA: O, falsely, falsely murdered?
EMILIA: O, Lord! what cry is that?
OTHELLO: That? What?
EMILIA: Out and alas! that was my lady's voice.   120
 Help! help, ho! help! O lady, speak again!
 Sweet Desdemona! O sweet mistress, speak!
DESDEMONA: A guiltless death I die.
EMILIA: O, who hath done this deed?
DESDEMONA: Nobody—I myself. Farewell.   125
 Commend° me to my kind lord. O, farewell!

(She dies.)

OTHELLO: Why, how should she be murd'red?
EMILIA: Alas, who knows?
OTHELLO: You heard her say herself, it was not I.
EMILIA: She said so. I must needs report the truth.
OTHELLO: She's like a liar gone to burning hell!   130
 'Twas I that killed her.
EMILIA: O, the more angel she,
 And you the blacker devil!
OTHELLO: She turned to folly, and she was a whore.
EMILIA: Thou dost belie her, and thou art a devil.
OTHELLO: She was false as water.°
EMILIA: Thou art rash as fire to say   135
 That she was false. O, she was heavenly true!
OTHELLO: Cassio did top her. Ask thy husband else.
 O, I were damned beneath all depth in hell
 But that I did proceed upon just grounds
 To this extremity. Thy husband knew it all.   140
EMILIA: My husband?
OTHELLO: Thy husband.
EMILIA: That she was false to wedlock?
OTHELLO: Ay, with Cassio. Nay, had she been true,
 If heaven would make me such another world   145
 Of one entire and perfect chrysolite,°
 I'ld not have sold her for it.
EMILIA: My husband?

126 Commend: Remember. **135 water:** (Which   is   yielding). **146 chrysolite:**
(Precious topaz).

OTHELLO: Ay 'twas he that told me first.
    An honest man he is, and hates the slime
    That sticks on filthy deeds.
EMILIA: My husband?   150
OTHELLO: What needs this iterance,° woman? I say thy husband.
EMILIA: O mistress, villainy hath made mocks with love!
    My husband say that she was false?
OTHELLO: He, woman.
    I say, thy husband. Dost understand the word?
    My friend, thy husband; honest, honest Iago.   155
EMILIA: If he say so, may his pernicious soul
    Rot half a grain a day! he lies to th' heart.
    She was too fond of her most filthy bargain.
OTHELLO: Ha!
EMILIA: Do thy worst.   160
    This deed of thine is no more worthy heaven
    Than thou wast worthy her.
OTHELLO: Peace, you were best.
EMILIA: Thou hast not half the power to do me harm
    As I have to be hurt.° O gull! O dolt!
    As ignorant as dirt! thou hast done a deed—   165
    I care not for thy sword; I'll make thee known,
    Though I lost twenty lives. Help! help! Ho! help!
    The Moor hath killed my mistress! Murder! murder!

Enter Montano, Gratiano, Iago, and others.

MONTANO: What is the matter? How now, general?
EMILIA: O, are you come, Iago? You have done well,   170
    That men must lay their murders on your neck.
GRATIANO: What is the matter?
EMILIA: Disprove this villain, if thou be'st a man.
    He says thou told'st him that his wife was false.
    I know thou didst not; thou'rt not such a villain.   175
    Speak, for my heart is full.
IAGO: I told him what I thought, and told no more
    Than what he found himself was apt and true.
EMILIA: But did you ever tell him she was false?
IAGO: I did.   180
EMILIA: You told a lie, an odious damnèd lie!
    Upon my soul, a lie! a wicked lie!
    She false with Cassio? Did you say with Cassio?
IAGO: With Cassio, mistress. Go to, charm° your tongue.

---

151 iterance: Repetition.   **164 to be hurt:** To endure hurt.   **184 charm:** Cast a spell on.

EMILIA: I will not charm my tongue; I am bound to speak: 185
   My mistress here lies murdered in her bed—
ALL: O heavens forfend!
EMILIA: And your reports have set the murder on.
OTHELLO: Nay, stare not, masters. It is true indeed.
GRATIANO: 'Tis a strange truth.   190
MONTANO: O monstrous act!
EMILIA: Villainy, villainy, villainy!
   I think upon't—I think I smell't!—O villainy!
   I thought so then.—I'll kill myself for grief.—
   O villainy, villainy!
IAGO: What, are you mad? I charge you get you home.   195
EMILIA: Good gentlemen, let me have leave to speak.
   'Tis proper I obey him, but not now.
   Perchance, Iago, I will ne'er go home.
OTHELLO: O! O! O!   *(Falls on the bed.)*
EMILIA: Nay, lay thee down and roar!
   For thou hast killed the sweetest innocent   200
   That e'er did lift up eye.
OTHELLO: O, she was foul!
[Rises.]
   I scarce did know you, uncle. There lies your niece,
   Whose breath, indeed, these hands have newly stopped.
   I know this act shows° horrible and grim.
GRATIANO: Poor Desdemon! I am glad thy father's dead.   205
   Thy match was mortal to him, and pure grief
   Shore his old thread in twain. Did he live now,
   This sight would make him do a desperate turn;°
   Yea, curse his better angel from his side,
   And fall to reprobation.°   210
OTHELLO: 'Tis pitiful; but yet Iago knows
   That she with Cassio hath the act of shame
   A thousand times committed. Cassio confessed it;
   And she did gratify° his amorous works
   With that recognizance° and pledge of love   215
   Which I first gave her. I saw it in his hand.
   It was a handkerchief, an antique token
   My father gave my mother.
EMILIA: O God! O heavenly God!
IAGO: Zounds, hold your peace!
EMILIA: 'Twill out, 'twill out! I peace?   220

---

204 shows: Appears.   **208 turn:** Act.   **210 reprobation:** Rejection by God, damnation.   **214 gratify:** Reward.   **215 recognizance:** Token.

No, I will speak as liberal as the north,°
Let heaven and men and devils, let them all,
All, all, cry shame against me, yet I'll speak.

IAGO: Be wise, and get you home.

EMILIA: I will not.

[Iago draws and threatens Emilia.]

GRATIANO: Fie!
    Your sword upon a woman?   225

EMILIA: O thou dull Moor, that handkerchief thou speak'st of
    I found by fortune, and did give my husband;
    For often with a solemn earnestness—
    More than indeed belonged to such a trifle—
    He begged of me to steal't.

IAGO: Villainous whore!   230

EMILIA: She give it Cassio? No, alas, I found it,
    And I did give't my husband.

IAGO: Filth, thou liest!

EMILIA: By heaven, I do not, I do not, gentlemen.
    O murd'rous coxcomb! what should such a fool
    Do with so good a wife?

OTHELLO: Are there no stones° in heaven   235
    But what serves for the thunder? Precious villain!

The Moor runs at Iago [but is disarmed by Montano].

Iago kills his wife.

GRATIANO: The woman falls. Sure he hath killed his wife.

EMILIA: Ay, ay. O, lay me by my mistress' side.   *Exit Iago.*

GRATIANO: He's gone, but his wife's killed.

MONTANO: 'Tis a notorious° villain. Take you this weapon,   240
    Which I have here recovered from the Moor.
    Come, guard the door without. Let him not pass,
    But kill him rather. I'll after that same villain,
    For 'tis a damnèd slave.

                        Exit [Montano, with all but Othello and Emilia].

OTHELLO: I am not valiant neither;
    But every puny whipster° gets my sword.   245
    But why should honor outlive honesty?
    Let it go all.

EMILIA: What did thy song bode, lady?
    Hark, canst thou hear me? I will play the swan,
    And die in music. *[Sings.]* "Willow, willow, willow."

---

221 liberal as the north: Unchecked as the north wind blows. **235 stones:** Bolts like those used for thunderbolts. **240 notorious:** Notable. **245 puny whipster:** Whippersnapper.

Moor, she was chaste. She loved thee, cruel Moor: 250
So come my soul to bliss as I speak true.
So speaking as I think, alas, I die.

(She dies.)

OTHELLO: I have another weapon in this chamber;
It is a sword of Spain, the ice brook's° temper.
O, here it is. — Uncle, I must come forth.   255
GRATIANO *(within)*:   If thou attempt it, it will cost thee dear.
Thou hast no weapon, and perforce must suffer.
OTHELLO: Look in upon me then and speak with me,
Or, naked° as I am, I will assault thee.

[Enter Gratiano.]

GRATIANO: What is the matter?
OTHELLO: Behold, I have a weapon;   260
A better never did itself sustain
Upon a soldier's thigh. I have seen the day
That with this little arm and this good sword
I have made my way through more impediments
Than twenty times your stop.° But O vain boast!   265
Who can control his fate? 'Tis not so now.
Be not afraid, though you do see me weaponed.
Here is my journey's end, here is my butt,°
And very seamark° of my utmost sail:
Do you go back dismayed? 'Tis a lost° fear.   270
Man but a rush° against Othello's breast,
And he retires. Where should Othello go?
Now, how dost thou look now? O ill-starred wench!
Pale as thy smock! When we shall meet at compt,°
This look of thine will hurl my soul from heaven,   275
And fiends will snatch at it. Cold, cold, my girl?
Even like thy chastity.
O cursèd, cursèd slave! Whip me, ye devils,
From the possession of this heavenly sight!
Blow me about in winds! roast me in sulphur!   280
Wash me in steep-down gulfs of liquid fire!
Oh Desdemon! dead Desdemon! dead! Oh! Oh!

Enter Lodovico, Montano, Iago [as prisoner], and Officers; Cassio in a chair.

LODOVICO: Where is this rash and most unfortunate man?
OTHELLO: That's he that was Othello. Here I am.

---

254 ice brook: I.e., a Spanish blade, tempered in cold running water.   **259 naked:**
Disarmed.   **265 stop:** Power   to   stop.   **268 butt:** Limit.   **269 seamark:** Beacon,
destination.   **270 lost:** Wasted.   **271 Man but a rush:** Wield   only   a   reed.   **274
compt:** Final accounting, Last Judgment.

LODOVICO: Where is that viper? Bring the villain forth.   285
OTHELLO: I look down towards his feet° — but that's a fable.
    If that thou be'st a devil, I cannot kill thee.

[Wounds Iago.]

LODOVICO: Wrench his sword from him.

[Othello is disarmed.]

IAGO: I bleed, sir, but not killed.
OTHELLO: I am not sorry neither. I'ld have thee live;
    For in my sense, 'tis happiness to die.   290
LODOVICO: O thou Othello that wert once so good,
    Fall'n in the practice° of a damnèd slave,
    What shall be said to thee?
OTHELLO: Why, anything;
    An honorable murderer, if you will;
    For naught did I in hate, but all in honor.   295
LODOVICO: This wretch hath part confessed his villainy.
    Did you and he consent in° Cassio's death?
OTHELLO: Ay.
CASSIO: Dear general, I never gave you cause.
OTHELLO: I do believe it, and I ask your pardon.   300
    Will you, I pray, demand that demi-devil
    Why he hath thus ensnared my soul and body?
IAGO: Demand me nothing. What you know, you know.
    From this time forth I never will speak word.
LODOVICO: What, not to pray?
GRATIANO: Torments will ope your lips.   305
OTHELLO: Well, thou dost best.
LODOVICO: Sir, you shall understand what hath befall'n,
    Which, as I think, you know not. Here is a letter
    Found in the pocket of the slain Roderigo;
    And here another. The one of them imports   310
    The death of Cassio to be undertook
    By Roderigo.
OTHELLO: O villain!
CASSIO: Most heathenish and most gross!
LODOVICO: Now here's another discontented paper
    Found in the pocket too; and this, it seems,   315
    Roderigo meant t' have sent this damnèd villain;
    But that, belike, Iago in the nick°
    Came in and satisfied him.
OTHELLO: O thou pernicious caitiff! —

---

286 I . . . feet: I.e., to see if they are cloven, like the Devil's.   **292 practice:** Plot.
297 consent in: Agree upon.   **317 nick:** Nick of time.

How came you, Cassio, by that handkerchief
That was my wife's?

CASSIO: I found it in my chamber;   320
And he himself confessed but even now
That there he dropped it for a special purpose
Which wrought to his desire.

OTHELLO: O fool! fool! fool!

CASSIO: There is besides in Roderigo's letter,
How he upbraids Iago that he made him   325
Brave me upon the watch; whereon it came
That I was cast;° and even but now he spake,
After long seeming dead—Iago hurt him,
Iago set him on.

LODOVICO: You must forsake this room and go with us.   330
Your power and your command is taken off,
And Cassio rules in Cyprus. For this slave,
If there be any cunning cruelty
That can torment him much and hold him long,
It shall be his. You shall close prisoner rest   335
Till that the nature of your fault be known
To the Venetian state. Come, bring away.

OTHELLO: Soft you! a word or two before you go.
I have done the state some service, and they know't.
No more of that. I pray you, in your letters,   340
When you shall these unlucky° deeds relate,
Speak of me as I am. Nothing extenuate,
Nor set down aught in malice. Then must you speak
Of one that loved not wisely, but too well;
Of one not easily jealous, but, being wrought,   345
Perplexed° in the extreme; of one whose hand,
Like the base Judean,° threw a pearl away
Richer than all his tribe; of one whose subdued° eyes,
Albeit unusèd to the melting mood,
Drop tears as fast as the Arabian trees   350
Their med'cinable gum. Set you down this.
And say besides that in Aleppo once,
Where a malignant and a turbaned Turk
Beat a Venetian and traduced the state,
I took by th' throat the circumcisèd dog   355
And smote him—thus.

(He stabs himself.)

---

327 cast: Dismissed.   **341 unlucky:** Fatal.   **346 Perplexed:** Distracted.   **347 Judean:** Judas Iscariot (?) (quarto reads "Indian").   **348 subdued:** I.e., conquered by grief.

LODOVICO: O bloody period!°
GRATIANO: All that's spoke is marred.
OTHELLO: I kissed thee ere I killed thee. No way but this,
    Killing myself, to die upon a kiss.

(He [falls upon the bed and] dies.)

CASSIO: This did I fear, but thought he had no weapon;   360
    For he was great of heart.
LODOVICO *[to Iago]*:   O Spartan dog,
    More fell° than anguish, hunger, or the sea!
    Look on the tragic loading of this bed.
    This is thy work. The object poisons sight;
    Let it be hid.° Gratiano, keep the house,   365
    And seize upon° the fortunes of the Moor,
    For they succeed on you. To you, lord governor,
    Remains the censure° of this hellish villain,
    The time, the place, the torture. O, enforce it!
    Myself will straight aboard, and to the state   370
    This heavy act with heavy heart relate.

                                          Exeunt.

357 period: Ending.   **362 fell:** Cruel.   **365 Let it be hid:** I.e., draw the bed curtains.   **366 seize upon:** Take legal possession of.   **368 censure:** Judicial sentence.

≡ THINKING ABOUT THE TEXT

1. Jealousy is one of the central motifs in this play. What characters are jealous and for what reasons?

2. Is Iago diabolically devious and clever, or is Othello especially gullible? How would you respond if a trusted friend made similar accusations against someone whom you cared for deeply?

3. Is Othello's tragic flaw — the quality that leads to his downfall — jealousy or something else, perhaps credulity?

4. Is it possible for Othello's love to turn so quickly into hate?

5. How might the end of the play and the final resolution of the characters' fates be seen as Shakespeare's commentary on jealousy?

A. C. BRADLEY
The Noble Othello

A. C. Bradley (1851–1935), a British literary critic and highly influential Shakespearean scholar, was the youngest boy among twenty-one children. His father was a well-regarded preacher. Bradley attended Balliol College at Oxford University and later was a professor at the University of Liverpool and at Oxford. His books include

Oxford Lectures on Poetry *(1909) and* Shakespearean Tragedy *(1904), where "The Noble Othello" appeared. The essays published in both books were originally lectures delivered by Bradley. Upon his death, Bradley's will established a fellowship for English literary scholars. Here, Bradley refutes the common notion that Othello was unjustifiably and easily jealous by considering how Othello's character diminishes only in light of the evidence Iago provides regarding Desdemona's supposed affair.*

This character is so noble, Othello's feelings and actions follow so inevitably from it and from the forces brought to bear on it, and his sufferings are so heart-rending, that he stirs, I believe, in most readers a passion of mingled love and pity which they feel for no other hero in Shakespeare, and to which not even Mr. Swinburne can do more than justice. Yet there are some critics and not a few readers who cherish a grudge against him. They do not merely think that in the later stages of his temptation he showed a certain obtuseness, and that, to speak pedantically, he acted with unjustifiable precipitance and violence; no one, I suppose, denies that. But, even when they admit that he was not of a jealous temper, they consider that he *was* "easily jealous"; they seem to think that it was inexcusable in him to feel any suspicion of his wife at all; and they blame him for never suspecting Iago or asking him for evidence. I refer to this attitude of mind chiefly in order to draw attention to certain points in the story. It comes partly from mere inattention (for Othello did suspect Iago and did ask him for evidence); partly from a misconstruction of the text which makes Othello appear jealous long before he really is so; and partly from failure to realise certain essential facts. I will begin with these.

(1) Othello, we have seen, was trustful, and thorough in his trust. He put entire confidence in the honesty of Iago, who had not only been his companion in arms, but, as he believed, had just proved his faithfulness in the matter of the marriage. This confidence was misplaced, and we happen to know it; but it was no sign of stupidity in Othello. For his opinion of Iago was the opinion of practically everyone who knew him: and that opinion was that Iago was before all things "honest," his very faults being those of excess in honesty. This being so, even if Othello had not been trustful and simple, it would have been quite unnatural in him to be unmoved by the warnings of so honest a friend, warnings offered with extreme reluctance and manifestly from a sense of a friend's duty. *Any* husband would have been troubled by them.

(2) Iago does not bring these warnings to a husband who had lived with a wife for months and years and knew her like his sister or his bosom-friend. Nor is there any ground in Othello's character for supposing that, if he had been such a man, he would have felt and acted as he does in the play. But he was newly married; in the circumstances he cannot have known much of Desdemona before his marriage; and further he was conscious of being under the spell of a feeling which can give glory to the truth but can also give it to a dream.

(3) This consciousness in any imaginative man is enough, in such circumstances, to destroy his confidence in his powers of perception. In Othello's case,

after a long and most artful preparation, there now comes, to reinforce its effect, the suggestions that he is not an Italian, nor even a European; that he is totally ignorant of the thoughts and the customary morality of Venetian women; that he had himself seen in Desdemona's deception of her father how perfect an actress she could be. As he listens in horror, for a moment at least the past is revealed to him in a new and dreadful light, and the ground seems to sink under his feet. These suggestions are followed by a tentative but hideous and humiliating insinuation of what his honest and much-experienced friend fears may be the true explanation of Desdemona's rejection of acceptable suitors, and of her strange, and naturally temporary, preference for a black man. Here Iago goes too far. He sees something in Othello's face that frightens him, and he breaks off. Nor does this idea take any hold of Othello's mind. But it is not surprising that his utter powerlessness to repel it on the ground of knowledge of his wife, or even of that instinctive interpretation of character which is possible between persons of the same race, should complete his misery, so that he feels he can bear no more, and abruptly dismisses his friend (III. iii. 238).

Now I repeat that *any* man situated as Othello was would have been disturbed by Iago's communications, and I add that many men would have been made wildly jealous. But up to this point, where Iago is dismissed, Othello, I must maintain, does not show jealousy. His confidence is shaken, he is confused and deeply troubled, he feels even horror; but he is not yet jealous in the proper sense of that word. In his soliloquy (III. iii. 258ff.) the beginning of this passion may be traced; but it is only after an interval of solitude, when he has had time to dwell on the idea presented to him, and especially after statements of fact, not mere general grounds of suspicion, are offered, that the passion lays hold of him. Even then, however, and indeed to the very end, he is quite unlike the essentially jealous man, quite unlike Leontes. No doubt the thought of another man's possessing the woman he loves is intolerable to him; no doubt the sense of insult and the impulse of revenge are at times most violent; and these are the feelings of jealousy proper. But these are not the chief or the deepest source of Othello's suffering. It is the wreck of his faith and his love. It is the feeling,

> If she be false, oh then Heaven mocks itself;

the feeling,

> O Iago, the pity of it, Iago!

the feeling,

> But there where I have garner'd up my heart,
> Where either I must live, or bear no life;
> The fountain from the which my current runs,
> Or else dries up—to be discarded thence....

You will find nothing like this in Leontes.

Up to this point, it appears to me, there is not a syllable to be said against Othello. But the play is a tragedy, and from this point we may abandon the ungrateful and undramatic task of awarding praise and blame. When Othello, after a brief interval, re-enters (III. iii. 329), we see at once that the poison has been at work, and "burns like the mines of sulphur."

> Look where he comes! Not poppy, nor mandragora,
> Nor all the drowsy syrups of the world,
> Shall ever medicine thee to that sweet sleep
> Which thou owedst yesterday.

He is "on the rack," in an agony so unbearable that he cannot endure the sight of Iago. Anticipating the probability that Iago has spared him the whole truth, he feels that in that case his life is over and his "occupation gone" with all its glories. But he has not abandoned hope. The bare possibility that his friend is deliberately deceiving him—though such a deception would be a thing so monstrously wicked that he can hardly conceive it credible—is a kind of hope. He furiously demands proof, ocular proof. And when he is compelled to see that he is demanding an impossibility he still demands evidence. He forces it from the unwilling witness, and hears the maddening tale of Cassio's dream. It is enough. And if it were not enough, has he not sometimes seen a handkerchief spotted with strawberries in his wife's hand? Yes, it was his first gift to her.

> I know not that; but such a handkerchief—
> I am sure it was your wife's—did I to-day
> See Cassio wipe his beard with.

"If it be that," he answers—but what need to test the fact? The "madness of revenge" is in his blood, and hesitation is a thing he never knew. He passes judgment, and controls himself only to make his sentence a solemn vow.

The Othello of the Fourth Act is Othello in his fall. His fall is never complete, but he is much changed. Towards the close of the Temptation-scene he becomes at times most terrible, but his grandeur remains almost undiminished. Even in the following scene (III. iv.), where he goes to test Desdemona in the matter of the handkerchief, and receives a fatal confirmation of her guilt, our sympathy with him is hardly touched by any feeling of humiliation. But in the Fourth Act "Chaos has come." A slight interval of time may be admitted here. It is but slight; for it was necessary for Iago to hurry on, and terribly dangerous to leave a chance for a meeting of Cassio with Othello; and his insight into Othello's nature taught him that his plan was to deliver blow on blow, and never to allow his victim to recover from the confusion of the first shock. Still there is a slight interval; and when Othello reappears we see at a glance that he is a changed man. He is physically exhausted, and his mind is dazed. He sees everything blurred through a mist of blood and tears. He has actually forgotten the incident of the handkerchief, and has to be reminded of it. When Iago, perceiving that he can now risk almost any lie, tells him that Cassio has confessed his guilt, Othello, the hero who has seemed to us only second to Coriolanus in physical power, trembles all over; he mutters disjointed words; a blackness suddenly intervenes between his eyes and the world; he takes it for the shuddering testimony of nature to the horror he has just heard, and he falls senseless to the ground. When he recovers it is to watch Cassio, as he imagines, laughing over his shame. It is an imposition so gross, and should have been one so perilous, that Iago would never have ventured it before. But he is safe now. The sight only adds to the confusion of intellect the madness of rage; and a ravenous thirst for revenge, contending with motions of infinite longing and regret, conquers them. The delay till night-fall is torture to him. His self-control has wholly deserted him, and he strikes his wife in the presence of the Venetian envoy. He is so lost to all sense of reality that he never asks himself what will follow the deaths of Cassio and his wife. An ineradicable instinct of justice, rather than any last quiver of hope, leads him to question Emilia; but nothing could convince him now, and there follows the dreadful scene of accusation; and then, to allow us the relief of burning hatred and burning tears, the interview of Desdemona with Iago, and that last talk of hers with Emilia, and her last song.

But before the end there is again a change. The supposed death of Cassio (V. i.) satiates the thirst for vengeance. The Othello who enters the bed-chamber with the words,

It is the cause, it is the cause, my soul,

is not the man of the Fourth Act. The deed he is bound to do is no murder, but a sacrifice. He is to save Desdemona from herself, not in hate but in honour; in honour, and also in love. His anger has passed; a boundless sorrow has taken its place; and

this sorrow's heavenly:
It strikes where it doth love.

Even when, at the sight of her apparent obduracy, and at the hearing of words which by a crowning fatality can only reconvince him of her guilt, these feelings give way to others, it is to righteous indignation they give way, not to rage; and, terribly painful as this scene is, there is almost nothing here to diminish the admiration and love which heighten pity. And pity itself vanishes, and love and admiration alone remain, in the majestic dignity and sovereign ascendancy of the close. Chaos has come and gone; and the Othello of the Council-chamber and the quay of Cyprus has returned, or a greater and nobler Othello still. As he speaks those final words in which all the glory and agony of his life — long ago in India and Arabia and Aleppo, and afterwards in Venice, and now in Cyprus — seem to pass before us, like the pictures that flash before the eyes of a drowning man, a triumphant scorn for the fetters of the flesh and the littleness of all the lives that must survive him sweeps our grief away, and when he dies upon a kiss the most painful of all tragedies leaves us for the moment free from pain, and exulting in the power of "love and man's unconquerable mind."

[1904]

MILLICENT BELL
Othello's Jealousy

Millicent Bell is a professor emerita in the English department at Boston University and a frequent contributor to The New York Review of Books. *She is the author of the books* Marquand: An American Life *(1979),* Meaning in Henry James *(1993), and* Shakespeare's Tragic Skepticism *(2002), where this essay appeared after first publication in the* Yale Review *(1997). In "Othello's Jealousy," Bell delves into how the notion of "seeing is believing" drives Othello to madness as what he sees in life and what he sees in his imagination are used by Iago to disturb his trust in Desdemona.*

Oh, yes, the chief subject of *Othello* is sexual jealousy. Most dramatic represen-tations seize upon and emphasize the way this condition, like a fatal disease, grows on the hero and destroys him until the recovery of sanity and dignity arrives at the tragic end. The more directly we see and hear him the more we almost share the madness that mounts in his mind until it reaches a point in which he appears to hallucinate, seeing what is not there, writhing before the inner vision of his wife's betrayal. In the recent Kenneth Branagh film this in-ner vision reaches the screen and the viewer is briefly unable to distinguish between what is and what is imagined as he or she sees—for a terrifying mo-ment, like a clip from a porn film—Cassio's lips meeting Desdemona's, their naked bodies twining together. Film's hallucinatory power, its ability to make virtual what words have only suggested, its ability to make us voyeurs who desire to witness the last detail of a scene, particularly an erotic scene, adds something that goes beyond stage presentation. The movie's powerful lan-guage of the visible provides—delusively even to us, though we know Othello is deluded—that ultimate visibility which goes beyond the evidence Iago has manipulated to "prove" Othello's love a whore.

But the greater reserve of the play as we read it, and even the reserve of stage presentation, which works such tricks awkwardly if at all, reminds us that jealousy feeds, precisely, upon what is *not* witnessed but only imagined. Othello, desperately swinging between belief in his wife's innocence and con-viction of her guilt, pleads for visible proof: "I'll see before I doubt," he cries. He thinks he can trust Desdemona, "for she had eyes and chose me," he tells Iago, who responds, "Look to your wife. Observe her well with Cassio; wear your eyes thus: not jealous, nor secure. . . . Look to't. . . . In Venice they do let God see the pranks / They dare not show their husbands." "Make me to see't," Othello pleads.

He groans, "Would I were satisfied!" but his tormentor observes—in an age before hidden video cameras and paparazzi—"but how? How satisfied, my Lord? / Would you the supervisor, grossly gape on? / Behold her topped?" and summons into inner view the dreadful vision, after all. But Iago says, at the same time,

It is impossible you should see this,
Were they as prime as goats, as hot as monkeys,
As salt as wolves in pride, and fools as gross
As Ignorance made drunk.

Iago will continue throughout the travail of Othello's jealousy to induce such hallucinations, to make Othello's own imagination set them forth on his inner stage. By the time we have reached the opening of the fourth act, the process is complete, and inner and outer vision are indistinguishable.

IAGO: Will you think so?
OTHELLO: Think so, Iago!
IAGO: What!
   To kiss in private?
OTHELLO: An unauthorized kiss!
IAGO: Or to be naked with her friend in bed
   An hour or more, not meaning any harm?
OTHELLO: Naked in bed, Iago, and not mean harm?

Othello is driven mad by what, by the force of suggestion, he *inwardly* sees, and yet he craves a certainty that can be satisfied only by outward sight — the sense that most convincingly assures us that we know what is before us. The central utterance in the play is, surely, Othello's anguished "Give me the ocular proof." But he craves confirmation of suspicion to end the agony aroused by what he cannot really see. For, as Iago says, "Her honor is an essence that's not seen." If he could witness the pair in bed together it might still not be enough. He is plagued by the realization that truth cannot be directly known; what we perceive is only *seeming.* "Seeing" and "seeming" are significantly repeated words that underline this problem throughout the play.

Othello, I want to argue against many of the play's critics, is the *most* intellectual of all Shakespeare's tragedies, including *Hamlet*, despite its concern with elementary personal emotion. In a genuine sense, the play is a "domestic tragedy," as it is frequently termed. But this is not at all to say that it simply shows the evolution of wife-murder, a version of the O. J. Simpson case. Harley Granville-Barker said it was "a tragedy without meaning," and A. C. Bradley thought it inferior to Shakespeare's other tragedies for lacking "the power of dilating the imagination by vague suggestions of huge universal powers working in the world of individual fate and passion." The editor of the New Cambridge Shakespeare edition, Norman Sanders, calls it "the most private of the great tragedies," though he insists that "to complain of its lack of supernatural reference or its limited metaphysical range is to miss the point." "The object poisons sight; / Let it be hid," says Lodovico when Othello and Desdemona lie dead together on their bed. Sanders says this "is the only possible end, because the arena for the struggle the protagonists have lived through is best symbolized by the curtained bed." But I shall insist that the play is not the less philosophical for that. "Sight" is indeed "poisoned" — yet not merely because of the spectacle of a love that has made such horror, but because this ending has shown the inadequacy of human vision.

Shakespeare, as is his habit, is always telling us a number of things at once. The power of the theme of sexual jealousy obscures other subjects in the play. Race and the divisive role of prejudice seem much more central than used to be conceded by critics who could not imagine how the Elizabethan world provided Shakespeare with so strong a sense of the most acute social problem of modern societies — expressed by the symbolic fantasy of miscegenation, the monstrous union of the socially separated. Shakespeare's treatment of marital violence also contains much that we respond to with recognition, seeing this problem rooted, then as now, in false notions of the differentiations of gender. Jealousy is also rooted in the unnaturalness of *any* love inordinate in its expectations, because each of us is just one and no more, and the single "beast with two backs" — that frightening visibility with which Iago arouses the rage of Brabantio — is a monster created only in an instant of sensual joy. Jealousy is evidence of the doubt that lies at the bottom of love's desire for knowledge of another, the doubt beneath love's refusal to accept the difference between one's perception and another's reality. The torment of Othello is epistemological, a condition of doubt of which sexual jealousy is only a specific illustration or consequence.

That Othello is so vulnerable to suggestion, passing so readily from hypothesis to certainty, has bothered those who have complained that he does not connect, as a character, with what happens; his noble strength, the slowness to anger that rules his early responses to Brabantio and to the drunken scuffle that awakens him from his wedded bliss in Cyprus, the majesty of his language — none of this prepares us for the speed with which he casts reason and refinement aside and becomes brutal and coarse. But it is precisely because jealousy cannot be satisfied by any degree of proof that it is a representation of the effect of skepticism, the specter that haunted the Renaissance imagination.

At the end of the sixteenth century, natural science was becoming more empirical. The view the educated person took of human history and of an individual life was apt to distinguish more consciously between certainty and probability, to discriminate among different kinds of evidence, whereas what "truth" was had become problematic. Though the truth of received religion was still a matter of faith, only a few kinds of certainty — like the certainty of mathematical proofs — were practically attainable. Shakespeare's great contemporary, Sir Francis Bacon, aspired with his grand inductive program to the ultimate restitution of "moral certainty," a concept borrowed from theology by which one might be sure about most things after observing and evaluating the facts. Bacon's effort was directed against the devastating view expressed by Montaigne that nothing could be known. A response to the problem of Montaigne's radical disbelief has been noted in Shakespeare's best writing — the sonnets and the great tragedies. Florio's translation into English of Montaigne's *Essais* was published in 1603, the year before *Othello* appeared on the stage. Perhaps, even, as Stanley Cavell argues, Shakespeare intuitively anticipated the terrifying culmination of Renaissance skepticism in René Descartes, who would make the issue "no longer, or not alone, as with earlier skepticism, how to conduct oneself in an uncertain world; the issue suggested is how to live at all in a groundless world."

In *Othello*, Iago is the source of skepticism; his nihilism links him in Shakespeare's works with Thersites and Edmund. But Othello's mind is the theater in which faith in the unseen and unseeable contends with the doubt that demands physical seeing and yet is never convinced it sees enough. Because Othello becomes the victim of his desire to know by seeing, his almost unbelievable collapse, his too-swift descent from composure and confidence to panic and disbelief, can be understood. But we are not meant to view him altogether in terms of realistic psychology — though nothing seems more real than his actual feelings when they overtake him.

If we do try to explain his fall realistically, we find ourselves in the crossfire   10
of critical tradition. F. R. Leavis was able to make a devastating case against Bradley's view that Othello's perfect nature — noble, strong-minded, self-disciplined — is destroyed by Iago's inhuman malice and intellect. Leavis discovered grounds for seeing Othello as a man infatuated with his own ideal view of himself, and *self*-destroyed. More recent psychological views suggest that Othello's great love, expressed in majestic, romantic hyperbole, may be the bluster of the untried bridegroom whose fear of inadequacy already rouses him from his nuptial bed along with the shouts of Iago and Roderigo in the opening scene. But neither a completely heroic nor a fatuous or secretly vulnerable Othello accounts adequately for the way this hero affects us. Perhaps Othello's improbable gullibility and precipitate fall depends, then, as E. E. Stoll claimed, on the literary convention of the "calumniator believed." We need to remember how commonplace and even farcical are some of the delusionary tricks that destroy Othello's faith in Desdemona; in Shakespeare's own *Much Ado About Nothing*, another ex-soldier, Claudio, is tricked by similar means into believing in the wantonness of his innocent betrothed. But Othello, unlike the lightweight Claudio, is really undone by an idea, though he is hardly philosopher enough himself to formulate it. Shakespeare makes us experience — through Othello's trauma — the absolute difference between a trust in appearances and the loss of that trust. . . .

Throughout *Othello*, Shakespeare's strong interest in the law is also evident in language full of legal terms drawn from the procedures of court trials that those who have hoped to detect more about his life from such elusive traces can suppose that he had had some training in the law. But English court trials were open to the public, forms of entertainment like the theater, and the audience for both was likely to contain persons who were amateur experts, like recent viewers of televised trials. Iago complains that Othello turned a deaf ear to those who urged his advancement; he "non-suites my Mediators," he says — that is, he rules their case out of court. When he refuses to tell Othello his private thoughts, he asks if anyone has "a breast so pure, / But some uncleanly apprehensions / Keep leets and law-days, and in sessions sit / With meditations lawful," "leets and law-days" being court sessions to certify the good behavior of a community. Pleading Cassio's case with Othello, Desdemona insists that the handkerchief business is but "a trick to put me from my suit." She chides herself for "Arraigning his unkindness with my soul; / But now I find I had suborned the witness / And he's indicted falsely," a reference to the crime of subornation of perjury. What is important to note, among these obscurities, is the way words that have a common usage as well as a specific legal sense seem to reverberate with a courtroom meaning—as when Othello's handkerchief, the central symbolic object that is the mark of the troth between him and Desdemona, is called "the recognizance and pledge of love," where "recognizance" is the *legal* word for a binding bond.

It is appropriate to the preoccupation of the play with a general epistemological crisis that the issue of proof is expressed as a legal question. The general evolution of thought in the sixteenth and seventeenth centuries is connected with the fact that English common law established in this period a foundation of rules of evidence that persists to this day. Brabantio's charges and Othello's refutation reflect current controversy over trials for witchcraft. In 1597, James I of England[1] had felt called upon to attempt in his *Demonologie* to refute Reginald Scott's attack (*Discoverie of Witchcraft,* 1584) on the procedures for trying those accused of witchcraft. Yet James I soon developed doubts and censured judges who rushed to judgment without adequate proof. A general movement had begun in the courts to develop proper modes of establishing this crime. Along with that skeptical doubt that caused some, like Montaigne, to doubt the existence of witchcraft altogether, the trial of witches was changing from the search for a hidden character—established only by confession, formerly extracted by torture, if necessary—to a weighing of visible effects, testified to by witnesses. The shift is epistemological.

The courtroom, like the stage, was for the Elizabethans a place where the dynamics of changing concepts of the self were being enacted, being tried. How might one argue from crime to criminal—or reverse the process? By what evidence might the play connect plot and character? In the courtroom it was not enough to argue from "reputation" in deciding probable guilt—as it is not enough for Iago to convict Desdemona by referring to her "Venetian" character—but the prosecution might add plausibility to its case by presenting, as Iago does, a narrative of events leading to her crime, by "imputation." Beyond this, how might guilt be proven? Circumstantial evidence in criminal cases was becoming the most usual basis of conviction. Iago protests that he cannot enable Othello to see his wife in her lover's arms, but adds,

> If imputation and strong circumstances,
> Which lead directly to the door of truth,
> Will give you satisfaction, you might have't.

---

[1] Before becoming James I of England in 1603, he was James VI of Scotland from 1567–1603. [Eds.]

The paradigm of a trial of law, invoked at the start by an actual trial, is replicated in the structure of the play, a trial of Desdemona that ends in her execution. In a terrible parody of judicial sentence, in the second scene of the last act, Othello enters with a speech of deliberate dignity:

> It is the cause, it is the cause, my soul:
> Let me not name it to you, you chaste stars.
> It is the cause. Yet I'll not shed her blood,
> Nor scar that whiter skin of hers than snow,
> And smooth as monumental alabaster —
> Yet she must die, else she'll betray more men.

"Cause" is a legal term in addition to meaning simply a reason for an oc-   15
currence. To seek a cause is to seek a motive to increase the probability of guilt, while the accused may claim for his deed that he had *just* cause. Iago has begun by telling Roderigo, "I hate the Moor. My cause is hearted; thine hath no less reason." He has begun the motive-hunting that Coleridge deemed motiveless; his search for his own motive is a legal procedure to reinforce belief. A cause may be a general purpose, even a high principle to which one is attached; the cause of a heavenly ideal of chastity for which, Othello declares, Desdemona must die. But a cause is also, simply, a suit, as Desdemona called her effort to win pardon for Cassio, acting as his "solicitor." And Othello's charge against Desdemona is a suit in which he becomes prosecutor, judge, and, finally, executioner under a rule of human law aimed not only at punishment but to protect society from further crimes by the criminal ("else she'll betray more men").

Proof as in a law court is what Othello so mistakenly has asked Iago to produce. When Othello says, "I'll see before I doubt; when I doubt prove," Iago says, "I speak not yet of proof," but urges him to watch Desdemona for some self-betrayal and sets forth, meanwhile, her record as a practiced deceiver who has known how to make seeing her directly impossible: "She that so young could give out such a seeming / To seal her father's eyes up close as oak." Perhaps this would not be enough—though Othello is already frantic—but prompt to his purpose, Desdemona reappears to drop the handkerchief that Iago will seize and enter into evidence. "Trifles light as air / Are to the jealous confirmations strong / As proofs of holy writ"—though a just judge and dispassionate jury might not take them so. The handkerchief, for Othello, is the exhibit brought into the courtroom, a piece of the accused's clothing found at the scene of the crime, "ocular proof"—not of the unseeable act but circumstantial evidence, so that "the probation [or determining test] bear no hinge nor loop to hang a doubt on."

Feebly, Othello clings to his faith that Desdemona is honest and asks for presumptive motive: "Give me a living reason she's disloyal," but Iago ignores this. He testifies that he has observed Cassio relive in sleep his secret moments with Desdemona. And when Othello protests that this was but a dream, Iago says, "this may help to thicken other proofs / That do demonstrate thinly." And what are these? Iago saw Cassio wipe his beard with the handkerchief. "It speaks against her with the other proofs."

So, as the fourth act opens, Iago provokingly drives the question of proof to its most paradoxical extreme — with the assurance that, although absolute knowledge is impossible, circumstances will convict. There is no direct witness to adultery between Cassio and Desdemona — but after all, how could there be? What if you found them naked and kissing in bed together for an hour or more? Would it *prove* they were "meaning any harm? . . . if they do nothing, 'tis a venial slip." As though the case would be similar, Iago asks if giving a handkerchief away need convict a woman of much — knowing that Othello will conclude that it is as circumstantially damning as a sight of the lovers flagrantly embracing. But the time has come for Iago to offer the confirming proof of confession, though, of course, it is confession reported at second hand — Cassio has supposedly confessed to *him*. It is not quite enough, and Iago will repair the defect in his case, or appear to; Othello will think he witnesses Cassio boasting how "he hath and is again to cope" Desdemona when Cassio really is talking about his mistress, who appears on cue, handkerchief in hand.

It is no use for Desdemona to defend herself. Or for Emilia to protest in a logical way, "Who keeps her company? What place, what time, what form, what likelihood?" But Emilia as defense witness arrives too late, discovering her husband's perfidy only after the death of her mistress. Before Othello executes his sentence, he asks Desdemona if she has repented of crime, as condemned criminals generally were asked, for the rescue of her soul and also to confirm the sentence by the strongest of proofs: "Take heed of perjury: thou art on thy death bed."

She maintains her innocence, having nothing to confess. Iago, who has   20
everything to tell, withholds *his* confession, but Emilia will dispose of the false evidence of the handkerchief by revealing that she stole it for him, and documentary proof, letters from Iago found on Roderigo, close the case — unnecessarily for the audience but in keeping with the judicial process that governs the play.

But if the legal conceptualization of *Othello* relates it to the whole issue of the nature of truth, it is really an ironic parody of real legal inquiry. The search for evidentiary proof is, in fact, constantly mocked despite all the talk of proofs and making the wronged husband "see." Iago's pseudo-legal demonstration of Cassio's and Desdemona's guilt is conducted in the Cyprus world ruled by "seeming" — a world that makes such deceptions possible by demonic magic. Emilia's "what place, what time, what form, what likelihood" reminds us of the sleights that the playwright has himself exercised, not the least by that famous deception of "double time" that allows no time or opportunity — though we fail to notice it — for an affair between Cassio and Desdemona. Iago has merely to repeat Brabantio's charges that there was something "unnatural" in Desdemona's love to get Othello's assent to an idea he had serenely rejected in the Venetian court. He says Cassio's declarations, in sleep, of his love for Desdemona, reported by Iago, "denoted a foregone conclusion," and it is enough for him to have heard that Cassio has the handkerchief to be convinced that she would betray him sexually, accepting the false analogy: may she not just as freely give away her invisible honor? Othello does not have to hear Cassio's actual conversation with Iago about Bianca to assume that his wife is the subject.

There is a subtle slippage that merges supposition with ascertained fact. When Iago says, "What if I had said I had seen him do you wrong?" or heard Cassio "blab" of his conquest, the "what if" glides by as though never uttered. Othello reaches vainly for his sanity: "Hath he said anything?" *Then,* Iago slips in the knife—"He hath my lord"—only to assure Othello that Cassio would deny it. When Othello asks, "What hath he said?" he receives the riddling answer "what he did—I know not what he did," and to Othello's "with her?" the reply is a verbal quibble that throws his victim into his swoon, "With her, on her, what you will."

As we attend this collapse of logic, the difference between the world of illusion and the real world in which fact and appearance are distinguishable dissolves, for we are ourselves swept along by the play's hypnotic persuasion to jealousy, which banishes such distinctions. When Desdemona wonders at the "cause" for Othello's rage, Emilia rightly says,

> . . . jealous souls will not be answered so.
> They are not ever jealous for the cause,
> But jealous for they're jealous. 'Tis a monster
> Begot upon itself, born on itself.

But as I have been suggesting, jealousy becomes, in this extraordinary play, just a way of exhibiting a change of mind that equalizes the effect of all impressions. Othello may well say that contentedness in deception is best; it annihilates the reality that gives pain: "He that is robbed, not wanting what is stolen, / Let him not know't and he's not robbed at all."

It is often pointed out that the play exhibits contrasted viewpoints in the language of Othello and Iago—there is the poetic "Othello music," as L. C. Knights called it, sounded in words that seem to arise from a sense of the ordered cosmos and the hero's place in it. And there is the language of Iago, prosaically intelligent without any element of the ideal. Only Leavis and a few others have felt that Iago had some right to complain of Othello as "loving his own pride and purposes" and apt to employ "bombast circumstance" and "stuff'd" epithets. But it must be said that Othello's is the half of language most vulnerable to skepticism. Iago's version of Othello's tragedy is not the one most readers and viewers of the play embrace—he sees it as comedy, the leveling of preposterous presumption. His view goes down in defeat, we assume, as we listen to Othello's last grand speech as he prepares to kill himself—even though one suspects that T. S. Eliot was right in pointing out that the "honorable murderer" whom Emilia has called a "gull" and a "dolt" is simply trying to cheer himself up. Where Shakespeare stood is, as usual, not evident.

But if we see Othello's fall as a telescoped representation of the mind overtaken by its own epistemological distrust of appearances—and the paradoxical trust *only* in appearances—we can see that what overcomes Othello, or

25

rather what is represented *through* Othello's mad jealousy, is a trembling of the universal spheres, a perturbation from which recovery comes only at the cost of deadly anguish. It is not mere hyperbole that causes him to tell Desdemona, out of her hearing, "When I love thee not, / Chaos is come again," to exclaim, "If she be false, O then heaven mocks itself," or to say, in later confirmation of this prediction,

> O heavy hour!
> Methinks it should be now a huge eclipse
> Of sun and moon, and that th'affrighted globe
> Should yawn at alteration.   *[1997]*

JEFFRIE G. MURPHY
Jealousy, Shame, and the Rival

Jeffrie G. Murphy (b. 1941) is a distinguished legal and moral philosopher. He has published a number of books, including Getting Even: Forgiveness and Mercy *(2004) and most recently* Punishment and the Moral Emotions: Essays in Law, Morality, and Religion *(2012). His essay, "Jealousy, Shame, and the Rival," which appeared in the journal* Philosophical Studies, *is essentially a critique of Jerome Neu's work on jealousy in* A Tear Is an Intellectual Thing *(2000). Murphy maintains that Othello's acts of jealousy stem not from a fear of loss of love (as Neu's definition of jealousy requires) but from a fear of the shame brought on by that loss.*

When Jerome Neu's essay "Jealous Thoughts" was published in 1980, jealousy was widely regarded—at least in leftist intellectual and cultural circles—as an irrational and even evil "bourgeois" passion—one tied to a capitalistic market conception of human relations. The jealous person—according to this view—regards the loved person as a kind of object—as owned property over which the lover has rights. Jealousy is thus a kind of property fear—analogous to the fear of theft. The fear intrinsically involves the belief that one risks losing a possessed loved object to whose love one has a right.

Neu—rightly in my judgment—rejects this account of jealousy as psychologically shallow. He argues—in "Jealous Thoughts" and in the later "Jealous Afterthoughts"—that psychoanalytic theory teaches us that love gets its initial life and draws its basic character from the Oedipal situation. The child so needs and depends upon the mother that loss of the mother's love would appear both as biological and psychological annihilation—psychological because the very self of the child is identified with that of the mother. Any perceived rival for the mother's affections (initially the father) is seen as a threat to security and thus provokes in the child a fear of loss of love. It is here that love and jealousy begin, develop through what Winnicott calls "transitional objects," and assume forms that will persist in adult life. To love is, at least in part, to be so identified with another person that the loss of that person's love will be perceived as loss or annihilation of one's very self or personality. Jealousy, then, is simply the fear that one will lose the love of a person with whom one is psychologically identified—an instance of the fear of annihilation. "If others do not love us," Neu writes, "we will disintegrate."

This fear is not, according to Neu, grounded in a bourgeois or possessive model of human relations, for one can fear the loss of love without believing that one owns the loved person or that one has a right to that person's love. All that is required is that one has the love. Love, then, in part involves self identification—when we lose it we lose ourselves, having our vulnerabilities open and unsupported. All human beings, regardless of social setting—bourgeois or communitarian—fear the exposure of vulnerabilities and the resulting loss of self. According to Neu, this fear is jealousy. Thus jealousy and love are necessarily connected—we cannot get rid of the former without losing the latter.

There are some questions that I immediately want to raise about this analysis. First, what about unrequited love? There are surely intense cases of jealousy where the jealous person knows full well that the love he feels is not returned. Not having it, he cannot fear its loss. Thus it cannot be literally true to say, as Neu does in the first essay, that "to be jealous over someone, you must believe that they love you or have loved you."

Unrequited love thus presents a problem for Neu's original analysis, but I think that the problem can be rather easily fixed. One might draw on some of the instructive things that Neu has to say in the later essay about the role of illusion and projection in erotic love, or one might suggest (think of the John Hinckley/Jodie Foster case) that what the jealous unrequited lover fears is not the loss of love (which he clearly does not have) but the loss of the *possibility* of love (which he may still hope for).

There is also, of course, the problem of jealousy over love that one believes is already hopelessly lost. Othello—often presented (as he is by Neu) as a paradigm of a jealous person—is frequently thought to be most jealous *after* he believes that he has lost Desdemona's love to Cassio. But surely this cannot be understood simply as the fear of loss of love, for how can one fear to lose what one has already lost?

In keeping with the spirit—if not the exact letter—of Neu's analysis, one might try to deal with the Othello case in this way: The fear that constitutes Othello's jealousy should not be seen as the fear of the loss of love (it is simply too late for *that* fear) but rather as the fear of the personal disintegration that may result from that loss.

Perhaps killing or other acts of revenge against the lost lover are strategies to defend against this possible consequence. Perhaps they are preventive strategies that seek the prevention, not of the loss of love, but rather of the dire consequences that—according to Neu—may flow from that loss. Or perhaps they are *retributive* strategies—seeking to inflict punishment on the person who has caused such personal disruption and pain at the core of one's very self. Thus it is possible that the jealous person who inflicts pain over love lost is somewhat like the lover of a murder victim who believes (sometimes rightly, sometimes wrongly) that a kind of closure will result from the execution of the killer.

We are all, alas, familiar with newspaper reports that read "He killed her in a jealous rage." Such a phrase might well describe Othello, but I am not sure. He was surely jealous when he suspected Desdemona of infidelity, but was he jealous at the time he murdered her? Perhaps he was simply vindictive. However, if such murderous rage is properly to be identified as "jealous," it surely cannot be motivated by the fear of losing love since the surest way permanently to lose love is to kill the lover. Dead people cannot love. So what goes on in these cases is either not jealousy at all but rather something else—vengeance perhaps—or it is jealousy motivated by something other than the fear of losing love. Perhaps it is motivated by a deep aversion to certain *consequences* of losing love. Neu would stress the consequence of annihilation or disintegration—since that is so integral to his analysis of love—but I shall later argue that one of these consequences may be *shame*. . . .

It is a perhaps sad but surely true claim that, to a substantial degree, people   10
derive their sense of self worth from the judgments of others. If we love a person, we tend to take that person's judgments in these matters quite seriously—i.e., we take them in some sense to be accurate judges of our own worth. (The mentally healthy among us—if there are any—would not follow Groucho Marx in contemptuously refusing to join any club that would have us for members; nor would we deeply mistrust the judgment of any person who could love us.) If we add to this the fact that non-moral judgments of worth are generally comparative, then the fact that a judge whom we trust prefers someone over us may make us doubt our own worth or value. So jealousy may stand as testimony, not merely to our need for love and attention, but also to our need for validation by another. We are thus shamed by rejection.

It is, of course, not merely the judgment of the loved person who matters. The judgment of a wider circle of people matters as well, for even the strongest of us needs validation from some relevant reference group. Consider Achilles. His rage over the loss of Briseis to Agamemnon is to a substantial degree based on his loss of honor—face and standing—in the eyes of his fellow warriors. He has been shamed by having the girl taken from him.

I think that similar shame may be found in many contemporary cases of jealousy and loss. The jilted lover is often ashamed to report this to others—thinking that it casts some bad reflection on his or her worth or standing. (Sometimes—for similar reasons I suspect—people are reluctant even to admit that they are divorced.) Being a victim of infidelity is, among other unpleasant things, shameful and embarrassing. Perhaps this in part explains the rage that is often found in those who have been jilted—a rage that may provoke expensive and vicious lawsuits, small or even major acts of retribution, and sometimes even murder. Why do people do these things? These acts will not get the love back, but they may go a long way—at least in the eyes of the perpetrator—toward saving face, restoring lost status and honor, and thus overcoming the shame of it all. If one believes that he has been brought down by another, he may find it therapeutic—or think he will find it therapeutic—to bring that person down as well. I am not, of course, saying that such a response is justified, only that it is—unfortunately—not unusual (particularly among men). As Norman Mailer (who ought to know) has asked: "Isn't human nature depressing?"

To summarize and conclude: I think that Neu has provided us with many profound insights on jealousy and its relation to love. Indeed, if I were asked to recommend just one philosophical essay on jealousy, it would be Neu's. It is, I think, the best place to start—for its insights, the framework it provides, and the provocative questions it forces us to raise.

In raising these questions, however, I have come to think that Neu's account of jealousy needs to be supplemented in certain ways. In particular, I have suggested that *shame* needs to be stressed in order fully to account for the role of the rival in jealousy.   *[2002]*

≡ MAKING COMPARISONS

1. Murphy focuses on jealousy as having a psychological basis, arguing that jealousy is "the fear that one will lose the love of a person with whom one is psychologically identified" (para. 2) and later adds shame into the mix of jealousy. Bell, however, seems to think jealousy has more to do with philosophy, with appearances and reality, with the distinction "between seeming and true seeing"—indeed, with the very nature of truth itself. Explain why one of these interpretations helps you understand *Othello* better.

2. Bradley claims that the true source of Othello's suffering is "the wreck of his faith and love" (para. 5). Do you think Bell and Murphy agree?

3. From each essay, choose a sentence or two that impresses you as offering an interesting insight into the play. How did each one deepen your understanding of *Othello*?

≡ WRITING ABOUT ISSUES

1. Research the nature of and causes for jealousy. In an essay, argue that the three scholars here do or do not do justice to the complexity of this emotion.

2. Bell claims that "sexual jealousy obscures other subjects in the play." Research what other issues might be in the play and argue, in an essay, that Bell's assertion is or is not correct.

3. Research a feminist or gender studies interpretation of *Othello*. Argue in an essay that this perspective is or is not a powerful tool in understanding the characters in the play.

4. Research either a postcolonial or New Historicism criticism on *Othello* and write an argument that one or a combination of these approaches gives us plausible insights into the play.

■ Arguments about an Issue: Is Marriage Worth It?

LAURA KIPNIS, "Against Love"

MEGHAN O'ROURKE, "The Marriage Trap"

Ever since Shakespeare's comedies, marriage has been one of the most popular endings for plays, novels, and films. And it is assumed by almost everybody, including both heterosexual and same-sex partners, that the happy couple, having found true love at last, will be lovers and friends for a lifetime. But according to some skeptics, the facts should make us believe otherwise. After all, the divorce rate has almost doubled since the 1960s, and considerably less than half of married couples say they are happy in their marriages. Some critics blame our inflated expectations about love's durability. Others see a kind of conspiracy to keep marriages together for economic reasons. And there are those who think we should give up the ghost and look for other less permanent arrangements. Laura Kipnis and Meghan O'Rourke develop witty, provocative, and often conflicting arguments about love and marriage.

■ BEFORE YOU READ

Why do you think true love should last forever? Why do you think love fades? Why do you think so many couples feel trapped in their marriages? Why do so many marriages end in divorce? Why do married people have affairs? Why might monogamy be unnatural?

LAURA KIPNIS

Against Love

Laura Kipnis (b. 1956) is a professor at Northwestern University outside of Chicago, where she teaches courses on gender, popular culture, and sexual politics. She has an M.F.A. from Nova Scotia College of Art and Design. The following essay appeared in the New York Times Magazine *in October 2001 as a prelude to her book* Against Love: A Polemic *(2003). Her latest book is* How to Become a Scandal: Adventures in Bad Behavior *(2010). She has been praised for her "sharp analysis" and "blistering wit" in challenging contemporary notions of love and sex.*

Love is, as we know, a mysterious and controlling force. It has vast power over our thoughts and life decisions. It demands our loyalty, and we, in turn, freely comply. Saying no to love isn't simply heresy; it is tragedy—the failure to achieve what is most essentially human. So deeply internalized is our obedience to this most capricious despot that artists create passionate odes to its cruelty, and audiences seem never to tire of the most deeply unoriginal mass spectacles devoted to rehearsing the litany of its torments, fixating their very beings on the narrowest glimmer of its fleeting satisfactions.

Yet despite near total compliance, a buzz of social nervousness attends the subject. If a society's lexicon of romantic pathologies reveals its particular anxieties, high on our own list would be diagnoses like "inability to settle down" or "immaturity," leveled at those who stray from the norms of domestic coupledom either by refusing entry in the first place or, once installed, pursuing various escape routes: excess independence, ambivalence, "straying," divorce. For the modern lover, "maturity" isn't a depressing signal of impending decrepitude but a sterling achievement, the sine qua non of a lover's qualifications to love and be loved.

This injunction to achieve maturity—synonymous in contemporary usage with 30-year mortgages, spreading waistlines, and monogamy—obviously finds its raison d'être in modern love's central anxiety, that structuring social contradiction the size of the San Andreas Fault: namely, the expectation that romance and sexual attraction can last a lifetime of coupled togetherness despite much hard evidence to the contrary.

Ever optimistic, heady with love's utopianism, most of us eventually pledge ourselves to unions that will, if successful, far outlast the desire that impelled them into being. The prevailing cultural wisdom is that even if sexual desire tends to be a short-lived phenomenon, "mature love" will kick in to save the day when desire flags. The issue that remains unaddressed is whether cutting off other possibilities of romance and sexual attraction for the more muted pleasures of mature love isn't similar to voluntarily amputating a healthy limb: a lot of anesthesia is required and the phantom pain never entirely abates. But if it behooves a society to convince its citizenry that wanting change means personal failure or wanting to start over is shameful or simply wanting more satisfaction than what you have is an illicit thing, clearly grisly acts of self-mutilation will be required.

There hasn't always been quite such optimism about love's longevity. For the Greeks, inventors of democracy and a people not amenable to being pushed around by despots, love was a disordering and thus preferably brief experience. During the reign of courtly love, love was illicit and usually fatal. Passion meant suffering: the happy ending didn't yet exist in the cultural imagination. As far as togetherness as an eternal ideal, the twelfth-century advice manual *De Amore et Amor is Remedio* (*On Love and the Remedies of Love*) warned that too many opportunities to see or chat with the beloved would certainly decrease love.

The innovation of happy love didn't even enter the vocabulary of romance until the seventeenth century. Before the eighteenth century—when the family was primarily an economic unit of production rather than a hothouse of Oedipal tensions—marriages were business arrangements between families; participants had little to say on the matter. Some historians consider romantic love a learned behavior that really only took off in the late eighteenth century along with the new fashion for reading novels, though even then affection between a husband and wife was considered to be in questionable taste.

5

Historians disagree, of course. Some tell the story of love as an eternal and unchanging essence; others, as a progress narrative over stifling social conventions. (Sometimes both stories are told at once; consistency isn't required.) But has modern love really set us free? Fond as we are of projecting our own emotional quandaries back through history, construing vivid costume dramas featuring medieval peasants or biblical courtesans sharing their feelings with the post-Freudian savvy of lifelong analysands, our amatory predecessors clearly didn't share all our particular aspirations about their romantic lives.

We, by contrast, feel like failures when love dies. We believe it could be otherwise. Since the cultural expectation is that a state of coupled permanence is achievable, uncoupling is experienced as crisis and inadequacy—even though such failures are more the norm than the exception.

As love has increasingly become the center of all emotional expression in the popular imagination, anxiety about obtaining it in sufficient quantities—and for sufficient duration—suffuses the population. Everyone knows that as the demands and expectations on couples escalated, so did divorce rates. And given the current divorce statistics (roughly 50 percent of all marriages end in divorce), all indications are that whomever you love today—your beacon of hope, the center of all your optimism—has a good chance of becoming your worst nightmare tomorrow. (Of course, that 50 percent are those who actually leave their unhappy marriages and not a particularly good indication of the happiness level or nightmare potential of those who remain.) Lawrence Stone, a historian of marriage, suggests—rather jocularly, you can't help thinking—that today's rising divorce rates are just a modern technique for achieving what was once taken care of far more efficiently by early mortality.

Love may or may not be a universal emotion, but clearly the social forms it   10 takes are infinitely malleable. It is our culture alone that has dedicated itself to allying the turbulence of romance and the rationality of the long-term couple, convinced that both love and sex are obtainable from one person over the course of decades, that desire will manage to sustain itself for 30 or 40 or 50 years, and that the supposed fate of social stability is tied to sustaining a fleeting experience beyond its given life span.

Of course, the parties involved must "work" at keeping passion alive (and we all know how much fun that is), the presumption being that even after living in close proximity to someone for a historically unprecedented length of time, you will still muster the requisite desire to achieve sexual congress on a regular basis. (Should passion fizzle out, just give up sex. Lack of desire for a mate is never an adequate rationale for "looking elsewhere.") And it is true, many couples do manage to perform enough psychic retooling to reshape the anarchy of desire to the confines of the marriage bed, plugging away at the task year after year (once a week, same time, same position) like diligent assembly-line workers, aided by the occasional fantasy or two to help get the old motor to turn over, or keep running, or complete the trip. And so we have the erotic life of a nation of workaholics: if sex seems like work, clearly you're not working hard enough at it.

But passion must not be allowed to die! The fear—or knowledge—that it does shapes us into particularly conflicted psychological beings, perpetually in search of prescriptions and professional interventions, regardless of cost or consequence. Which does have its economic upside, at least. Whole new sectors of the economy have been spawned, with massive social investment in new technologies from Viagra to couples' porn: capitalism's Lourdes for dying marriages.

There are assorted low-tech solutions to desire's dilemmas too. Take advice. In fact, take more and more advice. Between print, airwaves, and the therapy industry, if there were any way to quantify the G.N.P. in romantic counsel, it would be a staggering number. Desperate to be cured of love's temporality, a love-struck populace has molded itself into an advanced race of advice receptacles, like some new form of miracle sponge that can instantly absorb many times its own body weight in wetness.

Inexplicably, however, a rebellious breakaway faction keeps trying to leap over the wall and emancipate themselves, not from love itself—unthinkable!—but from love's domestic confinements. The escape routes are well trodden—love affairs, midlife crises—though strewn with the left-behind luggage of those who encountered unforeseen obstacles along the way (panic, guilt, self-engineered exposures) and beat self-abashed retreats to their domestic gulags, even after pledging body and soul to newfound loves in the balmy utopias of nondomesticated romances. Will all the adulterers in the audience please stand up? You know who you are. Don't be embarrassed! Adulterers aren't just "playing around." These are our home-grown closet social theorists, because adultery is not just a referendum on the sustainability of monogamy; it is a veiled philosophical discussion about the social contract itself. The question on the table is this: "How much renunciation of desire does society demand of us, versus the degree of gratification it provides?" Clearly, the adulterer's answer, following a long line of venerable social critics, would be, "Too much."

But what exactly is it about the actual lived experience of modern domestic   15
love that would make flight such a compelling option for so many? Let us briefly examine those material daily life conditions.

Fundamentally, to achieve love and qualify for entry into that realm of salvation and transcendence known as the couple (the secular equivalent of entering a state of divine grace), you must be a lovable person. And what precisely does being lovable entail? According to the tenets of modern love, it requires an advanced working knowledge of the intricacies of mutuality.

Mutuality means recognizing that your partner has needs and being prepared to meet them. This presumes, of course, that the majority of those needs can and should be met by one person. (Question this, and you question the very foundations of the institution. So don't.) These needs of ours run deep, a tangled underground morass of ancient, gnarled roots, looking to ensnarl any hapless soul who might accidentally trod upon their outer radices.

Still, meeting those needs is the most effective way to become the object of another's desire, thus attaining intimacy, which is required to achieve the state known as psychological maturity. (Despite how closely it reproduces the affective conditions of our childhoods, since trading compliance for love is the earliest social lesson learned; we learn it in our cribs.)

You, in return, will have your own needs met by your partner in matters large and small. In practice, many of these matters turn out to be quite small. Frequently, it is the tensions and disagreements over the minutiae of daily living that stand between couples and their requisite intimacy. Taking out the garbage, tone of voice, a forgotten errand—these are the rocky shoals upon which intimacy so often founders.

Mutuality requires communication, since in order to be met, these needs   20
must be expressed. (No one's a mind reader, which is not to say that many of us don't expect this quality in a mate. Who wants to keep having to tell someone what you need?) What you need is for your mate to understand you—your desires, your contradictions, your unique sensitivities, what irks you. (In practice, that means what about your mate irks you.) You, in turn, must learn to understand the mate's needs. This means being willing to hear what about yourself irks your mate. Hearing is not a simple physiological act performed with the ears, as you will learn. You may think you know how to hear, but that doesn't mean that you know how to listen.

With two individuals required to coexist in enclosed spaces for extended periods of time, domesticity requires substantial quantities of compromise and adaptation simply to avoid mayhem. Yet with the post-Romantic ideal of unconstrained individuality informing our most fundamental ideas of the self, this can prove a perilous process. Both parties must be willing to jettison whatever aspects of individuality might prove irritating while being simultaneously allowed to retain enough individuality to feel their autonomy is not being sacrificed, even as it is being surgically excised.

Having mastered mutuality, you may now proceed to advanced intimacy. Advanced intimacy involves inviting your partner "in" to your most interior self. Whatever and wherever our "inside" is, the widespread—if somewhat metaphysical—belief in its existence (and the related belief that whatever is in there is dying to get out) has assumed a quasi-medical status. Leeches once served a similar purpose. Now we "express our feelings" in lieu of our fluids because everyone knows that those who don't are far more prone to cancer, ulcers, or various dire ailments.

With love as our culture's patent medicine, prescribed for every ill (now even touted as a necessary precondition for that other great American obsession, longevity), we willingly subject ourselves to any number of arcane procedures in its quest. "Opening up" is required for relationship health, so lovers fashion themselves after doctors wielding long probes to penetrate the tender regions. Try to think of yourself as one big orifice: now stop clenching and relax. If the procedure proves uncomfortable, it just shows you're not open enough. Psychotherapy may be required before sufficient dilation can be achieved: the world's most expensive lubricant.

Needless to say, this opening-up can leave you feeling quite vulnerable, lying there psychically spread-eagled and shivering on the examining table of your relationship. (A favored suspicion is that your partner, knowing exactly where your vulnerabilities are, deliberately kicks you there—one reason this opening-up business may not always feel as pleasant as advertised.) And as anyone who has spent much time in—or just in earshot of—a typical couple knows, the "expression of needs" is often the Trojan horse of intimate warfare, since expressing needs means, by definition, that one's partner has thus far failed to meet them.

In any long-term couple, this lexicon of needs becomes codified over time   25 into a highly evolved private language with its own rules. Let's call this couple grammar. Close observation reveals this as a language composed of one recurring unit of speech: the interdiction—highly nuanced, mutually imposed commands and strictures extending into the most minute areas of household affairs, social life, finances, speech, hygiene, allowable idiosyncrasies, and so on. From bathroom to bedroom, car to kitchen, no aspect of coupled life is not subject to scrutiny, negotiation, and codes of conduct.

A sample from an inexhaustible list, culled from interviews with numerous members of couples of various ages, races, and sexual orientations:

You can't leave the house without saying where you're going. You can't not say what time you'll return. You can't go out when the other person feels like staying at home. You can't be a slob. You can't do less than 50 percent of the work around the house, even if the other person wants to do 100 percent more cleaning than you find necessary or even reasonable. You can't leave the dishes for later, load them the way that seems best to you, drink straight from the carton, or make crumbs. You can't leave the bathroom door open—it's offensive. You can't leave the bathroom door closed—your partner needs to get in. You can't not shave your underarms or legs. You can't gain weight. You can't watch soap operas. You can't watch infomercials or the pregame show or Martha Stewart. You can't eat what you want—goodbye Marshmallow Fluff; hello tofu meatballs. You can't spend too much time on the computer. And stay out of those chat rooms. You can't take risks, unless they are agreed-upon risks, which somewhat limits the concept of "risk." You can't make major purchases alone, or spend money on things the other person considers excesses. You can't blow money just because you're in a bad mood, and you can't be in a bad mood without being required to explain it. You can't begin a sentence with "You always. . . ." You can't begin a sentence with "I never. . . ." You can't be simplistic, even when things are simple. You can't say what you really think of that outfit or color combination or cowboy hat. You can't be cynical about things the other person is sincere about. You can't drink without the other person counting your drinks. You can't have the wrong laugh. You can't bum cigarettes when you're out because it embarrasses your mate, even though you've explained the unspoken fraternity between smokers. You can't tailgate, honk, or listen to talk radio in the car. And so on. The specifics don't matter. What matters is that the operative word is "can't."

Thus is love obtained.

Certainly, domesticity offers innumerable rewards: companionship, child-rearing convenience, reassuring predictability, and many other benefits too varied to list. But if love has power over us, domesticity is its enforcement wing:

the iron dust mop in the velvet glove. The historian Michel Foucault has argued that modern power made its mark on the world by inventing new types of enclosures and institutions, places like factories, schools, barracks, prisons, and asylums, where individuals could be located, supervised, processed, and subjected to inspection, order, and the clock. What current social institution is more enclosed than modern intimacy? What offers greater regulation of movement and time, or more precise surveillance of body and thought, to a greater number of individuals?

Of course, it is your choice—as if any of us could really choose not to desire   30
love or not to feel like hopeless losers should we fail at it. We moderns are beings yearning to be filled, yearning to be overtaken by love's mysterious power. We prostrate ourselves at love's portals, like social strivers waiting at the rope line outside some exclusive club hoping to gain admission and thereby confirm our essential worth. A life without love lacks an organizing narrative. A life without love seems so barren, and it might almost make you consider how empty the rest of the world is, as if love were vital plasma and everything else just tap water.

Exchanging obedience for love comes naturally—after all, we all were once children whose survival depended on the caprices of love. And there you have the template for future intimacies. If you love me, you'll do what I want—or need, or demand—and I'll love you in return. We all become household dictators, petty tyrants of the private sphere, who are, in our turn, dictated to.

And why has modern love developed in such a way as to maximize submission and minimize freedom, with so little argument about it? No doubt a citizenry schooled in renouncing desire instead of imagining there could be something more would be, in many respects, advantageous. After all, wanting more is the basis for utopian thinking, a path toward dangerous social demands, even toward imagining the possibilities for altogether different social arrangements. But if the most elegant forms of social control are those that came packaged in the guise of individual needs and satisfactions, so wedded to the individual psyche that any opposing impulse registers as the anxiety of unlovability, who needs a soldier on every corner? We are more than happy to police ourselves and those we love and call it living happily ever after. Perhaps a secular society needed another metaphysical entity to subjugate itself to after the death of God, and love was available for the job. But isn't it a little depressing to think we are somehow incapable of inventing forms of emotional life based on anything other than subjugation?

Steve (top): "When we got together, we immediately merged our finances. Chuck owned a lovely home in Sausalito, and to my total astonishment, he made me joint tenant with him. We have always maintained one checking account, and all of our investments and everything are in both our names. That is about as formal as a gay couple can get. And I think, like a lot of couples, it has helped us get through rough spots in life. When your lives are totally intertwined, it makes more sense to resolve issues than to start cutting things apart most of the time.

"At this point, after thirty years, Chuck and I have very few rules in our relationship. We don't have a rule, for instance, that you can never go out on the other one. We realized from time to time the opportunity would present itself, and we also realized that if we turned down every opportunity that presented itself to us, eventually we might begin to resent each other. So we said, O.K., you can go ahead and do it, but never make a date that leaves me sitting at home while you are out with someone else. And we have never done that. From time to time we have had affairs with other people, or moments of sexual release, but they were recreational."

Chuck: "Jealousy probably breaks up more gay people than anything in   35
the world. I guess that goes for all couples. And jealousy is caused by a lack of trust. The one who lacks trust the most and is accusing the other of cheating, he's usually the one who is cheating. Jealousy is based on guilt, an awful lot. But if you are absolutely convinced that the person you are with is totally open to you, that nothing is hidden, there won't be problems, ever. I know that Brad Pitt could not walk in this house and take Steve away from me. I am absolutely convinced of that.

I have total confidence in that. In my case, it is Michael York, but I go way back. And when you know that, sex is really an unimportant aspect, in terms of the deep emotions of your relationship. There is a movie called *Relax . . . It's Just Sex*—I love that title. It is only sex; it has no deep-seated meaning. It may seem to be a part of romance—certainly it jump-starts it—but as the years go by, it becomes more of a bonus to the relationship. There are no earthquakes that can happen as a result of sex."   [2001]

≣ THINKING ABOUT IDEAS

1. Clearly Kipnis believes love doesn't last. In what ways does your personal experience and your cultural experience (reading novels, watching television and films) confirm, deny, or make problematic this belief?

2. In what specific ways does Kipnis answer her own question: "But has modern love really set us free" (para. 7)? Describe how one can answer this question positively.

3. Kipnis uses a number of clever and provocative metaphors to bring home her point about love's temporality, including the claim that Viagra and pornography are "capitalism's Lourdes for dying marriages" (para. 12). What does she mean here? Explain her use of other metaphors, such as "like diligent assembly-line workers" (para. 11); "some new form of miracle sponge" (para. 13); "rocky shoals upon which intimacy so often founders" (para. 19); "leeches once served a similar purpose" (para. 22).

≣ THINKING ABOUT ARGUMENTATIVE MOVES

1. Kipnis claims "hard evidence to the contrary" (para. 3) that romance and sexual attraction can last a lifetime. What "evidence" does she cite? What does she mean by "hard"? Why might some of this "evidence" be considered interpretation or subjective?

2. Explain Kipnis's counterintuitive claim that adulterers are "our home-grown closet social theorists" (para. 14). How does this fit into her argument? Kipnis claims in several places that we learn about love in childhood. What specifically do we learn, and how does this play into her argument?

3. What alternatives does Kipnis provide to "a lifetime of coupled togetherness" (para. 3)? How does this help or hinder her argument? Look carefully at Kipnis's last question in paragraph 32 ("But isn't it. . ."). What answer would you give? What answer does she want you to give? How might someone opposed to Kipnis's point of view rephrase this question? How might subjugation be a "loaded" term?

MEGHAN O'ROURKE

The Marriage Trap

Meghan O'Rourke (b. 1976) is a poet and critic who has been widely published, winning numerous prizes and fellowships. She was a fiction editor at the New Yorker, *served as poetry editor at the* Paris Review, *and is a contributor to the* New York Times. *Her first book of poems,* Halflife *(2007), was published by W. W. Norton, and her memoir about the death of her mother,* The Long Goodbye *(2011), was critically acclaimed. She graduated from Yale University, has taught at New York University and Princeton University, and currently lives in Brooklyn, New York. O'Rourke posted her essay on* Slate *in September 2003 as a review of and response to Kipnis's* Against Love: A Polemic.

The classic 1960s feminist critique of marriage was that it suffocated women by tying them to the home and stifling their identity. The hope was that in a non-sexist society marriage could be a harmonious, genuine connection of minds. But forty years after Betty Friedan, Laura Kipnis has arrived with a new jeremiad, *Against Love: A Polemic,* to tell us that this hope was forlorn: Marriage, she suggests, belongs on the junk heap of human folly. It is an equal-opportunity oppressor, trapping men and women in a life of drudgery, emotional anesthesia, and a tug-of-war struggle to balance vastly different needs.

The numbers seem to back up her thesis: Modern marriage doesn't work for the majority of people. The rate of divorce has roughly doubled since the 1960s. Half of all marriages end in divorce. And as sketchy as poll data can be, a recent Rutgers University poll found that only 38 percent of married couples describe themselves as happy.

What's curious, though, is that even though marriage doesn't seem to make Americans very happy, they keep getting married (and remarried). Kipnis's essential question is: Why? Why, in what seems like an age of great social freedom, would anyone willingly consent to a life of constricting monogamy? Why has marriage (which she defines broadly as any long-term monogamous relationship) remained a polestar even as ingrained ideas about race, gender, and sexuality have been overturned?

Kipnis's answer is that marriage is an insidious social construct, harnessed by capitalism to get us to have kids and work harder to support them. Her quasi-Marxist argument sees desire as inevitably subordinated to economics. And the price of this subordination is immense: Domestic cohabitation is a "gulag"; marriage is the rough equivalent of a credit card with 0 percent APR that, upon first misstep, zooms to a punishing 30 percent and compounds daily. You feel you owe something, or you're afraid of being alone, and so you "work" at your relationship, like a prisoner in Siberia ice-picking away at the erotic permafrost.

Kipnis's ideological tack might easily have been as heavy as Frederick   5
Engels's in *The Origins of the Family, Private Property, and the State*, but she possesses the gleeful, viperish wit of a Dorothy Parker and the energetic charisma of a cheerleader. She is dead-on about the everyday exhaustion a relationship can produce. And she's diagnosed something interesting about the public discourse of marriage. People are more than happy to talk about how unhappy their individual marriages are, but public discussion assumes that in each case there is something wrong with *the* marriage—not marriage itself.

Take the way infidelity became a prime-time political issue in the '90s: Even as we wondered whether a politician who was not faithful to his or her spouse could be "faithful" to the country, no one was interested in asking whether marital fidelity was realistic or desirable.

Kipnis's answer to that question is a resounding no. The connection between sex and love, she argues, doesn't last as long as the need for each. And we probably shouldn't invest so much of *our own* happiness in the idea that someone else can help us sustain it—or spend so much time trying to make unhappy relationships "work." We should just look out for ourselves, perhaps mutually—more like two people gazing in the same general direction than two people expecting they want to look in each other's eyes for the rest of their (now much longer) lives. For this model to work, she argues, our social decisions need to start reflecting the reality of declining marriage rates—not the fairy-tale "happily ever after all" version.

Kipnis's vision of a good relationship may sound pretty vague. In fact, she doesn't really offer an alternative so much as diagnose the problems, hammering us into submission: Do we need a new way of thinking about love and domesticity? Marriage could be a form of renewable contract, as she idly wonders (and as Goethe proposed almost 200 years ago in *Elective Affinities*, his biting portrait of a marriage blighted by monogamy). Might it be possible to envision committed nonmonogamous heterosexual relationships?

Kipnis's book derives its *frisson* from the fact that she's asking questions no one seems that interested in entertaining. As she notes, even in a post-feminist age of loose social mores we are still encouraged, from the time we are children, to think of marriage as the proper goal of a well-lived life. I was first taught to play at the marriage fantasy in a Manhattan commune that had been formed explicitly to reject traditional notions of marriage; faced with a gaggle of eight-year-old girls, one of the women gave us a white wedding gown and invited us to imagine the heartthrob whom we wanted to devote ourselves to. Even radicals have a hard time banishing the dream of an enduring true love.

Let's accept that the resolute public emphasis on fixing ourselves, not marriage, can seem grim, and even sentimentally blinkered in its emphasis on ending divorce. Yet Kipnis's framing of the problem is grim, too. While she usefully challenges our assumptions about commitment, it's not evident that we'd be better off in the lust-happy world she envisions, or that men and women really want the exact same sexual freedoms. In its ideal form, marriage seems to reify all that's best about human exchange. Most people don't want to be alone at home with a cat, and everyone but Kipnis worries about the effects of divorce on children. "Work," in her lexicon, is always the drudgery of self-denial, not the challenge of extending yourself beyond what you knew you could do. But we usually mean two things when we say "work": The slog we endure purely to put food on the table, and the kind we do because we like it—are drawn to it, even.

While it's certainly true that people stay in an unhappy relationship longer than they should, it's not yet clear that monogamy is more "unnatural" than sleeping around but finding that the hum of your refrigerator is your most constant companion. And Kipnis spends scant time thinking about the fact that marriage is a hardy social institution several thousand years old, spanning many cultures—which calls into question, to say the least, whether its presence in our lives today has mostly to do with the insidious chokehold capitalism has on us.

While Kipnis's exaggerated polemic romp is wittily invigorating, it may not actually be as radical as it promises to be: These days, even sitcoms reflect her way of thinking. There's an old episode of *Seinfeld* in which Jerry and Kramer anticipate most of Kipnis's critique of domesticity; Kramer asks Jerry if he and his girlfriend are thinking about marriage and family, and then cuts him off: "They're prisons! Man-made prisons! You're doin' time! You get up in the morning—she's there. You go to sleep at night—she's there. It's like you gotta ask permission to, to use the bathroom: *Is it all right if I use the bathroom now?*" Still, love might indeed get a better name if we were as attentive to the intellectual dishonesties of the public debate over its failings as we are to the emotional dishonesties of adulterers.   *[2003]*

≡ **THINKING ABOUT IDEAS**

1. O'Rourke claims that as a culture we are happy to talk about unhappy individual marriages but not about marriage itself. In what ways do your personal experience and your cultural experience (reading novels, watching films and television) support or contradict this observation?

2. O'Rourke seems to agree with Kipnis that we are socialized to think of marriage as "the proper goal of a well-lived life" (para. 9). In what specific ways is this true from your personal and cultural experience?

3. In what ways does O'Rourke support marriage? What objections does she have to Kipnis's idea of working at a relationship? O'Rourke praises Kipnis for her "gleeful, viperish wit" (para. 5). Point out examples of where the same could be said of O'Rourke.

≡ THINKING ABOUT ARGUMENTATIVE MOVES

1. How does O'Rourke summarize the key elements of Kipnis's argument? What features of the argument does she seem most impressed with?

2. What are some objections O'Rourke has to Kipnis's essay? O'Rourke seems to save her main critique of Kipnis until the last paragraph. What is it? What is the rhetorical effect of "still" in the last sentence?

3. Kipnis's tone is often biting and ironic. How would you describe O'Rourke's tone? What are the advantages and disadvantages of using various tones, such as ironic, sarcastic, sincere, witty, clever, and confident?

≡ WRITING ABOUT ISSUES

1. Write an argument that agrees or disagrees with the idea that "marriage . . . belongs on the junk heap of human folly." Be sure to cite specific support and make reference to both Kipnis and O'Rourke.

2. Write an analysis of Kipnis's argument, focusing on the clarity of the claim, the adequacy of her supporting evidence, her attention to the opposition, and the idea of fairness.

3. Write an argument that focuses on the idea that our culture should be more honest about the failings of love. Give concrete suggestions about how this might happen and what the consequences might be.

4. In August 1989, the *New Republic* published Andrew Sullivan's "Here Comes the Groom," an influential essay that made (as the subtitle said) "a conservative case for gay marriage" that seemed radical to most readers. Now, decades later, a growing number of states have legalized same-sex marriage. And more and more Americans support such legislation. Read Sullivan's essay and write an analysis of his argument. Be sure to include contemporary voices both pro and con.

CHAPTER 9

===

Freedom and Confinement

Like most abstract and frequently used terms, *freedom* means many things to many people. In countries in the West, freedom is usually associated with political and religious choice, with the ability to dissent publicly from government policy, and even with an ability to dye our hair orange and paint our lips black. Indeed, freedom involves the right not to conform to conventional ideas about who we are and how we should behave as well as the right not to be stereotyped by a culture's demeaning, limiting, and distorted images and assumptions.

Readers of nineteenth-century fiction by women are familiar with the rigid cultural expectations that constricted the lives of most women. Excluded from public life and confined almost exclusively to domestic spaces, many women felt trapped in helping roles constructed for them by men. The consequences for the mental and physical health of thousands of would-be writers, artists, scientists, and intellectuals were often severe. Today many minorities in America also feel limited by the confining legacies of both racial and gender stereotypes. Children, who are especially vulnerable to the negative images that adults from the dominant culture have of them, have few defenses against internalizing damaging stereotypes that can adversely affect them well into adulthood. And when an entire culture constructs invidious stereotypes, as German Nazis did about European Jews, the consequences can be deadly. Although cultural prejudices against ethnic, religious, sexual, and gender minorities can be devastating, actual physical confinement can sorely test the limits of mind and body. Too often, minorities suffer from both prejudice and confinement when, like Martin Luther King Jr., they are jailed for protesting their lack of freedom.

This chapter brings together diverse literary texts that explore some of these issues of freedom and confinement, both physical and ideological—from the American internment of Japanese Americans during World War II to Langston Hughes's dreams of freedom, from Nora's refusal in *A Doll House* to a bizarre torture on a remote penal colony, and an amazing fantasy of girls raised by wolves. No less debilitating are the constraints tradition can have on human freedom, as honored customs and rituals are seen by some as inevitable and absolute and not subject to change, even when the reason for a tradition has long been lost to history. Even the very notion of freedom is deemed problematic, especially on college campuses where it is often liberals who urge constraints on free speech that demeans or intimidates. We hope you will be engaged by these imaginative and insightful writers as they explore the complex and moving ways that freedom is crucial in all of our lives.

The chapter opens with disturbing stories by Edgar Allan Poe and Ira Sher about fearsome incarcerations. Equally disturbing are stories by Ursula K. Le Guin and Shirley Jackson, who give us harrowing tales of traditions far removed from logic or compassion. Next is a modern re-visioning of the classic story of Little Red Riding Hood, followed by five poems that focus on animal stereotypes. These are followed by seven poems about human stereotypes. Langston Hughes is featured in the next cluster with four poems of freedom. Three plays from three distinct time periods come next, focusing on the struggle of wives to escape domestic prisons. Two essays by writers coping with the difficulties of negotiating two cultures in America are next. The issue of free speech on campus is the subject of the penultimate cluster, which is followed by a classic story of confinement and madness, "The Yellow Wallpaper," along with three essays that form a context for research.

EDGAR ALLAN POE, "The Cask of Amontillado"

IRA SHER, "The Man in the Well"

Most of us probably connect the word *incarceration* with prison or jail. That sounds terrible enough, given the reputation prisons have for killing the human spirit. Being isolated from society, family, and friends is a punishment that none of us would endure easily. But even worse would be to be incarcerated for no discernible crime, to find yourself confined by a madman or, perhaps even more frustrating, by accident. These would truly be dreadful incarcerations. The two authors presented here give us graphic examples of such nightmarish situations. Edgar Allan Poe's "The Cask of Amontillado" is perhaps the most famous and the most chilling of incarceration tales. The ironically named Fortunato surely does not deserve such a horrific fate, nor does the man trapped in a well in Ira Sher's eerie and troubling story.

▬ BEFORE YOU READ

Recount a time when you were temporarily trapped. How did you feel? Recall stories or movies about people being trapped or confined. What was your response?

EDGAR ALLAN POE
The Cask of Amontillado

The life of Edgar Allan Poe (1809–1849) was relatively brief, its end tragically hastened by his alcohol and drug abuse, but his contributions to literature were unique. As a book reviewer, he produced pieces of literary criticism and theory that are still widely respected. As a poet, he wrote such classics as "The Raven" (1845), "The Bells" (1849), and "Annabel Lee" (1849). Moreover, his short fiction was groundbreaking and continues to be popular, a source for many films and television shows. With works such as "The Murders in the Rue Morgue" (1841), "The Gold Bug" (1843), and "The Purloined Letter" (1844), he pioneered the modern detective story. Some of Poe's other tales are masterpieces of horror, including "The Fall of the House of Usher" (1842), "The Pit and the Pendulum" (1842), and the following story, one of Poe's most famous. It was first published in an 1846 issue of Godey's Lady's Book *and was then included in a posthumous 1850 collection of Poe's writings.*

The thousand injuries of Fortunato I had borne as I best could; but when he ventured upon insult, I vowed revenge. You, who so well know the nature of my soul, will not suppose, however, that I gave utterance to a threat. *At length* I

would be avenged; this was a point definitely settled—but the very definitive-
ness with which it was resolved precluded the idea of risk. I must not only punish, but punish with impunity. A wrong is unredressed when retribution
overtakes its redresser. It is equally unredressed when the avenger fails to make
himself felt as such to him who has done the wrong.

It must be understood, that neither by word nor deed had I given Fortunato
cause to doubt my good-will. I continued, as was my wont, to smile in his face,
and he did not perceive that my smile *now* was at the thought of his immolation.

He had a weak point—this Fortunato—although in other regards he was
a man to be respected and even feared. He prided himself on his connoisseur-
ship in wine. Few Italians have the true virtuoso spirit. For the most part their
enthusiasm is adopted to suit the time and opportunity—to practice impos-
ture upon the British and Austrian *millionnaires.* In painting and gemmary
Fortunato, like his countrymen, was a quack—but in the matter of old wines
he was sincere. In this respect I did not differ from him materially: I was skillful
in the Italian vintages myself, and bought largely whenever I could.

It was about dusk, one evening during the supreme madness of the carnival season, that I encountered my friend. He accosted me with excessive
warmth, for he had been drinking much. The man wore motley. He had on a
tight-fitting parti-striped dress, and his head was surmounted by the conical
cap and bells. I was so pleased to see him, that I thought I should never have
done wringing his hand.

I said to him: "My dear Fortunato, you are luckily met. How remarkably   5
well you are looking to-day! But I have received a pipe° of what passes for
Amontillado, and I have my doubts."

"How?" said he. "Amontillado? A pipe? Impossible! And in the middle of
the carnival!"

"I have my doubts," I replied; "and I was silly enough to pay the full Amontillado price without consulting you in the matter. You were not to be found,
and I was fearful of losing a bargain."

"Amontillado!"

"I have my doubts."

"Amontillado!"   10

"And I must satisfy them."

"Amontillado!"

"As you are engaged, I am on my way to Luchesi. If any one has a critical
turn, it is he. He will tell me——"

"Luchesi cannot tell Amontillado from Sherry."

"And yet some fools will have it that his taste is a match for your own."   15

"Come, let us go."

"Whither?"

"To your vaults."

"My friend, no; I will not impose upon your good nature. I perceive you
have an engagement. Luchesi——"

pipe: A large cask.

"I have no engagement;—come."   20

"My friend, no. It is not the engagement, but the severe cold with which I perceive you are afflicted. The vaults are insufferably damp. They are encrusted with nitre."

"Let us go, nevertheless. The cold is merely nothing. Amontillado! You have been imposed upon. And as for Luchesi, he cannot distinguish Sherry from Amontillado."

Thus speaking, Fortunato possessed himself of my arm. Putting on a mask of black silk, and drawing a *roquelaire*° closely about my person, I suffered him to hurry me to my palazzo.

There were no attendants at home; they had absconded to make merry in honor of the time. I had told them that I should not return until the morning, and had given them explicit orders not to stir from the house. These orders were sufficient, I well knew, to insure their immediate disappearance, one and all, as soon as my back was turned.

I took from their sconces two flambeaux, and giving one to Fortunato,   25
bowed him through several suites of rooms to the archway that led into the vaults. I passed down a long and winding staircase, requesting him to be cautious as he followed. We came at length to the foot of the descent, and stood together on the damp ground of the catacombs of the Montresors.

The gait of my friend was unsteady, and the bells upon his cap jingled as he strode.

"The pipe?" said he.

"It is farther on," said I; "but observe the white web-work which gleams from these cavern walls."

He turned toward me, and looked into my eyes with two filmy orbs that distilled the rheum of intoxication.

"Nitre?" he asked, at length.   30

"Nitre," I replied. "How long have you had that cough?"

"Ugh! ugh! ugh!—ugh! ugh! ugh!—ugh! ugh! ugh!—ugh! ugh! ugh!— ugh! ugh! ugh!"

My poor friend found it impossible to reply for many minutes.

"It is nothing," he said, at last.

"Come," I said, with decision, "we will go back; your health is precious.   35
You are rich, respected, admired, beloved; you are happy, as once I was. You are a man to be missed. For me it is no matter. We will go back; you will be ill, and I cannot be responsible. Besides, there is Luchesi ——"

"Enough," he said; "the cough is a mere nothing; it will not kill me. I shall not die of a cough."

"True—true," I replied; "and, indeed, I had no intention of alarming you unnecessarily; but you should use all proper caution. A draught of this Medoc will defend us from the damps."

Here I knocked off the neck of a bottle which I drew from a long row of its fellows that lay upon the mold.

roqueclaire: A short cloak.

"Drink," I said, presenting him the wine.

He raised it to his lips with a leer. He paused and nodded to me familiarly,   40
while his bells jingled.

"I drink," he said, "to the buried that repose around us."

"And I to your long life."

He again took my arm, and we proceeded.

"These vaults," he said, "are extensive."

"The Montresors," I replied, "were a great and numerous family."   45

"I forget your arms."

"A huge human foot d'or,° in a field azure; the foot crushes a serpent rampant whose fangs are imbedded in the heel."

"And the motto?"

"*Nemo me impune lacessit.*"°

"Good!" he said.   50

The wine sparkled in his eyes and the bells jingled. My own fancy grew warm
with the Medoc. We had passed through walls of piled bones, with casks and
puncheons intermingling into the inmost recesses of the catacombs. I paused
again, and this time I made bold to seize Fortunato by an arm above the elbow.

"The nitre!" I said; "see, it increases. It hangs like moss upon the vaults. We
are below the river's bed. The drops of moisture trickle among the bones. Come,
we will go back ere it is too late. Your cough——"

"It is nothing," he said; "let us go on. But first, another draught of the
Medoc."

I broke and reached him a flagon of De Grâve. He emptied it at a breath. His
eyes flashed with a fierce light. He laughed and threw the bottle upward with a
gesticulation I did not understand.

I looked at him in surprise. He repeated the movement—a grotesque one.   55

"You do not comprehend?" he said.

"Not I," I replied.

"Then you are not of the brotherhood."

"How?"

"You are not of the masons."   60

"Yes, yes," I said; "yes, yes."

"You? Impossible! A mason?"

"A mason," I replied.

"A sign," he said.

"It is this," I answered, producing a trowel from beneath the folds of my   65
roquelaire.

"You jest," he exclaimed, recoiling a few paces. "But let us proceed to the
Amontillado."

"Be it so," I said, replacing the tool beneath the cloak, and again offering
him my arm. He leaned upon it heavily. We continued our route in search of
the Amontillado. We passed through a range of low arches, descended, passed

d'or: Of gold.   ***nemo me impune lacessit:*** "No one wounds me with impunity" is the
motto on the royal arms of Scotland.

on, and descending again, arrived at a deep crypt, in which the foulness of the air caused our flambeaux rather to glow than flame.

At the most remote end of the crypt there appeared another less spacious. Its walls had been lined with human remains, piled to the vault overhead, in the fashion of the great catacombs of Paris. Three sides of this interior crypt were still ornamented in this manner. From the fourth the bones had been thrown down, and lay promiscuously upon the earth, forming at one point a mound of some size. Within the wall thus exposed by the displacing of the bones, we perceived a still interior recess, in depth about four feet, in width three, in height six or seven. It seemed to have been constructed for no especial use within itself, but formed merely the interval between two of the colossal supports of the roof of the catacombs, and was backed by one of their circumscribing walls of solid granite.

It was in vain that Fortunato, uplifting his dull torch, endeavored to pry into the depth of the recess. Its termination the feeble light did not enable us to see.

"Proceed," I said; "herein is the Amontillado. As for Luchesi ——" 70

"He is an ignoramus," interrupted my friend, as he stepped unsteadily forward, while I followed immediately at his heels. In an instant he had reached the extremity of the niche, and finding his progress arrested by the rock, stood stupidly bewildered. A moment more and I had fettered him to the granite. In its surface were two iron staples, distant from each other about two feet, horizontally. From one of these depended a short chain, from the other a padlock. Throwing the links about his waist, it was but the work of a few seconds to secure it. He was too much astounded to resist. Withdrawing the key I stepped back from the recess.

"Pass your hand," I said, "over the wall; you cannot help feeling the nitre. Indeed it is *very* damp. Once more let me *implore* you to return. No? Then I must positively leave you. But I must first render you all the little attentions in my power."

"The Amontillado!" ejaculated my friend, not yet recovered from his astonishment.

"True," I replied; "the Amontillado."

As I said these words I busied myself among the pile of bones of which 75 I have before spoken. Throwing them aside, I soon uncovered a quantity of building stone and mortar. With these materials and with the aid of my trowel, I began vigorously to wall up the entrance of the niche.

I had scarcely laid the first tier of the masonry when I discovered that the intoxication of Fortunato had in a great measure worn off. The earliest indication I had of this was a low moaning cry from the depth of the recess. It was *not* the cry of a drunken man. There was then a long and obstinate silence. I laid the second tier, and the third, and the fourth; and then I heard the furious vibrations of the chain. The noise lasted for several minutes, during which, that I might hearken to it with the more satisfaction, I ceased my labors and sat down upon the bones. When at last the clanking subsided, I resumed the trowel, and finished without interruption the fifth, the sixth, and the seventh tier. The wall was now nearly upon a level with my breast. I again paused, and holding the flambeaux over the masonwork, threw a few feeble rays upon the figure within.

A succession of loud and shrill screams, bursting suddenly from the throat of the chained form, seemed to thrust me violently back. For a brief moment I hesitated—I trembled. Unsheathing my rapier, I began to grope with it about the recess; but the thought of an instant reassured me. I placed my hand upon the solid fabric of the catacombs, and felt satisfied. I reapproached the wall. I replied to the yells of him who clamored. I reechoed—I aided—I surpassed them in volume and in strength. I did this, and the clamorer grew still.

It was now midnight, and my task was drawing to a close. I had completed the eighth, the ninth, and the tenth tier. I had finished a portion of the last and the eleventh; there remained but a single stone to be fitted and plastered in. I struggled with its weight; I placed it partially in its destined position. But now there came from out the niche a low laugh that erected the hairs upon my head. It was succeeded by a sad voice, which I had difficulty in recognizing as that of the noble Fortunato. The voice said—

"Ha! ha! ha!—he! he!—a very good joke indeed—an excellent jest. We will have many a rich laugh about it at the palazzo—he! he! he!—over our wine—he! he! he!"

"The Amontillado!" I said.   80

"He! he! he!—he! he! he!—yes, the Amontillado. But is it not getting late? Will not they be awaiting us at the palazzo, the Lady Fortunato and the rest? Let us be gone."

"Yes," I said, "let us be gone."

"*For the love of God, Montresor!*"

"Yes," I said, "for the love of God!"

But to these words I hearkened in vain for a reply. I grew impatient. I called   85
aloud:

"Fortunato!"

No answer. I called again:

"Fortunato!"

No answer still. I thrust a torch through the remaining aperture and let it fall within. There came forth in return only a jingling of the bells. My heart grew sick—on account of the dampness of the catacombs. I hastened to make an end of my labor. I forced the last stone into its position; I plastered it up. Against the new masonry I re-erected the old rampart of bones. For the half of a century no mortal has disturbed them. *In pace requiescat!*°   [1846]

In pace requiescat: In peace may he rest (Latin).

≡ THINKING ABOUT THE TEXT

1. Evidently Montresor is recounting the story of his revenge fifty years after it took place. To whom might he be speaking? With what purposes?

2. Montresor does not describe in detail any of the offenses that Fortunato has supposedly committed against him. In considering how to judge

Montresor, do you need such information? Why, or why not? State in your own words the principles of revenge he lays out in the first paragraph.

3. What, if anything, does Poe achieve by having this story take place during a carnival? By repeating the word *amontillado* so much?

4. What does Montresor mean when he echoes Fortunato's words "for the love of God" (para. 84)? What might Fortunato be attempting to communicate with his final "jingling of the bells" (para. 89)?

5. Do you sympathize with Montresor? With Fortunato? Explain. What emotion did you mainly feel as you read the story? Identify specific features of it that led to this emotion.

IRA SHER
The Man in the Well

Ira Sher (b. 1970) is a novelist and short-story writer. He received his M.F.A. from the University of Houston. His first novel, Gentlemen of Space *(2003), was called "beautiful and eloquent." A reviewer called his next novel,* Singer *(2009), "psychologically rich and stylistically assured." His fiction has appeared in a number of prestigious journals, including the* Gettysburg Review *and the* Chicago Review, *where the following story appeared. His work has been broadcast on National Public Radio's* This American Life. *He lives in Athens, New York.*

I was nine when I discovered the man in the well in an abandoned farm-lot near my home. I was with a group of friends, playing hide and go seek or something when I found the well, and then I heard the voice of the man in the well calling out for help.

I think it's important that we decided not to help him. Everyone, like myself, was probably on the verge of fetching a rope, or asking where we could find a ladder, but then we looked around at each other and it was decided. I don't remember if we told ourselves a reason why we couldn't help him, but we had decided then. Because of this, I never went very close to the lip of the well, or I only came up on my hands and knees, so that he couldn't see me; and just as we wouldn't allow him to see us, I know that none of us ever saw the man in the well—the well was too dark for that, too deep, even when the sun was high up, angling light down the stone sides like golden hair.

I remember that we were still full of games and laughter when we called down to him. He had heard us shouting while we were playing, and he had been hollering for us to come; he was so relieved at that moment.

"God, get me out. I've been here for days." He must have known we were children, because he immediately instructed us to "go get a ladder, get help."

At first afraid to disobey the voice from the man in the well, we turned around and actually began to walk toward the nearest house, which was   5

Arthur's. But along the way we slowed down, and then we stopped, and after waiting what seemed like a good while, we quietly came back to the well.

We stood or lay around the lip, listening for maybe half an hour, and then Arthur, after some hesitation, called down, "What's your name?" This, after all, seemed like the most natural question.

The man answered back immediately, "Do you have the ladder?"

We all looked at Arthur, and he called back down, "No, we couldn't find one."

Now that we had established some sort of a dialogue, everyone had questions he or she wanted to ask the man in the well, but the man wouldn't stop speaking:

"Go tell your parents there's someone in this well. If they have a rope or a   10
ladder . . ." he trailed off. His voice was raw and sometimes he would cough. "Just tell your parents."

We were quiet, but this time no one stood up or moved. Someone, I think little Jason, called down, "Hello. Is it dark?" and then, after a moment, "Can you see the sky?"

He didn't answer but instead told us to go again.

When we were quiet for a bit, he called to see if we had gone.

After a pause, Wendy crawled right to the edge so that her hair lifted slightly in the updraft. "Is there any water down there?"

"Have they gone for help?" he asked.   15

She looked around at us, and then she called down, "Yes, they're all gone now. Isn't there any water down there?" I don't think anyone smiled at how easy it was to deceive him—this was too important. "Isn't there?" she said again.

"No," he said. "It's very dry." He cleared his throat. "Do you think it will rain?" She stood up and took in the whole sky with her blue eyes, making sure. "No, I don't think so." We heard him coughing in the well, and we waited for a while, thinking about him waiting in the well.

Resting on the grass and cement by the well, I tried to picture him. I tried to imagine the gesture of his hand reaching to cover his mouth, each time he coughed. Or perhaps he was too tired to make that gesture, each time. After an hour, he began calling again, but for some reason we didn't want to answer. We got up and began running, filling up with panic as we moved, until we were racing across the ruts of the old field. I kept turning, stumbling as I looked behind. Perhaps he had heard us getting up and running away from the well. Only Wendy stayed by the well for a while, watching us run as his calling grew louder and wilder, until finally she ran, too, and then we were all far away.

The next morning we came back, most of us carrying bread or fruit or something to eat in our pockets. Arthur brought a canvas bag from his house and a plastic jug of water.

When we got to the well we stood around quietly for a moment listening   20
for him.

"Maybe he's asleep," Wendy said.

We sat down around the mouth of the well on the old concrete slab, warming in the sun and coursing with ants and tiny insects. Aaron called down then, when everyone was comfortable, and the man answered right away, as if he had been listening to us the whole time.

"Did your parents get help?"

Arthur kneeled at the edge of the well and called "Watch out," and then he let the bag fall after holding it out for a moment, maybe for the man to see. It hit the ground more quickly than I had expected; that, combined with a feeling that he could hear everything we said, made him suddenly closer, as if he might be able to see us. I wanted to be very quiet, so that if he heard or saw anyone, he would not notice me. The man in the well started coughing, and Arthur volunteered, "There's some water in the bag. We all brought something."

We could hear him moving around down there. After a few minutes he   25
asked us, "When are they coming? What did your parents say?"

We all looked at each other, aware that he couldn't address anyone in particular. He must have understood this, because he called out in his thin, groping voice, "What are your names?"

No one answered until Aaron, who was the oldest, said, "My father said he's coming, with the police. And he knows what to do." We admired Aaron very much for coming up with this, on the spot.

"Are they on their way?" the man in the well asked. We could hear that he was eating.

"My father said don't worry, because he's coming with the police."

Little Jason came up next to Aaron and asked, "What's your name?" be-   30
cause we still didn't know what to call him. When we talked among ourselves, he had simply become "the man."

He didn't answer, so Jason asked him how old he was, and then Grace came up too and asked him something, I don't remember. We all asked such stupid questions, and he wouldn't answer anyone. Finally, we all stopped talking, and we lay down on the cement.

It was a hot day, so after a while, Grace got up, and then Little Jason and another young boy, Robert I think, and went to town to sit in the cool movie theater. That was what we did most afternoons back then. After an hour everyone had left except Wendy and myself, and I was beginning to think I would go, too.

He called up to us all of a sudden. "Are they coming now?"

"Yes," Wendy said, looking at me, and I nodded my head. She sounded certain: "I think they're almost here. Aaron said his dad is almost here."

As soon as she said it she was sorry, because she'd broken one of the rules.   35
I could see it on her face, eyes filling with space as she moved back from the well. Now he had one of our names. She said "They're going to come" to cover up the mistake, but there it was, and there was nothing to do about it.

The man in the well didn't say anything for a few minutes. Then he surprised us again by asking, "Is it going to rain?"

Wendy stood up and turned around like she had done the other day, but the sky was clear. "No," she said.

Then he asked again, "They're coming, you said. Aaron's dad," and he shouted, "Right?" so that we jumped, and stood up, and began running away, just as we had the day before. We could hear him shouting for a while, and we were afraid someone might hear. I thought that toward the end maybe he had said he was sorry. But I never asked Wendy what she thought he'd said.

Everyone was there again on the following morning. It was all I could think about during supper the night before, and then the anticipation in the morning over breakfast. My mother was very upset with something at the time. I could hear her weeping at night in her room downstairs, and the stubborn murmur of my father. There was a feeling to those days, months actually, that I can't describe without resorting to the man in the well, as if through a great whispering, like a gathering of clouds, or the long sound, the turbulent wreck of the ocean.

At the well we put together the things to eat we had smuggled out, but we 40
hadn't even gotten them all in the bag when the voice of the man in the well soared out sharply, "They're on their way, now?"

We stood very still, so that he couldn't hear us, but I knew what was coming and I couldn't do anything to soften or blur the words of the voice.

"Aaron," he pronounced, and I had imagined him practicing that voice all night long, and holding it in his mouth so that he wouldn't let it slip away in his sleep. Aaron lost all the color in his face, and he looked at us with suspicion, as if we had somehow taken on a part of the man in the well. I didn't even glance at Wendy. We were both too embarrassed—neither of us said anything; we were all quiet then. Arthur finished assembling the bag, and we could see his hands shaking as he dropped it into the well. We heard the man in the well moving around.

After ten minutes or so, Grace called down to him, "What's your name?" but someone pulled her back from the well, and we became silent again. Today the question humiliated us with its simplicity.

There was no sound for a while from the well, except for the cloth noises and the scraping the man in the well made as he moved around. Then he called out, in a pleasant voice, "Aaron, what do you think my name is?"

Aaron, who had been very still this whole time, looked around at all of us 45
again. We knew he was afraid; his fingers were pulling with a separate life at the collar of his shirt, and maybe because she felt badly for him, Wendy answered instead: "Is your name Charles?" It sounded inane, but the man in the well answered.

"No," the man said.

She thought for a moment. "Edgar."

"No, no."

Little Jason called out, "David?"

"No," the man in the well said. 50

Then Aaron, who had been absolutely quiet, said "Arthur" in a small, clear voice, and we all started. I could see Arthur was furious, but Aaron was older and bigger than he was, and nothing could be said or done without giving himself, his name, away; we knew the man in the well was listening for the changes in our breath, anything. Aaron didn't look at Arthur, or anyone, and then he began giving all of our names, one at a time. We all watched him, trembling, our faces the faces I had seen pasted on the spectators in the freak tent when the circus had come to town. We were watching such a deformity take place before our eyes; and I remember the spasm of anger when he said my name, and felt the man in the well soak it up—because the man in the well understood. The man in the well didn't say anything, now.

When Aaron was done, we all waited for the man in the well to speak up. I stood on one leg, then the other, and eventually I sat down. We had to wait for an hour, and today no one wanted to leave to lie in the shade or hide in the velvet movie seats.

At last, the man in the well said, "All right, then. Arthur. What do you think I look like?" We heard him cough a couple of times, and then a sound like the smacking of lips. Arthur, who was sitting on the ground with his chin propped on his fists, didn't say anything. How could he—I knew I couldn't answer, myself, if the man in the well called me by name. He called a few of us, and I watched the shudder move from face to face.

Then he was quiet for a while. It was afternoon now, and the light was changing, withdrawing from the well. It was as if the well was filling up with earth. The man in the well moved around a bit, and then he called Jason. He asked, "How old do you think I am, Jason?" He didn't seem to care that no one would answer, or he seemed to expect that no one would. He said, "Wendy. Are they coming now? Is Aaron's dad coming now?" He walked around a bit, we heard him rummage in the bag of food, and he said, "All right. What's my name?" He used everyone's name; he asked everyone. When he said my name, I felt the water clouding my eyes, and I wanted to throw stones, dirt down the well to crush out his voice. But we couldn't do anything, none of us did—because then he would know.

In the evening we could tell he was getting tired. He wasn't saying much, and seemed to have lost interest in us. Before we left that day, as we were rising quietly and looking at the dark shadows of the trees we had to move through to reach our homes, he said, "Why didn't you tell anyone?" He coughed. "Didn't you want to tell anyone?" Perhaps he heard the hesitation in our breaths, but he wasn't going to help us now. It was almost night then, and we were spared the detail of having to see and read each other's faces.

That night it rained, and I listened to the rain on the roof and my mother sobbing, downstairs, until I fell asleep. After that we didn't play by the well anymore; even when we were much older, we didn't go back. I will never go back.

[1995]

≡ **THINKING ABOUT THE TEXT**

1. Maybe the most obvious question to ask is why the children don't help the man in the well, but perhaps there are a number of reasonable answers. What are some plausible explanations?

2. How would this story affect you differently if the children were five or six years old? What about fifteen or sixteen years old? And what if the parents of the children did nothing to help?

3. How does the narrator's assertion "I will never go back" affect your response or judgment of his behavior? Is it an assertion of innocence or denial or guilt or something else? Would the behavior of the narrator have been different if he were alone?

4. This story is plausible on the literal level; certainly people have fallen into wells. But on a symbolic or metaphorical level, the idea of a well that is deep and a disembodied mysterious voice speaking from the dark could suggest several things. What possibilities can you think of?

5. If you found out what the children did, what would you do? What if the police found out or the family of the man in the well?

≡ MAKING COMPARISONS

1. Although the man in the well appears to be there accidentally and Poe's Fortunato does not, presumably they both die. How might the children be seen as equally culpable as Montresor?

2. Compare the entreaties both men make to their possible rescuers. Are they employing the right strategies? Might each be more persuasive?

3. How does Montresor believe he is in some way justified in entombing Fortunato? How might the children also feel justified?

≡ WRITING ABOUT ISSUES

1. Write a brief argument that could account for either the behavior of the children in "The Man in the Well" or Fortunato in Poe's "The Cask of Amontillado."

2. Write a brief argument that focuses on the metaphorical possibilities of Ira Sher's story. Which interpretation makes the most sense to you and why?

3. Incarceration is the most common legal punishment for crimes in our country. Write an argument that first explains its benefits and drawbacks and then argue for either keeping or reforming our present system.

4. Research the incarceration systems of two other countries, say Sweden and Saudi Arabia (or perhaps Russia and Japan), comparing them to the United States, arguing that the prison system of a country does or does not reflect that country's values.

▤ Snares of Tradition: Stories

SHIRLEY JACKSON, "The Lottery"

URSULA K. LE GUIN, "The Ones Who Walk Away from Omelas"

Often our fondest memories of childhood involve family and community traditions, from public events like Thanksgiving, Halloween, and Fourth of July celebrations, to religious holidays like Christmas and Hanukkah, to private celebrations like birthdays and anniversaries. These rituals give our lives structure and create a sense of belonging. They give us psychological comfort and security and a ready-made identity of belonging with like-minded people who share our values. We acquire a sense of our adult roles, our goals, our understanding of the meaning of life, birth, death, love, and hate. Traditions and their accompanying rituals offer guidance as we address the complex question of how to "be" in the world.

Once a tradition starts, however, it may be difficult to change. Perhaps that is not so significant when we are thinking of birthday and graduation ceremonies, but it is life altering when traditions govern whom we may marry, what roles we can play in society, how we understand justice and freedom, and when our lives begin and end.

In some societies, traditions have been in place for thousands of years. They are difficult to change since they are woven into individuals' sense of self. People often feel that their own traditions are normal, even though anthropologists claim that few traditions are universal among cultures.

How does one change a time-honored tradition? What if the reason for the tradition has been lost to history? What if some members of the community feel their own values and morality are offended by the tradition? Can we look to the law for change? Or to community pressure? Maybe we just endure the ritual. Or maybe the sense of outrage is so great that we must leave the community. Then what? The two authors in this cluster confront these and other dilemmas when honored traditions are questioned. Sixty-five years after its publication, Shirley Jackson's "The Lottery" is still one of the most controversial stories ever printed in *The New Yorker*. When the story was banned in South Africa, Jackson said, "Well, at least they understood it." Ursula K. Le Guin's tale of a utopia with a terrible secret is an excellent example of the insidious snares of tradition.

▤ BEFORE YOU READ

Recall incidents from the past when you felt uncomfortable being involved in a tradition or ritual. How did you respond? What specific traditions in our culture could easily be eliminated? Are there harmful traditions in our culture that should be changed?

SHIRLEY JACKSON
The Lottery

Shirley Jackson (1916–1965) was born in San Francisco and grew up in the affluent suburb of Burlingame. Her family moved to Rochester, New York, in 1939, and she graduated from Syracuse University in 1940. Jackson wrote of her life: "I was married in 1940 to Stanley Edgar Hyman, critic and numismatist, and we live in Vermont, in a quiet rural community with fine scenery and comfortably away from city life. Our major export are books and children, both of which we produce in abundance." She received a National Book Award nomination for The Haunting of Hill House *(1959), which was adapted for film twice (1963 and 1999); this popular book is often cited as one of the best horror novels of the twentieth century and as an influence on contemporary masters of that genre such as Stephen King.*

The morning of June 27th was clear and sunny, with the fresh warmth of a full-summer day; the flowers were blossoming profusely and the grass was richly green. The people of the village began to gather in the square, between the post office and the bank, around ten o'clock; in some towns there were so many people that the lottery took two days and had to be started on June 26th, but in this village, where there were only about three hundred people, the whole lottery took less than two hours, so it could begin at ten o'clock in the morning and still be through in time to allow the villagers to get home for noon dinner.

The children assembled first, of course. School was recently over for the summer, and the feeling of liberty sat uneasily on most of them; they tended to gather together quietly for a while before they broke into boisterous play, and their talk was still of the classroom and teacher, of books and reprimands. Bobby Martin had already stuffed his pockets full of stones, and the other boys soon followed his example, selecting the smoothest and roundest stones; Bobby and Harry Jones and Dickie Delacroix—the villagers pronounced this name "Dellacroy"—eventually made a great pile of stones in one corner of the square and guarded it against the raids of the other boys. The girls stood aside, talking among themselves, looking over their shoulders at the boys, and the very small children rolled in the dust or clung to the hands of their older brothers or sisters.

Soon the men began to gather, surveying their own children, speaking of planting and rain, tractors and taxes. They stood together, away from the pile of stones in the corner, and their jokes were quiet and they smiled rather than laughed. The women, wearing faded house dresses and sweaters, came shortly after their menfolk. They greeted one another and exchanged bits of gossip as they went to join their husbands. Soon the women, standing by their husbands, began to call to their children, and the children came reluctantly, having to be called four or five times. Bobby Martin ducked under his mother's grasping hand and ran, laughing, back to the pile of stones. His father spoke up sharply, and Bobby came quickly and took his place between his father and his oldest brother.

The lottery was conducted—as were the square dances, the teenage club, the Halloween program—by Mr. Summers, who had time and energy to devote to civic activities. He was a round-faced, jovial man and he ran the coal business, and people were sorry for him, because he had no children and his wife was a scold. When he arrived in the square, carrying the black wooden box, there was a murmur of conversation among the villagers, and he waved and called, "Little late today, folks." The postmaster, Mr. Graves, followed him, carrying a three-legged stool, and the stool was put in the center of the square and Mr. Summers set the black box down on it. The villagers kept their distance, leaving a space between themselves and the stool, and when Mr. Summers said, "Some of you fellows want to give me a hand?" there was a hesitation before two men, Mr. Martin and his oldest son, Baxter, came forward to hold the box steady on the stool while Mr. Summers stirred up the papers inside it.

The original paraphernalia for the lottery had been lost long ago, and the   5
black box now resting on the stool had been put into use even before Old Man Warner, the oldest man in town, was born. Mr. Summers spoke frequently to the villagers about making a new box, but no one liked to upset even as much tradition as was represented by the black box. There was a story that the present box had been made with some pieces of the box that had preceded it, the one that had been constructed when the first people settled down to make a village here. Every year, after the lottery, Mr. Summers began talking again about a new box, but every year the subject was allowed to fade off without anything's being done. The black box grew shabbier each year; by now it was no longer completely black but splintered badly along one side to show the original wood color, and in some places faded or stained.

Mr. Martin and his oldest son, Baxter, held the black box securely on the stool until Mr. Summers had stirred the papers thoroughly with his hand. Because so much of the ritual had been forgotten or discarded, Mr. Summers had been successful in having slips of paper substituted for the chips of wood that had been used for generations. Chips of wood, Mr. Summers had argued, had been all very well when the village was tiny, but now that the population was more than three hundred and likely to keep on growing, it was necessary to use something that would fit more easily into the black box. The night before the lottery, Mr. Summers and Mr. Graves made up the slips of paper and put them in the box, and it was then taken to the safe of Mr. Summers's coal company and locked up until Mr. Summers was ready to take it to the square next morning. The rest of the year, the box was put away, sometimes one place, sometimes another; it had spent one year in Mr. Graves's barn and another year underfoot in the post office, and sometimes it was set on a shelf in the Martin grocery and left there.

There was a great deal of fussing to be done before Mr. Summers declared the lottery open. There were the lists to make up—of heads of families, heads of households in each family, members of each household in each family. There was the proper swearing-in of Mr. Summers by the postmaster, as the official of the lottery; at one time, some people remembered, there had been a recital of some sort, performed by the official of the lottery, a perfunctory, tuneless chant that had been rattled off duly each year; some people believed that the official of the lottery used to stand just so when he said or sang it, others believed that he was supposed to walk among the people, but years and years ago this part of the ritual had been allowed to lapse. There had been, also, a ritual salute, which the official of the lottery had had to use in addressing each person who came up to draw from the box, but this also had changed with time, until now it was felt necessary only for the official to speak to each person approaching. Mr. Summers was very good at all this; in his clean white shirt and blue jeans, with one hand resting carelessly on the black box, he seemed very proper and important as he talked interminably to Mr. Graves and the Martins.

Just as Mr. Summers finally left off talking and turned to the assembled villagers, Mrs. Hutchinson came hurriedly along the path to the square, her sweater thrown over her shoulders, and slid into place in the back of the crowd. "Clean forgot what day it was," she said to Mrs. Delacroix, who stood next to her, and they both laughed softly. "Thought my old man was out back stacking wood," Mrs. Hutchinson went on, "and then I looked out the window and the kids was gone, and then I remembered it was the twenty-seventh and came a-running." She dried her hands on her apron, and Mrs. Delacroix said, "You're in time, though. They're still talking away up there."

Mrs. Hutchinson craned her neck to see through the crowd and found her husband and children standing near the front. She tapped Mrs. Delacroix on the arm as a farewell and began to make her way through the crowd. The people separated good-humoredly to let her through; two or three people said, in voices just loud enough to be heard across the crowd, "Here comes your Missus, Hutchinson," and "Bill, she made it after all." Mrs. Hutchinson reached her husband, and Mr. Summers, who had been waiting, said cheerfully, "Thought we were going to have to get on without you, Tessie." Mrs. Hutchinson said, grinning, "Wouldn't have me leave m'dishes in the sink, now, would you, Joe?" and soft laughter ran through the crowd as the people stirred back into position after Mrs. Hutchinson's arrival.

"Well, now," Mr. Summers said soberly, "guess we better get started, get this over with, so's we can go back to work. Anybody ain't here?" 10

"Dunbar," several people said. "Dunbar; Dunbar."

Mr. Summers consulted his list. "Clyde Dunbar," he said. "That's right. He's broke his leg, hasn't he? Who's drawing for him?"

"Me, I guess," a woman said, and Mr. Summers turned to look at her. "Wife draws for her husband," Mr. Summers said. "Don't you have a grown boy to do it for you, Janey?" Although Mr. Summers and everyone else in the village knew the answer perfectly well, it was the business of the official of the lottery to ask such questions formally. Mr. Summers waited with an expression of polite interest while Mrs. Dunbar answered.

"Horace's not but sixteen yet," Mrs. Dunbar said regretfully. "Guess I gotta fill in for the old man this year."

"Right," Mr. Summers said. He made a note on the list he was holding.   15
Then he asked, "Watson boy drawing this year?"

A tall boy in the crowd raised his hand. "Here," he said. "I'm drawing for
m'mother and me." He blinked his eyes nervously and ducked his head as several voices in the crowd said things like "Good fellow, Jack," and "Glad to see
your mother's got a man to do it."

"Well," Mr. Summers said, "guess that's everyone. Old Man Warner
make it?"

"Here," a voice said, and Mr. Summers nodded.

A sudden hush fell on the crowd as Mr. Summers cleared his throat and
looked at the list. "All ready?" he called. "Now, I'll read the names — heads of
families first — and the men come up and take a paper out of the box. Keep the
paper folded in your hand without looking at it until everyone has had a turn.
Everything clear?"

The people had done it so many times that they only half listened to the   20
directions; most of them were quiet, wetting their lips, not looking around.
Then Mr. Summers raised one hand high and said, "Adams." A man disengaged himself from the crowd and came forward. "Hi, Steve," Mr. Summers
said, and Mr. Adams said, "Hi, Joe." They grinned at one another humorlessly
and nervously. Then Mr. Adams reached into the black box and took out a
folded paper. He held it firmly by one corner as he turned and went hastily back
to his place in the crowd, where he stood a little apart from his family, not looking down at his hand.

"Allen," Mr. Summers said, "Anderson. . . . Bentham."

"Seems like there's no time at all between lotteries any more," Mrs.
Delacroix said to Mrs. Graves in the back row. "Seems like we got through with
the last one only last week."

"Time sure goes fast," Mrs. Graves said.

"Clark. . . . Delacroix."

"There goes my old man," Mrs. Delacroix said. She held her breath while   25
her husband went forward.

"Dunbar," Mr. Summers said, and Mrs. Dunbar went steadily to the box
while one of the women said, "Go on, Janey," and another said, "There she goes."

"We're next," Mrs. Graves said. She watched while Mr. Graves came around
from the side of the box, greeted Mr. Summers gravely, and selected a slip of
paper from the box. By now, all through the crowd there were men holding the
small folded papers in their large hands, turning them over and over nervously.
Mrs. Dunbar and her two sons stood together, Mrs. Dunbar holding the slip of
paper.

"Harburt. . . . Hutchinson."

"Get up there, Bill," Mrs. Hutchinson said, and the people near her laughed.

"Jones."   30

"They do say," Mr. Adams said to Old Man Warner, who stood next to him,
"that over in the north village they're talking of giving up the lottery."

Old Man Warner snorted. "Pack of crazy fools," he said. "Listening to the
young folks, nothing's good enough for *them*. Next thing you know, they'll be

wanting to go back to living in caves, nobody work any more, live *that* way for a while. Used to be a saying about 'Lottery in June, corn be heavy soon.' First thing you know, we'd all be eating stewed chickweed and acorns. There's *always* been a lottery," he added petulantly. "Bad enough to see young Joe Summers up there joking with everybody."

"Some places have already quit lotteries," Mrs. Adams said.

"Nothing but trouble in *that*," Old Man Warner said stoutly. "Pack of young fools."

"Martin." And Bobby Martin watched his father go forward. "Overdyke. . . .   35
Percy."

"I wish they'd hurry," Mrs. Dunbar said to her older son. "I wish they'd hurry."

"They're almost through," her son said.

"You get ready to run tell Dad," Mrs. Dunbar said.

Mr. Summers called his own name and then stepped forward precisely and selected a slip from the box. Then he called, "Warner."

"Seventy-seventh year I been in the lottery," Old Man Warner said as he   40
went through the crowd. "Seventy-seventh time."

"Watson." The tall boy came awkwardly through the crowd. Someone said, "Don't be nervous, Jack," and Mr. Summers said, "Take your time, son."

"Zanini."

After that, there was a long pause, a breathless pause, until Mr. Summers, holding his slip of paper in the air, said, "All right, fellows." For a minute, no one moved, and then all the slips of paper were opened. Suddenly, all the women began to speak at once, saying, "Who is it?" "Who's got it?" "Is it the Dunbars?" "Is it the Watsons?" Then the voices began to say, "It's Hutchinson. It's Bill," "Bill Hutchinson's got it."

"Go tell your father," Mrs. Dunbar said to her older son.

People began to look around to see the Hutchinsons. Bill Hutchinson   45
was standing quiet, staring down at the paper in his hand. Suddenly, Tessie Hutchinson shouted to Mr. Summers, "You didn't give him time enough to take any paper he wanted. I saw you. It wasn't fair!"

"Be a good sport, Tessie," Mrs. Delacroix called, and Mrs. Graves said, "All of us took the same chance."

"Shut up, Tessie," Bill Hutchinson said.

"Well, everyone," Mr. Summers said, "that was done pretty fast, and now we've got to be hurrying a little more to get done in time." He consulted his next list. "Bill," he said, "you draw for the Hutchinson family. You got any other households in the Hutchinsons?"

"There's Don and Eva," Mrs. Hutchinson yelled. "Make *them* take their chance!"

"Daughters drew with their husbands' families, Tessie," Mr. Summers said   50
gently. "You know that as well as anyone else."

"It wasn't *fair*," Tessie said.

"I guess not, Joe," Bill Hutchinson said regretfully. "My daughter draws with her husband's family, that's only fair. And I've got no other family except the kids."

"Then, as far as drawing for families is concerned, it's you," Mr. Summers said in explanation, "and as far as drawing for households is concerned, that's you, too. Right?"

"Right," Bill Hutchinson said.

"How many kids, Bill?" Mr. Summers asked formally.   55

"Three," Bill Hutchinson said. "There's Bill Jr., and Nancy, and little Dave. And Tessie and me."

"All right, then," Mr. Summers said. "Harry, you got their tickets back?"

Mr. Graves nodded and held up the slips of paper. "Put them in the box, then," Mr. Summers directed. "Take Bill's and put it in."

"I think we ought to start over," Mrs. Hutchinson said, as quietly as she could. "I tell you it wasn't *fair.* You didn't give him time enough to choose. *Every*body saw that."

Mr. Graves had selected the five slips and put them in the box, and he   60
dropped all the papers but those onto the ground, where the breeze caught them and lifted them off.

"Listen, everybody," Mrs. Hutchinson was saying to the people around her.

"Ready, Bill?" Mr. Summers asked, and Bill Hutchinson, with one quick glance around at his wife and children, nodded.

"Remember," Mr. Summers said, "take the slips and keep them folded until each person has taken one. Harry, you help little Dave." Mr. Graves took the hand of the little boy, who came willingly with him up to the box. "Take a paper out of the box, Davy," Mr. Summers said. Davy put his hand into the box and laughed. "Take just *one* paper," Mr. Summers said. "Harry, you hold it for him." Mr. Graves took the child's hand and removed the folded paper from the tight fist and held it while little Dave stood next to him and looked up at him wonderingly.

"Nancy next," Mr. Summers said. Nancy was twelve, and her school friends breathed heavily as she went forward, switching her skirt, and took a slip daintily from the box. "Bill Jr.," Mr. Summers said, and Billy, his face red and his feet overlarge, nearly knocked the box over as he got a paper out. "Tessie," Mr. Summers said. She hesitated for a minute, looking around defiantly, and then set her lips and went up to the box. She snatched a paper out and held it behind her.

"Bill," Mr. Summers said, and Bill Hutchinson reached into the box and felt   65
around, bringing his hand out at last with the slip of paper in it.

The crowd was quiet. A girl whispered, "I hope it's not Nancy," and the sound of the whisper reached the edges of the crowd.

"It's not the way it used to be," Old Man Warner said clearly. "People ain't the way they used to be."

"All right," Mr. Summers said. "Open the papers. Harry, you open little Dave's."

Mr. Graves opened the slip of paper and there was a general sigh through the crowd as he held it up and everyone could see that it was blank. Nancy and Bill Jr. opened theirs at the same time, and both beamed and laughed, turning around to the crowd and holding their slips of paper above their heads.

"Tessie," Mr. Summers said. There was a pause, and then Mr. Summers 70 looked at Bill Hutchinson, and Bill unfolded his paper and showed it. It was blank.

"It's Tessie," Mr. Summers said, and his voice was hushed. "Show us her paper, Bill."

Bill Hutchinson went over to his wife and forced the slip of paper out of her hand. It had a black spot on it, the black spot Mr. Summers had made the night before with the heavy pencil in the coal-company office. Bill Hutchinson held it up and there was a stir in the crowd.

"All right, folks," Mr. Summers said. "Let's finish quickly."

Although the villagers had forgotten the ritual and lost the original black box, they still remembered to use stones. The pile of stones the boys had made earlier was ready; there were stones on the ground with the blowing scraps of paper that had come out of the box. Mrs. Delacroix selected a stone so large she had to pick it up with both hands and turned to Mrs. Dunbar. "Come on," she said. "Hurry up."

Mrs. Dunbar had small stones in both hands, and she said, gasping for 75 breath, "I can't run at all. You'll have to go ahead and I'll catch up with you."

The children had stones already, and someone gave little Davy Hutchinson a few pebbles.

Tessie Hutchinson was in the center of a cleared space by now, and she held her hands out desperately as the villagers moved in on her. "It isn't fair," she said. A stone hit her on the side of the head.

Old Man Warner was saying, "Come on, come on, everyone." Steve Adams was in the front of the crowd of villagers, with Mrs. Graves beside him.

"It isn't fair, it isn't right," Mrs. Hutchinson screamed and then they were upon her.   *[1948]*

☰ THINKING ABOUT THE TEXT

1. At what point in the story did you suspect that something was amiss in this bucolic village? How does Jackson both prepare you for and surprise you with her ending?

2. Make a list of the characters' names in the story. What symbolic significance might they have?

3. What do the phrase "Lottery in June, corn be heavy soon" and the pile of stones suggest about the origins of the lottery?

4. Critics often mention scapegoating, man's inherent evil, and the destructive consequence of hanging on to ancient and outdated rituals as the principal themes of this story. Do you agree? What are some other themes suggested by the story?

5. What contemporary issues does "The Lottery" bring to mind?

URSULA K. LE GUIN

The Ones Who Walk Away from Omelas

Ursula K. Le Guin (b. 1929) was born and raised in Berkeley, California, where she began writing at eleven, unsuccessfully submitting a story to Astounding Science Fiction. *She graduated from Radcliffe College (Phi Beta Kappa) in 1951 and received her M.A. from Columbia University a year later. She became famous with the publication of* The Left Hand of Darkness *(1969), an exploration of a hermaphroditic race that most critics see as a comment on contemporary gender politics. The novel won science fiction's highest awards: the Hugo and the Nebula. The Farthest Shore (1972) won the National Book Award, and* Tehanu: The Last Book of Earthsea *(1990) won the prestigious Nebula Award. More recently,* Powers *won the Nebula Award for 2008, and* Lavinia *won the 2009 Locus Award for Best Fantasy Novel. Besides her twenty novels, Le Guin has also published scores of short stories, books for children, nonfiction, and six volumes of poems. In 2000, Le Guin received the Library of Congress Living Legends award for her "significant contribution to America's heritage."*

With a clamor of bells that set the swallows soaring, the Festival of Summer came to the city Omelas, bright-towered by the sea. The rigging of the boats in harbor sparkled with flags. In the streets between houses with red roofs and painted walls, between old moss-grown gardens and under avenues of trees, past great parks and public buildings, processions moved. Some were decorous: old people in long stiff robes of mauve and gray, grave master workmen, quiet, merry women carrying their babies and chatting as they walked. In other streets the music beat faster, a shimmering of gong and tambourine, and the people went dancing, the procession was a dance. Children dodged in and out, their high calls rising like the swallows' crossing flights over the music and the singing. All the processions wound towards the north side of the city, where on the great water-meadow called the Green Fields boys and girls, naked in the bright air, with mudstained feet and ankles and long, lithe arms, exercised their restive horses before the race. The horses wore no gear at all but a halter without bit. Their manes were braided with streamers of silver, gold, and green. They flared their nostrils and pranced and boasted to one another; they were vastly excited, the horse being the only animal who has adopted our ceremonies as his own. Far off to the north and west the mountains stood up half encircling Omelas on her bay. The air of morning was so clear that the snow still crowning the Eighteen Peaks burned with white-gold fire across the miles of sunlit air, under the dark blue of the sky. There was just enough wind to make the banners that marked the racecourse snap and flutter now and then. In the silence of the broad green meadows one could hear the music winding through the city streets, farther and nearer and ever approaching, a cheerful faint sweetness of the air that from time to time trembled and gathered together and broke out into the great joyous clanging of the bells.

Joyous! How is one to tell about joy? How describe the citizens of Omelas?

They were not simple folk, you see, though they were happy. But we do not say the words of cheer much any more. All smiles have become archaic. Given a description such as this one tends to make certain assumptions. Given a description such as this one tends to look next for the King, mounted on a splendid stallion and surrounded by his noble knights, or perhaps in a golden litter borne by great-muscled slaves. But there was no king. They did not use swords, or keep slaves. They were not barbarians. I do not know the rules and laws of their society, but I suspect that they were singularly few. As they did without monarchy and slavery, so they also got on without the stock exchange, the advertisement, the secret police, and the bomb. Yet I repeat that these were not simple folk, not dulcet shepherds, noble savages, bland utopians. They were not less complex than us. The trouble is that we have a bad habit, encouraged by pedants and sophisticates, of considering happiness as something rather stupid. Only pain is intellectual, only evil interesting. This is the treason of the artist: a refusal to admit the banality of evil and the terrible boredom of pain. If you can't lick 'em, join 'em. If it hurts, repeat it. But to praise despair is to condemn delight, to embrace violence is to lose hold of everything else. We have almost lost hold, we can no longer describe a happy man, nor make any celebration of joy. How can I tell you about the people of Omelas? They were not naive and happy children—though their children were, in fact, happy. They were mature, intelligent, passionate adults whose lives were not wretched. O miracle! But I wish I could describe it better. I wish I could convince you. Omelas sounds in my words like a city in a fairy tale, long ago and far away, once upon a time. Perhaps it would be best if you imagined it as your own fancy bids, assuming it will rise to the occasion, for certainly I cannot suit you all. For instance, how about technology? I think that there would be no cars or helicopters in and above the streets; this follows from the fact that the people of Omelas are happy people. Happiness is based on a just discrimination of what is necessary, what is neither necessary nor destructive, and what is destructive. In the middle category, however—that of the unnecessary but undestructive, that of comfort, luxury, exuberance, etc.—they could perfectly well have central heating, subway trains, washing machines, and all kinds of marvelous devices not yet invented here, floating light-sources, fuelless power, a cure for the common cold. Or they could have none of that: it doesn't matter. As you like it. I incline to think that people from towns up and down the coast have been coming in to Omelas during the last days before the Festival on very fast little trains and double-decked trams, and that the train station of Omelas is actually the handsomest building in town, though plainer than the magnificent Farmers' Market. But even granted trains, I fear that Omelas so far strikes some of you as goody-goody. Smiles, bells, parades, horses, bleh. If so, please add an orgy. If an orgy would help, don't hesitate. Let us not, however, have temples from which issue beautiful nude priests and priestesses already half in ecstasy and ready to copulate with any man or woman, lover or stranger, who desires union with the deep godhead of the blood, although that was my first idea. But really it would be better not to have any temples in Omelas—at least, not manned temples. Religion yes, clergy no. Surely the beautiful nudes can just wander about, offering themselves like divine soufflés to the hunger of the needy and the rapture of the flesh. Let them join the processions. Let tambourines be struck above the copulations, and the glory of desire be proclaimed upon the gongs, and (a not unimportant point) let the offspring of these delightful rituals be beloved and looked after by all. One thing I know there is none of in Omelas is guilt. But what else should there be? I thought that first there were no drugs, but that is puritanical. For those who like it, the faint insistent sweetness of *drooz* may perfume the ways of the city, *drooz* which first brings a great lightness and brilliance to the mind and limbs, and then after some hours a dreamy languor, and wonderful visions at last of the very arcana and inmost secrets of the Universe, as well as exciting the pleasure of sex beyond all belief; and it is not habit-forming. For more modest tastes I think there ought to be beer. What else, what else belongs in the joyous city? The sense of victory, surely, the celebration of courage. But as we did without clergy, let us do without soldiers. The joy built upon successful slaughter is not the right kind of joy; it will not do; it is fearful and it is trivial. A boundless and generous contentment, a magnanimous triumph felt not against some outer enemy but in communion with the finest and fairest in the souls of all men everywhere and the splendor of the world's summer: this is what swells the hearts of the people of Omelas, and the victory they celebrate is that of life. I really don't think many of them need to take *drooz.*

Most of the processions have reached the Green Fields by now. A marvelous smell of cooking goes forth from the red and blue tents of the provisioners. The faces of small children are amiably sticky; in the benign grey beard of a man a couple of crumbs of rich pastry are entangled. The youths and girls have mounted their horses and are beginning to group around the starting line of the course. An old woman, small, fat, and laughing, is passing out flowers from a basket, and tall young men wear her flowers in their shining hair. A child of nine or ten sits at the edge of the crowd, alone, playing on a wooden flute. People pause to listen, and they smile, but they do not speak to him, for he never ceases playing and never sees them, his dark eyes wholly rapt in the sweet, thin magic of the tune.

He finishes, and slowly lowers his hands holding the wooden flute.   5

As if that little private silence were the signal, all at once a trumpet sounds from the pavilion near the starting line: imperious, melancholy, piercing. The horses rear on their slender legs, and some of them neigh in answer. Soberfaced, the young riders stroke the horses' necks and soothe them, whispering, "Quiet, quiet, there my beauty, my hope. . . ." They begin to form in rank along the starting line. The crowds along the racecourse are like a field of grass and flowers in the wind. The Festival of Summer has begun.

Do you believe? Do you accept the festival, the city, the joy? No? Then let me describe one more thing.

In a basement under one of the beautiful public buildings of Omelas, or perhaps in the cellar of one of its spacious private homes, there is a room. It has one locked door, and no window. A little light seeps in dustily between cracks in the boards, secondhand from a cobwebbed window somewhere across the cellar. In one corner of the little room a couple of mops, with stiff, clotted, foul-smelling heads, stand near a rusty bucket. The floor is dirt, a little damp to the touch, as cellar dirt usually is. The room is about three paces long and two wide: a mere broom closet or disused tool room. In the room a child is sitting. It could be a boy or a girl. It looks about six, but actually is nearly ten. It is feebleminded. Perhaps it was born defective, or perhaps it has become imbecile through fear, malnutrition, and neglect. It picks its nose and occasionally fumbles vaguely with its toes or genitals, as it sits hunched in the corner farthest from the bucket and the two mops. It is afraid of the mops. It finds them horrible. It shuts its eyes, but it knows the mops are still standing there: and the door is locked; and nobody will come. The door is always locked; and nobody ever comes, except that sometimes—the child has no understanding of time or interval—sometimes the door rattles terribly and opens, and a person, or several people, are there. One of them may come in and kick the child to make it stand up. The others never come close, but peer in at it with frightened, disgusted eyes. The food bowl and the water jug are hastily filled, the door is locked, the eyes disappear. The people at the door never say anything, but the child, who has not always lived in the tool room, and can remember sunlight and its mother's voice, sometimes speaks. "I will be good," it says. "Please let me out. I will be good!" They never answer. The child used to scream for help at night, and cry a good deal, but now it only makes a kind of whining, "eh-haa, eh-haa," and it speaks less and less often. It is so thin there are no calves to its legs; its belly protrudes; it lives on a half-bowl of corn meal and grease a day. It is naked. Its buttocks and thighs are a mass of festered sores, as it sits in its own excrement continually.

They all know it is there, all the people of Omelas. Some of them have come to see it, others are content merely to know it is there. They all know that it has to be there. Some of them understand why, and some do not, but they all understand that their happiness, the beauty of their city, the tenderness of their friendships, the health of their children, the wisdom of their scholars, the skill of their makers, even the abundance of their harvest and the kindly weathers of their skies, depend wholly on this child's abominable misery.

This is usually explained to children when they are between eight and   10
twelve, whenever they seem capable of understanding; and most of those who come to see the child are young people, though often enough an adult comes, or comes back, to see the child. No matter how well the matter has been explained to them, these young spectators are always shocked and sickened at the sight. They feel disgust, which they had thought themselves superior to. They feel anger, outrage, impotence, despite all the explanations. They would like to do something for the child. But there is nothing they can do. If the child were brought up into the sunlight out of that vile place, if it were cleaned and fed and comforted, that would be a good thing, indeed; but if it were done, in that day and hour all the prosperity and beauty and delight of Omelas would wither and be destroyed. Those are the terms. To exchange all the goodness and grace of every life in Omelas for that single, small improvement: to throw away the

happiness of thousands for the chance of the happiness of one: that would be to let guilt within the walls indeed.

The terms are strict and absolute; there may not even be a kind word spoken to the child.

Often the young people go home in tears, or in a tearless rage, when they have seen the child and faced this terrible paradox. They may brood over it for weeks or years. But as time goes on they begin to realize that even if the child could be released, it would not get much good of its freedom: a little vague pleasure of warmth and food, no doubt, but little more. It is too degraded and imbecile to know any real joy. It has been afraid too long ever to be free of fear. Its habits are too uncouth for it to respond to humane treatment. Indeed, after so long it would probably be wretched without walls about it to protect it, and darkness for its eyes, and its own excrement to sit in. Their tears at the bitter injustice dry when they begin to perceive the terrible justice of reality, and to accept it. Yet it is their tears and anger, the trying of their generosity and the acceptance of their helplessness, which are perhaps the true source of the splendor of their lives. Theirs is no vapid, irresponsible happiness. They know that they, like the child, are not free. They know compassion. It is the existence of the child, and their knowledge of its existence, that makes possible the nobility of their architecture, the poignancy of their music, the profundity of their science. It is because of the child that they are so gentle with children. They know that if the wretched one were not there snivelling in the dark, the other one, the flute-player, could make no joyful music as the young riders line up in their beauty for the race in the sunlight of the first morning of summer.

Now do you believe in them? Are they not more credible? But there is one more thing to tell, and this is quite incredible.

At times one of the adolescent girls or boys who go to see the child does not go home to weep or rage, does not, in fact, go home at all. Sometimes also a man or woman much older falls silent for a day or two, and then leaves home. These people go out into the street, and walk down the street alone. They keep walking, and walk straight out of the city of Omelas, through the beautiful gates. They keep walking across the farmlands of Omelas. Each one goes alone, youth or girl, man or woman. Night falls; the traveler must pass down village streets, between the houses with yellow-lit windows, and on out into the darkness of the fields. Each alone, they go west or north, towards the mountains. They go on. They leave Omelas, they walk ahead into the darkness, and they do not come back. The place they go towards is a place even less imaginable to most of us than the city of happiness. I cannot describe it at all. It is possible that it does not exist. But they seem to know where they are going, the ones who walk away from Omelas.   *[1973]*

≡ **THINKING ABOUT THE TEXT**

1. The opening three paragraphs make Omelas sound idyllic. Why might most people think of it as a utopia? What would you add or subtract? How might some aspects of our world be possible in Omelas?

2. Critics suggest that although many stories are set in the future or in an imaginary world, they are really about the present. How might this be true for this story?

3. How might you respond to the suffering child? How would you respond if you knew the happiness of a community of thousands was based on the suffering of this one individual?

4. Speculate about why some walk away from Omelas. Where are they going? Why do they seem so resolute?

5. What part does tradition play in the story? For example, if the people of Omelas didn't have such a tradition and someone proposed it, why would they be more or less likely to adopt the proposal (assuming that it would somehow work)?

≡ MAKING COMPARISONS

1. Give reasons why the citizens in both stories continue their rituals.

2. Give reasons why you think one of these writers has a darker view of humanity than the other.

3. If the rituals in both stories were reversed, how might the citizens in "The Lottery" respond to the outcast? How might the inhabitants of Omelas respond to the lottery?

≡ WRITING ABOUT ISSUES

1. Write an essay in which you argue that "The Lottery" is an apt allegory for some contemporary issue that you think is mired in tradition and needs change. Comment on the difficulties involved and possible solutions.

2. Write an essay that argues that "those who walk away from Omelas" can be seen as an allegory for a contemporary situation that you think needs to change. Suggest how this might be done.

3. Write an essay that recounts both pleasant and unpleasant experiences with traditional rituals. Argue that we would be better off continuing or discontinuing these rituals.

4. Look up Shirley Jackson's essay "The Morning of June 28, 1948, and 'The Lottery'" and write an essay that argues that if the story were published today, the response would be similar or different.

CHARLES PERRAULT, "Little Red Riding Hood"

JACOB AND WILHELM GRIMM, "Little Red Cap"

ANGELA CARTER, "The Company of Wolves"

The story of Little Red Riding Hood is still told to children throughout the world. Her adventure in facing mortal danger is part of their education. What, though, do they learn from this narrative? Scholars have suggested various interpretations, many of which hold that the tale helps its young readers face their own childhood fears. Among the best-known and most provocative interpreters of the story is the psychoanalyst Bruno Bettelheim, who sees it as a symbolic treatment of a girl's effort to understand her sexual development. In this view, the story teaches girls to work through adolescent anxieties. But whatever decoding the tale receives, two aspects of it remain important. First, it depicts a child's journey from innocence to experience, however these terms are defined. Little Red Riding Hood learns something from her encounters with the murderous wolf, and she does so largely on her own. Several versions of her story exist. Because this tale of a perilous journey is so popular and has circulated in various forms, we invite you to compare three versions of it: Charles Perrault's from the seventeenth century, the Brothers Grimm's from the nineteenth century, and Angela Carter's modern variation. Note that the Grimms' tale does not stray too far from Perrault's, at least not in representing Little Red Riding Hood as an innocent in need of male protection. Under the influence of contemporary feminism, however, Carter feels no need to conform to the fairy-tale tradition. As a result, Little Red Riding Hood is freed not only from genre conventions but also from a centuries-old stereotype about passive females.

■ BEFORE YOU READ

Write down what you remember about the story of Little Red Riding Hood, and then compare your version with those of your classmates. What elements of the story do your class's various renditions of it have in common? What differences, if any, emerge? Why do you think the story has been so popular?

CHARLES PERRAULT
Little Red Riding Hood

Along with the Brothers Grimm, Charles Perrault (1628–1703) was the most influential teller of the fairy tales many of us learned as children. Born in Paris to a fairly wealthy family, Perrault was trained as a lawyer. For his literary and philosophical

(Jacob and Wilhelm Grimm. © Bettmann/
Corbis.)

(Charles Perrault. The Granger Collection,
New York.)

(Angela Carter. © Sophie Bassouls/Sygma/
Corbis.)

achievements, however, Perrault was elected to the prestigious Académie Française in 1671. During his lifetime, he and others were involved in a major cultural dispute over the relative merits of ancient authors and modern ones, with Perrault favoring the more up-to-date group. Later generations remember him best, though, for his 1697 book Stories or Tales from Times Past, with Morals: Tales of Mother Goose. *This collection included "Le Petit Chaperon Rouge," which English-speaking readers have come to know as "Little Red Riding Hood." This story did not completely originate with Perrault; probably he had heard folktales containing some of its narrative elements. Nevertheless, his version became popular on publication and has remained so ever since.*

Once upon a time there lived in a certain village a little country girl, the prettiest creature who was ever seen. Her mother was excessively fond of her, and her grandmother doted on her still more. This good woman had a little red riding hood made for her. It suited the girl so extremely well that everybody called her Little Red Riding Hood.

One day her mother, having made some cakes, said to her, "Go, my dear, and see how your grandmother is doing, for I hear she has been very ill. Take her a cake, and this little pot of butter."

Little Red Riding Hood set out immediately to go to her grandmother, who lived in another village.

As she was going through the wood, she met with a wolf, who had a very great mind to eat her up, but he dared not, because of some woodcutters working nearby in the forest. He asked her where she was going. The poor child, who did not know that it was dangerous to stay and talk to a wolf, said to him, "I am going to see my grandmother and carry her a cake and a little pot of butter from my mother."

Does she live far off?" said the wolf.   5

"Oh I say," answered Little Red Riding Hood. "It is beyond that mill you see there, at the first house in the village."

"Well," said the wolf, "and I'll go and see her too. I'll go this way and go you that, and we shall see who will be there first."

The wolf ran as fast as he could, taking the shortest path, and the little girl took a roundabout way, entertaining herself by gathering nuts, running after butterflies, and gathering bouquets of little flowers. It was not long before the wolf arrived at the old woman's house. He knocked at the door: tap, tap.

"Who's there?"

"Your grandchild, Little Red Riding Hood," replied the wolf, counterfeiting   10
her voice, "who has brought you a cake and a little pot of butter sent you by Mother."

The good grandmother, who was in bed because she was somewhat ill, cried out, "Pull the bobbin, and the latch will go up."

The wolf pulled the bobbin, and the door opened, and then he immediately fell upon the good woman and ate her up in a moment, for it had been more than three days since he had eaten. He then shut the door and got into the grandmother's bed, expecting Little Red Riding Hood, who came some time afterwards and knocked at the door: tap, tap.

"Who's there?"

Little Red Riding Hood, hearing the big voice of the wolf, was at first afraid but, believing her grandmother had a cold and was hoarse, answered, "It is your grandchild Little Red Riding Hood, who has brought you a cake and a little pot of butter Mother sends you."

The wolf cried out to her, softening his voice as much as he could, "Pull the   15
bobbin, and the latch will go up."

Little Red Riding Hood pulled the bobbin, and the door opened.

The wolf, seeing her come in, said to her, hiding himself under the bedclothes, "Put the cake and the little pot of butter upon the stool, and come get into bed with me."

Little Red Riding Hood took off her clothes and got into bed. She was greatly amazed to see how her grandmother looked in her nightclothes and said to her, "Grandmother, what big arms you have!"

"All the better to hug you with, my dear."

"Grandmother, what big legs you have!"   20
"All the better to run with, my child."
"Grandmother, what big ears you have!"
"All the better to hear with, my child."
"Grandmother, what big eyes you have!"
"All the better to see with, my child."   25
"Grandmother, what big teeth you have got!"
"All the better to eat you up with."
And saying these words, this wicked wolf fell upon Little Red Riding Hood,
and ate her all up.

Moral: Children, especially attractive, well bred young ladies, should never talk
to strangers, for if they should do so, they may well provide dinner for a wolf. I
say "wolf," but there are various kinds of wolves. There are also those who
are charming, quiet, polite, unassuming, complacent, and sweet, who pursue
young women at home and in the streets. And unfortunately, it is these gentle
wolves who are the most dangerous ones of all.   *[1697]*

☰ THINKING ABOUT THE TEXT

1. To what extent does it matter to the story that Little Red Riding Hood is
   pretty? Would your reaction be the same if you learned she was homely
   or if you did not know how she looked? Explain.

2. The two main female characters are Little Red Riding Hood and her
   grandmother. Although the girl's mother appears briefly at the start,
   she then disappears from the narrative. What purposes are served by
   Perrault's leaving her out?

3. How would you describe Little Red Riding Hood as Perrault depicts her?
   Refer to specific details of the text.

4. In this version, Little Red Riding Hood dies. Would you draw different
   ideas from the text if she had lived? If so, what?

5. Does Perrault's moral seem well connected to the preceding story? Why,
   or why not? What metaphoric wolves might this moral apply to?

JACOB AND WILHELM GRIMM

Little Red Cap

*Jacob Grimm (1785–1863) and Wilhelm Grimm (1786–1859) were born in
Hanau, Germany, and studied law at Marburg University. They served as linguistics
professors at Göttingen University and made major contributions to the historical
study of language. The Grimms began to collect folktales from various oral European
traditions for their friends but later published their efforts for both children and
adults. Their methods became a model for the scientific collection of folktales and folk*

songs. Today they are known best for their volume Children's and Household Tales, *which was first published in 1812 and went through six more editions, the last in 1857. Their book included their version of the Little Red Riding Hood story, although their title for it was (in English translation) "Little Red Cap."*

Once upon a time there was a sweet little girl. Everyone who saw her liked her, but most of all her grandmother, who did not know what to give the child next. Once she gave her a little cap made of red velvet. Because it suited her so well, and she wanted to wear it all the time, she came to be known as Little Red Cap.

One day her mother said to her, "Come Little Red Cap. Here is a piece of cake and a bottle of wine. Take them to your grandmother. She is sick and weak, and they will do her well. Mind your manners, and give her my greetings. Behave yourself on the way, and do not leave the path, or you might fall down and break the glass, and then there will be nothing for your grandmother. And when you enter her parlor, don't forget to say 'Good morning,' and don't peer into all the corners first."

"I'll do everything just right," said Little Red Cap, shaking her mother's hand.

The grandmother lived out in the woods, a half hour from the village. When Little Red Cap entered the woods, a wolf came up to her. She did not know what a wicked animal he was and was not afraid of him.

"Good day to you, Little Red Cap." 5

"Thank you, wolf."

"Where are you going so early, Little Red Cap?"

"To Grandmother's."

"And what are you carrying under your apron?"

"Grandmother is sick and weak, and I am taking her some cake and wine. 10 We baked yesterday, and they should be good for her and give her strength."

"Little Red Cap, just where does your grandmother live?"

"Her house is a good quarter hour from here in the woods, under the three large oak trees. There's a hedge of hazel bushes there. You must know the place," said Little Red Cap.

The wolf thought to himself, "Now that sweet young thing is a tasty bite for me. She will taste even better than the old woman. You must be sly, and you can catch them both."

He walked along a little while with Little Red Cap. Then he said, "Little Red Cap, just look at the beautiful flowers that are all around us. Why don't you go and take a look? And I don't believe you can hear how beautifully the birds are singing. You are walking along as though you were on your way to school. It is very beautiful in the woods."

Little Red Cap opened her eyes, and when she saw the sunbeams dancing 15 to and fro through the trees and how the ground was covered with beautiful flowers, she thought, "If I take a fresh bouquet to Grandmother, she will be very pleased. Anyway, it is still early, and I'll be home on time." And she ran off the path into the woods looking for flowers. Each time she picked one, she

thought that she could see an even more beautiful one a little way off, and she ran after it, going farther and farther into the woods. But the wolf ran straight to the grandmother's house and knocked on the door.

"Who's there?"

"Little Red Cap. I'm bringing you some cake and wine. Open the door."

"Just press the latch," called out the grandmother. "I'm too weak to get up."

The wolf pressed the latch, and the door opened. He stepped inside, went straight to the grandmother's bed, and ate her up. Then he put on her clothes, put her cap on his head, got into her bed, and pulled the curtains shut.

Little Red Cap had run after the flowers. After she had gathered so many   20
that she could not carry any more, she remembered her grandmother and then continued on her way to her house. She found, to her surprise, that the door was open. She walked into the parlor, and everything looked so strange that she thought, "Oh, my God, why am I so afraid? I usually like it at Grandmother's."

She called out, "Good morning!" but received no answer.

Then she went to the bed and pulled back the curtains. Grandmother was lying there with her cap pulled down over her face and looking very strange.

"Oh, Grandmother, what big ears you have!"

"All the better to hear you with."

"Oh, Grandmother, what big eyes you have!"   25

"All the better to see you with."

"Oh, Grandmother, what big hands you have!"

"All the better to grab you with!"

"Oh, Grandmother, what a horribly big mouth you have!"

"All the better to eat you with!"   30

The wolf had scarcely finished speaking when he jumped from the bed with a single leap and ate up poor Little Red Cap. As soon as the wolf had satisfied his desires, he climbed back into bed, fell asleep, and began to snore very loudly.

A huntsman was just passing by. He thought, "The old woman is snoring so loudly. You had better see if something is wrong with her."

He stepped into the parlor, and when he approached the bed, he saw the wolf lying there. "So here I find you, you old sinner," he said. "I have been hunting for you a long time."

He was about to aim his rifle when it occurred to him that the wolf might have eaten the grandmother and that she still might be rescued. So instead of shooting, he took a pair of scissors and began to cut open the wolf's belly. After a few cuts he saw the red cap shining through, and after a few more cuts the girl jumped out, crying, "Oh, I was so frightened! It was so dark inside the wolf's body!"

And then the grandmother came out as well, alive but hardly able to   35
breathe. Then Little Red Cap fetched some large stones. She filled the wolf's body with them, and when he woke up and tried to run away, the stones were so heavy that he immediately fell down dead.

The three of them were happy. The huntsman skinned the wolf and went home with the pelt. The grandmother ate the cake and drank the wine that

Little Red Cap had brought. And Little Red Cap thought, "As long as I live, I will never leave the path and run off into the woods by myself if Mother tells me not to."

They also tell how Little Red Cap was taking some baked things to her grandmother another time, when another wolf spoke to her and wanted her to leave the path. But Little Red Cap took care and went straight to Grandmother's. She told her that she had seen the wolf and that he had wished her a good day but had stared at her in a wicked manner. "If we hadn't been on a public road, he would have eaten me up," she said.

"Come," said the grandmother. "Let's lock the door, so he can't get in."

Soon afterward the wolf knocked on the door and called out, "Open up, Grandmother. It's Little Red Cap, and I'm bringing you some baked things."

They remained silent and did not open the door. Gray-Head crept around 40 the house several times and finally jumped onto the roof. He wanted to wait until Little Red Cap went home that evening and then follow her and eat her up in the darkness. But the grandmother saw what he was up to. There was a large stone trough in front of the house.

"Fetch a bucket, Little Red Cap," she said to the child. "Yesterday I cooked some sausage. Carry the water that I boiled them with to the trough." Little Red Cap carried water until the large, large trough was clear full. The smell of sausage arose into the wolf's nose. He sniffed and looked down, stretching his neck so long that he could no longer hold himself, and he began to slide. He slid off the roof, fell into the trough, and drowned. And Little Red Cap returned home happily, and no one harmed her.   [1857]

≡ **THINKING ABOUT THE TEXT**

1. Why do you think that, at the beginning of the tale, the Grimms emphasize how sweet and likable Little Red Cap is?

2. To what extent do you blame Little Red Cap for being distracted by the beauty of nature? Explain your reasoning.

3. The Grimms have Little Red Cap and her grandmother rescued by a hunter. What would you say to someone who sees the Grimms as implying that women always need help from a man?

4. The wolf dies because Little Red Cap has filled his body with stones. Why do you think the Grimms did not have the huntsman simply shoot the wolf after freeing Little Red Cap and her grandmother?

5. Why do you think the Grimms added the second story? What is its effect?

≡ **MAKING COMPARISONS**

1. Does Little Red Riding Hood seem basically the same in both Perrault's version and the Grimms' version? Refer to specific details from both texts.

2. In Perrault's tale, the wolf persuades Little Red Riding Hood to take off her clothes and get into bed with him. In the Grimms' account, the wolf jumps up from the bed and eats her. How significant is this difference between the two versions?

3. In Perrault's version, Little Red Riding Hood and her grandmother die. In the Grimms' tale, on the other hand, they are rescued. Do you therefore see these two versions as putting forth different views of life? Explain.

ANGELA CARTER

The Company of Wolves

A native of Sussex, England, Angela Carter (1940–1991) worked in various genres, writing novels, short stories, screenplays, essays, and newspaper articles. Her fiction is most known for imaginatively refashioning classic tales of fantasy, including supernatural and gothic thrillers as well as fairy tales. Often, Carter rewrote these narratives from a distinctly female point of view, challenging what she saw as their patriarchal values and using them to explore the psychology of both genders. "The Company of Wolves," her version of the Little Red Riding Hood tale, was first published in the journal Bananas *in 1977. It then appeared in Carter's short-story volume* The Bloody Chamber *(1979) and was reprinted in* Burning Our Boats *(1995), a posthumous collection of all her stories. This tale also served as the basis for a 1984 film of the same title, which Carter wrote with director Neil Jordan.*

One beast and only one howls in the woods by night.

The wolf is carnivore incarnate, and he's as cunning as he is ferocious; once he's had a taste of flesh then nothing else will do.

At night, the eyes of wolves shine like candle flames, yellowish, reddish, but that is because the pupils of their eyes fatten on darkness and catch the light from your lantern to flash it back to you — red for danger; if a wolf's eyes reflect only moonlight, then they gleam a cold and unnatural green, a mineral, a piercing color. If the benighted traveler spies those luminous, terrible sequins stitched suddenly on the black thickets, then he knows he must run, if fear has not struck him stock-still.

But those eyes are all you will be able to glimpse of the forest assassins as they cluster invisibly round your smell of meat as you go through the wood unwisely late. They will be like shadows, they will be like wraiths, gray members of a congregation of nightmare; hark! his long, wavering howl . . . an aria of fear made audible.

The wolfsong is the sound of the rending you will suffer, in itself a murdering.   5

It is winter and cold weather. In this region of mountain and forest, there is now nothing for the wolves to eat. Goats and sheep are locked up in the

byre,° the deer departed for the remaining pasturage on the southern slopes—wolves grow lean and famished. There is so little flesh on them that you could count the starveling ribs through their pelts, if they gave you time before they pounced. Those slavering jaws; the lolling tongue; the rime of saliva on the grizzled chops—of all the teeming perils of the night and the forest, ghosts, hobgoblins, ogres that grill babies upon gridirons, witches that fatten their captives in cages for cannibal tables, the wolf is worst for he cannot listen to reason.

You are always in danger in the forest, where no people are. Step between the portals of the great pines where the shaggy branches tangle about you, trapping the unwary traveler in nets as if the vegetation itself were in a plot with the wolves who live there, as though the wicked trees go fishing on behalf of their friends—step between the gateposts of the forest with the greatest trepidation and infinite precautions, for if you stray from the path for one instant, the wolves will eat you. They are gray as famine, they are as unkind as plague.

The grave-eyed children of the sparse villages always carry knives with them when they go out to tend the little flocks of goats that provide the homesteads with acrid milk and rank, maggoty cheeses. Their knives are half as big as they are, the blades are sharpened daily.

But the wolves have ways of arriving at your own hearthside. We try and try but sometimes we cannot keep them out. There is no winter's night the cottager does not fear to see a lean, gray, famished snout questing under the door, and there was a woman once bitten in her own kitchen as she was straining the macaroni.

Fear and flee the wolf; for, worst of all, the wolf may be more than he seems. 10

There was a hunter once, near here, that trapped a wolf in a pit. This wolf had massacred the sheep and goats; eaten up a mad old man who used to live by himself in a hut halfway up the mountain and sing to Jesus all day; pounced on a girl looking after the sheep, but she made such a commotion that men came with rifles and scared him away and tried to track him into the forest but he was cunning and easily gave them the slip. So this hunter dug a pit and put a duck in it, for bait, all alive-oh; and he covered the pit with straw smeared with wolf dung. Quack, quack! went the duck and a wolf came slinking out of the forest, a big one, a heavy one, he weighed as much as a grown man, and the straw gave way beneath him—into the pit he tumbled. The hunter jumped down after him, slit his throat, cut off all his paws for a trophy.

And then no wolf at all lay in front of the hunter but the bloody trunk of a man, headless, footless, dying, dead.

A witch from up the valley once turned an entire wedding party into wolves because the groom had settled on another girl. She used to order them to visit her, at night, from spite, and they would sit and howl around her cottage for her, serenading her with their misery.

byre: Barn or shed.

Not so very long ago, a young woman in our village married a man who vanished clean away on her wedding night. The bed was made with new sheets and the bride lay down in it; the groom said, he was going out to relieve himself, insisted on it, for the sake of decency, and she drew the coverlet up to her chin and she lay there. And she waited and she waited and then she waited again—surely he's been gone a long time? Until she jumps up in bed and shrieks to hear a howling, coming on the wind from the forest.

That long-drawn, wavering howl has, for all its fearful resonance, some   15
inherent sadness in it, as if the beasts would love to be less beastly if only they knew how and never cease to mourn their own condition. There is a vast melancholy in the canticles° of the wolves, melancholy infinite as the forest, endless as these long nights of winter and yet that ghastly sadness, that mourning for their own, irremediable appetites, can never move the heart for not one phrase in it hints at the possibility of redemption; grace could not come to the wolf from its own despair, only through some external mediator, so that, sometimes, the beast will look as if he half welcomes the knife that dispatches him.

The young woman's brothers searched the outhouses and the haystacks but never found any remains, so the sensible girl dried her eyes and found herself another husband not too shy to piss into a pot who spent the nights indoors. She gave him a pair of bonny babies and all went right as a trivet until, one freezing night, the night of the solstice, the hinge of the year when things do not fit together as well as they should, the longest night, her first good man came home again.

A great thump on the door announced him as she was stirring the soup for the father of her children, and she knew him the moment she lifted the latch to him although it was years since she'd worn black for him and now he was in rags and his hair hung down his back and never saw a comb, alive with lice.

"Here I am again, missus," he said. "Get me my bowl of cabbage and be quick about it."

Then her second husband came in with wood for the fire and when the first one saw she'd slept with another man and, worse, clapped his red eyes on her little children who'd crept into the kitchen to see what all the din was about, he shouted: "I wish I were a wolf again, to teach this whore a lesson!" So a wolf he instantly became and tore off the eldest boy's left foot before he was chopped up with the hatchet they used for chopping logs. But when the wolf lay bleeding and gasping its last, the pelt peeled off again and he was just as he had been, years ago, when he ran away from his marriage bed, so that she wept and her second husband beat her.

They say there's an ointment the Devil gives you that turns you into a wolf the   20
minute you rub it on. Or that he was born feet first and had a wolf for his father and his torso is a man's but his legs and genitals are a wolf's. And he has a wolf's heart.

canticles: Songs or chants.

Seven years is a werewolf's natural span but if you burn his human clothing you condemn him to wolfishness for the rest of his life, so old wives hereabouts think it some protection to throw a hat or an apron at the werewolf, as if clothes made the man. Yet by the eyes, those phosphorescent eyes, you know him in all his shapes; the eyes alone unchanged by metamorphosis.

Before he can become a wolf, the lycanthrope° strips stark naked. If you spy a naked man among the pines, you must run as if the Devil were after you.

It is midwinter and the robin, the friend of man, sits on the handle of the gardener's spade and sings. It is the worst time in all the year for wolves, but this strong-minded child insists she will go off through the wood. She is quite sure the wild beasts cannot harm her although, well-warned, she lays a carving knife in the basket her mother has packed with cheeses. There is a bottle of harsh liquor distilled from brambles; a batch of flat oatcakes baked on the hearthstone; a pot or two of jam. The flaxen-haired girl will take these delicious gifts to a reclusive grandmother so old the burden of her years is crushing her to death. Granny lives two hours' trudge through the winter woods; the child wraps herself up in her thick shawl, draws it over her head. She steps into her stout wooden shoes; she is dressed and ready and it is Christmas Eve. The malign door of the solstice still swings upon its hinges, but she has been too much loved ever to feel scared.

Children do not stay young for long in this savage country. There are no toys for them to play with, so they work hard and grow wise, but this one, so pretty and the youngest of her family, a little late-comer, had been indulged by her mother and the grandmother who'd knitted her the red shawl that, today, has the ominous if brilliant look of blood on snow. Her breasts have just begun to swell; her hair is like lint, so fair it hardly makes a shadow on her pale forehead; her cheeks are an emblematic scarlet and white and she has just started her woman's bleeding, the clock inside her that will strike, henceforward, once a month.

She stands and moves within the invisible pentacle° of her own virginity.   25
She is an unbroken egg; she is a sealed vessel; she has inside her a magic space the entrance to which is shut tight with a plug of membrane; she is a closed system; she does not know how to shiver. She has her knife and she is afraid of nothing.

Her father might forbid her, if he were home, but he is away in the forest, gathering wood, and her mother cannot deny her.

The forest closed upon her like a pair of jaws.

There is always something to look at in the forest, even in the middle of winter — the huddled mounds of birds, succumbed to the lethargy of the season, heaped on the creaking boughs and too forlorn to sing; the bright frills of the winter fungi on the blotched trunks of the trees; the cuneiform° slots of rabbits and deer, the herringbone tracks of the birds, a hare as lean as a rasher of bacon streaking across the path where the thin sunlight dapples the russet brakes of last year's bracken.

---

lycanthrope: Werewolf.   **pentacle:** Five-pointed star; also called a pentagram.   **cuneiform:** Wedge-shaped.

When she heard the freezing howl of a distant wolf, her practiced hand sprang to the handle of her knife, but she saw no sign of a wolf at all, nor of a naked man, neither, but then she heard a clattering among the brushwood and there sprang on to the path a fully clothed one, a very handsome young one, in the green coat and wide-awake hat of a hunter, laden with carcasses of game birds. She had her hand on her knife at the first rustle of twigs, but he laughed with a flash of white teeth when he saw her and made her a comic yet flattering little bow; she'd never seen such a fine fellow before, not among the rustic clowns of her native village. So on they went together, through the thickening light of the afternoon.

Soon they were laughing and joking like old friends. When he offered to   30
carry her basket, she gave it to him although her knife was in it because he told her his rifle would protect them. As the day darkened, it began to snow again; she felt the first flakes settle on her eyelashes, but now there was only half a mile to go and there would be a fire, and hot tea, and a welcome, a warm one, surely, for the dashing huntsman as well as for herself.

This young man had a remarkable object in his pocket. It was a compass. She looked at the little round glass face in the palm of his hand and watched the wavering needle with a vague wonder. He assured her this compass had taken him safely through the wood on his hunting trip because the needle always told him with perfect accuracy where the north was. She did not believe it; she knew she should never leave the path on the way through the wood or else she would be lost instantly. He laughed at her again; gleaming trails of spittle clung to his teeth. He said, if he plunged off the path into the forest that surrounded them, he could guarantee to arrive at her grandmother's house a good quarter of an hour before she did, plotting his way through the undergrowth with his compass, while she trudged the long way, along the winding path.

I don't believe you. Besides, aren't you afraid of the wolves?

He only tapped the gleaming butt of his rifle and grinned.

Is it a bet? he asked her. Shall we make a game of it? What will you give me if I get to your grandmother's house before you?

What would you like? she asked disingenuously.   35

A kiss.

Commonplaces of a rustic seduction; she lowered her eyes and blushed.

He went through the undergrowth and took her basket with him but she forgot to be afraid of the beasts, although now the moon was rising, for she wanted to dawdle on her way to make sure the handsome gentleman would win his wager.

Grandmother's house stood by itself a little way out of the village. The freshly falling snow blew in eddies about the kitchen garden, and the young man stepped delicately up the snowy path to the door as if he were reluctant to get his feet wet, swinging his bundle of game and the girl's basket and humming a little tune to himself.

There is a faint trace of blood on his chin; he has been snacking on his catch.   40

He rapped upon the panels with his knuckles.

Aged and frail, granny is three-quarters succumbed to the mortality the ache in her bones promises her and almost ready to give in entirely. A boy came out from the village to build up her hearth for the night an hour ago and the kitchen crackles with busy firelight. She has her Bible for company, she is a pious old woman. She is propped up on several pillows in the bed set into the wall peasant-fashion, wrapped up in the patchwork quilt she made before she was married, more years ago than she cares to remember. Two china spaniels with liver-colored blotches on their coats and black noses sit on either side of the fireplace. There is a bright rug of woven rags on the pantiles. The grandfather clock ticks away her eroding time.

We keep the wolves outside by living well.

He rapped upon the panels with his hairy knuckles.

It is your granddaughter, he mimicked in a high soprano.   45

Lift up the latch and walk in, my darling.

You can tell them by their eyes, eyes of a beast of prey, nocturnal, devastating eyes as red as a wound; you can hurl your Bible at him and your apron after, granny, you thought that was a sure prophylactic against these infernal vermin . . . now call on Christ and his mother and all the angels in heaven to protect you but it won't do you any good.

His feral muzzle is sharp as a knife; he drops his golden burden of gnawed pheasant on the table and puts down your dear girl's basket, too. Oh, my God, what have you done with her?

Off with his disguise, that coat of forest-colored cloth, the hat with the feather tucked into the ribbon; his matted hair streams down his white shirt and she can see the lice moving in it. The sticks in the hearth shift and hiss; night and the forest has come into the kitchen with darkness tangled in its hair.

He strips off his shirt. His skin is the color and texture of vellum. A crisp   50
stripe of hair runs down his belly, his nipples are ripe and dark as poison fruit, but he's so thin you could count the ribs under his skin if only he gave you the time. He strips off his trousers and she can see how hairy his legs are. His genitals, huge. Ah! huge.

The last thing the old lady saw in all this world was a young man, eyes like cinders, naked as a stone, approaching her bed.

The wolf is carnivore incarnate.

When he had finished with her, he licked his chops and quickly dressed himself again, until he was just as he had been when he came through her door. He burned the inedible hair in the fireplace and wrapped the bones up in a napkin that he hid away under the bed in the wooden chest in which he found a clean pair of sheets. These he carefully put on the bed instead of the tell-tale stained ones he stowed away in the laundry basket. He plumped up the pillows and shook out the patchwork quilt, he picked up the Bible from the floor, closed it and laid it on the table. All was as it had been before except that grandmother was gone. The sticks twitched in the grate, the clock ticked and the young man sat patiently, deceitfully beside the bed in granny's nightcap.

Rat-a-tap-tap.

Who's there, he quavers in granny's antique falsetto.   55

Only your granddaughter.

So she came in, bringing with her a flurry of snow that melted in tears on the tiles, and perhaps she was a little disappointed to see only her grandmother sitting beside the fire. But then he flung off the blanket and sprang to the door, pressing his back against it so that she could not get out again.

The girl looked round the room and saw there was not even the indentation of a head on the smooth cheek of the pillow and how, for the first time she'd seen it so, the Bible lay closed on the table. The tick of the clock cracked like a whip. She wanted her knife from her basket, but she did not dare reach for it because his eyes were fixed upon her—huge eyes that now seemed to shine with a unique, interior light, eyes the size of saucers, saucers full of Greek fire, diabolic phosphorescence.

What big eyes you have.

All the better to see you with.   60

No trace at all of the old woman except for a tuft of white hair that had caught in the bark of an unburned log. When the girl saw that, she knew she was in danger of death.

Where is my grandmother?

There's nobody here but we two, my darling.

Now a great howling rose up all around them, near, very near, as close as the kitchen garden, the howling of a multitude of wolves; she knew the worst wolves are hairy on the inside and she shivered, in spite of the scarlet shawl she pulled more closely round herself as if it could protect her although it was as red as the blood she must spill.

Who has come to sing us carols, she said.   65

Those are the voices of my brothers, darling; I love the company of wolves. Look out of the window and you'll see them.

Snow half-caked the lattice and she opened it to look into the garden. It was a white night of moon and snow; the blizzard whirled round the gaunt, grey beasts who squatted on their haunches among the rows of winter cabbage, pointing their sharp snouts to the moon and howling as if their hearts would break. Ten wolves; twenty wolves—so many wolves she could not count them, howling in concert as if demented or deranged. Their eyes reflected the light from the kitchen and shone like a hundred candles.

It is very cold, poor things, she said; no wonder they howl so.

She closed the window on the wolves' threnody° and took off her scarlet shawl, the color of poppies, the color of sacrifices, the color of her menses, and, since her fear did her no good, she ceased to be afraid.

What shall I do with my shawl?   70

Throw it on the fire, dear one. You won't need it again.

She bundled up her shawl and threw it on the blaze, which instantly consumed it. Then she drew her blouse over her head; her small breasts gleamed as if the snow had invaded the room.

What shall I do with my blouse?

threnody: Lament or dirge.

Into the fire with it, too, my pet.

The thin muslin went flaring up the chimney like a magic bird and now 75
off came her skirt, her woolen stockings, her shoes, and on to the fire they went,
too, and were gone for good. The firelight shone through the edges of her skin;
now she was clothed only in her untouched integument° of flesh. This dazzling,
naked she combed out her hair with her fingers; her hair looked white as the snow
outside. Then went directly to the man with red eyes in whose unkempt mane the
lice moved; she stood up on tiptoe and unbuttoned the collar of his shirt.

What big arms you have.

All the better to hug you with.

Every wolf in the world now howled a prothalamion° outside the window
as she freely gave the kiss she owed him.

What big teeth you have!

She saw how his jaw began to slaver and the room was full of the clamor of 80
the forest's Liebestod° but the wise child never flinched, even when he answered:

All the better to eat you with.

The girl burst out laughing; she knew she was nobody's meat. She laughed
at him full in the face, she ripped off his shirt for him and flung it into the fire,
in the fiery wake of her own discarded clothing. The flames danced like dead
souls on Walpurgisnacht,° and the old bones under the bed set up a terrible
clattering, but she did not pay them any heed.

Carnivore incarnate, only immaculate flesh appeases him.

She will lay his fearful head on her lap and she will pick out the lice from
his pelt and perhaps she will put the lice into her mouth and eat them, as he
will bid her, as she would do in a savage marriage ceremony.

The blizzard will die down. 85

The blizzard died down, leaving the mountains as randomly covered with
snow as if a blind woman had thrown a sheet over them, the upper branches of
the forest pines limed, creaking, swollen with the fall.

Snowlight, moonlight, a confusion of paw-prints.

All silent, all still.

Midnight; and the clock strikes. It is Christmas Day, the werewolves' birthday, the door of the solstice stands wide open; let them all sink through.

See! sweet and sound she sleeps in granny's bed, between the paws of the 90
tender wolf.   [1977]

integument: Outer covering, such as animal skin or seed coat.   **prothalamion:** Wed-
ding song.   **Liebestod:** Final aria in Richard Wagner's opera *Tristan und Isolde,* in which
Isolde sings over Tristan's dead body and ultimately dies herself.   **Walpurgisnacht:** May
Day eve, the medieval witches' sabbath.

≡ THINKING ABOUT THE TEXT

1. The story begins with a section about wolves before it gets to the Little
   Red Riding Hood narrative. What image of wolves does this prologue
   convey? What in particular seems the purpose of the extended anecdote
   about the wife with two husbands?

2. Point out various places where Carter diverges from the conventions of the fairy tale.

3. Do you find it surprising that the girl does not get to her grandmother's house first? Do you suspect that the girl is not so innocent?

4. Obviously this is not a story for children. What traditional ideas about females and sexuality is Carter revising?

5. What do you conclude about the girl from her behavior at the end of the story? To what extent is "savage marriage ceremony" (para. 84) indeed an apt term for what occurs?

≡ MAKING COMPARISONS

1. To what extent is Carter's image of wolves different from Perrault's and the Grimms'? Refer to details from all three texts.

2. Several critics have described Carter's versions of fairy tales as feminist. To what extent can this term be applied to Perrault's and the Grimms' narratives as well as to hers? Define what you mean by *feminist*.

3. Would you say Carter's writing style is more realistic than that of Perrault and the Grimms? Or is the term *realism* completely irrelevant in the case of fairy tales? Explain.

≡ WRITING ABOUT ISSUES

1. Choose one of these versions of the Little Red Riding Hood story, and write an essay in which you elaborate a moral that modern *adults* might learn from. Or write an essay in which you explain what an adolescent might learn from Carter's version.

2. Does Carter's version radically depart from Perrault's and the Grimms', or does it basically resemble them? Write an essay that addresses this question by focusing on Carter's story and one of the other two.

3. Write an essay explaining what you think you learned from a fairy tale or other fictional story that you heard as a child. If you want to contrast your thinking about the story now with your thinking about it then, do so. Feel free to compare the story you focus on with any of the versions of Little Red Riding Hood in this cluster.

4. Write your own version of the story of Little Red Riding Hood, and on a separate piece of paper write the moral you think should be drawn from your text. Then give your version to a classmate, and see if he or she can guess your moral.

■ Freedom for Animals: Poems

WILLIAM BLAKE, "The Tyger"

D. H. LAWRENCE, "Snake"

ELIZABETH BISHOP, "The Fish"

THOMAS LUX, "To Help the Monkey Cross the River"

DEAN YOUNG, "Clam Ode"

Since before the Greeks, writers have used animals as symbols. The temptation to see in animal behavior human traits such as evil, sneakiness, tranquility, kindness, or cruelty seems too great for us to resist. The term *anthropomorphize* is used to describe how we superimpose human motives and attitudes on animals. But we are curtailing their freedom when we confine their lives to our assumptions and expectations. When we symbolize animals, we are almost always talking about ourselves. Although it is usually harmless and often insightful when poets anthropomorphize animals, the practice has nevertheless brought grievous harm to wolves, snakes, sharks, and other creatures that have been tortured for centuries by those who see them as irredeemably evil.

Certainly William Blake is talking about our own "deadly terrors" when he writes about tigers. And surely no one really thinks that snakes are inherently evil, even though D. H. Lawrence uses a biblical narrative to talk about temptation. When Elizabeth Bishop writes of the noble fish, or Thomas Lux the cute monkey, or Dean Young the calm clam, they are confining the freedom of these animals but giving us interesting and insightful comments on the human condition.

≡ BEFORE YOU READ

Describe at least one encounter you have had with wildlife, noting how you behaved at the time and what influenced your conduct. What is your attitude toward people who like to hunt or fish? What forms of wildlife, if any, do you think people are justified in fearing or despising? Do you think the notion of animal rights has merit? Identify particular values that your answers reflect.

WILLIAM BLAKE
The Tyger

William Blake (1757–1827) is today considered the major visionary poet, painter, and printmaker in Western culture, although his contemporaries thought him highly eccentric, even mad. A thinker and artist well ahead of his time, Blake is often cited as a forerunner of contemporary secular liberalism, feminism, and even birth control

and divorce. He was a philosophical anti-authoritarian, perhaps even an anarchist. He did brilliant paintings for many of his collections, including Marriage of Heaven and Hell. *"The Tyger," one of the most well-known poems in literature, has engaged critics and ordinary readers alike with its compelling imagery and its deep, mysterious questions.*

Tyger! Tyger! burning bright
In the forests of the night,
What immortal hand or eye
Could frame thy fearful symmetry?

In what distant deeps or skies   5
Burnt the fire of thine eyes?
On what wings dare he aspire?
What the hand, dare seize the fire?

And what shoulder, & what art,
Could twist the sinews of thy heart?   10
And when thy heart began to beat,
What dread hand? & what dread feet?

What the hammer? what the chain?
In what furnace was thy brain?
What the anvil? what dread grasp   15
Dare its deadly terrors clasp?

When the stars threw down their spears,
And water'd heaven with their tears,
Did he smile his work to see?
Did he who made the Lamb make thee?   20

Tyger! Tyger! burning bright
In the forests of the night,
What immortal hand or eye
Dare frame thy fearful symmetry?   *[1794]*

≡ THINKING ABOUT THE TEXT

1. What do you think Blake means in the first stanza by "fearful symmetry"?

2. What images does the poet use to describe the creation of the tiger? What is his purpose?

3. Why does the poet ask if the tiger's creator also made the lamb?

4. Why does Blake change the "could" of stanza 1 to "dare" in the last stanza?

5. Critics have argued over the meaning of this poem for centuries. How do you interpret Blake's question about the creation of the tiger? Is he really asking a more philosophical question?

D. H. LAWRENCE
Snake

David Herbert Lawrence (1885–1930) was a leading novelist and short-story writer in the first half of the twentieth century. The son of a coal miner and a former schoolteacher, he describes his English working-class upbringing in his autobiographical novel Sons and Lovers *(1913). Probably he remains best known for his 1928 novel* Lady Chatterley's Lover. *For many years, it was banned in England and the United States because it explicitly described the sexual relationship between an aristocratic woman and her husband's gamekeeper. In most of his work, Lawrence endorses human passion, although he argued that people needed to exist in harmony with nature as well as with one another. Besides writing fiction, he painted and wrote poetry. "Snake," published in 1913, is based on Lawrence's stay in Sicily, one of the many places he went as he searched for a land friendly to his ideals.*

A snake came to my water-trough
On a hot, hot day, and I in pyjamas for the heat,
To drink there.

In the deep, strange-scented shade of the great dark carob-tree
I came down the steps with my pitcher   5
And must wait, must stand and wait, for there he was at the trough
    before me.

He reached down from a fissure in the earth-wall in the gloom
And trailed his yellow-brown slackness soft-bellied down, over the edge
    of the stone trough
And rested his throat upon the stone bottom,
And where the water had dripped from the tap, in a small clearness,   10
He sipped with his straight mouth,
Softly drank through his straight gums, into his slack long body,
Silently.

Someone was before me at my water-trough,
And I, like a second comer, waiting.   15

He lifted his head from his drinking, as cattle do,
And looked at me vaguely, as drinking cattle do,
And flickered his two-forked tongue from his lips, and mused a moment,
And stooped and drank a little more,
Being earth-brown, earth-golden from the burning bowels of the earth   20
On the day of Sicilian July, with Etna smoking.

The voice of my education said to me
He must be killed,
For in Sicily the black, black snakes are innocent, the gold are
    venomous.

And voices in me said, If you were a man   25
You would take a stick and break him now, and finish him off.

But must I confess how I liked him,
How glad I was he had come like a guest in quiet, to drink at my
        water-trough
And depart peaceful, pacified, and thankless,
Into the burning bowels of this earth?   30

Was it cowardice, that I dared not kill him?
Was it perversity, that I longed to talk to him?
Was it humility, to feel so honoured?
I felt so honoured.

And yet those voices: 35
If you were not afraid, you would kill him!

And truly I was afraid, I was most afraid,
But even so, honoured still more
That he should seek my hospitality
From out the dark door of the secret earth.   40

He drank enough
And lifted his head, dreamily, as one who has drunken,
And flickered his tongue like a forked night on the air, so black;
Seeming to lick his lips,
And looked around like a god, unseeing, into the air,   45
And slowly turned his head,
And slowly, very slowly, as if thrice adream,
Proceeded to draw his slow length curving round
And climb again the broken bank of my wall-face.

And as he put his head into that dreadful hole,   50
And as he slowly drew up, snake-easing his shoulders, and entered
        farther,
A sort of horror, a sort of protest against his withdrawing into that
        horrid black hole,
Deliberately going into the blackness, and slowly drawing himself after,
Overcame me now his back was turned.

I looked round, I put down my pitcher,   55
I picked up a clumsy log
And threw it at the water-trough with a clatter.

I think it did not hit him,
But suddenly that part of him that was left behind convulsed in
        undignified haste,
Writhed like lightning, and was gone   60
Into the black hole, the earth-lipped fissure in the wall-front,
At which, in the intense still noon, I stared with fascination.

And immediately I regretted it.
I thought how paltry, how vulgar, what a mean act!
I despised myself and the voices of my accursed human education.   65

And I thought of the albatross,°
And I wished he would come back, my snake.

For he seemed to me again like a king,
Like a king in exile, uncrowned in the underworld,
Now due to be crowned again.   70

And so, I missed my chance with one of the lords
Of life.
And I have something to expiate;
A pettiness.   *[1913]*

66 albatross: In Samuel Taylor Coleridge's "Rime of the Ancient Mariner," a seaman brings misfortune to the crew of his ship by killing an albatross, an ocean bird.

≡ THINKING ABOUT THE TEXT

1. What did you associate with snakes before reading this poem? Does Lawrence push you to look at snakes differently, or does his poem endorse the view you already had? Develop your answer by referring to specific lines.

2. Discuss the poem as an argument involving various "voices." How do you think you would have reacted to the snake if you had been the speaker? What "voices" might you have heard inside your own mind? What people or institutions would these "voices" have come from?

3. Why does the speaker throw the log just as the snake is leaving? Note the explanation the speaker gives as well as the judgment he then makes about his act. Do both make sense to you? Why, or why not?

4. Lawrence begins many lines with the word *and*. What is the effect of his doing so?

5. In "Snake," Lawrence writes positively about an animal that is often feared. Think of a similar poem that you might write. What often-feared animal would you choose? What positive qualities would you point out or suggest in describing this animal? If you wish, try actually writing such a poem.

≡ MAKING COMPARISONS

1. Both tigers and snakes are feared. How do Blake and Lawrence use this idea?

2. Does Lawrence seem more self-conscious about his attitude toward his animal than Blake?

3. What assumptions about these poets' animals would you question?

ELIZABETH BISHOP
The Fish

Although she also wrote short stories, Elizabeth Bishop (1911–1979) is primarily known for her poetry, winning both the Pulitzer Prize and the National Book Award for it. Born in Worcester, Massachusetts, she spent much of her youth in Nova Scotia. As an adult, she lived in various places, including New York City, Florida, Mexico, and Brazil. Much of her poetry observes and reflects on a particular object or figure. Such is the case with "The Fish," which Bishop wrote in 1940 and then included in her 1946 book North and South.

I caught a tremendous fish
and held him beside the boat
half out of water, with my hook
fast in a corner of his mouth.
He didn't fight.   5
He hadn't fought at all.
He hung a grunting weight,
battered and venerable
and homely. Here and there
his brown skin hung in strips   10
like ancient wall-paper,
and its pattern of darker brown
was like wall-paper:
shapes like full-blown roses
stained and lost through age.   15
He was speckled with barnacles,
fine rosettes of lime,
and infested
with tiny white sea-lice,
and underneath two or three   20
rags of green weed hung down.
While his gills were breathing in
the terrible oxygen
— the frightening gills,
fresh and crisp with blood,   25
that can cut so badly —
I thought of the coarse white flesh
packed in like feathers,
the big bones and the little bones,
the dramatic reds and blacks   30
of his shiny entrails,
and the pink swim-bladder
like a big peony.
I looked into his eyes

which were far larger than mine   35
but shallower, and yellowed,
the irises backed and packed
with tarnished tinfoil
seen through the lenses
of old scratched isinglass.°   40
They shifted a little, but not
to return my stare.
— It was more like the tipping
of an object toward the light.
I admired his sullen face,   45
the mechanism of his jaw,
and then I saw
that from his lower lip
— if you could call it a lip —
grim, wet, and weapon-like,   50
hung five old pieces of fish-line,
or four and a wire leader
with the swivel still attached,
with all their five big hooks
grown firmly in his mouth.   55
A green line, frayed at the end
where he broke it, two heavier lines,
and a fine black thread
still crimped from the strain and snap
when it broke and he got away.   60
Like medals with their ribbons
frayed and wavering,
a five-haired beard of wisdom
trailing from his aching jaw.
I stared and stared   65
and victory filled up
the little rented boat,
from the pool of bilge
where oil had spread a rainbow
around the rusted engine   70
to the bailer rusted orange,
the sun-cracked thwarts,
the oarlocks on their strings,
the gunnels — until everything
was rainbow, rainbow, rainbow!   75
And I let the fish go.   *[1946]*

---

40 isinglass: A substitute for glass made from mica.

≡ THINKING ABOUT THE TEXT

1. Does the speaker change her attitude toward the fish, or does it stay pretty much the same? Support your reasoning by referring to specific lines. Are you surprised that the speaker lets the fish go? Why, or why not? How effective a conclusion is her release of the fish?

2. To what extent is the speaker describing the fish objectively? In what ways, if any, does her description of him seem to reflect her own particular values? Refer to specific lines.

3. The speaker reports that "victory filled up / the little rented boat" (lines 66–67). Whose victory might she have in mind? Why might she use this word? Often, a victory for one is a defeat for another. Is that the case here?

4. Where does the poem refer to acts and instruments of seeing? What conclusions might be drawn from these references?

5. How significant is it that the fish is male?

≡ MAKING COMPARISONS

1. What would you say to someone who argues that Bishop's speaker is more admirable than Lawrence's speaker because she lets the animal go free?

2. With each of these three poems, consider what you learn about the speaker's own state of mind. Does one of these poems tell you more about its speaker's thoughts than the other poems do? Support your answer by referring to specific lines.

3. Bishop's poem is one long, continuous stanza, whereas Blake and Lawrence divide theirs into several stanzas. Does this difference in strategy lead to a significant difference in effect? Do you consider one of these strategies better than the other? Explain your reasoning.

THOMAS LUX
To Help the Monkey Cross the River

Thomas Lux (b. 1946) was born in Northampton, Massachusetts, and attended Emerson College in Boston. He is the author of numerous volumes of poetry, including The Street of Clocks *(2001) and* The Cradle Place: Poems *(2004), as well as the recipient of prestigious grants and prizes. His latest collection is* God Particles *(2008). He has taught at Sarah Lawrence College; the University of California, Irvine; and Emerson College. He currently holds the Bourne Chair in poetry at Georgia Tech in Atlanta, where he lives. The following poem is from* The Cradle Place: Poems.

which he must
cross, by swimming, for fruits and nuts,
to help him
I sit with my rifle on a platform
high in a tree, same side of the river   5
as the hungry monkey. How does this assist
him? When he swims for it
I look first upriver: predators move faster with
the current than against it.
If a crocodile is aimed from upriver to eat the monkey   10
and an anaconda from downriver burns
with the same ambition, I do
the math, algebra, angles, rate-of-monkey,
croc- and snake-speed, and if, if
it looks as though the anaconda or the croc   15
will reach the monkey
before he attains the river's far bank,
I raise my rifle and fire
one, two, three, even four times into the river
just behind the monkey   20
to hurry him up a little.
Shoot the snake, the crocodile?
They're just doing their jobs,
but the monkey, the monkey
has little hands like a child's,   25
and the smart ones, in a cage, can be taught to smile.   [2004]

≡ THINKING ABOUT THE TEXT

1. Perhaps irony is not a strong enough notion for the juxtaposition between the title and the last line. Explain what, in fact, appears to be the
   speaker's intention for the monkey. How would you define the speaker's
   use of *help*?

2. Why might the speaker be sympathetic to the snake and the croc? Are
   you sympathetic to the speaker?

3. What is the effect of the repeated "if" in line 14 and "monkey" in line 24?

4. Lux plays with the reader's expectations. What did you assume Lux was
   going to do "to help" after you read the first nineteen lines (up to ". . . into
   the river")?

5. What is the effect of the phrase "in a cage" (line 26)? Does this change
   the meaning of the entire poem?

≡ MAKING COMPARISONS

1. Perhaps the speaker in Lux's poem is not what he appears to be at first. Which speaker in the three other poems does he most closely resemble? Why?

2. Do you think the speaker in Lawrence's poem would approve of a cute monkey in a cage?

3. Would the speaker in Bishop's poem be upset by Lux's speaker's tone and attitude toward the monkey?

DEAN YOUNG
Clam Ode

Dean Young (b. 1955) was born in Columbia, Pennsylvania. He is the author of ten books of poetry and poetics, most recently 7 Poets, 4 Days, 1 Book *(2009) and* The Art of Recklessness *(2010). He currently holds an endowed chair in poetry at the University of Texas at Austin. The following poem appeared in* The Best American Poetry 2006. *Somewhat tongue-in-cheek, Young writes, "One of the biggest challenges this poem presented was how not to confuse the spelling of clam and calm."*

One attempts to be significant on a grand scale
in the knock-down battle of life
but settles.
I love the expression "happy as a clam,"
how it imparts buoyant emotion   5
to a rather, when you get down to it,
nonexpressive creature: In piles of ice
it awaits its doom pretty much the same
as on the ocean's floor it awaits
life's banquet and bouquet and sexual joys.   10
Some barnacles we know are eggs dropped from outer space
but clams, who has a clue how they reproduce?
By trading clouds?
The Chinese thought them capable of prolonging life
while clams doubtlessly considered   15
the Chinese the opposite.
I remember the jawbreakers my dad would buy me
on the wharf at Stone Harbor,
every thirty seconds you'd take out
the one you were working on   20
to check what color it turned.

What does this have to do with clams?
A feeling.
States of feeling, unlike states of the upper Midwest,
are difficult to name.   25
That is why music was invented,
which caused a whole new slue of feelings
and is why ever since
people have had more feelings than they know what to do with
so you can see music sorta backfired   30
like a fire extinguisher that turns out to be a flame thrower.
They look somewhat alike, don't they?
If you're buying one be sure
you don't get the other,
the boys in the stockroom are stoners   35
who like to wear their pants falling down
and deserve their own island in *Gulliver's Travels*.
The clam however remains calm.
Green is the color of the kelp it rests on,
having a helluva wingding calm.   40
I am going to kill you in butter and white wine
so forgive me, great clam spirit,
join yourself to me through the emissary
of this al dente fettuccini
so I may be qualmless and happy as you.   *[2005]*   45

≡ THINKING ABOUT THE TEXT

1. Although the poem has a serious theme, the poet, not surprisingly in a poem about clams, uses humor. Point out some amusing lines.

2. What do you think the common expression "happy as a clam" means?

3. Why does the narrator start talking about feelings and music?

4. What does the poet mean when he says: "The clam however remains calm" (line 38)? Is this a positive response? Why does he use "however"?

5. Were you surprised by the word *qualmless* in the last line? Were you expecting *calmness* or perhaps *clamness*? What does he mean by this term?

≡ MAKING COMPARISONS

1. Why do you think there is humor in this poem and not in the others?

2. Young eats the clam. Does this make a significant difference in evaluating the poem?

3. Compare the theme of this poem with that of Bishop's poem.

≡ WRITING ABOUT ISSUES

1. Choose one of the poems in this cluster, and write an essay describing and evaluating its speaker. As you develop your judgment, acknowledge and address at least one other possible way of looking at this person: that is, a different judgment that someone might make of him or her.

2. Write an essay suggesting what one of the speakers in these poems might say about another. What, for example, might Bishop's speaker say about Lawrence's? Support your conjecture with details from both texts.

3. Write an essay arguing for or against how you treated a certain animal in a certain situation. Choose a situation in which you did, in fact, consider acting differently at the time. If you wish, you can draw analogies between your experience and any of those depicted in this cluster.

4. Argue that each of these poets is talking about human behavior, not animal behavior.

≣ Trapped in Stereotypes: Poems

CHRYSTOS, "Today Was a Bad Day like TB"

LOUISE ERDRICH, "Dear John Wayne"

DWIGHT OKITA, "In Response to Executive Order 9066"

DAVID HERNANDEZ, "Pigeons"

PAT MORA, "Legal Alien"

TOI DERRICOTTE, "Black Boys Play the Classics"

NAOMI SHIHAB NYE, "Blood"

When pressed, thoughtful people would agree that each of us has an individual personality and attributes that make us different from others. No one is an exact duplicate: even identical twins have both subtle and significant differences. Even so, cultures tend to lump together whole groups under dubious but convenient generalizations: used car dealers are dishonest, surfers are laid-back slackers, and computer geniuses are geeks. Usually based on limited, anecdotal, and often highly contextual historical and cultural evidence, these generalizations have a way of taking hold in a society long after the original context has disappeared (if there ever was one). Does anyone really think that dumb-blond jokes had any original validity? Is considering each person on his or her own merits too complicated?

When ethnic groups are stereotyped, their members may suffer consequences that are significantly more severe than those endured by, say, absent-minded professors. Some stereotypes are benign: as children growing up in New York, we routinely heard about industrious Chinese or hardworking Germans. But we also heard many negative generalizations that went hand in hand with racial discrimination and psychological damage. Members of the dominant groups in America are often oblivious to the ways that members of minority groups internalize destructive and distorted images of themselves, often seeing themselves as inferior to the dominant group and irredeemably other. They become trapped in images rampant in the culture and struggle daily to overcome the limited reality these stereotypes portray. The following seven poems represent aspects of this struggle in various ways — some with anger, resentment, and despair, others with thoughtful reflection, but all with an awareness of the pain that thoughtless stereotypes have on millions of Americans.

≣ BEFORE YOU READ

Do you think of yourself as an ethnic American? Have you ever seen the term *English American* or *Dutch American*? What's the difference between those terms and *African American* or *Irish American*? Do you think ethnic traditions should be preserved, or should they be replaced with American traditions? Can these traditions coexist?

CHRYSTOS
Today Was a Bad Day like TB

Born in San Francisco of a Lithuanian/Alsace-Lorraine mother and a Native American father of the Menominee tribe, Chrystos (b. 1946) writes in the outsider traditions of her ancestry, her lesbian perspective, and her geographical position on Bainbridge Island off the coast of the Pacific Northwest. She is a women's and native rights advocate, a working artist, and a poet. Her poetry collections include Not Vanishing *(1988),* Dream On *(1991),* In Her I Am *(1993),* Fire Power *(1995), and the 1994 winner of the Audre Lorde International Poetry Competition,* Fugitive Colors. *In 2007, she published* Some Poems by People I Like. *She is a Lannan Foundation fellow and the 1995 recipient of the Sappho Award of Distinction. The poem reprinted here is from* Not Vanishing.

> For Amanda White
>
> Saw whites clap during a sacred dance
> Saw young blond hippie boy with a red stone pipe°
>   My eyes burned him up
> He smiled   *This is a Sioux pipe* he said from his sportscar
>   *Yes*   I hiss   *I'm wondering how you got it*   5
>   *& the name is Lakota not Sioux*
> *I'll tell you* he said all friendly & liberal as only
>   those with no pain can be
>   I turned away   Can't charm me   can't bear to know
> thinking of the medicine bundle I saw opened up in a glass case   10
>   with a small white card beside it
>   naming the rich whites who say they
>   "own" it
> Maybe they have an old Indian grandma back in time
>   to excuse themselves   15
> Today was a day I wanted to beat up the smirking man wearing
> a pack with a Haida design from Moe's bookstore
> Listen Moe's   How many Indians do you have working there?
> How much money are you sending the Haida people
> to use their sacred Raven design?   20
>   You probably have an Indian grandma too
>   whose name you don't know
>   Today was a day like TB
>   you cough & cough trying to get it out
>   all that comes   25
>   is blood & spit   [1988]

---

2 red stone pipe: Traditionally, sacred peace pipes were made of red catlinite, a fine-grained stone.

≡ THINKING ABOUT THE TEXT

1. What argument about the ways whites relate to Native Americans is Chrystos making? What assumptions about whites does Chrystos seem to have? What stereotypes does she seem to harbor?

2. Might you have clapped during a Lakota dance? During a Catholic Mass? What is the "it" in line 24 that the poet is trying to get out? Do you think she is angry with her readers?

3. Is the ending too stark or perhaps too crude? Might the language have been more indirect and subtle, or is it appropriate to the theme?

4. Americans who are part of the "mainstream" — that is, white, male, middle class, or heterosexual — sometimes get annoyed when those who are not complain about bias, probably because the offense was inadvertent. (Think of Atlanta Braves fans doing "the tomahawk chop.") The young man in this poem, for example, seems quite oblivious of giving offense. Who determines who is right in these situations?

LOUISE ERDRICH
Dear John Wayne

Born in Little Falls, Minnesota, Louise Erdrich (b. 1954) is a member of the Turtle Mountain Band of the Chippewa tribe. Her parents taught at the Bureau of Indian Affairs Boarding School in North Dakota, where Erdrich worked as a beet weeder, waitress, and teacher. She earned a B.A. from Dartmouth College in 1976 and an M.A. from the writing program at Johns Hopkins University in 1979 and has won many awards and fellowships for her writing, including the National Book Critics Circle Award in 1984 for her first novel, Love Medicine. *Although she writes both poetry and nonfiction, she has received the most acclaim for her novels, which include* The Beet Queen *(1986),* Tracks *(1988),* The Bingo Palace *(1994), and* Tales of Burning Love *(1996). Some recent novels are* The Master Butchers Singing Club *(2003),* Four Souls *(2004), and* Shadow Fog *(2010).* The Game of Silence, *a children's book, was published in 2005. "Dear John Wayne" is taken from* Jacklight, *her 1984 collection of poems.*

August and the drive-in picture is packed.
We lounge on the hood of the Pontiac
surrounded by the slow-burning spirals they sell
at the window, to vanquish the hordes of mosquitoes.
Nothing works. They break through the smoke-screen for blood.   5

Always the look-out spots the Indians first,
spread north to south, barring progress.
The Sioux, or Cheyenne, or some bunch

in spectacular columns, arranged like SAC° missiles,
their feathers bristling in the meaningful sunset.   10

The drum breaks. There will be no parlance.
Only the arrows whining, a death-cloud of nerves
swarming down on the settlers
who die beautifully, tumbling like dust weeds
into the history that brought us all here   15
together: this wide screen beneath the sign of the bear.

The sky fills, acres of blue squint and eye
that the crowd cheers. His face moves over us,
a thick cloud of vengeance, pitted
like the land that was once flesh. Each rut,   20
each scar makes a promise: It is
not over, this fight, not as long as you resist.

Everything we see belongs to us.
A few laughing Indians fall over the hood
slipping in the hot spilled butter.   25
The eye sees a lot, John, but the heart is so blind.
How will you know what you own?

He smiles, a horizon of teeth
the credits reel over, and then the white fields
again blowing in the true-to-life dark.   30
The dark films over everything.
We get into the car
scratching our mosquito bites, speechless and small
as people are when the movie is done.
We are back in ourselves.   35

How can we help but keep hearing his voice,
the flip side of the sound-track, still playing:
Come on, boys, we've got them
where we want them, drunk, running.
They will give us what we want, what we need: 40
The heart is a strange wood inside of everything
we see, burning, doubling, splitting out of its skin.   *[1984]*

9 SAC: The Strategic Air Command was part of America's nuclear deterrent.

≡ THINKING ABOUT THE TEXT

1. While watching John Wayne fighting the Sioux or Cheyenne, Erdrich realizes she is not the intended audience for this mid-twentieth-century
   Western. Why not? Who is? What are the traditional assumptions
   about the Native Americans in the movies from this era?

2. When John Wayne and other movie heroes defeat "our" enemies, do you ever doubt that you are on the same side? Would Native Americans see these films differently than a mainstream audience? Have you seen recent films about Native Americans in which the conventional us-versus-them plot was disrupted in some way?

3. What do you think of Erdrich's transition from "hordes of mosquitoes" (line 4) to "Always the look-out spots the Indians first" (line 6)? What does "laughing Indians" mean in line 24?

4. Why does Erdrich say that "the heart is so blind" (line 26)? What does "They will give us what we want, what we need" refer to in line 40? Is that what John Wayne actually thought?

5. Movies give us a powerful sense of our history and our identity as Americans. Historical films about wars and heroes seem especially influential. Do you think Erdrich is overly sensitive? Do you think filmmakers have a responsibility to portray the ethnic diversity of America positively?

≣ MAKING COMPARISONS

1. If Chrystos's tone is bitter and angry, how might you characterize Erdrich's?

2. Compare the arguments both poets make about how whites perceive Native Americans. Which is more persuasive? Why?

3. How do you imagine Chrystos would respond to the movie? Erdrich to the dance?

DWIGHT OKITA

In Response to Executive Order 9066

A third-generation Japanese American, poet and playwright Dwight Okita (b. 1958) won an Illinois Art Council Fellowship for poetry in 1988. Although Crossing with the Light *(1992), from which this poem is taken, is his first book of poetry, Okita has been more active in promoting the performance of poetry than the printing of it, and he is well known as a "slam" poet at open-mike readings in Chicago. A member of the large Japanese American community that developed in Chicago as a result of the migration from the West after the bitter experience of the internment camps during World War II, Okita expresses his family history in his poetry and plays. His dramas include* The Rainy Season *(1992) and* The Salad Bowl Dance *(1993). His book* The Prospect of My Arrival *(2008) was nominated for the Amazon Breakthrough Novel Award.*

All Americans of Japanese Descent
Must Report to Relocation Centers

Dear Sirs:
Of course I'll come. I've packed my galoshes
and three packets of tomato seeds. Denise calls them
love apples. My father says where we're going
they won't grow.   5

I am a fourteen-year-old girl with bad spelling
and a messy room. If it helps any, I will tell you
I have always felt funny using chopsticks
and my favorite food is hot dogs.
My best friend is a white girl named Denise —   10
we look at boys together. She sat in front of me
all through grade school because of our names:
O'Connor, Ozawa. I know the back of Denise's head very well.

I tell her she's going bald. She tells me I copy on tests.
We're best friends.   15

I saw Denise today in Geography class.
She was sitting on the other side of the room.
"You're trying to start a war," she said, "giving secrets
away to the Enemy. Why can't you keep your big
mouth shut?"   20

I didn't know what to say.
I gave her a packet of tomato seeds
and asked her to plant them for me, told her
when the first tomato ripened
she'd miss me.   [1992]   25

≡ THINKING ABOUT THE TEXT

1. What claim is Okita making in the last stanza? On what assumption about friendship is it based?

2. During the U.S. government's internment of Japanese American citizens, thousands were told to leave their homes to live in relocation centers for the duration of the war. To represent this complex historical event, do you think it effective to have a young girl writing a letter about being shunned by her best friend?

3. Explain Okita's use of the tomato seeds throughout the poem (lines 3, 22). What about other concrete words: *galoshes* (line 2), *chopsticks* (line 8), *hot dogs* (line 9)?

4. Since there was no evidence that Japanese American citizens ever gave any "secrets / away to the Enemy" (lines 18–19) during World War II, why do you think Denise and millions of other Americans made that assumption?

≡ MAKING COMPARISONS

1. Compare the tone of Okita's poem with that of Chrystos's. What emotions do you see in each?

2. Okita creates a young female narrator to speak for him. Does this make his poem less direct than Chrystos's and Erdrich's? Who might be appropriate narrators in their poems?

3. Is the alienation described by Okita more or less painful than that described by Chrystos and Erdrich?

DAVID HERNANDEZ
Pigeons

An active member of Chicago's arts community, David Hernandez (b. 1946) has published several books of poetry, including Despertando / Waking Up *(1991),* Satin City Lullaby *(1986), and* Rooftop Piper *(1991), from which this poem is taken. He has written, recited, and taught poetry for more than thirty years and was commissioned to write a poem for Chicago's 150th anniversary in 1987. In addition to his own publications, Hernandez has edited three poetry anthologies. His recent work includes the poetry collections* Always Danger *(2006) and* Hoodwinked *(2011), and a young adult novel,* A House Waiting for Music *(2003).*

Pigeons are the spiks of Birdland.
   They are survivors of blood, fire and stone.
      They can't afford to fly south
        or a Florida winter home.

Most everybody passing up a pigeon pack   5
tries to break it up because they move funny
and seem to be dancing like young street thugs
with an 18-foot, 10-speaker Sanyo book box radio
on a 2-foot red shoulder strap.
                Pigeons have feathers of a different color.   10
                They are too bright to be dull
                and too dull to be bright
                so they are not accepted anywhere.
      Nobody wants to give pigeons a job.
      Parakeets, canaries and parrots   15
      have the market sewn up as far as that goes.
      They live in fancy cages, get 3 meals a day
      for a song and dance routine.
      When was the last time you saw a pigeon
      in someone's home?   20

/

Unless they bleach their feathers white
and try to pass off as doves,
you will never see pet pigeons.
Besides, their accents give them away
when they start cooing.   25

Once in a while, some creature will treat them decent.
    They are known as pigeon ladies, renegades,
        or bleeding-heart Liberals.
                        What they do is build these wooden cages
                            on rooftops that look like huge   30
                        pigeon housing projects
                    where they freeze during the winters
                and get their little claws stuck in tar
            on hot summer days
No wonder they are pigeon-toed.   35
I tell you,
            Pigeons are the spiks of Birdland.   [1991]

≡ THINKING ABOUT THE TEXT

1. Hernandez uses the pigeon simile to comment on the place of Latinos in Birdland/America. What specific comparisons does he make? What is his larger argument?

2. Is this poem a complaint or an accusation of Birdland/America? Do you see some validity in what Hernandez says?

3. Does he press the bird comparison too far? Not far enough? What about attempts to eradicate pigeons or their reputation as disease carriers? How far should a poet carry such similes or metaphors? How far should the reader?

4. Is *spiks* an appropriate word to use in a poem? What if a white person (a dove?) used the term? What does Hernandez mean by "pigeon-toed" (line 35)?

5. Is the poet being ironic about those who try to treat the pigeons decently? What would he have preferred?

≡ MAKING COMPARISONS

1. How would you compare Hernandez's complaint against the liberals with Chrystos's against the hippie?

2. Hernandez's poem seems more ambitious than some of the other poems. Do you think he is trying to paint a fuller picture of discrimination?

3. Which of the poetic devices in these first four poems strikes you as the most effective? The least? Why?

PAT MORA
Legal Alien

Pat Mora (b. 1942) was born in El Paso, Texas. She earned a B.A. from Texas Western College in 1963 and an M.A. from the University of Texas, El Paso, in 1967. She is a versatile writer of many children's books, essays, and poems. Her poems are, according to the New York Times, *"proudly bilingual." Her sixth collection,* Adobe Odes *(2006), was praised for turning its back on hopelessness, "finding a way to delight in the sensual world as well as its people," and a "must-have for libraries serving Latino communities." Her latest collection is* Dizzy in Your Eyes *(2010). Mora lives in Santa Fe, New Mexico. "Legal Alien" is from* Chants *(1984) and focuses on a common Chicana theme: the difficulties of living in two cultures simultaneously.*

Bi-lingual, Bi-cultural,
able to slip from "How's life?"
to *"Me'stan volviendo loca,"*°
able to sit in a paneled office
drafting memos in smooth English,   5
able to order in fluent Spanish
at a Mexican restaurant,
American but hyphenated,
viewed by Anglos as perhaps exotic,
perhaps inferior, definitely different,   10
viewed by Mexicans as alien,
(their eyes say, "You may speak
Spanish but you're not like me")
an American to Mexicans
a Mexican to Americans   15
a handy token
sliding back and forth
between the fringes of both worlds
by smiling
by masking the discomfort   20
of being pre-judged
Bi-laterally.   *[1984]*

≣ THINKING ABOUT THE TEXT

1. Was your first response to the opening line to think that such a situation is an advantage? Is that Mora's intent?

2. What advantages does being bicultural have? What disadvantages?

3 *"Me'stan volviendo loca"*: They're driving me crazy (Spanish).

3. What other Americans are referred to as "hyphenated"? Do you think the same pluses and minuses apply?

4. Is the title appropriate? Explain.

5. Explain the significance of the "token" metaphor in line 16.

≡ MAKING COMPARISONS

1. Mora sees some advantage to being bicultural. Do any of the other poets?

2. Compare Mora's tone with Chrystos's.

3. Which of the stereotypes in these poems seems the most psychologically damaging? Why?

TOI DERRICOTTE
Black Boys Play the Classics

Toi Derricotte (b. 1941) was born in Louisiana and was influenced as a child by her Creole and Catholic background. She graduated from Wayne State University in 1965. The first of her six books, The Empress of the Death House, *was published in 1978. Her latest collection of poems and stories,* Gathering Ground, *was published in 2006. Often compared to Sylvia Plath and Anne Sexton, Derricotte writes poems that, according to the poet and critic Marilyn Hacker, are "honest, fine-boned, deceptively simple . . . and deadly accurate." She is currently a professor of English at the University of Pittsburgh. The following poem is from* Tender *(1997).*

The most popular "act" in
Penn Station
is the three black kids in ratty
sneakers & T-shirts playing
two violins and a cello — Brahms.   5
White men in business suits
have already dug into their pockets
as they pass and they toss in
a dollar or two without stopping.
Brown men in work-soiled khakis   10
stand with their mouths open,
arms crossed on their bellies
as if they themselves have always
wanted to attempt those bars.
One white boy, three, sits   15
cross-legged in front of his

idols — in ecstasy —
their slick, dark faces,
their thin, wiry arms,
who must begin to look   20
like angels!
Why does this trembling
pull us?
A: *Beneath the surface we are one.*
B: *Amazing! I did not think that they could speak this tongue.*   [1997] 25

☰ THINKING ABOUT THE TEXT

1. Why do the "brown men" (line 10) respond as they do? Why do the "white men" (line 6)?

2. Why does the poet offer a description of the boys' clothes? Does it have to do with our stereotyped expectations?

3. What are some possible meanings for "pull us" (line 23)?

4. Explain what you think Derricotte means by the last line.

5. How would you state the theme of this poem? Do you agree with it? Who is the "we" in the next-to-last line?

☰ MAKING COMPARISONS

1. How does Derricotte's tone differ from Chrystos's tone? From Hernandez's?

2. How does the end of this poem differ from the ends of the other poems in this cluster? Is it more effective or less effective?

3. If you were to rewrite "Black Boys Play the Classics" as a first-person poem (as Okita's poem demonstrates), which character from this poem would you choose, and why? How would a different point of view change the poem?

NAOMI SHIHAB NYE

Blood

Naomi Shihab Nye (b. 1952) was born to a Lutheran German American mother and a Muslim Palestinian American father in St. Louis. Her parents moved to the Middle East near Jerusalem, where her father edited the Jerusalem Times, *for which Nye, at fourteen, wrote a weekly column. Eventually turmoil forced their return to America. They settled in Texas, and Nye graduated from Trinity University in San Antonio in 1974. She has published books for children and adolescents with subject matter she hopes will dispel stereotypes and foster an understanding of "difference." Her poetic*

focus is often on the Palestinian Diaspora and on themes of our common humanity. Her books include 19 Varieties of Gazelle *(2002) and* You and Yours: Poems *(2005). "Blood" is from* Yellow Glove *(1986).*

"A true Arab knows how to catch a fly in his hands,"
my father would say. And he'd prove it,
cupping the buzzer instantly
while the host with the swatter stared.

In the spring our palms peeled like snakes.   5
True Arabs believed watermelon could heal fifty ways.
I changed these to fit the occasion.

Years before, a girl knocked,
wanted to see the Arab.
I said we didn't have one.   10
After that, my father told me who he was,
"Shihab" — "shooting star" —
a good name, borrowed from the sky.
Once I said, "When we die, we give it back?"
He said that's what a true Arab would say.   15

Today the headlines clot in my blood.
A little Palestinian dangles a truck on the front page.
Homeless fig, this tragedy with a terrible root
is too big for us. What flag can we wave?
I wave the flag of stone and seed,   20
table mat stitched in blue.

I call my father, we talk around the news.
It is too much for him,
neither of his two languages can reach it.
I drive into the country to find sheep, cows,   25
to plead with the air:
Who calls anyone *civilized*?
Where can the crying heart graze?
What does a true Arab do now?   *[1986]*

≡ **THINKING ABOUT THE TEXT**

1. What is your response to the girl who comes looking "to see the Arab" (line 9)? What is the speaker's response?

2. What do you think the father means by "a true Arab"? Is there a true American? A true man? Woman? Texan?

3. What is the father's response to the news about the Middle East? What is the speaker's? What is yours?

4. What is the purpose of the speaker's drive into the country?

5. How would you answer the questions the speaker asks in the last stanza?

≡ MAKING COMPARISONS

1. Compare Nye's bicultural perspective to Mora's. Is Nye's status more precarious than Mora's in contemporary America?

2. Which of the speakers in all these poems seems angriest? Saddest? The most understanding?

3. What seems to be the most common theme among the poems?

≡ WRITING ABOUT ISSUES

1. Write a journal entry from either Chrystos's or Erdrich's perspective that comments on the writing of the poem, what you (as the author) were trying to do, how you feel about stereotyping, and what response you are hoping for from readers.

2. Write an essay that compares the stereotyping that occurs in "Pigeons" and "Dear John Wayne." Comment on its origins, consequences, and possible solutions.

3. Write an essay that explores the kind of stereotyping you were exposed to as a child and an adolescent in your family, in your peer group, or in the larger culture.

4. After doing research on an ethnic group not represented here, locate a poet from that group and write a brief report on his or her work.

≡ A Dream of Freedom: Poems by Langston Hughes

LANGSTON HUGHES, "Let America Be America Again"

LANGSTON HUGHES, "Open Letter to the South"

LANGSTON HUGHES, "Theme for English B"

LANGSTON HUGHES, "Harlem"

Inspired by two of the great poetic voices of American life, Walt Whitman and Carl Sandburg, Langston Hughes is often thought of as the African American poet laureate, a writer who is able to sing eloquently about the reality and idealism of democracy in America. He was committed to telling the truth about the lives of black people. In the introduction to *The Collected Poems of Langston Hughes*, it is noted that Hughes wrote of "the joys and sorrows, the trials and triumphs, of ordinary black folk, in the language of their typical speech and composed out of a genuine love of these people."

In response to the Depression of the 1930s, Hughes became radicalized by the poverty and injustice he saw everywhere in black America. His poems from this period are radical, indeed. "Open Letter to the South" calls for a socialist solidarity against oppression, and "Let America Be America Again" poignantly laments the wide gulf that often existed between the idealistic rhetoric of democracy and the appalling social reality of segregation. Although he later became less radical in his poetry, "Theme for English B" and "Harlem" still reflect his belief that poetry is a form of social action. At the heart of all Hughes's poetry was the deferred dream of African Americans to achieve the freedom and equality promised to all in America.

≡ BEFORE YOU READ

Can you imagine what would have happened to your personality if a dream of yours (perhaps going to college, playing a sport, or marrying someone you loved deeply) were denied? What would you do if America was not living up to its stated ideals or if those ideals were suddenly altered significantly? Would you express your disappointment publicly or only privately?

LANGSTON HUGHES
Let America Be America Again

Langston Hughes (1902–1967) has long been regarded as a major African American writer and is increasingly seen as an important contributor to American literature in general. Like Countee Cullen, Hughes was actively involved in the 1920s

(© Corbis)

movement called the Harlem Renaissance. Then and later, he worked in various genres, including fiction, drama, and autobiography. Nevertheless, he is primarily known for his poems. "Let America Be America Again" appeared in a 1938 pamphlet by Hughes entitled A New Song, *which was published by a socialist organization named the International Worker Order. At this point in his career, Hughes was critical of capitalism and sympathetic toward Communism, as were many other writers during the Great Depression. During the late 1930s, Communism in the United States entered a phase called the Popular Front, which linked Marxist principles to traditional American ideas and values. The title of Hughes's poem reflects this attempt at connection. Note, too, that within the poem Hughes sees African Americans as part of a larger population suffering from poverty and powerlessness. Indeed, the Depression led many writers to connect racism with other kinds of oppression, especially inequalities of class.*

Let America be America again.
Let it be the dream it used to be.
Let it be the pioneer on the plain

Seeking a home where he himself is free.
(America never was America to me.)   5

Let America be the dream the dreamers dreamed —
Let it be that great strong land of love
Where never kings connive nor tyrants scheme
That any man be crushed by one above.
(It never was America to me.)   10

O, let my land be a land where Liberty
Is crowned with no false patriotic wreath,
But opportunity is real, and life is free,
Equality is in the air we breathe.

(There's never been equality for me,   15
Nor freedom in this "homeland of the free.")

Say, who are you that mumbles in the dark?
And who are you that draws your veil across the stars?

I am the poor white, fooled and pushed apart,
I am the Negro bearing slavery's scars.   20
I am the red man driven from the land,
I am the immigrant clutching the hope I seek —
And finding only the same old stupid plan
Of dog eat dog, of mighty crush the weak.

I am the young man, full of strength and hope,   25
Tangled in that ancient endless chain
Of profit, power, gain, of grab the land!
Of grab the gold! Of grab the ways of satisfying need!
Of work the men! Of take the pay!
Of owning everything for one's own greed!   30

I am the farmer, bondsman to the soil.
I am the worker sold to the machine.
I am the Negro, servant to you all.
I am the people, humble, hungry, mean —
Hungry yet today despite the dream.   35
Beaten yet today — O, Pioneers!
I am the man who never got ahead,
The poorest worker bartered through the years.

Yet I'm the one who dreamt our basic dream
In that Old World while still a serf of kings,   40
Who dreamt a dream so strong, so brave, so true,
That even yet its mighty daring sings
In every brick and stone, in every furrow turned
That's made America the land it has become.

O, I'm the man who sailed those early seas   45
In search of what I meant to be my home —
For I'm the one who left dark Ireland's shore,
And Poland's plain, and England's grassy lea,
And torn from Black Africa's strand I came
To build a "homeland of the free."   50
The free?

Who said the free? Not me?
Surely not me? The millions on relief today?
The millions shot down when we strike?
The millions who have nothing for our pay?   55
For all the dreams we've dreamed
And all the songs we've sung
And all the hopes we've held
And all the flags we've hung,
The millions who have nothing for our pay —   60
Except the dream that's almost dead today.

O, let America be America again —
The land that never has been yet —
And yet must be — the land where *every* man is free.
The land that's mine — the poor man's, Indian's, Negro's, ME —   65
Who made America,
Whose sweat and blood, whose faith and pain,
Whose hand at the foundry, whose plow in the rain,
Must bring back our mighty dream again.

Sure, call me any ugly name you choose —   70
The steel of freedom does not stain.
From those who live like leeches on the people's lives,
We must take back our land again,
America!

O, yes,   75
I say it plain,
America never was America to me,
And yet I swear this oath —
America will be!

Out of the rack and ruin of our gangster death,   80
The rape and rot of graft, and stealth, and lies,
We, the people, must redeem
The land, the mines, the plants, the rivers.
The mountains and the endless plain —
All, all the stretch of these great green states —   85
And make America again!   *[1938]*

☰ THINKING ABOUT THE TEXT

1. In the title and in the first line comes the plea "Let America be America again." At several points in the poem, however, the speaker indicates that America has never lived up to its ideals, especially about freedom and equality. Identify these points. How can we reconcile them with the opening plea?

2. When this poem was written in 1938, what do you think the response to the poem would have been among poor blacks? Poor whites? Members of Congress? Intellectuals? Religious groups in the South? The North? How would you answer this question in today's America?

3. What other oppressed peoples does the speaker refer to besides African Americans? Does he succeed in convincing you that all these groups belong together in the poem? What significant differences among them, if any, do you think he overlooks?

4. Although the speaker uses "I" a lot, sometimes he refers to "we." What is the effect of this shift? Should he have used one of these pronouns more than he does? Explain.

5. What lines of this poem seem to reflect the specific period of the Depression? What lines, if any, strike you as still relevant today?

LANGSTON HUGHES

Open Letter to the South

This poem was originally published in New Masses *in 1932 as "Red Flag over Tuskegee." It clearly reflected the feeling among many working-class intellectuals and artists in the 1930s that solidarity among the workers of the world was the only sure path toward freedom and equality.*

White workers of the South
    Miners,
    Farmers,
    Mechanics,
    Mill hands,   5
    Shop girls,
    Railway men,
    Servants,
    Tobacco workers,
    Sharecroppers,   10
    GREETINGS!

I am the black worker,
    Listen:

That the land might be ours,
And the mines and the factories and the office towers   15
At Harlan, Richmond, Gastonia, Atlanta, New Orleans;
That the plants and the roads and the tools of power
Be ours:

Let us forget what Booker T. said,
"Separate as the fingers."   20

Let us become instead, you and I,
One single hand
That can united rise
To smash the old dead dogmas of the past —
To kill the lies of color   25
That keep the rich enthroned
And drive us to the time-clock and the plow
Helpless, stupid, scattered, and alone — as now —
Race against race,
Because one is black,   30
Another white of face.

Let us new lessons learn,
All workers,
New life-ways make,
One union form: 35
Until the future burns out
Every past mistake
Let us together, say:
"You are my brother, black or white,
You my sister — now — today!"   40
For me, no more, the great migration to the North.

Instead: migration into force and power —
Tuskegee with a new flag on the tower!
On every lynching tree, a poster crying FREE
Because, O poor white workers,   45
You have linked your hands with me.

We did not know that we were brothers.
Now we know!
Out of that brotherhood
Let power grow!   50
We did not know
That we were strong.
Now we see
In union lies our strength.
Let union be   55
The force that breaks the time-clock,

Smashes misery,
Takes land,
Takes factories,
Takes office towers,   60
Takes tools and banks and mines.
Railroads, ships and dams,
Until the forces of the world
Are ours!

White worker,   65
Here is my hand.

Today,
We're Man to Man.   *[1932]*

☰ THINKING ABOUT THE TEXT

1. Who does Hughes blame for "the lies of color" (line 25) that divide black from white? Do you agree?

2. Booker T. Washington (1856–1915), the most prominent African American of his day, is now often seen as an accommodationist who urged only gradual progress toward equality between blacks and whites. Why do you think Hughes tells his readers to "forget what Booker T. said" (line 19)?

3. If you think of this poem as an argument, what would be Hughes's claim? Who is his audience, and what is his evidence? Do you think he made the right choices for his argument?

4. What do you think Hughes meant by the following lines: "We did not know that we were brothers. / Now we know!" (lines 47–48).

5. Hughes is hoping that class solidarity is stronger than racial divisions. Was this the case in 1932? Is it the case today?

☰ MAKING COMPARISONS

1. "Open Letter to the South" was written six years earlier than "Let America Be America Again," yet it seems more optimistic. Was this your feeling? How might you account for this?

2. Compare the arguments of both poems. Is "Let America Be America Again" more ambitious? Less focused? More or less persuasive in terms of audience?

3. Is there a comparable line in "Open Letter to the South" to "We must take back our land again, / America!" (lines 73–74)?

LANGSTON HUGHES
Theme for English B

Langston Hughes wrote "Theme for English B" in 1949, when he was twenty-five years older than the poem's speaker. As a young man, he had attended a "college on the hill above Harlem": Columbia University.

The instructor said,
   Go home and write
   a page tonight.
   And let that page come out of you —
   Then, it will be true.   5

I wonder if it's that simple?
I am twenty-two, colored, born in Winston-Salem.
I went to school there, then Durham, then here
to this college on the hill above Harlem.
I am the only colored student in my class.   10
The steps from the hill lead down into Harlem,
through a park, then I cross St. Nicholas,
Eighth Avenue, Seventh, and I come to the Y,
the Harlem Branch Y, where I take the elevator
up to my room, sit down, and write this page: 15

It's not easy to know what is true for you or me
at twenty-two, my age. But I guess I'm what
I feel and see and hear, Harlem, I hear you:
hear you, hear me — we two — you, me, talk on this page.
(I hear New York, too.) Me — who?   20
Well, I like to eat, sleep, drink, and be in love.
I like to work, read, learn, and understand life.
I like a pipe for a Christmas present,
or records — Bessie,° bop, or Bach.
I guess being colored doesn't make me *not* like   25
the same things other folks like who are other races.
So will my page be colored that I write?
Being me, it will not be white.
But it will be
a part of you, instructor.   30
You are white —
yet a part of me, as I am part of you.
That's American.
Sometimes perhaps you don't want to be a part of me.
Nor do I often want to be a part of you.   35

---

24 Bessie: Bessie Smith (1898?–1937), the famous American blues singer.

But we are, that's true!
As I learn from you,
I guess you learn from me —
although you're older — and white —
and somewhat more free.   40
This is my page for English B.   *[1949]*

≡ THINKING ABOUT THE TEXT

1. What do you think the instructor's response to "my page" (line 41) would be? What would yours be?

2. What do you think the instructor was hoping for? On what basis does the narrator seem to critique the assignment?

3. What do you think the narrator means by "American" in line 33? After more than sixty years, does it mean something different?

4. What do you think he means by the line "It's not easy to know what is true for you or me / at twenty-two" (lines 16–17)? Do you agree?

5. The emphasis on freedom here seems more indirect than in the previous two poems. What do you think Hughes means by "free" in the next-to-last line? Would you agree with him then (1949)? Now?

≡ MAKING COMPARISONS

1. Although this poem, like the previous two, seems written to a white audience, its tone seems less aggressive. Is this your reading? What lines seem particularly diplomatic in contrast to "Let America Be America Again"?

2. Is there a line in this poem that might be comparable to "(America was never America to me)" (line 5) from "Let America Be America Again"?

3. Is "Today, / We're Man to Man" (lines 67–68) from "Open Letter to the South" the most hopeful (or naive) line in the three poems?

LANGSTON HUGHES
Harlem

Sometimes called "A Dream Deferred," "Harlem" is Hughes's most anthologized poem and has become synonymous with African Americans' long struggle for freedom and equality.

What happens to a dream deferred?

Does it dry up
like a raisin in the sun?

Or fester like a sore —
And then run?   5
Does it stink like rotten meat?
Or crust and sugar over —
like a syrupy sweet?

Maybe it just sags
like a heavy load.   10

Or does it explode?   [1951]

≡ THINKING ABOUT THE TEXT

1. The inspiration for Lorraine Hansberry's famous play, *A Raisin in the Sun*, Hughes's brief poem asks a question and then answers it with more questions. Is this effective? Should he have been more explicit?

2. What is the "dream deferred" (line 1)?

3. The alternatives given are specific and concrete metaphors presumably embodied in people. What kind of person would be "like a raisin in the sun" (line 3)?

4. How would you imagine a person who stank "like rotten meat" (line 6) would behave? One who "sags / like a heavy load" (lines 9–10)? One who is "like a syrupy sweet" (line 8)?

5. How do you read the last line?

≡ MAKING COMPARISONS

1. Why do you think "Harlem" is the most popular of the four poems presented here?

2. Are there hints in the previous three poems of the ideas developed in "Harlem"?

3. Which poem would you recommend to someone from another country who is trying to understand our racial history? Why?

≡ WRITING ABOUT ISSUES

1. Arguments are made in both "Let America Be America Again" and "Open Letter to the South." Choose one to analyze in terms of issue, claim, evidence, audience, and persuasion. (See the section on "Looking at Literature as Argument," p. 60.)

2. Write an essay that agrees or disagrees with Hughes's accusation in line 24 of "Let America Be America Again" that life in capitalist America is one of "dog eat dog, of mighty crush the weak."

3. Write an essay about your personal responses to these four poems. Include what you think the poems mean, whether you agree or not with the writer's points, and what emotions the poems provoked.

4. Both "Let America Be America Again" and "Open Letter to the South" were written in the 1930s, and we know that the civil rights movement didn't gain serious national attention until the mid-1960s. Since many other voices besides Hughes's were addressing the lack of freedom among America's minorities, especially African Americans, how can you account for the length of time it took for freedom and equality to become serious issues among white voters? Write an essay that addresses this issue.

■ Domestic Prisons: Plays

HENRIK IBSEN, *A Doll House*

SUSAN GLASPELL, *Trifles*

LYNN NOTTAGE, *POOF!*

The writer and scientist Loren Eiseley notes that "to grow is a gain, an enlargement of life. . . . Yet it is also a departure." Eiseley's seems a more sophisticated idea than one portraying personal and social progress as only positive. Life is more complicated than that. Most of us eagerly anticipate becoming adults and embracing adult responsibilities and privileges. But our literature is filled with nostalgia for the innocence and wonder of childhood. We have a sense that we have lost something as our culture, technology, and lifestyles have advanced. There is no going back, but to some the old ways sometimes seem simpler. Our grandparents longed to leave the limitations of small-town life, but fifty years later their urban grandchildren idealize small communities. Women agonized over the legal and personal restrictions of Victorian marriages, but contemporary women understand that divorce is often painful and difficult. No reasonable thinker would want women to return to the childlike position that wives were expected to inhabit a hundred years ago, but that does not mean we cannot acknowledge that divorce often comes with a steep emotional and practical price.

It appears that Henrik Ibsen understood this when he wrote *A Doll House* in 1879. It was an era of great political and social change, and Ibsen believed that writers could be instrumental in affecting the way people thought about the great issues of the day. His realistic problem plays confronted topical and controversial issues. Among the most debated was the status of women in society, especially their legal and emotional subjugation within marriage. To a contemporary audience, Nora, the main character of *A Doll House*, is treated like a child. Although that disturbs most women today, Ibsen's female audience tended not to sympathize with Nora. The play's unsettling conclusion outraged most men. Changes in accepted thinking are always contested. But although most critics today see Ibsen as a social visionary who championed equality in marriage, he was not naive enough to think that great sacrifice and pain would not also accompany freedom and equality. The solution of one problem often creates new problems. When Nora begins to question the old ways, her future starts to grow uncertain. Knowing what she knows, can she really remain in a marriage that seems to her a cruel and unjust trap?

Written almost forty years later, Susan Glaspell's *Trifles* explores similar feelings of confinement but in a different geographical context. Although the scene shifts from a comfortable middle-class home in Ibsen's Norway to rural America and the gloomy, abandoned kitchen of Minnie Wright, readers quickly get the feeling that the marriage of John and Minnie was also one of emotional domination. As the details surrounding John's death are cleverly and subtly

revealed to us, we also get the clear impression that we cannot look to the men in the play for insight and understanding of Minnie's situation. They are too concerned with a search for physical evidence to see the devastating emotional truth of this marriage that is in plain sight.

Written almost a hundred years after *Trifles*, *POOF!* deals with many of the same marriage problems of abuse and unequal status that were on Susan Glaspell's mind in 1916. That in itself should be cause for alarm since we like to think we have made great strides in gender equality over the past century. And, of course, in many significant ways that is the case. But because domestic abuse until the past twenty years or so was widely seen as a private matter, marriage is still a fertile ground for injustice. Verbal, physical, and emotional abuse is still a major issue in marriage, with women almost always the victims. And although the abuser in *POOF!* is punished for his crimes, that is more wishful thinking than a mirror of reality, as marriage for too many women is still a domestic prison.

≡ BEFORE YOU READ

Do you think a woman is ever justified in leaving her children? Do you think absolute equality is necessary for love to exist in a marriage? Do you think an abused wife who takes revenge on her husband deserves punishment?

HENRIK IBSEN
A Doll House

Translated by B. Farquharson Sharp

Henrik Ibsen (1828–1906) was born into a family with money in a small town in Norway, but his father soon went bankrupt. Ibsen later remembered this genteel poverty by writing about issues of social injustice that he experienced firsthand. At fifteen Ibsen was apprenticed to a pharmacist, a profession he had no interest in. He soon was drawn to the theater, working to establish a Norwegian national theater. But this led to frustration, and Ibsen spent almost thirty years in a self-imposed exile in Italy and Germany, where he wrote some of his most famous plays. Ibsen's plays are often performed today and still provoke controversy. They include Ghosts *(1881),* An Enemy of the People *(1882),* Hedda Gabler *(1890), and* When We Dead Awaken *(1899).*

DRAMATIS PERSONAE

TORVALD HELMER
NORA, *his wife*
DOCTOR *RANK*
MRS. LINDE

NILS KROGSTAD
Helmer's three young children
ANNE, *their nurse*
A Housemaid
A Porter

SCENE: *The action takes place in Helmer's house.*

ACT I

SCENE: *A room furnished comfortably and tastefully, but not extravagantly. At the back, a door to the right leads to the entrance-hall, another to the left leads to Helmer's study. Between the doors stands a piano. In the middle of the left-hand wall is a door, and beyond it a window. Near the window are a round table, arm-chairs and a small sofa. In the right-hand wall, at the farther end, another door; and on the same side, nearer the footlights, a stove, two easy chairs and a rocking-chair; between the stove and the door, a small table. Engravings on the walls; a cabinet with china and other small objects; a small book-case with well-bound books. The floors are carpeted, and a fire burns in the stove. It is winter.*

A bell rings in the hall; shortly afterwards the door is heard to open. Enter Nora, humming a tune and in high spirits. She is in outdoor dress and carries a number of parcels; these she lays on the table to the right. She leaves the outer door open after her, and through it is seen a Porter who is carrying a Christmas Tree and a basket, which he gives to the Maid who has opened the door.

NORA: Hide the Christmas Tree carefully, Helen. Be sure the children do not see it until this evening, when it is dressed. (*To the Porter, taking out her purse.*) How much?
PORTER: Sixpence.
NORA: There is a shilling. No, keep the change. (*The Porter thanks her, and goes out. Nora shuts the door. She is laughing to herself, as she takes off her hat and coat. She takes a packet of macaroons from her pocket and eats one or two; then goes cautiously to her husband's door and listens.*) Yes, he is in. (*Still humming, she goes to the table on the right.*)
HELMER (*calls out from his room*):   Is that my little lark twittering out there?
NORA (*busy opening some of the parcels*):   Yes, it is!
HELMER: Is it my little squirrel bustling about?
NORA: Yes!
HELMER: When did my squirrel come home?
NORA: Just now. (*Puts the bag of macaroons into her pocket and wipes her mouth.*) Come in here, Torvald, and see what I have bought.
HELMER: Don't disturb me. (*A little later, he opens the door and looks into the room, pen in hand.*) Bought, did you say? All these things? Has my little spendthrift been wasting money again?
NORA: Yes but, Torvald, this year we really can let ourselves go a little. This is the first Christmas that we have not needed to economise.

HELMER: Still, you know, we can't spend money recklessly.

NORA: Yes, Torvald, we may be a wee bit more reckless now, mayn't we? Just a tiny wee bit! You are going to have a big salary and earn lots and lots of money.

HELMER: Yes, after the New Year; but then it will be a whole quarter before the salary is due.

NORA: Pooh! we can borrow until then.

HELMER: Nora! (*Goes up to her and takes her playfully by the ear.*) The same little featherhead! Suppose, now, that I borrowed fifty pounds to-day, and you spent it all in the Christmas week, and then on New Year's Eve a slate fell on my head and killed me, and—

NORA (*putting her hands over his mouth*):   Oh! don't say such horrid things.

HELMER: Still, suppose that happened,—what then?

NORA: If that were to happen, I don't suppose I should care whether I owed money or not.

HELMER: Yes, but what about the people who had lent it?

NORA: They? Who would bother about them? I should not know who they were.

HELMER: That is like a woman! But seriously, Nora, you know what I think about that. No debt, no borrowing. There can be no freedom or beauty about a home life that depends on borrowing and debt. We two have kept bravely on the straight road so far, and we will go on the same way for the short time longer that there need be any struggle.

NORA (*moving towards the stove*):   As you please, Torvald.

HELMER (*following her*):   Come, come, my little skylark must not droop her wings. What is this! Is my little squirrel out of temper? (*Taking out his purse.*) Nora, what do you think I have got here?

NORA (*turning round quickly*):   Money!

HELMER: There you are. (*Gives her some money.*) Do you think I don't know what a lot is wanted for housekeeping at Christmas-time?

NORA (*counting*):   Ten shillings—a pound—two pounds! Thank you, thank you, Torvald; that will keep me going for a long time.

HELMER: Indeed it must.

NORA: Yes, yes, it will. But come here and let me show you what I have bought. And all so cheap! Look, here is a new suit for Ivar, and a sword; and a horse and a trumpet for Bob; and a doll and dolly's bedstead for Emmy,—they are very plain, but anyway she will soon break them in pieces. And here are dress-lengths and handkerchiefs for the maids; old Anne ought really to have something better.

HELMER: And what is in this parcel?

NORA (*crying out*):   No, no! you mustn't see that until this evening.

HELMER: Very well. But now tell me, you extravagant little person, what would you like for yourself?

NORA: For myself? Oh, I am sure I don't want anything.

HELMER: Yes, but you must. Tell me something reasonable that you would particularly like to have.

NORA: No, I really can't think of anything—unless, Torvald—

HELMER: Well?

NORA (*playing with his coat buttons, and without raising her eyes to his*):   If you really want to give me something, you might—you might—

HELMER: Well, out with it!

NORA (*speaking quickly*):   You might give me money, Torvald. Only just as much as you can afford; and then one of these days I will buy something with it.

HELMER: But, Nora—

NORA: Oh, do! dear Torvald; please, please do! Then I will wrap it up in beautiful gilt paper and hang it on the Christmas Tree. Wouldn't that be fun?

HELMER: What are little people called that are always wasting money?

NORA: Spendthrifts—I know. Let us do as you suggest, Torvald, and then I shall have time to think what I am most in want of. That is a very sensible plan, isn't it?

HELMER (*smiling*):   Indeed it is—that is to say, if you were really to save out of the money I give you, and then really buy something for yourself. But if you spend it all on the housekeeping and any number of unnecessary things, then I merely have to pay up again.

NORA: Oh but, Torvald—

HELMER: You can't deny it, my dear little Nora. (*Puts his arm round her waist.*) It's a sweet little spendthrift, but she uses up a deal of money. One would hardly believe how expensive such little persons are!

NORA: It's a shame to say that. I do really save all I can.

HELMER (*laughing*):   That's very true,—all you can. But you can't save anything!

NORA (*smiling quietly and happily*):   You haven't any idea how many expenses we skylarks and squirrels have, Torvald.

HELMER: You are an odd little soul. Very like your father. You always find some new way of wheedling money out of me, and, as soon as you have got it, it seems to melt in your hands. You never know where it has gone. Still, one must take you as you are. It is in the blood; for indeed it is true that you can inherit these things, Nora.

NORA: Ah, I wish I had inherited many of papa's qualities.

HELMER: And I would not wish you to be anything but just what you are, my sweet little skylark. But, do you know, it strikes me that you are looking rather—what shall I say—rather uneasy today?

NORA: Do I?

HELMER: You do, really. Look straight at me.

NORA (*looks at him*):   Well?

HELMER (*wagging his finger at her*):   Hasn't Miss Sweet Tooth been breaking rules in town today?

NORA: No; what makes you think that?

HELMER: Hasn't she paid a visit to the confectioner's?

NORA: No, I assure you, Torvald—

HELMER: Not been nibbling sweets?

NORA: No, certainly not.

HELMER: Not even taken a bite at a macaroon or two?

NORA: No, Torvald, I assure you really—

HELMER: There, there, of course I was only joking.

NORA (*going to the table on the right*):   I should not think of going against your wishes.

HELMER: No, I am sure of that; besides, you gave me your word—(*Going up to her.*) Keep your little Christmas secrets to yourself, my darling. They will all be revealed to-night when the Christmas Tree is lit, no doubt.

NORA: Did you remember to invite Doctor Rank?

HELMER: No. But there is no need; as a matter of course he will come to dinner with us. However, I will ask him when he comes in this morning. I have ordered some good wine. Nora, you can't think how I am looking forward to this evening.

NORA: So am I! And how the children will enjoy themselves, Torvald!

HELMER: It is splendid to feel that one has a perfectly safe appointment, and a big enough income. It's delightful to think of, isn't it?

NORA: It's wonderful!

HELMER: Do you remember last Christmas? For a full three weeks beforehand you shut yourself up every evening until long after midnight, making ornaments for the Christmas Tree, and all the other fine things that were to be a surprise to us. It was the dullest three weeks I ever spent!

NORA: I didn't find it dull.

HELMER (*smiling*):   But there was precious little result, Nora.

NORA: Oh, you shouldn't tease me about that again. How could I help the cat's going in and tearing everything to pieces?

HELMER: Of course you couldn't, poor little girl. You had the best of intentions to please us all, and that's the main thing. But it is a good thing that our hard times are over.

NORA: Yes, it is really wonderful.

HELMER: This time I needn't sit here and be dull all alone, and you needn't ruin your dear eyes and your pretty little hands—

NORA (*clapping her hands*):   No, Torvald, I needn't any longer, need I! It's wonderfully lovely to hear you say so! (*Taking his arm.*) Now I will tell you how I have been thinking we ought to arrange things, Torvald. As soon as Christmas is over—(*A bell rings in the hall.*) There's the bell. (*She tidies the room a little.*) There's some one at the door. What a nuisance!

HELMER: If it is a caller, remember I am not at home.

MAID (*in the doorway*):   A lady to see you, ma'am,—a stranger.

NORA: Ask her to come in.

MAID (*to Helmer*):   The doctor came at the same time, sir.

HELMER: Did he go straight into my room?

MAID: Yes, sir.

Helmer goes into his room. The Maid ushers in Mrs. Linde, who is in travelling dress, and shuts the door.

MRS. LINDE (*in a dejected and timid voice*):   How do you do, Nora?

NORA (*doubtfully*):   How do you do—

MRS. LINDE: You don't recognise me, I suppose.

NORA: No, I don't know—yes, to be sure, I seem to—(*Suddenly.*) Yes! Christine! Is it really you?

MRS. LINDE: Yes, it is I.

NORA: Christine! To think of my not recognising you! And yet how could I—
(*In a gentle voice.*) How you have altered, Christine!

MRS. LINDE: Yes, I have indeed. In nine, ten long years—

NORA: Is it so long since we met? I suppose it is. The last eight years have been
a happy time for me, I can tell you. And so now you have come into the town,
and have taken this long journey in winter—that was plucky of you.

MRS. LINDE: I arrived by steamer this morning.

NORA: To have some fun at Christmas-time, of course. How delightful! We will
have such fun together! But take off your things. You are not cold, I hope.
(*Helps her.*) Now we will sit down by the stove, and be cosy. No, take this
armchair; I will sit here in the rocking-chair. (*Takes her hands.*) Now you
look like your old self again; it was only the first moment—You are a little
paler, Christine, and perhaps a little thinner.

MRS. LINDE: And much, much older, Nora.

NORA: Perhaps a little older; very, very little; certainly not much. (*Stops suddenly and speaks seriously.*) What a thoughtless creature I am, chattering
away like this. My poor, dear Christine, do forgive me.

MRS. LINDE: What do you mean, Nora?

NORA (*gently*):   Poor Christine, you are a widow.

MRS. LINDE: Yes; it is three years ago now.

NORA: Yes, I knew; I saw it in the papers. I assure you, Christine, I meant ever
so often to write to you at the time, but I always put it off and something
always prevented me.

MRS. LINDE: I quite understand, dear.

NORA: It was very bad of me, Christine. Poor thing, how you must have suffered. And he left you nothing?

MRS. LINDE: No.

NORA: And no children?

MRS. LINDE: No.

NORA: Nothing at all, then.

MRS. LINDE: Not even any sorrow or grief to live upon.

NORA (*looking incredulously at her*):   But, Christine, is that possible?

MRS. LINDE (*smiles sadly and strokes her hair*):   It sometimes happens, Nora.

NORA: So you are quite alone. How dreadfully sad that must be. I have three
lovely children. You can't see them just now, for they are out with their
nurse. But now you must tell me all about it.

MRS. LINDE: No, no; I want to hear about you.

NORA: No, you must begin. I mustn't be selfish today; today I must only think
of your affairs. But there is one thing I must tell you. Do you know we have
just had a great piece of good luck?

MRS. LINDE: No, what is it?

NORA: Just fancy, my husband has been made manager of the Bank!

MRS. LINDE: Your husband? What good luck!

NORA:　Yes, tremendous! A barrister's profession is such an uncertain thing, especially if he won't undertake unsavoury cases; and naturally Torvald has never been willing to do that, and I quite agree with him. You may imagine how pleased we are! He is to take up his work in the Bank at the New Year, and then he will have a big salary and lots of commissions. For the future we can live quite differently—we can do just as we like. I feel so relieved and so happy, Christine! It will be splendid to have heaps of money and not need to have any anxiety, won't it?

MRS. LINDE:　Yes, anyhow I think it would be delightful to have what one needs.

NORA:　No, not only what one needs, but heaps and heaps of money.

MRS. LINDE (*smiling*):　Nora, Nora, haven't you learned sense yet? In our school-days you were a great spendthrift.

NORA (*laughing*):　Yes, that is what Torvald says now. (*Wags her finger at her.*) But "Nora, Nora" is not so silly as you think. We have not been in a position for me to waste money. We have both had to work.

MRS. LINDE:　You too?

NORA:　Yes; odds and ends, needlework, crotchet-work, embroidery, and that kind of thing. (*Dropping her voice.*) And other things as well. You know Torvald left his office when we were married? There was no prospect of promotion there, and he had to try and earn more than before. But during the first year he over-worked himself dreadfully. You see, he had to make money every way he could, and he worked early and late; but he couldn't stand it, and fell dreadfully ill, and the doctors said it was necessary for him to go south.

MRS. LINDE:　You spent a whole year in Italy, didn't you?

NORA:　Yes. It was no easy matter to get away, I can tell you. It was just after Ivar was born; but naturally we had to go. It was a wonderfully beautiful journey, and it saved Torvald's life. But it cost a tremendous lot of money, Christine.

MRS. LINDE:　So I should think.

NORA:　It cost about two hundred and fifty pounds. That's a lot, isn't it?

MRS. LINDE:　Yes, and in emergencies like that it is lucky to have the money.

NORA:　I ought to tell you that we had it from papa.

MRS. LINDE:　Oh, I see. It was just about that time that he died, wasn't it?

NORA:　Yes; and, just think of it, I couldn't go and nurse him. I was expecting little Ivar's birth every day and I had my poor sick Torvald to look after. My dear, kind father—I never saw him again, Christine. That was the saddest time I have known since our marriage.

MRS. LINDE:　I know how fond you were of him. And then you went off to Italy?

NORA:　Yes; you see we had money then, and the doctors insisted on our going, so we started a month later.

MRS. LINDE:　And your husband came back quite well?

NORA:　As sound as a bell!

MRS. LINDE:　But—the doctor?

NORA:　What doctor?

MRS. LINDE: I thought your maid said the gentleman who arrived here just as I did, was the doctor?

NORA: Yes, that was Doctor Rank, but he doesn't come here professionally. He is our greatest friend, and comes in at least once everyday. No, Torvald has not had an hour's illness since then, and our children are strong and healthy and so am I. (*Jumps up and claps her hands.*) Christine! Christine! it's good to be alive and happy!—But how horrid of me; I am talking of nothing but my own affairs. (*Sits on a stool near her, and rests her arms on her knees.*) You mustn't be angry with me. Tell me, is it really true that you did not love your husband? Why did you marry him?

MRS. LINDE: My mother was alive then, and was bedridden and helpless, and I had to provide for my two younger brothers; so I did not think I was justified in refusing his offer.

NORA: No, perhaps you were quite right. He was rich at that time, then?

MRS. LINDE: I believe he was quite well off. But his business was a precarious one; and, when he died, it all went to pieces and there was nothing left.

NORA: And then?—

MRS. LINDE: Well, I had to turn my hand to anything I could find—first a small shop, then a small school, and so on. The last three years have seemed like one long working-day, with no rest. Now it is at an end, Nora. My poor mother needs me no more, for she is gone; and the boys do not need me either; they have got situations and can shift for themselves.

NORA: What a relief you must feel it—

MRS. LINDE: No, indeed; I only feel my life unspeakably empty. No one to live for anymore. (*Gets up restlessly.*) That was why I could not stand the life in my little backwater any longer. I hope it may be easier here to find something which will busy me and occupy my thoughts. If only I could have the good luck to get some regular work—office work of some kind—

NORA: But, Christine, that is so frightfully tiring, and you look tired out now. You had far better go away to some watering-place.

MRS. LINDE (*walking to the window*):   I have no father to give me money for a journey, Nora.

NORA (*rising*):   Oh, don't be angry with me!

MRS. LINDE (*going up to her*):   It is you that must not be angry with me, dear. The worst of a position like mine is that it makes one so bitter. No one to work for, and yet obliged to be always on the lookout for chances. One must live, and so one becomes selfish. When you told me of the happy turn your fortunes have taken—you will hardly believe it—I was delighted not so much on your account as on my own.

NORA: How do you mean?—Oh, I understand. You mean that perhaps Torvald could get you something to do.

MRS. LINDE: Yes, that was what I was thinking of.

NORA: He must, Christine. Just leave it to me; I will broach the subject very cleverly—I will think of something that will please him very much. It will make me so happy to be of some use to you.

MRS. LINDE: How kind you are, Nora, to be so anxious to help me! It is doubly kind in you, for you know so little of the burdens and troubles of life.

NORA: I—? I know so little of them?

MRS. LINDE (*smiling*):   My dear! Small household cares and that sort of thing!—You are a child, Nora.

NORA (*tosses her head and crosses the stage*):   You ought not to be so superior.

MRS. LINDE: No?

NORA: You are just like the others. They all think that I am incapable of anything really serious—

MRS. LINDE: Come, come—

NORA: —that I have gone through nothing in this world of cares.

MRS. LINDE: But, my dear Nora, you have just told me all your troubles.

NORA: Pooh!—those were trifles. (*Lowering her voice.*) I have not told you the important thing.

MRS. LINDE: The important thing? What do you mean?

NORA: You look down upon me altogether, Christine—but you ought not to. You are proud, aren't you, of having worked so hard and so long for your mother?

MRS. LINDE: Indeed, I don't look down on anyone. But it is true that I am both proud and glad to think that I was privileged to make the end of my mother's life almost free from care.

NORA: And you are proud to think of what you have done for your brothers?

MRS. LINDE: I think I have the right to be.

NORA: I think so, too. But now, listen to this; I too have something to be proud and glad of.

MRS. LINDE: I have no doubt you have. But what do you refer to?

NORA: Speak low. Suppose Torvald were to hear! He mustn't on any account—no one in the world must know, Christine, except you.

MRS. LINDE: But what is it?

NORA: Come here. (*Pulls her down on the sofa beside her.*) Now I will show you that I too have something to be proud and glad of. It was I who saved Torvald's life.

MRS. LINDE: "Saved"? How?

NORA: I told you about our trip to Italy. Torvald would never have recovered if he had not gone there—

MRS. LINDE: Yes, but your father gave you the necessary funds.

NORA (*smiling*):   Yes, that is what Torvald and all the others think, but—

MRS. LINDE: But—

NORA: Papa didn't give us a shilling. It was I who procured the money.

MRS. LINDE: You? All that large sum?

NORA: Two hundred and fifty pounds. What do you think of that?

MRS. LINDE: But, Nora, how could you possibly do it? Did you win a prize in the Lottery?

NORA (*contemptuously*):   In the Lottery? There would have been no credit in that.

MRS. LINDE: But where did you get it from, then?

NORA (*humming and smiling with an air of mystery*):   Hm, hm! Aha!

MRS. LINDE: Because you couldn't have borrowed it.

NORA: Couldn't I? Why not?

MRS. LINDE: No, a wife cannot borrow without her husband's consent.

NORA (*tossing her head*):   Oh, if it is a wife who has any head for business—a wife who has the wit to be a little bit clever—

MRS. LINDE: I don't understand it at all, Nora.

NORA: There is no need you should. I never said I had borrowed the money. I may have got it some other way. (*Lies back on the sofa.*) Perhaps I got it from some other admirer. When anyone is as attractive as I am—

MRS. LINDE: You are a mad creature.

NORA: Now, you know you're full of curiosity, Christine.

MRS. LINDE: Listen to me, Nora dear. Haven't you been a little bit imprudent?

NORA (*sits up straight*):   Is it imprudent to save your husband's life?

MRS. LINDE: It seems to me imprudent, without his knowledge, to—

NORA: But it was absolutely necessary that he should not know! My goodness, can't you understand that? It was necessary he should have no idea what a dangerous condition he was in. It was to me that the doctors came and said that his life was in danger, and that the only thing to save him was to live in the south. Do you suppose I didn't try, first of all, to get what I wanted as if it were for myself? I told him how much I should love to travel abroad like other young wives; I tried tears and entreaties with him; I told him that he ought to remember the condition I was in, and that he ought to be kind and indulgent to me; I even hinted that he might raise a loan. That nearly made him angry, Christine. He said I was thoughtless, and that it was his duty as my husband not to indulge me in my whims and caprices—as I believe he called them. Very well, I thought, you must be saved—and that was how I came to devise a way out of the difficulty—

MRS. LINDE: And did your husband never get to know from your father that the money had not come from him?

NORA: No, never. Papa died just at that time. I had meant to let him into the secret and beg him never to reveal it. But he was so ill then—alas, there never was any need to tell him.

MRS. LINDE: And since then have you never told your secret to your husband?

NORA: Good Heavens, no! How could you think so? A man who has such strong opinions about these things! And besides, how painful and humiliating it would be for Torvald, with his manly independence, to know that he owed me anything! It would upset our mutual relations altogether; our beautiful happy home would no longer be what it is now.

MRS. LINDE: Do you mean never to tell him about it?

NORA (*meditatively, and with a half smile*):   Yes—someday, perhaps, after many years, when I am no longer as nice-looking as I am now. Don't laugh at me! I mean, of course, when Torvald is no longer as devoted to me as he is now; when my dancing and dressing-up and reciting have palled on him; then it may be a good thing to have something in reserve—(*Breaking off.*) What nonsense! That time will never come. Now, what do you think of my great secret, Christine? Do you still think I am of no use? I can tell you, too, that this affair has caused me a lot of worry. It has been by no means easy for me to meet my engagements punctually. I may tell you that there is something that is called, in business, quarterly interest, and another thing called payment in installments, and it is always so dreadfully difficult to manage them. I have had to save a little here and there, where I could, you understand. I have not been able to put aside much from my housekeeping money, for Torvald must have a good table. I couldn't let my children be shabbily dressed; I have felt obliged to use up all he gave me for them, the sweet little darlings!

MRS. LINDE: So it has all had to come out of your own necessaries of life, poor Nora?

NORA: Of course. Besides, I was the one responsible for it. Whenever Torvald has given me money for new dresses and such things, I have never spent more than half of it; I have always bought the simplest and cheapest things. Thank Heaven, any clothes look well on me, and so Torvald has never noticed it. But it was often very hard on me, Christine—because it is delightful to be really well dressed, isn't it?

MRS. LINDE: Quite so.

NORA: Well, then I have found other ways of earning money. Last winter I was lucky enough to get a lot of copying to do; so I locked myself up and sat writing every evening until quite late at night. Many a time I was desperately tired; but all the same it was a tremendous pleasure to sit there working and earning money. It was like being a man.

MRS. LINDE: How much have you been able to pay off in that way?

NORA: I can't tell you exactly. You see, it is very difficult to keep an account of a business matter of that kind. I only know that I have paid every penny that I could scrape together. Many a time I was at my wits' end. (*Smiles.*) Then I used to sit here and imagine that a rich old gentleman had fallen in love with me—

MRS. LINDE: What! Who was it?

NORA: Be quiet!—that he had died; and that when his will was opened it contained, written in big letters, the instruction: "The lovely Mrs. Nora Helmer is to have all I possess paid over to her at once in cash."

MRS. LINDE: But, my dear Nora—who could the man be?

NORA: Good gracious, can't you understand? There was no old gentleman at all; it was only something that I used to sit here and imagine, when I couldn't think of any way of procuring money. But it's all the same now; the tiresome old person can stay where he is, as far as I am concerned; I don't care about him or his will either, for I am free from care now. (*Jumps up.*) My goodness, it's delightful to think of, Christine! Free from care! To be able to be free from care, quite free from care; to be able to play and romp with the children; to be able to keep the house beautifully and have everything just as Torvald likes it! And, think of it, soon the spring will come and the big blue sky! Perhaps we shall be able to take a little trip—perhaps I shall see the sea again! Oh, it's a wonderful thing to be alive and be happy. (*A bell is heard in the hall.*)

MRS. LINDE (*rising*): There is the bell; perhaps I had better go.

NORA: No, don't go; no one will come in here; it is sure to be for Torvald.

SERVANT (*at the hall door*): Excuse me, ma'am—there is a gentleman to see the master, and as the doctor is with him—

NORA: Who is it?

KROGSTAD (*at the door*): It is I, Mrs. Helmer (*Mrs. Linde starts, trembles, and turns to the window.*)

NORA (*takes a step towards him, and speaks in a strained, low voice*): You? What is it? What do you want to see my husband about?

KROGSTAD: Bank business—in a way. I have a small post in the Bank, and I hear your husband is to be our chief now—

NORA: Then it is—

KROGSTAD: Nothing but dry business matters, Mrs. Helmer; absolutely nothing else.

NORA: Be so good as to go into the study, then. (*She bows indifferently to him and shuts the door into the hall; then comes back and makes up the fire in the stove.*)

MRS. LINDE: Nora—who was that man?

NORA: A lawyer, of the name of Krogstad.

MRS. LINDE: Then it really was he.

NORA: Do you know the man?

MRS. LINDE: I used to—many years ago. At one time he was a solicitor's clerk in our town.

NORA: Yes, he was.

MRS. LINDE: He is greatly altered.

NORA: He made a very unhappy marriage.

MRS. LINDE: He is a widower now, isn't he?

NORA: With several children. There now, it is burning up. (*Shuts the door of the stove and moves the rocking-chair aside.*)

MRS. LINDE: They say he carries on various kinds of business.

NORA: Really! Perhaps he does; I don't know anything about it. But don't let us think of business; it is so tiresome.

DOCTOR RANK (*comes out of Helmer's study. Before he shuts the door he calls to him*): No, my dear fellow, I won't disturb you; I would rather go in to your wife for a little while. (*Shuts the door and sees Mrs. Linde.*) I beg your pardon; I am afraid I am disturbing you too.

NORA: No, not at all. (*Introducing him.*) Doctor Rank, Mrs. Linde.

RANK: I have often heard Mrs. Linde's name mentioned here. I think I passed you on the stairs when I arrived, Mrs. Linde?

MRS. LINDE: Yes, I go up very slowly; I can't manage stairs well.

RANK: Ah! some slight internal weakness?

MRS. LINDE: No, the fact is I have been overworking myself.

RANK: Nothing more than that? Then I suppose you have come to town to amuse yourself with our entertainments?

MRS. LINDE: I have come to look for work.

RANK: Is that a good cure for overwork?

MRS. LINDE: One must live, Doctor Rank.

RANK: Yes, the general opinion seems to be that it is necessary.

NORA: Look here, Doctor Rank—you know you want to live.

RANK: Certainly. However wretched I may feel, I want to prolong the agony as long as possible. All my patients are like that. And so are those who are morally diseased; one of them, and a bad case too, is at this very moment with Helmer—

MRS. LINDE (*sadly*):   Ah!

NORA: Whom do you mean?

RANK: A lawyer of the name of Krogstad, a fellow you don't know at all. He suffers from a diseased moral character, Mrs. Helmer; but even he began talking of its being highly important that he should live.

NORA: Did he? What did he want to speak to Torvald about?

RANK: I have no idea; I only heard that it was something about the Bank.

NORA: I didn't know this—what's his name—Krogstad had anything to do with the Bank.

RANK: Yes, he has some sort of appointment there. (*To Mrs. Linde.*) I don't know whether you find also in your part of the world that there are certain people who go zealously snuffing about to smell out moral corruption, and, as soon as they have found some, put the person concerned into some lucrative position where they can keep their eye on him. Healthy natures are left out in the cold.

MRS. LINDE: Still I think the sick are those who most need taking care of.

RANK (*shrugging his shoulders*):   Yes, there you are. That is the sentiment that is turning Society into a sick-house.

Nora, who has been absorbed in her thoughts, breaks out into smothered laughter and claps her hands.

RANK: Why do you laugh at that? Have you any notion what Society really is?

NORA: What do I care about tiresome Society? I am laughing at something quite different, something extremely amusing. Tell me, Doctor Rank, are all the people who are employed in the Bank dependent on Torvald now?

RANK: Is that what you find so extremely amusing?

NORA (*smiling and humming*):   That's my affair! (*Walking about the room.*) It's perfectly glorious to think that we have—that Torvald has so much power over so many people. (*Takes the packet from her pocket.*) Doctor Rank, what do you say to a macaroon?

RANK: What, macaroons? I thought they were forbidden here.

NORA: Yes, but these are some Christine gave me.

MRS. LINDE: What! I?—

NORA: Oh, well, don't be alarmed! You couldn't know that Torvald had forbidden them. I must tell you that he is afraid they will spoil my teeth. But, bah!—once in a way—That's so, isn't it, Doctor Rank? By your leave! (*Puts a macaroon into his mouth.*) You must have one too, Christine. And I shall have one, just a little one—or at most two. (*Walking about.*) I am tremendously happy. There is just one thing in the world now that I should dearly love to do.

RANK: Well, what is that?

NORA: It's something I should dearly love to say, if Torvald could hear me.

RANK: Well, why can't you say it?

NORA: No, I daren't; it's so shocking.

MRS. LINDE: Shocking?

RANK: Well, I should not advise you to say it. Still, with us you might. What is it you would so much like to say if Torvald could hear you?

NORA: I should just love to say — Well, I'm damned!

RANK: Are you mad?

MRS. LINDE: Nora, dear — !

RANK: Say it, here he is!

NORA (*hiding the packet*):   Hush! Hush! Hush! (*Helmer comes out of his room, with his coat over his arm and his hat in his hand.*)

NORA: Well, Torvald dear, have you got rid of him?

HELMER: Yes, he has just gone.

NORA: Let me introduce you — this is Christine, who has come to town.

HELMER: Christine — ? Excuse me, but I don't know —

NORA: Mrs. Linde, dear; Christine Linde.

HELMER: Of course. A school friend of my wife's, I presume?

MRS. LINDE: Yes, we have known each other since then.

NORA: And just think, she has taken a long journey in order to see you.

HELMER: What do you mean?

MRS. LINDE: No, really, I —

NORA: Christine is tremendously clever at book-keeping, and she is frightfully anxious to work under some clever man, so as to perfect herself —

HELMER: Very sensible, Mrs. Linde.

NORA: And when she heard you had been appointed manager of the Bank — the news was telegraphed, you know — she travelled here as quick as she could. Torvald, I am sure you will be able to do something for Christine, for my sake, won't you?

HELMER: Well, it is not altogether impossible. I presume you are a widow, Mrs. Linde?

MRS. LINDE: Yes.

HELMER: And have had some experience of book-keeping?

MRS. LINDE: Yes, a fair amount.

HELMER: Ah! well, it's very likely I may be able to find something for you —

NORA (*clapping her hands*):   What did I tell you? What did I tell you?

HELMER: You have just come at a fortunate moment, Mrs. Linde.

MRS. LINDE: How am I to thank you?

HELMER: There is no need. (*Puts on his coat.*) But to-day you must excuse me —

RANK: Wait a minute; I will come with you. (*Brings his fur coat from the hall and warms it at the fire.*)

NORA: Don't be long away, Torvald dear.

HELMER: About an hour, not more.

NORA: Are you going too, Christine?

MRS. LINDE (*putting on her cloak*):   Yes, I must go and look for a room.

HELMER: Oh, well then, we can walk down the street together.

NORA (*helping her*):   What a pity it is we are so short of space here; I am afraid it is impossible for us—

MRS. LINDE: Please don't think of it! Good-bye, Nora dear, and many thanks.

NORA: Good-bye for the present. Of course you will come back this evening. And you too, Dr. Rank. What do you say? If you are well enough? Oh, you must be! Wrap yourself up well. (*They go to the door all talking together. Children's voices are heard on the staircase.*)

NORA: There they are! There they are! (*She runs to open the door. The Nurse comes in with the children.*) Come in! Come in! (*Stoops and kisses them.*) Oh, you sweet blessings! Look at them, Christine! Aren't they darlings?

RANK: Don't let us stand here in the draught.

HELMER: Come along, Mrs. Linde; the place will only be bearable for a mother now!

Rank, Helmer, and Mrs. Linde go downstairs. The Nurse comes forward with the children; Nora shuts the hall door.

NORA: How fresh and well you look! Such red cheeks like apples and roses. (*The children all talk at once while she speaks to them.*) Have you had great fun? That's splendid! What, you pulled both Emmy and Bob along on the sledge?—both at once?—that was good. You are a clever boy, Ivar. Let me take her for a little, Anne. My sweet little baby doll! (*Takes the baby from the Maid and dances it up and down.*) Yes, yes, mother will dance with Bob too. What! Have you been snowballing? I wish I had been there too! No, no, I will take their things off, Anne; please let me do it, it is such fun. Go in now, you look half frozen. There is some hot coffee for you on the stove.

The Nurse goes into the room on the left. Nora takes off the children's things and throws them about, while they all talk to her at once.

NORA: Really! Did a big dog run after you? But it didn't bite you? No, dogs don't bite nice little dolly children. You mustn't look at the parcels, Ivar. What are they? Ah, I daresay you would like to know. No, no—it's something nasty! Come, let us have a game! What shall we play at? Hide and Seek? Yes, we'll play Hide and Seek. Bob shall hide first. Must I hide? Very well, I'll hide first. (*She and the children laugh and shout, and romp in and out of the room; at last Nora hides under the table, the children rush in and out for her, but do not see her; they hear her smothered laughter, run to the table, lift up the cloth and find her. Shouts of laughter. She crawls forward and pretends to frighten them. Fresh laughter. Meanwhile there has been a knock at the hall door, but none of them has noticed it. The door is half opened, and Krogstad appears. He waits a little; the game goes on.*)

KROGSTAD: Excuse me, Mrs. Helmer.

NORA (*with a stifled cry, turns round and gets up on to her knees*):   Ah! what do you want?

KROGSTAD: Excuse me, the outer door was ajar; I suppose someone forgot to shut it.

NORA (*rising*):   My husband is out, Mr Krogstad.

KROGSTAD: I know that.

NORA: What do you want here, then?

KROGSTAD: A word with you.

NORA: With me?—(*To the children, gently.*) Go in to nurse. What? No, the strange man won't do mother any harm. When he has gone we will have another game. (*She takes the children into the room on the left, and shuts the door after them.*) You want to speak to me?

KROGSTAD: Yes, I do.

NORA: To-day? It is not the first of the month yet.

KROGSTAD: No, it is Christmas Eve, and it will depend on yourself what sort of a Christmas you will spend.

NORA: What do you mean? To-day it is absolutely impossible for me—

KROGSTAD: We won't talk about that until later on. This is something different. I presume you can give me a moment?

NORA: Yes—yes, I can—although—

KROGSTAD: Good. I was in Olsen's Restaurant and saw your husband going down the street—

NORA: Yes?

KROGSTAD: With a lady.

NORA: What then?

KROGSTAD: May I make so bold as to ask if it was a Mrs. Linde?

NORA: It was.

KROGSTAD: Just arrived in town?

NORA: Yes, to-day.

KROGSTAD: She is a great friend of yours, isn't she?

NORA: She is. But I don't see—

KROGSTAD: I knew her too, once upon a time.

NORA: I am aware of that.

KROGSTAD: Are you? So you know all about it; I thought as much. Then I can ask you, without beating about the bush—is Mrs. Linde to have an appointment in the Bank?

NORA: What right have you to question me, Mr. Krogstad?—You, one of my husband's subordinates! But since you ask, you shall know. Yes, Mrs. Linde *is* to have an appointment. And it was I who pleaded her cause, Mr. Krogstad, let me tell you that.

KROGSTAD: I was right in what I thought, then.

NORA (*walking up and down the stage*):   Sometimes one has a tiny little bit of influence, I should hope. Because one is a woman, it does not necessarily follow that—. When anyone is in a subordinate position, Mr. Krogstad, they should really be careful to avoid offending anyone who—who—

KROGSTAD: Who has influence?

NORA: Exactly.

KROGSTAD (*changing his tone*):   Mrs. Helmer, you will be so good as to use your influence on my behalf.

NORA: What? What do you mean?

KROGSTAD: You will be so kind as to see that I am allowed to keep my subordinate position in the Bank.

NORA: What do you mean by that? Who proposes to take your post away from you?

KROGSTAD: Oh, there is no necessity to keep up the pretence of ignorance. I can quite understand that your friend is not very anxious to expose herself to the chance of rubbing shoulders with me; and I quite understand, too, whom I have to thank for being turned off.

NORA: But I assure you—

KROGSTAD: Very likely; but, to come to the point, the time has come when I should advise you to use your influence to prevent that.

NORA: But, Mr. Krogstad, I *have* no influence.

KROGSTAD: Haven't you? I thought you said yourself just now—

NORA: Naturally I did not mean you to put that construction on it. What should make you think I have any influence of that kind with my husband?

KROGSTAD: Oh, I have known your husband from our student days. I don't suppose he is any more unassailable than other husbands.

NORA: If you speak slightingly of my husband, I shall turn you out of the house.

KROGSTAD: You are bold, Mrs. Helmer.

NORA: I am not afraid of you any longer. As soon as the New Year comes, I shall in a very short time be free of the whole thing.

KROGSTAD (*controlling himself*):   Listen to me, Mrs. Helmer. If necessary, I am prepared to fight for my small post in the Bank as if I were fighting for my life.

NORA: So it seems.

KROGSTAD: It is not only for the sake of the money; indeed, that weighs least with me in the matter. There is another reason—well, I may as well tell you. My position is this. I daresay you know, like everybody else, that once, many years ago, I was guilty of an indiscretion.

NORA: I think I have heard something of the kind.

KROGSTAD: The matter never came into court; but every way seemed to be closed to me after that. So I took to the business that you know of. I had to do something; and, honestly, I don't think I've been one of the worst. But now I must cut myself free from all that. My sons are growing up; for their sake I must try and win back as much respect as I can in the town. This post in the Bank was like the first step up for me—and now your husband is going to kick me downstairs again into the mud.

NORA: But you must believe me, Mr. Krogstad; it is not in my power to help you at all.

KROGSTAD: Then it is because you haven't the will; but I have means to compel you.

NORA: You don't mean that you will tell my husband that I owe you money?

KROGSTAD: Hm!—suppose I were to tell him?

NORA: It would be perfectly infamous of you. (*Sobbing.*) To think of his learning my secret, which has been my joy and pride, in such an ugly, clumsy way—that he should learn it from you! And it would put me in a horribly disagreeable position—

KROGSTAD: Only disagreeable?

NORA (*impetuously*):   Well, do it, then!—and it will be the worse for you. My husband will see for himself what a blackguard you are, and you certainly won't keep your post then.

KROGSTAD: I asked you if it was only a disagreeable scene at home that you were afraid of?

NORA: If my husband does get to know of it, of course he will at once pay you what is still owing, and we shall have nothing more to do with you.

KROGSTAD (*coming a step nearer*):   Listen to me, Mrs. Helmer. Either you have a very bad memory or you know very little of business. I shall be obliged to remind you of a few details.

NORA: What do you mean?

KROGSTAD: When your husband was ill, you came to me to borrow two hundred and fifty pounds.

NORA: I didn't know anyone else to go to.

KROGSTAD: I promised to get you that amount—

NORA: Yes, and you did so.

KROGSTAD: I promised to get you that amount, on certain conditions. Your mind was so taken up with your husband's illness, and you were so anxious to get the money for your journey, that you seem to have paid no attention to the conditions of our bargain. Therefore it will not be amiss if I remind you of them. Now, I promised to get the money on the security of a bond which I drew up.

NORA: Yes, and which I signed.

KROGSTAD: Good. But below your signature there were a few lines constituting your father a surety for the money; those lines your father should have signed.

NORA: Should? He did sign them.

KROGSTAD: I had left the date blank; that is to say, your father should himself have inserted the date on which he signed the paper. Do you remember that?

NORA: Yes, I think I remember—

KROGSTAD: Then I gave you the bond to send by post to your father. Is that not so?

NORA: Yes.

KROGSTAD: And you naturally did so at once, because five or six days afterwards you brought me the bond with your father's signature. And then I gave you the money.

NORA: Well, haven't I been paying it off regularly?

KROGSTAD: Fairly so, yes. But—to come back to the matter in hand—that must have been a very trying time for you, Mrs. Helmer.

NORA: It was, indeed.

KROGSTAD: Your father was very ill, wasn't he?

NORA: He was very near his end.

KROGSTAD: And he died soon afterwards?

NORA: Yes.

KROGSTAD: Tell me, Mrs. Helmer, can you by any chance remember what day your father died?—on what day of the month, I mean.

NORA: Papa died on the 29th of September.

KROGSTAD: That is correct; I have ascertained it for myself. And, as that is so, there is a discrepancy (*taking a paper from his pocket*) which I cannot account for.

NORA: What discrepancy? I don't know —

KROGSTAD: The discrepancy consists, Mrs. Helmer, in the fact that your father signed this bond three days after his death.

NORA: What do you mean? I don't understand —

KROGSTAD: Your father died on the 29th of September. But, look here; your father has dated his signature the 2nd of October. It is a discrepancy, isn't it? (*Nora is silent.*) Can you explain it to me? (*Nora is still silent.*) It is a remarkable thing, too, that the words "2nd of October," as well as the year, are not written in your father's handwriting but in one that I think I know. Well, of course it can be explained; your father may have forgotten to date his signature, and someone else may have dated it haphazard before they knew of his death. There is no harm in that. It all depends on the signature of the name; and *that* is genuine, I suppose, Mrs. Helmer? It was your father himself who signed his name here?

NORA (*after a short pause, throws her head up and looks defiantly at him*):   No, it was not. It was I that wrote papa's name.

KROGSTAD: Are you aware that is a dangerous confession?

NORA: In what way? You shall have your money soon.

KROGSTAD: Let me ask you a question; why did you not send the paper to your father?

NORA: It was impossible; papa was so ill. If I had asked him for his signature, I should have had to tell him what the money was to be used for; and when he was so ill himself I couldn't tell him that my husband's life was in danger — it was impossible.

KROGSTAD: It would have been better for you if you had given up your trip abroad.

NORA: No, that was impossible. That trip was to save my husband's life; I couldn't give that up.

KROGSTAD: But did it never occur to you that you were committing a fraud on me?

NORA: I couldn't take that into account; I didn't trouble myself about you at all. I couldn't bear you, because you put so many heartless difficulties in my way, although you knew what a dangerous condition my husband was in.

KROGSTAD: Mrs. Helmer, you evidently do not realise clearly what it is that you have been guilty of. But I can assure you that my one false step, which lost me all my reputation, was nothing more or nothing worse than what you have done.

NORA: You? Do you ask me to believe that you were brave enough to run a risk to save your wife's life?

KROGSTAD: The law cares nothing about motives.

NORA: Then it must be a very foolish law.

KROGSTAD: Foolish or not, it is the law by which you will be judged, if I produce this paper in court.

NORA: I don't believe it. Is a daughter not to be allowed to spare her dying father anxiety and care? Is a wife not to be allowed to save her husband's life?
I don't know much about law; but I am certain that there must be laws
permitting such things as that. Have you no knowledge of such laws —
you who are a lawyer? You must be a very poor lawyer, Mr. Krogstad.

KROGSTAD: Maybe. But matters of business — such business as you and I have
had together — do you think I don't understand that? Very well. Do as you
please. But let me tell you this — if I lose my position a second time, you
shall lose yours with me. (*He bows, and goes out through the hall.*)

NORA (*appears buried in thought for a short time, then tosses her head*):   Nonsense!
Trying to frighten me like that! — I am not so silly as he thinks. (*Begins
to busy herself putting the children's things in order.*) And yet — ? No, it's impossible! I did it for love's sake.

CHILDREN (*in the doorway on the left*):   Mother, the stranger man has gone out
through the gate.

NORA: Yes, dears, I know. But, don't tell anyone about the stranger man. Do
you hear? Not even papa.

CHILDREN: No, mother; but will you come and play again?

NORA: No, no, — not now.

CHILDREN: But, mother, you promised us.

NORA: Yes, but I can't now. Run away in; I have such a lot to do. Run away in,
my sweet little darlings. (*She gets them into the room by degrees and shuts the
door on them; then sits down on the sofa, takes up a piece of needlework and sews
a few stitches, but soon stops.*) No! (*Throws down the work, gets up, goes to the
hall door and calls out.*) Helen! bring the Tree in. (*Goes to the table on the left,
opens a drawer, and stops again.*) No, no! it is quite impossible!

MAID (*coming in with the Tree*):   Where shall I put it, ma'am?

NORA: Here, in the middle of the floor.

MAID: Shall I get you anything else?

NORA: No, thank you. I have all I want.   (*Exit Maid.*)

NORA (*begins dressing the tree*):   A candle here — and flowers here —. The horrible man! It's all nonsense — there's nothing wrong. The Tree shall be
splendid! I will do everything I can think of to please you, Torvald! — I will
sing for you, dance for you — (*Helmer comes in with some papers under his
arm.*) Oh! are you back already?

HELMER: Yes. Has anyone been here?

NORA: Here? No.

HELMER: That is strange. I saw Krogstad going out of the gate.

NORA: Did you? Oh yes, I forgot, Krogstad was here for a moment.

HELMER: Nora, I can see from your manner that he has been here begging you
to say a good word for him.

NORA: Yes.

HELMER: And you were to appear to do it of your own accord; you were to
conceal from me the fact of his having been here; didn't he beg that of
you too?

NORA: Yes, Torvald, but—

HELMER: Nora, Nora, and you would be a party to that sort of thing? To have any talk with a man like that, and give him any sort of promise? And to tell me a lie into the bargain?

NORA: A lie—?

HELMER: Didn't you tell me no one had been here? (*Shakes his finger at her.*) My little song-bird must never do that again. A song-bird must have a clean beak to chirp with—no false notes! (*Puts his arm around her waist.*) That is so, isn't it? Yes, I am sure it is. (*Lets her go.*) We will say no more about it. (*Sits down by the stove.*) How warm and snug it is here! (*Turns over his papers.*)

NORA (*after a short pause, during which she busies herself with the Christmas Tree*):   Torvald!

HELMER: Yes.

NORA: I am looking forward tremendously to the fancy-dress ball at the Stenborgs' the day after to-morrow.

HELMER: And I am tremendously curious to see what you are going to surprise me with.

NORA: It was very silly of me to want to do that.

HELMER: What do you mean?

NORA: I can't hit upon anything that will do; everything I think of seems so silly and insignificant.

HELMER: Does my little Nora acknowledge that at last?

NORA (*standing behind his chair with her arms on the back of it*):   Are you very busy, Torvald?

HELMER: Well—

NORA: What are all those papers?

HELMER: Bank business.

NORA: Already?

HELMER: I have got authority from the retiring manager to undertake the necessary changes in the staff and in the rearrangement of the work; and I must make use of the Christmas week for that, so as to have everything in order for the new year.

NORA: Then that was why this poor Krogstad—

HELMER: Hm!

NORA (*leans against the back of his chair and strokes his hair*):   If you hadn't been so busy I should have asked you a tremendously big favour, Torvald.

HELMER: What is that? Tell me.

NORA: There is no one has such good taste as you. And I do so want to look nice at the fancy-dress ball. Torvald, couldn't you take me in hand and decide what I shall go as, and what sort of a dress I shall wear?

HELMER: Aha! so my obstinate little woman is obliged to get someone to come to her rescue?

NORA: Yes, Torvald, I can't get along a bit without your help.

HELMER: Very well, I will think it over, we shall manage to hit upon something.

NORA: That is nice of you. (*Goes to the Christmas Tree. A short pause.*) How pretty the red flowers look—. But, tell me, was it really something very bad that this Krogstad was guilty of?

HELMER: He forged someone's name. Have you any idea what that means?

NORA: Isn't it possible that he was driven to do it by necessity?

HELMER: Yes; or, as in so many cases, by imprudence. I am not so heartless as to condemn a man altogether because of a single false step of that kind.

NORA: No, you wouldn't, would you, Torvald?

HELMER: Many a man has been able to retrieve his character, if he has openly confessed his fault and taken his punishment.

NORA: Punishment—?

HELMER: But Krogstad did nothing of that sort; he got himself out of it by a cunning trick, and that is why he has gone under altogether.

NORA: But do you think it would—?

HELMER: Just think how a guilty man like that has to lie and play the hypocrite with every one, how he has to wear a mask in the presence of those near and dear to him, even before his own wife and children. And about the children—that is the most terrible part of it all, Nora.

NORA: How?

HELMER: Because such an atmosphere of lies infects and poisons the whole life of a home. Each breath the children take in such a house is full of the germs of evil.

NORA (*coming nearer him*):   Are you sure of that?

HELMER: My dear, I have often seen it in the course of my life as a lawyer. Almost everyone who has gone to the bad early in life has had a deceitful mother.

NORA: Why do you only say—mother?

HELMER: It seems most commonly to be the mother's influence, though naturally a bad father's would have the same result. Every lawyer is familiar with the fact. This Krogstad, now, has been persistently poisoning his own children with lies and dissimulation; that is why I say he has lost all moral character. (*Holds out his hands to her.*) That is why my sweet little Nora must promise me not to plead his cause. Give me your hand on it. Come, come, what is this? Give me your hand. There now, that's settled. I assure you it would be quite impossible for me to work with him; I literally feel physically ill when I am in the company of such people.

NORA (*takes her hand out of his and goes to the opposite side of the Christmas Tree*):   How hot it is in here; and I have such a lot to do.

HELMER (*getting up and putting his papers in order*):   Yes, and I must try and read through some of these before dinner; and I must think about your costume, too. And it is just possible I may have something ready in gold paper to hang up on the Tree. (*Puts his hand on her head.*) My precious little singing-bird! (*He goes into his room and shuts the door after him.*)

NORA (*after a pause, whispers*):   No, no—it isn't true. It's impossible; it must be impossible.

The Nurse opens the door on the left.

NURSE: The little ones are begging so hard to be allowed to come in to mamma.

NORA: No, no, no! Don't let them come in to me! You stay with them, Anne.

NURSE: Very well, ma'am. (*Shuts the door.*)

NORA (*pale with terror*):   Deprave my little children? Poison my home? (*A short pause. Then she tosses her head.*) It's not true. It can't possibly be true.

ACT II

THE SAME SCENE: *The Christmas Tree is in the corner by the piano, stripped of its ornaments and with burnt-down candle-ends on its dishevelled branches. Nora's cloak and hat are lying on the sofa. She is alone in the room, walking about uneasily. She stops by the sofa and takes up her cloak.*

NORA (*drops her cloak*):   Someone is coming now! (*Goes to the door and listens.*) No — it is no one. Of course, no one will come to-day, Christmas Day — nor to-morrow either. But, perhaps — (*opens the door and looks out*). No, nothing in the letter-box; it is quite empty. (*Comes forward.*) What rubbish! of course he can't be in earnest about it. Such a thing couldn't happen; it is impossible — I have three little children.

Enter the Nurse from the room on the left, carrying a big cardboard box.

NURSE: At last I have found the box with the fancy dress.

NORA: Thanks; put it on the table.

NURSE (*doing so*):   But it is very much in want of mending.

NORA: I should like to tear it into a hundred thousand pieces.

NURSE: What an idea! It can easily be put in order — just a little patience.

NORA: Yes, I will go and get Mrs. Linde to come and help me with it.

NURSE: What, out again? In this horrible weather? You will catch cold, ma'am, and make yourself ill.

NORA: Well, worse than that might happen. How are the children?

NURSE: The poor little souls are playing with their Christmas presents, but —

NORA: Do they ask much for me?

NURSE: You see, they are so accustomed to have their mamma with them.

NORA: Yes, but, nurse, I shall not be able to be so much with them now as I was before.

NURSE: Oh well, young children easily get accustomed to anything.

NORA: Do you think so? Do you think they would forget their mother if she went away altogether?

NURSE: Good heavens! — went away altogether?

NORA: Nurse, I want you to tell me something I have often wondered about — how could you have the heart to put your own child out among strangers?

NURSE: I was obliged to, if I wanted to be little Nora's nurse.

NORA: Yes, but how could you be willing to do it?

NURSE: What, when I was going to get such a good place by it? A poor girl who has got into trouble should be glad to. Besides, that wicked man didn't do a single thing for me.

NORA: But I suppose your daughter has quite forgotten you.

NURSE: No, indeed she hasn't. She wrote to me when she was confirmed, and when she was married.

NORA (*putting her arms round her neck*):   Dear old Anne, you were a good mother to me when I was little.

NURSE: Little Nora, poor dear, had no other mother but me.

NORA: And if my little ones had no other mother, I am sure you would—What nonsense I am talking! (*Opens the box.*) Go in to them. Now I must—. You will see to-morrow how charming I shall look.

NURSE: I am sure there will be no one at the ball so charming as you, ma'am. (*Goes into the room on the left.*)

NORA (*begins to unpack the box, but soon pushes it away from her*):   If only I dared go out. If only no one would come. If only I could be sure nothing would happen here in the meantime. Stuff and nonsense! No one will come. Only I mustn't think about it. I will brush my muff. What lovely, lovely gloves! Out of my thoughts, out of my thoughts! One, two, three, four, five, six— (*Screams.*) Ah! there is someone coming—. (*Makes a movement towards the door, but stands irresolute.*)

Enter Mrs. Linde from the hall, where she has taken off her cloak and hat.

NORA: Oh, it's you, Christine. There is no one else out there, is there? How good of you to come!

MRS. LINDE: I heard you were up asking for me.

NORA: Yes, I was passing by. As a matter of fact, it is something you could help me with. Let us sit down here on the sofa. Look here. To-morrow evening there is to be a fancy-dress ball at the Stenborgs', who live above us; and Torvald wants me to go as a Neapolitan fisher-girl, and dance the Tarantella that I learned at Capri.

MRS. LINDE: I see; you are going to keep up the character.

NORA: Yes, Torvald wants me to. Look, here is the dress; Torvald had it made for me there, but now it is all so torn, and I haven't any idea—

MRS. LINDE: We will easily put that right. It is only some of the trimming come unsewn here and there. Needle and thread? Now then, that's all we want.

NORA: It *is* nice of you.

MRS. LINDE (*sewing*):   So you are going to be dressed up to-morrow, Nora. I will tell you what—I shall come in for a moment and see you in your fine feathers. But I have completely forgotten to thank you for a delightful evening yesterday.

NORA (*gets up, and crosses the stage*):   Well, I don't think yesterday was as pleasant as usual. You ought to have come to town a little earlier, Christine. Certainly Torvald does understand how to make a house dainty and attractive.

MRS. LINDE: And so do you, it seems to me; you are not your father's daughter for nothing. But tell me, is Doctor Rank always as depressed as he was yesterday?

NORA: No; yesterday it was very noticeable. I must tell you that he suffers from a very dangerous disease. He has consumption of the spine, poor creature. His father was a horrible man who committed all sorts of excesses; and that is why his son was sickly from childhood, do you understand?

MRS. LINDE (*dropping her sewing*):   But, my dearest Nora, how do you know anything about such things?

NORA (*walking about*): Pooh! When you have three children, you get visits now and then from—from married women, who know something of medical matters, and they talk about one thing and another.

MRS. LINDE: (*goes on sewing. A short silence*) Does Doctor Rank come here every-day?

NORA: Everyday regularly. He is Torvald's most intimate friend, and a great friend of mine too. He is just like one of the family.

MRS. LINDE: But tell me this—is he perfectly sincere? I mean, isn't he the kind of man that is very anxious to make himself agreeable?

NORA: Not in the least. What makes you think that?

MRS. LINDE: When you introduced him to me yesterday, he declared he had often heard my name mentioned in this house; but afterwards I noticed that your husband hadn't the slightest idea who I was. So how could Doctor Rank—?

NORA: That is quite right, Christine. Torvald is so absurdly fond of me that he wants me absolutely to himself, as he says. At first he used to seem almost jealous if I mentioned any of the dear folk at home, so naturally I gave up doing so. But I often talk about such things with Doctor Rank, because he likes hearing about them.

MRS. LINDE: Listen to me, Nora. You are still very like a child in many things, and I am older than you in many ways and have a little more experience. Let me tell you this—you ought to make an end of it with Doctor Rank.

NORA: What ought I to make an end of?

MRS. LINDE: Of two things, I think. Yesterday you talked some nonsense about a rich admirer who was to leave you money—

NORA: An admirer who doesn't exist, unfortunately! But what then?

MRS. LINDE: Is Doctor Rank a man of means?

NORA: Yes, he is.

MRS. LINDE: And has no one to provide for?

NORA: No, no one; but—

MRS. LINDE: And comes here everyday?

NORA: Yes, I told you so.

MRS. LINDE: But how can this well-bred man be so tactless?

NORA: I don't understand you at all.

MRS. LINDE: Don't prevaricate, Nora. Do you suppose I don't guess who lent you the two hundred and fifty pounds?

NORA: Are you out of your senses? How can you think of such a thing! A friend of ours, who comes here everyday! Do you realise what a horribly painful position that would be?

MRS. LINDE: Then it really isn't he?

NORA: No, certainly not. It would never have entered into my head for a moment. Besides, he had no money to lend then; he came into his money afterwards.

MRS. LINDE: Well, I think that was lucky for you, my dear Nora.

NORA: No, it would never have come into my head to ask Doctor Rank. Although I am quite sure that if I had asked him—

MRS. LINDE: But of course you won't.

NORA: Of course not. I have no reason to think it could possibly be necessary. But I am quite sure that if I told Doctor Rank—

MRS. LINDE: Behind your husband's back?

NORA: I must make an end of it with the other one, and that will be behind his back too. I *must* make an end of it with him.

MRS. LINDE: Yes, that is what I told you yesterday, but—

NORA (*walking up and down*):   A man can put a thing like that straight much easier than a woman—

MRS. LINDE: One's husband, yes.

NORA: Nonsense! (*Standing still.*) When you pay off a debt you get your bond back, don't you?

MRS. LINDE: Yes, as a matter of course.

NORA: And can tear it into a hundred thousand pieces, and burn it up—the nasty dirty paper!

MRS. LINDE (*looks hard at her, lays down her sewing and gets up slowly*):   Nora, you are concealing something from me.

NORA: Do I look as if I were?

MRS. LINDE: Something has happened to you since yesterday morning. Nora, what is it?

NORA (*going nearer to her*):   Christine! (*Listens.*) Hush! there's Torvald come home. Do you mind going in to the children for the present? Torvald can't bear to see dressmaking going on. Let Anne help you.

MRS. LINDE (*gathering some of the things together*):   Certainly—but I am not going away from here until we have had it out with one another. (*She goes into the room on the left, as Helmer comes in from the hall.*)

NORA (*going up to Helmer*):   I have wanted you so much, Torvald dear.

HELMER: Was that the dressmaker?

NORA: No, it was Christine; she is helping me to put my dress in order. You will see I shall look quite smart.

HELMER: Wasn't that a happy thought of mine, now?

NORA: Splendid! But don't you think it is nice of me, too, to do as you wish?

HELMER: Nice?—because you do as your husband wishes? Well, well, you little rogue, I am sure you did not mean it in that way. But I am not going to disturb you; you will want to be trying on your dress, I expect.

NORA: I suppose you are going to work.

HELMER: Yes. (*Shows her a bundle of papers.*) Look at that. I have just been into the bank. (*Turns to go into his room.*)

NORA: Torvald.

HELMER: Yes.

NORA: If your little squirrel were to ask you for something very, very prettily—?

HELMER: What then?

NORA: Would you do it?

HELMER: I should like to hear what it is, first.

NORA: Your squirrel would run about and do all her tricks if you would be nice, and do what she wants.

HELMER: Speak plainly.

NORA: Your skylark would chirp about in every room, with her song rising and falling—

HELMER: Well, my skylark does that anyhow.

NORA: I would play the fairy and dance for you in the moonlight, Torvald.

HELMER: Nora—you surely don't mean that request you made to me this morning?

NORA (*going near him*):   Yes, Torvald, I beg you so earnestly—

HELMER: Have you really the courage to open up that question again?

NORA: Yes, dear, you *must* do as I ask; you *must* let Krogstad keep his post in the bank.

HELMER: My dear Nora, it is his post that I have arranged Mrs. Linde shall have.

NORA: Yes, you have been awfully kind about that; but you could just as well dismiss some other clerk instead of Krogstad.

HELMER: This is simply incredible obstinacy! Because you chose to give him a thoughtless promise that you would speak for him, I am expected to—

NORA: That isn't the reason, Torvald. It is for your own sake. This fellow writes in the most scurrilous newspapers; you have told me so yourself. He can do you an unspeakable amount of harm. I am frightened to death of him—

HELMER: Ah, I understand; it is recollections of the past that scare you.

NORA: What do you mean?

HELMER: Naturally you are thinking of your father.

NORA: Yes—yes, of course. Just recall to your mind what these malicious creatures wrote in the papers about papa, and how horribly they slandered him. I believe they would have procured his dismissal if the Department had not sent you over to inquire into it, and if you had not been so kindly disposed and helpful to him.

HELMER: My little Nora, there is an important difference between your father and me. Your father's reputation as a public official was not above suspicion. Mine is, and I hope it will continue to be so, as long as I hold my office.

NORA: You never can tell what mischief these men may contrive. We ought to be so well off, so snug and happy here in our peaceful home, and have no cares—you and I and the children, Torvald! That is why I beg you so earnestly—

HELMER: And it is just by interceding for him that you make it impossible for me to keep him. It is already known at the Bank that I mean to dismiss Krogstad. Is it to get about now that the new manager has changed his mind at his wife's bidding—

NORA: And what if it did?

HELMER: Of course!—if only this obstinate little person can get her way! Do you suppose I am going to make myself ridiculous before my whole staff, to let people think that I am a man to be swayed by all sorts of outside influence? I should very soon feel the consequences of it, I can tell you! And besides, there is one thing that makes it quite impossible for me to have Krogstad in the Bank as long as I am manager.

NORA: Whatever is that?

HELMER: His moral failings I might perhaps have overlooked, if necessary—

NORA: Yes, you could—couldn't you?

HELMER: And I hear he is a good worker, too. But I knew him when we were boys. It was one of those rash friendships that so often prove an incubus in afterlife. I may as well tell you plainly, we were once on very intimate terms with one another. But this tactless fellow lays no restraint on himself when other people are present. On the contrary, he thinks it gives him the right to adopt a familiar tone with me, and every minute it is "I say, Helmer, old fellow!" and that sort of thing. I assure you it is extremely painful for me. He would make my position in the Bank intolerable.

NORA: Torvald, I don't believe you mean that.

HELMER: Don't you? Why not?

NORA: Because it is such a narrow-minded way of looking at things.

HELMER: What are you saying? Narrow-minded? Do you think I am narrow-minded?

NORA: No, just the opposite, dear—and it is exactly for that reason.

HELMER: It's the same thing. You say my point of view is narrow-minded, so I must be so too. Narrow-minded! Very well—I must put an end to this. (*Goes to the hall door and calls.*) Helen!

NORA: What are you going to do?

HELMER (*looking among his papers*):   Settle it. (*Enter Maid.*) Look here; take this letter and go downstairs with it at once. Find a messenger and tell him to deliver it, and be quick. The address is on it, and here is the money.

MAID: Very well, sir. (*Exit with the letter.*)

HELMER (*putting his papers together*):   Now then, little Miss Obstinate.

NORA (*breathlessly*):   Torvald—what was that letter?

HELMER: Krogstad's dismissal.

NORA: Call her back, Torvald! There is still time. Oh Torvald, call her back! Do it for my sake—for your own sake—for the children's sake! Do you hear me, Torvald? Call her back! You don't know what that letter can bring upon us.

HELMER: It's too late.

NORA: Yes, it's too late.

HELMER: My dear Nora, I can forgive the anxiety you are in, although really it is an insult to me. It is, indeed. Isn't it an insult to think that I should be afraid of a starving quill-driver's vengeance? But I forgive you nevertheless, because it is such eloquent witness to your great love for me. (*Takes her in his arms.*) And that is as it should be, my own darling Nora. Come what will, you may be sure I shall have both courage and strength if they be needed. You will see I am man enough to take everything upon myself.

NORA (*in a horror-stricken voice*):   What do you mean by that?

HELMER: Everything, I say—

NORA (*recovering herself*):   You will never have to do that.

HELMER: That's right. Well, we will share it, Nora, as man and wife should. That is how it shall be. (*Caressing her.*) Are you content now? There!

there!—not these frightened dove's eyes! The whole thing is only the wildest fancy!—Now, you must go and play through the Tarantella and practise with your tambourine. I shall go into the inner office and shut the door, and I shall hear nothing; you can make as much noise as you please. (*Turns back at the door.*) And when Rank comes, tell him where he will find me. (*Nods to her, takes his papers and goes into his room, and shuts the door after him.*)

NORA (*bewildered with anxiety, stands as if rooted to the spot, and whispers*):   He was capable of doing it. He will do it. He will do it in spite of everything.— No, not that! Never, never! Anything rather than that! Oh, for some help, some way out of it! (*The door-bell rings.*) Doctor Rank! Anything rather than that—anything, whatever it is! (*She puts her hands over her face, pulls herself together, goes to the door and opens it. Rank is standing without, hanging up his coat. During the following dialogue it begins to grow dark.*)

NORA: Good-day, Doctor Rank. I knew your ring. But you mustn't go in to Torvald now; I think he is busy with something.

RANK: And you?

NORA (*brings him in and shuts the door after him*):   Oh, you know very well I always have time for you.

RANK: Thank you. I shall make use of as much of it as I can.

NORA: What do you mean by that? As much of it as you can?

RANK: Well, does that alarm you?

NORA: It was such a strange way of putting it. Is anything likely to happen?

RANK: Nothing but what I have long been prepared for. But I certainly didn't expect it to happen so soon.

NORA (*gripping him by the arm*):   What have you found out? Doctor Rank, you must tell me.

RANK (*sitting down by the stove*):   It is all up with me. And it can't be helped.

NORA (*with a sigh of relief*):   Is it about yourself?

RANK: Who else? It is no use lying to one's self. I am the most wretched of all my patients, Mrs. Helmer. Lately I have been taking stock of my internal economy. Bankrupt! Probably within a month I shall lie rotting in the churchyard.

NORA: What an ugly thing to say!

RANK: The thing itself is cursedly ugly, and the worst of it is that I shall have to face so much more that is ugly before that. I shall only make one more examination of myself; when I have done that, I shall know pretty certainly when it will be that the horrors of dissolution will begin. There is something I want to tell you. Helmer's refined nature gives him an unconquerable disgust at everything that is ugly; I won't have him in my sick-room.

NORA: Oh, but, Doctor Rank—

RANK: I won't have him there. Not on any account. I bar my door to him. As soon as I am quite certain that the worst has come, I shall send you my card with a black cross on it, and then you will know that the loathsome end has begun.

NORA: You are quite absurd to-day. And I wanted you so much to be in a really good humour.

RANK: With death stalking beside me?—To have to pay this penalty for another man's sin? Is there any justice in that? And in every single family, in one way or another, some such inexorable retribution is being exacted—

NORA (*putting her hands over her ears*):   Rubbish! Do talk of something cheerful.

RANK: Oh, it's a mere laughing matter, the whole thing. My poor innocent spine has to suffer for my father's youthful amusements.

NORA (*sitting at the table on the left*):   I suppose you mean that he was too partial to asparagus and pâté de foie gras, don't you?

RANK: Yes, and to truffles.

NORA: Truffles, yes. And oysters too, I suppose?

RANK: Oysters, of course, that goes without saying.

NORA: And heaps of port and champagne. It is sad that all these nice things should take their revenge on our bones.

RANK: Especially that they should revenge themselves on the unlucky bones of those who have not had the satisfaction of enjoying them.

NORA: Yes, that's the saddest part of it all.

RANK (*with a searching look at her*):   Hm!—

NORA (*after a short pause*):   Why did you smile?

RANK: No, it was you that laughed.

NORA: No, it was you that smiled, Doctor Rank!

RANK (*rising*):   You are a greater rascal than I thought.

NORA: I am in a silly mood to-day.

RANK: So it seems.

NORA (*putting her hands on his shoulders*):   Dear, dear Doctor Rank, death mustn't take you away from Torvald and me.

RANK: It is a loss you would easily recover from. Those who are gone are soon forgotten.

NORA (*looking at him anxiously*):   Do you believe that?

RANK: People form new ties, and then—

NORA: Who will form new ties?

RANK: Both you and Helmer, when I am gone. You yourself are already on the high road to it, I think. What did that Mrs. Linde want here last night?

NORA: Oho!—you don't mean to say you are jealous of poor Christine?

RANK: Yes, I am. She will be my successor in this house. When I am done for, this woman will—

NORA: Hush! don't speak so loud. She is in that room.

RANK: To-day again. There, you see.

NORA: She has only come to sew my dress for me. Bless my soul, how unreasonable you are! (*Sits down on the sofa.*) Be nice now, Doctor Rank, and to-morrow you will see how beautifully I shall dance, and you can imagine I am doing it all for you—and for Torvald too, of course. (*Takes various things out of the box.*) Doctor Rank, come and sit down here, and I will show you something.

RANK (*sitting down*):   What is it?

NORA: Just look at those!

RANK: Silk stockings.

NORA: Flesh-coloured. Aren't they lovely? It is so dark here now, but to-morrow—. No, no, no! you must only look at the feet. Oh well, you may have leave to look at the legs too.

RANK: Hm!—

NORA: Why are you looking so critical? Don't you think they will fit me?

RANK: I have no means of forming an opinion about that.

NORA (*looks at him for a moment*):   For shame! (*Hits him lightly on the ear with the stockings.*) That's to punish you. (*Folds them up again.*)

RANK: And what other nice things am I to be allowed to see?

NORA: Not a single thing more, for being so naughty. (*She looks among the things, humming to herself.*)

RANK (*after a short silence*):   When I am sitting here, talking to you as intimately as this, I cannot imagine for a moment what would have become of me if I had never come into this house.

NORA (*smiling*):   I believe you do feel thoroughly at home with us.

RANK (*in a lower voice, looking straight in front of him*):   And to be obliged to leave it all—

NORA: Nonsense, you are not going to leave it.

RANK (*as before*):   And not be able to leave behind one the slightest token of one's gratitude, scarcely even a fleeting regret—nothing but an empty place which the first comer can fill as well as any other.

NORA: And if I asked you now for a—? No!

RANK: For what?

NORA: For a big proof of your friendship—

RANK: Yes, yes!

NORA: I mean a tremendously big favour.

RANK: Would you really make me so happy for once?

NORA: Ah, but you don't know what it is yet.

RANK: No—but tell me.

NORA: I really can't, Doctor Rank. It is something out of all reason; it means advice, and help, and a favour—

RANK: The bigger a thing it is the better. I can't conceive what it is you mean. Do tell me. Haven't I your confidence?

NORA: More than anyone else. I know you are my truest and best friend, and so I will tell you what it is. Well, Doctor Rank, it is something you must help me to prevent. You know how devotedly, how inexpressibly deeply Torvald loves me; he would never for a moment hesitate to give his life for me.

RANK (*leaning towards her*):   Nora—do you think he is the only one—?

NORA (*with a slight start*):   The only one—?

RANK: The only one who would gladly give his life for your sake.

NORA (*sadly*):   Is that it?

RANK: I was determined you should know it before I went away, and there will never be a better opportunity than this. Now you know it, Nora. And now you know, too, that you can trust me as you would trust no one else.

NORA (*rises, deliberately and quietly*):   Let me pass.

RANK (*makes room for her to pass him, but sits still*):   Nora!

NORA (*at the hall door*):   Helen, bring in the lamp. (*Goes over to the stove.*) Dear Doctor Rank, that was really horrid of you.

RANK: To have loved you as much as anyone else does? Was that horrid?

NORA: No, but to go and tell me so. There was really no need—

RANK: What do you mean? Did you know—? (*Maid enters with lamp, puts it down on the table, and goes out.*) Nora—Mrs. Helmer—tell me, had you any idea of this?

NORA: Oh, how do I know whether I had or whether I hadn't? I really can't tell you—To think you could be so clumsy, Doctor Rank! We were getting on so nicely.

RANK: Well, at all events you know now that you can command me, body and soul. So won't you speak out?

NORA (*looking at him*):   After what happened?

RANK: I beg you to let me know what it is.

NORA: I can't tell you anything now.

RANK: Yes, yes. You mustn't punish me in that way. Let me have permission to do for you whatever a man may do.

NORA: You can do nothing for me now. Besides, I really don't need any help at all. You will find that the whole thing is merely fancy on my part. It really is so—of course it is! (*Sits down in the rocking-chair, and looks at him with a smile.*) You are a nice sort of man, Doctor Rank!—don't you feel ashamed of yourself, now the lamp has come?

RANK: Not a bit. But perhaps I had better go—for ever?

NORA: No, indeed, you shall not. Of course you must come here just as before. You know very well Torvald can't do without you.

RANK: Yes, but you?

NORA: Oh, I am always tremendously pleased when you come.

RANK: It is just that, that put me on the wrong track. You are a riddle to me. I have often thought that you would almost as soon be in my company as in Helmer's.

NORA: Yes—you see there are some people one loves best, and others whom one would almost always rather have as companions.

RANK: Yes, there is something in that.

NORA: When I was at home, of course I loved papa best. But I always thought it tremendous fun if I could steal down into the maids' room, because they never moralised at all, and talked to each other about such entertaining things.

RANK: I see—it is *their* place I have taken.

NORA (*jumping up and going to him*):   Oh, dear, nice Doctor Rank, I never meant that at all. But surely you can understand that being with Torvald is a little like being with papa—

Enter Maid from the hall.

MAID: If you please, ma'am. (*Whispers and hands her a card.*)

NORA (*glancing at the card*):   Oh! (*Puts it in her pocket.*)

RANK: Is there anything wrong?

NORA: No, no, not in the least. It is only something—it is my new dress—

RANK: What? Your dress is lying there.

NORA: Oh, yes, that one; but this is another. I ordered it. Torvald mustn't know about it—

RANK: Oho! Then that was the great secret.

NORA: Of course. Just go in to him; he is sitting in the inner room. Keep him as long as—

RANK: Make your mind easy; I won't let him escape. (*Goes into Helmer's room.*)

NORA (*to the Maid*):   And he is standing waiting in the kitchen?

MAID: Yes; he came up the back stairs.

NORA: But didn't you tell him no one was in?

MAID: Yes, but it was no good.

NORA: He won't go away?

MAID: No; he says he won't until he has seen you, ma'am.

NORA: Well, let him come in—but quietly. Helen, you mustn't say anything about it to anyone. It is a surprise for my husband.

MAID: Yes, ma'am, I quite understand. (*Exit.*)

NORA: This dreadful thing is going to happen! It will happen in spite of me! No, no, no, it can't happen—it shan't happen! (*She bolts the door of Helmer's room. The Maid opens the hall door for Krogstad and shuts it after him. He is wearing a fur coat, high boots and a fur cap.*)

NORA (*advancing towards him*):   Speak low—my husband is at home.

KROGSTAD: No matter about that.

NORA: What do you want of me?

KROGSTAD: An explanation of something.

NORA: Make haste then. What is it?

KROGSTAD: You know, I suppose, that I have got my dismissal.

NORA: I couldn't prevent it, Mr. Krogstad. I fought as hard as I could on your side, but it was no good.

KROGSTAD: Does your husband love you so little, then? He knows what I can expose you to, and yet he ventures—

NORA: How can you suppose that he has any knowledge of the sort?

KROGSTAD: I didn't suppose so at all. It would not be the least like our dear Torvald Helmer to show so much courage—

NORA: Mr. Krogstad, a little respect for my husband, please.

KROGSTAD: Certainly—all the respect he deserves. But since you have kept the matter so carefully to yourself, I make bold to suppose that you have a little clearer idea, than you had yesterday, of what it actually is that you have done?

NORA: More than you could ever teach me.

KROGSTAD: Yes, such a bad lawyer as I am.

NORA: What is it you want of me?

KROGSTAD: Only to see how you were, Mrs. Helmer. I have been thinking about you all day long. A mere cashier, a quill-driver, a—well, a man like me— even he has a little of what is called feeling, you know.

NORA: Show it, then; think of my little children.

KROGSTAD: Have you and your husband thought of mine? But never mind about that. I only wanted to tell you that you need not take this matter too seriously. In the first place there will be no accusation made on my part.

NORA: No, of course not; I was sure of that.

KROGSTAD: The whole thing can be arranged amicably; there is no reason why anyone should know anything about it. It will remain a secret between us three.

NORA: My husband must never get to know anything about it.

KROGSTAD: How will you be able to prevent it? Am I to understand that you can pay the balance that is owing?

NORA: No, not just at present.

KROGSTAD: Or perhaps that you have some expedient for raising the money soon?

NORA: No expedient that I mean to make use of.

KROGSTAD: Well, in any case, it would have been of no use to you now. If you stood there with ever so much money in your hand, I would never part with your bond.

NORA: Tell me what purpose you mean to put it to.

KROGSTAD: I shall only preserve it—keep it in my possession. No one who is not concerned in the matter shall have the slightest hint of it. So that if the thought of it has driven you to any desperate resolution—

NORA: It has.

KROGSTAD: If you had it in your mind to run away from your home—

NORA: I had.

KROGSTAD: Or even something worse—

NORA: How could you know that?

KROGSTAD: Give up the idea.

NORA: How did you know I had thought of *that?*

KROGSTAD: Most of us think of that at first. I did, too—but I hadn't the courage.

NORA (*faintly*):   No more had I.

KROGSTAD (*in a tone of relief*):   No, that's it, isn't it—you hadn't the courage either?

NORA: No, I haven't—I haven't.

KROGSTAD: Besides, it would have been a great piece of folly. Once the first storm at home is over—. I have a letter for your husband in my pocket.

NORA: Telling him everything?

KROGSTAD: In as lenient a manner as I possibly could.

NORA (*quickly*):   He mustn't get the letter. Tear it up. I will find some means of getting money.

KROGSTAD: Excuse me, Mrs. Helmer, but I think I told you just now—

NORA: I am not speaking of what I owe you. Tell me what sum you are asking my husband for, and I will get the money.

KROGSTAD: I am not asking your husband for a penny.

NORA: What do you want, then?

KROGSTAD: I will tell you. I want to rehabilitate myself, Mrs. Helmer; I want to get on; and in that your husband must help me. For the last year and a half I have not had a hand in anything dishonourable, and all that time I have been struggling in most restricted circumstances. I was content to work my way up step by step. Now I am turned out, and I am not going to be satisfied with merely being taken into favour again. I want to get on, I tell you. I want to get into the Bank again, in a higher position. Your husband must make a place for me—

NORA: That he will never do!

KROGSTAD: He will; I know him; he dare not protest. And as soon as I am in there again with him, then you will see! Within a year I shall be the manager's right hand. It will be Nils Krogstad and not Torvald Helmer who manages the Bank.

NORA: That's a thing you will never see!

KROGSTAD: Do you mean that you will—?

NORA: I have courage enough for it now.

KROGSTAD: Oh, you can't frighten me. A fine, spoilt lady like you—

NORA: You will see, you will see.

KROGSTAD: Under the ice, perhaps? Down into the cold, coal-black water? And then, in the spring, to float up to the surface, all horrible and unrecognisable, with your hair fallen out—

NORA: You can't frighten me.

KROGSTAD: Nor you me. People don't do such things, Mrs. Helmer. Besides, what use would it be? I should have him completely in my power all the same.

NORA: Afterwards? When I am no longer—

KROGSTAD: Have you forgotten that it is I who have the keeping of your reputation? (*Nora stands speechlessly looking at him.*) Well, now, I have warned you. Do not do anything foolish. When Helmer has had my letter, I shall expect a message from him. And be sure you remember that it is your husband himself who has forced me into such ways as this again. I will never forgive him for that. Good-bye, Mrs. Helmer. (*Exit through the hall.*)

NORA (*goes to the hall door, opens it slightly and listens*):   He is going. He is not putting the letter in the box. Oh no, no! that's impossible! (*Opens the door by degrees.*) What is that? He is standing outside. He is not going downstairs. Is he hesitating? Can he—? (*A letter drops into the box; then Krogstad's footsteps are heard, till they die away as he goes downstairs. Nora utters a stifled cry, and runs across the room to the table by the sofa. A short pause.*)

NORA: In the letter-box. (*Steals across to the hall door.*) There it lies—Torvald, Torvald, there is no hope for us now!

Mrs. Linde comes in from the room on the left, carrying the dress.

MRS. LINDE: There, I can't see anything more to mend now. Would you like to try it on—?

NORA (*in a hoarse whisper*):   Christine, come here.

MRS. LINDE (*throwing the dress down on the sofa*):   What is the matter with you? You look so agitated!

NORA: Come here. Do you see that letter? There, look—you can see it through the glass in the letter-box.

MRS. LINDE: Yes, I see it.

NORA: That letter is from Krogstad.

MRS. LINDE: Nora—it was Krogstad who lent you the money!

NORA: Yes, and now Torvald will know all about it.

MRS. LINDE: Believe me, Nora, that's the best thing for both of you.

NORA: You don't know all. I forged a name.

MRS. LINDE: Good heavens—!

NORA: I only want to say this to you, Christine—you must be my witness.

MRS. LINDE: Your witness? What do you mean? What am I to—?

NORA: If I should go out of my mind—and it might easily happen—

MRS. LINDE: Nora!

NORA: Or if anything else should happen to me—anything, for instance, that might prevent my being here—

MRS. LINDE: Nora! Nora! you are quite out of your mind.

NORA: And if it should happen that there were some one who wanted to take all the responsibility, all the blame, you understand—

MRS. LINDE: Yes, yes—but how can you suppose—?

NORA: Then you must be my witness, that it is not true, Christine. I am not out of my mind at all! I am in my right senses now, and I tell you no one else has known anything about it; I, and I alone, did the whole thing. Remember that.

MRS. LINDE: I will, indeed. But I don't understand all this.

NORA: How should you understand it? A wonderful thing is going to happen!

MRS. LINDE: A wonderful thing?

NORA: Yes, a wonderful thing!—But it is so terrible, Christine; it *mustn't* happen, not for all the world.

MRS. LINDE: I will go at once and see Krogstad.

NORA: Don't go to him; he will do you some harm.

MRS. LINDE: There was a time when he would gladly do anything for my sake.

NORA: He?

MRS. LINDE: Where does he live?

NORA: How should I know—? Yes (*feeling in her pocket*), here is his card. But the letter, the letter—!

HELMER (*calls from his room, knocking at the door*):   Nora!

NORA (*cries out anxiously*):   Oh, what's that? What do you want?

HELMER: Don't be so frightened. We are not coming in; you have locked the door. Are you trying on your dress?

NORA: Yes, that's it. I look so nice, Torvald.

MRS. LINDE (*who has read the card*):   I see he lives at the corner here.

NORA: Yes, but it's no use. It is hopeless. The letter is lying there in the box.

MRS. LINDE: And your husband keeps the key?

NORA: Yes, always.

MRS. LINDE: Krogstad must ask for his letter back unread, he must find some pretence—

NORA: But it is just at this time that Torvald generally—

MRS. LINDE: You must delay him. Go in to him in the meantime. I will come back as soon as I can. (*She goes out hurriedly through the hall door.*)

NORA (*goes to Helmer's door, opens it and peeps in*):   Torvald!

HELMER (*from the inner room*):   Well? May I venture at last to come into my own room again? Come along, Rank, now you will see—(*Halting in the doorway.*) But what is this?

NORA: What is what, dear?

HELMER: Rank led me to expect a splendid transformation.

RANK (*in the doorway*):   I understood so, but evidently I was mistaken.

NORA: Yes, nobody is to have the chance of admiring me in my dress until to-morrow.

HELMER: But, my dear Nora, you look so worn out. Have you been practising too much?

NORA: No, I have not practised at all.

HELMER: But you will need to—

NORA: Yes, indeed I shall, Torvald. But I can't get on a bit without you to help me; I have absolutely forgotten the whole thing.

HELMER: Oh, we will soon work it up again.

NORA: Yes, help me, Torvald. Promise that you will! I am so nervous about it—all the people—. You must give yourself up to me entirely this evening. Not the tiniest bit of business—you mustn't even take a pen in your hand. Will you promise, Torvald dear?

HELMER: I promise. This evening I will be wholly and absolutely at your service, you helpless little mortal. Ah, by the way, first of all I will just—(*Goes towards the hall door.*)

NORA: What are you going to do there?

HELMER: Only see if any letters have come.

NORA: No, no! don't do that, Torvald!

HELMER: Why not?

NORA: Torvald, please don't. There is nothing there.

HELMER: Well, let me look. (*Turns to go to the letter-box. Nora, at the piano, plays the first bars of the Tarantella. Helmer stops in the doorway.*) Aha!

NORA: I can't dance tomorrow if I don't practise with you.

HELMER (*going up to her*):   Are you really so afraid of it, dear?

NORA: Yes, so dreadfully afraid of it. Let me practise at once; there is time now, before we go to dinner. Sit down and play for me, Torvald dear; criticise me, and correct me as you play.

HELMER: With great pleasure, if you wish me to. (*Sits down at the piano.*)

NORA (*takes out of the box a tambourine and a long variegated shawl. She hastily drapes the shawl round her. Then she springs to the front of the stage and calls out*):   Now play for me! I am going to dance!

Helmer plays and Nora dances. Rank stands by the piano behind Helmer, and looks on.

HELMER (*as he plays*):   Slower, slower!

NORA: I can't do it any other way.

HELMER: Not so violently, Nora!

NORA: This is the way.

HELMER (*stops playing*):   No, no—that is not a bit right.

NORA (*laughing and swinging the tambourine*):   Didn't I tell you so?

RANK: Let me play for her.

HELMER (*getting up*):   Yes, do. I can correct her better then.

Rank sits down at the piano and plays. Nora dances more and more wildly. Helmer has taken up a position beside the stove, and during her dance gives her frequent instructions. She does not seem to hear him; her hair comes down and falls over her shoulders; she pays no attention to it, but goes on dancing. Enter Mrs. Linde.

MRS. LINDE (*standing as if spell-bound in the doorway*):   Oh!—

NORA (*as she dances*):   Such fun, Christine!

HELMER: My dear darling Nora, you are dancing as if your life depended on it.

NORA: So it does.

HELMER: Stop, Rank; this is sheer madness. Stop, I tell you! (*Rank stops playing, and Nora suddenly stands still. Helmer goes up to her.*) I could never have believed it. You have forgotten everything I taught you.

NORA (*throwing away the tambourine*):   There, you see.

HELMER: You will want a lot of coaching.

NORA: Yes, you see how much I need it. You must coach me up to the last minute. Promise me that, Torvald!

HELMER: You can depend on me.

NORA: You must not think of anything but me, either to-day or to-morrow; you mustn't open a single letter—not even open the letter-box—

HELMER: Ah, you are still afraid of that fellow—

NORA: Yes, indeed I am.

HELMER: Nora, I can tell from your looks that there is a letter from him lying there.

NORA: I don't know; I think there is; but you must not read anything of that kind now. Nothing horrid must come between us until this is all over.

RANK (*whispers to Helmer*):   You mustn't contradict her.

HELMER (*taking her in his arms*):   The child shall have her way. But to-morrow night, after you have danced—

NORA: Then you will be free. (*The Maid appears in the doorway to the right.*)

MAID: Dinner is served, ma'am.

NORA: We will have champagne, Helen.

MAID: Very good, ma'am.   [*Exit.*]

HELMER: Hullo!—are we going to have a banquet?

NORA: Yes, a champagne banquet until the small hours. (*Calls out.*) And a few macaroons, Helen—lots, just for once!

HELMER: Come, come, don't be so wild and nervous. Be my own little skylark, as you used.

NORA: Yes, dear, I will. But go in now and you too, Doctor Rank. Christine, you must help me to do up my hair.

RANK (*whispers to Helmer as they go out*):   I suppose there is nothing—she is not expecting anything?

HELMER: Far from it, my dear fellow; it is simply nothing more than this childish nervousness I was telling you of. (*They go into the right-hand room.*)

NORA: Well!

MRS. LINDE: Gone out of town.

NORA: I could tell from your face.

MRS. LINDE: He is coming home to-morrow evening. I wrote a note for him.

NORA: You should have let it alone; you must prevent nothing. After all, it is splendid to be waiting for a wonderful thing to happen.

MRS. LINDE: What is it that you are waiting for?

NORA: Oh, you wouldn't understand. Go in to them, I will come in a moment. (*Mrs. Linde goes into the dining-room. Nora stands still for a little while, as if to compose herself. Then she looks at her watch.*) Five o'clock. Seven hours until midnight; and then four-and-twenty hours until the next midnight. Then the Tarantella will be over. Twenty-four and seven? Thirty-one hours to live.

HELMER (*from the doorway on the right*):   Where's my little skylark?

NORA (*going to him with her arms outstretched*):   Here she is!

ACT III

THE SAME SCENE: *The table has been placed in the middle of the stage, with chairs round it. A lamp is burning on the table. The door into the hall stands open. Dance music is heard in the room above. Mrs. Linde is sitting at the table idly turning over the leaves of a book; she tries to read, but does not seem able to collect her thoughts. Every now and then she listens intently for a sound at the outer door.*

MRS. LINDE (*looking at her watch*):   Not yet—and the time is nearly up. If only he does not—. (*Listens again.*) Ah, there he is. (*Goes into the hall and opens the outer door carefully. Light footsteps are heard on the stairs. She whispers.*) Come in. There is no one here.

KROGSTAD (*in the doorway*):   I found a note from you at home. What does this mean?

MRS. LINDE: It is absolutely necessary that I should have a talk with you.

KROGSTAD: Really? And is it absolutely necessary that it should be here?

MRS. LINDE: It is impossible where I live; there is no private entrance to my rooms. Come in; we are quite alone. The maid is asleep, and the Helmers are at the dance upstairs.

KROGSTAD (*coming into the room*):   Are the Helmers really at a dance to-night?

MRS. LINDE: Yes, why not?

KROGSTAD: Certainly—why not?

MRS. LINDE: Now, Nils, let us have a talk.

KROGSTAD: Can we two have anything to talk about?

MRS. LINDE: We have a great deal to talk about.

KROGSTAD: I shouldn't have thought so.

MRS. LINDE: No, you have never properly understood me.

KROGSTAD: Was there anything else to understand except what was obvious to all the world—a heartless woman jilts a man when a more lucrative chance turns up?

MRS. LINDE: Do you believe I am as absolutely heartless as all that? And do you believe that I did it with a light heart?

KROGSTAD: Didn't you?

MRS. LINDE: Nils, did you really think that?

KROGSTAD: If it were as you say, why did you write to me as you did at the time?

MRS. LINDE: I could do nothing else. As I had to break with you, it was my duty also to put an end to all that you felt for me.

KROGSTAD (*wringing his hands*):   So that was it. And all this — only for the sake of money!

MRS. LINDE: You must not forget that I had a helpless mother and two little brothers. We couldn't wait for you, Nils; your prospects seemed hopeless then.

KROGSTAD: That may be so, but you had no right to throw me over for anyone else's sake.

MRS. LINDE: Indeed I don't know. Many a time did I ask myself if I had the right to do it.

KROGSTAD (*more gently*):   When I lost you, it was as if all the solid ground went from under my feet. Look at me now — I am a shipwrecked man clinging to a bit of wreckage.

MRS. LINDE: But help may be near.

KROGSTAD: It *was* near; but then you came and stood in my way.

MRS. LINDE: Unintentionally, Nils. It was only to-day that I learned it was your place I was going to take in the Bank.

KROGSTAD: I believe you, if you say so. But now that you know it, are you not going to give it up to me?

MRS. LINDE: No, because that would not benefit you in the least.

KROGSTAD: Oh, benefit, benefit — I would have done it whether or no.

MRS. LINDE: I have learned to act prudently. Life, and hard, bitter necessity have taught me that.

KROGSTAD: And life has taught me not to believe in fine speeches.

MRS. LINDE: Then life has taught you something very reasonable. But deeds you must believe in?

KROGSTAD: What do you mean by that?

MRS. LINDE: You said you were like a shipwrecked man clinging to some wreckage.

KROGSTAD: I had good reason to say so.

MRS. LINDE: Well, I am like a shipwrecked woman clinging to some wreckage — no one to mourn for, no one to care for.

KROGSTAD: It was your own choice.

MRS. LINDE: There was no other choice — then.

KROGSTAD: Well, what now?

MRS. LINDE: Nils, how would it be if we two shipwrecked people could join forces?

KROGSTAD: What are you saying?

MRS. LINDE: Two on the same piece of wreckage would stand a better chance than each on their own.

KROGSTAD: Christine!

MRS. LINDE: What do you suppose brought me to town?

KROGSTAD: Do you mean that you gave me a thought?

MRS. LINDE: I could not endure life without work. All my life, as long as I can remember, I have worked, and it has been my greatest and only pleasure. But now I am quite alone in the world — my life is so dreadfully empty and I feel so forsaken. There is not the least pleasure in working for one's self. Nils, give me someone and something to work for.

KROGSTAD: I don't trust that. It is nothing but a woman's overstrained sense of generosity that prompts you to make such an offer of yourself.

MRS. LINDE: Have you ever noticed anything of the sort in me?

KROGSTAD: Could you really do it? Tell me — do you know all about my past life?

MRS. LINDE: Yes.

KROGSTAD: And do you know what they think of me here?

MRS. LINDE: You seemed to me to imply that with me you might have been quite another man.

KROGSTAD: I am certain of it.

MRS. LINDE: Is it too late now?

KROGSTAD: Christine, are you saying this deliberately? Yes, I am sure you are. I see it in your face. Have you really the courage, then — ?

MRS. LINDE: I want to be a mother to someone, and your children need a mother. We two need each other. Nils, I have faith in your real character — I can dare anything together with you.

KROGSTAD (*grasps her hands*):   Thanks, thanks, Christine! Now I shall find a way to clear myself in the eyes of the world. Ah, but I forgot —

MRS. LINDE (*listening*):   Hush! The Tarantella! Go, go!

KROGSTAD: Why? What is it?

MRS. LINDE: Do you hear them up there? When that is over, we may expect them back.

KROGSTAD: Yes, yes — I will go. But it is all no use. Of course you are not aware what steps I have taken in the matter of the Helmers.

MRS. LINDE: Yes, I know all about that.

KROGSTAD: And in spite of that have you the courage to — ?

MRS. LINDE: I understand very well to what lengths a man like you might be driven by despair.

KROGSTAD: If I could only undo what I have done!

MRS. LINDE: You cannot. Your letter is lying in the letter-box now.

KROGSTAD: Are you sure of that?

MRS. LINDE: Quite sure, but —

KROGSTAD (*with a searching look at her*):   Is that what it all means? — that you want to save your friend at any cost? Tell me frankly. Is that it?

MRS. LINDE: Nils, a woman who has once sold herself for another's sake, doesn't do it a second time.

KROGSTAD: I will ask for my letter back.

MRS. LINDE: No, no.

KROGSTAD: Yes, of course I will. I will wait here until Helmer comes; I will tell him he must give me my letter back—that it only concerns my dismissal—that he is not to read it—

MRS. LINDE: No, Nils, you must not recall your letter.

KROGSTAD: But, tell me, wasn't it for that very purpose that you asked me to meet you here?

MRS. LINDE: In my first moment of fright, it was. But twenty-four hours have elapsed since then, and in that time I have witnessed incredible things in this house. Helmer must know all about it. This unhappy secret must be disclosed; they must have a complete understanding between them, which is impossible with all this concealment and falsehood going on.

KROGSTAD: Very well, if you will take the responsibility. But there is one thing I can do in any case, and I shall do it at once.

MRS. LINDE (*listening*):   You must be quick and go! The dance is over; we are not safe a moment longer.

KROGSTAD: I will wait for you below.

MRS. LINDE: Yes, do. You must see me back to my door.

KROGSTAD: I have never had such an amazing piece of good fortune in my life! (*Goes out through the outer door. The door between the room and the hall remains open.*)

MRS. LINDE (*tidying up the room and laying her hat and cloak ready*):   What a difference! what a difference! Some-one to work for and live for—a home to bring comfort into. That I will do, indeed. I wish they would be quick and come—(*Listens.*) Ah, there they are now. I must put on my things. (*Takes up her hat and cloak. Helmer's and Nora's voices are heard outside; a key is turned, and Helmer brings Nora almost by force into the hall. She is in an Italian costume with a large black shawl around her; he is in evening dress, and a black domino which is flying open.*)

NORA (*hanging back in the doorway, and struggling with him*):   No, no, no!— don't take me in. I want to go upstairs again; I don't want to leave so early.

HELMER: But, my dearest Nora—

NORA: Please, Torvald dear—please, *please*—only an hour more.

HELMER: Not a single minute, my sweet Nora. You know that was our agreement. Come along into the room; you are catching cold standing there. (*He brings her gently into the room, in spite of her resistance.*)

MRS. LINDE: Good-evening.

NORA: Christine!

HELMER: You here, so late, Mrs. Linde?

MRS. LINDE: Yes, you must excuse me; I was so anxious to see Nora in her dress.

NORA: Have you been sitting here waiting for me?

MRS. LINDE: Yes, unfortunately I came too late, you had already gone upstairs; and I thought I couldn't go away again without having seen you.

HELMER (*taking off Nora's shawl*):   Yes, take a good look at her. I think she is worth looking at. Isn't she charming, Mrs. Linde?

MRS. LINDE: Yes, indeed she is.

HELMER: Doesn't she look remarkably pretty? Everyone thought so at the dance. But she is terribly self-willed, this sweet little person. What are we to do with her? You will hardly believe that I had almost to bring her away by force.

NORA: Torvald, you will repent not having let me stay, even if it were only for half an hour.

HELMER: Listen to her, Mrs. Linde! She had danced her Tarantella, and it had been a tremendous success, as it deserved—although possibly the performance was a trifle too realistic—a little more so, I mean, than was strictly compatible with the limitations of art. But never mind about that! The chief thing is, she had made a success—she had made a tremendous success. Do you think I was going to let her remain there after that, and spoil the effect? No, indeed! I took my charming little Capri maiden—my capricious little Capri maiden, I should say—on my arm; took one quick turn round the room; a curtsey on either side, and, as they say in novels, the beautiful apparition disappeared. An exit ought always to be effective, Mrs. Linde; but that is what I cannot make Nora understand. Pooh! this room is hot. (*Throws his domino on a chair, and opens the door of his room.*) Hullo! it's all dark in here. Oh, of course—excuse me—. (*He goes in, and lights some candles.*)

NORA (*in a hurried and breathless whisper*):   Well?

MRS. LINDE (*in a low voice*):   I have had a talk with him.

NORA: Yes, and—

MRS. LINDE: Nora, you must tell your husband all about it.

NORA (*in an expressionless voice*):   I knew it.

MRS. LINDE: You have nothing to be afraid of as far as Krogstad is concerned; but you must tell him.

NORA: I won't tell him.

MRS. LINDE: Then the letter will.

NORA: Thank you, Christine. Now I know what I must do. Hush—!

HELMER (*coming in again*):   Well, Mrs. Linde, have you admired her?

MRS. LINDE: Yes, and now I will say good-night.

HELMER: What, already? Is this yours, this knitting?

MRS. LINDE (*taking it*):   Yes, thank you, I had very nearly forgotten it.

HELMER: So you knit?

MRS. LINDE: Of course.

HELMER: Do you know, you ought to embroider.

MRS. LINDE: Really? Why?

HELMER: Yes, it's far more becoming. Let me show you. You hold the embroidery thus in your left hand, and use the needle with the right—like this—with a long, easy sweep. Do you see?

MRS. LINDE: Yes, perhaps—

HELMER: But in the case of knitting—that can never be anything but ungraceful; look here—the arms close together, the knitting-needles going up and down—it has a sort of Chinese effect—. That was really excellent champagne they gave us.

MRS. LINDE: Well,—good-night, Nora, and don't be self-willed any more.

HELMER: That's right, Mrs. Linde.

MRS. LINDE: Good-night, Mr. Helmer.

HELMER (*accompanying her to the door*):   Good-night, good-night. I hope you will get home all right. I should be very happy to—but you haven't any great distance to go. Good-night, good-night. (*She goes out; he shuts the door after her, and comes in again.*) Ah!—at last we have got rid of her. She is a frightful bore, that woman.

NORA: Aren't you very tired, Torvald?

HELMER: No, not in the least.

NORA: Nor sleepy?

HELMER: Not a bit. On the contrary, I feel extraordinarily lively. And you?—you really look both tired and sleepy.

NORA: Yes, I am very tired. I want to go to sleep at once.

HELMER: There, you see it was quite right of me not to let you stay there any longer.

NORA: Everything you do is quite right, Torvald.

HELMER (*kissing her on the forehead*):   Now my little skylark is speaking reasonably. Did you notice what good spirits Rank was in this evening?

NORA: Really? Was he? I didn't speak to him at all.

HELMER: And I very little, but I have not for a long time seen him in such good form. (*Looks for a while at her and then goes nearer to her.*) It is delightful to be at home by ourselves again, to be all alone with you—you fascinating, charming little darling!

NORA: Don't look at me like that, Torvald.

HELMER: Why shouldn't I look at my dearest treasure?—at all the beauty that is mine, all my very own?

NORA (*going to the other side of the table*):   You mustn't say things like that to me to-night.

HELMER (*following her*):   You have still got the Tarantella in your blood, I see. And it makes you more captivating than ever. Listen—the guests are beginning to go now. (*In a lower voice.*) Nora—soon the whole house will be quiet.

NORA: Yes, I hope so.

HELMER: Yes, my own darling Nora. Do you know, when I am out at a party with you like this, why I speak so little to you, keep away from you, and only send a stolen glance in your direction now and then?—do you know why I do that? It is because I make believe to myself that we are secretly in love, and you are my secretly promised bride, and that no one suspects there is anything between us.

NORA: Yes, yes—I know very well your thoughts are with me all the time.

HELMER: And when we are leaving, and I am putting the shawl over your beautiful young shoulders—on your lovely neck—then I imagine that you are my young bride and that we have just come from the wedding, and I am bringing you for the first time into our home—to be alone with you for the first time—quite alone with my shy little darling! All this evening I have longed for nothing but you. When I watched the seductive figures of the Tarantella, my blood was on fire; I could endure it no longer, and that was why I brought you down so early—

NORA: Go away, Torvald! You must let me go. I won't—

HELMER: What's that? You're joking, my little Nora! You won't—you won't? Am I not your husband—? (*A knock is heard at the outer door.*)

NORA (*starting*):   Did you hear—?

HELMER (*going into the hall*):   Who is it?

RANK (*outside*):   It is I. May I come in for a moment?

HELMER (*in a fretful whisper*):   Oh, what does he want now? (*Aloud.*) Wait a minute! (*Unlocks the door.*) Come, that's kind of you not to pass by our door.

RANK: I thought I heard your voice, and felt as if I should like to look in. (*With a swift glance round.*) Ah, yes!—these dear familiar rooms. You are very happy and cosy in here, you two.

HELMER: It seems to me that you looked after yourself pretty well upstairs too.

RANK: Excellently. Why shouldn't I? Why shouldn't one enjoy everything in this world?—at any rate as much as one can, and as long as one can. The wine was capital—

HELMER: Especially the champagne.

RANK: So you noticed that too? It is almost incredible how much I managed to put away!

NORA: Torvald drank a great deal of champagne to-night too.

RANK: Did he?

NORA: Yes, and he is always in such good spirits afterwards.

RANK: Well, why should one not enjoy a merry evening after a well-spent day?

HELMER: Well spent? I am afraid I can't take credit for that.

RANK (*clapping him on the back*):   But I can, you know!

NORA: Doctor Rank, you must have been occupied with some scientific investigation to-day.

RANK: Exactly.

HELMER: Just listen!—little Nora talking about scientific investigations!

NORA: And may I congratulate you on the result?

RANK: Indeed you may.

NORA: Was it favourable, then?

RANK: The best possible, for both doctor and patient—certainty.

NORA (*quickly and searchingly*):   Certainty?

RANK: Absolute certainty. So wasn't I entitled to make a merry evening of it after that?

NORA: Yes, you certainly were, Doctor Rank.

HELMER: I think so too, so long as you don't have to pay for it in the morning.

RANK: Oh well, one can't have anything in this life without paying for it.

NORA: Doctor Rank—are you fond of fancy-dress balls?

RANK: Yes, if there is a fine lot of pretty costumes.

NORA: Tell me—what shall we two wear at the next?

HELMER: Little featherbrain!—are you thinking of the next already?

RANK: We two? Yes, I can tell you. You shall go as a good fairy—

HELMER: Yes, but what do you suggest as an appropriate costume for that?

RANK: Let your wife go dressed just as she is in everyday life.

HELMER: That was really very prettily turned. But can't you tell us what you will be?

RANK: Yes, my dear friend, I have quite made up my mind about that.

HELMER: Well?

RANK: At the next fancy-dress ball I shall be invisible.

HELMER: That's a good joke!

RANK: There is a big black hat — have you never heard of hats that make you invisible? If you put one on, no one can see you.

HELMER (*suppressing a smile*):   Yes, you are quite right.

RANK: But I am clean forgetting what I came for. Helmer, give me a cigar — one of the dark Havanas.

HELMER: With the greatest pleasure. (*Offers him his case.*)

RANK (*takes a cigar and cuts off the end*):   Thanks.

NORA (*striking a match*):   Let me give you a light.

RANK: Thank you. (*She holds the match for him to light his cigar.*) And now good-bye!

HELMER: Good-bye, good-bye, dear old man!

NORA: Sleep well, Doctor Rank.

RANK: Thank you for that wish.

NORA: Wish me the same.

RANK: You? Well, if you want me to sleep well! And thanks for the light. (*He nods to them both and goes out.*)

HELMER (*in a subdued voice*):   He has drunk more than he ought.

NORA (*absently*):   Maybe. (*Helmer takes a bunch of keys out of his pocket and goes into the hall.*) Torvald! what are you going to do there?

HELMER: Empty the letter-box; it is quite full; there will be no room to put the newspaper in to-morrow morning.

NORA: Are you going to work to-night?

HELMER: You know quite well I'm not. What is this? Someone has been at the lock.

NORA: At the lock —?

HELMER: Yes, someone has. What can it mean? I should never have thought the maid —. Here is a broken hairpin. Nora, it is one of yours.

NORA (*quickly*):   Then it must have been the children —

HELMER: Then you must get them out of those ways. There, at last I have got it open. (*Takes out the contents of the letter-box, and calls to the kitchen.*) Helen! — Helen, put out the light over the front door. (*Goes back into the room and shuts the door into the hall. He holds out his hand full of letters.*) Look at that — look what a heap of them there are. (*Turning them over.*) What on earth is that?

NORA (*at the window*):   The letter — No! Torvald, no!

HELMER: Two cards — of Rank's.

NORA: Of Doctor Rank's?

HELMER (*looking at them*):   Doctor Rank. They were on the top. He must have put them in when he went out.

NORA: Is there anything written on them?

HELMER:　There is a black cross over the name. Look there—what an uncomfortable idea! It looks as if he were announcing his own death.

NORA:　It is just what he is doing.

HELMER:　What? Do you know anything about it? Has he said anything to you?

NORA:　Yes. He told me that when the cards came it would be his leave-taking from us. He means to shut himself up and die.

HELMER:　My poor old friend! Certainly I knew we should not have him very long with us. But so soon! And so he hides himself away like a wounded animal.

NORA:　If it has to happen, it is best it should be without a word—don't you think so, Torvald?

HELMER (*walking up and down*):　He had so grown into our lives. I can't think of him as having gone out of them. He, with his sufferings and his loneliness, was like a cloudy background to our sunlit happiness. Well, perhaps it is best so. For him, anyway. (*Standing still.*) And perhaps for us too, Nora. We two are thrown quite upon each other now. (*Puts his arms round her.*) My darling wife, I don't feel as if I could hold you tight enough. Do you know, Nora, I have often wished that you might be threatened by some great danger, so that I might risk my life's blood, and everything, for your sake.

NORA (*disengages herself, and says firmly and decidedly*):　Now you must read your letters, Torvald.

HELMER:　No, no; not to-night. I want to be with you, my darling wife.

NORA:　With the thought of your friend's death—

HELMER:　You are right, it has affected us both. Something ugly has come between us—the thought of the horrors of death. We must try and rid our minds of that. Until then—we will each go to our own room.

NORA (*hanging on his neck*):　Good-night, Torvald—Good-night!

HELMER (*kissing her on the forehead*):　Good-night, my little singing-bird. Sleep sound, Nora. Now I will read my letters through. (*He takes his letters and goes into his room, shutting the door after him.*)

NORA (*gropes distractedly about, seizes Helmer's domino, throws it round her, while she says in quick, hoarse, spasmodic whispers*):　Never to see him again. Never! Never! (*Puts her shawl over her head.*) Never to see my children again either—never again. Never! Never!—Ah! the icy, black water—the unfathomable depths—If only it were over! He has got it now—now he is reading it. Good-bye, Torvald and my children! (*She is about to rush out through the hall, when Helmer opens his door hurriedly and stands with an open letter in his hand.*)

HELMER:　Nora!

NORA:　Ah!—

HELMER:　What is this? Do you know what is in this letter?

NORA:　Yes, I know. Let me go! Let me get out!

HELMER (*holding her back*):　Where are you going?

NORA (*trying to get free*):　You shan't save me, Torvald!

HELMER (*reeling*):　True? Is this true, that I read here? Horrible! No, no—it is impossible that it can be true.

NORA: It is true. I have loved you above everything else in the world.

HELMER: Oh, don't let us have any silly excuses.

NORA (*taking a step towards him*):   Torvald—!

HELMER: Miserable creature—what have you done?

NORA: Let me go. You shall not suffer for my sake. You shall not take it upon yourself.

HELMER: No tragedy airs, please. (*Locks the hall door.*) Here you shall stay and give me an explanation. Do you understand what you have done? Answer me! Do you understand what you have done?

NORA (*looks steadily at him and says with a growing look of coldness in her face*):   Yes, now I am beginning to understand thoroughly.

HELMER (*walking about the room*):   What a horrible awakening! All these eight years—she who was my joy and pride—a hypocrite, a liar—worse, worse—a criminal! The unutterable ugliness of it all!—For shame! For shame! (*Nora is silent and looks steadily at him. He stops in front of her.*) I ought to have suspected that something of the sort would happen. I ought to have foreseen it. All your father's want of principle—be silent!—all your father's want of principle has come out in you. No religion, no morality, no sense of duty—. How I am punished for having winked at what he did! I did it for your sake, and this is how you repay me.

NORA: Yes, that's just it.

HELMER: Now you have destroyed all my happiness. You have ruined all my future. It is horrible to think of! I am in the power of an unscrupulous man; he can do what he likes with me, ask anything he likes of me, give me any orders he pleases—I dare not refuse. And I must sink to such miserable depths because of a thoughtless woman!

NORA: When I am out of the way, you will be free.

HELMER: No fine speeches, please. Your father had always plenty of those ready, too. What good would it be to me if you were out of the way, as you say? Not the slightest. He can make the affair known everywhere; and if he does, I may be falsely suspected of having been a party to your criminal action. Very likely people will think I was behind it all—that it was I who prompted you! And I have to thank you for all this—you whom I have cherished during the whole of our married life. Do you understand now what it is you have done for me?

NORA (*coldly and quietly*):   Yes.

HELMER: It is so incredible that I can't take it in. But we must come to some understanding. Take off that shawl. Take it off, I tell you. I must try and appease him some way or another. The matter must be hushed up at any cost. And as for you and me, it must appear as if everything between us were just as before—but naturally only in the eyes of the world. You will still remain in my house, that is a matter of course. But I shall not allow you to bring up the children; I dare not trust them to you. To think that I should be obliged to say so to one whom I have loved so dearly, and whom I still—. No, that is all over. From this moment happiness is not the question; all that concerns us is to save the remains, the fragments, the appearance—

A ring is heard at the front-door bell.

HELMER (*with a start*):   What is that? So late! Can the worst —? Can he —? Hide
yourself, Nora. Say you are ill.

Nora stands motionless. Helmer goes and unlocks the hall door.

MAID (*half-dressed, comes to the door*):   A letter for the mistress.
HELMER: Give it to me. (*Takes the letter, and shuts the door.*) Yes, it is from him.
You shall not have it; I will read it myself.
NORA: Yes, read it.
HELMER (*standing by the lamp*):   I scarcely have the courage to do it. It may mean
ruin for both of us. No, I must know. (*Tears open the letter, runs his eye over a
few lines, looks at a paper enclosed, and gives a shout of joy.*) Nora! (*She looks at
him questioningly.*) Nora! — No, I must read it once again —. Yes, it is true!
I am saved! Nora, I am saved!
NORA: And I?
HELMER: You too, of course; we are both saved, both you and I. Look, he sends
you your bond back. He says he regrets and repents — that a happy change
in his life — never mind what he says! We are saved, Nora! No one can do
anything to you. Oh, Nora, Nora! — no, first I must destroy these hateful
things. Let me see —. (*Takes a look at the bond.*) No, no, I won't look at it.
The whole thing shall be nothing but a bad dream to me. (*Tears up the bond
and both letters, throws them all into the stove, and watches them burn.*)
There — now it doesn't exist any longer. He says that since Christmas Eve
you —. These must have been three dreadful days for you, Nora.
NORA: I have fought a hard fight these three days.
HELMER: And suffered agonies, and seen no way out but —. No, we won't call
any of the horrors to mind. We will only shout with joy, and keep saying,
"It's all over! It's all over!" Listen to me, Nora. You don't seem to realise that
it is all over. What is this? — such a cold, set face! My poor little Nora, I
quite understand; you don't feel as if you could believe that I have forgiven
you. But it is true, Nora, I swear it; I have forgiven you everything. I know
that what you did, you did out of love for me.
NORA: That is true.
HELMER: You have loved me as a wife ought to love her husband. Only you
had not sufficient knowledge to judge of the means you used. But do
you suppose you are any the less dear to me, because you don't understand
how to act on your own responsibility? No, no; only lean on me; I will advise you and direct you. I should not be a man if this womanly helplessness
did not just give you a double attractiveness in my eyes. You must not think
anymore about the hard things I said in my first moment of consternation,
when I thought everything was going to overwhelm me. I have forgiven
you, Nora; I swear to you I have forgiven you.
NORA: Thank you for your forgiveness. (*She goes out through the door to the
right.*)
HELMER: No, don't go —. (*Looks in.*) What are you doing in there?

NORA (*from within*):   Taking off my fancy dress.

HELMER (*standing at the open door*):   Yes, do. Try and calm yourself, and make your mind easy again, my frightened little singing-bird. Be at rest, and feel secure; I have broad wings to shelter you under. (*Walks up and down by the door.*) How warm and cosy our home is, Nora. Here is shelter for you; here I will protect you like a hunted dove that I have saved from a hawk's claws; I will bring peace to your poor beating heart. It will come, little by little, Nora, believe me. To-morrow morning you will look upon it all quite differently; soon everything will be just as it was before. Very soon you won't need me to assure you that I have forgiven you; you will yourself feel the certainty that I have done so. Can you suppose I should ever think of such a thing as repudiating you, or even reproaching you? You have no idea what a true man's heart is like, Nora. There is something so indescribably sweet and satisfying, to a man, in the knowledge that he has forgiven his wife—forgiven her freely, and with all his heart. It seems as if that had made her, as it were, doubly his own; he has given her a new life, so to speak; and she has in a way become both wife and child to him. So you shall be for me after this, my little scared, helpless darling. Have no anxiety about anything, Nora; only be frank and open with me, and I will serve as will and conscience both to you—. What is this? Not gone to bed? Have you changed your things?

NORA (*in everyday dress*):   Yes, Torvald, I have changed my things now.

HELMER: But what for?—so late as this.

NORA: I shall not sleep to-night.

HELMER: But, my dear Nora—

NORA (*looking at her watch*):   It is not so very late. Sit down here, Torvald. You and I have much to say to one another. (*She sits down at one side of the table.*)

HELMER: Nora—what is this?—this cold, set face?

NORA: Sit down. It will take some time; I have a lot to talk over with you.

HELMER (*sits down at the opposite side of the table*):   You alarm me, Nora!—and I don't understand you.

NORA: No, that is just it. You don't understand me, and I have never understood you either—before to-night. No, you mustn't interrupt me. You must simply listen to what I say. Torvald, this is a settling of accounts.

HELMER: What do you mean by that?

NORA (*after a short silence*):   Isn't there one thing that strikes you as strange in our sitting here like this?

HELMER: What is that?

NORA: We have been married now eight years. Does it not occur to you that this is the first time we two, you and I, husband and wife, have had a serious conversation?

HELMER: What do you mean by serious?

NORA: In all these eight years—longer than that—from the very beginning of our acquaintance, we have never exchanged a word on any serious subject.

HELMER: Was it likely that I would be continually and forever telling you about worries that you could not help me to bear?

NORA: I am not speaking about business matters. I say that we have never sat down in earnest together to try and get at the bottom of anything.

HELMER: But, dearest Nora, would it have been any good to you?

NORA: That is just it; you have never understood me. I have been greatly wronged, Torvald—first by papa and then by you.

HELMER: What! By us two—by us two, who have loved you better than anyone else in the world?

NORA (*shaking her head*):   You have never loved me. You have only thought it pleasant to be in love with me.

HELMER: Nora, what do I hear you saying?

NORA: It is perfectly true, Torvald. When I was at home with papa, he told me his opinion about everything, and so I had the same opinions; and if I differed from him I concealed the fact, because he would not have liked it. He called me his doll-child, and he played with me just as I used to play with my dolls. And when I came to live with you—

HELMER: What sort of an expression is that to use about our marriage?

NORA (*undisturbed*):   I mean that I was simply transferred from papa's hands into yours. You arranged everything according to your own taste, and so I got the same tastes as you—or else I pretended to, I am really not quite sure which—I think sometimes the one and sometimes the other. When I look back on it, it seems to me as if I had been living here like a poor woman—just from hand to mouth. I have existed merely to perform tricks for you, Torvald. But you would have it so. You and papa have committed a great sin against me. It is your fault that I have made nothing of my life.

HELMER: How unreasonable and how ungrateful you are, Nora! Have you not been happy here?

NORA: No, I have never been happy. I thought I was, but it has never really been so.

HELMER: Not—not happy!

NORA: No, only merry. And you have always been so kind to me. But our home has been nothing but a playroom. I have been your doll-wife, just as at home I was papa's doll-child; and here the children have been my dolls. I thought it great fun when you played with me, just as they thought it great fun when I played with them. That is what our marriage has been, Torvald.

HELMER: There is some truth in what you say—exaggerated and strained as your view of it is. But for the future it shall be different. Playtime shall be over, and lesson-time shall begin.

NORA: Whose lessons? Mine, or the children's?

HELMER: Both yours and the children's, my darling Nora.

NORA: Alas, Torvald, you are not the man to educate me into being a proper wife for you.

HELMER: And you can say that!

NORA: And I—how am I fitted to bring up the children?

HELMER: Nora!

NORA: Didn't you say so yourself a little while ago—that you dare not trust me to bring them up?

HELMER: In a moment of anger! Why do you pay any heed to that?

NORA: Indeed, you were perfectly right. I am not fit for the task. There is another task I must undertake first. I must try and educate myself — you are not the man to help me in that. I must do that for myself. And that is why I am going to leave you now.

HELMER (*springing up*):   What do you say?

NORA: I must stand quite alone, if I am to understand myself and everything about me. It is for that reason that I cannot remain with you any longer.

HELMER: Nora, Nora!

NORA: I am going away from here now, at once. I am sure Christine will take me in for the night —

HELMER: You are out of your mind! I won't allow it! I forbid you!

NORA: It is no use forbidding me anything any longer. I will take with me what belongs to myself. I will take nothing from you, either now or later.

HELMER: What sort of madness is this!

NORA: To-morrow I shall go home — I mean, to my old home. It will be easiest for me to find something to do there.

HELMER: You blind, foolish woman!

NORA: I must try and get some sense, Torvald.

HELMER: To desert your home, your husband and your children! And you don't consider what people will say!

NORA: I cannot consider that at all. I only know that it is necessary for me.

HELMER: It's shocking. This is how you would neglect your most sacred duties.

NORA: What do you consider my most sacred duties?

HELMER: Do I need to tell you that? Are they not your duties to your husband and your children?

NORA: I have other duties just as sacred.

HELMER: That you have not. What duties could those be?

NORA: Duties to myself.

HELMER: Before all else, you are a wife and a mother.

NORA: I don't believe that any longer. I believe that before all else I am a reasonable human being, just as you are — or, at all events, that I must try and become one. I know quite well, Torvald, that most people would think you right, and that views of that kind are to be found in books; but I can no longer content myself with what most people say, or with what is found in books. I must think over things for myself and get to understand them.

HELMER: Can you not understand your place in your own home? Have you not a reliable guide in such matters as that? — have you no religion?

NORA: I am afraid, Torvald, I do not exactly know what religion is.

HELMER: What are you saying?

NORA: I know nothing but what the clergyman said, when I went to be confirmed. He told us that religion was this, and that, and the other. When I am away from all this, and am alone, I will look into that matter too. I will see if what the clergyman said is true, or at all events if it is true for me.

HELMER: This is unheard of in a girl of your age! But if religion cannot lead you aright, let me try and awaken your conscience. I suppose you have some moral sense? Or — answer me — am I to think you have none?

NORA: I assure you, Torvald, that is not an easy question to answer. I really don't know. The thing perplexes me altogether. I only know that you and I look at it in quite a different light. I am learning, too, that the law is quite another thing from what I supposed; but I find it impossible to convince myself that the law is right. According to it a woman has no right to spare her old dying father, or to save her husband's life. I can't believe that.

HELMER: You talk like a child. You don't understand the conditions of the world in which you live.

NORA: No, I don't. But now I am going to try. I am going to see if I can make out who is right, the world or I.

HELMER: You are ill, Nora; you are delirious; I almost think you are out of your mind.

NORA: I have never felt my mind so clear and certain as to-night.

HELMER: And is it with a clear and certain mind that you forsake your husband and your children?

NORA: Yes, it is.

HELMER: Then there is only one possible explanation.

NORA: What is that?

HELMER: You do not love me anymore.

NORA: No, that is just it.

HELMER: Nora!—and you can say that?

NORA: It gives me great pain, Torvald, for you have always been so kind to me, but I cannot help it. I do not love you any more.

HELMER (*regaining his composure*):   Is that a clear and certain conviction too?

NORA: Yes, absolutely clear and certain. That is the reason why I will not stay here any longer.

HELMER: And can you tell me what I have done to forfeit your love?

NORA: Yes, indeed I can. It was to-night, when the wonderful thing did not happen; then I saw you were not the man I had thought you.

HELMER: Explain yourself better. I don't understand you.

NORA: I have waited so patiently for eight years; for, goodness knows, I knew very well that wonderful things don't happen every day. Then this horrible misfortune came upon me; and then I felt quite certain that the wonderful thing was going to happen at last. When Krogstad's letter was lying out there, never for a moment did I imagine that you would consent to accept this man's conditions. I was so absolutely certain that you would say to him: Publish the thing to the whole world. And when that was done—

HELMER: Yes, what then?—when I had exposed my wife to shame and disgrace?

NORA: When that was done, I was so absolutely certain, you would come forward and take everything upon yourself, and say: I am the guilty one.

HELMER: Nora—!

NORA: You mean that I would never have accepted such a sacrifice on your part? No, of course not. But what would my assurances have been worth against yours? That was the wonderful thing which I hoped for and feared; and it was to prevent that, that I wanted to kill myself.

HELMER: I would gladly work night and day for you, Nora—bear sorrow and want for your sake. But no man would sacrifice his honour for the one he loves.

NORA: It is a thing hundreds of thousands of women have done.

HELMER: Oh, you think and talk like a heedless child.

NORA: Maybe. But you neither think nor talk like the man I could bind myself to. As soon as your fear was over—and it was not fear for what threatened me, but for what might happen to you—when the whole thing was past, as far as you were concerned it was exactly as if nothing at all had happened. Exactly as before, I was your little skylark, your doll, which you would in future treat with doubly gentle care, because it was so brittle and fragile. (*Getting up.*) Torvald—it was then it dawned upon me that for eight years I had been living here with a strange man, and had borne him three children—. Oh, I can't bear to think of it! I could tear myself into little bits!

HELMER (*sadly*): I see, I see. An abyss has opened between us—there is no denying it. But, Nora, would it not be possible to fill it up?

NORA: As I am now, I am no wife for you.

HELMER: I have it in me to become a different man.

NORA: Perhaps—if your doll is taken away from you.

HELMER: But to part!—to part from you! No, no, Nora, I can't understand that idea.

NORA (*going out to the right*): That makes it all the more certain that it must be done. (*She comes back with her cloak and hat and a small bag which she puts on a chair by the table.*)

HELMER: Nora, Nora, not now! Wait until to-morrow.

NORA (*putting on her cloak*): I cannot spend the night in a strange man's room.

HELMER: But can't we live here like brother and sister—?

NORA (*putting on her hat*): You know very well that would not last long. (*Puts the shawl round her.*) Good-bye, Torvald. I won't see the little ones. I know they are in better hands than mine. As I am now, I can be of no use to them.

HELMER: But some day, Nora—some day?

NORA: How can I tell? I have no idea what is going to become of me.

HELMER: But you are my wife, whatever becomes of you.

NORA: Listen, Torvald. I have heard that when a wife deserts her husband's house, as I am doing now, he is legally freed from all obligations towards her. In any case, I set you free from all your obligations. You are not to feel yourself bound in the slightest way, any more than I shall. There must be perfect freedom on both sides. See, here is your ring back. Give me mine.

HELMER: That too?

NORA: That too.

HELMER: Here it is.

NORA: That's right. Now it is all over. I have put the keys here. The maids know all about everything in the house—better than I do. To-morrow, after I have left her, Christine will come here and pack up my own things that I brought with me from home. I will have them sent after me.

HELMER: All over! All over!—Nora, shall you never think of me again?

NORA: I know I shall often think of you, the children, and this house.

HELMER: May I write to you, Nora?

NORA: No—never. You must not do that.

HELMER: But at least let me send you—

NORA: Nothing—nothing—

HELMER: Let me help you if you are in want.

NORA: No. I can receive nothing from a stranger.

HELMER: Nora—can I never be anything more than a stranger to you?

NORA (*taking her bag*):   Ah, Torvald, the most wonderful thing of all would have to happen.

HELMER: Tell me what that would be!

NORA: Both you and I would have to be so changed that—. Oh, Torvald, I don't believe any longer in wonderful things happening.

HELMER: But I will believe in it. Tell me! So changed that—?

NORA: That our life together would be a real wedlock. Good-bye. (*She goes out through the hall.*)

HELMER (*sinks down on a chair at the door and buries his face in his hands*):   Nora! Nora! (*Looks round, and rises.*) Empty. She is gone. (*A hope flashes across his mind.*) The most wonderful thing of all—?

The sound of a door shutting is heard from below.   [1879]

≡ THINKING ABOUT THE TEXT

1. Critics disagree about the necessity for Nora's leaving. What would your advice to her be? One critic thinks she has to leave because Torvald is impossible. What do you think?

2. Do you find credible the change in Nora's character from the first scene to the last? Do you know people who have transformed themselves?

3. Is Torvald in love with Nora in the first act? Explain. Is Nora in love with him in the first act? What is your idea of love in a marriage?

4. An early critic of the play claims that it is a comedy. Is this possible? How would you characterize it? Is it an optimistic or a pessimistic play? Is it tragic?

5. A few critics think Nora will return. Do you think this is possible? Under what conditions would you counsel her to do so? Do you think the "door heard 'round the world" had a positive or a negative effect on marriage?

SUSAN GLASPELL
Trifles

Susan Glaspell (1876–1948) is best known for the frequently anthologized play Trifles *and its short-story version, "A Jury of Her Peers." Surprisingly modern, Glaspell's work is in harmony with contemporary feminist concerns of identity, the difficulty of female expression in a patriarchal culture, the disillusionment of marriage for gifted women, and the necessity for female support and understanding.*

Glaspell graduated from Drake University in 1899 and first worked as a journalist in Des Moines, Iowa. She soon began to publish short stories in prestigious magazines like Harper's *and* The American. *After she married novelist and playwright George Cram Cook, they moved to Greenwich Village, where they felt more comfortable with its freethinking attitudes. Glaspell continued to publish both stories and novels. She also began writing plays, and in 1916 she and her husband founded the Provincetown Players, an important source for innovative American drama. During the 1920s and 1930s, Glaspell published a number of best-selling novels, including* Brook Evans *(1928), which was turned into a successful movie. Her play* Alison's House *won the Pulitzer Prize in 1931, and her novel* The Morning Is Near *(1939) sold more than one hundred thousand copies. Today her significant successes in two genres, drama and fiction, are considered remarkable.*

CHARACTERS

GEORGE HENDERSON, *county attorney*
HENRY PETERS, *sheriff*
LEWIS HALE, *a neighboring farmer*
MRS. PETERS
MRS. HALE

SCENE: *The kitchen in the now-abandoned farmhouse of John Wright, a gloomy kitchen, and left without having been put in order — the walls covered with a faded wallpaper. Down right is a door leading to the parlor. On the right wall above this door is a built-in kitchen cupboard with shelves in the upper portion and drawers below. In the rear wall at right, up two steps is a door opening onto stairs leading to the second floor. In the rear wall at left is a door to the shed and from there to the outside. Between these two doors is an old-fashioned black iron stove. Running along the left wall from the shed door is an old iron sink and sink shelf, in which is set a hand pump. Downstage of the sink is an uncurtained window. Near the window is an old wooden rocker. Center stage is an unpainted wooden kitchen table with straight chairs on either side. There is a small chair down right. Unwashed pans under the sink, a loaf of bread outside the breadbox, a dish towel on the table — other signs of incompleted work. At the rear the shed door opens and the Sheriff comes in followed by the County Attorney and Hale. The Sheriff and Hale are men in middle life, the County Attorney is a young man; all are much bundled up and go at once to the stove. They are followed by the two women — the Sheriff's wife, Mrs. Peters, first; she is a slight wiry woman,* *a thin nervous face. Mrs. Hale is larger and would ordinarily be called more comfortable looking, but she is disturbed now and looks fearfully about as she enters. The women have come in slowly, and stand close together near the door.*

COUNTY ATTORNEY *(at stove rubbing his hands)*:   This feels good. Come up to the fire, ladies.

MRS. PETERS *(after taking a step forward)*:   I'm not — cold.

SHERIFF *(unbuttoning his overcoat and stepping away from the stove to right of table as if to mark the beginning of official business)*:   Now, Mr. Hale, before we move things about, you explain to Mr. Henderson just what you saw when you came here yesterday morning.

COUNTY ATTORNEY *(crossing down to left of the table)*:   By the way, has anything been moved? Are things just as you left them yesterday?

SHERIFF *(looking about)*:   It's just about the same. When it dropped below zero last night I thought I'd better send Frank out this morning to make a fire for us — *(sits right of center table)* no use getting pneumonia with a big case on, but I told him not to touch anything except the stove — and you know Frank.

COUNTY ATTORNEY: Somebody should have been left here yesterday.

SHERIFF: Oh — yesterday. When I had to send Frank to Morris Center for that man who went crazy — I want you to know I had my hands full yesterday. I knew you could get back from Omaha by today and as long as I went over everything here myself ——

COUNTY ATTORNEY: Well, Mr. Hale, tell just what happened when you came here yesterday morning.

HALE *(crossing down to above table)*:   Harry and I had started to town with a load of potatoes. We came along the road from my place and as I got here I said, "I'm going to see if I can't get John Wright to go in with me on a party telephone." I spoke to Wright about it once before and he put me off, saying folks talked too much anyway, and all he asked was peace and quiet — I guess you know about how much he talked himself; but I thought maybe if I went to the house and talked about it before his wife, though I said to Harry that I didn't know as what his wife wanted made much difference to John ——

COUNTY ATTORNEY: Let's talk about that later, Mr. Hale. I do want to talk about that, but tell now just what happened when you got to the house.

HALE: I didn't hear or see anything; I knocked at the door, and still it was all quiet inside. I knew they must be up, it was past eight o'clock. So I knocked again, and I thought I heard somebody say, "Come in." I wasn't sure, I'm not sure yet, but I opened the door — this door *(indicating the door by which the two women are still standing)* and there in that rocker — *(pointing to it)* sat Mrs. Wright. *(They all look at the rocker down left.)*

COUNTY ATTORNEY: What — was she doing?

HALE: She was rockin' back and forth. She had her apron in her hand and was kind of — pleating it.

COUNTY ATTORNEY: And how did she — look?

HALE: Well, she looked queer.

COUNTY ATTORNEY: How do you mean — queer?

HALE: Well, as if she didn't know what she was going to do next. And kind of done up.

COUNTY ATTORNEY *(takes out notebook and pencil and sits left of center table)*:   How did she seem to feel about your coming?

HALE: Why, I don't think she minded — one way or other. She didn't pay much attention. I said, "How do, Mrs. Wright, it's cold, ain't it?" And she said, "Is it?" — and went on kind of pleating at her apron. Well, I was surprised; she didn't ask me to come up to the stove, or to set down, but just sat there, not even looking at me, so I said, "I want to see John." And then she — laughed. I guess you would call it a laugh. I thought of Harry and the team outside, so I said a little sharp: "Can't I see John?" "No," she says, kind o' dull like. "Ain't he home?" says I. "Yes," says she, "he's home." "Then why can't I see him?" I asked her, out of patience. " 'Cause he's dead," says she. "*Dead?*" says I. She just nodded her head, not getting a bit excited, but rockin' back and forth. "Why — where is he?" says I, not knowing what to say. She just pointed upstairs — like that. *(Himself pointing to the room above.)* I started for the stairs, with the idea of going up there. I walked from there to here — then I says, "Why, what did he die of?" "He died of a rope round his neck," says she, and just went on pleatin' at her apron. Well, I went out and called Harry. I thought I might — need help. We went upstairs and there he was lyin' ——

COUNTY ATTORNEY: I think I'd rather have you go into that upstairs, where you can point it all out. Just go on now with the rest of the story.

HALE: Well, my first thought was to get that rope off. It looked . . . *(stops; his face twitches)* . . . but Harry, he went up to him, and he said, "No, he's dead all right, and we'd better not touch anything." So we went back downstairs. She was still sitting that same way. "Has anybody been notified?" I asked. "No," says she, unconcerned. "Who did this, Mrs. Wright?" said Harry. He said it businesslike — and she stopped pleatin' of her apron. "I don't know," she says. "You don't *know*?" says Harry. "No," says she. "Weren't you sleepin' in the bed with him?" says Harry. "Yes," says she, "but I was on the inside." "Somebody slipped a rope round his neck and strangled him and you didn't wake up?" says Harry. "I didn't wake up," she said after him. We must 'a' looked as if we didn't see how that could be, for after a minute she said, "I sleep sound." Harry was going to ask her more questions but I said maybe we ought to let her tell her story first to the coroner, or the sheriff, so Harry went fast as he could to Rivers's place, where there's a telephone.

COUNTY ATTORNEY: And what did Mrs. Wright do when she knew that you had gone for the coroner?

HALE: She moved from the rocker to that chair over there *(pointing to a small chair in the down right corner)* and just sat there with her hands held together and looking down. I got a feeling that I ought to make some conversation, so I said I had come in to see if John wanted to put in a telephone, and at that she started to laugh, and then she stopped and looked at me—scared. *(The County Attorney, who has had his notebook out, makes a note.)* I dunno, maybe it wasn't scared. I wouldn't like to say it was. Soon Harry got back, and then Dr. Lloyd came and you, Mr. Peters, and so I guess that's all I know that you don't.

COUNTY ATTORNEY *(rising and looking around):*   I guess we'll go upstairs first—and then out to the barn and around there. *(To the Sheriff.)* You're convinced that there was nothing important here—nothing that would point to any motive?

SHERIFF: Nothing here but kitchen things. *(The County Attorney, after again looking around the kitchen, opens the door of a cupboard closet in right wall. He brings a small chair from right—gets on it and looks on a shelf. Pulls his hand away, sticky.)*

COUNTY ATTORNEY: Here's a nice mess. *(The women draw nearer up center.)*

MRS. PETERS *(to the other woman):*   Oh, her fruit; it did freeze. *(To the Lawyer.)* She worried about that when it turned so cold. She said the fire'd go out and her jars would break.

SHERIFF *(rises):*   Well, can you beat the woman! Held for murder and worryin' about her preserves.

COUNTY ATTORNEY *(getting down from chair):*   I guess before we're through she may have something more serious than preserves to worry about. *(Crosses down right center.)*

HALE: —Well, women are used to worrying over trifles. *(The two women move a little closer together.)*

COUNTY ATTORNEY *(with the gallantry of a young politician):*   And yet, for all their worries, what would we do without the ladies? *(The women do not unbend. He goes below the center table to the sink, takes a dipperful of water from the pail, and pouring it into a basin, washes his hands. While he is doing this the Sheriff and Hale cross to cupboard, which they inspect. The County Attorney starts to wipe his hands on the roller towel, turns it for a cleaner place.)* Dirty towels! *(Kicks his foot against the pans under the sink.)* Not much of a housekeeper, would you say, ladies?

MRS. HALE *(stiffly):*   There's a great deal of work to be done on a farm.

COUNTY ATTORNEY: To be sure. And yet *(with a little bow to her)* I know there are some Dickson County farmhouses which do not have such roller towels. *(He gives it a pull to expose its full-length again.)*

MRS. HALE: Those towels get dirty awful quick. Men's hands aren't always as clean as they might be.

COUNTY ATTORNEY: Ah, loyal to your sex, I see. But you and Mrs. Wright were neighbors. I suppose you were friends, too.

MRS. HALE *(shaking her head):*   I've not seen much of her of late years. I've not been in this house—it's more than a year.

COUNTY ATTORNEY *(crossing to women up center):*   And why was that? You didn't like her?

MRS. HALE: I liked her all well enough. Farmers' wives have their hands full, Mr. Henderson. And then——

COUNTY ATTORNEY: Yes —— ?

MRS. HALE *(looking about)*:   It never seemed a very cheerful place.

COUNTY ATTORNEY: No — it's not cheerful. I shouldn't say she had the home-making instinct.

MRS. HALE: Well, I don't know as Wright had, either.

COUNTY ATTORNEY: You mean that they didn't get on very well?

MRS. HALE: No, I don't mean anything. But I don't think a place'd be any cheerfuller for John Wright's being in it.

COUNTY ATTORNEY: I'd like to talk more of that a little later. I want to get the lay of things upstairs now. *(He goes past the women to up right where steps lead to a stair door.)*

SHERIFF: I suppose anything Mrs. Peters does'll be all right. She was to take in some clothes for her, you know, and a few little things. We left in such a hurry yesterday.

COUNTY ATTORNEY: Yes, but I would like to see what you take, Mrs. Peters, and keep an eye out for anything that might be of use to us.

MRS. PETERS: Yes, Mr. Henderson. *(The men leave by up right door to stairs. The women listen to the men's steps on the stairs, then look about the kitchen.)*

MRS. HALE *(crossing left to sink)*:   I'd hate to have men coming into my kitchen, snooping around and criticizing. *(She arranges the pans under sink which the lawyer had shoved out of place.)*

MRS. PETERS: Of course it's no more than their duty. *(Crosses to cupboard up right.)*

MRS. HALE: Duty's all right, but I guess that deputy sheriff that came out to make the fire might have got a little of this on. *(Gives the roller towel a pull.)* Wish I'd thought of that sooner. Seems mean to talk about her for not having things slicked up when she had to come away in such a hurry. *(Crosses right to Mrs. Peters at cupboard.)*

MRS. PETERS *(who has been looking through cupboard, lifts one end of towel that covers a pan)*:   She had bread set. *(Stands still.)*

MRS. HALE *(eyes fixed on a loaf of bread beside the breadbox, which is on a low shelf of the cupboard)*:   She was going to put this in there. *(Picks up loaf, abruptly drops it. In a manner of returning to familiar things.)* It's a shame about her fruit. I wonder if it's all gone. *(Gets up on the chair and looks.)* I think there's some here that's all right, Mrs. Peters. Yes — here; *(holding it toward the window)* this is cherries, too. *(Looking again.)* I declare I believe that's the only one. *(Gets down, jar in her hand. Goes to the sink and wipes it off on the outside.)* She'll feel awful bad after all her hard work in the hot weather. I remember the afternoon I put up my cherries last summer. *(She puts the jar on the big kitchen table, center of the room. With a sigh, is about to sit down in the rocking chair. Before she is seated realizes what chair it is; with a slow look at it, steps back. The chair which she has touched rocks back and forth. Mrs. Peters moves to center table and they both watch the chair rock for a moment or two.)*

MRS. PETERS *(shaking off the mood which the empty rocking chair has evoked. Now in a businesslike manner she speaks)*:   Well I must get those things from the front room closet. *(She goes to the door at the right but, after looking into the other room, steps back.)* You coming with me, Mrs. Hale? You could help me carry them. *(They go in the other room; reappear, Mrs. Peters carrying a dress, petticoat, and skirt, Mrs. Hale following with a pair of shoes.)* My, it's cold in there. *(She puts the clothes on the big table and hurries to the stove.)*

MRS. HALE *(right of center table examining the skirt):* Wright was close. I think maybe that's why she kept so much to herself. She didn't even belong to the Ladies' Aid. I suppose she felt she couldn't do her part, and then you don't enjoy things when you feel shabby. I heard she used to wear pretty clothes and be lively, when she was Minnie Foster, one of the town girls singing in the choir. But that — oh, that was thirty years ago. This all you want to take in?

MRS. PETERS: She said she wanted an apron. Funny thing to want, for there isn't much to get you dirty in jail, goodness knows. But I suppose just to make her feel more natural. *(Crosses to cupboard.)* She said they was in the top drawer in this cupboard. Yes, here. And then her little shawl that always hung behind the door. *(Opens stair door and looks.)* Yes, here it is. *(Quickly shuts door leading upstairs.)*

MRS. HALE *(abruptly moving toward her):* Mrs. Peters?

MRS. PETERS: Yes, Mrs. Hale? *(At up right door.)*

MRS. HALE: Do you think she did it?

MRS. PETERS *(in a frightened voice):* Oh, I don't know.

MRS. HALE: Well, I don't think she did. Asking for an apron and her little shawl. Worrying about her fruit.

MRS. PETERS *(starts to speak, glances up, where footsteps are heard in the room above. In a low voice):* Mr. Peters says it looks bad for her. Mr. Henderson is awful sarcastic in a speech and he'll make fun of her sayin' she didn't wake up.

MRS. HALE: Well, I guess John Wright didn't wake when they was slipping that rope under his neck.

MRS. PETERS *(crossing slowly to table and placing shawl and apron on table with other clothing):* No, it's strange. It must have been done awful crafty and still. They say it was such a — funny way to kill a man, rigging it all up like that.

MRS. HALE *(crossing to left of Mrs. Peters at table):* That's just what Mr. Hale said. There was a gun in the house. He says that's what he can't understand.

MRS. PETERS: Mr. Henderson said coming out that what was needed for the case was a motive; something to show anger, or — sudden feeling.

MRS. HALE *(who is standing by the table):* Well, I don't see any signs of anger around here. *(She puts her hand on the dish towel, which lies on the table, stands looking down at table, one-half of which is clean, the other half messy.)* It's wiped to here. *(Makes a move as if to finish work, then turns and looks at loaf of bread outside the breadbox. Drops towel. In that voice of coming back to familiar things.)* Wonder how they are finding things upstairs. *(Crossing below table to down right.)* I hope she had it a little more red-up° up there. You know, it seems kind of *sneaking.* Locking her up in town and then coming out here and trying to get her own house to turn against her!

red-up: To get ready or clean up.

MRS. PETERS: But, Mrs. Hale, the law is the law.

MRS. HALE: I s'pose 'tis. *(Unbuttoning her coat.)* Better loosen up your things, Mrs. Peters. You won't feel them when you go out. *(Mrs. Peters takes off her fur tippet, goes to hang it on chair back left of table, stands looking at the work basket on floor near down left window.)*

MRS. PETERS: She was piecing a quilt. *(She brings the large sewing basket to the center table and they look at the bright pieces, Mrs. Hale above the table and Mrs. Peters left of it.)*

MRS. HALE: It's a log cabin pattern. Pretty, isn't it? I wonder if she was goin' to quilt it or just knot it? *(Footsteps have been heard coming down the stairs. The Sheriff enters followed by Hale and the County Attorney.)*

SHERIFF: They wonder if she was going to quilt it or just knot it! *(The men laugh, the women look abashed.)*

COUNTY ATTORNEY *(rubbing his hands over the stove)*:   Frank's fire didn't do much up there, did it? Well, let's go out to the barn and get that cleared up. *(The men go outside by up left door.)*

MRS. HALE *(resentfully)*:   I don't know as there's anything so strange, our takin' up our time with little things while we're waiting for them to get the evidence. *(She sits in chair right of table smoothing out a block with decision.)* I don't see as it's anything to laugh about.

MRS. PETERS *(apologetically)*:   Of course they've got awful important things on their minds. *(Pulls up a chair and joins Mrs. Hale at the left of the table.)*

MRS. HALE *(examining another block)*:   Mrs. Peters, look at this one. Here, this is the one she was working on, and look at the sewing! All the rest of it has been so nice and even. And look at this! It's all over the place! Why, it looks as if she didn't know what she was about! *(After she has said this they look at each other, then start to glance back at the door. After an instant Mrs. Hale has pulled at a knot and ripped the sewing.)*

MRS. PETERS: Oh, what are you doing, Mrs. Hale?

MRS. HALE *(mildly)*:   Just pulling out a stitch or two that's not sewed very good. *(Threading a needle.)* Bad sewing always made me fidgety.

MRS. PETERS *(with a glance at door, nervously)*:   I don't think we ought to touch things.

MRS. HALE: I'll just finish up this end. *(Suddenly stopping and leaning forward.)* Mrs. Peters?

MRS. PETERS: Yes, Mrs. Hale?

MRS. HALE: What do you suppose she was so nervous about?

MRS. PETERS: Oh — I don't know. I don't know as she was nervous. I sometimes sew awful queer when I'm just tired. *(Mrs. Hale starts to say something, looks at Mrs. Peters, then goes on sewing.)* Well, I must get these things wrapped up. They may be through sooner than we think. *(Putting apron and other things together.)* I wonder where I can find a piece of paper, and string. *(Rises.)*

MRS. HALE: In that cupboard, maybe.

MRS. PETERS *(crosses right looking in cupboard)*:   Why, here's a bird-cage. *(Holds it up.)* Did she have a bird, Mrs. Hale?

MRS. HALE: Why, I don't know whether she did or not — I've not been here for so long. There was a man around last year selling canaries cheap, but I don't know as she took one; maybe she did. She used to sing real pretty herself.

MRS. PETERS *(glancing around)*:   Seems funny to think of a bird here. But she must have had one, or why would she have a cage? I wonder what happened to it?

MRS. HALE: I s'pose maybe the cat got it.

MRS. PETERS: No, she didn't have a cat. She's got that feeling some people have about cats — being afraid of them. My cat got in her room and she was real upset and asked me to take it out.

MRS. HALE: My sister Bessie was like that. Queer, ain't it?

MRS. PETERS *(examining the cage)*:   Why, look at this door. It's broke. One hinge is pulled apart. *(Takes a step down to Mrs. Hale's right.)*

MRS. HALE *(looking too)*:   Looks as if someone must have been rough with it.

MRS. PETERS: Why, yes. *(She brings the cage forward and puts it on the table.)*

MRS. HALE *(glancing toward up left door)*:   I wish if they're going to find any evidence they'd be about it. I don't like this place.

MRS. PETERS: But I'm awful glad you came with me, Mrs. Hale. It would be lonesome for me sitting here alone.

MRS. HALE: It would, wouldn't it? *(Dropping her sewing.)* But I tell you what I do wish, Mrs. Peters. I wish I had come over sometimes when *she* was here. I — *(looking around the room)* — wish I had.

MRS. PETERS: But of course you were awful busy, Mrs. Hale — your house and your children.

MRS. HALE *(rises and crosses left)*:   I could've come. I stayed away because it weren't cheerful — and that's why I ought to have come. I — *(looking out left window)* — I've never liked this place. Maybe because it's down in a hollow and you don't see the road. I dunno what it is, but it's a lonesome place and always was. I wish I had come over to see Minnie Foster sometimes. I can see now — *(Shakes her head.)*

MRS. PETERS *(left of table and above it)*:   Well, you mustn't reproach yourself, Mrs. Hale. Somehow we just don't see how it is with other folks until — something turns up.

MRS. HALE: Not having children makes less work — but it makes a quiet house, and Wright out to work all day, and no company when he did come in. *(Turning from window.)* Did you know John Wright, Mrs. Peters?

MRS. PETERS: Not to know him; I've seen him in town. They say he was a good man.

MRS. HALE: Yes — good; he didn't drink, and kept his word as well as most, I guess, and paid his debts. But he was a hard man, Mrs. Peters. Just to pass the time of day with him — *(Shivers.)* Like a raw wind that gets to the bone. *(Pauses, her eye falling on the cage.)* I should think she would 'a' wanted a bird. But what do you suppose went with it?

MRS. PETERS: I don't know, unless it got sick and died. *(She reaches over and swings the broken door, swings it again, both women watch it.)*

MRS. HALE: You weren't raised round here, were you? *(Mrs. Peters shakes her head.)* You didn't know — her?

MRS. PETERS: Not till they brought her yesterday.

MRS. HALE: She — come to think of it, she was kind of like a bird herself — real sweet and pretty, but kind of timid and — fluttery. How — she — did — change. *(Silence: then as if struck by a happy thought and relieved to get back to everyday things. Crosses right above Mrs. Peters to cupboard, replaces small chair used to stand on to its original place down right.)* Tell you what, Mrs. Peters, why don't you take the quilt in with you? It might take up her mind.

MRS. PETERS: Why, I think that's a real nice idea, Mrs. Hale. There couldn't possibly be any objection to it could there? Now, just what would I take? I wonder if her patches are in here — and her things. *(They look in the sewing basket.)*

MRS. HALE *(crosses to right of table)*:   Here's some red. I expect this has got sewing things in it. *(Brings out a fancy box.)* What a pretty box. Looks like something somebody would give you. Maybe her scissors are in here. *(Opens box. Suddenly puts her hand to her nose.)* Why —— *(Mrs. Peters bends nearer, then turns her face away.)* There's something wrapped up in this piece of silk.

MRS. PETERS: Why, this isn't her scissors.

MRS. HALE *(lifting the silk)*:   Oh, Mrs. Peters — it's —— *(Mrs. Peters bends closer.)*

MRS. PETERS: It's the bird.

MRS. HALE: But, Mrs. Peters — look at it! Its neck! Look at its neck! It's all — other side *to.*

MRS. PETERS: Somebody — wrung — its — neck. *(Their eyes meet. A look of growing comprehension, of horror. Steps are heard outside. Mrs. Hale slips box under quilt pieces, and sinks into her chair. Enter Sheriff and County Attorney. Mrs. Peters steps down left and stands looking out of window.)*

COUNTY ATTORNEY *(as one turning from serious things to little pleasantries)*:   Well, ladies, have you decided whether she was going to quilt it or knot it? *(Crosses to center above table.)*

MRS. PETERS: We think she was going to — knot it. *(Sheriff crosses to right of stove, lifts stove lid, and glances at fire, then stands warming hands at stove.)*

COUNTY ATTORNEY: Well, that's interesting, I'm sure. *(Seeing the bird-cage.)* Has the bird flown?

MRS. HALE *(putting more quilt pieces over the box)*:   We think the — cat got it.

COUNTY ATTORNEY *(preoccupied)*:   Is there a cat? *(Mrs. Hale glances in a quick covert way at Mrs. Peters.)*

MRS. PETERS *(turning from window takes a step in)*:   Well, not *now.* They're superstitious, you know. They leave.

COUNTY ATTORNEY *(to Sheriff Peters, continuing an interrupted conversation)*:   No sign at all of anyone having come from the outside. Their own rope. Now let's go up again and go over it piece by piece. *(They start upstairs.)* It would have to have been someone who knew just the —— *(Mrs. Peters sits down left of table. The two women sit there not looking at one another, but as if peering into something and at the same time holding back. When they talk now it is in the manner of feeling their way over strange ground, as if afraid of what they are saying, but as if they cannot help saying it.)*

MRS. HALE *(hesitatively and in hushed voice)*:   She liked the bird. She was going to bury it in that pretty box.

MRS. PETERS *(in a whisper)*:   When I was a girl — my kitten — there was a boy took a hatchet, and before my eyes — and before I could get there ——— *(Covers her face an instant.)* If they hadn't held me back I would have — *(catches herself, looks upstairs where steps are heard, falters weakly)* — hurt him.

MRS. HALE *(with a slow look around her)*:   I wonder how it would seem never to have had any children around. *(Pause.)* No, Wright wouldn't like the bird — a thing that sang. She used to sing. He killed that, too.

MRS. PETERS *(moving uneasily)*:   We don't know who killed the bird.

MRS. HALE: I knew John Wright.

MRS. PETERS: It was an awful thing was done in this house that night, Mrs. Hale. Killing a man while he slept, slipping a rope around his neck that choked the life out of him.

MRS. HALE: His neck. Choked the life out of him. *(Her hand goes out and rests on the bird-cage.)*

MRS. PETERS *(with rising voice)*:   We don't know who killed him. We don't *know.*

MRS. HALE *(her own feeling not interrupted)*:   If there'd been years and years of nothing, then a bird to sing to you, it would be awful — still, after the bird was still.

MRS. PETERS *(something within her speaking)*:   I know what stillness is. When we homesteaded in Dakota, and my first baby died — after he was two years old, and me with no other then ———

MRS. HALE *(moving)*:   How soon do you suppose they'll be through looking for the evidence?

MRS. PETERS: I know what stillness is. *(Pulling herself back.)* The law has got to punish crime, Mrs. Hale.

MRS. HALE *(not as if answering that)*:   I wish you'd seen Minnie Foster when she wore a white dress with blue ribbons and stood up there in the choir and sang. *(A look around the room.)* Oh, I *wish* I'd come over here once in a while! That was a crime! That was a crime! Who's going to punish that?

MRS. PETERS *(looking upstairs)*:   We mustn't — take on.

MRS. HALE: I might have known she needed help! I know how things can be — for women. I tell you, it's queer, Mrs. Peters. We live close together and we live far apart. We all go through the same things — it's all just a different kind of the same thing. *(Brushes her eyes, noticing the jar of fruit, reaches out for it.)* If I was you I wouldn't tell her her fruit was gone. Tell her it *ain't.* Tell her it's all right. Take this in to prove it to her. She — she may never know whether it was broke or not.

MRS. PETERS *(takes the jar, looks about for something to wrap it in; takes petticoat from the clothes brought from the other room, very nervously begins winding this around the jar. In a false voice)*:   My, it's a good thing the men couldn't hear us. Wouldn't they just laugh! Getting all stirred up over a little thing like a — dead canary. As if that could have anything to do with — with — wouldn't they *laugh!* *(The men are heard coming downstairs.)*

MRS. HALE *(under her breath)*:   Maybe they would — maybe they wouldn't.

COUNTY ATTORNEY: No, Peters, it's all perfectly clear except a reason for doing it. But you know juries when it comes to women. If there was some definite thing. *(Crosses slowly to above table. Sheriff crosses down right. Mrs. Hale*

and Mrs. Peters remain seated at either side of table.) Something to show —
something to make a story about — a thing that would connect up with
this strange way of doing it —— *(The women's eyes meet for an instant. Enter
Hale from outer door.)*

HALE *(remaining by door)*:   Well, I've got the team around. Pretty cold out there.

COUNTY ATTORNEY: I'm going to stay awhile by myself. *(To the Sheriff.)* You can
send Frank out for me, can't you? I want to go over everything. I'm not
satisfied that we can't do better.

SHERIFF: Do you want to see what Mrs. Peters is going to take in? *(The Lawyer
picks up the apron, laughs.)*

COUNTY ATTORNEY: Oh, I guess they're not very dangerous things the ladies
have picked out. *(Moves a few things about, disturbing the quilt pieces which
cover the box. Steps back.)* No, Mrs. Peters doesn't need supervising. For that
matter a sheriff's wife is married to the law. Ever think of it that way, Mrs.
Peters?

MRS. PETERS: Not — just that way.

SHERIFF *(chuckling)*:   Married to the law. *(Moves to down right door to the other
room.)* I just want you to come in here a minute, George. We ought to take
a look at these windows.

COUNTY ATTORNEY *(scoffingly)*:   Oh, windows!

SHERIFF: We'll be right out, Mr. Hale. *(Hale goes outside. The Sheriff follows the
County Attorney into the room. Then Mrs. Hale rises, hands tight together, looking intensely at Mrs. Peters, whose eyes make a slow turn, finally meeting Mrs.
Hale's. A moment Mrs. Hale holds her, then her own eyes point the way to where
the box is concealed. Suddenly Mrs. Peters throws back quilt pieces and tries to
put the box in the bag she is carrying. It is too big. She opens box, starts to take
bird out, cannot touch it, goes to pieces, stands there helpless. Sound of a knob
turning in the other room. Mrs. Hale snatches the box and puts it in the pocket
of her big coat. Enter County Attorney and Sheriff, who remains down right.)*

COUNTY ATTORNEY *(crosses to up left door facetiously)*:   Well, Henry, at least we
found out that she was not going to quilt it. She was going to — what is it
you call it, ladies?

MRS. HALE *(standing center below table facing front, her hand against her pocket)*:
We call it — knot it, Mr. Henderson.

Curtain.   *[1916]*

≡ **THINKING ABOUT THE TEXT**

1. Although much of this play is about Minnie Wright, Glaspell keeps her
    offstage. Why, do you think?

2. What does Glaspell imply about differences between men and women?
    Support your inference with details from the text.

3. What do Mrs. Hale and Mrs. Peters realize about themselves during the
    course of the play? To what extent should they feel guilty about their
    own past behavior?

4. Ultimately, Mrs. Hale and Mrs. Peters cover up evidence to protect Minnie Wright. They seem to act out of loyalty to their sex. How sympathetic are you to their stand? Do you feel there are times when you should be someone's ally because that person is of the same gender as you?

5. Is this play about freedom and confinement? About the injustice of male domination? About the bonds that hold women together? Or something else? Explain your answer.

≡ MAKING COMPARISONS

1. Does class or socioeconomic level play a significant role in the freedom of the women in these two plays?

2. Compare Torvald and John Wright.

3. Both endings were controversial in their day. Would they be today? Why, or why not?

LYNN NOTTAGE
POOF!

Lynn Nottage (b. 1964) is an American playwright and an activist focused on preventing violence against women. She grew up in New York City and attended Brown University and the Yale School of Drama. She then worked for four years at Amnesty International. Ruined, *a play about Congolese women during civil war was awarded the Pulitzer Prize for Drama in 2009. Her plays have been performed in dozens of theaters. She has received a Guggenheim Fellowship and a MacArthur Grant. Her latest play is* By the Way, Meet Vera Stark *(2011).*

CHARACTERS

SAMUEL, *Loureen's husband*
LOUREEN, *a demure housewife, early thirties*
FLORENCE, *Loureen's best friend, early thirties*

TIME: *The present*
PLACE: *Kitchen*

A NOTE: *Nearly half the women on death row in the United States were convicted of killing abusive husbands. Spontaneous combustion is not recognized as a capital crime.*

Darkness.

SAMUEL (*In the darkness*):   WHEN I COUNT TO TEN I DON' WANT TO SEE YA! I DON' WANT TO HEAR YA! ONE, TWO, THREE, FOUR —
LOUREEN (*In the darkness*):   DAMN YOU TO HELL, SAMUEL!

A bright flash.

> *Lights rise. A huge pile of smoking ashes rests in the middle of the kitchen. Loureen, a demure housewife in her early thirties, stares down at the ashes incredulously. She bends and lifts a pair of spectacles from the remains. She ever so slowly backs away.*

Samuel? Uh! (*Places the spectacles on the kitchen table*) Uh! . . . Samuel? (*Looks around*) Don't fool with me now. I'm not in the mood. (*Whispers*) Samuel? I didn't mean it really. I'll be good if you come back . . . Come on now, dinner's waiting. (*Chuckles, then stops abruptly*) Now stop your foolishness . . . And let's sit down. (*Examines the spectacles*) Uh! (*Softly*) Don't be cross with me. Sure I forgot to pick up your shirt for tomorrow. I can wash another, I'll do it right now. Right now! Sam? . . . (*Cautiously*) You hear me! (*Awaits a response*) Maybe I didn't ever intend to wash your shirt. (*Pulls back as though about to receive a blow; a moment*) Uh! (*Sits down and dials the telephone*) Florence, honey, could you come on down for a moment. There's been a . . . little . . . accident . . . Quickly please. Uh!

Loureen hangs up the phone. She gets a broom and a dust pan. She hesitantly approaches the pile of ashes. She gets down on her hands and knees and takes a closer look. A fatuous grin spreads across her face. She is startled by a sudden knock on the door. She slowly walks across the room like a possessed child. Loureen lets in Florence, her best friend and upstairs neighbor. Florence, also a housewife in her early thirties, wears a floral housecoat and a pair of oversized slippers. Without acknowledgment Loureen proceeds to saunter back across the room.

FLORENCE: HEY!

LOUREEN (*Pointing at the ashes*): Uh! . . . (*She struggles to formulate words, which press at the inside of her mouth, not quite realized*) Uh! . . .

FLORENCE: You all right? What happened? (*Sniffs the air*) Smells like you burned something? (*Stares at the huge pile of ashes*) What the devil is that?

LOUREEN (*Hushed*): Samuel . . . It's Samuel, I think.

FLORENCE: What's he done now?

LOUREEN: It's him. It's him. (*Nods her head repeatedly*)

FLORENCE: Chile, what's wrong with you? Did he finally drive you out your mind? I knew something was going to happen sooner or later.

LOUREEN: Dial 911, Florence!

FLORENCE: Why? You're scaring me!

LOUREEN: Dial 911!

Florence picks up the telephone and quickly dials.

I think I killed him.

Florence hangs up the telephone.

FLORENCE: What?

LOUREEN (*Whimpers*): I killed him! I killed Samuel!

FLORENCE: Come again? . . . He's dead dead?

Loureen wrings her hands and nods her head twice, mouthing "dead dead." Florence backs away.

No, stop it, I don't have time for this. I'm going back upstairs. You know how Samuel hates to find me here when he gets home. You're not going to get me this time. (*Louder*) Y'all can have your little joke, I'm not part of it! (*A moment. She takes a hard look into Loureen's eyes; she squints*) Did you really do it this time?

LOUREEN (*Hushed*):   I don't know how or why it happened, it just did.

FLORENCE: Why are you whispering?

LOUREEN: I don't want to talk too loud—something else is liable to disappear.

FLORENCE: Where's his body?

LOUREEN (*Points to the pile of ashes*):   There! . . .

FLORENCE: You burned him?

LOUREEN: I DON'T KNOW! (*Covers her mouth as if to muffle her words; hushed*) I think so.

FLORENCE: Either you did or you didn't, what you mean you don't know? We're talking murder, Loureen, not oven settings.

LOUREEN: You think I'm playing?

FLORENCE: How many times have I heard you talk about being rid of him. How many times have we sat at this very table and laughed about the many ways we could do it and how many times have you done it? None.

LOUREEN (*Lifting the spectacles*):   A pair of cheap spectacles, that's all that's left. And you know how much I hate these. You ever seen him without them, no! . . . He counted to four and disappeared. I swear to God!

FLORENCE: Don't bring the Lord into this just yet! Sit down now . . . What you got to sip on?

LOUREEN: I don't know whether to have a stiff shot of scotch or a glass of champagne.

Florence takes a bottle of sherry out of the cupboard and pours them each a glass. Loureen downs hers, then holds out her glass for more.

He was . . .

FLORENCE: Take your time.

LOUREEN: Standing there.

FLORENCE: And?

LOUREEN: He exploded.

FLORENCE: Did that muthafucka hit you again?

LOUREEN: No . . . he exploded. Boom! Right in front of me. He was shouting like he does, being all colored, then he raised up that big crusty hand to hit me, and poof, he was gone . . . I barely got words out and I'm looking down at a pile of ash.

Florence belts back her sherry. She wipes her forehead and pours them both another.

FLORENCE: Chile, I'll give you this, in terms of color you've matched my husband Edgar, the story king. He came in at six Sunday morning, talking about he'd hit someone with his car, and had spent all night trying to out-run the police. I felt sorry for him. It turns out he was playing poker with his paycheck no less. You don't want to know how I found out . . . But I did.

LOUREEN: You think I'm lying?

FLORENCE: I certainly hope so, Loureen. For your sake and my heart's.

LOUREEN: Samuel always said if I raised my voice something horrible would happen. And it did. I'm a witch . . . the devil spawn!

FLORENCE: You've been watching too much television.

LOUREEN: Never seen anything like this on television. Wish I had, then I'd know what to do . . . There's no question, I'm a witch. (*Looks at her hands with disgust*)

FLORENCE: Chile, don't tell me you've been messing with them mojo women again? What did I tell ya.

Loureen, agitated, stands and sits back down.

LOUREEN: He's not coming back. Oh no, how could he? It would be a miracle! Two in one day . . . I could be canonized. Worse yet, he could be . . . All that needs to happen now is for my palms to bleed and I'll be eternally re-membered as Saint Loureen, the patron of battered wives. Women from across the country will make pilgrimages to me, laying pies and pot roast at my feet and asking the good saint to make their husbands turn to dust. How often does a man like Samuel get damned to hell, and go?

She breaks down. Florence moves to console her friend, then realizes that Loureen is actually laughing hysterically.

FLORENCE: You smoking crack?

LOUREEN: Do I look like I am?

FLORENCE: Hell, I've seen old biddies creeping out of crack houses, talking about they were doing church work.

LOUREEN: Florence, please be helpful, I'm very close to the edge! . . . I don't know what to do next! Do I sweep him up? Do I call the police? Do I . . .

The phone rings.

Oh God.

FLORENCE: You gonna let it ring?

Loureen reaches for the telephone slowly.

LOUREEN: NO! (*Holds the receiver without picking it up, paralyzed*) What if it's his mother? . . . She knows!

The phone continues to ring. They sit until it stops. They both breathe a sigh of relief.

I should be mourning, I should be praying, I should be thinking of the burial, but all that keeps popping into my mind is what will I wear on tele-vision when I share my horrible and wonderful story with a studio audi-ence . . . (*Whimpers*) He's made me a killer, Florence, and you remember what a gentle child I was. (*Whispers*) I'm a killer, I'm a killer, I'm a killer.

FLORENCE: I wouldn't throw that word about too lightly even in jest. Talk like that gets around.

LOUREEN: You think they'll lock me up? A few misplaced words and I'll probably get the death penalty, isn't that what they do with women like me, murderesses?

FLORENCE: Folks have done time for less.

LOUREEN: Thank you, just what I needed to hear!

FLORENCE: What did you expect, that I was going to throw up my arms and congratulate you? Why'd you have to go and lose your mind at this time of day, while I got a pot of rice on the stove and Edgar's about to walk in the door and wonder where his goddamn food is. (*Losing her cool*) And he's going to start in on me about all the nothing I've been doing during the day and why I can't work and then he'll mention how clean you keep your home. And I don't know how I'm going to look him in the eye without . . .

LOUREEN: I'm sorry, Florence. Really. It's out of my hands now.

She takes Florence's hand and squeezes it.

FLORENCE (*Regaining her composure*):   You swear on your right tit?

LOUREEN (*Clutching both breasts*):   I swear on both of them!

FLORENCE: Both your breasts, Loureen! You know what will happen if you're lying. (*Loureen nods; hushed*) Both your breasts Loureen?

LOUREEN: Yeah!

FLORENCE (*Examines the pile of ashes, then shakes her head*):   Oh sweet, sweet Jesus. He must have done something truly terrible.

LOUREEN: No more than usual. I just couldn't take being hit one more time.

FLORENCE: You've taken a thousand blows from that man, couldn't you've turned the cheek and waited? I'd have helped you pack. Like we talked about.

A moment.

LOUREEN: Uh! . . . I could blow on him and he'd disappear across the linoleum. (*Snaps her fingers*) Just like that. Should I be feeling remorse or regret or some other "R" word? I'm strangely jubilant, like on prom night when Samuel and I first made love. That's the feeling! (*The women lock eyes*) Uh!

FLORENCE: Is it . . .

LOUREEN: Like a ton of bricks been lifted from my shoulders, yeah.

FLORENCE: Really?

LOUREEN: Yeah!

Florence walks to the other side of the room.

FLORENCE: You bitch!

LOUREEN: What?

FLORENCE: We made a pact.

LOUREEN: I know.

FLORENCE: You've broken it . . . We agreed that when things got real bad for both of us we'd . . . you know . . . together . . . Do I have to go back upstairs to that? . . . What next?

LOUREEN: I thought you'd tell me! . . . I don't know!

FLORENCE: I don't know!

LOUREEN: I don't know!

Florence begins to walk around the room, nervously touching objects. Loureen sits, wringing her hands and mumbling softly to herself.

FLORENCE: Now you got me, Loureen, I'm truly at a loss for words.

LOUREEN: Everybody always told me, "Keep your place, Loureen." My place, the silent spot on the couch with a wine cooler in my hand and a pleasant smile that warmed the heart. All this time I didn't know why he was so afraid for me to say anything, to speak up. Poof! . . . I've never been by myself, except for them two weeks when he won the office pool and went to Reno with his cousin Mitchell. He wouldn't tell me where he was going until I got that postcard with the cowboy smoking a hundred cigarettes . . . Didn't Sonny Larkin look good last week at Caroline's? He looked good, didn't he . . .

Florence nods. She nervously picks up Samuel's jacket, which is hanging on the back of the chair. She clutches it unconsciously.

NO! No! Don't wrinkle that, that's his favorite jacket. He'll kill me. Put it back!

Florence returns the jacket to its perch. Loureen begins to quiver.

I'm sorry. (*She grabs the jacket and wrinkles it up*) There! (*She then digs into the coat pockets and pulls out his wallet and a movie stub*) Look at that, he said he didn't go to the movies last night. Working late. (*Frantically thumbs through his wallet*) Picture of his motorcycle, Social Security card, driver's license, and look at that from our wedding. (*Smiling*) I looked good, didn't I? (*She puts the pictures back in the wallet and holds the jacket up to her face*) There were some good things. (*She then sweeps her hand over the jacket to remove the wrinkles, and folds it ever so carefully, and finally throws it in the garbage*) And out of my mouth those words made him disappear. All these years and just words, Florence. That's all they were.

FLORENCE: I'm afraid I won't ever get those words out. I'll start resenting you, honey. I'm afraid won't anything change for me.

LOUREEN: I been to that place.

FLORENCE: Yeah? But now I wish I could relax these old lines (*Touches her forehead*) for a minute maybe. Edgar has never done me the way Samuel did you, but he sure did take the better part of my life.

LOUREEN: Not yet, Florence.

FLORENCE (*Nods*):   I have the children to think of . . . right?

LOUREEN: You can think up a hundred things before . . .

FLORENCE: Then come upstairs with me . . . we'll wait together for Edgar and then you can spit out your words and . . .

LOUREEN: I can't do that.

FLORENCE: Yes you can. Come on now.

Loureen shakes her head no.

Well, I guess my mornings are not going to be any different.

LOUREEN: If you can say for certain, then I guess they won't be. I couldn't say that.

FLORENCE: But you got a broom and a dust pan, you don't need anything more than that . . . He was a bastard and nobody will care that he's gone.

LOUREEN: Phone's gonna start ringing soon, people are gonna start asking soon, and they'll care.

FLORENCE: What's your crime? Speaking your mind?

LOUREEN: Maybe I should mail him to his mother. I owe her that. I feel bad for her, she didn't understand how it was. I can't just throw him away and pretend like it didn't happen. Can I?

FLORENCE: I didn't see anything but a pile of ash. As far as I know you got a little careless and burned a chicken.

LOUREEN: He was always threatening not to come back.

FLORENCE: I heard him.

LOUREEN: It would've been me eventually.

FLORENCE: Yes.

LOUREEN: I should call the police, or someone.

FLORENCE: Why? What are you gonna tell them? About all those times they refused to help, about all those nights you slept in my bed 'cause you were afraid to stay down here? About the time he nearly took out your eye 'cause you flipped the television channel?

LOUREEN: No.

FLORENCE: You've got it, girl!

LOUREEN: Good-bye to the fatty meats and the salty food. Good-bye to the bourbon and the bologna sandwiches. Good-bye to the smell of his feet, his breath and his bowel movements . . . (*A moment. She closes her eyes and, reliving a horrible memory, she shudders*) Good-bye. (*Walks over to the pile of ashes*) Samuel? . . . Just checking.

FLORENCE: Good-bye Samuel.

They both smile.

LOUREEN: I'll let the police know that he's missing tomorrow . . .

FLORENCE: Why not the next day?

LOUREEN: Chicken's warming in the oven, you're welcome to stay.

FLORENCE: Chile, I got a pot of rice on the stove, kids are probably acting out . . . and Edgar, well . . . Listen, I'll stop in tomorrow.

LOUREEN: For dinner?

FLORENCE: Edgar wouldn't stand for that. Cards maybe.

LOUREEN: Cards.

The women hug for a long moment. Florence exits. Loureen stands over the ashes for a few moments contemplating what to do. She finally decides to sweep them under the carpet, and then proceeds to set the table and sit down to eat her dinner.

END OF PLAY   [1993]

☰ WRITING ABOUT THE TEXT

1. How would you describe Loureen's relationship to her husband Samuel? What reason can you suggest for Loureen staying in that relationship?

2. What specific offenses does Samuel commit? Which would be violations of wedding vows? Which would be legal issues?

3. Describe the progression of Loureen's response to Samuel's death.

4. What evidence might there be that Loureen could become a model for battered women? What do you think about Edgar's future?

5. Even though Samuel dies, the play doesn't seem tragic. Point out the comic element. How does Nottage get away with using humor in a play where someone loses his life?

☰ MAKING COMPARISONS

1. Compare the marital situations of Nora, Minnie, and Loureen.

2. Explain the justification each woman has for her behavior. Which seems the most compelling? The least?

3. How would contemporary audiences judge Torvald, John Wright, and Samuel?

☰ WRITING ABOUT ISSUES

1. Write an essay that argues that justice was or was not served in either *A Doll House*, *Trifles*, or *POOF!*

2. Based on these three plays, write an essay that argues that the relationship problems in marriages have changed or remained the same since 1879.

3. One could argue that a mystical intervention killed Samuel. Argue that such a device would or would not be tolerated in Ibsen's play in 1879 or Glaspell's in 1916. How do you account for these responses?

4. Write an argument that sets out your view of what a contemporary relationship between equals would be.

RICHARD RODRIGUEZ, "Aria"

JOSE ANTONIO VARGAS, "My Life as an Undocumented Immigrant"

Although both Richard Rodriguez and Jose Antonio Vargas grew up in immigrant families around San Francisco, their responses to the cultural and language boundaries each had to negotiate were quite different. Rodriguez agonized over his childhood fluency in English. He felt Spanish was the comforting and solidifying language of family life. As he learned the public language of the majority, he felt his family life changed. In a way, his growing proficiency in English and gradual socialization into American culture distanced him from the family life he so loved as a child. His progress was also a loss. Despite this sense of loss, Rodriguez opposes bi-lingual education and affirmative action and favors immersing students in English. As a result of this controversial position against students using their native languages in school, he was widely criticized as a traitor to Mexican Americans. Caught between two cultures, not belonging completely in either, Rodriguez claims he is "a comic victim of two cultures."

Jose Vargas also has a foothold in both cultures, but he seems not to have suffered the emotional family turmoil that Rodriguez recounts. Vargas has assimilated into American culture with eloquence and excellence. His problem is a technical one. As he explains, "I am an American. I just don't have the right papers." Vargas's essay tells of his attempts to cross the boundary from immigrant to American citizen without official approval. That he is so successful is in itself an example of the American Dream.

■ BEFORE YOU READ

Recall incidents from your past when you felt you had to cross or negotiate various boundaries. How did you feel? Recall stories or films about people crossing boundaries, whether geographical, linguistic, class, religious, or other. How did you respond?

RICHARD RODRIGUEZ
Aria

A native of San Francisco, California, Richard Rodriguez (b. 1944) is the son of Mexican immigrants. Until he entered school at the age of six, he spoke primarily Spanish. His 1982 memoir, Hunger of Memory, *describes how English-language instruction distanced him from his parents' native culture. Rodriguez went on to attend Stanford University and the University of California at Berkeley, where he earned a doctorate in English Renaissance literature. He is also the author of* Days of Obligation: An Argument with My Mexican Father *(1992) and* Brown: The

Last Discovery of America *(2003). His essay "The God of the Desert" was published in* Best American Essays 2009. *Currently Rodriguez is a contributing editor for* Harper's *magazine and a commentator on public television's* NewsHour.

1

I remember to start with that day in Sacramento — a California now nearly thirty years past — when I first entered a classroom, able to understand some fifty stray English words.

The third of four children, I had been preceded to a neighborhood Roman Catholic school by an older brother and sister. But neither of them had revealed very much about their classroom experiences. Each afternoon they returned, as they left in the morning, always together, speaking in Spanish as they climbed the five steps of the porch. And their mysterious books, wrapped in shopping-bag paper, remained on the table next to the door, closed firmly behind them.

An accident of geography sent me to a school where all my classmates were white, many the children of doctors and lawyers and business executives. All my classmates certainly must have been uneasy on that first day of school — as most children are uneasy — to find themselves apart from their families in the first institution of their lives. But I was astonished.

The nun said, in a friendly but oddly impersonal voice, "Boys and girls, this is Richard Rodriguez." (I heard her sound out: *Rich-heard Road-ree-guess.*) It was the first time I had heard anyone name me in English. "Richard," the nun repeated more slowly, writing my name down in her black leather book. Quickly I turned to see my mother's face dissolve in a watery blur behind the pebbled glass door.

Many years later there is something called bilingual education — a scheme proposed in the late 1960s by Hispanic-American social activists, later endorsed by a congressional vote. It is a program that seeks to permit non-English-speaking children, many from lower-class homes, to use their family language as the language of school. (Such is the goal its supporters announce.) I hear them and am forced to say no: it is not possible for a child — any child — ever to use his family's language in school. Not to understand this is to misunderstand the public uses of schooling and to trivialize the nature of intimate life — a family's "language." 5

Memory teaches me what I know of these matters; the boy reminds the adult. I was a bilingual child, a certain kind — socially disadvantaged — the son of working-class parents, both Mexican immigrants.

In the early years of my boyhood, my parents coped very well in America. My father had steady work. My mother managed at home. They were nobody's victims. Optimism and ambition led them to a house (our home) many blocks from the Mexican south side of town. We lived among *gringos* and only a block from the biggest, whitest houses. It never occurred to my parents that they couldn't live wherever they chose. Nor was the Sacramento of the fifties bent on teaching them a contrary lesson. My mother and father were more annoyed than intimidated by those two or three neighbors who tried initially to make us unwelcome. ("Keep your brats away from my sidewalk!") But despite all they achieved, perhaps because they had so much to achieve, any deep feeling of ease, the confidence of "belonging" in public was withheld from them both. They regarded the people at work, the faces in crowds, as very distant from us. They were the others, *los gringos*. That term was interchangeable in their speech with another, even more telling, *los americanos*.

I grew up in a house where the only regular guests were my relations. For one day, enormous families of relatives would visit and there would be so many people that the noise and the bodies would spill out to the backyard and front porch. Then, for weeks, no one came by. (It was usually a salesman who rang the doorbell.) Our house stood apart. A gaudy yellow in a row of white bungalows. We were the people with the noisy dog. The people who raised pigeons and chickens. We were the foreigners on the block. A few neighbors smiled and waved. We waved back. But no one in the family knew the names of the old couple who lived next door; until I was seven years old, I did not know the names of the kids who lived across the street.

In public, my father and mother spoke a hesitant, accented, not always grammatical English. And they would have to strain — their bodies tense — to catch the sense of what was rapidly said by *los gringos*. At home they spoke Spanish. The language of their Mexican past sounded in counterpoint to the English of public society. The words would come quickly, with ease. Conveyed through those sounds was the pleasing, soothing, consoling reminder of being at home.

During those years when I was first conscious of hearing, my mother and   10
father addressed me only in Spanish; in Spanish I learned to reply. By contrast, English (*inglés*), rarely heard in the house, was the language I came to associate with *gringos*. I learned my first words of English overhearing my parents speak to strangers. At five years of age, I knew just enough English for my mother to trust me on errands to stores one block away. No more.

I was a listening child, careful to hear the very different sounds of Spanish and English. Wide-eyed with hearing, I'd listen to sounds more than words. First, there were English (*gringo*) sounds. So many words were still unknown that when the butcher or the lady at the drugstore said something to me, exotic polysyllabic sounds would bloom in the midst of their sentences. Often, the speech of people in public seemed to me very loud, booming with confidence. The man behind the counter would literally ask, "What can I do for you?" But by being so firm and so clear, the sound of his voice said that he was a *gringo*; he belonged in public society.

I would also hear then the high nasal notes of middle-class American speech. The air stirred with sound. Sometimes, even now, when I have been traveling abroad for several weeks, I will hear what I heard as a boy. In hotel lobbies or airports, in Turkey or Brazil, some Americans will pass, and suddenly I will hear it again — the high sound of American voices. For a few seconds I will hear it with pleasure, for it is now the sound of *my* society — a reminder of home. But inevitably — already on the flight headed for home — the sound fades with repetition. I will be unable to hear it anymore.

When I was a boy, things were different. The accent of *los gringos* was never pleasing nor was it hard to hear. Crowds at Safeway or at bus stops would be noisy with sound. And I would be forced to edge away from the chirping chatter above me.

I was unable to hear my own sounds, but I knew very well that I spoke English poorly. My words could not stretch far enough to form complete thoughts. And the words I did speak I didn't know well enough to make into distinct sounds. (Listeners would usually lower their heads, better to hear what I was trying to say.) But it was one thing for *me* to speak English with difficulty. It was more troubling for me to hear my parents speak in public: their high-whining vowels and guttural consonants; their sentences that got stuck with "eh" and "ah" sounds; the confused syntax; the hesitant rhythm of sounds so different from the way *gringos* spoke. I'd notice, moreover, that my parents' voices were softer than those of *gringos* we'd meet.

I am tempted now to say that none of this mattered. In adulthood I am   15 embarrassed by childhood fears. And in a way, it didn't matter very much that my parents could not speak English with ease. Their linguistic difficulties had no serious consequences. My mother and father made themselves understood at the county hospital clinic and at government offices. And yet, in another way, it mattered very much — it was unsettling to hear my parents struggle with English. Hearing them, I'd grow nervous, my clutching trust in their protection and power weakened.

There were many times like the night at a brightly lit gasoline station (a blaring white memory) when I stood uneasily, hearing my father. He was talking to a teenaged attendant. I do not recall what they were saying, but I cannot forget the sounds my father made as he spoke. At one point his words slid together to form one word — sounds as confused as the threads of blue and green oil in the puddle next to my shoes. His voice rushed through what he had left to say. And, toward the end, reached falsetto notes, appealing to his listener's understanding. I looked away to the lights of passing automobiles. I tried not to hear anymore. But I heard only too well the calm, easy tones in the attendant's reply. Shortly afterward, walking toward home with my father, I shivered when he put his hand on my shoulder. The very first chance that I got, I evaded his grasp and ran on ahead into the dark, skipping with feigned boyish exuberance.

But then there was Spanish. *Español*: my family's language. *Español*: the language that seemed to me a private language. I'd hear strangers on the radio and in the Mexican Catholic church across town speaking in Spanish, but I couldn't really believe that Spanish was a public language, like English. Spanish speakers, rather, seemed related to me, for I sensed that we shared — through our language — the experience of feeling apart from *los gringos*. It was thus a ghetto Spanish that I heard and I spoke. Like those whose lives are bound by a barrio, I was reminded by Spanish of my separateness from *los otros, los gringos* in power. But more intensely than for most barrio children — because I did not live in a barrio — Spanish seemed to me the language of home. (Most days it was only at home that I'd hear it.) It became the language of joyful return.

A family member would say something to me and I would feel myself specially recognized. My parents would say something to me and I would feel embraced by the sounds of their words. Those sounds said: *I am speaking with ease in Spanish. I am addressing you in words I never use with* los gringos. *I recognize you as someone special, close, like no one outside. You belong with us. In the family.*

(*Ricardo.*)

At the age of five, six, well past the time when most other children no   20
longer easily notice the difference between sounds uttered at home and words spoken in public, I had a different experience. I lived in a world magically compounded of sounds. I remained a child longer than most; I lingered too long, poised at the edge of language — often frightened by the sounds of *los gringos,* delighted by the sounds of Spanish at home. I shared with my family a language that was startlingly different from that used in the great city around us.

For me there were none of the gradations between public and private society so normal to a maturing child. Outside the house was public society; inside the house was private. Just opening or closing the screen door behind me was an important experience. I'd rarely leave home all alone or without reluctance. Walking down the sidewalk, under the canopy of tall trees, I'd warily notice the — suddenly — silent neighborhood kids who stood warily watching me. Nervously, I'd arrive at the grocery store to hear there the sounds of the *gringo* — foreign to me — reminding me that in this world so big, I was a foreigner. But then I'd return. Walking back toward our house, climbing the steps from the sidewalk, when the front door was open in summer, I'd hear voices beyond the screen door talking in Spanish. For a second or two, I'd stay, linger there, listening. Smiling, I'd hear my mother call out, saying in Spanish (words): "Is that you, Richard?" All the while her sounds would assure me: *You are home now; come closer; inside. With us.*

"*Sí,*" I'd reply.

Once more inside the house I would resume (assume) my place in the family. The sounds would dim, grow harder to hear. Once more at home, I would grow less aware of that fact. It required, however, no more than the blurt of the doorbell to alert me to listen to sounds all over again. The house would turn instantly still while my mother went to the door. I'd hear her hard English sounds. I'd wait to hear her voice return to soft-sounding Spanish, which assured me, as surely as did the clicking tongue of the lock on the door, that the stranger was gone.

Plainly, it is not healthy to hear such sounds so often. It is not healthy to distinguish public words from private sounds so easily. I remained cloistered by sounds, timid and shy in public, too dependent on voices at home. And yet it needs to be emphasized: I was an extremely happy child at home. I remember many nights when my father would come back from work, and I'd hear him call out to my mother in Spanish, sounding relieved. In Spanish, he'd sound light and free notes he never could manage in English. Some nights I'd jump up just at hearing his voice. With *mis hermanos* I would come running into the room where he was with my mother. Our laughing (so deep was the pleasure!) became screaming. Like others who know the pain of public alienation, we transformed the knowledge of our public separateness and made it consoling — the reminder of intimacy. Excited, we joined our voices in a celebration of sounds. *We are speaking now the way we never speak out in public. We are alone — together,* voices sounded, surrounded to tell me. Some nights, no one seemed willing to loosen the hold sounds had on us. At dinner, we invented new words. (Ours sounded Spanish, but made sense only to us.) We pieced together new words by taking, say, an English verb and giving it Spanish endings. My mother's instructions at bedtime would be lacquered with mock-urgent tones. Or a word like *sí* would become, in several notes, able to convey added measures of feeling. Tongues explored the edges of words, especially the fat vowels. And we happily sounded that military drum roll, the twirling roar of the Spanish *r.* Family language: my family's sounds. The voices of my parents and sisters and brother. Their voices insisting: *You belong here. We are family members. Related. Special to one another. Listen!* Voices singing and sighing, rising, straining, then surging, teeming with pleasure that burst syllables into fragments of laughter. At times it seemed there was steady quiet only when, from another room, the rustling whispers of my parents faded and I moved closer to sleep.

2

Supporters of bilingual education today imply that students like me miss a great deal by not being taught in their family's language. What they seem not to recognize is that, as a socially disadvantaged child, I considered Spanish to be a private language. What I needed to learn in school was that I had the right — and the obligation — to speak the public language of *los gringos.* The odd truth is that my first-grade classmates could have become bilingual, in the conventional sense of that word, more easily than I. Had they been taught (as upper-middle-class children are often taught early) a second language like Spanish or French, they could have regarded it simply as that: another public language. In my case such bilingualism could not have been so quickly achieved. What I did not believe was that I could speak a single public language.

    Without question, it would have pleased me to hear my teachers address me in Spanish when I entered the classroom. I would have felt much less afraid. I would have trusted them and responded with ease. But I would have delayed — for how long postponed? — having to learn the language of public society. I would have evaded — and for how long could I have afforded to delay? — learning the great lesson of school, that I had a public identity.

    Fortunately, my teachers were unsentimental about their responsibility. What they understood was that I needed to speak a public language. So their voices would search me out, asking me questions. Each time I'd hear them, I'd look up in surprise to see a nun's face frowning at me. I'd mumble, not really meaning to answer. The nun would persist, "Richard, stand up. Don't look at the floor. Speak up. Speak to the entire class, not just to me!" But I couldn't believe that the English language was mine to use. (In part, I did not want to believe it.) I continued to mumble. I resisted the teacher's demands. (Did I somehow suspect that once I learned public language my pleasing family life would be changed?) Silent, waiting for the bell to sound, I remained dazed, diffident, afraid.

Because I wrongly imagined that English was intrinsically a public language and Spanish an intrinsically private one, I easily noted the difference between classroom language and the language of home. At school, words were directed to a general audience of listeners. ("Boys and girls.") Words were meaningfully ordered. And the point was not self-expression alone but to make oneself understood by many others. The teacher quizzed: "Boys and girls, why do we use that word in this sentence? Could we think of a better word to use there? Would the sentence change its meaning if the words were differently arranged? And wasn't there a better way of saying much the same thing?" (I couldn't say. I wouldn't try to say.)

Three months. Five. Half a year passed. Unsmiling, ever watchful, my teachers noted my silence. They began to connect my behavior with the difficult progress my older sister and brother were making. Until one Saturday morning three nuns arrived at the house to talk to our parents. Stiffly, they sat on the blue living room sofa. From the doorway of another room, spying the visitors, I noted the incongruity — the clash of two worlds, the faces and voices of school intruding upon the familiar setting of home. I overheard one voice gently wondering, "Do your children speak only Spanish at home, Mrs. Rodriguez?" While another voice added, "That Richard especially seems so timid and shy."

That Rich-heard!   30

With great tact the visitors continued, "Is it possible for you and your husband to encourage your children to practice their English when they are home?" Of course, my parents complied. What would they not do for their children's well-being? And how could they have questioned the Church's authority which those women represented? In an instant, they agreed to give up the language (the sounds) that had revealed and accentuated our family's closeness. The moment after the visitors left, the change was observed. "*Ahora,* speak to us *en inglés,*" my father and mother united to tell us.

At first, it seemed a kind of game. After dinner each night, the family gathered to practice "our" English. (It was still then *inglés,* a language foreign to us, so we felt drawn as strangers to it.) Laughing, we would try to define words we could not pronounce. We played with strange English sounds, often overanglicizing our pronunciations. And we filled the smiling gaps of our sentences with familiar Spanish sounds. But that was cheating, somebody shouted. Everyone laughed. In school, meanwhile, like my brother and sister, I was required to attend a daily tutoring session. I needed a full year of special attention. I also needed my teachers to keep my attention from straying in class by calling out, *Rich-heard* — their English voices slowly prying loose my ties to my other name, its three notes, *Ri-car-do.* Most of all I needed to hear my mother and father speak to me in a moment of seriousness in broken — suddenly heartbreaking — English. The scene was inevitable: one Saturday morning I entered the kitchen where my parents were talking in Spanish. I did not realize that they were talking in Spanish however until, at the moment they saw me, I heard their voices change to speak English. Those *gringo* sounds they uttered startled me. Pushed me away. In that moment of trivial misunderstanding and profound insight, I felt my throat twisted by unsounded grief. I turned quickly and left the room. But I had no place to escape to with Spanish. (The spell was broken.) My brother and sisters were speaking English in another part of the house.

Again and again in the days following, increasingly angry, I was obliged to hear my mother and father: "Speak to us *en inglés.*" (*Speak.*) Only then did I determine to learn classroom English. Weeks after, it happened: one day in school I raised my hand to volunteer an answer. I spoke out in a loud voice. And I did not think it remarkable when the entire class understood. That day, I moved very far from the disadvantaged child I had been only days earlier. The belief, the calming assurance that I belonged in public, had at last taken hold.

Shortly after, I stopped hearing the high and loud sounds of *los gringos.* A more and more confident speaker of English, I didn't trouble to listen to *how* strangers sounded, speaking to me. And there simply were too many English-speaking people in my day for me to hear American accents anymore. Conversations quickened. Listening to persons who sounded eccentrically pitched voices, I usually noted their sounds for an initial few seconds before I concentrated on *what* they were saying. Conversations became content-full. Transparent. Hearing someone's *tone* of voice — angry or questioning or sarcastic or happy or sad — I didn't distinguish it from the words it expressed. Sound and word were thus tightly wedded. At the end of a day, I was often bemused, always relieved, to realize how "silent," though crowded with words, my day in public had been. (This public silence measured and quickened the change in my life.)

At last, seven years old, I came to believe what had been technically true   35 since my birth: I was an American citizen.

But the special feeling of closeness at home was diminished by then. Gone was the desperate, urgent, intense feeling of being at home; rare was the experience of feeling myself individualized by family intimates. We remained a loving family, but one greatly changed. No longer so close; no longer bound tight by the pleasing and troubling knowledge of our public separateness. Neither my older brother nor sister rushed home after school anymore. Nor did I. When I arrived home there would often be neighborhood kids in the house. Or the house would be empty of sounds.

Following the dramatic Americanization of their children, even my parents grew more publicly confident. Especially my mother. She learned the names of all the people on our block. And she decided we needed to have a telephone installed in the house. My father continued to use the word *gringo.* But it was no longer charged with the old bitterness or distrust. (Stripped of any emotional content, the word simply became a name for those Americans not of Hispanic descent.) Hearing him, sometimes, I wasn't sure if he was pronouncing the Spanish word *gringo* or saying gringo in English.

Matching the silence I started hearing in public was a new quiet at home. The family's quiet was partly due to the fact that, as we children learned more and more English, we shared fewer and fewer words with our parents. Sentences needed to be spoken slowly when a child addressed his mother or father. (Often the parent wouldn't understand.) The child would need to repeat himself. (Still the parent misunderstood.) The young voice, frustrated, would end up saying, "Never mind" — the subject was closed. Dinners would be noisy with the clinking of knives and forks against dishes. My mother would smile softly between her remarks; my father at the other end of the table would chew and chew at his food, while he stared over the heads of his children.

My *mother*! My *father*! After English became my primary language, I no longer knew what words to use in addressing my parents. The old Spanish words (those tender accents of sound) I had used earlier — *mamá* and *papá* — I couldn't use anymore. They would have been too painful reminders of how much had changed in my life. On the other hand, the words I heard neighborhood kids call *their* parents seemed equally unsatisfactory. *Mother* and *Father*; *Ma*, *Papa*, *Pa*, *Dad*, *Pop* (how I hated the all-American sound of that last word especially) — all these terms I felt were unsuitable, not really terms of address for *my* parents. As a result, I never used them at home. Whenever I'd speak to my parents, I would try to get their attention with eye contact alone. In public conversations, I'd refer to "my parents" or "my mother and father."

My mother and father, for their part, responded differently, as their chil-   40
dren spoke to them less. She grew restless, seemed troubled and anxious at the scarcity of words exchanged in the house. It was she who would question me about my day when I came home from school. She smiled at small talk. She pried at the edges of my sentences to get me to say something more. (What?) She'd join conversations she overheard, but her intrusions often stopped her children's talking. By contrast, my father seemed reconciled to the new quiet. Though his English improved somewhat, he retired into silence. At dinner he spoke very little. One night his children and even his wife helplessly giggled at his garbled English pronunciation of the Catholic Grace before Meals. Thereafter he made his wife recite the prayer at the start of each meal, even on formal occasions, when there were guests in the house. Hers became the public voice of the family. On official business, it was she, not my father, one would usually hear on the phone or in stores, talking to strangers. His children grew so accustomed to his silence that, years later, they would speak routinely of his shyness. (My mother would often try to explain: both his parents died when he was eight. He was raised by an uncle who treated him like little more than a menial servant. He was never encouraged to speak. He grew up alone. A man of few words.) But my father was not shy, I realized, when I'd watch him speaking Spanish with relatives. Using Spanish, he was quickly effusive. Especially when talking with other men, his voice would spark, flicker, flare alive with sounds. In Spanish, he expressed ideas and feelings he rarely revealed in English. With firm Spanish sounds, he conveyed confidence and authority English would never allow him.

The silence at home, however, was finally more than a literal silence. Fewer words passed between parent and child, but more profound was the silence that resulted from my inattention to sounds. At about the time I no longer bothered to listen with care to the sounds of English in public, I grew careless about listening to the sounds family members made when they spoke. Most of the time I heard someone speaking at home and didn't distinguish his sounds from the words people uttered in public. I didn't even pay much attention to my parents' accented and ungrammatical speech. At least not at home. Only when I was with them in public would I grow alert to their accents. Though, even then, their sounds caused me less and less concern. For I was increasingly confident of my own public identity.

I would have been happier about my public success had I not sometimes recalled what it had been like earlier, when my family had conveyed its intimacy through a set of conveniently private sounds. Sometimes in public, hearing a stranger, I'd hark back to my past. A Mexican farmworker approached me downtown to ask directions to somewhere. "*¿Hijito . . . ?*" he said. And his voice summoned deep longing. Another time, standing beside my mother in the visiting room of a Carmelite convent, before the dense screen which rendered the nuns shadowy figures, I heard several Spanish-speaking nuns — their busy, singsong overlapping voices — assure us that yes, yes, we were remembered, all our family was remembered in their prayers. (Their voices echoed faraway family sounds.) Another day, a dark-faced old woman — her hand light on my shoulder — steadied herself against me as she boarded a bus. She murmured something I couldn't quite comprehend. Her Spanish voice came near, like the face of a never-before-seen relative in the instant before I was kissed. Her voice, like so many of the Spanish voices I'd hear in public, recalled the golden age of my youth. Hearing Spanish then, I continued to be a careful, if sad, listener to sounds. Hearing a Spanish-speaking family walking behind me, I turned to look. I smiled for an instant, before my glance found the Hispanic-looking faces of strangers in the crowd going by.

Today I hear bilingual educators say that children lose a degree of "individuality" by becoming assimilated into public society. (Bilingual schooling was popularized in the seventies, that decade when middle-class ethnics began to resist the process of assimilation — the American melting pot.) But the bilingualists simplistically scorn the value and necessity of assimilation. They do not seem to realize that there are *two* ways a person is individualized. So they do not realize that while one suffers a diminished sense of *private* individuality by becoming assimilated into public society, such assimilation makes possible the achievement of *public* individuality.

The bilingualists insist that a student should be reminded of his difference from others in mass society, his heritage. But they equate mere separateness with individuality. The fact is that only in private — with intimates — is separateness from the crowd a prerequisite for individuality. (An intimate draws me apart, tells me that I am unique, unlike all others.) In public, by contrast, full individuality is achieved, paradoxically, by those who are able to consider themselves members of the crowd. Thus it happened for me: only when I was able to think of myself as an American, no longer an alien in *gringo* society, could I seek the rights and opportunities necessary for full public individuality.

The social and political advantages I enjoy as a man result from the day that I came to believe that my name, indeed, is *Rich-heard Road-ree-guess*. It is true that my public society today is often impersonal. (My public society is usually mass society.) Yet despite the anonymity of the crowd and despite the fact that the individuality I achieve in public is often tenuous — because it depends on my being one in a crowd — I celebrate the day I acquired my new name. Those middle-class ethnics who scorn assimilation seem to me filled with decadent self-pity, obsessed by the burden of public life. Dangerously, they romanticize public separateness and they trivialize the dilemma of the socially disadvantaged.

My awkward childhood does not prove the necessity of bilingual education. My story discloses instead an essential myth of childhood — inevitable pain. If I rehearse here the changes in my private life after my Americanization, it is finally to emphasize the public gain. The loss implies the gain: the house I returned to each afternoon was quiet. Intimate sounds no longer rushed to the door to greet me. There were other noises inside. The telephone rang. Neighborhood kids ran past the door of the bedroom where I was reading my schoolbooks — covered with shopping-bag paper. Once I learned public language, it would never again be easy for me to hear intimate family voices. More and more of my day was spent hearing words. But that may only be a way of saying that the day I raised my hand in class and spoke loudly to an entire roomful of faces, my childhood started to end.   *[1982]*

45

☰ THINKING ABOUT THE TEXT

1. What distinctions does Rodriguez make between the "private" and "public" worlds of his childhood? Ultimately, he brings up the possibility of "*public* individuality" (para. 43). What does he mean by this? Does this concept make sense to you?

2. What, according to Rodriguez, were the changes he experienced? With what tone does he recall these changes? Consider in particular the way he describes his changing relationship to his parents.

3. Do you agree with Rodriguez that the changes he went through were necessary? To what extent is your answer influenced by your own social position?

4. Rodriguez declares, "Those middle-class ethnics who scorn assimilation seem to me filled with decadent self-pity, obsessed by the burden of public life. Dangerously, they romanticize public separateness and they trivialize the dilemma of the socially disadvantaged" (para. 44). Evaluate this claim. Would you say that you are a "middle-class ethnic"? Why, or why not?

5. Rodriguez suggests that a student must speak up in class to succeed in school. Do you agree? Rodriguez indicates that matters of language play a crucial role in a child's education. Have you found this true? Be specific.

JOSE ANTONIO VARGAS

My Life as an Undocumented Immigrant

Jose Antonio Vargas (b. 1981) is a journalist, filmmaker, and immigrant activist. He was born in the Philippines and at the age of twelve was sent to America to live with his grandparents, but without official authorization. He became interested in journalism in high school and became a copy boy with the San Francisco Chronicle. *After graduating from San Francisco State University, he began writing at the* Washington Post. *Vargas was part of a team working on the story of the Virginia Tech shootings that earned him a Pulitzer Prize. In 2009 he joined the staff of the* Huffington Post. *The following essay was published in the* New York Times Sunday Magazine *and won the June 2011 Sidney Award as an "outstanding piece of socially conscious journalism." He continues to be an activist for immigrant issues.*

One August morning nearly two decades ago, my mother woke me and put me in a cab. She handed me a jacket. *"Baka malamig doon"* were among the few words she said. ("It might be cold there.") When I arrived at the Philippines' Ninoy Aquino International Airport with her, my aunt, and a family friend, I was introduced to a man I'd never seen. They told me he was my uncle. He held my hand as I boarded an airplane for the first time. It was 1993, and I was twelve.

My mother wanted to give me a better life, so she sent me thousands of miles away to live with her parents in America — my grandfather (*Lolo* in Tagalog) and grandmother (*Lola*). After I arrived in Mountain View, California, in the San Francisco Bay Area, I entered sixth grade and quickly grew to love my new home, family, and culture. I discovered a passion for language, though it was hard to learn the difference between formal English and American slang. One of my early memories is of a freckled kid in middle school asking me, "What's up?" I replied, "The sky," and he and a couple of other kids laughed. I won the eighth-grade spelling bee by memorizing words I couldn't properly pronounce. (The winning word was "indefatigable.")

One day when I was sixteen, I rode my bike to the nearby D.M.V. office to get my driver's permit. Some of my friends already had their licenses, so I figured it was time. But when I handed the clerk my green card as proof of U.S. residency, she flipped it around, examining it. "This is fake," she whispered. "Don't come back here again."

Confused and scared, I pedaled home and confronted Lolo. I remember him sitting in the garage, cutting coupons. I dropped my bike and ran over to him, showing him the green card. *"Peke ba ito?"* I asked in Tagalog. ("Is this fake?") My grandparents were naturalized American citizens — he worked as a security guard, she as a food server — and they had begun supporting my mother and me financially when I was three, after my father's wandering eye and inability to properly provide for us led to my parents' separation. Lolo was a proud man, and I saw the shame on his face as he told me he purchased the card, along with other fake documents, for me. "Don't show it to other people," he warned.

I decided then that I could never give anyone reason to doubt I was an 5
American. I convinced myself that if I worked enough, if I achieved enough, I would be rewarded with citizenship. I felt I could earn it.

I've tried. Over the past fourteen years, I've graduated from high school and college and built a career as a journalist, interviewing some of the most famous people in the country. On the surface, I've created a good life. I've lived the American dream.

But I am still an undocumented immigrant. And that means living a different kind of reality. It means going about my day in fear of being found out. It means rarely trusting people, even those closest to me, with who I really am. It means keeping my family photos in a shoebox rather than displaying them on shelves in my home, so friends don't ask about them. It means reluctantly, even painfully, doing things I know are wrong and unlawful. And it has meant relying on a sort of twenty-first-century underground railroad of supporters, people who took an interest in my future and took risks for me.

Last year I read about four students who walked from Miami to Washington to lobby for the Dream Act, a nearly decade-old immigration bill that would provide a path to legal permanent residency for young people who have been educated in this country. At the risk of deportation—the Obama administration has deported almost 800,000 people in the last two years—they are speaking out. Their courage has inspired me.

There are believed to be 11 million undocumented immigrants in the United States. We're not always who you think we are. Some pick your strawberries or care for your children. Some are in high school or college. And some, it turns out, write news articles you might read. I grew up here. This is my home. Yet even though I think of myself as an American and consider America my country, my country doesn't think of me as one of its own.

My first challenge was the language. Though I learned English in the Philip- 10
pines, I wanted to lose my accent. During high school, I spent hours at a time watching television (especially *Frasier*, *Home Improvement*, and reruns of *The Golden Girls*) and movies (from *Goodfellas* to *Anne of Green Gables*), pausing the VHS to try to copy how various characters enunciated their words. At the local library, I read magazines, books, and newspapers—anything to learn how to write better. Kathy Dewar, my high-school English teacher, introduced me to journalism. From the moment I wrote my first article for the student paper, I convinced myself that having my name in print—writing in English, interviewing Americans—validated my presence here.

The debates over "illegal aliens" intensified my anxieties. In 1994, only a year after my flight from the Philippines, Governor Pete Wilson was re-elected in part because of his support for Proposition 187, which prohibited undocumented immigrants from attending public school and accessing other services. (A federal court later found the law unconstitutional.) After my encounter at the D.M.V. in 1997, I grew more aware of anti-immigrant sentiments and stereotypes:

they don't want to assimilate, they are a drain on society. They're not talking about me, I would tell myself. I have something to contribute.

To do that, I had to work—and for that, I needed a Social Security number. Fortunately, my grandfather had already managed to get one for me. Lolo had always taken care of everyone in the family. He and my grandmother emigrated legally in 1984 from Zambales, a province in the Philippines of rice fields and bamboo houses, following Lolo's sister, who married a Filipino American serving in the American military. She petitioned for her brother and his wife to join her. When they got here, Lolo petitioned for his two children—my mother and her younger brother—to follow them. But instead of mentioning that my mother was a married woman, he listed her as single. Legal residents can't petition for their married children. Besides, Lolo didn't care for my father. He didn't want him coming here too.

But soon Lolo grew nervous that the immigration authorities reviewing the petition would discover my mother was married, thus derailing not only her chances of coming here but those of my uncle as well. So he withdrew her petition. After my uncle came to America legally in 1991, Lolo tried to get my mother here through a tourist visa, but she wasn't able to obtain one. That's when she decided to send me. My mother told me later that she figured she would follow me soon. She never did.

The "uncle" who brought me here turned out to be a coyote, not a relative, my grandfather later explained. Lolo scraped together enough money—I eventually learned it was $4,500, a huge sum for him—to pay him to smuggle me here under a fake name and fake passport. (I never saw the passport again after the flight and have always assumed that the coyote kept it.) After I arrived in America, Lolo obtained a new fake Filipino passport, in my real name this time, adorned with a fake student visa, in addition to the fraudulent green card.

Using the fake passport, we went to the local Social Security Administration office and applied for a Social Security number and card. It was, I remember, a quick visit. When the card came in the mail, it had my full, real name, but it also clearly stated: "Valid for work only with I.N.S. authorization."   15

When I began looking for work, a short time after the D.M.V. incident, my grandfather and I took the Social Security card to Kinko's, where he covered the "I.N.S. authorization" text with a sliver of white tape. We then made photocopies of the card. At a glance, at least, the copies would look like copies of a regular, unrestricted Social Security card.

Lolo always imagined I would work the kind of low-paying jobs that undocumented people often take. (Once I married an American, he said, I would get my real papers, and everything would be fine.) But even menial jobs require documents, so he and I hoped the doctored card would work for now. The more documents I had, he said, the better.

While in high school, I worked part time at Subway, then at the front desk of the local Y.M.C.A., then at a tennis club, until I landed an unpaid internship at the *Mountain View Voice*, my hometown newspaper. First I brought coffee and helped around the office; eventually I began covering city-hall meetings and other assignments for pay.

For more than a decade of getting part-time and full-time jobs, employers have rarely asked to check my original Social Security card. When they did, I showed the photocopied version, which they accepted. Over time, I also began checking the citizenship box on my federal I-9 employment eligibility forms. (Claiming full citizenship was actually easier than declaring permanent resident "green card" status, which would have required me to provide an alien registration number.)

This deceit never got easier. The more I did it, the more I felt like an impostor, the more guilt I carried—and the more I worried that I would get caught. But I kept doing it. I needed to live and survive on my own, and I decided this was the way. 20

Mountain View High School became my second home. I was elected to represent my school at school-board meetings, which gave me the chance to meet and befriend Rich Fischer, the superintendent for our school district. I joined the speech and debate team, acted in school plays, and eventually became co-editor of the *Oracle*, the student newspaper. That drew the attention of my principal, Pat Hyland. "You're at school just as much as I am," she told me. Pat and Rich would soon become mentors, and over time, almost surrogate parents for me.

After a choir rehearsal during my junior year, Jill Denny, the choir director, told me she was considering a Japan trip for our singing group. I told her I couldn't afford it, but she said we'd figure out a way. I hesitated, and then decided to tell her the truth. "It's not really the money," I remember saying. "I don't have the right passport." When she assured me we'd get the proper documents, I finally told her. "I can't get the right passport," I said. "I'm not supposed to be here."

She understood. So the choir toured Hawaii instead, with me in tow. (Mrs. Denny and I spoke a couple of months ago, and she told me she hadn't wanted to leave any student behind.)

Later that school year, my history class watched a documentary on Harvey Milk, the openly gay San Francisco city official who was assassinated. This was 1999, just six months after Matthew Shepard's body was found tied to a fence in Wyoming. During the discussion, I raised my hand and said something like: "I'm sorry Harvey Milk got killed for being gay. . . . I've been meaning to say this. . . . I'm gay."

I hadn't planned on coming out that morning, though I had known that I was gay for several years. With that announcement, I became the only openly gay student at school, and it caused turmoil with my grandparents. Lolo kicked me out of the house for a few weeks. Though we eventually reconciled, I had disappointed him on two fronts. First, as a Catholic, he considered homosexuality a sin and was embarrassed about having "*ang apo na bakla*" ("a grandson who is gay"). Even worse, I was making matters more difficult for myself, he said. I needed to marry an American woman in order to gain a green card. 25

Tough as it was, coming out about being gay seemed less daunting than coming out about my legal status. I kept my other secret mostly hidden.

While my classmates awaited their college acceptance letters, I hoped to get a full-time job at the *Mountain View Voice* after graduation. It's not that I didn't want to go to college, but I couldn't apply for state and federal financial aid. Without that, my family couldn't afford to send me.

But when I finally told Pat and Rich about my immigration "problem" — as we called it from then on — they helped me look for a solution. At first, they even wondered if one of them could adopt me and fix the situation that way, but a lawyer Rich consulted told him it wouldn't change my legal status because I was too old. Eventually they connected me to a new scholarship fund for high-potential students who were usually the first in their families to attend college. Most important, the fund was not concerned with immigration status. I was among the first recipients, with the scholarship covering tuition, lodging, books, and other expenses for my studies at San Francisco State University.

As a college freshman, I found a job working part time at the *San Francisco Chronicle*, where I sorted mail and wrote some freelance articles. My ambition was to get a reporting job, so I embarked on a series of internships. First I landed at the *Philadelphia Daily News*, in the summer of 2001, where I covered a drive-by shooting and the wedding of the 76ers star Allen Iverson. Using those articles, I applied to the *Seattle Times* and got an internship for the following summer.

But then my lack of proper documents became a problem again. The   30 *Times*'s recruiter, Pat Foote, asked all incoming interns to bring certain paperwork on their first day: a birth certificate, or a passport, or a driver's license plus an original Social Security card. I panicked, thinking my documents wouldn't pass muster. So before starting the job, I called Pat and told her about my legal status. After consulting with management, she called me back with the answer I feared: I couldn't do the internship.

This was devastating. What good was college if I couldn't then pursue the career I wanted? I decided then that if I was to succeed in a profession that is all about truth-telling, I couldn't tell the truth about myself.

After this episode, Jim Strand, the venture capitalist who sponsored my scholarship, offered to pay for an immigration lawyer. Rich and I went to meet her in San Francisco's financial district.

I was hopeful. This was in early 2002, shortly after Senators Orrin Hatch, the Utah Republican, and Dick Durbin, the Illinois Democrat, introduced the Dream Act — Development, Relief, and Education for Alien Minors. It seemed like the legislative version of what I'd told myself: If I work hard and contribute, things will work out.

But the meeting left me crushed. My only solution, the lawyer said, was to go back to the Philippines and accept a ten-year ban before I could apply to return legally.

If Rich was discouraged, he hid it well. "Put this problem on a shelf," he   35 told me. "Compartmentalize it. Keep going."

And I did. For the summer of 2003, I applied for internships across the country. Several newspapers, including the *Wall Street Journal*, the *Boston Globe*, and the *Chicago Tribune*, expressed interest. But when the *Washington Post* offered me a spot, I knew where I would go. And this time, I had no intention of acknowledging my "problem."

The *Post* internship posed a tricky obstacle: It required a driver's license. (After my close call at the California D.M.V., I'd never gotten one.) So I spent an afternoon at the Mountain View Public Library, studying various states' requirements. Oregon was among the most welcoming—and it was just a few hours' drive north.

Again, my support network came through. A friend's father lived in Portland, and he allowed me to use his address as proof of residency. Pat, Rich, and Rich's longtime assistant, Mary Moore, sent letters to me at that address. Rich taught me how to do three-point turns in a parking lot, and a friend accompanied me to Portland.

The license meant everything to me—it would let me drive, fly, and work. But my grandparents worried about the Portland trip and the Washington internship. While Lola offered daily prayers so that I would not get caught, Lolo told me that I was dreaming too big, risking too much.

I was determined to pursue my ambitions. I was twenty-two, I told them, 40 responsible for my own actions. But this was different from Lolo's driving a confused teenager to Kinko's. I knew what I was doing now, and I knew it wasn't right. But what was I supposed to do?

I was paying state and federal taxes, but I was using an invalid Social Security card and writing false information on my employment forms. But that seemed better than depending on my grandparents or on Pat, Rich, and Jim— or returning to a country I barely remembered. I convinced myself all would be O.K. if I lived up to the qualities of a "citizen": hard work, self-reliance, love of my country.

At the D.M.V. in Portland, I arrived with my photocopied Social Security card, my college I.D., a pay stub from the *San Francisco Chronicle*, and my proof of state residence—the letters to the Portland address that my support network had sent. It worked. My license, issued in 2003, was set to expire eight years later, on my thirtieth birthday, on February 3, 2011. I had eight years to succeed professionally, and to hope that some sort of immigration reform would pass in the meantime and allow me to stay.

It seemed like all the time in the world.

My summer in Washington was exhilarating. I was intimidated to be in a major newsroom but was assigned a mentor—Peter Perl, a veteran magazine writer—to help me navigate it. A few weeks into the internship, he printed out one of my articles, about a guy who recovered a long-lost wallet, circled the first two paragraphs, and left it on my desk. "Great eye for details—awesome!" he wrote. Though I didn't know it then, Peter would become one more member of my network.

At the end of the summer, I returned to the *San Francisco Chronicle*. My 45 plan was to finish school—I was now a senior—while I worked for the *Chronicle* as a reporter for the city desk. But when the *Post* beckoned again, offering me a full-time, two-year paid internship that I could start when I graduated in June 2004, it was too tempting to pass up. I moved back to Washington.

About four months into my job as a reporter for the *Post*, I began feeling increasingly paranoid, as if I had "illegal immigrant" tattooed on my forehead— and in Washington, of all places, where the debates over immigration seemed never-ending. I was so eager to prove myself that I feared I was annoying some colleagues and editors—and worried that any one of these professional journalists could discover my secret. The anxiety was nearly paralyzing. I decided I had to tell one of the higher-ups about my situation. I turned to Peter.

By this time, Peter, who still works at the *Post*, had become part of management as the paper's director of newsroom training and professional development. One afternoon in late October, we walked a couple of blocks to Lafayette Square, across from the White House. Over some twenty minutes, sitting on a bench, I told him everything: the Social Security card, the driver's license, Pat and Rich, my family.

Peter was shocked. "I understand you 100 times better now," he said. He told me that I had done the right thing by telling him, and that it was now our shared problem. He said he didn't want to do anything about it just yet. I had just been hired, he said, and I needed to prove myself. "When you've done enough," he said, "we'll tell Don and Len together." (Don Graham is the chairman of the Washington Post Company; Leonard Downie Jr. was then the paper's executive editor.) A month later, I spent my first Thanksgiving in Washington with Peter and his family.

In the five years that followed, I did my best to "do enough." I was promoted to staff writer, reported on video-game culture, wrote a series on Washington's H.I.V./AIDS epidemic, and covered the role of technology and social media in the 2008 presidential race. I visited the White House, where I interviewed senior aides and covered a state dinner—and gave the Secret Service the Social Security number I obtained with false documents.

I did my best to steer clear of reporting on immigration policy but couldn't   50
always avoid it. On two occasions, I wrote about Hillary Clinton's position on driver's licenses for undocumented immigrants. I also wrote an article about Senator Mel Martinez of Florida, then the chairman of the Republican National Committee, who was defending his party's stance toward Latinos after only one Republican presidential candidate—John McCain, the coauthor of a failed immigration bill—agreed to participate in a debate sponsored by Univision, the Spanish-language network.

It was an odd sort of dance: I was trying to stand out in a highly competitive newsroom, yet I was terrified that if I stood out too much, I'd invite unwanted scrutiny. I tried to compartmentalize my fears, distract myself by reporting on the lives of other people, but there was no escaping the central conflict in my life. Maintaining a deception for so long distorts your sense of self. You start wondering who you've become, and why.

In April 2008, I was part of a *Post* team that won a Pulitzer Prize for the paper's coverage of the Virginia Tech shootings a year earlier. Lolo died a year earlier, so it was Lola who called me the day of the announcement. The first thing she said was, "*Anong mangyayari kung malaman ng mga tao?*"

What will happen if people find out?

I couldn't say anything. After we got off the phone, I rushed to the bathroom on the fourth floor of the newsroom, sat down on the toilet, and cried.

In the summer of 2009, without ever having had that follow-up talk with   55
top *Post* management, I left the paper and moved to New York to join the

Huffington Post. I met Arianna Huffington at a Washington Press Club Foundation dinner I was covering for the *Post* two years earlier, and she later recruited me to join her news site. I wanted to learn more about Web publishing, and I thought the new job would provide a useful education.

Still, I was apprehensive about the move: many companies were already using E-Verify, a program set up by the Department of Homeland Security that checks if prospective employees are eligible to work, and I didn't know if my new employer was among them. But I'd been able to get jobs in other newsrooms, I figured, so I filled out the paperwork as usual and succeeded in landing on the payroll.

While I worked at the *Huffington Post*, other opportunities emerged. My H.I.V./AIDS series became a documentary film called "The Other City," which opened at the Tribeca Film Festival last year and was broadcast on Showtime. I began writing for magazines and landed a dream assignment: profiling Facebook's Mark Zuckerberg for *The New Yorker*.

The more I achieved, the more scared and depressed I became. I was proud of my work, but there was always a cloud hanging over it, over me. My old eight-year deadline—the expiration of my Oregon driver's license—was approaching.

After slightly less than a year, I decided to leave the *Huffington Post*. In part, this was because I wanted to promote the documentary and write a book about online culture—or so I told my friends. But the real reason was, after so many years of trying to be a part of the system, of focusing all my energy on my professional life, I learned that no amount of professional success would solve my problem or ease the sense of loss and displacement I felt. I lied to a friend about why I couldn't take a weekend trip to Mexico. Another time I concocted an excuse for why I couldn't go on an all-expenses-paid trip to Switzerland. I have been unwilling, for years, to be in a long-term relationship because I never wanted anyone to get too close and ask too many questions. All the while, Lola's question was stuck in my head: What will happen if people find out?

Early this year, just two weeks before my thirtieth birthday, I won a small reprieve: I obtained a driver's license in the state of Washington. The license is valid until 2016. This offered me five more years of acceptable identification—but also five more years of fear, of lying to people I respect and institutions that trusted me, of running away from who I am.

I'm done running. I'm exhausted. I don't want that life anymore.

So I've decided to come forward, own up to what I've done, and tell my story to the best of my recollection. I've reached out to former bosses and employers and apologized for misleading them—a mix of humiliation and liberation coming with each disclosure. All the people mentioned in this article gave me permission to use their names. I've also talked to family and friends about my situation and am working with legal counsel to review my options. I don't know what the consequences will be of telling my story.

I do know that I am grateful to my grandparents, my Lolo and Lola, for giving me the chance for a better life. I'm also grateful to my other family—the support network I found here in America—for encouraging me to pursue my dreams.

It's been almost eighteen years since I've seen my mother. Early on, I was mad at her for putting me in this position, and then mad at myself for being angry and ungrateful. By the time I got to college, we rarely spoke by phone. It became too painful; after a while it was easier to just send money to help support her and my two half-siblings. My sister, almost two years old when I left, is almost twenty now. I've never met my fourteen-year-old brother. I would love to see them.

Not long ago, I called my mother. I wanted to fill the gaps in my memory   65
about that August morning so many years ago. We had never discussed it. Part of me wanted to shove the memory aside, but to write this article and face the facts of my life, I needed more details. Did I cry? Did she? Did we kiss goodbye?

My mother told me I was excited about meeting a stewardess, about getting on a plane. She also reminded me of the one piece of advice she gave me for blending in: If anyone asked why I was coming to America, I should say I was going to Disneyland.   *[2011]*

≡ WRITING ABOUT THE TEXT

1. Who is the audience for this essay? What response do you think Vargas wants? What likely response will he get? What is your response to this confession?

2. Why does Vargas mention the incident where he asserts that he is gay? Do you think this will make him more or less sympathetic?

3. Comment on the tension between Vargas telling the truth and fulfilling his dream. Mention at least three specific examples and say why you think he made the right or wrong choice.

4. If this essay were to be considered an attempt at persuasion, point out two or three incidents and say why you think they are persuasive.

5. Why do you think Vargas opens and closes with accounts of his mother? What significance do you think should be attributed to Vargas's mention of Disneyland in the last sentence?

≡ MAKING COMPARISONS

1. Compare Rodriguez's and Vargas's childhood views of English.

2. Rodriguez has generally been criticized by the immigrant activists while Vargas has been praised. Point to attitudes in these two essays that might account for such a difference.

3. What lessons have Rodriguez's and Vargas's childhoods taught them?

≡ WRITING ABOUT ISSUES

1. Argue that either Rodriguez or Vargas has more successfully crossed the boundary between immigrant and mainstream culture.

2. Write an essay that argues that Vargas should or should not be allowed to become an American citizen.

3. There is a complex and emotional debate in Congress over illegal immigrants. What seems to you to be the most cogent arguments on both sides? Explain why.

4. Locate Vargas's cover story for *Time* (June 15, 2012) on undocumented immigrants and argue that he does or does not offer a compelling solution.

■ Arguments about an Issue: What Are the Bounds of Free Speech on Campus?

GERALD UELMEN, "The Price of Free Speech"

CHARLES R. LAWRENCE III, "The Debates over Placing Limits on Racist Speech Must Not Ignore the Damage It Does to Its Victims"

GREG LUKIANOFF, "Feigning Free Speech on Campus"

Nothing is more contentious than the definition of "free" in the debate over First Amendment rights. Is "free speech" really free? Can you say anything, however offensive, insulting, or hateful? Many countries believe that prohibiting "hate speech" is a "necessary evil" to protect minority and religious groups against emotional and psychological harm. This is especially relevant at universities, where speech codes are enacted to foster productive learning environments that may be destroyed by verbal attacks against groups that historically have faced discrimination or subjugation. These students, it is argued, may not be able to compete fairly in academics, thereby justifying speech limitations. Further it is argued that the university should be an ideal forum where rational argument prevails, not the irrational hate speech of bigotry. The right of a student to an education is seen, then, as more important than the "free speech" rights of others.

Those who argue against university speech codes maintain that nothing should trump the fundamental human right of freedom of speech. Their thinking is that the First Amendment demands tolerance for the intolerant. For them, no laws should regulate what is permissible or not. From the point of view of free speech advocate David Cole, "the path to equality of the civil rights movement, the women's rights movement, and the gay rights movement was paved by more and more free speech, not by the suppression of racist, sexist, or homophobic comments." Our three essayists provide interesting commentary on these issues.

Gerald Uelmen's essay tries to fairly set out the issues involved in both sides of the debate, while Charles Lawrence III and Greg Lukianoff clearly stake out territory on opposite ends of the intellectual and emotional fields.

■ BEFORE YOU READ

What do you think "free" means in the First Amendment's right to freedom of speech? What exceptions do you think might be reasonable? Are you constrained to use your free speech rights responsibly by laws and regulations or by social norms and ethics? Are you aware of speech codes at your college? What issues are dealt with in the university's code of conduct for students?

GERALD UELMEN

The Price of Free Speech

Gerald Uelmen (b. 1941) is a professor at Santa Clara University School of Law where he specializes in criminal law and procedure. He participated in the defense of Daniel Ellsberg and the Pentagon Papers and has argued cases before the United States and the California Supreme Courts. He previously taught law at Loyola Law School in Los Angeles where he was also an associate dean. He has law degrees from George-town Law Center. He published an account of the O. J. Simpson trial, entitled Lessons from the Trial *(1996). The following essay appeared in* Issues in Ethics *(Summer 1992).*

At Emory University, certain conduct that is permissible off campus is not al-lowed on campus. Specifically, some speech and behaviors are prohibited in Emory's version of what are derogatorily labeled "politically correct" codes but are more commonly known as hate speech codes. Emory's code begins with its definition of banned behavior.

Discriminatory harassment includes conduct (oral, written, graphic, or physical) directed against any person or group of persons because of their race, color, national origin, religion, sex, sexual orientation, age, disability, or veter-an's status and that has the purpose or reasonably foreseeable effect of creating an offensive, demeaning, intimidating, or hostile environment for that person or group of persons.

There were approximately 75 hate speech codes in place at U.S. colleges and universities in 1990; by 1991, the number grew to over 300. School ad-ministrators institute codes primarily to foster productive learning environ-ments in the face of rising racially motivated and other offensive incidents on many campuses. According to a recent study, reports of campus harassment increased 400 percent between 1985 and 1990. Moreover, 80 percent of cam-pus harassment incidents go unreported.

Hate speech codes follow several formats. Some codes, including Emory's, prohibit speech or conduct that creates an intimidating, hostile, or offensive educational environment. Others ban behavior that intentionally inflicts emo-tional distress. Still others outlaw "general harassment and threats," without clarifying what constitutes such conduct. Court rulings have prohibited public (state-run) colleges and universities from enacting codes that restrict the con-stitutional right to free speech based on content. Private institutions, in con-trast, are not subject to these decisions. Emory, for example, as a private university, can ignore public law rulings and draft whatever hate speech policy it chooses.

Hate speech codes raise important ethical questions. When civil liberties are pitted against the right to freedom of speech, which does justice favor? Do the costs of hate speech codes outweigh their benefits? Is the harm that results from hate speech so serious that codes to restrict freedom of speech are morally required? 5

Arguments against Campus Hate Speech Codes

The most fundamental argument against hate speech codes rests on the idea that they violate a fundamental human right, freedom of speech. Such a fundamental right, it is argued, should not be limited except to prevent serious harm to others. Libel or shouting "Fire!" in a movie theater, for example, can cause serious harm and, therefore, are legitimately banned. In contrast, what campuses prohibit as "hate speech" is primarily opinion that, while often offensive and unpopular, does not cause serious harm. The fundamental right to free speech should not be restricted merely to prevent hate speech.

Additionally, critics assert that the costs of hate speech codes far outweigh their benefits. Threatened by "politically correct" students who are backed by hate speech codes, students who have reasonable yet nonconforming points of view will be afraid to speak in classes. As a social institution, a university should be open to all opinions, popular and unpopular. As Oliver Wendell Holmes commented, "The very aim and end of our institutions is just this: that we may think what we like and say what we think." Hate speech codes thus inflict a major harm on our social institutions.

Censorship is only one example of how hate speech codes undercut the benefits of higher education. If these codes shield students from dissenting opinions, how will they learn to respond to such opinions after they graduate? Hate speech codes encourage an artificial reality on campus that prevents students from learning effectively to tolerate diversity.

Hate speech codes may obstruct the kind of education that promotes tolerance of diversity in other ways. Over time, the same fervor that brought hate speech codes will bring further restrictions by administrators eager to create egalitarian institutions in a nonegalitarian world.

The law school at the State University of New York, Buffalo, for example, 10 seeks out and ask state bars to deny admission to former students who violate its hate speech code. And following the 1988 passage of the Civil Rights Restoration Act, which denies federal aid to students of private colleges and universities that violate federal anti-discrimination rules, legislators are considering a law that would force private institutions to require courses on racial sensitivity and ethnic history. From defining what specifically constitutes "hate speech" to choosing the manner in which policies are enforced, codes clearly cause or invite more trouble than they are worth.

In Defense of Campus Hate Speech Codes

Those who advocate hate speech codes believe that the harm codes prevent is more important than the freedom they restrict. When hate speech is directed at a student from a protected group, like those listed in Emory University's code, the effect is much more than hurt feelings. The verbal attack is a symptom of an oppressive history of discrimination and subjugation that plagues the harmed student and hinders his or her ability to compete fairly in the academic arena. The resulting harm is clearly significant and, therefore, justifies limiting speech rights.

In addition to minimizing harm, hate speech codes result in other benefits. The university is ideally a forum where views are debated using rational argumentation; part of a student's education is learning how to derive and rationally defend an opinion. The hate speech that codes target, in contrast, is not presented rationally or used to provoke debate. In fact, hate speech often intends to provoke violence. Hate speech codes emphasize the need to support convictions with facts and reasoning while protecting the rights of potential victims.

As a society we reason that it is in the best interest of the greatest number of citizens to sometimes restrict speech when it conflicts with the primary purpose of an event. A theater owner, for example, has a right to remove a heckler when the heckler's behavior conflicts with the primary purpose of staging a play — to entertain an audience. Therefore, if the primary purpose of an academic institution is to educate students, and hate speech obstructs the educational process by reducing students' abilities to learn, then it is permissible to extend protection from hate speech to students on college or university campuses.

Hate speech codes also solve the conflict between the right to freely speak and the right to an education. A student attending a college or university clearly has such a right. But students exercising their "free speech" right may espouse hateful or intimidating words that impede other students' abilities to learn and thereby destroy their chances to earn an education.

Finally, proponents of hate speech codes see them as morally essential to a   15
just resolution of the conflict between civil rights (e.g., freedom from harmful stigma and humiliation) and civil liberties (e.g., freedom of speech). At the heart of the conflict is the fact that under-represented students cannot claim fair and equal access to freedom of speech and other rights when there is an imbalance of power between them and students in the majority. If a black student, for example, shouts an epithet at a white student, the white student may become upset or feel enraged, but he or she has little reason to feel terror or intimidation. Yet when a white student directs an epithet toward a black student or a Jewish student, an overt history of subjugation intensifies the verbal attack that humiliates and strikes institutional fear in the victim. History shows that words of hatred are amplified when they come from those in power and abridged when spoken by the powerless.

Discrimination on college and university campuses is a growing problem with an uncertain future. Whether hate speech codes are morally just responses to campus intolerance depends on how society interprets the harms of discriminatory harassment, the benefits and costs of restricting free speech, and the just balance between individual rights and group rights.   *[1992]*

Further Reading

Feinberg, Joel. *Social Philosophy.* Englewood Cliffs, N.J.: Prentice Hall, 1973.
Grey, Thomas C. "Civil Rights vs. Civil Liberties: The Case of Discriminatory Harassment." *Social Philosophy & Policy* 8 (August 1991): 81–107.
Hentoff, Nat. "The New Jacobins." *Reason* 23 (November 1991): 30–33.
Rieff, David. "The Case Against Sensitivity." *Esquire* 114 (November 1990): 120–31.

≡ THINKING ABOUT IDEAS

1. Several democratic countries, including England, Germany, France, and Canada, prohibit hate speech, although with differing definitions of what hate speech is. Paraphrase Uelmen's definition. What would you add or delete?

2. What is the most compelling argument against speech codes? What is the most compelling argument for them? In his last paragraph, Uelmen claims that whether speech codes are "morally just" or not depends on one's interpretation of the "harm" hate speech does and the "cost" of restricting free speech. What are some of the serious harms that might result from hate speech, and what might be some "benefits" of restricting free speech?

3. Uelmen's fifth paragraph raises some ethical questions. How would an advocate for codes answer them? How would someone opposed to speech codes answer them?

≡ THINKING ABOUT ARGUMENTATIVE MOVES

1. Uelmen wants to render objectively the opposing sides in the speech code debate. What reasons does he give for enacting codes? What is the reasoning behind prohibiting verbal attacks against those with "a history of discrimination and subjugation"? What kind of evidence would he need to support this position?

2. Give a specific example of what Uelmen means when he says speech codes target irrational speech. Presumably when someone is accused of hate speech she could try to support her convictions with facts and reasoning. Give a possible example that would illustrate this idea.

3. Freedom of speech advocates argue that serious harm is not done even with hate speech. What other objections do they have against codes? Give a concrete example of what is meant by the contention that codes "encourage an artificial reality on campus" that prevents future tolerance of diversity.

CHARLES R. LAWRENCE III

The Debates over Placing Limits on Racist Speech Must Not Ignore the Damage It Does to Its Victims

Charles R. Lawrence III (b. 1943) graduated from Yale Law School in 1969 and has taught at a number of leading law schools, including Harvard, Berkeley, Stanford, and Georgetown. He is well known for his work in anti-discrimination law, equal protection, and critical race theory. He is the author of the influential text We Won't Go Back: Making the Case for Affirmative Action *(1997). He has won numerous teaching awards and fellowships and is currently Centennial University Professor at the University of Hawai'i. Lawrence's essay on racist speech was first published in an October 1989 issue of the* Chronicle of Higher Education.

I have spent the better part of my life as a dissenter. As a high-school student, I was threatened with suspension for my refusal to participate in a civil-defense drill, and I have been a conspicuous consumer of my First Amendment liberties ever since. There are very strong reasons for protecting even racist speech. Perhaps the most important of these is that such protection reinforces our society's commitment to tolerance as a value, and that by protecting bad speech from government regulation, we will be forced to combat it as a community.

But I also have a deeply felt apprehension about the resurgence of racial violence and the corresponding rise in the incidence of verbal and symbolic assault and harassment to which blacks and other traditionally subjugated and excluded groups are subjected. I am troubled by the way the debate has been framed in response to the recent surge of racist incidents on college and university campuses and in response to some universities' attempts to regulate harassing speech. The problem has been framed as one in which the liberty of free speech is in conflict with the elimination of racism. I believe this has placed the bigot on the moral high ground and fanned the rising flames of racism.

Above all, I am troubled that we have not listened to the real victims, that we have shown so little understanding of their injury, and that we have abandoned those whose race, gender, or sexual preference continues to make them second-class citizens. It seems to me a very sad irony that the first instinct of civil libertarians has been to challenge even the smallest, most narrowly framed efforts by universities to provide black and other minority students with the protection the Constitution guarantees them.

The landmark case of *Brown v. Board of Education* is not a case that we normally think of as a case about speech. But *Brown* can be broadly read as articulating the principle of equal citizenship. *Brown* held that segregated schools were inherently unequal because of the message that segregation conveyed—that black children were an untouchable caste, unfit to go to school with white children. If we understand the necessity of eliminating the system of signs and symbols that signal the inferiority of blacks, then we should hesitate before proclaiming that all racist speech that stops short of physical violence must be defended.

University officials who have formulated policies to respond to incidents of racial harassment have been characterized in the press as "thought police," but such policies generally do nothing more than impose sanctions against intentional face-to-face insults. When racist speech takes the form of face-to-face insults, catcalls, or other assaultive speech aimed at an individual or small group of persons, it falls directly within the "fighting words" exception to First Amendment protection. The Supreme Court has held that words which "by their very utterance inflict injury or tend to incite an immediate breach of the peace" are not protected by the First Amendment.

5

If the purpose of the First Amendment is to foster the greatest amount of speech, racial insults disserve that purpose. Assaultive racist speech functions as a preemptive strike. The invective is experienced as a blow, not as a proffered idea, and once the blow is struck, it is unlikely that a dialogue will follow. Racial insults are particularly undeserving of First Amendment protection because the perpetrator's intention is not to discover truth or initiate dialogue but to injure the victim. In most situations, members of minority groups realize that they are likely to lose if they respond to epithets by fighting and are forced to remain silent and submissive.

Courts have held that offensive speech may not be regulated in public forums such as streets where the listener may avoid the speech by moving on, but the regulation of otherwise protected speech has been permitted when the speech invades the privacy of the unwilling listener's home or when the unwilling listener cannot avoid the speech. Racist posters, fliers, and graffiti in dormitories, bathrooms, and other common living spaces would seem to clearly fall within the reasoning of these cases. Minority students should not be required to remain in their rooms in order to avoid racial assault. Minimally, they should find a safe haven in their dorms and in all other common rooms that are a part of their daily routine.

I would also argue that the university's responsibility for insuring that these students receive an equal educational opportunity provides a compelling justification for regulations that insure them safe passage in all common areas. A minority student should not have to risk becoming the target of racially assaulting speech every time he or she chooses to walk across campus. Regulating vilifying speech that cannot be anticipated or avoided would not preclude announced speeches and rallies—situations that would give minority-group members and their allies the chance to organize counter-demonstrations or avoid the speech altogether.

The most commonly advanced argument against the regulation of racist speech proceeds something like this: We recognize that minority groups suffer pain and injury as the result of racist speech, but we must allow this hate mongering for the benefit of society as a whole. Freedom of speech is the lifeblood of our democratic system. It is especially important for minorities because often it is their only vehicle for rallying support for the redress of their grievances. It will be impossible to formulate a prohibition so precise that it will prevent the racist speech you want to suppress without catching in the same net all kinds of speech that it would be unconscionable for a democratic society to suppress.

Whenever we make such arguments, we are striking a balance on the one 10 hand between our concern for the continued free flow of ideas and the democratic process dependent on that flow, and, on the other, our desire to further the cause of equality. There can be no meaningful discussion of how we should reconcile our commitment to equality and our commitment to free speech until it is acknowledged that there is real harm inflicted by racist speech and that this harm is far from trivial.

To engage in a debate about the First Amendment and racist speech without a full understanding of the nature and extent of that harm is to risk making the First Amendment an instrument of domination rather than a vehicle of liberation. We have not all known the experience of victimization by racist, misogynist, and homophobic speech, nor do we equally share the burden of the societal harm it inflicts. We are often quick to say that we have heard the cry of the victims when we have not.

The *Brown* case is again instructive because it speaks directly to the psychic injury inflicted by racist speech by noting that the symbolic message of segregation affected "the hearts and minds" of Negro children "in a way unlikely ever to be undone." Racial epithets and harassment often cause deep emotional scarring and feelings of anxiety and fear that pervade every aspect of a victim's life.

Brown also recognized that black children did not have an equal opportunity to learn and participate in the school community if they bore the additional burden of being subjected to the humiliation and psychic assault contained in the message of segregation. University students bear an analogous burden when they are forced to live and work in an environment where at any moment they may be subjected to denigrating verbal harassment and assault. The same injury was addressed by the Supreme Court when it held that sexual harassment that creates a hostile or abusive work environment violates the ban on sex discrimination in employment of Title VII of the Civil Rights Act of 1964.

Carefully drafted university regulations would bar the use of words as assault weapons and leave unregulated even the most heinous of ideas when those ideas are presented at times and places and in manners that provide an opportunity for reasoned rebuttal or escape from immediate injury. The history of the development of the right to free speech has been one of carefully evaluating the importance of free expression and its effects on other important societal interests. We have drawn the line between protected and unprotected speech before without dire results. (Courts have, for example, exempted from the protection of the First Amendment obscene speech and speech that disseminates official secrets, that defames or libels another person, or that is used to form a conspiracy or monopoly.)

Blacks and other people of color are skeptical about the argument that even the most injurious speech must remain unregulated because, in an unregulated marketplace of ideas, the best ones will rise to the top and gain acceptance. Our experience tells us quite the opposite. We have seen too many demagogues elected by appealing to America's racism. We have seen too many good liberal politicians shy away from the issues that might brand them as being too closely allied with us.

Whenever we decide that racist speech must be tolerated because of the importance of maintaining societal tolerance for all unpopular speech, we are asking blacks and other subordinated groups to bear the burden for the good of all. We must be careful that the ease with which we strike the balance against the regulation of racist speech is in no way influenced by the fact that the cost will be borne by others. We must be certain that those who will pay that price are fairly represented in our deliberations and that they are heard.

At the core of the argument that we should resist all government regulation of speech is the ideal that the best cure for bad speech is good, that ideas that affirm equality and the worth of all individuals will ultimately prevail. This is an empty ideal unless those of us who would fight racism are vigilant and unequivocal in that fight. We must look for ways to offer assistance and support to students whose speech and political participation are chilled in a climate of racial harassment.

Civil-rights lawyers might consider suing on behalf of blacks whose right to an equal education is denied by a university's failure to insure a non-discriminatory educational climate or conditions of employment. We must embark upon the development of a First Amendment jurisprudence grounded in the reality of our history and our contemporary experience. We must think hard about how best to launch legal attacks against the most indefensible forms of hate speech. Good lawyers can create exceptions and narrow interpretations that limit the harm of hate speech without opening the floodgates of censorship.

Everyone concerned with these issues must find ways to engage actively in actions that resist and counter the racist ideas that we would have the First Amendment protect. If we fail in this, the victims of hate speech must rightly assume that we are on the oppressors' side.   *[1989]*

≡ THINKING ABOUT IDEAS

1. What specifically is Lawrence referring to when he says we need to "eliminat[e] the system of signs and symbols that signal the inferiority of blacks" (para. 4)? What examples can you give for other "traditionally subjugated and excluded groups" (para. 2)? Who should get to judge whether certain words or symbols are hate speech or not? Does the intention of the speaker matter, or is it the interpretation of the hearer that dictates?

2. How would you define the "real harm" and "trivial harm" that might result from hate speech? How does your college encourage both freedom of speech and civil discourse? What is Lawrence's proposal in the last two paragraphs?

3. Under what conditions might you allow "even the most heinous of ideas" (para. 14) in public? What guidelines would you set up if you were on a committee responsible for monitoring the appearance on campus of the Ku Klux Klan? A Holocaust denial speaker? Groups that exclude gays and lesbians?

≡ THINKING ABOUT ARGUMENTATIVE MOVES

1. How might Lawrence's personal testimony in the first paragraph help or hinder his credibility? What is Lawrence's argumentative strategy in the last sentence of the first paragraph? What are the advantages of such a

move? What move does he then make using "but" in the following paragraph?

2. What are the exceptions to the First Amendment that Lawrence notes? How does Lawrence think racist speech "disserves" the purpose of fostering more speech? Which one of the reasons Lawrence gives for his claim that speech codes are necessary is the most compelling? Why? How might he have made it even stronger?

3. Analyze the ways Lawrence deals with the opposition to speech codes. For example, why specifically is he upset at "civil libertarians"? What is his response to accusations of being "thought police"? Why does he say the idea that injurious speech must be "unregulated" is an empty ideal? How does Lawrence's conclusion help or hinder his larger argument? Suggest another approach that might be more effective.

GREG LUKIANOFF

Feigning Free Speech on Campus

Greg Lukianoff (b. 1975) is an attorney specializing in First Amendment rights. He is president of the Foundation for Individual Rights in Education. He has published dozens of articles and essays in leading newspapers and magazines and is a regular columnist for the Huffington Post. *He received the 2008 Playboy Foundation Freedom of Expression Award. He graduated from Stanford Law School. His latest book,* Unlearning Liberty: Campus Censorship and the End of American Debate *(2012), was praised by Nat Hentoff as a "must read" in the debate over free speech on campus. Lukianoff's op-ed article that follows appeared in the* New York Times *in October 2012.*

Despite high youth voter turnout in 2008 — 48.5 percent of 18- to 24-year-olds cast ballots that year — levels are expected to return to usual lows this year, and with that the usual hand-wringing about disengagement and apathy among young voters.

Colleges and universities are supposed to be bastions of unbridled inquiry and expression, but they probably do as much to repress free speech as any other institution in young people's lives. In doing so, they discourage civic engagement at a time when debates over deficits and taxes should make young people pay more attention, not less.

Since the 1980s, in part because of "political correctness" concerns about racially insensitive speech and sexual harassment, and in part because of the dramatic expansion in the ranks of nonfaculty campus administrators, colleges have enacted stringent speech codes. These codes are sometimes well intended but, outside of the ivory tower, would violate the constitutional guarantee of freedom of speech. From protests and rallies to displays of posters and flags, students have been severely constrained in their ability to demonstrate their beliefs. The speech codes are at times intended to enforce civility, but they often backfire, suppressing free expression instead of allowing for open debate of controversial issues.

Last month, Christopher Newport University in Newport News, Virginia, forbade students to protest an appearance by Representative Paul D. Ryan, the Republican vice-presidential nominee. Why? According to university policy, students must apply ten business days in advance to demonstrate in the college's tiny "free speech zone" — and Mr. Ryan's visit was announced on a Sunday, two days before his Tuesday visit.

Also last month, a student at Ohio University in Athens, Ohio, was blocked   5
from putting a notice on her door arguing that neither President Obama nor Mitt Romney was fit for office. (She successfully appealed.) And over the summer, a federal judge struck down the University of Cincinnati's "free speech zone," which had limited demonstrations to 0.1 percent of the campus.

In a study of 392 campus speech codes last year, the Foundation for Individual Rights in Education, where I work, found that 65 percent of the colleges had policies that in our view violated the Constitution's guarantee of the right to free speech. (While the First Amendment generally prohibits public universities from restricting nondisruptive free speech, private colleges are not state actors and therefore have more leeway to establish their own rules.)

Some elite colleges in particular have Orwellian speech codes that are so vague and broad that they would never pass constitutional muster at state-financed universities. Harvard is a particularly egregious example. Last year, incoming Harvard freshmen were pressured by campus officials to sign an oath promising to act with "civility" and "inclusiveness" and affirming that "kindness holds a place on par with intellectual attainment." Harry R. Lewis, a computer science professor and a former dean of Harvard College, was quick to criticize the oath. "For Harvard to 'invite' people to pledge to kindness is unwise, and sets a terrible precedent," he wrote on his blog. "It is a promise to control one's thoughts."

Civility is nice, but on college campuses it often takes on a bizarre meaning. In 2009, Yale banned students from making a T-shirt with an F. Scott Fitzgerald quotation — "I think of all Harvard men as sissies," from his 1920 novel *This Side of Paradise* — to mock Harvard at their annual football game. The T-shirt was blocked after some gay and lesbian students argued that "sissies" amounted to a homophobic slur. "What purports to be humor by targeting a group through slurs is not acceptable," said Mary Miller, a professor of art history and the dean of Yale College.

Elsewhere, rules that aim for inclusiveness do more to confuse students than to encourage debate. Earlier this year, Vanderbilt prohibited student groups (if they wished to receive university support and financing) from barring students from leadership positions based on their beliefs. The apparent goal was to prevent evangelical Christian groups from excluding gay students from leadership positions — but the policy also means that a Democrat could be elected as an officer of the College Republicans.

A 2010 study by the American Association of Colleges and Universities of 24,000 college students and 9,000 faculty and staff members found that only 35.6 percent of the students—and only 18.5 percent of the faculty and staff—strongly agreed that it was "safe to hold unpopular positions on campus."

For reasons both good and bad—and sometimes for mere administrative convenience—colleges have promulgated speech codes that are not only absurd in their results but also detrimental to the ideals of free inquiry. Students can't learn how to navigate democracy and engage with their fellow citizens if they are forced to think twice before they speak their mind.   [2012]

≡ THINKING ABOUT IDEAS

1. When Lukianoff says that speech codes are "sometimes well intended" (para. 3), what is he implying? What might the not-well-intended administrator be trying to accomplish? Lukianoff's opposition to speech codes is obvious in the last sentence, but how might "thinking twice" be both a good and a bad idea?

2. When Lukianoff's foundation found that 65 percent of colleges it looked at had policies that violated free speech, what is this evidence of? Suggest alternative ways the foundation might have supported its position. Give an example of a possible free speech violation you have experienced on campus.

3. Comment on the appropriateness of the two examples Lukianoff gives of "Orwellian speech codes" (para. 7) from Harvard and Yale. How specifically might Lawrence respond to these examples? How, for example, might the "'pledge to kindness'" be "'a promise to control one's thoughts'" (para. 7)? How might his Vanderbilt example "do more to confuse students than to encourage debate" (para. 9)?

≡ THINKING ABOUT ARGUMENTATIVE MOVES

1. In arguing against speech codes, Lukianoff comments on the motivation of his opponents. Why does he say they instituted these codes? (What might Lawrence say about his own reasons for supporting speech codes?) What is the rhetorical effect of Lukianoff's use of terms such as "repress," "discourage," "severely constrained," "suppressing free expression," "bizarre meaning," "absurd," and "detrimental"?

2. What kind of evidence does Lukianoff supply for his claims that colleges "do as much to repress free speech as any other institution" (para. 2)? What kind of additional evidence does this assertion call for?

3. In his third, fourth, and fifth paragraphs, Lukianoff gives examples of ways students have been "severely constrained in their ability to demonstrate their beliefs" (para. 3). How might this be the case? How might it not? What is problematic about the term "beliefs"? For example, is he

talking just about mainstream beliefs? What about those who believe gay and lesbian organizations should not be funded by student fees? What about Holocaust deniers or Students Against Contraception or Students United to Ban Military Recruiters? Why might all or some of these groups be given equal opportunity to demonstrate their beliefs?

≡ WRITING ABOUT ISSUES

1. Write an argument that agrees or disagrees with Oliver Wendell Holmes's comment: "The very aim and end of our institutions is just this: that we may think what we like and say what we think."

2. Write an argument that agrees with, disagrees with, or qualifies the following idea: Limits on free speech should be enforced by social norms and ethics and by discussion and dialogue, not by laws. Be sure to include the views of both Lawrence and Lukianoff.

3. Write an essay that argues that hate speech codes do or do not promote tolerance for diversity.

4. One of the most respected defenders of prohibitions on hate speech is Jeremy Waldron whose book, *The Harm of Hate Speech* (2012), was reviewed by Justice John Paul Stevens in the *New York Review of Books*. Locate and read this review and summarize Stevens's points of agreement and disagreement with Waldron's position. Then write an argument setting forth your own points of agreement and disagreement with Stevens and Waldron. On balance, is your position closer to Stevens's or Waldron's? Explain your position and why it matters.

CHARLOTTE PERKINS GILMAN, "The Yellow Wallpaper"

CULTURAL CONTEXTS:
CHARLOTTE PERKINS GILMAN, "Why I Wrote 'The Yellow Wallpaper'"

S. WEIR MITCHELL, From "The Evolution of the Rest Treatment"

JOHN HARVEY KELLOGG, From *The Ladies' Guide in Health and Disease*

When doctors make a medical or psychiatric diagnosis, they pinpoint their patient's condition but also often accept or reject their society's definition of *health*. The social context of diagnoses seems especially worth considering when a particular condition afflicts one gender much more than the other. Today, many more women than men appear to suffer from depression, anorexia, bulimia, and dissociative identity disorder. Why? Perhaps traditional female roles encourage these illnesses; perhaps gender bias affects how doctors label and treat them. Charlotte Perkins Gilman raised both these possibilities in her 1892 short story "The Yellow Wallpaper." In her own life, the consequences from her egregious treatment were not as serious as she depicts in her story. But Gilman was the exception. Many women suffered terribly from doctors who ignored the cultural causes of depression. Besides Gilman's story, we include her account of why she wrote it, an excerpt from a lecture by Mitchell about his cure, and some advice about motherhood from John Kellogg, another influential doctor of the time.

≡ **BEFORE YOU READ**

How is mental illness depicted in movies and television shows you have seen? Which representations of mental illness have you appreciated the most? Which have you especially disliked? State your criteria for these judgments.

CHARLOTTE PERKINS GILMAN
The Yellow Wallpaper

Charlotte Perkins Gilman (1860–1935) was a major activist and theorist in America's first wave of feminism. During her lifetime, she was chiefly known for her 1898 book Women and Economics. *In it she argued that women should not be confined to the household and made economically dependent on men. Gilman also advanced such ideas through her many public-speaking appearances and her magazine* The Forerunner, *which she edited from 1909 to 1916. Gilman wrote many articles and works of fiction for* The Forerunner, *including a tale called* Herland *(1915) in*

(Charlotte Perkins Gilman. The Granger Collection. New York.)

which she envisioned an all-female utopia. Today, however, Gilman is best known for her short story "The Yellow Wallpaper," which she published first in an 1892 issue of the New England Magazine. *The story is based on Gilman's struggle with depression after the birth of her daughter Katharine in 1885. Seeking help for emotional turmoil, Gilman consulted the eminent neurologist Silas Weir Mitchell, who prescribed his famous "rest cure." This treatment, which forbade Gilman to work, actually worsened her distress. She improved only after she moved to California, divorced her husband, let him raise Katharine with his new wife, married someone else, and plunged fully into a literary and political career. As Gilman noted in her posthumously published autobiography,* The Living of Charlotte Perkins Gilman *(1935), she never fully recovered from the debilitation that had led her to Dr. Mitchell, but she ultimately managed to be enormously productive. Although "The Yellow Wallpaper" is a work of fiction rather than a factual account of her experience with Mitchell, Gilman used the story to criticize the doctor's patriarchal approach as well as society's efforts to keep women passive.*

It is very seldom that mere ordinary people like John and myself secure ancestral halls for the summer.

A colonial mansion, a hereditary estate, I would say a haunted house and reach the height of romantic felicity—but that would be asking too much of fate!

Still I will proudly declare that there is something queer about it.

Else, why should it be let so cheaply? And why have stood so long untenanted?

John laughs at me, of course, but one expects that in marriage.   5

John is practical in the extreme. He has no patience with faith, an intense horror of superstition, and he scoffs openly at any talk of things not to be felt and seen and put down in figures.

John is a physician, and *perhaps*—(I would not say it to a living soul, of course, but this is dead paper and a great relief to my mind)—*perhaps* that is one reason I do not get well faster.

You see, he does not believe I am sick!

And what can one do?

If a physician of high standing, and one's own husband, assures friends   10 and relatives that there is really nothing the matter with one but temporary nervous depression—a slight hysterical tendency° — what is one to do?

My brother is also a physician, and also of high standing, and he says the same thing.

So I take phosphates or phosphites—whichever it is, and tonics, and journeys, and air, and exercise, and am absolutely forbidden to "work" until I am well again.

Personally, I disagree with their ideas.

Personally, I believe that congenial work, with excitement and change, would do me good.

But what is one to do?   15

I did write for a while in spite of them; but it *does* exhaust me a good deal— having to be so sly about it, or else meet with heavy opposition.

I sometimes fancy that in my condition if I had less opposition and more society and stimulus—but John says the very worst thing I can do is to think about my condition, and I confess it always makes me feel bad.

So I will let it alone and talk about the house.

The most beautiful place! It is quite alone, standing well back from the road, quite three miles from the village. It makes me think of English places that you read about, for there are hedges and walls and gates that lock, and lots of separate little houses for the gardeners and people.

There is a *delicious* garden! I never saw such a garden—large and shady,   20 full of box-bordered paths, and lined with long grape-covered arbors with seats under them.

There were greenhouses, too, but they are all broken now.

There was some legal trouble, I believe, something about the heirs and co-heirs; anyhow, the place has been empty for years.

hysterical tendency: It was common among Victorian doctors to believe women had an innate tendency to be overly emotional; now a discredited assumption.

That spoils my ghostliness, I am afraid, but I don't care—there is something strange about the house—I can feel it.

I even said so to John one moonlight evening, but he said what I felt was a *draught*, and shut the window.

I get unreasonably angry with John sometimes. I'm sure I never used to be so sensitive. I think it is due to this nervous condition.

But John says if I feel so, I shall neglect proper self-control; so I take pains to control myself—before him, at least, and that makes me very tired.

I don't like our room a bit. I wanted one downstairs that opened on the piazza and had roses all over the window, and such pretty old-fashioned chintz hangings! but John would not hear of it.

He said there was only one window and not room for two beds, and no near room for him if he took another.

He is very careful and loving, and hardly lets me stir without special direction.

I have a schedule prescription for each hour in the day; he takes all care from me, and so I feel basely ungrateful not to value it more.

He said we came here solely on my account, that I was to have perfect rest and all the air I could get. "Your exercise depends on your strength, my dear," said he, "and your food somewhat on your appetite; but air you can absorb all the time." So we took the nursery at the top of the house.

It is a big, airy room, the whole floor nearly, with windows that look all ways, and air and sunshine galore. It was nursery first and then playroom and gymnasium, I should judge; for the windows are barred for little children, and there are rings and things in the walls.

The paint and paper look as if a boys' school had used it. It is stripped off — the paper—in great patches all around the head of my bed, about as far as I can reach, and in a great place on the other side of the room low down. I never saw a worse paper in my life.

One of those sprawling flamboyant patterns committing every artistic sin.

It is dull enough to confuse the eye in following, pronounced enough to constantly irritate and provoke study, and when you follow the lame uncertain curves for a little distance they suddenly commit suicide—plunge off at outrageous angles, destroy themselves in unheard of contradictions.

The color is repellant, almost revolting; a smouldering unclean yellow, strangely faded by the slow-turning sunlight.

It is a dull yet lurid orange in some places, a sickly sulphur tint in others.

No wonder the children hated it! I should hate it myself if I had to live in this room long.

There comes John, and I must put this away,—he hates to have me write a word.

We have been here two weeks, and I haven't felt like writing before, since that first day.

I am sitting by the window now, up in this atrocious nursery, and there is nothing to hinder my writing as much as I please, save lack of strength.

John is away all day, and even some nights when his cases are serious.

I am glad my case is not serious!

But these nervous troubles are dreadfully depressing.

John does not know how much I really suffer. He knows there is no *reason*   45
to suffer, and that satisfies him.

Of course it is only nervousness. It does weigh on me so not to do my duty
in any way!

I meant to be such a help to John, such a real rest and comfort, and here I
am a comparative burden already!

Nobody would believe what an effort it is to do what little I am able,—to
dress and entertain, and order things.

It is fortunate Mary is so good with the baby. Such a dear baby!

And yet I *cannot* be with him, it makes me so nervous.   50

I suppose John never was nervous in his life. He laughs at me so about this
wallpaper!

At first he meant to repaper the room, but afterward he said that I was letting it get the better of me, and that nothing was worse for a nervous patient
than to give way to such fancies.

He said that after the wallpaper was changed it would be the heavy bedstead, and then the barred windows, and then that gate at the head of the
stairs, and so on.

"You know the place is doing you good," he said, "and really, dear, I don't
care to renovate the house just for a three months' rental."

"Then do let us go downstairs," I said, "there are such pretty rooms there."   55

Then he took me in his arms and called me a blessed little goose, and said
he would go down cellar, if I wished, and have it whitewashed into the bargain.

But he is right enough about the beds and windows and things.

It is an airy and comfortable room as anyone need wish, and, of course, I
would not be so silly as to make him uncomfortable just for a whim.

I'm really getting quite fond of the big room, all but that horrid paper.

Out of one window I can see the garden, those mysterious deep-shaded   60
arbors, the riotous old-fashioned flowers, and bushes and gnarly trees.

Out of another I get a lovely view of the bay and a little private wharf belonging to the estate. There is a beautiful shaded lane that runs down there
from the house. I always fancy I see people walking in these numerous paths
and arbors, but John has cautioned me not to give way to fancy in the least. He
says that with my imaginative power and habit of story-making, a nervous
weakness like mine is sure to lead to all manner of excited fancies, and that I
ought to use my will and good sense to check the tendency. So I try.

I think sometimes that if I were only well enough to write a little it would
relieve the press of ideas and rest me.

But I find I get pretty tired when I try.

It is so discouraging not to have any advice and companionship about my
work. When I get really well, John says we will ask Cousin Henry and Julia
down for a long visit; but he says he would as soon put fireworks in my pillow-
case as to let me have those stimulating people about now.

I wish I could get well faster. 65

But I must not think about that. This paper looks to me as if it *knew* what a vicious influence it had!

There is a recurrent spot where the pattern lolls like a broken neck and two bulbous eyes stare at you upside down.

I get positively angry with the impertinence of it and the everlastingness. Up and down and sideways they crawl, and those absurd, unblinking eyes are everywhere. There is one place where two breadths didn't match, and the eyes go all up and down the line, one a little higher than the other.

I never saw so much expression in an inanimate thing before, and we all know how much expression they have! I used to lie awake as a child and get more entertainment and terror out of blank walls and plain furniture than most children could find in a toy-store.

I remember what a kindly wink the knobs of our big, old bureau used to 70 have, and there was one chair that always seemed like a strong friend.

I used to feel that if any of the other things looked too fierce I could always hop into that chair and be safe.

The furniture in this room is no worse than inharmonious, however, for we had to bring it all from downstairs. I suppose when this was used as a play-room they had to take the nursery things out, and no wonder! I never saw such ravages as the children have made here.

The wallpaper, as I said before, is torn off in spots, and it sticketh closer than a brother—they must have had perseverance as well as hatred.

Then the floor is scratched and gouged and splintered, the plaster itself is dug out here and there, and this great heavy bed, which is all we found in the room, looks as if it had been through the wars.

But I don't mind it a bit—only the paper. 75

There comes John's sister. Such a dear girl as she is, and so careful of me! I must not let her find me writing.

She is a perfect and enthusiastic housekeeper, and hopes for no better profession. I verily believe she thinks it is the writing which made me sick!

But I can write when she is out, and see her a long way off from these windows.

There is one that commands the road, a lovely shaded winding road, and one that just looks off over the country. A lovely country, too, full of great elms and velvet meadows.

This wallpaper has a kind of sub-pattern in a different shade, a particularly 80 irritating one, for you can only see it in certain lights, and not clearly then.

But in the places where it isn't faded and where the sun is just so—I can see a strange, provoking, formless sort of figure, that seems to skulk about behind that silly and conspicuous front design.

There's sister on the stairs!

Well, the Fourth of July is over! The people are all gone and I am tired out. John thought it might do me good to see a little company, so we just had mother and Nellie and the children down for a week.

Of course I didn't do a thing. Jennie sees to everything now.

But it tired me all the same.

John says if I don't pick up faster he shall send me to Weir Mitchell° in the fall. 85

But I don't want to go there at all. I had a friend who was in his hands once, and she says he is just like John and my brother, only more so!

Besides, it is such an undertaking to go so far.

I don't feel as if it was worthwhile to turn my hand over for anything, and I'm getting dreadfully fretful and querulous.

I cry at nothing, and cry most of the time. 90

Of course I don't when John is here, or anybody else, but when I am alone.

And I am alone a good deal just now. John is kept in town very often by serious cases, and Jennie is good and lets me alone when I want her to.

So I walk a little in the garden or down that lovely lane, sit on the porch under the roses, and lie down up here a good deal.

I'm getting really fond of the room in spite of the wallpaper. Perhaps *because* of the wallpaper.

It dwells in my mind so! 95

I lie here on this great immovable bed—it is nailed down, I believe—and follow that pattern about by the hour. It is as good as gymnastics, I assure you. I start, we'll say, at the bottom, down in the corner over there where it has not been touched, and I determine for the thousandth time that I *will* follow that pointless pattern to some sort of a conclusion.

I know a little of the principle of design, and I know this thing was not arranged on any laws of radiation, or alternation, or repetition, or symmetry, or anything else that I ever heard of.

It is repeated, of course, by the breadths, but not otherwise.

Looked at in one way each breadth stands alone, the bloated curves and flourishes—a kind of "debased Romanesque" with *delirium tremens*—go waddling up and down in isolated columns of fatuity.

But, on the other hand, they connect diagonally, and the sprawling outlines run off in great slanting waves of optic horror, like a lot of wallowing seaweeds in full chase. 100

The whole thing goes horizontally, too, at least it seems so, and I exhaust myself in trying to distinguish the order of its going in that direction.

They have used a horizontal breadth for a frieze, and that adds wonderfully to the confusion.

There is one end of the room where it is almost intact, and there, when the crosslights fade and the low sun shines directly upon it, I can almost fancy radiation after all,—the interminable grotesques seem to form around a common center and rush off in headlong plunges of equal distraction.

It makes me tired to follow it. I will take a nap I guess.

Weir Mitchell: Dr. S. Weir Mitchell (1829–1914) was an eminent Philadelphia neurologist who advocated "rest cures" for nervous disorders. He was the author of *Diseases of the Nervous System, Especially of Women* (1881).

*   *   *

I don't know why I should write this.   105

I don't want to.

I don't feel able.

And I know John would think it absurd. But I *must* say what I feel and think in some way—it is such a relief!

But the effort is getting to be greater than the relief.

Half the time now I am awfully lazy, and lie down ever so much.   110

John says I mustn't lose my strength, and has me take cod liver oil and lots of tonics and things, to say nothing of ale and wine and rare meat.

Dear John! He loves me very dearly, and hates to have me sick. I tried to have a real earnest reasonable talk with him the other day, and tell him how I wish he would let me go and make a visit to Cousin Henry and Julia.

But he said I wasn't able to go, nor able to stand it after I got there; and I did not make out a very good case for myself, for I was crying before I had finished.

It is getting to be a great effort for me to think straight. Just this nervous weakness I suppose.

And dear John gathered me up in his arms, and just carried me upstairs   115
and laid me on the bed, and sat by me and read to me till it tired my head.

He said I was his darling and his comfort and all he had, and that I must take care of myself for his sake, and keep well.

He says no one but myself can help me out of it, that I must use my will and self-control and not let any silly fancies run away with me.

There's one comfort, the baby is well and happy, and does not have to occupy this nursery with the horrid wallpaper.

If we had not used it, that blessed child would have! What a fortunate escape! Why, I wouldn't have a child of mine, an impressionable little thing, live in such a room for worlds.

I never thought of it before, but it is lucky that John kept me here after all, 120
I can stand it so much easier than a baby, you see.

Of course I never mention it to them any more—I am too wise, but I keep watch of it all the same.

There are things in the wallpaper that nobody knows but me, or ever will.

Behind that outside pattern the dim shapes get clearer every day.

It is always the same shape, only very numerous.

And it is like a woman stooping down and creeping about behind that pat-   125
tern. I don't like it a bit. I wonder—I begin to think—I wish John would take me away from here!

It is so hard to talk with John about my case, because he is so wise, and because he loves me so.

But I tried it last night.

It was moonlight. The moon shines in all around just as the sun does.

I hate to see it sometimes, it creeps so slowly, and always comes in by one window or another.

John was asleep and I hated to waken him, so I kept still and watched the   130
moonlight on that undulating wallpaper till I felt creepy.

The faint figure behind seemed to shake the pattern, just as if she wanted
to get out.

I got up softly and went to feel and see if the paper *did* move, and when I
came back John was awake.

"What is it, little girl?" he said. "Don't go walking about like that—you'll
get cold."

I thought it was a good time to talk, so I told him that I really was not gaining here, and that I wished he would take me away.

"Why, darling!" said he, "our lease will be up in three weeks, and I can't see   135
how to leave before.

"The repairs are not done at home, and I cannot possibly leave town just
now. Of course if you were in any danger, I could and would, but you really are
better, dear, whether you can see it or not. I am a doctor, dear, and I know. You
are gaining flesh and color, your appetite is better, I feel really much easier
about you."

"I don't weigh a bit more," said I, "nor as much; and my appetite may be
better in the evening when you are here but it is worse in the morning when
you are away!"

"Bless her little heart!" said he with a big hug, "she shall be as sick as she
pleases! But now let's improve the shining hours by going to sleep, and talk
about it in the morning!"

"And you won't go away?" I asked gloomily.

"Why, how can I, dear? It is only three weeks more and then we will take a   140
nice little trip of a few days while Jennie is getting the house ready. Really dear
you are better!"

"Better in body perhaps —" I began, and stopped short, for he sat up
straight and looked at me with such a stern, reproachful look that I could not
say another word.

"My darling," said he, "I beg you, for my sake and for our child's sake, as well
as for your own, that you will never for one instant let that idea enter your mind!
There is nothing so dangerous, so fascinating, to a temperament like yours. It is
a false and foolish fancy. Can you trust me as a physician when I tell you so?"

So of course I said no more on that score, and we went to sleep before long.
He thought I was asleep first, but I wasn't, and lay there for hours trying to
decide whether that front pattern and the back pattern really did move together
or separately.

On a pattern like this, by daylight, there is a lack of sequence, a defiance of law,
that is a constant irritant to a normal mind.

The color is hideous enough, and unreliable enough, and infuriating   145
enough, but the pattern is torturing.

You think you have mastered it, but just as you get well underway in following, it turns a back-somersault and there you are. It slaps you in the face,
knocks you down, and tramples upon you. It is like a bad dream.

The outside pattern is a florid arabesque, reminding one of a fungus. If you can imagine a toadstool in joints, an interminable string of toadstools, budding and sprouting in endless convolutions — why, that is something like it.

That is, sometimes!

There is one marked peculiarity about this paper, a thing nobody seems to notice but myself, and that is that it changes as the light changes.

When the sun shoots in through the east window — I always watch for   150
that first long, straight ray — it changes so quickly that I never can quite believe it.

That is why I watch it always.

By moonlight — the moon shines in all night when there is a moon — I wouldn't know it was the same paper.

At night in any kind of light, in twilight, candlelight, lamplight, and worst of all by moonlight, it becomes bars! The outside pattern I mean, and the woman behind it is as plain as can be.

I didn't realize for a long time what the thing was that showed behind, that dim sub-pattern, but now I am quite sure it is a woman.

By daylight she is subdued, quiet. I fancy it is the pattern that keeps her so   155
still. It is so puzzling. It keeps me quiet by the hour.

I lie down ever so much now. John says it is good for me, and to sleep all I can.

Indeed he started the habit by making me lie down for an hour after each meal.

It is a very bad habit I am convinced, for you see I don't sleep.

And that cultivates deceit, for I don't tell them I'm awake — O, no!

The fact is I am getting a little afraid of John.   160

He seems very queer sometimes, and even Jennie has an inexplicable look.

It strikes me occasionally, just as a scientific hypothesis, — that perhaps it is the paper!

I have watched John when he did not know I was looking, and come into the room suddenly on the most innocent excuses, and I've caught him several times *looking at the paper*! And Jennie too. I caught Jennie with her hand on it once.

She didn't know I was in the room, and when I asked her in a quiet, a very quiet voice, with the most restrained manner possible, what she was doing with the paper — she turned around as if she had been caught stealing, and looked quite angry — asked me why I should frighten her so!

Then she said that the paper stained everything it touched, that she had   165
found yellow smooches on all my clothes and John's, and she wished we would be more careful!

Did not that sound innocent? But I know she was studying that pattern, and I am determined that nobody shall find it out but myself!

Life is very much more exciting now than it used to be. You see I have something more to expect, to look forward to, to watch. I really do eat better, and am more quiet than I was.

John is so pleased to see me improve! He laughed a little the other day, and said I seemed to be flourishing in spite of my wallpaper.

I turned it off with a laugh. I had no intention of telling him it was *because* of the wallpaper — he would make fun of me. He might even want to take me away.

I don't want to leave now until I have found it out. There is a week more, 170 and I think that will be enough.

I'm feeling ever so much better! I don't sleep much at night, for it is so interesting to watch developments; but I sleep a good deal in the daytime.

In the daytime it is tiresome and perplexing.

There are always new shoots on the fungus, and new shades of yellow all over it. I cannot keep count of them, though I have tried conscientiously.

It is the strangest yellow, that wallpaper! It makes me think of all the yellow things I ever saw — not beautiful ones like buttercups, but old foul, bad yellow things.

But there is something else about that paper — the smell! I noticed it the 175 moment we came into the room, but with so much air and sun it was not bad. Now we have had a week of fog and rain, and whether the windows are open or not, the smell is here.

It creeps all over the house.

I find it hovering in the dining-room, skulking in the parlor, hiding in the hall, lying in wait for me on the stairs.

It gets into my hair.

Even when I go to ride, if I turn my head suddenly and surprise it — there is that smell!

Such a peculiar odor, too! I have spent hours in trying to analyze it, to find 180 what it smelled like.

It is not bad — at first, and very gentle, but quite the subtlest, most enduring odor I ever met.

In this damp weather it is awful, I wake up in the night and find it hanging over me.

It used to disturb me at first. I thought seriously of burning the house — to reach the smell.

But now I am used to it. The only thing I can think of that it is like is the *color* of the paper! A yellow smell.

There is a very funny mark on this wall, low down, near the mopboard. 185 A streak that runs round the room. It goes behind every piece of furniture, except the bed, a long, straight, even *smooch*, as if it had been rubbed over and over.

I wonder how it was done and who did it, and what they did it for. Round and round and round — round and round and round — it makes me dizzy!

I really have discovered something at last.

Through watching so much at night, when it changes so, I have finally found out.

The front pattern *does* move — and no wonder! The woman behind shakes it!

Sometimes I think there are a great many women behind, and sometimes   190
only one, and she crawls around fast, and her crawling shakes it all over.

Then in the very bright spots she keeps still, and in the very shady spots she
just takes hold of the bars and shakes them hard.

And she is all the time trying to climb through. But nobody could climb
through that pattern — it strangles so; I think that is why it has so many heads.

They get through, and then the pattern strangles them off and turns them
upside down, and makes their eyes white!

If those heads were covered or taken off it would not be half so bad.

I think that woman gets out in the daytime!   195

And I'll tell you why — privately — I've seen her!

I can see her out of every one of my windows!

It is the same woman, I know, for she is always creeping, and most women
do not creep by daylight.

I see her in that long shaded lane, creeping up and down. I see her in those
dark grape arbors, creeping all around the garden.

I see her on that long road under the trees, creeping along, and when a   200
carriage comes she hides under the blackberry vines.

I don't blame her a bit. It must be very humiliating to be caught creeping
by daylight!

I always lock the door when I creep by daylight. I can't do it at night, for I
know John would suspect something at once.

And John is so queer now, that I don't want to irritate him. I wish he would
take another room! Besides, I don't want anybody to get that woman out at
night but myself.

I often wonder if I could see her out of all the windows at once.

But, turn as fast as I can, I can only see out of one at one time.   205

And though I always see her, she *may* be able to creep faster than I can turn!

I have watched her sometimes away off in the open country, creeping as
fast as a cloud shadow in a high wind.

If only that top pattern could be gotten off from the under one! I mean to try it,
little by little.

I have found out another funny thing, but I shan't tell it this time! It does
not do to trust people too much.

There are only two more days to get this paper off, and I believe John is be-   210
ginning to notice. I don't like the look in his eyes.

And I heard him ask Jennie a lot of professional questions, about me. She
had a very good report to give.

She said I slept a good deal in the daytime.

John knows I don't sleep very well at night, for all I'm so quiet!

He asked me all sorts of questions too, and pretended to be very loving
and kind.

As if I couldn't see through him!   215

Still, I don't wonder he acts so, sleeping under this paper for three months.

It only interests me, but I feel sure John and Jennie are secretly affected by it.

*   *   *

Hurrah! This is the last day, but it is enough. John is to stay in town over night, and won't be out until this evening.

Jennie wanted to sleep with me—the sly thing! But I told her I should undoubtedly rest better for a night all alone.

That was clever, for really I wasn't alone a bit! As soon as it was moonlight and   220
that poor thing began to crawl and shake the pattern, I got up and ran to help her.

I pulled and she shook, I shook and she pulled, and before morning we had peeled off yards of that paper.

A strip about as high as my head and half around the room.

And then when the sun came and that awful pattern began to laugh at me, I declared I would finish it to-day!

We go away to-morrow, and they are moving all my furniture down again to leave things as they were before.

Jennie looked at the wall in amazement, but I told her merrily that I did it   225
out of pure spite at the vicious thing.

She laughed and said she wouldn't mind doing it herself, but I must not get tired.

How she betrayed herself that time!

But I am here, and no person touches this paper but me,—not *alive*!

She tried to get me out of the room—it was too patent! But I said it was so quiet and empty and clean now that I believed I would lie down again and sleep all I could, and not to wake me even for dinner—I would call when I woke.

So now she is gone, and the servants are gone, and the things are gone,   230
and there is nothing left but that great bedstead nailed down, with the canvas mattress we found on it.

We shall sleep downstairs to-night, and take the boat home to-morrow.

I quite enjoy the room, now it is bare again.

How those children did tear about here!

This bedstead is fairly gnawed!

But I must get to work.   235

I have locked the door and thrown the key down into the front path.

I don't want to go out, and I don't want to have anybody come in, till John comes.

I want to astonish him.

I've got a rope up here that even Jennie did not find. If that woman does get out, and tries to get away, I can tie her!

But I forgot I could not reach far without anything to stand on!   240

This bed will *not* move!

I tried to lift and push it until I was lame, and then I got so angry I bit off a little piece at one corner—but it hurt my teeth.

Then I peeled off all the paper I could reach standing on the floor. It sticks horribly and the pattern just enjoys it! All those strangled heads and bulbous eyes and waddling fungus growths just shriek with derision!

I am getting angry enough to do something desperate. To jump out of the window would be admirable exercise, but the bars are too strong even to try.

Besides I wouldn't do it. Of course not. I know well enoug that is improper and might be misconstrued.

I don't like to *look* out of the windows even—there are creeping women, and they creep so fast.

I wonder if they all come out of that wallpaper as I did?

But I am securely fastened now by my well-hidden rope—you don't get *me* out in the road there!

I suppose I shall have to get back behind the pattern when it comes night, and that is hard!

It is so pleasant to be out in this great room and creep around as I please!   250

I don't want to go outside. I won't, even if Jennie asks me to.

For outside you have to creep on the ground, and everything is green instead of yellow.

But here I can creep smoothly on the floor, and my shoulder just fits in that long smooch around the wall, so I cannot lose my way.

Why, there's John at the door!

It is no use, young man, you can't open it!   255

How he does call and pound!

Now he's crying for an axe.

It would be a shame to break down that beautiful door!

"John dear!" said I in the gentlest voice, "the key is down by the front steps, under a plantain leaf!"

That silenced him for a few moments.   260

Then he said—very quietly indeed, "Open the door, my darling!"

"I can't," said I. "The key is down by the front door under a plantain leaf!"

And then I said it again, several times, very gently and slowly, and said it so often that he had to go and see, and he got it of course, and came in. He stopped short by the door.

"What is the matter?" he cried. "For God's sake, what are you doing!"

I kept on creeping just the same, but I looked at him over my shoulder.   265

"I've got out at last," said I, "in spite of you and Jane. And I've pulled off most of the paper, so you can't put me back!"

Now why should that man have fainted? But he did, and right across my path by the wall, so that I had to creep over him every time!   [1892]

≡ THINKING ABOUT THE TEXT

1. What psychological stages does the narrator go through as the story progresses?

2. How does the wallpaper function as a symbol in this story? What do you conclude about the narrator when she becomes increasingly interested in the woman she finds there?

3. Explain your ultimate view of the narrator, by using specific details of the story and by identifying some of the warrants or assumptions behind

your opinion. Do you admire her? Sympathize with her? Recoil from her? What would you say to someone who simply dismisses her as crazy?

4. The story is narrated in the present tense. Would its effect be different if it were narrated in the past tense? Why, or why not?

5. In real life, Gilman's husband and her doctor were two separate people. In the story, the narrator's husband is her doctor as well. Why do you think Gilman made this change? What is the effect of her combining husband and doctor?

CHARLOTTE PERKINS GILMAN
Why I Wrote "The Yellow Wallpaper"

Gilman published the following piece in the October 1913 issue of her magazine, The Forerunner.

Many and many a reader has asked that. When the story first came out, in the *New England Magazine* about 1891, a Boston physician made protest in *The Transcript.* Such a story ought not to be written, he said; it was enough to drive anyone mad to read it.

Another physician, in Kansas I think, wrote to say that it was the best description of incipient insanity he had ever seen, and — begging my pardon — had I been there?

Now the story of the story is this:

For many years I suffered from a severe and continuous nervous breakdown tending to melancholia — and beyond. During about the third year of this trouble I went, in devout faith and some faint stir of hope, to a noted specialist in nervous diseases, the best known in the country. This wise man put me to bed and applied the rest cure, to which a still good physique responded so promptly that, he concluded there was nothing much the matter with me, and sent me home with solemn advice to "live as domestic a life as far as possible," to "have but two hours' intellectual life a day," and "never to touch pen, brush, or pencil again as long as I lived." This was in 1887.

I went home and obeyed those directions for some three months, and came so near the border line of utter mental ruin that I could see over.

Then, using the remnants of intelligence that remained, and helped by a wise friend, I cast the noted specialist's advice to the winds and went to work again — work, the normal life of every human being; work, in which is joy and growth and service, without which one is a pauper and a parasite; ultimately recovering some measure of power.

Being naturally moved to rejoicing by this narrow escape, I wrote *The Yellow Wallpaper*, with its embellishments and additions to carry out the ideal (I never had hallucinations or objections to my mural decorations) and sent a copy to the physician who so nearly drove me mad. He never acknowledged it.

The little book is valued by alienists° and as a good specimen of one kind of literature. It has to my knowledge saved one woman from a similar fate — so terrifying her family that they let her out into normal activity and she recovered.

But the best result is this. Many years later I was told that the great specialist had admitted to friends of his that he had altered his treatment of neurasthenia since reading *The Yellow Wallpaper.*

It was not intended to drive people crazy, but to save people from being   10
driven crazy, and it worked.   *[1913]*

alienists: Nineteenth-century term for psychiatrists.

≣ THINKING ABOUT THE TEXT

1. S. Weir Mitchell was the "noted specialist in nervous diseases" (para. 4) whom Gilman mentions. Yet she does not identify him by name. Why not, do you think? Some historians argue that, contrary to Gilman's claim here, Mitchell continued to believe his "rest cure" valid. Does this issue of fact matter to your judgment of her piece? Why, or why not?

2. Look again at Gilman's last sentence. Do you believe that her story could indeed "save people from being driven crazy"? Why, or why not?

3. Does this piece as a whole affect your interpretation and opinion of Gilman's story? Why, or why not? In general, how much do you think readers of a story should know about its author's life?

S. WEIR MITCHELL
From The Evolution of the Rest Treatment

Charlotte Perkins Gilman sought help from Silas Weir Mitchell (1829–1914) because he was a well-known and highly respected physician who had treated many women's mental problems. Mitchell developed his "rest cure" while serving as an army surgeon during the Civil War. Ironically, like Gilman he was also a writer. Besides producing numerous monographs on medical subjects, he published many short stories and novels. The following is an excerpt from a lecture that Mitchell gave to the Philadelphia Neurological Society in 1904, twelve years after "The Yellow Wallpaper" appeared. As you will see, Mitchell was still enthusiastic about his "rest cure," although he had changed it in certain respects since devising it.

I have been asked to come here to-night to speak to you on some subject connected with nervous disease. I had hoped to have had ready a fitting paper for so notable an occasion, but have been prevented by public engagements and private business so as to make it quite impossible. I have, therefore, been driven to ask whether it would be agreeable if I should speak in regard to the mode in which the treatment of disease by rest was evolved. This being favorably received, I am here this evening to say a few words on that subject.

You all know full well that the art of cure rests upon a number of sciences, and that what we do in medicine, we cannot always explain, and that our methods are far from having the accuracy involved in the term scientific. Very often, however, it is found that what comes to us through some accident or popular use and proves of value, is defensible in the end by scientific explanatory research. This was the case as regards the treatment I shall briefly consider for you to-night.

The first indication I ever had of the great value of mere rest in disease, was during the Civil War, when there fell into the hands of Doctors Morehouse, Keen, and myself, a great many cases of what we called acute exhaustion. These were men, who, being tired by much marching, gave out suddenly at the end of some unusual exertion, and remained for weeks, perhaps months, in a pitiable state of what we should call today, Neurasthenia. In these war cases, it came on with strange abruptness. It was more extreme and also more certainly curable than are most of the graver male cases which now we are called on to treat.

I have seen nothing exactly like it in civil experience, but the combination of malaria, excessive exertion, and exposure provided cases such as no one sees today. Complete rest and plentiful diet usually brought these men up again and in many instances enabled them to return to the front.

In 1872 I had charge of a man who had locomotor ataxia° with extreme pain in the extremities, and while making some unusual exertion, he broke his right thigh. This confined him to his bed for three months, and the day he got up, he broke his left thigh. This involved another three months of rest. At the end of that time he confessed with satisfaction that his ataxia was better, and that he was, as he remained thereafter, free from pain. I learned from this, and two other cases, that in ataxia the bones are brittle, and I learned also that rest in bed is valuable in a proportion of such cases. You may perceive that my attention was thus twice drawn towards the fact that mere rest had certain therapeutic values.

In 1874 Mrs. G., of B ——, Maine, came to see me in the month of January. I have described her case elsewhere, so that it is needless to go into detail here, except to say that she was a lady of ample means, with no special troubles or annoyances, but completely exhausted by having had children in rapid succession and from having undertaken to do charitable and other work to an extent far beyond her strength. When first I saw this tall woman, large, gaunt, weighing under a hundred pounds, her complexion pale and acneous, and heard her story, I was for a time in a state of such therapeutic despair as usually fell upon physicians of that day when called upon to treat such cases. She had been to Spas, to physicians of the utmost eminence, passed through the hands

ataxia: An inability to control muscular movements that is symptomatic of some nervous diseases.

of gynecologists, worn spinal supporters, and taken every tonic known to the books. When I saw her she was unable to walk up stairs. Her exercise was limited to moving feebly up and down her room, a dozen times a day. She slept little and, being very intelligent, felt deeply her inability to read or write. Any such use of the eyes caused headache and nausea. Conversation tired her, and she had by degrees accepted a life of isolation. She was able partially to digest and retain her meals if she lay down in a noiseless and darkened room. Any disturbance or the least excitement, in short, any effort, caused nausea and immediate rejection of her meal. With care she could retain enough food to preserve her life and hardly to do more. Anemia, which we had then no accurate means of measuring, had been met by half a dozen forms of iron, all of which were said to produce headache, and generally to disagree with her. Naturally enough, her case had been pronounced to be hysteria, but calling names may relieve a doctor and comfort him in failure, but does not always assist the patient, and to my mind there was more of a general condition of nervous excitability due to the extreme of weakness than I should have been satisfied to label with the apologetic label hysteria.

I sat beside this woman day after day, hearing her pitiful story, and distressed that a woman, young, once handsome, and with every means of enjoyment in life should be condemned to what she had been told was a state of hopeless invalidism. After my third or fourth visit, with a deep sense that everything had been done for her that able men could with reason suggest, and many things which reason never could have suggested, she said to me that I appeared to have nothing to offer which had not been tried over and over again. I asked her for another day before she gave up the hope which had brought her to me. The night brought counsel. The following morning I said to her, if you are at rest you appear to digest your meals better. "Yes," she said. "I have been told that on that account I ought to lie in bed. It has been tried, but when I remain in bed for a few days, I lose all appetite, have intense constipation, and get up feeling weaker than when I went to bed. Please do not ask me to go to bed." Nevertheless, I did, and a week in bed justified her statements. She threw up her meals undigested, and was manifestly worse for my experiment. Sometimes the emesis° was mere regurgitation, sometimes there was nausea and violent straining, with consequent extreme exhaustion. She declared that unless she had the small exercise of walking up and down her room, she was infallibly worse. I was here between two difficulties. That she needed rest I saw, that she required some form of exercise I also saw. How could I unite the two?

As I sat beside her, with a keen sense of defeat, it suddenly occurred to me that some time before, I had seen a man, known as a layer on of hands, use very rough rubbing for a gentleman who was in a state of general paresis.° Mr. S. had asked me if I objected to this man rubbing him. I said no, and that I should like to see him do so, as he had relieved, to my knowledge, cases of rheumatic stiffness. I was present at two sittings and saw this man rub my patient. He kept him sitting in a chair at the time and was very rough and violent like

---

emesis: Vomiting.   **paresis:** Brain syphilis.

the quacks now known as osteopaths. I told him he had injured my patient by his extreme roughness, and that if he rubbed him at all he must be more gentle. He took the hint and as a result there was every time a notable but temporary gain. Struck with this, I tried to have rubbing used on spinal cases, but those who tried to do the work were inefficient, and I made no constant use of it. It remained, however, on my mind, and recurred to me as I sat beside this wreck of a useful and once vigorous woman. The thought was fertile. I asked myself why rubbing might not prove competent to do for the muscles and tardy circulation what voluntary exercise does. I said to myself, this may be exercise without exertion, and wondered why I had not long before had this pregnant view of the matter.

Suffice it to say that I brought a young woman to Mrs. G.'s bedside and told her how I thought she ought to be rubbed. The girl was clever, and developed talent in that direction, and afterwards became the first of that great number of people who have since made a livelihood by massage. I watched the rubbing two or three times, giving instructions, in fact developing out of the clumsy massage I had seen, the manual of a therapeutic means, at that time entirely new to me. A few days later I fell upon the idea of giving electric passive exercise and cautiously added this second agency. Meanwhile, as she had always done best when secluded, I insisted on entire rest and shut out friends, relatives, books, and letters. I had some faith that I should succeed. In ten days I was sure the woman had found a new tonic, hope, and blossomed like a rose. Her symptoms passed away one by one. I was soon able to add to her diet, to feed her between meals, to give her malt daily, and, after a time, to conceal in it full doses of pyro-phosphates of iron. First, then, I had found two means which enabled me to use rest in bed without causing the injurious effects of unassisted rest; secondly, I had discovered that massage was a tonic of extraordinary value; thirdly, I had learned that with this combination of seclusion, massage, and electricity, I could overfeed the patient until I had brought her into a state of entire health. I learned later the care which had to be exercised in getting these patients out of bed. But this does not concern us now. In two months she gained forty pounds and was a cheerful, blooming woman, fit to do as she pleased. She has remained, save for time's ravage, what I made her.

It may strike you as interesting that for a while I was not fully aware of the enormous value of a therapeutic discovery which employed no new agents, but owed its usefulness to a combination of means more or less well known.

Simple rest as a treatment had been suggested, but not in this class of cases. Massage has a long history. Used, I think, as a luxury by the Orientals for ages, it was employed by Ling in 1813. It never attained perfection in the hands of the Swedes, nor do they to-day understand the proper use of this agent. It was over and over recognized in Germany, but never generally accepted. In France, at a later period, Dreyfus, in 1841, wrote upon it and advised its use, as did Recamier and Lainé in 1868. Two at least of these authors thought it useful as a general agent, but no one seems to have accepted their views, nor was its value as a tonic spoken of in the books on therapeutics or recommended on any text-book as a powerful toning agent. It was used here in the Rest

Treatment, and this, I think, gave it vogue and caused the familiar use of this invaluable therapeutic measure.

A word before I close. My first case left me in May, 1874, and shortly afterwards I began to employ the same method in other cases, being careful to choose only those which seemed best suited to it. My first mention in print of the treatment was in 1875, in the Sequin Lectures, Vol. 1, No. 4, "Rest in the Treatment of Disease." In that paper I first described Mrs. G.'s case. My second paper was in 1877, an address before the Medico-Chirurgical faculty of Maryland, and the same year I printed my book on "Rest Treatment." The one mistake in the book was the title. I was, however, so impressed at the time by the extraordinary gain in flesh and blood under this treatment that I made it too prominent in the title of the book. Let me say that for a long time the new treatment was received with the utmost incredulity. When I spoke in my papers of the people who had gained half a pound a day or more, my results were questioned and ridiculed in this city as approaching charlatanism. At a later date in England some physicians were equally wanting in foresight and courtesy. It seems incredible that any man who was a member of the British Medical Association could have said that he would rather see his patients not get well than have them cured by such a method as that. It was several years before it was taken up by Professor Goodell, and it was a longer time in making its way in Europe when by mere accident it came to be first used by Professor William Playfair.

I suffered keenly at that time from this unfair criticism, as any sensitive man must have done, for some who were eminent in the profession said of it and of me things which were most inconsiderate. Over and over in consultation I was rejected with ill-concealed scorn. I made no reply to my critics. I knew that time would justify me: I have added a long since accepted means of helping those whom before my day few helped. This is a sufficient reward for silence, patience, and self-faith. I fancy that there are in this room many who have profited for themselves and their patients by the thought which evolved the Rest Treatment as I sat by the bedside of my first rest case in 1874. Playfair said of it at the British Association that he had nothing to add to it and nothing to omit, and to this day no one has differed as to his verdict.

How fully the use of massage has been justified by the later scientific studies of Lauder Brunton, myself, and others you all know. It is one of the most scientific of remedial methods.   *[1904]*

≡ **THINKING ABOUT THE TEXT**

1. How would you describe Mitchell's tone in this lecture? What self-image does he seem to cultivate? Support your answers by referring to specific words in the text.

2. Why does Mitchell consider Mrs. G.'s case significant? In what ways does she resemble Gilman and the narrator of Gilman's story?

3. Mitchell indicates that his patients have included male as well as female hysterics. Are we therefore justified in concluding that gender did not matter much in his application of the "rest cure"? Why, or why not?

JOHN HARVEY KELLOGG

From *The Ladies' Guide in Health and Disease*

John Harvey Kellogg (1852–1943) was an American physician who wrote much advice about how to discipline one's sexual desires and, in the case of women, how to be a good mother. As founder and superintendent of the Battle Creek Sanitarium in Michigan, Dr. Kellogg urged that his patients eat cereals as part of their treatment, and eventually his brother established the cereal company that bears their family name. Dr. Kellogg's keen interest in cereals and health foods is satirized in T. Coraghessan Boyle's 1993 novel, The Road to Wellville, *and the film based on that book. The following piece is an excerpt from Kellogg's 1882* Ladies' Guide in Health and Disease: Girlhood, Maidenhood, Wifehood, Motherhood. *In this selection, he virtually equates womanhood with motherhood and discusses what a woman must do to produce outstanding children. Kellogg's advice reflects the view that much of his society held about women—or at least about middle- and upper-class white women. His discussion of "puerperal mania" is especially relevant to Gilman's story.*

The special influence of the mother begins with the moment of conception. In fact it is possible that the mental condition at the time of the generative act has much to do with determining the character of the child, though it is generally conceded that at this time the influence of the father is greater than that of the mother. Any number of instances have occurred in which a drunken father has impressed upon his child the condition of his nervous system to such a degree as to render permanent in the child the staggering gait and maudlin manner which in his own case was a transient condition induced by the poisonous influence of alcohol. A child born as the result of a union in which both parents were in a state of beastly intoxication was idiotic.

Another fact might be added to impress the importance that the new being should be supplied from the very beginning of its existence with the very best conditions possible. Indeed, it is desirable to go back still further, and secure a proper preparation for the important function of maternity. The qualities which go to make up individuality of character are the result of the summing up of a long line of influences, too subtle and too varied to admit of full control, but still, to some degree at least, subject to management. The dominance of law is nowhere more evident than in the relation of ante-natal influences to character.

The hap-hazard way in which human beings are generated leaves no room for surprise that the race should deteriorate. No stock-breeder would expect anything but ruin should he allow his animals to propagate with no attention to their physical conditions or previous preparation.

Finding herself in a pregnant condition, the mother should not yield to the depressing influences which often crowd upon her. The anxieties and fears which women sometimes yield themselves to, grow with encouragement, until they become so absorbed as to be capable of producing a profoundly evil impression on the child. The true mother who is prepared for the functions of maternity, will welcome the evidence of pregnancy, and joyfully enter upon the Heaven-given task of molding a human character, of bringing into the world a new being whose life-history may involve the destinies of nations, or change the current of human thought for generations to come.

The pregnant mother should cultivate cheerfulness of mind and calmness of temper, but should avoid excitements of all kinds, such as theatrical performances, public contests of various descriptions, etc. Anger, envy, irritability of temper, and, in fact, all the passions and propensities should be held in check. The fickleness of desire and the constantly varying whims which characterize the pregnant state in some women should not be regarded as uncontrollable, and to be yielded to as the only means of appeasing them. The mother should be gently encouraged to resist such tendencies when they become at all marked, and to assist her in the effort, her husband should endeavor to engage her mind by interesting conversation, reading, and various harmless and pleasant diversions.   5

If it is desired that the child should possess a special aptitude for any particular art or pursuit, during the period of pregnancy the mother's mind should be constantly directed in this channel. If artistic taste or skill is the trait desired, the mother should be surrounded by works of art of a high order of merit. She should read art, think art, talk, and write about art, and if possible, herself engage in the close practical study of some one or more branches of art, as painting, drawing, etching, or modeling. If ability for authorship is desired, then the mother should devote herself assiduously to literature. It is not claimed that by following these suggestions any mother can make of her children great artists or authors at will; but it is certain that by this means the greatest possibilities in individual cases can be attained; and it is certain that decided results have been secured by close attention to the principles laid down. It should be understood, however, that not merely a formal and desultory effort on the part of the mother is what is required. The theme selected must completely absorb her mind. It must be the one idea of her waking thoughts and the model on which is formed the dreams of her sleeping hours.

The question of diet during pregnancy as before stated is a vitally important one as regards the interests of the child. A diet into which enters largely such unwholesome articles as mustard, pepper, hot sauces, spices, and other stimulating condiments, engenders a love for stimulants in the disposition of the infant. Tea and coffee, especially if used to excess, undoubtedly tend in the same direction. We firmly believe that we have, in the facts first stated, the key to the constant increase in the consumption of ardent spirits. The children of the present generation inherit from their condiment-consuming, tea-, coffee-, and liquor-drinking, and tobacco-using parents, not simply a readiness for the acquirement of the habits mentioned, but a propensity for the use of stimulants which in persons of weak will-power and those whose circumstances are not the most favorable, becomes irresistible.

The present generation is also suffering in consequence of the impoverished diet of its parents. The modern custom of bolting the flour from the different grains has deprived millions of infants and children of the necessary supply of bone-making material, thus giving rise to a greatly increased frequency of the various diseases which arise from imperfect bony structure, as rickets, caries, premature decay of the teeth, etc. The proper remedy is the disuse of fine-flour bread and all other bolted grain preparations. Graham-flour bread, oatmeal, cracked wheat, and similar preparations, should be relied upon as the leading articles of diet. Supplemented by milk, the whole-grain preparations constitute a complete form of nourishment, and render a large amount of animal food not only unnecessary but really harmful on account of its stimulating character. It is by no means so necessary as is generally supposed that meat, fish, fowl, and flesh in various forms should constitute a large element of the dietary of the pregnant or nursing mother in order to furnish adequate nourishment for the developing child. We have seen the happiest results follow the employment of a strictly vegetarian dietary, and do not hesitate to advise moderation in the use of flesh food, though we do not recommend the entire discontinuance of its use by the pregnant mother who has been accustomed to use it freely.

A nursing mother should at once suspend nursing if she discovers that pregnancy has again occurred. The continuance of nursing under such circumstances is to the disadvantage of three individuals, the mother, the infant at the breast, and the developing child.

Sexual indulgence during pregnancy may be suspended with decided benefit to both mother and child. The most ancient medical writers call attention to the fact that by the practice of continence° during gestation, the pains of childbirth are greatly mitigated. The injurious influences upon the child of the gratification of the passions during the period when its character is being formed, is undoubtedly much greater than is usually supposed. We have no doubt that this is a common cause of the transmission of libidinous tendencies to the child; and that the tendency to abortion is induced by sexual indulgence has long been a well-established fact. The females of most animals resolutely resist the advances of the males during this period, being guided in harmony with natural law by their natural instincts which have been less perverted in them than in human beings. The practice of continence during pregnancy is also enforced in the harems of the East, which fact leads to the practice of abortion among women of this class who are desirous of remaining the special favorites of the common husband.

The general health of the mother must be kept up in every way. It is especially important that the regularity of the bowels should be maintained. Proper diet and as much physical exercise as can be taken are the best means for ac-

continence: Chastity, abstinence, or restraint.

complishing this. When constipation is allowed to exist, the infant as well as the mother suffers. The effete products which should be promptly removed from the body, being long retained, are certain to find their way back into the system again, poisoning not only the blood of the mother but that of the developing fetus. . . .

Puerperal Mania. —This form of mental disease is most apt to show itself about two weeks after delivery. Although, fortunately, of not very frequent occurrence, it is a most serious disorder when it does occur, and hence we may with propriety introduce the following somewhat lengthy, but most graphic description of the disease from the pen of Dr. Ramsbotham, an eminent English physician: —

"In mania there is almost always, at the very commencement, a troubled, agitated, and hurried manner, a restless eye, an unnaturally anxious, suspicious, and unpleasing expression of face; —sometimes it is pallid, at others more flushed than usual; —an unaccustomed irritability of temper, and impatience of control or contradiction; a vacillation of purpose, or loss of memory; sometimes a rapid succession of contradictory orders are issued, or a paroxysm of excessive anger is excited about the merest trifle. Occasionally, one of the first indications will be a sullen obstinacy, or listlessness and stubborn silence. The patient lies on her back, and can by no means be persuaded to reply to the questions of her attendants, or she will repeat them, as an echo, until, all at once, without any apparent cause, she will break out into a torrent of language more or less incoherent, and her words will follow each other with surprising rapidity. These symptoms will sometimes show themselves rather suddenly, on the patient's awakening from a disturbed and unrefreshing sleep, or they may supervene more slowly when she has been harassed with wakefulness for three or four previous nights in succession, or perhaps ever since her delivery. She will very likely then become impressed with the idea that some evil has befallen her husband, or, what is still more usual, her child; that it is dead or stolen; and if it be brought to her, nothing can persuade her it is her own; she supposes it to belong to somebody else; or she will fancy that her husband is unfaithful to her, or that he and those about her have conspired to poison her. Those persons who are naturally the objects of her deepest and most devout affection, are regarded by her with jealousy, suspicion, and hatred. This is particularly remarkable with regard to her newly born infant; and I have known many instances where attempts have been made to destroy it when it has been incautiously left within her power. Sometimes, though rarely, may be observed a great anxiety regarding the termination of her own case, or a firm conviction that she is speedily about to die. I have observed upon occasions a constant movement of the lips, while the mouth was shut; or the patient is incessantly rubbing the inside of her lips with her fingers, or thrusting them far back into her mouth; and if questions are asked, particularly if she be desired to put out her tongue, she will often compress the lips forcibly together, as if with an obstinate determination of resistance. One peculiarity attending some cases of puerperal mania is the immorality and obscenity of the expressions uttered; they are often such, indeed, as to excite our astonishment that women in a respectable station of society could ever have become acquainted with such language."

The insanity of childbirth differs from that of pregnancy in that in the latter cases the patient is almost always melancholy,° while in the former there is active mania. Derangement of the digestive organs is a constant accompaniment of the disease.

If the patient has no previous or hereditary tendency to insanity, the prospect of a quite speedy recovery is good. The result is seldom immediately fatal, but the patient not infrequently remains in a condition of mental unsoundness for months or even years, and sometimes permanently.

Treatment: When there is reason to suspect a liability to puerperal mania from previous mental disease or from hereditary influence, much can be done to ward off an attack. Special attention must be paid to the digestive organs, which should be regulated by proper food and simple means to aid digestion. The tendency to sleeplessness must be combatted by careful nursing, light massage at night, rubbing of the spine, alternate hot and cold applications to the spine, cooling the head by cloths wrung out of cold water, and the use of the warm bath at bed time. These measures are often successful in securing sleep when all other measures fail.

The patient must be kept very quiet. Visitors, even if near relatives, must not be allowed when the patient is at all nervous or disturbed, and it is best to exclude nearly every one from the sick-room with the exception of the nurse, who should be a competent and experienced person.

When the attack has really begun, the patient must have the most vigilant watchcare, not being left for a moment. It is much better to care for the patient at home, when possible to do so efficiently, than to take her to an asylum.

When evidences of returning rationality appear, the greatest care must be exercised to prevent too great excitement. Sometimes a change of air, if the patient is sufficiently strong, physically, will at this period prove eminently beneficial. A visit from a dear friend will sometimes afford a needed stimulus to the dormant faculties. Such cases as these of course require intelligent medical supervision.   *[1882]*

melancholy: Mental state characterized by severe depression, somatic problems, and hallucinations or delusions.

☰ THINKING ABOUT THE TEXT

1. What specific responsibilities does Kellogg assign to women? What are some key assumptions he makes about them?

2. Quite possibly Kellogg would have said that the narrator of Gilman's story suffers from puerperal mania. What details of the story would support this diagnosis? What significant details of the narrator's life, if

any, would Kellogg be ignoring if he saw her as *merely* a case of puerperal mania?

3. If Kellogg's advice were published today, what parts of it do you think readers would accept? What parts do you think many readers would reject?

☰ WRITING ABOUT ISSUES

1. After reading the three essays given here, research women's psychological disorders of the nineteenth century and write an essay that argues that those "disorders" were the result of mule attitudes toward women.

2. Research the term "female hysteria" and write a report that includes the ideas of S. Weir Mitchell and other prominent nineteenth-century doctors. Include in your report your evaluation of their credibility.

3. Research mental illness in America from the Puritans to the present. Write an essay that argues that mental illness is connected to the culture it occurs in.

4. Research such contemporary psychological problems as depression, bulimia, anorexia, and dissociative identity disorders. Write an essay that tries to explain why these diseases seem to affect mostly women.

CHAPTER 10

Doing Justice

Thinking about literature involves people making judgments about other people's views. Throughout your course, you have been making judgments as you interpret and evaluate written works, including the texts in this book and those produced by the class. You have been deciding also how you feel about positions expressed by your teacher and classmates. In all these acts of judgment, you have considered where you stand on general issues of aesthetics, ethics, politics, religion, and law.

Outside school, you judge things all the time, though you may not always be aware that you are doing so. You may be more conscious of your judgments when other people disagree with you, when you face multiple options, when you are trying to understand something complex, when your decisions will have significant consequences, or when you must review an act you have already committed. Some people are quite conscious that they make judgments because they have the political, professional, or institutional authority to enforce their will. Of course, these people may wind up being judged by whomever they dominate, and they may even face active revolt.

A term closely related to *judgment* is *justice*, which many people associate with judgments that are wise, fair, and sensitive to the parties involved. In this sense, justice is an ideal, which may not always be achieved in real life. Indeed, though communities hope their police departments and courts will act soundly, sometimes representatives of our legal institutions are accused of violating justice instead of upholding it. Much, of course, depends on how *justice* is defined in any particular case, and equally crucial is who defines it. Many works of literature have challenged laws of the society in which they were written, while others have at least questioned or complicated the notions of justice prevailing in their culture. Often, literature has probed the complexities of situations that in real life are resolved as clear victories for one particular party. In this respect, literature draws attention to issues that we may normally oversimplify or overlook.

This chapter begins by juxtaposing Nathaniel Hawthorne's famous tale, "Young Goodman Brown," and a modern-day story by Toni Cade Bambara that focuses on the psychological effects of young people confronting injustice for the first time. Poems of racial injustice by Countee Cullen and Natasha Trethewey follow. Next, poems by William Blake, Martín Espada, and Mark Jarman imagine what a world of ideal justice would be like. Then we present four poems that examine the responsibility of people who inflict, witness, or learn about punishments. In Robert Browning's classic poem "My Last Duchess," the speaker takes revenge against his wife; we add Gabriel Spera's contemporary poem "My Ex-Husband," which presents the reverse perspective. In the subsequent cluster, we turn to Sophocles' ancient Greek tragedy *Antigone*, a classic conflict between an individual's and a state's visions of justice. We accompany this drama with two newspaper accounts of contemporary women who can be seen as present-day Antigones insofar as they, too, challenge governments they deem oppressive. The next cluster also treats the issue of what to do when faced with laws one considers unjust. More specifically, Henry David Thoreau's classic essay "Civil Disobedience," Rebecca Solnit's commentary on the text, and Martin Luther King Jr.'s well-known "Letter from Birmingham Jail" argue for nonviolent resistance. After this cluster is one centered on Flannery O'Connor's troubling story "A Good Man Is Hard to Find," in which a character called The Misfit becomes homicidal in the cause of cosmic justice. O'Connor's explanation of this story follows with comments by three critics who argue over her analysis. We then present two contemporary essayists arguing over the influence of brain research on our justice system. We conclude with Ida Fink's play *The Table*, as Holocaust survivors prepare for a trial of their Nazi persecutors. To create a larger context, we include an account of an essay from the Nazi deportation along with a reflection on Holocaust survivors' capacity to recall facts from their horrific past.

NATHANIEL HAWTHORNE, "Young Goodman Brown"

TONI CADE BAMBARA, "The Lesson"

Much fiction depicts characters learning about injustice they had not been aware of before. They move from relative innocence to knowledge of corruption. Moreover, they must now figure out what to do about the wrongdoing they have found. They must also decide how, in general, they will live in a world where virtue mixes with vice. The title character of Nathaniel Hawthorne's classic tale "Young Goodman Brown" comes to believe that his New England community is satanic, and therefore he grows alienated from it. But does he thereby become excessively self-righteous? In Toni Cade Bambara's modern-day story "The Lesson," the narrator is an African American girl who must decide what to think when a woman of her race tries to teach her that whites monopolize society's wealth. On issues of justice, the protagonists of both stories undergo discovery and reflection. Readers of their narratives are encouraged to do the same.

▬ BEFORE YOU READ

In his memoir *Fatheralong* (1994), John Edgar Wideman notes that his father's attitude toward society differs from that of his late mother. "The first rule of my father's world," Wideman writes, "is that you stand alone. Alone, alone, alone. . . . Accept the bottom line, icy clarity, of the one thing you can rely on: nothing" (50). On the other hand, "My mother's first rule was love. She refused to believe she was alone. *Be not dismayed, what e'er betides / God will take care of you*" (51). What were you taught about society as you were growing up? What specific messages were you given about it by your parents or the people who raised you? How did they convey these messages to you?

NATHANIEL HAWTHORNE

Young Goodman Brown

Nathaniel Hawthorne (1804–1864) was born in Salem, Massachusetts, into a family that was founded by New England's Puritan colonists. This lineage troubled Hawthorne, especially because his ancestor John Hathorne was involved as a judge in the Salem witch trials. After graduating from Maine's Bowdoin College in 1825, Hawthorne returned to Salem and began his career as a writer. In 1832, he self-published his first novel, Fanshawe, *but considered it an artistic as well as a commercial failure and tried to destroy all unsold copies of it. He was more successful* with his *1832 short-story collection* Twice-Told Tales *(reprinted and enlarged in 1842). In the early 1840s, Hawthorne worked as a surveyor in the Boston Custom House, briefly joined the Utopian community of Brook Farm, and then moved to Concord. There he published several children's books and lived with his wife, Sophia, in writer Ralph Waldo Emerson's former home, the Old Manse. In 1846, he produced a second collection of short stories,* Mosses from an Old Manse. *For the next three years, Hawthorne worked in a custom house in his hometown of Salem before publishing his most famous analysis of Puritan culture,* The Scarlet Letter *(1850). Later novels included* The House of the Seven Gables *(1851),* The Blithedale Romance *(an 1852 satire on Brook Farm), and* The Marble Faun *(1860). When his friend Franklin Pierce became president of the United States, Hawthorne served as American consul in Liverpool, England, for four years and then traveled in Italy for two more. At his death in 1864, he was already highly respected as a writer. Much of his fiction deals with conflicted characters whose hearts and souls are torn by sin, guilt, pride, and isolation. Indeed, his good friend Herman Melville, author of* Moby-Dick, *praised "the power of blackness" he found in Hawthorne's works. The allegorical story "Young Goodman Brown" is an especially memorable example of this power. Hawthorne wrote the tale in 1835 and later included it in* Mosses *from an Old Manse.*

Young Goodman Brown came forth at sunset into the street at Salem village; but put his head back, after crossing the threshold, to exchange a parting kiss with his young wife. And Faith, as the wife was aptly named, thrust her own pretty head into the street, letting the wind play with the pink ribbons of her cap while she called to Goodman Brown.

"Dearest heart," whispered she, softly and rather sadly, when her lips were close to his ear, "prithee put off your journey until sunrise and sleep in your own bed to-night. A lone woman is troubled with such dreams and such thoughts that she's afeared of herself sometimes. Pray tarry with me this night, dear husband, of all nights in the year."

"My love and my Faith," replied young Goodman Brown, "of all nights in the year, this one night must I tarry away from thee. My journey, as thou callest it, forth and back again, must needs be done 'twixt now and sunrise. What, my sweet, pretty wife, dost thou doubt me already, and we but three months married?"

"Then God bless you!" said Faith, with the pink ribbons; "and may you find all well when you come back."

"Amen!" cried Goodman Brown. "Say thy prayers, dear Faith, and go to bed   5
at dusk, and no harm will come to thee."

So they parted; and the young man pursued his way until, being about to turn the corner by the meeting-house, he looked back and saw the head of Faith still peeping after him with a melancholy air, in spite of her pink ribbons.

"Poor little Faith!" thought he, for his heart smote him. "What a wretch am I to leave her on such an errand! She talks of dreams, too. Methought as she spoke there was trouble in her face, as if a dream had warned her what work is to be done to-night. But no, no; 't would kill her to think it. Well, she's a blessed angel on earth, and after this one night I'll cling to her skirts and follow her to heaven."

With this excellent resolve for the future, Goodman Brown felt himself justified in making more haste on his present evil purpose. He had taken a dreary road, darkened by all the gloomiest trees of the forest, which barely stood aside to let the narrow path creep through, and closed immediately behind. It was all as lonely as could be; and there is this peculiarity in such a solitude, that the traveller knows not who may be concealed by the innumerable trunks and the thick boughs overhead; so that with lonely footsteps he may yet be passing through an unseen multitude.

"There may be a devilish Indian behind every tree," said Goodman Brown to himself; and he glanced fearfully behind him as he added, "What if the devil himself should be at my very elbow!"

His head being turned back, he passed a crook of the road, and, looking   10 forward again, beheld the figure of a man, in grave and decent attire, seated at the foot of an old tree. He arose at Goodman Brown's approach and walked onward side by side with him.

"You are late, Goodman Brown," said he. "The clock of the Old South was striking as I came through Boston, and that is full fifteen minutes agone."

"Faith kept me back a while," replied the young man, with a tremor in his voice, caused by the sudden appearance of his companion, though not wholly unexpected.

It was now deep dusk in the forest, and deepest in that part of it where these two were journeying. As nearly as could be discerned, the second traveller was about fifty years old, apparently in the same rank of life as Goodman Brown, and bearing a considerable resemblance to him, though perhaps more in expression than features. Still they might have been taken for father and son. And yet, though the elder person was as simply clad as the younger, and as simple in manner too, he had an indescribable air of one who knew the world, and who would not have felt abashed at the governor's dinner table or in King William's court, were it possible that his affairs should call him thither. But the only thing about him that could be fixed upon as remarkable was his staff, which bore the likeness of a great black snake, so curiously wrought that it might almost be seen to twist and wriggle itself like a living serpent. This, of course, must have been an ocular deception, assisted by the uncertain light.

"Come, Goodman Brown," cried his fellow-traveller, "this is a dull pace for the beginning of a journey. Take my staff, if you are so soon weary."

"Friend," said the other, exchanging his slow pace for a full stop, "having   15 kept covenant by meeting thee here, it is my purpose now to return whence I came. I have scruples touching the matter thou wot'st of."

"Sayest thou so?" replied he of the serpent, smiling apart. "Let us walk on, nevertheless, reasoning as we go; and if I convince thee not thou shalt turn back. We are but a little way in the forest yet."

"Too far! too far!" exclaimed the goodman, unconsciously resuming his walk. "My father never went into the woods on such an errand, nor his father before him. We have been a race of honest men and good Christians since the days of the martyrs; and shall I be the first of the name of Brown that ever took this path and kept"—

"Such company, thou wouldst say," observed the elder person, interpreting his pause. "Well said, Goodman Brown! I have been as well acquainted with your family as with ever a one among the Puritans; and that's no trifle to say. I helped your grandfather, the constable, when he lashed the Quaker woman so smartly through the streets of Salem; and it was I that brought your father a pitch-pine knot, kindled at my own hearth, to set fire to an Indian village, in King Philip's war.° They were my good friends, both; and many a pleasant walk have we had along this path, and returned merrily after midnight. I would fain be friends with you for their sake."

"If it be as thou sayest," replied Goodman Brown, "I marvel they never spoke of these matters; or, verily, I marvel not, seeing that the least rumor of the sort would have driven them from New England. We are a people of prayer, and good works to boot, and abide no such wickedness."

"Wickedness or not," said the traveller with the twisted staff, "I have a very   20
general acquaintance here in New England. The deacons of many a church have drunk the communion wine with me; the selectmen of divers towns make me their chairman; and a majority of the Great and General Court are firm supporters of my interest. The governor and I, too—But these are state secrets."

"Can this be so?" cried Goodman Brown, with a stare of amazement at his undisturbed companion. "Howbeit, I have nothing to do with the governor and council; they have their own ways, and are no rule for a simple husbandman like me. But, were I to go on with thee, how should I meet the eye of that good old man, our minister, at Salem village? Oh, his voice would make me tremble both Sabbath day and lecture day."

Thus far the elder traveller had listened with due gravity; but now burst into a fit of irrepressible mirth, shaking himself so violently that his snake-like staff actually seemed to wriggle in sympathy.

"Ha! ha! ha!" shouted he again and again; then composing himself, "Well, go on, Goodman Brown, go on; but, prithee, don't kill me with laughing."

"Well, then, to end the matter at once," said Goodman Brown, considerably nettled, "there is my wife, Faith. It would break her dear little heart; and I'd rather break my own."

"Nay, if that be the case," answered the other, "e'en go thy ways, Goodman   25
Brown. I would not for twenty old women like the one hobbling before us that Faith should come to any harm."

As he spoke he pointed his staff at a female figure on the path, in whom Goodman Brown recognized a very pious and exemplary dame, who had taught him his catechism in youth, and was still his moral and spiritual adviser, jointly with the minister and Deacon Gookin.

King Philip's war: King Philip, a Wampanoag chief, waged a bloody war against the New England colonists from 1675 to 1676.

"A marvel, truly that Goody Cloyse should be so far in the wilderness at nightfall," said he. "But with your leave, friend, I shall take a cut through the woods until we have left this Christian woman behind. Being a stranger to you, she might ask whom I was consorting with and whither I was going."

"Be it so," said his fellow-traveller. "Betake you to the woods, and let me keep the path."

Accordingly the young man turned aside, but took care to watch his companion, who advanced softly along the road until he had come within a staff's length of the old dame. She, meanwhile, was making the best of her way, with singular speed for so aged a woman, and mumbling some indistinct words — a prayer, doubtless — as she went. The traveller put forth his staff and touched her withered neck with what seemed the serpent's tail.

"The devil!" screamed the pious old lady.   30

"Then Goody Cloyse knows her old friend?" observed the traveller, confronting her and leaning on his writhing stick.

"Ah, forsooth, and is it your worship indeed?" cried the good dame. "Yea, truly is it, and in the very image of my old gossip, Goodman Brown, the grandfather of the silly fellow that now is. But — would your worship believe it? — my broomstick hath strangely disappeared, stolen, as I suspect, by that unhanged witch, Goody Cory, and that, too, when I was all anointed with the juice of smallage, and cinquefoil, and wolf's bane" —

"Mingled with fine wheat and the fat of a new-born babe," said the shape of old Goodman Brown.

"Ah, your worship knows the recipe," cried the old lady, cackling aloud. "So, as I was saying, being all ready for the meeting, and no horse to ride on, I made up my mind to foot it; for they tell me there is a nice young man to be taken into communion to-night. But now your good worship will lend me your arm, and we shall be there in a twinkling."

"That can hardly be," answered her friend. "I may not spare you my arm,   35 Goody Cloyse; but here is my staff, if you will."

So saying, he threw it down at her feet, where, perhaps, it assumed life, being one of the rods which its owner had formerly lent to the Egyptian magi. Of this fact, however, Goodman Brown could not take cognizance. He had cast up his eyes in astonishment, and, looking down again, beheld neither Goody Cloyse nor the serpentine staff, but his fellow-traveller alone, who waited for him as calmly as if nothing had happened.

"That old woman taught me my catechism," said the young man; and there was a world of meaning in this simple comment.

They continued to walk onward, while the elder traveller exhorted his companion to make good speed and persevere in the path, discoursing so aptly that his arguments seemed rather to spring up in the bosom of his auditor than to be suggested by himself. As they went, he plucked a branch of maple to serve for a walking stick, and began to strip it of the twigs and little boughs, which were wet with evening dew. The moment his fingers touched them they became strangely withered and dried up as with a week's sunshine. Thus the pair proceeded, at a good free pace, until suddenly, in a gloomy hollow of the road,

Goodman Brown sat himself down on the stump of a tree and refused to go any farther.

"Friend," he said, stubbornly, "my mind is made up. Not another step will I budge on this errand. What if a wretched old woman do choose to go to the devil when I thought she was going to heaven: is that any reason why I should quit my dear Faith and go after her?"

"You will think better of this by and by," said his acquaintance, compos- 40
edly. "Sit here and rest yourself a while; and when you feel like moving again, there is my staff to help you along."

Without more words, he threw his companion the maple stick, and was as speedily out of sight as if he had vanished into the deepening gloom. The young man sat a few moments by the roadside, applauding himself greatly, and think-ing with how clear a conscience he should meet the minister in his morning walk, nor shrink from the eye of good old Deacon Gookin. And what calm sleep would be his that very night, which was to have been spent so wickedly, but so purely and sweetly now, in the arms of Faith! Amidst these pleasant and praise-worthy meditations, Goodman Brown heard the tramp of horses along the road, and deemed it advisable to conceal himself within the verge of the forest, conscious of the guilty purpose that had brought him thither, though now so happily turned from it.

On came the hoof tramps and the voices of the riders, two grave old voices, conversing soberly as they drew near. These mingled sounds appeared to pass along the road, within a few yards of the young man's hiding-place; but, owing doubtless to the depth of the gloom at that particular spot, neither the travel-lers nor their steeds were visible. Though their figures brushed the small boughs by the wayside, it could not be seen that they intercepted, even for a moment, the faint gleam from the strip of bright sky athwart which they must have passed. Goodman Brown alternately crouched and stood on tiptoe, pull-ing aside the branches and thrusting forth his head as far as he durst without discerning so much as a shadow. It vexed him the more, because he could have sworn, were such a thing possible, that he recognized the voices of the minister and Deacon Gookin, jogging along quietly, as they were wont to do, when bound to some ordination or ecclesiastical council. While yet within hearing, one of the riders stopped to pluck a switch.

"Of the two, reverend sir," said the voice like the deacon's, "I had rather miss an ordination dinner than to-night's meeting. They tell me that some of our community are to be here from Falmouth and beyond, and others from Connecticut and Rhode Island, besides several of the Indian powwows, who, after their fashion, know almost as much deviltry as the best of us. Moreover, there is a goodly young woman to be taken into communion."

"Mighty well, Deacon Gookin!" replied the solemn old tones of the minis-ter. "Spur up, or we shall be late. Nothing can be done, you know, until I get on the ground."

The hoofs clattered again; and the voices, talking so strangely in the empty 45
air, passed on through the forest, where no church had ever been gathered or solitary Christian prayed. Whither, then, could these holy men be journeying

so deep into the heathen wilderness? Young Goodman Brown caught hold of a tree for support, being ready to sink down on the ground, faint and overburdened with the heavy sickness of his heart. He looked up to the sky, doubting whether there really was a heaven above him. Yet there was the blue arch, and the stars brightening in it.

"With heaven above and Faith below, I will yet stand firm against the devil!" cried Goodman Brown.

While he still gazed upward into the deep arch of the firmament and had lifted his hands to pray, a cloud, though no wind was stirring, hurried across the zenith and hid the brightening stars. The blue sky was still visible, except directly overhead, where this black mass of cloud was sweeping swiftly northward. Aloft in the air, as if from the depths of the cloud, came a confused and doubtful sound of voices. Once the listener fancied that he could distinguish the accents of towns-people of his own, men and women, both pious and ungodly, many of whom he had met at the communion table, and had seen others rioting at the tavern. The next moment, so indistinct were the sounds, he doubted whether he had heard aught but the murmur of the old forest, whispering without a wind. Then came a stronger swell of those familiar tones, heard daily in the sunshine at Salem village, but never until now from a cloud of night. There was one voice, of a young woman, uttering lamentations, yet with an uncertain sorrow, and entreating for some favor, which, perhaps, it would grieve her to obtain; and all the unseen multitude, both saints and sinners, seemed to encourage her onward.

"Faith!" shouted Goodman Brown, in a voice of agony and desperation; and the echoes of the forest mocked him, crying, "Faith! Faith!" as if bewildered wretches were seeking her all through the wilderness.

The cry of grief, rage, and terror was yet piercing the night, when the unhappy husband held his breath for a response. There was a scream, drowned immediately in a louder murmur of voices, fading into far-off laughter, as the dark cloud swept away, leaving the clear and silent sky above Goodman Brown. But something fluttered lightly down through the air and caught on the branch of a tree. The young man seized it, and beheld a pink ribbon.

"My Faith is gone!" cried he after one stupefied moment. "There is no good on earth; and sin is but a name. Come, devil; for to thee is this world given." 50

And, maddened with despair, so that he laughed loud and long, did Goodman Brown grasp his staff and set forth again, at such a rate that he seemed to fly along the forest path rather than to walk or run. The road grew wilder and drearier and more faintly traced, and vanished at length, leaving him in the heart of the dark wilderness, still rushing onward with the instinct that guides mortal man to evil. The whole forest was peopled with frightful sounds—the creaking of the trees, the howling of wild beasts, and the yell of Indians; while sometimes the wind tolled like a distant church bell, and sometimes gave a broad roar around the traveller, as if all Nature were laughing him to scorn. But he was himself the chief horror of the scene, and shrank not from its other horrors.

"Ha! ha! ha!" roared Goodman Brown when the wind laughed at him. "Let us hear which will laugh loudest. Think not to frighten me with your deviltry.

Come witch, come wizard, come Indian powwow, come devil himself, and here comes Goodman Brown. You may as well fear him as he fear you."

In truth, all through the haunted forest there could be nothing more frightful than the figure of Goodman Brown. On he flew among the black pines, brandishing his staff with frenzied gestures, now giving vent to an inspiration of horrid blasphemy, and now shouting forth such laughter as set all the echoes of the forest laughing like demons around him. The fiend in his own shape is less hideous than when he rages in the breast of man. Thus sped the demoniac on his course, until, quivering among the trees, he saw a red light before him, as when the felled trunks and branches of a clearing have been set on fire, and throw up their lurid blaze against the sky, at the hour of midnight. He paused, in a lull of the tempest that had driven him onward, and heard the swell of what seemed a hymn, rolling solemnly from a distance with the weight of many voices. He knew the tune; it was a familiar one in the choir of the village meeting-house. The verse died heavily away, and was lengthened by a chorus, not of human voices, but of all the sounds of the benighted wilderness pealing in awful harmony together. Goodman Brown cried out, and his cry was lost to his own ear by its unison with the cry of the desert.

In the interval of silence he stole forward until the light glared full upon his eyes. At one extremity of an open space, hemmed in by the dark wall of the forest, arose a rock, bearing some rude, natural resemblance either to an altar or a pulpit, and surrounded by four blazing pines, their tops aflame, their stems untouched, like candles at an evening meeting. The mass of foliage that had overgrown the summit of the rock was all on fire, blazing high into the night and fitfully illuminating the whole field. Each pendent twig and leafy festoon was in a blaze. As the red light arose and fell, a numerous congregation alternately shone forth, then disappeared in shadow, and again grew, as it were, out of the darkness, peopling the heart of the solitary woods at once.

"A grave and dark-clad company," quoth Goodman Brown.   55

In truth they were such. Among them, quivering to and fro between gloom and splendor, appeared faces that would be seen next day at the council board of the province, and others which, Sabbath after Sabbath, looked devoutly heavenward, and benignantly over the crowded pews, from the holiest pulpits in the land. Some affirm that the lady of the governor was there. At least there were high dames well known to her, and wives of honored husbands, and widows, a great multitude, and ancient maidens, all of excellent repute, and fair young girls, who trembled lest their mothers should espy them. Either the sudden gleams of light flashing over the obscure field bedazzled Goodman Brown, or he recognized a score of the church members of Salem village famous for their especial sanctity. Good old Deacon Gookin had arrived, and waited at the skirts of that venerable saint, his revered pastor. But, irreverently consorting with these grave, reputable, and pious people, these elders of the church, these chaste dames and dewy virgins, there were men of dissolute lives and women of spotted fame, wretches given over to all mean and filthy vice, and suspected even of horrid crimes. It was strange to see that the good shrank not from the wicked, nor were the sinners abashed by the saints. Scattered also among their pale-faced enemies were the Indian priests, or powwows, who had often scared their native forest with more hideous incantations than any known to English witchcraft.

"But where is Faith?" thought Goodman Brown; and, as hope came into his heart, he trembled.

Another verse of the hymn arose, a slow and mournful strain, such as the pious love, but joined to words which expressed all that our nature can conceive of sin, and darkly hinted at far more. Unfathomable to mere mortals is the lore of fiends. Verse after verse was sung; and still the chorus of the desert swelled between like the deepest tone of a mighty organ; and with the final peal of that dreadful anthem there came a sound, as if the roaring wind, the rushing streams, the howling beasts, and every other voice of the unconcerted wilderness were mingling and according with the voice of guilty man in homage to the prince of all. The four blazing pines threw up a loftier flame, and obscurely discovered shapes and visages of horror on the smoke wreaths above the impious assembly. At the same moment the fire on the rock shot redly forth and formed a flowing arch above its base, where now appeared a figure. With reverence be it spoken, the figure bore no slight similitude, both in garb and manner, to some grave divine of the New England churches.

"Bring forth the converts!" cried a voice that echoed through the field and rolled into the forest.

At the word, Goodman Brown stepped forth from the shadow of the trees   60 and approached the congregation, with whom he felt a loathful brotherhood by the sympathy of all that was wicked in his heart. He could have well-nigh sworn that the shape of his own dead father beckoned him to advance, looking downward from a smoke wreath, while a woman, with dim features of despair, threw out her hand to warn him back. Was it his mother? But he had no power to retreat one step, nor to resist, even in thought, when the minister and good old Deacon Gookin seized his arms and led him to the blazing rock. Thither came also the slender form of a veiled female, led between Goody Cloyse, that pious teacher of the catechism, and Martha Carrier, who had received the devil's promise to be queen of hell. A rampant hag was she. And there stood the proselytes beneath the canopy of fire.

"Welcome, my children," said the dark figure, "to the communion of your race. Ye have found thus young your nature and your destiny. My children, look behind you!"

They turned; and flashing forth, as it were, in a sheet of flame, the fiend worshippers were seen; the smile of welcome gleamed darkly on every visage.

"There," resumed the sable form, "are all whom ye have reverenced from youth. Ye deemed them holier than yourselves and shrank from your own sin, contrasting it with their lives of righteousness and prayerful aspirations heavenward. Yet here are they all in my worshipping assembly. This night it shall be granted you to know their secret deeds: how hoary-bearded elders of the church have whispered wanton words to the young maids of their households; how many a woman, eager for widows' weeds, has given her husband a drink at bedtime and let him sleep his last sleep in her bosom; how beardless youths have made haste to inherit their fathers' wealth; and how fair damsels—blush not, sweet ones—have dug little graves in the garden, and bidden me, the sole guest, to an infant's funeral. By the sympathy of your human hearts for sin ye shall scent out all the places—whether in church, bedchamber, street, field, or forest—where crime has been committed, and shall exult to behold the whole earth one stain of guilt, one mighty blood spot. Far more than this. It shall be yours to penetrate, in every bosom, the deep mystery of sin, the fountain of all wicked arts, and which inexhaustibly supplies more evil impulses than human power—than my power at its utmost—can make manifest in deeds. And now, my children, look upon each other."

They did so; and, by the blaze of the hell-kindled torches, the wretched man beheld his Faith, and the wife her husband, trembling before that unhallowed altar.

"Lo, there ye stand, my children," said the figure, in a deep and solemn 65 tone, almost sad with its despairing awfulness, as if his once angelic nature could yet mourn for our miserable race. "Depending upon one another's hearts, ye had still hoped that virtue were not all a dream. Now are ye undeceived. Evil is the nature of mankind. Evil must be your only happiness. Welcome again, my children, to the communion of your race."

"Welcome," repeated the fiend worshippers, in one cry of despair and triumph.

And there they stood, the only pair, as it seemed, who were yet hesitating on the verge of wickedness in this dark world. A basin was hallowed, naturally, in the rock. Did it contain water, reddened by the lurid light? or was it blood? or, perchance, a liquid flame? Herein did the shape of evil dip his hand and prepare to lay the mark of baptism upon their foreheads, that they might be partakers of the mystery of sin, more conscious of the secret guilt of others, both in deed and thought, than they could now be of their own. The husband cast one look at his pale wife, and Faith at him. What polluted wretches would the next glance show them to each other, shuddering alike at what they disclosed and what they saw!

"Faith! Faith!" cried the husband, "look up to heaven, and resist the wicked one."

Whether Faith obeyed he knew not. Hardly had he spoken when he found himself amid calm night and solitude, listening to a roar of the wind which died heavily away through the forest. He staggered against the rock, and felt it chill and damp; while a hanging twig, that had been all on fire, besprinkled his cheek with the coldest dew.

The next morning young Goodman Brown came slowly into the street 70 of Salem village, staring around him like a bewildered man. The good old minister was taking a walk along the graveyard to get an appetite for breakfast and meditate his sermon, and bestowed a blessing, as he passed, on Goodman Brown. He shrank from the venerable saint as if to avoid an anathema. Old Deacon Gookin was at domestic worship, and the holy words of his prayer were heard through the open window. "What God doth the wizard pray to?" quoth Goodman Brown. Goody Cloyse, that excellent old Christian, stood in the early sunshine at her own lattice, catechizing a little girl who had brought her a pint of morning's milk. Goodman Brown snatched away the child as from the grasp of the fiend himself. Turning the corner by the meeting-house, he spied the head of Faith, with the pink ribbons, gazing anxiously forth, and bursting into such joy at sight of him that she skipped along the street and almost kissed her husband before the whole village. But Goodman Brown looked sternly and sadly into her face, and passed on without a greeting.

Had Goodman Brown fallen asleep in the forest and only dreamed a wild dream of a witch-meeting?

Be it so if you will; but, alas! it was a dream of evil omen for young Goodman Brown. A stern, a sad, a darkly meditative, a distrustful, if not a desperate man did he become from the night of that fearful dream. On the Sabbath day, when the congregation were singing a holy psalm, he could not listen because an anthem of sin rushed loudly upon his ear and drowned all the blessed strain. When the minister spoke from the pulpit with power and fervid eloquence, and, with his hand on the open Bible, of the sacred truths of our religion, and of saint-like lives and triumphant deaths, and of future bliss or misery unutterable, then did Goodman Brown turn pale, dreading lest the roof should thunder down upon the gray blasphemer and his hearers. Often, awaking suddenly at midnight, he shrank from the bosom of Faith; and at morning or eventide, when the family knelt down at prayer, he scowled and muttered to himself, and gazed sternly at his wife, and turned away. And when he had lived long, and was borne to his grave a hoary corpse, followed by Faith, an aged woman, and children and grandchildren, a goodly procession, besides neighbors not a few, they carved no hopeful verse upon his tombstone, for his dying hour was gloom.   *[1835]*

≡ THINKING ABOUT THE TEXT

1. "Young Goodman Brown" seems quite allegorical, with journeys in the night woods and statements like "My Faith is gone!" (para. 50). How would you explain this allegorical story? What is Brown looking for? What does he find out? How does he deal with his discoveries?

2. If you were a good friend of Brown's, what might you tell him to try to save him from a life of gloom?

3. The devil suggests that there is more evil in the human heart "than my power at its utmost" (para. 63). Do you agree? If so, is this a message to despair about?

4. The devil says he is well acquainted with Brown's family. What has his family done? Is Brown innocent and naive, or perhaps stubborn and arrogant, in his refusal to admit that evil exists all around us?

5. Do you suspect that Brown merely dreamed or imagined his experience in the woods? Or do you think it really took place? Refer to specific details of the text.

TONI CADE BAMBARA

The Lesson

Toni Cade Bambara (1939–1995) taught at various colleges and worked as a community activist. She edited The Black Woman *(1970), a collection of essays that became a landmark of contemporary black feminism. Bambara wrote two novels:* The Salt Eaters *(1980), which won the American Book Award, and* These Bones Are Not My Child *(2000), a posthumously published work about the murders of several African American children in late 1970s Atlanta. She also produced several collections of short stories. "The Lesson" comes from her first,* Gorilla, My Love *(1972).*

Back in the days when everyone was old and stupid or young and foolish and me and Sugar were the only ones just right, this lady moved on our block with nappy hair and proper speech and no makeup. And quite naturally we laughed at her, laughed the way we did at the junk man who went about his business like he was some big-time president and his sorry-ass horse his secretary. And we kinda hated her too, hated the way we did the winos who cluttered up our parks and pissed on our handball walls and stank up our hallways and stairs so you couldn't halfway play hide-and-seek without a goddamn gas mask. Miss Moore was her name. The only woman on the block with no first name. And she was black as hell, cept for her feet, which were fish-white and spooky. And she was always planning these boring-ass things for us to do, us being my cousin, mostly, who lived on the block cause we all moved North the same time and to the same apartment then spread out gradual to breathe. And our parents would yank our heads into some kinda shape and crisp up our clothes so we'd be presentable for travel with Miss Moore, who always looked like she was going to church, though she never did. Which is just one of the things the grownups talked about when they talked behind her back like a dog. But when she came calling with some sachet she'd sewed up or some gingerbread she'd made or some book, why then they'd all be too embarrassed to turn her down and we'd get handed over all spruced up. She'd been to college and said it was only right that she should take responsibility for the young ones' education, and she not even related by marriage or blood. So they'd go for it. Specially Aunt Gretchen. She was the main gofer in the family. You got some ole dumb shit foolishness you want somebody to go for, you send for Aunt Gretchen. She been screwed into the go-along for so long, it's a blood-deep natural thing with her. Which is how she got saddled with me and Sugar and Junior in the first place while our mothers were in a la-de-da apartment up the block having a good ole time.

So this one day, Miss Moore rounds us all up at the mailbox and it's puredee hot and she's knockin herself out about arithmetic. And school suppose to let up in summer I heard, but she don't never let up. And the starch in my pinafore scratching the shit outta me and I'm really hating this nappy-head bitch and her goddamn college degree. I'd much rather go to the pool or to the show where it's cool. So me and Sugar leaning on the mailbox being surly, which is a Miss Moore word. And Flyboy checking out what everybody brought for lunch. And Fat Butt already wasting his peanut-butter-and-jelly sandwich like the pig he is. And Junebug punchin on Q.T.'s arm for potato chips. And Rosie Giraffe shifting from one hip to the other waiting for somebody to step on her foot or ask her if she from Georgia so she can kick ass, preferably Mercedes's. And Miss Moore asking us do we know what money is, like we a bunch of retards. I mean real money, she say, like it's only poker chips or monopoly papers we lay on the grocer. So right away I'm tired of this and say so. And would much rather snatch Sugar and go to the Sunset and terrorize the West Indian kids and take their hair ribbons and their money too. And Miss Moore files that remark away for next week's lesson on brotherhood, I can tell. And finally I say we oughta get to the subway cause it's cooler and besides we might meet some cute boys. Sugar done swiped her mama's lipstick, so we ready.

So we heading down the street and she's boring us silly about what things cost and what our parents make and how much goes for rent and how money ain't divided up right in this country. And then she gets to the part about we all poor and live in the slums, which I don't feature. And I'm ready to speak on that, but she steps out in the street and hails two cabs just like that. Then she hustles half the crew in with her and hands me a five-dollar bill and tells me to calculate 10 percent tip for the driver. And we're off. Me and Sugar and Junebug and Flyboy hangin out the window and hollering to everybody, putting lipstick on each other cause Flyboy a faggot anyway, and making farts with our sweaty armpits. But I'm mostly trying to figure how to spend this money. But they all fascinated with the meter ticking and Junebug starts laying bets as to how much it'll read when Flyboy can't hold his breath no more. Then Sugar lays bets as to how much it'll be when we get there. So I'm stuck. Don't nobody want to go for my plan, which is to jump out at the next light and run off to the first bar-b-que we can find. Then the driver tells us to get the hell out cause we there already. And the meter reads eighty-five cents. And I'm stalling to figure out the tip and Sugar say give him a dime. And I decide he don't need it bad as I do, so later for him. But then he tries to take off with Junebug foot still in the door so we talk about his mama something ferocious. Then we check out that we on Fifth Avenue and everybody dressed up in stockings. One lady in a fur coat, hot as it is. White folks crazy.

"This is the place," Miss Moore say, presenting it to us in the voice she uses at the museum. "Let's look in the windows before we go in."

"Can we steal?" Sugar asks very serious like she's getting the ground rules   5
squared away before she plays. "I beg your pardon," say Miss Moore, and we fall out. So she leads us around the windows of the toy store and me and Sugar screamin, "This is mine, that's mine, I gotta have that, that was made for me, I was born for that," till Big Butt drowns us out.

"Hey, I'm goin to buy that there."

"That there? You don't even know what it is, stupid."

"I do so," he say punchin on Rosie Giraffe. "It's a microscope."

"Whatcha gonna do with a microscope, fool?"

"Look at things." 10

"Like what, Ronald?" ask Miss Moore. And Big Butt ain't got the first notion. So here go Miss Moore gabbing about the thousands of bacteria in a drop of water and the somethinorother in a speck of blood and the million and one living things in the air around us is invisible to the naked eye. And what she say that for? Junebug go to town on that "naked" and we rolling. Then Miss Moore ask what it cost. So we all jam into the window smudgin it up and the price tag say $300. So then she ask how long'd take for Big Butt and Junebug to save up their allowances. "Too long," I say. "Yeh," adds Sugar, "outgrown it by that time." And Miss Moore say no, you never outgrow learning instruments. "Why, even medical students_and interns and," blah, blah, blah. And we ready to choke Big Butt for bringing it up in the first damn place.

"This here costs four hundred eighty dollars," says Rosie Giraffe. So we pile up all over her to see what she pointin out. My eyes tell me it's a chunk of glass cracked with something heavy, and different-color inks dripped into the splits, then the whole thing put into a oven or something. But for $480 it don't make sense.

"That's a paperweight made of semi-precious stones fused together under tremendous pressure," she explains slowly, with her hands doing the mining and all the factory work.

"So what's a paperweight?" asks Rosie Giraffe.

"To weigh paper with, dumbbell," say Flyboy, the wise man from the East. 15

"Not exactly," say Miss Moore, which is what she say when you warm or way off too. "It's to weigh paper down so it won't scatter and make your desk untidy." So right away me and Sugar curtsy to each other and then to Mercedes who is more the tidy type.

"We don't keep paper on top of the desk in my class," say Junebug, figuring Miss Moore crazy or lyin one.

"At home, then," she say. "Don't you have a calendar and pencil case and a blotter and a letter-opener on your desk at home where you do your homework?" And she know damn well what our homes look like cause she nosys around in them every chance she gets.

"I don't even have a desk," say Junebug. "Do we?"

"No. And I don't get no homework neither," says Big Butt. 20

"And I don't even have a home," say Flyboy like he do at school to keep the white folks off his back and sorry for him. Send this poor kid to camp posters, is his specialty.

"I do," says Mercedes. "I have a box of stationery on my desk and a picture of my cat. My godmother bought the stationery and the desk. There's a big rose on each sheet and the envelopes smell like roses."

"Who wants to know about your smelly-ass stationery," say Rosie Giraffe fore I can get my two cents in.

"It's important to have a work area all your own so that . . ."

"Will you look at this sailboat, please," say Flyboy, cuttin her off and 25 pointin to the thing like it was his. So once again we tumble all over each other to gaze at this magnificent thing in the toy store which is just big enough to maybe sail two kittens across the pond if you strap them to the posts tight. We all start reciting the price tag like we in assembly. "Handcrafted sailboat of fiberglass at one thousand one hundred ninety-five dollars."

"Unbelievable," I hear myself say and am really stunned. I read it again for myself just in case the group recitation put me in a trance. Same thing. For some reason this pisses me off. We look at Miss Moore and she lookin at us, waiting for I dunno what.

"Who'd pay all that when you can buy a sailboat set for a quarter at Pop's, a tube of glue for a dime, and a ball of string for eight cents? It must have a motor and a whole lot else besides," I say. "My sailboat cost me about fifty cents."

"But will it take water?" say Mercedes with her smart ass.

"Took mine to Alley Pond Park once," say Flyboy. "String broke. Lost it. Pity."

"Sailed mine in Central Park and it keeled over and sank. Had to ask my   30
father for another dollar."

"And you got the strap," laugh Big Butt. "The jerk didn't even have a string on it. My old man wailed on his behind."

Little Q.T. was staring hard at the sailboat and you could see he wanted it bad. But he too little and somebody'd just take it from him. So what the hell. "This boat for kids, Miss Moore?"

"Parents silly to buy something like that just to get all broke up," say Rosie Giraffe.

"That much money it should last forever," I figure.

"My father'd buy it for me if I wanted it."   35

"Your father, my ass," say Rosie Giraffe getting a chance to finally push Mercedes.

"Must be rich people shop here," say Q.T.

"You are a very bright boy," say Flyboy. "What was your first clue?" And he rap him on the head with the back of his knuckles, since Q.T. the only one he could get away with. Though Q.T. liable to come up behind you years later and get his licks in when you half expect it.

"What I want to know is," I says to Miss Moore though I never talk to her, I wouldn't give the bitch that satisfaction, "is how much a real boat costs? I figure a thousand'd get you a yacht any day."

"Why don't you check that out," she says, "and report back to the group?"   40
Which really pains my ass. If you gonna mess up a perfectly good swim day least you could do is have some answers. "Let's go in," she say like she got something up her sleeve. Only she don't lead the way. So me and Sugar turn the corner to where the entrance is, but when we get there I kinda hang back. Not that I'm scared, what's there to be afraid of, just a toy store. But I feel funny, shame. But what I got to be shamed about? Got as much right to go in as anybody. But somehow I can't seem to get hold of the door, so I step away from Sugar to lead. But she hangs back too. And I look at her and she looks at me and this is ridiculous. I mean, damn, I have never ever been shy about doing nothing or going nowhere. But then Mercedes steps up and then Rosie Giraffe and Big Butt crowd in behind and shove, and next thing we all stuffed into the

doorway with only Mercedes squeezing past us, smoothing out her jumper and walking right down the aisle. Then the rest of us tumble in like a glued-together jigsaw done all wrong. And people lookin at us. And it's like the time me and Sugar crashed into the Catholic church on a dare. But once we got in there and everything so hushed and holy and the candles and the bowin and the hand-kerchiefs on all the drooping heads, I just couldn't go through with the plan. Which was for me to run up to the altar and do a tap dance while Sugar played the nose flute and messed around in the holy water. And Sugar kept givin me the elbow. Then later teased me so bad I tied her up in the shower and turned it on and locked her in. And she'd be there till this day if Aunt Gretchen hadn't finally figured I was lying about the boarder takin a shower.

Same thing in the store. We all walkin on tiptoe and hardly touchin the games and puzzles and things. And I watched Miss Moore who is steady watchin us like she waitin for a sign. Like Mama Drewery watches the sky and sniffs the air and takes note of just how much slant is in the bird formation. Then me and Sugar bump smack into each other, so busy gazing at the toys, 'specially the sailboat. But we don't laugh and go into our fat-lady bump-stomach routine. We just stare at that price tag. Then Sugar run a finger over the whole boat. And I'm jealous and want to hit her. Maybe not her, but I sure want to punch somebody in the mouth.

"Watcha bring us here for, Miss Moore?"

"You sound angry, Sylvia. Are you mad about something?" Givin me one of them grins like she tellin a grown-up joke that never turns out to be funny. And she's lookin very closely at me like maybe she plannin to do my portrait from memory. I'm mad, but I won't give her that satisfaction. So I slouch around the store bein very bored and say, "Let's go."

Me and Sugar at the back of the train watchin the tracks whizzin by large then small then getting gobbled up in the dark. I'm thinkin about this tricky toy I saw in the store. A clown that somersaults on a bar then does chin-ups just cause you yank lightly at his leg. Cost $35. I could see me askin my mother for a $35 birthday clown. "You wanna who that costs what?" she'd say, cocking her head to the side to get a better view of the hole in my head. Thirty-five dollars could buy new bunk beds for Junior and Gretchen's boy. Thirty-five dollars and the whole household could go visit Grand-daddy Nelson in the country. Thirty-five dollars would pay for the rent and the piano bill too. Who are these people that spend that much for performing clowns and $1000 for toy sailboats? What kinda work they do and how they live and how come we ain't in on it? Where we are is who we are, Miss Moore always pointin out. But it don't necessarily have to be that way, she always adds then waits for somebody to say that poor people have to wake up and demand their share of the pie and don't none of us know what kind of pie she talking about in the first damn place. But she ain't so smart cause I still got her four dollars from the taxi and she sure ain't gettin it. Messin up my day with this shit. Sugar nudges me in my pocket and winks.

Miss Moore lines us up in front of the mailbox where we started from, seem like years ago, and I got a headache for thinkin so hard. And we lean all over   45 each other so we can hold up under the draggy-ass lecture she always finishes us off with at the end before we thank her for borin us to tears. But she just looks at us like she readin tea leaves. Finally she say, "Well, what did you think of F. A. O. Schwarz?"

Rosie Giraffe mumbles, "White folks crazy."

"I'd like to go there again when I get my birthday money," says Mercedes, and we shove her out the pack so she has to lean on the mailbox by herself.

"I'd like a shower. Tiring day," say Flyboy.

Then Sugar surprises me by sayin, "You know, Miss Moore, I don't think all of us here put together eat in a year what that sailboat costs." And Miss Moore lights up like somebody goosed her. "And?" she say, urging Sugar on. Only I'm standin on her foot so she don't continue.

"Imagine for a minute what kind of society it is in which some people   50
can spend on a toy what it would cost to feed a family of six or seven. What do you think?"

"I think," say Sugar pushing me off her feet like she never done before, cause I whip her ass in a minute, "that this is not much of a democracy if you ask me. Equal chance to pursue happiness means an equal crack at the dough, don't it?" Miss Moore is beside herself and I am disgusted with Sugar's treachery. So I stand on her foot one more time to see if she'll shove me. She shuts up, and Miss Moore looks at me, sorrowfully I'm thinkin. And somethin weird is goin on, I can feel it in my chest.

"Anybody else learn anything today?" lookin dead at me. I walk away and Sugar has to run to catch up and don't even seem to notice when I shrug her arm off my shoulder.

"Well, we got four dollars anyway," she says.

"Uh hunh."

"We could go to Hascombs and get half a chocolate layer and then go to   55
the Sunset and still have plenty money for potato chips and ice cream sodas."

"Un hunh."

"Race you to Hascombs," she say.

We start down the block and she gets ahead which is O.K. by me cause I'm going to the West End and then over to the Drive to think this day through. She can run if she want to and even run faster. But ain't nobody gonna beat me at nuthin.   *[1972]*

≣ THINKING ABOUT THE TEXT

1. Bambara's story begins with "Back in the days," which suggests that Sylvia is significantly older now than she was then. How much time do you think has passed since the events she recalls? Does it matter to you how old she is now? Why, or why not?

2. Miss Moore is not officially a teacher. Nor is she a relative of the children she instructs. Is it right, then, for her to "take responsibility for the young ones' education" (para. 1)? Make arguments for and against her doing so.

3. Consider Miss Moore herself as making an argument. What are her claims? Which of her strategies, if any, seem effective in persuading her audience? Which, if any, seem ineffective?

4. What statements by the children articulate the lesson that Miss Moore teaches? Are all these statements saying pretty much the same thing? At the end of the story, is Sylvia ready to agree with all of them? Explain.

5. Do class and race seem equally important in this story, or does one seem more important than the other? Elaborate your reasoning.

≡ MAKING COMPARISONS

1. "The Lesson" is more humorous than "Young Goodman Brown." Does its humor lead you to take Bambara's story of injustice less seriously than you do Hawthorne's? Why, or why not?

2. Whereas "Young Goodman Brown" has an omniscient narrator, "The Lesson" is narrated in the first person, by Sylvia herself. To what extent does this difference matter as you read the two stories together?

3. Sylvia is younger in age than Goodman Brown is. How significant is this difference to you as you consider their responses to injustice?

≡ WRITING ABOUT ISSUES

1. Write an essay about "Young Goodman Brown" or "The Lesson" in which you identify the extent to which the protagonist changes over the course of the story. What signs of change, if any, does this character show? In what ways might he or she remain the same?

2. Write an essay comparing Miss Moore with an adult character in Hawthorne's story (someone other than Goodman Brown himself). To what extent do both of these characters serve as helpful "teachers"?

3. Write an essay recalling an occasion when someone you knew or read about was intent on branding someone else a sinner or wrongdoer. Moreover, let this occasion be one that left you with mixed feelings. Then write an essay that identifies the issues you thought were at stake and also expresses and supports your view of the outcome. If you wish, refer to one or both of the stories in this cluster.

4. Imagine that you are giving a brief speech about "Young Goodman Brown" to a college class studying issues of religion, or a brief speech about "The Lesson" to a group of elementary-school teachers. Write this speech, making clear the main point that you are using the story to illustrate.

≣ Racial Injustice: Poems

COUNTEE CULLEN, "Incident"

NATASHA TRETHEWEY, "Incident"

Throughout literary history, writers have called attention to the injustices of racial oppression. The following pair of poems, both entitled "Incident," remind us that racial prejudice could be blatant and vicious both early in the twentieth century and toward its end. Indeed, the subject is not likely to die out even now, when laws blatantly permitting slavery or segregation have ceased to exist. Racism continues in various forms, though perhaps subtler ones. As you read these poems, consider what recent "incidents" might be topics of similar texts.

> ### ≣ BEFORE YOU READ
>
> How do you define *racism*? What, for you, are possible signs of it?

COUNTEE CULLEN
Incident

Countee Cullen (1903–1946) was one of the leading writers of the Harlem Renaissance, a New York–based movement of African American authors, artists, and intellectuals that flourished from World War I to the Great Depression. Cullen's place of birth may have been Baltimore, Louisville, or New York, but by 1918 he was living in New York as the adopted son of a Methodist minister. Cullen wrote poetry and received prizes for it even as he attended New York University. In 1925, while pursuing a master's degree from Harvard, he published his first book of poems, Color, *which contained "Incident." His later books include* Copper Sun *(1927),* The Black Christ and Other Poems *(1929), a translation of Euripides' play* Medea *(1935), and a children's book,* The Lost Zoo *(1940). Cullen gained much attention when, in 1928, he wed the daughter of famed African American writer and scholar W. E. B. DuBois, but their marriage ended just two years later. During the 1930s, Cullen's writing did not earn him enough to live on, so he taught English and French at Frederick Douglass High School. At the time of his death in 1946, he was collaborating on the Broadway musical* St. Louis Woman. *In part because he died relatively young, Cullen's reputation faded. Langston Hughes became much better known as a Harlem Renaissance figure. "Incident," however, has been consistently anthologized, and today Cullen is being rediscovered along with other contributors to African American literature.*

Once riding in old Baltimore
   Heart-filled, head-filled with glee,
I saw a Baltimorean
   Keep looking straight at me.

Now I was eight and very small,   5
   And he was no whit bigger,
And so I smiled, but he poked out
   His tongue and called me, "Nigger."

I saw the whole of Baltimore
   From May until December: 10
Of all the things that happened there
   That's all that I remember.   *[1925]*

≡ THINKING ABOUT THE TEXT

1. Why do you think the speaker calls attention to his heart *and* his head in the second line? Might referring to just one of these things have been enough?

2. "Baltimorean" (line 3) seems a rather unusual and abstract term for the boy that the speaker encountered. How do you explain its presence in the poem? How important is it that the speaker name the city where the incident occurred?

3. Although the incident that the speaker recalls must have been painful for him, why do you think he does not state his feelings about it more explicitly? What is the effect of his relative reticence about it?

4. The rhythm of this poem is rather singsongy. Why do you think Cullen made it so?

5. The speaker states that he was eight at the time of the incident. How old might he be now? How important is his age?

NATASHA TRETHEWEY
Incident

The child of an interracial marriage, Natasha Trethewey (b. 1966) graduated from the University of Georgia and earned a master's degree at Hollins College in Virginia. Currently the U.S. poet laureate, she teaches creative writing at Emory University in Atlanta, Georgia. She is the author of four volumes of poetry: Domestic Work *(2000);* Bellocq's Ophelia *(2002);* Native Guard *(2006), which won the Pulitzer Prize and includes the following poem; and* Thrall *(2012).* Beyond Katrina: A Meditation on the Mississippi Gulf Coast *(2010), is a combination of memoir and reportage that also mixes prose with verse.*

We tell the story every year—
how we peered from the windows, shades drawn—
though nothing really happened,
the charred grass now green again.

We peered from the windows, shade drawn,   5
at the cross trussed like a Christmas tree,
the charred grass still green. Then
we darkened our rooms, lit the hurricane lamps.

At the cross trussed like a Christmas tree,
a few men gathered, white as angels in their gowns.   10
We darkened our room and lit hurricane lamps,
the wicks trembling in their fonts of oil.

It seemed the angels had gathered, white men in their gowns.
When they were done, they left quietly. No one came.
The wicks trembled all night in their fonts of oil;   15
by morning the flames had all dimmed.

When they were done, the men left quietly. No one came.
Nothing really happened.
By morning all the flames had dimmed.
We tell the story every year.   *[2006]*   20

≡ THINKING ABOUT THE TEXT

1. Trethewey has acknowledged that this poem is a *pantoum*. This form of verse consists of *quatrains* (stanzas of four lines each); also, the second and fourth lines of a quatrain are repeated as the first and third lines of the following quatrain, with the final line of the entire poem repeating its very first line. It's a difficult type of poem to write. Why do you think Trethewey attempted it here?

2. How does the poem use religious imagery?

3. What information does the poet leave out? Why do you think she omits it?

4. Why do you think the "we" of the poem "tell[s] the story every year"? Why tell the story at all? Why not tell it more often?

5. Twice, the speaker claims that "nothing really happened." Do you agree with her? Why, or why not?

≡ MAKING COMPARISONS

1. In giving her poem the title "Incident," Trethewey is surely aware of Cullen's poem. What other connections between these two texts do you feel encouraged by her to make?

2. Which of the two poems, Cullen's or Trethewey's, strikes you as more abstract? Does this difference lead to a difference in effect? Why, or why not?

3. Do the speakers in these two poems strike you as using pretty much the same tone? Refer to specific lines in each work.

≡ **WRITING ABOUT ISSUES**

1. Choose either Cullen's poem or Trethewey's, and write an essay in which you examine what the poem suggests about the act of *remembering* an incident of race-related injustice.

2. Cullen's poem is famous; does Trethewey's deserve to be equally well known? Write an essay addressing this question for your audience, making clear your criteria for artistic success.

3. Take a line from either Cullen's poem or Trethewey's, and write an essay showing how the line is applicable to an "incident" that you recently witnessed or saw being reported in the media.

4. Find and read at least three articles on racial discrimination in early twentieth-century Baltimore or on American laws against interracial marriage. Then write an essay explaining how these articles illuminate the "incident" described in Cullen's or Trethewey's poem.

≡ Envisioning a More Just World: Poems

WILLIAM BLAKE, "The Chimney Sweeper"

MARTÍN ESPADA, "Imagine the Angels of Bread"

MARK JARMAN, "If I Were Paul"

The next three poems invite their readers to imagine what a more just world than the current one would be like. Such a vision involves defining what *justice* means in the first place. It also involves identifying what the leading examples of present injustice are. Directly or indirectly, each poem in this cluster points to moral blights that its speaker hopes to cure. Whether or not utopia can ever be achieved, these literary works encourage their audiences to identify and challenge existing social ills.

≡ BEFORE YOU READ

When you think about major types of injustice today, what specifically comes to your mind?

WILLIAM BLAKE
The Chimney Sweeper

His contemporaries largely dismissed him as eccentric, even mad, but William Blake (1757–1827) is now regarded as a major figure in British Romanticism. In part, Blake was a printer and an engraver, lavishly illustrating his own editions of his poems. Through both his visual and his verbal art, Blake promoted his own self-devised religion, which incorporated stories and characters from the Bible. The following poem appears in his 1789 collection Songs of Innocence. *In 1794, he produced a counterpart volume,* Songs of Experience.

When my mother died I was very young,
And my father sold me while yet my tongue
Could scarcely cry "'weep! 'weep! 'weep! 'weep!"
So your chimneys I sweep & in soot I sleep.

There's little Tom Dacre, who cried when his head   5
That curled like a lamb's back, was shaved, so I said,
"Hush, Tom! never mind it, for when your head's bare,
You know that the soot cannot spoil your white hair."

And so he was quiet, & that very night,
As Tom was a-sleeping he had such a sight!   10
That thousands of sweepers, Dick, Joe, Ned, & Jack,
Were all of them locked up in coffins of black;

And by came an Angel who had a bright key,
And he opened the coffins & set them all free;
Then down a green plain, leaping, laughing they run,   15
And wash in a river and shine in the Sun.

Then naked & white, all their bags left behind,
They rise upon clouds, and sport in the wind.
And the Angel told Tom, if he'd be a good boy,
He'd have God for his father & never want joy.   20

And so Tom awoke; and we rose in the dark
And got with our bags & our brushes to work.
Though the morning was cold, Tom was happy & warm;
So if all do their duty, they need not fear harm.   [1789]

≡ THINKING ABOUT THE TEXT

1. How do colors matter in this poem?
2. What is the effect of the poem's obvious rhyming?
3. Why do you think that Blake made the dream Tom's rather than the speaker's?
4. As an imaginative vision of a better world, how unusual does Tom's dream strike you?
5. Do you assume that the author himself agrees with the last line? Why, or why not? In general, how much of what the speaker says do you think Blake wants his readers to accept? Explain.

MARTÍN ESPADA
Imagine the Angels of Bread

Originally from Brooklyn, New York, Martín Espada (b. 1957) is a widely published poet, essayist, and translator whose work often reflects on his Puerto Rican heritage. Though currently a professor of English at the University of Massachusetts–Amherst, he has also practiced as a tenant lawyer. His collections of verse include The Trouble Ball *(2011),* The Republic of Poetry *(2006),* A Mayan Astronomer in Hell's Kitchen *(2000), and* City of Coughing and Dead Radiators *(1993). The following is the title poem of his book* Imagine the Angels of Bread *(1996), which won the American Book Award.*

This is the year that squatters evict landlords,
gazing like admirals from the rail
of the roofdeck
or levitating hands in praise
of steam in the shower;   5

this is the year
that shawled refugees deport judges
who stare at the floor
and their swollen feet
as files are stamped   10
with their destination;
this is the year that police revolvers,
stove-hot, blister the fingers
of raging cops,
and nightsticks splinter   15
in their palms;
this is the year
that darkskinned men
lynched a century ago
return to sip coffee quietly   20
with the apologizing descendants
of their executioners.

This is the year that those
who swim the border's undertow
and shiver in boxcars   25
are greeted with trumpets and drums
at the first railroad crossing
on the other side;
this is the year that the hands
pulling tomatoes from the vine   30
uproot the deed to the earth that sprouts the vine,
the hands canning tomatoes
are named in the will
that owns the bedlam of the cannery;
this is the year that the eyes   35
stinging from the poison that purifies toilets
awaken at last to the sight
of a rooster-loud hillside,
pilgrimage of immigrant birth;
this is the year that cockroaches   40
become extinct, that no doctor
finds a roach embedded
in the ear of an infant;
this is the year that the food stamps
of adolescent mothers   45
are auctioned like gold doubloons,
and no coin is given to buy machetes
for the next bouquet of severed heads
in coffee plantation country.

If the abolition of slave-manacles   50
began as a vision of hands without manacles,

then this is the year;
if the shutdown of extermination camps
began as imagination of a land
without barbed wire or the crematorium,   55
then this is the year;
if every rebellion begins with the idea
that conquerors on horseback
are not many-legged gods, that they too drown
if plunged in the river,   60
then this is the year.

So may every humiliated mouth,
teeth like desecrated headstones,
fill with the angels of bread.   *[1997]*

☰ THINKING ABOUT THE TEXT

1. Identify the patterns of repetition in this poem. What is their effect?

2. The poem is divided into four stanzas. What is the function of each?

3. What are the specific types of injustice that the speaker seems concerned about?

4. What are the various kinds of actions that the speaker envisions the victims of injustice performing? To what extent does he imagine them taking revenge?

5. What action does the speaker encourage the poem's readers to take?

☰ MAKING COMPARISONS

1. Angels figure in both Espada's poem and Blake's. Do they play the same role in these poems, however? Refer to specific lines in each text.

2. Espada's poem refers to a greater number of injustices than Blake's does. Does this difference produce a significant difference in effect? Explain.

3. What do you think Espada's speaker would say about the last line uttered by Blake's speaker?

MARK JARMAN
If I Were Paul

Mark Jarman (b. 1952) is Centennial Professor of English at Vanderbilt University in Nashville, Tennessee. The author of two essay collections, The Secret of Poetry *(2001) and* Body and Soul *(2002), he has also produced several books of verse, including* Questions for Ecclesiastes *(1998),* Unholy Sonnets *(2000),* To the Green Man *(2004), and* Epistles *(2007), which begins with the following poem. In the Bible, the genre of the epistle is associated with Paul of Tarsus. It is a type of letter that he supposedly wrote to the people of various cities, urging them to become Christians. Martin Luther King Jr.'s "Letter from Birmingham Jail" (see this chapter's "Civil Disobedience" cluster) has been viewed as a modern-day Pauline epistle.*

Consider how you were made.

Consider the loving geometry that sketched your bones, the passionate symmetry that sewed flesh to your skeleton, and the cloudy zenith whence your soul descended in shimmering rivulets across pure granite to pour as a single braided stream into the skull's cup.

Consider the first time you conceived of justice, engendered mercy, brought parity into being, coaxed liberty like a marten from its den to uncoil its limber spine in a sunny clearing, how you understood the inheritance of first principles, the legacy of noble thought, and built a city like a forest in the forest, and erected temples like thunderheads.

Consider, as if it were penicillin or the speed of light, the discovery of another's hands, his oval field of vision, her muscular back and hips, his nerve-jarred neck and shoulders, her bleeding gums and dry elbows and knees, his baldness and cauterized skin cancers, her lucid and forgiving gaze, his healing touch, her mind like a prairie. Consider the first knowledge of otherness. How it felt.

Consider what you were meant to be in the egg, in your parents' arms, under a sky full of stars.   5

Now imagine what I have to say when I learn of your enterprising viciousness, the discipline with which one of you turns another into a robot or a parasite or a maniac or a body strapped to a chair. Imagine what I have to say.

Do the impossible. Restore life to those you have killed, wholeness to those you have maimed, goodness to what you have poisoned, trust to those you have betrayed.

Bless each other with the heart and soul, the hand and eye, the head and foot, the lips, tongue, and teeth, the inner ear and the outer ear, the flesh and spirit, the brain and bowels, the blood and lymph, the heel and toe, the muscle and bone, the waist and hips, the chest and shoulders, the whole body, clothed and naked, young and old, aging and growing up.

I sent you this not knowing if you will receive it, or if having received it, you will read it, or if having read it, you will know that it contains my blessing.   *[2008]*

≡ **THINKING ABOUT THE TEXT**

1. Paul was an early Christian. Do you see Jarman's poem as addressed primarily to people of this faith? Why, or why not?

2. Note the first line. Why, in order to correct injustice, might it be important to "Consider how you were made"?

3. The next three stanzas are pretty dense in their language. Try to express in your own words the main ideas they convey. Should Jarman have used much simpler wording than he does? Why, or why not?

4. In the sixth stanza, the speaker accuses his audience of "enterprising viciousness." In the next stanza, he says that they have "killed," "maimed," "poisoned," and "betrayed" people. What would you say to someone who argues that language like this would merely offend readers rather than persuade them to share the speaker's ideals?

5. What, in general, does the speaker emphasize in his next-to-last stanza when he calls for things to be blessed?

☰ MAKING COMPARISONS

1. Both Espada's poem and Jarman's use the word *imagine*. Do you think that the poems are inviting their readers to imagine the same sorts of things? Refer to specific lines in each text.

2. Does Jarman's speaker seem angrier than Espada's? Do you detect any anger in Blake's speaker? Explain.

3. Can Espada's poem and Blake's also be considered epistles? Why, or why not?

☰ WRITING ABOUT ISSUES

1. Choose one of the poems in this cluster, and write an essay in which you identify what are, in general, the injustice(s) that the poem considers. Refer to specific lines.

2. The three poems in this cluster differ markedly in the number and kinds of stanzas they use. Choose two of the poems, and write an essay in which you explain how the different ways they use stanzas produce major differences in effect.

3. Write your own epistle, in prose or verse, to a specific group of people who in your view have committed a particular injustice. In your letter, do not simply accuse your readers of a moral failing and demand that they correct it; explain *why* you are disturbed by something they have done, as well as *how* it amounts to an injustice in your definition of the term. If you wish, refer to any of the poems in this cluster.

4. Choose a recent speech, editorial, or blog entry that you see as identifying an injustice and as imagining a world in which it no longer exists. Write an essay analyzing the strategies of persuasion the speaker or writer uses. If you wish, refer to any of the poems in this cluster.

SEAMUS HEANEY, "Punishment"

CAROLYN FORCHÉ, "The Colonel"

C. K. WILLIAMS, "The Nail"

SHERMAN ALEXIE, "Capital Punishment"

Acts of punishment may be just or unjust: in any case, a punishment reflects the decisions and values of the person ordering it and the ethics of the person willing to carry it out. Even people who merely learn about a punishment wind up judging it. Consciously or unconsciously, they choose to praise it, criticize it, or passively tolerate it. Each of these four poems deals with judgments made by punishers and by those who are, in some sense, their audience. Think about the actions you are taking and the principles you are expressing as you judge the people you encounter here.

≡ BEFORE YOU READ

Recall a particular punishment that you considered unjust. What were the circumstances? What experiences, values, and reasoning led you to disapprove of the punishment? Could you have done anything to prevent it or to see that similarly unfair punishments did not recur? If so, what?

SEAMUS HEANEY
Punishment

For his distinguished career as a poet, Seamus Heaney (1939–2013) won the Nobel Prize for literature in 1995. He was raised as a Catholic in Northern Ireland, where Protestants remained in the majority and frequently conflicted with Catholics. Until the Peace Accord of 1997, the region was controlled by the British government, whereas now it is ruled by a mixed body representing both religions. Several of Heaney's poems deal with Catholic resistance to the longtime British domination of his native land. Heaney moved to Dublin, in the Republic of Ireland, in the early 1970s, but he often visited the United States, even holding an appointment as Boylston Professor of Rhetoric at Harvard University. The following poem appears in Heaney's 1975 book North. *It is part of a whole sequence of poems based on P. V. Glob's 1969 book* The Bog People. *Heaney was drawn to Glob's photographs of Iron Age people whose preserved bodies were discovered in bogs of Denmark and other European countries.*

I can feel the tug
of the halter at the nape
of her neck, the wind
on her naked front.

It blows her nipples   5
to amber beads,
it shakes the frail rigging
of her ribs.

I can see her drowned
body in the bog,   10
the weighing stone,
the floating rods and boughs.

Under which at first
she was a barked sapling
that is dug up   15
oak-bone, brain-firkin:

her shaved head
like a stubble of black corn,
her blindfold a soiled bandage,
her noose a ring   20

to store
the memories of love.
Little adulteress,
before they punished you

you were flaxen-haired,   25
undernourished, and your
tar-black face was beautiful.
My poor scapegoat,

I almost love you
but would have cast, I know,   30
the stones of silence.°
I am the artful voyeur

of your brain's exposed
and darkened combs,
your muscles' webbing   35
and all your numbered bones:

30–31 would have cast ... of silence: In John 8:7–9, Jesus confronts a mob about to
stone an adulterous woman and makes the famous statement "He that is without sin among
you, let him first cast a stone at her." The crowd retreats, "being convicted by their own
conscience."

I who have stood dumb
when your betraying sisters,
cauled in tar,
wept by the railings,°   40

who would connive
in civilized outrage
yet understand the exact
and tribal, intimate revenge.   *[1975]*

37–40 I who . . . by the railings: In 1969, the British army became highly visible occu-
piers of Northern Ireland. In Heaney's native city of Belfast, the Irish Republican Army
retaliated against Irish Catholic women who dated British soldiers. Punishments included
shaving the women's heads, stripping and tarring them, and handcuffing them to the city's
railings.

≡ THINKING ABOUT THE TEXT

1. Summarize your impression of the bog woman. Where does the speaker
   begin addressing her directly? Why do you suppose Heaney has him refrain from addressing her right away?

2. Who is the main subject of this poem? The bog woman? The "betraying
   sisters" (line 38)? The speaker? Some combination of these people?

3. The speaker refers to himself as a "voyeur" (line 32). Consult a dictionary definition of this word. How might it apply to the speaker? Do you
   think it is ultimately the best label for him? Explain. Do you feel like a
   voyeur reading this poem? Why, or why not?

4. What are the speaker's thoughts in the last stanza? What connotation
   do you attach to the word *connive*? (You might want to consult a dictionary definition of it.) What is the speaker's attitude toward "the exact /
   and tribal, intimate revenge"? Do you see him as tolerating violence?

5. What words in this poem, if any, are unfamiliar to you? What is their
   effect on you? Each stanza has four lines. Does this pattern create a
   steady rhythm or one more fragmented than harmonious? Try reading it
   aloud.

CAROLYN FORCHÉ
The Colonel

*In her poetry, Carolyn Forché (b. 1950) often addresses contemporary abuses of
power. Her first book of poems,* Gathering the Tribes *(1976), won the Yale Series
of Younger Poets competition. The following poem is from her second,* The Country
between Us *(1981), which won the Lamont Award from the Academy of American
Poets. Much of this book is based on Forché's experiences during her stay in El Salvador,*

which at the time was beset by civil war. She has edited a collection entitled Against
Forgetting: Twentieth-Century Poetry of Witness *(1993), and her latest book of
poetry is* The Blue Hour *(2003). She is currently a professor of English at George-
town University in Washington, D.C.*

What you have heard is true. I was in his house. His wife carried a tray of coffee
and sugar. His daughter filed her nails, his son went out for the night. There
were daily papers, pet dogs, a pistol on the cushion beside him. The moon
swung bare on its black cord over the house. On the television was a cop show.
It was in English. Broken bottles were embedded in the walls around the house   5
to scoop the kneecaps from a man's legs or cut his hands to lace. On the
windows there were gratings like those in liquor stores. We had dinner, rack of
lamb, good wine, a gold bell was on the table for calling the maid. The maid
brought green mangoes, salt, a type of bread. I was asked how I enjoyed the
country. There was a brief commercial in Spanish. His wife took everything   10
away. There was some talk then of how difficult it had become to govern. The
parrot said hello on the terrace. The colonel told it to shut up, and pushed himself from the table. My friend said to me with his eyes: say nothing. The colonel
returned with a sack used to bring groceries home. He spilled many human
ears on the table. They were like dried peach halves. There is no other way to   15
say this. He took one of them in his hands, shook it in our faces, dropped it into
a water glass. It came alive there. I am tired of fooling around he said. As for the
rights of anyone, tell your people they can go fuck themselves. He swept the
ears to the floor with his arm and held the last of his wine in the air. Something
for your poetry, no? he said. Some of the ears on the floor caught this scrap of   20
his voice. Some of the ears on the floor were pressed to the ground.   *[1978]*

☰ THINKING ABOUT THE TEXT

1. How do you characterize the colonel? List a number of specific adjectives and supporting details. Does your impression of him change as you
   read, or does it stay pretty much the same? Explain.

2. Forché calls this text a poem, and yet it seems to consist of one long
   prose paragraph. Here is an issue of genre: Is it *really* a poem? Support
   your answer by identifying what you think are characteristics of poetry.
   What is the effect of Forché's presenting the text as a poem? Note what
   the colonel says about poetry. How might this text be considered a response to him?

3. Forché uses many short sentences here. What is the effect of this strategy? Even though she quotes the colonel, she does not use quotation
   marks. What is the effect of this choice?

4. The poem begins, "What you have heard is true." Do you think the situation it describes really occurred? Identify some warrants or assumptions

that influence your answer. Where else does the poem refer to hearing? How might it be seen as being about audiences and their responses?

5. Forché wrote "The Colonel" after a stay in El Salvador, and so it is reasonable for her audience to conclude that the poem is set in that country. Yet she does not actually specify the setting. Should she have done so? Why, or why not?

≡ MAKING COMPARISONS

1. Do you find the punishments alluded to in Heaney's and Forché's poems equally disturbing? Note specific details that influence your impressions.

2. To what extent does each of these two poems seem an effort to imagine the mind of someone who inflicts punishment?

3. Which, if any, of the situations referred to in these two poems could happen in the contemporary United States?

C. K. WILLIAMS
The Nail

Originally from Newark, New Jersey, C. K. Williams (b. 1936) has taught for many years at Princeton University while also spending much time in France. His most recent books include Writers Writing Dying: Poems *(2012),* In Time: Poets, Poems, and the Rest *(2012),* Collected Poems *(2006), and* On Whitman *(2010), a study of Walt Whitman. During his long career as a poet, he has won several major prizes, including the National Book Award for* The Singing *(2003), the National Book Critics Circle Award for* Flesh and Blood *(1987), and the Pulitzer Prize for* Repair *(1999), which includes the following selection.*

Some dictator or other had gone into exile, and now reports were coming
　　about his regime,
the usual crimes, torture, false imprisonment, cruelty and corruption,
　　but then a detail:
that the way his henchmen had disposed of enemies was by hammering
　　nails into their skulls.
Horror, then, what mind does after horror, after that first feeling that
　　you'll never catch your breath,
mind imagines—how not be annihilated by it?—the preliminary tap,　　　5
　　feels it in the tendons of the hand,
feels the way you do with *your* nail when you're fixing something,
　　making something, shelves, a bed;
the first light tap to set the slant, and then the slightly harder tap, to
　　embed the tip a little more . . .

No, no more: this should be happening in myth, in stone, or paint, not in
    reality, not here;
it should be an emblem of itself, not itself, something that would *mean*,
    not really have to happen,
something to go out, expand in implication from that unmoved mass of   10
    matter in the breast;
as in the image of an anguished face, in grief for us, not us as us, us as in
    a myth, a moral tale,
a way to tell the truth that grief is limitless, a way to tell us we must
    always understand
it's we who do such things, we who set the slant, embed the tip, lift the
    sledge and drive the nail,
drive the nail which is the axis upon which turns the brutal human world
    upon the world.   *[1999]*

≡ THINKING ABOUT THE TEXT

1. If not for the "detail" of the nailing, do you think the speaker would have been greatly bothered by what he refers to as "the usual crimes, torture, false imprisonment, cruelty and corruption" (line 2)? Explain your reasoning.

2. Although the first stanza begins by referring to people other than the speaker ("Some dictator or other," "his henchmen"), it then refers to "you." What is the effect of this shift? The second stanza then brings up "we" and "us." Why does Williams make this change in pronouns, do you think?

3. In line 5, the speaker suggests that the mind can be "annihilated." In what sense might this be so?

4. The speaker seems to compare the dictator's punishment of his foes— his "hammering nails into their skulls" (line 3)—to ordinary carpentry that the poem's readers might perform. What would you say to a reader who argues that this comparison trivializes the barbarity of the dictator's act?

5. At the beginning of the second stanza, the speaker understandably expresses a wish that the dictator's act take place "not in reality, not here." Explain the alternative he imagines. What does he mean when he says that "this should be happening in myth, in stone, or paint" (line 8)— that "it should be an emblem of itself, not itself, something that would *mean*" (line 9)?

6. What would you say to a reader who sees references to Christ's crucifixion in the last few lines? How helpful do you find this association for an understanding of the poem? How should non-Christian readers feel about it?

☰ MAKING COMPARISONS

1. Williams's title, "The Nail," suggests that his poem depends heavily on imagery. Does imagery play as big a role in Heaney's and Forché's poems as it does in Williams's? Explain by referring to specific lines in each.

2. Are Williams's and Heaney's poems more about the speaker's *reaction* to punishment than Forché's is? Refer to specific lines in all three texts.

3. In what ways does each of the three poems turn the physical punishment it focuses on into a metaphor? What would you say to someone who argues that a poem should never do this—that making punishment metaphorical is insensitive to the pain of those it actually hurts?

SHERMAN ALEXIE
Capital Punishment

Born in Spokane, Washington, Sherman Alexie (b. 1966) is a member of the Spokane/ Coeur d'Alene tribe. His fiction includes the novels Reservation Blues *(1996),* Indian Killer *(1997),* Flight *(2007), and* The Absolutely True Diary of a Part-Time Indian *(2007). He has also produced four collections of short stories:* Blasphemy: New and Selected Stories *(2013),* Ten Little Indians *(2003),* The Toughest Indian in the World *(2001), and* The Lone Ranger and Tonto Fistfight in Heaven *(1994), which he adapted for the acclaimed 1998 film* Smoke Signals. *Alexie is a poet, too, with his collections of verse including* The Business of Fancy Dancing *(1992),* Old Shirts and New Skins *(1993),* First Indian on the Moon *(1993),* Drums like This *(1996),* One Stick Song *(2000), and* Face *(2009). "Capital Punishment" appeared in a 1996 issue of* Indiana Review *and, that same year, in Alexie's collection* The Summer of Black Widows. *It was also selected for the 1996 edition of the volume* Best American Poetry. *Alexie wrote the poem after reading media coverage of an actual execution in the state of Washington.*

I prepare the last meal
for the Indian man to be executed

but this killer doesn't want much:
baked potato, salad, tall glass of ice water.

(I am not a witness)   5

It's mostly the dark ones
who are forced to sit in the chair

especially when white people die.
It's true, you can look it up

and this Indian killer pushed   10
his fists all the way down

a white man's throat, just to win a bet
about the size of his heart.

Those Indians are always gambling.
Still, I season this last meal   15

with all I have. I don't have much
but I send it down the line

with the handsome guard
who has fallen in love

with the Indian killer.   20
I don't care who loves whom.

(I am not a witness)

I don't care if I add too much
salt or pepper to the warden's stew.

He can eat what I put in front of him.   25
I just cook for the boss

but I cook just right
for the Indian man to be executed.

The temperature is the thing.
I once heard a story   30

about a black man who was electrocuted
in that chair and lived to tell about it

before the court decided to sit him back down
an hour later and kill him all over again.

I have an extra sandwich hidden away   35
in the back of the refrigerator

in case this Indian killer survives
that first slow flip of the switch

and gets hungry while he waits
for the engineers to debate the flaws.   40

(I am not a witness)

I prepare the last meal for free
just like I signed up for the last war.

I learned how to cook
by lasting longer than any of the others.   45

Tonight, I'm just the last one left
after the handsome guard takes the meal away.

I turn off the kitchen lights
and sit alone in the dark

because the whole damn prison dims   50
when the chair is switched on.

You can watch a light bulb flicker
on a night like this

and remember it too clearly
like it was your first kiss   55

or the first hard kick to your groin.
It's all the same

when I am huddled down here
trying not to look at the clock

look at the clock, no, don't   60
look at the clock, when all of it stops

making sense: a salad, a potato
a drink of water all taste like heat.

(I am not a witness)

I want you to know I tasted a little   65
of that last meal before I sent it away.

It's the cook's job, to make sure
and I was sure I ate from the same plate

and ate with the same fork and spoon
that the Indian killer used later   70

in his cell. Maybe a little bit of me
lodged in his stomach, wedged between

his front teeth, his incisors, his molars
when he chewed down on the bit

and his body arced like modern art   75
curving organically, smoke rising

from his joints, wispy flames decorating
the crown of his head, the balls of his feet.

(I am not a witness)

I sit here in the dark kitchen   80
when they do it, meaning

when they kill him, kill
and add another definition of the word

to the dictionary. American fills
its dictionary. We write down *kill* and everybody   85

in the audience shouts out exactly how
they spell it, what it means to them

and all of the answers are taken down
by the pollsters and secretaries

who take care of the small details: 90
time of death, pulse rate, press release.

I heard a story once about some reporters
at a hanging who wanted the hood removed

from the condemned's head, so they could look
into his eyes and tell their readers   95

what they saw there. What did they expect?
All of the stories should be simple.

1 death + 1 death = 2 deaths.
But we throw the killers in one grave

and victims in another. We form sides   100
and have two separate feasts.

(I am a witness)

I prepared the last meal
for the Indian man who was executed

and have learned this: If any of us   105
stood for days on top of a barren hill

during an electrical storm
then lightning would eventually strike us

and we'd have no idea for which of our sins
we were reduced to headlines and ash.   *[1996]*   110

≣ THINKING ABOUT THE TEXT

1. Alexie reports that in writing this poem, he aimed "to call for the abolition of the death penalty." In reading the poem, do you sense that this
   is his aim? Why, or why not? In what respects might the poem be seen
   as arguing against the death penalty? State how you viewed capital punishment before and after you read it. Did Alexie affect your attitude? If
   so, how?

2. Why do you think Alexie cast the speaker as the condemned man's
   cook? How do you explain the speaker's shift from denying that he is a

witness to acknowledging that he is one? Identify how he seems to define the term *witness*. What would you say to someone who argues that the speaker is unreasonably stretching the meaning of this word because apparently he didn't directly observe the execution?

3. How does race figure in this poem? Should people consider race when discussing capital punishment? If so, what about race should they especially ponder? In examining Alexie's poem, should readers bear in mind that the author is Native American? Why, or why not?

4. The film *Dead Man Walking* (1995), which deals with arguments about capital punishment, shows in chilling detail an execution by injection. Yet at the moment the condemned man dies, the film also shows the faces of his two victims. By contrast, Alexie doesn't refer to the victim of the executed man after line 12. Should he have mentioned this victim again? Identify some of the values reflected in your answer.

5. Summarize and evaluate the lesson delivered by the speaker at the end of the poem. What do you think headlines might say about you if you were killed in the manner he describes?

≡ MAKING COMPARISONS

1. Forché's first sentence is "What you have heard is true." After noting that "It's mostly the dark ones / who are forced to sit in the chair / especially when white people die" (lines 6–8), Alexie's speaker declares, "It's true, you can look it up" (line 9). What do these lines imply about each poem's readers?

2. In his last three lines, Alexie's speaker refers to "us." Williams's last stanza also uses this pronoun and goes so far as to say, "it's we who do such things" (line 13). Do you take both speakers, as well as Forché's and Heaney's, to be making the same observation about their society in general? Why, or why not?

3. Of all the punishments mentioned in these four poems, only the one discussed in Alexie's — capital punishment — is currently authorized by law in the United States. Should this fact make his poem the most relevant to American readers? Why, or why not?

≡ WRITING ABOUT ISSUES

1. Choose one of the poems in this cluster. Then write an essay explaining how it can be seen as a poem about witnessing *or* about how people may be somehow involved with events that they haven't directly observed. If your essay refers to witnessing, make clear your definition of the term.

2. Even when people are not literally guilty of a crime or an atrocity, they may still *feel* guilty in a psychological sense. Choose two of the poems in

this cluster, and write an essay arguing that one poem's main speaker evidently feels more guilt than the other poem's main speaker does. Refer to specific lines in both texts.

3. Write an essay in which you discuss whether the phrase "cruel and unusual punishment" applies to the event described in this paragraph from the March 26, 1997, issue of the *Washington Post*:

> Moments after convicted killer Pedro Medina was strapped into Florida's electric chair and 2,000 volts of electricity surged into his body this morning, flames leapt from the inmate's head, filling the death chamber with smoke and horrifying two dozen witnesses.

Does Medina's execution amount to "cruel and unusual punishment"? If you need additional information before firmly deciding, what do you need to know?

4. Today, Amnesty International and PEN International, a writers' organization, regularly bring to the American public's attention cases of what they deem unjust punishment. In fact, Amnesty International has criticized all instances of capital punishment in the United States. Research one of the cases reported by these organizations. Then write an article for your school newspaper in which you (a) present the basic facts of the case, (b) identify values and principles you think your audience should apply to it, and (c) point out anything you believe can and should be done about it. If you wish, refer to any of the poems in this cluster.

He Said/She Said: Re-Visions of a Poem

ROBERT BROWNING, "My Last Duchess"

GABRIEL SPERA, "My Ex-Husband"

Although the terms *justice* and *injustice* are most often applied to developments that affect entire groups, these words can also prove relevant to personal relationships. In particular, two people may quit being a couple because at least one of them feels that the other has done an injustice to him or her. Of course, the two parties may define *justice* differently, and they may disagree as well about which of them is in the wrong. Together, the following poems illustrate such a conflict of views. Indeed, they present a he said/she said scenario. In the first poem, Robert Browning's famous "My Last Duchess," the speaker explains how his wife's allegedly unjust behavior forced him to get rid of her. In the second poem, Gabriel Spera's more recent "My Ex-Husband," the speaker recalls how her former spouse's injustices drove her to divorce him. Notice the specific ways that Spera's re-vision of Browning's poem forces us to consider differences in perspective.

≡ BEFORE YOU READ

Think of two people you know who have broken off a relationship they had with each other. To what extent do these people see the breakup the same way? How, if at all, do their views of it differ?

ROBERT BROWNING
My Last Duchess

Today, Robert Browning (1812–1889) is regarded as one of the greatest poets of nineteenth-century England, but in his own time he was not nearly as celebrated as his wife, the poet Elizabeth Barrett Browning. He is chiefly known for his achievements with the dramatic monologue, *a genre of poetry that emphasizes the speaker's own distinct personality. Often Browning's speakers are his imaginative re-creations of people who once existed in real life. He was especially interested in religious, political, and artistic figures from the Renaissance. The following poem, perhaps Browning's most famous, was written in 1842, and its speaker, the Duke of Ferrara, was an actual man.*

(© Bettmann/Corbis.)

Ferrara°

That's my last Duchess painted on the wall,
Looking as if she were alive. I call
That piece a wonder, now: Frà Pandolf's° hands
Worked busily a day, and there she stands.
Will't please you sit and look at her? I said   5
"Frà Pandolf" by design, for never read
Strangers like you that pictured countenance,
The depth and passion of its earnest glance,
But to myself they turned (since none puts by
The curtain I have drawn for you, but I)   10
And seemed as they would ask me, if they durst,
How such a glance came there; so, not the first
Are you to turn and ask thus. Sir, 'twas not
Her husband's presence only, called that spot
Of joy into the Duchess' cheek: perhaps   15

Epigraph Ferrara: In the sixteenth century, the duke of this Italian city arranged to marry a second time after the mysterious death of his very young first wife.   **3 Frà Pandolf:** A fictitious artist.

Frà Pandolf chanced to say "Her mantle laps
Over my lady's wrist too much," or "Paint
Must never hope to reproduce the faint
Half-flush that dies along her throat": such stuff
Was courtesy, she thought, and cause enough   20
For calling up that spot of joy. She had
A heart—how shall I say?—too soon made glad,
Too easily impressed; she liked whate'er
She looked on, and her looks went everywhere.
Sir, 'twas all one! My favor at her breast,   25
The dropping of the daylight in the West,
The bough of cherries some officious fool
Broke in the orchard for her, the white mule
She rode with round the terrace—all and each
Would draw from her alike the approving speech,   30
Or blush, at least. She thanked men,—good! but thanked
Somehow—I know not how—as if she ranked
My gift of a nine-hundred-years-old name
With anybody's gift. Who'd stoop to blame
This sort of trifling? Even had you skill   35
In speech—which I have not—to make your will
Quite clear to such an one, and say, "Just this
Or that in you disgusts me; here you miss,
Or there exceed the mark"—and if she let
Herself be lessoned so, nor plainly set   40
Her wits to yours, forsooth, and made excuse,
—E'en then would be some stooping; and I choose
Never to stoop. Oh sir, she smiled, no doubt,
Whene'er I passed her; but who passed without
Much the same smile? This grew; I gave commands;   45
Then all smiles stopped together. There she stands
As if alive. Will't please you rise? We'll meet
The company below, then. I repeat,
The Count your master's known munificence
Is ample warrant that no just pretense   50
Of mine for dowry will be disallowed;
Though his fair daughter's self, as I avowed
At starting, is my object. Nay, we'll go
Together down, sir. Notice Neptune, though,
Taming a sea-horse, thought a rarity,   55
Which Claus of Innsbruck° cast in bronze for me!   *[1842]*

---

56 Claus of Innsbruck: A fictitious artist.

≡ THINKING ABOUT THE TEXT

1. The duke offers a history of his first marriage. Summarize his story in your own words, including the reasons he gives for his behavior. How would you describe him? Do you admire anything about him? If so, what?

2. Try to reconstruct the rhetorical situation in which the duke is making his remarks. Who might be his audience? What might be his goals? What strategies is he using to accomplish them? Cite details that support your conjectures.

3. When you read the poem aloud, how conscious are you of its rhymes? What is its rhyme scheme? What is the effect of Browning's using just one stanza rather than breaking the poem into several?

4. Going by this example of the genre, what are the advantages of writing a poem as a dramatic monologue? What are the disadvantages?

5. Browning suggests that the setting of this poem is Renaissance Italy. What relevance might his poem have had for readers in mid-nineteenth-century England? What relevance might it have for audiences in the United States today?

GABRIEL SPERA
My Ex-Husband

Raised in New Jersey, Gabriel Spera (b. 1966) graduated from Cornell University and earned an M.F.A. from the University of North Carolina at Greensboro. He has worked as a technical writer for several years, most recently for a California aerospace firm. At the same time, he has published many poems, including the following one, which first appeared in the journal Poetry *in 1992. It also appears in his book* The Standing Wave *(2003), which was chosen for the National Poetry Series and also won the PEN-USA West Literary Book Award for Poetry. Spera's second book of Poetry,* The Rigid Body, *was published in 2012.*

That's my ex-husband pictured on the shelf,
Smiling as if in love. I took it myself
With his Leica, and stuck it in that frame
We got for our wedding. Kind of a shame
To waste it on him, but what could I do?   5
(Since I haven't got a photograph of you.)
I know what's on your mind—you want to know
Whatever could have made me let him go—
He seems like any woman's perfect catch,
What with his ruddy cheeks, the thin mustache,   10
Those close-set, baggy eyes, that tilted grin.

(Photo by Rachel Lee.)

But snapshots don't show what's beneath the skin!
He had a certain charm, charisma, style,
That passionate, earnest glance he struck, meanwhile
Whispering the sweetest things, like "Your lips   15
Are like plump rubies, eyes like diamond chips,"
Could flush the throat of any woman, not
Just mine. He blew the most romantic spots
In town, where waiters, who all knew his face,
Reserved an intimately dim-lit place   20
Half-hidden in a corner nook. Such stuff
Was all too well rehearsed, I soon enough
Found out. He had an attitude—how should
I put it—smooth, self-satisfied, too good
For the rest of the world, too easily   25
Impressed with his officious self. And he
flirted—fine! but flirted somehow a bit
Too ardently, too blatantly, as if,

If someone ever noticed, no one cared
How slobbishly he carried on affairs.   30
Who'd lower herself to put up with shit
Like that? Even if you'd the patience—which
I have not—to go and see some counsellor
And say, "My life's a living hell," or
"Everything he does disgusts, the lout!"—   35
And even if you'd somehow worked things out,
Took a long trip together, made amends,
Let things get back to normal, even then
You'd still be on the short end of the stick;
And I choose never ever to get stuck.   40
Oh, no doubt, it always made my limbs go
Woozy when he kissed me, but what bimbo
In the steno pool went without the same
Such kisses? So, I made some calls, filed some claims,
All kisses stopped together. There he grins,   45
Almost lovable. Shall we go? I'm in
The mood for Chez Pierre's, perhaps, tonight,
Though anything you'd like would be all right
As well, of course, though I'd prefer not to go
To any place with checkered tables. No,   50
We'll take my car. By the way, have I shown
You yet these lovely champagne flutes, hand blown,
Imported from Murano, Italy,
Which Claus got in the settlement for me!   *[1992]*

≡ THINKING ABOUT THE TEXT

1. Why, evidently, did the speaker get divorced? What would you say to someone who argues that because she still thinks about her former husband, keeps his photograph on the shelf, and clearly has not forgiven him, she remains "stuck" (line 40) in that relationship?

2. How reliable do you think the speaker's account of her former husband is?

3. Where does the speaker shift the kind of language she's been using? Do you think her feelings are consistent despite this shifting? Explain.

4. Who do you think the "you" (line 6) in this poem is? In what ways, if any, does the presence of this "you" seem to influence what the speaker says and how she says it?

5. Although the speaker is a woman, poet Gabriel Spera is a man. Does this poem lead you to believe that a man can, in fact, write from a woman's point of view? Why, or why not?

≡ MAKING COMPARISONS

1. Where in his poem does Spera closely echo Browning's poem? Refer to specific lines in both texts. What is the effect of the changes in wording that Spera makes?

2. Do you sympathize more with Spera's speaker than with Browning's? Why, or why not? Explain.

3. Do the listeners in these two poems both seem passive? Refer to specific details of both texts.

≡ WRITING ABOUT ISSUES

1. Choose either of the poems in this cluster, and write an essay analyzing what you consider to be its most significant line. Be sure to explain why you find your chosen line important.

2. To what extent and in what ways does Spera's poem seem more "modern" than Browning's? Write an essay in which you answer this question. Refer to specific details from both poems, and define clearly what you mean by *modern*.

3. Write an essay analyzing a relationship that you broke off because you thought the other person had acted unjustly. To what extent do you still brood about this relationship? How much have you forgiven the other person? What meaning of the term *justice* seems applicable here?

4. Write a dialogue between the speakers of these two poems, or write a dialogue between the listeners in them. Shape the dialogue so that it emphasizes ideas and principles that the two people have in common. Then write a brief essay in which you analyze the conversation you have constructed. What do you want your readers to conclude from it?

Women Resisting Injustice: A Play in the News

SOPHOCLES, *Antigone*

IN THE NEWS:
PETER BEAUMONT AND SAEED KAMALI DEHGHAN, "Iran: Women on the Frontline of the Fight for Rights"

ISABEL HILTON, "A Triumph for Moral Authority"

We began this chapter with the topic of civil disobedience, nonviolent dissent that assumes that moral law can require violation of human law. For recent examples, we pointed to Myanmar, Iran, and China, where advocates of democracy dare to resist dictators. For most Americans, these are distant places. By studying the protests in them, however, you can better understand how literature has depicted similar acts. The reverse is true as well: literary works about such defiance can shed light on its current role in these nations. So, here we connect Sophocles' ancient tragedy *Antigone* with accounts of protests in these countries.

Think in particular about how the following texts center on women, shown as fighting unjust rule. Of course, history has seen countless women oppose their governments, whether through peaceful or violent means. In the United States, for example, Harriet Tubman helped slaves escape their owners. American and British suffragists militantly campaigned to win the vote. Later, Algerian women joined in their country's revolt against French control. In the Philippines, Corazon Aquino led a revolt against the corrupt Marcos government. And when the regime of Argentina arrested alleged subversives — often proceeding to torture and kill them — mothers of "the disappeared" protested through daily marches. Nevertheless, many people still feel that politics has been — and should be — the domain of men. The texts we feature here challenge this belief, even as their heroines emerge as complex and perhaps even flawed in fighting oppressive leaders.

≡ BEFORE YOU READ

Around the world today, many female protesters — and many male ones, too — claim to be working on behalf of "human rights," a term that was the subject of a United Nations declaration in 1948. What does this term mean to you? What specific "rights" do you associate with it?

SOPHOCLES

Antigone

Translated by Robert Fagles

Antigone was first produced in 441 B.C.E., more than a decade before Oedipus the King was first produced. Just before the action of Antigone begins, the heroine's two brothers have killed each other in battle. One, Eteocles, was defending Thebes; the other, Polynices, was leading an army against it. The current ruler of Thebes, Antigone's uncle Creon, now forbids burial of Polynices—a command that Antigone will defy.

CHARACTERS

ANTIGONE, *daughter of Oedipus and Jocasta*
ISMENE, *sister of Antigone*
A CHORUS *of old Theban citizens and their* LEADER
CREON, *king of Thebes, uncle of Antigone and Ismene*
A SENTRY
HAEMON, *son of Creon and Eurydice*
TIRESIAS, *a blind prophet*
A MESSENGER
EURYDICE, *wife of Creon*
GUARDS, ATTENDANTS, AND A BOY

TIME AND SCENE: *The royal house of Thebes. It is still night, and the invading armies of Argos have just been driven from the city. Fighting on opposite sides, the sons of Oedipus, Eteocles and Polynices, have killed each other in combat. Their uncle, Creon, is now king of Thebes.*

    Enter Antigone, slipping through the central doors of the palace. She motions to her sister, Ismene, who follows her cautiously toward an altar at the center of the stage.

ANTIGONE: My own flesh and blood—dear sister, dear Ismene,
      how many griefs our father Oedipus handed down!
      Do you know one, I ask you, one grief
      that Zeus° will not perfect for the two of us
      while we still live and breathe? There's nothing,   5
      no pain—our lives are pain—no private shame,
      no public disgrace, nothing I haven't seen
      in your griefs and mine. And now this:
      an emergency decree, they say, the Commander
      has just declared for all of Thebes.   10

4 Zeus: The highest Olympian deity.

(© Bettmann/Corbis.)

What, haven't you heard? Don't you see?
The doom reserved for enemies
marches on the ones we love the most.
ISMENE: Not I, I haven't heard a word, Antigone.
Nothing of loved ones,   15
no joy or pain has come my way, not since
the two of us were robbed of our two brothers,
both gone in a day, a double blow—
not since the armies of Argos vanished,
just this very night. I know nothing more,   20
whether our luck's improved or ruin's still to come.
ANTIGONE: I thought so. That's why I brought you out here,
past the gates, so you could hear in private.
ISMENE: What's the matter? Trouble, clearly . . .
you sound so dark, so grim.   25
ANTIGONE: Why not? Our own brothers' burial!

Hasn't Creon graced one with all the rites,
disgraced the other? Eteocles, they say,
has been given full military honors,
rightly so—Creon's laid him in the earth   30
and he goes with glory down among the dead.
But the body of Polynices, who died miserably—
why, a city-wide proclamation, rumor has it,
forbids anyone to bury him, even mourn him.
He's to be left unwept, unburied, a lovely treasure   35
for birds that scan the field and feast to their heart's content.

Such, I hear, is the martial law our good Creon
lays down for you and me—yes, me, I tell you—
and he's coming here to alert the uninformed
in no uncertain terms,   40
and he won't treat the matter lightly. Whoever
disobeys in the least will die, his doom is sealed:
stoning to death inside the city walls!

There you have it. You'll soon show what you are,
worth your breeding, Ismene, or a coward—   45
for all your royal blood.
ISMENE: My poor sister, if things have come to this,
who am I to make or mend them, tell me,
what good am I to you?
ANTIGONE: Decide.
Will you share the labor, share the work?   50
ISMENE: What work, what's the risk? What do you mean?
ANTIGONE:

Raising her hands.

Will you lift up his body with these bare hands
and lower it with me?
ISMENE: What? You'd bury him—
when a law forbids the city?
ANTIGONE: Yes!
He is my brother and—deny it as you will—   55
your brother too.
No one will ever convict me for a traitor.
ISMENE: So desperate, and Creon has expressly—
ANTIGONE: No,
he has no right to keep me from my own.
ISMENE: Oh my sister, think—   60
think how our own father died, hated,
his reputation in ruins, driven on
by the crimes he brought to light himself
to gouge out his eyes with his own hands—

then mother . . . his mother and wife, both in one,   65
mutilating her life in the twisted noose—
and last, our two brothers dead in a single day,
both shedding their own blood, poor suffering boys,
battling out their common destiny hand-to-hand.
Now look at the two of us, left so alone . . .   70
think what a death we'll die, the worst of all
if we violate the laws and override
the fixed decree of the throne, its power—
we must be sensible. Remember we are women,
we're not born to contend with men. Then too,   75
we're underlings, ruled by much stronger hands,
so we must submit in this, and things still worse.

I, for one, I'll beg the dead to forgive me—
I'm forced, I have no choice—I must obey
the ones who stand in power. Why rush to extremes?   80
It's madness, madness.
ANTIGONE: I won't insist,
no, even if you should have a change of heart,
I'd never welcome you in the labor, not with me.
So, do as you like, whatever suits you best—
I'll bury him myself.   85
And even if I die in the act, that death will be a glory.
I'll lie with the one I love and loved by him—
an outrage sacred to the gods! I have longer
to please the dead than please the living here:
in the kingdom down below I'll lie forever.   90
Do as you like, dishonor the laws
the gods hold in honor.
ISMENE: I'd do them no dishonor . . .
but defy the city? I have no strength for that.
ANTIGONE: You have your excuses. I am on my way,
I'll raise a mound for him, for my dear brother.   95
ISMENE: Oh Antigone, you're so rash—I'm so afraid for you!
ANTIGONE: Don't fear for me. Set your own life in order.
ISMENE: Then don't, at least, blurt this out to anyone.
Keep it a secret. I'll join you in that, I promise.
ANTIGONE: Dear god, shout it from the rooftops. I'll hate you   100
all the more for silence—tell the world!
ISMENE: So fiery—and it ought to chill your heart.
ANTIGONE: I know I please where I must please the most.
ISMENE: Yes, if you can, but you're in love with impossibility.
ANTIGONE: Very well then, once my strength gives out   105
I will be done at last.
ISMENE: You're wrong from the start,

you're off on a hopeless quest.

ANTIGONE: If you say so, you will make me hate you,
    and the hatred of the dead, by all rights,
    will haunt you night and day.   110
    But leave me to my own absurdity, leave me
    to suffer this—dreadful thing. I'll suffer
    nothing as great as death without glory.

Exit to the side.

ISMENE: Then go if you must, but rest assured,
    wild, irrational as you are, my sister,   115
    you are truly dear to the ones who love you.

Withdrawing to the palace. Enter a Chorus, the old citizens of Thebes, chanting as the sun begins to rise.

CHORUS: Glory!—great beam of sun, brightest of all
    that ever rose on the seven gates of Thebes,
        you burn through night at last!
                Great eye of the golden day,   120
    mounting the Dirce's° banks you throw him back—
    the enemy out of Argos, the white shield, the man of bronze—
    he's flying headlong now
        the bridle of fate stampeding him with pain!

    And he had driven against our borders,   125
    launched by the warring claims of Polynices—
    like an eagle screaming, winging havoc
    over the land, wings of armor
    shielded white as snow,
    a huge army massing,   130
    crested helmets bristling for assault.

He hovered above our roofs, his vast maw gaping
closing down around our seven gates,
    his spears thirsting for the kill
                but now he's gone, look,   135
before he could glut his jaws with Theban blood
or the god of fire put our crown of towers to the torch.

He grappled the Dragon none can master—Thebes—
    the clang of our arms like thunder at his back!

    Zeus hates with a vengeance all bravado,   140
    the mighty boasts of men. He watched them
    coming on in a rising flood, the pride
    of their golden armor ringing shrill—

---

121 the Dirce: A river near Thebes.

and brandishing his lightning
blasted the fighter just at the goal,   145
rushing to shout his triumph from our walls.

Down from the heights he crashed, pounding down on the earth!
And a moment ago, blazing torch in hand—
   mad for attack, ecstatic
he breathed his rage, the storm   150
 of his fury hurling at our heads!
But now his high hopes have laid him low
and down the enemy ranks the iron god of war
  deals his rewards, his stunning blows—Ares°
rapture of battle, our right arm in the crisis.   155

  Seven captains marshaled at seven gates
seven against their equals, gave
their brazen trophies up to Zeus,
god of the breaking rout of battle,
all but two: those blood brothers,   160
one father, one mother—matched in rage,
spears matched for the twin conquest—
clashed and won the common prize of death.

But now for Victory! Glorious in the morning,
joy in her eyes to meet our joy   165
  she is winging down to Thebes,
our fleets of chariots wheeling in her wake—
  Now let us win oblivion from the wars,
thronging the temples of the gods
in singing, dancing choirs through the night!   170
  Lord Dionysus,° god of the dance
that shakes the land of Thebes, now lead the way!

Enter Creon from the palace, attended by his guard.
  But look, the king of the realm is coming,
Creon, the new man for the new day,
whatever the gods are sending now . . .   175
what new plan will he launch?
Why this, this special session?
Why this sudden call to the old men
summoned at one command?
CREON: My countrymen,
the ship of state is safe. The gods who rocked her,   180
after a long, merciless pounding in the storm,
have righted her once more.

154 Ares: God of war. **171 Dionysus:** God of fertility and wine.

                    Out of the whole city
I have called you here alone. Well I know,
first, your undeviating respect
for the throne and royal power of King Laius.   185
Next, while Oedipus steered the land of Thebes,
and even after he died, your loyalty was unshakable,
you still stood by their children. Now then,
since the two sons are dead—two blows of fate
in the same day, cut down by each other's hands,   190
both killers, both brothers stained with blood—
as I am next in kin to the dead,
I now possess the throne and all its powers.

Of course you cannot know a man completely,
his character, his principles, sense of judgment,   195
not till he's shown his colors, ruling the people,
making laws. Experience, there's the test.
As I see it, whoever assumes the task,
the awesome task of setting the city's course,
and refuses to adopt the soundest policies   200
but fearing someone, keeps his lips locked tight,
he's utterly worthless. So I rate him now,
I always have. And whoever places a friend
above the good of his own country, he is nothing:
I have no use for him. Zeus my witness,   205
Zeus who sees all things, always—
I could never stand by silent, watching destruction
march against our city, putting safety to rout,
nor could I ever make that man a friend of mine
who menaces our country. Remember this: 210
our country *is* our safety.
Only while she voyages true on course
can we establish friendships, truer than blood itself.
Such are my standards. They make our city great.

Closely akin to them I have proclaimed,   215
just now, the following decree to our people
concerning the two sons of Oedipus.
Eteocles, who died fighting for Thebes,
excelling all in arms: he shall be buried,
crowned with a hero's honors, the cups we pour   220
to soak the earth and reach the famous dead.

But as for his blood brother, Polynices,
who returned from exile, home to his father-city
and the gods of his race, consumed with one desire—

to burn them roof to roots—who thirsted to drink   225
his kinsmen's blood and sell the rest to slavery:
that man—a proclamation has forbidden the city
to dignify him with burial, mourn him at all.
No, he must be left unburied, his corpse
carrion for the birds and dogs to tear,   230
an obscenity for the citizens to behold!
These are my principles. Never at my hands
will the traitor be honored above the patriot.
But whoever proves his loyalty to the state:
I'll prize that man in death as well as life.   235
LEADER: If this is your pleasure, Creon, treating
our city's enemy and our friend this way . . .
The power is yours, I suppose, to enforce it
with the laws, both for the dead and all of us,
the living.
CREON: Follow my orders closely then,   240
be on your guard.
LEADER: We're too old.
Lay that burden on younger shoulders.
CREON: No, no,
I don't mean the body—I've posted guards already.
LEADER: What commands for us then? What other service?
CREON: See that you never side with those who break my orders.   245
LEADER: Never. Only a fool could be in love with death.
CREON: Death is the price—you're right. But all too often
the mere hope of money has ruined many men.

A Sentry enters from the side.

SENTRY: My lord,
I can't say I'm winded from running, or set out
with any spring in my legs either—no sir,   250
I was lost in thought, and it made me stop, often,
dead in my tracks, wheeling, turning back,
and all the time a voice inside me muttering,
"Idiot, why? You're going straight to your death."
Then muttering, "Stopped again, poor fool?   255
If somebody gets the news to Creon first,
what's to save your neck?"
                          And so,
mulling it over, on I trudged, dragging my feet,
you can make a short road take forever . . .
but at last, look, common sense won out,   260
I'm here, and I'm all yours,
and even though I come empty-handed
I'll tell my story just the same, because

I've come with a good grip on one hope,
what will come will come, whatever fate —   265

CREON: Come to the point!
What's wrong — why so afraid?

SENTRY: First, myself, I've got to tell you,
I didn't do it, didn't see who did —
Be fair, don't take it out on me.   270

CREON: You're playing it safe, soldier,
barricading yourself from any trouble.
It's obvious, you've something strange to tell.

SENTRY: Dangerous too, and danger makes you delay
for all you're worth.   275

CREON: Out with it — then dismiss!

SENTRY: All right, here it comes. The body —
someone's just buried it, then run off . . .
sprinkled some dry dust on the flesh,
given it proper rites.

CREON: What?   280
What man alive would dare —

SENTRY: I've no idea, I swear it.
There was no mark of a spade, no pickaxe there,
no earth turned up, the ground packed hard and dry,
unbroken, no tracks, no wheelruts, nothing,
the workman left no trace. Just at sunup   285
the first watch of the day points it out —
it was a wonder! We were stunned . . .
a terrific burden too, for all of us, listen:
you can't see the corpse, not that it's buried,
really, just a light cover of road-dust on it,   290
as if someone meant to lay the dead to rest
and keep from getting cursed.
Not a sign in sight that dogs or wild beasts
had worried the body, even torn the skin.

But what came next! Rough talk flew thick and fast,   295
guard grilling guard — we'd have come to blows
at last, nothing to stop it; each man for himself
and each the culprit, no one caught red-handed,
all of us pleading ignorance, dodging the charges,
ready to take up red-hot iron in our fists,   300
go through fire, swear oaths to the gods —
"I didn't do it, I had no hand in it either,
not in the plotting, not in the work itself!"

Finally, after all this wrangling came to nothing,
one man spoke out and made us stare at the ground,   305

hanging our heads in fear. No way to counter him,
no way to take his advice and come through
safe and sound. Here's what he said:
"Look, we've got to report the facts to Creon,
we can't keep this hidden." Well, that won out,   310
and the lot fell on me, condemned me,
unlucky as ever, I got the prize. So here I am,
against my will and yours too, well I know—
no one wants the man who brings bad news.

LEADER: My king,
ever since he began I've been debating in my mind,   315
could this possibly be the work of the gods?

CREON: Stop—
before you make me choke with anger—the gods!
You, you're senile, must you be insane?
You say—why it's intolerable—say the gods
could have the slightest concern for that corpse?   320
Tell me, was it for meritorious service
they proceeded to bury him, prized him so? The hero
who came to burn their temples ringed with pillars,
their golden treasures—scorch their hallowed earth
and fling their laws to the winds.   325
Exactly when did you last see the gods
celebrating traitors? Inconceivable!

No, from the first there were certain citizens
who could hardly stand the spirit of my regime,
grumbling against me in the dark, heads together,   330
tossing wildly, never keeping their necks beneath
the yoke, loyally submitting to their king.
These are the instigators, I'm convinced—
they've perverted my own guard, bribed them
to do their work.

                    Money! Nothing worse   335
in our lives, so current, rampant, so corrupting.
Money—you demolish cities, root men from their homes,
you train and twist good minds and set them on
to the most atrocious schemes. No limit,
you make them adept at every kind of outrage,   340
every godless crime—money!
                              Everyone—
the whole crew bribed to commit this crime,
they've made one thing sure at least:
sooner or later they will pay the price.

Wheeling on the Sentry.

You—   345
I swear to Zeus as I still believe in Zeus,
if you don't find the man who buried that corpse,
the very man, and produce him before my eyes,
simple death won't be enough for you,
not till we string you up alive   350
and wring the immorality out of you.
Then you can steal the rest of your days,
better informed about where to make a killing.
You'll have learned, at last, it doesn't pay
to itch for rewards from every hand that beckons.   355
Filthy profits wreck most men, you'll see—
they'll never save your life.

SENTRY: Please,
may I say a word or two, or just turn and go?

CREON: Can't you tell? Everything you say offends me.

SENTRY: Where does it hurt you, in the ears or in the heart?   360

CREON: And who are you to pinpoint my displeasure?

SENTRY: The culprit grates on your feelings,
I just annoy your ears.

CREON: Still talking?
You talk too much! A born nuisance—

SENTRY: Maybe so,
but I never did this thing, so help me!

CREON: Yes you did—   365
what's more, you squandered your life for silver!

SENTRY: Oh it's terrible when the one who does the judging
judges things all wrong.

CREON: Well now,
you just be clever about your judgments—
if you fail to produce the criminals for me,   370
you'll swear your dirty money brought you pain.

Turning sharply, reentering the palace.

SENTRY: I hope he's found. Best thing by far.
But caught or not, that's in the lap of fortune;
I'll never come back, you've seen the last of me.
I'm saved, even now, and I never thought,   375
I never hoped—
dear gods, I owe you all my thanks!

Rushing out.

CHORUS: Numberless wonders
terrible wonders walk the world but none the match for man—
that great wonder crossing the heaving gray sea,
                   driven on by the blasts of winter   380

on through breakers crashing left and right,
    holds his steady course
and the oldest of the gods he wears away—
the Earth, the immortal, the inexhaustible—
as his plows go back and forth, year in, year out   385
    with the breed of stallions turning up the furrows.
And the blithe, lightheaded race of birds he snares,
the tribes of savage beasts, the life that swarms the depths—
        with one fling of his nets
woven and coiled tight, he takes them all,   390
    man the skilled, the brilliant!
He conquers all, taming with his techniques
the prey that roams the cliffs and wild lairs,
training the stallion, clamping the yoke across
    his shaggy neck, and the tireless mountain bull.   395
And speech and thought, quick as the wind
and the mood and mind for law that rules the city—
    all these he has taught himself
and shelter from the arrows of the frost
when there's rough lodging under the cold clear sky   400
and the shafts of lashing rain—
        ready, resourceful man!
            Never without resources
never an impasse as he marches on the future—
only Death, from Death alone he will find no rescue   405
but from desperate plagues he has plotted his escapes.

Man the master, ingenious past all measure
past all dreams, the skills within his grasp—
    he forges on, now to destruction
now again to greatness. When he weaves in   410
the laws of the land, and the justice of the gods
that binds his oaths together
        he and his city rise high—
            but the city casts out
that man who weds himself to inhumanity   415
thanks to reckless daring. Never share my hearth
never think my thoughts, whoever does such things.

Enter Antigone from the side, accompanied by the Sentry.

    Here is a dark sign from the gods—
    what to make of this? I know her,
    how can I deny it? That young girl's Antigone!   420
    Wretched, child of a wretched father,
    Oedipus. Look, is it possible?
    They bring you in like a prisoner—

why? did you break the king's laws?
Did they take you in some act of mad defiance?   42⁵

SENTRY: She's the one, she did it single-handed—
we caught her burying the body. Where's Creon?

Enter Creon from the palace.

LEADER: Back again, just in time when you need him.
CREON: In time for what? What is it?
SENTRY: My king,
there's nothing you can swear you'll never do—   43⁰
second thoughts make liars of us all.
I could have sworn I wouldn't hurry back
(what with your threats, the buffeting I just took),
but a stroke of luck beyond our wildest hopes,
what a joy, there's nothing like it. So,   43⁵
back I've come, breaking my oath, who cares?
I'm bringing in our prisoner—this young girl—
we took her giving the dead the last rites.
But no casting lots this time; this is *my* luck,
my prize, no one else's.
                              Now, my lord,   44⁰
here she is. Take her, question her,
cross-examine her to your heart's content.
But set me free, it's only right—
I'm rid of this dreadful business once for all.
CREON: Prisoner! Her? You took her—where, doing what?   44⁵
SENTRY: Burying the man. That's the whole story.
CREON: What?
You mean what you say, you're telling me the truth?
SENTRY: She's the one. With my own eyes I saw her
bury the body, just what you've forbidden.
There. Is that plain and clear?   45⁰
CREON: What did you see? Did you catch her in the act?
SENTRY: Here's what happened. We went back to our post,
those threats of yours breathing down our necks—
we brushed the corpse clean of the dust that covered it,
stripped it bare . . . it was slimy, going soft,   45⁵
and we took to high ground, backs to the wind
so the stink of him couldn't hit us;
jostling, baiting each other to keep awake,
shouting back and forth—no napping on the job,
not this time. And so the hours dragged by   46⁰
until the sun stood dead above our heads,
a huge white ball in the noon sky, beating,
blazing down, and then it happened—
suddenly, a whirlwind!

Twisting a great dust-storm up from the earth,   465
a black plague of the heavens, filling the plain,
ripping the leaves off every tree in sight,
choking the air and sky. We squinted hard
and took our whipping from the gods.

And after the storm passed—it seemed endless—   470
there, we saw the girl!
And she cried out a sharp, piercing cry,
like a bird come back to an empty nest,
peering into its bed, and all the babies gone . . .
Just so, when she sees the corpse bare   475
she bursts into a long, shattering wail
and calls down withering curses on the heads
of all who did the work. And she scoops up dry dust,
handfuls, quickly, and lifting a fine bronze urn,
lifting it high and pouring, she crowns the dead   480
with three full libations.
                  Soon as we saw
we rushed her, closed on the kill like hunters,
and she, she didn't flinch. We interrogated her,
charging her with offenses past and present—
she stood up to it all, denied nothing. I tell you,   485
it made me ache and laugh in the same breath.
It's pure joy to escape the worst yourself,
it hurts a man to bring down his friends.
But all that, I'm afraid, means less to me
than my own skin. That's the way I'm made.

CREON:

Wheeling on Antigone.

                          You,   490
    with your eyes fixed on the ground—speak up.
    Do you deny you did this, yes or no?

ANTIGONE: I did it. I don't deny a thing.

CREON:

To the Sentry.

    You, get out, wherever you please—
    you're clear of a very heavy charge.   495

He leaves; Creon turns back to Antigone.

    You, tell me briefly, no long speeches—
    were you aware a decree had forbidden this?

ANTIGONE: Well aware. How could I avoid it? It was public.

CREON: And still you had the gall to break this law?

ANTIGONE: Of course I did. It wasn't Zeus, not in the least,   500
    who made this proclamation—not to me.
    Nor did that Justice, dwelling with the gods
    beneath the earth, ordain such laws for men.
    Nor did I think your edict had such force
    that you, a mere mortal, could override the gods,   505
    the great unwritten, unshakable traditions.
    They are alive, not just today or yesterday:
    they live forever, from the first of time,
    and no one knows when they first saw the light.

    These laws—I was not about to break them,   510
    not out of fear of some man's wounded pride,
    and face the retribution of the gods.
    Die I must, I've known it all my life—
    how could I keep from knowing?—even without
    your death-sentence ringing in my ears.   515
    And if I am to die before my time
    I consider that a gain. Who on earth,
    alive in the midst of so much grief as I,
    could fail to find his death a rich reward?
    So for me, at least, to meet this doom of yours   520
    is precious little pain. But if I had allowed
    my own mother's son to rot, an unburied corpse—
    that would have been an agony! This is nothing.
    And if my present actions strike you as foolish,
    let's just say I've been accused of folly   525
    by a fool.
LEADER: Like father like daughter,
    passionate, wild . . .
    she hasn't learned to bend before adversity.
CREON: No? Believe me, the stiffest stubborn wills
    fall the hardest; the toughest iron,   530
    tempered strong in the white-hot fire,
    you'll see it crack and shatter first of all.
    And I've known spirited horses you can break
    with a light bit—proud, rebellious horses.
    There's no room for pride, not in a slave,   535
    not with the lord and master standing by.

    This girl was an old hand at insolence
    when she overrode the edicts we made public.
    But once she'd done it—the insolence,
    twice over—to glory in it, laughing,   540
    mocking us to our face with what she'd done.

I'm not the man, not now: she is the man
if this victory goes to her and she goes free.

Never! Sister's child or closer in blood
than all my family clustered at my altar   545
worshiping Guardian Zeus—she'll never escape,
she and her blood sister, the most barbaric death.
Yes, I accuse her sister of an equal part
in scheming this, this burial.

To his attendants.

                              Bring her here!
I just saw her inside, hysterical, gone to pieces.   550
It never fails: the mind convicts itself
in advance, when scoundrels are up to no good,
plotting in the dark. Oh but I hate it more
when a traitor, caught red-handed,
tries to glorify his crimes.   555
ANTIGONE: Creon, what more do you want
than my arrest and execution?
CREON: Nothing. Then I have it all.
ANTIGONE: Then why delay? Your moralizing repels me,
every word you say—pray god it always will.   560
So naturally all I say repels you too.
                              Enough.
Give me glory! What greater glory could I win
than to give my own brother decent burial?
These citizens here would all agree,

To the Chorus.

they'd praise me too   565
if their lips weren't locked in fear.

Pointing to Creon.

Lucky tyrants—the perquisites of power!
Ruthless power to do and say whatever pleases *them.*
CREON: You alone, of all the people in Thebes,
see things that way.
ANTIGONE: They see it just that way   570
but defer to you and keep their tongues in leash.
CREON: And you, aren't you ashamed to differ so from them?
So disloyal!
ANTIGONE: Not ashamed for a moment,
not to honor my brother, my own flesh and blood.
CREON: Wasn't Eteocles a brother too—cut down, facing him?   575
ANTIGONE: Brother, yes, by the same mother, the same father.

CREON: Then how can you render his enemy such honors,
    such impieties in his eyes?

ANTIGONE: He'll never testify to that,
    Eteocles dead and buried.

CREON: He will—   580
    if you honor the traitor just as much as him.

ANTIGONE: But it was his brother, not some slave that died—

CREON: Ravaging our country!—
    but Eteocles died fighting in our behalf.

ANTIGONE: No matter—Death longs for the same rites for all.   585

CREON: Never the same for the patriot and the traitor.

ANTIGONE: Who, Creon, who on earth can say the ones below
    don't find this pure and uncorrupt?

CREON: Never. Once an enemy, never a friend,
    not even after death.   590

ANTIGONE: I was born to join in love, not hate—
    that is my nature.

CREON: Go down below and love,
    if love you must—love the dead! While I'm alive,
    no woman is going to lord it over me.

Enter Ismene from the palace, under guard.

CHORUS: Look,
    Ismene's coming, weeping a sister's tears,   595
    loving sister, under a cloud . . .
    her face is flushed, her cheeks streaming.
    Sorrow puts her lovely radiance in the dark.

CREON: You—
    in my house, you viper, slinking undetected,
    sucking my life-blood! I never knew   600
    I was breeding twin disasters, the two of you
    rising up against my throne. Come, tell me,
    will you confess your part in the crime or not?
    Answer me. Swear to me.

ISMENE: I did it, yes—
    if only she consents—I share the guilt,   605
    the consequences too.

ANTIGONE: No,
    Justice will never suffer that—not you,
    you were unwilling. I never brought you in.

ISMENE: But now you face such dangers . . . I'm not ashamed
    to sail through trouble with you,   610
    make your troubles mine.

ANTIGONE: Who did the work?
    Let the dead and the god of death bear witness!
    I've no love for a friend who loves in words alone.

ISMENE: Oh no, my sister, don't reject me, please,
  let me die beside you, consecrating   615
  the dead together.
ANTIGONE: Never share my dying,
  don't lay claim to what you never touched.
  My death will be enough.
ISMENE: What do I care for life, cut off from you?
ANTIGONE: Ask Creon. Your concern is all for him.   620
ISMENE: Why abuse me so? It doesn't help you now.
ANTIGONE: You're right—
  if I mock you, I get no pleasure from it,
  only pain.
ISMENE: Tell me, dear one,
  what can I do to help you, even now?
ANTIGONE: Save yourself. I don't grudge you your survival. 625
ISMENE: Oh no, no, denied my portion in your death?
ANTIGONE: You chose to live, I chose to die.
ISMENE: Not, at least,
  without every kind of caution I could voice.
ANTIGONE: Your wisdom appealed to one world—mine, another.
ISMENE: But look, we're both guilty, both condemned to death. 630
ANTIGONE: Courage! Live your life. I gave myself to death,
  long ago, so I might serve the dead.
CREON: They're both mad, I tell you, the two of them.
  One's just shown it, the other's been that way
  since she was born.
ISMENE: True, my king,   635
  the sense we were born with cannot last forever . . .
  commit cruelty on a person long enough
  and the mind begins to go.
CREON: Yours did,
  when you chose to commit your crimes with her.
ISMENE: How can I live alone, without her?
CREON: Her?   640
  Don't even mention her—she no longer exists.
ISMENE: What? You'd kill your own son's bride?
CREON: Absolutely:
  there are other fields for him to plow.
ISMENE: Perhaps,
  but never as true, as close a bond as theirs.
CREON: A worthless woman for my son? It repels me.   645
ISMENE: Dearest Haemon, your father wrongs you so!
CREON: Enough, enough—you and your talk of marriage!
ISMENE: Creon—you're really going to rob your son of Antigone?
CREON: Death will do it for me—break their marriage off.
LEADER: So, it's settled then? Antigone must die?   650

CREON: Settled, yes—we both know that.

To the guards.

> Stop wasting time. Take them in.
> From now on they'll act like women.
> Tie them up, no more running loose;
> even the bravest will cut and run,   655
> once they see Death coming for their lives.

The guards escort Antigone and Ismene into the palace. Creon remains while the old citizens form their chorus.

CHORUS: Blest, they are the truly blest who all their lives
> have never tasted devastation. For others, once
> the gods have rocked a house to its foundations
>   the ruin will never cease, cresting on and on   660
> from one generation on throughout the race—
> like a great mounting tide
> driven on by savage northern gales,
>   surging over the dead black depths
> roiling up from the bottom dark heaves of sand   665
> and the headlands, taking the storm's onslaught full-force,
> roar, and the low moaning
>   echoes on and on
>   and now
> as in ancient times I see the sorrows of the house,
> the living heirs of the old ancestral kings,
> piling on the sorrows of the dead   670
>   and one generation cannot free the next—
> some god will bring them crashing down,
> the race finds no release.
> And now the light, the hope
>   springing up from the late last root   675
> in the house of Oedipus, that hope's cut down in turn
> by the long, bloody knife swung by the gods of death
> by a senseless word
>   by fury at the heart.
>   Zeus,
> yours is the power, Zeus, what man on earth
> can override it, who can hold it back?   680
> Power that neither Sleep, the all-ensnaring
>   no, nor the tireless months of heaven
> can ever overmaster—young through all time,
> mighty lord of power, you hold fast
>   the dazzling crystal mansions of Olympus.   685
> And throughout the future, late and soon
> as through the past, your law prevails:

no towering form of greatness
   enters into the lives of mortals
       free and clear of ruin.
                              True,   690
our dreams, our high hopes voyaging far and wide
bring sheer delight to many, to many others
   delusion, blithe, mindless lusts
and the fraud steals on one slowly . . . unaware
till he trips and puts his foot into the fire.   695
   He was a wise old man who coined
the famous saying: "Sooner or later
foul is fair, fair is foul
to the man the gods will ruin"—
   He goes his way for a moment only   700
       free of blinding ruin.

Enter Haemon from the palace.

   Here's Haemon now, the last of all your sons.
   Does he come in tears for his bride,
   his doomed bride, Antigone—
   bitter at being cheated of their marriage?   705
CREON: We'll soon know, better than seers could tell us.

Turning to Haemon.

   Son, you've heard the final verdict on your bride?
   Are you coming now, raving against your father?
   Or do you love me, no matter what I do?
HAEMON: Father, I'm your *son* . . . you in your wisdom   710
set my bearings for me—I obey you.
No marriage could ever mean more to me than you,
whatever good direction you may offer.
CREON: Fine, Haemon.
That's how you ought to feel within your heart,
subordinate to your father's will in every way.   715
That's what a man prays for: to produce good sons—
households full of them, dutiful and attentive,
so they can pay his enemy back with interest
and match the respect their father shows his friend.
But the man who rears a brood of useless children,   720
what has he brought into the world, I ask you?
Nothing but trouble for himself, and mockery
from his enemies laughing in his face.
                         Oh Haemon,
never lose your sense of judgment over a woman.
The warmth, the rush of pleasure, it all goes cold   725
in your arms, I warn you . . . a worthless woman

in your house, a misery in your bed.
What wound cuts deeper than a loved one
turned against you? Spit her out,
like a mortal enemy—let the girl go.   730
Let her find a husband down among the dead.

Imagine it: I caught her in naked rebellion,
the traitor, the only one in the whole city.
I'm not about to prove myself a liar,
not to my people, no, I'm going to kill her!   735
That's right—so let her cry for mercy, sing her hymns
to Zeus who defends all bonds of kindred blood.
Why, if I bring up my own kin to be rebels,
think what I'd suffer from the world at large.
Show me the man who rules his household well: 740
I'll show you someone fit to rule the state.
That good man, my son,
I have every confidence he and he alone
can give commands and take them too. Staunch
in the storm of spears he'll stand his ground,   745
a loyal, unflinching comrade at your side.

But whoever steps out of line, violates the laws
or presumes to hand out orders to his superiors,
he'll win no praise from me. But that man
the city places in authority, his orders   750
must be obeyed, large and small,
right and wrong.
                           Anarchy—
show me a greater crime in all the earth!
She, she destroys cities, rips up houses,
breaks the ranks of spearmen into headlong rout.   755
But the ones who last it out, the great mass of them
owe their lives to discipline. Therefore
we must defend the men who live by law,
never let some woman triumph over us.
Better to fall from power, if fall we must,   760
at the hands of a man—never be rated
inferior to a woman, never.
LEADER: To us,
    unless old age has robbed us of our wits,
    you seem to say what you have to say with sense.
HAEMON: Father, only the gods endow a man with reason,   765
    the finest of all their gifts, a treasure.
    Far be it from me—I haven't the skill,
    and certainly no desire, to tell you when,
    if ever, you make a slip in speech . . . though

someone else might have a good suggestion.   770
Of course it's not for you,
in the normal run of things, to watch
whatever men say or do, or find to criticize.
The man in the street, you know, dreads your glance,
he'd never say anything displeasing to your face.   775
But it's for me to catch the murmurs in the dark,
the way the city mourns for this young girl.
"No woman," they say, "ever deserved death less,
and such a brutal death for such a glorious action.
She, with her own dear brother lying in his blood—   780
she couldn't bear to leave him dead, unburied,
food for the wild dogs or wheeling vultures.
Death? She deserves a glowing crown of gold!"
So they say, and the rumor spreads in secret,
darkly . . .
    I rejoice in your success, father—   785
nothing more precious to me in the world.
What medal of honor brighter to his children
than a father's growing glory? Or a child's
to his proud father? Now don't, please,
be quite so single-minded, self-involved,   790
or assume the world is wrong and you are right.
Whoever thinks that he alone possesses intelligence,
the gift of eloquence, he and no one else,
and character too . . . such men, I tell you,
spread them open—you will find them empty.
        No,   795
it's no disgrace for a man, even a wise man,
to learn many things and not to be too rigid.
You've seen trees by a raging winter torrent,
how many sway with the flood and salvage every twig,
but not the stubborn—they're ripped out, roots and all.   800
Bend or break. The same when a man is sailing:
haul your sheets too taut, never give an inch,
you'll capsize, go the rest of the voyage
keel up and the rowing-benches under.

Oh give way. Relax your anger—change!   805
I'm young, I know, but let me offer this:
it would be best by far, I admit,
if a man were born infallible, right by nature.
If not—and things don't often go that way,
it's best to learn from those with good advice.   810
LEADER: You'd do well, my lord, if he's speaking to the point,
  to learn from him,

Turning to Haemon.

and you, my boy, from him.
You both are talking sense.

CREON: So,
men our age, we're to be lectured, are we?—
schooled by a boy his age?   815

HAEMON: Only in what is right. But if I seem young,
look less to my years and more to what I do.

CREON: Do? Is admiring rebels an achievement?

HAEMON: I'd never suggest that you admire treason.

CREON: Oh?—
isn't that just the sickness that's attacked her?   820

HAEMON: The whole city of Thebes denies it, to a man.

CREON: And is Thebes about to tell me how to rule?

HAEMON: Now, you see? Who's talking like a child?

CREON: Am I to rule this land for others—or myself?

HAEMON: It's no city at all, owned by one man alone.   825

CREON: What? The city *is* the king's—that's the law!

HAEMON: What a splendid king you'd make of a desert island—
you and you alone.

CREON:

To the Chorus.

                              This boy, I do believe,
is fighting on her side, the woman's side.

HAEMON: If you are a woman, yes;   830
my concern is all for you.

CREON: Why, you degenerate—bandying accusations,
threatening me with justice, your own father!

HAEMON: I see my father offending justice—wrong.

CREON: Wrong?
To protect my royal rights?

HAEMON: Protect your rights?   835
When you trample down the honors of the gods?

CREON: You, you soul of corruption, rotten through—
woman's accomplice!

HAEMON: That may be,
but you'll never find me accomplice to a criminal.

CREON: That's what *she* is,   840
and every word you say is a blatant appeal for her—

HAEMON: And you, and me, and the gods beneath the earth.

CREON: You'll never marry her, not while she's alive.

HAEMON: Then she'll die . . . but her death will kill another.

CREON: What, brazen threats? You go too far!

HAEMON: What threat?   845
Combating your empty, mindless judgments with a word?

CREON: You'll suffer for your sermons, you and your empty wisdom!

HAEMON: If you weren't my father, I'd say you were insane.
CREON: Don't flatter me with Father—you woman's slave!
HAEMON: You really expect to fling abuse at me   850
    and not receive the same?
CREON: Is that so!
    Now, by heaven, I promise you, you'll pay—
    taunting, insulting me! Bring her out,
    that hateful—she'll die now, here,
    in front of his eyes, beside her groom!   855
HAEMON: No, no, she will never die beside me—
    don't delude yourself. And you will never
    see me, never set eyes on my face again.
    Rage your heart out, rage with friends
    who can stand the sight of you.   860

Rushing out.

LEADER: Gone, my king, in a burst of anger.
    A temper young as his . . . hurt him once,
    he may do something violent.
CREON: Let him do—
    dream up something desperate, past all human limit!
    Good riddance. Rest assured,   865
    he'll never save those two young girls from death.
LEADER: Both of them, you really intend to kill them both?
CREON: No, not her, the one whose hands are clean;
    you're quite right.
LEADER: But Antigone—
    what sort of death do you have in mind for her?   870
CREON: I'll take her down some wild, desolate path
    never trod by men, and wall her up alive
    in a rocky vault, and set out short rations,
    just a gesture of piety
    to keep the entire city free of defilement.   875
    There let her pray to the one god she worships:
    Death—who knows?—may just reprieve her from death.
    Or she may learn at last, better late than never,
    what a waste of breath it is to worship Death.

Exit to the palace.

CHORUS: Love, never conquered in battle   880
    Love the plunderer laying waste the rich!
    Love standing the night-watch
            guarding a girl's soft cheek,
    you range the seas, the shepherds' steadings off in the wilds—
    not even the deathless gods can flee your onset,   885
    nothing human born for a day—

whoever feels your grip is driven mad.
                              Love
you wrench the minds of the righteous into outrage,
swerve them to their ruin—you have ignited this,
this kindred strife, father and son at war   890
                              and Love alone the victor—
warm glance of the bride triumphant, burning with desire!
Throned in power, side-by-side with the mighty laws!
Irresistible Aphrodite,° never conquered—
Love, you mock us for your sport.   895

Antigone is brought from the palace under guard.

        But now, even I'd rebel against the king,
        I'd break all bounds when I see this—
        I fill with tears, can't hold them back,
        not any more . . . I see Antigone make her way
        to the bridal vault where all are laid to rest.   900
ANTIGONE: Look at me, men of my fatherland,
        setting out on the last road
    looking into the last light of day
    the last I'll ever see . . .
    the god of death who puts us all to bed   905
    takes me down to the banks of Acheron° alive—
        denied my part in the wedding-songs,
    no wedding-song in the dusk has crowned my marriage—
    I go to wed the lord of the dark waters.
CHORUS: Not crowned with glory, crowned with a dirge,   910
        you leave for the deep pit of the dead.
        No withering illness laid you low,
        no strokes of the sword—a law to yourself,
        alone, no mortal like you, ever, you go down
        to the halls of Death alive and breathing.   915
ANTIGONE: But think of Niobe°—well I know her story—
        think what a living death she died,
    Tantalus's daughter, stranger queen from the east:
    there on the mountain heights, growing stone
    binding as ivy, slowly walled her round   920
    and the rains will never cease, the legends say
    the snows will never leave her . . .
        wasting away, under her brows the tears
    showering down her breasting ridge and slopes—
    a rocky death like hers puts me to sleep.   925

---

894 Aphrodite: Goddess of love.   **906 Acheron:** A river in the underworld, to which the dead go.   **916 Niobe:** A queen of Thebes who was punished by the gods for her pride and was turned into stone.

CHORUS: But she was a god, born of gods,
         and we are only mortals born to die.
         And yet, of course, it's a great thing
         for a dying girl to hear, just hear
         she shares a destiny equal to the gods,   930
         during life and later, once she's dead.
ANTIGONE: O you mock me!
       Why, in the name of all my fathers' gods
       why can't you wait till I am gone—
          must you abuse me to my face?
       O my city, all your fine rich sons!   935
       And you, you springs of the Dirce,
       holy grove of Thebes where the chariots gather,
                you at least, you'll bear me witness, look,
       unmourned by friends and forced by such crude laws
       I go to my rockbound prison, strange new tomb—   940
          always a stranger, O dear god,
          I have no home on earth and none below,
             not with the living, not with the breathless dead.
CHORUS: You went too far, the last limits of daring—
             smashing against the high throne of Justice!   945
                Your life's in ruins, child—I wonder . . .
             do you pay for your father's terrible ordeal?
ANTIGONE: There—at last you've touched it, the worst pain
       the worst anguish! Raking up the grief for father
             three times over, for all the doom   950
       that's struck us down, the brilliant house of Laius.
       O mother, your marriage-bed
       the coiling horrors, the coupling there—
             you with your own son, my father—doomstruck mother!
       Such, such were my parents, and I their wretched child.   955
       I go to them now, cursed, unwed, to share their home—
             I am a stranger! O dear brother, doomed
             in your marriage—your marriage murders mine,
             your dying drags me down to death alive!

Enter Creon.

CHORUS: Reverence asks some reverence in return—   960
             but attacks on power never go unchecked,
                not by the man who holds the reins of power.
             Your own blind will, your passion has destroyed you.
ANTIGONE: No one to weep for me, my friends,
             no wedding-song—they take me away   965
       in all my pain . . . the road lies open, waiting.
       Never again, the law forbids me to see
       the sacred eye of day. I am agony!

No tears for the destiny that's mine,
no loved one mourns my death.

CREON: Can't you see?   970
If a man could wail his own dirge *before* he dies,
he'd never finish.

To the guards.

Take her away, quickly!
Wall her up in the tomb, you have your orders.
Abandon her there, alone, and let her choose—
death or a buried life with a good roof for shelter.   975
As for myself, my hands are clean. This young girl—
dead or alive, she will be stripped of her rights,
her stranger's rights, here in the world above.

ANTIGONE: O tomb, my bridal-bed—my house, my prison
cut in the hollow rock, my everlasting watch!   980
I'll soon be there, soon embrace my own,
the great growing family of our dead
Persephone° has received among her ghosts.

I,
the last of them all, the most reviled by far,
go down before my destined time's run out.   985
But still I go, cherishing one good hope:
my arrival may be dear to father,
dear to you, my mother,
dear to you, my loving brother, Eteocles—
When you died I washed you with my hands,   990
I dressed you all, I poured the cups
across your tombs. But now, Polynices,
because I laid your body out as well,
this, this is my reward. Nevertheless
I honored you—the decent will admit it—   995
well and wisely too.

Never, I tell you,
if I had been the mother of children
or if my husband died, exposed and rotting—
I'd never have taken this ordeal upon myself,
never defied our people's will. What law,   1000
you ask, do I satisfy with what I say?
A husband dead, there might have been another.
A child by another too, if I had lost the first.
But mother and father both lost in the halls of Death,
no brother could ever spring to light again.   1005
For this law alone I held first in honor.
For this, Creon, the king, judges me a criminal

---

983 Persephone: Queen of the underworld.

guilty of dreadful outrage, my dear brother!
And now he leads me off, a captive in his hands,
with no part in the bridal-song, the bridal-bed,   1010
denied all joy of marriage, raising children—
deserted so by loved ones, struck by fate,
I descend alive to the caverns of the dead.
What law of the mighty gods have I transgressed?
Why look to the heavens any more, tormented as I am?   1015
Whom to call, what comrades now? Just think,
my reverence only brands me for irreverence!
Very well: if this is the pleasure of the gods,
once I suffer I will know that I was wrong.
But if these men are wrong, let them suffer   1020
nothing worse than they mete out to me—
these masters of injustice!
LEADER: Still the same rough winds, the wild passion
     raging through the girl.
CREON:

To the guards.

                         Take her away.
     You're wasting time—you'll pay for it too.   1025
ANTIGONE: Oh god, the voice of death. It's come, it's here.
CREON: True. Not a word of hope—your doom is sealed.
ANTIGONE: Land of Thebes, city of all my fathers—
               O you gods, the first gods of the race!
               They drag me away, now, no more delay.   1030
               Look on me, you noble sons of Thebes—
               the last of a great line of kings,
               I alone, see what I suffer now
               at the hands of what breed of men—
               all for reverence, my reverence for the gods!   1035

She leaves under guard; the Chorus gathers.

CHORUS: Danaë, Danaë°—
     even she endured a fate like yours,
          in all her lovely strength she traded
     the light of day for the bolted brazen vault—
     buried within her tomb, her bridal-chamber,   1040
     wed to the yoke and broken.
          But she was of glorious birth
                    my child, my child
     and treasured the seed of Zeus within her womb,
     the cloudburst streaming gold!   1045

1036 Danaë: Locked in a cell by her father because it was prophesied that her son would
kill him, but visited by Zeus in the form of a shower of gold. Their son was Perseus.

The power of fate is a wonder,
dark, terrible wonder—
neither wealth nor armies
towered walls nor ships
black hulls lashed by the salt   1050
can save us from that force.
The yoke tamed him too
     young Lycurgus° flaming in anger
king of Edonia, all for his mad taunts
Dionysus clamped him down, encased   1055
in the chain-mail of rock
     and there his rage
                         his terrible flowering rage burst—
sobbing, dying away . . . at last that madman
came to know his god—   1060
          the power he mocked, the power
          he taunted in all his frenzy
          trying to stamp out
          the women strong with the god—
          the torch, the raving sacred cries—   1065
          enraging the Muses° who adore the flute.

And far north where the Black Rocks
          cut the sea in half
and murderous straits
split the coast of Thrace   1070
     a forbidding city stands
where once, hard by the walls
the savage Ares thrilled to watch
a king's new queen, a Fury rearing in rage
against his two royal sons—   1075
          her bloody hands, her dagger-shuttle
stabbing out their eyes—cursed, blinding wounds—
their eyes blind sockets screaming for revenge!

They wailed in agony, cries echoing cries
          the princes doomed at birth . . .   1080
and their mother doomed to chains,
walled off in a tomb of stone—
          but she traced her own birth back
to a proud Athenian line and the high gods
and off in caverns half the world away,   1085
born of the wild North Wind
          she sprang on her father's gales,

1053 **Lycurgus:** Punished by Dionysus because he would not worship him. **1066 Muses:** Goddesses of the arts.

racing stallions up the leaping cliffs—
child of the heavens. But even on her the Fates
the gray everlasting Fates rode hard   1090
my child, my child.

Enter Tiresias, the blind prophet, led by a boy.

TIRESIAS: Lords of Thebes,
I and the boy have come together,
hand in hand. Two see with the eyes of one . . .
so the blind must go, with a guide to lead the way.
CREON: What is it, old Tiresias? What news now?   1095
TIRESIAS: I will teach you. And you obey the seer.
CREON: I will,
I've never wavered from your advice before.
TIRESIAS: And so you kept the city straight on course.
CREON: I owe you a great deal, I swear to that.
TIRESIAS: Then reflect, my son: you are poised,   1100
once more, on the razor-edge of fate.
CREON: What is it? I shudder to hear you.
TIRESIAS: You will learn
when you listen to the warnings of my craft.
As I sat on the ancient seat of augury,°
in the sanctuary where every bird I know   1105
will hover at my hands—suddenly I heard it,
a strange voice in the wingbeats, unintelligible,
barbaric, a mad scream! Talons flashing, ripping,
they were killing each other—that much I knew—
the murderous fury whirring in those wings   1110
made that much clear!
                        I was afraid,
I turned quickly, tested the burnt-sacrifice,
ignited the altar at all points—but no fire,
the god in the fire never blazed.
Not from those offerings . . . over the embers   1115
slid a heavy ooze from the long thighbones,
smoking, sputtering out, and the bladder
puffed and burst—spraying gall into the air—
and the fat wrapping the bones slithered off
and left them glistening white. No fire!   1120
The rites failed that might have blazed the future
with a sign. So I learned from the boy here;
he is my guide, as I am guide to others.
                            And it's you—
your high resolve that sets this plague on Thebes.
The public altars and sacred hearths are fouled,   1125

1104 seat of augury: Where Tiresias looked for omens among birds.

one and all, by the birds and dogs with carrion
torn from the corpse, the doomstruck son of Oedipus!
And so the gods are deaf to our prayers, they spurn
the offerings in our hands, the flame of holy flesh.
No birds cry out an omen clear and true—   1130
they're gorged with the murdered victim's blood and fat.
Take these things to heart, my son, I warn you.
All men make mistakes, it is only human.
But once the wrong is done, a man
can turn his back on folly, misfortune too,   1135
if he tries to make amends, however low he's fallen,
and stops his bullnecked ways. Stubbornness
brands you for stupidity—pride is a crime.
No, yield to the dead!
Never stab the fighter when he's down.   1140
Where's the glory, killing the dead twice over?

I mean you well. I give you sound advice.
It's best to learn from a good adviser
when he speaks for your own good:
it's pure gain.
CREON: Old man—all of you! So,   1145
you shoot your arrows at my head like archers at the target—
I even have *him* loosed on me, this fortune-teller.
Oh his ilk has tried to sell me short
and ship me off for years. Well,
drive your bargains, traffic—much as you like—   1150
in the gold of India, silver-gold of Sardis.
You'll never bury that body in the grave,
not even if Zeus's eagles rip the corpse
and wing their rotten pickings off to the throne of god!
Never, not even in fear of such defilement   1155
will I tolerate his burial, that traitor.
Well I know, we can't defile the gods—
no mortal has the power.
                         No,
reverend old Tiresias, all men fall,
it's only human, but the wisest fall obscenely   1160
when they glorify obscene advice with rhetoric—
all for their own gain.
TIRESIAS: Oh god, is there a man alive
who knows, who actually believes . . .
CREON: What now?
What earth-shattering truth are you about to utter?   1165
TIRESIAS: . . . just how much a sense of judgment, wisdom
is the greatest gift we have?

CREON: Just as much, I'd say,
  as a twisted mind is the worst affliction going.
TIRESIAS: You are the one who's sick, Creon, sick to death.
CREON: I am in no mood to trade insults with a seer.   1170
TIRESIAS: You have already, calling my prophecies a lie.
CREON: Why not?
  You and the whole breed of seers are mad for money!
TIRESIAS: And the whole race of tyrants lusts to rake it in.
CREON: This slander of yours—
  are you aware you're speaking to the king?   1175
TIRESIAS: Well aware. Who helped you save the city?
CREON: You—
  you have your skills, old seer, but you lust for injustice!
TIRESIAS: You will drive me to utter the dreadful secret in my heart.
CREON: Spit it out! Just don't speak it out for profit.
TIRESIAS: Profit? No, not a bit of profit, not for you.   1180
CREON: Know full well, you'll never buy off my resolve.
TIRESIAS: Then know this too, learn this by heart!
  The chariot of the sun will not race through
  so many circuits more, before you have surrendered
  one born of your own loins, your own flesh and blood,   1185
  a corpse for corpses given in return, since you have thrust
  to the world below a child sprung for the world above,
  ruthlessly lodged a living soul within the grave—
  then you've robbed the gods below the earth,
  keeping a dead body here in the bright air,   1190
  unburied, unsung, unhallowed by the rites.

  You, you have no business with the dead,
  nor do the gods above—this is violence
  you have forced upon the heavens.
  And so the avengers, the dark destroyers late   1195
  but true to the mark, now lie in wait for you,
  the Furies sent by the gods and the god of death
  to strike you down with the pains that you perfected!

  There. Reflect on that, tell me I've been bribed.
  The day comes soon, no long test of time, not now,   1200
  that wakes the wails for men and women in your halls.
  Great hatred rises against you—
  cities in tumult, all whose mutilated sons
  the dogs have graced with burial, or the wild beasts,
  some wheeling crow that wings the ungodly stench of carrion   1205
  back to each city, each warrior's hearth and home.

  These arrows for your heart! Since you've raked me
  I loose them like an archer in my anger,

arrows deadly true. You'll never escape
their burning, searing force.   1210

Motioning to his escort.

> Come, boy, take me home.
> So he can vent his rage on younger men,
> and learn to keep a gentler tongue in his head
> and better sense than what he carries now.

Exit to the side.

LEADER: The old man's gone, my king—   1215
terrible prophecies. Well I know,
since the hair on this old head went gray,
he's never lied to Thebes.

CREON: I know it myself—I'm shaken, torn.
It's a dreadful thing to yield . . . but resist now?   1220
Lay my pride bare to the blows of ruin?
That's dreadful too.

LEADER: But good advice,
Creon, take it now, you must.

CREON: What should I do? Tell me . . . I'll obey.

LEADER: Go! Free the girl from the rocky vault   1225
and raise a mound for the body you exposed.

CREON: That's your advice? You think I should give in?

LEADER: Yes, my king, quickly. Disasters sent by the gods
cut short our follies in a flash.

CREON: Oh it's hard,
giving up the heart's desire . . . but I will do it—   1230
no more fighting a losing battle with necessity.

LEADER: Do it now, go, don't leave it to others.

CREON: Now—I'm on my way! Come, each of you,
take up axes, make for the high ground,
over there, quickly! I and my better judgment   1235
have come round to this—I shackled her,
I'll set her free myself. I am afraid . . .
it's best to keep the established laws
to the very day we die.

Rushing out, followed by his entourage. The Chorus clusters around the altar.

CHORUS: God of a hundred names!
                                Great Dionysus—   1240
                Son and glory of Semele! Pride of Thebes—
Child of Zeus whose thunder rocks the clouds—
Lord of the famous lands of evening—
King of the Mysteries!
                    King of Eleusis, Demeter's plain°

1244 Demeter's plain: The goddess of grain was worshipped at Eleusis, near Athens.

her breasting hills that welcome in the world—   1245
Great Dionysus!
              Bacchus,° living in Thebes
the mother-city of all your frenzied women—
                         Bacchus
       living along the Ismenus's° rippling waters
standing over the field sown with the Dragon's teeth!

You—we have seen you through the flaring smoky fires,   1250
     your torches blazing over the twin peaks
where nymphs of the hallowed cave climb onward
                fired with you, your sacred rage—
we have seen you at Castalia's running spring°
and down from the heights of Nysa° crowned with ivy   1255
the greening shore rioting vines and grapes
        down you come in your storm of wild women
          ecstatic, mystic cries—
                    Dionysus—
down to watch and ward the roads of Thebes!

First of all cities, Thebes you honor first   1260
you and your mother, bride of the lightning—
come, Dionysus! now your people lie
in the iron grip of plague,
come in your racing, healing stride
            down Parnassus's° slopes   1265
or across the moaning straits.
              Lord of the dancing—
dance, dance the constellations breathing fire!
Great master of the voices of the night!
Child of Zeus, God's offspring, come, come forth!
Lord, king, dance with your nymphs, swirling, raving   1270
arm-in-arm in frenzy through the night
      they dance you, Iacchus°—
               Dance, Dionysus
giver of all good things!

Enter a Messenger from the side.

MESSENGER: Neighbors,
friends of the house of Cadmus° and the kings,
there's not a thing in this life of ours   1275

1246 **Bacchus:** Another name for Dionysus.   1248 **Ismenus:** A river near Thebes where the founders of the city were said to have sprung from a dragon's teeth. **1254 Castalia's running spring:** The sacred spring of Apollo's oracle at Delphi. **1255 Nysa:** A mountain where Dionysus was worshipped.   **1265 Parnassus:** A mountain in Greece that was sacred to Dionysus as well as other gods and goddesses. **1272 Iacchus:** Dionysus.   **1274 Cadmus:** The legendary founder of Thebes.

I'd praise or blame as settled once for all.
Fortune lifts and Fortune fells the lucky
and unlucky every day. No prophet on earth
can tell a man his fate. Take Creon:
there was a man to rouse your envy once,   1280
as I see it. He saved the realm from enemies;
taking power, he alone, the lord of the fatherland,
he set us true on course—flourished like a tree
with the noble line of sons he bred and reared . . .
and now it's lost, all gone.
                    Believe me,   1285
when a man has squandered his true joys,
he's good as dead, I tell you, a living corpse.
Pile up riches in your house, as much as you like—
live like a king with a huge show of pomp,
but if real delight is missing from the lot,   1290
I wouldn't give you a wisp of smoke for it,
not compared with joy.
LEADER: What now?
What new grief do you bring the house of kings?
MESSENGER: Dead, dead—and the living are guilty of their death!
LEADER: Who's the murderer? Who is dead? Tell us.   1295
MESSENGER: Haemon's gone, his blood spilled by the very hand—
LEADER: His father's or his own?
MESSENGER: His own . . .
raging mad with his father for the death—
LEADER: Oh great seer,
you saw it all, you brought your word to birth!
MESSENGER: Those are the facts. Deal with them as you will.   1300

As he turns to go, Eurydice enters from the palace.

LEADER: Look, Eurydice. Poor woman, Creon's wife,
so close at hand. By chance perhaps,
unless she's heard the news about her son.
EURYDICE: My countrymen,
all of you—I caught the sound of your words
as I was leaving to do my part,   1305
to appeal to queen Athena° with my prayers.
I was just loosing the bolts, opening the doors,
when a voice filled with sorrow, family sorrow,
struck my ears, and I fell back, terrified,
into the women's arms—everything went black.   1310
Tell me the news, again, whatever it is . . .
sorrow and I are hardly strangers;
I can bear the worst.

1306 Athena: Goddess of wisdom and protector of Greek cities.

MESSENGER: I—dear lady,
  I'll speak as an eye-witness. I was there.
  And I won't pass over one word of the truth.   1315
  Why should I try to soothe you with a story,
  only to prove a liar in a moment?
  Truth is always best.
                          So,
  I escorted your lord, I guided him
  to the edge of the plain where the body lay,   1320
  Polynices, torn by the dogs and still unmourned.
  And saying a prayer to Hecate of the Crossroads,
  Pluto° too, to hold their anger and be kind,
  we washed the dead in a bath of holy water
  and plucking some fresh branches, gathering . . .   1325
  what was left of him, we burned them all together
  and raised a high mound of native earth, and then
  we turned and made for that rocky vault of hers,
  the hollow, empty bed of the bride of Death.
  And far off, one of us heard a voice,   1330
  a long wail rising, echoing
  out of that unhallowed wedding-chamber;
  he ran to alert the master and Creon pressed on,
  closer—the strange, inscrutable cry came sharper,
  throbbing around him now, and he let loose   1335
  a cry of his own, enough to wrench the heart,
  "Oh god, am I the prophet now? going down
  the darkest road I've ever gone? My son—
  it's *his* dear voice, he greets me! Go, men,
  closer, quickly! Go through the gap,   1340
  the rocks are dragged back—
  right to the tomb's very mouth—and look,
  see if it's Haemon's voice I think I hear,
  or the gods have robbed me of my senses."

  The king was shattered. We took his orders,   1345
  went and searched, and there in the deepest,
  dark recesses of the tomb we found her . . .
  hanged by the neck in a fine linen noose,
  strangled in her veils—and the boy,
  his arms flung around her waist,   1350
  clinging to her, wailing for his bride,
  dead and down below, for his father's crimes
  and the bed of his marriage blighted by misfortune.
  When Creon saw him, he gave a deep sob,

1322–23 Hecate, Pluto: Gods of the underworld.

he ran in, shouting, crying out to him,   1355
"Oh my child—what have you done? what seized you,
what insanity? what disaster drove you mad?
Come out, my son! I beg you on my knees!"
But the boy gave him a wild burning glance,
spat in his face, not a word in reply,   1360
he drew his sword—his father rushed out,
running as Haemon lunged and missed!—
and then, doomed, desperate with himself,
suddenly leaning his full weight on the blade,
he buried it in his body, halfway to the hilt.   1365
And still in his senses, pouring his arms around her,
he embraced the girl and breathing hard,
released a quick rush of blood,
bright red on her cheek glistening white.
And there he lies, body enfolding body . . .   1370
he has won his bride at last, poor boy,
not here but in the houses of the dead.

Creon shows the world that of all the ills
afflicting men the worst is lack of judgment.

Eurydice turns and reenters the palace.

LEADER: What do you make of that? The lady's gone,   1375
        without a word, good or bad.
MESSENGER: I'm alarmed too
        but here's my hope—faced with her son's death,
        she finds it unbecoming to mourn in public.
        Inside, under her roof, she'll set her women
        to the task and wail the sorrow of the house.   1380
        She's too discreet. She won't do something rash.
LEADER: I'm not so sure. To me, at least,
        a long heavy silence promises danger,
        just as much as a lot of empty outcries.
MESSENGER: We'll see if she's holding something back,   1385
        hiding some passion in her heart.
        I'm going in. You may be right—who knows?
        Even too much silence has its dangers.

Exit to the palace. Enter Creon from the side, escorted by attendants carrying Haemon's body on a bier.

LEADER: The king himself! Coming toward us,
            look, holding the boy's head in his hands.   1390
            Clear, damning proof, if it's right to say so—
            proof of his own madness, no one else's,
                no, his own blind wrongs.
CREON: Ohhh,

so senseless, so insane . . . my crimes,
my stubborn, deadly — 1395
Look at us, the killer, the killed,
father and son, the same blood — the misery!
My plans, my mad fanatic heart,
my son, cut off so young!
Ai, dead, lost to the world, 1400
not through your stupidity, no, my own.

LEADER: Too late,
too late, you see what justice means.

CREON: Oh I've learned
through blood and tears! Then, it was then,
when the god came down and struck me — a great weight
shattering, driving me down that wild savage path, 1405
ruining, trampling down my joy. Oh the agony,
the heartbreaking agonies of our lives.

Enter the Messenger from the palace.

MESSENGER: Master,
what a hoard of grief you have, and you'll have more.
The grief that lies to hand you've brought yourself —

Pointing to Haemon's body.

the rest, in the house, you'll see it all too soon. 1410

CREON: What now? What's worse than this?

MESSENGER: The queen is dead.
The mother of this dead boy . . . mother to the end —
poor thing, her wounds are fresh.

CREON: No, no,
harbor of Death, so choked, so hard to cleanse! —
why me? why are you killing me? 1415
Herald of pain, more words, more grief?
I died once, you kill me again and again!
What's the report, boy . . . some news for me?
My wife dead? O dear god!
Slaughter heaped on slaughter?

The doors open; the body of Eurydice is brought out on her bier.

MESSENGER: See for yourself: 1420
now they bring her body from the palace.

CREON: Oh no,
another, a second loss to break the heart.
What next, what fate still waits for me?
I just held my son in my arms and now,
look, a new corpse rising before my eyes — 1425
wretched, helpless mother — O my son!

MESSENGER: She stabbed herself at the altar,
    then her eyes went dark, after she'd raised
    a cry for the noble fate of Megareus,° the hero
    killed in the first assault, then for Haemon,   1430
    then with her dying breath she called down
    torments on your head—you killed her sons.
CREON: Oh the dread,
    I shudder with dread! Why not kill me too?—
    run me through with a good sharp sword?
    Oh god, the misery, anguish—   1435
    I, I'm churning with it, going under.
MESSENGER: Yes, and the dead, the woman lying there,
    piles the guilt of all their deaths on you.
CREON: How did she end her life, what bloody stroke?
MESSENGER: She drove home to the heart with her own hand,   1440
    once she learned her son was dead . . . that agony.
CREON: And the guilt is all mine—
    can never be fixed on another man,
    no escape for me. I killed you,
    I, god help me, I admit it all!   1445

To his attendants.

    Take me away, quickly, out of sight.
    I don't even exist—I'm no one. Nothing.
LEADER: Good advice, if there's any good in suffering.
    Quickest is best when troubles block the way.
CREON:

Kneeling in prayer.

    Come, let it come!—that best of fates for me   1450
    that brings the final day, best fate of all.
    Oh quickly, now—
    so I never have to see another sunrise.
LEADER: That will come when it comes;
    we must deal with all that lies before us.   1455
    The future rests with the ones who tend the future.
CREON: That prayer—I poured my heart into that prayer!
LEADER: No more prayers now. For mortal men
    there is no escape from the doom we must endure.
CREON: Take me away, I beg you, out of sight.   1460
    A rash, indiscriminate fool!
    I murdered you, my son, against my will—
    you too, my wife . . .

1429 Megareus: A son of Creon and Eurydice; he died when Thebes was attacked.

> Wailing wreck of a man,
> whom to look to? where to lean for support?

Desperately turning from Haemon to Eurydice on their biers.

> Whatever I touch goes wrong—once more   1465
> a crushing fate's come down upon my head.

The Messenger and attendants lead Creon into the palace.

CHORUS: Wisdom is by far the greatest part of joy,
and reverence toward the gods must be safeguarded.
The mighty words of the proud are paid in full
with mighty blows of fate, and at long last   1470
those blows will teach us wisdom.

The old citizens exit to the side.   [c. 441 B.C.E.]

☰ THINKING ABOUT THE TEXT

1. Describe Antigone with at least three adjectives of your own. How much do you sympathize with her? Do you consider her morally superior to Creon? Identify specific things that influence your view of her. Do your feelings about her shift during the course of the play? If so, when and how?

2. Do you feel any sympathy for Creon? For Ismene? Explain your reasoning. What values seem to be in conflict as Antigone argues with each?

3. Where, if anywhere, do you see the chorus as expressing wisdom? Where, if anywhere, do the members of the chorus strike you as imperfect people?

4. Here is an issue of genre: Ever since the ancient Greek philosopher Aristotle analyzed tragedy in his *Poetics*, a common definition of this kind of play is that its central character has a fatal flaw. How well does this definition fit *Antigone*? Must it be altered to accommodate Sophocles' play? Explain. Here is another issue of genre: In the *Poetics*, Aristotle also argued that a tragedy ends in catharsis. After arousing pity and fear in the audience, a tragedy relieves the audience of these feelings. How well does Aristotle's observation apply in the case of *Antigone*?

5. As was customary in Greek tragedy, the violent events in this play occur offstage and are merely reported. Had they occurred onstage, how might the audience's reaction have been different? Today, many films and television shows directly confront their audience with violence. Do you prefer this directness to Greek tragedy's way of dealing with violence? Support your answer by comparing some contemporary presentations of violence with *Antigone*'s.

In the News

The following two articles, drawn from London-based newspapers, examine present-day fights by women against governmental injustice. The first piece, which appeared in the September 12, 2010, issue of the *Observer*, reports on female activists and judicial victims in Iran. Since the deposing of the shah of Iran in 1979, the country has been ruled by Islamic clerics (ayatollahs), although its citizens supposedly choose the president and other officials. Notable opponents of the regime have included Shirin Ebadi, whose campaign for human rights in her nation won her the Nobel Peace Prize in 2003. Women also figured prominently in the mass demonstrations against the government that broke out in June 2009, when the highly conservative president Mahmoud Ahmadinejad won reelection in a vote that was clearly rigged. This large-scale protest is sometimes called the "Green Movement," a term that the authors of the article use.

The second piece, essentially an opinion column, was published in the November 15, 2010, issue of the *Independent*. Author Isabel Hilton is responding to the appearance in public of Aung San Suu Kyi, another female winner of the Nobel Peace Prize. She had recently been freed after several years of house arrest in her native country of Myanmar, formerly known as Burma. Basically, she had been sentenced for demanding more democracy from the military officers who now rule her nation. Hilton uses the occasion of her release to consider whether an individual protester's moral authority can lead to significant political change. In pondering this issue, she refers to other famous activists, including Corazon Aquino (who led a movement that overthrew the dictator Ferdinand Marcos in the Philippines), Nelson Mandela (who became prime minister of South Africa after a long imprisonment by its formerly white-supremacist regime), Václav Havel (a Czech playwright who became president of his country after helping to topple its Communist leaders), the Dalai Lama (who still fights for the liberation of Tibet from Chinese control), and Liu Xiabo, a jailed pro-democracy activist in China who had won the Nobel Peace Prize just before Hilton wrote this article.

PETER BEAUMONT AND SAEED KAMALI DEHGHAN

Iran: Women on the Frontline of the Fight for Rights

When Shahrzad Kariman finally saw her imprisoned daughter Shiva Nazar Ahari earlier this month, it was for a brief moment outside the Tehran courtroom where the 26-year-old human rights campaigner had been brought. "We could see her for a few minutes," Kariman told the International Campaign for Human Rights in Iran last week. "Just enough to hug her. But we couldn't ask her how the court session went. . . . We didn't know what the charges were prior to the court session."

The charges against Nazar Ahari are among the most serious that can be levelled in Iran: *muharebeh* (enmity against God), a crime, in theory punishable by death, originally intended to be used against armed gangs and pirates, not dissidents.

Nazar Ahari is also charged with assembly and collusion aiming to commit a crime, propagating against the regime, and disrupting public order. But perhaps most dangerous among the allegations — strongly denied both by her family and her organization, the Committee for Human Rights Reporters — is of "relations" with the banned Mojahedin e-Khalq group, which is accused by the Iranian regime of terrorist activities. Her family says that she deplores the organization.

Arrested twice since the disputed Iranian elections in June 2009 and held in the notorious Evin prison, in north-west Tehran, Nazar Ahari has been kept largely incommunicado since December, when she was arrested with several other women activists on her way to the funeral of Grand Ayatollah Hossein Ali Montazeri in the city of Qom. Also detained was Mahboubeh Abbasgholizadeh, another prominent women's rights activist and film-maker, who has since left Iran and was sentenced in absentia to two-and-a-half years in jail and thirty lashes for her part in a 2007 protest.

For the fifteen months since Iran's stolen elections, the faces of these   5 women and others like them have been visible from Paris to New York, in London, Berlin, Sydney, and the Hague.

Their pictures have been held aloft at demonstrations, appeared on human rights Web sites, and are plastered almost daily across newspapers and television screens. They have joined the faces of other Iranian women who, through their activism or by dint of becoming victims of the regime, have come to be the most visible symbols in the west of the wider political and social oppression in Iran under its conservative president, Mahmoud Ahmadinejad.

Then there are the images of the dead, such as Neda Agha Soltan, shot on 20 June 2009 while attending an opposition demonstration to protest at the theft of the Iranian election by Ahmadinejad and his supporters.

If female activists have been prominent, so too have women threatened with death, such as Sakineh Mohammadi Ashtiani, the 43-year-old mother-of-two thrust to international attention after she was sentenced to being stoned to death for adultery.

And if Mohammadi Ashtiani is not an activist but a victim, her shocking case has become a lightning rod for activism for Iranian human rights, an example of how women are treated in the Islamic republic and the failure of its judicial system. This has been seized on by film stars and celebrities such as Colin Firth, Emma Thompson, and Carla Bruni, the wife of France's president, Nicolas Sarkozy, by politicians such as foreign secretary William Hague, and by institutions such as the European parliament and the Vatican.

The consequence has been that some names and pictures have become as   10 recognizable as those Iranian women internationally renowned before 2009, such as Shirin Ebadi, the Nobel Prize–winning human rights activist.

There is a simple reason why the cases of those women being persecuted for their activism and the case of Mohammadi Ashtiani are connected. Their stories reflect different aspects of the same confrontation in Iran: the place of women — and how women who fall foul of the regime can be accused and charged with anything, with no guarantee of a fair trial.

While the existence of this faultline long predates the events surrounding the 2009 election and the rise of the Green Movement, what is true is that Iran's opposition, for a while at least, has amplified the calls for women's rights which have come to define both the international anxiety about and protest against Ahmadinejad's regime.

Dr. Ziba Mir-Hosseini, a Cambridge-based activist and scholar, argues that the current thrusting of women to the fore of the struggle between "despotism and democracy," as she calls it, has been inevitable given the history of women's rights in Iran.

It is a tension, she argues, that has been exacerbated by the contradictory attitude of the 1979 Islamic revolution towards women's political rights. For while the family protection law, introduced by the shah to give women equal rights in issues such as divorce, was quickly revoked after his downfall, the Islamic revolution allowed women to continue voting — a political right, ironically, that was invested with more meaning after the revolution, even as women's human rights were being eroded again under the pretense of the revolution's "protection of women's honor."

The reformists also opened up political space for women to operate, according to Mir-Hosseini. "Mohammad Khatami, during the eight years of his reformist presidency, set up a Centre for Women's Participation that saw the number of women's NGOs in Iran increase from around 45 to over 500."   15

The consequence, she believes, was that feminism — a word that could not even be uttered in the early 1980s — and a feminism linked strongly to notions of wider human rights, took hold in a new generation of Iranian women.

But even during the period when the country's women were actively encouraged to participate, conservative elements of the regime were working to silence them.

With the birth of the One Million Signature campaign, set up by veteran women's rights activists in 2006, a year after the election of Ahmadinejad for the first time, the scene was set for a confrontation.

And while the campaign was successful in forcing the temporary shelving of Ahmadinejad's own new family protection law, which would have made polygamy easier for men and divorce more difficult for women, the emerging power of women activists, who became leaders of the street protests against the 2009 election result, set them on a collision course with the increasingly hardline regime.

"I think part of the reason there has been so much focus on women's rights   20 since the election is the important role women had in the protests [in 2009]," says Maryam Namazie of the international support group Iran Solidarity. "They were at the very forefront, leading the chanting of the slogans. It is also a fact that women's rights are very much the target of this government."

If the face of that activism went largely unnoticed in the international media before the 2009 election protests, confined to the figure of Shirin Ebadi, the violent sweeping up of those protests catapulted a wider group of women to global attention, both as prisoners of conscience and campaigners on an international stage.

This was partly due to the Neda effect, which drew attention to the role of women activists after Neda Agha Soltan was gunned down, with her death recorded on video and viewed around the world.

But if that event created a climate of intense interest in the often young women protestors, the response of the Ahmadinejad regime in clamping down on female campaigners drew even more attention.

A final component is the global attention paid to the stoning sentence delivered against Sakineh Mohammadi Ashtiani, which has served to underline what the women activists had long been saying about the broader attempt to dismantle women's rights.

Another prominent case is that of Shadi Sadr, who ran Rahai, a women's legal advice center, campaigning against stoning, and acted as defense lawyer for Nazar Ahari.

Arrested in July last year walking to Tehran University, where she had been planning to attend the Friday prayers led by the reformist former president Ayatollah Akbar Hashemi Rafsanjani, Shadi Sadr was bundled into an unmarked car and taken to Evin prison. Here she was held in solitary confinement and interrogated about other women's rights activists and the election, before being informed that she would be charged with endangering national security by causing riots.

In court, she was named as a leader of a women's rights movement accused of attempting to overthrow the Islamic republic. Shadi Sadr fled to Turkey two days later.

Describing her attempts to defend Nazar Ahari last week, Shadi Sadr said: "I was never given the permission to meet Shiva [Nazar Ahari] until the day I myself was arrested and, ironically, taken to the same cell Shiva was kept in until the day before I was taken in.

"On the wall of the cell she had written her stories and the charges she thought she was facing. Can you imagine that? The lawyer and her client both kept in one cell within a day? I was not allowed to meet her to hear what she had to say in her defense but that day I read it all on a cell wall.

"Shiva's arrest and especially charging her with *muharebeh*, which is punishable by death, is a clear message to all women's rights activists in Iran and the message is that they face execution if they continue."

The fate of Shadi Sadr, Shiva Nazar Ahari, and Mahboubeh Abbasgholizadeh since 2009 is deeply instructive. Their cases, as the Iran Human Rights Documentation Centre (IHRDC) argued last month in a report entitled "Silencing the Women's Rights Movement in Iran," have been used to attempt to dismantle the women's rights movement, and to cow it into silence under the cover of national security concerns.

That has included claims of links with "terrorism," as in Nazar Ahari's case, or collaboration with foreign countries, which was the explicit claim made by the Iranian authorities last year when they identified the women's rights movement as being one of six groups behind an attempted "velvet revolution."

Whether the regime really believes that or not, the aim since then, says Parisa Kakaee, a veteran women's rights activist quoted in the IHRDC report, is to present women activists with three options: "to become inactive, to go to prison, or to leave the country."

There is no indication that the campaign against women activists is letting up. Last month it was the turn of Nasrin Sotoudeh, 45, an outspoken lawyer and colleague of Shirin Ebadi who has defended a number of opposition activists and protesters. A member of the One Million Signatures campaign, she had been threatened by intelligence service officials that she would be arrested if she continued representing Shirin Ebadi, who left Iran a day before the election for a conference in Spain and didn't return for fear of harassment.

Ebadi said of Sotoudeh's arrest: "The only reason she was arrested is be-   35
cause of her human rights activities, because of defending her clients without any fear. Since the election last summer, a new move of intimidating and putting pressures on lawyers and especially women lawyers has emerged.

"Many have been forced to leave Iran and some are in jail. In this situation, Sotoudeh was one of the very few lawyers and women's right activists who was still working in Iran."

Ebadi is certain why the present Iranian regime is so afraid of women. In an article in the *Guardian*, she declared: "Mark my words, it will be women who bring democracy to Iran."

That socially potent coincidence of women's rights and democratic reform is something Ahmadinejad and his supporters are determined should not be permitted to arise.

It had been hoped that U.S. citizen Sarah Shourd would be released to mark the end of Ramadan, but she remains in custody. Shourd is one of three American hikers who crossed into Iran from Iraq's northern Kurdish region in July 2009.

Iran has threatened to put Shourd and her two male companions on trial   40
for spying. Their families say they were hiking in the largely peaceful region of Iraq and that, if they did cross the border, it was accidental.

Clotilde Reiss, a French teaching assistant, was released earlier this year after being initially accused, like Shourd and her companions, of espionage. Reiss was arrested during the mass protests in 2009, when she was 24, and given two five-year jail sentences. Two Iranian men tried on the same day were hanged.

Found to have attended a demonstration and sent photographs of Iran to contacts at home, Reiss was put on trial with more than 100 others accused of trying to topple the regime and spent a month and a half in Evin prison before she was freed on bail and transferred to the French embassy.   [2010]

ISABEL HILTON
A Triumph for Moral Authority

All who watched Aung San Suu Kyi's short walk to freedom on Saturday had waited a long time for a moment that was full of both joy and uncertainty about the future.

As millions around the world caught their first glimpse of this resolute and courageous woman, who has borne her nearly two decades of confinement with dignity and integrity of purpose, other moments in recent history inevitably came to mind: would her release signal that change is coming to Burma, as that of Nelson Mandela did in South Africa? Would she be able to lead a people-power revolution, as Corazon Aquino did in the Philippines in 1986, or Vaclav Havel in Czechoslovakia in 1989? Would her return to public life in Burma bring the first rays of a political dawn, or will darkness return?

There are as many reasons to hope as to fear a new disappointment, but whatever the final impact of her release, there is no questioning the power of her presence. However we marshal the many arguments against the likelihood of a restoration of democracy to Burma, the mesmerizing impact of those first images reminds us of the exemplary catalyzing force of personal courage and moral purpose.

It is not a good time for politics: In America, politics has descended into a destructive, dysfunctional condition in which popular frustration is channeled into a corporate-funded, poisonous populism. The conduct of the wars in Iraq and Afghanistan has fatally damaged the West's ability to argue for human rights elsewhere: how can Washington lecture Beijing or Burma on human rights when it has itself embraced torture and imprisonment without trial? Western governments still wave their rhetorical moral flags, but they are too tarnished to be convincing.

Yet the desire to believe that political leaders can embody the moral values essential to fair, equitable, and tolerant societies refuses to die. We continue to hope for a politics that upholds humanity and justice against greed and violence. For many, the prospects of such a leadership seem unbearably distant. Most of us struggle to match the moral claims of our leaders with political reality. Out of this disappointment comes the extraordinary power of those individuals who display personal courage against overwhelming odds.

The government of Burma's giant neighbor, China, has spent more than two decades hoping the world—and its own citizens—will forget the devastating brutality of its suppression of the student demonstrators in Tiananmen Square in 1989. But the unforgettable image of that tragic episode is one unidentified man in a white shirt and dark trousers, a shopping bag in one hand, facing down an advancing column of tanks and bringing it to a standstill with nothing more than unshakeable individual courage. To this day, Chinese contemporary art works are scrutinised by the security forces for images that might be read as coded references to that iconic moment.

We measure political power in material terms: how strong is the party, how big the army, how full the coffers, how secure the grip on the levers of state? By those measures, the Burmese generals hold all the cards, just as the apartheid regime did in South Africa when Nelson Mandela made his walk to freedom. But that assessment leaves out of account the unmeasurable power of moral authority, a power that derives from the ability not to coerce or to marshal fear, but to inspire citizens to acts of individual and collective courage, to keep hope alive, and to engender actions that may bring tragedy to the individual but that can create an unstoppable collective force.

Who would have predicted that an unarmed Czech playwright would catalyse a peaceful revolution against the armed might of the Soviet Union, or that an Indian campaigner for non-violence would drive the British from India? Such symbols take root in our memories and endure, long after the tanks have rusted. Does anyone doubt that the Dalai Lama is able to inspire — or that Hu Jintao° is not? How many citizens would shout for joy at the sight of one of Burma's military dictators? Would any real tears be shed if they were never seen again?

No doubt the Burmese regime does not seek to be loved, as long as it is sufficiently feared. Nevertheless, it has shown that it is not immune to the need to pretend that its mission is the general good. The election that the generals staged last month was an empty attempt to paint a coat of popular assent on coercion. That a regime that holds all the material cards needs to indulge in such pretence reveals both the limits of force and the fragility of a power that must suspect subversion everywhere. By every conventional measure, Aung San Suu Kyi is weak: a 65-year-old widow with no troops, few funds, and, formally at least, no party. When strong regimes show their fear of weak individuals their own vulnerability stands revealed.

Aung San Suu Kyi's release is one of those universal moments that resonate far beyond the borders of her suffering country. When she won the Nobel Peace Prize in 1991, she was already in detention. Her late husband, Michael Aris, and her two sons accepted the prize on her behalf. A photograph of the imprisoned laureate sat in the centre of the stage, a reminder to all of the regime's brutal intransigence.

On 10 December, China will undergo a similar moral rebuke when the Nobel Peace Prize is awarded to Liu Xiaobo, the Chinese public intellectual currently imprisoned for calling, amongst other things, for the Chinese government to respect its own constitution and to respect its own laws.

China is both Burma's neighbor and economic mainstay. China's official news agency, Xinhua, reported Aung San Suu Kyi's release in a few short paragraphs that led with her willingness to work for "national reconciliation." China's state television news led their report with the Burmese government's announcement of her release. Neither mentioned that she, like Liu Xiaobo, is a Nobel Peace Prize laureate.

Hu Jintao: Leader of the People's Republic of China.

Liu is not someone who inspires a mass following in China as Aung San Suu Kyi does in Burma, but his moral courage, like hers, serves as a mirror that magnifies the lack of it in his jailers. Ever since the Nobel announcement in October, Beijing has been on the horns of a painful dilemma: they cannot release Liu to attend the ceremony without acknowledging the injustice of his imprisonment, but his absence at a ceremony makes the case against them even more powerfully.

Beijing has been attempting to coerce other countries into boycotting the ceremony, while detaining, or restricting the travel, of an ever wider circle of friends and sympathizers who might be suspected of planning to represent him in Oslo. The greater the effort to limit the impact of the Nobel prize, the worse the Chinese government looks; their impotence eats away at the one thing that no regime can enforce — the abstract but potent qualities of credibility and legitimacy.

Without the legitimacy of popular consent, even a lone, unarmed, impris-   15
oned individual is a potential threat. Their example shows us that we can decline to believe in a lie and that fear can be conquered. Once a people conquers its fears, the outcome is no longer in doubt. It is only a matter of time.   *[2010]*

≡ THINKING ABOUT THE TEXTS

1. In the first of these two articles, authors Beaumont and Dehghan suggest it makes sense to connect female activists with female victims of the Iranian justice system who are not necessarily protesting the overall government. To what extent do you accept the authors' linking of the two groups? Do you see Antigone as both activist *and* victim, or are you more inclined to give her just one of these labels? Explain.

2. In the second article, Hilton argues that Aung San Suu Kyi and other protesters she discusses carry "moral authority." How would *you* define this term? Do you see it as applicable to Antigone? Why, or why not?

3. Do you see Antigone as more flawed than the main women mentioned in the news articles? Why, or why not?

≡ WRITING ABOUT ISSUES

1. Write an essay that analyzes a character in Sophocles' play *other* than Antigone or Creon: examples include the chorus (which you can treat as one character), Ismene, Haemon, Tiresias, and Eurydice. Concentrate on explaining the relation between your chosen character and an issue that Antigone must deal with, too. (Remember that it's useful to phrase an issue as a question with more than one possible answer.)

2. Imagine that you are producing a contemporary staging of *Antigone* and must advertise it with a poster depicting one of the women mentioned in the news articles. Write an essay explaining your selection of the

particular woman you choose. Feel free to do further research on her if necessary.

3. Write an essay about a woman you know, directly or indirectly, whom you see as a fighter against injustice. Although you can use some of the essay to praise her, spend most of it explaining how she has had to confront at least one difficult issue — that is, a question with more than one possible answer. If you wish, refer to any of the texts in this cluster.

4. Write an essay or a script in which you imagine how Antigone would behave if she were transported to contemporary Iran, Myanmar, or China. If you wish, refer to one or both of the news articles in this cluster.

▤ Civil Disobedience: Essays

HENRY DAVID THOREAU, "Civil Disobedience"

REBECCA SOLNIT, "The Thoreau Problem"

MARTIN LUTHER KING JR., "Letter from Birmingham Jail"

Many people assume that the legal systems they live under are fair and moral. At various times and places, however, individuals and social movements have objected to certain laws, declaring them unethical and perhaps even condemning the entire government behind them. History has seen numerous occasions when such criticism has turned violent, even becoming outright revolt. At other moments, though, the protest has taken the form of civil disobedience. This is usually defined as the use of relatively *non*violent means to defy a law, on behalf of what the protesters claim is a higher principle. Contemporary examples in the United States have included mass demonstrations by foes of capitalism at economic summits, as well as the blocking of abortion clinics by right-to-life groups. Of course, civil disobedience has also occurred in other countries. Mahatma Gandhi famously practiced it in working for the independence of India. More recently, rallies have defied oppressive regimes in Myanmar (Burma) and Iran, while smaller circles of dissidents continue to challenge the leaders of Communist China.

Featured in this cluster are two of the most well-known and inspirational arguments for civil disobedience, Henry David Thoreau's essay of that title and Martin Luther King Jr.'s "Letter from Birmingham Jail." Also here is a commentary by Rebecca Solnit that ponders the implications of Thoreau's text. All three pieces leave you, the reader, having to decide how *you* would identify and deal with the differences between "just" and "unjust" laws.

▤ BEFORE YOU READ

Civil disobedience is usually defined as a form of protest: specifically, the use of nonviolent means to defy a law on behalf of a supposedly higher moral principle. In Thoreau's classic essay on this subject, for example, he relates that he refused to pay taxes because he opposed the U.S. government's tolerance of slavery and also its war against Mexico. Under what circumstances, if any, do you think civil disobedience is justified? What particular historical and contemporary events come to your mind when you consider this issue?

HENRY DAVID THOREAU
Civil Disobedience

Henry David Thoreau (1817–1862) spent his life in the area of Concord, Massachusetts. But since his death, he has been acclaimed worldwide as a major contributor to American thought and literature. His writings on ecology, philosophy, theology, and agriculture inspire many people even today. His most well-known text is his book Walden *(1854). A classic argument for plain, simple living in harmony with nature, it grew out of the journal that Thoreau kept during the two years he spent in a cabin at Walden Pond, on land owned by his friend Ralph Waldo Emerson. Also renowned, however, is the following essay, which has influenced such important civic activists as Mahatma Gandhi and Martin Luther King Jr. It was first a public lecture that Thoreau gave locally on January 26, 1848. With the title "Resistance to Civil Government," it was then published in May 1849 in* Aesthetic Papers, *a periodical that lasted for only one issue. "Civil Disobedience" acquired its present title in an 1866 volume of Thoreau's works. Although the essay expresses a theory of law and politics that he held throughout his life, in part Thoreau was moved to write it by hatred of two then-current U.S. government policies. One was the system of slavery, which federal law permitted to exist in the southern states. The other was the Mexican-American War, which to Thoreau was an immoral conflict sparked by his nation's lust for territory. The chief form of civil disobedience that Thoreau discusses in the essay is his own refusal to pay taxes. As he recalls, this once resulted in his being jailed for a night.*

I heartily accept the motto, "That government is best which governs least"; and I should like to see it acted up to more rapidly and systematically. Carried out, it finally amounts to this, which also I believe — "That government is best which governs not at all"; and when men are prepared for it, that will be the kind of government which they will have. Government is at best but an expedient; but most governments are usually, and all governments are sometimes, inexpedient. The objections which have been brought against a standing army, and they are many and weighty, and deserve to prevail, may also at last be brought against a standing government. The standing army is only an arm of the standing government. The government itself, which is only the mode which the people have chosen to execute their will, is equally liable to be abused and perverted before the people can act through it. Witness the present Mexican war, the work of comparatively a few individuals using the standing government as their tool; for, in the outset, the people would not have consented to this measure.

This American government — what is it but a tradition, though a recent one, endeavoring to transmit itself unimpaired to posterity, but each instant losing some of its integrity? It has not the vitality and force of a single living man; for a single man can bend it to his will. It is a sort of wooden gun to the people themselves. But it is not the less necessary for this; for the people must have some complicated machinery or other, and hear its din, to satisfy that idea of government which they have. Governments show thus how successfully men can be imposed on, even impose on themselves, for their own advantage. It is excellent, we must all allow. Yet this government never of itself furthered any enterprise, but by the alacrity with which it got out of its way. It does not keep the country free. It does not settle the West. It does not educate. The character inherent in the American people has done all that has been accomplished; and it would have done somewhat more, if the government had not sometimes got in its way. For government is an expedient by which men would fain succeed in letting one another alone; and, as has been said, when it is most expedient, the governed are most let alone by it. Trade and commerce, if they were not made of india-rubber, would never manage to bounce over the obstacles which legislators are continually putting in their way; and, if one were to judge these men wholly by the effects of their actions and not partly by their intentions, they would deserve to be classed and punished with those mischievous persons who put obstructions on the railroads.

But, to speak practically and as a citizen, unlike those who call themselves no-government men, I ask for, not at once no government, but at once a better government. Let every man make known what kind of government would command his respect, and that will be one step toward obtaining it.

After all, the practical reason why, when the power is once in the hands of the people, a majority are permitted, and for a long period continue, to rule is not because they are most likely to be in the right, nor because this seems fairest to the minority, but because they are physically the strongest. But a government in which the majority rule in all cases cannot be based on justice, even as far as men understand it. Can there not be a government in which majorities do not virtually decide right and wrong, but conscience? — in which majorities decide only those questions to which the rule of expediency is applicable? Must the citizen ever for a moment, or in the least degree, resign his conscience to the legislation? Why has every man a conscience, then? I think that we should be men first, and subjects afterward. It is not desirable to cultivate a respect for the law, so much as for the right. The only obligation which I have a right to assume is to do at any time what I think right. It is truly enough said that a corporation has no conscience; but a corporation of conscientious men is a corporation with a conscience. Law never made men a whit more just; and, by means of their respect for it, even the well-disposed are daily made the agents of injustice. A common and natural result of an undue respect for law is, that you may see a file of soldiers, colonel, captain, corporal, privates, powder-monkeys, and all, marching in admirable order over hill and dale to the wars, against their wills, ay, against their common sense and consciences, which makes it very steep marching indeed, and produces a palpitation of the heart. They have no doubt that it is a damnable business in which they are concerned; they are all peaceably inclined. Now, what are they? Men at all? or small movable forts and magazines, at the service of some unscrupulous man in power? Visit the Navy-Yard, and behold a marine, such a man as an American government can make, or such as it can make a man with its black arts — a mere shadow and reminiscence of humanity, a man laid out alive and standing, and already, as one may say, buried under arms with funeral accompaniments, though it may be,

> "Not a drum was heard, not a funeral note,
> As his corse to the rampart we hurried;
> Not a soldier discharged his farewell shot
> O'er the grave where our hero we buried."

The mass of men serve the state thus, not as men mainly, but as machines, with their bodies. They are the standing army, and the militia, jailers, constables, posse comitatus, etc. In most cases there is no free exercise whatever of the judgment or of the moral sense; but they put themselves on a level with wood and earth and stones; and wooden men can perhaps be manufactured that will serve the purpose as well. Such command no more respect than men of straw or a lump of dirt. They have the same sort of worth only as horses and dogs. Yet such as these even are commonly esteemed good citizens. Others — as most legislators, politicians, lawyers, ministers, and office-holders — serve the state chiefly with their heads; and, as they rarely make any moral distinctions, they are as likely to serve the devil, without intending it, as God. A very few — as heroes, patriots, martyrs, reformers in the great sense, and men — serve the state with their consciences also, and so necessarily resist it for the most part; and they are commonly treated as enemies by it. A wise man will only be useful as a man, and will not submit to be "clay," and "stop a hole to keep the wind away," but leave that office to his dust at least: 5

> "I am too high-born to be propertied,
> To be a secondary at control,
> Or useful serving-man and instrument
> To any sovereign state throughout the world."

He who gives himself entirely to his fellow-men appears to them useless and selfish; but he who gives himself partially to them is pronounced a benefactor and philanthropist.

How does it become a man to behave toward this American government today? I answer, that he cannot without disgrace be associated with it. I cannot for an instant recognize that political organization as my government which is the slave's government also.

All men recognize the right of revolution; that is, the right to refuse allegiance to, and to resist, the government, when its tyranny or its inefficiency are great and unendurable. But almost all say that such is not the case now. But such was the case, they think, in the Revolution of '75. If one were to tell me that this was a bad government because it taxed certain foreign commodities brought to its ports, it is most probable that I should not make an ado about it, for I can do without them. All machines have their friction; and possibly this does enough good to counterbalance the evil. At any rate, it is a great evil to make a stir about it. But when the friction comes to have its machine, and oppression and robbery are organized, I say, let us not have such a machine any longer. In other words, when a sixth of the population of a nation which has undertaken to be the refuge of liberty are slaves, and a whole country is un-justly overrun and conquered by a foreign army, and subjected to military law, I think that it is not too soon for honest men to rebel and revolutionize. What makes this duty the more urgent is the fact that the country so overrun is not our own, but ours is the invading army.

Paley, a common authority with many on moral questions, in his chapter on the "Duty of Submission to Civil Government," resolves all civil obligation into expediency; and he proceeds to say that "so long as the interest of the whole society requires it, that is, so long as the established government cannot be resisted or changed without public inconveniency, it is the will of God . . . that the established government be obeyed — and no longer. This principle be-ing admitted, the justice of every particular case of resistance is reduced to a computation of the quantity of the danger and grievance on the one side, and of the probability and expense of redressing it on the other." Of this, he says, every man shall judge for himself. But Paley appears never to have contem-plated those cases to which the rule of expediency does not apply, in which a people, as well as an individual, must do justice, cost what it may. If I have un-justly wrested a plank from a drowning man, I must restore it to him though I drown myself. This, according to Paley, would be inconvenient. But he that would save his life, in such a case, shall lose it. This people must cease to hold slaves, and to make war on Mexico, though it cost them their existence as a people.

In their practice, nations agree with Paley; but does any one think that   10
Massachusetts does exactly what is right at the present crisis?

"A drab of state, a cloth-o'-silver slut,
To have her train borne up, and her soul trail in the dirt."

Practically speaking, the opponents to a reform in Massachusetts are not a hundred thousand politicians at the South, but a hundred thousand mer-chants and farmers here, who are more interested in commerce and agricul-ture than they are in humanity, and are not prepared to do justice to the slave and to Mexico, cost what it may. I quarrel not with far-off foes, but with those who, near at home, cooperate with, and do the bidding of those far away, and without whom the latter would be harmless. We are accustomed to say, that the mass of men are unprepared; but improvement is slow, because the few are not materially wiser or better than the many. It is not so important that many should be as good as you, as that there be some absolute goodness somewhere; for that will leaven the whole lump. There are thousands who are in opinion opposed to slavery and to the war, who yet in effect do nothing to put an end to them; who, esteeming themselves children of Washington and Franklin, sit down with their hands in their pockets, and say that they know not what to do, and do nothing; who even postpone the question of freedom to the question of free trade, and quietly read the prices-current along with the latest advices from Mexico, after dinner, and, it may be, fall asleep over them both. What is the price-current of an honest man and patriot today? They hesitate, and they regret, and sometimes they petition; but they do nothing in earnest and with effect. They will wait, well disposed, for others to remedy the evil, that they may no longer have it to regret. At most, they give only a cheap vote, and a feeble countenance and God-speed, to the right, as it goes by them. There are nine hundred and ninety-nine patrons of virtue to one virtuous man. But it is easier to deal with the real possessor of a thing than with the temporary guardian of it.

All voting is a sort of gaming, like checkers or backgammon, with a slight moral tinge to it, a playing with right and wrong, with moral questions; and betting naturally accompanies it. The character of the voters is not staked. I cast my vote, perchance, as I think right; but I am not vitally concerned that that right should prevail. I am willing to leave it to the majority. Its obligation, therefore, never exceeds that of expediency. Even voting for the right is doing nothing for it. It is only expressing to men feebly your desire that it should prevail. A wise man will not leave the right to the mercy of chance, nor wish it to prevail through the power of the majority. There is but little virtue in the action of masses of men. When the majority shall at length vote for the abolition of slavery, it will be because they are indifferent to slavery, or because there is but little slavery left to be abolished by their vote. They will then be the only slaves. Only his vote can hasten the abolition of slavery who asserts his own freedom by his vote.

I hear of a convention to be held at Baltimore, or elsewhere, for the selection of a candidate for the Presidency, made up chiefly of editors, and men who are politicians by profession; but I think, what is it to any independent, intelligent, and respectable man what decision they may come to? Shall we not have the advantage of his wisdom and honesty, nevertheless? Can we not count upon some independent votes? Are there not many individuals in the country who do not attend conventions? But no: I find that the respectable man, so called, has immediately drifted from his position, and despairs of his country, when his country has more reason to despair of him. He forthwith adopts one of the candidates thus selected as the only available one, thus proving that he is himself available for any purposes of the demagogue. His vote is of no more worth than that of any unprincipled foreigner or hireling native, who may have been bought. O for a man who is a man, and, as my neighbor says, has a bone in his back which you cannot pass your hand through! Our statistics are at fault: the population has been returned too large. How many men are there to a square thousand miles in this country? Hardly one. Does not America offer any inducement for men to settle here? The American has dwindled into an Odd Fellow — one who may be known by the development of his organ of gregariousness, and a manifest lack of intellect and cheerful self-reliance; whose first and chief concern, on coming into the world, is to see that the almshouses are in good repair; and, before yet he has lawfully donned the virile garb, to collect a fund for the support of the widows and orphans that may be; who, in short, ventures to live only by the aid of the Mutual Insurance company, which has promised to bury him decently.

It is not a man's duty, as a matter of course, to devote himself to the eradication of any, even the most enormous, wrong; he may still properly have other concerns to engage him; but it is his duty, at least, to wash his hands of it, and, if he gives it no thought longer, not to give it practically his support. If I devote myself to other pursuits and contemplations, I must first see, at least, that I do not pursue them sitting upon another man's shoulders. I must get off him first, that he may pursue his contemplations too. See what gross inconsistency is tolerated. I have heard some of my townsmen say, "I should like to have them order me out to help put down an insurrection of the slaves, or to march to Mexico; — see if I would go"; and yet these very men have each, directly by their allegiance, and so indirectly, at least, by their money, furnished a substitute. The soldier is applauded who refuses to serve in an unjust war by those who do not refuse to sustain the unjust government which makes the war; is applauded by those whose own act and authority he disregards and sets at naught; as if the state were penitent to that degree that it differed one to scourge it while it sinned, but not to that degree that it left off sinning for a moment. Thus, under the name of Order and Civil Government, we are all made at last to pay homage to and support our own meanness. After the first blush of sin comes its indifference; and from immoral it becomes, as it were, unmoral, and not quite unnecessary to that life which we have made.

The broadest and most prevalent error requires the most disinterested   15
virtue to sustain it. The slight reproach to which the virtue of patriotism is commonly liable, the noble are most likely to incur. Those who, while they disapprove of the character and measures of a government, yield to it their allegiance and support are undoubtedly its most conscientious supporters, and so frequently the most serious obstacles to reform. Some are petitioning the State to dissolve the Union, to disregard the requisitions of the President. Why do they not dissolve it themselves — the union between themselves and the State — and refuse to pay their quota into its treasury? Do not they stand in the same relation to the State that the State does to the Union? And have not the same reasons prevented the State from resisting the Union which have prevented them from resisting the State?

How can a man be satisfied to entertain an opinion merely, and enjoy it? Is there any enjoyment in it, if his opinion is that he is aggrieved? If you are cheated out of a single dollar by your neighbor, you do not rest satisfied with knowing that you are cheated, or with saying that you are cheated, or even with petitioning him to pay you your due; but you take effectual steps at once to obtain the full amount, and see that you are never cheated again. Action from principle, the perception and the performance of right, changes things and relations; it is essentially revolutionary, and does not consist wholly with anything which was. It not only divides States and churches, it divides families; ay, it divides the individual, separating the diabolical in him from the divine.

Unjust laws exist: shall we be content to obey them, or shall we endeavor to amend them, and obey them until we have succeeded, or shall we transgress them at once? Men generally, under such a government as this, think that they ought to wait until they have persuaded the majority to alter them. They think that, if they should resist, the remedy would be worse than the evil. But it is the fault of the government itself that the remedy is worse than the evil. It makes it worse. Why is it not more apt to anticipate and provide for reform? Why does it not cherish its wise minority? Why does it cry and resist before it is hurt? Why does it not encourage its citizens to be on the alert to point out its faults, and do better than it would have them? Why does it always crucify Christ, and excommunicate Copernicus and Luther, and pronounce Washington and Franklin rebels?

One would think, that a deliberate and practical denial of its authority was the only offence never contemplated by government; else, why has it not assigned its definite, its suitable and proportionate, penalty? If a man who has no property refuses but once to earn nine shillings for the State, he is put in prison for a period unlimited by any law that I know, and determined only by the discretion of those who placed him there; but if he should steal ninety times nine shillings from the State, he is soon permitted to go at large again.

If the injustice is part of the necessary friction of the machine of government, let it go, let it go: perchance it will wear smooth — certainly the machine will wear out. If the injustice has a spring, or a pulley, or a rope, or a crank, exclusively for itself, then perhaps you may consider whether the remedy will not be worse than the evil; but if it is of such a nature that it requires you to be the agent of injustice to another, then, I say, break the law. Let your life be a counter-friction to stop the machine. What I have to do is to see, at any rate, that I do not lend myself to the wrong which I condemn.

As for adopting the ways which the State has provided for remedying the evil, I know not of such ways. They take too much time, and a man's life will be gone. I have other affairs to attend to. I came into this world, not chiefly to make this a good place to live in, but to live in it, be it good or bad. A man has not everything to do, but something; and because he cannot do everything, it is not necessary that he should do something wrong. It is not my business to be petitioning the Governor or the Legislature any more than it is theirs to petition me; and if they should not bear my petition, what should I do then? But in this case the State has provided no way: its very Constitution is the evil. This may seem to be harsh and stubborn and unconciliatory; but it is to treat with the utmost kindness and consideration the only spirit that can appreciate or deserves it. So is all change for the better, like birth and death, which convulse the body.

I do not hesitate to say, that those who call themselves Abolitionists should at once effectually withdraw their support, both in person and property, from the government of Massachusetts, and not wait till they constitute a majority of one, before they suffer the right to prevail through them. I think that it is enough if they have God on their side, without waiting for that other one. Moreover, any man more right than his neighbors constitutes a majority of one already.

I meet this American government, or its representative, the State government, directly, and face to face, once a year — no more — in the person of its

20

tax-gatherer; this is the only mode in which a man situated as I am necessarily meets it; and it then says distinctly, Recognize me; and the simplest, the most effectual, and, in the present posture of affairs, the indispensablest mode of treating with it on this head, of expressing your little satisfaction with and love for it, is to deny it then. My civil neighbor, the tax-gatherer, is the very man I have to deal with — for it is, after all, with men and not with parchment that I quarrel — and he has voluntarily chosen to be an agent of the government. How shall he ever know well what he is and does as an officer of the government, or as a man, until he is obliged to consider whether he shall treat me, his neighbor, for whom he has respect, as a neighbor and well-disposed man, or as a maniac and disturber of the peace, and see if he can get over this obstruction to his neighborliness without a ruder and more impetuous thought or speech corresponding with his action. I know this well, that if one thousand, if one hundred, if ten men whom I could name — if ten honest men only — ay, if one HONEST man, in this State of Massachusetts, ceasing to hold slaves, were actually to withdraw from this copartnership, and be locked up in the county jail therefor, it would be the abolition of slavery in America. For it matters not how small the beginning may seem to be: what is once well done is done forever. But we love better to talk about it: that we say is our mission. Reform keeps many scores of newspapers in its service, but not one man. If my esteemed neighbor, the State's ambassador, who will devote his days to the settlement of the question of human rights in the Council Chamber, instead of being threatened with the prisons of Carolina, were to sit down the prisoner of Massachusetts, that State which is so anxious to foist the sin of slavery upon her sister — though at present she can discover only an act of inhospitality to be the ground of a quarrel with her — the Legislature would not wholly waive the subject the following winter.

Under a government which imprisons any unjustly, the true place for a just man is also a prison. The proper place today, the only place which Massachusetts has provided for her freer and less desponding spirits, is in her prisons, to be put out and locked out of the State by her own act, as they have already put themselves out by their principles. It is there that the fugitive slave, and the Mexican prisoner on parole, and the Indian come to plead the wrongs of his race should find them; on that separate, but more free and honorable, ground, where the State places those who are not with her, but against her — the only house in a slave State in which a free man can abide with honor. If any think that their influence would be lost there, and their voices no longer afflict the ear of the State, that they would not be as an enemy within its walls, they do not know by how much truth is stronger than error, nor how much more eloquently and effectively he can combat injustice who has experienced a little in his own person. Cast your whole vote, not a strip of paper merely, but your whole influence. A minority is powerless while it conforms to the majority; it is not even a minority then; but it is irresistible when it clogs by its whole weight. If the alternative is to keep all just men in prison, or give up war and slavery, the State will not hesitate which to choose. If a thousand men were not to pay their tax-bills this year, that would not be a violent and bloody measure, as it would be to pay them, and enable the State to commit violence and shed innocent blood. This is, in fact, the definition of a peaceable revolution, if any such is possible. If the tax-gatherer, or any other public officer, asks me, as one has done, "But what shall I do?" my answer is, "If you really wish to do anything, resign your office." When the subject has refused allegiance, and the officer has resigned his office, then the revolution is accomplished. But even suppose blood should flow. Is there not a sort of blood shed when the conscience is wounded? Through this wound a man's real manhood and immortality flow out, and he bleeds to an everlasting death. I see this blood flowing now.

I have contemplated the imprisonment of the offender, rather than the seizure of his goods — though both will serve the same purpose — because they who assert the purest right, and consequently are most dangerous to a corrupt State, commonly have not spent much time in accumulating property. To such the State renders comparatively small service, and a slight tax is wont to appear exorbitant, particularly if they are obliged to earn it by special labor with their hands. If there were one who lived wholly without the use of money, the State itself would hesitate to demand it of him. But the rich man — not to make any invidious comparison — is always sold to the institution which makes him rich. Absolutely speaking, the more money, the less virtue; for money comes between a man and his objects, and obtains them for him; and it was certainly no great virtue to obtain it. It puts to rest many questions which he would otherwise be taxed to answer; while the only new question which it puts is the hard but superfluous one, how to spend it. Thus his moral ground is taken from under his feet. The opportunities of living are diminished in proportion as what are called the "means" are increased. The best thing a man can do for his culture when he is rich is to endeavor to carry out those schemes which he entertained when he was poor. Christ answered the Herodians according to their condition. "Show me the tribute-money," said he; — and one took a penny out of his pocket; — if you use money which has the image of Caesar on it, and which he has made current and valuable, that is, if you are men of the State, and gladly enjoy the advantages of Caesar's government, then pay him back some of his own when he demands it. "Render therefore to Caesar that which is Caesar's, and to God those things which are God's" — leaving them no wiser than before as to which was which; for they did not wish to know.

When I converse with the freest of my neighbors, I perceive that, whatever 25 they may say about the magnitude and seriousness of the question, and their regard for the public tranquility, the long and the short of the matter is, that they cannot spare the protection of the existing government, and they dread the consequences to their property and families of disobedience to it. For my own part, I should not like to think that I ever rely on the protection of the State. But, if I deny the authority of the State when it presents its tax-bill, it will soon take and waste all my property, and so harass me and my children without end. This is hard. This makes it impossible for a man to live honestly, and at the same time comfortably, in outward respects. It will not be worth the while to accumulate property; that would be sure to go again. You must hire or squat somewhere, and raise but a small crop, and eat that soon. You must live within yourself, and depend upon yourself always tucked up and ready for a start, and not have many affairs. A man may grow rich in Turkey even, if he will be in all respects a good subject of the Turkish government. Confucius said: "If a state is governed by the principles of reason, poverty and misery are subjects of shame; if a state is not governed by the principles of reason, riches and honors are the subjects of shame." No: until I want the protection of Massachusetts to be extended to me in some distant Southern port, where my liberty is endangered, or until I am bent solely on building up an estate at home by peaceful enterprise, I can afford to refuse allegiance to Massachusetts, and her right to my property and life. It costs me less in every sense to incur the penalty of disobedience to the State than it would to obey. I should feel as if I were worth less in that case.

Some years ago, the State met me in behalf of the Church, and commanded me to pay a certain sum toward the support of a clergyman whose preaching my father attended, but never I myself. "Pay," it said, "or be locked up in the jail." I declined to pay. But, unfortunately, another man saw fit to pay it. I did not see why the schoolmaster should be taxed to support the priest, and not the priest the schoolmaster; for I was not the State's schoolmaster, but I supported myself by voluntary subscription. I did not see why the lyceum should not present its tax-bill, and have the State to back its demand, as well as the Church. However, at the request of the selectmen, I condescended to make some such statement as this in writing: — "Know all men by these presents, that I, Henry Thoreau, do not wish to be regarded as a member of any incorporated society which I have not joined." This I gave to the town clerk; and he has it. The State, having thus learned that I did not wish to be regarded as a member of that church, has never made a like demand on me since; though it said that it must adhere to its original presumption that time. If I had known how to name them, I should then have signed off in detail from all the societies which I never signed on to; but I did not know where to find a complete list.

I have paid no poll-tax for six years. I was put into a jail once on this account, for one night; and, as I stood considering the walls of solid stone, two or three feet thick, the door of wood and iron, a foot thick, and the iron grating which strained the light, I could not help being struck with the foolishness of that institution which treated me as if I were mere flesh and blood and bones, to be locked up. I wondered that it should have concluded at length that this was the best use it could put me to, and had never thought to avail itself of my services in some way. I saw that, if there was a wall of stone between me and my townsmen, there was a still more difficult one to climb or break through before they could get to be as free as I was. I did not for a moment feel confined, and the walls seemed a great waste of stone and mortar. I felt as if I alone of all my townsmen had paid my tax. They plainly did not know how to treat me, but behaved like persons who are underbred. In every threat and in every compliment there was a blunder; for they thought that my chief desire was to stand the other side of that stone wall. I could not but smile to see how industriously they locked the door on my meditations, which followed them out again without let or hindrance, and they were really all that was dangerous. As they could not reach me, they had resolved to punish my body; just as boys, if they cannot come at some person against whom they have a spite, will abuse his dog. I saw that the State was half-witted, that it was timid as a lone woman with her silver spoons, and that it did not know its friends from its foes, and I lost all my remaining respect for it, and pitied it.

Thus the State never intentionally confronts a man's sense, intellectual or moral, but only his body, his senses. It is not armed with superior wit or honesty, but with superior physical strength. I was not born to be forced. I will breathe after my own fashion. Let us see who is the strongest. What force has a multitude? They only can force me who obey a higher law than I. They force me to become like themselves. I do not hear of men being forced to have this way or that by masses of men. What sort of life were that to live? When I meet a government which says to me, "Your money or your life," why should I be in haste to give it my money? It may be in a great strait, and not know what to do: I cannot help that. It must help itself; do as I do. It is not worth the while to snivel about it. I am not responsible for the successful working of the machinery of society. I am not the son of the engineer. I perceive that, when an acorn and a chestnut fall side by side, the one does not remain inert to make way for the other, but both obey their own laws, and spring and grow and flourish as best they can, till one, perchance, overshadows and destroys the other. If a plant cannot live according to its nature, it dies; and so a man.

The night in prison was novel and interesting enough. The prisoners in their shirt-sleeves were enjoying a chat and the evening air in the doorway, when I entered. But the jailer said, "Come, boys, it is time to lock up"; and so they dispersed, and I heard the sound of their steps returning into the hollow apartments. My room-mate was introduced to me by the jailer as "a first-rate fellow and a clever man." When the door was locked, he showed me where to hang my hat, and how he managed matters there. The rooms were whitewashed once a month; and this one, at least, was the whitest, most simply furnished, and probably the neatest apartment in the town. He naturally wanted to know where I came from, and what brought me there; and, when I had told him, I asked him in my turn how he came there, presuming him to be an honest man, of course; and, as the world goes, I believe he was. "Why," said he, "they accuse me of burning a barn; but I never did it." As near as I could discover, he had probably gone to bed in a barn when drunk, and smoked his pipe there; and so a barn was burnt. He had the reputation of being a clever man, had been there some three months waiting for his trial to come on, and would have to wait as much longer; but he was quite domesticated and contented, since he got his board for nothing, and thought that he was well treated.

He occupied one window, and I the other; and I saw that if one stayed there long, his principal business would be to look out the window. I had soon read all the tracts that were left there, and examined where former prisoners had broken out, and where a grate had been sawed off, and heard the history of the various occupants of that room; for I found that even here there was a history and a gossip which never circulated beyond the walls of the jail. Probably this is the only house in the town where verses are composed, which are afterward

30

printed in a circular form, but not published. I was shown quite a long list of verses which were composed by some young men who had been detected in an attempt to escape, who avenged themselves by singing them.

I pumped my fellow-prisoner as dry as I could, for fear I should never see him again; but at length he showed me which was my bed, and left me to blow out the lamp.

It was like travelling into a far country, such as I had never expected to behold, to lie there for one night. It seemed to me that I never had heard the town clock strike before, nor the evening sounds of the village; for we slept with the windows open, which were inside the grating. It was to see my native village in the light of the Middle Ages, and our Concord was turned into a Rhine stream, and visions of knights and castles passed before me. They were the voices of old burghers that I heard in the streets. I was an involuntary spectator and auditor of whatever was done and said in the kitchen of the adjacent village inn — a wholly new and rare experience to me. It was a closer view of my native town. I was fairly inside of it. I never had seen its institutions before. This is one of its peculiar institutions; for it is a shire town. I began to comprehend what its inhabitants were about.

In the morning, our breakfasts were put through the hole in the door, in small oblong-square tin pans, made to fit, and holding a pint of chocolate, with brown bread, and an iron spoon. When they called for the vessels again, I was green enough to return what bread I had left; but my comrade seized it, and said that I should lay that up for lunch or dinner. Soon after he was let out to work at haying in a neighboring field, whither he went every day, and would not be back till noon; so he bade me good-day, saying that he doubted if he should see me again.

When I came out of prison — for some one interfered, and paid that tax — I did not perceive that great changes had taken place on the common, such as he observed who went in a youth and emerged a tottering and gray-headed man; and yet a change had to my eyes come over the scene — the town, and State, and country — greater than any that mere time could effect. I saw yet more distinctly the State in which I lived. I saw to what extent the people among whom I lived could be trusted as good neighbors and friends; that their friendship was for summer weather only; that they did not greatly propose to do right; that they were a distinct race from me by their prejudices and superstitions, as the Chinamen and Malays are; that in their sacrifices to humanity they ran no risks, not even to their property; that after all they were not so noble but they treated the thief as he had treated them, and hoped, by a certain outward observance and a few prayers, and by walking in a particular straight though useless path from time to time, to save their souls. This may be to judge my neighbors harshly; for I believe that many of them are not aware that they have such an institution as the jail in their village.

It was formerly the custom in our village, when a poor debtor came out of jail, for his acquaintances to salute him, looking through their fingers, which were crossed to represent the grating of a jail window, "How do ye do?" My neighbors did not thus salute me, but first looked at me, and then at one

35

another, as if I had returned from a long journey. I was put into jail as I was going to the shoemaker's to get a shoe which was mended. When I was let out the next morning, I proceeded to finish my errand, and, having put on my mended shoe, joined a huckleberry party, who were impatient to put themselves under my conduct; and in half an hour — for the horse was soon tackled — was in the midst of a huckleberry field, on one of our highest hills, two miles off, and then the State was nowhere to be seen.

This is the whole history of "My Prisons."

I have never declined paying the highway tax, because I am as desirous of being a good neighbor as I am of being a bad subject; and as for supporting schools, I am doing my part to educate my fellow-countrymen now. It is for no particular item in the tax-bill that I refuse to pay it. I simply wish to refuse allegiance to the State, to withdraw and stand aloof from it effectually. I do not care to trace the course of my dollar, if I could, till it buys a man or a musket to shoot one with — the dollar is innocent — but I am concerned to trace the effects of my allegiance. In fact, I quietly declare war with the State, after my fashion, though I will still make what use and get what advantage of her I can, as is usual in such cases.

If others pay the tax which is demanded of me, from a sympathy with the State, they do but what they have already done in their own case, or rather they abet injustice to a greater extent than the State requires. If they pay the tax from a mistaken interest in the individual taxed, to save his property, or prevent his going to jail, it is because they have not considered wisely how far they let their private feelings interfere with the public good.

This, then, is my position at present. But one cannot be too much on his guard in such a case, lest his action be biased by obstinacy or an undue regard for the opinions of men. Let him see that he does only what belongs to himself and to the hour.

I think sometimes, Why, this people mean well, they are only ignorant; they would do better if they knew how: why give your neighbors this pain to treat you as they are not inclined to? But I think again, This is no reason why I should do as they do, or permit others to suffer much greater pain of a different kind. Again, I sometimes say to myself, When many millions of men, without heat, without ill will, without personal feeling of any kind, demand of you a few shillings only, without the possibility, such is their constitution, of retracting or altering their present demand, and without the possibility, on your side, of appeal to any other millions, why expose yourself to this overwhelming brute force? You do not resist cold and hunger, the winds and the waves, thus obstinately; you quietly submit to a thousand similar necessities. You do not put your head into the fire. But just in proportion as I regard this as not wholly a brute force, but partly a human force, and consider that I have relations to those millions as to so many millions of men, and not of mere brute or inanimate things, I see that appeal is possible, first and instantaneously, from them to the Maker of them, and, secondly, from them to themselves. But if I put my head deliberately into the fire, there is no appeal to fire or to the Maker of fire, and I have only myself to blame. If I could convince myself that I have any

40

right to be satisfied with men as they are, and to treat them accordingly, and not according, in some respects, to my requisitions and expectations of what they and I ought to be, then, like a good Mussulman° and fatalist, I should endeavor to be satisfied with things as they are, and say it is the will of God. And, above all, there is this difference between resisting this and a purely brute or natural force, that I can resist this with some effect; but I cannot expect, like Orpheus, to change the nature of the rocks and trees and beasts.

I do not wish to quarrel with any man or nation. I do not wish to split hairs, to make fine distinctions, or set myself up as better than my neighbors. I seek rather, I may say, even an excuse for conforming to the laws of the land. I am but too ready to conform to them. Indeed, I have reason to suspect myself on this head; and each year, as the tax-gatherer comes round, I find myself disposed to review the acts and position of the general and State governments, and the spirit of the people, to discover a pretext for conformity.

> "We must affect our country as our parents,
>   And if at any time we alienate
>   Our love or industry from doing it honor,
> We must respect effects and teach the soul
>   Matter of conscience and religion,
>   And not desire of rule or benefit."

I believe that the State will soon be able to take all my work of this sort out of my hands, and then I shall be no better a patriot than my fellow-countrymen. Seen from a lower point of view, the Constitution, with all its faults, is very good; the law and the courts are very respectable; even this State and this American government are, in many respects, very admirable, and rare things, to be thankful for, such as a great many have described them; but seen from a point of view a little higher, they are what I have described them; seen from a higher still, and the highest, who shall say what they are, or that they are worth looking at or thinking of at all? However, the government does not concern me much, and I shall bestow the fewest possible thoughts on it. It is not many moments that I live under a government, even in this world. If a man is thought-free, fancy-free, imagination-free, that which is not never for a long time appearing to be to him, unwise rulers or reformers cannot fatally interrupt him.

I know that most men think differently from myself; but those whose lives are by profession devoted to the study of these or kindred subjects content me as little as any. Statesmen and legislators, standing so completely within the institution, never distinctly and nakedly behold it. They speak of moving society, but have no resting-place without it. They may be men of a certain experience and discrimination, and have no doubt invented ingenious and even useful systems, for which we sincerely thank them; but all their wit and usefulness lie within certain not very wide limits. They are wont to forget that the world is not governed by policy and expediency. Webster° never goes behind

---

Mussulman: Muslim. **Daniel Webster (1782–1852):** Celebrated U.S. Senator and Secretary of State who advocated compromise between slave and free states.

government, and so cannot speak with authority about it. His words are wisdom to those legislators who contemplate no essential reform in the existing government; but for thinkers, and those who legislate for all time, he never once glances at the subject. I know of those whose serene and wise speculations on this theme would soon reveal the limits of his mind's range and hospitality. Yet, compared with the cheap professions of most reformers, and the still cheaper wisdom and eloquence of politicians in general, his are almost the only sensible and valuable words, and we thank Heaven for him. Comparatively, he is always strong, original, and, above all, practical. Still, his quality is not wisdom, but prudence. The lawyer's truth is not Truth, but consistency or a consistent expediency. Truth is always in harmony with herself, and is not concerned chiefly to reveal the justice that may consist with wrong-doing. He well deserves to be called, as he has been called, the Defender of the Constitution. There are really no blows to be given by him but defensive ones. He is not a leader, but a follower. His leaders are the men of '87 — "I have never made an effort," he says, "and never propose to make an effort; I have never countenanced an effort, and never mean to countenance an effort, to disturb the arrangement as originally made, by which the various States came into the Union." Still thinking of the sanction which the Constitution gives to slavery, he says, "Because it was a part of the original compact — let it stand." Notwithstanding his special acuteness and ability, he is unable to take a fact out of its merely political relations, and behold it as it lies absolutely to be disposed of by the intellect — what, for instance, it behooves a man to do here in America today with regard to slavery — but ventures, or is driven, to make some such desperate answer as the following, while professing to speak absolutely, and as a private man — from which what new and singular code of social duties might be inferred? "The manner," says he, "in which the governments of those States where slavery exists are to regulate it is for their own consideration, under their responsibility to their constituents, to the general laws of propriety, humanity, and justice, and to God. Associations formed elsewhere, springing from a feeling of humanity, or any other cause, have nothing whatever to do with it. They have never received any encouragement from me, and they never will."

They who know of no purer sources of truth, who have traced up its stream no higher, stand, and wisely stand, by the Bible and the Constitution, and drink at it there with reverence and humility; but they who behold where it comes trickling into this lake or that pool, gird up their loins once more, and continue their pilgrimage toward its fountain-head.

No man with a genius for legislation has appeared in America. They are   45
rare in the history of the world. There are orators, politicians, and eloquent men, by the thousand; but the speaker has not yet opened his mouth to speak who is capable of settling the much-vexed questions of the day. We love eloquence for its own sake, and not for any truth which it may utter, or any heroism it may inspire. Our legislators have not yet learned the comparative value of free trade and of freedom, of union, and of rectitude, to a nation. They have no genius or talent for comparatively humble questions of taxation and finance, commerce and manufactures and agriculture. If we were left solely to

the wordy wit of legislators in Congress for our guidance, uncorrected by the seasonable experience and the effectual complaints of the people, America would not long retain her rank among the nations. For eighteen hundred years, though perchance I have no right to say it, the New Testament has been written; yet where is the legislator who has wisdom and practical talent enough to avail himself of the light which it sheds on the science of legislation?

The authority of government, even such as I am willing to submit to — for I will cheerfully obey those who know and can do better than I, and in many things even those who neither know nor can do so well — is still an impure one: to be strictly just, it must have the sanction and consent of the governed. It can have no pure right over my person and property but what I concede to it. The progress from an absolute to a limited monarchy, from a limited monarchy to a democracy, is a progress toward a true respect for the individual. Even the Chinese philosopher was wise enough to regard the individual as the basis of the empire. Is a democracy, such as we know it, the last improvement possible in government? Is it not possible to take a step further towards recognizing and organizing the rights of man? There will never be a really free and enlightened State until the State comes to recognize the individual as a higher and independent power, from which all its own power and authority are derived, and treats him accordingly. I please myself with imagining a State at least which can afford to be just to all men, and to treat the individual with respect as a neighbor; which even would not think it inconsistent with its own repose if a few were to live aloof from it, not meddling with it, nor embraced by it, who fulfilled all the duties of neighbors and fellow-men. A State which bore this kind of fruit, and suffered it to drop off as fast as it ripened, would prepare the way for a still more perfect and glorious State, which also I have imagined, but not yet anywhere seen.

[1849]

≡ THINKING ABOUT THE TEXT

1. What is Thoreau's view of government in general? Identify specific passages that relate his major points about it. Do any groups or individuals put forth this view today? Consider the theories of government expressed by various public figures, political parties, and personal relatives or friends.

2. What would you say to someone who argues that Thoreau is encouraging anyone who disagrees with a law to break it? Identify specific passages that support this inference or complicate it.

3. Two words that Thoreau repeats in various forms are *machine* and *expediency*. What ideas is he emphasizing by using these words multiple times? Note the specific passages where *machine* or *expediency* appear.

4. Note where Thoreau refers to "man." Writers of his time often used this word in a generic sense, intending it to mean women as well as men. Do you assume that this is always Thoreau's intent, or are there moments when you think that he has only the male gender in mind? Explain.

5. What specific points does Thoreau seem most concerned to make as he describes his night in jail? Why do you suppose he held off describing it until near the end of the essay?

REBECCA SOLNIT
The Thoreau Problem

Rebecca Solnit (b. 1961) writes chiefly about politics, ecology, human rights, and the visual arts. Her books include As Eve Said to the Serpent: On Landscape, Gender, and Art *(2001);* River of Shadows: Eadweard Muybridge and the Technological Wild West *(2003), for which she won a National Book Critics Circle Award;* A Field Guide to Getting Lost *(2006);* The Faraway Nearby *(2013); and* A Paradise Built in Hell: The Extraordinary Communities That Arise in Disaster *(2009), a study of people's resilience in the wake of calamities like Hurricane Katrina. Solnit regularly contributes commentaries to the Web site Tomdispatch.com and to* Orion, *an environmental magazine, which published the following essay in its May/June 2007 issue.*

Thoreau was emphatic about the huckleberries. In one of his two most famous pieces of writing, "Civil Disobedience," he concluded his account of a night in Concord's jail with, "I was put in jail as I was going to the shoemaker's to get a shoe which was mended. When I was let out the next morning, I proceeded to finish my errand, and having put on my mended shoe, joined a huckleberry party." He told the same story again in *Walden*, this time saying that he "returned to the woods in season to get my dinner of huckleberries on Fair-Haven Hill." That he told it twice suggests that he considered the conjunction of prisons and berry parties, of the landscape of incarceration and of pastoral pleasure, significant. But why?

The famous night in jail took place about halfway through his stay on Emerson's woodlot at Walden Pond. His two-year stint in the small cabin he built himself is often portrayed as a monastic retreat from the world of human affairs into the world of nature, though he went back to town to eat and talk with friends and family and to pick up money doing odd jobs that didn't fit into *Walden*'s narrative. He went to jail not only because he felt passionately enough about national affairs — slavery and the war on Mexico — to refuse to pay his tax, but also because the town jailer ran into him while he was getting his shoe mended.

Says the introduction to my paperback edition of *Walden* and "Civil Disobedience": "As much as Thoreau wanted to disentangle himself from other people's problems so he could get on with his own life, he sometimes found that the issue of black slavery spoiled his country walks. His social conscience impinged on his consciousness, even though he believed that his duty was not to eradicate social evils but to live his life independently." To believe this is to believe that the woods were far from Concord jail not merely by foot but by thought. To believe that conscience is an imposition upon consciousness is to regard engagement as a hijacker rather than a rudder, interference with one's true purpose rather than perhaps at least part of that purpose.

Thoreau did not believe so or wish that it were so, and he contradicted this isolationist statement explicitly in "Civil Disobedience" (completed, unlike *Walden*, shortly after those years in the woods), but many who have charge of his reputation do. These scholars and critics permit no conversation, let alone any unity, between Thoreau the rebel, intransigent muse to Gandhi and Martin Luther King, and that other Thoreau who wrote about autumnal tints, ice, light, color, grasses, woodchucks, and other natural histories, essays easily and often defanged and diced up into inspiring extracts. But for Thoreau, any subject was a good enough starting point to travel any distance, toward any destination.

This compartmentalizing of Thoreau is a microcosm of a larger partition   5
in American thought, a fence built in the belief that places in the imagination can be contained. Those who deny that nature and culture, landscape and politics, the city and the country are inextricably interfused have undermined the connections for all of us (so few have been able to find Thoreau's short, direct route between them since). This makes politics dreary and landscape trivial, a vacation site. It banishes certain thoughts, including the thought that much of what the environmental movement dubbed wilderness was or is indigenous homeland — a very social and political space indeed, then and now — and especially the thought that Thoreau in jail must have contemplated the following day's huckleberry party, and Thoreau among the huckleberries must have ruminated on his stay in jail.

If "black slavery spoiled his country walks," it spoiled the slaves' country walks even more. Thus the unresisting walk to jail. "Eastward, I go only by force; but westward I go free," Thoreau wrote. His thoughts on the matter might be summed up this way: You head for the hills to enjoy the best of what the world is at this moment; you head for confrontation, for resistance, for picket lines to protect it, to liberate it. Thus it is that the road to paradise often runs through prison, thus it is that Thoreau went to jail to enjoy a better country, and thus it is that one of his greatest students, Martin Luther King Jr., found himself in jail and eventually in the way of a bullet on what got called the long road to freedom, whose goal he spoke of as the mountaintop.

Conventional environmental writing has often maintained a strict silence on or even an animosity toward the city, despite its importance as a lower-impact place for the majority to live, its intricate relations to the rural, and the direct routes between the two. Imagining the woods or any untrammeled landscape as an unsocial place, an outside, also depends on erasing those who dwelt and sometimes still dwell there, the original Americans — and one more thing that can be said in favor of Thoreau is that he spent a lot of time imaginatively repopulating with Indians the woods around Concord, and even prepared quantities of notes for a never-attempted history of Native America.

Not that those woods were unsocial even after the aboriginal population was driven out. "Visitors" was one of the chapters of *Walden*, and in it he describes meeting in the woods and guiding farther on the road to freedom runaway slaves. Rather than ruining his country walks, some slaves joined him on them, or perhaps he joined them in the act of becoming free. Some of those he guided were on the Underground Railroad, in which his mother and sisters in Concord were deeply involved, and a few months after that famous night in jail Thoreau hosted a meeting of Concord's most important abolitionist group, the Concord Female Anti-Slavery Society, at his Walden Pond hut. What kind of a forest was this, with slaves, rebels, and the ghosts of the original inhabitants all moving through the trees?

If he went to jail to demonstrate his commitment to the freedom of others, he went to the berries to exercise his own recovered freedom, the liberty to do whatever he wished, and the evidence in all his writing is that he very often wished to pick berries. There's a widespread belief, among both activists and those who cluck disapprovingly over insufficiently austere activists, that idealists should not enjoy any pleasure denied to others, that beauty, sensuality, delight all ought to be stalled behind some dam that only the imagined revolution will break. This schism creates, as the alternative to a life of selfless devotion, a life of flight from engagement, which seems to be one way those years at Walden Pond are sometimes portrayed. But change is not always by revolution, the deprived don't generally wish that the rest of us would join them in deprivation, and a passion for justice and pleasure in small things are not incompatible. That's part of what the short jaunt from jail to hill says.

Perhaps prison is anything that severs and alienates, paradise is the reclaimed commons with the fences thrown down, and so any step toward connection and communion is a step toward paradise, even if the route detours through jail. Thoreau was demonstrating on that one day in Concord in June of 1847 both what dedication to freedom was and what enjoyment of freedom might look like — free association, free roaming, the picking of the fruits of the Earth for free, free choice of commitments. That is the direct route to paradise, the one road worth traveling.   *[2007]*

≡ **THINKING ABOUT THE TEXT**

1. What, according to Solnit, *is* "the Thoreau problem," and for whom does it exist? What larger problem in American thinking does she think it illustrates?

2. What does Solnit emphasize about the woods surrounding Thoreau? How is this emphasis part of her effort to solve "the Thoreau problem"?

3. How do prisons and journeys function as metaphors in Solnit's argument? Trace the passages where these references appear.

4. Solnit wrote this essay for *Orion*, a magazine whose readers are generally interested in environmental issues and are likely to be fond of Thoreau's *Walden* as well as other writings of his about nature. At what moments does she seem to have this specific audience very much in mind?

5. To what extent do you agree with Solnit's claim that "a passion for justice and pleasure in small things are not incompatible" (para. 9)? Whom, if anyone, do you see combining such "passion" and "pleasure" today?

≡ MAKING COMPARISONS

1. As an analysis of Thoreau's essay, Solnit's is rather brief. What major points of his does she *not* touch on? Should she have referred to any of these? Why, or why not?

2. What aspects of Thoreau's life and world does Solnit discuss *more* than he does in "Civil Disobedience"?

3. Should Solnit have told us about how she personally tries to implement the values and ideas of Thoreau's that she admires? Explain.

MARTIN LUTHER KING JR.
Letter from Birmingham Jail°

A native of Atlanta, Martin Luther King Jr. (1929–1968) was the son of a Baptist minister and a schoolteacher. After graduating from Morehouse College in Atlanta, he studied at several universities before receiving a Ph.D. in theology from Boston University. He married Coretta Scott in 1955 and had four children. In 1959, he resigned his position as pastor of a church in Alabama to move back to Atlanta to direct the activities of the Southern Christian Leadership Conference. From 1960 until his death, he was copastor with his father at Ebenezer Baptist Church in Atlanta.

Dr. King was a central figure in the civil rights movement. Pivotal in the successful Montgomery bus boycott in 1956, he was arrested more than thirty times for his participation in nonviolent demonstrations. His charismatic leadership and eloquent speeches stirred and inspired the conscience of a generation. Dr. King's idea of "somebodiness" gave black and poor people a new sense of worth and dignity, and his philosophy of nonviolent direct action helped change the nation's attitudes and priorities. His famous "I have a dream" speech at the Lincoln Memorial in 1963 and the classic "Letter" printed here are among the most important documents in American history. At thirty-five, he was the youngest person to win the Nobel Prize for peace. His assassination in 1968 set off riots in more than a hundred cities. Today the nation honors his birthday as a holiday.

Letter from Birmingham Jail: This response to a published statement by eight fellow clergymen from Alabama (Bishop C. C. J. Carpenter, Bishop Joseph A. Durick, Rabbi Hilton L. Grafman, Bishop Paul Hardin, Bishop Holan B. Harmon, the Reverend George M. Murray, the Reverend Edward V. Ramage, and the Reverend Earl Stallings) was composed under somewhat constricting circumstances. Begun on the margins of the newspaper in which the statement appeared while I was in jail, the letter was continued on scraps of writing paper supplied by a friendly Negro trusty, and concluded on a pad my attorneys were eventually permitted to leave me. Although the text remains in substance unaltered, I have indulged in the author's prerogative of polishing it for publication. [King's note.]

My Dear Fellow Clergymen:

While confined here in the Birmingham city jail, I came across your recent statement calling my present activities "unwise and untimely." Seldom do I pause to answer criticism of my work and ideas. If I sought to answer all the criticisms that cross my desk, my secretaries would have little time for anything other than such correspondence in the course of the day, and I would have no time for constructive work. But since I feel that you are men of genuine good will and that your criticisms are sincerely set forth, I want to try to answer your statement in what I hope will be patient and reasonable terms.

I think I should indicate why I am here in Birmingham, since you have been influenced by the view which argues against "outsiders coming in." I have the honor of serving as president of the Southern Christian Leadership Conference, an organization operating in every southern state, with headquarters in Atlanta, Georgia. We have some eighty-five affiliated organizations across the South, and one of them is the Alabama Christian Movement for Human Rights. Frequently we share staff, educational, and financial resources with our affiliates. Several months ago the affiliate here in Birmingham asked us to be on call to engage in a nonviolent direct-action program if such were deemed necessary. We readily consented, and when the hour came we lived up to our promise. So I, along with several members of my staff, am here because I was invited here. I am here because I have organizational ties here.

But more basically, I am in Birmingham because injustice is here. Just as the prophets of the eighth century B.C. left their villages and carried their "thus saith the Lord" far beyond the boundaries of their home towns, and just as the Apostle Paul left his village of Tarsus° and carried the gospel of Jesus Christ to the far corners of the Greco-Roman world, so am I compelled to carry the gospel of freedom beyond my own home town. Like Paul, I must constantly respond to the Macedonian call for aid.°

Moreover, I am cognizant of the interrelatedness of all communities and states. I cannot sit idly by in Atlanta and not be concerned about what happens in Birmingham. Injustice anywhere is a threat to justice everywhere. We are caught in an inescapable network of mutuality, tied in a single garment of destiny. Whatever affects one directly, affects all indirectly. Never again can we afford to live with the narrow, provincial "outside agitator" idea. Anyone who lives inside the United States can never be considered an outsider anywhere within its bounds.

You deplore the demonstrations taking place in Birmingham. But your statement, I am sorry to say, fails to express a similar concern for the conditions that brought about the demonstrations. I am sure that none of you would want to rest content with the superficial kind of social analysis that deals merely with effects and does not grapple with the underlying causes. It is unfortunate that demonstrations are taking place in Birmingham, but it is even more unfortunate that the city's white power structure left the Negro community with no alternative.

Tarsus: Present-day Turkey, birthplace of St. Paul.   **Macedonian . . . aid:** The Christian community in Macedonia often called on Paul for aid.

In any nonviolent campaign there are four basic steps: collection of the facts to determine whether injustices exist; negotiation; self-purification; and direct action. We have gone through all these steps in Birmingham. There can be no gainsaying the fact that racial injustice engulfs this community. Birmingham is probably the most thoroughly segregated city in the United States. Its ugly record of brutality is widely known. Negroes have experienced grossly unjust treatment in the courts. There have been more unsolved bombings of Negro homes and churches in Birmingham than in any other city in the nation. These are the hard, brutal facts of the case. On the basis of these conditions, Negro leaders sought to negotiate with the city fathers. But the latter consistently refused to engage in good-faith negotiation.

Then, last September, came the opportunity to talk with leaders of Birmingham's economic community. In the course of the negotiations, certain promises were made by the merchants — for example, to remove the stores' humiliating racial signs. On the basis of these promises, the Reverend Fred Shuttlesworth and the leaders of the Alabama Christian Movement for Human Rights agreed to a moratorium on all demonstrations. As the weeks and months went by, we realized that we were the victims of a broken promise. A few signs, briefly removed, returned; the others remained.

As in so many past experiences, our hopes had been blasted, and the shadow of deep disappointment settled upon us. We had no alternative except to prepare for direct action, whereby we would present our very bodies as a means of laying our case before the conscience of the local and the national community. Mindful of the difficulties involved, we decided to undertake a process of self-purification. We began a series of workshops on nonviolence, and we repeatedly asked ourselves: "Are you able to accept blows without retaliating?" "Are you able to endure the ordeal of jail?" We decided to schedule our direct-action program for the Easter season, realizing that except for Christmas, this is the main shopping period of the year. Knowing that a strong economic-withdrawal program would be the by-product of direct action, we felt that this would be the best time to bring pressure to bear on the merchants for the needed change.

Then it occurred to us that Birmingham's mayoral election was coming up in March, and we speedily decided to postpone action until after election-day. When we discovered that the Commissioner of Public Safety, Eugene "Bull" Connor, had piled up enough votes to be in the run-off, we decided again to postpone action until the day after the run-off so that the demonstrations could not be used to cloud the issues. Like many others, we waited to see Mr. Connor defeated, and to this end we endured postponement after postponement. Having aided in this community need, we felt that our direct-action program could be delayed no longer.

You may well ask, "Why direct action? Why sit-ins, marches, and so forth? Isn't negotiation a better path?" You are quite right in calling for negotiation. Indeed, this is the very purpose of direct action. Nonviolent direct action seeks to create such a crisis and foster such a tension that a community which has constantly refused to negotiate is forced to confront the issue. It seeks so to dramatize the issue that it can no longer be ignored. My citing the creation of

10

tension as part of the work of the nonviolent-resister may sound rather shocking. But I must confess that I am not afraid of the word "tension." I have earnestly opposed violent tension, but there is a type of constructive, nonviolent tension which is necessary for growth. Just as Socrates° felt that it was necessary to create a tension in the mind so that individuals could rise from the bondage of myths and half-truths to the unfettered realm of creative analysis and objective appraisal, so must we see the need for nonviolent gadflies to create the kind of tension in society that will help men rise from the dark depths of prejudice and racism to the majestic heights of understanding and brotherhood.

The purpose of our direct-action program is to create a situation so crisis-packed that it will inevitably open the door to negotiation. I therefore concur with you in your call for negotiation. Too long has our beloved Southland been bogged down in a tragic effort to live in monologue rather than dialogue.

One of the basic points in your statement is that the action that I and my associates have taken in Birmingham is untimely. Some have asked: "Why didn't you give the new city administration time to act?" The only answer that I can give to this query is that the new Birmingham administration must be prodded about as much as the outgoing one, before it will act. We are sadly mistaken if we feel that the election of Albert Boutwell as mayor will bring the millennium to Birmingham. While Mr. Boutwell is a much more gentle person than Mr. Connor, they are both segregationists, dedicated to maintenance of the status quo. I have hoped that Mr. Boutwell will be reasonable enough to see the futility of massive resistance to desegregation. But he will not see this without pressure from devotees of civil rights. My friends, I must say to you that we have not made a single gain in civil rights without determined legal and nonviolent pressure. Lamentably, it is an historical fact that privileged groups seldom give up their privileges voluntarily. Individuals may see the moral light and voluntarily give up their unjust posture; but, as Reinhold Niebuhr° has reminded us, groups tend to be more immoral than individuals.

We know through painful experience that freedom is never voluntarily given by the oppressor; it must be demanded by the oppressed. Frankly, I have yet to engage in a direct-action campaign that was "well timed" in the view of those who have not suffered unduly from the disease of segregation. For years now I have heard the word "Wait!" It rings in the ear of every Negro with piercing familiarity. This "Wait" has almost always meant "Never." We must come to see, with one of our distinguished jurists, that "justice too long delayed is justice denied."

We have waited for more than 340 years for our constitutional and God-given rights. The nations of Asia and Africa are moving with jetlike speed toward gaining political independence, but we still creep at horse-and-buggy pace toward gaining a cup of coffee at a lunch counter. Perhaps it is easy for

---

Socrates (469–399 B.C.E.): The Greek philosopher would feign ignorance to expose the errors in his opponent's arguments.   **Reinhold Niebuhr (1892–1971):** American theologian.

those who have never felt the stinging darts of segregation to say, "Wait." But when you have seen vicious mobs lynch your mothers and fathers at will and drown your sisters and brothers at whim; when you have seen hate-filled policemen curse, kick, and even kill your black brothers and sisters; when you see the vast majority of your twenty million Negro brothers smothering in an airtight cage of poverty in the midst of an affluent society; when you suddenly find your tongue twisted and your speech stammering as you seek to explain to your six-year-old daughter why she can't go to the public amusement park that has just been advertised on television, and see tears welling up in her eyes when she is told that Funtown is closed to colored children, and see ominous clouds of inferiority beginning to form in her little mental sky, and see her beginning to distort her personality by developing an unconscious bitterness toward white people; when you have to concoct an answer for a five-year-old son who is asking, "Daddy, why do white people treat colored people so mean?"; when you take a cross-country drive and find it necessary to sleep night after night in the uncomfortable corners of your automobile because no motel will accept you; when you are humiliated day in and day out by nagging signs reading "white" and "colored"; when your first name becomes "nigger," your middle name becomes "boy" (however old you are), and your last name becomes "John," and your wife and mother are never given the respected title "Mrs."; when you are harried by day and haunted by night by the fact that you are a Negro, living constantly at tiptoe stance, never quite knowing what to expect next, and are plagued with inner fears and outer resentments; when you are forever fighting a degenerating sense of "nobodiness" — then you will understand why we find it difficult to wait. There comes a time when the cup of endurance runs over, and men are no longer willing to be plunged into the abyss of despair. I hope, sirs, you can understand our legitimate and unavoidable impatience.

You express a great deal of anxiety over our willingness to break laws. This 15 is certainly a legitimate concern. Since we so diligently urge people to obey the Supreme Court's decision of 1954 outlawing segregation in the public schools, at first glance it may seem rather paradoxical for us consciously to break laws. One may well ask: "How can you advocate breaking some laws and obeying others?" The answer lies in the fact that there are two types of laws: just and unjust. I would be the first to advocate obeying just laws. One has not only a legal but a moral responsibility to obey just laws. Conversely, one has a moral responsibility to disobey unjust laws. I would agree with St. Augustine that "an unjust law is no law at all."

Now, what is the difference between the two? How does one determine whether a law is just or unjust? A just law is a man-made code that squares with the moral law or the law of God. An unjust law is a code that is out of harmony with the moral law. To put it in the terms of St. Thomas Aquinas: An unjust law is a human law that is not rooted in eternal law and natural law. Any law that uplifts human personality is just. Any law that degrades human personality is unjust. All segregation statutes are unjust because segregation distorts the soul and damages the personality. It gives the segregator a false sense of superiority and the segregated a false sense of inferiority. Segregation, to use the terminology of the Jewish philosopher Martin Buber, substitutes an "I-it" relationship for an "I-thou" relationship and ends up relegating persons to the status of things. Hence segregation is not only politically, economically, and sociologically unsound, it is morally wrong and sinful. Paul Tillich has said that sin is separation. Is not segregation an existential expression of man's tragic separation, his awful estrangement, his terrible sinfulness? Thus it is that I can urge men to obey the 1954 decision of the Supreme Court, for it is morally right; and I can urge them to disobey segregation ordinances, for they are morally wrong.

Let us consider a more concrete example of just and unjust laws. An unjust law is a code that a numerical or power majority group compels a minority group to obey but does not make binding on itself. This is *difference* made legal. By the same token, a just law is a code that a majority compels a minority to follow and that it is willing to follow itself. This is *sameness* made legal.

Let me give another explanation. A law is unjust if it is inflicted on a minority that, as a result of being denied the right to vote, had no part in enacting or devising the law. Who can say that the legislature of Alabama which set up that state's segregation laws was democratically elected? Throughout Alabama all sorts of devious methods are used to prevent Negroes from becoming registered voters, and there are some counties in which, even though Negroes constitute a majority of the population, not a single Negro is registered. Can any law enacted under such circumstances be considered democratically structured?

Sometimes a law is just on its face and unjust in its application. For instance, I have been arrested on a charge of parading without a permit. Now, there is nothing wrong in having an ordinance which requires a permit for a parade. But such an ordinance becomes unjust when it is used to maintain segregation and to deny citizens the First-Amendment privilege of peaceful assembly and protest.

I hope you are able to see the distinction I am trying to point out. In no sense   20 do I advocate evading or defying the law, as would the rabid segregationist. That would lead to anarchy. One who breaks an unjust law must do so openly, lovingly, and with a willingness to accept the penalty. I submit that an individual who breaks a law that conscience tells him is unjust, and who willingly accepts the penalty of imprisonment in order to arouse the conscience of the community over its injustice, is in reality expressing the highest respect for law.

Of course, there is nothing new about this kind of civil disobedience. It was evidenced sublimely in the refusal of Shadrach, Meshach, and Abednego to obey the laws of Nebuchadnezzar, on the ground that a higher moral law was at stake.° It was practiced superbly by the early Christians, who were willing to face hungry lions and the excruciating pain of chopping blocks rather than submit to certain unjust laws of the Roman Empire. To a degree, academic freedom is a reality today because Socrates practiced civil disobedience. In our own nation, the Boston Tea Party represented a massive act of civil disobedience.

Shadrach . . . : See the book of Daniel in the Hebrew Scriptures (1:7–3:30).

We should never forget that everything Adolf Hitler did in Germany was "legal" and everything the Hungarian freedom fighters did in Hungary was "illegal." It was "illegal" to aid and comfort a Jew in Hitler's Germany. Even so, I am sure that, had I lived in Germany at the time, I would have aided and comforted my Jewish brothers. If today I lived in a Communist country where certain principles dear to the Christian faith are suppressed, I would openly advocate disobeying that country's anti-religious laws.

I must make two honest confessions to you, my Christian and Jewish brothers. First, I must confess that over the past few years I have been gravely disappointed with the white moderate. I have almost reached the regrettable conclusion that the Negro's great stumbling block in his stride toward freedom is not the white Citizen's Counciler° or the Ku Klux Klanner, but the white moderate, who is more devoted to "order" than to justice; who prefers a negative peace which is the absence of tension to a positive peace which is the presence of justice; who constantly says, "I agree with you in the goal you seek, but I cannot agree with your methods of direct action"; who paternalistically believes he can set the timetable for another man's freedom; who lives by a mythical concept of time and who constantly advises the Negro to wait for a "more convenient season." Shallow understanding from people of good will is more frustrating than absolute misunderstanding from people of ill will. Lukewarm acceptance is much more bewildering than outright rejection.

I had hoped that the white moderate would understand that law and order exist for the purpose of establishing justice and that when they fail in this purpose they become the dangerously structured dams that block the flow of social progress. I had hoped that the white moderate would understand that the present tension in the South is a necessary phase of the transition from an obnoxious negative peace, in which the Negro passively accepted his unjust plight, to a substantive and positive peace, in which all men will respect the dignity and worth of human personality. Actually, we who engage in nonviolent direct action are not the creators of tension. We merely bring to the surface the hidden tension that is already alive. We bring it out in the open, where it can be seen and dealt with. Like a boil that can never be cured so long as it is covered up but must be opened with all its ugliness to the natural medicines of air and light, injustice must be exposed, with all the tension its exposure creates, to the light of human conscience and the air of national opinion, before it can be cured.

In your statement you assert that our actions, even though peaceful, must   25
be condemned because they precipitate violence. But is this a logical assertion? Isn't this like condemning a robbed man because his possession of money precipitated the evil act of robbery? Isn't this like condemning Socrates because his unswerving commitment to truth and his philosophical inquiries precipitated the act by the misguided populace in which they made him drink hemlock? Isn't this like condemning Jesus because his unique God-consciousness

White Citizen's Councils: Resisted desegregation after the U.S. Supreme Court declared segregated education unconstitutional in 1954.

and never-ceasing devotion to God's will precipitated the evil act of crucifixion? We must come to see that, as the federal courts have consistently affirmed, it is wrong to urge an individual to cease his efforts to gain his basic constitutional rights because the quest may precipitate violence. Society must protect the robbed and punish the robber.

I had also hoped that the white moderate would reject the myth concerning time in relation to the struggle for freedom. I have just received a letter from a white brother in Texas. He writes: "All Christians know that the colored people will receive greater equal rights eventually, but it is possible that you are in too great a religious hurry. It has taken Christianity almost two thousand years to accomplish what it has. The teachings of Christ take time to come to earth." Such an attitude stems from a tragic misconception of time, from the strangely irrational notion that there is something in the very flow of time that will inevitably cure all ills. Actually, time itself is neutral; it can be used either destructively or constructively. More and more I feel that the people of ill will have used time much more effectively than have the people of good will. We will have to repent in this generation not merely for the hateful words and actions of the bad people, but for the appalling silence of the good people. Human progress never rolls in on wheels of inevitability; it comes through the tireless efforts of men willing to be co-workers with God, and without this hard work, time itself becomes an ally of the forces of social stagnation. We must use time creatively, in the knowledge that the time is always ripe to do right. Now is the time to make real the promise of democracy and transform our pending national elegy into a creative psalm of brotherhood. Now is the time to lift our national policy from the quicksand of racial injustice to the solid rock of human dignity.

You speak of our activity in Birmingham as extreme. At first I was rather disappointed that fellow clergymen would see my nonviolent efforts as those of an extremist. I began thinking about the fact that I stand in the middle of two opposing forces in the Negro community. One is a force of complacency, made up in part of Negroes, who, as a result of long years of oppression, are so drained of self-respect and a sense of "somebodiness" that they have adjusted to segregation; and in part of a few middle-class Negroes who, because of a degree of academic and economic security and because in some ways they profit by segregation, have become insensitive to the problems of the masses. The other force is one of bitterness and hatred, and it comes perilously close to advocating violence. It is expressed in the various black nationalist groups that are springing up across the nation, the largest and best-known being Elijah Muhammad's Muslim movement.° Nourished by the Negro's frustration over the continued existence of racial discrimination, this movement is made up of people who have lost faith in America, who have absolutely repudiated Christianity, and who have concluded that the white man is an incorrigible "devil."

Elijah Muhammad (1897–1975): Leader of the Nation of Islam, a Muslim religious group that called on African Americans to reject integration and establish their own nation.

I have tried to stand between these two forces, saying that we need emulate neither the "do-nothingism" of the complacent nor the hatred and despair of the black nationalist. For there is the more excellent way of love and nonviolent protest. I am grateful to God that, through the influence of the Negro church, the way of nonviolence became an integral part of our struggle.

If this philosophy had not emerged, by now many streets of the South would, I am convinced, be flowing with blood. And I am further convinced that if our white brothers dismiss as "rabble-rousers" and "outside agitators" those of us who employ nonviolent direct action, and if they refuse to support our nonviolent efforts, millions of Negroes will, out of frustration and despair, seek solace and security in black-nationalist ideologies — a development that would inevitably lead to a frightening racial nightmare.

Oppressed people cannot remain oppressed forever. The yearning for free-   30
dom eventually manifests itself, and that is what has happened to the American Negro. Something within has reminded him of his birthright of freedom, and something without has reminded him that it can be gained. Consciously or unconsciously, he has been caught up by the *Zeitgeist*,° and with his black brothers of Africa and his brown and yellow brothers of Asia, South America, and the Caribbean, the United States Negro is moving with a sense of great urgency toward the promised land of racial justice. If one recognizes this vital urge that has engulfed the Negro community, one should readily understand why public demonstrations are taking place. The Negro has many pent-up resentments and latent frustrations, and he must release them. So let him march; let him make prayer pilgrimages to the city hall; let him go on freedom rides° — and try to understand why he must do so. If his repressed emotions are not released in nonviolent ways, they will seek expression through violence; this is not a threat but a fact of history. So I have not said to my people, "Get rid of your discontent." Rather, I have tried to say that this normal and healthy discontent can be channeled into the creative outlet of nonviolent direct action. And now this approach is being termed extremist.

But though I was initially disappointed at being categorized as an extremist, as I continued to think about the matter I gradually gained a measure of satisfaction from the label. Was not Jesus an extremist for love: "Love your enemies, bless them that curse you, do good to them that hate you, and pray for them that despitefully use you, and persecute you." Was not Amos an extremist for justice: "Let justice roll down like waters and righteousness like an everflowing stream." Was not Paul an extremist for the Christian gospel: "I bear in my body the marks of the Lord Jesus." Was not Martin Luther an extremist: "Here I stand; I cannot do otherwise, so help me God." And John Bunyan: "I will stay in jail to the end of my days before I make a butchery of my conscience." And Abraham Lincoln: "This nation cannot survive half slave and half free." And Thomas Jefferson: "We hold these truths to be self-evident, that

---

Zeitgeist: The spirit of the age (German).   **freedom rides:** In 1961, the Congress of Racial Equality (CORE) directed activists to flout race laws in the South that mandated segregation in buses and bus terminals.

all men are created equal. . . ." So the question is not whether we will be extremists, but what kind of extremists we will be. Will we be extremists for the preservation of injustice or for the extension of justice? In that dramatic scene on Calvary's hill three men were crucified. We must never forget that all three were crucified for the same crime — the crime of extremism. Two were extremists for immorality, and thus fell below their environment. The other, Jesus Christ, was an extremist for love, truth, and goodness, and thereby rose above his environment. Perhaps the South, the nation, and the world are in dire need of creative extremists.

I had hoped that the white moderate would see this need. Perhaps I was too optimistic; perhaps I expected too much. I suppose I should have realized that few members of the oppressor race can understand the deep groans and passionate yearnings of the oppressed race, and still fewer have the vision to see that injustice must be rooted out by strong, persistent, and determined action. I am thankful, however, that some of our white brothers in the South have grasped the meaning of this social revolution and committed themselves to it. They are still all too few in quantity, but they are big in quality. Some — such as Ralph McGill, Lillian Smith, Harry Golden, James McBride Dabbs, Ann Braden, and Sarah Patton Boyle — have written about our struggle in eloquent and prophetic terms. Others have marched with us down nameless streets of the South. They have languished in filthy, roach-infested jails, suffering the abuse and brutality of policemen who view them as "dirty nigger-lovers." Unlike so many of their moderate brothers and sisters, they have recognized the urgency of the moment and sensed the need for powerful "action" antidotes to combat the disease of segregation.

Let me take note of my other major disappointment. I have been so greatly disappointed with the white church and its leadership. Of course, there are some notable exceptions. I am not unmindful of the fact that each of you has taken some significant stands on this issue. I commend you, Reverend Stallings, for your Christian stand on this past Sunday, in welcoming Negroes to your worship service on a nonsegregated basis. I commend the Catholic leaders of this state for integrating Spring Hill College several years ago.

But despite these notable exceptions, I must honestly reiterate that I have been disappointed with the church. I do not say this as one of those negative critics who can always find something wrong with the church. I say this as a minister of the gospel, who loves the church; who was nurtured in its bosom; who has been sustained by its spiritual blessings and who will remain true to it as long as the cord of life shall lengthen.

When I was suddenly catapulted into the leadership of the bus protest in   35
Montgomery, Alabama, a few years ago, I felt we would be supported by the white church. I felt that the white ministers, priests, and rabbis of the South would be among our strongest allies. Instead, some have been outright opponents, refusing to understand the freedom movement and misrepresenting its leaders; all too many others have been more cautious than courageous and have remained silent behind the anesthetizing security of stained-glass windows.

In spite of my shattered dreams, I came to Birmingham with the hope that the white religious leadership of this community would see the justice of our cause and, with deep moral concern, would serve as the channel through which our just grievances could reach the power structure. I had hoped that each of you would understand. But again I have been disappointed.

I have heard numerous southern religious leaders admonish their worshipers to comply with a desegregation decision because it is the law, but I have longed to hear white ministers declare: "Follow this decree because integration is morally right and because the Negro is your brother." In the midst of blatant injustices inflicted upon the Negro, I have watched white churchmen stand on the sideline and mouth pious irrelevancies and sanctimonious trivialities. In the midst of a mighty struggle to rid our nation of racial and economic injustice, I have heard many ministers say: "Those are social issues, with which the gospel has no real concern." And I have watched many churches commit themselves to a completely otherworldly religion which makes a strange, unbiblical distinction between body and soul, between the sacred and the secular.

I have traveled the length and breadth of Alabama, Mississippi, and all the other southern states. On sweltering summer days and crisp autumn mornings I have looked at the South's beautiful churches with their lofty spires pointing heavenward. I have beheld the impressive outlines of her massive religious-education buildings. Over and over I have found myself asking: "What kind of people worship here? Who is their God? Where were their voices when the lips of Governor Barnett dripped with words of interposition and nullification? Where were they when Governor Wallace gave a clarion call for defiance and hatred? Where were their voices of support when bruised and weary Negro men and women decided to rise from the dark dungeons of complacency to the bright hills of creative protest?"

Yes, these questions are still in mind. In deep disappointment I have wept over the laxity of the church. But be assured that my tears have been tears of love. There can be no deep disappointment where there is not deep love. Yes, I love the church. How could I do otherwise? I am in the rather unique position of being the son, the grandson, and the great-grandson of preachers. Yes, I see the church as the body of Christ. But, oh! How we have blemished and scarred the body through social neglect and through fear of being nonconformists.

There was a time when the church was very powerful — in the time when 40 the early Christians rejoiced at being deemed worthy to suffer for what they believed. In those days the church was not merely a thermometer that transformed the mores of society. Whenever the early Christians entered a town, the people in power became disturbed and immediately sought to convict the Christians for being "disturbers of the peace" and "outside agitators." But the Christians pressed on, in the conviction that they were "a colony of heaven," called to obey God rather than man. Small in number, they were big in commitment. They were too God-intoxicated to be "astronomically intimidated." By their effort and example they brought an end to such ancient evils as infanticide and gladiatorial contests.

Things are different now. So often the contemporary church is a weak, ineffectual voice with an uncertain sound. So often it is an archdefender of the status quo. Far from being disturbed by the presence of the church, the power structure of the average community is consoled by the church's silent — and often even vocal — sanction of things as they are.

But the judgment of God is upon the church as never before. If today's church does not recapture the sacrificial spirit of the early church, it will lose its authenticity, forfeit the loyalty of millions, and be dismissed as an irrelevant social club with no meaning for the twentieth century. Every day I meet young people whose disappointment with the church has turned into outright disgust.

Perhaps I have once again been too optimistic. Is organized religion too inextricably bound to the status quo to save our nation and the world? Perhaps I must turn my faith to the inner spiritual church, the church within the church, as the true *ekklesia*° and the hope of the world. But again I am thankful to God that some noble souls from the ranks of organized religion have broken loose from the paralyzing chains of conformity and joined us as active partners in the struggle for freedom. They have left their secure congregations and walked the streets of Albany, Georgia, with us. They have gone down the highways of the South on tortuous rides for freedom. Yes, they have gone to jail with us. Some have been dismissed from their churches, have lost the support of their bishops and fellow ministers. But they have acted in the faith that right defeated is stronger than evil triumphant. Their witness has been the spiritual salt that has preserved the true meaning of the gospel in these troubled times. They have carved a tunnel of hope through the dark mountain of disappointment.

I hope that the church as a whole will meet the challenge of this decisive hour. But even if the church does not come to the aid of justice, I have no despair about the future. I have no fear about the outcome of our struggle in Birmingham, even if our motives are at present misunderstood. We will reach the goal of freedom in Birmingham and all over the nation, because the goal of America is freedom. Abused and scorned though we may be, our destiny is tied up with America's destiny. Before the pilgrims landed at Plymouth, we were here. Before the pen of Jefferson etched the majestic words of the Declaration of Independence across the pages of history, we were here. For more than two centuries our forebears labored in this country without wages; they made cotton king; they built the homes of their masters while suffering gross injustice and shameful humiliation — and yet out of a bottomless vitality they continued to thrive and develop. If the inexpressible cruelties of slavery could not stop us, the opposition we now face will surely fail. We will win our freedom because the sacred heritage of our nation and the eternal will of God are embodied in our echoing demands.

Before closing I feel impelled to mention one other point in your statement that has troubled me profoundly. You warmly commended the Birmingham police force for keeping "order" and "preventing violence." I doubt that you   45

---

ekklesia: The ancient Greek term for "people's assembly." It was chosen by early Christians to describe their gatherings or church.

would have so warmly commended the police force if you had seen its dogs sinking their teeth into unarmed, nonviolent Negroes. I doubt that you would so quickly commend the policemen if you were to observe their ugly and inhumane treatment of Negroes here in the city jail; if you were to watch them push and curse old Negro women and young Negro girls; if you were to see them slap and kick old Negro men and young boys; if you were to observe them, as they did on two occasions, refuse to give us food because we wanted to sing our grace together. I cannot join you in your praise of the Birmingham police department.

It is true that the police have exercised a degree of discipline in handling the demonstrators. In this sense they have conducted themselves rather "nonviolently" in public. But for what purpose? To preserve the evil system of segregation. Over the past few years I have consistently preached that nonviolence demands that the means we use must be as pure as the ends we seek. I have tried to make clear that it is wrong to use immoral means to attain moral ends. But now I must affirm that it is just as wrong, or perhaps even more so, to use moral means to preserve immoral ends. Perhaps Mr. Connor and his policemen have been rather nonviolent in public, as was Chief Pritchett in Albany, Georgia, but they have used the moral means of nonviolence to maintain the immoral end of racial injustice. As T. S. Eliot° has said, "The last temptation is the greatest treason: to do the right deed for the wrong reason."

I wish you had commended the Negro sit-inners and demonstrators of Birmingham for their sublime courage, their willingness to suffer, and their amazing discipline in the midst of great provocation. One day the South will recognize its real heroes. They will be the James Merediths,° with the noble sense of purpose that enables them to face jeering and hostile mobs, and with the agonizing loneliness that characterizes the life of the pioneer. They will be old, oppressed, battered Negro women, symbolized in a seventy-two-year-old woman in Montgomery, Alabama, who rose up with a sense of dignity and with her people decided not to ride segregated buses, and who responded with ungrammatical profundity to one who inquired about her weariness: "My feets is tired, but my soul is at rest." They will be the young high school and college students, the young ministers of the gospel and a host of their elders, courageously and nonviolently sitting in at lunch counters and willingly going to jail for conscience' sake. One day the South will know that when these disinherited children of God sat down at lunch counters, they were in reality standing up for what is best in the American dream and for the most sacred values in our Judaeo-Christian heritage, thereby bringing our nation back to those great wells of democracy which were dug deep by the founding fathers in their formulation of the Constitution and the Declaration of Independence.

Never before have I written so long a letter. I'm afraid it is much too long to take your precious time. I can assure you that it would have been much shorter

---

Thomas Stearns Eliot (1888–1965): American-born poet and literary critic.   **James Meredith (b. 1933):** The first African American student to be admitted to the University of Mississippi.

if I had been writing from a comfortable desk, but what else can one do when he is alone in a narrow jail cell, other than write long letters, think long thoughts, and pray long prayers?

If I have said anything in this letter that overstates the truth and indicates an unreasonable impatience, I beg you to forgive me. If I have said anything that understates the truth and indicates my having a patience that allows me to settle for anything less than brotherhood, I beg God to forgive me.

I hope this letter finds you strong in the faith. I hope that circumstances   50
will soon make it possible for me to meet each of you, not as an integrationist or a civil-rights leader but as a fellow clergyman and a Christian brother. Let us all hope that the dark clouds of a racial prejudice will soon pass away and the deep fog of misunderstanding will be lifted from our fear-drenched communities, and in some not too distant tomorrow the radiant stars of love and brotherhood will shine over our great nation with all their scintillating beauty.

Yours for the cause of Peace and Brotherhood,
Martin Luther King Jr.   *[1963]*

≡ THINKING ABOUT THE TEXT

1. King wrote his letter in response to a published statement by eight clergymen from Alabama, who — as he points out in his first sentence — felt that his actions in Birmingham were "unwise and untimely." In what passages does he seem to be addressing this particular audience of religious leaders, referring to their specific accusation as well as to other ideas and texts that they would be especially familiar with? What are some passages where he seems to be addressing a larger audience, perhaps American society as a whole?

2. In one of the letter's most famous sections, King distinguishes between just and unjust laws (paras. 16–22). How does he define each of these two categories? To what extent do you find helpful the differences he draws between them?

3. In the middle of his letter (beginning in para. 23), King criticizes at length "the white moderate." What are his main observations about this kind of person? Why, apparently, does he devote his central section to *this* figure rather than to the extreme segregationist, who many people would think is his biggest enemy?

4. How would you describe King's tone? What impression of himself does he evidently seek to convey with it? Identify specific passages where you are especially conscious of his tone, perhaps because you are aware that another writer in his situation might have used a different one.

5. Among the rhetorical devices that King employs is anaphora, a pattern of repetition in which consecutive sentences all start with the same word or words. For example, in paragraph 25, King begins three sentences in a row with the words "Isn't this." Where else in his letter does he use the technique? How effective do you find it?

≡ MAKING COMPARISONS

1. How do Thoreau, Solnit, and King refer to prison not just as a physical structure but also as a psychological condition?

2. In her paragraph 4, Solnit suggests that despite what certain "scholars and critics" have said, the Thoreau who inspired King is connected to "that other Thoreau who wrote about autumnal tints, ice, light, color, grasses, woodchucks, and other natural histories." After reading King's letter, do you think that he might see himself as resembling "that other Thoreau"? Explain.

3. King's text is more overtly religious in its references than Thoreau's and Solnit's are. Do you think this is a significant difference? Why, or why not?

≡ WRITING ABOUT ISSUES

1. Choose one of the texts in this cluster and write an essay in which you explain how it attempts to solve a conceptual problem, which in Solnit's case might be what her title refers to as "the Thoreau problem." Whatever the problem you choose to discuss, phrase it as a question to which there could be more than one answer. For example, you might ask: How can one determine when civil disobedience is justified? or How can one make the best use of one's time? At some point in your essay, you may want to evaluate the writer's approach to solving the problem, but focus for the most part on identifying what the approach and the problem are in the first place.

2. Is civic disobedience for King a more active, dramatic, and sustained process than it seems to be for Thoreau and Solnit? Write an essay that addresses this question by comparing King's letter to at least one of the other two texts.

3. Write an essay in which you recall and analyze an occasion when you were inclined to disobey a law, rule, or regulation that you thought was unjust. Perhaps you did engage in disobedience; then again, perhaps you ultimately decided not to. Besides giving details of the incident, explain what criteria you used in determining the "right" thing to do. If you wish, refer to one or more texts in this cluster. Especially helpful may be the distinctions they draw between "just" and "unjust" government politics.

4. Choose a recent case of civil disobedience that the media have reported on, and read some opinion columns that have been published about it. Then, write an essay in which you analyze and evaluate at least two of these arguments. If you wish, refer to one or more texts in this cluster. Again, you may want to consider the distinctions they draw between "just" and "unjust" government policies.

▤ Arguments about a Story: Flannery O'Connor's "A Good Man Is Hard to Find"

FLANNERY O'CONNOR, "A Good Man Is Hard to Find"

CRITICAL COMMENTARIES:
FLANNERY O'CONNOR, From *Mystery and Manners*

MARTHA STEPHENS, From *The Question of Flannery O'Connor*

STEPHEN BANDY, From " 'One of My Babies': The Misfit and the Grandmother"

JOHN DESMOND, From "Flannery O'Connor's Misfit and the Mystery of Evil"

Most of us are social beings; we long to fit in. The communities we form sustain us, giving us our moral compasses and our psychological bearings. But sometimes people voluntarily remove themselves from all traditional communities. Indeed, literature is filled with misfits. Their decisions may intrigue us but also perplex and trouble us, perhaps because they represent antisocial impulses in all of us. Especially interesting are those literary misfits who demand that their own sense of justice be satisfied. Probably the most notable example in post–World War II American fiction is a character in Flannery O'Connor's 1953 short story "A Good Man Is Hard to Find." This man actually calls himself The Misfit, and he turns violent as he challenges Christianity's belief in Jesus' ability to raise the dead. O'Connor's story has been widely read, in part because it is subject to various interpretations. Here, in addition to the story and O'Connor's own remarks about it, we present three critical commentaries that respond to her analysis.

▤ BEFORE YOU READ

What do you think you might find in a story by a practicing Roman Catholic author? What topics, themes, characters, and events might she write about?

FLANNERY O'CONNOR
A Good Man Is Hard to Find

Flannery O'Connor (1925–1964) spent most of her life in Millidgeville, Georgia, where she raised peacocks on a farm with her mother. She died of lupus at the age of thirty-nine, when she was at the peak of her creative powers. All of her fiction reflects her Roman Catholic faith and Southern heritage, as do her nonfiction writings, which were collected after her death in Mystery and Manners *(1969). Critics have often seen in her work Christian parables of grace and redemption in the face of random violence. Like other Southern writers such as William Faulkner and Carson McCullers,*

(Apic/Hulton Archive/
Getty Images.)

*she uses grotesque characters to suggest our own morally flawed humanity. O'Connor's
early stories won her a scholarship to the University of Iowa, where she received an
M.F.A. She went on to produce two novels,* Wise Blood *(1952) and* The Violent
Bear It Away *(1960), but she is known and admired mostly for her short fiction. The
following story was first published in the volume* Modern Writing 1 *in 1953.
O'Connor then included it in her 1955 collection entitled* A Good Man Is Hard to
Find and Other Stories. *The book won her national acclaim, as did a later collection,
the posthumously published* Everything That Rises Must Converge *(1965). These
two volumes were combined in 1979 as* The Complete Stories of Flannery
O'Connor, *which won the National Book Award for fiction.*

> The dragon is by the side of the road, watching those who pass. Beware
> lest he devour you. We go to the Father of Souls, but it is necessary to pass
> by the dragon.
> — St. Cyril of Jerusalem

The grandmother didn't want to go to Florida. She wanted to visit some of her
connections in east Tennessee and she was seizing at every chance to change

Bailey's mind. Bailey was the son she lived with, her only boy. He was sitting on the edge of his chair at the table, bent over the orange sports section of the *Journal.* "Now look here, Bailey," she said, "see here, read this," and she stood with one hand on her thin hip and the other rattling the newspaper at his bald head. "Here this fellow that calls himself The Misfit is aloose from the Federal Pen and headed toward Florida and you read here what it says he did to these people. Just you read it. I wouldn't take my children in any direction with a criminal like that aloose in it. I couldn't answer to my conscience if I did." *Misfit*

Bailey didn't look up from his reading so she wheeled around then and faced the children's mother, a young woman in slacks, whose face was as broad and innocent as a cabbage and was tied around with a green head-kerchief that had two points on the top like rabbit's ears. She was sitting on the sofa, feeding the baby his apricots out of a jar. "The children have been to Florida before," the old lady said. "You all ought to take them somewhere else for a change so they would see different parts of the world and be broad. They never have been to east Tennessee."

The children's mother didn't seem to hear her but the eight-year-old boy, John Wesley, a stocky child with glasses, said, "If you don't want to go to Florida, why dontcha stay at home?" He and the little girl, June Star, were reading the funny papers on the floor.

"She wouldn't stay at home to be queen for a day," June Star said without raising her yellow head.

"Yes and what would you do if this fellow, The Misfit, caught you?" the 5
grandmother asked.

"I'd smack his face," John Wesley said.

"She wouldn't stay at home for a million bucks," June Star said. "Afraid she'd miss something. She has to go everywhere we go."

"All right, Miss," the grandmother said. "Just remember that the next time you want me to curl your hair."

June Star said her hair was naturally curly.

The next morning the grandmother was the first one in the car, ready to 10
go. She had her big black valise that looked like the head of a hippopotamus in one corner, and underneath it she was hiding a basket with Pitty Sing, the cat, in it. She didn't intend for the cat to be left alone in the house for three days because he would miss her too much and she was afraid he might brush against one of the gas burners and accidentally asphyxiate himself. Her son, Bailey, didn't like to arrive at a motel with a cat.

She sat in the middle of the back seat with John Wesley and June Star on either side of her. Bailey and the children's mother and the baby sat in front and they left Atlanta at eight forty-five with the mileage on the car at 55890. The grandmother wrote this down because she thought it would be interesting to say how many miles they had been when they got back. It took them twenty minutes to reach the outskirts of the city.

The old lady settled herself comfortably, removing her white cotton gloves and putting them up with her purse on the shelf in front of the back window. The children's mother still had on slacks and still had her head tied up in a green kerchief, but the grandmother had on a navy blue straw sailor hat with a bunch of white violets on the brim and a navy blue dress with a small white dot in the print. Her collars and cuffs were white organdy trimmed with lace and at her neckline she had pinned a purple spray of cloth violets containing a sachet. In case of an accident, anyone seeing her dead on the highway would know at once that she was a lady.

She said she thought it was going to be a good day for driving, neither too hot nor too cold, and she cautioned Bailey that the speed limit was fifty-five miles an hour and that the patrolmen hid themselves behind billboards and small clumps of trees and sped out after you before you had a chance to slow down. She pointed out interesting details of the scenery: Stone Mountain; the blue granite that in some places came up to both sides of the highway; the brilliant red clay banks slightly streaked with purple; and the various crops that made rows of green lace-work on the ground. The trees were full of silver-white sunlight and the meanest of them sparkled. The children were reading comic magazines and their mother had gone back to sleep.

"Let's go through Georgia fast so we won't have to look at it much," John Wesley said.

"If I were a little boy," said the grandmother, "I wouldn't talk about my native state that way. Tennessee has the mountains and Georgia has the hills."   15

"Tennessee is just a hillbilly dumping ground," John Wesley said, "and Georgia is a lousy state too."

"You said it," June Star said.

"In my time," said the grandmother, folding her thin veined fingers, "children were more respectful of their native states and their parents and everything else. People did right then. Oh look at the cute little pickaninny!" she said and pointed to a Negro child standing in the door of a shack. "Wouldn't that make a picture, now?" she asked and they all turned and looked at the little Negro out of the back window. He waved.

"He didn't have any britches on," June Star said.

"He probably didn't have any," the grandmother explained. "Little niggers   20 in the country don't have things like we do. If I could paint, I'd paint that picture," she said.

The children exchanged comic books.

The grandmother offered to hold the baby and the children's mother passed him over the front seat to her. She set him on her knee and bounced him and told him about the things they were passing. She rolled her eyes and screwed up her mouth and stuck her leathery thin face into his smooth bland one. Occasionally he gave her a faraway smile. They passed a large cotton field with five or six graves fenced in the middle of it, like a small island. "Look at the graveyard!" the grandmother said, pointing it out. "That was the old family burying ground. That belonged to the plantation."

"Where's the plantation?" John Wesley asked.

"Gone with the Wind," said the grandmother. "Ha. Ha."

When the children finished all the comic books they had brought, they   25 opened the lunch and ate it. The grandmother ate a peanut butter sandwich and an olive and would not let the children throw the box and the paper napkins out the window. When there was nothing else to do they played a game by choosing a cloud and making the other two guess what shape it suggested. John Wesley took one the shape of a cow and June Star guessed a cow and John Wesley said, no, an automobile, and June Star said he didn't play fair, and they began to slap each other over the grandmother.

The grandmother said she would tell them a story if they would keep quiet. When she told a story, she rolled her eyes and waved her head and was very dramatic. She said once when she was a maiden lady she had been courted by a Mr. Edgar Atkins Teagarden from Jasper, Georgia. She said he was a very good-looking man and a gentleman and that he brought her a watermelon every Saturday afternoon with his initials cut in it, E. A. T. Well, one Saturday, she said, Mr. Teagarden brought the watermelon and there was nobody at home and he left it on the front porch and returned in his buggy to Jasper, but she never got the watermelon, she said, because a nigger boy ate it when he saw the initials, E. A. T.! This story tickled John Wesley's funny bone and he giggled and giggled but June Star didn't think it was any good. She said she wouldn't marry a man that just brought her a watermelon on Saturday. The grandmother said she would have done well to marry Mr. Teagarden because he was a gentleman and had bought Coca-Cola stock when it first came out and that he had died only a few years ago, a very wealthy man.

They stopped at The Tower for barbecued sandwiches. The Tower was a part stucco and part wood filling station and dance hall set in a clearing outside of Timothy. A fat man named Red Sammy Butts ran it and there were signs stuck here and there on the building and for miles up and down the highway saying, TRY RED SAMMY'S FAMOUS BARBECUE. NONE LIKE FAMOUS RED SAMMY'S! RED SAM! THE FAT BOY WITH THE HAPPY LAUGH. A VETERAN! RED SAMMY'S YOUR MAN!

Red Sammy was lying on the bare ground outside The Tower with his head under a truck while a gray monkey about a foot high, chained to a small chinaberry tree, chattered nearby. The monkey sprang back into the tree and got on the highest limb as soon as he saw the children jump out of the car and run toward him.

Inside, The Tower was a long dark room with a counter at one end and tables at the other and dancing space in the middle. They all sat down at a board table next to the nickelodeon and Red Sam's wife, a tall burnt-brown woman with hair and eyes lighter than her skin, came and took their order. The children's mother put a dime in the machine and played "The Tennessee Waltz," and the grandmother said that tune always made her want to dance. She asked Bailey if he would like to dance but he only glared at her. He didn't have a naturally sunny disposition like she did and trips made him nervous. The grandmother's brown eyes were very bright. She swayed her head from side to side and pretended she was dancing in her chair. June Star said play something she could tap to so the children's mother put in another dime and played a fast number and June Star stepped out onto the dance floor and did her tap routine.

"Ain't she cute?" Red Sam's wife said, leaning over the counter. "Would you like to come be my little girl?"   30

"No I certainly wouldn't," June Star said. "I wouldn't live in a broken-down place like this for a million bucks!" and she ran back to the table.

"Ain't she cute?" the woman repeated, stretching her mouth politely.

"Aren't you ashamed?" hissed the grandmother.

Red Sam came in and told his wife to quit lounging on the counter and hurry up with these people's order. His khaki trousers reached just to his hip bones and his stomach hung over them like a sack of meal swaying under his shirt. He came over and sat down at a table nearby and let out a combination sigh and yodel. "You can't win," he said. "You can't win," and he wiped his sweating red face off with a gray handkerchief. "These days you don't know who to trust," he said. "Ain't that the truth?" *What good*.

"People are certainly not nice like they used to be," said the grandmother.   35

"Two fellers come in here last week," Red Sammy said, "driving a Chrysler. It was a old beat-up car but it was a good one and these boys looked all right to me. Said they worked at the mill and you know I let them fellers charge the gas they bought? Now why did I do that?"

"Because you're a good man!" the grandmother said at once.

"Yes'm, I suppose so," Red Sam said as if he were struck with this answer.

His wife brought the orders, carrying the five plates all at once without a tray, two in each hand and one balanced on her arm. "It isn't a soul in this green world of God's that you can trust," she said. "And I don't count nobody out of that, not nobody," she repeated, looking at Red Sammy.

"Did you read about that criminal, The Misfit, that's escaped?" asked the   40
grandmother.

"I wouldn't be a bit surprised if he didn't attack this place right here," said the woman. "If he hears about it being here, I wouldn't be none surprised to see him. If he hears it's two cent in the cash register, I wouldn't be a tall surprised if he . . ."

"That'll do," Red Sam said. "Go bring these people their Co'-Colas," and the woman went off to get the rest of the order.

"A good man is hard to find," Red Sammy said. "Everything is getting terrible. I remember the day you could go off and leave your screen door unlatched. Not no more."

He and the grandmother discussed better times. The old lady said that in her opinion Europe was entirely to blame for the way things were now. She said the way Europe acted you would think we were made of money and Red Sam said it was no use talking about it, she was exactly right. The children ran outside into the white sunlight and looked at the monkey in the lacy chinaberry tree. He was busy catching fleas on himself and biting each one carefully between his teeth as if it were a delicacy.

They drove off again into the hot afternoon. The grandmother took cat   45
naps and woke up every few minutes with her own snoring. Outside of Toombsboro she woke up and recalled an old plantation that she had visited in this neighborhood once when she was a young lady. She said the house had six white columns across the front and that there was an avenue of oaks leading up to it and two little wooden trellis arbors on either side in front where you sat

down with your suitor after a stroll in the garden. She recalled exactly which road to turn off to get to it. She knew that Bailey would not be willing to lose any time looking at an old house, but the more she talked about it, the more she wanted to see it once again and find out if the little twin arbors were still standing. "There was a secret panel in this house," she said craftily, not telling the truth but wishing that she were, "and the story went that all the family silver was hidden in it when Sherman came through but it was never found . . ."

"Hey!" John Wesley said. "Let's go see it! We'll find it! We'll poke all the woodwork and find it! Who lives there? Where do you turn off at? Hey Pop, can't we turn off there?"

"We never have seen a house with a secret panel!" June Star shrieked. "Let's go to the house with the secret panel! Hey Pop, can't we go see the house with the secret panel!"

"It's not far from here, I know," the grandmother said. "It wouldn't take over twenty minutes."

Bailey was looking straight ahead. His jaw was as rigid as a horseshoe. "No," he said.

The children began to yell and scream that they wanted to see the house   50
with the secret panel. John Wesley kicked the back of the front seat and June Star hung over her mother's shoulder and whined desperately into her ear that they never had any fun even on their vacation, that they could never do what THEY wanted to do. The baby began to scream and John Wesley kicked the back of the seat so hard that his father could feel the blows in his kidney.

"All right!" he shouted and drew the car to a stop at the side of the road. "Will you all shut up? Will you all just shut up for one second? If you don't shut up, we won't go anywhere."

"It would be very educational for them," the grandmother murmured.

"All right," Bailey said, "but get this: this is the only time we're going to stop for anything like this. This is the one and only time."

"The dirt road that you have to turn down is about a mile back," the grandmother directed. "I marked it when we passed."

"A dirt road," Bailey groaned.   55

After they had turned around and were headed toward the dirt road, the grandmother recalled other points about the house, the beautiful glass over the front doorway and the candle-lamp in the hall. John Wesley said that the secret panel was probably in the fireplace.

"You can't go inside this house," Bailey said. "You don't know who lives there."

"While you all talk to the people in front, I'll run around behind and get in a window," John Wesley suggested.

"We'll all stay in the car," his mother said.

They turned onto the dirt road and the car raced roughly along in a swirl   60
of pink dust. The grandmother recalled the times when there were no paved roads and thirty miles was a day's journey. The dirt road was hilly and there were sudden washes in it and sharp curves on dangerous embankments. All at once they would be on a hill, looking down over the blue tops of trees for

miles around, then the next minute, they would be in a red depression with the dust-coated trees looking down on them.

"This place had better turn up in a minute," Bailey said, "or I'm going to turn around."

The road looked as if no one had traveled on it in months.

"It's not much farther," the grandmother said and just as she said it, a horrible thought came to her. The thought was so embarrassing that she turned red in the face and her eyes dilated and her feet jumped up, upsetting her valise in the corner. The instant the valise moved, the newspaper top she had over the basket under it rose with a snarl and Pitty Sing, the cat, sprang onto Bailey's shoulder.

The children were thrown to the floor and their mother, clutching the baby, was thrown out the door onto the ground; the old lady was thrown into the front seat. The car turned over once and landed right-side-up in a gulch off the side of the road. Bailey remained in the driver's seat with the cat—gray-striped with a broad white face and an orange nose—clinging to his neck like a caterpillar.

As soon as the children saw they could move their arms and legs, they scrambled out of the car, shouting, "We've had an ACCIDENT!" The grandmother was curled up under the dashboard, hoping she was injured so that Bailey's wrath would not come down on her all at once. The horrible thought she had had before the accident was that the house she had remembered so vividly was not in Georgia but in Tennessee.

Bailey removed the cat from his neck with both hands and flung it out the window against the side of a pine tree. Then he got out of the car and started looking for the children's mother. She was sitting against the side of the red gutted ditch, holding the screaming baby, but she only had a cut down her face and a broken shoulder. "We've had an ACCIDENT!" the children screamed in a frenzy of delight.

"But nobody's killed," June Star said with disappointment as the grandmother limped out of the car, her hat still pinned to her head but the broken front brim standing up at a jaunty angle and the violet spray hanging off the side. They all sat down in the ditch, except the children, to recover from the shock. They were all shaking.

"Maybe a car will come along," said the children's mother hoarsely.

"I believe I have injured an organ," said the grandmother, pressing her side, but no one answered her. Bailey's teeth were clattering. He had on a yellow sport shirt with bright blue parrots designed in it and his face was as yellow as the shirt. The grandmother decided that she would not mention that the house was in Tennessee.

The road was about ten feet above and they could only see the tops of the trees on the other side of it. Behind the ditch they were sitting in there were more woods, tall and dark and deep. In a few minutes they saw a car some distance away on top of a hill, coming slowly as if the occupants were watching them. The grandmother stood up and waved both arms dramatically to attract their attention. The car continued to come on slowly, disappeared around

65

70

a bend and appeared again, moving even slower, on top of the hill they had gone over. It was a big black battered hearse-like automobile. There were three men in it.

It came to a stop just over them and for some minutes, the driver looked down with a steady expressionless gaze to where they were sitting, and didn't speak. Then he turned his head and muttered something to the other two and they got out. One was a fat boy in black trousers and a red sweat shirt with a silver stallion embossed on the front of it. He moved around on the right side of them and stood staring, his mouth partly open in a kind of loose grin. The other had on khaki pants and a blue striped coat and a gray hat pulled very low, hiding most of his face. He came around slowly on the left side. Neither spoke.

The driver got out of the car and stood by the side of it, looking down at them. He was an older man than the other two. His hair was just beginning to gray and he wore silver-rimmed spectacles that gave him a scholarly look. He had a long creased face and didn't have on any shirt or undershirt. He had on blue jeans that were too tight for him and was holding a black hat and a gun. The two boys also had guns.

"We've had an ACCIDENT!" the children screamed.

The grandmother had the peculiar feeling that the bespectacled man was someone she knew. His face was as familiar to her as if she had known him all her life but she could not recall who he was. He moved away from the car and began to come down the embankment, placing his feet carefully so that he wouldn't slip. He had on tan and white shoes and no socks, and his ankles were red and thin. "Good afternoon," he said. "I see you all had you a little spill."

"We turned over twice!" said the grandmother.   75

"Oncet," he corrected. "We seen it happen. Try their car and see will it run, Hiram," he said quietly to the boy with the gray hat.

"What you got that gun for?" John Wesley asked. "Whatcha gonna do with that gun?"

"Lady," the man said to the children's mother, "would you mind calling them children to sit down by you? Children make me nervous. I want all you all to sit down right together there where you're at."

"What are you telling US what to do for?" June Star asked.

Behind them the line of woods gaped like a dark open mouth. "Come here,"   80
said the mother.

"Look here now," Bailey began suddenly, "we're in a predicament! We're in . . ."

The grandmother shrieked. She scrambled to her feet and stood staring. "You're The Misfit!" she said. "I recognized you at once!"

"Yes'm," the man said, smiling slightly as if he were pleased in spite of himself to be known, "but it would have been better for all of you, lady, if you hadn't of reckernized me."

Bailey turned his head sharply and said something to his mother that shocked even the children. The old lady began to cry and The Misfit reddened.

"Lady," he said, "don't you get upset. Sometimes a man says things he   85
don't mean. I don't reckon he meant to talk to you thataway."

"You wouldn't shoot a lady, would you?" the grandmother said and removed a clean handkerchief from her cuff and began to slap at her eyes with it.

The Misfit pointed the toe of his shoe into the ground and made a little hole and then covered it up again. "I would hate to have to," he said.

"Listen," the grandmother almost screamed, "I know you're a good man. You don't look a bit like you have common blood. I know you must come from nice people!"

"Yes mam," he said, "finest people in the world." When he smiled he showed a row of strong white teeth. "God never made a finer woman than my mother and my daddy's heart was pure gold," he said. The boy with the red sweat shirt had come around behind them and was standing with his gun at his hip. The Misfit squatted down on the ground. "Watch them children, Bobby Lee," he said. "You know they make me nervous." He looked at the six of them huddled together in front of him and he seemed to be embarrassed as if he couldn't think of anything to say. "Ain't a cloud in the sky," he remarked, looking up at it. "Don't see no sun but don't see no cloud neither."

"Yes, it's a beautiful day," said the grandmother. "Listen," she said, "you   90
shouldn't call yourself The Misfit because I know you're a good man at heart. I can just look at you and tell."

"Hush!" Bailey yelled. "Hush! Everybody shut up and let me handle this!" He was squatting in the position of a runner about to sprint forward but he didn't move.

"I pre-chate that, lady," The Misfit said and drew a little circle in the ground with the butt of his gun.

"It'll take a half a hour to fix this here car," Hiram called, looking over the raised hood of it.

"Well, first you and Bobby Lee get him and that little boy to step over yonder with you," The Misfit said, pointing to Bailey and John Wesley. "The boys want to ast you something," he said to Bailey. "Would you mind stepping back in them woods there with them?"

"Listen," Bailey began, "we're in a terrible predicament! Nobody realizes   95
what this is," and his voice cracked. His eyes were as blue and intense as the parrots in his shirt and he remained perfectly still.

The grandmother reached up to adjust her hat brim as if she were going to the woods with him but it came off in her hand. She stood staring at it and after a second she let it fall on the ground. Hiram pulled Bailey up by the arm as if he were assisting an old man. John Wesley caught hold of his father's hand and Bobby Lee followed. They went off toward the woods and just as they reached the dark edge, Bailey turned and supporting himself against a gray naked pine trunk, he shouted, "I'll be back in a minute, Mamma, wait on me!"

"Come back this instant!" his mother shrilled but they all disappeared into the woods.

"Bailey Boy!" the grandmother called in a tragic voice but she found she was looking at The Misfit squatting on the ground in front of her. "I just know you're a good man," she said desperately. "You're not a bit common!"

"Nome, I ain't a good man," The Misfit said after a second as if he had considered her statement carefully, "but I ain't the worst in the world neither. My daddy said I was a different breed of dog from my brothers and sisters. 'You know,' Daddy said, 'it's some that can live their whole life out without asking about it and it's others has to know why it is, and this boy is one of the latters. He's going to be into everything!' " He put on his black hat and looked up suddenly and then away deep into the woods as if he were embarrassed again. "I'm sorry I don't have on a shirt before you ladies," he said, hunching his shoulders slightly. "We buried our clothes that we had on when we escaped and we're just making do until we can get better. We borrowed these from some folks we met," he explained.

"That's perfectly all right," the grandmother said. "Maybe Bailey has an   100
extra shirt in his suitcase."

"I'll look and see terrectly," The Misfit said.

"Where are they taking him?" the children's mother screamed.

"Daddy was a card himself," The Misfit said. "You couldn't put anything over on him. He never got in trouble with the Authorities though. Just had the knack of handling them."

"You could be honest too if you'd only try," said the grandmother. "Think how wonderful it would be to settle down and live a comfortable life and not have to think about somebody chasing you all the time."

The Misfit kept scratching in the ground with the butt of his gun as if he   105
were thinking about it. "Yes'm, somebody is always after you," he murmured.

The grandmother noticed how thin his shoulder blades were just behind his hat because she was standing up looking down at him. "Do you ever pray?" she asked.

He shook his head. All she saw was the black hat wiggle between his shoulder blades. "Nome," he said.

There was a pistol shot from the woods, followed closely by another. Then silence. The old lady's head jerked around. She could hear the wind move through the tree tops like a long satisfied insuck of breath. "Bailey Boy!" she called.

"I was a gospel singer for a while," The Misfit said. "I been most everything. Been in the arm service, both land and sea, at home and abroad, been twict married, been an undertaker, been with the railroads, plowed Mother Earth, been in a tornado, seen a man burnt alive oncet," and he looked up at the children's mother and the little girl who were sitting close together, their faces white and their eyes glassy; "I even seen a woman flogged," he said.

"Pray, pray," the grandmother began, "pray, pray . . ."   110

"I never was a bad boy that I remember of," The Misfit said in an almost dreamy voice, "but somewheres along the line I done something wrong and got sent to the penitentiary. I was buried alive," and he looked up and held her attention to him by a steady stare.

"That's when you should have started to pray," she said. "What did you do to get sent to the penitentiary, that first time?"

"Turn to the right, it was a wall," The Misfit said, looking up again at the cloudless sky. "Turn to the left, it was a wall. Look up it was a ceiling, look down it was a floor. I forgot what I done, lady. I set there and set there, trying to re-member what it was I done and I ain't recalled it to this day. Oncet in a while, I would think it was coming to me, but it never come."

"Maybe they put you in by mistake," the old lady said vaguely.

"Nome," he said. "It wasn't no mistake. They had the papers on me." 115

"You must have stolen something," she said.

The Misfit sneered slightly. "Nobody had nothing I wanted," he said. "It was a head-doctor at the penitentiary said what I had done was kill my daddy but I known that for a lie. My daddy died in nineteen ought nineteen of the epidemic flu and I never had a thing to do with it. He was buried in the Mount Hopewell Baptist churchyard and you can go there and see for yourself."

"If you would pray," the old lady said, "Jesus would help you."

"That's right," The Misfit said.

"Well then, why don't you pray?" she asked trembling with delight 120 suddenly.

"I don't want no hep," he said. "I'm doing all right by myself."

Bobby Lee and Hiram came ambling back from the woods. Bobby Lee was dragging a yellow shirt with bright blue parrots in it.

"Thow me that shirt, Bobby Lee," The Misfit said. The shirt came flying at him and landed on his shoulder and he put it on. The grandmother couldn't name what the shirt reminded her of. "No, lady," The Misfit said while he was buttoning it up, "I found out the crime don't matter. You can do one thing or you can do another, kill a man or take a tire off his car, because sooner or later you're going to forget what it was you done and just be punished for it."

The children's mother had begun to make heaving noises as if she couldn't get her breath. "Lady," he asked, "would you and that little girl like to step off yonder with Bobby Lee and Hiram and join your husband?"

"Yes, thank you," the mother said faintly. Her left arm dangled helplessly 125 and she was holding the baby, who had gone to sleep, in the other. "Hep that lady up, Hiram," The Misfit said as she struggled to climb out of the ditch, "and Bobby Lee, you hold onto that little girl's hand."

"I don't want to hold hands with him," June Star said. "He reminds me of a pig."

The fat boy blushed and laughed and caught her by the arm and pulled her off into the woods after Hiram and her mother.

Alone with The Misfit, the grandmother found that she had lost her voice. There was not a cloud in the sky nor any sun. There was nothing around her but woods. She wanted to tell him that he must pray. She opened and closed her mouth several times before anything came out. Finally she found herself say-ing, "Jesus. Jesus," meaning, Jesus will help you, but the way she was saying it, it sounded as if she might be cursing.

"Yes'm," The Misfit said as if he agreed. "Jesus thown everything off bal-ance. It was the same case with Him as with me except He hadn't committed any crime and they could prove I had committed one because they had the pa-pers on me. Of course," he said, "they never shown me my papers. That's why I sign myself now. I said long ago, you get you a signature and sign everything you do and keep a copy of it. Then you'll know what you done and you can hold up the crime to the punishment and see do they match and in the end you'll have something to prove you ain't been treated right. I call myself The Misfit," he said, "because I can't make what all I done wrong fit what all I gone through in punishment."

There was a piercing scream from the woods, followed closely by a pistol report. "Does it seem right to you, lady, that one is punished a heap and another ain't punished at all?"   130

"Jesus!" the old lady cried. "You've got good blood! I know you wouldn't shoot a lady! I know you come from nice people! Pray! Jesus, you ought not to shoot a lady. I'll give you all the money I've got!"

"Lady," The Misfit said, looking beyond her far into the woods, "there never was a body that give the undertaker a tip."

There were two more pistol reports and the grandmother raised her head like a parched old turkey hen crying for water and called, "Bailey Boy, Bailey Boy!" as if her heart would break.

"Jesus was the only One that ever raised the dead," The Misfit continued, "and He shouldn't have done it. He thown everything off balance. If He did what He said, then it's nothing for you to do but thow away everything and follow Him, and if He didn't, then it's nothing for you to do but enjoy the few minutes you got left the best you can — by killing somebody or burning down his house or doing some other meanness to him. No pleasure but meanness," he said and his voice had become almost a snarl.

"Maybe He didn't raise the dead," the old lady mumbled, not knowing what she was saying and feeling so dizzy that she sank down in the ditch with her legs twisted under her.   135

"I wasn't there so I can't say He didn't," The Misfit said. "I wisht I had of been there," he said, hitting the ground with his fist. "It ain't right I wasn't there because if I had of been there I would of known. Listen lady," he said in a high voice, "if I had of been there I would of known and I wouldn't be like I am now." His voice seemed about to crack and the grandmother's head cleared for an instant. She saw the man's face twisted close to her own as if he were going to cry and she murmured, "Why you're one of my babies. You're one of my own children!" She reached out and touched him on the shoulder. The Misfit sprang back as if a snake had bitten him and shot her three times through the chest. Then he put his gun down on the ground and took off his glasses and began to clean them.

Hiram and Bobby Lee returned from the woods and stood over the ditch, looking down at the grandmother who half sat and half lay in a puddle of blood with her legs crossed under her like a child's and her face smiling up at the cloudless sky.

Without his glasses, The Misfit's eyes were red-rimmed and pale and defenseless-looking. "Take her off and thow her where you thown the others," he said, picking up the cat that was rubbing itself against his leg.

"She was a talker, wasn't she?" Bobby Lee said, sliding down the ditch with a yodel.

⟨"She would of been a good woman," The Misfit said, "if it had been some-   140
body there to shoot her every minute of her life."⟩

"Some fun!" Bobby Lee said.

"Shut up, Bobby Lee," The Misfit said. "It's no real pleasure in life."

[1955]

☰ THINKING ABOUT THE TEXT

1. Although this story begins with comedy, ultimately it shocks many readers. Did it shock you? Why, or why not? What would you say to someone who argues that the shift in tone is a flaw in the story?

2. Note places where the word *good* comes up in this story. How is it defined? Do the definitions change? Do you think the author has in mind a definition that does not occur to the characters? If so, what might that definition be?

3. What in his life history is The Misfit unsure about? Why do you think he is hazy about these matters? Should O'Connor have resolved for us all the issues of fact that bother him? Why, or why not?

4. Does The Misfit have any redeeming qualities? Does the grandmother? Explain. What do you think the grandmother means when she murmurs, "Why you're one of my babies. You're one of my own children!" (para. 136)? Why do you think The Misfit responds as he does?

5. There is much talk about Jesus and Christianity in this story. Should O'Connor have done more to help non-Christian readers see the story as relevant to them? Explain your reasoning.

FLANNERY O'CONNOR
From *Mystery and Manners*

For public presentations at colleges and other places, Flannery O'Connor often chose to read and comment on "A Good Man Is Hard to Find." The following remarks come from her introduction to the story when she read it at Hollins College in Virginia in 1963. After her death, the introduction was published as "On Her Own Work" in Mystery and Manners, *a 1969 collection of O'Connor's nonfiction pieces. Her comments on "A Good Man Is Hard to Find" encourage a religious analysis of it. How helpful, though, is her own interpretation? Many critics who have subsequently written about the story have raised and addressed this issue.*

It is true that the old lady is a hypocritical old soul; her wits are no match for the Misfit's, nor is her capacity for grace equal to his; yet I think the unprejudiced reader will feel that the Grandmother has a special kind of triumph in this story which instinctively we do not allow to someone altogether bad.

I often ask myself what makes a story work and what makes it hold up as a story, and I have decided that it is probably some action, some gesture of a character that is unlike any other in the story, one which indicates where the real heart of the story lies. This would have to be an action or a gesture which was both totally right and totally unexpected; it would have to be one that was both in character and beyond character; it would have to suggest both the world and eternity. The action or gesture I'm talking about would have to be on the anagogical level, that is, the level which has to do with the Divine life and our participation in it. It would be a gesture that transcended any neat allegory that might have been intended or any pat moral categories a reader could make. It would be a gesture which somehow made contact with mystery.

There is a point in this story where such a gesture occurs. The Grandmother is at last alone, facing the Misfit. Her head clears for an instant and she realizes, even in her limited way, that she is responsible for the man before her and joined to him by ties of kinship which have their roots deep in the mystery she has been merely prattling about so far. And at this point, she does the right thing, she makes the right gesture.

I find that students are often puzzled by what she says and does here, but I think myself that if I took out this gesture and what she says with it, I would have no story. What was left would not be worth your attention. Our age not only does not have a very sharp eye for the almost imperceptible intrusions of grace, it no longer has much feeling for the nature of the violences which precede and follow them. The devil's greatest wile, Baudelaire has said, is to convince us that he does not exist.

I suppose the reasons for the use of so much violence in modern fiction will   5
differ with each writer who uses it, but in my own stories I have found that violence is strangely capable of returning my characters to reality and preparing them to accept their moment of grace. Their heads are so hard that almost nothing else will do the work. This idea, that reality is something to which we must be returned at considerable cost, is one which is seldom understood by the casual reader, but it is one which is implicit in the Christian view of the world.

I don't want to equate the Misfit with the devil. I prefer to think that, however unlikely this may seem, the old lady's gesture, like the mustard-seed, will grow to be a great crow-filled tree in the Misfit's heart and will be enough of a pain to him there to turn him into the prophet he was meant to become. But that's another story.

This story has been called grotesque, but I prefer to call it literal. A good story is literal in the same sense that a child's drawing is literal. When a child draws, he doesn't intend to distort but to set down exactly what he sees, and as his gaze is direct, he sees the lines that create motion. Now the lines of motion that interest the writer are usually invisible. They are lines of spiritual motion. And in this story you should be on the lookout for such things as the action of grace in the Grandmother's soul, and not for the dead bodies.   *[1963]*

MARTHA STEPHENS

From *The Question of Flannery O'Connor*

Martha Stephens is professor emeritus of English and comparative literature at the University of Cincinnati. After Flannery O'Connor's religious explanation of "A Good Man Is Hard to Find" was published in the 1969 volume Mystery and Manners, *other readers of the story began responding to her comments. Stephens's 1973 book* The Question of Flannery O'Connor *includes one of the earliest attempts to gauge the helpfulness of O'Connor's analysis. Stephens is disturbed by the story's apparent shift of tone as it moves from farce to violent tragedy. O'Connor's remarks clarify this shift, Stephens thinks, but the religious doctrine reflected in them is severe.*

An ordinary and undistinguished family, a family even comical in its dullness, ill-naturedness, and triviality, sets out on a trip to Florida and on an ordinary summer day meets with a terrible fate. In what would the interest of such a story normally lie? Perhaps, one might think, in something that is revealed about the family in the way it meets its death, in some ironical or interesting truth about the nature of those people or those relationships — something we had been prepared unbeknownst to see, at the end plainly dramatized by their final common travail and death. But obviously, as regards the family as a whole, no such thing happens. The family is shown to be in death just as ordinary and ridiculous as before. With the possible exception of the grandmother, we know them no better; nothing about them of particular significance is brought forth.

The grandmother, being as we have seen the last to die, suffers the deaths of all her family while carrying on the intermittent conversation with the Misfit, and any reader will have some dim sense that it is through this encounter that the story is trying to transform and justify itself. One senses that this conversation — even though our attention is in reality fastened upon the horrible acts that are taking place in the background (and apparently against the thrust of the story) — is meant to be the real center of the story and the part in which the "point," as it were, of the whole tale lies.

But what is the burden of that queer conversation between the Misfit and the grandmother; what power does it have, even when we retrospectively sift and weigh it line by line, to transform our attitude towards the seemingly gratuitous — in terms of the art of the tale — horror of the massacre? The uninitiated reader will not, most likely, be able to unravel the strange complaint of the killer without some difficulty, but when we see the convict's peculiar dilemma in the context of O'Connor's whole work and what is known of her religious thought, it is not difficult to explain.

The Misfit's most intriguing statement — the line that seemingly the reader must ponder, set as it is as the final pronouncement on the grandmother after her death — is from the final passage . . . : "She would of been a good woman if it had been somebody there to shoot her every minute of her life." Certainly we know from the first half of the story that the grandmother has seen herself as a good woman — and a good woman in a day when good men and women are hard to find, when people are disrespectful and dishonest, when they are not nice like they used to be. The grandmother is not common but a lady; and at the end of the story we know that she will be found dead just as we know she wanted to be—in the costume of a lady. She was not common, and the Misfit, with his "scholarly spectacles," his courtly apology for not wearing a shirt, his yes ma'ams and no ma'ams, was not common either—she had believed, wanted to believe, or pretended to believe. "Why I can see you come from good people," she said, "not common at all." Yet the Misfit says of her that she *would* have been a good woman if somebody had been there to shoot her all her life. And if we take the Misfit's statement as the right one about the grandmother, how was she a good woman in her death?

A good woman, perhaps we are given to believe, is one who understands   5
the worthlessness and emptiness of being or not being a "lady," of having or not having Coca-Cola stock, of "being broad" and seeing the world, of good manners and genteel attire. "Woe to them," said Isaiah, "that are wise in their own eyes, and prudent in their own sight." The futility of all the grandmother's values, the story strives to encapsulate in this image of her disarray after the car has overturned and she has recognized the Misfit: "The grandmother reached up to adjust her hat brim as if she were going to the woods with him but it came off in her hand. She stood staring at it and after a second she let it fall on the ground."

The Misfit is a figure that seems, one must say to the story's credit, to have fascinated more readers than any other single O'Connor character, and it is by contrast with the tormented spiritual state of this seeming monster that the nature of the grandmother's futile values becomes evident. We learn that the center of the Misfit's thought has always been Jesus Christ, and what becomes clear as we study over the final scene is that the Misfit has, in the eyes of the author, the enormous distinction of having at least faced up to the problem of Christian belief. And everything he has done—everything he so monstrously does here—proceeds from his inability to accept Christ, to truly believe. This is the speech which opens the narrow and emotionally difficult route into the meaning of the story:

> "Jesus was the only One that ever raised the dead," The Misfit continued, "and He shouldn't have done it. He thown everything off balance. If He did what He said, then it's nothing for you to do but thow away everything and follow Him, and if He didn't, then it's nothing for you to do but enjoy the few minutes you got left the best way you can—by killing somebody or burning down his house or doing some other meanness to him. No pleasure but meanness," he said and his voice had become almost a snarl.

The Misfit has chosen, at least, whom he would serve—has followed the injunction of the prophet in I Kings 18:21: "And Elijah came unto all the people, and said, How long halt ye between two opinions? if the Lord be God, follow him: but if Baal, then follow him." The crucial modern text for the authorial view here, which belongs to a tradition in religio-literary thought sometimes referred to as the sanctification of the sinner, is T. S. Eliot's essay on Baudelaire, in which he states: "So far as we are human, what we do must be either evil or good; so far as we do evil or good, we are human; and it is better, in a paradoxical way, to do evil than to do nothing; at least, we exist. It is true that the glory of man is his capacity for salvation; it is also true to say that his glory is his capacity for damnation."

Thus observe how, in the context of these statements, "A Good Man Is Hard to Find" begins to yield its meaning. What O'Connor has done is to take, in effect, Eliot's maxim—"It is better, in a paradoxical way, to do evil than to do nothing"—and to stretch our tolerance of this idea to its limits. The conclusion that one cannot avoid is that the story depends, for its final effect, on our being able to appreciate—even to be startled by, to be pleasurably struck with—the notion of the essential moral superiority of the Misfit over his victims, who have lived without choice or commitment of any kind, who have in effect not "lived" at all.

But again, in what sense is the grandmother a "good woman" in her death, as the Misfit claims? Here even exegesis falters. Because in her terror she calls on the name of Jesus, because she exhorts the Misfit to pray? Is she "good" because as the old lady sinks fainting into the ditch, after the Misfit's Jesus speech recorded above, she mumbles, "Maybe he didn't raise the dead"? Are we to see her as at last beginning to face the central question of human existence: did God send his son to save the world? Perhaps there is a clue in the dead grandmother's final image: she is said to half lie and half sit "in a puddle of blood with her legs crossed under her like a child's and her face smiling up at the cloudless sky." For Christ said, after all, that "whosoever shall not receive the kingdom of God as a little child shall in no wise enter herein."

To see that the Misfit is really the one courageous and admirable figure in the story; that the grandmother was perhaps—even as he said—a better woman in her death than she had ever been; to see that the pain of the other members of the family, that any godless pain or pleasure that human beings may experience is, beside the one great question of existence, *unimportant*—to see all these things is to enter fully into the experience of the story. Not to see them is to find oneself pitted not only against the forces that torture and destroy the wretched subjects of the story, but against the story itself and its attitude of indifference to and contempt for human pain.

Now as it happens, "A Good Man Is Hard to Find" was a favorite story of O'Connor's. It was the story she chose to read whenever she was asked to read from her work, and clearly it held a meaning for her that was particularly important. Whenever she read the story, she closed by reading a statement giving her own explanation of it. (One version of that statement can now be read in the collection of O'Connor's incidental prose edited by Robert and Sally Fitzgerald titled *Mystery and Manners*.) She had come to realize that it was a story that readers found difficult, and she said in her statement that she felt that the reason the story was misunderstood was that the present age "not only does not have a very sharp eye for the almost imperceptible intrusions of grace, it no longer has much feeling for the nature of the violences which precede and follow them." The intrusion of grace in "A Good Man Is Hard to Find" comes, Miss O'Connor said, in that much-discussed passage in which the

10

grandmother, her head suddenly clearing for a moment, murmurs to the Misfit, "Why, you're one of my babies. You're one of my own children!" and is shot just as she reaches out to touch him. The grandmother's gesture here is what, according to O'Connor, makes the story work; it shows that the grandmother realizes that "she is responsible for the man before her and joined to him by ties of kinship which have their roots deep in the mystery she has been merely prattling about so far," and it affords the grandmother "a special kind of triumph . . . which we instinctively do not allow to someone altogether bad."

This explanation does solve, in a sense, one of the riddles of this odd story—although, of course, one must say that while it is interesting to know the intent of the author, speaking outside the story and after the fact, such knowledge does not change the fact that the intent of the narrator manifested strictly within the story is damagingly unclear on this important point. And what is even more important here is that O'Connor's statement about the story, taken as a whole, only further confirms the fact that the only problem in this tale is really a function of our difficulty with O'Connor's formidable doctrine. About the Misfit, O'Connor says that while he is not to be seen as the hero of the story, yet his capacity for grace is far greater than the grandmother's and that the author herself prefers to think "that the old lady's gesture, like the mustard-seed, will grow to be a great crow-filled tree in the Misfit's heart, and will be enough of a pain to him there to turn him into the prophet he was meant to become." The capacity for grace of the other members of the family is apparently zero, and hence—Christian grace in O'Connor, one cannot help noting, is rather an expensive process—it is proper that their deaths should have no spiritual context whatever.   [1973]

STEPHEN BANDY
From "One of My Babies":
The Misfit and the Grandmother

In an article published in a 1996 issue of Studies in Short Fiction, *Stephen Bandy strongly disagrees with O'Connor's interpretation of "A Good Man Is Hard to Find." In particular, he thinks that the grandmother is sentimental and vindictive, whereas O'Connor is sympathetic to the character and believes that she manifests grace. Following are excerpts from Bandy's analysis.*

Grasping at any appeal, and hardly aware of what she is saying, the Grandmother declares to the Misfit: " 'Why you're one of my babies. You're one of my own children!' " As she utters these shocking words, "She reached out and touched him on the shoulder. The Misfit sprang back as if a snake had bitten him and shot her three times through the chest" (p. 950).

Noting that some squeamish readers had found this ending too strong, O'Connor defended the scene in this way: "If I took out this gesture and what she says with it, I would have no story. What was left would not be worth your attention" (*Mystery and Manners* 112).[1] Certainly the scene is crucial to the story, and most readers, I think, grant its dramatic "rightness" as a conclusion. What is arguable is the meaning to the Grandmother's final words to the Misfit, as well as her "gesture," which seemed equally important to O'Connor. One's interpretation depends on one's opinion of the Grandmother.

What *are* we to think of this woman? At the story's beginning, she seems a harmless busybody, utterly self-absorbed but also amusing, in her way. And, in her way, she provides a sort of human Rorschach test of her readers. We readily forgive her so much, including her mindless racism—she points at the "cute little pickaninny" by the roadside, and entertains her grandchildren with a story in which a watermelon is devoured by "a nigger boy." She is filled with the prejudices of her class and her time. And so, some readers conclude, she is in spite of it all a "good" person. Somewhat more ominously, the Misfit—after he has fired three bullets into her chest—pronounces that she might have been "'a good woman . . . if it had been somebody there to shoot her every minute of her life'" (p. 951). We surmise that in the universe of this story, the quality of what is "good" (which is after all the key word of the story's title) depends greatly on who is using the term. I do not think the Misfit is capable of irony—he truly means what he says about her, even though he finds it necessary to kill her. Indeed, the opposing categories of "good" and "evil" are very much in the air throughout this story. But like most supposed opposites, they have an alarming tendency to merge. It is probably worth noting that the second line of the once-popular song that gave O'Connor her title is "You always get the other kind."

Much criticism of the story appears to take a sentimental view of the Grandmother largely because she *is* a grandmother. Flannery O'Connor herself, as we shall see shortly, found little to blame in this woman, choosing to wrap her in the comfortable mantle of elderly Southern womanhood. O'Connor applies this generalization so uncritically that we half suspect she is pulling our leg. In any case, we can be sure that such sentimentality (in the mind of either the writer or her character) is fatal to clear thinking. If the Grandmother is old (although she does not seem to be *that* old), grey-haired, and "respectable," it follows that she must be weak, gentle, and benevolent—precisely the Grandmother's opinion of herself, and she is not shy of letting others know it. Intentionally or not, O'Connor has etched the Grandmother's character with wicked irony, which makes it all the more surprising to read the author's response to a frustrated teacher whose (Southern) students persisted in favoring the Grandmother, despite his strenuous efforts to point out her flaws. O'Connor said,

> I had to tell him that they resisted . . . because they all had grand-
> mothers or great-aunts just like her at home, and they knew, from

---

[1]Flannery O'Connor, *Mystery and Manners: Occasional Prose*. Selected and Edited by Sally and Robert Fitzgerald (New York: Farrar, Straus, and Giroux, 1969).

personal experience, that the old lady lacked comprehension, but that she had a good heart.

O'Connor continued,

> The Southerner is usually tolerant of those weaknesses that proceed from innocence, and he knows that a taste for self-preservation can be readily combined with the missionary spirit. (*Mystery and Manners* 110)

What is most disappointing in this moral summary of the Grandmother,   5
and her ilk, is its disservice to the spiky, vindictive woman of the story. There may be a purpose to O'Connor's betrayal of her own character: her phrase "missionary spirit" gives the game away. O'Connor is determined that the Grandmother shall be the Misfit's savior, even though she may not seem so in the story.

The Grandmother's role as grace-bringer is by now a received idea, largely because the author said it is so. But one must question the propriety of such tinkering with the character, after the fact. It reduces the fire-breathing woman who animates this story to nothing much more than a cranky maiden aunt. On the contrary, the Grandmother is a fierce fighter, never more so than in her final moments, nose-to-nose with the Misfit.

Granted, the Grandmother is not a homicidal monster like the Misfit, and she certainly does not deserve to die for her minor sins. And yet, does she quite earn absolution from any moral weakness beyond that of "a hypocritical old soul" (111)? For every reader who sees the image of his or her own grand-mother printed on this character's cold face, as O'Connor suggested we might do, there are surely many others who can only be appalled by a calculating opportunist who is capable of embracing her family's murderer, to save her own skin. Where indeed is the "good heart" which unites this unprincipled woman with all those "grandmothers or great-aunts just like her at home"? The answer to that question can only be an affirmation of the "banality of evil," to use Hannah Arendt's well-known phrase. . . .

What does in fact happen in this part of the story is quite straightforward: the Grandmother, having exhausted all other appeals to the Misfit, resorts to her only remaining (though certainly imperfect) weapon: motherhood. Declaring to the Misfit that he is one of her babies, she sets out to conquer him. Perhaps she hopes that this ultimate flattery will melt his heart, and he will collapse in her comforting motherly embrace. Such are the stratagems of sentimentality. The moral shoddiness of her action is almost beyond description. If we had not already guessed the depths to which the Grandmother might sink, now we know. It is not easy to say who is the more evil, the Misfit or the Grand-mother, and indeed that is the point. Her behavior is the manifest of her character.

It has been said that no action is without its redeeming aspect. Could this unspeakable act of selfishness carry within it the seeds of grace, acting, as it were, above the Grandmother? So Flannery O'Connor believed. But what is the precise movement of grace in this scene? It is surely straining the text to propose that the Grandmother has in this moment "seen the light." Are we to regard her as the unwitting agent of divine grace whose selfish intentions are somehow transfigured into a blessing? Such seems to have been O'Connor's opinion:

> ... however unlikely this may seem, the old lady's gesture, like the mustard-seed, will grow to be a great crow-filled tree in the Misfit's heart, and will be enough of a pain to him there to turn him into the prophet he was meant to become. (*Mystery and Manners* 113)

We are almost persuaded to forget that none of this happens in the story itself. If this can be so, then we can just as easily attribute any interpretation we like to the scene. But in fact he is in no way changed. There is no "later on" in fiction. We do not, and will not, see "created grace" in the spirit of the Misfit.

But more important, this is not the way grace works. As we read in the *New*   10
Catholic Encyclopedia:

> ... the spiritual creature must respond to this divine self-donation freely. Hence, the doctrine of grace supposes a creature already constituted in its own being in such wise that it has the possibility of entering into a free and personal relationship with the Divine Persons or of rejecting that relationship. (6:661)

If grace was extended to the Misfit, he refused it and that is the end. There can be no crow-filled tree, nor can there be the "lines of spiritual motion" leading to that tree, however attractive the image may be. Prudently, O'Connor added, "But that's another story" (*Mystery and Manners* 113)   [1996]

JOHN DESMOND
From Flannery O'Connor's Misfit and the Mystery of Evil

In an article published in a 2004 issue of Renascence, *a journal that examines religious issues in literature, John Desmond tends to support O'Connor's interpretation of "A Good Man Is Hard to Find." For help in understanding the climactic scene between The Misfit and the grandmother, he turns to the late French Catholic philosopher Simone Weil. The following is an excerpt from his analysis.*

This climactic scene, full of ambiguity, has occasioned a wealth of critical comment. O'Connor herself argued that the grandmother's final words and actions represent the mysterious action of grace (5). Some readers have viewed it more skeptically, even arguing that the grandmother's gesture may be a final desperate attempt to save her own life. Other critics have argued a middle ground, granting O'Connor's right to her theological view, while judging the scene as satisfactory or not on the basis of strictly literary criteria. My focus here is on what this climactic scene suggests about the mysterious interpenetration of good and evil.

What initially strikes the reader about the scene is the enormous gap or lacuna between the grandmother's statement of doubt — "Maybe He didn't raise the dead. . ." — and her reaching out fatally to touch the Misfit and embrace him as "one of my babies. . . ," one of "my own children." O'Connor explains nothing of what happens in the grandmother's mind and heart to bring her to this touch of kinship with the criminal, except to say that "her head cleared for an instant." The gap is mysterious, perhaps supernatural, yet also exactly right in the human sense. Such acts of metanoia,° while inexplicable, are totally within the range of human behavior. What is significant about her calling him "one of my babies. . . ," one of "my own children," and "touching him" is that her actions threaten to undermine his self-designation of himself as the Misfit, the name he chose to signify his difference from ordinary humanity. The Misfit rejects the communal world, just as his sense of "justice" is individualistic rather than communal. Significantly, he remarked earlier in that story that "children make me nervous." The grandmother's claim of kinship rejects his solitary identity, and instead places him within the community as a child of man, like any other. So also, her touching him threatens his proud, isolated self-created role as the Misfit, a threat he cannot tolerate. After all, if he is not the Misfit, what is he? An ordinary, frail, suffering creature. So what we view from the grandmother's perspective as a good act — her recognition of her own bond with an evil man, her complicity, yet also her compassion for his suffering — is viewed by the Misfit as evil: he springs back from her touch "as if a snake had bitten him. . . ."

Why does the Misfit regard the touch as evil, and then answer it with evil? We recall Simone Weil's maxim: "Evil is to love, what mystery is to the intelligence." The grandmother's touch brings the Misfit into direct contact with the good of charity. The touch of charity measures the gap between him and the good. He cannot abide such threatening contact because it would mean opening himself to an admission of failure, and more importantly, to the possibility of good within the human community. Instead, he chooses the "hell" of isolation and despair. The truth of compassion, and being named a child of the human community, is for the Misfit an "evil" he must escape. Once again, Weil's comments are insightful:

> The sin against the Spirit consists of knowing a thing to be good, and hating it because it is good. We experience the equivalent of it in the form of resistance every time we set our faces in the direction of good. For every contact with good leads to a knowledge of the distance between good and evil and the commencement of a painful effort of assimilation. It is something which hurts and we are afraid. This fear is perhaps the sign of the reality of the contact. The corresponding sin cannot come about unless a lack of hope makes the consciousness of the distance intolerable and changes the pain into hatred. (*Gravity and Grace* 67)

---

metanoia: A Greek term meaning repentance or spiritual conversion.

The Misfit's pain at the grandmother's touch is instantly transformed into a hatred of the gratuitous act of charity, which he then answers with a brutal execution. What the Misfit fears is the mystery of love, the demands of love which the grandmother mysteriously responded to when faced with the criminal's suffering, and her own impending death. In her case, evil issued finally in good, or as Weil expressed it, evil exposed the good. But if the encounter with evil exposed the good in the grandmother, the final predicament of the Misfit is more complicated, more mysterious.

As I noted earlier, the Misfit acts under the delusion that his actions are somehow good, i.e., good for him. Since he cannot make sense of his spiritual condition, he now tries to reduce ethical mystery to a perverse pleasure-pain principle. Initially he told the grandmother: "No pleasure but meanness." Yet his encounter with her touch has exposed his need, his human vulnerability. In his crucial final remark, he shifts from the earlier "No pleasure but meanness" to "It's no real pleasure in life." He has again failed to liberate himself from his predicament through violence, failed to "balance out" his deeds and find the meaning of his life. He himself is his own deepest mystery, a profoundly human condition which he can neither fathom nor abide. His last statement, that there is no "real pleasure" in life, shows that what he thought might bring pleasure, i.e., acts of meanness, has also proven to be bankrupt, a hollow illusion.

In the end, the Misfit's spiritual and mental suffering continues and intensifies, for with the failure of his code, his awareness of the gap between good and evil has widened. His violence is projected back onto himself as self-hatred. Perhaps at some future time his knowledge of this interior chasm will bring about the collapse of his self-begotten identity as a "Misfit," and an acceptance of his broken humanity. O'Connor suggested the possibility that he might ultimately be brought to such a conversion. She called the Misfit a "prophet gone wrong," and referred to the grandmother's touching him as "like the mustard-seed," which "will grow to be a great crow-filled tree in the Misfit's heart, and will be enough of a pain to him there to turn him into the prophet he was meant to become" (*Mystery and Manners* 110, 112–13). The grandmother's touch may bring him to the point where the mystery of good and evil is finally subsumed in the mystery of love. For the Misfit, evil may, in the end, through the grace of charity, bring about his ultimate good.

≡ MAKING COMPARISONS

1. Stephens believes that her interpretation of "A Good Man Is Hard to Find" is compatible with O'Connor's. Do you accept both? Why, or why not?

2. In what ways, if any, does Desmond's use of Simone Weil go beyond O'Connor's view of her story or complicate it? Do the other two critics, Stephens and Bandy, make you hesitate to accept O'Connor's account? In general, do you think readers should accept an author's interpretation of his or her work? Explain your reasoning.

3. All of these commentaries on the story focus on religious aspects of it, though not all of them agree on how much of a role, and what kind of a role, religion plays in it. Are you similarly inclined to put the story in a religious framework? Why, or why not?

≡ **WRITING ABOUT ISSUES**

1. The Misfit says that the grandmother " 'would of been a good woman . . . if it had been somebody there to shoot her every minute of her life' " (para. 140). Write an essay in which you argue for your own understanding of this claim. Is The Misfit right or just cruel? How should we define *good* in this context?

2. Choose one of the critics' interpretations featured in this cluster, and write an essay in which you imagine how O'Connor would respond to its points. Feel free to express and support your own views, too.

3. The man in O'Connor's story calls himself The Misfit " 'because I can't make what all I done wrong fit what all I gone through in punishment' " (para. 129). But plainly he is also a misfit in the sense that he has become alienated from society. Write an essay recalling someone you knew who seemed to be a misfit in this sense. More specifically, speculate on and try to describe this person's own perspective — what the person believed, how the person viewed the world, why he or she acted in certain ways. If you wish, your essay can be in the form of a letter to this person.

4. O'Connor promoted her version of Christianity in "A Good Man Is Hard to Find" and in her commentary on the story. On the basis of both texts, list various principles and concepts that she associates with her religion. Then do research on another religion, perhaps by reading two or three articles on it. Write an essay in which you compare O'Connor's theology with the religion you have researched. If you wish, you can focus your comparison by imagining what adherents to the other religion would say about "A Good Man Is Hard to Find."

Arguments about an Issue: Should Brain Science Influence the Law?

DAVID EAGLEMAN, From "The Brain on Trial"

RAYMOND TALLIS, "Why Blame Me? It Was All My Brain's Fault"

One of the oldest debates in philosophy and sociology, and indeed in society at large, is that between the influence of nature and nurture on our behavior. The equally contentious debate about free will versus determinism is just another way of getting at the perplexing question of why we are the way we are. Traditionally, conservative thought in all fields held that we were captains of our souls, steering our own boats. The debate over the past several generations, however, has tipped the scales toward nurture as the dominant force influencing our consciousness. The influential disciplines of psychology and sociology have provided credible evidence that free will is not as absolute as previously thought. And now emerging technological advances in science have provided fresh support for the significant influence of genes and environment on our actions. Neuroscience, for example, is offering new insights into the psychology and cognition of the brain through such technological advances as functional magnetic resonance imaging. Brain imaging has allowed us a deeper understanding of thought processes and the effect defects might have on criminal behavior. And so the debate surrounding free will, choice, and genetic blueprints has become an especially vital one in law schools throughout the world. As we learn more about the interaction between our brain and our behavior, the implications for a radical shift in law are significant.

≡ BEFORE YOU READ

To what extent might a tumor or brain injury affect criminal punishment? Should sentencing or rehabilitation be influenced by recent findings of neuroscience? How might nature or nurture affect our behavior? How might our biological inheritance affect our free will?

DAVID EAGLEMAN

From The Brain on Trial

Born in New Mexico in 1971 and educated at Rice University and Baylor College of Medicine where he earned a Ph.D. in neuroscience, David Eagleman is the founder of Baylor College of Medicine's Initiative on Neuroscience and Law. His latest book, Incognito: The Secret Lives of the Brain *(2011), was a* New York Times *best-seller and was widely praised as a "book that will leave you looking at yourself—and the world—differently." He is currently working on a textbook entitled* Cognitive Neuroscience. *Eagleman is also a fiction writer.* Sum: Forty Tales from *the Afterlives was a best-seller published in twenty-seven languages. Critics called the book inventive, imaginative, thought-provoking, and haunting. The excerpt below is from an Eagleman essay that appeared in the July 2011 issue of the* Atlantic.

On the steamy first day of August 1966, Charles Whitman took an elevator to the top floor of the University of Texas Tower in Austin. The 25-year-old climbed the stairs to the observation deck, lugging with him a footlocker full of guns and ammunition. At the top, he killed a receptionist with the butt of his rifle. Two families of tourists came up the stairwell; he shot at them at point-blank range. Then he began to fire indiscriminately from the deck at people below. The first woman he shot was pregnant. As her boyfriend knelt to help her, Whitman shot him as well. He shot pedestrians in the street and an ambulance driver who came to rescue them.

The evening before, Whitman had sat at his typewriter and composed a suicide note:

> I don't really understand myself these days. I am supposed to be an average reasonable and intelligent young man. However, lately (I can't recall when it started) I have been a victim of many unusual and irrational thoughts.

By the time the police shot him dead, Whitman had killed 13 people and wounded 32 more. The story of his rampage dominated national headlines the next day. And when police went to investigate his home for clues, the story became even stranger: in the early hours of the morning on the day of the shooting, he had murdered his mother and stabbed his wife to death in her sleep.

> It was after much thought that I decided to kill my wife, Kathy, tonight . . . I love her dearly, and she has been as fine a wife to me as any man could ever hope to have. I cannot rationa[l]ly pinpoint any specific reason for doing this . . .

Along with the shock of the murders lay another, more hidden, surprise: the juxtaposition of his aberrant actions with his unremarkable personal life. Whitman was an Eagle Scout and a former marine, studied architectural engineering at the University of Texas, and briefly worked as a bank teller and volunteered as a scoutmaster for Austin's Boy Scout Troop 5. As a child, he'd scored 138 on the Stanford-Binet IQ test, placing in the 99th percentile. So after his shooting spree from the University of Texas Tower, everyone wanted answers.

For that matter, so did Whitman. He requested in his suicide note that an autopsy be performed to determine if something had changed in his brain — because he suspected it had.   5

> I talked with a Doctor once for about two hours and tried to convey to him my fears that I felt [overcome by] overwhelming violent impulses. After one session I never saw the Doctor again, and since then I have been fighting my mental turmoil alone, and seemingly to no avail.

Whitman's body was taken to the morgue, his skull was put under the bone saw, and the medical examiner lifted the brain from its vault. He discovered that Whitman's brain harbored a tumor the diameter of a nickel. This tumor, called a glioblastoma, had blossomed from beneath a structure called the thalamus, impinged on the hypothalamus, and compressed a third region called the amygdala. The amygdala is involved in emotional regulation, especially of fear and aggression. By the late 1800s, researchers had discovered that damage to the amygdala caused emotional and social disturbances. In the 1930s, the researchers Heinrich Klüver and Paul Bucy demonstrated that damage to the amygdala in monkeys led to a constellation of symptoms, including lack of fear, blunting of emotion, and overreaction. Female monkeys with amygdala damage often neglected or physically abused their infants. In humans, activity in the amygdala increases when people are shown threatening faces, are put into frightening situations, or experience social phobias. Whitman's intuition about himself — that something in his brain was changing his behavior — was spot-on.

Stories like Whitman's are not uncommon: legal cases involving brain damage crop up increasingly often. As we develop better technologies for probing the brain, we detect more problems, and link them more easily to aberrant behavior. Take the 2000 case of a 40-year-old man we'll call Alex, whose sexual preferences suddenly began to transform. He developed an interest in child pornography — and not just a little interest, but an overwhelming one. He poured his time into child-pornography Web sites and magazines. He also solicited prostitution at a massage parlor, something he said he had never previously done. He reported later that he'd wanted to stop, but "the pleasure principle overrode" his restraint. He worked to hide his acts, but subtle sexual advances toward his prepubescent stepdaughter alarmed his wife, who soon discovered his collection of child pornography. He was removed from his house, found guilty of child molestation, and sentenced to rehabilitation in lieu of prison. In the rehabilitation program, he made inappropriate sexual advances toward the staff and other clients, and was expelled and routed toward prison.

At the same time, Alex was complaining of worsening headaches. The night before he was to report for prison sentencing, he couldn't stand the pain anymore, and took himself to the emergency room. He underwent a brain scan, which revealed a massive tumor in his orbitofrontal cortex. Neurosurgeons removed the tumor. Alex's sexual appetite returned to normal.

The year after the brain surgery, his pedophilic behavior began to return. The neuroradiologist discovered that a portion of the tumor had been missed in the surgery and was regrowing — and Alex went back under the knife. After the removal of the remaining tumor, his behavior again returned to normal.

When your biology changes, so can your decision-making and your desires. The drives you take for granted ("I'm a heterosexual/homosexual," "I'm attracted to children/adults," "I'm aggressive/not aggressive," and so on) depend on the intricate details of your neural machinery. Although acting on such drives is popularly thought to be a free choice, the most cursory examination of the evidence demonstrates the limits of that assumption.   10

Alex's sudden pedophilia illustrates that hidden drives and desires can lurk undetected behind the neural machinery of socialization. When the frontal lobes are compromised, people become disinhibited, and startling behaviors can emerge. Disinhibition is commonly seen in patients with frontotemporal dementia, a tragic disease in which the frontal and temporal lobes degenerate. With the loss of that brain tissue, patients lose the ability to control their hidden impulses. To the frustration of their loved ones, these patients violate social norms in endless ways: shoplifting in front of store managers, removing their clothes in public, running stop signs, breaking out in song at inappropriate times, eating food scraps found in public trash cans, being physically aggressive or sexually transgressive. Patients with frontotemporal dementia commonly end up in courtrooms, where their lawyers, doctors, and embarrassed adult children must explain to the judge that the violation was not the perpetrator's *fault*, exactly: much of the brain has degenerated, and medicine offers no remedy. Fifty-seven percent of frontotemporal-dementia patients violate social norms, as compared with only 27 percent of Alzheimer's patients.

Changes in the balance of brain chemistry, even small ones, can also cause large and unexpected changes in behavior. Victims of Parkinson's disease offer an example. In 2001, families and caretakers of Parkinson's patients began to notice something strange. When patients were given a drug called pramipexole, some of them turned into gamblers. And not just casual gamblers, but pathological gamblers. These were people who had never gambled much before, and now they were flying off to Vegas. One 68-year-old man amassed losses of more than $200,000 in six months at a series of casinos. Some patients became consumed with Internet poker, racking up unpayable credit-card bills. For several, the new addiction reached beyond gambling, to compulsive eating, excessive alcohol consumption, and hypersexuality.

What was going on? Parkinson's involves the loss of brain cells that produce a neurotransmitter known as dopamine. Pramipexole works by impersonating dopamine. But it turns out that dopamine is a chemical doing double duty in the brain. Along with its role in motor commands, it also mediates the reward systems, guiding a person toward food, drink, mates, and other things useful for survival. Because of dopamine's role in weighing the costs and benefits of decisions, imbalances in its levels can trigger gambling, overeating, and drug addiction—behaviors that result from a reward system gone awry. Physicians now watch for these behavioral changes as a possible side effect of drugs like pramipexole. Luckily, the negative effects of the drug are reversible—the physician simply lowers the dosage, and the compulsive gambling goes away.

The lesson from all these stories is the same: human behavior cannot be separated from human biology. If we like to believe that people make free choices about their behavior (as in, "I don't gamble, because I'm strong-willed"), cases like Alex the pedophile, the frontotemporal shoplifters, and the gambling Parkinson's patients may encourage us to examine our views more carefully. Perhaps not everyone is equally "free" to make socially appropriate choices.

Does the discovery of Charles Whitman's brain tumor modify your feelings about the senseless murders he committed? Does it affect the sentence you   15 would find appropriate for him, had he survived that day? Does the tumor change the degree to which you consider the killings "his fault"? Couldn't you just as easily be unlucky enough to develop a tumor and lose control of your behavior?

On the other hand, wouldn't it be dangerous to conclude that people with a tumor are free of guilt, and that they should be let off the hook for their crimes?

As our understanding of the human brain improves, juries are increasingly challenged with these sorts of questions. When a criminal stands in front of the judge's bench today, the legal system wants to know whether he is *blameworthy*. Was it his fault, or his biology's fault?

I submit that this is the wrong question to be asking. The choices we make are inseparably yoked to our neural circuitry, and therefore we have no meaningful way to tease the two apart. The more we learn, the more the seemingly simple concept of blameworthiness becomes complicated, and the more the foundations of our legal system are strained.

If I seem to be heading in an uncomfortable direction—toward letting criminals off the hook—please read on, because I'm going to show the logic of a new argument, piece by piece. The upshot is that we can build a legal system more deeply informed by science, in which we will continue to take criminals off the streets, but we will customize sentencing, leverage new opportunities for rehabilitation, and structure better incentives for good behavior. Discoveries in neuroscience suggest a new way forward for law and order—one that will lead to a more cost-effective, humane, and flexible system than the one we have today. When modern brain science is laid out clearly, it is difficult to justify how our legal system can continue to function without taking what we've learned into account.

Many of us like to believe that all adults possess the same capacity to make   20
sound choices. It's a charitable idea, but demonstrably wrong. People's brains are vastly different.

Who you even have the possibility to be starts at conception. If you think genes don't affect how people behave, consider this fact: if you are a carrier of a particular set of genes, the probability that you will commit a violent crime is four times as high as it would be if you lacked those genes. You're three times as likely to commit robbery, five times as likely to commit aggravated assault, eight times as likely to be arrested for murder, and thirteen times as likely to be arrested for a sexual offense. The overwhelming majority of prisoners carry these genes; 98.1 percent of death-row inmates do. These statistics alone indicate that we cannot presume that everyone is coming to the table equally equipped in terms of drives and behaviors.

And this feeds into a larger lesson of biology: *we* are not the ones steering the boat of our behavior, at least not nearly as much as we believe. *Who we are* runs well below the surface of our conscious access, and the details reach back in time to before our birth, when the meeting of a sperm and an egg granted us certain attributes and not others. *Who we can be* starts with our molecular blueprints—a series of alien codes written in invisibly small strings of acids— well before we have anything to do with it. Each of us is, in part, a product of our inaccessible, microscopic history. By the way, as regards that dangerous set of genes, you've probably heard of them. They are summarized as the Y chromosome. If you're a carrier, we call you a male.

Genes are part of the story, but they're not the whole story. We are likewise influenced by the environments in which we grow up. Substance abuse by a mother during pregnancy, maternal stress, and low birth weight all can influence how a baby will turn out as an adult. As a child grows, neglect, physical abuse, and head injury can impede mental development, as can the physical environment. (For example, the major public-health movement to eliminate lead-based paint grew out of an understanding that ingesting lead can cause brain damage, making children less intelligent and, in some cases, more impulsive and aggressive.) And every experience throughout our lives can modify genetic expression—activating certain genes or switching others off—which in turn can inaugurate new behaviors. In this way, genes and environments intertwine.

When it comes to nature and nurture, the important point is that we choose neither one. We are each constructed from a genetic blueprint, and then born into a world of circumstances that we cannot control in our most-formative years. The complex interactions of genes and environment mean that all citizens—equal before the law—possess different perspectives, dissimilar personalities, and varied capacities for decision-making. The unique patterns of neurobiology inside each of our heads cannot qualify as *choices*; these are the cards we're dealt.

Because we did not choose the factors that affected the formation and structure of our brain, the concepts of free will and personal responsibility begin to sprout question marks. Is it meaningful to say that Alex made bad *choices*, even though his brain tumor was not his fault? Is it justifiable to say that the patients with frontotemporal dementia or Parkinson's should be *punished* for their bad behavior?

It is problematic to imagine yourself in the shoes of someone breaking the law and conclude, "Well, *I* wouldn't have done that"—because if you weren't exposed to in utero cocaine, lead poisoning, and physical abuse, and he was, then you and he are not directly comparable. You cannot walk a mile in his shoes.

The legal system rests on the assumption that we are "practical reasoners," a term of art that presumes, at bottom, the existence of free will. The idea is that we use conscious deliberation when deciding how to act—that is, in the absence of external duress, we make free decisions. This concept of the practical reasoner is intuitive but problematic.

The existence of free will in human behavior is the subject of an ancient debate. Arguments in support of free will are typically based on direct subjective experience ("I *feel* like I made the decision to lift my finger just now"). But evaluating free will requires some nuance beyond our immediate intuitions.

Consider a decision to move or speak. It feels as though free will leads you to stick out your tongue, or scrunch up your face, or call someone a name. But free will is not *required* to play any role in these acts. People with Tourette's syndrome, for instance, suffer from involuntary movements and vocalizations. A typical Touretter may stick out his tongue, scrunch up his face, or call someone a name—all without *choosing* to do so.

We immediately learn two things from the Tourette's patient. First, actions 30 can occur in the absence of free will. Second, the Tourette's patient has no *free won't*. He cannot use free will to override or control what subconscious parts of his brain have decided to do. What the lack of free will and the lack of free won't have in common is the lack of "free." Tourette's syndrome provides a case in which the underlying neural machinery does its thing, and we all agree that the person is not responsible.

This same phenomenon arises in people with a condition known as chorea, for whom actions of the hands, arms, legs, and face are involuntary, even though they certainly *look* voluntary: ask such a patient why she is moving her fingers up and down, and she will explain that she has no control over her hand. She cannot *not* do it. Similarly, some split-brain patients (who have had the two hemispheres of the brain surgically disconnected) develop alien-hand syndrome: while one hand buttons up a shirt, the other hand works to unbutton it. When one hand reaches for a pencil, the other bats it away. No matter how hard the patient tries, he cannot make his alien hand *not* do what it's doing. The movements are not "his" to freely start or stop.

Unconscious acts are not limited to unintended shouts or wayward hands; they can be surprisingly sophisticated. Consider Kenneth Parks, a 23-year-old Canadian with a wife, a five-month-old daughter, and a close relationship with his in-laws (his mother-in-law described him as a "gentle giant"). Suffering from financial difficulties, marital problems, and a gambling addiction, he made plans to go see his in-laws to talk about his troubles.

In the wee hours of May 23, 1987, Kenneth arose from the couch on which he had fallen asleep, but he did not awaken. Sleepwalking, he climbed into his car and drove the 14 miles to his in-laws' home. He broke in, stabbed his mother-in-law to death, and assaulted his father-in-law, who survived. Afterward, he drove himself to the police station. Once there, he said, "I think I have killed some people . . . My hands," realizing for the first time that his own hands were severely cut.

Over the next year, Kenneth's testimony was remarkably consistent, even in the face of attempts to lead him astray: he remembered nothing of the incident. Moreover, while all parties agreed that Kenneth had undoubtedly committed the murder, they also agreed that he had no motive. His defense attorneys argued that this was a case of killing while sleepwalking, known as homicidal somnambulism.

Although critics cried "Faker!," sleepwalking is a verifiable phenomenon. 35 On May 25, 1988, after lengthy consideration of electrical recordings from Kenneth's brain, the jury concluded that his actions had indeed been involuntary, and declared him not guilty.

As with Tourette's sufferers, split-brain patients, and those with choreic movements, Kenneth's case illustrates that high-level behaviors can take place in the absence of free will. Like your heartbeat, breathing, blinking, and swallowing, even your mental machinery can run on autopilot. The crux of the question is whether *all* of your actions are fundamentally on autopilot or whether some little bit of you is "free" to choose, independent of the rules of biology.

This has always been the sticking point for philosophers and scientists alike. After all, there is no spot in the brain that is not densely interconnected with—and driven by—other brain parts. And that suggests that no part is independent and therefore "free." In modern science, it is difficult to find the gap into which to slip free will—the uncaused causer—because there seems to be no part of the machinery that does not follow in a causal relationship from the other parts.

Free will *may* exist (it may simply be beyond our current science), but one thing seems clear: if free will *does* exist, it has little room in which to operate. It can at best be a small factor riding on top of vast neural networks shaped by genes and environment. In fact, free will may end up being so small that we eventually think about bad decision-making in the same way we think about any physical process, such as diabetes or lung disease.   *[2011]*

≡ THINKING ABOUT IDEAS

1. In what way might Eagleman's claim that not everyone is equally free to make socially appropriate choices be true? In what ways does your socialization (by parents, school, religious community) suggest that this is not true? Why might it not be surprising that previous generations mostly held firm convictions about the strength of our free will?

2. What does Eagleman mean when he says that we did not choose either nature or nurture? If we are not steering the boat of our behavior, how might this affect criminal sentencing? What about rehabilitation? In what ways does Eagleman complicate or call into question the idea of choice?

3. What might the implications be for religion or law if traditional notions of free will were modified? What support might there be for Eagleman's contention that "many of us like to believe that all adults possess the same capacity to make sound choices" (para. 20)?

≡ THINKING ABOUT ARGUMENTATIVE MOVES

1. Instead of the more typical deductive argument that begins with a thesis, Eagleman begins his argument inductively with a detailed example. What might be the advantages and disadvantages of such a move?

2. Eagleman begins paragraph 7 by saying that technology turns up problems linked to behavior. He then gives us the Alex example. In what ways is this an effective strategy? What does this example illustrate? What does the example of the 68-year-old gambler illustrate? What is Eagleman's purpose in using questions in paragraph 15?

3. How does Eagleman's strategy shift in paragraph 16 with "On the other hand . . ."? Why does Eagleman claim that focusing on the issue of blameworthiness" is the wrong tactic? How does Eagleman's calling into question traditional notions of free will influence his recommendation that neuroscience should have an impact on the law? Where in the essay is the most effective statement of Eagleman's main point?

RAYMOND TALLIS

Why Blame Me? It Was All My Brain's Fault

Raymond Tallis (b. 1946) was born in Liverpool, England. He received a medical degree from Oxford University and later became professor of geriatric medicine at the University of Manchester. He has diverse scholarly interests and has published widely as a philosopher, poet, novelist, clinical neurologist, and literary critic. He is well known in England as a critic of contemporary intellectual trends. In 2011 he published Aping Mankind: Neuromania, Darwinists, and the Misrepresentation of Humanity, *in which he critiques what he takes to be the exaggerated claims of neuroscience to explain human behavior and consciousness. He is currently Visiting Professor of English at the University of Liverpool. Tallis's essay was printed in* The Times *of London in October 2007.*

Imagine this futuristic courtroom scene. The defense barrister stands up, and pointing to his client in the dock, makes this plea: "The case against Mr. X must be dismissed. He cannot be held responsible for smashing Mr. Y's face into a pulp. He is not guilty, it was his brain that did it. Blame not Mr. X, but his overactive amygdala."

The legal profession in America is taking an increasing interest in neuroscience. There is a flourishing academic discipline of "neurolaw" and neurolawyers are penetrating the legal system. Vanderbilt University recently opened a $27 million neuroimaging center and hopes to enroll students in a program in the law and neuroscience. In the courts, as in the trial of serial rapist and murderer Bobby Joe Long, brain-scan evidence is being invoked in support of pleas of diminished responsibility. The idea is abroad that developments in neuroscience—in particular the observation of activity in the living brain, using techniques such as functional magnetic resonance imaging—have shown us that we are not as free, or as accountable for our actions, as we traditionally thought.

Defense lawyers are licking their lips at the possibility of (to use law professor Jeffrey Rosen's succinct phrase) placing "the brain on the stand" to take the rap on behalf of the client. Though they failed to cut much ice in Long's case, arguments that blame lies not with the defendant but with his overactive amygdala (supposedly responsible for aggressive emotions) or his underactive frontal lobes (supposedly responsible for inhibiting the expression of such emotions) are being deployed with increasing frequency. If our brains are in charge, and bad behavior is due to them, our attitude to criminal responsibility, to punishment (the balance between rehabilitation and retribution), and to preventive detention of individuals thought to have criminal tendencies may all have to change.

Before we invest millions in "neurolaw" centers, however, we need to remind ourselves that observations of brain activity in the laboratory can explain very few things about us. We have no neural explanation for: sensations; the differences between sensations; the way our consciousness coheres at any particular time and over time; our relationship to an explicit past and an explicit future; our sense of being a self; and our awareness of other people as having minds like ourselves. All of these are involved in ordinary, waking behavior. The confident assertion that "his brain made him do it," except in well-attested cases—such as the automatisms associated with certain forms of epilepsy or the disinhibited behavior that may follow severe brain injury— therefore goes beyond our current knowledge or understanding.

Those who blame the brain should be challenged as to why they stop at the   5
brain when they seek the causes of bad behavior. Since the brain is a physical object, it is wired into nature at large. "My brain made me do it" must mean (ultimately) that "The Big Bang" made me do it. Neurodeterminism quickly slides into determinism tout court.°

And there is a contradiction built into the plea of neuromitigation. The claim "my brain made me do it" suggests that I am not my brain; even that my brain is some kind of alien force. One of the founding notions of neurolaw, however, is that the person is the brain. If I were my brain, then "My brain made me do it" would boil down to "I made me do it" and that would hardly get me off the hook.

And yet, if I am not identical with my brain, why should a brain make me do anything? Why should this impersonal bit of matter single me out?

The brain is, of course, the final common pathway of all actions. You can't do much without a brain. Decapitation is, in most instances, associated with a decline in IQ. Nevertheless, there is a difference between events that owe their origin to the stand-alone brain—for example the twitching associated with an epileptic fit—and actions that do not. While we do not hold someone responsible for an epileptic fit, we do hold them responsible for driving against medical advice and causing a fatal crash. The global excuse "my brain made me do it" would reduce life to a condition of status epilepticus.

In practice, most brain-blamers are not prepared to deny everyone's responsibility for anything and everything. While the brain is blamed for actions that attract moral disapprobation or legal sanction, people do not normally pass responsibility on to their brains for good actions or for neutral actions such as pouring a cup of tea or just getting up for a stretch after a long sit down. When asked why he is defending a particular client, a barrister is unlikely to

---

tout court: French, literally "in short"; used to mean "nothing else" or "only that."

say: "My brain made me do it, your honor." This pick-and-mix neurodeterminism is grounds for treating a plea of "neuromitigation" with caution.

So we still retain the distinction between events such as epileptic fits that   10
can be attributed to brain activity and those that we attribute to persons who are more than mere neural activity. Deciding on the boundaries of our responsibility for events in which we are implicated cannot be handed over to neuroscientists examining the activity of the isolated brain in the laboratory. As Stephen Morse, a professor of law, has reminded us, it is people, not brains, who commit crimes and "neuroscience . . . can never identify the mysterious point at which people should be excused responsibility for their actions." That moral, legal question must be answered not in laboratories but in courtrooms and legislatures.

Meanwhile, the neuromitigation of blame has to be treated with suspicion except in those instances where there is unambiguous evidence of grossly abnormal brain function or abnormal mental function due to clearcut illness that may have its origin in brain disease. Our knowledge of the relationship between brain and consciousness, brain and self, and brain and agency is so weak and so conceptually confused that the appeal to neuroscience in the law courts, the police station, or anywhere else is premature and usually inappropriate. And, I would suggest, it will remain both premature and inappropriate. Neurolaw is just another branch of neuromythology.   *[2007]*

≣ THINKING ABOUT IDEAS

1. Why does Tallis suggest that we should pause before spending millions on neurolaw centers? If our current knowledge about brains is insufficient, how might we change that situation? What might be Eagleman's response to Tallis's thinking about the efficacy of research?

2. If you were skeptical of Tallis's logic, how might you answer the questions he poses in paragraph 7? Likewise how would you counter Tallis's claim that "pick-and-mix neurodeterminism" (para. 9) is cause for us to doubt the influence of the brain on our behavior? How might you counter Stephen Morse's claim that "people, not brains . . . commit crimes" (para. 10)?

3. In his concluding paragraph, Tallis seems willing to hold a criminal blameless only "where there is unambiguous evidence of grossly abnormal brain function or abnormal mental function due to clearcut illness that may have its origin in brain disease." How reasonable does this standard of proof strike you? Do you think Eagleman would agree to it? Why, or why not?

≣ THINKING ABOUT ARGUMENTATIVE MOVES

1. Tallis clearly states his thesis in the last sentence. How might it have been more effective to begin with this claim? In the course of his argument, does Tallis ever qualify this question?

2. Where specifically does Tallis concern himself with his opposition? What kinds of evidence do you think would have been necessary for Tallis to mitigate this stance? How might Tallis's assertion that "neurodeterminism quickly slides into determinism tout court" (para. 5) be an example of the slippery slope fallacy?

3. Comment on how the last two sentences affect Tallis's argument, especially his claim that "it will remain both premature and inappropriate" (para. 11). How might Eagleman comment?

≡ WRITING ABOUT THE ISSUES

1. Although a cliché, the saying that you should not judge a person until you have walked a mile in his or her shoes is a helpful guide to tolerance and understanding difference. Write an essay that agrees or disagrees with this expression, including the ways Eagleman problematizes this old adage.

2. Write an essay that critiques Tallis's argument, including his thesis, his support, his way of dealing with the logic of the opposition, and the credibility of his persona or ethos.

3. Agree with, disagree with, or qualify Eagleman's assertion that "human behavior cannot be separated from human biology" (para. 14). Be sure to include Tallis's perspective.

4. After searching online for relevant articles on neurolaw or neuroscience and the law, write an essay that explains how at least two essays either support or fail to support the argument of Eagleman or Tallis.

≡ Contexts for Research: Ida Fink's *The Table* and Wartime Atrocities

IDA FINK, *The Table*

CULTURAL CONTEXTS:

WLADYSLAW SZPILMAN, "The *Umschlagplatz*"

DORI LAUB AND SHOSHANA FELMAN, "Testimony and Historical Truth"

Most people from the Western world would say that among the worst injustices of the twentieth century were the mass killings of Jews and other groups perpetrated by Nazi Germany and its collaborators during World War II. Indeed, many of the people responsible for this genocide were eventually found guilty of war crimes. Nevertheless, several of the murderers eluded efforts to track them down. Moreover, others were not arrested and tried in court until decades after the war. Even when they were brought to trial, their conviction was by no means assured. On various occasions, Holocaust survivors who testified against them could not remember exact details of the atrocities the perpetrators had committed. Inevitably, these eyewitnesses had to rely on fading and tormented memories, which defense lawyers were quick to criticize. Ida Fink's short play *The Table* explores the limits, as well as the strengths, of such recollections by showing a prosecutor for one of the trials interrogating his own team of witnesses. To help you think about the play and the issues it raises, we provide background texts. The first—a chapter from Wladyslaw Szpilman's celebrated memoir, *The Pianist*—is an eyewitness account of a deadly Nazi roundup in Warsaw. Then, we present Dori Laub's analysis of a Holocaust survivor's testimony.

≡ BEFORE YOU READ

Think of an occasion when your memory of an event conflicted with someone else's memory of it. What, if anything, about the event were the two of you able to agree on? What did you disagree about, and what do you think produced this disagreement? Do you now believe that one of you remembered the event more accurately? If so, why do you believe this?

IDA FINK
The Table

A Play for Four Voices and Basso Ostinato

Translated by Francine Prose and Madeline G. Levine

Originally from Zbaraz, Poland (now part of the Ukraine), Ida Fink (1921–2011) wrote in Polish about the Holocaust. During the Nazi occupation of her country, she was confined along with other Jews to a ghetto in her hometown but then escaped to

(Ulf Andersen/Hulton Archive/
Getty Images.)

its "Aryan" section and hid there using false identity papers. In 1957, she moved to
Israel, where she lived until her death at the age of ninety. Her works of fiction include a novel, The Journey (1990), as well as the short-story collections Traces
(1997) and A Scrap of Time (1987), a book that also contains the following play.
Fink wrote The Table for Israeli radio in 1970. "At that time," she reported, "I was
working as an interpreter and a clerk of the court during hearings of witnesses at the
trials of Nazi criminals." Eleven years later, the play was performed on German television. Fink identified it as being "for four voices and basso ostinato," a term that literally means "obstinate bass" and that in music refers to a continuously repeating
bass line. Here, Fink evidently associated the term with the prosecutor's voice.

CHARACTERS:

FIRST MAN, 50 years old
FIRST WOMAN, 45 years old
SECOND MAN, 60 years old
SECOND WOMAN, 38 years old
PROSECUTOR, 35–40 years old

The stage is empty and dark. Spotlights only on the witness, seated in a chair, and the prosecutor, seated at a desk.

PROSECUTOR: Have you recovered, Mr. Grumbach? Can we go on? Where did we stop? . . . Oh, yes. So you remember precisely that there was a table there.

FIRST MAN: Yes. A small table.

PROSECUTOR: A *small* table? How small? How many people could sit at a table that size?

FIRST MAN: Do I know? It's hard for me to say now.

PROSECUTOR: How long was it? A meter? Eight centimeters? Fifty centimeters?

FIRST MAN: A table. A regular table—not too small, not too big. It's been so many years . . . And at a time like that, who was thinking about a table?

PROSECUTOR: Yes, of course, I understand. But you have to understand me, too, Mr. Grumbach: every detail is crucial. You must understand that it's for a good purpose that I'm tormenting you with such details.

FIRST MAN: *(resigned)* All right, let it be eighty centimeters. Maybe ninety.

PROSECUTOR: Where did that table—that small table—stand? On the right side or the left side of the marketplace as you face the town hall?

FIRST MAN: On the left. Yes.

PROSECUTOR: Are you certain?

FIRST MAN: Yes . . . I saw them carry it out.

PROSECUTOR: That means that at the moment you arrived at the marketplace the table was not there yet.

FIRST MAN: No . . . Or maybe it was. You know, I don't remember. Maybe I saw them carrying it from one place to another. But is it so important if they were bringing it out or just moving it?

PROSECUTOR: Please concentrate.

FIRST MAN: How many years has it been? Twenty-five? And you want me to remember such details? I haven't thought about that table once in twenty-five years.

PROSECUTOR: And yet today, while you were telling your story, on your own, without prompting, you said, "He was sitting at a table." Please concentrate and tell me what you saw as you entered the square.

FIRST MAN: What did I see? I was coming from Rozana Street, from the opposite direction, because Rozana is on the other side of the market. I was struck by the silence. That was my first thought: so many people, and so quiet. I noticed a group of people I knew; among them was the druggist, Mr. Weidel, and I asked Weidel, "What do you think, Doctor, what will they do with us?" And he answered me, "My dear Mr. Grumbach . . ."

PROSECUTOR: You already mentioned that, please stick to the point. What did you see in the square?

FIRST MAN: The square was black with people.

PROSECUTOR: Earlier you said that the people assembled in the marketplace were standing at the rear of the square, facing the town hall, and that there was an empty space between the people and the town hall.

FIRST MAN: That's right.

PROSECUTOR: In other words, to say, "The square was black with people," is not completely accurate. That empty space was, shall we say, white — especially since, as you've mentioned, fresh snow had fallen during the night.

FIRST MAN: Yes, that's right.

PROSECUTOR: Now please think, Mr. Grumbach. Did you notice anything or anyone in that empty white space?

FIRST MAN: Kiper was sitting in a chair and striking his boots with a riding crop.

PROSECUTOR: I would like to call your attention to the fact that none of the witnesses until now has mentioned that Kiper was walking around with a riding crop. Are you certain that Kiper was striking his boots with a riding crop?

FIRST MAN: Maybe it was a stick or a branch. In any case, he was striking his boots — *that* I remember. Sometimes you remember such tiny details. Hamke and Bondke were standing next to him, smoking cigarettes. There were policemen and Ukrainians standing all around the square — a lot of them, one next to the other.

PROSECUTOR: Yes, we know that already. So, you remember that Kiper was sitting in a chair.

FIRST MAN: Absolutely.

PROSECUTOR: So if there was a chair in the marketplace, wouldn't there have been a table as well?

FIRST MAN: A table . . . just a minute . . . a table . . . no. Because that chair seemed so . . . wait a minute . . . No, there wasn't any table there. But they carried out a small table later. Now I remember exactly. Two policemen brought a small table out from the town hall.

PROSECUTOR: *(relieved)* Well, something concrete at last. What time would that have been?

FIRST MAN: *(reproachfully)* Really, I . . .

PROSECUTOR: Please, think about it.

FIRST MAN: The time? . . . God knows, I have no idea. I left the house at 6:15, that I know. I stopped in at my aunt's on Poprzeczna Street, that took ten minutes, then I walked down Miodna, Krotka, Okolna, and Mickiewicza streets. On Mickiewicza I hid for a few minutes inside the gate of one of the houses because I heard shots. It must have taken me about half an hour to walk there.

PROSECUTOR: How much time elapsed from the moment you arrived in the square to the moment when you noticed the policemen carrying the table out from the town hall?

FIRST MAN: Not a long time. Let's say half an hour.

PROSECUTOR: In other words, the policemen carried a table into the marketplace around 7:15. A small table.

FIRST MAN: That's right. Now I recall that Kiper pointed with his riding crop to the place where they were supposed to set the table down.

PROSECUTOR: Please indicate on the map you drew for us the exact place where the policemen set the table down. With a cross or a circle. Thank you. *(satisfied)* Excellent. Kiper is sitting in a chair, the policemen carry in the table, the length of the table is about eighty centimeters. How was the table placed? I mean, in front of Kiper? Next to him?

FIRST MAN: I don't know. That I couldn't see.

PROSECUTOR: If you could see them carrying in the table you could see that, too—perhaps you just don't remember. But maybe you can remember where Kiper sat? At the table? Beside it? In front of it?

FIRST MAN: Obviously, at the table. When someone waits for a table, it's so he can sit at it. He was sitting at the table. Of course. That's what people do.

PROSECUTOR: Alone?

FIRST MAN: In the beginning? I don't know. I wasn't looking that way the whole time. But later—this I know—they were all there: Kiper, Hamke, Bondke, Rossel, Kuntz, and Wittelmann.

PROSECUTOR: *(slowly)* Kiper, Hamke, Bondke, Rossel, Kuntz, and Wittelmann. When you testified a year ago you didn't mention either Rossel or Wittelmann.

FIRST MAN: I must have forgotten about them then. Now I remember that they were there, too.

PROSECUTOR: Were they all sitting at the table?

FIRST MAN: No. Not all of them. Some of them were standing next to it.

PROSECUTOR: Who was sitting?

FIRST MAN: What I saw was that Kiper, Hamke, Bondke, and Kuntz were sitting. The rest were standing. There were more than a dozen of them, I don't remember all the names.

PROSECUTOR: How were they seated, one beside the other?

FIRST MAN: Yes.

PROSECUTOR: Is it possible that four grown men could sit one beside the other at a table that is eighty centimeters long?

FIRST MAN: I don't know. Maybe the table was longer than that; or maybe it wasn't big enough for all of them. In any event, they were sitting in a row.

PROSECUTOR: Who read the names from the list?

FIRST MAN: Hamke or Bondke.

PROSECUTOR: How did they do it?

FIRST MAN: People walked up to the table, showed their *Arbeitskarten,*° and Kiper looked them over and pointed either to the right or to the left. The people who had good *Arbeitskarten* went to the right, and those whose work wasn't considered important, or who didn't have any *Arbeitskarten,* they went to the left.

PROSECUTOR: Was Kiper the one who conducted the selection?

FIRST MAN: Yes, I'm positive about that.

PROSECUTOR: Did Kiper stay in that spot during the whole time the names were read? Or did he get up from the table?

FIRST MAN: I don't know. Maybe he got up. I wasn't looking at him every minute. It took a very long time. And anyway, is it that important?

Arbeitskarten: Identity cards.

PROSECUTOR: I'm sorry to be tormenting you with these seemingly unimportant details . . . In other words, is it possible that Kiper got up and walked
away from the table, or even left the square?

FIRST MAN: I can't give a definite answer. I wasn't watching Kiper every minute. It's possible that he did get up from the table. That's not out of the
question. Still, he was the one in charge at the marketplace. Kiper — and
no one else. And he was the one who shot the mother and child.

PROSECUTOR: Did you see this with your own eyes?

FIRST MAN: Yes.

PROSECUTOR: Please describe the incident.

FIRST MAN: The woman wasn't from our town, so I don't know her name. She
was young, she worked in the brickworks. She had a ten-year-old daughter,
Mala. I remember the child's name; she was a pretty little girl. When this
woman's name was called she walked up to the table with her daughter.
She was holding the child by the hand. Kiper gave her back her *Arbeitskarte*
and ordered her to go to the right. But he ordered the child to go to the left.
The mother started begging him to leave the child with her, but he wouldn't
agree. Then she placed her *Arbeitskarte* on the table and walked to the left
side with the child. Kiper called her back and asked her if she knew the
penalty for disobeying an order, and then he shot them — first the girl, and
then the mother.

PROSECUTOR: Did you actually see Kiper shoot?

FIRST MAN: I saw the woman approach the table with the child. I saw them
standing in front of Kiper. A moment later I heard two shots.

PROSECUTOR: Where were you standing at that moment? Please mark it on the
map. With a cross or a circle. Thank you. So, you were standing near the
pharmacy. How far was it from the table to the pharmacy?

FIRST MAN: Thirty meters, maybe fifty.

PROSECUTOR: Then you couldn't have heard the conversation between Kiper
and the mother.

FIRST MAN: No, obviously. I didn't hear what they said, but I saw that the
mother exchanged several sentences with Kiper. It was perfectly clear what
they were talking about. Everyone understood what the mother was asking. Then I saw the mother place her *Arbeitskarte* on the table and go to the
left with the child. I heard Kiper call her back. They went back.

PROSECUTOR: They went back and stood in front of the table, correct?

FIRST MAN: That's correct.

PROSECUTOR: In other words, they were blocking your view of the men who
were sitting at the table, or at least of some of the men sitting at the table.

FIRST MAN: It's possible. I don't remember exactly. In any case, I saw them
come back to the table, and a moment later there were two shots, and then
I saw them lying on the ground. People who stood closer to them clearly
heard Kiper ask her if she knew the penalty for disobeying an order.

PROSECUTOR: Was Kiper standing or sitting at that moment?

FIRST MAN: I don't remember.

PROSECUTOR: So, you didn't see him at the exact moment you heard the shots. Did you see a gun in his hand? What kind of gun? A pistol? A machine gun?

FIRST MAN: He must have shot them with a pistol. Those were pistol shots.

PROSECUTOR: Did you see a pistol in Kiper's hand?

FIRST MAN: No . . . perhaps the mother and child were blocking my view; or maybe I was looking at the victims and not at the murderer. I don't know. But in any case, I did see something that told me it was Kiper who shot them, and no one else.

PROSECUTOR: Namely?

FIRST MAN: Namely . . . immediately after the shots, when the mother and child were lying on the ground, I saw with my own eyes how Kiper rubbed his hands together with a disgusted gesture, as if to cleanse them of filth. I won't forget that gesture.

PROSECUTOR: *(summarizing)* And so, Mr. Grumbach, you saw Kiper sitting at a table in the company of Hamke, Bondke, Rossel, and Kuntz. Then you saw Kiper carrying out the selection and Kiper brushing off his hands immediately after you heard the shots that killed the mother and child. But you didn't see a gun in Kiper's hand nor the shooting itself. Is that correct?

FIRST MAN: Still, I assert with absolute confidence that the murderer of the mother and child was Kiper.

PROSECUTOR: Was Kiper sitting behind the table when your name was called?

FIRST MAN: *(hesitating)* I was one of the last to be called. My *Arbeitskarte* was taken and returned by Bondke. I don't remember if Kiper was present or not. By then I was already half dead.

PROSECUTOR: Of course. What time would it have been when your name was called?

FIRST MAN: What time? My God, I don't know, it was already past noon.

PROSECUTOR: Did you witness any other murders committed that day?

FIRST MAN: That day more than four hundred people were shot in the town. Another eight hundred at the cemetery.

PROSECUTOR: Did you see any member of the Gestapo shoot someone?

FIRST MAN: No.

PROSECUTOR: Were you one of the group that buried the victims in the cemetery?

FIRST MAN: No.

PROSECUTOR: Is there anything else that you would like to say in connection with that day?

FIRST MAN: Yes.

PROSECUTOR: Please, go ahead.

FIRST MAN: It was a sunny, cold day. There was snow in the streets. The snow was red.

FIRST WOMAN: It was a Sunday. I remember it perfectly. As I was walking to the square, the church bells were ringing. It was a Sunday. Black Sunday.

PROSECUTOR: Is that what the day was called afterwards?

FIRST WOMAN: Yes.

PROSECUTOR: Some of the witnesses have testified that the day was called Bloody Sunday.

FIRST WOMAN: *(dryly)* I should think the name would be unimportant. It was certainly bloody. Four hundred corpses on the streets of the town.

PROSECUTOR: How do you know the exact figure?

FIRST WOMAN: From those who buried the victims. The *Ordnungsdienst*° did that. Later they told us, four hundred murdered in the town alone. A hard, packed snow lay on the streets; it was red with blood. The worst one was Kiper.

PROSECUTOR: Slow down. Please describe the events in the square as they occurred.

FIRST WOMAN: At six they ordered us to leave our houses and go to the marketplace. First I decided not to go, and I ran up to the attic. There was a window there, so I looked out. I saw people pouring down Rozana, Kwiatowa, Piekna, and Mickiewicza streets towards the square. Suddenly I noticed two SS entering the house next door. They stayed inside for a moment, then came out leading an elderly couple, the Weintals. Mrs. Weintal was crying. I saw that. They were elderly people. They owned a paper goods store. The SS-men ordered them to stand facing the wall of the house, and then they shot them.

PROSECUTOR: Do you know the names of the two SS-men?

FIRST WOMAN: No. One was tall and thin. He had a terrifying face. I might be able to recognize him in a photograph. You don't forget such a face. But they were local SS, because there were no outside SS in town that day. *They* did it, the locals. Four hundred murdered on the spot, twice that number in the cemetery.

PROSECUTOR: Let's take it slowly now. So, you saw two SS leading the Weintal couple out of the building and putting them against the wall. You lived on Kwiatowa Street. Was their house also located on Kwiatowa?

FIRST WOMAN: I lived on Kwiatowa at number 1; it was the corner building. The Weintals lived in a building on Rozana.

PROSECUTOR: What number?

FIRST WOMAN: I don't know, I don't remember . . .

PROSECUTOR: Did you see which of the two SS shot them? The tall one or the other one?

FIRST WOMAN: That I didn't see, because when they ordered them to stand facing the wall, I knew what would happen next and I couldn't watch. I was afraid. I moved away from the window. I was terribly afraid.

PROSECUTOR: Afterwards, did you see the Weintal couple lying on the ground dead?

FIRST WOMAN: They shot them from a distance of two meters; I assume they knew how to aim.

PROSECUTOR: Did you see the bodies afterwards?

Ordnungsdienst: Jewish police forces controlled by the Nazis.

FIRST WOMAN: No, I ran downstairs from the attic, I was afraid—with good reason—I was afraid that they would search the houses for people who were trying to hide, but I didn't go out into the street, I took the back exit to the garden and made my way to the marketplace by a roundabout route.

PROSECUTOR: Would you recognize those two SS in photos?

FIRST WOMAN: Perhaps. I'm fairly certain I could recognize the tall thin one. You don't forget such a face.

PROSECUTOR: Please look through this album. It contains photographs of members of the Gestapo who were in your town; but there are also photographs here of people who were never there.

FIRST WOMAN: *(she turns the pages; a pause)* Oh, that's him.

PROSECUTOR: Is that one of the men you saw from the window?

FIRST WOMAN: No, it's that awful murderer. It's Kiper. Yes, I remember, it's definitely him.

PROSECUTOR: Please look through all the photographs.

FIRST WOMAN: *(a pause)* No, I can't find that face. Unfortunately.

PROSECUTOR: You said "awful murderer." Did you ever witness a murder committed by Kiper?

FIRST WOMAN: *(laughs)* Witness? You're joking. The witnesses to his murders aren't alive.

PROSECUTOR: But there are people who saw him shoot.

FIRST WOMAN: I did, too. Sure—in the square, he fired into the crowd. Just like that.

PROSECUTOR: Do you know who he killed then?

FIRST WOMAN: I don't know. There were fifteen hundred of us in the square. But I saw him rushing around like a wild man and shooting. Not just him, others, too. Bendke, for example.

PROSECUTOR: When was that?

FIRST WOMAN: In the morning. Before the selection. But it's possible it also went on during the selection. I don't remember. I know that they fired into the crowd. Just like that.

PROSECUTOR: Who read the names from the list?

FIRST WOMAN: An SS-man. I don't know his name.

PROSECUTOR: How did they do it?

FIRST WOMAN: Very simply. Names were called out, some people went to the right and others to the left. The left meant death.

PROSECUTOR: Who conducted the selection?

FIRST WOMAN: They were all there: Kiper, Bendke, Hamm, Rosse.

PROSECUTOR: Which one of them reviewed the *Arbeitskarten?*

FIRST WOMAN: I don't remember.

PROSECUTOR: Who ordered you to go to the right? Kiper? Bendke? Hamm? Rosse?

FIRST WOMAN: I don't remember. At such a time, you know . . . at such a time, when you don't know . . . life or death . . . I didn't look at their faces. To me, they all had the same face. All of them! What difference does it make whether it was Kiper or Bendke or Hamm or Rosse? They were all there.

There were ten or maybe fifteen of those murderers. They stood in a semi-circle, with their machine guns across their chests. What difference does it make which one? They all gave orders, they all shot! All of them!

PROSECUTOR: Please calm yourself. I am terribly sorry that I have to provoke you with such questions. But you see, we can only convict people if we can *prove* that they committed murder. You say that all the members of the local Gestapo were there. But it could be that one of them was on leave, or possibly on duty in the *Dienststelle*.° And didn't shoot.

FIRST WOMAN: Every one of them shot. If not that day, then another. During the second or third action, during the liquidation.

PROSECUTOR: The law requires proof. And I, as the prosecuting attorney, am asking you for proof. I am asking for the names of the murderers, the names of the victims, the circumstances in which they were murdered. Otherwise, I can do nothing.

FIRST WOMAN: *(quietly)* My God . . .

PROSECUTOR: Excuse me?

FIRST WOMAN: Nothing, nothing.

PROSECUTOR: Please think: which one of them was in charge of the selection in the square?

FIRST WOMAN: They all participated in the selection. Kiper, Bendke, Hamm, Rosse. They were standing in a semicircle.

PROSECUTOR: Standing? Were all of them standing? Or perhaps some of them were seated?

FIRST WOMAN: No, they were standing. Is it that important?

PROSECUTOR: It's very important. Do you remember seeing a table in the marketplace at which several Gestapo men were seated? The others were standing near the table.

FIRST WOMAN: A table? I don't remember. There was no table there.

SECOND MAN: Here's the map. The marketplace was shaped like a trapezoid. At the top was the town hall, a beautiful old building that had been built by a Polish nobleman in the seventeenth century. The jewel of the town. The square sloped down towards the actual market where the stores were, as if the town hall reigned over the place. On the left, by the ruins of the old ramparts, stood those whose *Arbeitskarten* were taken away and also those who did not have *Arbeitskarten*. Note that the streets radiate out like a star. Here's Rozana, then Sienkiewicza, then Piekna, then Male Targi, then Nadrzeczna. There was no river in the town, but maybe once upon a time there was one, and that's why it was called Nadrzeczna—Riverside. Then came Zamkowa Street. All the streets I've named were later included in the ghetto, with the exception of Piekna. Beyond Male Targi there was a cemetery. Yes. That's where they were shot. Nadrzeczna was adjacent to the cemetery. Most of the people who lived on Nadrzeczna were Poles, but it was incorporated into the ghetto nonetheless, because of the cemetery. Be-

---

***Dienststelle*:** Police station.

cause the cemetery played a major role in our life then. Between Rozana and Sienkiewicza there were shops. First, Weidel's pharmacy—he was killed in the camp; then Rosenzweig's iron shop—he was shot during the second action. Then Kreitz's dry goods store, the Haubers' restaurant and hotel—they were the wealthiest people among us, their daughter lives in Canada—and then two groceries, one beside the other, Blumenthal's and Hochwald's. They were rivals all their lives, and now they're lying in the same grave. Oh yes, I can draw every single stone for you, describe every single person. Do you know how many of us survived?

PROSECUTOR: Forty.

SECOND MAN: How do you know?

PROSECUTOR: They are my witnesses.

SECOND MAN: And have you found all of them? And taken their testimony?

PROSECUTOR: I have found almost all of them, but I still haven't taken testimony from everyone. Several witnesses live in America; they will be questioned by our consular officials, and if necessary, subpoenaed for the trial. Two live in Australia, one in Venezuela. Now I would like to ask you about the details of the selection that took place during the first action. When was it, do you remember?

SECOND MAN: Of course. It was a Sunday, in December, towards the end of the month. It was a sunny, cold day. Nature, you see, was also against us. She was mocking us. Yes, indeed. If it had rained, or if there had been a storm, who knows, perhaps they wouldn't have kept shooting from morning till night. Darkness was already falling when they led those people to the cemetery. Oh, you want proof, don't you? The snow on the town's streets was red. Red! Does that satisfy you?

PROSECUTOR: Unfortunately, Mr. Zachwacki, snow doesn't constitute proof for judges, especially snow that melted twenty-five years ago.

SECOND MAN: The snow was red. Bloody Sunday. Four hundred fifty corpses on the streets. That's not proof? Then go there and dig up the mass graves.

PROSECUTOR: I'm interested in the selection. Who was in charge of it?

SECOND MAN: Kiper. A thug, a murderer. The worst sort. I can't talk about this calmly. No. Do you mind if I smoke? These are things . . . I'm sixty, my blood pressure shoots right up. A cutthroat like that . . .

PROSECUTOR: How do you know that Kiper was in charge of the selection?

SECOND MAN: What do you mean, how? I gave him my *Arbeitskarte* myself. He peered at me from under his brows and snarled, "*Rechts!*" I went to the right. Saved. Saved until the next time.

PROSECUTOR: Please describe the scene in more detail.

SECOND MAN: I was standing some distance away. We all tried to stand as far away from them as possible, as if that could have helped. I was standing near the Haubers' hotel. It was one in the afternoon. The church bell struck one, and since it was quiet in the square, you could hear the bell clearly even though the church was in a different part of town, near Waly Ksiazece. By then they had been calling out names for about an hour. Suddenly I hear, "Zachwacki!"

PROSECUTOR: Who called your name?

SECOND MAN: One of the Gestapo, but I don't know which one.

PROSECUTOR: Didn't you notice which of them was holding the list?

SECOND MAN: No, you're asking too much. There was a list, because they read the names from a list, but I didn't see it. If a person saw a scene like that in the theater, maybe he could describe it in detail. This here, that there, and so on. But when a tragedy like this is being played in real life? You expect me to look at a list when my life is hanging by a thread? I was standing there with my wife. She had an *Arbeitskarte* from the sawmill—that was a good place to work—and I had one from the cement works. Also a good place. When they called my name, my wife grabbed my arm. "Let's stay together!" she cried. Dr. Gluck was standing nearby, a kind old doctor. He told my wife, "Mrs. Zachwacki, calm down, your husband has a good *Arbeitskarte*, you have a good *Arbeitskarte*, get a grip on yourself." But she kept saying, "I want to stay together, if we don't we won't see each other ever again. Albert," she said, "I'm afraid." I literally had to tear myself away, she was holding on to me so tight. There, you see, so much for instinct, intuition . . . I never saw her again. All the women who worked in the sawmill were sent to the left. *(he clears his throat)*

PROSECUTOR: *(a short pause)* Then what happened?

SECOND MAN: I dashed through the crowd. There was an empty space between us and them, you had to walk about thirty meters to cross the empty square. First—I remember this—someone kicked me, who I don't know. I took a deep breath and ran as hard as I could to get to the town hall as fast as possible. When I handed them my *Arbeitskarte* my hand was trembling like an aspen leaf, although I'm not a coward. Not at all!

PROSECUTOR: To whom did you hand your *Arbeitskarte*?

SECOND MAN: I already told you, to Kiper. He opened it, read it, handed it back to me and snarled, "*Rechts!*" I was young, tall, strong. He gave me a reprieve.

PROSECUTOR: At the moment that you handed him your *Arbeitskarte*, was Kiper standing or sitting?

SECOND MAN: He was standing with his legs apart, his machine gun across his chest. His face was swollen, red.

PROSECUTOR: And the rest of the Gestapo?

SECOND MAN: I didn't see. I don't remember if any of them were standing next to Kiper.

PROSECUTOR: Did you see a table?

SECOND MAN: Yes, there was a table, but it was further to the right, as if it had nothing to do with what was happening there.

PROSECUTOR: A small table?

SECOND MAN: No, not at all. It was a big, long oak table, like one of those trestle tables you see in monasteries. It was probably one of those antique tables from the old town hall.

PROSECUTOR: Long, you say. What were its dimensions, more or less?

SECOND MAN: How should I know? Two, three meters. The Gestapo sat in a row on one side of the table; and there was quite a large group of them sitting there. Bondke was sitting, Rossel was sitting—them I remember. And there were at least six others.

PROSECUTOR: Did you by any chance notice whether Kiper was sitting at the table earlier and whether the reviewing of the *Arbeitskarten* took place at the table?

SECOND MAN: I didn't notice. When I was called, Kiper was standing several meters from the table.

PROSECUTOR: Who do you think was in charge of the action?

SECOND MAN: Kuntze. He had the highest rank.

PROSECUTOR: Did you see him in the square?

SECOND MAN: I don't remember if I saw Kuntze. Presumably he was sitting at the table. But I only remember Bondke and Rossel.

PROSECUTOR: Was the table already there when you got to the square?

SECOND MAN: Yes.

PROSECUTOR: Who was seated at it?

SECOND MAN: No one.

PROSECUTOR: Some people claim that Kiper was sitting in a chair even before the table was brought out and that afterwards he sat at the head of the table. That he took the *Arbeitskarten* while he was sitting.

SECOND MAN: It's possible. Everything is possible. When I was called, Kiper was standing.

PROSECUTOR: Mr. Zachwacki, do you recall an incident with a mother and child who were shot in the square?

SECOND MAN: Yes, I do. It was Rosa Rubinstein and her daughter Ala. They were from another town and had lived in our town only since the beginning of the war. I knew them.

PROSECUTOR: Who shot them, and under what circumstances?

SECOND MAN: I was standing in the group of workers on the right side of the square, beside the well.

PROSECUTOR: Please indicate the place on the map. With a circle or a cross. Thank you. There was a well there, you say. No one has yet mentioned that well.

SECOND MAN: It was an old well, wooden, with a wooden fence around it. All around it, in a semicircle, there were trees, poplars. At one moment I heard a shot, and people who were standing somewhat closer said that Rosa Rubinstein and her daughter had been shot. It seems that both of them had been sent to the left, but they went to the right. People said that Kiper ran after them and shot them.

PROSECUTOR: You said, "I heard a shot." Do you mean you heard a single shot?

SECOND MAN: Those were my words, but it's hard for me to say if I heard one shot, or two, or three. No doubt he fired at least twice.

PROSECUTOR: Did you see the shooting with your own eyes?

SECOND MAN: No. I saw the bodies lying on the ground. They were lying next to each other. Then the *Ordnungsdienst* picked them up. A red stain was left on the snow.

PROSECUTOR: You were part of the group that helped to bury the victims afterwards?

SECOND MAN: That's correct. There were so many victims that the *Ordnungs-dienst* had to take twenty men to help. Four hundred and fifty people were killed in the town—in the square and in the house searches—and eight hundred and forty were shot in the cemetery. My wife was one of them.

PROSECUTOR: *(pause)* But you didn't see any murders with your own eyes? Can you say, "I saw with my own eyes that this one or that one shot so-and-so or so-and-so?"

SECOND MAN: I saw thirteen hundred victims. The mass grave was thirty meters long, three meters wide, five meters deep.

SECOND WOMAN: No, I wasn't in the square. Because I worked as a cleaning woman for the Gestapo, and in the morning, when everyone was going to the marketplace, Mama said to me, "See if they'll let you stay at work." I took my pail and a rag and a brush and said goodbye to my parents on the corner of Mickiewicza and Rozana. We lived on Mickiewicza Street. My parents kept going straight, and I turned onto Rozana. I had gone a few steps when suddenly I caught sight of Rossel and Hamke; they were walking towards me and I got terribly frightened, so I ran into the first gate, and they passed by, they didn't notice me. Later I saw them entering the building at number 13. I kept going.

PROSECUTOR: Who lived in the house?

SECOND WOMAN: I don't know, I was young, I was thirteen years old, but I said I was sixteen because children, you know, were killed. I was well developed, so I said I was sixteen and they let me work for them. That was good luck. That day the Gestapo were going around to all the houses looking for people who hadn't gone to the square, and if they found someone, they shot him either in his apartment or on the street.

PROSECUTOR: Was there a family named Weintal in the house at number 13?

SECOND WOMAN: Weintal? No, I never heard of anyone with that name. I stayed at the Gestapo all day long, hiding. I knew the building, I knew where I could hide. Well, I must say, I certainly was lucky.

PROSECUTOR: Which Gestapo members were in the building that day?

SECOND WOMAN: I don't know. I was hiding in an alcove next to the stairway to the cellar, at the very end of the corridor. Once I thought I heard Wittelmann's voice; he seemed to be on the telephone and was yelling something awful.

PROSECUTOR: Did you ever witness an execution while you worked there?

SECOND WOMAN: I know that they took place, and I know where. But I never saw them shoot anyone. I was afraid, and as soon as they brought someone in, I would hide, get out of their way. I was afraid that they might shoot me, too. They killed them against the fence.

PROSECUTOR: Which fence?

SECOND WOMAN: There was a courtyard at the back surrounded by a fence, and behind the fence there was a trench. That's where they were shot. I know, because afterwards the *Ordnungsdienst* would come and collect the bodies. Once I saw them carrying a doctor whom they had killed. His name was

Gluck. But that was after the first action, in the spring. Another time I saw a group of Gestapo men walk out into the courtyard and immediately afterwards I heard a burst of machine-gun fire.

PROSECUTOR: Who did you see then?

SECOND WOMAN: Bondke, Rossel, Hamke, and Wittelmann.

PROSECUTOR: All together?

SECOND WOMAN: Yes. All together. I was washing the stairs to the cellar then.

PROSECUTOR: Were they all armed? Did each of them have a weapon?

SECOND WOMAN: Yes.

PROSECUTOR: Those shots you heard then, were they from a single machine gun or from several?

SECOND WOMAN: I don't know. I didn't pay attention. I wasn't thinking that someday someone would ask me about that. Maybe one of them shot, maybe two. Maybe they took turns. How should I know?

PROSECUTOR: When was that?

SECOND WOMAN: That was even before the first action, probably in the fall.

PROSECUTOR: Do you know how many people were shot then? Do you know their names?

SECOND WOMAN: I don't. I didn't see their bodies being taken away. I saw them collect the dead only once or twice. I don't know who was killed then.

PROSECUTOR: And you never saw a Gestapo man fire a gun?

SECOND WOMAN: No. I only worked there until the second action. I couldn't stand it any longer, I preferred to go to a camp. In general they were nice to me and never did anything bad. Once Bondke gave me cigarettes. The best-mannered was Kiper. He was an educated man, like Kuntze. But the others, no. Kiper had a lot of books in his room. He wanted fresh flowers in a vase every day. Once, when I didn't bring flowers, he yelled at me. Once he broke the vase because the flowers were wilted. On the desk in his room was a photograph of an elegant woman with a dog. But it was Hamke who had a dog. I used to prepare food for the dog. His name was Roosevelt. A wolfhound, very well trained. He tore the druggist Weidel's child to pieces. I heard Hamke boasting about him: *"Roosevelt hat heute ein Jüdlein zum Frühstück bekommen"* — Roosevelt had a little Jew for breakfast today. He said that to Kiper, and Kiper screwed up his face in disgust. Kiper couldn't stand Hamke and used to quarrel with Bondke. In general, he kept to himself. He didn't drink. That Sunday he was the first to come back from the marketplace.

PROSECUTOR: How do you know it was Kiper? Did you see him?

SECOND WOMAN: I heard his voice.

PROSECUTOR: Who was he talking to?

SECOND WOMAN: He was talking to himself. I thought he was reciting a poem. Anyway, that's what it sounded like. Then he went to his room and played his violin — I forgot to say that he was a trained musician. Bondke used to make fun of him and call him *Gestapogeiger* — Gestapo-fiddler. I don't know much about music, but I think he played very well. I heard him play several times. Always the same thing. I don't know what melody it was, I don't know much about music.

PROSECUTOR: Did you see him that day?

SECOND WOMAN: No, I only heard him playing.

PROSECUTOR: What time would that have been?

SECOND WOMAN: I don't know. It was growing dark.

PROSECUTOR: Could you hear the shots from the cemetery inside the Gestapo building?

SECOND WOMAN: I don't know. Maybe not. The cemetery is on Male Targi, and the Gestapo headquarters was on St. Jerzy Square. That's quite a distance. But maybe in the silence, in the clear air . . .

PROSECUTOR: Did you hear any shots when Kiper returned?

SECOND WOMAN: I can't say. Because the way I felt that Sunday and for several days afterwards, I was hearing shots all the time, and my parents thought I had lost my mind. I kept saying, "Listen, they're shooting . . . ," and I'd run and hide. Mama took me to Gluck, who gave me a powder, but it didn't help. I kept on hearing shots for a week. It was my nerves.

PROSECUTOR: When did the other Gestapo men come back?

SECOND WOMAN: I don't know. When it got dark, I sneaked out through the courtyard and returned home. The city was empty, as if no one was left alive. I was astonished: the snow was black. That was the blood. The most blood was on Sienkiewicza Street, and on Rozana. I didn't meet anyone in the marketplace either. It was empty. In the center of the square, lying on its back with its legs in the air, was a small, broken table.   *[1970]*

☰ THINKING ABOUT THE TEXT

1. Is the prosecutor being reasonable when he seeks to know facts about the table? In general, how fair is he in his questioning of the witnesses? Why do you think Fink decided to focus on a prosecutor as the interrogator, rather than confronting them with the defense attorney for the person or persons they are testifying against?

2. What sorts of details do the witnesses recall?

3. How much does the order of the witnesses matter in this play? Would the play have the same effect if their testimonies appeared in a different order? Why, or why not?

4. This play was originally written for radio, which is evidently the reason that Fink does not provide any description of the set. Describe the kind of set you would use if you were staging the play in a theater. What props and pieces of furniture, if any, would you employ?

5. Fink herself has stated that this play "is a protest against the law which tries genocide according to the code intended for trivial crimes." What do you think she means? Refer to specific lines in the script.

WLADYSLAW SZPILMAN
The *Umschlagplatz*

Translated by Anthea Bell

Born in Sosnowiec, Poland, Wladyslaw Szpilman (1911–2000) became one of his nation's leading pianists and composers, especially celebrated for his performances on Polish radio. As Jews living in Warsaw, he and his family were forced into the ghetto of that city during its Nazi occupation. Indeed, his parents and siblings ultimately perished in the death camps, while he himself was rescued from deportation to them and managed to hide in Warsaw for the rest of the war. Afterward, Szpilman returned to his musical career. He also wrote a memoir of his wartime experience, Death of a City. *Published in Poland in 1946, it was quickly withdrawn by the country's Communist leaders, who were disturbed by its references to Poles and members of the Soviet army who helped the Nazi cause. In 1999, the book was republished in Poland as* The Pianist, *and with the same title it was made into an Oscar-winning film in 2002. In the following chapter from the book, Szpilman recollects a scene similar to the one recalled by the witnesses in Fink's play. It is set in a big public area of Warsaw called the* Umschlagplatz, *where the Nazis assembled the city's Jews for shipment to extinction.*

The *Umschlagplatz* lay on the border of the ghetto. A compound by the railway sidings, it was surrounded by a network of dirty streets, alleys, and pathways. Despite its unprepossessing appearance, it had contained riches before the war. One of the sidings had been the destination of large quantities of goods from all over the world. Jewish businessmen bargained over them, later supplying them to the Warsaw shops from depots in Nalewki Street and Simon Passage. The place was a huge oval, partly surrounded by buildings, partly fenced, with a number of roads running into it like streams into a lake, useful links with the city. The area had been closed off with gates where the streets reached it, and could now contain up to eight thousand people.

When we arrived it was still quite empty. People were walking up and down, searching in vain for water. It was a hot, fine day in late summer. The sky was blue-grey, as if it would turn to ashes in the heat rising from the trodden ground and the dazzling walls of the buildings, and the blazing sun squeezed the last drops of sweat from exhausted bodies.

At the edge of the compound, where one of the streets ran into it, there was an unoccupied space. Everyone was giving this spot a wide berth, never lingering there but casting glances of horror at it. Bodies lay there: the bodies of those killed yesterday for some crime or other, perhaps even for attempting to escape. Among the bodies of men were the corpses of a young woman and two girls with their skulls smashed to pieces. The wall under which the corpses lay showed clear traces of bloodstains and brain tissue. The children had been murdered by a favorite German method: seized by the legs, their heads swung violently against the wall. Large black flies were walking over the dead and the pools of spilt blood on the ground, and the bodies were almost visibly bloating and decaying in the heat.

We had settled down reasonably comfortably, waiting for the train. Mother was sitting on the bundle of our things, Regina was on the ground beside her, I was standing, and Father was walking nervously up and down, his hands behind his back, four steps one way, four steps back. Only now, in the glaring sunlight, when there was no point in worrying about any useless plans to save us any more, did I have time to examine Mother closely. She looked dreadful, although she was apparently fully in control of herself. Her hair, once beautiful and always carefully tended, had hardly any color left in it and was hanging down in strands over her careworn, wrinkled face. The light in her bright black eyes seemed to have gone out, and a nervous twitch ran down from her right temple and over her cheek to the corner of her mouth. I had never noticed it before, and it showed how distressed Mother was by the scene around us. Regina was weeping, with her hands in front of her face, the tears running through her fingers.

At intervals vehicles drove up to the gates of the *Umschlagplatz* and crowds of people destined for resettlement were herded in. These new arrivals did not conceal their despair. The men were talking in raised voices, and women whose children had been taken away from them were wailing and sobbing convulsively. But soon the atmosphere of leaden apathy reigning over the compound began to affect them too. They quietened down, and only occasionally was there a brief outbreak of panic when it entered the head of a passing SS man to shoot someone who did not get out of his way quickly enough, or whose expression was not sufficiently humble.

A young woman sat on the ground not far away from us. Her dress was torn and her hair disheveled, as if she had been fighting someone. Now, however, she sat there quite calmly, her face like death, her eyes fixed on some point in space. Her fingers spread wide, clutching her throat, and from time to time she asked, with monotonous regularity, "Why did I do it? Why did I do it?"

A young man standing beside her, obviously her husband, was trying to comfort her and convince her of something, speaking softly, but it did not seem to penetrate her mind.

We kept meeting acquaintances among the people driven into the compound. They came over to us, greeted us, and out of sheer habit tried to make some kind of conversation, but it was not long before these conversations broke off. They moved away, preferring to try to master their anxiety alone.

The sun rose higher and higher, blazing down, and we suffered increasing torments of hunger and thirst. We had eaten the last of our bread and soup the evening before. It was difficult to stay put in one place, and I decided to walk about; that might be an improvement.

As more and more people arrived the place became increasingly crowded, and you had to avoid groups of people standing and lying around. They were all discussing the same subject: where we would be taken, and if we were really going to be sent to do labor, as the Jewish police tried to convince everyone.

I saw a group of old people lying down in one part of the compound, men and women probably evacuated from an old people's home. They were dreadfully thin, exhausted by hunger and the heat, and obviously at the very limit of their strength. Some of them were lying there with their eyes closed, and you could not tell if they were already dead or just dying. If we were going to be a labor force, then what were these old people doing here?

Women carrying children dragged themselves from group to group, begging for a drop of water. The Germans had turned off the water supply to the *Umschlagplatz* on purpose. The children's eyes were lifeless, their lids already drooping over them: their little heads nodded on thin necks, and their dry lips were open like the mouths of small fish discarded on the bank by the fishermen.

When I came back to my family they were not alone. A friend of Mother's was sitting beside her, and her husband, once the owner of a large shop, had joined my father and another acquaintance of theirs. The businessman was in quite good spirits. However, their other companion, a dentist who used to practice in Śliska Street not far from our flat, saw everything in very dark hues. He was nervous and bitter.

"It's a disgrace to us all!" he almost screamed. "We're letting them take us to our death like sheep to the slaughter! If we attacked the Germans, half a million of us, we could break out of the ghetto, or at least die honorably, not as a stain on the face of history!"

Father listened. Rather embarrassed, but with a kindly smile, he shrugged his shoulders slightly and asked, "How can you be absolutely certain they're sending us to our death?"

The dentist clasped his hands. "Well, of course I don't know for certain. How could I? Are they about to tell us? But you can be ninety percent sure they plan to wipe us all out!"

Father smiled again, as if he were even more sure of himself after this reply. "Look," he said, indicating the crowd at the *Umschlagplatz*. "We're not heroes! We're perfectly ordinary people, which is why we prefer to risk hoping for that ten percent chance of living."

The businessman agreed with Father. His opinion too was diametrically opposite to the dentist's: the Germans couldn't be so stupid as to squander the huge potential labor force represented by the Jews. He thought we were going to labor camps, perhaps very strictly run labor camps, but surely they would not kill us.

Meanwhile the businessman's wife was telling Mother and Regina how she had left her silverware walled up in the cellar. It was beautiful, valuable silver, and she expected to find it again on her return from deportation.

It was already afternoon when we saw a new group for resettlement being herded into the compound. We were horrified to see Halina and Henryk among them. So they were to share our fate too—and it had been such a comfort to think that at least the two of them would be safe.

I hurried to meet Henryk, certain that his idiotically upright attitude was to blame for bringing him and Halina here. I bombarded him with questions and reproaches before he could get a word of explanation in, but he was not going to deign to answer me anyway. He shrugged his shoulders, took a small

Oxford edition of Shakespeare out of his pocket, moved over to one side of us and began to read.

It was Halina who told us what had happened. They heard at work that we had been taken away, and they simply volunteered to go to the *Umschlagplatz* because they wanted to be with us.

What a stupid emotional reaction on their part! I decided to get them away from here at any price. After all, they were not on the list for resettlement. They could stay in Warsaw.

The Jewish policeman who had brought them knew me from the Sztuka café, and I was counting on being able to soften his heart quite easily, particularly as there was no formal reason for the two of them to be here. Unfortunately I had miscalculated: he wouldn't hear of letting them go. Like every policeman, he was duty bound to deliver five people to the *Umschlagplatz* every day personally, on pain of being resettled himself if he did not comply. Halina and Henryk made up today's quota of five. He was tired and had no intention of letting them go and setting out to chase up two more people, God knew where. In his opinion these hunts were not an easy assignment, since people would not come when the police called them but hid instead, and anyway he was sick of the whole thing.

I went back to my family empty-handed. Even this last attempt to save at least a couple of us had failed, like all my earlier attempts. I sat down beside Mother in a very downcast mood.

It was now five in the afternoon, but as hot as ever, and the crowd grew greater with every passing hour. People got lost in the crush and called to one another in vain. We heard the shots and shouting which meant raids were going on in the nearby streets. Agitation grew as the hour approached at which the train was supposed to come.

The woman next to us who kept asking, "Why did I do it?" got on our nerves more than anyone else. We knew what she was talking about by now. Our friend the businessman had found out. When everyone was told to leave their building this woman, her husband, and their child had hidden in a place prepared in advance. As the police were passing it the baby began crying, and in her fear the mother smothered it with her own hands. Unfortunately even that did not help. The baby's crying and then its death rattle were heard, and the hiding place was discovered.

At one point a boy made his way through the crowd in our direction with a box of sweets on a string round his neck. He was selling them at ridiculous prices, although heaven knows what he thought he was going to do with the money. Scraping together the last of our small change, we bought a single cream caramel. Father divided it into six parts with his penknife. That was our last meal together.

Around six o'clock a sense of nervous tension came over the compound. Several German cars had driven up, and the police were inspecting those destined to be taken away, picking out the young and strong. These lucky ones were obviously to be used for other purposes. A crowd of many thousands began pressing that way; people were shouting, trying to drown each other out, get to the front and display their physical advantages. The Germans responded

by firing. The dentist, still with our group, could scarcely contain his indignation. He snapped furiously at my father, as if it were all his fault. "So now do
you believe me when I say they're going to kill us all? People fit for work will
stay here. Death lies that way!"

His voice broke as he tried to shout this above the noise of the crowd and   30
the shooting, pointing the way the transports were to go.

Downcast and grief-stricken, Father did not reply. The businessman
shrugged his shoulders and smiled ironically; he was still in good spirits. He did
not think the selection of a few hundred people meant anything.

The Germans had finally picked their labor force and now drove off, but the
crowd's agitation did not die down. Soon afterwards we heard the whistle of a
locomotive in the distance and the sound of trucks rattling over the rails as
they came closer. A few more minutes, and the train came into sight: more
than a dozen cattle trucks and goods trucks rolling slowly towards us. The evening breeze, blowing in the same direction, wafted a suffocating wave of chlorine our way.

At the same time the cordon of Jewish police and SS men surrounding the
compound became denser and began making its way towards its center. Once
again we heard shots fired to frighten us. Loud wailing from the women and the
sound of children weeping rose from the close-packed crowd.

We got ready to leave. Why wait? The sooner we were in the trucks the better. A line of police was stationed a few paces away from the train, leaving a
broad path open for the crowd. The path led to the open doors of the chlorinated trucks.

By the time we had made our way to the train the first trucks were already   35
full. People were standing in them pressed close to each other. SS men were still
pushing with their rifle butts, although there were loud cries from inside and
complaints about the lack of air. And indeed the smell of chlorine made breathing difficult, even some distance from the trucks. What went on in there if the
floors had to be so heavily chlorinated? We had gone about halfway down the
train when I suddenly heard someone shout, "Here! Here, Szpilman!" A hand
grabbed me by the collar, and I was flung back and out of the police cordon.

Who dared do such a thing? I didn't want to be parted from my family.
I wanted to stay with them!

My view was now of the closed ranks of the policemen's backs. I threw
myself against them, but they did not give way. Peering past the policemen's
heads I could see Mother and Regina, helped by Halina and Henryk, clamber-
ing into the trucks, while Father was looking around for me.

"Papa!" I shouted.

He saw me and took a couple of steps my way, but then hesitated and
stopped. He was pale, and his lips trembled nervously. He tried to smile, helplessly, painfully, raised his hand and waved goodbye, as if I were setting out into
life and he was already greeting me from beyond the grave. Then he turned and
went towards the trucks.

I flung myself at the policemen's shoulders again with all my might.   40
"Papa! Henryk! Halina!"

I shouted like someone possessed, terrified to think that now, at the last vital moment, I might not get to them and we would be parted for ever.

One of the policemen turned and looked angrily at me.

"What the hell do you think you're doing? Go on, save yourself!"

Save myself? From what? In a flash I realized what awaited the people in the cattle trucks. My hair stood on end. I glanced behind me. I saw the open compound, the railway lines and platforms, and beyond them the streets. Driven by compulsive animal fear, I ran for the streets, slipped in among a column of Council workers just leaving the place, and got through the gate that way.

When I could think straight again, I was on a pavement among buildings. An SS man came out of one of the houses with a Jewish policeman. The SS man had an impassive, arrogant face; the policeman was positively crawling to him, smiling, dancing attendance. He pointed to the train standing at the *Umschlagplatz* and said to the German, with comradely familiarity and in a sarcastic tone, "Well, off they go for meltdown!"

I looked the way he was pointing. The doors of the trucks had been closed, and the train was starting off, slowly and laboriously.

I turned away and staggered down the empty street, weeping out loud, pursued by the fading cries of the people shut up in those trucks. It sounded like the twittering of caged birds in deadly peril.   [*1946*]

☰ THINKING ABOUT THE TEXT

1. Imagine Szpilman's being interrogated about this scene by Fink's prosecutor. What would this dialogue be like? Try writing it. How credible do *you* find Szpilman's recollection? Refer to specific details of his account.

2. Should Szpilman have felt guilty that he was rescued from the train while his family was not? Why, or why not?

3. The last sentence of this chapter in Szpilman's memoir refers to "the twittering of caged birds in deadly peril." To what extent, and in what ways, can these words be applied to the roundup described by the witnesses in Fink's play?

DORI LAUB AND SHOSHANA FELMAN
Testimony and Historical Truth

Originally from Czernowitz, Romania, Dori Laub (b. 1937) is a clinical professor of psychiatry at the Yale University School of Medicine and a private psychoanalyst. A specialist in psychological trauma, he cofounded the Holocaust Survivors Film Project in 1979. Eventually, this turned into Yale's Fortunoff Video Archive for Holocaust Testimonies, many of which Laub participated in gathering. The following is a section from a book he wrote with literary critic Shoshana Felman, Testimony: Crises of Witnessing in Literature, Psychoanalysis, and History *(1992). He is concerned here with the relationship between personal memory and historical truth.*

A woman in her late sixties was narrating her Auschwitz experience to inter-viewers from the Video Archive for Holocaust Testimonies at Yale. She was slight, self-effacing, almost talking in whispers, mostly to herself. Her presence was indeed barely noteworthy in spite of the overwhelming magnitude of the catastrophe she was addressing. She tread lightly, leaving hardly a trace.

She was relating her memories as an eyewitness of the Auschwitz upris-ing; a sudden intensity, passion, and color were infused into the narrative. She was fully there. "All of sudden," she said, "we saw four chimneys going up in flames, exploding. The flames shot into the sky, people were running. It was unbelievable." There was a silence in the room, a fixed silence against which the woman's words reverberated loudly, as though carrying along an echo of the jubilant sounds exploding from behind barbed wires, a stampede of people breaking loose, screams, shots, battle cries, explosions. It was no longer the deadly timelessness of Auschwitz. A dazzling, brilliant moment from the past swept through the frozen stillness of the muted, grave-like landscape with dash-ing meteoric speed, exploding it into a shower of sights and sounds. Yet the meteor from the past kept moving on. The woman fell silent and the tumults of the moment faded. She became subdued again and her voice resumed the un-eventful, almost monotonous and lamenting tone. The gates of Auschwitz closed and the veil of obliteration and of silence, at once oppressive and repres-sive, descended once again. The comet of intensity and of aliveness, the explo-sion of vitality and of resistance faded and receded into the distance.

Many months later, a conference of historians, psychoanalysts, and art-ists, gathered to reflect on the relation of education to the Holocaust, watched the videotaped testimony of the woman, in an attempt to better understand the era. A lively debate ensued. The testimony was not accurate, historians claimed. The number of chimneys was misrepresented. Historically, only one chimney was blown up, not all four. Since the memory of the testifying woman turned out to be, in this way, fallible, one could not accept—nor give credence to— her whole account of the events. It was utterly important to remain accurate, lest the revisionists in history discredit everything.

A psychoanalyst who had been one of the interviewers of this woman, profoundly disagreed. "The woman was testifying," he insisted, "not to the number of the chimneys blown up, but to something else, more radical, more crucial: the reality of an unimaginable occurrence. One chimney blown up in Auschwitz was as incredible as four. The number mattered less than the fact of the occurrence. The event itself was almost inconceivable. The woman testified to an event that broke the all-compelling frame of Auschwitz, where Jewish armed revolts just did not happen, and had no place. She testified to the break-age of a framework. That was historical truth."

The psychoanalyst who had interviewed that woman happened to have been myself, and though my attitude vis-à-vis her testimony was different than the attitude of the historians, I had myself the opportunity of encountering— during the very process of the interviewing—questions similar in nature to those that the historians were now raising. And yet I had to deal with those objections and those questions in a different manner.

5

I figured from the woman's testimony that in Auschwitz she had been a member of what is known as "the Canada commando," a group of inmates chosen to sort out the belongings of those who had been gassed, so that those belongings could be recuperated by the Nazis and sent back to Germany. The testifying woman spoke indeed at length of her work in a commando that would leave each morning, separately from the others, and return every night with various items of clothes and shoes in excellent condition. She emphasized with pride the way in which, upon returning, she would supply these items to her fellow inmates, thus saving the lives of some of them who literally had no shoes to walk in and no clothes to protect them from the frost. She was perking up again as she described these almost breathtaking exploits of rescue. I asked her if she knew of the name of the commando she was serving on. She did not. Does the term "Canada commando" mean anything to her? I followed up. "No," she said, taken aback, as though startled by my question. I asked nothing more about her work. I had probed the limits of her knowledge and decided to back off; to respect, that is, the silence out of which this testimony spoke. We did not talk of the sorting out of the belongings of the dead. She did not think of them as the remainings of the thousands who were gassed. She did not ask herself where they had come from. The presents she brought back to her fellow inmates, the better, newer clothes and shoes, had for her no origin.

My attempt as interviewer and as listener was precisely to respect — not to upset, not to trespass — the subtle balance between what the woman *knew* and what she *did not,* or *could not, know.* It was only at the price of this respect, I felt, this respect of the constraints and of the boundaries of silence, that what the woman *did know* in a way that none of us did — what she came to testify about — could come forth and could receive, indeed, a hearing. The historians' stance, however, differed from my way of listening, in their firm conviction that the limits of the woman's knowledge in effect called into question the validity of her whole testimony.

"Don't you see," one historian passionately exclaimed, "that the woman's eyewitness account of the uprising that took place at Auschwitz is hopelessly misleading in its incompleteness? She had no idea what was going on. She ascribes importance to an attempt that, historically, made no difference. Not only was the revolt put down and all the inmates executed; the Jewish underground was, furthermore, betrayed by the Polish resistance, which had promised to assist in the rebellion, but failed to do so. When the attempt to break out of the camps began, the Jewish inmates found themselves completely alone. No one joined their ranks. They flung themselves into their death, alone and in desperation."

When I interviewed the woman, I knew, of course, that the Auschwitz uprising was put down, but I myself did not know the specific contribution of the Polish underground to the defeat: I did not know of the extent of the betrayal.

Had I known, however, would I have questioned her about it? Probably   10
not, since such questions might have in effect suppressed her message, suppressed what she was there to tell me.

Had I known, moreover, I might have had an agenda of my own that might have interfered with my ability to listen, and to hear. I might have felt driven to confirm my knowledge, by asking questions that could have derailed the testimony, and by proceeding to hear everything she had to say in light of what I knew already. And whether my agenda would have been historical or psychoanalytical, it might unwittingly have interfered with the process of the testimony. In this respect, it might be useful, sometimes, not to know too much.

Of course, it is by no means ignorance that I espouse. The listener must be quite well informed if he is to be able to hear — to be able to pick up the cues. Yet knowledge should not hinder or obstruct the listening with foregone conclusions and preconceived dismissals, should not be an obstacle or a foreclosure to new, diverging, unexpected information.

In the process of the testimony to a trauma, as in psychoanalytic practice, in effect, you often do not want to know anything except what the patient tells you, because what is important is the situation of *discovery* of knowledge — its evolution, and its very *happening.* Knowledge in the testimony is, in other words, not simply a factual given that is reproduced and replicated by the testifier, but a genuine advent, an event in its own right. In a case such as this witness, for example, I had to be particularly careful that what I knew would not affect — would not obstruct, coerce, or overshadow — what she was there to tell me. I had, in fact, to be all the more cautious because this testifying woman did not simply come to convey knowledge that was already safely, and exhaustively, in her possession. On the contrary, it was her very talk to me, the very process of her bearing witness to the trauma she had lived through, that helped her now to come to know of the event. And it was through my listening to her that I in turn came to understand not merely her subjective truth, but the very historicity of the event, in an entirely new dimension.

She was testifying not simply to empirical historical facts, but to the very secret of survival and of resistance to extermination. The historians could not hear, I thought, the way in which her silence was itself part of her testimony, an essential part of the historical truth she was precisely bearing witness to. She saw four chimneys blowing up in Auschwitz: she saw, in other words, the unimaginable taking place right in front of her own eyes. And she came to testify to the unbelievability, precisely, of what she had eyewitnessed — this bursting open of the very frame of Auschwitz. The historians' testifying to the fact that only one chimney was blown up in Auschwitz, as well as to the fact of the betrayal of the Polish underground, does not break the frame. The woman's testimony, on the other hand, is breaking the frame of the concentration camp by and through her very testimony: she is breaking out of Auschwitz even by her very talking. She had come, indeed, to testify, not to the empirical number of the chimneys, but to resistance, to the affirmation of survival, to the breakage of the frame of death; in the same way, she had come to testify not to betrayal, nor to her actual removal of the belongings of the dead, but to her vital memory of helping people, to her effective rescuing of lives. This was her way of being, of surviving, of resisting. It is not merely her speech, but the very boundaries of silence which surround it, which attest, today as well as in the past, to this assertion of resistance.

There is thus a subtle dialectic between what the survivor did not know   15 and what she knew; between what I as interviewer did not know and what I knew; between what the historians knew and what they did not know. Because the testifier did not know the number of the chimneys that blew up; because she did not know of the betrayal of the Polish underground and of the violent and desperate defeat of the rebellion of the Auschwitz inmates, the historians said that she knew nothing. I thought that she knew more, since she knew about the breakage of the frame, that her very testimony was now reenacting.   [1992]

≡ THINKING ABOUT THE TEXT

1. In part, Laub writes about what it means to be a "good" listener for a Holocaust survivor. Would Fink's prosecutor meet Laub's standards? Why, or why not?

2. How might the responsibility of a prosecutor or judge listening to a Holocaust survivor differ from that of a psychoanalyst? Refer to details of both Fink's play and Laub's text.

3. Do any of the witnesses in Fink's play seem to go through the "breakage of the frame" that Laub refers to? Explain.

≡ WRITING ABOUT ISSUES

1. Do research on the Nuremberg trials held after World War II. Describe the charges, the defendants, and the purpose and procedures of these trials, and argue that justice was or was not served.

2. Do research on the Eichmann trial in Jerusalem in the early 1960s. Describe the circumstances, procedures, and outcome, and argue that justice was or was not served.

3. Do research on war atrocities since World War II and the role of the World Court in The Hague. Write an essay that argues that such an institution is necessary or not. Include such ideas as what concept of justice is at work here. Is justice a universal concept? Can those accused be held accountable if they didn't violate their own country's values?

4. Do research on the concept of restorative justice in South Africa after the abolition of apartheid. Write an essay that argues that this concept is or is not a better way to deal with such gross injustices as the Holocaust.

CHAPTER 11

Journeys

Perhaps no impulse is as ancient and as natural as the desire to leave one's home, to journey out of the village to unknown lands. Ancient epics like the *Iliad* and the *Odyssey* and more modern tales like Mark Twain's *Adventures of Huckleberry Finn* and Jack Kerouac's *On the Road* are narratives of wandering, encountering the strange and the wondrous. Sometimes the journey has a specific goal, a quest for riches, for fame, or for adventure. Sometimes the journey is simply for escape, for curiosity's sake, for an understanding of the wider world. Of course the idea of the journey easily lends itself to both the literal and the metaphorical, to quests external and internal. We all take journeys of self-discovery from childhood to adolescence to adulthood and eventually to death. Life as a journey is a notion deeply woven into our cultural understanding from Greek mythology, epics, novels, religious beliefs, and popular culture.

It is no surprise then that writers for thousands of years have written about their perilous journeys to dangerous places, their contemplative journeys to self-reflection and wisdom, as well as their imaginative treks to dystopic futures. Our selections in this chapter work with an expansive idea of the journey, featuring work from Eudora Welty's classic short story "A Worn Path" to Kurt Vonnegut's journey to a harrowing future. For some the journey is quite literal; for others the path is decidedly metaphorical. Like the dancers in the Eagles' song "Hotel California," some writers journey to remember, others to forget. Whether the journey is the writer's own or a fictional one a character takes, the creative leap is always thoughtful, illuminating, and moving.

The chapter begins with two story clusters. The first pairs classic tales about adults apparently making journeys to help sick children. The second, which follows the burdened steps of a soldier and his comrades during the American war in Vietnam, is echoed in a mother's accompanying news article about her son's deploying to a more recent war. Then four poetry clusters ensue: three famous journey poems by Robert Frost; three poetic responses to William Stafford's haunting poem "Traveling through the Dark"; three metaphorical meditations on ferry rides; and four poems that wrestle with the final journey we all take. The next cluster presents two essays that argue about journeys we make—or don't make—in our digitally connected environments. Finally, a story presents a difficult stop on the narrator's journey to adulthood in pre–civil rights America; accompanying historical documents draw out some of the issues on the hard road to racial equality and suggest avenues for further research and writing.

WILLIAM CARLOS WILLIAMS, "The Use of Force"

EUDORA WELTY, "A Worn Path"

Although both of the well-known stories in this cluster start out as errands of mercy, they have quite different endings. Doctors are almost always portrayed in a favorable light in popular culture. And because they are sometimes the difference between life and death, they enjoy an elevated status in the culture. We think highly of them and expect them, perhaps unfairly, to be both paragons of compassion and professionally dispassionate. William Carlos Williams's story, however, reminds us that doctors are also human and can act in unprofessional ways, even with the best of intentions. "The Use of Force" is a disturbing tale that typically elicits a wide range of responses from readers. Perhaps Eudora Welty's tale of mercy, "A Worn Path," is not as unsettling as Williams's story, but it is as open to widely different interpretation. Phoenix Jackson, one of literature's most memorable characters, endures her difficult trek at Christmastime to buy medicine for her grandson, who may or may not be alive. Seen as everything from religious pilgrimage to civil rights allegory, Phoenix is a symbol for many things to many readers.

≣ BEFORE YOU READ

In what ways does our popular culture portray doctors? What specific guidance were you given as a child in regard to mercy or compassion or self-sacrifice? How does our culture reward mercy and compassion? Recount an incident where you were forced to do something "for your own good." What was your response?

WILLIAM CARLOS WILLIAMS
The Use of Force

William Carlos Williams (1883–1963) was an American poet and fiction writer usually thought of as a modernist closely associated with the imagists. His brief poem, "The Red Wheelbarrow," is one of the most famous in literature. Williams was born in New Jersey and received his medical degree from the University of Pennsylvania in 1906. His first book, Poems, *was published in 1909. Williams's main occupation was as a family doctor, but he had a successful literary career and was well known and respected among the leading writers of the day. He championed poetry as "equipment for living" and felt his own career was overshadowed by the highly intellectual and allusive style of T. S. Eliot, especially the highly influential "The Waste Land." Williams also wrote a number of novels and short story and essay collections. The following popular story was published on the eve of World War II and explores themes of responsibility, restraint, domination, submission, and the consequences of violence.*

They were new patients to me, all I had was the name, Olson. Please come down as soon as you can, my daughter is very sick. When I arrived I was met by the mother, a big startled looking woman, very clean and apologetic who merely said, Is this the doctor? and let me in. In the back, she added. You must excuse us, doctor, we have her in the kitchen where it is warm. It is very damp here sometimes.

The child was fully dressed and sitting on her father's lap near the kitchen table. He tried to get up, but I motioned for him not to bother, took off my overcoat and started to look things over. I could see that they were all very nervous, eyeing me up and down distrustfully. As often, in such cases, they weren't telling me more than they had to, it was up to me to tell them; that's why they were spending three dollars on me.

The child was fairly eating me up with her cold, steady eyes, and no expression to her face whatever. She did not move and seemed, inwardly, quiet; an unusually attractive little thing, and as strong as a heifer in appearance. But her face was flushed, she was breathing rapidly, and I realized that she had a high fever. She had magnificent blond hair, in profusion. One of those picture children often reproduced in advertising leaflets and the photogravure sections of the Sunday papers.

She's had a fever for three days, began the father and we don't know what it comes from. My wife has given her things, you know, like people do, but it don't do no good. And there's been a lot of sickness around. So we tho't you'd better look her over and tell us what is the matter.

As doctors often do I took a trial shot at it as a point of departure. Has she had a sore throat?   5

Both parents answered me together, No . . . No, she says her throat don't hurt her.

Does your throat hurt you? added the mother to the child. But the little girl's expression didn't change nor did she move her eyes from my face.

Have you looked?

I tried to, said the mother, but I couldn't see.

As it happens we had been having a number of cases of diphtheria in the   10 school to which the child went during that month and we were all, quite apparently, thinking of that, though no one had as yet spoken of the thing.

Well, I said, suppose we take a look at the throat first. I smiled in my best professional manner and asking for the child's first name I said, come on, Mathilda, open your mouth and let's take a look at your throat.

Nothing doing.

Aw, come on, I coaxed, just open your mouth wide and let me take a look. Look, I said opening both hands wide, I haven't anything in my hands. Just open up and let me see.

Such a nice man, put in the mother. Look how kind he is to you. Come on, do what he tells you to, he won't hurt you.

At that I ground my teeth in disgust. If only they wouldn't use the word   15 "hurt" I might be able to get somewhere. But I did not allow myself to be hurried or disturbed but speaking quietly and slowly I approached the child again.

As I moved my chair a little nearer suddenly with one catlike movement both her hands clawed instinctively for my eyes and she almost reached them too. In fact she knocked my glasses flying and they fell, though unbroken, several feet away from me on the kitchen floor.

Both the mother and father almost turned themselves inside out in embarrassment and apology. You bad girl, said the mother, taking her and shaking her by one arm. Look what you've done. The nice man . . .

For heaven's sake, I broke in. Don't call me a nice man to her. I'm here to look at her throat on the chance that she might have diphtheria and possibly die of it. But that's nothing to her. Look here, I said to the child, we're going to look at your throat. You're old enough to understand what I'm saying. Will you open it now by yourself or shall we have to open it for you?

Not a move. Even her expression hadn't changed. Her breaths however were coming faster and faster. Then the battle began. I had to do it. I had to have a throat culture for her own protection. But first I told the parents that it was entirely up to them. I explained the danger but said that I would not insist on a throat examination so long as they would take the responsibility.

If you don't do what the doctor says you'll have to go to the hospital, the   20
mother admonished her severely.

Oh yeah? I had to smile to myself. After all, I had already fallen in love with the savage brat, the parents were contemptible to me. In the ensuing struggle they grew more and more abject, crushed, exhausted while she surely rose to magnificent heights of insane fury of effort bred of her terror of me.

The father tried his best, and he was a big man but the fact that she was his daughter, his shame at her behavior and his dread of hurting her made him release her just at the critical times when I had almost achieved success, till I wanted to kill him. But his dread also that she might have diphtheria made him tell me to go on, go on though he himself was almost fainting, while the mother moved back and forth behind us raising and lowering her hands in an agony of apprehension.

Put her in front of you on your lap, I ordered, and hold both her wrists.

But as soon as he did the child let out a scream. Don't, you're hurting me. Let go of my hands. Let them go I tell you. Then she shrieked terrifyingly, hysterically. Stop it! Stop it! You're killing me!

Do you think she can stand it, doctor! said the mother.   25

You get out, said the husband to his wife. Do you want her to die of diphtheria?

Come on now, hold her, I said.

Then I grasped the child's head with my left hand and tried to get the wooden tongue depressor between her teeth. She fought, with clenched teeth, desperately! But now I also had grown furious — at a child. I tried to hold myself down but I couldn't. I know how to expose a throat for inspection. And I did my best. When finally I got the wooden spatula behind the last teeth and just the point of it into the mouth cavity, she opened up for an instant but before I could see anything she came down again and gripped the wooden blade between her molars. She reduced it to splinters before I could get it out again.

Aren't you ashamed, the mother yelled at her. Aren't you ashamed to act like that in front of the doctor?

Get me a smooth-handled spoon of some sort, I told the mother. We're go-   30
ing through with this. The child's mouth was already bleeding. Her tongue was cut and she was screaming in wild hysterical shrieks. Perhaps I should have desisted and come back in an hour or more. No doubt it would have been better. But I have seen at least two children lying dead in bed of neglect in such cases, and feeling that I must get a diagnosis now or never I went at it again. But the worst of it was that I too had got beyond reason. I could have torn the child apart in my own fury and enjoyed it. It was a pleasure to attack her. My face was burning with it.

The damned little brat must be protected against her own idiocy, one says to one's self at such times. Others must be protected against her. It is a social necessity. And all these things are true. But a blind fury, a feeling of adult shame, bred of a longing for muscular release are the operatives. One goes on to the end.

In the final unreasoning assault I overpowered the child's neck and jaws. I forced the heavy silver spoon back of her teeth and down her throat till she gagged. And there it was—both tonsils covered with membrane. She had fought valiantly to keep me from knowing her secret. She had been hiding that sore throat for three days at least and lying to her parents in order to escape just such an outcome as this.

Now truly she was furious. She had been on the defensive before but now she attacked. Tried to get off her father's lap and fly at me while tears of defeat blinded her eyes.   *[1938]*

≣ THINKING ABOUT THE TEXT

1. Describe the conflicting emotions of the doctor and the little girl.

2. What can be said to justify the doctor's actions? What can be said to criticize the doctor's actions? What can be said to justify the girl's actions? What can be said to criticize the girl's actions?

3. Why would some critics think the idea of being blind in all its literal and metaphorical meanings is a key idea in this story?

4. Explain the doctor's relationship to the child's parents. Why at one point does the doctor say about the father, "I wanted to kill him" (para. 22)?

5. What possible comment on human nature does the story make? What might the story be saying about the consequence of violence?

EUDORA WELTY
A Worn Path

Eudora Welty (1909–2001)—who was born, raised, and died in Jackson, Missis-
sippi—is considered one of the twentieth century's most gifted short-story writ-
ers. She studied at the University of Wisconsin and Columbia University and worked
for the New York Times Book Review *during World War II. During this time, she*
began writing stories for the Southern Review. *Soon after one of her stories ap-*
peared in the Atlantic Monthly, *she published her first collection in 1941,* A Curtain of Green, *which was followed by* The Wide Net and Other Stories *(1943).*
Her first novel was Delta Wedding *(1946). Another novel,* The Optimist's Daughter *(1972), won the Pulitzer Prize. Although Welty herself admitted that she led a*
sheltered life, her critics have always been impressed by her lyrical portrayal of the
complexities of the heart's emotional truths. "A Worn Path" received an O. Henry
Award in 1941.

It was December—a bright frozen day in the early morning. Far out in the
country there was an old Negro woman with her head tied in a red rag, coming
along a path through the pinewoods. Her name was Phoenix Jackson. She was
very old and small and she walked slowly in the dark pine shadows, moving a
little from side to side in her steps, with the balanced heaviness and lightness of
a pendulum in a grandfather clock. She carried a thin, small cane made from
an umbrella, and with this she kept tapping the frozen earth in front of her.
This made a grave and persistent noise in the still air, that seemed meditative
like the chirping of a solitary little bird.

She wore a dark striped dress reaching down to her shoe tops, and an
equally long apron of bleached sugar sacks, with a full pocket: all neat and tidy,
but every time she took a step she might have fallen over her shoelaces, which
dragged from her unlaced shoes. She looked straight ahead. Her eyes were blue
with age. Her skin had a pattern all its own of numberless branching wrinkles
and as though a whole little tree stood in the middle of her forehead, but a
golden color ran underneath, and the two knobs of her cheeks were illumined
by a yellow burning under the dark. Under the red rag her hair came down on
her neck in the frailest of ringlets, still black, and with an odor like copper.

Now and then there was a quivering in the thicket. Old Phoenix said, "Out
of my way, all you foxes, owls, beetles, jack rabbits, coons, and wild animals! . . .
Keep out from under these feet, little bobwhites. . . . Keep the big wild hogs out
of my path. Don't let none of those come running my direction. I got a long
way." Under her small black-freckled hand her cane, limber as a buggy whip,
would switch at the brush as if to rouse up any hiding things.

On she went. The woods were deep and still. The sun made the pine needles
almost too bright to look at, up where the wind rocked. The cones dropped as
light as feathers. Down in the hollow was the mourning dove—it was not too
late for him.

The path ran up a hill. "Seem like there is chains about my feet, time I   5
get this far," she said, in the voice of argument old people keep to use with
themselves. "Something always take a hold of me on this hill—pleads I
should stay."

After she got to the top she turned and gave a full, severe look behind her
where she had come. "Up through pines," she said at length. "Now down
through oaks."

Her eyes opened their widest, and she started down gently. But before she
got to the bottom of the hill a bush caught her dress.

Her fingers were busy and intent, but her skirts were full and long, so that
before she could pull them free in one place they were caught in another. It was
not possible to allow the dress to tear. "I in the thorny bush," she said. "Thorns,
you doing your appointed work. Never want to let folks pass, no sir. Old eyes
thought you was a pretty little *green* bush."

Finally, trembling all over, she stood free, and after a moment dared to
stoop for her cane.

"Sun so high!" she cried, leaning back and looking, while the thick tears   10
went over her eyes. "The time getting all gone here."

At the foot of this hill was a place where a log was laid across the creek.

"Now comes the trial," said Phoenix.

Putting her right foot out, she mounted the log and shut her eyes. Lifting
her skirt, leveling her cane fiercely before her, like a festival figure in some parade, she began to march across. Then she opened her eyes and she was safe on
the other side.

"I wasn't as old as I thought," she said.

But she sat down to rest. She spread her skirts on the bank around her and   15
folded her hands over her knees. Up above her was a tree in a pearly cloud of
mistletoe. She did not dare to close her eyes, and when a little boy brought her
a plate with a slice of marble-cake on it she spoke to him. "That would be acceptable," she said. But when she went to take it there was just her own hand
in the air.

So she left that tree, and had to go through a barbed-wire fence. There she
had to creep and crawl, spreading her knees and stretching her fingers like a
baby trying to climb the steps. But she talked loudly to herself: she could not let
her dress be torn now, so late in the day, and she could not pay for having her
arm or her leg sawed off if she got caught fast where she was.

At last she was safe through the fence and risen up out in the clearing. Big
dead trees, like black men with one arm, were standing in the purple stalks of
the withered cotton field. There sat a buzzard.

"Who you watching?"

In the furrow she made her way along.

"Glad this not the season for bulls," she said, looking sideways, "and the   20
good Lord made his snakes to curl up and sleep in the winter. A pleasure I don't
see no two-headed snake coming around that tree, where it come once. It took
a while to get by him, back in the summer."

She passed through the old cotton and went into a field of dead corn. It whispered and shook and was taller than her head. "Through the maze now," she said, for there was no path.

Then there was something tall, black, and skinny there, moving before her.

At first she took it for a man. It could have been a man dancing in the field. But she stood still and listened, and it did not make a sound. It was as silent as a ghost.

"Ghost," she said sharply, "who be you the ghost of? For I have heard of nary death close by."

But there was no answer—only the ragged dancing in the wind.   25

She shut her eyes, reached out her hand, and touched a sleeve. She found a coat and inside that an emptiness, cold as ice.

"You scarecrow," she said. Her face lighted. "I ought to be shut up for good," she said with laughter. "My senses is gone. I too old. I the oldest people I ever know. Dance, old scarecrow," she said, "while I dancing with you."

She kicked her foot over the furrow, and with mouth drawn down, shook her head once or twice in a little strutting way. Some husks blew down and whirled in streamers about her skirts.

Then she went on, parting her way from side to side with the cane, through the whispering field. At last she came to the end, to a wagon track where the silver grass blew between the red ruts. The quail were walking around like pullets, seeming all dainty and unseen.

"Walk pretty," she said. "This the easy place. This the easy going."   30

She followed the track, swaying through the quiet bare fields, through the little strings of trees silver in their dead leaves, past cabins silver from weather, with the doors and windows boarded shut, all like old women under a spell sitting there. "I walking in their sleep," she said, nodding her head vigorously.

In a ravine she went where a spring was silently flowing through a hollow log. Old Phoenix bent and drank. "Sweet-gum makes the water sweet," she said, and drank more. "Nobody know who made this well, for it was here when I was born."

The track crossed a swampy part where the moss hung as white as lace from every limb. "Sleep on, alligators, and blow your bubbles." Then the track went into the road.

Deep, deep the road went down between the high green-colored banks. Overhead the live-oaks met, and it was as dark as a cave.

A black dog with a lolling tongue came up out of the weeds by the ditch.   35
She was meditating, and not ready, and when he came at her she only hit him a little with her cane. Over she went in the ditch, like a little puff of milkweed.

Down there, her senses drifted away. A dream visited her, and she reached her hand up, but nothing reached down and gave her a pull. So she lay there and presently went to talking. "Old woman," she said to herself, "that black dog come up out of the weeds to stall you off, and now there he sitting on his fine tail, smiling at you."

A white man finally came along and found her—a hunter, a young man, with his dog on a chain.

"Well, Granny!" he laughed. "What are you doing there?"

"Lying on my back like a June-bug waiting to be turned over, mister," she said, reaching up her hand.

He lifted her up, gave her a swing in the air, and set her down. "Anything broken, Granny?"   40

"No sir, them old dead weeds is springy enough," said Phoenix, when she had got her breath. "I thank you for your trouble."

"Where do you live, Granny?" he asked, while the two dogs were growling at each other.

"Away back yonder, sir, behind the ridge. You can't even see it from here."

"On your way home?"

"No sir, I going to town."   45

"Why, that's too far! That's as far as I walk when I come out myself, and I get something for my trouble." He patted the stuffed bag he carried, and there hung down a little closed claw. It was one of the bobwhites, with its beak hooked bitterly to show it was dead. "Now you go on home, Granny!"

"I bound to go to town, mister," said Phoenix. "The time come around."

He gave another laugh, filling the whole landscape. "I know you old colored people! Wouldn't miss going to town to see Santa Claus!"

But something held old Phoenix very still. The deep lines in her face went into a fierce and different radiation. Without warning, she had seen with her own eyes a flashing nickel fall out of the man's pocket onto the ground.

"How old are you, Granny?" he was saying.   50

"There is no telling, mister," she said, "no telling."

Then she gave a little cry and clapped her hands and said, "Git on away from here, dog! Look! Look at that dog!" She laughed as if in admiration. "He ain't scared of nobody. He a big black dog." She whispered, "Sic him!"

"Watch me get rid of that cur," said the man. "Sic him, Pete! Sic him!"

Phoenix heard the dogs fighting, and heard the man running and throwing sticks. She even heard a gunshot. But she was slowly bending forward by that time, further and further forward, the lid stretched down over her eyes, as if she were doing this in her sleep. Her chin was lowered almost to her knees. The yellow palm of her hand came out from the fold of her apron. Her fingers slid down and along the ground under the piece of money with the grace and care they would have in lifting an egg from under a setting hen. Then she slowly straightened up, she stood erect, and the nickel was in her apron pocket. A bird flew by. Her lips moved. "God watching me the whole time. I come to stealing."

The man came back, and his own dog panted about them. "Well, I scared   55
him off that time," he said, and then he laughed and lifted his gun and pointed it at Phoenix.

She stood straight and faced him.

"Doesn't the gun scare you?" he said, still pointing it.

"No, sir, I seen plenty go off closer by, in my day, and for less than what I done," she said, holding utterly still.

He smiled, and shouldered the gun. "Well, Granny," he said, "you must be a hundred years old, and scared of nothing. I'd give you a dime if I had any money with me. But you take my advice and stay home, and nothing will happen to you."

"I bound to go on my way, mister," said Phoenix. She inclined her head in the red rag. Then they went in different directions, but she could hear the gun shooting again and again over the hill.

She walked on. The shadows hung from the oak trees to the road like curtains. Then she smelled wood-smoke, and smelled the river, and she saw a steeple and the cabins on their steep steps. Dozens of little black children whirled around her. There ahead was Natchez shining. Bells were ringing. She walked on.

In the paved city it was Christmas time. There were red and green electric lights strung and crisscrossed everywhere, and all turned on in the daytime. Old Phoenix would have been lost if she had not distrusted her eyesight and depended on her feet to know where to take her.

She paused quietly on the sidewalk where people were passing by. A lady came along in the crowd, carrying an armful of red-, green-, and silver-wrapped presents; she gave off perfume like the red roses in hot summer, and Phoenix stopped her.

"Please, missy, will you lace up my shoe?" She held up her foot.

"What do you want, Grandma?"

"See my shoe," said Phoenix. "Do all right for out in the country, but wouldn't look right to go in a big building."

"Stand still then, Grandma," said the lady. She put her packages down on the sidewalk beside her and laced and tied both shoes tightly.

"Can't lace 'em with a cane," said Phoenix. "Thank you, missy. I doesn't mind asking a nice lady to tie up my shoe, when I gets out on the street."

Moving slowly and from side to side, she went into the big building, and into a tower of steps, where she walked up and around and around until her feet knew to stop.

She entered a door, and there she saw nailed up on the wall the document that had been stamped with the gold seal and framed in the gold frame, which matched the dream that was hung up in her head.

"Here I be," she said. There was a fixed and ceremonial stiffness over her body.

"A charity case, I suppose," said an attendant who sat at the desk before her.

But Phoenix only looked above her head. There was sweat on her face, the wrinkles in her skin shone like a bright net.

"Speak up, Grandma," the woman said. "What's your name? We must have your history, you know. Have you been here before? What seems to be the trouble with you?"

Old Phoenix only gave a twitch to her face as if a fly were bothering her.

"Are you deaf?" cried the attendant.

But then the nurse came in.

"Oh, that's just old Aunt Phoenix," she said. "She doesn't come for herself — she has a little grandson. She makes these trips just as regular as clockwork. She lives away back off the Old Natchez Trace." She bent down. "Well, Aunt Phoenix, why don't you just take a seat? We won't keep you standing after your long trip." She pointed.

The old woman sat down, bolt upright in the chair.

"Now, how is the boy?" asked the nurse.   80

Old Phoenix did not speak.

"I said, how is the boy?"

But Phoenix only waited and stared straight ahead, her face very solemn and withdrawn into rigidity.

"Is his throat any better?" asked the nurse. "Aunt Phoenix, don't you hear me? Is your grandson's throat any better since the last time you came for the medicine?"

With her hands on her knees, the old woman waited, silent, erect, and mo-   85
tionless, just as if she were in armor.

"You mustn't take up our time this way, Aunt Phoenix," the nurse said. "Tell us quickly about your grandson, and get it over. He isn't dead, is he?"

At last there came a flicker and then a flame of comprehension across her face, and she spoke.

"My grandson. It was my memory had left me. There I sat and forgot why I made my long trip."

"Forgot?" The nurse frowned. "After you came so far?"

Then Phoenix was like an old woman begging a dignified forgiveness for   90
waking up frightened in the night. "I never did go to school, I was too old at the Surrender,"° she said in a soft voice. "I'm an old woman without an education. It was my memory fail me. My little grandson, he is just the same, and I forgot it in the coming."

"Throat never heals, does it?" said the nurse, speaking in a loud, sure voice to old Phoenix. By now she had a card with something written on it, a little list. "Yes. Swallowed lye. When was it?—January—two, three years ago—"

Phoenix spoke unasked now. "No, missy, he not dead, he just the same. Every little while his throat began to close up again, and he not able to swallow. He not get his breath. He not able to help himself. So the time come around, and I go on another trip for the soothing medicine."

"All right. The doctor said as long as you came to get it, you could have it," said the nurse. "But it's an obstinate case."

"My little grandson, he sit up there in the house all wrapped up, waiting by himself," Phoenix went on. "We is the only two left in the world. He suffer and it don't seem to put him back at all. He got a sweet look. He going to last. He wear a little patch quilt and peep out holding his mouth open like a little bird. I remembers so plain now. I not going to forget him again, no, the whole enduring time. I could tell him from all the others in creation."

"All right." The nurse was trying to hush her now. She brought her a bottle   95
of medicine. "Charity," she said, making a check mark in a book.

---

the Surrender: On April 9, 1865, General Robert E. Lee surrendered to General Ulysses S. Grant, at Appomattox, Virginia, ending the Civil War.

Old Phoenix held the bottle close to her eyes, and then carefully put it into her pocket.

"I thank you," she said.

"It's Christmas time, Grandma," said the attendant. "Could I give you a few pennies out of my purse?"

"Five pennies is a nickel," said Phoenix stiffly.

"Here's a nickel," said the attendant.

Phoenix rose carefully and held out her hand. She received the nickel and then fished the other nickel out of her pocket and laid it beside the new one. She stared at her palm closely, with her head on one side.

Then she gave a tap with her cane on the floor.

"This is what come to me to do," she said. "I going to the store and buy my child a little windmill they sells, made out of paper. He going to find it hard to believe there such a thing in the world. I'll march myself back where he waiting, holding it straight up in this hand."

She lifted her free hand, gave a little nod, turned around, and walked out of the doctor's office. Then her slow step began on the stairs, going down.

[1941]

≡ THINKING ABOUT THE TEXT

1. Comment on the old woman's name; in a tale about a journey, it seems to have allegorical significance.

2. Phoenix meets a hunter on her trek. Comment on the significant details of their encounter.

3. Phoenix speaks directly to a number of things. What are they, and what allegorical significance might they have?

4. Welty has claimed that the most frequent question she was asked about this story was whether Phoenix's grandson is really dead. Her answer is that, either way, the meaning of this story would not be affected. What do you think she means?

5. Google "A Worn Path" and look at the scores of images associated with the story. Describe three of them and explain why they are apt.

≡ MAKING COMPARISONS

1. Compare the errands of mercy of Phoenix and the doctor.

2. In "The Use of Force" the doctor says, "One goes on to the end" (para. 31). Compare the significance of this idea in both stories.

3. Both Phoenix and the doctor start their journey with the best of intentions. It may be that Phoenix's specific mission is in vain. It may also be that the doctor's mission has mixed results. Explain these ideas.

≡ **WRITING ABOUT ISSUES**

1. Argue that the doctor is or is not at fault in "The Use of Force."

2. Write an essay that sees symbolic significance in the journey of Phoenix Jackson. Be sure to use specific incidents from the story to support your position.

3. Write an essay that compares the errands of mercy of Phoenix and the doctor. Make a judgment about their goals, their ethics, their missions, their characters, and anything else that seems relevant.

4. Locate and read Eudora Welty's essay, "Is Phoenix Jackson's Grandson Really Dead?" and write an argumentative essay that either agrees or disagrees with her conclusion. (The essay originally appeared in the September 1974 issue of *Critical Inquiry*.)

A Journey to War: A Story in the News

TIM O'BRIEN, "The Things They Carried"

IN THE NEWS:
VALERIE SEILING JACOBS, "Packing for the Ineffable"

Throughout history, soldiers have had to defend their native regions against invaders. Just as commonly, armies have journeyed far from home, to wage war in distant countries. And upon arriving there, they have wandered even farther, their sites of battle shifting as they engage their enemy. During these various physical treks, many of them have displayed incredible endurance and bravery. But some have become mentally dislocated, finding themselves on a confusing and unpredictable journey of the mind. This can be especially true when the soldier is barely mature and the war's aim is unclear. Such was the case for many Americans who fought in Vietnam, as Tim O'Brien suggests in his now-classic story "The Things They Carried." Its characters risk becoming psychologically lost as they roam a land strange and dangerous to them, serving missions whose aims are vague. Decades later, Americans sent to fight in Iraq and Afghanistan have often faced similar stress. To help you compare *their* journeys with the ones that O'Brien depicts, we pair his story with a 2007 newspaper column in which the author reflects on the things her stepson carried off to war.

≡ BEFORE YOU READ

What do you associate with the United States' war in Vietnam? List specific details that come to mind. To what extent do the present wars in Iraq and Afghanistan strike you as similar to that one?

TIM O'BRIEN
The Things They Carried

A native of Minnesota, Tim O'Brien (b. 1946) was drafted after he graduated from Macalester College. Subsequently, he served in the Vietnam War, during which he received a Purple Heart. In one way or another, practically all of his fiction deals with the war, although he has been repeatedly ambiguous about how and when his work incorporates his own Vietnam experiences. O'Brien's novels include If I Die in a Combat Zone *(1973),* Going After Cacciato *(which won the National Book Award in 1978),* In the Lake of the Woods *(a 1994 book that touches on the massacre at My Lai),* Tomcat in Love *(1998), and* July *(2002). Originally published in* Esquire *magazine, the following story was reprinted in* The Best American Short Stories 1987. *It then appeared along with related stories by O'Brien in a 1990 book also entitled* The Things They Carried.

(Bill Giduz Photo.)

First Lieutenant Jimmy Cross carried letters from a girl named Martha, a junior at Mount Sebastian College in New Jersey. They were not love letters, but Lieutenant Cross was hoping, so he kept them folded in plastic at the bottom of his rucksack. In the late afternoon, after a day's march, he would dig his foxhole, wash his hands under a canteen, unwrap the letters, hold them with the tips of his fingers, and spend the last hour of light pretending. He would imagine romantic camping trips into the White Mountains in New Hampshire. He would sometimes taste the envelope flaps, knowing her tongue had been there. More than anything, he wanted Martha to love him as he loved her, but the letters were mostly chatty, elusive on the matter of love. She was a virgin, he was almost sure. She was an English major at Mount Sebastian, and she wrote beautifully about her professors and roommates and midterm exams, about her respect for Chaucer and her great affection for Virginia Woolf. She often quoted lines of poetry; she never mentioned the war, except to say, Jimmy, take care of yourself. The letters weighed ten ounces. They were signed "Love, Martha," but Lieutenant Cross understood that "Love" was only a way of signing and did not mean what he sometimes pretended it meant. At dusk, he would carefully return the letters to his rucksack. Slowly, a bit distracted, he would get up and move among his men, checking the perimeter, then at full dark he would return to his hole and watch the night and wonder if Martha was a virgin.

The things they carried were largely determined by necessity. Among the necessities or near necessities were P-38 can openers, pocket knives, heat tabs, wrist watches, dog tags, mosquito repellant, chewing gum, candy, cigarettes, salt tablets, packets of Kool-Aid, lighters, matches, sewing kits, Military Payment Certificates, C rations, and two or three canteens of water. Together, these items weighed between fifteen and twenty pounds, depending upon a man's habits or rate of metabolism. Henry Dobbins, who was a big man, carried extra rations; he was especially fond of canned peaches in heavy syrup over pound cake. Dave Jensen, who practiced field hygiene, carried a toothbrush, dental floss, and several hotel-size bars of soap he'd stolen on R&R in Sydney, Australia. Ted Lavender, who was scared, carried tranquilizers until he was shot in the head outside the village of Than Khe in mid-April. By necessity and because it was SOP,° they all carried steel helmets that weighed five pounds including the liner and camouflage cover. They carried the standard fatigue jackets and trousers. Very few carried underwear. On their feet they carried jungle boots — 2.1 pounds — and Dave Jensen carried three pairs of socks and a can of Dr. Scholl's foot powder as a precaution against trench foot. Until he was shot, Ted Lavender carried six or seven ounces of premium dope, which for him was a necessity. Mitchell Sanders, the RTO,° carried condoms. Norman Bowker carried a diary. Rat Kiley carried comic books. Kiowa, a devout Baptist, carried an illustrated New Testament that had been presented to him by his father, who taught Sunday school in Oklahoma City, Oklahoma. As a hedge against bad times, however, Kiowa also carried his grandmother's distrust of the white man, his grandfather's old hunting hatchet. Necessity dictated. Because the land was mined and booby-trapped, it was SOP for each man to carry a steel-centered, nylon-covered flak jacket, which weighed 6.7 pounds, but which on hot days seemed much heavier. Because you could die so quickly, each man carried at least one large compress bandage, usually in the helmet band for easy access. Because the nights were cold, and because the monsoons were wet, each carried a green plastic poncho that could be used as a raincoat or ground sheet or makeshift tent. With its quilted liner, the poncho weighed almost two pounds, but it was worth every ounce. In April, for instance, when Ted Lavender was shot, they used his poncho to wrap him up, then to carry him across the paddy, then to lift him into the chopper that took him away.

They were called legs or grunts.

To carry something was to "hump" it, as when Lieutenant Jimmy Cross humped his love for Martha up the hills and through the swamps. In its intransitive form, "to hump" meant "to walk," or "to march," but it implied burdens far beyond the intransitive.

Almost everyone humped photographs. In his wallet, Lieutenant Cross   5
carried two photographs of Martha. The first was a Kodachrome snapshot signed "Love," though he knew better. She stood against a brick wall. Her eyes were gray and neutral, her lips slightly open as she stared straight-on at the camera. At night, sometimes, Lieutenant Cross wondered who had taken the picture, because he knew she had boyfriends, because he loved her so much, and because he could see the shadow of the picture taker spreading out against

SOP: Standard operating procedure.   **RTO:** Radiotelephone operator.

the brick wall. The second photograph had been clipped from the 1968 Mount Sebastian yearbook. It was an action shot—women's volleyball—and Martha was bent horizontal to the floor, reaching, the palms of her hands in sharp focus, the tongue taut, the expression frank and competitive. There was no visible sweat. She wore white gym shorts. Her legs, he thought, were almost certainly the legs of a virgin, dry and without hair, the left knee cocked and carrying her entire weight, which was just over one hundred pounds. Lieutenant Cross remembered touching that left knee. A dark theater, he remembered, and the movie was *Bonnie and Clyde*, and Martha wore a tweed skirt, and during the final scene, when he touched her knee, she turned and looked at him in a sad, sober way that made him pull his hand back, but he would always remember the feel of the tweed skirt and the knee beneath it and the sound of the gunfire that killed Bonnie and Clyde, how embarrassing it was, how slow and oppressive. He remembered kissing her good night at the dorm door. Right then, he thought, he should've done something brave. He should've carried her up the stairs to her room and tied her to the bed and touched that left knee all night long. He should've risked it. Whenever he looked at the photographs, he thought of new things he should've done.

What they carried was partly a function of rank, partly of field specialty.

As a first lieutenant and platoon leader, Jimmy Cross carried a compass, maps, code books, binoculars, and a .45-caliber pistol that weighed 2.9 pounds fully loaded. He carried a strobe light and the responsibility for the lives of his men.

As an RTO, Mitchell Sanders carried the PRC-25 radio, a killer, twenty-six pounds with its battery.

As a medic, Rat Kiley carried a canvas satchel filled with morphine and plasma and malaria tablets and surgical tape and comic books and all the things a medic must carry, including M&M's for especially bad wounds, for a total weight of nearly twenty pounds.

As a big man, therefore a machine gunner, Henry Dobbins carried the M-60, which weighed twenty-three pounds unloaded, but which was almost always loaded. In addition, Dobbins carried between ten and fifteen pounds of ammunition draped in belts across his chest and shoulders.

As PFCs or Spec 4s, most of them were common grunts and carried the standard M-16 gas-operated assault rifle. The weapon weighed 7.5 pounds unloaded, 8.2 pounds with its full twenty-round magazine. Depending on numerous factors, such as topography and psychology, the riflemen carried anywhere from twelve to twenty magazines, usually in cloth bandoliers, adding on another 8.4 pounds at minimum, fourteen pounds at maximum. When it was available, they also carried M-16 maintenance gear—rods and steel brushes and swabs and tubes of LSA on—all of which weighed about a pound. Among the grunts, some carried the M-79 grenade launcher, 5.9 pounds unloaded, a reasonably light weapon except for the ammunition, which was heavy. A single round weighed ten ounces. The typical load was twenty-five rounds. But Ted Lavender, who was scared, carried thirty-four rounds when he was shot and killed outside Than Khe, and he went down under an exceptional burden, more than twenty pounds of ammunition, plus the flak jacket and helmet and rations and water and toilet paper and tranquilizers and all the rest, plus the unweighed fear. He was dead weight. There was no twitching or flopping. Kiowa, who saw it happen, said it was like watching a rock fall, or a big sandbag or something—just boom, then down—not like the movies where the dead guy rolls around and does fancy spins and goes ass over teakettle—not like that, Kiowa said, the poor bastard just flats fuck fell Boom. Down. Nothing else. It was a bright morning in mid-April Lieutenant Cross felt the pain. He blamed himself. They stripped off Lavender's canteens and ammo, all the heavy things, and Rat Kiley said the obvious, the guy's dead, and Mitchell Sanders used his radio to report one U.S. KIA° and to request a chopper. Then they wrapped Lavender in his poncho. They carried him out to a dry paddy, established security, and sat smoking the dead man's dope until the chopper came. Lieutenant Cross kept to himself. He pictured Martha's smooth young face, thinking he loved her more than anything, more than his men, and now Ted Lavender was dead because he loved her so much and could not stop thinking about her. When the dust-off arrived, they carried Lavender aboard. Afterward they burned Than Khe. They marched until dusk, then dug their holes, and that night Kiowa kept explaining how you had to be there, how fast it was, how the poor guy just dropped like so much concrete. Boom-down, he said. Like cement.

In addition to the three standard weapons—the M-60, M-16, and M-79—they carried whatever presented itself, or whatever seemed appropriate as a means of killing or staying alive. They carried catch-as-catch-can. At various times, in various situations, they carried M-14s and CAR-15s and Swedish Ks and grease guns and captured AK-47s and Chi-Coms and RPGs and Simonov carbines and black-market Uzis and .38-caliber Smith & Wesson handguns and 66 mm LAWs and shotguns and silencers and blackjacks and bayonets and C-4 plastic explosives. Lee Strunk carried a slingshot; a weapon of last resort, he called it. Mitchell Sanders carried brass knuckles. Kiowa carried his grandfather's feathered hatchet. Every third or fourth man carried a Claymore antipersonnel mine—3.5 pounds with its firing device. They all carried fragmentation grenades—fourteen ounces each. They all carried at least one M-18 colored smoke grenade—twenty-four ounces. Some carried CS or tear-gas grenades. Some carried white-phosphorus grenades. They carried all they could bear, and then some, including a silent awe for the terrible power of the things they carried.

In the first week of April, before Lavender died, Lieutenant Jimmy Cross received a good-luck charm from Martha. It was a simple pebble, an ounce at most. Smooth to the touch, it was a milky-white color with flecks of orange and violet, oval-shaped, like a miniature egg. In the accompanying letter, Martha wrote that she had found the pebble on the Jersey shoreline, precisely where the land touched water at high tide, where things came together but also separated.

KIA: Killed in action.

It was this separate-but-together quality, she wrote, that had inspired her to pick up the pebble and to carry it in her breast pocket for several days, where it seemed weightless, and then to send it through the mail, by air, as a token of her truest feelings for him. Lieutenant Cross found this romantic. But he wondered what her truest feelings were, exactly, and what she meant by separate-but-together. He wondered how the tides and waves had come into play on that afternoon along the Jersey shoreline when Martha saw the pebble and bent down to rescue it from geology. He imagined bare feet. Martha was a poet, with the poet's sensibilities, and her feet would be brown and bare, the toenails unpainted, the eyes chilly and somber like the ocean in March, and though it was painful, he wondered who had been with her that afternoon. He imagined a pair of shadows moving along the strip of sand where things came together but also separated. It was phantom jealousy, he knew, but he couldn't help himself. He loved her so much. On the march, through the hot days of early April, he carried the pebble in his mouth, turning it with his tongue, tasting sea salts and moisture. His mind wandered. He had difficulty keeping his attention on the war. On occasion he would yell at his men to spread out the column, to keep their eyes open, but then he would slip away into daydreams, just pretending, walking barefoot along the Jersey shore, with Martha, carrying nothing. He would feel himself rising. Sun and waves and gentle winds, all love and lightness.

What they carried varied by mission.

When a mission took them to the mountains, they carried mosquito netting, machetes, canvas tarps, and extra bug juice.

If a mission seemed especially hazardous, or if it involved a place they knew to be bad, they carried everything they could. In certain heavily mined AOs,° where the land was dense with Toe Poppers and Bouncing Betties, they took turns humping a twenty-eight-pound mine detector. With its headphones and big sensing plate, the equipment was a stress on the lower back and shoulders, awkward to handle, often useless because of the shrapnel in the earth, but they carried it anyway, partly for safety, partly for the illusion of safety.

On ambush, or other night missions, they carried peculiar little odds and ends. Kiowa always took along his New Testament and a pair of moccasins for silence. Dave Jensen carried night-sight vitamins high in carotin. Lee Strunk carried his slingshot; ammo, he claimed, would never be a problem. Rat Kiley carried brandy and M&M's. Until he was shot, Ted Lavender carried the starlight scope, which weighed 6.3 pounds with its aluminum carrying case. Henry Dobbins carried his girlfriend's pantyhose wrapped around his neck as a comforter. They all carried ghosts. When dark came, they would move out single file across the meadows and paddies to their ambush coordinates, where they would quietly set up the Claymores and lie down and spend the night waiting.

Other missions were more complicated and required special equipment. In mid-April, it was their mission to search out and destroy the elaborate tunnel

AOs: Areas of operations.

complexes in the Than Khe area south of Chu Lai. To blow the tunnels, they carried one-pound blocks of pentrite high explosives, four blocks to a man, sixty-eight pounds in all. They carried wiring, detonators, and battery-powered clackers. Dave Jensen carried earplugs. Most often, before blowing the tunnels, they were ordered by higher command to search them, which was considered bad news, but by and large they just shrugged and carried out orders. Because he was a big man, Henry Dobbins was excused from tunnel duty. The others would draw numbers. Before Lavender died there were seventeen men in the platoon, and whoever drew the number seventeen would strip off his gear and crawl in head first with a flashlight and Lieutenant Cross's .45-caliber pistol. The rest of them would fan out as security. They would sit down or kneel, not facing the hole, listening to the ground beneath them, imagining cobwebs and ghosts, whatever was down there—the tunnel walls squeezing in—how the flashlight seemed impossibly heavy in the hand and how it was tunnel vision in the very strictest sense, compression in all ways, even time, and how you had to wiggle in—ass and elbows—a swallowed-up feeling—and how you found yourself worrying about odd things—will your flashlight go dead? Do rats carry rabies? If you screamed, how far would the sound carry? Would your buddies hear it? Would they have the courage to drag you out? In some respects, though not many, the waiting was worse than the tunnel itself. Imagination was a killer.

On April 16, when Lee Strunk drew the number seventeen, he laughed and muttered something and went down quickly. The morning was hot and very still. Not good, Kiowa said. He looked at the tunnel opening, then out across a dry paddy toward the village of Than Khe. Nothing moved. No clouds or birds or people. As they waited, the men smoked and drank Kool-Aid, not talking much, feeling sympathy for Lee Strunk but also feeling the luck of the draw. You win some, you lose some, said Mitchell Sanders, and sometimes you settle for a rain check. It was a tired line and no one laughed.

Henry Dobbins ate a tropical chocolate bar. Ted Lavender popped a tranquilizer and went off to pee.   20

After five minutes, Lieutenant Jimmy Cross moved to the tunnel, leaned down, and examined the darkness. Trouble, he thought—a cave-in maybe. And then suddenly, without willing it, he was thinking about Martha. The stresses and fractures, the quick collapse, the two of them buried alive under all that weight. Dense, crushing love. Kneeling, watching the hole, he tried to concentrate on Lee Strunk and the war, all the dangers, but his love was too much for him, he felt paralyzed, he wanted to sleep inside her lungs and breathe her blood and be smothered. He wanted her to be a virgin and not a virgin, all at once. He wanted to know her. Intimate secrets—why poetry? Why so sad? Why the grayness in her eyes? Why so alone? Not lonely, just alone—riding her bike across campus or sitting off by herself in the cafeteria. Even dancing, she danced alone—and it was the aloneness that filled him with love. He remembered telling her that one evening. How she nodded and looked away. And how, later, when he kissed her, she received the kiss without returning it, her eyes wide open, not afraid, not a virgin's eyes, just flat and uninvolved.

Lieutenant Cross gazed at the tunnel. But he was not there. He was buried with Martha under the white sand at the Jersey shore. They were pressed together, and the pebble in his mouth was her tongue. He was smiling. Vaguely, he was aware of how quiet the day was, the sullen paddies, yet he could not bring himself to worry about matters of security. He was beyond that. He was just a kid at war, in love. He was twenty-two years old. He couldn't help it.

A few moments later Lee Strunk crawled out of the tunnel. He came up grinning, filthy but alive. Lieutenant Cross nodded and closed his eyes while the others clapped Strunk on the back and made jokes about rising from the dead.

Worms, Rat Kiley said. Right out of the grave. Fuckin' zombie.

The men laughed. They all felt great relief.   25

Spook City, said Mitchell Sanders.

Lee Strunk made a funny ghost sound, a kind of moaning, yet very happy, and right then, when Strunk made that high happy moaning sound, when he went *Ahhooooo*, right then Ted Lavender was shot in the head on his way back from peeing. He lay with his mouth open. The teeth were broken. There was a swollen black bruise under his left eye. The cheekbone was gone. Oh shit, Rat Kiley said, the guy's dead. The guy's dead, he kept saying, which seemed profound — the guy's dead. I mean really.

The things they carried were determined to some extent by superstition. Lieutenant Cross carried his good-luck pebble. Dave Jensen carried a rabbit's foot. Norman Bowker, otherwise a very gentle person, carried a thumb that had been presented to him as a gift by Mitchell Sanders. The thumb was dark brown, rubbery to the touch, and weighed four ounces at most. It had been cut from a VC corpse, a boy of fifteen or sixteen. They'd found him at the bottom of an irrigation ditch, badly burned, flies in his mouth and eyes. The boy wore black shorts and sandals. At the time of his death he had been carrying a pouch of rice, a rifle, and three magazines of ammunition.

You want my opinion, Mitchell Sanders said, there's a definite moral here.

He put his hand on the dead boy's wrist. He was quiet for a time, as if   30
counting a pulse, then he patted the stomach, almost affectionately, and used Kiowa's hunting hatchet to remove the thumb.

Henry Dobbins asked what the moral was.

Moral?

You know. *Moral.*

Sanders wrapped the thumb in toilet paper and handed it across to Norman Bowker. There was no blood. Smiling, he kicked the boy's head, watched the flies scatter, and said, It's like with that old TV show — Paladin. Have gun, will travel.

Henry Dobbins thought about it.   35

Yeah, well, he finally said. I don't see no moral.

There it *is*, man.

Fuck off.

They carried USO stationery and pencils and pens. They carried Sterno, safety pins, trip flares, signal flares, spools of wire, razor blades, chewing tobacco, liberated joss sticks and statuettes of the smiling Buddha, candles, grease pencils, *The Stars and Stripes*, fingernail clippers, Psy Ops° leaflets, bush hats, bolos, and much more. Twice a week, when the resupply choppers came in, they carried hot chow in green Mermite cans and large canvas bags filled with iced beer and soda pop. They carried plastic water containers, each with a two-gallon capacity. Mitchell Sanders carried a set of starched tiger fatigues for special occasions. Henry Dobbins carried Black Flag insecticide. Dave Jensen carried empty sandbags that could be filled at night for added protection. Lee Strunk carried tanning lotion. Some things they carried in common. Taking turns, they carried the big PRC-77 scrambler radio, which weighed thirty pounds with its battery. They shared the weight of memory. They took up what others could no longer bear. Often, they carried each other, the wounded or weak. They carried infections. They carried chess sets, basketballs, Vietnamese-English dictionaries, insignia of rank, Bronze Stars and Purple Hearts, plastic cards imprinted with the Code of Conduct. They carried diseases, among them malaria and dysentery. They carried lice and ringworm and leeches and paddy algae and various rots and molds. They carried the land itself — Vietnam, the place, the soil — a powdery orange-red dust that covered their boots and fatigues and faces. They carried the sky. The whole atmosphere, they carried it, the humidity, the monsoons, the stink of fungus and decay, all of it, they carried gravity. They moved like mules. By daylight they took sniper fire, at night they were mortared, but it was not battle, it was just the endless march, village to village, without purpose, nothing won or lost. They marched for the sake of the march. They plodded along slowly, dumbly, leaning forward against the heat, unthinking, all blood and bone, simple grunts, soldiering with their legs, toiling up the hills and down into the paddies and across the rivers and up again and down, just humping, one step and then the next and then another, but no volition, no will, because it was automatic, it was anatomy, and the war was entirely a matter of posture and carriage, the hump was everything, a kind of inertia, a kind of emptiness, a dullness of desire and intellect and conscience and hope and human sensibility. Their principles were in their feet. Their calculations were biological. They had no sense of strategy or mission. They searched the villages without knowing what to look for, not caring, kicking over jars of rice, frisking children and old men, blowing tunnels, sometimes setting fires and sometimes not, then forming up and moving on to the next village, then other villages, where it would always be the same. They carried their own lives. The pressures were enormous. In the heat of early afternoon, they would remove their helmets and flak jackets, walking bare, which was dangerous but which helped ease the strain. They would often discard things along the route of march. Purely for comfort, they would throw away rations, blow their Claymores and grenades, no matter, because by nightfall the resupply choppers would arrive with more of the same, then a day or two later still more, fresh watermelons and crates of ammunition and sunglasses and woolen sweaters — the resources were stunning — sparklers for the Fourth of July, colored eggs for Easter. It was the great American war chest — the fruits of science, the

Psy Ops: Psychological operations.

smokestacks, the canneries, the arsenals at Hartford, the Minnesota forests, the machine shops, the vast fields of corn and wheat—they carried like freight trains, they carried it on their backs and shoulders—and for all the ambiguities of Vietnam, all the mysteries and unknowns, there was at least the single abiding certainty that they would never be at a loss for things to carry.

After the chopper took Lavender away, Lieutenant Jimmy Cross led his men   40
into the village of Than Khe. They burned everything. They shot chickens and dogs, they trashed the village well, they called in artillery and watched the wreckage, then they marched for several hours through the hot afternoon, and then at dusk, while Kiowa explained how Lavender died, Lieutenant Cross found himself trembling.

He tried not to cry. With his entrenching tool, which weighed five pounds, he began digging a hole in the earth.

He felt shame. He hated himself. He had loved Martha more than his men, and as a consequence Lavender was now dead, and this was something he would have to carry like a stone in his stomach for the rest of the war.

All he could do was dig. He used his entrenching tool like an ax, slashing, feeling both love and hate, and then later, when it was full dark, he sat at the bottom of his foxhole and wept. It went on for a long while. In part, he was grieving for Ted Lavender, but mostly it was for Martha, and for himself, because she belonged to another world, which was not quite real, and because she was a junior at Mount Sebastian College in New Jersey, a poet and a virgin and uninvolved, and because he realized she did not love him and never would.

Like cement, Kiowa whispered in the dark. I swear to God—boom-down. Not a word.

I've heard this, said Norman Bowker.   45

A pisser, you know? Still zipping himself up. Zapped while zipping.

All right, fine. That's enough.

Yeah, but you had to see it, the guy just —

I *heard*, man. Cement. So why not shut the fuck *up*?

Kiowa shook his head sadly and glanced over at the hole where Lieutenant   50
Jimmy Cross sat watching the night. The air was thick and wet. A warm, dense fog had settled over the paddies and there was the stillness that precedes rain.

After a time Kiowa sighed.

One thing for sure, he said. The Lieutenant's in some deep hurt. I mean that crying jag—the way he was carrying on—it wasn't fake or anything, it was real heavy-duty hurt. The man cares.

Sure, Norman Bowker said.

Say what you want, the man does care.

We all got problems.   55

Not Lavender.

No, I guess not, Bowker said. Do me a favor, though.

Shut up?

That's a smart Indian. Shut up.

Shrugging, Kiowa pulled off his boots. He wanted to say more, just to   6(
lighten up his sleep, but instead he opened his New Testament and arranged it
beneath his head as a pillow. The fog made things seem hollow and unattached.
He tried not to think about Ted Lavender, but then he was thinking how fast it
was, no drama, down and dead, and how it was hard to feel anything except
surprise. It seemed un-Christian. He wished he could find some great sadness,
or even anger, but the emotion wasn't there and he couldn't make it happen.
Mostly he felt pleased to be alive. He liked the smell of the New Testament under
his cheek, the leather and ink and paper and glue, whatever the chemicals
were. He liked hearing the sounds of night. Even his fatigue, it felt fine, the stiff
muscles and the prickly awareness of his own body, a floating feeling. He enjoyed not being dead. Lying there, Kiowa admired Lieutenant Jimmy Cross's
capacity for grief. He wanted to share the man's pain, he wanted to care as
Jimmy Cross cared. And yet when he closed his eyes, all he could think was
Boom-down, and all he could feel was the pleasure of having his boots off and
the fog curling in around him and the damp soil and the Bible smells and the
plush comfort of night.

After a moment Norman Bowker sat up in the dark.

What the hell, he said. You want to talk, *talk*. Tell it to me.

Forget it.

No, man, go on. One thing I hate, it's a silent Indian.

For the most part they carried themselves with poise, a kind of dignity. Now   65
and then, however, there were times of panic, when they squealed or wanted to
squeal but couldn't, when they twitched and made moaning sounds and covered their heads and said Dear Jesus and flopped around on the earth and fired
their weapons blindly and cringed and sobbed and begged for the noise to stop
and went wild and made stupid promises to themselves and to God and to their
mothers and fathers, hoping not to die. In different ways, it happened to all of
them. Afterward, when the firing ended, they would blink and peek up. They
would touch their bodies, feeling shame, then quickly hiding it. They would
force themselves to stand. As if in slow motion, frame by frame, the world
would take on the old logic—absolute silence, then the wind, then sunlight,
then voices. It was the burden of being alive. Awkwardly, the men would reas-
semble themselves, first in private, then in groups, becoming soldiers again.
They would repair the leaks in their eyes. They would check for casualties, call
in dust-offs, light cigarettes, try to smile, clear their throats and spit and begin
cleaning their weapons. After a time someone would shake his head and say,
No lie, I almost shit my pants, and someone else would laugh, which meant it
was bad, yes, but the guy had obviously not shit his pants, it wasn't that bad,
and in any case nobody would ever do such a thing and then go ahead and talk
about it. They would squint into the dense, oppressive sunlight. For a few moments, perhaps, they would fall silent, lighting a joint and tracking its passage
from man to man, inhaling, holding in the humiliation. Scary stuff, one of
them might say. But then someone else would grin or flick his eyebrows and
say, Roger-dodger, almost cut me a new asshole, *almost*.

There were numerous such poses. Some carried themselves with a sort of wistful resignation, others with pride or stiff soldierly discipline or good humor or macho zeal. They were afraid of dying but they were even more afraid to show it.

They found jokes to tell.

They used a hard vocabulary to contain the terrible softness. *Greased,* they'd say. *Offed, lit up, zapped while zipping.* It wasn't cruelty, just stage presence. They were actors and the war came at them in 3-D. When someone died, it wasn't quite dying, because in a curious way it seemed scripted, and because they had their lines mostly memorized, irony mixed with tragedy, and because they called it by other names, as if to encyst and destroy the reality of death itself. They kicked corpses. They cut off thumbs. They talked grunt lingo. They told stories about Ted Lavender's supply of tranquilizers, how the poor guy didn't feel a thing, how incredibly tranquil he was.

There's a moral here, said Mitchell Sanders.

They were waiting for Lavender's chopper, smoking the dead man's dope.   70

The moral's pretty obvious, Sanders said, and winked. Stay away from drugs. No joke, they'll ruin your day every time.

Cute, said Henry Dobbins.

Mind-blower, get it? Talk about wiggy—nothing left, just blood and brains.

They made themselves laugh.

There it is, they'd say, over and over, as if the repetition itself were an act of   75
poise, a balance between crazy and almost crazy, knowing without going. There it is, which meant be cool, let it ride, because oh yeah, man, you can't change what can't be changed, there it is, there it absolutely and positively and fucking well *is.*

They were tough.

They carried all the emotional baggage of men who might die. Grief, terror, love, longing—these were intangibles, but the intangibles had their own mass and specific gravity, they had tangible weight. They carried shameful memories. They carried the common secret of cowardice barely restrained, the instinct to run or freeze or hide, and in many respects this was the heaviest burden of all, for it could never be put down, it required perfect balance and perfect posture. They carried their reputations. They carried the soldier's greatest fear, which was the fear of blushing. Men killed, and died, because they were embarrassed not to. It was what had brought them to the war in the first place, nothing positive, no dreams of glory or honor, just to avoid the blush of dishonor. They died so as not to die of embarrassment. They crawled into tunnels and walked point and advanced under fire. Each morning, despite the unknowns, they made their legs move. They endured. They kept humping. They did not submit to the obvious alternative, which was simply to close the eyes and fall. So easy, really. Go limp and tumble to the ground and let the muscles unwind and not speak and not budge until your buddies picked you up and lifted you into the chopper that would roar and dip its nose and carry you off to the world. A mere matter of falling, yet no one ever fell. It was not courage, exactly; the object was not valor. Rather, they were too frightened to be cowards.

By and large they carried these things inside, maintaining the masks of composure. They sneered at sick call. They spoke bitterly about guys who had found release by shooting off their own toes or fingers. Pussies, they'd say. Candyasses. It was fierce, mocking talk, with only a trace of envy or awe, but even so, the image played itself out behind their eyes.

They imagined the muzzle against flesh. They imagined the quick, sweet pain, then the evacuation to Japan, then a hospital with warm beds and cute geisha nurses.

They dreamed of freedom birds.   80

At night, on guard, staring into the dark, they were carried away by jumbo jets. They felt the rush of takeoff. *Gone!* they yelled. And then velocity, wings and engines, a smiling stewardess—but it was more than a plane, it was a real bird, a big sleek silver bird with feathers and talons and high screeching. They were flying. The weights fell off, there was nothing to bear. They laughed and held on tight, feeling the cold slap of wind and altitude, soaring, thinking *It's over, I'm gone!*—they were naked, they were light and free—it was all lightness, bright and fast and buoyant, light as light, a helium buzz in the brain, a giddy bubbling in the lungs as they were taken up over the clouds and the war, beyond duty, beyond gravity and mortification and global entanglements—*Sin loi!°* they yelled, *I'm sorry, motherfuckers, but I'm out of it. I'm goofed, I'm on a space cruise, I'm gone!*—and it was a restful, disencumbered sensation, just riding the light waves, sailing that big silver freedom bird over the mountains and oceans, over America, over the farms and great sleeping cities and cemeteries and highways and the golden arches of McDonald's. It was flight, a kind of fleeing, a kind of falling, falling higher and higher, spinning off the edge of the earth and beyond the sun and through the vast, silent vacuum where there were no burdens and where everything weighed exactly nothing. *Gone!* they screamed, *I'm sorry but I'm gone!* And so at night, not quite dreaming, they gave themselves over to lightness, they were carried, they were purely borne.

On the morning after Ted Lavender died, First Lieutenant Jimmy Cross crouched at the bottom of his foxhole and burned Martha's letters. Then he burned the two photographs. There was a steady rain falling, which made it difficult, but he used heat tabs and Sterno to build a small fire, screening it with his body, holding the photographs over the tight blue flame with the tips of his fingers.

He realized it was only a gesture. Stupid, he thought. Sentimental, too, but mostly just stupid.

Lavender was dead. You couldn't burn the blame.

Besides, the letters were in his head. And even now, without photographs,   85
Lieutenant Cross could see Martha playing volleyball in her white gym shorts and yellow T-shirt. He could see her moving in the rain.

When the fire died out, Lieutenant Cross pulled his poncho over his shoulders and ate breakfast from a can.

There was no great mystery, he decided.

Sin loi!: "Sorry about that."

In those burned letters Martha had never mentioned the war, except to say, Jimmy, take care of yourself. She wasn't involved. She signed the letters "Love," but it wasn't love, and all the fine lines and technicalities did not matter.

The morning came up wet and blurry. Everything seemed part of everything else, the fog and Martha and the deepening rain.

It was a war, after all.   90

Half smiling, Lieutenant Jimmy Cross took out his maps. He shook his head hard, as if to clear it, then bent forward and began planning the day's march. In ten minutes, or maybe twenty, he would rouse the men and they would pack up and head west, where the maps showed the country to be green and inviting. They would do what they had always done. The rain might add some weight, but otherwise it would be one more day layered upon all the other days.

He was realistic about it. There was that new hardness in his stomach.

No more fantasies, he told himself.

Henceforth, when he thought about Martha, it would be only to think that she belonged elsewhere. He would shut down the daydreams. This was not Mount Sebastian, it was another world, where there were no pretty poems or midterm exams, a place where men died because of carelessness and gross stupidity. Kiowa was right. Boom-down, and you were dead, never partly dead.

Briefly, in the rain, Lieutenant Cross saw Martha's gray eyes gazing back   95
at him.

He understood.

It was very sad, he thought. The things men carried inside. The things men did or felt they had to do.

He almost nodded at her, but didn't.

Instead he went back to his maps. He was now determined to perform his duties firmly and without negligence. It wouldn't help Lavender, he knew that, but from this point on he would comport himself as a soldier. He would dispose of his good-luck pebble. Swallow it, maybe, or use Lee Strunk's slingshot, or just drop it along the trail. On the march he would impose strict field discipline. He would be careful to send out flank security, to prevent straggling or bunching up, to keep his troops moving at the proper pace and at the proper interval. He would insist on clean weapons. He would confiscate the remainder of Lavender's dope. Later in the day, perhaps, he would call the men together and speak to them plainly. He would accept the blame for what had happened to Ted Lavender. He would be a man about it. He would look them in the eyes, keeping his chin level, and he would issue the new SOPs in a calm, impersonal tone of voice, an officer's voice, leaving no room for argument or discussion. Commencing immediately, he'd tell them, they would no longer abandon equipment along the route of march. They would police up their acts. They would get their shit together, and keep it together, and maintain it neatly and in good working order.

He would not tolerate laxity. He would show strength, distancing himself.   100

Among the men there would be grumbling, of course, and maybe worse, because their days would seem longer and their loads heavier, but Lieutenant

Cross reminded himself that his obligation was not to be loved but to lead. He would dispense with love; it was not now a factor. And if anyone quarreled or complained, he would simply tighten his lips and arrange his shoulders in the correct command posture. He might give a curt little nod. Or he might not. He might just shrug and say Carry on, then they would saddle up and form into a column and move out toward the villages of Than Khe.   [1986]

≡ THINKING ABOUT THE TEXT

1. This story does not depict events in chronological order. Instead, it moves around in time. Why do you think O'Brien structured the story this way?

2. In various places, the narrator refers to things that the men carried. In each of these sections, what *kind* of things does the narrator focus on? Does the order of these sections matter? Why, or why not?

3. What are some significant differences, if any, among the soldiers under Jimmy Cross's command?

4. What is your attitude toward Jimmy Cross's apparent obsession with Martha?

5. Jimmy Cross seems to feel guilty about Ted Lavender's death. To what extent does his feeling seem rational? *Should* he feel guilty, in your view? Why, or why not? In the final two paragraphs, he makes a number of resolutions. Which, if any, do you think that he is capable of keeping?

In the News

The following piece appeared as an op-ed column in the April 11, 2007, issue of the *New York Times*. Its author, Valerie Seiling Jacobs, was a practicing attorney for many years. She has published several essays and is pursuing an M.F.A. degree at Columbia University in New York. She also leads workshops on legal writing. "Packing for the Ineffable" is part of a memoir that she is working on, *Waiting for Greg*, which is about her family's life during her stepson's service in Iraq.

VALERIE SEILING JACOBS
Packing for the Ineffable

I have a photograph of the guns he packed. Apparently, it is true that a rifle is a marine's best friend. Greg will travel, indeed sleep, with his weapons. My husband snapped the photo and e-mailed it from North Carolina, right after he put Greg on the bus that took him to the airstrip where he began his journey to Iraq.

We are 48 hours into a 210-day tour. I write "we," though it is Greg, our 19-year-old son, who will actually serve the time. And I include myself in the equation, although I am not related to Greg by blood, having met and married his father only six years ago.

Each soldier is limited to a knapsack and two sea bags—what civilians would call duffels. Space is tight. Once Greg packed his firearms, there was hardly room for any of the other paraphernalia that might make seven months in Iraq bearable, assuming that such a thing is possible.

I am not there for the send-off, but confident that he made room for his iPod. "I would lose my mind without it," he told me during his last visit home. "What makes you think you won't lose your mind anyway?" I wanted to ask. But that is exactly the kind of thing I can never say.

My husband reports that Greg took a stack of DVDs to play on his laptop,   5
another piece of electronic equipment that he presumably managed to cram into his bags. But I have few details. I do not know, for example, whether he chose comedies or combat films to while away the downtime, if such a thing exists.

And I know precious little about what else he stuffed into his bags. Just as well, I think. It would be all too reminiscent of Tim O'Brien's *The Things They Carried*, a book that I picked up and then put down somewhere around page 10. Right after the nervous guy who carried the tranquilizers took a bullet in the head. Besides, if he doesn't make it, we'll know soon enough what he carried. Don't they send the stuff home?

Sometimes, however, curiosity gets the better of me. And then I wonder if the three items I sent made the cut.

Choosing those articles was tricky. What do you give to a young man who has decided to put himself in harm's way? It must be small, it must be light, and it must be thoughtful. And because I am only his stepmother, it cannot be overly sentimental. Technically speaking, I do not have a place card at this party. I would be wise to tread lightly. So I opt for a prayer, a book, and a journal, which, in a lighter moment, my husband predicts will come home still encased in its shrink wrap. I accept the teasing with good humor, and laugh. That's O.K., as long as Greg doesn't come home wrapped in anything.

At Christmas, Greg casually mentioned that when this is all over, he wants to climb Mount Everest. "Sounds like a good plan," my husband replied. Sounds like another ridiculously dangerous decision.

But I keep quiet, switch lenses, and focus on my stepson's optimism and on   10
his unspoken assumption that he will come home in one piece. Healthy enough to undertake such an arduous expedition. And that premise makes selecting a book easy.

"Great choice," says the cashier at the bookstore, when I plunk down a paperback copy of Jon Krakauer's *Into Thin Air*.°

But Ari, my 17-year-old daughter, is cautious. "Do they all make it?" she asks, examining the book jacket.

"Of course," I answer.

Into Thin Air: A 1999 nonfiction best-seller about a disastrous 1996 climbing expedition on Mount Everest in which five people died when a blizzard hit.

But later, I am not so sure. After the book is gift-wrapped, and it's too late to retrieve it from my husband's luggage, I suddenly recall the image of empty oxygen bottles and frozen corpses littering the path to the summit. But then, that little voice in my brain—the one that excuses bad behavior and stupid decisions—begins to rationalize: "Oh, well, better that he knows the risks up front. Besides, it's a page-turner. It will help to kill time in Iraq." Assuming of course, that Iraq doesn't kill him.

The prayer I pick is neither Christian, Jewish, nor Muslim. Perfect for a member of this hodgepodge of a family, a patchwork of people, faiths, and traditions. It is an old Celtic blessing, famous for its entreaty for the safekeeping of a loved one. An ideal choice. If anyone needs to be held in the hollow of God's hand, then it is this sweet boy, who by some combination of fate and ill luck has pulled the short straw. The one that requires him to man the machine gun in the Humvee. Isn't that the most dangerous job? Do they know that he is 6-foot-4? How will he be able to keep his head down? But that is exactly the kind of thing I can never say.

Instead, I type and retype the prayer, playing with the format and font until it is the size of a small card. Tiny enough to fit in a pocket—or hold in a private moment of panic. And then, at the last minute, I decide to laminate the slip of paper. I remember how my children loved that wonder film when they were young. How they coated everything they could lay their hands on. I still carry their shiny library cards in my wallet, tangible proof of their enthusiasm and wobbly beginner signatures. So I dig out the roll of plastic from the closet. This way, it won't get torn. And he can still read the prayer if it gets wet, in case anybody spills anything on it. "Like blood," a scary voice whispers.

By now, Greg is halfway around the world. Most likely in Kuwait, cooling his heels and waiting for transport to the real action. Already, he is lucky not to have been on that helicopter that was shot down by a missile. The one I read about in the morning while I sipped my coffee—and did not mention to my husband.

But my efforts to shield my spouse proved futile. Of course he spotted that headline. How could he miss it? We are now on red alert. No detail about Iraq goes unnoticed. We listen to the evening news like bloodhounds, thirsty for the scent of our beloved son.

"Don't worry," I tell my husband. "Bad news travels on wings. We will know soon enough if there is a problem."

But silently, I worry. What if I am wrong? What if, in our upper-middle-class complacency, we assume the best and suffer the worst? What if the death notification squad arrives late, after we have read the newspaper? How will we bear it? But that is exactly the kind of thing I can never say.

Two hundred and eight days to go.   *[2007]*

■ THINKING ABOUT THE TEXTS

1. Jacobs reports that she could read only a little of O'Brien's *The Things They Carried*, a book of interrelated short stories that includes the one you have just read. What, if anything, about that story might conceivably have helped her cope at home with her stepson's dangerous service in the Middle East?

2. Do any of O'Brien's characters rely on items similar to Greg's iPod and DVD collection (entertainment technology that developed well after the Vietnam War)? Explain.

3. Although Jacobs spends two paragraphs discussing the prayer she sent along with her stepson, she does not actually reveal what it is. Should she have done so? Why, or why not? What, if anything, are significant details that O'Brien withholds from his story?

■ WRITING ABOUT ISSUES

1. Write an essay analyzing "The Things They Carried" as a depiction of a *psychological* journey. Feel free to concentrate for the most part on just one or two characters. Be sure to make clear what the term *psychological journey* means to you — the specific sorts of changes it involves.

2. Take a word from Jacobs's article, and write an essay in which you explain how it does or does not apply to a specific character in O'Brien's story. Be sure to make clear how Jacobs and you define the term (your definitions might differ). Some possible words of hers include "thoughtful" (para. 8), "sentimental" (para. 8), "ridiculously" (para. 9), "optimism" (para. 10), "rationalize" (para. 14), and "complacency" (para. 20).

3. Write an essay in which you show how a particular book, movie, or television show about war includes at least one physical journey that is not *just* physical. Support your claims with specific details of the work, and be sure to specify the other kind(s) of journey that it depicts. If you wish, refer to one or both of the texts in this cluster.

4. Write an essay about the journey *back* from war taken by a recent combat veteran whom you know or have read about. More specifically, explain how this person's return home and subsequent life need to be placed in a particular context in order to be understood. The assignment might include research, such as reading various general accounts of the conditions that today's veterans face. If you wish, refer to one or both of the texts in this cluster.

■ Roads Taken: Poems by Robert Frost

ROBERT FROST, "Stopping by Woods on a Snowy Evening"

ROBERT FROST, "The Road Not Taken"

ROBERT FROST, "Acquainted with the Night"

Critic Randall Jarrell saw Robert Frost as "the subtlest and saddest of poets." Although many readers thought of this esteemed, pastoral poet as the optimistic voice of the common man, his lyrical vision is actually quite tragic, a quality President Kennedy thought helped strengthen his own presidential character. Alert readers should be careful about equating Frost's simple language and rural settings with lack of depth. The three poems assembled here (and "Mending Wall," p. 61) use the common motif of an external journey to comment on the internal burdens of adult responsibility, the anxiety inherent in making choices, and the loneliness of the human heart. The language of these journeys is beautifully crafted and evocative, able to be read profitably by both schoolchildren and sophisticated critics.

■ BEFORE YOU READ

Do you remember reading a Frost poem in high school? What is your memory of that reading and discussion in class?

ROBERT FROST

Stopping by Woods on a Snowy Evening

Robert Frost (1874–1963) was perhaps the best-known poet of the twentieth century: winning four Pulitzer Prizes, garnering more than forty honorary degrees, and being widely anthologized throughout the world. His popular image, perhaps forever fixed by his reading at John Kennedy's inauguration, is of a white-haired New Englander fond of simple, homey descriptions of nature. Actually, Frost was born in San Francisco, and most critics think his poetry is anything but simple.

Frost spent his childhood in California and later moved with his mother to eastern Massachusetts, where he grew up in the small city of Lawrence. He briefly attended Dartmouth College and married in 1895. Frost and his wife taught school together, but they soon moved to a farm in New Hampshire, where he worked and wrote poetry. In 1912, he moved to a town outside London and soon published his first book of poetry, A Boy's Will, in 1913. The book was well received, and a few years later Frost moved to Franconia, New Hampshire, and began a lifelong career of writing and teaching. For more than twenty years, he was a professor at Amherst College and for decades taught summers at the Bread Loaf School in Vermont.

(© Bettmann/Corbis.)

Frost's most popular poems—"Mending Wall," "After Apple-Picking," "Birches," and "Fire and Ice"—and those printed here deal with complex social issues in a seemingly natural manner. But even a casual search of essays interpreting "Mending Wall," for example, demonstrates that critics see in Frost's poems a sophisticated, searching, and often dark commentary on the human condition.

Whose woods these are I think I know.
His house is in the village, though;
He will not see me stopping here
To watch his woods fill up with snow.

My little horse must think it queer
To stop without a farmhouse near   5
Between the woods and frozen lake
The darkest evening of the year.

He gives his harness bells a shake
To ask if there is some mistake.   10

The only other sound's the sweep
Of easy wind and downy flake.

The woods are lovely, dark and deep,
But I have promises to keep,
And miles to go before I sleep,   1
And miles to go before I sleep.   *[1923]*

≡ THINKING ABOUT THE TEXT

1. Why does the narrator seem so concerned that someone will notice him watching "woods fill up with snow" (line 4)?

2. Is the "darkest evening" (line 8) meant literally or metaphorically or both?

3. Notice the alliteration in lines 11–12. What effect is Frost trying to achieve with this poetic device?

4. Some critics see the narrator's pause and the lure of woods that "are lovely, dark and deep" (line 13) as something like a death wish. Do you agree?

5. How do you interpret the last lines? Are they a literal or a figurative statement? Why the repetition?

ROBERT FROST
The Road Not Taken

Two roads diverged in a yellow wood,
And sorry I could not travel both
And be one traveler, long I stood
And looked down one as far as I could
To where it bent in the undergrowth;   5

Then took the other, as just as fair,
And having perhaps the better claim,
Because it was grassy and wanted wear;
Though as for that the passing there
Had worn them really about the same,   10

And both that morning equally lay
In leaves no step had trodden black.
Oh, I kept the first for another day!
Yet knowing how way leads on to way,
I doubted if I should ever come back.   15

I shall be telling this with a sigh
Somewhere ages and ages hence:

Two roads diverged in a wood, and I—
I took the one less traveled by,
And that has made all the difference.   *[1916]*   20

≡ THINKING ABOUT THE TEXT

1. Is it odd that the title would refer to a road *not* taken?

2. This is clearly a poem about a journey. Did you ever think of your life as a journey on a particular path? How far can you see your future on this path?

3. Critics have noticed that although the narrator says he has taken the path less traveled, he also says the paths were worn about the same. How might you account for this?

4. The conventional interpretation of this poem is that it is about nonconformity. Does this make sense? Why? Given the issue in the previous question, might there be other interpretations?

5. Why does the narrator "sigh" in the last stanza? Is it due to boredom? Regret? Resignation? Nostalgia?

≡ MAKING COMPARISONS

1. Compare the moods of the speakers in both poems.

2. Both poems touch on the future. In what ways?

3. Is the focus of "Stopping by Woods on a Snowy Evening" more pessimistic than that of "The Road Not Taken"?

ROBERT FROST

Acquainted with the Night

I have been one acquainted with the night.
I have walked out in rain—and back in rain.
I have outwalked the furthest city light.

I have looked down the saddest city lane.
I have passed by the watchman on his beat   5
And dropped my eyes, unwilling to explain.

I have stood still and stopped the sound of feet
When far away an interrupted cry
Came over houses from another street,

But not to call me back or say good-by;   10
And further still at an unearthly height
One luminary clock against the sky

Proclaimed the time was neither wrong nor right.
I have been one acquainted with the night.   *[1928]*

≡ THINKING ABOUT THE TEXT

1. When the narrator passes the watchman, he drops his eyes (lines 5–6). Why?
2. It seems that the cry (line 8) has nothing to do with the narrator. Is this detail a key to his psychological and emotional state?
3. The narrator says the "time was neither wrong nor right" (line 13). What is he trying to suggest? What might the "time was right" suggest?
4. Why does the narrator choose the night for his walks? Why not walk during the day?
5. Although the first and last lines are identical, do you sense a difference in meaning?

≡ MAKING COMPARISONS

1. Which of these three journeys in Frost's poems seems the most hopeful?
2. Is the speaker in "Acquainted with the Night" more honest than the other speakers? Why?
3. Which line in the three poems seems the most enigmatic? Why?

≡ WRITING ABOUT ISSUES

1. Write an essay about a decision you made that you assumed would make a difference in your life.
2. All three poems involve journeys. Write an essay that compares the three journeys in terms of purpose, mood, and meaning.
3. Write an essay about a significant and recent journey that you have taken. Did you learn something about yourself? Did you change?
4. Another Frost poem, "Mending Wall," appears in the first part of this book (p. 61). Write an essay that compares the attitude of that speaker with the three speakers in this cluster.

≡ Travels through the Dark: Re-Visions of a Poem

WILLIAM STAFFORD, "Traveling through the Dark"

JOHN BURNSIDE, "Penitence"

ROBERT WRIGLEY, "Highway 12, Just East of Paradise, Idaho"

LOREN GOODMAN, "Traveling through the Dark (2005)"

One of life's more disturbing events is hitting an animal as you drive alone on a dark night. Perhaps not in the city, but unfortunately in many suburban and rural sections of the country, it is an all too familiar occurrence. Depending on the context, it can test our ethical and social responsibility. Perhaps the temptation to flee is too great for many. But others will do more, seeing their predicament as a call to action, however ineffective. Given our cultural inclinations, hurting a deer seems particularly horrific. A surprising number of writers have dealt with just this situation, none more famously than William Stafford in "Traveling through the Dark." It seems reasonable to assume that the three other poets in this cluster are familiar with Stafford's poignant and ethically resonant poem. But as with many iconic texts, some writers will treat it satirically and others seriously. And perhaps others—like Wrigley—want to parody the darkness of Stafford's ethical dilemma. Certainly the controversy surrounding the publication of Goodman's almost identical poem testifies to the esteemed place Stafford's text has in the literary canon.

≡ BEFORE YOU READ

Do you believe our interactions with animals should be influenced by ethical concerns? Do you see contradictions in our culture's treatment of animals?

WILLIAM STAFFORD
Traveling through the Dark

Besides being a poet himself, William Stafford (1914–1995) was a mentor to many others. During World War II, he was a conscientious objector. Later, he wrote and taught poetry at a variety of places in the United States, eventually settling in Oregon. The following poem was written in 1960 and subsequently appeared in a 1962 collection of Stafford's poems, also entitled Traveling through the Dark, *which won the National Book Award in 1963. He went on to publish over fifty more volumes of poetry and prose. He taught at Lewis and Clark College until his retirement in 1980. Like those of Robert Frost, to whom Stafford is often compared, his poems are deceptively simple. On closer examination, however, they reveal themselves to be complex and highly suggestive of deeper concerns.*

(Photo by Kim Stafford.)

(© Ulf Andersen/Getty Images.)

(Photo by Matt Valentine. Courtesy Robert Wrigley.)

(Courtesy Loren Goodman.)

Traveling through the dark I found a deer
dead on the edge of the Wilson River road.
It is usually best to roll them into the canyon:
that road is narrow; to swerve might make more dead.

By glow of the tail-light I stumbled back of the car   5
and stood by the heap, a doe, a recent killing;
she had stiffened already, almost cold.
I dragged her off; she was large in the belly.

My fingers touching her side brought me the reason—
her side was warm; her fawn lay there waiting,   10
alive, still, never to be born.
Beside that mountain road I hesitated.

The car aimed ahead its lowered parking lights;
under the hood purred the steady engine.
I stood in the glare of the warm exhaust turning red;   15
around our group I could hear the wilderness listen.

I thought hard for us all—my only swerving—
then pushed her over the edge into the river.   *[1962]*

☰ THINKING ABOUT THE TEXT

1. Depending on where readers have grown up, the narrative of this poem might seem exotic or routine. Some readers have, in fact, faced exactly this situation. Have you any experience with such an event? Have you ever hit an animal with your car? What was your response?

2. How do you read "I could hear the wilderness listen" (line 16)? Why do you think the speaker uses "purred" in line 14?

3. What are some possible readings of the title? Of the word *dark*?

4. Why do you think the narrator "hesitated"? How would you define "swerve" as used in line 4? How about as it is used in the penultimate line?

5. This is, in part, a poem about decisions. Do you agree with the narrator's choice at the end? Would you have wanted to do otherwise?

JOHN BURNSIDE
Penitence

John Burnside (b. 1955) grew up in Dunfermline, Scotland. He studied English at Cambridge College and worked as a computer-software engineer. He currently teaches at the University of St. Andrews. His books of poetry have won numerous awards, including the Whitbread Poetry Award for Asylum Dance *(2000). The* Light Trap *(2002) was also short-listed for the T. S. Eliot Prize. His recent publications include his memoir,* A Lie about My Father *(2006); the poetry collections* Gift Songs *(2007),* The Hunt in the Forest *(2009), and* Black Cat Bone *(2011); and the novels* Glister *(2008) and* Something Like Happy *(2013). The critic George Szirtes has said that Burnside's "antennae are tuned to the buzz and flow of nature."*

I was driving into the wind
on a northern road,
the redwoods swaying around me like a black
ocean.
     I'd drifted off: I didn't see the deer   5
till it bounced away,
the back legs swinging outwards as I braked
and swerved into the tinder
of the verge.
        Soon as I stopped   10
the headlamps filled with moths
and something beyond the trees was tuning in,
a hard attention
boring through my flesh
to stroke the bone.   15
        That shudder took so long

to end, I thought the animal had slipped
beneath the wheels, and lay there
quivering.
       I left the engine running; stepped outside;   2
away, at the edge of the light, a body
shifted amongst the leaves
and I wanted to go, to help, to make it well,
but every step I took
pushed it away.   2
       Or—no; that's not the truth,
or all the truth:
now I admit my own fear held me back,
not fear of the dark or that presence
bending the trees;   3
not even fear, exactly, but the dread
of touching, of colliding with that pain.
I stood there, in the river of the wind,
for minutes; then I walked back to the car
and drove away.   3
       I want to think that deer
survived; or, if it died,
it slipped into the blackness unawares.
But now and then I drive out to the woods
and park the car: the headlamps fill with moths;   4
the woods tune in; I listen to the night
and hear an echo, fading through the trees,
my own flesh in the body of the deer
still resonant, remembered through the fender.   [1997]

≡ THINKING ABOUT THE TEXT

1. The narrator is more responsible for the deer's death than the speaker in the previous poem. Do you think this affects his behavior?

2. What specific words echo those in Stafford's poem?

3. This narrator says "the woods tune in" (line 41). Is this different from "I could hear the wilderness listen" in Stafford's poem?

4. Like Stafford's narrator, the driver here leaves the engine running and steps outside. Describe the differences in their subsequent behaviors.

5. This narrator walks away from the deer. Can you understand why? What would you have done?

≡ MAKING COMPARISONS

1. Compare the narrators of both poems. Does one seem more ethical than the other?

2. What are the similarities and differences in these two poems?

3. What seems the strongest first evidence that Burnside was thinking of the Stafford poem?

ROBERT WRIGLEY
Highway 12, Just East of Paradise, Idaho

Robert Wrigley (b. 1951) is the director of the M.F.A. program in creative writing at the University of Idaho. He received his M.A. from the University of Utah and has written six volumes of poetry, including Lives of Animals *(2003). He has won numerous awards, including a Guggenheim Fellowship and a National Endowment of the Arts Fellowship. Wrigley lives in Moscow, Idaho, with the writer Kim Barnes. His most recent book is* Anatomy of Melancholy and Other Poems *(2013).*

The doe, at a dead run, was dead
the instant the truck hit her.
In the headlights I saw her tongue
extend and her eyes go shocked and vacant.
Launched at a sudden right angle — say   5
from twenty miles per hour south to fifty
miles per hour east — she skated
many yards on the slightest toe-edge tips
of her dainty deer hooves, then fell
slowly, inside the speed of her new trajectory,   10
not pole-axed but stunned, away
from me and the truck's decelerating pitch.
She skidded along the right lane's
fog line true as a cue ball,
until her neck caught a sign post   15
that spun her across both lanes and out of sight
beyond the edge. For which, I admit, I was grateful,
the road there being dark, narrow, and shoulderless,
and home, with its lights, not far away.   *[2003]*

☰ THINKING ABOUT THE TEXT

1. Does the narrator seem too matter-of-fact or perhaps too indifferent to the deer's death? What are some other ways he might have responded? How would you?

2. Are you surprised that most of this poem is a quite detailed account of the deer's demise? What effect do you think the poet is after? Is it effective?

3. Does the phrase "her dainty deer hooves" (line 9) seem a bit odd with respect to the general tone and language of the poem? Are there other words or phrases that caught your attention?

4. Were you surprised by the term "grateful" (line 17)? Do you think the speaker is insensitive, honest, or simply practical and unsentimental?

5. Do you think Wrigley wrote this poem with "Traveling through the Dark" in the background; that is, is this yet another way of dealing with the death of a deer on a dark road?

☰ MAKING COMPARISONS

1. What specific similarities do you see among the poems?

2. Is Wrigley more practical or less heartless than Stafford and Burnside?

3. Which response to hitting a deer do you imagine would be closest to yours? Why?

LOREN GOODMAN
Traveling through the Dark (2005)

Loren Goodman (b. 1969) was raised in Wichita, Kansas, and graduated from Columbia University in 1991. He later received an M.A. from SUNY-Buffalo. Critics see his book of poems, Famous Americans *(2006), which was published in the prestigious Yale Younger Poets Series, as sophisticated comic art. His most recent work is* Suppository Writing *(2008). The poet W. S. Merwin notes that Goodman seems to love nonsense for its own sake but that his work is also clever, spontaneous, playful, and surreal. Others are not so sure. When the controversial poem presented here appeared in the prestigious journal* Poetry *(July/August 2005), some readers were surprised, some outraged. Others saw this poem, an intriguing and surprising reworking of William Stafford's classic verse, as provocative and serious.*

Traveling through the dark I found a deer
dead on the edge of the Wilson River road.
It is usually best to roll them into the canyon:
that road is narrow; to swerve might make more dead.

By glow of the tail-light I stumbled back of the car   5
and stood by the heap, a doe, a recent killing;
she had stiffened already, almost cold.
I dragged her off; she was large in the belly.

My fingers touching her side brought me the reason —
her side was warm; her fawn lay there waiting,   10
alive, still, never to be born.
Beside that mountain road I hesitated.

The car aimed ahead its lowered parking lights;
under the hood purred the steady engine.
I stood in the glare of the warm exhaust turning red;   15
around our group I could hear the wilderness listen.

I thought hard for us all — my only swerving —,
then pushed myself over the edge into the river.   *[2005]*

≡ THINKING ABOUT THE TEXT

1. Assuming this parody is also meant to be serious, how does "myself" change the meaning of the poem?

2. If this were the first time you were reading this poem, might you be surprised by the last line? Why?

3. Is it possible to read the poem as leading logically to "myself"? Why?

4. Goodman is probably trying for multiple effects. What might they be?

5. Can you think of other plausible ways to change the last lines? What effect does your change make on the meaning of the poem? What would be the effect if you changed "deer" to a person — say, a friend, a lover, or an enemy?

≡ MAKING COMPARISONS

1. Both the Wrigley and Goodman poems can be seen as parodies. Which do you prefer?

2. Of the four "takes" on accidents with animals, which seems the most insightful? Why?

3. Which of the three poems do you think Stafford would be most impressed by? The most surprised by?

≡ WRITING ABOUT ISSUES

1. Argue that the title of Stafford's poem is the key to understanding the verse's meaning.

2. Argue that Goodman's poem is not plagiarism.

3. Write a brief critique of these poems, choosing one as the response to hitting a deer that you feel most resembles your own.

4. Argue that there are or are not ethical issues in the situation Stafford and the others deal with.

KATIA KAPOVICH, "The Ferry"

LINDA PASTAN, "Leaving the Island"

MARK DOTY, "Night Ferry"

For some reason, journeys on ferries seem to put us in a wistful, meditative frame of mind. Especially for a writer, this trip seems more symbolic than those in cars or on planes. It often brings to mind previous outings, perhaps from childhood, or sometimes it might remind us that "all life," as Arthur Miller wrote, is a "leave taking." And, of course, there is the larger metaphor that our life is a kind of ferry ride between the shores of life and death. The three poets included here take advantage of these notions, adding their own lyrical perspectives. Katia Kapovich, for example, muses on time passing, Linda Pastan on rituals repeated, and Mark Doty on mysteries as deep as the seas. As Pastan writes, "The ferry is no simple pleasure boat."

≡ BEFORE YOU READ

Why do you think ferries evoke meditative responses that planes or cars usually do not elicit? Have you ever taken a ferry ride? What was your response?

KATIA KAPOVICH
The Ferry

Katia Kapovich (b. 1960) was born in Moldova in the former Soviet Union, where as a young intellectual artist she was under considerable pressure to conform. As a member of an underground literary dissident movement, she was in constant conflict with an oppressive government. During a demonstration for intellectual freedom at a university in Leningrad, she was arrested after clashing with police. She was briefly confined and later immigrated to America. For the past twenty years, she has lived in Cambridge, Massachusetts, where she teaches Russian literature and writes in both Russian and English. Her poems have been described as exquisitely crafted and quite complex. She and her husband edit the journal Fulcrum. *Her latest book of poems is* Cossacks and Bandits *(2008). The following poem is from* Best American Poetry 2006.

> I'm jotting down these lines,
> having borrowed a pen from a waitress
> in this roadside restaurant. Three rusty pines

prod up the sky in the windows.
My soup gets cold, which implies   5

I'll eat it cold. Soon I too
will leave a tip on the table, merge
into the beehive of travelers
and board one of the ferries,
where there's always a line to the loo   10
and no one knows where the captain is.

Slightly seasick, I keep on writing
of the wind rose and lobster traps,
seagulls, if any—and there always are.
Check the air and you'll see them   15
above straw hats and caps.
The sun at noon glides like a monstrous star-

fish through clouds. Others drink iced tea,
training binoculars on a tugboat.
When I finish this letter, I'll take a gulp   20
from the flask you gave me for the road
in days when I was too young to care about
those on the pier who waved goodbye.

I miss them now: cousins in linen dresses,
my mother, you, boys in light summer shirts.   25
Life is too long. The compass needle dances.
Everything passes by. The ferry passes
by ragged yellow shores.   *[2006]*

≡ THINKING ABOUT THE TEXT

1. Who might the "you" referred to in lines 21 and 25 be? Is there a difference between missing one's mother and missing "cousins in linen
   dresses" (line 24) and "boys in light summer shirts" (line 25)?

2. How do the details in the first three stanzas (rusty pines, cold soup, long
   lines, seasickness) suggest the narrator's mood?

3. The poem shifts from the present to the past in stanza 4. What thought
   comes first to the narrator's mind? How old do you think the narrator is?

4. Is the claim that "[l]ife is too long" (line 26) surprising? Are the following two sentences (lines 26–27) evidence of this?

5. Do ferry rides (as opposed to bridge crossings or tunnel passages) seem
   to make you reflective or nostalgic? Why?

LINDA PASTAN
Leaving the Island

Linda Pastan (b. 1932) was born in the Bronx and graduated from Radcliffe College; she later received her M.A. from Brandeis University. The recipient of numerous prestigious awards and nominations for the National Book Award, Pastan has published several volumes of poetry, including Cardinal Evening: New and Selected Poems 1968–1998 *(1998),* Queen of a Rainy Country *(2006), and* Traveling Light *(2011). The poet May Sarton praised Pastan for her integrity, noting her "unsentimental acceptance of hard work." Pastan was poet laureate of Maryland (1991–1995) and for twenty years taught at the noted Bread Loaf Writers Conference sponsored by Middlebury College in Vermont.*

> We roll up rugs and strip the beds by rote,
> summer expires as it has done before.
> The ferry is no simple pleasure boat
>
> nor are we simply cargo, though we'll float
> alongside heavy trucks — their stink and roar.
> We roll up rugs and strip the beds by rote.
>
> This bit of land whose lines the glaciers wrote
> becomes the muse of memory once more;
> the ferry is no simple pleasure boat.
>
> I'll trade my swimsuit for a woolen coat;
> the torch of autumn has but small allure.
>
> We roll up rugs and strip the beds by rote.
>
> The absences these empty shells denote
> suggest the losses winter has in store.
> The ferry is no simple pleasure boat.
>
> The songs of summer dwindle to one note:
> the fog horn's blast (which drowns this closing door).
> We rolled up rugs and stripped the beds by rote.
> The ferry is no simple pleasure boat.   *[2004]*

≡ **THINKING ABOUT THE TEXT**

1. How would you describe the narrator's mood? Is it temporary? What effects does the repetition of "We roll up rugs and strip the beds by rote" and "The ferry is no simple pleasure boat" have on the reader?

2. Is this a poem about summer's passing or about something more general — say, time passing or aging?

3. Why does summer seem the best of times for the narrator? Is it for you? Do losses happen mostly in the winter?

4. Do you remember a childhood vacation? Is your memory positive? Were you sad when it ended?

5. How would you expand on the refrain "The ferry is no simple pleasure boat"? Is "simple" the key idea?

≡ MAKING COMPARISONS

1. Compare the mood or the tone of the speakers in these two poems.

2. Is nostalgia part of the poems? How does a poet avoid being too sentimental about the past? Do these poets succeed in that regard?

3. Note the rhyme scheme in both poems. Does the pattern work better in Pastan's poem than in Kapovich's? Why?

MARK DOTY
Night Ferry

Mark Doty (b. 1953) was born in Tennessee, but his father, who was a builder working for the Army Corps of Engineers, was a man who could not get along with supervisors and often moved the family. In the autobiographical Firebird *(1999), Doty describes growing up as "a sissy" in a Southern Gothic family. He attended high school in Tucson, Arizona, where he first developed an interest in writing. Then he briefly attended the University of Tucson, but dropped out and married when he was eighteen. In the 1970s, he attended Drake University in Iowa, where he and his wife published chapbooks of poetry together. In 1981, he dissolved his marriage when he acknowledged his homosexuality. He received his M.F.A. at Goddard College in Vermont and taught there, eventually moving with his partner to Provincetown, Massachusetts. After his partner died from complications of AIDS in 1984, Doty's poetry took on a new intensity and significance. Doty has taught at several universities and now teaches at Rutgers University. His awards and fellowships include the National Book Critics Award and the T. S. Eliot Prize in 1993 for* My Alexandria. *His many publications include the poetry collections* Sweet Machine *(1998),* School of the Arts *(2005),* Fire to Fire *(2008), and* Paragon Park *(2012), as well as the memoirs* Heaven's Coast *(1997) and* Dog Years *(2007).*

> We're launched into the darkness,
> half a load of late passengers
>   gliding onto the indefinite
>   black surface, a few lights vague
>
>   and shimmering on the island shore.   5
> Behind us, between the landing's twin flanks

(wooden pylons strapped with old tires),
        the docklights shatter in our twin,

    folding wakes, their colors
on the roughened surface combed   1
    like the patterns of Italian bookpaper,
        lustrous and promising. The narrative

    of the ferry begins and ends brilliantly,
and its text is this moving out
    into what is soon before us   1
        and behind: the night going forward,

    sentence by sentence, as if on faith,
into whatever takes place.
    It's strange how we say things *take place*,
        as if occurrence were a location—   2

    the dark between two shores,
for instance, where for a little while
    we're on no solid ground. Twelve minutes,
        precisely, the night ferry hurries

    across the lake. And what happens   2
is always the body of water,
    its skin like the wrong side of satin.
        I love to stand like this,

    where the prow pushes blunt into the future,
knowing, more than seeing, how   3
    the surface rushes and doesn't even break
        but simply slides under us.

    Lake melds into shoreline,
one continuous black moiré;°
    the boatmen follow the one course they know   3
        toward a dock nearly the mirror

    of the first, mercury lamps vaporing
over the few late birds
    attending the pier. Even the bored men
        at the landing, who wave   4

    their flashlights for the last travelers,
steering us toward the road, will seem
    the engineers of our welcome,
        their red-sheathed lights marking

    the completion of our, or anyone's, crossing.   4
Twelve dark minutes. Love,

34 *moiré*: Wavy pattern.

we are between worlds, between
        unfathomed water and I don't know how much

light-flecked black sky, the fogged circles
of island lamps. I am almost not afraid   50
      on this good boat, breathing its good smell
           of grease and kerosene,

warm wind rising up the stairwell
from the engine's serious study.
      There's no beautiful binding   55
           for this story, only the temporary,

liquid endpapers of the hurried water,
shot with random color. But in the gliding forward's
      a scent so quick and startling
           it might as well be blowing   60

off the stars. Now, just before we arrive,
the wind carries a signal and a comfort,
      lovely, though not really meant for us:
           woodsmoke risen from the chilly shore.   *[1993]*

≡ THINKING ABOUT THE TEXT

1. The poem seems to be a sustained metaphor for life's journey. In what ways does this comparison make sense? What other significant metaphor is developed?

2. As symbols, what do the following images suggest — "a few lights vague / and shimmering" (lines 4–5), "like the patterns of Italian bookpaper, / lustrous and promising" (lines 11–12), "no beautiful binding / for this story, only the temporary, / liquid endpapers of the hurried water, / shot with random color" (lines 55–58)?

3. How did you evaluate the speaker's attitude when he says, "I am almost not afraid / on this good boat, breathing its good smell" (lines 50–51)?

4. Does the image of "a scent . . . / . . . blowing / off the stars" (lines 59–61) seem more mysterious than Doty's other images? What idea might the poet be after with such imagery?

5. Can we sustain the journey-of-life metaphor into the last stanza? Where might the passengers be arriving? What is the signal "not really meant for us" (line 63)? Why woodsmoke? Why "the chilly shore" (line 64)?

≡ MAKING COMPARISONS

1. Is Doty's poem more melancholy than the other poems? Why?

2. Is Doty's poem more metaphorical than the others? Why?

3. Which line or lines in these four poems do you find the most lyrical? The most mysterious? The most suggestive?

≡ WRITING ABOUT ISSUES

1. Which of these three poems most closely reflects your own sense of what life's journey is like? Write an essay in which you make the case for your poem in comparison with one or both of the other poems.

2. Write a brief essay defending the idea that ferry rides in literature often have symbolic value. Use the poems here as evidence.

3. Write a brief personal essay about a ferry trip you took, noting your thoughts about it.

4. Read Walt Whitman's famous poem "Crossing Brooklyn Ferry," and write a brief analysis of Whitman's response to his ride.

≡ A Journey to Death: Poems

MARY OLIVER, "When Death Comes"

JOHN DONNE, "Death Be Not Proud"

DYLAN THOMAS, "Do Not Go Gentle into That Good Night"

EMILY DICKINSON, "Because I could not stop for Death"

For many cultures, death seems more than a metaphorical journey. This is especially true of the Greeks, in whose mythology Charon, the ferryman of the underworld, is literally charged with taking the dead across the river Styx, where they will continue their trek for better or worse. Contemporary poets tend to see death's journey differently than the ancients did, but their appreciation of the mysteries and power of death is enduring. And poets reflect on death's presence in our lives in lyrical and illuminating ways.

Mary Oliver uses a series of interesting similes both to describe death's arrival ("like the hungry bear") and to prepare herself for its inevitability. John Donne sneers at death, perhaps to demonstrate its power, and Dylan Thomas wants to resist that power. Reducing the significance of death was probably on Emily Dickinson's mind when she describes Death as a civil carriage driver who kindly stops for her on the way to eternity. Death has intrigued and puzzled poets for centuries perhaps because, as Shakespeare reminds us, it is a country from which no traveler returns.

≡ BEFORE YOU READ

Does our society have a particular attitude toward death? Can you point to films that might reveal such a cultural inclination? Does your religion have a specific take on death? What is your general attitude toward death, and where does it come from?

MARY OLIVER
When Death Comes

Mary Oliver (b. 1935) was born in Maple Heights, Ohio, and briefly attended Ohio State University. She was strongly influenced by the poet Edna St. Vincent Millay. Her collection No Voyage and Other Poems *(1963) was the first of numerous volumes, including* New and Selected Poems *(1992), which won the National Book Award, and* American Primitive *(1984), which won the Pulitzer Prize for poetry. She has taught at Bucknell University and Sweet Briar College. Her most recent poetry collections are* Dog Songs *(2013) and* A Thousand Mornings *(2012). The poet Maxine Kumin calls Oliver "an undefatigable guide to the natural world."*

When death comes
like the hungry bear in autumn;
when death comes and takes all the bright coins from his purse

to buy me, and snaps the purse shut;
when death comes
like the measles-pox;

when death comes
like an iceberg between the shoulder blades,

I want to step through the door full of curiosity, wondering:
what is it going to be like, that cottage of darkness?   1

And therefore I look upon everything
as a brotherhood and a sisterhood,
and I look upon time as no more than an idea,
and I consider eternity as another possibility,

and I think of each life as a flower, as common   1
as a field daisy, and as singular,
and each name a comfortable music in the mouth
tending as all music does, toward silence,

and each body a lion of courage, and something
precious to the earth.   2

When it's over, I want to say: all my life
I was a bride married to amazement.
I was the bridegroom, taking the world into my arms.

When it is over, I don't want to wonder
if I have made of my life something particular, and real.   2
I don't want to find myself sighing and frightened,
or full of argument.

I don't want to end up simply having visited this world.   *[1992]*

≡ **THINKING ABOUT THE TEXT**

1. How would you describe what the narrator wants to avoid when death comes?

2. The poet uses a number of similes to describe death's coming. Explain why any one of these seems particularly apt.

3. How does Oliver's view of death influence the way she lives her life?

4. Unpack "visited" in the last line.

5. Does our culture have a particular view of death? What might that be? Does your religion have an attitude toward death that may have influenced you? Is there evidence for a cultural view of death in movies? In popular songs? On TV shows?

JOHN DONNE
Death Be Not Proud

Long regarded as a major English writer, John Donne (1572–1631) was also trained as a lawyer and clergyman. Around 1594, he converted from Catholicism to Anglicanism; in 1615, he was ordained; and in 1621, he was appointed to the prestigious position of dean of St. Paul's Cathedral in London. Today, his sermons continue to be studied as literature, yet he is more known for his poetry. When he was a young man, he often wrote about love, but later he focused on religious themes. The following poem, one of Donne's "holy sonnets," is from 1611.

Death be not proud, though some have callèd thee
Mighty and dreadful, for thou art not so;
For those whom thou think'st thou dost overthrow
Die not, poor Death, nor yet canst thou kill me.
From rest and sleep, which but thy pictures° be,   *images*   5
Much pleasure; then from thee much more must flow,
And soonest our best men with thee do go,
Rest of their bones, and soul's delivery.°   *deliverance*
Thou art slave to Fate, Chance, kings, and desperate men,
And dost with Poison, War, and Sickness dwell;   10
And poppy or channs can make us sleep as well,
And better than thy stroke; why swell'st° thou then?   *swell with pride*
One short sleep past, we wake eternally
And death shall be no more; Death, thou shalt die.   [1611]

≣ THINKING ABOUT THE TEXT

1. In a sense, Death is the speaker's audience. But presumably Donne expected the living to read his poem. What reaction might he have wanted from this audience?

2. Is the speaker proud? Define what you mean by the term.

3. Evidently the speaker believes in an afterlife. What would you say to people who consider the speaker naive and the poem irrelevant because they don't believe that "we wake eternally" (line 13)? How significant is this warrant or assumption? Do you share it?

4. What are the arguments the narrator uses to diminish Death?

5. Imagine Death writing a sonnet in response to the speaker. Perhaps it would be entitled "Life Be Not Proud." What might Death say in it?

≣ MAKING COMPARISONS

1. Is death more or less fearsome in Donne's poem than in Oliver's?

2. Do both speakers refuse to be afraid of death?

3. What optimistic note do both speakers take?

DYLAN THOMAS
Do Not Go Gentle into That Good Night

Dylan Thomas (1914–1953) was a Welsh poet, short-story writer, and playwright. Among his most enduring works are his radio dramas Under Milk Wood *(1954) and* A Child's Christmas in Wales *(1955). A frequent visitor to the United States, Thomas built a devoted audience in this country through his electrifying public readings. Unfortunately, he was also well known for his alcoholism, which killed him at a relatively young age. He wrote the following poem in 1952, not long before his own death. It takes the form of a villanelle, which consists of nineteen lines: five tercets (three-line stanzas) followed by a quatrain (four-line stanza). The first and third lines of the opening tercet are used alternately to conclude each succeeding tercet, and they are joined to form a rhyme at the poem's end.*

Do not go gentle into that good night,
Old age should burn and rave at close of day;
Rage, rage against the dying of the light.

Though wise men at their end know dark is right,
Because their words had forked no lightning they
Do not go gentle into that good night.

Good men, the last wave by, crying how bright
Their frail deeds might have danced in a green bay,
Rage, rage against the dying of the light.

Wild men who caught and sang the sun in flight,
And learn, too late, they grieved it on its way,
Do not go gentle into that good night.

Grave men, near death, who see with blinding sight
Blind eyes could blaze like meteors and be gay,
Rage, rage against the dying of the light.

And you, my father, there on the sad height,
Curse, bless, me now with your fierce tears, I pray.
Do not go gentle into that good night.
Rage, rage against the dying of the light.

[1952]

☰ THINKING ABOUT THE TEXT

1. In what sense could the night possibly be "good," given that people are supposed to "rage" at it?

2. Why do you think Thomas has his speaker refer to "the dying of the light" instead of simply to "dying"? What other parts of the poem relate to the word *light*?

3. The speaker refers to four kinds of "men." Restate in your own words the description given of each. Should Thomas's language about them have been less abstract? Why, or why not?

4. What is the effect of climaxing the poem with a reference to "you, my father" (line 16)? If the father had been introduced in the first or second stanzas, would the effect have been quite different? If so, how?

5. What is the effect of the villanelle form? Judging by Thomas's poem, do you think it is worthwhile for a poet to write in this way, despite the technical challenges of the form? Should teachers of poetry writing push their students to write a villanelle? Explain your reasoning.

≡ MAKING COMPARISONS

1. Is this poem an affirmation of life? Could Oliver's or Donne's poem be considered as such?

2. Compare the speaker's attitude in this poem to that in Oliver's.

3. Which poet seems most at peace with death?

EMILY DICKINSON
Because I could not stop for Death

Although Emily Dickinson (1830–1886) was considered an eccentric recluse by many of her provincial neighbors, history has interpreted Emily Dickinson's life in various ways, according to the thinking of the times. Once considered isolated, she is now seen by many critics as connected to the issues and literature of her age. And feminist and queer studies scholars now see the once shy figure as an active champion of defying gender stereotypes. Although she has often been described as a nunlike, passive figure, critics today see her as a nonconformist mistrustful of power and dogma and as someone who questioned any kind of received opinion, even popular views on religion and the afterlife.

The following much-discussed poem has intrigued and puzzled critics for generations. Its elusive meaning and its combination of Christian promises and Gothic imagery has allowed critics to see the poem as everything from an acceptance of New England Protestant dogma to a rejection of religion in favor of the immortality of art. The poem was originally published in 1890 as "The Chariot."

Because I could not stop for Death —
He kindly stopped for me —
The Carriage held but just Ourselves —
And Immortality.

We slowly drove — He knew no haste   5
And I had put away

My labor and my leisure too,
For His Civility—

We passed the School, where Children strove
At Recess—in the Ring—
We passed the Fields of Gazing Grain—
We passed the Setting Sun—

Or rather—He passed us—
The Dews drew quivering and chill—
For only Gossamer, my Gown—
My Tippet—only Tulle—

We paused before a House that seemed
A Swelling of the Ground—
The Roof was scarcely visible—
The Cornice—in the Ground—

Since then—'tis Centuries—and yet
Feels shorter than the Day
I first surmised the Horses' Heads
Were toward Eternity—

[1890]

≡ THINKING ABOUT THE TEXT

1. Who are the passengers in the carriage? What is the effect of "kindly" in line 2? How might we imagine Immortality? Fear of death was a common theme in nineteenth-century sermons. How might this poem be a rejection of that fear?

2. How might the second stanza be an acceptance of death? Why does Death drive slowly?

3. What might the three images in the third stanza stand for?

4. Critics have debated the reference for "He" in stanza 4. What do you think she means? What do "gossamer," "tippet," and "tulle" mean?

5. What suggests that the narrator might already be dead? What might "House" in the fifth stanza refer to?

≡ MAKING COMPARISONS

1. Using just a phrase or a word, how would you characterize the attitude of these four poems toward death?

2. What do you assume Donne's response to Dickinson's poem would be? How about Oliver?

3. Explain which of the four poems seem the most religious and which seem the most secular.

☰ WRITING ABOUT ISSUES

1. Choose one of the four poems about death, and write an essay analyzing it as an argument for a certain position on death. Specify the main claim and the evidence given in support of it. Feel free to evaluate the argument you discuss, although keep in mind that the artistic success of the poem may or may not depend on whether its argument is fully developed.

2. Write an essay comparing two of the poems in this cluster, focusing on the issue of whether they are basically similar or significantly different in the ideas and feelings they express. Refer to specific lines from each text.

3. Write an essay recalling a specific occasion when you had difficulty deciding whether to accept something as inevitable. In your essay, give details of the occasion, the difficulty, and your ultimate reasoning. Indicate as well what your final decision revealed about you. Perhaps you will want to distinguish between the self you were then and the self you are now. If you wish, refer to any of the poems in this cluster.

4. Imagine that you are on the staff of a nursing home. At a staff meeting, the chief administrator asks you and your colleagues to consider framing and hanging one of these four poems in the recreation room. Write a letter to the administrator in which you favor one of these poems or reject them all as inappropriate. Be sure to give reasons for your view.

SHERRY TURKLE, "The Flight from Conversation"

NATHAN JURGENSON, "The IRL Fetish"

It is now commonplace to see three or four students walking together on campus, each staring intently at a smartphone, texting, returning e-mails, and surfing the Web. To older generations, such behavior is puzzling, perhaps even harmful. Of course, to the present generation, being constantly online is casually woven into the fabric of life. It is not odd or puzzling and certainly not negative. But theorists of social media like Sherry Turkle worry that young people are "alone together," hiding from one another in a bubble, existing as a "tribe of one." For Turkle, "connecting" has taken the place of conversation. And conversation, she contends, teaches us self-reflection. Simply connecting online dumbs down our communication, increases our sense of isolation, and provides only the illusion of companionship. She suggests that we take steps to alter the growing trend toward mere connection by embracing the real, that is, offline reality.

But other critics disagree, claiming that there is no longer a disconnect between online and offline; we are now so interconnected in our lives that we are never really offline. Nathan Jurgenson, for example, asserts that "social media is more than something we log into; it is something we carry within us. We can't log off." Arguing that we are actually more interested in the real than ever before, Jurgenson sees critics like Turkle as myopic in their gloomy take on social media. Such debates are growing as thinkers try to understand a technological world in constant transition.

■ BEFORE YOU READ

If it were possible, would you seek dating advice from an artificial intelligence program rather than from your parents or peers? What might be the advantages? What are the pluses and minuses of being on Facebook? What would be the benefits of locking away your cell phone or smartphone for a week?

SHERRY TURKLE
The Flight from Conversation

Sherry Turkle (b. 1948) is a professor in the Program of Science, Technology and Society at the Massachusetts Institute of Technology. She was born in Brooklyn, New York, and in 1976 received her Ph.D. from Harvard in sociology and personality psychology. She has written eight books, the most recent of which focus on human-technology interaction. Her widely praised 1984 book, The Second Self, *analyzes our relationship with computers and comes to the conclusion that they are more than tools; they are part of ourselves, altering how we think and who we are. In her latest book,* Alone Together: Why We Expect More from Technology and Less from Each Other *(2011), she focuses on technology's effect on the present generation, especially the ways face-to-face relationships are being devalued by electronic devices. She worries about the illusion of companionship these devices give and suggests that we think of solitude as a desirable way to get to know ourselves. Her op-ed piece on "the flight from conversation" appeared in the* New York Times *in April 2012.*

We live in a technological universe in which we are always communicating. And yet we have sacrificed conversation for mere connection.

At home, families sit together, texting and reading e-mail. At work executives text during board meetings. We text (and shop and go on Facebook) during classes and when we're on dates. My students tell me about an important new skill: it involves maintaining eye contact with someone while you text someone else; it's hard, but it can be done.

Over the past fifteen years, I've studied technologies of mobile connection and talked to hundreds of people of all ages and circumstances about their plugged-in lives. I've learned that the little devices most of us carry around are so powerful that they change not only what we do, but also who we are.

We've become accustomed to a new way of being "alone together." Technology-enabled, we are able to be with one another, and also elsewhere, connected to wherever we want to be. We want to customize our lives. We want to move in and out of where we are because the thing we value most is control over where we focus our attention. We have gotten used to the idea of being in a tribe of one, loyal to our own party.

Our colleagues want to go to that board meeting but pay attention only to what interests them. To some this seems like a good idea, but we can end up hiding from one another, even as we are constantly connected to one another.   5

A businessman laments that he no longer has colleagues at work. He doesn't stop by to talk; he doesn't call. He says that he doesn't want to interrupt them. He says they're "too busy on their e-mail." But then he pauses and corrects himself. "I'm not telling the truth. I'm the one who doesn't want to be interrupted. I think I should. But I'd rather just do things on my Black-Berry."

A sixteen-year-old boy who relies on texting for almost everything says almost wistfully, "Someday, someday, but certainly not now, I'd like to learn how to have a conversation."

In today's workplace, young people who have grown up fearing conversation show up on the job wearing earphones. Walking through a college library or the campus of a high-tech start-up, one sees the same thing: we are together, but each of us is in our own bubble, furiously connected to keyboards and tiny touch screens. A senior partner at a Boston law firm describes a scene in his office. Young associates lay out their suite of technologies: laptops, iPods, and multiple phones. And then they put their earphones on. "Big ones. Like pilots.

They turn their desks into cockpits." With the young lawyers in their cockpits, the office is quiet, a quiet that does not ask to be broken.

In the silence of connection, people are comforted by being in touch with a lot of people—carefully kept at bay. We can't get enough of one another if we can use technology to keep one another at distances we can control: not too close, not too far, just right. I think of it as a Goldilocks effect.

Texting and e-mail and posting let us present the self we want to be. This means we can edit. And if we wish to, we can delete. Or retouch: the voice, the flesh, the face, the body. Not too much, not too little—just right.

Human relationships are rich; they're messy and demanding. We have learned the habit of cleaning them up with technology. And the move from conversation to connection is part of this. But it's a process in which we short-change ourselves. Worse, it seems that over time we stop caring, we forget that there is a difference.

We are tempted to think that our little "sips" of online connection add up to a big gulp of real conversation. But they don't. E-mail, Twitter, Facebook, all of these have their places—in politics, commerce, romance, and friendship. But no matter how valuable, they do not substitute for conversation.

Connecting in sips may work for gathering discrete bits of information or for saying, "I am thinking about you." Or even for saying, "I love you." But connecting in sips doesn't work as well when it comes to understanding and knowing one another. In conversation we tend to one another. (The word itself is kinetic; it's derived from words that mean to move, together.) We can attend to tone and nuance. In conversation, we are called upon to see things from another's point of view.

Face-to-face conversation unfolds slowly. It teaches patience. When we communicate on our digital devices, we learn different habits. As we ramp up the volume and velocity of online connections, we start to expect faster answers. To get these, we ask one another simpler questions; we dumb down our communications, even on the most important matters. It is as though we have all put ourselves on cable news. Shakespeare might have said, "We are consum'd with that which we were nourish'd by."

And we use conversation with others to learn to converse with ourselves. So our flight from conversation can mean diminished chances to learn skills of self-reflection. These days, social media continually asks us what's "on our mind," but we have little motivation to say something truly self-reflective. Self-reflection in conversation requires trust. It's hard to do anything with 3,000 Facebook friends except connect.

As we get used to being shortchanged on conversation and to getting by with less, we seem almost willing to dispense with people altogether. Serious people muse about the future of computer programs as psychiatrists. A high school sophomore confides to me that he wishes he could talk to an artificial intelligence program instead of his dad about dating; he says the A.I. would have so much more in its database. Indeed, many people tell me they hope that as Siri, the digital assistant on Apple's iPhone, becomes more advanced, "she" will be more and more like a best friend—one who will listen when others won't.

During the years I have spent researching people and their relationships with technology, I have often heard the sentiment "No one is listening to me." I believe this feeling helps explain why it is so appealing to have a Facebook page or a Twitter feed—each provides so many automatic listeners. And it helps explain why—against all reason—so many of us are willing to talk to machines that seem to care about us. Researchers around the world are busy inventing sociable robots, designed to be companions to the elderly, to children, to all of us.

One of the most haunting experiences during my research came when I brought one of these robots, designed in the shape of a baby seal, to an elder-care facility, and an older woman began to talk to it about the loss of her child. The robot seemed to be looking into her eyes. It seemed to be following the conversation. The woman was comforted.

And so many people found this amazing. Like the sophomore who wants advice about dating from artificial intelligence and those who look forward to computer psychiatry, this enthusiasm speaks to how much we have confused conversation with connection and collectively seem to have embraced a new kind of delusion that accepts the simulation of compassion as sufficient unto the day. And why would we want to talk about love and loss with a machine that has no experience of the arc of human life? Have we so lost confidence that we will be there for one another?

We expect more from technology and less from one another and seem increasingly drawn to technologies that provide the illusion of companionship without the demands of relationship. Always-on/always-on-you devices provide three powerful fantasies: that we will always be heard; that we can put our attention wherever we want it to be; and that we never have to be alone. Indeed our new devices have turned being alone into a problem that can be solved. 20

When people are alone, even for a few moments, they fidget and reach for a device. Here connection works like a symptom, not a cure, and our constant, reflexive impulse to connect shapes a new way of being.

Think of it as "I share, therefore I am." We use technology to define ourselves by sharing our thoughts and feelings as we're having them. We used to think, "I have a feeling; I want to make a call." Now our impulse is, "I want to have a feeling; I need to send a text."

So, in order to feel more, and to feel more like ourselves, we connect. But in our rush to connect, we flee from solitude, our ability to be separate and gather ourselves. Lacking the capacity for solitude, we turn to other people but don't experience them as they are. It is as though we use them, need them as spare parts to support our increasingly fragile selves.

We think constant connection will make us feel less lonely. The opposite is true. If we are unable to be alone, we are far more likely to be lonely. If we don't teach our children to be alone, they will know only how to be lonely.

I am a partisan for conversation. To make room for it, I see some first, de-   2
liberate steps. At home, we can create sacred spaces: the kitchen, the dining
room. We can make our cars "device-free zones." We can demonstrate the
value of conversation to our children. And we can do the same thing at work.
There we are so busy communicating that we often don't have time to talk to
one another about what really matters. Employees asked for casual Fridays;
perhaps managers should introduce conversational Thursdays. Most of all, we
need to remember — in between texts and e-mails and Facebook posts — to listen to one another, even to the boring bits, because it is often in unedited moments, moments in which we hesitate and stutter and go silent, that we reveal
ourselves to one another.

I spend the summers at a cottage on Cape Cod, and for decades I walked the
same dunes that Thoreau once walked. Not too long ago, people walked with
their heads up, looking at the water, the sky, the sand, and at one another, talking. Now they often walk with their heads down, typing. Even when they are
with friends, partners, children, everyone is on their own devices.

So I say, look up, look at one another, and let's start the conversation.

[2012]

≡ THINKING ABOUT IDEAS

1. In lamenting our excessive reliance on technology, Turkle gives the example of a seal-shaped "sociable robot" (para. 17). In what ways might
   such a sociable robot be a bad thing? How might it be seen as something positive? Compare this example to the sophomore who wishes for
   AI advice.

2. Based on your experience and observations, in what ways is Turkle's
   claim that we lack "the capacity for solitude" (para. 23) accurate? How
   might it be an overstatement? According to Turkle, what are the consequences of fleeing from solitude? In your experience, how do people
   present idealized versions of themselves online? How is this different
   from offline versions?

3. What steps does Turkle suggest for an increase in conversations? If you
   were in charge of arranging a "conversational Thursday" (para. 25) at
   your dorm or off campus among your friends, what specific activities
   would you plan? What would be your goal? What other steps can you
   suggest that might be effective in reaching Turkle's goals?

≡ THINKING ABOUT ARGUMENTATIVE MOVES

1. According to Turkle, what are some of the qualitative differences between connecting and conversation? What is her support for this contention? How could we see them as not so different? What kind of
   evidence could you assemble to support the ideas that conversation fos-
   ters "self-reflection" and "requires trust" (para. 15)?

2. What does Turkle mean when she suggests that real conversations can't happen online? In what ways might this not be true? In what ways is Turkle's assumption that we connect online "to feel more like ourselves" (para. 23) true? How might it also be false? How could this assumption be supported?

3. In trying to persuade readers, writers construct a persona, a version of themselves they hope will convince readers of their credibility and trust-worthiness. How does Turkle succeed in creating a persuasive voice? One of her critics hears Turkle saying, "I am real. I am the thoughtful human. You are the automaton." Where in the essay do you think this critic got this impression? How does her Cape Cod anecdote add or detract from her persona?

NATHAN JURGENSON
The IRL Fetish

Nathan Jurgenson (b. 1980s) is a social media theorist and sociologist. He received his B.A. from Northern Illinois University in 2004, as well as an M.A. in 2007. He lives in Washington, D.C., and is currently a doctoral student in social media at the University of Maryland, where he teaches. He has published articles and book chapters on social media in scholarly and popular publications. His essay below was published in the New Inquiry *in June 2012.*

The deep infiltration of digital information into our lives has created a fervor around the supposed corresponding loss of logged-off *real life*. Each moment is oversaturated with digital potential: Texts, status updates, photos, check-ins, tweets, and e-mails are just a few taps away or pushed directly to your buzzing and chirping pocket computer—anachronistically still called a "phone." Count the folks using their devices on the train or bus or walking down the sidewalk or, worse, crossing the street oblivious to drivers who themselves are bouncing back and forth between the road and their digital distractor. Hanging out with friends and family increasingly means also hanging out with their technology. While eating, defecating, or resting in our beds, we are rubbing on our glowing rectangles, seemingly lost within the infostream.

If the hardware has spread virally within physical space, the software is even more insidious. Thoughts, ideas, locations, photos, identities, friendships, memories, politics, and almost everything else are finding their way to social media. The power of "social" is not just a matter of the time we're spending checking apps, nor is it the data that for-profit media companies are gathering; it's also that the *logic* of the sites has burrowed far into our consciousness. Smartphones and their symbiotic social media give us a surfeit of options to tell the truth about who we are and what we are doing, and an audience for it all, reshaping norms around mass exhibitionism and voyeurism. Twitter lips and

Instagram eyes: Social media is part of ourselves; the Facebook source code becomes our own code.

Predictably, this intrusion has created a backlash. Critics complain that people, especially young people, have logged on and checked out. Given the addictive appeal of the infostream, the masses have traded *real* connection for the virtual. They have traded human friends for Facebook friends. Instead of being present at the dinner table, they are lost in their phones. Writer after writer laments the loss of a sense of disconnection, of boredom (now redeemed as a respite from anxious info-cravings), of sensory peace in this age of always-on information, omnipresent illuminated screens, and near-constant self-documentation. Most famously, there is Sherry Turkle, who is amassing fame for decrying the loss of real, offline connection. In the *New York Times*, Turkle writes that "in our rush to connect, we flee from solitude . . . we seem almost willing to dispense with people altogether." She goes on:

> I spend the summers at a cottage on Cape Cod, and for decades I walked the same dunes that Thoreau once walked. Not too long ago, people walked with their heads up, looking at the water, the sky, the sand, and at one another, talking. Now they often walk with their heads down, typing. Even when they are with friends, partners, children, everyone is on their own devices. So I say, look up, look at one another.

While the Cape Cod example is Kerry/Romney–level unrelatable, we can grasp her point: Without a device, we are heads up, eyes to the sky, left to ponder and appreciate. Turkle leads the chorus that insists that taking time out is becoming dangerously difficult and that we need to follow their lead and log off.

This refrain is repeated just about any time someone is forced to detether   5 from a digital appendage. Forgetting one's phone causes a sort of existential crisis. Having to navigate without a maps app, eating a delicious lunch and not being able to post a photograph, having a witty thought without being able to tweet forces reflection on how different our modern lives really are. To spend a moment of boredom without a glowing screen, perhaps while waiting in line at the grocery store, can propel people into a *This American Life*–worthy self-exploration about how profound the experience was.

Fueled by such insights into our lost "reality," we've been told to resist technological intrusions and aspire to consume less information: turn off your phones, log off social media, and learn to reconnect offline. Books like Turkle's *Alone Together*, William Powers's *Hamlet's Blackberry*, and the whole Digital Sabbath movement plead with us to close the Facebook tab so we can focus on one task undistracted. We should go out into the "real" world, lift our chins, and breathe deep the wonders of the offline (which, presumably, smells of Cape Cod).

But as the proliferation of such essays and books suggests, we are far from forgetting about the offline; rather we have become obsessed with being offline more than ever before. We have never appreciated a solitary stroll, a camping trip, a face-to-face chat with friends, or even our boredom better than we do now. Nothing has contributed more to our collective appreciation for being logged off and technologically disconnected than the very technologies of connection. The ease of digital distraction has made us appreciate solitude with a new intensity. We savor being face-to-face with a small group of friends or family in one place and one time far more thanks to the digital sociality that so fluidly rearranges the rules of time and space. In short, we've never cherished being alone, valued introspection, and treasured information disconnection more than we do now. Never has being disconnected—even if for just a moment—felt so profound.

The current obsession with the analog, the vintage, and the retro has everything to do with this fetishization of the offline. The rise of the mp3 has been coupled with a resurgence in vinyl. Vintage cameras and typewriters dot the apartments of Millennials. Digital photos are cast with the soft glow, paper borders, and scratches of Instagram's faux-vintage filters. The ease and speed of the digital photo resists itself, creating a new appreciation for slow film photography. "Decay porn" has become a thing.

Many of us, indeed, have always been quite happy to occasionally log off and appreciate stretches of boredom or ponder printed books—even though books themselves were regarded as a deleterious distraction as they became more prevalent. But our immense self-satisfaction in disconnection is new. How proud of ourselves we are for fighting against the long reach of mobile and social technologies! One of our new hobbies is patting ourselves on the back by demonstrating how much we *don't* go on Facebook. People boast about not having a profile. We have started to congratulate ourselves for keeping our phones in our pockets and fetishizing the offline as something more real to be nostalgic for. While the offline is said to be increasingly difficult to access, it is simultaneously easily obtained—if, of course, you are the "right" type of person.

Every other time I go out to eat with a group, be it family, friends, or acquaintances of whatever age, conversation routinely plunges into a discussion of when it is appropriate to pull out a phone. People boast about their self-control over not checking their device, and the table usually reaches a self-congratulatory consensus that we should all just keep it in our pants. The pinnacle of such abstinence-only smartphone education is a game that is popular to talk about (though I've never actually seen it played) wherein the first person at the dinner table to pull out their device has to pay the tab. Everyone usually agrees this is awesome.

What a ridiculous state of affairs this is. To obsess over the offline and deny all the ways we routinely remain disconnected is to fetishize this disconnection. Author after author pretends to be a lone voice, taking a courageous stand in support of the offline in precisely the moment it has proliferated and become over-valorized. For many, maintaining the fiction of the collective loss of the offline *for everyone else* is merely an attempt to construct their own personal time-outs as more special, as allowing them to rise above those social forces of distraction that have ensnared the masses. "I am real. I am the thoughtful human. You are the automaton." I am reminded of a line from a recent essay by Sarah Nicole Prickett: that we are "so obsessed with the real that it's unrealistic, atavistic, and just silly." How have we come to make the error of collectively mourning the loss of that which is proliferating?

In great part, the reason is that we have been taught to mistakenly view *online* as meaning *not offline*. The notion of the offline as real and authentic is a recent invention, corresponding with the rise of the online. If we can fix this false separation and view the digital and physical as enmeshed, we will understand that what we do while connected is inseparable from what we do when disconnected. That is, disconnection from the smartphone and social media isn't really disconnection at all: The logic of social media follows us long after we log out. There was and is no offline; it is a lusted-after fetish object that some claim special ability to attain, and it has always been a phantom.

Digital information has long been portrayed as an elsewhere, a new and different cyberspace, a tendency I have coined the term "digital dualism" to describe: the habit of viewing the online and offline as largely distinct. The common (mis)understanding is experience is zero-sum: time spent online means less spent offline. We are either jacked into the Matrix or not; we are either looking at our devices or not. When camping, I have service or not, and when out to eat, my friend is either texting or not. The smartphone has come to be "the perfect symbol" of leaving the here and now for something digital, some other, *cyber*, space. To be clear, the digital and physical *are not the same*, but we should aim to better understand the relationship of different combinations of information, be they analog or digital, whether using the technologies of stones, transistors, or flesh and blood. Also, technically, bits *are* atoms, but the language can still be conceptually useful.

But this idea that we are trading the offline for the online, though it dominates how we think of the digital and the physical, is myopic. It fails to capture the plain fact that our lived reality is the result of the constant interpenetration of the online and offline. That is, we live in an augmented reality that exists at the intersection of materiality and information, physicality and digitality, bodies and technology, atoms and bits, the off and the online. It is wrong to say "IRL" to mean offline: *Facebook is real life*.

Facebook doesn't curtail the offline but depends on it. What is most crucial   15
to our time spent logged on is what happened when logged off; it is the fuel that runs the engine of social media. The photos posted, the opinions expressed, the check-ins that fill our streams are often anchored by what happens when disconnected and logged-off. The Web has everything to do with reality; it comprises real people with real bodies, histories, and politics. It is the fetish objects of the offline and the disconnected that are not real.

Those who mourn the loss of the offline are blind to its prominence online. When Turkle was walking Cape Cod, she breathed in the air, felt the breeze, and watched the waves with Facebook in mind. The appreciation of this moment of so-called disconnection was, in part, a product of online connection. The stroll ultimately was understood as and came to be fodder for her op-ed, just as our own time spent not looking at Facebook becomes the status updates and photos we will post later. Turkle takes for granted not only her Cape Cod cottage but also her access to high-profile op-ed space, blinding her to others' similar need for media to declare how meaningful our lives are.

The clear distinction between the on and offline, between human and technology, is queered beyond tenability. It's not real unless it's on Google; pics or it didn't happen. We aren't friends until we are Facebook friends. We have come to understand more and more of our lives through the logic of digital connection. Social media is more than something we log into; it is something we carry within us. We can't log off.

Solving this digital dualism also solves the contradiction: We may never fully log off, but this in no way implies the loss of the face-to-face, the slow, the analog, the deep introspection, the long walks, or the subtle appreciation of life sans screen. We enjoy all of this more than ever before. Let's not pretend we are in some special, elite group with access to the pure offline, turning the real into a fetish and regarding everyone else as a little less real and a little less human.

[2012]

≡ THINKING ABOUT IDEAS

1. Although he agrees that technology has burrowed deep into our consciousness, Jurgenson does not accept Turkle's large distinction between online and offline. Why is this? Why does he think "real" is such a dubious and questionable term?

2. According to Jurgenson, why do some people "boast about their self-control over not checking their device" (para. 10)? Is this the same as "boasting about not having a [Facebook] profile" (para. 9)? From your experience, who might these people be? What might be the positive and negative consequences of turning off all of your digital technology for a day? For a week?

3. According to Jurgenson, what is "digital dualism" (para. 13), and how can we solve it? What are Jurgenson's objections to Turkle's ideas? How might some of his criticisms be considered ad hominem — that is, an attack on the person rather than the person's ideas?

≡ THINKING ABOUT ARGUMENTATIVE MOVES

1. Who exactly is Jurgenson's opposition? How fairly does he state their positions? How does Jurgenson's use of sarcasm and irony affect his credibility?

2. Although Jurgenson's position might be inferred from his use of "supposed" in the first sentence, his position doesn't become obvious until he says in paragraph 11, "what a ridiculous state of affairs this is." What exactly is he complaining about, and how does he hope to correct these mistaken views?

3. Rather than being obsessed with being online, Jurgenson surprisingly claims "we have become obsessed with being offline more than ever"

(para. 7). What evidence does he provide? What additional evidence might there be?

≡ WRITING ABOUT ISSUES

1. In an essay, agree with, disagree with, or qualify Jurgenson's contention that "Facebook is real life" (para. 14).

2. Write an essay in which you analyze the differences between communicating online and offline, taking into consideration Turkle's distinction between connecting and communicating and Jurgenson's digital dualism.

3. Based on your own experience and observations, write an essay that takes issue with Turkle's Cape Cod anecdote. You may partly or fully disagree or agree with her. Be sure to include Jurgenson's response to this example.

4. Search online for information about the Digital Sabbath movement and Decay porn. Write an essay that explains how these ideas either support or call into question Turkle's and Jurgenson's positions.

▤ Contexts for Research: Ralph Ellison's "Battle Royal" and the Pursuit of Equality

RALPH ELLISON, "Battle Royal"

CULTURAL CONTEXTS:
BOOKER T. WASHINGTON, "Atlanta Exposition Address (The Atlanta Compromise)"

W. E. B. DU BOIS, "Of Mr. Booker T. Washington"

GUNNAR MYRDAL, "Social Equality"

More than forty years after the civil rights movement of the 1960s, our national awareness of how brutal discrimination was against African Americans is diminished. Although educational and economic equality has not been completely attained, progress has been made, especially in eliminating official policies and gestures of bias. Before World War II, however, overt discrimination was common, especially in the small towns of the segregated South and the rural Midwest. African Americans were rarely allowed to hold anything other than menial jobs in small towns, and most middle-class whites knew African Americans only as maids, gardeners, and servants. African Americans were completely outside the established power structure and rarely able to complain about or obtain justice for their many grievances. Public protest was out of the question. Many African Americans even avoided private protest against their outsider status because they feared that it would worsen their situation. Among African American intellectuals and ordinary citizens, debates raged about which strategy to pursue: to cooperate with the white establishment, hoping to modify hostility, or to agitate for change. Generations of blacks followed the first course until the 1960s, when the nonviolent sit-ins of the civil rights movement ushered in the public protests that ended state-sanctioned segregation. Ralph Ellison's story takes place in the era of segregation and graphically portrays how marginalized African Americans were and how difficult they found it to decide on an effective strategy for progress. At the story's end, the main character, like Ellison himself, begins a lifelong journey from racism toward social justice.

▤ BEFORE YOU READ

Have you ever been in a situation in which you felt discriminated against because of your race, religion, gender, sexual orientation, or age? Did you ever see someone else suffer discrimination? Did you feel powerless? What was your strategy for dealing with this feeling?

(National Archives.)

RALPH ELLISON
Battle Royal

Born in Oklahoma to an activist mother and an intellectual father, Ralph Ellison (1914–1994) was well grounded in literary and social matters by the time he entered Tuskegee Institute to study music in 1933. Finding the conservatism and accommodationism of Tuskegee limiting, Ellison read modernist poets like T. S. Eliot and in 1936 moved to New York, where he met writers Langston Hughes and Richard Wright. Inspired by Wright and by the works of Conrad, Dostoyevsky, and other writers of fiction, Ellison began drafting his novel Invisible Man *(1952) while he was serving in the merchant marine during World War II. Published as a short story in 1947, "Battle Royal" became the first chapter of this National Book Award–winning novel.*

It goes a long way back, some twenty years. All my life I had been looking for something, and everywhere I turned someone tried to tell me what it was. I accepted their answers too, though they were often in contradiction and even self-contradictory. I was naive. I was looking for myself and asking everyone except myself questions which I, and only I, could answer. It took me a long time and much painful boomeranging of my expectations to achieve a realization everyone else appears to have been born with: that I am nobody but myself. But first I had to discover that I am an invisible man!

And yet I am no freak of nature, not of history. I was in the cards, other things having been equal (or unequal) eighty-five years ago. I am not ashamed of my grandparents for having been slaves. I am only ashamed of myself for having at one time been ashamed. About eighty-five years ago they were told that they were free, united with others of our country in everything pertaining to the common good, and, in everything social, separate like the fingers of the hand. And they believed it. They exulted in it. They stayed in their place, worked hard, and brought up my father to do the same. But my grandfather is the one. He was an odd old guy, my grandfather, and I am told I take after him. It was he who caused the trouble. On his deathbed he called my father to him and said, "Son, after I'm gone I want you to keep up the good fight. I never told you, but our life is a war and I have been a traitor all my born days, a spy in the enemy's country ever since I give up my gun back in the Reconstruction. Live with your head in the lion's mouth. I want you to overcome 'em with yeses, undermine 'em with grins, agree 'em to death and destruction, let 'em swoller you till they vomit or bust wide open." They thought the old man had gone out of his mind. He had been the meekest of men. The younger children were rushed from the room, the shades drawn and the flame of the lamp turned so low that it sputtered on the wick like the old man's breathing. "Learn it to the younguns," he whispered fiercely; then he died.

But my folks were more alarmed over his last words than over his dying. It was as though he had not died at all, his words caused so much anxiety. I was warned emphatically to forget what he had said and, indeed, this is the first time it has been mentioned outside the family circle. It had a tremendous effect upon me, however. I could never be sure of what he meant. Grandfather had been a quiet old man who never made any trouble, yet on his deathbed he had called himself a traitor and a spy, and he had spoken of his meekness as a dangerous activity. It became a constant puzzle which lay unanswered in the back of my mind. And whenever things went well for me I remembered my grandfather and felt guilty and uncomfortable. It was as though I was carrying out his advice in spite of myself. And to make it worse, everyone loved me for it. I was praised by the most lily-white men of the town. I was considered an example of desirable conduct—just as my grandfather had been. And what puzzled me was that the old man had defined it as *treachery*. When I was praised for my conduct I felt a guilt that in some way I was doing something that was really against the wishes of the white folks, that if they had understood they would have desired me to act just the opposite, that I should have been sulky and mean, and that that really would have been what they wanted, even though they were fooled and thought they wanted me to act as I did. It made me afraid that some day they would look upon me as a traitor and I would be lost. Still I was more afraid to act any other way because they didn't like that at all. The old man's words were like a curse. On my graduation day I delivered an oration in which I showed that humility was the secret, indeed, the very essence of progress.

(Not that I believed this—how could I, remembering my grandfather?—I only believed that it worked.) It was a great success. Everyone praised me and I was invited to give the speech at a gathering of the town's leading white citizens. It was a triumph for our whole community.

It was in the main ballroom of the leading hotel. When I got there I discovered that it was on the occasion of a smoker, and I was told that since I was to be there anyway I might as well take part in the battle royal to be fought by some of my schoolmates as part of the entertainment. The battle royal came first.

All of the town's big shots were there in their tuxedoes, wolfing down the buffet foods, drinking beer and whiskey and smoking black cigars. It was a large room with a high ceiling. Chairs were arranged in neat rows around three sides of a portable boxing ring. The fourth side was clear, revealing a gleaming space of polished floor. I had some misgivings over the battle royal, by the way. Not from a distaste for fighting, but because I didn't care too much for the other fellows who were to take part. They were tough guys who seemed to have no grandfather's curse worrying their minds. No one could mistake their toughness. And besides, I suspected that fighting a battle royal might detract from the dignity of my speech. In those pre-invisible days I visualized myself as a potential Booker T. Washington. But the other fellows didn't care too much for me either, and there were nine of them. I felt superior to them in my way, and I didn't like the manner in which we were all crowded together into the servants' elevator. Nor did they like my being there. In fact, as the warmly lighted floors flashed past the elevator we had words over the fact that I, by taking part in the fight, had knocked one of their friends out of a night's work.

We were led out of the elevator through a rococo hall into an anteroom and told to get into our fighting togs. Each of us was issued a pair of boxing gloves and ushered out into the big mirrored hall, which we entered looking cautiously about us and whispering, lest we might accidentally be heard above the noise of the room. It was foggy with cigar smoke. And already the whiskey was taking effect. I was shocked to see some of the most important men of the town quite tipsy. They were all there—bankers, lawyers, judges, doctors, fire chiefs, teachers, merchants. Even one of the more fashionable pastors. Something we could not see was going on up front. A clarinet was vibrating sensuously and the men were standing up and moving eagerly forward. We were a small tight group, clustered together, our bare upper bodies touching and shining with anticipatory sweat; while up front the big shots were becoming increasingly excited over something we still could not see. Suddenly I heard the school superintendent, who had told me to come, yell, "Bring up the shines, gentlemen! Bring up the little shines!"

We were rushed up to the front of the ballroom, where it smelled even more strongly of tobacco and whiskey. Then we were pushed into place. I almost wet my pants. A sea of faces, some hostile, some amused, ringed around us, and in the center, facing us, stood a magnificent blonde—stark naked. There was dead silence. I felt a blast of cold air chill me. I tried to back away, but they were behind me and around me. Some of the boys stood with lowered heads, trembling. I felt a wave of irrational guilt and fear. My teeth chattered, my skin turned to goose flesh, my knees knocked. Yet I was strongly attracted and looked in spite of myself. Had the price of looking been blindness, I would have looked. The hair was yellow like that of a circus kewpie doll, the face heavily powdered and rouged, as though to form an abstract mask, the eyes hollow and smeared a cool blue, the color of a baboon's butt. I felt a desire to spit upon her as my eyes brushed slowly over her body. Her breasts were firm and round as the domes of East Indian temples, and I stood so close as to see the fine skin texture and beads of pearly perspiration glistening like dew around the pink and erected buds of her nipples. I wanted at one and the same time to run from the room, to sink through the floor, or go to her and cover her from my eyes and the eyes of the others with my body; to feel the soft thighs, to caress her and destroy her, to love her and murder her, to hide from her, and yet to stroke where below the small American flag tattooed upon her belly her thighs formed a capital V. I had a notion that of all in the room she saw only me with her impersonal eyes.

And then she began to dance, a slow sensuous movement; the smoke of a hundred cigars clinging to her like the thinnest of veils. She seemed like a fair bird-girl girdled in veils calling to me from the angry surface of some gray and threatening sea. I was transported. Then I became aware of the clarinet playing and the big shots yelling at us. Some threatened us if we looked and others if we did not. On my right I saw one boy faint. And now a man grabbed a silver pitcher from a table and stepped close as he dashed ice water upon him and stood him up and forced two of us to support him as his head hung and moans issued from his thick bluish lips. Another boy began to plead to go home. He was the largest of the group, wearing dark red fighting trunks much too small to conceal the erection which projected from him as though in answer to the insinuating low-registered moaning of the clarinet. He tried to hide himself with his boxing gloves.

And all the while the blonde continued dancing, smiling faintly at the big shots who watched her with fascination, and faintly smiling at our fear. I noticed a certain merchant who followed her hungrily, his lips loose and drooling. He was a large man who wore diamond studs in a shirtfront which swelled with the ample paunch underneath, and each time the blonde swayed her undulating hips he ran his hand through the thin hair of his bald head and, with his arms upheld, his posture clumsy like that of an intoxicated panda, wound his belly in a slow and obscene grind. This creature was completely hypnotized. The music had quickened. As the dancer flung herself about with a detached expression on her face, the men began reaching out to touch her. I could see their beefy fingers sink into the soft flesh. Some of the others tried to stop them as she began to move around the floor in graceful circles, as they gave chase, slipping and sliding over the polished floor. It was mad. Chairs went crashing, drinks were spilt, as they ran laughing and howling after her. They caught her just as she reached a door, raised her from the floor, and tossed her as college boys are tossed at a hazing, and above her red, fixed-smiling lips I saw the terror and disgust in her eyes, almost like my own terror and that which I saw in some of the other boys. As I watched, they tossed her twice and her soft breasts seemed to flatten against the air and her legs flung wildly as she spun. Some of the more sober ones helped her to escape. And I started off the floor, heading for the anteroom with the rest of the boys.

Some were still crying in hysteria. But as we tried to leave we were stopped and ordered to get into the ring. There was nothing to do but what we were told. All ten of us climbed under the ropes and allowed ourselves to be blindfolded with broad bands of white cloth. One of the men seemed to feel a bit sympathetic and tried to cheer us up as we stood with our backs against the ropes. Some of us tried to grin. "See that boy over there?" one of the men said. "I want you to run across at the bell and give it to him right in the belly. If you don't get him, I'm going to get you. I don't like his looks." Each of us was told the same. The blindfolds were put on. Yet even then I had been going over my speech. In my mind each word was as bright as flame. I felt the cloth pressed into place, and frowned so that it would be loosened when I relaxed.

But now I felt a sudden fit of blind terror. I was unused to darkness. It was as though I had suddenly found myself in a dark room filled with poisonous cotton-mouths. I could hear the bleary voices yelling insistently for the battle royal to begin.

"Get going in there!"

"Let me at that big nigger!"

I strained to pick up the school superintendent's voice, as though to squeeze some security out of that slightly more familiar sound.

"Let me at those black sonsabitches!" someone yelled.

"No, Jackson, no!" another voice yelled. "Here, somebody, help me hold Jack."

"I want to get at that ginger-colored nigger. Tear him limb from limb," the first voice yelled.

I stood against the ropes trembling. For in those days I was what they called ginger-colored, and he sounded as though he might crunch me between his teeth like a crisp ginger cookie.

Quite a struggle was going on. Chairs were being kicked about and I could hear voices grunting as with a terrific effort. I wanted to see, to see more desperately than ever before. But the blindfold was tight as a thick skin-puckering scab and when I raised my gloved hands to push the layers of white aside a voice yelled, "Oh, no you don't, black bastard! Leave that alone!"

"Ring the bell before Jackson kills him a coon!" someone boomed in the sudden silence. And I heard the bell clang and the sound of the feet scuffling forward.

A glove smacked against my head. I pivoted, striking out stiffly as someone went past, and felt the jar ripple along the length of my arm to my shoulder. Then it seemed as though all nine of the boys had turned upon me at once. Blows pounded me from all sides while I struck out as best I could. So many blows landed upon me that I wondered if I were not the only blindfolded fighter in the ring, or if the man called Jackson hadn't succeeded in getting me after all.

Blindfolded, I could no longer control my motions. I had no dignity. I stumbled about like a baby or a drunken man. The smoke had become thicker and with each new blow it seemed to sear and further restrict my lungs. My saliva became like hot bitter glue. A glove connected with my head, filling my mouth with warm blood. It was everywhere. I could not tell if the moisture I felt upon my body was sweat or blood. A blow landed hard against the nape of my neck. I felt myself going over, my head hitting the floor. Streaks of blue light filled the black world behind the blindfold. I lay prone, pretending that I was knocked out, but felt myself seized by hands and yanked to my feet. "Get going, black boy! Mix it up!" My arms were like lead, my head smarting from blows. I managed to feel my way to the ropes and held on, trying to catch my breath. A glove landed in my mid-section and I went over again, feeling as though the smoke had become a knife jabbed into my guts. Pushed this way and that by the legs milling around me, I finally pulled erect and discovered that I could see the black, sweat-washed forms weaving in the smoky-blue atmosphere like drunken dancers weaving to the rapid drumlike thuds of blows.

Everyone fought hysterically. It was complete anarchy. Everybody fought everybody else. No group fought together for long. Two, three, four, fought one, then turned to fight each other, were themselves attacked. Blows landed below the belt and in the kidney, with the gloves open as well as closed, and with my eye partly opened now there was not so much terror. I moved carefully, avoiding blows, although not too many to attract attention, fighting from group to group. The boys groped about like blind, cautious crabs crouching to protect their mid-sections, their heads pulled in short against their shoulders, their arms stretched nervously before them, with their fists testing the smoke-filled air like the knobbed feelers of hypersensitive snails. In one corner I glimpsed a boy violently punching the air and heard him scream in pain as he smashed his hand against a ring post. For a second I saw him bent over holding his hand, then going down as a blow caught his unprotected head. I played one group against the other, slipping in and throwing a punch then stepping out of range while pushing the others into the melee to take the blows blindly aimed at me. The smoke was agonizing and there were no rounds, no bells at three minute intervals to relieve our exhaustion. The room spun round me, a swirl of lights, smoke, sweating bodies surrounded by tense white faces. I bled from both nose and mouth, the blood spattering upon my chest.

The men kept yelling, "Slug him, black boy! Knock his guts out!"

"Uppercut him! Kill him! Kill that big boy!"

25

Taking a fake fall, I saw a boy going down heavily beside me as though we were felled by a single blow, saw a sneaker-clad foot shoot into his groin as the two who had knocked him down stumbled upon him. I rolled out of range, feeling a twinge of nausea.

The harder we fought the more threatening the men became. And yet, I had begun to worry about my speech again. How would it go? Would they recognize my ability? What would they give me?

I was fighting automatically when suddenly I noticed that one after another of the boys was leaving the ring. I was surprised, filled with panic, as though I had been left alone with an unknown danger. Then I understood. The boys had arranged it among themselves. It was the custom for the two men left in the ring to slug it out for the winner's prize. I discovered this too late. When the bell sounded two men in tuxedoes leaped into the ring and removed the blindfold. I found myself facing Tatlock, the biggest of the gang. I felt sick at my stomach. Hardly had the bell stopped ringing in my ears than it clanged again and I saw him moving swiftly toward me. Thinking of nothing else to do I hit him smash on the nose. He kept coming, bringing the rank sharp violence of stale sweat. His face was a black blank of a face, only his eyes alive — with hate of me and aglow with a feverish terror from what had happened to us all. I became anxious. I wanted to deliver my speech and he came at me as though he meant to beat it out of me. I smashed him again and again, taking his blows as they came. Then on a sudden impulse I struck him lightly and as we clinched, I whispered, "Fake like I knocked you out, you can have the prize."

"I'll break your behind," he whispered hoarsely.

"For *them?*"   30

"For *me*, sonofabitch!"

They were yelling for us to break it up and Tatlock spun me half around with a blow, and as a joggled camera sweeps in a reeling scene, I saw the howling red faces crouching tense beneath the cloud of blue-gray smoke. For a moment the world wavered, unraveled, flowed, then my head cleared and Tatlock bounced before me. That fluttering shadow before my eyes was his jabbing left hand. Then falling forward, my head against his damp shoulder, I whispered,

"I'll make it five dollars more."

"Go to hell!"

But his muscles relaxed a trifle beneath my pressure and I breathed, "Seven?"   35

"Give it to your ma," he said, ripping me beneath the heart.

And while I still held him I butted him and moved away. I felt myself bombarded with punches. I fought back with hopeless desperation. I wanted to deliver my speech more than anything else in the world, because I felt that only these men could judge truly my ability, and now this stupid clown was ruining my chances. I began fighting carefully now, moving in to punch him and out again with my greater speed. A lucky blow to his chin and I had him going too — until I heard a loud voice yell, "I got my money on the big boy."

Hearing this, I almost dropped my guard. I was confused: Should I try to win against the voice out there? Would not this go against my speech, and was not this a moment for humility, for nonresistance? A blow to my head as I danced about sent my right eye popping like a jack-in-the-box and settled my dilemma. The room went red as I fell. It was a dream fall, my body languid and fastidious as to where to land, until the floor became impatient and smashed up to meet me. A moment later I came to. An hypnotic voice said FIVE, emphatically. And I lay there, hazily watching a dark red spot of my own blood shaping itself into a butterfly, glistening and soaking into the soiled gray world of the canvas.

When the voice drawled TEN I was lifted up and dragged to a chair. I sat dazed. My eye pained and swelled with each throb of my pounding heart and I wondered if now I would be allowed to speak. I was wringing wet, my mouth still bleeding. We were grouped along the wall now. The other boys ignored me as they congratulated Tatlock and speculated as to how much they would be paid. One boy whimpered over his smashed hand. Looking up front, I saw attendants in white jackets rolling the portable ring away and placing a small square rug in the vacant space surrounded by chairs. Perhaps, I thought, I will stand on the rug to deliver my speech.

Then the M.C. called to us, "Come on up here boys and get your money." 40 We ran forward to where the men laughed and talked in their chairs, waiting. Everyone seemed friendly now.

"There it is on the rug," the man said. I saw the rug covered with coins of all dimensions and a few crumpled bills. But what excited me, scattered here and there, were the gold pieces.

"Boys, it's all yours," the man said. "You get all you grab."

"That's right, Sambo," a blond man said, winking at me confidentially.

I trembled with excitement, forgetting my pain. I would get the gold and the bills, I thought. I would use both hands. I would throw my body against the boys nearest me to block them from the gold.

"Get down around the rug now," the man commanded, "and don't anyone 45 touch it until I give the signal."

"This ought to be good," I heard.

As told, we got around the square rug on our knees. Slowly the man raised his freckled hand as we followed it upward with our eyes.

I heard, "These niggers look like they're about to pray!"

Then, "Ready," the man said. "Go!"

I lunged for a yellow coin lying on the blue design of the carpet, touching 50 it and sending a surprised shriek to join those rising around me. I tried frantically to remove my hand but could not let go. A hot, violent force tore through my body, shaking me like a wet rat. The rug was electrified. The hair bristled up on my head as I shook myself free. My muscles jumped, my nerves jangled, writhed. But I saw that this was not stopping the other boys. Laughing in fear and embarrassment, some were holding back and scooping up the coins knocked off by the painful contortions of the others. The men roared above us as we struggled.

"Pick it up, goddamnit, pick it up!" someone called like a bass-voiced parrot. "Go on, get it!"

I crawled rapidly around the floor, picking up the coins, trying to avoid the coppers and to get greenbacks and the gold. Ignoring the shock by laughing, as I brushed the coins off quickly, I discovered that I could contain the electricity—a contradiction, but it works. Then the men began to push us onto the rug. Laughing embarrassedly, we struggled out of their hands and kept after the coins. We were all wet and slippery and hard to hold. Suddenly I saw a boy lifted into the air, glistening with sweat like a circus seal, and dropped, his wet back landing flush upon the charged rug, heard him yell and saw him literally dance upon his back, his elbows beating a frenzied tattoo upon the floor, his muscles twitching like the flesh of a horse stung by many flies. When he finally rolled off, his face was gray and no one stopped him when he ran from the floor amid booming laughter.

"Get the money," the M.C. called. "That's good hard American cash!"

And we snatched and grabbed, snatched and grabbed. I was careful not to come too close to the rug now, and when I felt the hot whiskey breath descend upon me like a cloud of foul air I reached out and grabbed the leg of a chair. It was occupied and I held on desperately.

"Leggo, nigger! Leggo!"   5[...]

The huge face wavered down to mine as he tried to push me free. But my body was slippery and he was too drunk. It was Mr. Colcord, who owned a chain of movie houses and "entertainment palaces." Each time he grabbed me I slipped out of his hands. It became a real struggle. I feared the rug more than I did the drunk, so I held on, surprising myself for a moment by trying to topple *him* upon the rug. It was such an enormous idea that I found myself actually carrying it out. I tried not to be obvious, yet when I grabbed his leg, trying to tumble him out of the chair, he raised up roaring with laughter, and, looking at me with soberness dead in the eye, kicked me viciously in the chest. The chair leg flew out of my hand and I felt myself going and rolled. It was as though I had rolled through a bed of hot coals. It seemed a whole century would pass before I would roll free, a century in which I was seared through the deepest levels of my body to the fearful breath within me and the breath seared and heated to the point of explosion. It'll all be over in a flash, I thought as I rolled clear. It'll all be over in a flash.

But not yet, the men on the other side were waiting, red faces swollen as though from apoplexy as they bent forward in their chairs. Seeing their fingers coming toward me I rolled away as a fumbled football rolls off the receiver's fingertips, back into the coals. That time I luckily sent the rug sliding out of place and heard the coins ringing against the floor and the boys scuffling to pick them up and the M.C. calling, "All right, boys, that's all. Go get dressed and get your money."

I was limp as a dish rag. My back felt as though it had been beaten with wires.

When we had dressed the M.C. came in and gave us each five dollars, except Tatlock, who got ten for being last in the ring. Then he told us to leave. I was not to get a chance to deliver my speech, I thought. I was going out into the dim alley in despair when I was stopped and told to go back. I returned to the ballroom, where the men were pushing back their chairs and gathering in groups to talk.

The M.C. knocked on a table for quiet. "Gentlemen," he said, "we almost   60[...]
forgot an important part of the program. A most serious part, gentlemen. This boy was brought here to deliver a speech which he made at his graduation yesterday . . ."

"Bravo!"

"I'm told that he is the smartest boy we've got out there in Greenwood. I'm told that he knows more big words than a pocket-sized dictionary."

Much applause and laughter.

"So now, gentlemen, I want you to give him your attention."

There was still laughter as I faced them, my mouth dry, my eye throbbing. I began slowly, but evidently my throat was tense, because they began shouting, "Louder! Louder!"

"We of the younger generation extol the wisdom of that great leader and educator," I shouted, "who first spoke these flaming words of wisdom: 'A ship lost at sea for many days suddenly sighted a friendly vessel. From the mast of the unfortunate vessel was seen a signal: "Water, water; we die of thirst!" The answer from the friendly vessel came back: "Cast down your bucket where you are." The captain of the distressed vessel, at last heeding the injunction, cast down his bucket, and it came up full of fresh sparkling water from the mouth of the Amazon River.' And like him I say, and in his words, 'To those of my race who depend upon bettering their condition in a foreign land, or who underestimate the importance of cultivating friendly relations with the Southern white man, who is his next-door neighbor, I would say: "Cast down your bucket where you are" — cast it down in making friends in every manly way of the people of all races by whom we are surrounded . . .' "

I spoke automatically and with such fervor that I did not realize that the men were still talking and laughing until my dry mouth, filling up with blood from the cut, almost strangled me. I coughed, wanting to stop and go to one of the tall brass, sand-filled spittoons to relieve myself, but a few of the men, especially the superintendent, were listening and I was afraid. So I gulped it down, blood, saliva, and all, and continued. (What powers of endurance I had during those days! What enthusiasm! What a belief in the rightness of things!) I spoke even louder in spite of the pain. But still they talked and still they laughed, as though deaf with cotton in dirty ears. So I spoke with greater emotional emphasis. I closed my ears and swallowed blood until I was nauseated. The speech seemed a hundred times as long as before, but I could not leave out a single word. All had to be said, each memorized nuance considered, rendered. Nor was that all. Whenever I uttered a word of three or more syllables a group of voices would yell for me to repeat it. I used the phrase "social responsibility" and they yelled:

"What's that word you say, boy?"

"Social responsibility," I said.

"What?"

"Social . . ."

"Louder."

". . . responsibility."

"More!"

"Respon —"

"Repeat!"

"— sibility."

The room filled with the uproar of laughter until, no doubt, distracted by having to gulp down my blood, I made a mistake and yelled a phrase I had often seen denounced in newspaper editorials, heard debated in private.

"Social . . ."

"What?" they yelled.   8(

". . . equality—"

The laughter hung smokelike in the sudden stillness. I opened my eyes, puzzled. Sounds of displeasure filled the room. The M.C. rushed forward. They shouted hostile phrases at me. But I did not understand.

A small dry mustached man in the front row blared out, "Say that slowly, son!"

"What, sir?"

"What you just said!"   85

"Social responsibility, sir," I said.

"You weren't being smart, were you, boy?" he said, not unkindly.

"No, sir!"

"You sure that about 'equality' was a mistake?"

"Oh, yes, sir," I said. "I was swallowing blood."   90

"Well, you had better speak more slowly so we can understand. We mean to do right by you, but you've got to know your place at all times. All right, now, go on with your speech."

I was afraid. I wanted to leave but I wanted also to speak and I was afraid they'd snatch me down.

"Thank you, sir," I said, beginning where I had left off, and having them ignore me as before.

Yet when I finished there was a thunderous applause. I was surprised to see the superintendent come forth with a package wrapped in white tissue paper, and, gesturing for quiet, address the men.

"Gentlemen, you see that I did not overpraise this boy. He makes a good   95 speech and some day he'll lead his people in the proper paths. And I don't have to tell you that that is important in these days and times. This is a good, smart boy, and so to encourage him in the right direction, in the name of the Board of Education I wish to present him a prize in the form of this . . ."

He paused, removing the tissue paper and revealing a gleaming calfskin brief case.

". . . in the form of this first-class article from Shad Whitmore's shop."

"Boy," he said, addressing me, "take this prize and keep it well. Consider it a badge of office. Prize it. Keep developing as you are and some day it will be filled with important papers that will help shape the destiny of your people."

I was so moved that I could hardly express my thanks. A rope of bloody saliva forming a shape like an undiscovered continent drooled upon the leather and I wiped it quickly away. I felt an importance that I had never dreamed.

"Open it and see what's inside," I was told.   100

My fingers a-tremble, I complied, smelling the fresh leather and finding an official-looking document inside. It was a scholarship to the state college for Negroes. My eyes filled with tears and I ran awkwardly off the floor.

I was overjoyed; I did not even mind when I discovered that the gold pieces I had scrambled for were brass pocket tokens advertising a certain make of automobile.

When I reached home everyone was excited. Next day the neighbors came to congratulate me. I even felt safe from grandfather, whose deathbed curse usually spoiled my triumphs. I stood beneath his photograph with my brief case in hand and smiled triumphantly into his stolid black peasant's face. It was a face that fascinated me. The eyes seemed to follow everywhere I went.

That night I dreamed I was at a circus with him and that he refused to laugh at the clowns no matter what they did. Then later he told me to open my brief case and read what was inside and I did, finding an official envelope stamped with the state seal; and inside the envelope I found another and another, endlessly, and I thought I would fall of weariness. "Them's years," he said. "Now open that one." And I did and in it I found an engraved document containing a short message in letters of gold. "Read it," my grandfather said. "Out loud!"

"To Whom It May Concern," I intoned. "Keep This Nigger-Boy Running."   105
I awoke with the old man's laughter ringing in my ears.

(It was a dream I was to remember and dream again for many years after. But at that time I had no insight into its meaning. First I had to attend college.)   *[1947]*

≡ THINKING ABOUT THE TEXT

1. Some critics have seen the events at the smoker as symbolic or perhaps as an allegory of the plight of African Americans in the segregated South. Pick at least two specific events from the story. How are they meant to explain certain aspects of the African American experience before the civil rights movement of the 1960s?

2. Some readers are surprised by the bizarre and cruel behavior of the town's leaders. Are you? How do you explain what goes on there?

3. How do you interpret the narrator's dream (paras. 104–06)? Why would his grandfather be laughing?

4. Reread paragraphs 1 through 3. How is this opening section connected to the story? To the last paragraph? What might Ellison's narrator mean when he says in paragraph 1 that he is "an invisible man"?

5. The grandfather's deathbed advice in paragraph 2 causes quite a stir. In your own words, what is his advice? Why are his relatives surprised? What might be some alternatives for dealing with oppression? Which "solution" sounds like the one you would have promoted for our society during Ellison's boyhood?

BOOKER T. WASHINGTON

Atlanta Exposition Address (The Atlanta Compromise)

Recognized in his time as the major spokesman for his race, Booker T. Washington (1856–1915) is often seen today as an accommodationist whose insistence on gradual progress and vocational rather than intellectual education played into the hands of the white power structure, delaying racial equality. He founded and served as president of Tuskegee Institute, wrote twelve books (including the autobiographical Up from Slavery *in 1901), controlled much of the Negro press, and spoke in cities throughout the nation. His speech at the Atlanta Cotton States and International Exposition in 1895, in which he praised the South, condoned segregation and the glory of "common labor" for his race, and called for harmony and cooperation between the races, is often called "The Atlanta Compromise."*

One-third of the population of the South is of the Negro race. No enterprise seeking the material, civil, or moral welfare of this section can disregard this element of our population and reach the highest success. I but convey to you, Mr. President and Directors, the sentiment of the masses of my race when I say that in no way have the value and manhood of the American Negro been more fittingly and generously recognized than by the managers of this magnificent Exposition at every stage of its progress. It is a recognition that will do more to cement the friendship of the two races than any occurrence since the dawn of our freedom.

Not only this, but the opportunity here afforded will awaken among us a new era of industrial progress. Ignorant and inexperienced, it is not strange that in the first years of our new life we began at the top instead of at the bottom; that a seat in Congress or the state legislature was more sought than real estate or industrial skill; that the political convention or stump speaking had more attractions than starting a dairy farm or truck garden.

A ship lost at sea for many days suddenly sighted a friendly vessel. From the mast of the unfortunate vessel was seen a signal, "Water, water; we die of thirst!" The answer from the friendly vessel at once came back, "Cast down your bucket where you are." A second time the signal, "Water, water, send us water!" ran up from the distressed vessel, and was answered, "Cast down your bucket where you are." And a third and fourth signal for water was answered, "Cast down your bucket where you are." The captain of the distressed vessel, at last heeding the injunction, cast down his bucket, and it came up full of fresh, sparkling water from the mouth of the Amazon River. To those of my race who depend on bettering their condition in a foreign land or who underestimate the importance of cultivating friendly relations with the Southern white man, who is their next-door neighbor, I would say: "Cast down your bucket where you are"—cast it down in making friends in every manly way of the people of all races by whom we are surrounded.

Cast it down in agriculture, mechanics, in commerce, in domestic service, and in the professions. And in this connection it is well to bear in mind that whatever other sins the South may be called to bear, when it comes to business, pure and simple, it is in the South that the Negro is given a man's chance in the commercial world, and in nothing is this Exposition more eloquent than in emphasizing this chance. Our greatest danger is that in the great leap from slavery to freedom we may overlook the fact that the masses of us are to live by the productions of our hands, and fail to keep in mind that we shall prosper in proportion as we learn to dignify and glorify common labor and put brains and skill into the common occupations of life; shall prosper in proportion as we learn to draw the line between the superficial and the substantial, the ornamental gewgaws of life and the useful. No race can prosper till it learns that there is as much dignity in tilling a field as in writing a poem. It is at the bottom of life we must begin, and not at the top. Nor should we permit our grievances to overshadow our opportunities.

To those of the white race who look to the incoming of those of foreign birth and strange tongue and habits for the prosperity of the South, were I permitted I would repeat what I say to my own race, "Cast down your bucket where you are." Cast it down among the eight millions of Negroes whose habits you know, whose fidelity and love you have tested in days when to have proved treacherous meant the ruin of your firesides. Cast down your bucket among these people who have, without strikes and labor wars, tilled your fields, cleared your forests, builded your railroads and cities, and brought forth treasures from the bowels of the earth, and helped make possible this magnificent representation of the progress of the South. Casting down your bucket among my people, helping and encouraging them as you are doing on these grounds, and to education of head, hand, and heart, you will find that they will buy your surplus land, make blossom the waste places in your fields, and run your factories. While doing this, you can be sure in the future, as in the past, that you and your families will be surrounded by the most patient, faithful, law-abiding, and unresentful people that the world has seen. As we have proved our loyalty to you in the past, in nursing your children, watching by the sick-bed of your mothers and fathers, and often following them with tear-dimmed eyes to their graves, so in the future, in our humble way, we shall stand by you with a devotion that no foreigner can approach, ready to lay down our lives, if need be, in defense of yours, interlacing our industrial, commercial, civil, and religious life with yours in a way that shall make the interests of both races one. In all things that are purely social we can be as separate as the fingers, yet one as the hand in all things essential to mutual progress.

There is no defense or security for any of us except in the highest intelligence and development of all. If anywhere there are efforts tending to curtail the fullest growth of the Negro, let these efforts be turned into stimulating, encouraging, and making him the most useful and intelligent citizen. Effort or means so invested will pay a thousand per cent interest. These efforts will be twice blessed—"blessing him that gives and him that takes."

There is no escape through law of man or God from the inevitable:—

> The laws of changeless justice bind
> Oppressor with oppressed;

5

> And close as sin and suffering joined
> We march to fate abreast.

Nearly sixteen millions of hands will aid you in pulling the load upward, or they will pull against you the load downward. We shall constitute one-third and more of the ignorance and crime of the South, or one-third its intelligence and progress; we shall contribute one-third to the business and industrial prosperity of the South, or we shall prove a veritable body of death, stagnating, depressing, retarding every effort to advance the body politic.

Gentlemen of the Exposition, as we present to you our humble effort at an exhibition of our progress, you must not expect overmuch. Starting thirty years ago with ownership here and there in a few quilts and pumpkins and chickens (gathered from miscellaneous sources), remember the path that has led from these to the inventions and production of agricultural implements, buggies, steam-engines, newspapers, books, statuary, carving, paintings, the management of drug-stores and banks, has not been trodden without contact with thorns and thistles. While we take pride in what we exhibit as a result of our independent efforts, we do not for a moment forget that our part in this exhibition would fall far short of your expectations but for the constant help that has come to our educational life, not only from the Southern states, but especially from Northern philanthropists who have made their gifts a constant stream of blessing and encouragement.

The wisest among my race understand that the agitation of questions of social equality is the extremest folly, and that progress in the enjoyment of all the privileges that will come to us must be the result of severe and constant struggle rather than of artificial forcing. No race that has anything to contribute to the markets of the world is long in any degree ostracized. It is important and right that all privileges of the law be ours, but it is vastly more important that we be prepared for the exercises of these privileges. The opportunity to earn a dollar in a factory just now is worth infinitely more than the opportunity to spend a dollar in an opera-house.

In conclusion, may I repeat that nothing in thirty years has given us more hope and encouragement, and drawn us so near to you of the white race, as this opportunity offered by the Exposition; and here bending, as it were, over the altar that represents the results of the struggles of your race and mine, both starting practically empty-handed three decades ago, I pledge that in your effort to work out the great and intricate problem which God has laid at the doors of the South, you shall have at all times the patient, sympathetic help of my race; only let this be constantly in mind, that, while from representations in these buildings of the product of field, of forest, of mine, of factory, letters, and art, much good will come, yet far above and beyond material benefits will be that higher good, that, let us pray God, will come, in a blotting out of sectional differences and racial animosities and suspicions, in a determination to administer absolute justice, in a willing obedience among all classes to the mandates of law. This, this, coupled with our material prosperity, will bring into our beloved South a new heaven and a new earth.   [1895]

≣ **THINKING ABOUT THE TEXT**

1. Cite two passages from Washington's speech that would probably have had an impact on the African American characters in "Battle Royal."

2. Do you think Washington is right in saying, "No race can prosper till it learns that there is as much dignity in tilling a field as in writing a poem" (para. 4)?

3. Are you surprised that Washington pledges "the patient, sympathetic help of my race" as those whites in power "work out the great and intricate problem which God has laid at the doors of the South" (para. 11)? What might contemporary black leaders think of this attitude?

W. E. B. DU BOIS
Of Mr. Booker T. Washington

W. E. B. Du Bois (1868–1963) was a driving force in the movement for equality for people of color in America and throughout the world well into his nineties. He was born in Massachusetts soon after the Civil War, and his death in Africa coincided with the March on Washington in 1963. Du Bois was educated at Fisk, Berlin, and Harvard universities, receiving a Ph.D. from Harvard in 1895 for his dissertation on the history of the slave trade. He is best known for his work with the National Association for the Advancement of Colored People (NAACP), serving as editor of The Crisis *from 1910 to 1932. As a scholar, writer, and intellectual, Du Bois openly opposed policies such as those supported by Booker T. Washington that kept social, political, and educational opportunities from most African Americans.* The Souls of Black Folk *(1903), from which our reading is taken, is perhaps the most influential of his many writings.*

Easily the most striking thing in the history of the American Negro since 1876 is the ascendancy of Mr. Booker T. Washington. It began at the time when war memories and ideals were rapidly passing; a day of astonishing commercial development was dawning; a sense of doubt and hesitation overtook the freedmen's sons,—then it was that his leading began. Mr. Washington came, with a simple definite programme, at the psychological moment when the nation was a little ashamed of having bestowed so much sentiment on Negroes, and was concentrating its energies on Dollars. His programme of industrial education, conciliation of the South, and submission and silence as to civil and political rights, was not wholly original; the Free Negroes from 1830 up to wartime had striven to build industrial schools, and the American Missionary Association had from the first taught various trades; and Price° and others had sought a way of honorable alliance with the best of the Southerners. But

Price: Joseph C. Price (1854–1893), founder of Zion Wesley College and Livingstone College, was a prominent African American educator and championed liberal-arts education.

Mr. Washington first indissolubly linked these things; he put enthusiasm, unlimited energy, and perfect faith into this programme, and changed it from a by-path into a veritable Way of Life. And the tale of the methods by which he did this is a fascinating study of human life.

It startled the nation to hear a Negro advocating such a programme after many decades of bitter complaint; it startled and won the applause of the South, it interested and won the admiration of the North; and after a confused murmur of protest, it silenced if it did not convert the Negroes themselves.

To gain the sympathy and cooperation of the various elements comprising the white South was Mr. Washington's first task; and this, at the time Tuskegee was founded, seemed, for a black man, well-nigh impossible. And yet ten years later it was done in the word spoken at Atlanta: "In all things purely social we can be as separate as the five fingers, and yet one as the hand in all things essential to mutual progress." This "Atlanta Compromise" is by all odds the most notable thing in Mr. Washington's career. The South interpreted it in different ways: the radicals received it as a complete surrender of the demand for civil and political equality; the conservatives, as a generously conceived working basis for mutual understanding. So both approved it, and today its author is certainly the most distinguished Southerner since Jefferson Davis, and the one with the largest personal following. . . .

Mr. Washington represents in Negro thought the old attitude of adjustment and submission; but adjustment at such a peculiar time as to make his programme unique. This is an age of unusual economic development, and Mr. Washington's programme naturally takes an economic cast, becoming a gospel of Work and Money to such an extent as apparently almost completely to over-shadow the higher aims of life. Moreover, this is an age when the more advanced races are coming in closer contact with the less developed races, and the race-feeling is therefore intensified; and Mr. Washington's programme practically accepts the alleged inferiority of the Negro races. Again, in our own land, the reaction from the sentiment of war time has given impetus to race-prejudice against Negroes, and Mr. Washington withdraws many of the high demands of Negroes as men and American citizens. In other periods of intensified prejudice all the Negro's tendency to self-assertion has been called forth; at this period a policy of submission is advocated. In the history of nearly all other races and people the doctrine preached at such crises has been that manly self-respect is worth more than lands and houses, and that a people who voluntarily surrender such respect, or cease striving for it, are not worth civilizing.

In answer to this, it has been claimed that the Negro can survive only   5
through submission. Mr. Washington distinctly asks that black people give up, at least for the present, three things—

First, political power,
Second, insistence on civil rights,
Third, higher education of Negro youth,—

and concentrate all their energies on industrial education, the accumulation of wealth, and the conciliation of the South. This policy has been courageously and insistently advocated for over fifteen years, and has been triumphant for perhaps ten years. As a result of this tender of the palm-branch, what has been the return? In these years there have occurred:

1. The disfranchisement of the Negro.
2. The legal creation of a distinct status of civil inferiority for the Negro.
3. The steady withdrawal of aid from institutions for the higher training of the Negro.

These movements are not, to be sure, direct results of Mr. Washington's teachings; but his propaganda has, without a shadow of doubt, helped their speedier accomplishment. The question then comes: Is it possible, and probable, that nine millions of men can make effective progress in economic lines if they are deprived of political rights, made a servile caste, and allowed only the most meager chance for developing their exceptional men? If history and reason give any distinct answer to these questions, it is an emphatic *No*. . . .

In failing thus to state plainly and unequivocally the legitimate demands of their people, even at the cost of opposing an honored leader the thinking classes of American Negroes would shirk a heavy responsibility,—a responsibility to themselves, a responsibility to struggling masses, a responsibility to the darker races of men whose future depends so largely on this American experiment, but especially a responsibility to this nation,—this common Fatherland. It is wrong to encourage a man or a people in evil-doing; it is wrong to aid and abet a national crime simply because it is unpopular not to do so. The growing spirit of kindliness and reconciliation between the North and South after the frightful differences of a generation ago ought to be a source of deep congratulation to all, and especially to those whose mistreatment caused the war; but if that reconciliation is to be marked by the industrial slavery and civic death of those same black men, with permanent legislation into a position of inferiority, then those black men, if they are really men, are called upon by every consideration of patriotism and loyalty to oppose such a course by all civilized methods, even though such opposition involves disagreement with Mr. Booker T. Washington. We have no right to sit silently by while the inevitable seeds are sown for a harvest of disaster to our children, black and white.

First, it is the duty of black men to judge the South discriminatingly. The present generation of Southerners are not responsible for the past, and they should not be blindly hated or blamed for it. Furthermore, to no class is the indiscriminate endorsement of the recent course of the South toward Negroes more nauseating than to the best thought of the South. The South is not "solid"; it is a land in the ferment of social change, wherein forces of all kinds are fighting for supremacy; and to praise the ill the South is today perpetrating is just as wrong as to condemn the good. Discriminating and broad-minded criticism is what the South needs,—needs it for the sake of her own white sons and daughters, and for the insurance of robust, healthy mental and moral development.

Today even the attitude of the Southern whites toward the blacks is not, as so many assume, in all cases the same; the ignorant Southerner hates the

Negro, the workingmen fear his competition, the money-makers wish to use him as a laborer, some of the educated see a menace in his upward development, while others, — usually the sons of the masters — wish to help him to rise. National opinion has enabled this last class to maintain the Negro common schools, and to protect the Negro partially in property, life, and limb. Through the pressure of the money-makers, the Negro is in danger of being reduced to semi-slavery, especially in the country districts; the workingmen, and those of the educated who fear the Negro, have united to disfranchise him, and some have urged his deportation; while the passions of the ignorant are easily aroused to lynch and abuse any black man. To praise this intricate whirl of thought and prejudice is nonsense, to inveigh indiscriminately against "the South" is unjust; but to use the same breath in praising Governor Aycock, exposing Senator Morgan, arguing with Mr. Thomas Nelson Page, and denouncing Senator Ben Tillman, is not only sane, but the imperative duty of thinking black men.

It would be unjust to Mr. Washington not to acknowledge that in several instances he has opposed movements in the South which were unjust to the Negro; he sent memorials to the Louisiana and Alabama constitutional conventions, he has spoken against lynching, and in other ways has openly or silently set his influence against sinister schemes and unfortunate happenings. Notwithstanding this, it is equally true to assert that on the whole the distinct impression left by Mr. Washington's propaganda is, first, that the South is justified in its present attitude toward the Negro because of the Negro's degradation; secondly, that the prime cause of the Negro's failure to rise more quickly is his wrong education in the past; and, thirdly, that his future rise depends primarily on his own efforts. Each of these propositions is a dangerous half-truth. The supplementary truths must never be lost sight of: first, slavery and race-prejudice are potent if not sufficient causes of the Negro's position; second, industrial and common-school training were necessarily slow in planting because they had to await the black teachers trained by higher institutions, — it being extremely doubtful if any essentially different development was possible, and certainly a Tuskegee was unthinkable before 1880; and, third, while it is a great truth to say that the Negro must strive and strive mightily to help himself, it is equally true that unless his striving be not simply seconded, but rather aroused and encouraged, by the initiative of the richer and wiser environing group, he cannot hope for great success.

In his failure to realize and impress this last point, Mr. Washington is especially to be criticized. His doctrine has tended to make the whites, North and South, shift the burden of the Negro problem to the Negro's shoulders and stand aside as critical and rather pessimistic spectators; when in fact the burden belongs to the nation, and the hands of none of us are clean if we bend not our energies to righting these great wrongs.

The South ought to be led, by candid and honest criticism, to assert her better self and do her full duty to the race she has cruelly wronged and is still wronging. The North — her copartner in guilt — cannot salve her conscience by plastering it with gold. We cannot settle this problem by diplomacy and suaveness, by "policy" alone. If worse come to worst, can the moral fiber of this country survive the slow throttling and murder of nine millions of men?

The black men of America have a duty to perform, a duty stern and delicate, — a forward movement to oppose a part of the work of their greatest leader. So far as Mr. Washington preaches Thrift, Patience, and Industrial Training for the masses, we must hold up his hands and strive with him, rejoicing in his honors and glorying in the strength of this Joshua called of God and of man to lead the headless host. But so far as Mr. Washington apologizes for injustice, North or South, does not rightly value the privilege and duty of voting, belittles the emasculating effects of caste distinctions, and opposes the higher training and ambition of our brighter minds, — so far as he, the South, or the Nation, does this, — we must unceasingly and firmly oppose them. By every civilized and peaceful method we must strive for the rights which the world accords to men, clinging unwaveringly to those great words which the sons of the Fathers would fain forget: "We hold these truths to be self-evident: that all men are created equal; that they are endowed by their Creator with certain unalienable rights; that among these are life, liberty, and the pursuit of happiness."

[1903]

≡ THINKING ABOUT THE TEXT

1. Du Bois is clearly upset with Washington. What is his main objection to the Atlanta Compromise? Do you agree with him?

2. Is the narrator of "Battle Royal" still under Washington's influence, or has the thinking of Du Bois made some inroads?

3. What might the grandfather in "Battle Royal" think of Du Bois's last paragraph?

GUNNAR MYRDAL
Social Equality

A Swedish economist who with his wife, Alva Myrdal (winner of the 1982 Nobel Peace Prize), established a model social-welfare system for Sweden in the 1930s, Gunnar Myrdal (1898–1987) was asked by the Carnegie Foundation in 1938 to study racism in the United States. "Social Equality" is an excerpt from the book that elaborated on the results of his study, An American Dilemma: The Negro Problem and Modern Democracy *(1944). In* Cultural Contexts for Ralph Ellison's "Invisible Man," *historian Eric Sundquist points out that for the white men in "Battle Royal," the term* social equality *would have included sexual relations and marriage between black men and white women, which was then an important cultural taboo.*

In his first encounter with the American Negro problem, perhaps nothing perplexes the outside observer more than the popular term and the popular theory of "no social equality." He will be made to feel from the start that it has concrete implications and a central importance for the Negro problem in America. But, nevertheless, the term is kept vague and elusive, and the theory loose and ambiguous. One moment it will be stretched to cover and justify every form of social segregation and discrimination, and, in addition, all the inequalities in justice, politics, and breadwinning. The next moment it will be narrowed to express only the denial of close personal intimacies and intermarriage. The very lack of precision allows the notion of "no social equality" to rationalize the rather illogical and wavering system of color caste in America.

The kernel of the popular theory of "no social equality" will, when pursued, be presented as a firm determination on the part of the whites to block amalgamation and preserve "the purity of the white race." The white man identifies himself with "the white race" and feels that he has a stake in resisting the dissipation of its racial identity. Important in this identification is the notion of "the absolute and unchangeable superiority of the white race." From this racial dogma will often be drawn the *direct* inference that the white man shall dominate in all spheres. But when the logic of this inference is inquired about, the inference will be made *indirect* and will be made to lead over to the danger of amalgamation, or, as it is popularly expressed, "intermarriage."

It is further found that the ban on intermarriage is focused on white women. For them it covers both formal marriage and illicit intercourse. In regard to white men it is taken more or less for granted that they would not stoop to marry Negro women, and that illicit intercourse does not fall under the same intense taboo. Their offspring, under the popular doctrine that maternity is more certain than paternity, become Negroes anyway, and the white race easily avoids pollution with Negro blood. To prevent "intermarriage" in this specific sense of sex relations between white women and Negro men, it is not enough to apply legal and social sanctions against it—so the popular theory runs. In using the danger of intermarriage as a defense for the whole caste system, it is assumed both that Negro men have a strong desire for "intermarriage," and that white women would be open to proposals from Negro men, *if* they are not guarded from even meeting them on an equal plane. The latter assumption, of course, is never openly expressed, but is logically implicit in the popular theory. The conclusion follows that the whole system of segregation and discrimination is justified. Every single measure is defended as necessary to block "social equality" which in its turn is held necessary to prevent "intermarriage."

The basic role of the fear of amalgamation in white attitudes to the race problem is indicated by the popular magical concept of "blood." Educated white Southerners, who know everything about modern genetic and biological research, confess readily that they actually feel an irrational or "instinctive" repugnance in thinking of "intermarriage." These measures of segregation and discrimination are often of the type found in the true taboos, and in the notion "not to be touched" of primitive religion. The specific taboos are characterized, further, by a different degree of excitement which attends their violation and a different degree of punishment to the violator: the closer the act to sexual association, the more furious is the public reaction. Sexual association itself is punished by death and is accompanied by tremendous public excitement; the other social relations meet decreasing degrees of public fury. Sex becomes in this popular theory the principle around which the whole structure of segregation of the Negroes—down to disfranchisement and denial of equal opportunities on the labor market—is organized. The reasoning is this: "For, say what we will, may not all the equalities be ultimately based on potential social equality, and that in turn on intermarriage? Here we reach the real *crux* of the question." In cruder language, but with the same logic, the Southern man on the street responds to any plea for social equality: "Would you like to have your daughter marry a Negro?"

This theory of color caste centering around the aversion to amalgamation   5
determines, as we have just observed, the white man's rather definite rank order of the various measures of segregation and discrimination against Negroes. The relative significance attached to each of those measures is dependent upon their degree of expediency or necessity—in the view of white people—as means of upholding the ban on "intermarriage." In this rank order, (1) the ban on intermarriage and other sex relations involving white women and colored men takes precedence before everything else. It is the end for which the other restrictions are arranged as means. Thereafter follow: (2) all sorts of taboos and etiquettes in personal contacts; (3) segregation in schools and churches; (4) segregation in hotels, restaurants, and theaters, and other public places where people meet socially; (5) segregation in public conveyances; (6) discrimination in public services; and, finally, inequality in (7) politics, (8) justice, and (9) breadwinning and relief.

The degree of liberalism on racial matters in the white South can be designated mainly by the point on this rank order where a man stops because he believes further segregation and discrimination are not necessary to prevent "intermarriage." We have seen that white liberals in the South of the present day, as a matter of principle, rather unanimously stand up against inequality in breadwinning, relief, justice, and politics. These fields of discrimination form the chief battleground and considerable changes in them are, as we have seen, on the way. When we ascend to the higher ranks which concern social relations in the narrow sense, we find the Southern liberals less prepared to split off from the majority opinion of the region. Hardly anybody in the South is prepared to go the whole way and argue that even the ban on intermarriage should be lifted. Practically all agree, not only upon the high desirability of preventing "intermarriage," but also that a certain amount of separation between the two groups is expedient and necessary to prevent it. Even the one who has his philosophical doubts on the point must, if he is reasonable, abstain from ever voicing them. The social pressure is so strong that it would be foolish not to conform. Conformity is a political necessity for having any hope of influence; it is, in addition, a personal necessity for not meeting social ostracism. . . .

The fixation on the purity of white womanhood, and also part of the intensity of emotion surrounding the whole sphere of segregation and discrimination, are to be understood as the backwashes of the sore conscience on the part of white men for their own or their compeers' relations with, or desires for, Negro women. These psychological effects are greatly magnified because of the puritan *milieu* of America and especially of the South. The upper class men in a less puritanical people could probably have indulged in sex relations with, and sexual day-dreams of, lower caste women in a more matter-of-course way and without generating so much pathos about white womanhood. The Negro people have to carry the burden not only of the white men's sins but also of their virtues. The virtues of the honest, democratic, puritan white Americans in the South are great, and the burden upon the Negroes becomes ponderous.

Our practical conclusion is that it would have cleansing effects on race relations in America, and particularly in the South, to have an open and sober discussion in rational terms of this ever present popular theory of "intermarriage" and "social equality," giving matters their factual ground, true proportions and logical relations. Because it is, to a great extent, an opportunistic rationalization, and because it refers directly and indirectly to the most touchy spots in American life and American morals, tremendous inhibitions have been built up against a detached and critical discussion of this theory. But such inhibitions are gradually overcome when, in the course of secularized education, people become rational about their life problems. It must never be forgotten that in our increasingly intellectualized civilization even the plain citizen feels an urge for truth and objectivity, and that this rationalistic urge is increasingly competing with the opportunistic demands for rationalization and escape.

There are reasons to believe that a slow but steady cleansing of the American mind is proceeding as the cultural level is raised. The basic racial inferiority doctrine is being undermined by research and education. For a white man to have illicit relations with Negro women is increasingly meeting disapproval. Negroes themselves are more and more frowning upon such relations. This all must tend to dampen the emotional fires around "social equality." Sex and race fears are, however, even today the main defense for segregation and, in fact, for the whole caste order. The question shot at the interviewer touching any point of this order is still: "Would you like to have your daughter (sister) marry a Negro?"   *[1944]*

≡ **THINKING ABOUT THE TEXT**

1. Look back at the smoker section in "Battle Royal," especially when the narrator during his speech says "social equality" instead of "social responsibility." Why do you think there was a "sudden stillness" in the room?

2. Based on his ideas about white sexual fears, how might Myrdal read the part of the smoker dealing with the naked dancer?

3. Myrdal writes that "conformity is a political necessity for having any hope of influence; it is, in addition, a personal necessity for not meeting social ostracism" (para. 6). Does this insight help your understanding of the world of the smoker?

☰ WRITING ABOUT ISSUES

1. Argue that the episode at the smoker is or is not evidence that the grandfather's advice in "Battle Royal" to "'overcome 'em with yeses, undermine 'em with grins, agree 'em to death and destruction'" (para. 2) will not work.

2. Analyze the arguments of Washington and Du Bois in terms of the claims they both make, the assumptions they base their claims on, the evidence they use as support for their assumptions, and the effectiveness of their claims with the intended audience. Which writer do you find more persuasive?

3. Write a personal narrative detailing an experience either when you were the victim of bias because of your race, sex, age, religion, ethnicity, sexual preference, or any other personal dynamic or when you were part of a group that held biased views. Be specific about what happened, how you felt then, how you feel now, and what you learned from the experience.

APPENDIX

Critical Approaches to Literature

Exploring the topics of literary criticism can help readers understand the various ways literature can matter. One popular way to investigate critical approaches to literature is to group critics into schools. Critics who are concerned primarily with equality for women, for example, are often classified as feminist critics, and those concerned with the responses of readers are classified as reader-response critics. Likewise, critics who focus on the unconscious are said to belong to the psychoanalytic school, and those who analyze class conflicts belong to the Marxist school.

Classifying critics in this way is probably more convenient than precise. Few critics like to be pigeonholed or thought predictable, and many professional readers tend to be eclectic — that is, they use ideas from various schools to help them illuminate the text. Nevertheless, knowing something about contemporary schools of criticism can make you a more informed reader and help literature matter to you even more.

There is a commonsense belief that words mean just what they say — that to understand a certain passage in a text a reader simply needs to know what the words mean. But meaning is rarely straightforward. Scholars have been arguing over the meaning of passages in the Bible, in the Constitution, and in Shakespeare's plays for centuries without reaching agreement. Pinning down the exact meaning of words like *sin, justice,* and *love* is almost impossible, but even more daunting is the unacknowledged theory of reading that each person brings to any text, including literature. Some people who read the Bible or the Constitution, for example, believe in the literal meaning of the words, and some think the real meaning lies in the original intention of the writer, while others believe that the only meaning we can be sure of is our own perspective. For these latter readers, there is no objective meaning, and no absolutely true meaning is possible.

Indeed, a good deal of what a text means depends on the perspective that readers bring with them. Passages can be read effectively from numerous points of view. A generation ago most English professors taught their students to pay attention to the internal aspects of a poem and not to the poem's larger social and political contexts. So oppositions, irony, paradox, and coherence — not gender equality or social justice — were topics of discussion. Proponents of this approach were said to belong to the New Critical school. In the last twenty-five years or so, however, professors have put much more emphasis on the external aspects of interpretation, stressing social, political, cultural, sexual, and gender-based perspectives. Each one of these perspectives can give us a valuable window on a text, helping us see the rich possibilities of literature. Even though each approach can provide insights into a text, it can also be blind to other textual elements. When we read in too focused a way, we can sometimes miss the opportunity to see what others see.

In this appendix, however, we want to present our interpretation in a clear, logical, and reflective manner as we take a position and try to persuade others of its reasonableness. Since there are many possible lenses to see a text through, you can be sure your classmates will see things differently. Part of the excitement and challenge of making arguments that matter is your ability to analyze and clarify your ideas, gather and organize your evidence, and present your claim in carefully revised and edited prose.

Contemporary Schools of Criticism

The following eight approaches are just a few of the many different literary schools or perspectives a reader can use in engaging a text. Think of them as intellectual tools or informed lenses that you can employ to enhance your interpretation of a particular literary text:

- New Criticism
- Feminist criticism
- Psychoanalytic criticism
- Marxist criticism
- Deconstruction
- Reader-response criticism
- Postcolonial criticism
- New Historicism

NEW CRITICISM

New Criticism was developed about seventy years ago as a way to focus on "the text itself." Although it is no longer as popular as it once was, some of its principles are still widely accepted, especially the use of specific examples from the text as evidence for a particular interpretation. Sometimes called *close reading*, this approach does not see either the writer's intention or the reader's personal response as relevant. It is also uninterested in the text's social context, the spirit of the age, or its relevance to issues of gender, social justice, or oppression. These critics are interested, for example, in a poem's internal structure, images, symbols, metaphors, point of view, plot, and characterizations. Emphasis is placed on literary language—on the ways connotation, ambiguity, irony, and paradox all reinforce the meaning. In fact, *how* a poem means is inseparable from *what* it means. The primary method for judging the worth of a piece of literature is its organic unity or the complex way all the elements of a text contribute to the poem's meaning.

Critics often argue that their interpretations are the most consistent with textual evidence. A popular approach is to note the oppositions in the text and to focus on tensions, ironies, and paradoxes. Typically a paradox early in the text is shown at the end not to be that contradictory after all. The critic then argues that all the elements of the text can be seen as contributing to this resolution.

FEMINIST CRITICISM

Feminist criticism developed during the 1970s as an outgrowth of a resurgent women's movement. The goals of the feminist critic and the feminist political activist are similar—to contest the patriarchal point of view as the standard for all moral, aesthetic, political, and intellectual judgments and to assert that gender roles are primarily learned, not universal. They hope to uncover and challenge essentialist attitudes that hold it is normal for women to be kept in domestic, secondary, and subservient roles, and they affirm the value of a woman's experiences and perspectives in understanding the world. Recently both female and male critics have become interested in gender studies, a branch of theory concerned with the ways cultural practices socialize us to act in certain ways because of our gender. Focused primarily on issues of identity, gender criticism looks at the ways characters in literary texts are represented, or how they are constructed in a particular culture as feminine or masculine. Like the broader area of feminism, many gender specialists hope that studying the arbitrary ways we are expected to dress, walk, talk, and behave can help us widen the conventional notions of gender.

PSYCHOANALYTIC CRITICISM

Psychoanalytic criticism began with Sigmund Freud's theories of the unconscious, especially the numerous repressed wounds, fears, unresolved conflicts, and guilty desires from childhood that can significantly affect behavior and mental health in our adult lives. Freud developed the tripart division of the mind into the ego (the conscious self), the superego (the site of what our culture has taught us about good and bad), and the id (the primitive unconscious and source of our sexual drive). Psychoanalytic critics often see literature as a kind of dream filled with symbolic elements that often mask their real meaning. Freud also theorized that young males were threatened by their fathers in the competition for the affection of their mothers. Critics are alert to the complex ways this Oedipal drama unfolds in literature.

MARXIST CRITICISM

Marxist criticism is based on the political and economic theories of Karl Marx. Marxists think that a society is propelled by its economy, which is manipulated by a class system. Most people, especially blue-collar workers (the proletariat), do not understand the complex ways their lives are subject to economic forces beyond their control. This false consciousness about history and material well-being prevents workers from seeing that their values have been socially constructed to keep them in their place. What most interests contemporary Marxists is the way ideology shapes our consciousness. And since literature both represents and projects ideology, Marxist critics see it as a way to unmask our limited view of society's structures.

DECONSTRUCTION

Deconstruction is really more a philosophical movement than a school of literary criticism, but many of its techniques have been used by Marxist and feminist literary critics to uncover important concepts they believe are hidden in texts. Made famous by the French philosopher Jacques Derrida, deconstruction's main tenet is that Western thought has divided the world into binary opposites. To gain a semblance of control over the complexity of human experience, we have constructed a worldview in which good is clearly at one end of a continuum and bad at the other. Additional examples of binary opposites include masculine and feminine, freedom and slavery, objective and subjective, mind and body, and presence and absence. According to Derrida, however, this arbitrary and illusory construct simply reflects the specific ideology of one culture. Far from being opposed to each other, masculinity and femininity, for example, are intimately interconnected, and traces of the feminine are to be found within the masculine. The concepts need each other for meaning to occur, an idea referred to as *différance*. Derrida also notes that language, far from being a neutral medium of communication, is infused with our biases, assumptions, and values—which leads some of us to refer to sexually active women as "sluts" and to sexually active men as "studs." One term ("sluts") is marginalized, and the other ("studs") is privileged because our culture grants men more power than women in shaping the language that benefits them.

Thus, language filters, distorts, and alters our perception of the world. For deconstructors or deconstructive critics, language is not stable or reliable, and when closely scrutinized, it becomes slippery and ambiguous, constantly overflowing with implications, associations, and contradictions. For Derrida, this endless freeplay of meaning suggests that language is always changing, always in flux—especially so when we understand that words can be viewed from almost endless points of view or contexts. That is why deconstructionists claim that texts (or individuals or systems of thought) have no fixed definition, no center, no absolute meaning. And so one way to deconstruct or lay bare the arbitrary construction of a text is to show that the oppositions in the text are not really absolutely opposed, that outsiders can be seen to be insiders, and that words that seem to mean one thing can mean many things.

READER-RESPONSE CRITICISM

Reader-response criticism is often misunderstood to be simply giving one's opinion about a text: "I liked it," "I hate happy endings," "I think the characters were unrealistic." But reader-response criticism is actually more interested in why readers have certain responses. The central assumption is that texts do not come alive and do not mean anything until active readers engage them with specific assumptions about what reading is. New Critics think a reader's response is irrelevant because a text's meaning is timeless. But response critics, including feminists and Marxists, maintain that what a text means cannot be separated from the reading process used by readers as they draw on personal and literary experiences to make meaning. In other words, the text is not an object but an event that occurs in readers over time.

Response criticism includes critics who think that the reader's contribution to the making of meaning is quite small as well as critics who think that readers play a primary role in the process. Louise Rosenblatt is a moderate response critic since she thinks the contributions are about equal. Her transactive theory claims that the text guides our response, like a printed musical score that we adjust as we move through the text. She allows for a range of acceptable meanings as long as she can find reasonable textual support in the writing.

Response critics like Stanley Fish downplay individual responses, focusing instead on how communities influence our responses to texts. We probably all belong to a number of these interpretive communities (such as churches, universities, neighborhoods, political parties, and social class) and have internalized their interpretive strategies, their discourse, or their way of reading texts of all kinds. Fish's point is that we all come to texts already predisposed to read them in a certain way: we do not interpret stories, but we create them by using the reading tools and cultural assumptions we bring with us. Our reading then reveals what is in us more than what is in the text. We find what we expect to see.

POSTCOLONIAL CRITICISM

Postcolonial criticism, like feminist criticism, has developed because of the dramatic shrinking of the world and the increasing multicultural cast of our own country. It is mainly interested in the ways nineteenth-century European political domination affects the lives of people living in former colonies, especially the way the dominant culture becomes the norm and those without power are portrayed as inferior. Postcolonial critics often look for stereotypes in texts as well as in characters whose self-image has been damaged by being forced to see themselves as Other, as less than. As oppressed people try to negotiate life in both the dominant and the oppressed cultures, they can develop a double consciousness that leads to feelings of alienation and deep conflicts.

Literary critics often argue that being caught between the demands of two cultures — one dominant and privileged, the other marginalized and scorned — causes a character to be "unhomed," a psychological refugee who is uncomfortable everywhere.

NEW HISTORICISM

New Historicism was developed because critics were dissatisfied with the old historicism, a long-standing traditional approach that viewed history simply as a background for understanding the literary text. History was thought to be an accurate record of what happened because the professional historian used objective and proven methods. But most literary critics no longer hold to this view of history. Instead, history is now thought to be just one perspective among many possibilities, inevitably subjective and biased. Influenced by the theorist Michel Foucault, history is seen as one of many discourses that can shed light on the past. But the dominant view is that all of us, including historians, writers, and critics, live in a particular culture and cannot escape its influences. And since these social, cultural, literary, economic, and political influences are all interrelated, all texts can tell us something important. Stories, histories, diaries, laws, speeches, newspapers, and magazines are all relevant. Culture permeates all texts, influencing everyone to see society's view of reality, of what's right and wrong and which values, assumptions, and truths are acceptable. Critics and historians try to interpret a vast web of interconnected discourses and forces in order to understand an era. Naturally, since many of these forces are competing for power, critics are always looking for power struggles among discourses. Think of the present struggle over the amount of influence religion should have in politics or who has the right to marry. Literature is one of the texts in a culture that shapes our views and which critics investigate to unearth these competing ideas.

Working with the Critical Approaches

Keep these brief descriptions of the critical approaches in mind as you read the following story by James Joyce, one of the most important writers of the twentieth century. Joyce (1882–1941) was born in Ireland, although he spent most of his life in self-imposed exile on the European continent. "Counterparts" is from *Dubliners* (1914), a collection of stories set in the Irish city of his childhood years. (For more on James Joyce, see his story "Araby," on p. 378.)

JAMES JOYCE
Counterparts

The bell rang furiously and, when Miss Parker went to the tube, a furious voice called out in a piercing North of Ireland accent:

— Send Farrington here!

Miss Parker returned to her machine, saying to a man who was writing at a desk:

— Mr Alleyne wants you upstairs.

The man muttered *Blast him!* under his breath and pushed back his chair to stand up. When he stood up he was tall and of great bulk. He had a hanging face, dark wine-coloured, with fair eyebrows and moustache: his eyes bulged forward slightly and the whites of them were dirty. He lifted up the counter and, passing by the clients, went out of the office with a heavy step.

5

He went heavily upstairs until he came to the second landing, where a door bore a brass plate with the inscription *Mr Alleyne.* Here he halted, puffing with labor and vexation, and knocked. The shrill voice cried:

— Come in!

The man entered Mr Alleyne's room. Simultaneously Mr Alleyne, a little man wearing gold-rimmed glasses on a cleanshaven face, shot his head up over a pile of documents. The head itself was so pink and hairless that it seemed like a large egg reposing on the papers. Mr Alleyne did not lose a moment:

— Farrington? What is the meaning of this? Why have I always to complain of you? May I ask you why you haven't made a copy of that contract between Bodley and Kirwan? I told you it must be ready by four o'clock.

— But Mr Shelley said, sir —   10

— *Mr Shelley said, sir.* . . . Kindly attend to what I say and not to what *Mr Shelley says, sir.* You have always some excuse or another for shirking work. Let me tell you that if the contract is not copied before this evening I'll lay the matter before Mr Crosbie. . . . Do you hear me now?

— Yes, sir.

— Do you hear me now? . . . Ay and another little matter! I might as well be talking to the wall as talking to you. Understand once for all that you get a half an hour for your lunch and not an hour and a half. How many courses do you want, I'd like to know. . . . Do you mind me, now?

— Yes, sir.

Mr Alleyne bent his head again upon his pile of papers. The man stared   15 fixedly at the polished skull which directed the affairs of Crosbie & Alleyne, gauging its fragility. A spasm of rage gripped his throat for a few moments and then passed, leaving after it a sharp sensation of thirst. The man recognized the sensation and felt that he must have a good night's drinking. The middle of the month was passed and, if he could get the copy done in time, Mr Alleyne might give him an order on the cashier. He stood still, gazing fixedly at the head upon the pile of papers. Suddenly Mr Alleyne began to upset all the papers, searching for something. Then, as if he had been unaware of the man's presence till that moment, he shot up his head again, saying:

— Eh? Are you going to stand there all day? Upon my word, Farrington, you take things easy!

— I was waiting to see . . .

— Very good, you needn't wait to see. Go downstairs and do your work.

The man walked heavily towards the door and, as he went out of the room, he heard Mr Alleyne cry after him that if the contract was not copied by evening Mr Crosbie would hear of the matter.

He returned to his desk in the lower office and counted the sheets which   20 remained to be copied. He took up his pen and dipped it in the ink but he continued to stare stupidly at the last words he had written: *In no case shall the said Bernard Bodley be.* . . . The evening was falling and in a few minutes they would be lighting the gas: then he could write. He felt that he must slake the thirst in his throat. He stood up from his desk and, lifting the counter as before, passed out of the office. As he was passing out the chief clerk looked at him inquiringly.

—It's all right, Mr Shelley, said the man, pointing with his finger to indicate the objective of his journey.

The chief clerk glanced at the hat-rack but, seeing the row complete, offered no remark. As soon as he was on the landing the man pulled a shepherd's plaid cap out of his pocket, put it on his head and ran quickly down the rickety stairs. From the street door he walked on furtively on the inner side of the path towards the corner and all at once dived into a doorway. He was now safe in the dark snug of O'Neill's shop, and, filling up the little window that looked into the bar with his inflamed face, the color of dark wine or dark meat, he called out:

—Here, Pat, give us a g.p., like a good fellow.

The curate brought him a glass of plain porter. The man drank it at a gulp and asked for a caraway seed. He put his penny on the counter and, leaving the curate to grope for it in the gloom, retreated out of the snug as furtively as he had entered it.

Darkness, accompanied by a thick fog, was gaining upon the dusk of   25
February and the lamps in Eustace Street had been lit. The man went up by the houses until he reached the door of the office, wondering whether he could finish his copy in time. On the stairs a moist pungent odor of perfumes saluted his nose: evidently Miss Delacour had come while he was out in O'Neill's. He crammed his cap back again into his pocket and re-entered the office assuming an air of absent-mindedness.

—Mr Alleyne has been calling for you, said the chief clerk severely. Where were you?

The man glanced at the two clients who were standing at the counter as if to intimate that their presence prevented him from answering. As the clients were both male the chief clerk allowed himself a laugh.

—I know that game, he said. Five times in one day is a little bit. . . . Well, you better look sharp and get a copy of our correspondence in the Delacour case for Mr Alleyne.

This address in the presence of the public, his run upstairs, and the porter he had gulped down so hastily confused the man and, as he sat down at his desk to get what was required, he realized how hopeless was the task of finishing his copy of the contract before half past five. The dark damp night was coming and he longed to spend it in the bars, drinking with his friends amid the glare of gas and the clatter of glasses. He got out the Delacour correspondence and passed out of the office. He hoped Mr Alleyne would not discover that the last two letters were missing.

The moist pungent perfume lay all the way up to Mr Alleyne's room. Miss   30
Delacour was a middle-aged woman of Jewish appearance. Mr Alleyne was said to be sweet on her or on her money. She came to the office often and stayed a long time when she came. She was sitting beside his desk now in an aroma of perfumes, smoothing the handle of her umbrella, and nodding the great black feather in her hat. Mr Alleyne had swivelled his chair round to face her and thrown his right foot jauntily upon his left knee. The man put the correspondence on the desk and bowed respectfully but neither Mr Alleyne nor Miss Delacour took any notice of his bow. Mr Alleyne tapped a finger on the

correspondence and then flicked it towards him as if to say: *That's all right: you can go.*

The man returned to the lower office and sat down again at his desk. He stared intently at the incomplete phrase: *In no case shall the said Bernard Bodley be . . .* and thought how strange it was that the last three words began with the same letter. The chief clerk began to hurry Miss Parker, saying she would never have the letters typed in time for post. The man listened to the clicking of the machine for a few minutes and then set to work to finish his copy. But his head was not clear and his mind wandered away to the glare and rattle of the public-house. It was a night for hot punches. He struggled on with his copy, but when the clock struck five he had still fourteen pages to write. Blast it! He couldn't finish it in time. He longed to execrate aloud, to bring his fist down on something violently. He was so enraged that he wrote *Bernard Bernard* instead of *Bernard Bodley* and had to begin again on a clean sheet.

He felt strong enough to clear out the whole office singlehanded. His body ached to do something, to rush out and revel in violence. All the indignities of his life enraged him. . . . Could he ask the cashier privately for an advance? No, the cashier was no good, no damn good: he wouldn't give an advance. . . . He knew where he would meet the boys: Leonard and O'Halloran and Nosey Flynn. The barometer of his emotional nature was set for a spell of riot.

His imagination had so abstracted him that his name was called twice before he answered. Mr Alleyne and Miss Delacour were standing outside the counter and all the clerks had turned round in anticipation of something. The man got up from his desk. Mr Alleyne began a tirade of abuse, saying that two letters were missing. The man answered that he knew nothing about them, that he had made a faithful copy. The tirade continued: it was so bitter and violent that the man could hardly restrain his fist from descending upon the head of the manikin before him.

—I know nothing about any other two letters, he said stupidly.

— *You — know — nothing.* Of course you know nothing, said Mr Alleyne.   35
Tell me, he added, glancing first for approval to the lady beside him, do you take me for a fool? Do you think me an utter fool?

The man glanced from the lady's face to the little egg-shaped head and back again; and, almost before he was aware of it, his tongue had found a felicitous moment:

—I don't think, sir, he said, that that's a fair question to put to me.

There was a pause in the very breathing of the clerks. Everyone was astounded (the author of the witticism no less than his neighbors) and Miss Delacour, who was a stout amiable person, began to smile broadly. Mr Alleyne flushed to the hue of a wild rose and his mouth twitched with a dwarf's passion. He shook his fist in the man's face till it seemed to vibrate like the knob of some electric machine:

—You impertinent ruffian! You impertinent ruffian! I'll make short work of you! Wait till you see! You'll apologize to me for your impertinence or you'll quit the office instanter! You'll quit this, I'm telling you, or you'll apologize to me!

He stood in a doorway opposite the office watching to see if the cashier would 40
come out alone. All the clerks passed out and finally the cashier came out with
the chief clerk. It was no use trying to say a word to him when he was with the
chief clerk. The man felt that his position was bad enough. He had been obliged
to offer an abject apology to Mr Alleyne for his impertinence but he knew what
a hornet's nest the office would be for him. He could remember the way in
which Mr Alleyne had hounded little Peake out of the office in order to make
room for his own nephew. He felt savage and thirsty and revengeful, annoyed
with himself and with everyone else. Mr Alleyne would never give him an
hour's rest; his life would be a hell to him. He had made a proper fool of himself
this time. Could he not keep his tongue in his cheek? But they had never pulled
together from the first, he and Mr Alleyne, ever since the day Mr Alleyne had
overheard him mimicking his North of Ireland accent to amuse Higgins and
Miss Parker: that had been the beginning of it. He might have tried Higgins for
the money, but sure Higgins never had anything for himself. A man with two
establishments to keep up, of course he couldn't. . . .

He felt his great body again aching for the comfort of the public-house.
The fog had begun to chill him and he wondered could he touch Pat in O'Neill's.
He could not touch him for more than a bob — and a bob was no use. Yet he
must get money somewhere or other: he had spent his last penny for the g.p.
and soon it would be too late for getting money anywhere. Suddenly, as he was
fingering his watch-chain, he thought of Terry Kelly's pawn-office in Fleet
Street. That was the dart! Why didn't he think of it sooner?

He went through the narrow alley of Temple Bar quickly, muttering to
himself that they could all go to hell because he was going to have a good night
of it. The clerk in Terry Kelly's said *A crown!* but the consignor held out for six
shillings; and in the end the six shillings was allowed him literally. He came out
of the pawn-office joyfully, making a little cylinder of the coins between his
thumb and fingers. In Westmoreland Street the footpaths were crowded with
young men and women returning from business and ragged urchins ran here
and there yelling out the names of the evening editions. The man passed
through the crowd, looking on the spectacle generally with proud satisfaction
and staring masterfully at the office-girls. His head was full of the noises of
tram-gongs and swishing trolleys and his nose already sniffed the curling
fumes of punch. As he walked on he preconsidered the terms in which he
would narrate the incident to the boys:

— So, I just looked at him — coolly, you know, and looked at her. Then
I looked back at him again — taking my time, you know. *I don't think that that's
a fair question to put to me, says I.*

Nosey Flynn was sitting up in his usual corner of Davy Byrne's and, when
he heard the story, he stood Farrington a half-one, saying it was as smart a
thing as ever he heard. Farrington stood a drink in his turn. After a while
O'Halloran and Paddy Leonard came in and the story was repeated to them.
O'Halloran stood tailors of malt, hot, all round and told the story of the retort
he had made to the chief clerk when he was in Callan's of Fownes's Street; but,

as the retort was after the manner of the liberal shepherds in the eclogues, he had to admit that it was not so clever as Farrington's retort. At this Farrington told the boys to polish off that and have another.

Just as they were naming their poisons who should come in but Higgins! 4 Of course he had to join in with the others. The men asked him to give his version of it, and he did so with great vivacity for the sight of five small hot whiskies was very exhilarating. Everyone roared laughing when he showed the way in which Mr Alleyne shook his fist in Farrington's face. Then he imitated Farrington, saying, *And here was my nabs, as cool as you please*, while Farrington looked at the company out of his heavy dirty eyes, smiling and at times drawing forth stray drops of liquor from his moustache with the aid of his lower lip.

When that round was over there was a pause. O'Halloran had money but neither of the other two seemed to have any; so the whole party left the shop somewhat regretfully. At the corner of Duke Street Higgins and Nosey Flynn bevelled off to the left while the other three turned back towards the city. Rain was drizzling down on the cold streets and, when they reached the Ballast Office, Farrington suggested the Scotch House. The bar was full of men and loud with the noise of tongues and glasses. The three men pushed past the whining match-sellers at the door and formed a little party at the corner of the counter. They began to exchange stories. Leonard introduced them to a young fellow named Weathers who was performing at the Tivoli as an acrobat and knockabout *artiste*. Farrington stood a drink all round. Weathers said he would take a small Irish and Apollinaris. Farrington, who had definite notions of what was what, asked the boys would they have an Apollinaris too; but the boys told Tim to make theirs hot. The talk became theatrical. O'Halloran stood a round and then Farrington stood another round, Weathers protesting that the hospitality was too Irish. He promised to get them in behind the scenes and introduce them to some nice girls. O'Halloran said that he and Leonard would go but that Farrington wouldn't go because he was a married man; and Farrington's heavy dirty eyes leered at the company in token that he understood he was being chaffed. Weathers made them all have just one little tincture at his expense and promised to meet them later on at Mulligan's in Poolbeg Street.

When the Scotch House closed they went round to Mulligan's. They went into the parlor at the back and O'Halloran ordered small hot specials all round. They were all beginning to feel mellow. Farrington was just standing another round when Weathers came back. Much to Farrington's relief he drank a glass of bitter this time. Funds were running low but they had enough to keep them going. Presently two young women with big hats and a young man in a check suit came in and sat at a table close by. Weathers saluted them and told the company that they were out of the Tivoli. Farrington's eyes wandered at every moment in the direction of one of the young women. There was something striking in her appearance. An immense scarf of peacock-blue muslin was wound round her hat and knotted in a great bow under her chin; and she wore bright yellow gloves, reaching to the elbow. Farrington gazed admiringly at the plump arm which she moved very often and with much grace; and when, after a little time, she answered his gaze he admired still more her large dark brown eyes. The oblique staring expression in them fascinated him. She glanced at him once or twice and, when the party was leaving the room, she brushed against his chair and said O, pardon! in a London accent. He watched her leave the room in the hope that she would look back at him, but he was disappointed. He cursed his want of money and cursed all the rounds he had stood, particularly all the whiskies and Apollinaris which he had stood to Weathers. If there was one thing that he hated it was a sponge. He was so angry that he lost count of the conversation of his friends.

When Paddy Leonard called him he found that they were talking about feats of strength. Weathers was showing his biceps muscle to the company and boasting so much that the other two had called on Farrington to uphold the national honor. Farrington pulled up his sleeve accordingly and showed his biceps muscle to the company. The two arms were examined and compared and finally it was agreed to have a trial of strength. The table was cleared and the two men rested their elbows on it, clasping hands. When Paddy Leonard said Go! each was to try to bring down the other's hand on to the table. Farrington looked very serious and determined.

The trial began. After about thirty seconds Weathers brought his opponent's hand slowly down on to the table. Farrington's dark wine-coloured face flushed darker still with anger and humiliation at having been defeated by such a stripling.

— You're not to put the weight of your body behind it. Play fair, he said.   50

— Who's not playing fair? said the other.

— Come on again. The two best out of three.

The trial began again. The veins stood out on Farrington's forehead, and the pallor of Weathers' complexion changed to peony. Their hands and arms trembled under the stress. After a long struggle Weathers again brought his opponent's hand slowly on to the table. There was a murmur of applause from the spectators. The curate, who was standing beside the table, nodded his red head towards the victor and said with loutish familiarity:

— Ah! that's the knack!

— What the hell do you know about it? said Farrington fiercely, turning on   55
the man. What do you put in your gab for?

— Sh, sh! said O'Halloran, observing the violent expression of Farrington's face. Pony up, boys. We'll have just one little smahan more and then we'll be off.

A very sullen-faced man stood at the corner of O'Connell Bridge waiting for the little Sandymount tram to take him home. He was full of smouldering anger and revengefulness. He felt humiliated and discontented; he did not even feel drunk; and he had only twopence in his pocket. He cursed everything. He had done for himself in the office, pawned his watch, spent all his money; and he had not even got drunk. He began to feel thirsty again and he longed to be back again in the hot reeking public-house. He had lost his reputation as a strong man, having been defeated twice by a mere boy. His heart swelled with fury and, when he thought of the woman in the big hat who had brushed against him and said Pardon! his fury nearly choked him.

His tram let him down at Shelbourne Road and he steered his great body along in the shadow of the wall of the barracks. He loathed returning to his home. When he went in by the side-door he found the kitchen empty and the kitchen fire nearly out. He bawled upstairs:

— Ada! Ada!

His wife was a little sharp-faced woman who bullied her husband when he   60 was sober and was bullied by him when he was drunk. They had five children. A little boy came running down the stairs.

— Who is that? said the man, peering through the darkness.

— Me, pa.

— Who are you? Charlie?

— No, pa. Tom.

— Where's your mother?   65

— She's out at the chapel.

— That's right. . . . Did she think of leaving any dinner for me?

— Yes, pa. I —

— Light the lamp. What do you mean by having the place in darkness? Are the other children in bed?

The man sat down heavily on one of the chairs while the little boy lit the   70 lamp. He began to mimic his son's flat accent, saying half to himself: *At the chapel. At the chapel, if you please!* When the lamp was lit he banged his fist on the table and shouted:

— What's for my dinner?

— I'm going . . . to cook it, pa, said the little boy.

The man jumped up furiously and pointed to the fire.

— On that fire! You let the fire out! By God, I'll teach you to do that again!

He took a step to the door and seized the walking-stick which was standing   75 behind it.

— I'll teach you to let the fire out! he said, rolling up his sleeve in order to give his arm free play.

The little boy cried *O, pa!* and ran whimpering round the table, but the man followed him and caught him by the coat. The little boy looked about him wildly but, seeing no way of escape fell upon his knees.

— Now, you'll let the fire out the next time! said the man, striking at him viciously with the stick. Take that, you little whelp!

The boy uttered a squeal of pain as the stick cut his thigh. He clasped his hands together in the air and his voice shook with fright.

— O, pa! he cried. Don't beat me, pa! And I'll . . . I'll say a *Hail Mary* for   80 you. . . . I'll say a *Hail Mary* for you, pa, if you don't beat me. . . . I'll say a *Hail Mary*. . . .   *[1914]*

A thorough critical analysis of "Counterparts" using any one of these approaches would take dozens of pages. The following are brief suggestions for how such a reading might proceed.

NEW CRITICISM

A New Critic might want to demonstrate the multiple ways the title holds the narrative together, giving it unity and coherence — for example, Farrington and his son Tom are counterparts since Tom is the victim of his father's bullying just as Farrington is bullied by Mr. Alleyne at work. You can also probably spot other counterparts: Farrington and his wife, for example, trade off bullying each other, and their means of escaping from the drudgery of their lives, the bar and the church, are also parallel. And naturally when Weathers, the acrobat, defeats the much larger Farrington in arm wrestling, we are reminded of the verbal beating Farrington must endure from his equally diminutive boss, Mr. Alleyne. New Critics are fond of finding the ways all the elements of a text reinforce one another.

A New Critic might argue that these counterparts or oppositions introduce tensions into the story from the first few lines when the "bell rang furiously" for Farrington to report to Mr. Alleyne for a dressing-down. The irony is that Farrington is big and Alleyne is small, that Farrington is powerful and Alleyne is fragile as an egg. But it is Mr. Alleyne who breaks Farrington; it is Farrington who is weak. Throughout the story, tensions, oppositions, and ironies continue, for example, when Farrington is defeated by the smaller Weathers. In the last scene, the tension is finally resolved when the larger Farrington beats his small son, making him a counterpart to both Alleyne and Weathers in oppressing the weak. The final evidence that Farrington is ethically powerless is cruelly obvious as the son promises to pray for his abusing father.

FEMINIST CRITICISM

Feminist critics and their first cousins, gender critics, would naturally be struck by the violent masculinity of Farrington, his fantasies of riot and abuse, his savage feelings of revenge, and his "smouldering anger" (para. 57). Farrington is depicted not only as crude and brutish but also as a kind of perverse stereotype of male vanity, self-centeredness, and irresponsibility. His obsession with obtaining money for drinking completely disregards his role as the provider for a large family, and, of course, the beatings of his son are a cruel parody of his role as paternal protector. And if he had not wasted his money on drink, Farrington would also be a womanizer ("Farrington's eyes wandered at every moment in the direction of one of the young women," para. 47). Gender critics would be interested in the social and cultural mechanisms that could construct such primitive masculinity.

A reasonable argument might focus on the representation of women in the story. Miss Parker, Miss Delacour, Farrington's wife, and the performer Farrington sees in the bar are marginal characters. One student made the following claim: "The women in Farrington's world, and Irish society in general, have no agency: they are prevented from taking an active part in determining their lives and futures." Another student argued differently, saying, "While women in general are oppressed by the raw and brutal masculinity represented by Farrington, the women in this story do hold a degree of power over men." Based on their own analysis and interpretations, these students demonstrated that there was reasonable textual evidence to support their claims.

PSYCHOANALYTIC CRITICISM

A psychoanalytic critic would first notice the extreme pattern of behavior Farrington exhibits, as he repeatedly withdraws from his adult work responsibilities and as he fantasizes about being physically violent against his supervisors. Critics would argue that such behavior is typical of Farrington's repressed wounds and his unresolved conflicts with his own father. Farrington seems to be playing out painful childhood experiences. Given the violent displacement (taking it out on someone else) visited on Tom, we can imagine that Farrington is beating not only his boss, Mr. Alleyne, but also perhaps his own abusive father. The fantasies at work in Farrington also suggest the psychological defense of projection, since Farrington is blaming his problems on Mr. Alleyne and his job. Although his tasks do seem to be tedious, they certainly cannot account for his "spasm of rage" (para. 15) or his desire "to clear out the whole office single-handed" (para. 32). When Farrington feels "humiliated and discontented" (para. 57), it is only in part because of his immediate context. It is the return of the repressed that plagues Farrington, a resurfacing of a buried pain. These ideas should also be tied to Farrington's death wish, especially his stunningly self-destructive behavior at work. Freudian critics would also argue that these specific actions are related to other core issues that would include intense loss of self-esteem, fear of intimacy, and betrayal.

MARXIST CRITICISM

A Marxist critic would be interested in focusing on the specific historical moment of "Counterparts" and not on Farrington's individual psyche, which can only distract us from the real force that affects human experience — the economic system in which Farrington is trapped. Economic power — not the Oedipal drama or gender — is the crucial human motivator. Farrington's material circumstances and not timeless values are the key to understanding his behavior. The real battle lines are drawn between Crosbie and Alleyne (the "haves") and Farrington (a "have-not") — that is, between the bourgeoisie and the proletariat, between those who control economic resources and those who perform the labor that fills the coffers of the rich. In a Marxist analysis, critics would argue that Farrington is a victim of class warfare. His desperation, his humiliation, his rage, his cruel violence are all traceable to classism — an ideology that determines people's worth according to their economic class. Although Farrington does appear shiftless and irresponsible, it is not because of his class; it is because of the meaninglessness of his work and the demeaning hierarchy that keeps him at the bottom. In his alienation, he reverts to a primitive physical masculinity, a false consciousness that only further diminishes his sense of his worth.

Marxists are often interested in what lies beneath the text in its political unconscious. To get at the unconscious, Marxists, like psychoanalytic critics, look for symptoms on the surface that suggest problems beneath. Typically, such symptomatic readings reveal class conflicts that authors are sometimes unaware of themselves. Marxist critics might debate whether Joyce himself understood that the root cause of Farrington's aberrant behavior was economic and not psychological. This makes sense since for Marxists both reader and writer are under the sway of the same ideological system that they see as natural.

One student made the following claim: "Farrington's role as proletarian results in his feelings of inferiority, resentment over lack of entitlement, and an expectation of disappointment." This same student, like many Marxist critics who see the function of literature through a pragmatic lens, concluded her essay with an appeal toward change, arguing that "The remedy does not lie in changing Farrington's consciousness, but rather in changing the economic and political discourse of power that has constituted him."

DECONSTRUCTION

One of many possible deconstructions of "Counterparts" would involve focusing on a troubling or puzzling point called an *aporia*. Some deconstructive critics have looked at the incomplete phrase that Farrington copies, *"In no case shall the said Bernard Bodley be . . ."* as an aporia, an ambiguous and not completely understandable textual puzzle but one that might be a way into the story's meaning. The oppositions that are being deconstructed or laid bare here are *presence* and *absence, word* and *reality.* Working off the implications of the title "Counterparts," Bernard Bodley can be seen as a double or counterpart for Farrington, a character like Bodley whose existence is in doubt. Although Farrington's size suggests that he is very much physically present, his behavior might suggest otherwise. He spends his time copying other people's words and has a compelling need to repeat the narrative of his encounter with Mr. Alleyne, as if he must demonstrate his own existence through repetition. He does not have a viable inner life, an authentic identity. Farrington's essence is not present but absent. His identity is insubstantial. He tries to fill the emptiness at the center of his being with camaraderie and potency, but his efforts produce the opposite — escape, loneliness, and weakness. In other words, the said Farrington does not really exist and cannot be. In this way, we can deconstruct "Counterparts" as a story in which presence is absence, strength is weakness, Farrington's actions lead only to paralysis and repetition, and Farrington's frustration with his impotence makes his oppressors more powerful.

One student working with similar interpretations of "Counterparts" noted other oppositions, especially between male and female, escape and confinement. She argued that Farrington spends most of his time trying to avoid being thought of as stereotypically feminine. However, the more exaggerated his masculine aggression, drinking, violence, and irresponsibility become, the weaker, the more stereotypically feminine he becomes. Similarly, the more

Farrington tries to escape, the more ensnared he is. In this way, the student argued, our conventional understandings of these opposing terms are deconstructed, so that we are no longer confident about the meaning of escape, masculinity, or strength.

READER-RESPONSE CRITICISM

Willa Ervinman, a student, was asked to respond to the story by using Stanley Fish's ideas and noting the conflicts between the interpretive or discourse communities Willa belonged to and those depicted in the story. The following are excerpts from her response journal:

> I was upset by Farrington's lack of responsibility at work. He is completely unreliable and demonstrates very little self-esteem. He must know that the people he works with consider him a slacker and a fake. I was raised in a middle-class home where both my parents worked hard in a bank from 9 to 5. Just the idea that they would sneak out of work to drink in dark bars is absurd. My belief in the discourse of middle-class responsibility or perhaps the Protestant work ethic makes it almost impossible for me to see Farrington with sympathy even though I can see that his work is probably completely mechanical and unfulfilling. . . .
>
> Farrington's domestic violence against his son is such a violation of the discourse of domesticity that it is hard to understand any other response. Someone in my response group thought that Farrington was a victim of his working-class discourse of masculinity. I can see how he was humiliated by the smaller men, Mr. Alleyne and Weathers, but beating his innocent son as a kind of revenge cannot be forgiven. My grandmother tells me that it was common for children to be physically punished in her day, but in the interpretive community I was raised in, there is no excuse for domestic violence. It is more than a character flaw; it is criminal behavior, and I judge Farrington to be a social menace, beyond compassion.

Willa went on to argue that Farrington's violent behavior is inexcusable, interpreting our current understandings of domestic violence and responsible masculinity as evidence. She blended this personal view with textual support. Her warrant for her claim was that historical circumstances and norms should not be used to excuse reprehensible behavior.

POSTCOLONIAL CRITICISM

"Counterparts" was written in the early twentieth century at a time when the Ireland Joyce writes about was still a colony of the British Empire. Farrington is, then, a colonial subject and subject to political domination. At the story's opening, Farrington, a Catholic from the south of Ireland, is summoned by a "furious voice" from Northern Ireland, a stronghold of British sympathy and Protestant domination. The tension is announced early because it is crucial to Farrington's behavior and his internalized and colonized mindset. Many colonials have a negative self-image because they are alienated from their own indigenous culture. Indeed, Farrington seems completely ill suited to the office copying task he is relegated to. He seems more suited to some physical endeavor, but given the difficult economics of Dublin, he probably has few career options.

Farrington is the Other in the discourse of colonialism, and he is made to seem inferior at every turn, from the verbal lashing of Mr. Alleyne to the physical defeat by Weathers, who is probably British. Symbolically, Farrington tries to resist his subjugation by the British establishment but fails. He is what postcolonial theorists refer to as *unhomed* or *displaced*. He is uncomfortable at work, in the bars where he seeks solace, and finally in his ultimate refuge, a place unprepared even to feed him. Indeed, in an act likely to perpetuate abuse upon future generations, Farrington turns on his own family, becoming, through his enraged attack on his child Tom, a metaphor for the conflicted, tormented, and defeated Ireland. When a colonial is not "at home" even in his own home, he is truly in psychological agony and exile. Joyce represents the trauma of British domination through one subject's self-destructive and self-hating journey, a journey made even more cruelly ironic by Farrington's attack — in a mimicry of British aggression and injustice — on his own subjected son.

NEW HISTORICISM

A critic influenced by Foucault and New Historicism might argue that Farrington is a victim of an inflexible discourse of masculinity, that he has been socialized by working-class norms of how a man should behave to such an extent that he cannot change. Growing up in a working-class culture, Farrington would have received high marks among his peers for his size and strength, just as Mr. Alleyne would be diminished in status for his. And in another context, say, on a construction site, Farrington's sense of masculinity might be a plus. But in an office, his aggressive masculinity is a liability. In all cultures, people are subject to multiple discourses that pull them one way then another. Farrington's sarcasm, his drinking, his longing for camaraderie, and his resorting to violence to solve problems are the results of being too enmeshed in a discourse of masculinity from working-class Dublin and not enough in the middle-class business assumptions about discipline, responsibility, and concentration. Farrington is defeated at work, in the pubs, and at home because he is unable to move from one discourse to another. He is stuck in a subject position that only reinforces his powerlessness. His self-esteem is so damaged by the end of the story that he even violates his own code of masculinity by beating a defenseless child.

Sample Student Essay

The following essay was written by a first-year student using a postcolonial perspective.

Molly Frye
Prof. Christine Hardee
English 102
10 May - - - -

A Refugee at Home

It is difficult to argue that Farrington, the main character in James Joyce's "Counterparts," should be seen in a sympathetic light. After all, he seems an extreme stereotype of an aggressive, irresponsible drinker. Although his character traits certainly do not conform to our modern standards of mature masculinity, I want to argue that although we do not want to condone Farrington's brutal behavior, we can find it understandable. As an Irish subject in the British Empire, Farrington is more sinned against than sinner, more victim than victimizer. Farrington is not simply an obnoxious male since his actions can be understood as stemming from his colonial consciousness in struggling vainly against his powerlessness. His frustrations are especially clear in the three spaces Farrington inhabits: his office, the bars, and his home.

Farrington's first appearance is telling. Because of his poor job performance, his boss demands to see him: "Send Farrington here!" Farrington, who most often is referred to as "the man," mutters his first words, "Blast him!" This typical antagonistic relationship in a colonial context foreshadows the rest of the story. Farrington is the working-class subject caught in a menial and unsatisfying job he can never complete under a boss who has social and cultural power. This counterpart relationship is similar to the positions of Ireland and England where the colony is disparaged and oppressed by the empire. In his office run by Protestants loyal to the British, Farrington is ironically "tall and of great bulk," while his boss, Mr. Alleyne, is "a little man" whose head, "pink and hairless," resembles a "large egg." Farrington's only asset, his size and strength, is irrelevant because he is so economically and socially weak. This disparity only increases Farrington's frustration and precipitates fantasies of violence against his oppressor. When Mr. Alleyne rebukes him, "Do you mind me now," Farrington is sent into a "spasm of rage." He cannot, of course, act on his aggressive urges, so he represses these feelings by rationalizing that he must have a "good night's drinking." Thus begins a pattern of self-destructive behavior that only increases Farrington's marginal position in society.

Farrington is so uncomfortable at work, a postcolonial condition known as being unhomed, that he cannot concentrate on anything but drinking. He seems quite unsuited for the tedious task of copying legal documents, staring "stupidly at the last words he has written," knowing he will never finish his task, never advance, never get anywhere. Farrington is paralyzed by his alienation. He feels his only recourse is sneaking out to drink, which only exacerbates his poverty and powerlessness. When he attempts to cover up his inability to concentrate and finish copying letters for Mr. Alleyne, he is caught and confronted. Instead of acknowledging his underling position, he attempts a witticism which, of course, backfires. Even though he is forced to apologize, his job now seems in jeopardy. Mr. Alleyne humiliates him by calling him an "impertinent ruffian," a status that seems to him the most he can hope for. As a colonial subject, Farrington is plagued by a double consciousness. He longs for the masculine status his physical strength should give him in his working-class culture, but he must suffer indignities at the hands of Mr. Alleyne because of his inability to perform a simple task a competent child could do. Farrington should probably be working in construction as a laborer, not an office worker where discipline, patience, and mental concentration are necessary.

When Farrington finally leaves work, he expects to find some solace in the Dublin pubs. He has hocked his watch for drinking money, a clear indication of how desperate he is to escape the confines of regimented office work. The camaraderie of Paddy Leonard and Nosey Flynn is temporary, and Farrington is not at home in these public spaces either. He runs out of money he would have spent drinking and womanizing, and he is finally humiliated by another small British man. Called on to "uphold the national honor," Farrington's loss in an arm-wrestling contest with Weathers leaves him "full of smouldering anger and revengefulness. He is humiliated and discontented . . . His heart swelled with fury. . . ." His longing for escape from the confinement and disappointment of work has taken a disastrous turn. Farrington's already damaged self-esteem is degraded, and his repressed anger at his oppressor is near the breaking point. Perhaps his self-destructive behavior can be redirected at his home, his last possibility for comfort and acceptance.

For the unhomed colonized, however, this is not to be. Farrington enters the kitchen to find it symbolically empty, "the fire nearly out." His wife is at chapel, his five children in bed, and his dinner is cold. His agonies continue. Having internalized the humiliations suffered at work and in the pubs, Farrington has no resources left. And so in a bitter irony, he beats his son for not attending to the fire, "striking at him viciously with a stick. 'Take that, you little whelp!'" Farrington the oppressed becomes Farrington the oppressor. His role as provider and protector is cruelly turned upside-down. Farrington compensates for his defeats at the hands of Mr. Alleyne and Weathers by beating his son, and in doing so, mimics the cycle of oppression prevalent in countries dominated by the empire. Farrington is not only a cog in the bureaucratic wheel at work; he is also a pathetic, but understandable cog crushed by the wheel of power even in his own home.

≡ FOR THINKING AND WRITING

1. Using a feminist critique of Joyce, one student claimed that "Joyce's text indulges dominance over submission." Do you think there is textual evidence to support this assertion?

2. How might various critics (postcolonial, feminist, Marxist, psychoanalytical) interpret these lines from "Counterparts"?

   ■ "The man passed through the crowd, looking on the spectacle generally with proud satisfaction and staring masterfully at the office-girls" (para. 42).

   ■ "His heart swelled with fury and, when he thought of the woman in the big hat who had brushed against him and said *Pardon!* his fury nearly choked him" (para. 57).

   ■ "What's for my dinner?" (para. 71).

3. Influenced by New Critical ideas, one student wrote, "'Counterparts' is filled with parallel scenes and emotions that reflect one another." What textual evidence would help support this notion?

4. Engaging in a Marxist critique, one student wrote, "His unfair work conditions so distract him that he does not even know the names of his children." What is the warrant behind such an assertion? What work conditions might the student think "fair"?

5. Using a New Historicist approach, what might you learn about this story from doing research on the elementary-school curriculum in Dublin, the pay scale in a law office, the legal rights of women, the laws on domestic violence, the unemployment rate? What other practices and texts do you think would illuminate the story?

Acknowledgments continued from p. iv

Rane Arroyo. "My Transvestite Uncle Is Missing" by Rane Arroyo from *The Singing Shark* by Rane Arroyo. Copyright © 1996. Reprinted by permission of Bilingual Press/Editorial Bilingue, Arizona State University, Tempe, AZ.

W. H. Auden. "Funeral Blues" copyright 1940 and renewed 1968 by W. H. Auden, from *Collected Poems of W. H. Auden* by W. H. Auden. Used by permission of Random House, Inc. Any third party use of this material, outside of this publication, is prohibited. Interested parties must apply directly to Random House, Inc. for permission.

Steven Gould Axelrod. *Sylvia Plath: The Wound and the Cure of Words*, pages 1–8. © 1990 The Johns Hopkins University Press. Reprinted with permission of The Johns Hopkins University Press.

James Baldwin. "Sonny's Blues" © 1957 by James Baldwin, was originally published in *Partisan Review*. Copyright renewed. Collected in *Going to Meet the Man*, published by Vintage Books. Used by arrangement with the James Baldwin Estate.

Toni Cade Bambara. "The Lesson," copyright © 1972 by Toni Cade Bambara, from *Gorilla, My Love* by Toni Cade Bambara. Used by permission of Random House, Inc.

Stephen Bandy. Excerpt from " 'One of My Babies': The Misfit and the Grandmother." Originally published in *Studies in Short Fiction*. Copyright © 1996 by Stephen Bandy. Reprinted with permission.

David Barno. "A New Moral Compact." © 2012, Foreign Policy.

Peter Beaumont and Saeed Kamali Dehghan. "Iran: Women on the frontline of the fight for rights" by Peter Beaumont and Saeed Kamali Dehghan. Copyright Guardian News & Media Ltd. 2010.

Millicent Bell. "Othello's Jealousy" by Millicent Bell from *The Yale Review*, Vol. 85, No. 2, 1997. Copyright 1997 by Yale University. Reproduced with permission of Yale University via Copyright Clearance Center.

Gerald Eades Bentley. "Notes & Commentary" by Gerald Eades Bentley from *Othello* by William Shakespeare, edited by Gerald Eades Bentley, copyright © 1958, 1970 by Penguin Books. Used by permission of Penguin, a division of Penguin Group (USA) LLC.

Elizabeth Bishop. "The Fish" from *The Complete Poems: 1927–1979* by Elizabeth Bishop. Copyright © 1979, 1983 by Alice Helen Methfessel. Reprinted by permission of Farrar, Straus and Giroux, LLC.

T. Coraghessan Boyle. "The Love of My Life" from *After the Plague* by T. Coraghessan Boyle, copyright © 2001 by T. Coraghessan Boyle. Used by permission of Viking Penguin, a division of Penguin Group (USA) Inc.

Mary Lynn Broe. Reprinted from *Protean Poetic: The Poetry of Sylvia Plath* by Mary Lynn Broe, by permission of the University of Missouri Press. Copyright © 1980 by the Curators of the University of Missouri.

Lynda K. Bundtzen. From *Plath's Incarnations: Woman and the Creative Process* by Lynda K. Bundtzen, published by The University of Michigan Press in 1989. Reprinted by permission of The University of Michigan Press.

John Burnside. "Penitence" from *A Normal Skin* by John Burnside, published by Jonathan Cape. Reprinted by permission of The Random House Group Ltd.

Angela Carter. "The Company of Wolves." © Angela Carter 1979. Reproduced by permission of the author c/o Rogers, Coleridge & White Ltd., 20 Powis Mews, London W11 1JN.

Raymond Carver. "What We Talk About When We Talk About Love" from *What We Talk About When We Talk About Love: Stories* by Raymond Carver, copyright © 1974, 1976, 1978, 1980, 1981 by Raymond Carver. Used by permission of Alfred A. Knopf, an imprint of the Knopf Doubleday Publishing Group, a division of Random House LLC. All rights reserved. Any third party use of this material, outside of this publication, is prohibited. Interested parties must apply directly to Random House LLC for permission.

Martín Espada. "Imagine the Angels of Bread" from *Imagine the Angels of Bread* by Martín Espada. Copyright © 1996 by Martín Espada. Used by permission of W.W. Norton & Company, Inc.

William Faulkner. "A Rose For Emily," copyright 1930 and renewed 1958 by William Faulkner, from *Collected Stories of William Faulkner* by William Faulkner. Used by permission of Random House, Inc. Any third party use of this material, outside of this publication, is prohibited. Interested parties must apply directly to Random House, Inc. for permission.

Ida Fink. "The Table" from *A Scrap of time and Other Stories*. Translated by Madeline Levine and Francine Prose. Copyright © 1983 by Ida Fink. Evanston: Northwestern University Press, 1995, pages 139–65. Reprinted by permission of Northwestern University Press.

Carolyn Forché. All text [prose poem] from "The Colonel" from *The Country Between Us* by Carolyn Forché. Copyright © 1981 by Carolyn Forché. Originally appeared in *Women's International Resource Exchange*. Reprinted by permission of HarperCollins Publishers.

Carlos Fraenkel. "In Praise of the Clash of Cultures." Reprinted by permission of the author.

Robert Frost. "Stopping by Woods on a Snowy Evening" and "Acquainted with the Night" from *The Poetry of Robert Frost* edited by Edward Connery Lathem. Copyright ©1923, 1928, 1969 by Henry Holt and Company, copyright © 1944, 1951, 1956 by Robert Frost. Reprinted by permission of Henry Holt and Company, LLC.

Nikki Giovanni. "Legacies" from *My House* by Nikki Giovanni. Copyright © 1972 by Nikki Giovanni, renewed 2000 by Nikki Giovanni. Reprinted by permission of HarperCollins Publishers.

Paul Goldberger. "Disconnected Urbanism." Reprinted by permission of the author.

Loren Goodman. "Traveling through the Dark (2005)." Reproduced by permission of the author.

Michael S. Harper. "Discovery" from *Songlines in Michaeltree: New and Collected Poems*. Copyright 2000 by Michael S. Harper. Used with permission of the poet and the University of Illinois Press.

Robert Hayden. "Those Winter Sundays." Copyright © 1966 by Robert Hayden, from *Collected Poems of Robert Hayden* by Robert Hayden, edited by Frederick Glaysher. Used by Permission of Liveright Publishing Corporation.

Seamus Heaney. "Punishment" from *Opened Ground: Selected Poems 1966–1996* by Seamus Heaney. Copyright © 1998 by Seamus Heaney. Reprinted by permission of Farrar, Straus and Giroux, LLC and Faber and Faber Ltd.

Ernest Hemingway. "Hills Like White Elephants." Reprinted with the permission of Scribner Publishing Group from *The Short Stories of Ernest Hemingway* by Ernest Hemingway. Copyright © 1927 by Charles Scribner's Sons. Copyright renewed © 1955 by Ernest Hemingway. All rights reserved.

Essex Hemphill. "Commitments" from *Ceremonies* by Essex Hemphill, copyright © 1992 by Essex Hemphill. Used by permission of Plume, a division of Penguin Group (USA) Inc.

David Hernandez. "Pigeons." Reprinted by permission of Batya Hernandez.

Isabel Hilton. "A Triumph for Moral Authority" by Isabel Hilton, copyright © 2010 by *The Independent* (*The Independent*, November 15, 2010).

Linda Hogan. "Heritage." Reprinted by permission of Linda Hogan for Greenfield Review Press.

Langston Hughes. "Harlem (2)," "Let America Be America Again," "Open Letter to the South," and "Theme for English B" from *The Collected Poems of Langston Hughes* by Langston Hughes, edited by Arnold Rampersad with David Roessel, Associate Editor, copyright © 1994 by the Estate of Langston Hughes. Used by permission of Alfred A. Knopf, a division of Random House LLC. Any third party use of this material, outside of this publication, is prohibited. Interested parties must apply directly to Random House LLC for permission.

Lynda Hull. "Night Waitress" from *Collected Poems*. Copyright © 1986 by Lynda Hull. Reprinted by permission of The Permissions Company, Inc., on behalf of Graywolf Press, Minneapolis, Minnesota, www.graywolfpress.org.

Rolando Perez. "Office at Night" from *The Lining of Our Souls: Excursion into Selected Paintings of Edward Hopper* by Rolando Perez (Cool Grove Press).

Sylvia Plath. All lines from "Daddy" from *Ariel* by Sylvia Plath. Copyright © 1963 by Ted Hughes. Reprinted by permission of HarperCollins Publishers. From *Collected Poems* by Sylvia Plath. Reprinted by the permission of Faber and Faber Limited.

Minnie Bruce Pratt. "Two Small-Sized Girls" from *Crime Against Nature* by Minnie Bruce Pratt © 1992.

Francine Prose. "Why Are Poor Kids Paying for School Security?" by Francine Prose. Copyright © 2012 by Francine Prose. First appeared in NYRblog (*The New York Review of Books*). Reprinted with permission of the Denise Shannon Literary Agency, Inc. All rights reserved.

Alberto Ríos. "Mi Abuelo." Sheep Meadow Press.

Richard Rodriguez. "Aria." From *Aria: A Memoir of a Bilingual Childhood* by Richard Rodriguez. Copyright © 1980 by Richard Rodriguez. Originally appeared in *The American Scholar*. Reprinted by permission of Georges Borchardt, Inc., on behalf of the author.

Theodore Roethke. "My Papa's Waltz," copyright 1942 by Hearst Magazines, Inc., from *Collected Poems of Theodore Roethke* by Theodore Roethke. Used by permission of Doubleday, a division of Random House, Inc. Any third party use of this material, outside of this publication, is prohibited. Interested parties must apply directly to Random House, Inc. for permission. "Elegy for Jane," copyright © 1950 by Theodore Roethke, from *Collected Poems of Theodore Roethke* by Theodore Roethke. Used by permission of Doubleday, a division of Random House, Inc. Any third party use of this material, outside of this publication, is prohibited. Interested parties must apply directly to Random House, Inc. for permission.

Anne Sexton. "Sylvia's Death" from *Live or Die* by Anne Sexton. Copyright © 1966 by Anne Sexton, renewed 1994 by Linda G. Sexton. Reprinted by permission of Houghton Mifflin Harcourt Publishing Company. All rights reserved.

Ira Sher. "The Man in the Well." Copyright © 1995 by Ira Sher. This story first appeared in *The Chicago Review* (Vol. 41, no. 4).

Naomi Shihab. "Blood." By permission of the author, Naomi Shihab Nye, 2013.

Lee Siegel. "The Perils of Parenting in the Digital Age" from *Newsweek*, October 8, 2012. © 2012 The Newsweek/Daily Beast Company LLC. All rights reserved. Used by permission and protected by the Copyright Laws of the United States. The printing, copying, redistribution, or re-transmission of the Material without express written permission is prohibited.

Rebecca Solnit. "The Thoreau Problem." © Rebecca Solnit from *Storming the Gates of Paradise: Landscapes for Politics* (UC Press, 2007).

Sophocles. "Antigone" from *Three Theban Plays* by Sophocles, translated by Robert Fagles, translation copyright © 1982 by Robert Fagles. Used by permission of Viking Penguin, a division of Penguin Group (USA) Inc.

Gary Soto. "Behind Grandma's House" from *New and Selected Poems*. © 1995 by Garry Soto. Used by permission of Chronicle Books LLC, San Francisco. Visit ChronicleBooks.com.

Gabriel Spera. "My Ex-Husband." Reprinted by permission of the author.

William Stafford. "Traveling through the Dark" from *The Way It Is: New & Selected Poems*. Copyright © 1998 by the Estate of William Stafford. Reprinted with the permission of The Permissions Company, Inc. on behalf of Graywolf Press, Minneapolis, Minnesota. www.graywolfpress.org.

Martha Stephens. From "The Question of Flannery O'Connor." Reprinted by permission of Louisiana State University Press.

Wladyslaw Szpilman. "The Umschlagplatz" from *The Pianist: The Extraordinary True Story of One Man's Survival in Warsaw, 1939–1945* by Wladyslaw Szpilman, translated by Anthea Bell. © Wladyslaw Szpilman 1998. Translation copyright © 1999 by Victor Golancz Ltd. Reprinted by permission of Picador and Christopher Little Literary Agency LLP.

Index of Authors, Titles, First Lines, and Key Terms

Key terms page numbers are in bold.